THE HILLIER GARDENER'S GUIDE TO TREES & SHRUBS

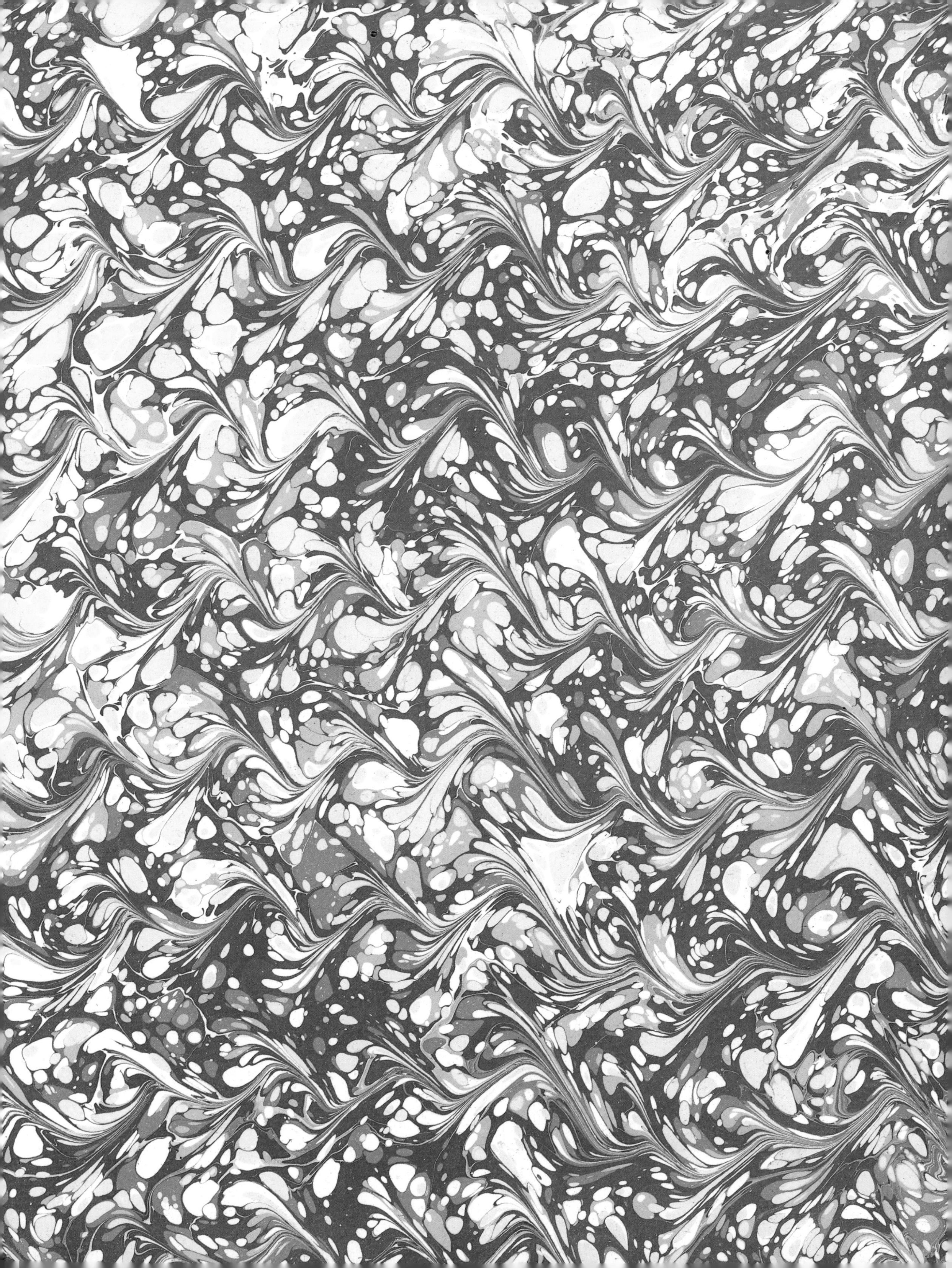

The HILLIER GARDENER'S GUIDE TO TREES & SHRUBS

Editor JOHN KELLY

Consultant Editor JOHN G. HILLIER VMH

THE READER'S DIGEST ASSOCIATION, INC.

Pleasantville, New York/Montreal

A READER'S DIGEST BOOK
EDITED AND PRODUCED BY
DAVID & CHARLES PUBLISHERS

North American edition.

First published in Great Britain in 1995

Acknowledgments
The inspiration for this book was the catalog of plants prepared by Sir Harold Hillier, Desmond Clarke, Roy Lancaster, and Mr. P.H.B. Gardner and first published in 1972 as the *Hillier Manual of Trees & Shrubs*. The original text was revised, edited, and updated for *The Hillier Gardener's Guide to Trees and Shrubs* and contains a substantial amount of new material. The North American edition was produced with the help of Trevor Cole, consultant; Rosemary Rennicke, editor; and Nancy Stabile, copy editor.

The Hillier gardener's guide to trees & shrubs/editor, John Kelly;
consultant editor John Hillier.
p. cm.
Rev., edited, and updated ed. of: Hillier manual of trees & shrubs. 6th ed. 1991.
Includes index.
ISBN 0-89577-973-0
1. Ornamental trees. 2. Ornamental shrubs. I. Kelly, John.
II. Hillier manual of trees & shrubs.
SB435.H54 1997
635.9'77--dc21 97-4282

Book design by Michael Whitehead and Ian Muggeridge
Line illustrations by Coral Mula
Printed in Italy

CONTENTS

How to Use the Guide

Descriptions

The descriptions in the following guide have, where possible, been based on typical plants growing in the United Kingdom. Many, however, originated and are widely available in North America. Because of natural variations in species and varieties, such key characteristics as leaf shape, color and texture, flower color, occurrence of flower and fruit, growth habit, and autumn color may differ (within the limitations of the species) from those described. Autumn colors are particularly influenced by various local and seasonal conditions, but some clones of a species are more reliable than others.

Genus descriptions The genus heading provides the genus name, family name, and common name (when it applies to the whole genus) in the following style:

Acer *Aceraceae*
Maple

The genus description sets out distinctive generic characteristics, including size, period of bloom, flower and leaf characteristics, hardiness tolerance, soil preferences, pruning advice, and the region of origin. Where no information is given on a particular subject, it may be assumed that no relevant information exists on that topic for that plant.

Plant descriptions The plant heading may describe a species, subspecies, variety, form, cultivar, or hybrid. It includes the common name in parentheses when specific to the species in the following style:

A. saccharum (Sugar maple)

When a plant has a synonym it is included in the plant description (*see p.9*). The plant description details the characteristics for which the plant is renowned and any special growing descriptions that differ from those of the genus (in the case of a species) and from those of the species (in the case of subspecies, varieties, forms, cultivars, and hybrids). The plant is denoted as deciduous or evergreen only when the genus comprises a mix of evergreen and deciduous specimens; refer otherwise to the genus description. Region of origin and date of introduction into Western gardens are given when known; when this information is not available, the guide gives the earliest known date of cultivation. Finally, the plant description includes a hardiness zone ratings based on the Plant Hardiness Zone Map published in 1990 by the United States Department of Agriculture (USDA) and the plant hardiness map from Agriculture Canada.

The flaming orange-red blossom color of this *Rhododendron* 'Balzac' is typical of many of the Exbury azaleas.

Heights The ultimate height of a tree or shrub depends on a number of key factors, including soil, siting, local weather conditions, and seasonal variations. The following scale defines the terms *large, medium,* and *small* as used throughout the guide and indicates the probable range of heights for each plant grown under average conditions. However, allowances must be made for specimens growing in shade, against walls, and in any other exceptional growing conditions.

Trees

Large	over 60 ft (18 m)
Medium	35 to 60 ft (10 to 18 m)
Small	up to 35 ft (10 m)

Shrubs

Large	over 10 ft (3 m)
Medium	6 to 10 ft (1.5 to 3 m)
Small	3 to 5 ft (1 to 1.5 m)
Dwarf	1 to $2^1/_2$ ft (30 cm to 75 cm)
Prostrate	creeping

Seasons and months Within the continent of North America, each region experiences spring and fall at different times of the calendar year. For this reason, the guide employs the widely used seasonal system that requires the reader to apply experience gained from knowledge of local weather patterns and seasonality to roughly allocate a period of the calendar year to each of the four seasons, and within those seasons to subdivide further into early, mid-, and late. Once understood, this system allows the most accurate application of seasonally relevant information over the widest area.

Award of Garden Merit 🏆 In Britain the Award of Garden Merit (AGM) is given by the Royal Horticultural Society to recognize plants of outstanding excellence for garden use. The AGM is of practical value for gardeners in that it highlights exceptional plants among the tens of thousands currently offered in the international horticultural trade.

Hardiness The hardiness of plants is a subject full of pitfalls, surprises, disappointments, and exceptions to the rule. In this book, hardiness in North America is rated according to two maps *(see pp.14–15)*: the USDA Plant Hardiness Zone Map and the official Canadian map developed by Agriculture Canada. The USDA map, which covers the United States, plus Canada and Mexico, divides the countries into 11 zones dependent on their minimum temperatures, zone 1 being the coldest and zone 11 being frost-free. Only the United States portion of the USDA map is shown here because the Canadian map — with its 10 zones, most of which are further subdivided into *a* (colder) and *b* (warmer) regions — is widely used in Canadian nurseries and publications. The two maps overlap occasionally but generally are different. Be sure you know which map is being referred to when selecting plants for your garden.

Every plant in the guide is given a hardiness rating that indicates its ability to survive in a particular environment given average conditions. Exceptional weather conditions or unusual sites may cause discrepancies.

For example, a plant in zone 4 that is generally hardy may be encouraged into growth by a midwinter thaw, only to be killed back with the return of cold weather. This is particularly common in areas just east of the Rockies, where warm chinook winds can raise the temperature from well below freezing to a springlike high in a few hours. In addition to cold killing new growth, the soil is still frozen and water lost by developing leaves cannot be replaced by the roots. Thus desiccation also plays a part in the plant's demise.

Nomenclature and Classification

Plant nomenclature is controlled by two internationally accepted codes. The botanical names of plants (necessary for both wild and cultivated plants) are covered by the International Code of Botanical Nomenclature, while the use of cultivar and group epithets as well as the names of graft hybrids (required only for cultivated plants) are governed by the International Code of Nomenclature for Cultivated Plants.

As our knowledge of both plant variation and plant relationships has developed, we have been forced to review the earlier classification of many plants. This, along with the application of the "Rule of Priority" (that is, the obligatory use of the earliest legitimate name), has necessitated a number of name changes over the years. Not all of these changes have been accepted in the guide, but when a plant has been renamed, it also appears under its old name with a cross-reference referring the reader to the new name for full information. The old name is generally included as a synonym *(see p.9)* after the new name.

Use of Botanical Names in the Guide

The conventions governing the naming of plants may appear complex, but they are in fact extremely logical and intuitive once some basic principles are grasped. A full treatment of the subject can be found on p.80; for now, however, it will suffice to understand the significance of the various elements of a given plant name.

Plants are referred to scientifically by at least two names, generally written in italics. The first name, which is always written with an initial capital, is that of the genus (plural, *genera*), a group of related species that share various characteristics. The second is the species name, or specific epithet. Members of a species are closely related and often very similar.

Genera are themselves classified into groupings called families on the basis of botanical similarities that are often not immediately apparent to the gardener. Indeed, some families contain genera with quite different external characteristics: the Caprifoliaceae, for example, includes such outwardly dissimilar plants as *Abelia*, *Lonicera*, and *Viburnum*.

Throughout the guide, certain typestyles have been used consistently to denote the hierarchical ordering of plant name elements, and these are reproduced below:

Acer	genus name
Aceraceae	family name
Maple	genus common name
Acer saccharum	species
(Sugar maple)	species common name

Subspecies, varietas, and forma In nature, species often show greater or lesser degrees of variation in character, and these variants are denoted by a third scientific name. The botanically recognized subdivisions of a species (that is, distinct forms occurring in the wild) are the **subspecies (subsp.)**, the **varietas (var.)**, and the **forma (f.)**, denoted in the guide in the following style:

Acer saccharum* subsp. *grandidentatum	subspecies
Acer grosseri* var. *hersii	varietas
Acer rufinerve* f. *albolimbatum	forma

(Note: Although varietas is a recognized botanical category, the term *variety* is often used to refer to a varietas or cultivar, and by the same token the botanical category forma is not to be confused with the term *form*, often used colloquially to refer to a variety, subspecies, or cultivar.)

Groups, cultivars, and specific hybrids In status, the group falls somewhere between the botanical subdivisions of the species and the cultivar. Whereas a cultivar (from *culti*vated *var*iety) should show little or no variation from plant to plant, the members of a group can vary considerably. Cultivars are distinct forms, often with considerable horticultural merit for their flower color, attractive leaf form, or some other garden-worthy characteristic. Selected either from the wild or from garden plants, they are grown in cultivation and their characteristics are maintained by controlled propagation. Cultivars can also be produced as the result of deliberately crossing two or more related plants. The product of interbreeding between two species of the same genus is called a specific hybrid or specific cross, and the resulting offspring normally shows characteristics from both parents. The hybrid plant is given a new Latin name preceded by "×" (cross); for example, *Gleditsia* × *texana* is a specific hybrid of *Gleditsia aquatica* and *Gleditsia triacanthos*. These subdivisions are indicated in the following style:

***Acer saccharinum* Laciniatum group**	group
***Acer saccharinum* 'Lutescens'**	cultivar
Acer* × *hillieri	specific hybrid

Synonyms One consequence of the continuing reclassification of plants is that many names by which they were previously known are now no longer valid. These old names, together with names not accepted in the guide, are shown in italics after the accepted name and prefixed by the abbreviation *syn.*

Acer maximowiczianum, syn. *A. nikoense*	synonym

ABBREVIATIONS

Genus and species names These are abbreviated to an initial capital (for the genus) and lowercase letter (for the species) after their first mention; in order to establish the full name, refer back to the first preceding generic or specific name beginning with that letter. For example:

Paeonia *Paeoniaceae*
Peony

***P.* × *lemoinii* 'Chromatella'**
(the *P.* refers to the generic name *Paeonia*)

***P.* × *l.* 'Souvenir de Maxime Cornu'**
(the *P.* refers to the generic name *Paeonia* and the *l.* to the specific name *lemoinii*)

General abbreviations

c	circa
yd	yard
ft	foot
in	inch
m	meter
cm	centimeter
mm	millimeter
sp	species (singular)
spp	species (plural)
subsp	subspecies (singular)
subspp	subspecies (plural)
var	variety
cv	cultivar
cvs	cultivars (plural)
f	form

GLOSSARY

Acicular Needle-shaped
Acuminate Tapering at the end, long-pointed
Acute Sharp-pointed
Adpressed Lying close and flat against
Alternate (Leaves) borne singly at each node on opposite sides of the stem
Anther Pollen-bearing part of the stamen
Aristate Bearded, bristle-tipped
Articulate Jointed
Ascending Rising somewhat obliquely and curving upward
Auricle Ear-shaped projection or appendage
Auriculate Shaped like an ear
Awl-shaped Tapering from the base to a slender and stiff point
Axil Angle formed by a leaf or lateral branch with the stem, or that formed by a vein with the midrib
Axillary Produced in the axil
Bearded Furnished with long or stiff hairs
Berry Strictly a pulpy, normally several-seeded, indehiscent fruit
Bifid Divided in two by a deep cleft
Bipinnate Twice pinnate
Bisexual Both male and female organs in the same flower
Blade Expanded part of a leaf or petal
Bloom A fine, powderlike, waxy deposit
Bole Trunk, of a tree
Bract Modified, usually reduced leaf at the base of a flower stalk, flower cluster, or shoot
Bullate Blistered or puckered
Calcareous Containing carbonate of lime or limestone; chalky or limy
Calyx Outer part of a flower, the sepals
Campanulate Bell-shaped
Capitate Headlike, collected in a dense cluster
Capsule Dry, several-celled pod
Catkin Normally dense spike or spikelike raceme of tiny, scaly-bracted flowers or fruits
Ciliate Fringed with hairs
Cladode Flattened leaflike stem
Clone Group of individuals derived originally from a single specimen and maintained in cultivation by vegetative propagation. All cloned specimens are exactly alike and identical to the original. The majority of cultivars are clonal in origin and are normally propagated vegetatively.
Columnar Tall and cylindrical or tapering
Compound Composed of two or more similar parts
Compressed Flattened
Conical Cone-shaped
Cordate Shaped like a heart (leaf base)
Coriaceous Leathery
Corolla Inner, normally conspicuous part of a flower, the petals
Corymb Flat-topped or dome-shaped flower head with the outer flowers opening first
Corymbose Having flowers in corymbs
Crenate Toothed with shallow, rounded teeth; scalloped
Crenulate Minutely crenate
Cultivar Cultivated variety selected either from wild or garden plants and produced and maintained by propagation
Cuneate Wedge-shaped
Cuspidate Abruptly sharp-pointed
Cyme Flat-topped or dome-shaped flower head with the inner flowers opening first
Cymose Having flowers in cymes
Deciduous (Of tree or shrub) that sheds its leaves each year at the end of the period of growth; not persistent
Decumbent Reclining, the tips ascending
Decurrent Extending down the stem
Deltoid Triangular
Dentate Toothed with teeth directed outward
Denticulate Minutely dentate
Depressed Flattened from above
Diffuse Loosely or widely spreading
Digitate With the members arising from one point like fingers (as in a digitate leaf)
Dioecious Bearing male and female flowers on different plants
Dissected Divided into many narrow segments
Distichous Arranged in two vertical ranks
Divaricate Spreading far apart
Divergent Spreading
Divided Separated to the base
Double (Flowers) with more than the usual number of petals, often with the style and stamens changed to petals
Doubly serrate Large teeth and small teeth alternating
Downy Covered with soft hair or down
Elliptic Widest at or about the middle, narrowing equally at both ends
Elongate Lengthened
Emarginate With a shallow notch at the apex
Entire Undivided and without teeth
Evergreen Remaining green during winter
Exfoliating Peeling off in thin strips
Falcate Sickle-shaped
Fascicle Dense cluster
Fastigiate With branches erect and close together
Ferruginous Rust-colored
Fertile Of stamens producing good pollen or fruit containing good seeds, or of stems with flowering organs
Filament Stalk of a stamen
Filiform Threadlike
Fimbriate Fringed
Flexuous Wavy or zigzag
Floccose Clothed with flocks of soft hair or wool
Florets Small, individual flowers of a dense inflorescence
Floriferous Flower-bearing, usually used to indicate profuse flowering
Gibbous Swollen, usually at the base (as in corolla)
Glabrous Hairless, smooth
Glandular With secreting organs
Glaucous Covered with a bloom; bluish white or bluish gray
Glutinous Sticky
Hastate Shaped like a spearhead
Hermaphrodite Bisexual, bearing both male and female organs in the same flower
Hirsute With rather coarse or stiff hairs
Hispid Beset with rigid hairs or bristles
Hoary Covered with a close whitish or grayish white pubescence
Hybrid Plant resulting from a cross between different species
Imbricate Overlapping, as tiles on a roof
Impressed Sunken (as in veins)
Incised Sharply and usually deeply and irregularly cut
Indehiscent (Of fruits) that do not (burst) open
Indumentum Dense hairy covering
Inflorescence Flowering part of the plant
Internode Portion of stem between two nodes or joints
Involucre Whorl of bracts surrounding a flower or flower cluster
Keel Central ridge

Lacerate Torn; irregularly cut or cleft
Laciniate Cut into narrow-pointed lobes
Lanceolate Lance-shaped, widening above the base and long-tapering to the apex
Lanuginous Woolly or cottony
Lateral On or at the side
Lax Loose
Leaflet Part of a compound leaf
Linear Long and narrow with nearly parallel margins
Lip One of the parts of an unequally divided flower
Lobe Any protruding part of an organ (as in leaf, corolla, or calyx)
Lustrous Shining
Membranous Thin and rather soft
Midrib Central vein or rib of a leaf
Monoecious Bearing male and female flowers separately, but on the same plant
Monotypic Of a single species (genus)
Mucronate Terminated abruptly by a spiny tip
Nectary Nectar-secreting gland, usually a small pit or protuberance
Node Point on the stem where the leaves are attached, the "joint"
Nut Nonsplitting, one-seeded, hard or bony fruit
Oblanceolate Inversely lanceolate
Oblique Unequal-sided
Oblong Longer than it is broad, with nearly parallel sides
Obovate Inversely ovate
Obtuse Blunt (as in apex of leaf or petal)
Opposite (Leaves) borne two to each node, opposite each other
Orbicular Almost circular in outline
Oval Broadest at the middle
Ovary Basal "box" part of the pistil, containing the ovules
Ovate Broadest below the middle
Ovule Female germ cell in flowering plant
Palmate Lobed or divided in handlike fashion, usually five- or seven-lobed
Panicle Branching raceme
Paniculate Bearing flowers in panicles
Parted Cut or cleft almost to the base
Pea flower Shaped like a sweet-pea blossom
Pectinate Comblike (of leaf margin)
Pedicel Stalk of an individual flower in an inflorescence
Peduncle Stalk of a flower cluster or of a solitary flower
Pellucid Clear, transparent (as in gland)
Pendulous Hanging, weeping
Perfoliate Of leaves in pairs fused at the base whose stem appears to pass through them
Perianth Calyx and corolla together; also commonly used for a flower in which there is no distinction between corolla and calyx
Persistent Remaining attached
Petal One of the separate segments of a corolla
Petaloid Petallike (as in stamen)
Petiole Leaf stalk
Pilose With long, soft, straight hairs
Pinnate With leaflets arranged on either side of a central stalk
Pinnatifid Cleft or parted in a pinnate way
Pistil Female organ of a flowering plant comprising ovary, style, and stigma
Plumose Feathery, as the down of a thistle
Pollen Spores or grains contained in the anther, containing the male element
Polygamous Bearing bisexual and unisexual flowers on the same plant
Procumbent Lying or creeping
Prostrate Lying flat on the ground
Pruinose Bloomy
Puberulent Minutely pubescent
Pubescent Covered with short, soft hairs; downy
Punctate With translucent or colored dots or depressions
Pungent Ending in a stiff, sharp point; also acid (to the taste) or strong-smelling
Pyramidal Pyramid-shaped (broad at the base and tapering to a point)
Raceme Simple elongated inflorescence with stalked flowers
Racemose Bearing flowers in racemes
Rachis Axis bearing flowers or leaflets
Recurved Curved downward or backward
Reflexed Abruptly turned downward
Reniform Kidney-shaped
Reticulate Like a network (as in veins)
Retuse Round-ended with central notch
Revolute Rolled backward; margin rolled under (as in leaf)
Rib Prominent vein in a leaf
Rotund Nearly circular
Rufous Reddish brown
Rugose Wrinkled or rough
Runner Trailing shoot taking root at the nodes
Sagittate Shaped like an arrowhead
Scabrous Rough to the touch
Scale Minute leaf or bract, or a flat glandlike appendage on the surface of a leaf, flower, or shoot
Scandent With climbing stems
Scarious Thin and dry, not green
Semievergreen Normally evergreen but losing some or all of its leaves in a cold winter or cold area
Sepal One of the segments of a calyx
Serrate Saw-toothed (teeth pointing forward)
Serrulate Minutely serrate
Sessile Attached without a stalk
Setose Clothed with bristles
Sheath Tubular envelope
Shrub Woody plant that branches from the base with no obvious trunk
Simple (Of a leaf or an unbranched inflorescence) that is not compound
Sinuate Strongly waved (as in leaf margin)
Sinus Recess or space between two lobes or divisions of a leaf, calyx, or corolla
Spathulate Spoon-shaped
Spicate Flowers in spikes
Spike Simple, elongated inflorescence with sessile flowers
Spine Sharp-pointed end of a leaf or branch
Spur Tubular projection from a flower; short, stiff branchlet
Stamen Male organ of a flowering plant comprising filament and anther
Staminode Sterile stamen, or structure resembling a stamen, sometimes petallike
Standard Largest, normally uppermost petal in a pea flower; tall, clear-stemmed young tree; shrub (often rose) trained in this fashion
Stellate Star-shaped
Stigma Summit of the pistil that receives the pollen, often sticky or feathery
Stipule Appendage (normally two) at the base of some petioles
Stolon Shoot at or below the surface of the ground that produces a new plant at its tip
Striate With fine, longitudinal lines
Strigose Clothed with flattened, fine, bristlelike hairs
Style Middle part of the pistil, often elongated between the ovary and stigma
Subulate Awl-shaped
Succulent Juicy, fleshy, soft, and thickened in texture
Sucker Vertical shoot growing from plant roots or stems where no buds are present; also shoot from the stock of a grafted plant
Tendril Twining threadlike appendage
Tepal Subdivision of a perianth that cannot be clearly differentiated into sepal or petal
Ternate In threes
Tessellated Mosaic-like (as in veins)
Tomentose With dense, woolly pubescence
Tomentum Dense covering of matted hairs
Tree Woody plant that normally produces a single trunk and an elevated head of branches
Trifoliate Three-leaved
Trifoliolate Leaf with three separate leaflets
Truncate Cut short (of leaf base)
Turbinate Top-shaped
Type Strictly the original (type) specimen, but often used in a general sense to indicate the typical form in cultivation
Umbel Normally flat-topped inflorescence in which the pedicels or peduncles all arise from a common point
Umbellate With flowers in umbels
Undulate With wavy margins
Unisexual Of one sex
Urceolate Urn-shaped
Velutinous Clothed with a velvety indumentum
Venation Arrangement of veins
Verrucose Having a wartlike or nodular surface
Verticillate Arranged in a whorl or ring
Villous Bearing long, soft hairs
Viscid Sticky
Whorl Three or more flowers or leaves arranged in a ring

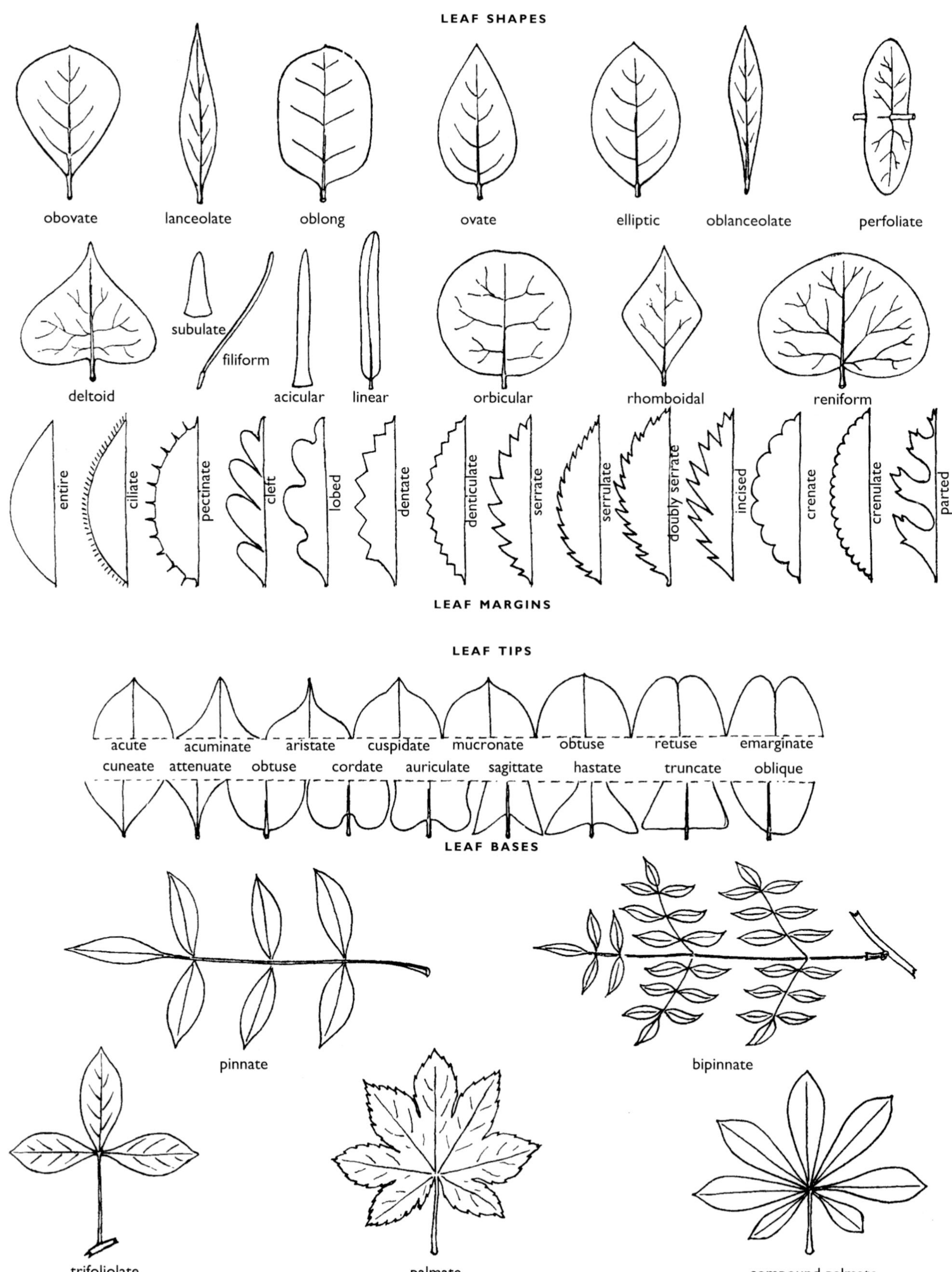
LEAF SHAPES
obovate
lanceolate
oblong
ovate
elliptic
oblanceolate
perfoliate
deltoid
subulate
filiform
acicular
linear
orbicular
rhomboidal
reniform
entire
ciliate
pectinate
cleft
lobed
dentate
denticulate
serrate
serrulate
doubly serrate
incised
crenate
crenulate
parted
LEAF MARGINS
LEAF TIPS
acute
acuminate
aristate
cuspidate
mucronate
obtuse
retuse
emarginate
cuneate
attenuate
obtuse
cordate
auriculate
sagittate
hastate
truncate
oblique
LEAF BASES
pinnate
bipinnate
trifoliolate
palmate
compound palmate

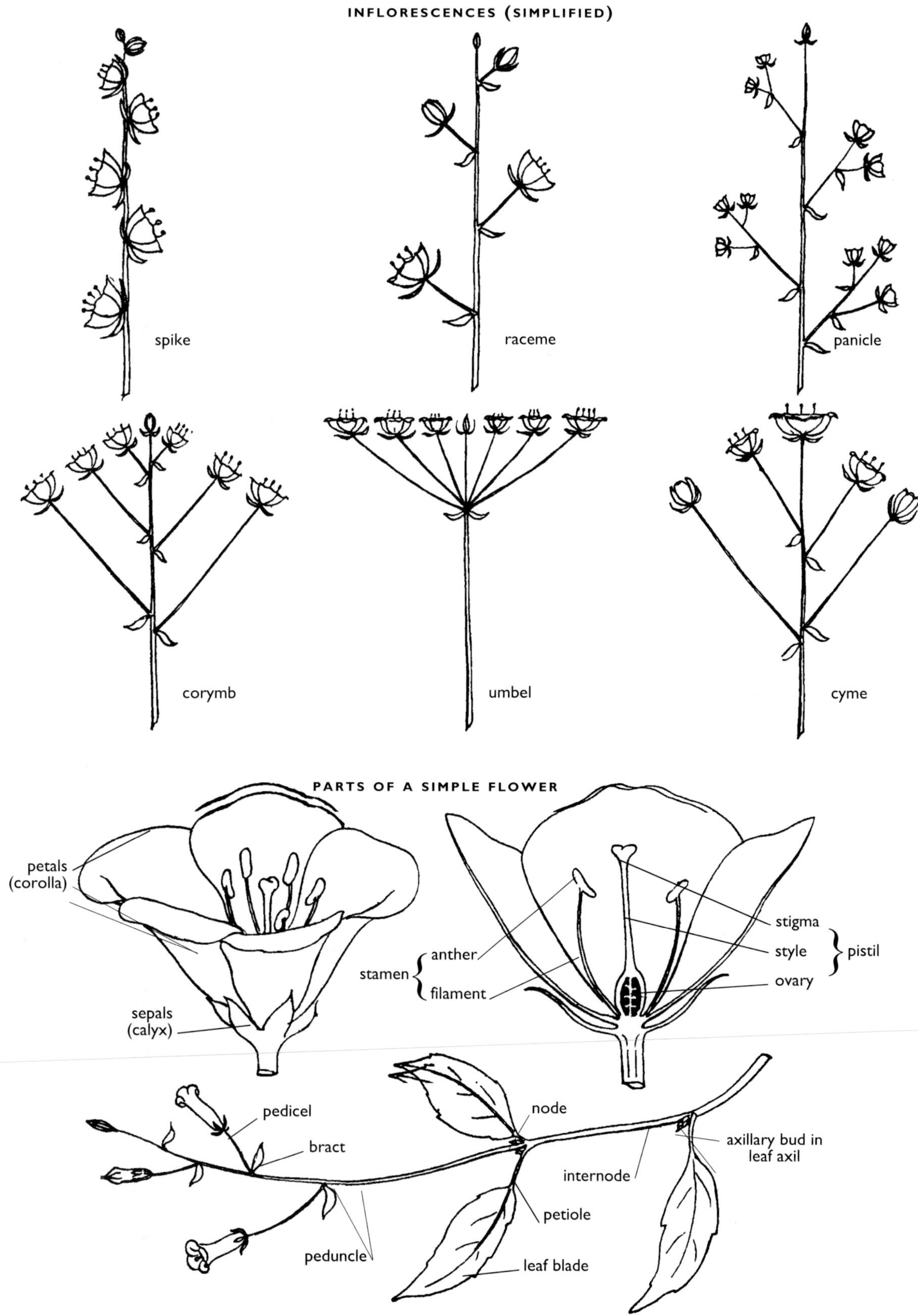
INFLORESCENCES (SIMPLIFIED)
spike
raceme
panicle
corymb
umbel
cyme
PARTS OF A SIMPLE FLOWER
petals (corolla)
sepals (calyx)
stamen
anther
filament
stigma
style
ovary
pistil
pedicel
bract
peduncle
node
internode
petiole
leaf blade
axillary bud in leaf axil

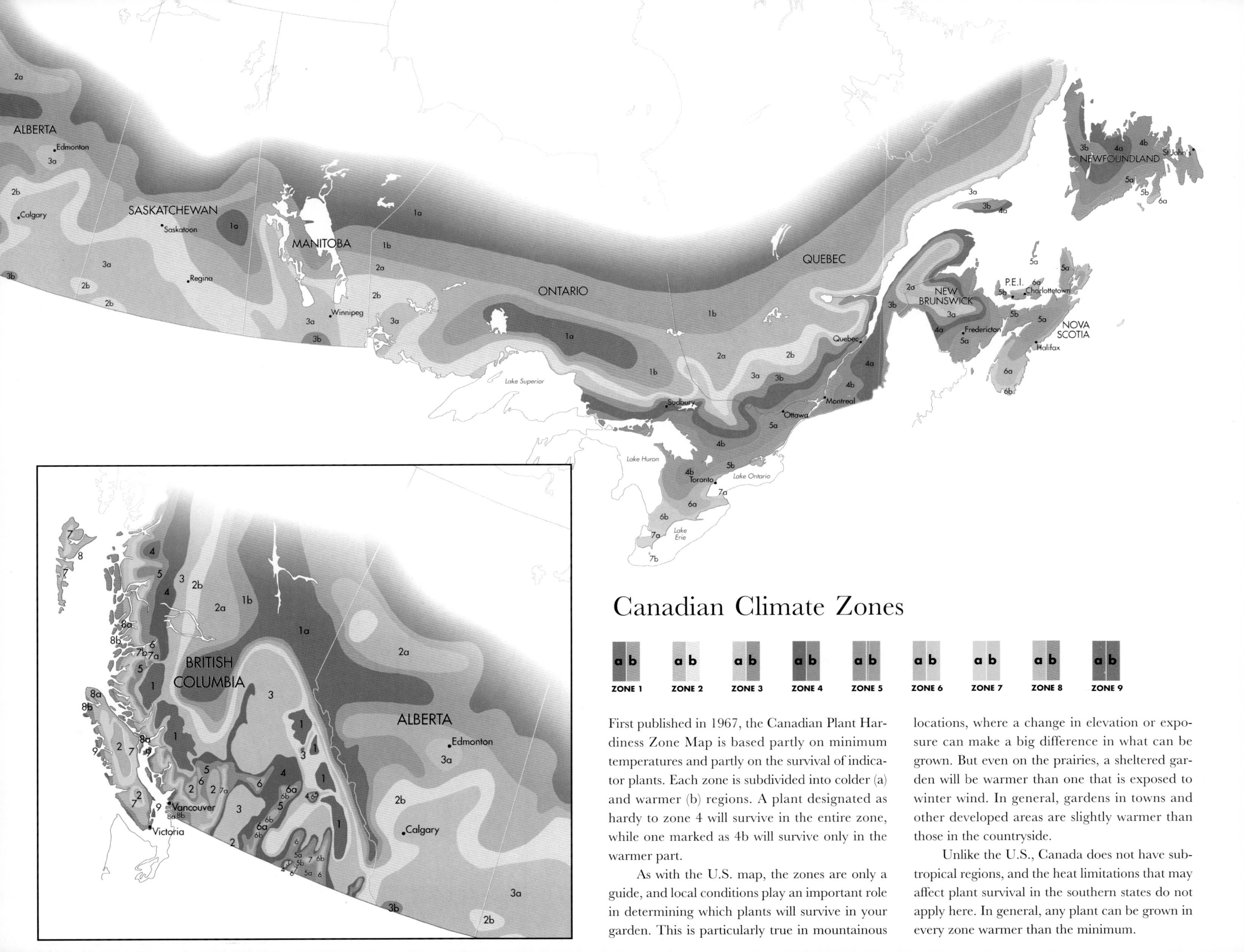

Canadian Climate Zones

First published in 1967, the Canadian Plant Hardiness Zone Map is based partly on minimum temperatures and partly on the survival of indicator plants. Each zone is subdivided into colder (a) and warmer (b) regions. A plant designated as hardy to zone 4 will survive in the entire zone, while one marked as 4b will survive only in the warmer part.

As with the U.S. map, the zones are only a guide, and local conditions play an important role in determining which plants will survive in your garden. This is particularly true in mountainous locations, where a change in elevation or exposure can make a big difference in what can be grown. But even on the prairies, a sheltered garden will be warmer than one that is exposed to winter wind. In general, gardens in towns and other developed areas are slightly warmer than those in the countryside.

Unlike the U.S., Canada does not have subtropical regions, and the heat limitations that may affect plant survival in the southern states do not apply here. In general, any plant can be grown in every zone warmer than the minimum.

U. S. Climate Zones

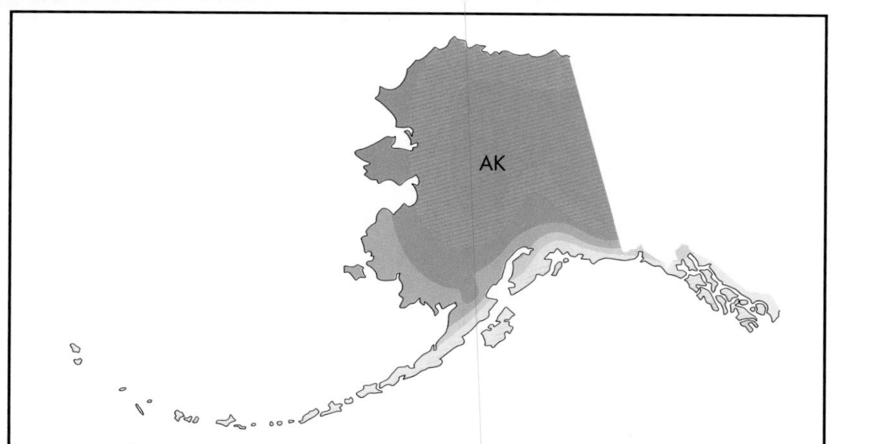

Published in 1990, this hardiness map was developed by the U.S. Department of Agriculture; it replaces an earlier version published in 1965 and a hardiness map developed by the Arnold Arboretum in 1967. It is becoming the standard used in the trade, but some nurseries and books may still use one of the older versions.

Each hardiness zone is based on average minimum winter temperatures, and the plants in this book are zoned accordingly. The map, however, is only a guide. Microclimates within each zone may mean you can grow plants from a warmer zone, or conversely, some plants hardy to your zone may not survive in your garden. This is particularly true toward the upper and lower limits of each zone. In addition, the zone boundaries blend into one another — there is no definite line indicating where a particular plant can or cannot be grown.

Summer heat and humidity can also limit the ability of a plant to survive, especially plants that tolerate very low temperatures. This is much harder to predict, and a zone map based on maximum temperatures has not yet been devised. Local nurseries and other gardeners can advise you if a hardy plant will survive hot summers.

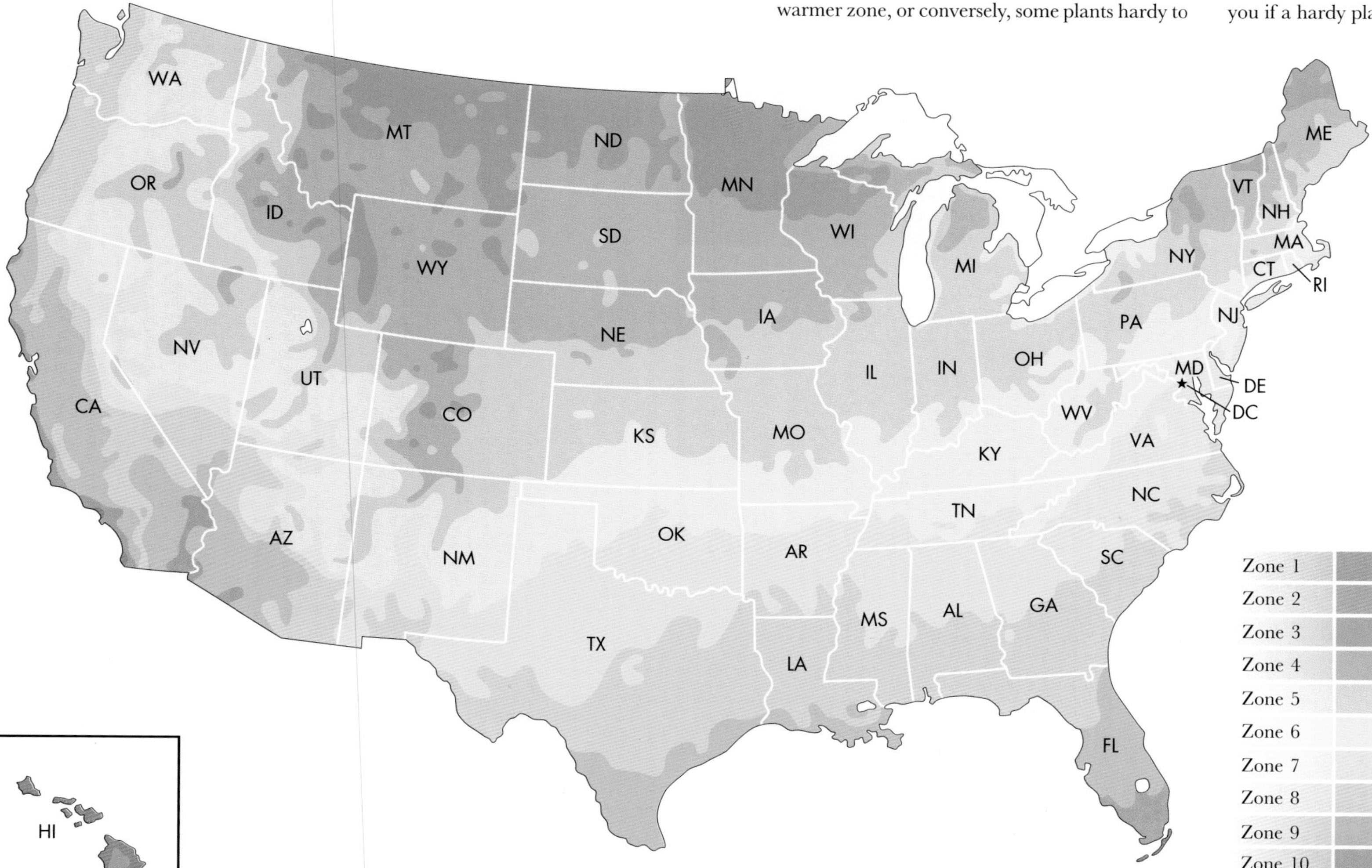

	Fahrenheit	Celsius
Zone 1	below -50°	below -46°
Zone 2	-50° to -40°	-46° to -40°
Zone 3	-40° to -30°	-40° to -34°
Zone 4	-30° to -20°	-34° to -29°
Zone 5	-20° to -10°	-29° to -23°
Zone 6	-10° to 0°	-23° to -18°
Zone 7	0° to 10°	-18° to -12°
Zone 8	10° to 20°	-12° to -7°
Zone 9	20° to 30°	-7° to -1°
Zone 10	30° to 40°	-1° to 4°
Zone 11	above 40°	above 4°

INTRODUCTION

IF YOU WANT TO CREATE A GARDEN FOR A YEAR, THEN FILL THE BORDERS WITH FLOWERS. BUT IF YOU WANT TO CREATE A GARDEN FOR A LIFETIME, THEN PLANT IT WITH TREES AND SHRUBS. ONE OF the delights of trees and shrubs is that they let a garden develop from year to year rather than merely repeat itself. As a leaf canopy fills out or a tree gains in height, new focal points appear, views change, and the character of the garden matures. Trees and shrubs add a new dimension to the garden, allowing leaves, flowers, and fruit to be carried far above the heights that can be reached by the soft stems of herbaceous perennials, and lift the garden from the limitations of the flower border.

The characteristic woodiness of trees and shrubs, which allows these plants to remain above ground long after herbaceous plants have retreated, provides a garden with its permanent framework not only from year to year but also throughout the year. In a bare winter garden the mere presence of the tree skeleton — perhaps with elegant boughs or brilliant bark — is pleasure enough, but there is also a host of bonuses. Long-lived woody plants provide the garden with an enormous range of interest throughout the year: from the wonderful scent of the winter flowers of witch hazel borne on naked stems, through the flamboyant blooms of spring viburnum and summer hydrangea, to the dazzling leaf displays of Japanese maple in fall.

Woody plants — trees and shrubs — dominate and control the garden. On gaining maturity they often define it much more surely than the shape of the land itself and may encompass the garden so thoroughly that an entirely new, private world is created. To a large extent they determine the climate of the garden and, to an overwhelming degree, its microclimates. By providing shelter from wind, they allow a wider range of plants to be grown, and by casting shade in varying degrees, from the dense shadow of a holly or rhododendron to the dappled shade found under an oak tree, they influence the choice of plant material.

The qualities of atmosphere and mood created by trees and shrubs are almost infinitely variable, not merely because of the effect on them of such things as the weather, the season, and the time of day. Gardeners should be as aware of the intangible, mood-creating attributes of woody plants as they are of their tangible ones and plan for these effects. It is only with trees and shrubs that such long-term considerations come into play, so the gardener needs to spend some time learning about the characteristics of individual plants.

Above The bare outline of a well-established oak makes a powerful impact when little other plant life is above ground on a foggy winter's day. *Opposite* When summer is over, this *Betula pendula* 'Youngii' will still provide a focal point of interest because of its magnificent branch structure and bark.

Having evolved for over 100 million years and adapted to a variety of different habitats, trees and shrubs provide today's gardeners with an unbelievable selection of plants drawn from all over the world. Their ability to produce wood tissue within their cells has allowed trees and shrubs to reach high above other plants to compete for sunlight. All green plants produce their own food by taking energy from sunlight, carbon dioxide from the air, and water and nutrients from the soil. Then within the chlorophyll, a green pigment found in leaves, they produce carbohydrates, giving off oxygen as a by-product. This self-contained factory has enabled plants to colonize all but the harshest regions of the world, and it has enabled trees, in particular, to excel in the art of survival. Trees and shrubs have the unique ability to produce a living framework of wood tissue, where energy produced throughout the growing season can be stored, enhancing survival throughout severe climatic conditions. This stored energy is also used for the formation of trunks, branches, stems, shoots, new leaves, roots, and, on reaching sexual maturity, flowers.

Our gardens today are a mix of plants that have been collected from many regions of the world, and today's gardeners owe much to the plant collectors who scoured the earth in search of nature's treasures. From the early 1600s until the mid-1900s, plant collectors, funded by botanical gardens or famous nurseries, actively sought plants from the temperate zones of the world. Such dedicated plant hunters as Robert Fortune, Sir Joseph Hooker, Ernest Wilson, George Forrest, and Frank Kingdon-Ward have provided gardeners with specimens from across the globe. China and the Himalayas have yielded a tremendous volume of new plant material. Other countries have also offered great treasures, as expeditions widened to Japan, Chile, Korea, Europe, and Russia, and contributed plants to the almost unbelievable range that we see today. Modern plant collectors are constantly exploring new areas in search of garden-worthy plants. New acquisitions are complemented by new forms produced by plant breeders throughout the world, creating a supply of plants that is truly global. Garden centers and nurseries now have the ability, skill, and systems to bring a diverse and breathtaking supply of high-quality and affordable plants virtually to our doorsteps.

Tree and shrub definitions

The principal difference between a tree and a shrub is that the former has a distinct main stem, or trunk, branching some significant distance from the ground, while the latter consists of a number of stems arising at or close to ground level. Apart from this formal definition, the word *tree* has other implications. It suggests an altogether larger plant, evoking a mental picture of a certain massiveness of structure — a thick, more or less tapering, tall trunk; heavy load-bearing branches; and a high, substantial canopy of foliage.

For most of us, "tree" means a big, leafy, imposing presence, while the words *shrub* and *scrub* are not very far apart. For a great many of us, the climates in which we live have encouraged the development of large forest trees on the one hand and short, scrubby shrubs on the other. It is important to remember, however, that our garden plants are gathered from all over the world; in some places shrubs grow as large as many of our native trees, while in others there are trees that are not just small but quite dwarf. Large rhododendrons with multiple stems can easily grow as big as small trees, such as the mountain ash, and demonstrate that the difference between a tree and a shrub is not necessarily one of size. Differences in garden climates also induce changes of habit; what might be thought of as a tree in one garden may be considered a shrub farther north.

Opposite Forsythia exhibits the classic shrublike shape in which a number of stems rise from close to ground level. *Above* A rhododendron illustrates how some shrubs develop the height and trunklike stems that give them treelike proportions.

Generally speaking, we use the terms *tree* and *shrub* in a practical sense, sometimes with little regard to their strict definitions. Thus, in anything but the very smallest garden, trees are the largest plants that dominate the rest and form the uppermost canopy of the garden, while shrubs, occupying a lower level, complement them. In fact, they fulfill subtly different roles.

Trees and shrubs in small gardens

To an extent, all gardens are "small," especially in light of the enormous number of plants available to gardeners. In recent years the choice of plants has greatly increased, as we have experienced a new age of plant hunters and witnessed great advances in the techniques of hybridization and propagation. For example, in its first four editions during the 1970s, *The Hillier Manual of Trees & Shrubs* listed — fairly comprehensively — about 30 cultivars of the Japanese maple *Acer palmatum*. By 1995, *The RHS Plant Finder* (which did not exist in those earlier years) cited an incredible 185.

The gardener is faced with an overwhelming problem of choice. Even the largest garden can hold only a small proportion of the plants available; for the owner of a small garden, selection can seem quite impossible. A good way of setting about the task is to look for plants with more than one main feature. A plant in a small garden needs to give the best account of itself for as much of the year as possible. Anything with pretty flowers for a month or so but ordinary foliage and a dumpy shape should be left for those with more space.

It is, however, too much to hope for — and actually not really desirable — that every plant should live up to the ideal of beautiful flowers, lovely foliage, striking bark, long-lasting berries, and a sweet scent. In practice, two or possibly three attractive features are enough. If there are too many stars, none of them will shine and the garden will become a muddle with too many accents, contrasts, and focal points all defeating one another. For this reason, plain green foliage should not be considered a deficiency. As long as it is combined with an interesting shape or an intangible quality, such as elegance, it will play an important supporting role.

In the small garden, statements should be simple and not repeated too often. Purple foliage, for example, is all too easily overdone; one "purple" accent is usually enough. Even in a large garden, three may be one too many. The use of plants with variegated foliage should be similarly restrained. A single variegated plant combined with plants of differing shades of solid green will provide an accent without losing the restfulness for which any garden, but especially a small one, should be designed.

The best possible combination of features is at its most important when choosing trees. Most small gardens have room for very few trees, and some may be restricted to one. Something such as the Japanese cherry *Prunus* 'Kanzan', which so often appears in gardens far too small for it and has but one short season of stardom, is far from ideal. It would be much better to plant a cherry with the versatility of *Prunus sargentii*, which has daintier flowers and a shining, rich chestnut bark. Its foliage emerges bronze-red, turns green, and then flames into orange and crimson in early fall. It is the smallest of trees, but it is beautiful throughout the year and takes a long time to become at all large.

Finally, the overall shape and outline of a tree or a shrub is as important as any of its other characteristics. For much of the time we see plants in silhouette, and a series of formless shapes can be very uninteresting. The interplay of domed crowns, flat heads of branches, the cones and cylinders of conifers, and the skeletal outlines of deciduous trees in winter can be effectively achieved on any scale from the intimate to the grand.

Trees and Shrubs in This Book

The range of trees and shrubs that can be found in gardens, parks, and arboretums in cool temperate regions is extensive. However, many are found only in large collections, and a number of woody plants are of more academic than horticultural interest. Some, while beautiful and highly desirable, are of such marginal hardiness that they may be destroyed by weather, even in the mildest areas, before they reach the stage at which their aesthetic qualities have properly developed. Of course, such trees and shrubs should be grown, but their inclusion is justified only in very large or academically oriented gardens. This book is concerned primarily with those woody plants that appeal to gardeners, bearing in mind that the selection is inclined toward those that offer the most beauty for the greatest possible part of the year.

Many of the plants in this book have received awards for their garden-worthiness, while those that have not are nevertheless recognized as deserving space in gardens. There are evergreen and deciduous trees and shrubs, climbers, conifers, and bamboos. There are mighty oaks, as well as dwarf conifers that grow as little as a few feet in 30 years. You will find trees and shrubs suitable for the seaside, industrial areas, cold places, and areas deep in shade. There are brilliantly colored leaves, vivid berries, beautiful barks, and sweet, subtle fragrances. Whether you garden in the deepest, best loam or have to contend with less-than-ideal conditions — from impenetrable clay to thin sand — you will find more than enough choices of woody plants with which to create a garden that is truly individually yours.

Prunus sargentii is an excellent tree for the small garden, offering dainty spring flowers *(below left)* followed in fall by striking red and orange foliage *(below right)*. Popular for its fall foliage and graceful leaf shape, *Acer palmatum (opposite)* is becoming available in an increasing number of varieties each year.

Basic Biology

An understanding of the biological characteristics of trees and shrubs and of their growth pattern can only enhance our cultivation skills as we move plants away from their native environments. All plants are native to at least one part of the globe, and to cultivate them successfully we must know their origins and their native environment in order to satisfy each plant's growing requirements in our own gardens.

The origins of plants

All plants are autotrophs, or "self-feeders." In other words, they (along with algae and some bacteria) manufacture their own food or energy by the process of photosynthesis, which involves using sunlight to convert water and carbon dioxide into sugar. That food, in turn, is available to other organisms, called heterotrophs, which depend on plants for their energy; humans, animals, and fungi are typical examples. The first fossil evidence shows that self-feeders colonized the oceans 3.4 billion years ago, but it is possible that primitive organisms with the ability to photosynthesize appeared much earlier. It was not until around 100 million years ago that the first flowering plants began to appear. Once flowering plants colonized the soil, the great diversity that we witness today began to evolve.

FIG. I HOW TREES AND SHRUBS WORK

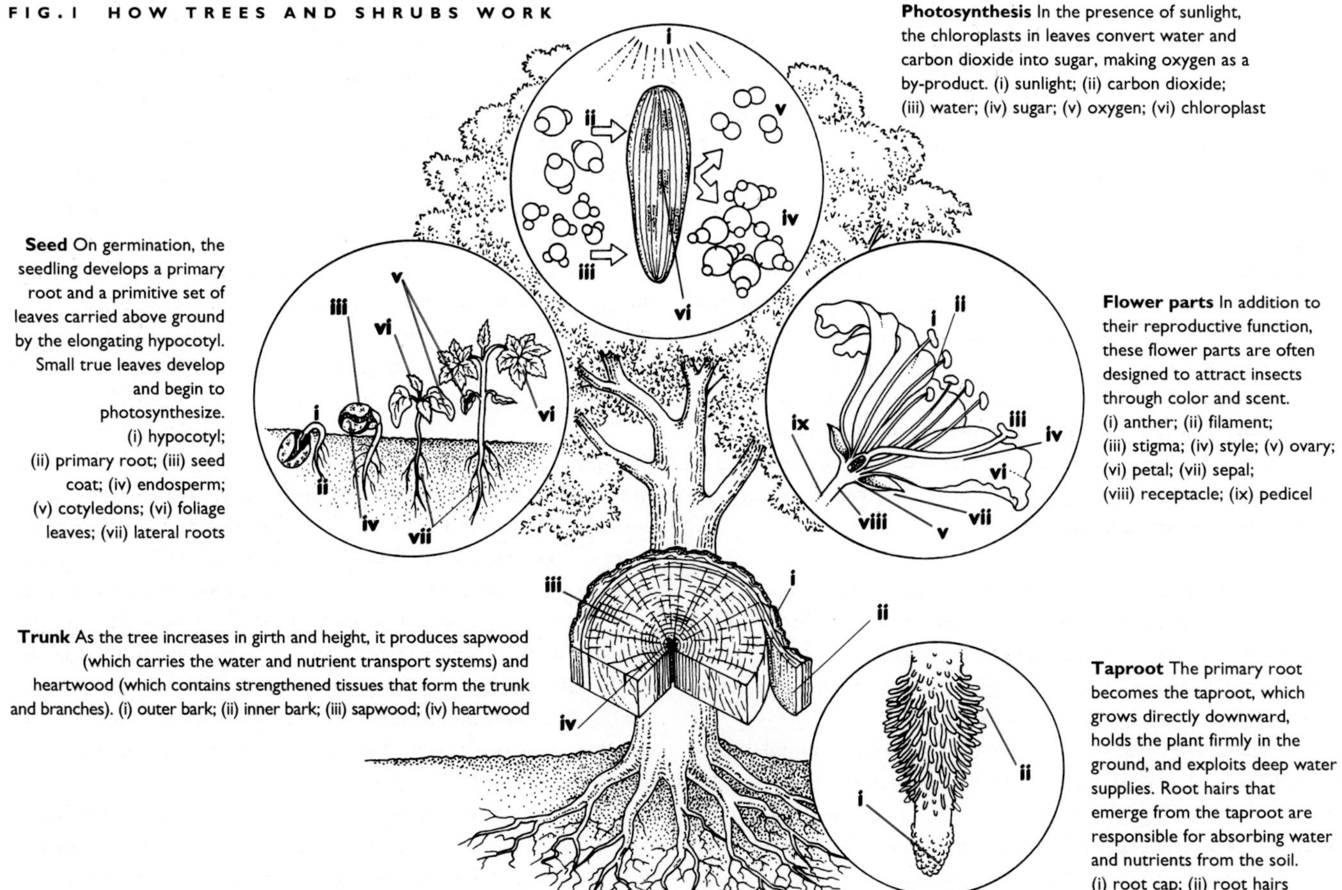

Photosynthesis In the presence of sunlight, the chloroplasts in leaves convert water and carbon dioxide into sugar, making oxygen as a by-product. (i) sunlight; (ii) carbon dioxide; (iii) water; (iv) sugar; (v) oxygen; (vi) chloroplast

Seed On germination, the seedling develops a primary root and a primitive set of leaves carried above ground by the elongating hypocotyl. Small true leaves develop and begin to photosynthesize. (i) hypocotyl; (ii) primary root; (iii) seed coat; (iv) endosperm; (v) cotyledons; (vi) foliage leaves; (vii) lateral roots

Flower parts In addition to their reproductive function, these flower parts are often designed to attract insects through color and scent. (i) anther; (ii) filament; (iii) stigma; (iv) style; (v) ovary; (vi) petal; (vii) sepal; (viii) receptacle; (ix) pedicel

Trunk As the tree increases in girth and height, it produces sapwood (which carries the water and nutrient transport systems) and heartwood (which contains strengthened tissues that form the trunk and branches). (i) outer bark; (ii) inner bark; (iii) sapwood; (iv) heartwood

Taproot The primary root becomes the taproot, which grows directly downward, holds the plant firmly in the ground, and exploits deep water supplies. Root hairs that emerge from the taproot are responsible for absorbing water and nutrients from the soil. (i) root cap; (ii) root hairs

How trees and shrubs work

As gardeners we need to understand how trees and shrubs germinate, develop, and reproduce in order to care for them effectively. The following section is a brief look at the parts and processes of woody plants *(Fig. 1)*.

Germination Most woody plants begin their lives as seeds, which require water, oxygen, and warmth to germinate. They do not usually require sunlight, because at this stage a new plant is not photosynthesizing but rather using stored reserves of sugar within its seed to develop.

On germination, the seedling develops a root and then a primitive set of leaves, which for the first time allows it to produce its own energy. These first "leaves," or cotyledons, are then followed by small true leaves. As the plant develops, so do the transport systems for energy and water. These develop from single cells into a series of tubes running the whole length of the plant. The water and nutrients are transported from the roots to the leaves in the xylem (water transport system), and the energy produced by photosynthesis is transported to the growing points of the plants by the phloem (energy transport system).

Photosynthesis Using solar power to convert the sun's energy into electricity is probably the closest people will ever come to reproducing photosynthesis. Just as we harvest crops, plants harvest water and carbon dioxide in the presence of sunlight, converting them into sugar. The energy state of these compounds is changed so that the chemical bonds are broken and the ions are re-formed into new molecules. This final sugar produced is the plant's food.

Photosynthesis can be broken down into two separate processes: light reaction and carbon dioxide fixation. The first of these occurs when light enters the chloroplast (a single unit of chlorophyll) through the surface of the leaf, creating energy that is used to split water molecules into hydrogen and oxygen to create simple sugars. The oxygen is released back into the atmosphere.

Carbon dioxide fixation is the process by which carbon dioxide is absorbed into the leaf through small openings called stomata. The carbon dioxide then bonds with the processed sugar to make more-elaborate molecules, such as glucose and starch, which are used to feed the growing plant.

Leaves Leaves are the factories of food production in which the plant makes maximum use of the raw materials of sunlight, water, and carbon dioxide. The production of a growing structure above ground enables woody plants to hold their leaves high above competitors and take the lion's share of sunlight.

The shape, size, and foliage pattern of leaves are carefully considered by gardeners in terms of their ornamental value, but the characteristics of leaves are often also the means by which they survive. The needle-shaped leaves of conifers are small, compared with the leaves of deciduous trees, and covered with a tough cuticle to keep water loss to a minimum. This is especially important in winter when frozen ground may make water replacement difficult

In the uncultivated environment of a beech woods, fallen leaves enrich the soil with nutrients and organic matter for the coming year.

or even impossible. Their shape also minimizes the harsh effects of cold winds and sheds snow more easily than do broader leaves. Furthermore, the stomata of conifers are deeply set into the underside of the leaf, again minimizing moisture loss. These simple factors have allowed conifers to survive in harsh environments. These same harsh environments also explain the evergreen nature of most conifers. Quite simply, conifers are indigenous to regions in which a yearly loss of leaves is pointless, since by the time new ones have grown, summer has ended.

Deciduous plants lose their leaves as a response to falling temperatures and lower light levels in order to minimize moisture loss in winter. As their growth slows, the green pigment remaining in the leaves breaks down, leaving the autumnal tints. Once the leaves have fallen, soil organisms break down the remaining tissues into the soil, providing recycled nutrients for our trees and shrubs. In spring, deciduous trees grow new green leaves whose characteristics enable them to excel at photosynthesis and make the most of the long hours of sunshine.

Wood production At the end of the first season following germination, growth begins to slow and energy is stored in the stems and roots. At this point, the inner, actively dividing cambium meristem — the tissue located directly below the bark on trees and shrubs — divides to produce wood on the inner side and bark on the outer side. The wood is made up of fibers called lignin; this strengthens the stem or trunk and creates the woody framework. Bark is developed from fibers of cork, which protect the stem of trees and shrubs from damage and reduce water loss from the stem. As the tree or shrub ages, the cork will split and be replaced by a new layer, giving bark its familiar knobbly texture.

With future development, the tree or shrub will increase in girth and height. In doing so it will produce sapwood (which contains the cambium and the transport systems) and heartwood (which contains strengthened tissues that form the trunk, stems, and branches). This is known as secondary thickening and can be thought of

FIG.2 WOOD PRODUCTION

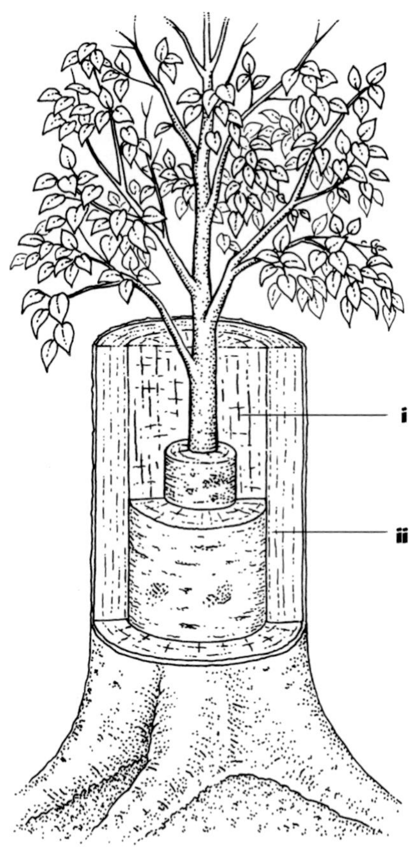

Every growth period, a tree develops new heartwood (i) and sapwood (ii), which envelops the tree like a new skin.

as the woody plant growing a new layer of skin over its entirety, including the roots. It can be clearly seen in the annual rings of temperate woody plants, which display two distinct growth rings: one large ring in the spring, and a smaller one in fall as growth slows down and finally stops.

Water Trees and shrubs have certain requirements for best growth. Gardeners can help with some of these, such as providing water and nutrients.

Water is used in many ways within a plant. It keeps the living cells turgid so that they can carry out their function of producing energy. It also keeps the leaves cool on hot summer days. Water movement within the stems and leaves reduces the risk of damage from freezing, because as water moves out of the plant cells, the remaining sap thickens and has a lower freezing point.

It is estimated that a mature beech tree can absorb 200–300 gal (900–1,200 L) of water per day. This water is transported by an underground system that is made up of two different types of roots. The big structural roots anchor the plant in the soil. At their ends and along their length are tiny absorption roots, called root hairs. These are delicate and brittle and are constantly broken off as the root cap grows through the soil. Root hairs absorb water and nutrients, which are essential to a plant's healthy growth. Once water has been absorbed into the main root system, it moves up the stem into the leaves through the xylem, aiding in the production of energy. Excess water is carried on to the surface of the leaves, where it evaporates and cools the leaves. This process is called transpiration, and the transpiration stream created between the roots and shoots draws more water through the system.

A tree depends on its roots for anchorage and for the uptake of water and nutrients for the stems, branches, and leaves.

The ability to recognize a plant in water stress is important when transplanting or planting. If a plant cannot replace lost water, it will die. During transplanting, particularly of evergreens, it is important to spray the foliage at regular intervals to cool down the leaves until damaged roots hairs have regrown. When planting, it is important to prevent dehydration of both the potting mix in which the plant has been established and the surrounding soil. Leaves should always feel cool during the growing season; if they feel warm, the plant is suffering water stress.

Roots The leaves, branches, and stems of all plants depend on the roots for anchorage, the uptake of water and nutrients, and the storage of food reserves. The extent of the root system depends on the type of plant, its growing environment, and its management through cultivation. The root systems of most plants grow mainly within the top 3 ft (1 m) of soil, with the majority of the absorption roots within the first 6 in (15 cm). The depth of roots is influenced by the availability of water, oxygen, and nutrients and ease of soil penetration. In heavily compacted soils, the lack of oxygen to the roots will force them to grow near the surface, whereas deeply cultivated soils with a high organic content will allow a much deeper root system.

The roots of individual specimen trees may grow two to three times wider than the edge of the leaf canopy. Trees grown in groups, on the other hand, may compete with each other, decreasing the overall extent of the root system. If competition is reduced, roots grow wherever there is sufficient oxygen, moisture, temperature, and nutrients, invariably in directions in which there is the least resistance to the advancing root system.

Tree and shrub root systems are often misunderstood. Willows, poplars, and alders, in particular, are often blamed for developing massive root systems that block drains, lift pavement, or cause problems with the foundations of nearby buildings. In fact, tree root systems will only stray where they are not wanted when they are not provided with satisfactory conditions in their normal root zone. When roots enter a land drain that carries water or grow under pavement on which water condenses or against a building beneath which water collects, they are suddenly provided with perfect conditions. Inevitably, roots exploit this by growing rapidly and, therefore, split or block the drainage pipe, lift the pavement, and exert pressure on the side of a building. If the roots are severed, the new developing roots will soon find their way back to their oasis. The way to prevent problems of this sort is to make the conditions within the normal root zone as inviting as possible, by irrigation, aeration, and fertilization.

The root-to-shoot balance The roots, stems, branches, and leaves of healthy trees and shrubs grow in harmony; there is enough energy being produced by the leaves to support the whole plant, while the root system absorbs sufficient water to support the aboveground tissues. After transplanting shrubs, it is advisable to reduce the leaf area in proportion to the damaged root system *(see p.49)*. Remember to water the plant thoroughly a few weeks before lifting and after transplanting.

Trees react dramatically to damage suffered by roots and shoots. If a tree is damaged in a storm or even heavily pruned, it will use stored energy to replace lost leaf area as quickly as possible. The resulting mass of new shoots arising from the stem are called epicormic or adventitious shoots. Removing these important new shoots will only stimulate the growth of replacements. If the tree does not re-create the balance of shoot to root successfully, areas of the root system may die until the balance is recovered.

Sexual maturity Both trees and shrubs have a period of non-flowering growth before reaching sexual maturity. Some of the tree magnolias, such as *Magnolia campbellii*, may take up to 30 years from seed to flower. This period allows the tree time to attain sufficient height so that it can display its flowers high above its competitors.

Plants consume massive amounts of energy stored within the stems, roots, and shoots in order to produce their flowers. Even during periods of drought, when trees and shrubs may drop some of their flowering buds in order to preserve their energy balance, they will always produce some flowers. This is typical of camellias, which produce thousands of flower buds, some of which simply fail to open and drop to the ground. This is perfectly healthy, and gardeners should simply regard it as a sign of the plant restoring its natural balance. Many species are pruned directly after flowering. This allows the maximum amount of time for the production of more vegetative shoots, thus increasing the area available to store energy for the following season's blooms.

Flowers Living things naturally seek to perpetuate themselves, and plants use up considerable energy to ensure that their species survives. The flowers of some trees are wind-pollinated, and these are usually quite insignificant blooms. However, the majority of trees and shrubs that we cultivate in our gardens carry bold, attractive flowers. These have evolved to attract not gardeners but pollinators. The brightly colored petals of these flowers serve as an advertisement to the right pollinator, whose reward for pollen collection is supplied in the form of nectar.

Flowers are highly complex and have a huge number of individual characteristics. The nature and arrangement of their various parts have enabled botanists to select common features that can be used to place closely related plants into families. While the individual characteristics of a flower vary from species to species, the main parts of a flower are common to all species and serve roughly similar functions.

The flower is connected to the stem by the pedicel or flower stalk, which holds it above the foliage. Before the flower opens, it is protected by the sepals or flower buds. When these open they reveal the brightly colored petals — the plant's attraction to pollinators. On entering the flower the pollinator must take pollen from the male parts (the stamens, which comprise anthers and filament) and pass on the pollen it is already carrying to the female parts (the stigma and style) in order to fertilize the ovary. Once fertilization is complete, the seeds will develop and the plant has ensured its survival by perpetuating its species.

Seeds In the same way that flower production costs the plant dearly in reserves of stored energy, so seed production eats into the plant's energy store. All the elements that the offspring needs to survive until it germinates are present in each seed. As the seed develops on the parent plant, it builds up a store of food within the seed leaves, or cotyledons, which surround the embryo. The seed may be covered in a fruit, which is itself no more than a mechanism to ensure efficient dispersal. In the case of the cherry, for example, the fruits containing the seeds are carried away from the plant by birds. They are eaten, pass unharmed through the host's digestive system, and are then excreted, returning to the soil, where, if conditions are right, they will germinate. From the earliest stage of germination until it develops leaves, the embryonic plant relies totally on reserves of stored energy.

UNDERSTANDING INDIVIDUAL REQUIREMENTS

While all woody plants develop in essentially the same way, their individual requirements for light and shade, water, nutrients, soil, and shelter vary enormously from genus to genus and, indeed, within a particular genus. Today, our gardens play host to millions of plants from all areas of the world. A garden plant is often selected for its ornamental value alone with little consideration given to its native habit. Ideally, plant selection should include other considerations if the specimens are to thrive. Fortunately, most of the trees and shrubs available from garden centers and nurseries have been in cultivation for a long time, and their growth requirements are well understood.

However, new introductions have not endured the test of time and may require careful siting. For example, *Choisya ternata* 'Sundance' is a recently introduced yellow-leaved form of the Mexican orange blossom. Its cultivar name suggests that it likes to "dance" in the sun. However, its lack of chlorophyll means that it scorches if placed in direct sunlight, an environment in which the green-leaved form thrives. A poorly sited, stressed plant will succumb to pests and diseases and be a poor addition to the garden. Therefore it is important to understand your garden's different habitats and microclimates and plant appropriately.

The flamboyant, colorful blooms of deciduous azaleas appeal to many gardeners and also attract insects for pollination.

Theory & Practice

It is tempting to consider only the aesthetic values of trees and shrubs when using them in the garden landscape, looking no further than attractive leaves, beautiful flowers, intricate bark patterns, and a fascinating variety of fruit and seed shapes. However, this is a very small part of the overall picture, as a well-designed and carefully planned garden will do much more than simply look pretty. Trees and shrubs within a garden control the prevailing climate by creating a unique microclimate. This may be achieved quite simply by protecting the garden from cold wind or by cooling the area by providing shade. They also have positive effects on atmospheric pollution and noise, provide increased security, and define boundaries. The first part of this chapter considers the ways in which trees and shrubs contribute in physical ways to the local environment; the second part shows how practical considerations often merge into aesthetics; and the third part focuses on two key practical considerations prior to planting — hardiness and soil requirements.

Physical benefits of trees and shrubs

How many of us stop and think about the shelter and shade that plants provide, their ability to improve the soil by preventing erosion, or the way they trap the dust and pollutants that float in the atmosphere? Just imagine how unbearable life in our cities and towns would be if there were no trees or shrubs.

Pollution We can characterize trees as the lungs of the planet: they release much of the oxygen in our atmosphere as a by-product of photosynthesis and absorb huge volumes of the greenhouse gas carbon dioxide in the process. But trees contribute in other ways to cleaning up the air we breathe.

In treeless cities, the annual dust fall may be as high as 0.03 oz per square yard (850 mg/m^2) per day. A 1-acre (0.5 ha) plantation of spruces can intercept as much as 16 tons of dust in a year. A thick foliage screen, such as a copse or woodland planting, will also effectively filter the air for atmospheric pollutants, accumulating particulate or gaseous material on and sometimes in plant leaves.

Temperature Trees and shrubs cool the air; think of the difference in temperature between a busy city street and a nearby park, which can be several degrees cooler than the surrounding urban environment. This is due not only to a reduction in sunlight but also to increased transpiration. All plants absorb heat as they transpire, and this brings about significant temperature reduction even at relatively low planting densities: it is estimated that a 30 percent cover of vegetation will give two-thirds of the cooling effect of complete plant cover. This natural air-conditioning property is an often overlooked benefit of tree planting.

The lowering of temperatures is accompanied by a rise in relative humidity as water vapor is transferred from the leaf surface to the surrounding atmosphere. The air in towns and cities may be unpleasantly dry; wooded parks and tree-lined streets can increase relative humidity in their immediate vicinity by 18 percent or more, thus contributing to the comfort level as well as providing better air quality and cool surroundings in summer.

Noise reduction Noise is not significantly reduced by the foliage and trunks of trees; the actual amount of sound energy absorbed results in a reduction of only a few decibels. Where trees can help is in concealing the source of the sound, which may bring some relief. In addition, the movement of leaves and branches can disguise other sounds simply by creating distracting "white noise": the rustling leaves of trees such as *Populus tremula* (aspen), for example, can help mask the hum of traffic.

Trees improve the quality of our environment in many ways, such as providing shade and reducing atmospheric pollution.

Soil erosion Large quantities of soil can be eroded if exposed to rain, running water, or wind. Water erosion accounts for the highest loss of topsoil, something that few of us can spare. Trees and shrubs influence soil erosion in two main ways. First, the foliage can intercept raindrops and reduce their impact on the soil. Second, the root systems of trees and shrubs physically bind the soil together, stopping or reducing the runoff caused when particles of soil are picked up by rainwater.

Drainage and nutrients The consistency and moisture content of garden soil are profoundly affected by the trees and shrubs planted in it. On a warm summer's day, hundreds of gallons of water are transferred from the soil via the systems of a large tree to the air by transpiration. This means that a dry soil may become drier, but, more important, it also means that wet soils are rendered less wet. It does not imply, however, that trees by themselves can convert bad drainage to good.

The dropping of deciduous leaves is, in part, nature's way of returning nutrients to the soil. In larger plantings the soil will gradually be changed by the annual mulches of fallen leaves. In the garden this rarely happens, simply because the quantity of leaves involved is so much smaller. But if you gather up the fallen leaves, compost them, and use them for mulch, the return of this material to the ground will be highly beneficial.

Protection An immediately apparent effect of trees and shrubs is that they provide protection from wind, although exactly how the wind is affected by them is not quite so obvious as it might first seem. Fences and walls offer shelter from wind only within a short distance from their base. Farther away they create violent swirls and eddies that can cause severe damage to plants and also make the garden less than comfortable for the gardener.

A 50 percent permeable screen that filters, rather than blocks, the wind creates virtually no swirling and provides effective protection over a distance of 10 times its own height. However, at the farther reaches, protection is afforded only close to ground level, and the maximum protection is of an area only about 6 times its height. The wind speed returns to its original velocity after 30 times the height of the screen.

The best permeable screens consist of trees and shrubs. Ideally, a windy site is best protected by a shelter belt 65 ft (20 m) deep, but this is obviously practicable only on large properties. Nevertheless, the average garden will receive more than adequate protection from hedges or even simply from ornamental plantings of trees and shrubs. In this case, there should be a good balance between deciduous and evergreen specimens so that enough protection is given in winter.

In really windy gardens, hedges can be planted so that they reinforce one another. For example, a hedge 6 ft (2 m) high will provide excellent protection for 40 ft (12 m) downwind. If a second hedge of the same height is planted at this distance from the first, maximum protection is provided over 80 ft (24 m). In practice, such perfect solutions are seldom sought, and the spacing of hedges can be considerably greater. Where more than the prevailing wind gives trouble, a system of boundary and internal hedges or plantings of trees and shrubs can be devised relatively easily.

Screening The use of trees and shrubs for visual screening should not be forgotten. Whereas a fence or wall may well shut out an offensive view or provide much-needed privacy, it always introduces strong, straight lines that, in an urban environment, merely add to the sort of unsightliness you are trying to exclude. Trees and shrubs provide natural lines with flowing shapes and tend to soften urban geometry or blend in with country landscapes.

Remember that the closer the screen is to you, the more effectively you will be screened. A tree or shrub planted close to your viewpoint can be quite small but still highly effective. If another house overlooks yours, for example, a small tree with a fairly open branch structure, such as the autumn cherry (*Prunus subhirtella* 'Autumnalis'), planted only a short distance away will protect you from prying eyes just as effectively as a larger, denser tree planted much farther away.

Unlike tree flowers, which appear above eye level and are best viewed at a distance for their combined effect, shrub flowers generally bloom at or below eye level and can be appreciated individually from close up.

Aesthetic considerations

Shrubs are appreciated primarily for their flowers, which are near eye level, while trees often appeal mainly for their foliage and silhouette. There are, of course, exceptions: the larger magnolias, for example, are worth growing for their flowers alone, and there are many shrubs grown principally for their foliage. Nevertheless, it can be said that the higher the tree, the less important its flowers, and the lower the shrub, the more significant its flowers.

It is the whole foliage mass of a large tree, rather than the individual leaves, that is effective. This is because the eye's ability to distinguish individual leaves diminishes with distance. The taller the tree and the longer the clean length of its trunk, the more important the general shape and overall color and character of the foliage become. The foliage on shrubs, on the other hand, is around eye level, and each leaf therefore has greater significance. A shrub whose overall silhouette is more attractive than its leaves is worthy of space in a large garden, where it is seen from a greater distance, but is not a wise choice for a small one.

Trees with interesting, arresting, or beautiful leaves should not be planted closely. If they are, the outcome will be long trunks and high, distant crowns, and the leaf characteristics will be lost. The variegated tulip tree (*Liriodendron tulipifera* 'Aureomarginata'), for example, has beautifully sculpted leaves with yellow margins. When planted in an open position, which allows it to produce foliage almost to ground level, it is quite magnificent. Grown too close to other trees, however, it ultimately forms a long, leafless bole, above which is carried a head of branches whose individual leaves can be appreciated only with the aid of binoculars.

Gardening in layers There are three distinct layers in a mature garden: the tree canopy forms the top; the middle layer is composed partly of the lower foliage of trees but mainly of shrubs and small trees; and the lowest layer is inhabited largely by a mixture of herbaceous perennials, evergreen perennials, ground covers, bulbs, and small shrubs.

For successful gardening, it is more useful to think in terms of plants that are suitable for the three layers than to become overly concerned with the academic distinctions between a tree and a shrub. In this book, therefore, a "large shrub" or a "small tree" is used to describe a plant suitable for the middle layer.

Tree and shrub silhouettes The outline of a tree or a shrub is an important quality, too. The plant's shape can be thought of as a natural sculpture, which can be used to hide, frame, or create focal points. Upright, fastigiate, or tapering trees have many uses. For example, an upright conifer, such as *Cupressus sempervirens* 'Green Pencil', can be used to hide a streetlight or frame a view. Contorted trees or shrubs make an interesting feature within a garden. The twisted branches of Harry Lauder's walking stick (*Corylus avellana* 'Contorta') create an intricate sculpture in the winter, especially if illuminated at night. Weeping or pendulous trees are important, allowing for the understory to be filled with contrasting plants or features.

Opposite The trim, symmetrical *Carpinus betulus* 'Fastigiata' takes on a graceful vase shape as it matures. *Top* Trees constitute the top layer and shrubs the middle layer of the garden, with bulbs, perennials, and annuals filling the understory. *Bottom* Fragrant flowering shrubs are particularly welcome in a seating area, where the gardener pauses to relax and enjoy the landscape.

Hardiness

The word *hardy* has many shades of meaning between two extremes. At one extreme is the Australian interpretation, in which a plant's hardiness relates to its ability to withstand heat; at the other extreme is the definition common in most other parts of the English-speaking world that indicates a plant's ability to resist cold.

The provenance of a plant — the wild locality from which it

Garrya elliptica, from California and Oregon, performs best when given the protection of a north- or northeast-facing wall, which will greatly enhance the production of decorative catkins in late winter.

was introduced — can be a major factor in determining hardiness. For many species it is not very important, but for others, those from large areas with considerable differences in climate, it can be, horticulturally speaking, vital.

For example, beginning in the late 1980s the areas in which eucalyptus species could be grown increased dramatically. This was largely the result of work done at the Australian National Botanic Gardens, Canberra, in developing a bank of seeds collected from the coldest provenance. Consequently, a species such as *Eucalyptus nicholii*, previously thought to be one of the more tender, was found capable of surviving severe frosts for short periods better than the mountain snow gum, *E. pauciflora* subsp. *niphophila*, which was supposedly one of the hardiest.

Hardiness can be considered a form of environmental stress. To understand it, you must comprehend a plant's native growing conditions and then manipulate these within the garden landscape. The climate of North America is very diverse; thus the range of plants that can be grown is vast. The plants described in this book are best suited to the northern part of the continent and especially the West Coast, rather than the warm Gulf region and adjoining states. Many need a period below freezing to grow well. A number of these plants are uncommon in cultivation in North America, and their hardiness has not always been fully determined. There is much we still do not understand about whether a certain plant will survive and, more important, flourish.

The hardiness of plants is also related to the amount of sun they receive and the wetness of the soil in winter. Thus two identical plants situated at the same altitude but on opposing sides of a range of coastal hills might exhibit quite different hardiness characteristics. The one on the side receiving the incoming, moisture-laden, prevailing wind will experience more rain and less sun. The other, on the rain-shadow side, will be subject to less rain and more sun and is likely to appear to be appreciably hardier. Altitude, of course, makes a significant difference. All things being equal, a plant growing at 500 ft (150 m) experiences an average temperature about 3°F (1.5°C) lower than one at sea level.

Windchill — the perceived lowering of the temperature due to a combination of cold and wind — also affects hardiness, even though plants do not "feel" the difference in cold the same way humans do. Wind causes moisture loss, thus placing plants under more stress than from the cold alone. Many trees and shrubs that can tolerate very low temperatures in still air may nonetheless perish from wind exposure even when the thermometer reading is not much below freezing.

Microclimates

Microclimate is an often misunderstood concept. It is not the climate of a particular river valley or the surroundings of a specific town, but that of an area so small that there may be several microclimates within a single garden. An individual plant can be supplied with its own microclimate simply by giving it a burlap or netting shelter against wind. A valuable microclimate can be provided at the base of a warm wall, where the extra heat will help plants ripen their wood. A small barrel, sunk in the soil and kept full of water, will provide increased humidity. A slight fall in level, even over just a short distance, may be sufficient to allow cold air to flow downward, letting warm air take its place. A sandy strip passing naturally through a clay garden allows drainage and proves a haven for plants on the margin of local hardiness.

Exploring the variables Plants often set puzzles for gardeners in their resistance to winter weather. You may find, for instance, that a *Convolvulus cneorum*, whose home is in the Mediterranean, will survive a winter that kills a nearby weigela, which is native to eastern Asia. Alternatively, a shrub from New Zealand may now shrug off conditions that would have destroyed it a few years before. Hardiness is subject to so many variables that

For the beautiful *Camellia japonica* 'Lady Vansittart' *(below right),* as for all camellias, avoid a site that gets early morning sun, as rapid thawing will damage any blooms touched by frost overnight.

gardeners must learn to be flexible. There is science enough, but there is also room for experimentation. "Science" simply means "knowledge"; who cares how we acquire it as long as it works in the garden. If you want to experiment, go ahead. Other gardeners will be the first to offer their congratulations.

SOIL

Land plants are remarkable organisms in that they inhabit two different environments, one above and one below ground. The conditions affecting the aerial parts of plants have a profound effect on the roots and vice versa. It is essential that you understand your growing medium before buying or planting.

The term *soil* means many different things to people, reflected in the various words used to describe it: earth, ground, dirt, and mud. When growing plants, our main concern is always the care and management of what we seek to cultivate. However, it is equally important to understand and respect the medium in which plants "live" — the soil. It is, perhaps, best regarded as shorthand for "an environment that teems with life."

In looking at the components of soil and how each contributes to plant growth, bear in mind that the nature and the proportion of the components vary greatly from one area to another. No two soils are identical. This makes generalization difficult. Similarly, always remember that soil structure is much easier to destroy than to restore.

Structure Soils differ in their makeup and behavior depending on the underlying geology of the area and on its cultivation history. They are composed of minute particles of weathered rock of different types and sizes together with accumulated organic material and microorganisms. When we talk of soil types in gardening we are interested mainly in a relatively shallow band of soil where the plant roots will grow, and this is referred to as topsoil.

Most soil is classified according to the varying proportions of each of the three components — clay, silt, and sand — present in the mix. The size of these mineral particles varies widely, from coarse grits up to 1/8 in (2 mm) in diameter to fine clay particles too small to be visible to the naked eye, and their relative proportions determine the physical and chemical characteristics of the soil, from drainage to fertility.

Types of soils Clay soils are defined as those with more than 25 percent clay particles; soils with less than 8 percent clay are classified as silty or sandy, depending on the predominant mineral. Soils with a good balance of sand, silt, and clay particles are known as loams. Where clay particles predominate, we speak of a clay loam, and where sand is the dominant mineral, a sandy loam.

Sandy loams have poor retention ability, which means that water and nutrients are leached quickly from the soil. This has led to their being known as "hungry soils." However, sandy loams drain freely, so they warm up quickly in spring and cool down quickly in winter. They are easily worked at any time of year but require frequent supervision and, because they are less fertile than clays, copious amounts of organic matter. A sandy loam can contain up to 75 percent sand, with the remainder made up of silt and clay in approximately equal proportions.

Silt loams have a high water-retaining capacity, although the very fine particles (several hundred times smaller than sand grains) tend to compact and may cause the surface to crust and puddle easily. They warm up and cool down relatively slowly and are prone to erosion by water and wind, especially when dry. A silt loam may contain up to 80 percent silt, 5 percent sand, and 15 percent clay.

Clay loams are very sticky when wet. They compact easily and, once dry, can crack and become almost impenetrable. They may have serious drainage problems, making them cool down and warm up slowly. However, clay particles are chemically charged, so they hold nutrients and organic matter.

Because of their dense structure, both clay and silt loams may require installation of adequate drainage systems to remove surface water. Additionally, these soils should be amended with quantities of coarse sand, grit, or gypsum (calcium sulfate), which helps to keep the particles separate and aid air and water circulation. Only after this has been done should organic matter be added. Digging in rotted manure or other material first will just bind the soil tighter.

Soil pH and fertility The acidity or alkalinity of soil is measured on a scale of 1–14. Neutral soil has a pH of 7; values below this are considered acidic, and values above, alkaline. The reason soil pH is so important is that it directly affects the solubility of certain soil minerals, and hence their availability to plants. These nutrients, essential for healthy growth, fall into two groups.

There are nine so-called macronutrients, all of which plants need in relatively large quantities. Carbon, hydrogen, and oxygen are obtained from air and water, while nitrogen, phosphorus, potassium, calcium, magnesium, and sulfur are normally absorbed through the roots. Macronutrients are present in most soils, but their levels require careful management since deficiencies do sometimes occur.

The seven micronutrients — iron, manganese, zinc, boron, molybdenum, copper, and chlorine — are required in smaller quantities. Soils are rarely deficient in micronutrients, but these elements may occur in forms that make them unusable to plants.

When the pH of a soil falls below 4.5, zinc, iron, and manganese dissolve readily and occur in such concentrations that they become toxic to certain plants. The activity of bacteria, earthworms, and fungi is also greatly decreased as soil pH drops. As soil pH rises, ions of zinc, iron, and manganese are bound up in insoluble compounds and become less available, which may lead to a deficiency in these elements at a pH of 7 and above.

A soil that falls between a pH of 6.5 and 7.5 is favorable for most plant growth. Within this range, the essential nutrient elements are readily available to most plants, the microorganisms of the soil can carry on their beneficial functions, and mineral toxicity is not a problem. However, some species of plants grow best under acid conditions (calcifuges), while others grow best under alkaline conditions (calcicoles).

This delightful garden, with its inventive and varied planting, is thriving in alkaline soil, demonstrating that a soil characteristic does not have to be regarded as a soil problem.

Modifying soil pH The biggest single determinant of soil pH is its calcium level. Calcium is a strongly alkaline element that occurs naturally in chalk and limestone. Because it is readily soluble, however, it tends to leach out of many types of free-draining soil, especially sandy ones, causing them to become gradually more acidic.

If the soil pH is too acidic for optimum plant growth, the pH can be raised by applying calcium in the form of lime, either ordinary (calcium carbonate) or dolomitic (calcium carbonate and magnesium carbonate). How much lime to add depends on the amount of change required, soil texture, organic-matter content, and the form in which it is added.

If the soil is too alkaline, the pH can be lowered with sulfur or aluminum sulfate. The latter, however, is required in relatively larger quantities and is best suited to small areas.

It is also possible to grow plants outside their pH range by treating nutrient deficiencies directly. The most common example of this is the use of chelated iron compounds to prevent chlorosis (calcium-induced iron deficiency) in alkaline soil.

It is generally more effective to manipulate the pH for a particular plant or crop in a confined area than to attempt large-scale treatment. This may be done by using raised beds, containers, or other methods of creating small planting pockets that can then be filled with the desired soil type. For instance, to grow acid-loving rhododendrons in an alkaline area, you can dig out a bed to the appropriate depth, lay a geotextile liner, and fill with soil that has a pH of 4.5 to 6.5.

It is, however, far wiser to select the right plant for the right place, as opposed to fighting nature. There are woody plant varieties suited to every type of soil.

Selection & Purchase

It is very common to approach garden planning by deciding, apparently for no real reason, to have a tree here and a group of shrubs there. The thought process leading to this decision may have been complex or subconscious but quite possibly also accurate. However, whether you plan "properly" or allow your intuition some sway, the next questions carry the real weight. Which tree? What kind of shrubs?

The key is to ask yourself, "What do I want the tree or shrub for?" A tree is planted for one or, more likely, several reasons. You may want a tree to screen your living room from the neighbors' view, to give a vertical component to an otherwise horizontal landscape, or to cast some welcome shade in summer. These considerations involve matters of height, spread, shape, density of foliage, and type, whether deciduous or evergreen. Your attention should turn next to what is possible culturally — in terms of climate, soil, and drainage.

Just by thinking about what you want the tree for, you have begun to describe it. Now ask yourself the same question — "What do I want the tree for?" — but this time in terms of its performance as an ornamental object. Is your first priority beauty of foliage or the need for a year-round presence? Perhaps you feel a garden tree should have a spectacular display of flowers. Maybe you have already gone through this process when selecting other plants, and you want a tree that will complement them, contrast with them, or relate to them in some other way.

This sort of process brings to bear the knowledge you have gained from garden visits, reading, and chatting with other gardeners. As you think about each criterion, different kinds of trees come to mind. Foliage? Maples! Flowers? Magnolias! Colored stems? Birches! And so on. You can then start to shop around to find the best all-round performers. White stems, graceful branches, pretty foliage, good fall color, not too large: the birch *Betula utilis jacquemontii* 'Doorenbos'. Pretty foliage for spring and summer, the finest red fall color, the longest-lasting berries for winter: the mountain ash *Sorbus hupehensis*.

Asking yourself these questions leads to clear thinking, and gardening is generally a matter of thinking in a fairly logical way while still allowing your imagination to exercise itself.

Spacing trees and shrubs

Knowing the mature sizes of the trees and shrubs will save you time, trouble, and money later on. If you can visualize their height and spread in about 20 years' time and plant accordingly, you will avoid a great deal of disappointment. It is helpful, too, to know roughly what they will be like after 5, 10, and 15 years, but 20 should be the benchmark for deciding on the location and spacing of woody plants. By visiting gardens and arboretums and becoming

Sorbus hupehensis boasts pretty foliage on purple-brown branches in spring and summer *(below left)*, followed by a striking display in fall *(below right)*. *Opposite* Care with spacing allows each plant to develop its natural shape and individual character.

reasonably familiar with trees of different sizes, you will soon be able to translate general descriptions, such as "small to medium-sized tree," into useful information.

Trees and shrubs are often planted too close together to achieve a short-term effect, which ultimately leads to their removal. Many plants can be pruned to prevent their growth from becoming too rampant, untidy, or unbalanced and, even to some extent, to slow down the rate at which they occupy space. However, the time will come when further pruning begins to spoil them, and they become overclipped, overcrowded, and unhealthy. Flowering ceases except on patchy groups of branches, leaf formation stops where the shrubs meet, and the ground beneath them becomes worn out and starved of moisture. Overrestricting growth on such a scale is desirable only in the formation of hedges and topiary features.

If the trees and shrubs intended to form the framework of your garden are planted at their proper spacing, they can be looked on as a long-term investment. Proper spacing means something like their approximate 20-year span, plus about 10 percent for trees. The space between them can, of course, still be used while you are allowing for the annual increase in size. For example, you can interplant with shrubs that are naturally short-lived but are good performers in their early years. Brooms provide quick growth and flower in their youth. Cultivars of *Cytisus scoparius* are among the many shrubs that can be used for short-term height. Others, such as daphnes, ceanothus, cistus, genistas, halimiums, and hebes, will do a similar job. Meanwhile, some of the framework shrubs of medium longevity, such as forsythias, spireas, cotoneasters, laburnums, hydrangeas, and hypericums, will begin to occupy their permanent spaces. They may, if necessary, be sacrificed or transplanted later. You may also complement the scheme with perennials, bulbs, and annuals, creating what is, in effect, a mixed border.

The advantages of this system are that you can reduce the area covered by a particular herbaceous perennial merely by dividing it and replanting fewer pieces. Eventually you can move it to somewhere else entirely; the same thing goes for bulbs. What is clear, however, is the wrong-headedness of the oft-heard advice concerning a shrub (not so often a tree) that goes, "Of course, you can always move it later." Frequently this is next to impossible (many magnolias), dependent on fairly precise timing (hollies and many other evergreens), a backbreaking job needing hardy assistants (the majority), or lethal to the plant (brooms, ceanothus, evergreen oaks, and others). The question also arises of where to move it to. If everything else has also grown and you have not suffered any major losses, there will be no room.

Opposite Interplanting with suitable shrubs and underplanting with perennials, annuals, and bulbs provides interest in the garden while young trees develop to fill their intended space. *Below* Although plant choice is largely determined by climate, a good balance of deciduous and evergreen plants brings great rewards, particularly in fall.

Deciduous and Evergreen

The proportion of evergreen to deciduous trees and shrubs in your garden will be partly determined by climate. In very cold areas,

the number of broad-leaved evergreens will have to be fewer than where it is warmer, and in really mild areas they may constitute a high proportion of the woody plants. The evergreen component in cold-climate gardens will necessarily contain a higher level of conifers, whose foliage can tolerate frosty and windy conditions. An evergreen tree or shrub will lose far more water in winter through wind and wind-frost than will a deciduous one. This moisture may be difficult to replace, especially when the soil is frozen. Conifers reduce the water lost from their leaves by having needlelike foliage or tiny leaves closely pressed to the stems, giving them an advantage over broad-leaved evergreens *(see p.23)*.

The balance between deciduous and evergreen is also a matter of taste and design, and it affects the mood and atmosphere of the garden. Try to make the plantings relate to one another. A dark blob of green will seem out of place among the bare twigs of deciduous shrubs unless there is a specific reason for it to be there. The new red growths of the evergreen *Photinia* × *fraseri* 'Red Robin', for example, would complement the rosy pink bark of the Chinese birch *Betula albo-sinensis* var. *septentrionalis*. The neatly shaped cone of the blue Lawson false cypress *Chamaecyparis lawsoniana* 'Pembury Blue' could be placed to give background and substance to a group of deciduous azaleas, while leading you to anticipate the bright flowers against its steely blue foliage. Whatever valid and valuable links, contrasts, and comparisons are made will create a planting that holds together in a balanced and interesting way.

Buying trees and shrubs

The first approach for most gardeners is to visit a local garden center. There you will find interesting species and cultivars with excellent qualities, and the additional advantage is that it caters to local conditions. Looking through their stock will provide a good survey of the plants that do well in your area. Even so, this may represent only a small proportion of the trees and shrubs that you might be able to grow; you may need to look further afield for a wider variety. Larger garden centers carry a wide selection of both garden plants and sundries. They also have plant displays that suggest ideas for companion plants and may introduce you to interesting new possibilities for planting combinations. Displays, however, should be been seen only as a starting point to plant selection. Before any on-the-spot purchase, make sure that you check the plant's compatibility with your site and its growing requirements; a garden center bookshop is a good place to do this.

Buying by mail order These days, nurseries send plants great distances; their skill in preparing and packing plants, together with the efficiency of delivery services, makes the transportation of plants safe across the country. Well-established nursery firms can be relied on to provide well-grown, disease-free plants. Their quality control is usually first class, as it is bad for business if plants have to be replaced because of complaint. It is common sense for nurseries to send plants in the best condition; those who fail to do so will not last long. Many mail-order nurseries tend to carry more specialized plants, and some concentrate on a particular range of plants. There are nurseries that specialize in bamboos, Japanese maples, oaks, and even architectural foliage plants.

Top A nursery presents a "balled-and-burlapped" magnolia for sale — that is, the roots are surrounded with the soil in which they grew and wrapped in burlap. *Above* A bare-rooted specimen is literally that and must be quickly planted or heeled in *(see p.43)*.

If you do have difficulty in locating a certain plant, it is worth consulting the Anderson Horticultural Library's *Source List of Plants and Seeds*, produced by the University of Minnesota. It lists thousands of plants and the nurseries that sell them.

When trees and shrubs arrive, they will be containerized, bare-rooted, or balled-and-burlapped, with their roots surrounded by much of the original soil ball in which they were grown in the field and wrapped in burlap or something similar. Those in containers are easily dealt with on arrival: they can be watered and sheltered until you are ready to plant them. Balled-and-burlapped and bare-rooted trees and shrubs should be planted immediately if the conditions are right, or they may be heeled in *(see p.43)*.

WHAT TO LOOK FOR WHEN BUYING

It is important to select quality-grown plants, as this could mean the difference between success and failure in the garden. The most important places to examine are the root and shoot areas.

Appearance A well-developed and healthy root system is essential to the survival of a plant. Watch out for roots that emerge from the surface of the growing medium at acute angles; this is an indication of two evils. First, the plant may have been grown in too small a container for too long, causing the root system to grow unnaturally. Second, if a root girdling the stem was not noticed and removed when young, it will place great pressure on the stem. Both will result in problems after planting, causing the tree or shrub to be unstable.

Also watch for and avoid plants that have root fibers poking through the pot's drainage holes or coiled inside the pot base (depending on plant size, you may be able to slip the plant carefully from the pot for inspection). These plants have been confined to a container too long and are rootbound; their roots may not spread out and grow into the soil once transplanted. Small plants in large pots are equally suspect, as they have probably been potted very recently to make them look like better value for the money.

The presence of a few weeds on the surface of the potting mix is excusable. But copious weed growth, especially if the weeds are perennial, flowering, and seeding, should be cause enough for you to reject the plant.

Trees should have a clear taper along the stem, that is, the top of the trunk should be much thinner than the base. Trees naturally produce reaction timber on load-bearing areas, the main one being the base of the trunk at soil level. This allows stress within the trunk to be evenly distributed along the lower two-thirds of the stem, thus reducing the risk of breakage or cracking. Trees without a clear taper should be avoided. Trees that have been permanently staked along their trunks do not generally produce reaction timber, so once the stake is removed they have difficulty supporting themselves and are vulnerable to breakage.

Vigor is a good guide to the health and well-being of a tree or shrub. Check this by looking at the extension growth. The current and previous season's growth is a good indicator of health. The spacing between nodes should be equal along the stem, regardless of species. The plants should look healthy and well grown. They should be free from pests and diseases; always look for insect pests on the underside of leaves and around soft new tips. Inspect areas of the trunk, stems, and branches for any visual damage.

Foliage Green foliage should be green. It may be a light, yellowish green, but the color should be appropriate to the variety and should look healthy. Foliage that has turned yellow through starvation or deficiency looks distinctly ill. The veins may remain green while the rest of the leaf is bright, or the leaf may be patchy yellow and green. Unseasonal leaf drop may be a sign that all is not well. Remember, however, that evergreens shed some leaves in summer. More than just a very few fallen leaves means that the plant has not been properly maintained.

Labeling If you ask for a specific tree or shrub, you cannot complain later that you really meant something else. On the other hand, you have the right to expect that the label means what it says. Commonsense checks can be made easily in many cases. A plant called 'Goldleaf' should not have blue foliage, for instance, or one called 'Variegata' should not have plain green leaves. The best course of action with flowering trees and shrubs is to go and see the plant when it is in flower. If you are still in doubt, ask; a good garden center will have knowledgeable and reliable staff.

Healthy foliage, absence of weeds on the soil surface, and suitable-sized containers in relation to the plant indicate that these rhododendrons are acceptable candidates for purchase.

Clear labeling of these *Choisya ternata* 'Sundance' specimens leaves customers with no doubt about what they are buying. The reverse of the label often carries useful facts on care and planting.

Care & Maintenance

Woody plants contribute greatly to our living environment, providing endless hours of pleasure as we cultivate them. Cultivation is the art of manipulating plants by furnishing them with the most suitable growing conditions so that they perform to their utmost potential. Gardeners require the appropriate knowledge so that they can preserve and care for the well-being of their garden plants and provide the conditions they require. The following chapter contains information for doing just that, through planting, staking, pruning, and correct aftercare.

Heeling-in and planting

Heeling-in is a simple procedure for holding plants for a short period before proper planting. Bare-rooted trees and shrubs should be soaked thoroughly first. Make a trench in a shady part of the garden, preferably where the soil is light and quick draining. "Plant" the plants in it very lightly, laying their roots in the trench and covering them with soil, peat moss, compost, or whatever suitable material you have on hand — even moist sand will do. This method allows you to delay planting for two to three weeks and protects the fragile roots from frost and dehydration.

Opposite Trees and shrubs are a long-term commitment, bringing years of pleasure if they are well cared for. *Above* If you do not want to plant bare-rooted specimens immediately, they may be heeled in to prevent damage from cold or dehydration.

Planting is a very different matter from heeling-in. By this stage, you should have acquired adequate knowledge about the plant, its height and spread, and, of course, its growing requirements. The most important factors to consider before planting are the condition of the plant, its requirements, and the current weather.

Plant bare-rooted deciduous trees and shrubs in the open ground during the dormant season — that is, after leaf fall and before spring leaf growth. Plant balled-and-burlapped evergreen trees and shrubs either between early and midfall or between mid- and late spring. Some gardeners prefer fall planting — to allow roots to establish before spring growth — while others plant in spring, once the threat of chill winds has passed. Newly planted evergreens should always be given wind protection while they establish, regardless of planting season *(Fig. 10)*.

Well-established containerized plants can be planted at any time, except in frosty conditions or during a drought, although even then they can be planted if adequate water is supplied. In sandy soils, which warm up quickly, there are advantages to planting from mid- to late spring; however, as sandy soils drain freely some experts favor fall planting. Experts recommend mid- to late fall planting in heavier soils, which warm up late in the year but retain their heat longer into fall.

Container-grown plants are the most difficult to establish after planting. Potting mixes contain optimum levels of nutrients and offer little resistance to developing roots, which can make it difficult for the plant to "take" once set in the ground. This is especially true in heavy clay soils, where the sides of the planting hole can create an almost impenetrable barrier. Bare-rooted trees and shrubs do not suffer in quite the same way because there is little of their native soil remaining; all new roots will develop in the new soil. In easy-to-cultivate soils, a conventional planting hole may suffice, but in heavier soils, a wider planting area may be needed.

Prepare the planting hole Remove any perennial weed cover before planting. This may involve applying an herbicide or digging out deep-rooted weeds. The next step is to prepare the planting site well in advance.

In light, sandy soils, dig in organic matter at a rate of 20–30 lb per square yard (9–15 kg/m^2). Good soil conditioners include compost, leaf mold, rotted manure, peat moss, or spent hops — all of

FIG. 3 PREPARING THE PLANTING HOLE

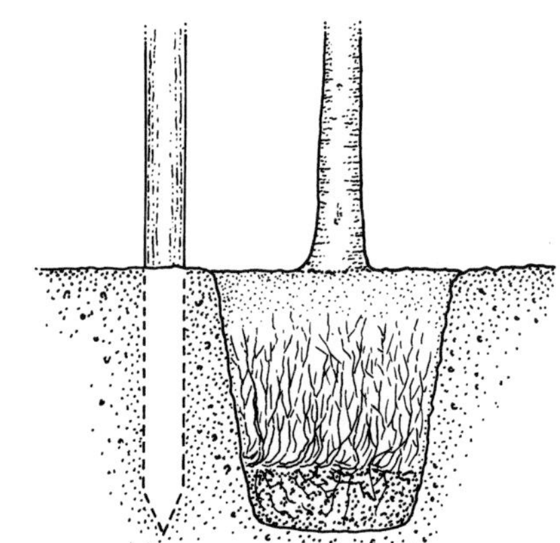

Prepare the planting hole by cultivating a sufficiently large area for the roots to become established. In figure (i) the roots have been unable to force their way through the sides of the hole.

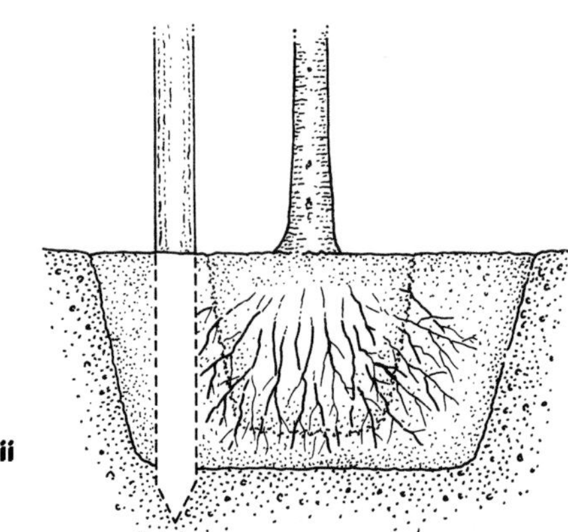

Figure (ii) illustrates how the roots are able to spread in a well-prepared planting hole, exploiting the larger area of well-cultivated soil to develop outward rapidly.

which will improve the soil's ability to retain water and nutrients.

In heavy clay soils, correct any drainage problems before adding organic matter to improve the tilth and fertility of the soil. Add material at a rate of 4–6 lb per square yard (2–3 kg/m²), preferably in late fall, so that frost can help break it down until spring. Letting the soil settle will improve its aeration and texture.

Once these preparations have been completed, dig a planting hole three times the width and twice the depth of the existing root system. Although providing a hole of this size may not always be practical, it is worth getting as close to it as possible, as the rapid establishment of your tree or shrub depends largely on the quality of the planting hole.

Staking Almost all trees and a few shrubs need to be staked. This is primarily to allow the roots to become established as anchors. Once they have gained a firm hold in the soil, the chances of the plant being blown over are slim. Until then, however, the constant movement of the stem under the influence of even light breezes will prevent the roots from growing into the surrounding soil.

Until experiments showed the importance of movement to stem development, tree stakes had always extended to just below the head of branches. Many people still use long stakes, but increasingly the short stake, 20 in (50 cm) in height, has been adopted. A long stake immobilizes the tree stem throughout its length. This does not inhibit growth but encourages the stem to develop a tubelike shape. If a short stake is used, the upper portion of the stem moves and in doing so produces reaction timber that reinforces the trunk *(see p.41)*. Single short stakes can be used for bare-rooted plants, but you can also use a short stake consisting of two uprights and a crossbar for containerized trees and shrubs and large specimen shrubs.

Tall or slender shrubs and those that move readily with the wind will also need staking. A short, angled stake is best, as shrubs have many stems and there is seldom a straight one among them. If you use a short stake and drive it in at an angle that neither interferes with the root ball nor chafes any branches, you will achieve sufficient stability for the shrub to become anchored.

One or more proper tree ties should always be used when staking trees and shrubs. It is a false economy to use strips of old pantyhose or lengths of garden hose and wire. Not only do they look ugly and untidy, but they are also inefficient, causing damage to the stem and leading to the entry of disease organisms. A commercial tree tie costs only pennies and may well make the difference between success and failure. It should consist of a strap with a buckle and one or more buffer blocks. It should grip the stem and the stake snugly. You can fasten it into the stake with a light nail to keep it from sliding down.

Very large tree specimens are difficult to establish because of anchorage problems, and even expert growers sometimes fail. Specialized systems of guying are the best solution. In most cases, three guy wires, passing through rubber antifriction tubes, are fastened to strong posts driven into the ground.

Stakes are frequently left in the ground and attached to the plants they are supporting for far too long. You should check them at least twice a year and be prepared to remove the stakes from established trees and shrubs after two years. The majority of trees, except perhaps those bought as large specimens, should be capable of standing on their own after three years.

Neglecting the tree tie can easily lead to the formation of a groove in the stem, and this "tight collar" effect often results in the stem's snapping later on. It is especially easy to forget that you staked a shrub, as the stake may become hidden. It is an unpleasant reminder to find a fine camellia in full flower, for example, suddenly reduced to half its height.

Planting bare-rooted trees and shrubs Bare-rooted trees and shrubs should have been properly packed and the roots safely protected by the nursery immediately after being lifted from the ground. You should either keep the roots moist within their

FIG. 4 STAKING METHODS

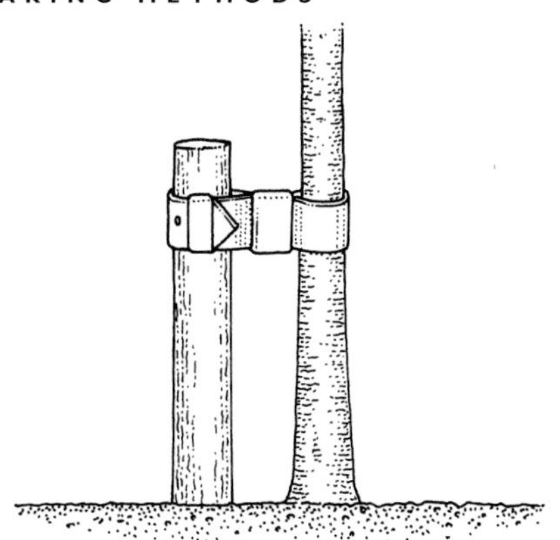

Short stakes allow the upper portion of the tree or shrub stem to move, producing reaction timber that reinforces the trunk.

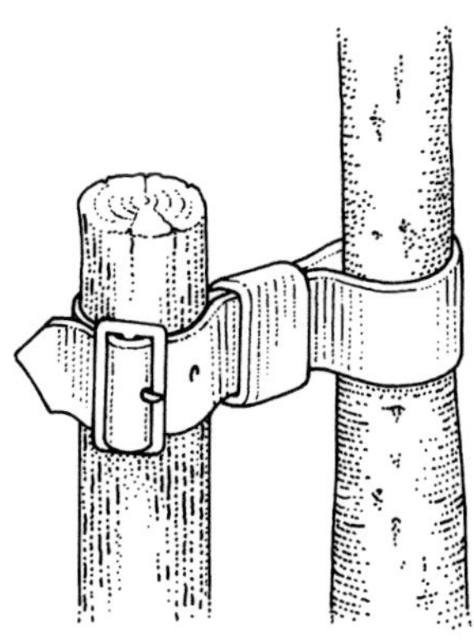

Commercial tree ties not only look more professional but also prevent chafing, which may provide an entry point for pests and diseases.

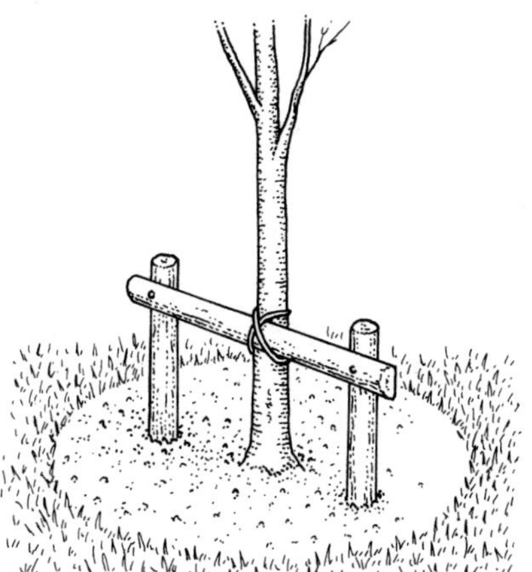

Short stakes and crossbar Two short stakes linked with a crossbar that is tied to the tree trunk is a particularly good way to support container-grown specimens and prevent damage to the root ball.

Guy-wire staking Commercial guying systems are recommended for the staking of large tree specimens.

wrappings or heel them in immediately upon bringing them home.

After preparing the soil, make a hole wide enough to accommodate the roots without their being bent or forced, then make a firm cone of soil in the bottom of the hole *(Fig. 5)*. The stem can rest on the apex of the cone as the roots fan downward. It is a good idea to have an assistant on hand, as it is very difficult to ensure that the tree or shrub is planted upright when you are also concerned with filling in the hole properly.

Find the point where the roots end and the stem or stems begin on each tree or shrub you plant. This is called the "nursery mark" — a dark band across the bottom of the stem where the soil level was. You should also look for any graft union and make sure it is not buried but remains 2–2½ in (5–6 cm) above soil level. (The opposite is true for roses, whose graft union would have been below ground level at the nursery and should remain so when you plant.) The way to ensure that the mark stays at the right level is to place a wooden stake or pole across the hole and align the nursery mark with its lower edge. It is part of your assistant's job to see that it is still aligned at the end of the planting process.

Before putting the plant (let us assume it is a tree) in the hole, position the stake and drive it into the bottom of the hole. Next, have your assistant hold the stem while you check the alignment. As you backfill the hole, your helper should give the tree a vertical shake from time to time to help settle the soil around the roots. It is important to prevent air pockets from forming, and this action, along with firming the soil with your feet, hands, and spade, will ensure that they do not.

It is not recommended to firm the soil around the roots with your heel, as the pressure concentrated on this small area is enough to damage roots. The sole, having a larger area, transmits less pressure and tends to firm rather than ram the soil. However, as the hole is filled further and the cushion of soil between your foot and the roots deepens, then the full pressure of your body weight can be applied through the heel. This firming is essential, as

FIG. 5 HOW TO PLANT A BARE-ROOTED TREE OR SHRUB

2 Line up the nursery mark using a wooden stake or pole to ensure that the tree is planted at the correct level.

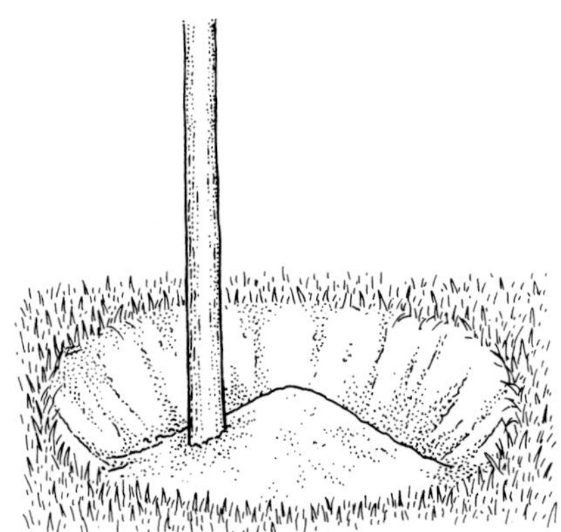

3 Remove the tree. Position the stake and drive it into the bottom of the hole.

1 Make a firm pyramid of soil at the bottom of the hole and rest the tree on top to make sure that the height is sufficient for the roots to fan down unrestricted.

4 With stake in position, replace the tree and begin backfilling the hole, giving the tree an occasional vertical shake to settle the soil around its roots.

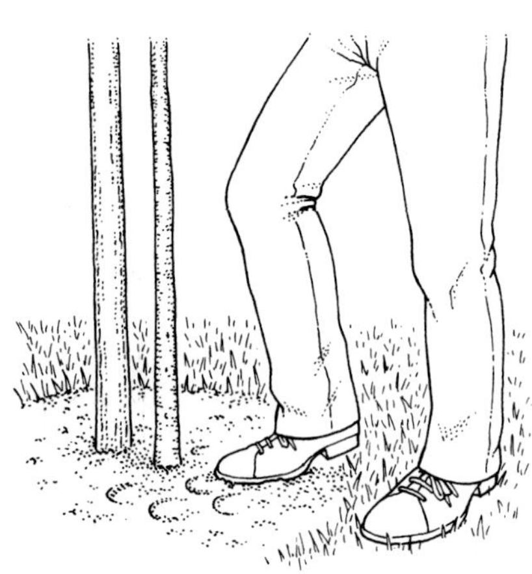

5 Firm the soil around the trunk of the tree, first with the sole of your foot, then with the heel.

without it the soil will settle into the hole and may leave the top of the root system exposed.

Planting balled-and-burlapped trees and shrubs Shrubs and trees with masses of fibrous roots are often sold with their root balls intact and tied up, or "balled," in natural or synthetic burlap. You need to know what the material is, as only a biodegradable substance should be allowed to remain on the root ball; nondegradable plastics must be removed. Even burlap should be untied, loosened, and cut away from the top of the root ball.

Use the crossbar method for staking *(Fig. 4)*, since you do not want to damage the root ball by driving a stake through it. Alternatively, large trees can be guyed at three points or double staked. Double staking *(Fig. 6)* is the only method that allows the use of flexible ties, such as strips of rubber, because the two strips oppose one another and keep the trunk firm but allow it to sway. The stakes are driven in opposite one another and to the sides of the root ball. The rubber strips are an alternative to attaching a crossbar and using a tree tie, a method that may not be practical in the case of heavier trees with thicker stems.

Planting container-grown trees and shrubs In many ways it is much easier to plant a containerized tree or shrub than one grown in the field. It is important to soak the root ball thoroughly before planting, as peat moss and several peat-substitute potting mixes will not to take up water once they have dried out. To ensure that the center of the root ball is wet, sink the container in a bucket of water and let it soak for an hour or two — certainly until bubbles have finished rising from the soil. Let it drain properly before you remove the pot, otherwise a rush of water might disturb the root ball and cause damage.

Placing the nursery mark correctly is important, and it is still a

FIG. 6 DOUBLE STAKING

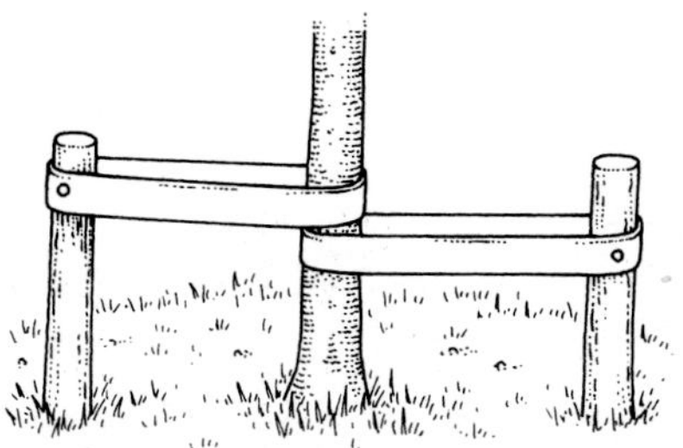

With this method, the stakes are linked by looped strips of rubber that hold the tree firm but allow it to sway. It is a particularly good choice for heavy, thick-stemmed trees unsuited to the short-stake-and-crossbar technique.

FIG. 7 THE NURSERY MARK

The nursery mark on trees and shrubs, which indicates the original planting depth, should be level with the soil surface.

good idea to have an assistant when planting large specimens. It is essential that the soil be properly cultivated and enriched around the planting hole. Containerized trees and shrubs are unforgiving toward gardeners who expect them to force their way through dense, impenetrable soil. Firm the soil thoroughly around the root ball.

Planting hedges It is often asserted that planting containerized plants is safe at any time of year, but the dangers from drought are ever present. When just a few trees or shrubs are planted in late spring or summer, it is no problem to keep an eye on them and water as necessary. Hedges, which consist of large numbers of young plants, are often located at property boundaries and are therefore far removed from water sources. Unless you are particularly vigilant, they are best planted between fall and spring, even when container grown. Plant bare-rooted deciduous hedging plants after leaf drop and before spring is under way. Plant evergreens in midfall or late spring, when the soil is warm enough for the roots to replenish water lost by the leaves. You can plant in dry conditions as long as the plant roots are soaked prior to planting and generously watered in.

It is often supposed that because hedges are generally the best defense against wind, they need no protection when young. Nothing could be farther from the truth, especially because hedges are frequently planted in exposed positions. Lack of protection during the first three or four winters is one of the most common causes of loss, resulting in gaps that have to be filled with replacement plants. Setting up screens made with fine-mesh plastic netting or burlap will provide protection from the wind, allow the hedge to grow stronger and more quickly, and may save you from having to buy new plants. In addition, make sure when planting that you have firmed the soil well around the roots. Check the plants after strong winds for soil movement throughout their first year.

Transplanting

Transplanting is simply a matter of moving trees and shrubs from one place to another within the garden. In practice it usually involves only smaller shrubs and young, small trees, as anything larger becomes a matter for professional skill and machinery.

The root hairs — the part of the root system that absorbs nutrients and water from the soil — are easily damaged and only rapidly repaired or replaced when the soil is warm and moist. The younger the root, the more root hairs it bears, and the younger the root system, the more young roots it has. Therefore the younger the plant, the better its chance of surviving a move. It follows, too, that the greater the proportion of the root system you manage to transplant intact, the more likely it is that the plant will be relatively unaffected.

Plants that have closely massed, highly fibrous roots, such as rhododendrons, can be moved at almost any time of the year except during periods of drought or when the soil is frozen.

Deciduous trees and shrubs can be moved during their dormant season — between leaf drop and bud break. The sooner after leaf drop, the better, so that damaged roots can regrow while the soil is still warm. Transplantation late in the dormant season may lead to trouble, as icy or drying winds can still blow in early spring.

There is often a short spell after the dormant season, in spring, during which soft showers fall and the soil has warmed up enough to activate the roots. This provides an extension to the transplanting season for deciduous specimens. A few tricky ones, including the deciduous magnolias, can be moved with the greatest safety at this time.

Evergreen trees and shrubs, with few exceptions, are not so easily moved, as the leaves lose water during the winter and a damaged root system cannot replace it. No matter how careful you are to retain the root balls intact, some degree of damage is inevitable, and this will adversely affect the water balance.

Evergreens are best moved just after the autumnal equinox in milder areas and just before it in colder regions. In places where spring is characterized by early spells of dry, cold winds, transplanting should be delayed until warmer, moister weather arrives. In regions where spring is short and swift, transplant as soon as the soil warms up. No matter when evergreen trees or shrubs are moved, they should, if possible, be protected from wind for the first season or two.

FIG. 8 TRANSPLANTING

1 Establish the outer edge of the root system and mark out a circle. Then cut a trench around the plant using the inner edge of the circle as a guide.

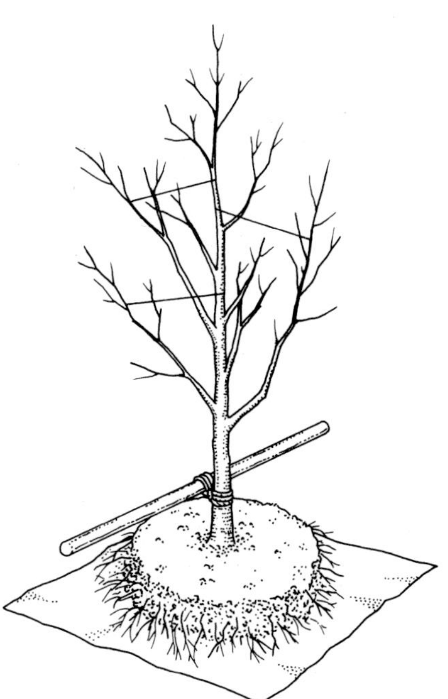

2 Tie a stout pole to the bottom of the main stem so that the pole is horizontal. With at least one assistant, lift the pole at each end and carry the plant onto a sheet of strong burlap or plastic. With a helper holding each corner of the sheet, carry the plant to its already prepared planting site.

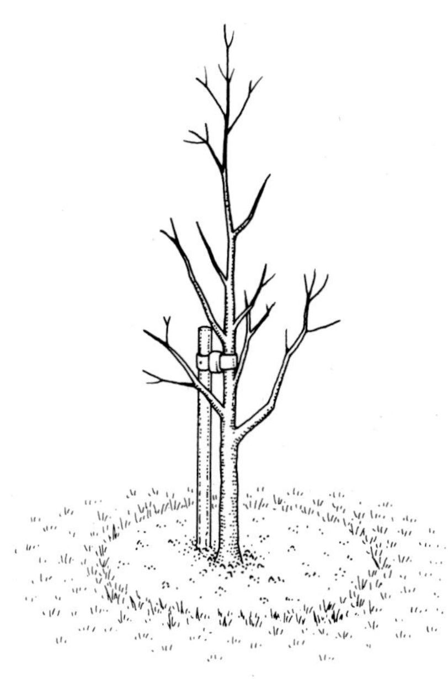

3 To counteract root damage, which is almost inevitable during transplanting, reduce the plant's top growth by up to one-third. Remove any damaged and crossing branches, but retain the leader.

How to transplant *(Fig. 8)* Before lifting a tree or shrub, you need to locate the outer limits of the root system, which may extend farther from the plant than you would expect. As a general guide, you can use the drip line, an imaginary line drawn from the outer edge of the canopy to the soil level. Tie a line to the base of the plant and extend it out to the drip line; attach a stake to the free end of the line and walk it around the plant to mark out a circle in the soil. Insert a spade one spade's width outside the marked circle. Rock the spade backward and forward without loosening the root ball. Continue around the plant and then cut out a trench using the inner edge of the circle as a guide. Cut through any exposed roots with an old but sharp saw. Finally, undercut the root ball to free it.

Tie a stout pole to the bottom of the main stem, looping the rope securely around both the stem and the pole so that the pole is held horizontal. Lift the plant onto a sheet of strong burlap or plastic and carry it by the four corners of this support to the planting site. Then follow Fig. 5.

Hedges are often planted in exposed, windblown locations along property boundaries, so particular care with watering is required while the young plants are getting established.

No matter how carefully you transplant a tree or shrub, you are almost certain to cause some root damage. Even when the damage is not apparent, it is still a good idea to reduce the top growth to balance the root loss. Otherwise the plant may not be able to balance water loss from the foliage and dieback may occur. A reduction of up to one-third of the top growth is possible in many cases; simply remove all crossing branches, open the framework up a little, and cut back the main branches by a relatively small amount. Take care, however, to maintain the leader.

Tree guards

Tree guards aid the growth of very young trees and are commonly used by professional landscapers. They not only provide a microclimate around the trunk, which can speed the establishment of the plant, but also protect against damage caused by lawn equipment and animals. Deer, rabbits, squirrels, and other wildlife — even family pets — can severely injure tree bark, which is unsightly and allows entry of diseases and pests.

Commercial tree guards are available in plastic tubes and strips in varying sizes. Look for strips that are perforated to permit air circulation around the trunk and check under any guard regularly for insects or diseases. You can also fashion a guard from wire

FIG. 9 TREE GUARDS

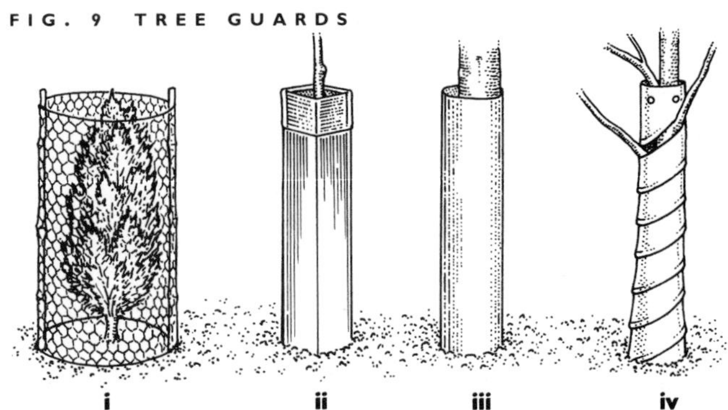

The following defenses offer some degree of protection against animals: (i) Homemade chicken wire guard, held with bamboo stakes, that extends 12 in (30 cm) deep below the soil surface to deter rabbits; (ii) commercial flat-sided plastic tube available in a range of lengths; (iii) commercial cylindrical plastic tube available in a range of lengths; (iv) commercial spiral wrap.

FIG. 10 PROTECTION FROM WIND

For the first few winters after planting, erect a V-shaped screen that points into the wind, providing shelter for the young tree behind it.

or plastic mesh, either simply winding it securely around the tree or around stakes set a short distance from the trunk.

Against rabbits, guards should be 2 ft (60 cm) high, but for deer they should be 6 ft (2 m) tall. If wild animals are a persistent nuisance, however, more expensive and elaborate alternatives, such as double fences or electrified fences, may be required.

Protection from wind and cold

Many hardy trees and shrubs are particularly vulnerable to damage from wind and cold during their first few winters. Protection, therefore, should, be on two fronts. Temper the prevailing wind by erecting a *V*-shaped shelter *(Fig. 10)*, made from fine plastic mesh or burlap, with the angle of the *V* pointing into the wind and the plant snugly behind it.

Protect against cold by erecting a triangular or rectangular burlap screen held on stakes around the plant, filling the interior loosely with dead leaves or straw to create an insulating muff. Prevent frost heaving and stabilize soil temperature around the roots by spreading a deep mulch of shredded bark or chopped leaves.

Watering

Once established, woody plants generally need little supplemental watering — providing they have been given a proper start. The first critical watering comes immediately after planting, when you should water in new specimens deeply and thoroughly. The purpose of this is not only to provide plants with the moisture they need but also to dispel air pockets and help soil make good contact with the roots.

Thereafter you need to monitor all trees and shrubs carefully during their first three years for signs of water stress, such as drooping or wilted foliage or poor flower production. Most woody plants need about 1 in (2.5 cm) of water per week and should be watched particularly closely during periods of drought, extreme heat, or high winds.

Whenever you water, be sure to soak the soil sufficiently, so that water reaches the full depth and spread of the root zone. Deep watering encourages deep roots, which are then better able to seek out moisture from the soil. In sandy soil, water will penetrate but also dry out quickly and may need to be replenished more frequently; the opposite is true of clay soil.

Weed control

Pay special attention to weed control around newly planted trees and shrubs. Weeds and grass rob moisture and nutrients from the soil, especially the nitrogen that young specimens need. Some woody plants compete better than others: young oaks, for example, can thrive amid weeds or grass, whereas birches will not. Nevertheless, garden plants should not have to compete with undesirables, so it is good practice to keep weeds down.

Routine use of herbicides, especially around young plants, is not recommended; hand weeding or hoeing is environmentally friendlier and safer. Controlling weeds need not be a time-consuming or heavy job, as long as you do not let them become established. If you hoe often, you will not need to hoe roughly or deeply and risk damaging the plant roots. Furthermore, you can stop hoeing at the onset of dry weather. The loose soil on top dries quickly, making it unsuitable for weed-seed germination; it also forms an insulating mulch to the soil beneath it. If you stir it up during dry weather, you bring moist soil to the surface, where it dries out. Weed germination is unlikely during dry spells, and if you have prepared the ground properly, there will be no up-growth of perennial weeds.

Mulches

Any material placed on the surface of the soil is considered a mulch. It may be organic, such as pine needles, shredded bark, grass clippings, or leaf mold, or inorganic, such as geotextile landscape fabric or black plastic. Applied correctly, mulches conserve soil moisture, reduce soil erosion, and suppress weed growth. Organic mulches also improve fertility and tilth and stabilize soil temperature.

To use organic mulch, spread it to a depth of 2–6 in (5–15 cm) around the plant, leaving about 6 in (15 cm) clear space around the stem to avoid problems with pests and diseases. The mulch can remain in place year-round; simply refresh the top as required.

For an extra barrier against weeds, you can lay down a piece of inorganic mulch and cover it with an ornamental organic mulch. However, use only geotextile landscape fabric, which permits air and water circulation, never plastic mulch, which is impermeable and can suffocate or otherwise injure roots. To mulch one plant, cut a sheet of fabric to the desired size and arrange it around the already planted specimen. With a large shrub border, lay the fabric over prepared soil first, then cut slits for setting in the plants.

Disease prevention

Tree care is a specialized subject, but accurate information can go a long way toward avoiding bad practices. It is advisable to consult the experts when dealing with large trees. The International Society of Arboriculture will provide a list of certified arborists on request. Contact the society at P.O. Box GG, Savoy IL 61874, (217) 355-9411.

Some tree problems can be controlled with sprays, injections, and judicious pruning, but others persist. Dutch elm disease, declines and diebacks, and root rots are only a few of the continuous problems. Perhaps too much time is spent looking at the disease or decay organism and not enough studying the "patient" — the tree. Without diminishing the other efforts, it may be helpful to look more closely at preventive measures that keep the tree in good health and help it resist disease. When compared with the well-balanced habitat provided in a forest, the stresses and strains placed on a tree within a hostile urban environment are immense. So how can we improve this in order to help trees help themselves?

Trees have been self-reliant for thousands of years, long before the arrival of the chain saw, wound dressings, and tree-care experts. Given half a chance, they will continue to survive long into the future without our intervention.

Trees are highly complex plants, built up of "compartments." When they break down, they do so compartment by compartment. Trees survive after injury or infection by "walling off" the affected wood in as small an area as possible. Some individual trees do this rapidly and effectively and can live in a healthy state with hundreds or even thousands of infections walled off in pockets. Other trees do not wall off rapidly and effectively; the force of the infection quickly leads to a large volume of injured wood. Such a tree will not live for long. The ability of a tree to wall off an infection depends on its health and genetic makeup.

Walling off, or compartmentalization, is a boundary-setting process that restricts the spread of infection or wounding. Wounding can be caused by a bad pruning cut or damage from a lawn mower, animals, broken limbs, lightning, and so on. When this first happens, the next season's growth is not yet present; the infection cannot spread to wood that has not yet formed. The tree responds to the injury or infection by setting firm chemical boundaries above the infected cells to resist the spread of fungi or pathogens. If the tree is very fast with its boundary-setting defenses, the infection will not spread but remain localized. If the tree is less effective, then rapid spread will occur. In that case, the entire tree may die, as it does with Dutch elm disease.

Wound dressings Studies have shown that no material entirely stops decay, and that in many instances trees close and compartmentalize wounds very rapidly, regardless of any treatment. Wound dressings certainly reduce discoloration, but this is not necessarily indicative of decay and some discoloration is normal. Many products stimulate the production of wound tissue (callus formation), but callus formation is not associated with the process of decay. Large wounds seldom close properly, and even when they appear closed, they have fine hairline cracks. This situation favors the growth of decay-forming organisms. When insects infect wounds, they usually bore into the dying tissue around the wound, so dressings directly on the wound are of no benefit. Putting fungicides into the wound dressings has also been considered, but decay-causing fungi are seldom the primary invader.

Many types of wound dressing have been developed, and the principle in the past was to provide a physical barrier to infection and prevent decay. It was also thought that protection of the callus was necessary to stop it from drying out. Wound dressings were often used to hide bad workmanship or to show the tree owner that the work had been completed. The ideal wound dressing does not exist, so it is better to let the tree heal itself.

Pruning

Proper pruning is one of the best things you can do to help a tree stay healthy. Conversely, bad pruning is one of the worst things you can do to a tree.

Proper pruning means removing dead, dying, or living branches in such a way that the branch bark collar is not injured or

FIG. 11 A PROPER PRUNING CUT

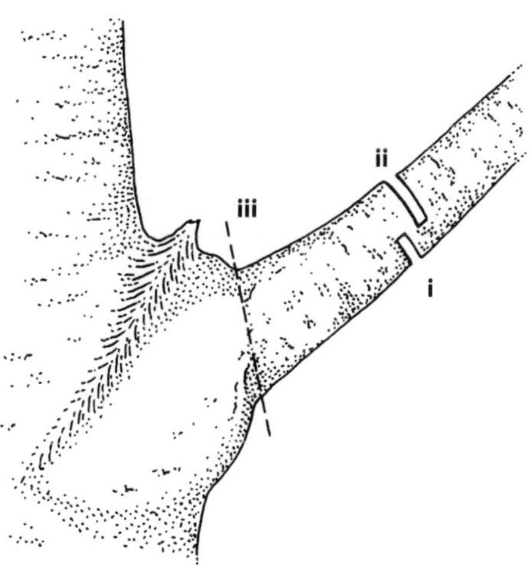

A proper pruning cut leaves no branch protruding from the branch collar and ensures that no damage is done to the branch collar. Make the first cut (i) 12 in (30 cm) from the trunk and one-third of the way through the branch underside. Make the second cut (ii) 1 in (2.5 cm) farther from the trunk and cut through from above to remove the bulk of the branch . Make the third cut (iii) just outside the branch collar.

removed *(Fig. 11)*. The branch bark ridge is the key to proper pruning, and no cut should start behind it. The slightly swollen branch collar that is present on some branches is not a stub. A stub is a projection of the branch, whereas a branch bark collar is part of the trunk. A proper cut does not leave any projection from the branch but allows the tree to heal itself naturally.

The most common question about branch pruning is whether it is better to err on the side of leaving a small stub or of cutting too close to the trunk. The answer is to adopt natural target pruning, so called because the lines of the cut follow those that a tree forms when it naturally sheds a branch. These points are target points.

Natural target pruning First reduce the weight of the branch. A small undercut about 12 in (30 cm) from the trunk followed by a finishing top cut 1 in (2.5 cm) farther out will stop the bark from tearing down the trunk. Next locate the targets. The first is on the outer side of the branch bark ridge, where the branch meets the main stem. The second is where the lower part of the branch meets the branch collar. These target points are obvious on most branches, especially dead and dying branches, because as the branch begins to die, the branch collar usually begins to swell and form a "doughnut" around the base of the branch.

Codominant stems Much of the main canopy on mature trees is made of codominant stems, of which there are two types. The normal type has a strong connection and can easily be identified by its bark, which points upward *(Fig. 14i)*. The second type has a potentially hazardous connection, recognizable by its downward-pointing bark *(Fig. 14ii)*. This kind has a connection farther down the stem that hides a long tapering crack. Where the two areas of the stem grow together, bark forms and pushes against the other side of the stem. If the connection is not identified early in a tree's life, it may have disastrous implications later. The correct removal of a codominant stem is shown in Fig. 13, but on large trees professional advice should be sought.

FIG. 12 TREE WITH CODOMINANT STEMS

Rival leaders produce an acute-angled fork. The tighter the angle of the fork, the more likely the development of a weak union, which may shear in high winds.

FIG. 13 PRUNING A WEAK CODOMINANT-STEMMED TREE

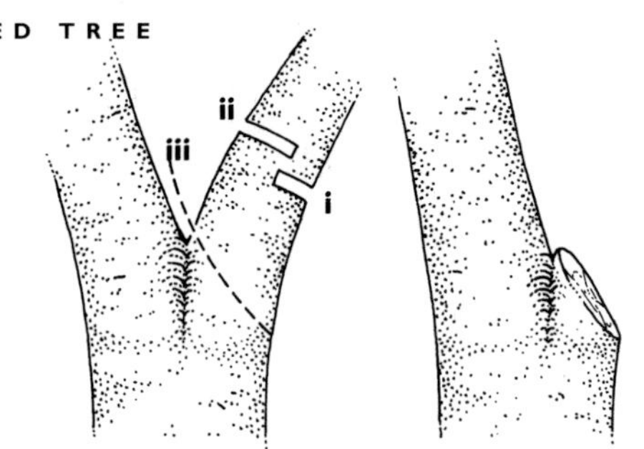

Make the first cut (i) 12 in (30 cm) from the trunk and one-third of the way through the branch underside. Make the second cut (ii) 1 in (2.5 cm) farther from the trunk and cut through from above to remove the bulk of the branch. Finally, make the third cut (iii) close to the apex but without damaging the branch collar.

FIG. 14 BARK ON CODOMINANT STEMS

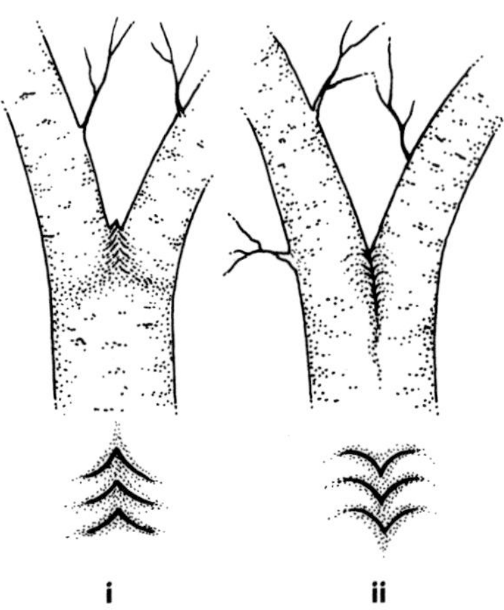

(i) illustrates a codominant-stemmed tree on which the bark points upward, signifying a strong union that is unlikely to break. (ii) illustrates a codominant-stemmed tree on which the bark points downward, signifying a weak union that should be remedied by removal of one of the branches *(Fig. 13)*.

When to prune The question most frequently asked by buyers of woody plants is "How and when do I prune?" The answer that should often be given is, "Don't."

This may seem a bit extreme, but the truth of the matter is that far too much attention is given to the mechanics of pruning and far too little to understanding the growth of plants. When you understand plants, pruning becomes much less of a mystery.

The main reason for pruning trees and shrubs is to remove dead or diseased wood and weak or crossing branches. While clearing these out, it is sometimes a good idea to remove some of the branches from the center of a bushy shrub, too, in order to allow more light and air to reach the foliage.

As gardeners, we try to grow each of our specimens as perfectly as we can. This means that we must either forestall or swiftly repair the ravages of nature and that we need to look forward into the future of each tree or shrub to help it on its way toward fulfilling its true potential. Apart from repair, there are two main purposes for pruning: producing plants in desired shapes and sizes and encouraging the maximum yield of flowers or fruit. In general, it can be said that winter pruning is for growth, while summer pruning is for flowers.

There are two ways of pruning trees and shrubs for shape and size: wrong and right. It is wrong to try to control the size of a shrub by constantly cutting it back. If you find yourself doing this, you have either chosen the wrong plant or planted it in the wrong place. It is right to prune wayward or unbalanced branches to train or encourage the specimen to achieve its natural shape for the species or variety.

Shaping trees One of the most obvious features of a tree is a length of clean trunk. It is often thought that this just happens. So it does in nature, but the process is not pretty, as the lowest, spindliest branches die off when they become shaded and remain as dead wood until they drop away, leaving a scar. When you buy a young tree you may find that the trunk is furnished with short, slender branches. They are there to bear leaves that feed the young tree until the head of branches has expanded enough to do the job without their help and the trunk is able to support it. A year after planting, you can remove about one-third of them with pruning shears, cutting close to the stem *(Fig. 15i)*. The rest can be removed over the next two years *(Fig. 15ii)*. It is unwise to trim up the entire stem in one operation.

FIG. 15 REMOVAL OF LOWER BRANCHES

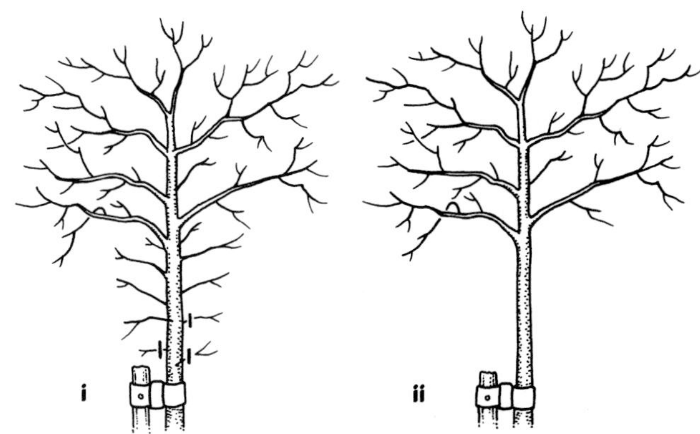

The lower branches on young trees are there to bear leaves that feed the tree until it is established. One year after planting, one-third of them may be removed with pruning shears (i). The remaining lower branches may be removed over the next two years (ii).

Some garden trees can be manipulated by annual pruning to create a pollarded effect, that is, pruning branches back to the same point each year *(Fig. 16)*. These are often quick-growing trees, such as *Eucalyptus gunnii*, which may be pollarded annually to attain a compact, bushy shrub.

An alternative method is to produce a multistemmed tree. This is undertaken early in its life with the removal of the main leader, resulting in a tree with many branches arising from near ground

FIG. 16 ANNUAL POLLARDING

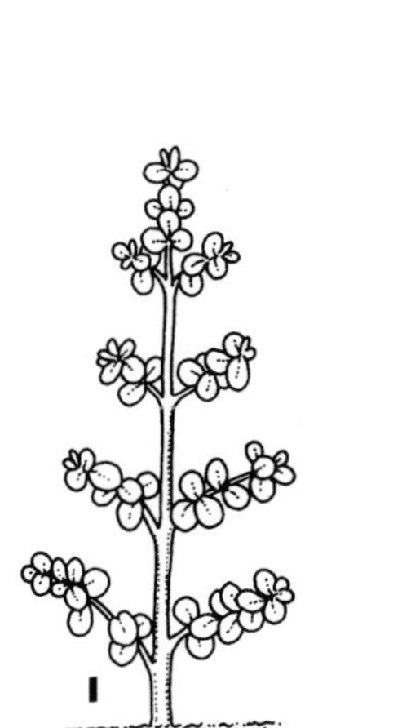

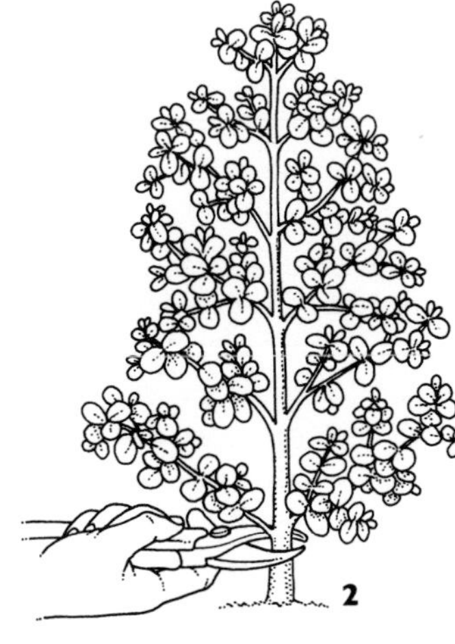

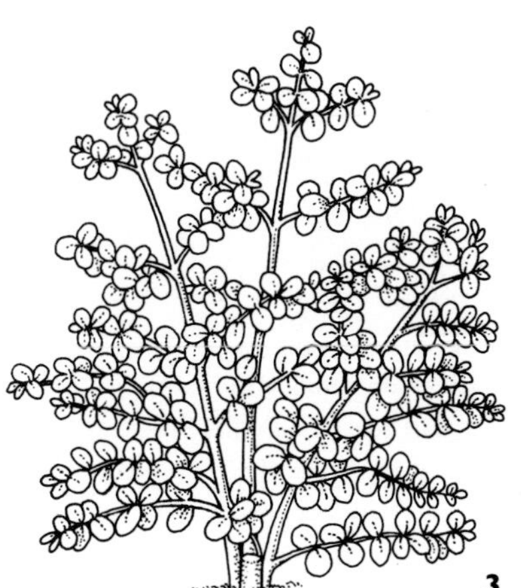

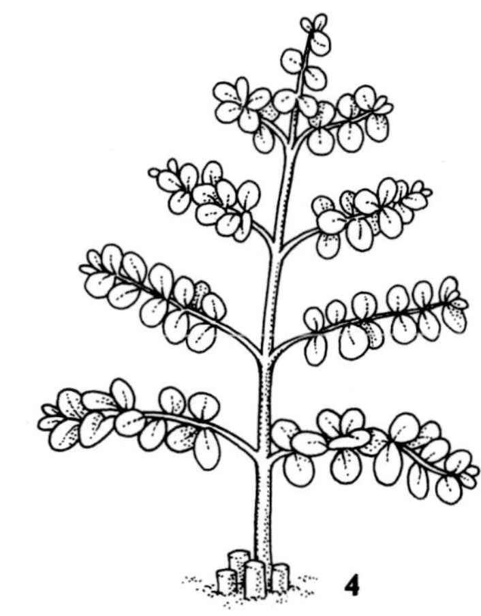

1 A young eucalyptus shortly after planting.
2 In early fall at least one year after planting, cut the plant back to ground level.
3 Two years after planting, choose a new leader from the many new shoots.
4 Remove all shoots other than the chosen leader and allow it to develop as the main stem. To maintain the pollarded effect, repeat step 2 annually.

FIG. 17 SHAPING UNBALANCED SHRUBS

1 An unbalanced shrub.

2 Prune the strong side lightly in summer.

3 Prune the weak side hard in winter.

level. The tree is then pruned every two years to produce a domed head. Examples of this are *Acer pensylvanicum* 'Erythrocladum', *A. negundo* 'Flamingo', *Prunus serrula*, and *Betula utilis*.

Birches, maples, and walnuts produce a heavy sap flow in the spring. Pruning at this time will cause the plant to bleed profusely and it is difficult to stop the flow. It is much wiser to prune trees in early fall, which allows them to heal before winter. This is also the best time to identify dead branches.

Shaping shrubs With shrubs, the tendency for a strong leader to emerge is usually considerably less noticeable, or even absent. Encourage a regular bushy shape in the early days by pinching back the tips of the young shoots. This slows their further growth outward from the center but encourages them to branch. It is also useful for stopping potentially rival leaders or any branches that may be growing in an unruly, unbalanced way.

If you prune hard in winter, you encourage growth. Where things can go wrong is if one side of a plant — whether a tree, shrub, or climber — has for some reason become suppressed while the other has grown strongly. To cut back the strong side in winter will only make it grow more vigorously. The correct procedure, paradoxical though it may seem, is to prune the less vigorous side hard in winter and the strong side lightly in summer *(Fig. 17)*.

Reversion Reversion is when leaves lose their variegation. Green leaves contain more chlorophyll, which is responsible for the food-making activity of the leaves, but variegated leaves contain little chlorophyll in those parts that are not green and so feed the branch less efficiently. A green, reverted branch can, therefore, grow at an alarming rate and completely unbalance the tree or shrub, as well as begin to take over the growth of the entire plant.

Examples of enthusiastic reverters are *Spiraea japonica* 'Goldflame', *Elaeagnus pungens* 'Maculata', *Acer platanoides* 'Drummondii', and *A. negundo* 'Variegatum'. The spirea can be a perfect nuisance in this regard, but it is such a pretty shrub that a constant program of pinching the green shoots is worth the trouble. Variegated trees may revert at any time. Luckily, they usually do so in comparative youth, when the rogue shoots can be reached from the ground at best or a ladder at worst.

Reverted shoots must be removed in their entirety or they will just grow again. Small, soft shoots on shrubs may be cut back with a little of the old wood or even with a small heel. A reverted tree branch must be taken back as close as possible to the main limb or trunk, following the targets for pruning *(see p.52)*.

Pruning climbers Climbers need to be pruned for size and for neatness rather than for shape. Many are also pruned to encourage flowering. In nature, a typical climber may grow up a tree or scramble over shrubs and eventually consist of long, bare, rope-like stems with flowers and foliage at their ends. This accurately describes the habit of some species of clematis, the garden versions of which, when grown into trees and large shrubs, need no pruning at all.

However, we do not want to see long lengths of bare stem on trellises and walls, so we prune to encourage flowering from the ground upward on a shorter, neater plant that may also be kept within the bounds of a porch or one pillar of a pergola.

Clematis that flower on the previous season's wood should be pruned after flowering *(Fig. 18)*. With clematis that flower on the new wood made in the current year, cutting away the whole top of the plant to within 1 ft (30 cm) of the ground in early spring maximizes the production of flowering wood and low-level flowers *(Fig. 19)*.

Other climbers, notably wisterias, are pruned by a different method to encourage flowers lower than where they would bloom if they grew into tall trees. Prune wisteria in high summer. The long growths of the current year, which are like whips, should be pruned right back to two or three buds from the main stem. The resulting

To create a relaxed, informal style, this *Vitis vinifera purpurea* has been allowed to scramble through surrounding plants without being pruned.

FIG. 18 CLEMATIS VARIETIES THAT FLOWER ON OLD WOOD

Remove all flower stems immediately after flowering.

FIG. 19 CLEMATIS VARIETIES THAT FLOWER ON NEW WOOD

Prune to within 12 in (30 cm) of the ground in early spring.

FIG. 20 WISTERIA

For maximum flower production, prune the current year's growth back to 2–3 buds from the main stem in summer.

spurs will develop flower buds, and the plants will flower much more profusely and all along the main stems *(Fig. 20)*.

Cutting back There is one type of shrub pruning, however, that can be carried out without concern for the loss of a season's flowers. This is cuttting back — a drastic measure taken when a shrub has become old, unsightly, or so leggy that the number of flowers it carries is of no great decorative value *(Fig. 21)*.

If shrubs have been dealt with properly from the start and given good light and adequate space, few really need cutting back, but it is occasionally necessary even in the best-regulated gardens. The beautiful French hybrid lilacs, *Syringa vulgaris* hybrids, are a good example of deciduous shrubs that benefit from this treatment from time to time. At its simplest, the entire shrub is cut down by half or even more, and weak or badly crossing branches can be removed at the same time. Do not be afraid to cut back hard, as new growth usually starts from just below the cut. As the plant will put so much energy into growth the following year, flowers are unlikely anyway. Nevertheless, the best time to carry out this operation is in late winter. Note that many shrubs, including several brooms, cannot be treated in this way, as they will not "break" into new growth from old wood. Rhododendrons, on the other hand, will break from buds that have been concealed beneath their bark.

Pruning evergreens Evergreens are generally pruned for shape and size, and as such, decisions about when and how much are largely up to the individual. Cutting back may also be required, but it should be done carefully. Broad-leaved evergreens can be cut back hard, but many coniferous plants will not regrow if cut back into the old wood. Late winter or early spring is the best time for most broad-leaved types; coniferous evergreens can be lightly trimmed, if required, in early summer as the new growth starts to elongate.

Pruning deciduous shrubs Generally speaking, pruning deciduous shrubs depends on when they flower and whether they do so on wood produced in the previous or current year. Those that flower earlier usually do so on the previous year's wood; there is no new wood on which to flower. Those that flower later do so on wood produced in the current year. The best rule is always to prune so that you provide the longest possible period of growth between pruning and flowering.

Shrubs that flower on new wood It makes sense to prune shrubs that flower on new wood *(Fig. 22)* in late winter or early spring for two reasons. The first is because winter pruning is for growth, and it is on new growths that flowers will be borne. The second is that this gives them the longest period of growth before flowering, which is late in the summer or in fall. Pruning immediately after flowering has little point, as no growth is made during the winter and plants also become susceptible to dieback caused by frost, so that another pruning might well be necessary.

Pruning does not need to be severe, just enough to stimulate good

FIG. 21 CUTTING BACK

Remove all dead, diseased, and crossing branches (i) and cut back the remainder by half (ii). This operation may be carried out at any time of year but is best done in late winter.

quantities of new shoots for bearing the best possible crop of flowers. Exactly how hard you cut back depends on the particular shrub. However, once you step onto the treadmill of keeping the shrub to a set size by hard pruning, you may end up producing an ugly duckling that will take months to turn into a swan again. A typical shrub to which this happens is *Hydrangea paniculata*, which is all too often reduced to a tangle of shorn stumps in the mistaken idea that this is necessary annually for it to put on a good show of flowers. (The correct pruning method is illustrated in Fig. 23.) Forms of *Buddleia davidii*, on the other hand, really do need to be cut back drastically each year *(Fig. 24)*. They are best grown where their pollarded stumps are hidden but where their stems, which can grow well over 7 ft (2 m) in a season, can reach into the light and put on their show for you and the butterflies.

Shrubs that flower later on new wood but that partly renew themselves from the base each year can be pruned in late winter or early spring in a somewhat different manner. Mophead and lacecap hydrangeas, for example, are best pruned first from the bottom upward, with old, weak, or overcrowded stems being removed entirely at ground level. This stimulates strong, straight growths that will grow right up through the bush in the first year. The second step is to prune from the top downward, an operation that consists of cutting back the old flowering growths to the first strong pair of buds.

Shrubs that flower on old wood The majority of shrubs that flower on the wood of the previous year are pruned immediately after flowering to allow the longest period of growth before the next flowering. However, those that flower in early spring are pruned differently from those that flower later on. This is because the early ones flower before the formation of any new wood and,

FIG. 22 SHRUBS THAT FLOWER ON NEW WOOD

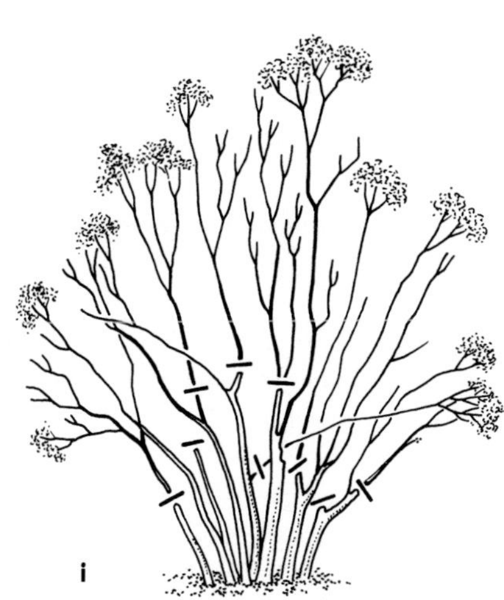

Prune shrubs that flower on new wood in late winter or early spring (i) to maximize growth and resultant flowering (ii).

FIG. 23 HYDRANGEA PANICULATA

Less vigorous shrubs that flower on new wood, like *H. paniculata*, should be pruned carefully in late winter or early spring. First remove all old, weak, and overcrowded growth from the base; then cut back flowered growths to the first pair of strong buds (i). Careful pruning will result in good flowering and a compact shape (ii).

FIG. 24 BUDDLEIA DAVIDII

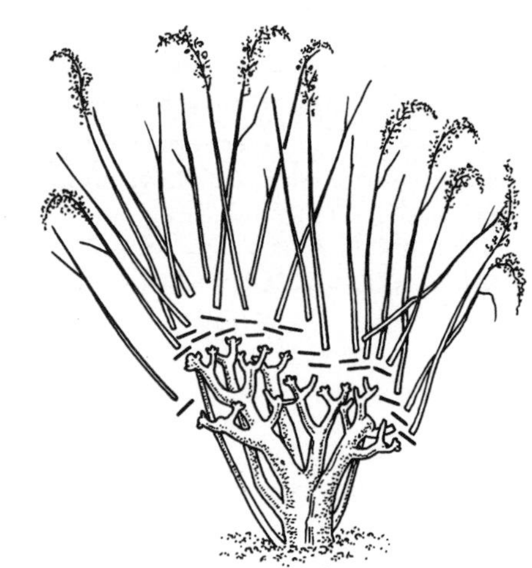

Vigorous shrubs that flower on new wood, like *B. davidii*, should be pruned hard in early spring. Remove the entire length of the previous year's flowering shoot (i) to achieve good flowering at an attractive height in the summer (ii).

therefore, can be cut back with only the old flowering wood being removed. This stimulates the formation of new wood and leads to a better crop of flowers the following year. It is the method used for forsythias *(Fig. 25)*.

If simple cutting back is performed directly after flowering on shrubs that flower later, when formation of new wood is under way, the new wood will be removed or badly shortened and the next flowering will be more or less severely curtailed. They should, therefore, be much more selectively pruned, so that just the old flowering stems are cut away. At the same time, any crossing or overcrowded branches can be removed at their points of origin. If this method is used on mock oranges and deutzias, for example, they will be greatly improved *(Fig. 26)*.

Clipping formal hedges The object of clipping hedges is to create a neat, attractive barrier, but patience is essential. If the hedge is allowed to grow too quickly in height, it will become thin and sparse. It may require clipping when young, sacrificing height for the formation of a dense, wide base. Once established, a hedge may require only one or two cuts each year. There are

FIG. 25 SHRUBS THAT FLOWER EARLY ON OLD WOOD

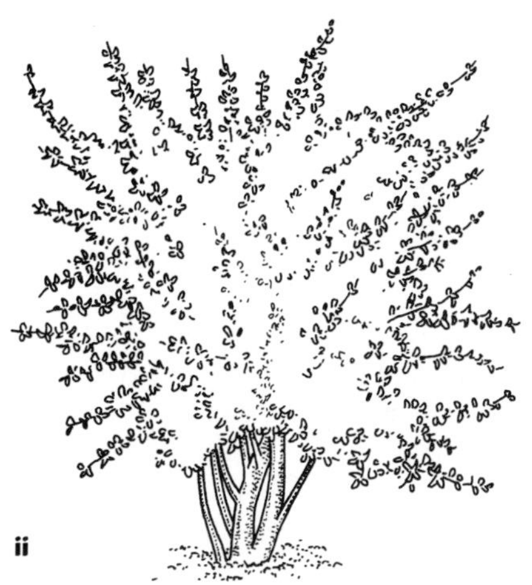

Shrubs such as forsythia that flower early in the year on wood produced the previous year should be pruned immediately after flowering. As no new growth will have formed, simply remove the old flowered stems (i) to maintain a good shape and promote flowering the next year (ii).

FIG. 26 SHRUBS THAT FLOWER LATE ON OLD WOOD

Shrubs such as mock orange that flower later in the year on wood produced the previous year should have flowered stems, crossing branches, and overcrowded branches removed carefully immediately after flowering, avoiding the current year's growth (i). This procedure will ensure that the wood is retained in good shape to maximize flowering the following year (ii).

exceptions, however, such as *Ulmus pumila*, which needs clipping every few weeks.

All clipping should be delayed until early summer and completed by late summer. This allows spring growth to take place but also lets new shoots harden off before winter. Hedge plants that need only one clipping, such as hornbeam and beech, should be trimmed in late summer. Those that flower late on wood of the current year, such as caryopteris, should be clipped in early to midspring. With several kinds of flowering hedges, a different pruning regimen may be needed. For example, pyracanthas may be clipped any time after spring, but flowering will be cut short. If you want to enjoy the decorative fruits, you should prune with pruning shears just after flowering, allowing chosen clusters of young berries to remain, and then clip between with hand shears.

Young hedges should be clipped with hand shears, while pruning shears may well prove to be the best tool for early shaping. Power hedge trimmers may be used on strong, mature hedges that are not required to flower or fruit.

Pruning for snow damage Although most trees and shrubs are tough and capable of standing up to the rigors of winter, they still may require vigilance after heavy snowfalls. Evergreens, and particularly conifers, may be "opened up" by snow — a process by which heavily laden branches are torn from the main body of the plant. If this occurs, it is necessary to neaten the tear with a clean pruning cut in order to avoid any potential problems with pests and diseases. However, it is preferable to prevent the possibility of such damage by gently shaking snow off affected plants.

Propagation

The methods described in this chapter for propagating plants are simple, yet rewarding, and represent the most effective ways to raise modest numbers of new specimens for the garden. They do not require specialized equipment and take up little room. Indeed, most gardeners already have the necessary tools, such as knives, pruning shears, and pots, and can find space, whether in a sunroom, cold frame, or even a window.

The two main techniques covered — cutting and layering — are widely used for the production of trees and shrubs and are forms of vegetative (or asexual) propagation, whereby shoots are rooted either after being removed from or while remaining attached to the parent or stock plant. Because the shoots carry material from the parent, there is no change in the genetic makeup of the new plant.

Cuttings

It is important that the material selected for any method of vegetative propagation is true to type, free from pests and diseases, and

Cornus alba (red-twig dogwood) is grown for its bright red stems, which create rich clumps of color in the landscape. The plant can be propagated from hardwood cuttings.

Populus nigra 'Italica' (Lombardy poplar) forms an effective screen, and its rustling leaves are useful in disguising traffic noise. It may be propagated from root cuttings.

FIG. 27 HARDWOOD CUTTINGS

1 Take hardwood cuttings between late fall and late winter.

2 Select well-ripened, vigorous, pencil-thick shoots.

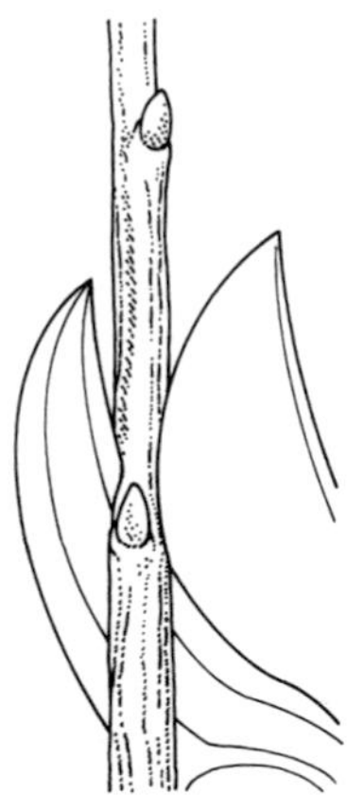

3 At the top of the cutting, make a sloping cut just above the proposed top bud.

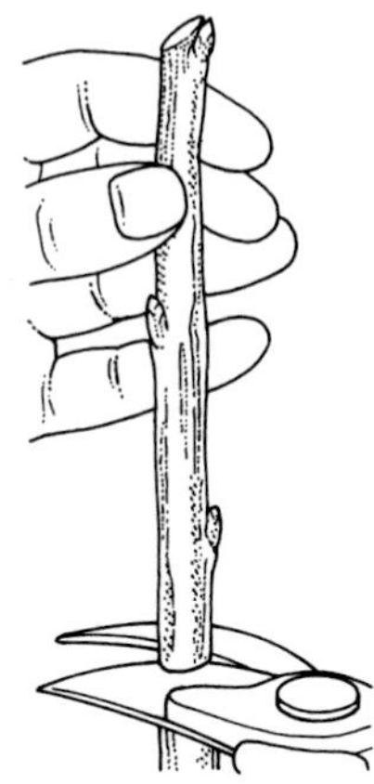

4 Then make a flat cut 6 in (15 cm) below the top cut.

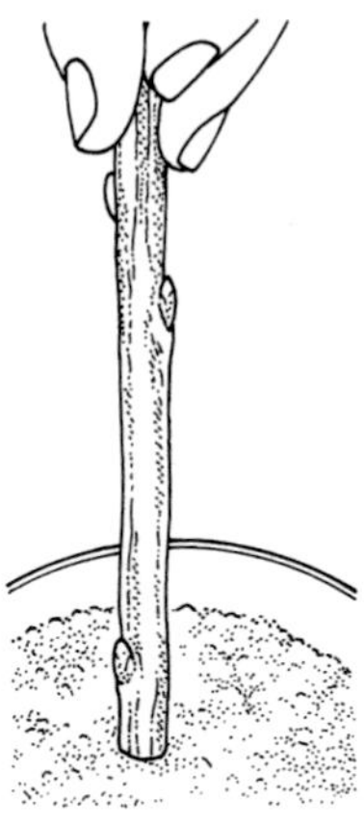

5 Dip the base of the cutting into rooting hormone powder.

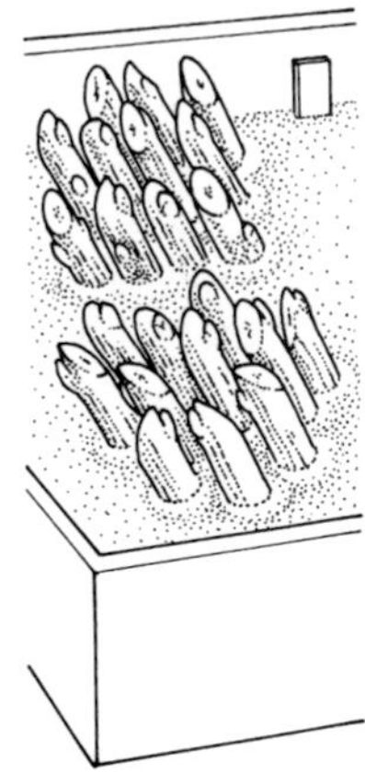

6 Bundle the cuttings together and place in a box of sand with the top third above the surface.

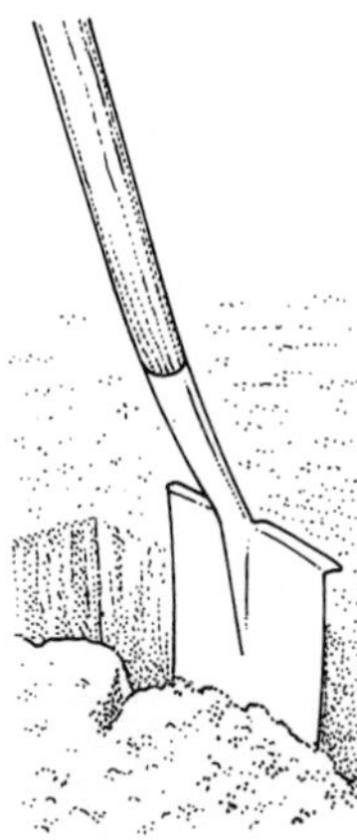

7 In spring, before bud break, prepare a 5 in (12 cm) trench in a propagation bed or a cold frame.

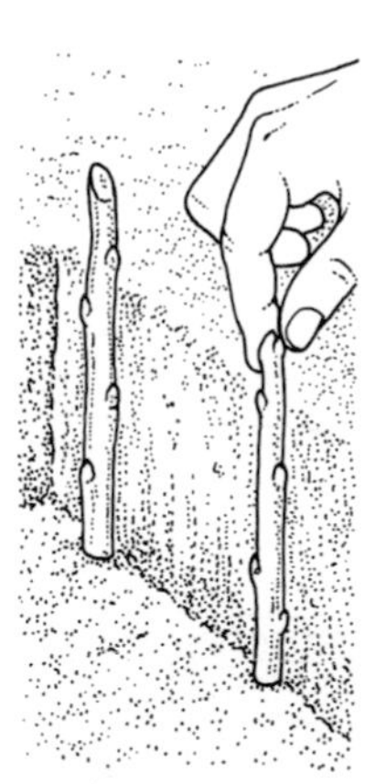

8 Plant cuttings vertically in the trenches at 4–6 in (10–15 cm) intervals.

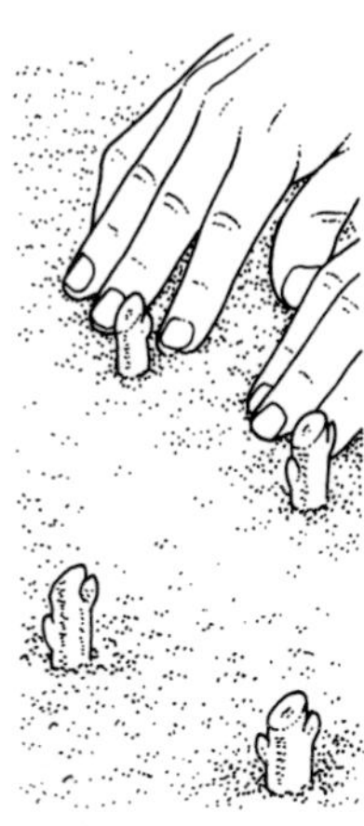

9 Leave 12–18 in (30–45 cm) between rows in open ground and 4 in (10 cm) in the cold frame.

10 Firm down the soil, leaving 1 in (2 cm) of cutting exposed.

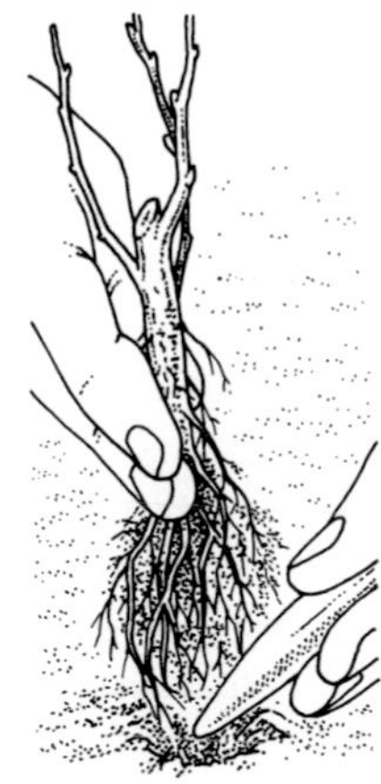

11 In fall, lift the rooted cuttings and plant in the final site.

not flowering. If flowering material is selected, all flower buds must be removed, as the plant will use energy to produce flowers rather than to develop a new root system.

In propagation by cuttings, a portion of stem, root, or leaf is cut from the parent or stock plant and induced to form roots and shoots. Taking cuttings, in all its variations, is the most widely practiced method of vegetative propagation. The list of plants that can be propagated by cuttings is endless, and the method has many advantages. First, many cuttings can be taken from a single parent and propagated in a small area. They can be rooted quickly and inexpensively and do not require complicated equipment. Plants raised by vegetative propagation exhibit greater uniformity, something that is not present in seed propagation.

It is important that the rooting medium is firm and dense so that it will hold the cuttings upright. Its volume must be fairly constant, whether wet or dry, although it must retain enough moisture not to need constant watering. It must also be sufficiently porous to allow excess water to drain freely so that oxygen can reach the

FIG. 28 SEMIHARDWOOD CUTTINGS

1 Cut off a shoot with all its current season's growth in late summer.

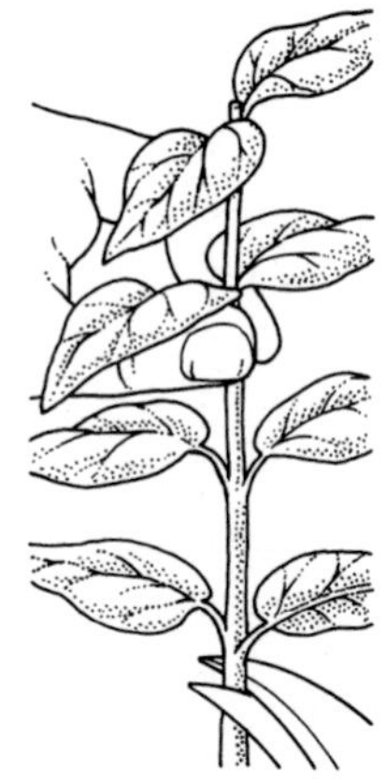

2 Make a flat cut at the bottom of the shoot below a leaf node, and wound *(Fig. 29)* if the bark is thick.

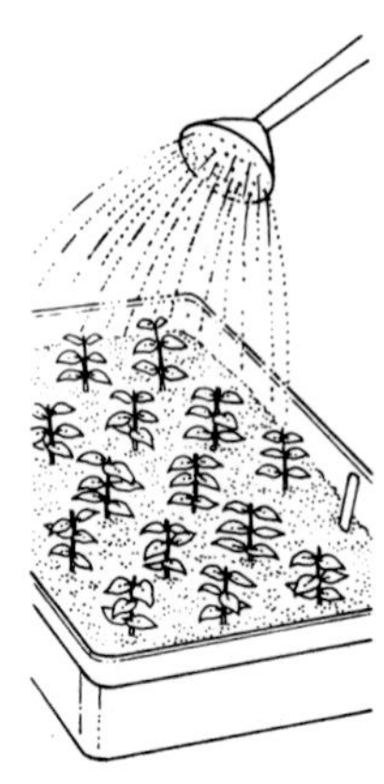

3 Dip cuttings into rooting hormone powder and insert into a flat. Water well and spray with fungicide.

FIG. 29 WOUNDING

Making a heavy single slice wound on a semihardwood cutting.

roots. Finally, it must be free from pests and diseases. Commonly used mixes for rooting medium are as follows: 50 percent ground bark (fine grade) and 50 percent perlite (fine); 50 percent sharp sand or silver sand and 50 percent peat moss or coconut fiber; 50 percent peat moss or coconut fiber and 50 percent ground bark; and equal parts peat moss, bark, and perlite. All these ratios are by volume and not by weight.

Rooting hormones Cuttings are treated with a rooting hormone (auxin) to increase their propensity to form roots, to hasten root initiation, and to increase the uniformity and quality of rooting. Plants that root easily do not benefit from an external supply of auxin. It is best to save rooting hormones for those that are difficult to root. In the late 1930s the substance now known as auxin was identified as indoleacetic acid. Of simple formation, it was soon being artificially manufactured. Today the most reliable rooting agents contain indolebutyric acid (IBA) or naphthaleneacetic acid (NAA), both available in liquid and powder form.

Deciduous hardwood cuttings *(Fig. 27)* are taken through the winter from matured material. The aim of this method is to induce the cutting to produce roots before the buds grow in spring. As there are no leaves when the cutting is taken, water loss is greatly reduced. Hardwoods are the easiest and least expensive to propagate from cuttings. The range of plants successfully propagated from deciduous hardwood cuttings is smaller than those suited to softwood or semihardwood propagation, but it includes the following: *Buddleia davidii*, *Clematis montana*, *Cornus alba*, *Cornus stolonifera*, *Deutzia*, *Euonymus*, *Forsythia*, *Hibiscus*, *Hypericum*, *Kerria japonica*, *Laburnum*, *Lonicera periclymenum*, *Metasequoia glyptostroboides*, *Philadelphus*, *Physocarpus*, *Platanus*, *Polygonum*, *Populus*, *Prunus cerasifera*, *Rosa rugosa*, *Salix*, *Sambucus*, *Spiraea*, *Symphoricarpos*, *Vitis*, and *Weigela*.

Take cuttings from well-ripened, vigorous, one-year-old shoots of roughly pencil thickness. Discard weak and bent shoots along with the shoot tip. Begin at the top of the cutting by making a sloping cut away from the bud, then make a flat cut at the bud closest to 6 in (15 cm) from the top of the cutting. Bundle the cuttings together and tie with string or an elastic band. The cuttings may then be heeled into the ground, or placed in a cold frame or in a bucket of sand with the top third above the surface; the latter allows them to form a callus before being planted out in spring. Keep the cuttings in a location that is cool but that will not get below about 14°F (-10°C). In spring, carefully lift them, separate the individual specimens, and plant in a propagation bed or a cold frame prior to planting in their final locations in fall.

The final planting depth varies for trees and shrubs. For trees,

The *Deutzia* species, including *D. scabra* 'Punctata' illustrated here, are suitable for propagation from softwood cuttings.

FIG. 30 SOFTWOOD CUTTINGS

1 Cut off the soft tip in the early morning when the cells are fully turgid.

2 Trim the stem at 1/8 in (2 mm) below the leaf node, using a sharp knife.

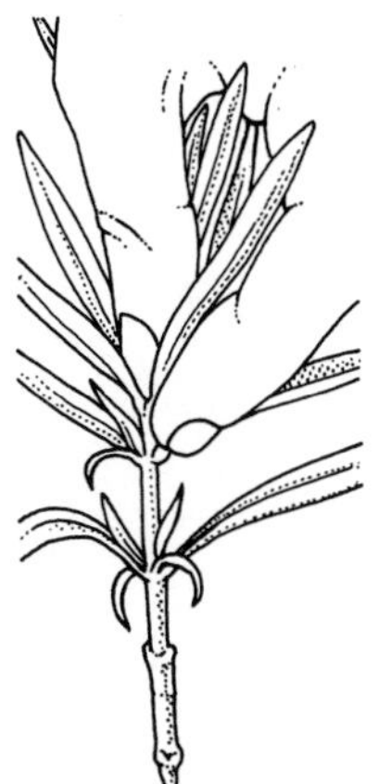

3 Remove the lower third of leaf cover and dip the stem into rooting hormone powder.

4 Insert the cuttings into the rooting medium up to the lowest leaves.

5 Label clearly and water.

6 Spray with a liquid fungicide at least once a week.

insert the cutting so only one or two buds are left above soil level. For shrubs, leave two to four buds above the soil to create a multistemmed specimen.

Semihardwood cuttings *(Fig. 28)* are taken from evergreens once they have started to build up wood tissue toward the end of the growing season. Material is collected between late summer and midwinter. Some of the plants commonly propagated using this method are *Abelia*, *Akebia trifoliata*, *Aucuba*, *Berberis*, *Buxus*, *Calocedrus decurrens*, *Calycanthus floridus*, *Camellia*, *Cephalotaxus fortunei*, *Chamaecyparis*, *Clematis armandii*, *Cryptomeria japonica*, × *Cupressocyparis leylandii*, *Cupressus*, *Elaeagnus*, *Euonymus*, *Garrya elliptica*, *Hedera*, *Ilex*, *Jasminum*, *Juniperus*, *Kalmia latifolia*, *Lapageria rosea*, *Mahonia*, *Microbiota decusata*, *Nandina domestica*, *Osmanthus*, *Picea*, *Pieris*, *Pileostegia hydrangoides*, *Pittosporum*, *Podocarpus*, *Prunus laurocerasus*, *Rhododendron*, *Sarcococca*, *Skimmia*, *Smilax*, *Taxus*, *Thuja*, *Torreya californica*, and *Trachelospermum jasminoides*.

Cut off a shoot with all its current season's growth in late summer. Because the stems have begun to produce bark, some semihardwood cuttings may require wounding *(Fig. 29)*. Greater emphasis is placed on the use of rooting hormone powders, too. The optimum cutting size is 4–7 in (10–17 cm). Remove the lower foliage so that it does not come in contact with the rooting medium. Make a flat cut below a node. If the bark is thick, wound the specimen, then apply the rooting hormone. Insert the cuttings into seed flats, label, water well, spray with a fungicide, and place in a cold frame and cover with plastic.

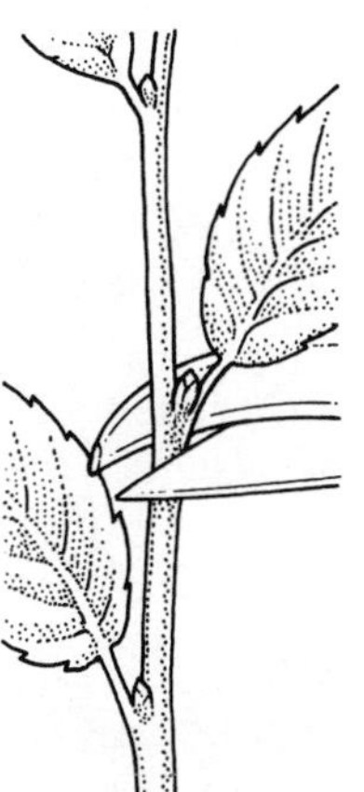

A nodal cutting is taken by cutting the soft tip just below a leaf node.

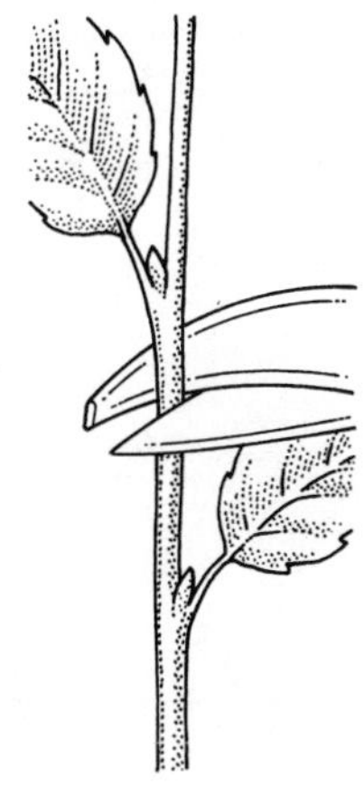

An internodal cutting is taken by cutting the soft tip halfway between two leaf nodes.

Softwood cuttings *(Fig. 30)* are taken from very soft growth between midspring and midsummer in the early morning when the cells are still turgid. The cuttings are extremely soft, so they must be taken quickly and placed in a humid environment before they wilt.

Listed here are some of the plants propagated in this way: *Acer*, *Actinidia kolomikta*, *Buddleia*, *Campsis radicans*, *Catalpa*, *Clematis*, *Cornus*, *Cotinus*, *Deutzia*, *Forsythia*, *Fuchsia*, *Hebe*, *Hydrangea*, *Hypericum*, *Kolkwitzia amabilis*, *Lonicera*, *Magnolia*, *Parthenocissus*, *Perovskia*, *Philadelphus*, *Potentilla*, *Pyracantha*, *Ribes*, *Schisandra*, *Schizophragma hydrangeoides*, *Spiraea*, *Stewartia*, *Syringa*, *Viburnum*, *Vitis*, and *Wisteria*.

Softwood cuttings can be divided into two groups: those taken nodally and those taken internodally. Nodal — cutting the soft tip just below a leaf node — is the most common method. The optimum cutting length is 2–4 in (5–10 cm). Strip or cut off the leaves from the cutting and remove the top rosette of leaves at the soft tip to prevent wilting. Make a clean cut just below a node with a sharp knife.

Internodal cuttings are used for plants, such as *Buddleia davidii*, that have large internodal spacing. If nodal cuttings were used, then the rooted cutting would develop with a clear, short stem, whereas taking the cutting internodally allows shoots to break close to the base. The method is identical to that for nodal cuttings, except for the fact that the cut is made at a point roughly halfway between two nodes.

FIG. 31 ROOT CUTTINGS

1 Lift the plant from mid- to late winter.

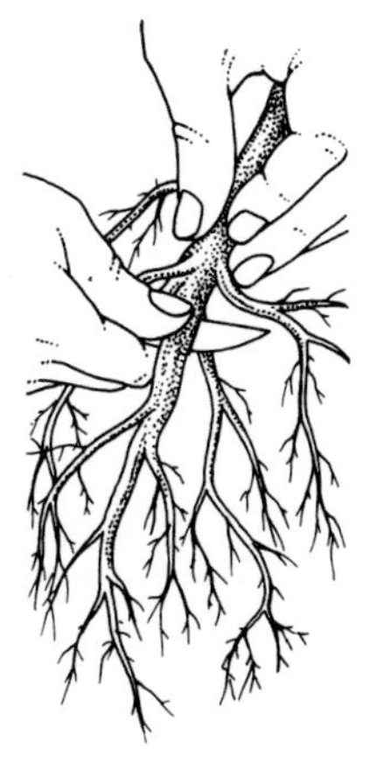

2 Carefully wash the roots and then with a sharp knife remove pencil-thick ones close to the crown.

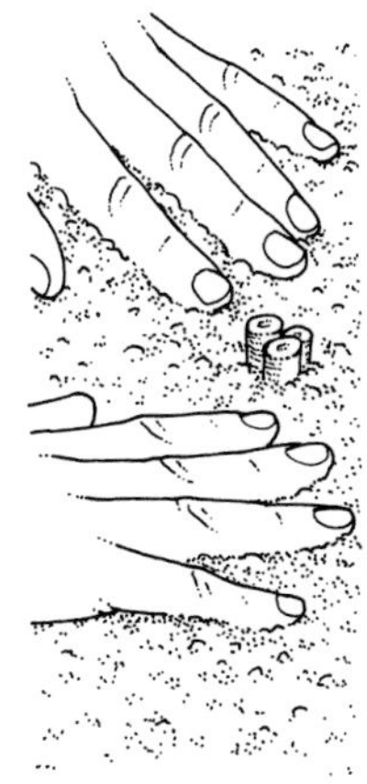

3 Return the plant to its position in the garden.

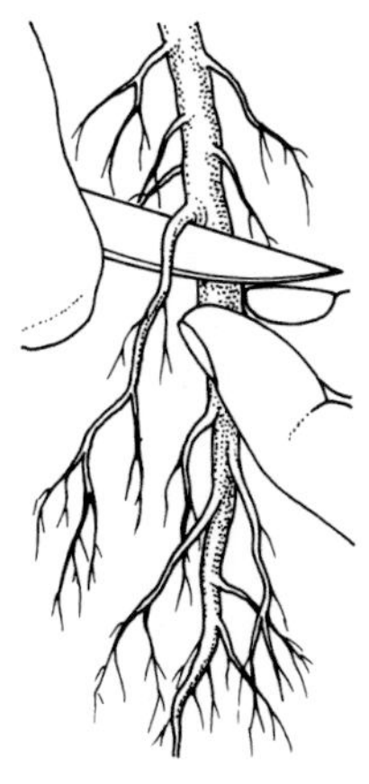

4 Remove any fibrous lateral roots from the cuttings.

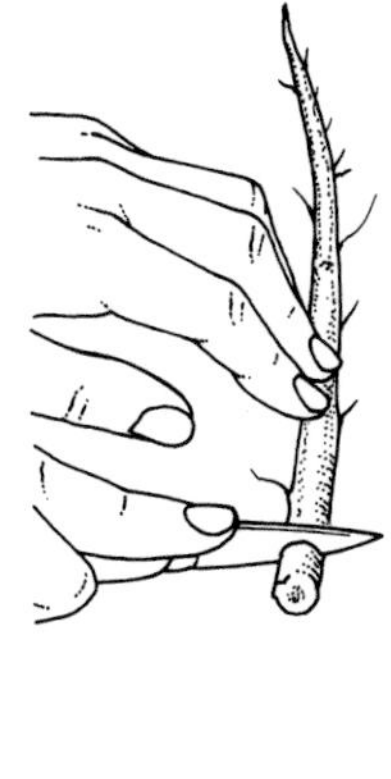

5 Make a flat cut at the top of the root (the end nearest to the stem).

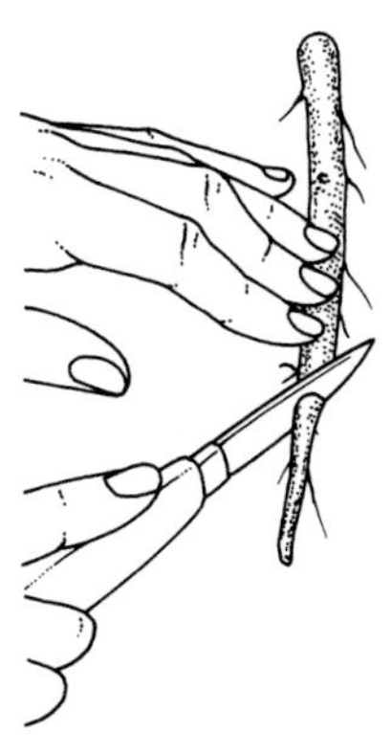

6 Make a sloping cut at the bottom of the root.

7 Insert the bottom end of the root cutting into a seed flat so that the top of the root cutting is level with the surface of the rooting medium. **8** Label and water regularly.

Root cuttings *(Fig. 31)* are taken less often in the nursery trade because of the advances in and economics of softwood and semihardwood propagation. It remains, however, a suitable propagation technique for the home garden. Listed here are some of the plants that can be raised with this method: *Ailanthus altissima*, *Albizia*, *Amelanchier*, *Aralia*, *Bignonia capreolata*, *Campsis radicans*, *Catalpa*, *Chaenomeles*, *Cladrastis lutea*, *Daphne*, *Decaisnea fargesii*, *Embothrium coccineum*, *Gymnocladus dioica*, *Indigofera*, *Koelreuteria paniculata*, *Paulownia tomentosa*, *Phellodendron amurense*, *Populus*, *Rhus*, *Robinia*, *Rosa*, *Rubus*, *Sambucus*, *Sassafras albidum*, *Syringa*, and *Xanthoceras sorbifolium*.

Take root cuttings from mid- to late winter (depending on your climate) while the plant is dormant. First, lift the parent plant and expose and carefully wash some of the roots. Remove pencil-thick roots to make into cuttings 2 in (5 cm) long. Make a sloping cut at the bottom of the cutting, the distal end (the end farthest away from the stem), and a flat cut at the top, the proximal end. Dip the prepared cuttings into a fungicide; there is no need to use a rooting hormone. Insert the distal end into the rooting medium until the tip is covered. The cuttings may also be laid flat and lightly covered with rooting medium. Label and water well. Place the cuttings in a cold frame or a greenhouse or just cover with plastic. Do not forget to return the parent plant to the garden.

Prunus cerasifera 'Nigra' makes an excellent, dense hedge shrub and is suitable for propagation by layering.

LAYERING

Propagation by means of layering differs from other methods of asexual propagation in that the "new addition" is induced to produce new roots while it is still attached to the parent plant. Once rooted, this "new" plant is then severed from its parent, or stock, plant and allowed to grow on its own roots unaided. The easiest plants to propagate with this technique are those that naturally produce suckers. Many, such as *Rubus fruticosus* (blackberry), naturally reproduce themselves by this method. In fact, tip layering is the only method of propagation for the blackberry.

The first known record of the layering technique dates to 1608, but it was probably practiced much earlier. During the 18th, 19th, and early 20th centuries, layering was widely used and, in many cases, was the primary method of propagation. The main problem with layering as a commercial production method is the amount of space occupied by the stock plants. However, it remains an excellent way to raise small numbers of plants for the gardener.

The following factors are required if layering is to succeed. In all types of layering the plant being layered is attached to the parent plant during the production of roots. This produces a larger plant in a much shorter time compared with other methods of propagation. Constriction must be induced within the stem to

FIG. 32 SIMPLE LAYERING

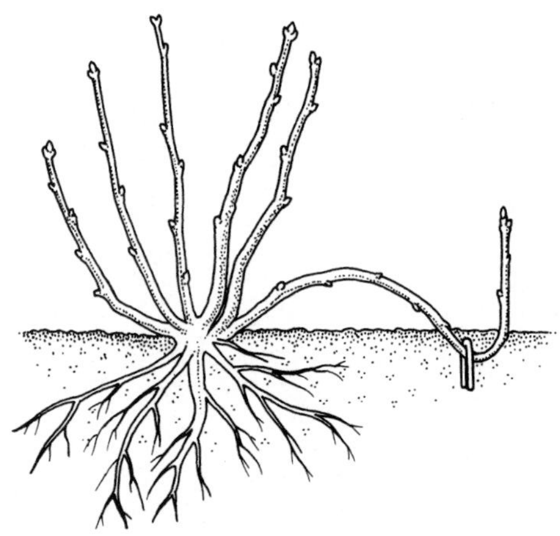

1 Bend a flexible stem to the ground and pin a section of it just below the surface of the soil.

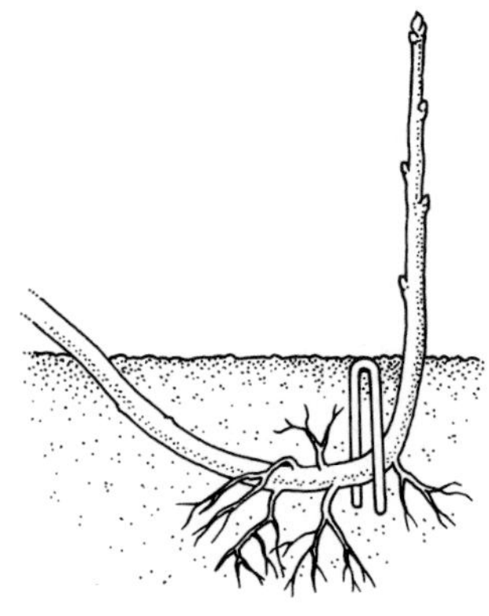

2 After one year, sufficient roots will have developed to allow the layered shoot to be severed from the parent plant.

restrict the natural flow of auxin, which acts as a rooting hormone at the point of restriction. The exclusion of light is thought to speed up the production of wound tissue and hence increase the speed of rooting.

Simple layering *(Fig. 32)* There are three main periods when simple layering can be undertaken: fall, late winter, and early spring. Spring or summer may be preferable if the stems, such as those of the flowering dogwoods *(Cornus kousa, C. nuttallii,* and *C. florida),* are too brittle during the winter months.

FIG. 33 STEM CONSTRICTION

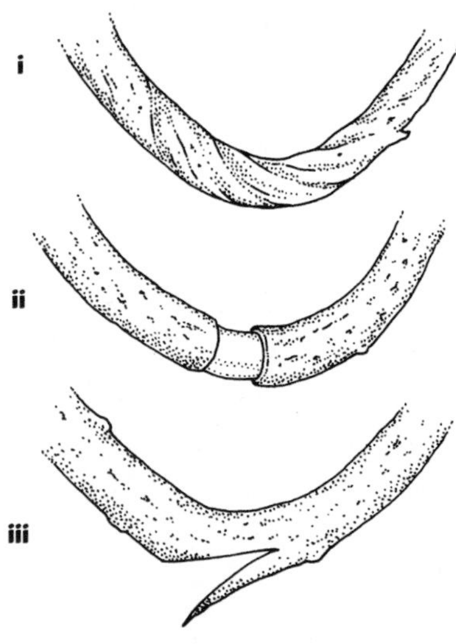

Methods of stem constriction required for simple, serpentine, and air layering: (i) twisting is achieved by rotating each end of the stem in opposite directions and pinning down; (ii) girdling involves removing the top layer of bark as shown with a sharp knife; (iii) creating a tongue requires making an incision into a third of the thickness of the stem.

The method involves bending a stem and pegging it just below the surface of the soil. A mixture of peat moss and sand is often used as a rooting medium, although just peat, sand, sawdust, coconut fiber, or even the native soil can also be used. The stem is then constricted and staked; this can be accomplished by twisting the stem, girdling it, or creating a tongue *(Fig. 33).*

The constricted stem is pegged down into the soil; a stake may be used to keep it vertical. The layered shoot should produce sufficient root growth within a year, although in some cases two years may be required. The shoot should be severed from the stock plant as close to the parent as possible. Four to six weeks later, carefully lift it. The shoot can either be placed in its permanent location or containerized and allowed to develop further.

Mound or stool layering *(Fig. 34)* is undertaken in late winter. The stem of the parent plant is cut back hard to within 1 in (2.5 cm) of the soil to encourage shoots to develop near the base. Soil is then mounded up around the plant, usually in two or three stages to avoid suffocating the parent plant. When the stems reach 6–8 in (15–20 cm), soil is mounded up to approximately 2–3 in (5–7.5 cm). This is repeated in midsummer, mounding the soil up to half the height of the stem. Another mounding can be done in late summer so that the total depth of the mound is about 6–8 in (15–20 cm). The first rooted shoots can be severed from the parent plant one to two years after mounding, in late winter.

French or continuous layering *(Fig. 35)* is often used if more than one plant is required. Selected shoots of the parent plant

Cornus florida Rubra group is grown for its beautiful rosy pink flower bracts, which are borne in late spring. Layering is best carried out in spring and summer when the plant stems are less brittle.

FIG. 34 MOUND OR STOOL LAYERING

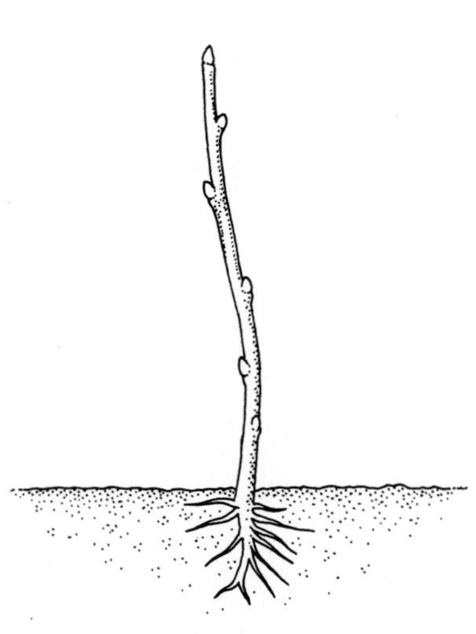

1 Plant the parent plant in winter and allow it to establish during spring and summer.

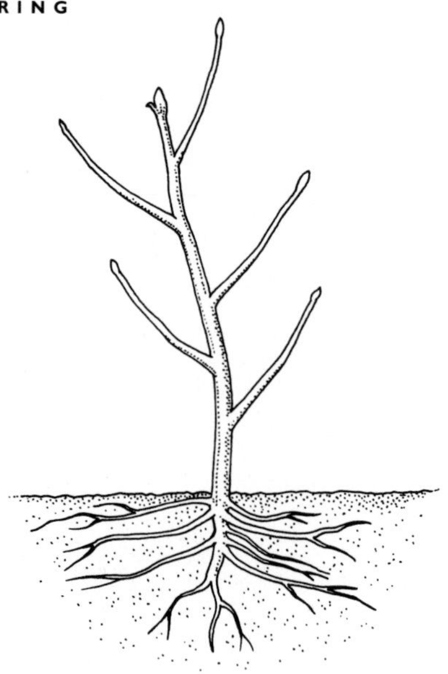

2 A substantial root system will have developed by one year after planting.

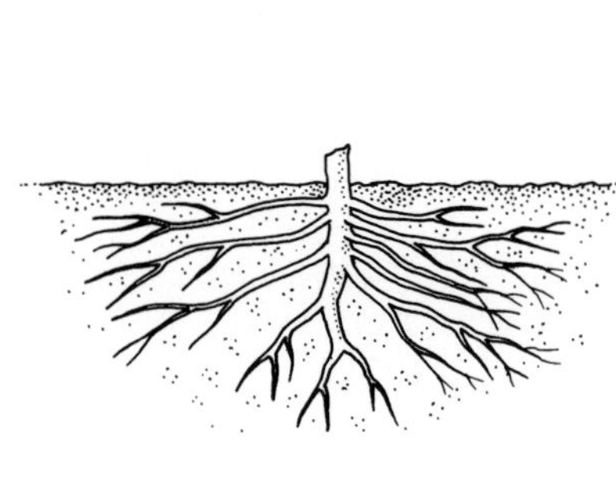

3 In late winter, a year after planting, cut the stem back to 1 in (2.5 cm) above soil level to encourage shoots to develop at the base of the stem.

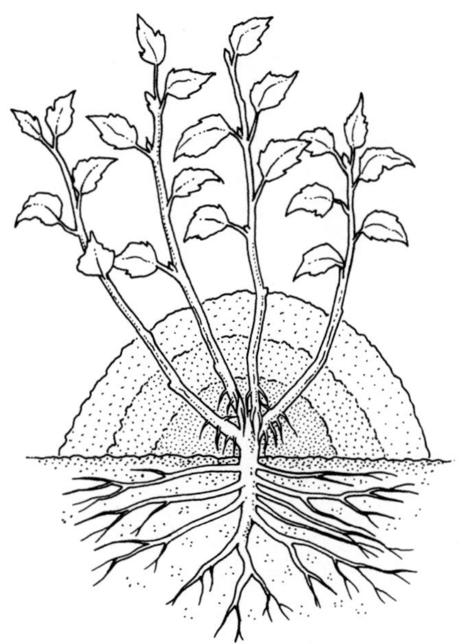

4 Mound the soil up in three stages: when the shoots are 6–8 in (15–20 cm) tall; in midsummer; and in late summer.

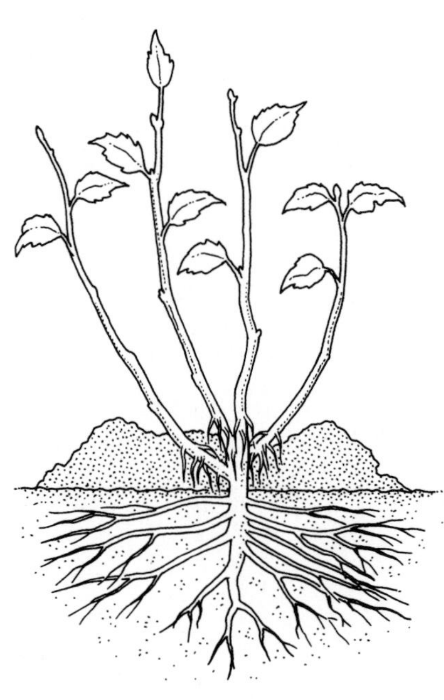

5 The first crop of rooted shoots is ready for harvesting one year after the parent plant was cut back.

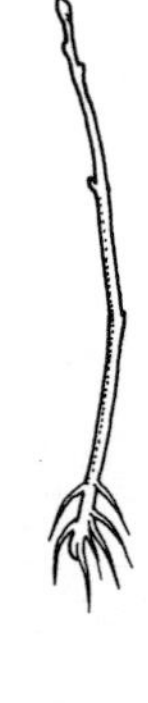

6 A single shoot is removed, ready for planting in a new site.

FIG. 35 FRENCH OR CONTINUOUS LAYERING

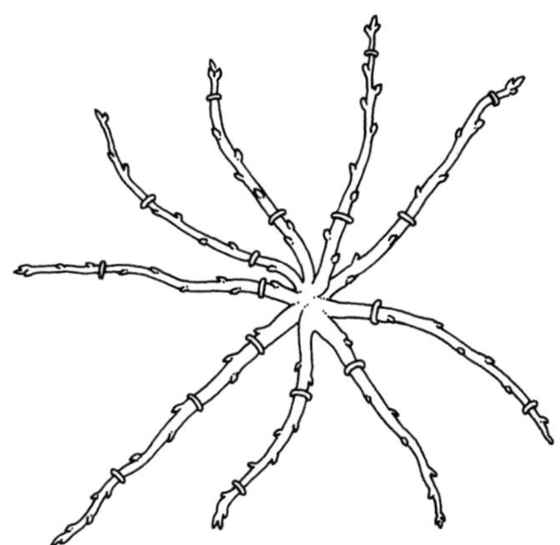

1 Select shoots of the parent plant and peg them down in winter.

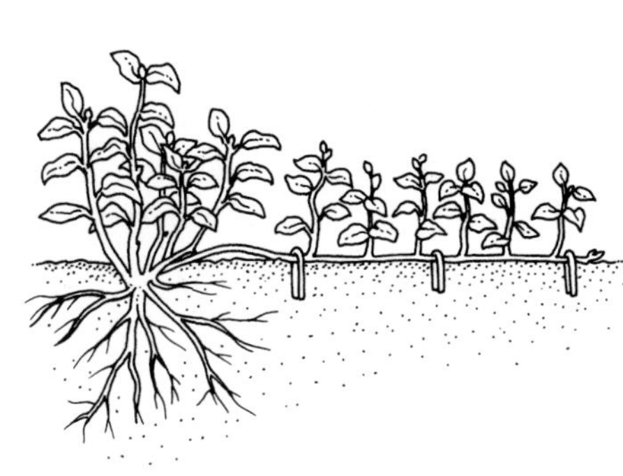

2 New growth will develop uniformly along the pegged-down stem.

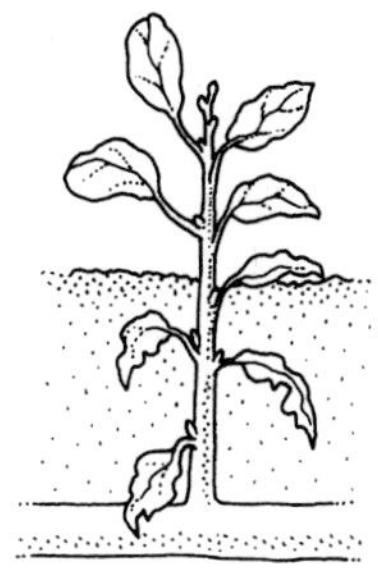

3 When new growth reaches 4 in (10 cm) high, in early summer, remove the pegs and mound soil up 2 in (5 cm).

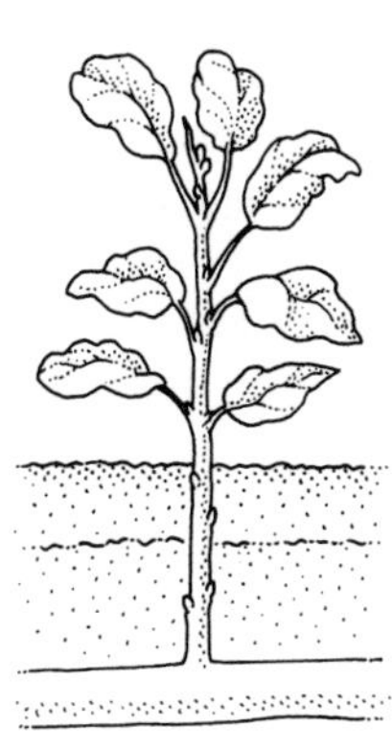

4 Mound up the developing shoots again in midsummer, adding 1 in (2.5 cm) of soil.

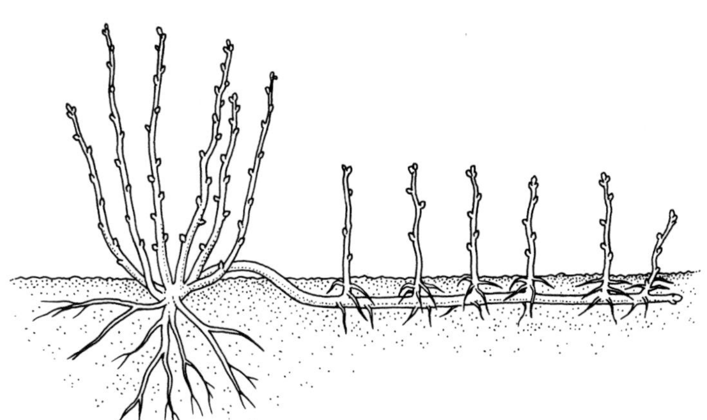

5 Substantial root growth will have developed by the end of the growing season.

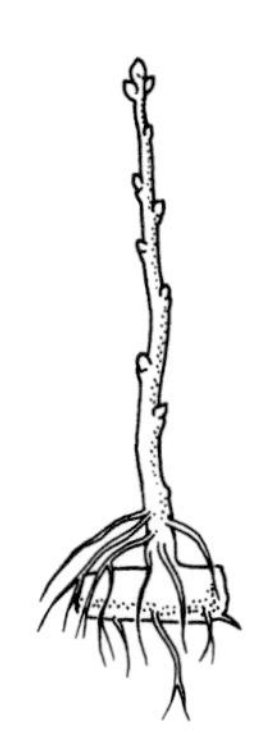

6 Sever the individual shoots in winter and plant out.

FIG. 36 SERPENTINE LAYERING

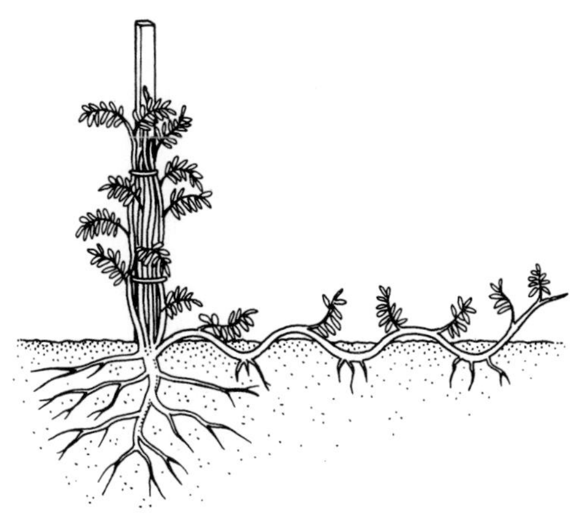

In spring, bury a long, flexible stem at intervals along its length. Sufficient roots will develop after one year to allow the stem to be severed from the parent plant, lifted, cut in sections, and replanted in spring or fall.

FIG. 37 AIR LAYERING

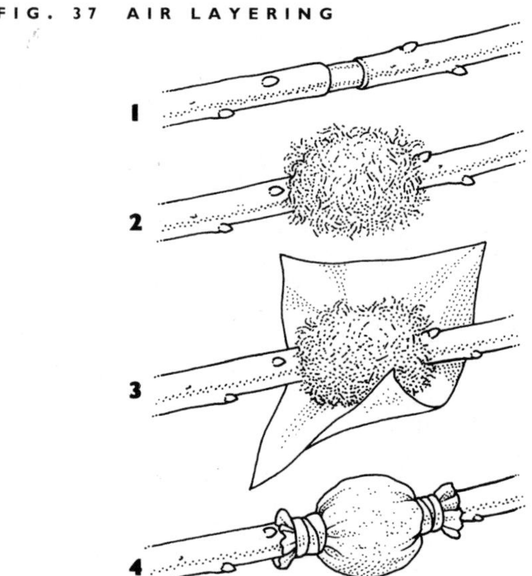

1 Girdle the stem or constrict it using an alternative method *(Fig. 33)*. **2** Apply a powdered rooting hormone to the cut surface and cover with damp sphagnum moss. **3** Wrap a square of black or opaque plastic around the sphagnum moss. **4** Secure the plastic at both ends to the stem.

are pegged down into the soil during winter. New growth develops along the stem. It should be uniform in habit, and once it has reached a height of 4 in (10 cm), the pegs can be removed. Developing shoots are mounded with soil to half their height in early summer; in midsummer, the shoots are mounded again, with 1 in (2.5 cm) of soil. Substantial root growth should have developed along the stem

Perhaps the most spectacular of all vines, *Vitis coignetiae* gives a magnificent fall display. Propagation is best achieved by serpentine layering.

by the end of the growing season. The horizontal stem is then severed from the parent plant during winter, and the individual shoots can be potted or field grown.

Serpentine layering *(Fig. 36)* was once widely used in the commercial production of climbing plants such as wisteria and clematis and remains a valuable technique for the home gardener. It looks similar to French layering, but multiple shoots are produced without burying the entire stem. This method is undertaken in spring. The stems are girdled, twisted, or tongued *(Fig. 33)* at regular intervals before being bent. The constricted parts are then buried in the ground; they are often arranged in a circular pattern to save space. The stem is severed from the parent plant after one year for lifting and replanting in spring or fall.

Air layering *(Fig. 37)*, also known as Chinese layering, is one of the oldest methods of vegetative propagation, dating back some 4,000–5,000 years. It differs from other methods of layering in that the rooting medium is brought to the stem, not vice versa. Air layering is done in spring, using stems from the previous year's growth. A constriction is made 5–12 in (12–30 cm) from the tip *(Fig. 33)* and a rooting hormone is applied to the cut surface to encourage root production. This area is then covered with damp sphagnum moss. A square of black or opaque plastic is wrapped around the moss to conserve moisture and improve humidity and is secured on both sides to the stem. Rooting may take up to two years. The layer can then be removed from the parent plant.

Propagation by Layering

Simple layering
Amelanchier
Arbutus
Azara
Camellia
Carpenteria
Chimonanthus
Corylopsis
Corylus
Daphne
Davidia
Disanthus
Distylium
Drimys
Enkianthus
Erica
Eucryphia
Fothergilla
Halesia
Hamamelis
Ilex
Kalmia
Laurus
Liquidambar
Magnolia
Nothofagus
Parrotia
Photinia
Pieris
Rhododendron
Schizophragma
Syringa

Mound layering
Castanea
Chaenomeles
Daphne
Prunus
Pterocarya
Rhododendron
Syringa
Tilia

French layering
Acer cappadocicum
Acer rubrum
Acer saccharinum
Alnus
Amelanchier
Cercidiphyllum
Cornus
Cotinus
Hoheria
Hydrangea
Prunus
Stachyurus
Syringa
Viburnum

Serpentine layering
Celastrus
Clematis
Jasminum
Lapageria
Smilax
Vitis
Wisteria

Air layering
Daphne
Drimys
Ficus
Hamamelis
Magnolia
Rhododendron

Pests & Diseases

Trees and shrubs are constantly at risk from organisms — animal, fungal, viral, or bacterial — that cause damage or disease. To understand and control them, the gardener must first recognize the symptoms that betray their presence, and often these are all he or she has to go on. Most pathogens (disease-causing agents) are invisible to the naked eye, and insect pests rapidly move on once the damage is done.

Even if you were to keep your plants in optimum conditions, they would still be attacked. So should pests and diseases be clinically eradicated at first sight? No, for this would harm the many beneficial organisms that coexist with the plant. The key to successful control is an integrated system, whereby the cause is identified, monitored, and dealt with in a measured way when visible damage begins to occur. At the same time, control measures should be put in place to prevent a repeat invasion, identifying the conditions that create the opportunity and acting accordingly. Here, as elsewhere, prevention is better than cure. This chapter covers all the major pest and disease problems commonly associated with trees and shrubs, with information on identification and control.

Pests

The term *pest* encompasses all animals that cause damage to plants, including vertebrates, such as rabbits, deer, mice, moles, and birds, as well as invertebrates, such as mites, snails, slugs, aphids, and caterpillars. If a pest is seen causing damage to a plant, then identification is relatively easy. Very often, especially with smaller pests such as mites, it is the symptoms that identify a problem. These symptoms vary from plant to plant but are generally related to the damage the pests cause.

Some insects, such as aphids, have needlelike mouthparts that they push into the soft tissues of the plant and use very much like straws to suck sugars from the living plant. Insects usually feed on the undersides of leaves and on the stems of soft growth. Many insects inject fluid into the plant that may transmit viral disorders. In this case the pest is known as a vector. Nematodes are virus vectors and in many cases deal the plant a double blow, as they not only live in the tissue and feed on the sap but also introduce a disease and reduce plant vigor. The final group of pests have mouthparts that bite or rasp at plant foliage. These include caterpillars, slugs, snails, and many of the beetles, and they may cause a lot of localized and conspicuous damage. Both the adults and the larvae are capable of causing serious damage.

Rabbits, squirrels, and other small rodents can cause a great deal of damage to trees and shrubs. Deer or elk may be a serious problem in gardens. Unfortunately, the various countermeasures usually recommended are seldom successful. Bundles of human hair, lights, music, scent repellents, and soap, for example, may chase away deer for a while, but that is all. Other similar traditional deterrents are equally ineffective. The only defenses that work over time are an electric fence or a high deer fence (6 ft/2 m) and cattle grids in any openings, such as a driveway. Rabbits can be excluded with a fence 2 ft (60 cm) tall made of wire netting and dug into the ground to a depth of about 1 ft (30 cm) *(see p.50)*.

Aphids and adelgids Aphids are small sap-feeding insects that can be found feeding on soft stems and on the undersides of leaves. Their presence weakens and distorts growth, resulting in loss of vigor, and they often introduce viruses. There are several hundred species of aphid, many of which are restricted to just a few host plants. It is possible to control aphids, even on large trees, but it is particularly important on a young plant, whose development may be affected. If young trees and shrubs are attacked, use a systemic insecticide or an insecticidal soap or handpick every three weeks from early spring to midsummer to prevent serious damage. Beneficial insects, such as ladybugs, may also be effective.

Larger trees can also be treated with a systemic insecticide, as it will be translocated throughout the tissues, but this is expensive. Applying insecticides to medium-sized or large trees is a specialized job; contact your local arborist for advice.

Adelgids are sap-sucking insects $^1/_{16}$–$^1/_8$ in (1–2 mm) long that are covered with a woolly, waxy, usually white substance. They are serious pests on larches, spruce, and silver firs. They also occur on Scotch pines and some other members of the genus but do less damage: on dwarf pines they merely look unsightly. They can be treated with malathion or a systemic insecticide in spring.

Spruce gall adelgids produce small galls on Norway spruce, which may persist for many years. These interfere with normal growth and produce misshapen trees. Control of the hemlock adelgid, which is a serious pest of *Tsuga canadensis*, has been achieved using horticultural oils and insecticidal soaps.

Caterpillars Generally speaking, the best method of dealing with caterpillars within reach is to pick them off, together with any eggs, and crush them or drop them into alchohol or kerosene. But any short-term contact insecticide, including rotenone, will kill them. Systemic insecticides are not particularly effective, but the natural bacterium *Bacillus thuringiensis* will control many caterpillars. While every effort should be made to control caterpillars on young or small plants, there is not much you can do when they occur on larger trees.

Vine weevil Vine weevils are small, black beetles with fine yellow hairs. The larvae eat the roots of a wide range of plants, and the adults make notches in the edges of leaves. The adults are active at night in late spring and early summer, hiding in the ground by day. Spray with a contact insecticide if they are visible. The larvae produce symptoms of apparently inexplicable wilt during summer. Closer inspection reveals that the plant's roots have been completely eaten, and plump, white grubs with copper-colored heads can be seen. On the West Coast in particular, rhododendrons are seriously affected. Adult grape and strawberry vine weevils can almost defoliate plants, while the grubs often girdle stems at or below ground level, causing plants to die.

Control of the adults is by systemic pesticides, whereas the larvae can be controlled using a wormlike predatory nematode, which "swims" through the soil and attacks the grubs. The nematode can be used outdoors only in warm weather.

Diseases

Diseases are caused by parasitic organisms, including fungi, bacteria, and viruses. Many of them are secondary pathogens, that is, they require an entry point, such as a wound or tissue damaged by an aphid (primary pathogen).

Fungi

The most important secondary pathogens are fungi. They do not have chlorophyll (the green energy-producing pigment found in plants), so they must find their food from another source — by breaking down plant tissues. Fungi absorb plant nutrients through their threadlike "roots," called hyphae (in mass they are termed mycelium). The mushrooms or toadstools that are produced are the fruiting bodies; it is these we use to help identify the pathogen.

Fungi are divided into two groups: obligate parasites, which develop specialized hyphae able to drain nutrients from plant cells without killing the host; and facultative parasites, which are far more destructive and grow into and between the plant cells. These produce toxic enzymes that seriously damage plant tissues.

Rusts, phytophthora root rot, mildews, anthracnose, blights, and wilts are examples of fungi pathogens.

Rusts These diseases are distinguished by reddish brown spores on plant leaves and result in distorted or stunted growth and dieback. While some rusts have a simple life cycle, others require two different, and usually unrelated, host plants. White pine blister, for example, affects several pine species, then attacks currants and gooseberries. Cedar-apple rust is found on apple, crab apple, hawthorn, and serviceberry, with the alternate host being red cedar and other junipers. Infection can be controlled by spraying with ferbam or sulfur. The most effective control measure, however, is to remove the alternate host from the area. In some states and in Canada, there are legislated distances that must be observed between commercial plantings and the alternate host, and the growing of some host plants has been banned outright.

Phytophthora root rot *(Phytophthora cinnamomi)* This is a major cause of rot in conifers, heathers, rhododendrons, maples, chestnuts, lilacs, camellias, and other woody plants. Phytophthora is a soilborne fungus transmitted through soil water. The fungi infect roots and quickly disturb the water supply to the plant, resulting in foliage wilt, loss of normal color, and desiccation and causing the foliage to turn rusty brown. This color change is most commonly seen during hot, dry, windy, or freezing conditions, when plants are under water stress. The disease is prevalent in soils that waterlog easily and where plants are suffering for other reasons. Infected plants should be removed and so, too, should any plants showing symptoms.

Anthracnose Several closely related diseases causing leaf spots and twig dieback in spring are collectively known as anthracnose. The native sycamore is commonly attacked, but many other trees, including maples, oaks, crab apples, dogwoods, and walnuts, are also susceptible. Symptoms include brown patches on leaves and premature defoliation. Twigs and small branches often die later in the season, and cankers may appear lower down the branch. Good hygiene — raking up and disposing of leaves as they fall — helps to reduce this disease, which is more prevalent in rainy springs. In addition to good hygiene, plants can be sprayed with maneb or zineb, with the first spray given as the leaves unfurl, the second when they are fully open, and a third 14 days later.

Rose rust and blackspot Rose rust has become more prevalent over recent years and is now a major debilitating fungal disease of roses. Orange pustules develop on the leafy stalks and particularly on the undersides of the leaves. Bushes can die quite rapidly. The pustules turn black in autumn and emit countless spores.

Blackspot is characterized by black patches on the leaves and appears especially in humid weather. It rapidly defoliates roses but is relatively easy to keep in check with a regular spraying program and by mulching in winter, which prevents spores from the previous year from being splashed up on the stems by rain.

Verticillium wilt This fungal disease causes dieback in spring. The foliage suddenly collapses and turns brown, and the tree or shrub may suffer a severe setback to growth. It is spread in infected soil and penetrates the slightest wounds in the fine roots, such as those caused by the entry of nematodes. It persists in the tissues for only one year, so an older plant that has survived stands a reasonable chance of recovering. Young plants, however, are usually killed because their conducting tissues become totally blocked by the fungus. The organism may persist in the soil in the form of spores. Avoid planting susceptible plants in the same location.

Treatment is difficult, but a systemic fungicide, made up in sufficient quantities to apply as a root drench, may alleviate the problems. The most frequently affected woody plant genera are *Acer*, *Catalpa*, *Tilia*, and *Syringa*. It does not affect conifers.

BACTERIA

Bacteria are much smaller than fungi. Each one usually consists of a single, microscopic cell that may be rod-shaped, spherical, or threadlike. They reproduce by simple division and can multiply rapidly, especially under warm conditions. They can cause high levels of damage to certain crops. Symptoms are very similar to those of fungal infection. It is worth stressing that bacterial infections are very difficult to control, for few chemicals are effective against them.

Bacteria are responsible for diseases such as fireblight, canker, dieback, gall, and leaf curl.

Fireblight *(Erwinia amylovora)* This is a serious disease of apples, hawthorns, cotoneasters, pyracanthas, pears, photinias, whitebeams, and mountain ash. The bacterium usually enters the plant via the flowers or through open wounds. The infected branch then dies, with the leaves turning brown and remaining on the branch, looking as though they have been burned. In severe cases, reinfection occurs, leading to the death of the entire plant. Cut out infected material immediately by removing the whole branch. Seriously infected shrubs or trees should be removed completely and burned. Any equipment used in such an operation must be sterilized afterward.

VIRUSES

Viruses and viruslike microscopic organisms are responsible for a wide range of diseases and disorders, such as cucumber mosaic, but are also responsible for creating aesthetic effects on ornamental plants, such as variegation, mottles, flower breaking, and the production of green blooms.

Viruses are difficult to trace, as they can mask themselves within the plant; the virus is present, but no obvious symptoms exist. It may be that the plant simply shows reduced vigor. Viruses are easily transported by propagation or by virus vectors.

It is important to keep garden tools clean, particularly those with which you prune, trim, or take cuttings. A virus that occurs among camellias — yellow mottle virus — produces irregular yellow patches on the leaves. It is known that it is not carried by insects in Europe, and the same is probably true in North America and Australia. It is, however, easily transmitted on garden tools. Some people have propagated it for ornament, but this is a mistake, as an infected knife or shears can set up yellow mottle virus in healthy, green cuttings.

Examples of viral diseases are mosaic virus, malformation, ring spots, necrosis, leaf pucker, dwarfing, and green flower.

PEST AND DISEASE CONTROL

Integrated pest management (IPM) This is a strategy for keeping pests and diseases at a tolerable level by treating the garden as an ecosystem, in which every component is related to and affects every other. IPM requires an understanding not only of the pest organism, but also of its environment and the most effective methods of prevention and control. Control may be cultural, physical, or biological; chemical control is used only as a last resort, and the least-toxic chemical is always chosen first.

Cultural control Good cultural practices lead to stronger, healthier plants that are better able to withstand pests and diseases. These include correct planting methods, adequate watering and drainage, the use of organic fertilizers, mulching, weeding, and the removal of dead and diseased material. It also involves good hygiene with garden tools, which can spread diseases.

Physical or mechanical control This type of control requires the use of mechanical traps and barriers, as well as the physical removal of pests from a plant. For example, many pests can be dislodged with a strong blast of water from a garden hose. Caterpillars can be picked off plants by hand and dropped into alcohol or can be trapped with sticky bands fastened around trees. Yellow sticky traps can be used to control whitefly, while red sticky traps attract apple maggots. Slugs and snails can be deterred with copper strips set around susceptible plants.

Biological control This method employs a range of organisms, such as beneficial insects and pathogens, that prey on pests. The most common biological controls are predator insects, including ladybugs, green lacewings, assassin bugs, and hoverflies, which feed on aphids, mealybugs, mites, and many other pests. Other effective predators are birds, bats, and toads.

Parasitoids are organisms that lay eggs in insect hosts, primarily at the larval stage, and thereby destroy them. Most are tiny wasps, usually less than 1/4 in (5 mm) long, that can barely be seen, although their work is sometimes visible. A grub covered with little ricelike pouches (which are the wasp eggs) indicates that a parasitic wasp has been in the garden. The most common wasps are *Encarsia formosa*, which controls whitefly, and *Trichogramma minuta*, which controls many moths. They are often used indoors, in the greenhouse, but they are effective outdoors in warm weather.

Other parasitic insects include beneficial nematodes *(Heterorhabditis)*, which are especially useful in destroying the larvae of Japanese beetles and various weevils.

Fungi, bacteria, and other pathogens have been formulated into highly selective insecticides that target only certain pests, leaving others — and the environment — unharmed. The bacterium *Bacillus thuringiensis* is the mostly widely used pathogen and is available in various strains. One strain, for instance, controls caterpillars, while another is effective against elm leaf beetles. Another bacterium is *Bacillus popilliae*, which kills beetle grubs.

Chemical control While synthetic chemicals have a place in the arsenal against garden problems, indiscriminate use of high-toxicity pesticides and fungicides has serious consequences. Chemicals not only destroy beneficial organisms, but have also resulted in the development of pests and diseases that are resistant to the very agents meant to control them. In IPM, chemicals are used only after other methods have failed, and gardeners begin with the least-toxic chemical available and appropriate to the problem. Controls are applied only where needed, in spot treatments.

Low-toxicity chemicals offer several advantages, although they also require more vigilance and patience. For example, they biodegrade quickly in the environment, leaving no harmful residues, but must be reapplied more frequently than products with high toxicity. They also work more slowly and are generally more selective in the problems they control.

Several types of chemical controls are available and they work in various ways. Insecticidal soaps and dusts destroy the protective coating on the pests' bodies and horticultural oils suffocate insects. Botanically based chemicals, such as neem, pyrethrum, and rotenone, and insect-growth regulators affect the organisms' major systems. Pheromones are sex-attractant chemicals used to lure pests into traps and interfere with the insects' ability to reproduce.

Although low-toxicity chemicals are safe, the use of any chemical control requires caution. Be sure to follow the manufacturer's instructions for dosage and application intervals and wear protective clothing. Reserve a separate sprayer or applicator for pesticides. Store chemicals away from children and pets and keep them in their original containers.

Although generally easy and rewarding to cultivate, maple trees are susceptible to attack from a variety of pests and diseases, including scale, aphids, gall mites, anthracnose, and verticillium wilt.

Pests and Diseases of Woody Plants

Genus	Pest or disease	Symptoms
Acer	Norway maple aphids infest leaves (spring) Gall mites (summer) Coral spot Tar spot Phytophthora root rot Powdery mildew (summer) Verticillium wilt	Leaf curl, loss of vigor. Honeydew and sooty mold present Small red pimples on the upper leaf surface Dieback of branches. Small pink pimples appear on dead branches Black tarlike spots on leaves may cause premature defoliation Foliage wilts, becomes brown, and dies. Sudden death of tree White powdery coating on leaves and stems Sudden wilting, withering, and dieback of stems. Wood stained greenish brown
Aesculus	Japanese beetle (summer) Bleeding canker of the stems Leaf blotch	Entire crown — or just the south side — rapidly defoliated Stems ooze a yellow-brown liquid that dries brown-black Leaves become brown and brittle and fall early
Amelanchier	Rust	Leaves and fruit show small pinkish fruiting bodies
Berberis	Rust	Bright orange spots on the foliage
Betula	Leaf miner Bronze birch borer	Leaves get transparent areas, turn brown and fall early Sections of the tree crown die out
Buxus	Canker	Branches are slow to leaf out, leaves turn brown, branches die
Camellia	Scale insect Leaf blotch Flower blight Canker dieback Phytophthora root rot	Brown or red scale insects found on twigs and under leaves Blotches may run together and upper leaf may look silvery Buds and/or flowers turn brown and fall prematurely Canker growth girdles the stem, resulting in rapid death Foliage wilts, becomes brown, and dies. Sudden death of tree
Carya	Leaf spots	Irregular reddish brown spots cover much of the leaves
Castanea	Blight	Entire branches die. If trunk becomes infected, tree dies
Catalpa	Midge	Inside of leaf is eaten, leaving papery surface. Leaves become distorted
Cercis	Dieback	Small cankers grow to girdle stem, causing wilting
Clematis	Clematis wilt (spring-summer)	Shoots die back rapidly often at the base of the plant. Stems turn black and rot
Conifers	Needle blight Juniper scale Juniper webworm (summer) Red spider mite Spruce aphid Spruce gall adelgid Woolly aphid Spruce budworm (summer) White pine weevil Rusts Black vine (Taxus) weevil Taxus mealybug Arborvitae leaf miner	Fungus causes foliage to yellow, then turn brown, leading to dieback or death Small white scales cover the needles and stems Small brown caterpillars bind shoots together and feed. Needles turn brown Needles turn brown Small, green-eyed aphid feeds on needles, causing yellowing and leaf drop Causes pineapple-shaped galls on several species White, woolly insects cover the shoots or bark of plants, causing yellowing Brown caterpillars eat new growth. May kill trees Leader and branch tips of white pines and some spruce turn brown Pines, spruce, and junipers are attacked. Pustules on bark or shoots Root feeding causes yew needles to turn yellow Waxy insects may cover branches and trunk, causing stunting Tips of shoots turn brown and look transparent
Cornus	Crown canker Borer	Leaves are small and twigs may die after planting Sudden wilting of shoots or small branches
Cotinus	Verticillium wilt	Sudden wilting, withering, and dieback of stems. Wood stained greenish brown
Crataegus	Tent caterpillar (late spring) Leaf blight Rust Fireblight (summer)	Weblike tents and rapid defoliation by a brown caterpillar Small reddish spots on leaves run together and leaves fall Pinkish fruiting bodies on fruit, leaves, and even stems Entire branch dies, with brown shriveled leaves still attached
Daphne	Leaf spots	Causes loss of vigor and defoliation
Euonymus	Anthracnose Scale insect (summer-fall)	Brown areas on leaves can cause early leaf drop 1/16 in (2 mm) long, whitish brown scale on stems and leaves, causing loss of vigor
Fagus	Beech bark disease (summer) Beech scale (summer) Woolly aphid (summer) Leaf mottle	Large areas of bark lift off the stem. Branches die, tree becomes unstable White powdery insects inhabit natural cracks in the trunk and branches Grayish white, powdery insect on underside of leaves and shoot tips Small clear spots on new leaves turn brown and leaves fall in midsummer
Fraxinus	Borer Flower gall Rust Leaf spots (spring)	Stems and branches wilt and may die back Small mites feed on flowers, which form persistent galls Swollen twigs and twisted foliage may have yellow pustules Leaf margins turn brown and foliage falls early
Gleditsia	Borer Pod gall midge Honey locust plant bug Leaf spots (summer)	Gum exuded from bark. Shoots wilt and may die Leaflets become swollen and podlike Stunted new growth, discolored foliage, and early defoliation Brown spots with black fruiting bodies
Hibiscus	Japanese beetle	Metallic green beetles devour open flowers and buds
Hydrangea	Red spider mite (summer) Powdery mildew (summer)	Foliage speckled with small white blotches. Characteristic webbing on top leaves Brown spots with white coating on upper and lower surface of leaves
Ilex	Leaf miner Tar spot (spring) Leaf spots	Irregular, purple-yellow blotches on leaves. Maggots feed inside leaf Yellow spots on leaves turn brown then black Persistent brown spots on leaves may cause defoliation
Juglans	Walnut caterpillar (summer) Leaf spots (summer) Canker	White-haired caterpillar can defoliate trees Irregular brown spots may cause leaf drop Sunken or flattened areas of bark. Branch dies if girdled
Kalmia	Leaf spot	Irregular grayish spots edged brown. Badly infected leaves may fall early
Koelreuteria	Coral spot canker (fall)	Small areas of bark have pink fruiting bodies
Laurus	Laurel psyllid	Leaf edges curl and twist upward

Genus	Pest or disease	Symptoms
Ligustrum	Thrips (summer) Japanese weevil Anthracnose	1/16 in (2 mm) long, yellow or brown-black. Feed on upper leaf, causing a dull silver sheen Small brown beetles eating new shoots cause stunting Leaves die but don't fall. Cankers occur on stems
Liriodendron	Aphid Scale	Small green aphid reduces plant vigor and gives copious honeydew Oval brown scales can cover branches, causing death
Lonicera	Russian aphid (spring) 4-lined plant bug Powdery mildew (late summer)	Small green aphid feeds on new growth, causing tasseling Orange-red nymphs feed on leaves, causing brown spots Foliage is coated with gray felt and may fall early
Magnolia	Magnolia scale	Circular scales with a waxy covering cause poor growth
Mahonia	Powdery mildew (summer) Rusts	White powdery coating on young leaves Red pimples appear on upper surface; powdery, brown spots on undersurface
Malus	Canker Fireblight (summer) Powdery mildew (summer) Scab (summer-fall) Rust Tent caterpillar (late spring)	Sunken zones of bark around branches and stems, occasional death of branches Entire branch dies, with brown shriveled leaves still attached White powdery coating on young leaves Fruits become spotted and distorted Brown to orange spots on leaves or fruit cause leaf drop Weblike tents and rapid defoliation by a brown caterpillar
Nyssa	Leaf spots	Irregular blotches up to 1 in (2.5 cm) across on upper surface
Parthenocissus	Grape flea beetle	Leaves become riddled with numerous small holes
Photinia	Powdery mildew (summer)	White powdery coating on young leaves
Pieris	Phytophthora root rot	Foliage wilts, becomes brown, and dies. Sudden death of tree
Platanus	Anthracnose Canker stain	Failure of buds to open in spring, stem death, wood stained orange-yellow Sunken areas on trunk and main branches. Discolored wood
Populus	Leaf spots Canker Dieback Borer Yellow leaf blister	Small, blackish brown spots on foliage, which falls prematurely Darker sunken areas on branches cause death of shoots Top of tree dies first, then progressively lower down Blackened and swollen regions on branches. May be sawdust Foliage bears bright yellow blisters, which cause distortion
Prunus	Borer Tent caterpillar (late spring) Black knot Peach leaf curl (spring-summer) Powdery mildew (summer) Shothole	Poor growth, yellowing leaves, and gummy exudations in crown Weblike tents and rapid defoliation by a brown caterpillar Cylindrical black galls on small branches, eventual death of shoot Young foliage is thick and tinged orange, old leaves are distorted, red and white White powdery coating on young leaves Holes appear in foliage, ragged edge in deciduous spp., round edge in evergreen
Pyracantha	Fireblight (summer)	Entire branch dies, with brown shriveled leaves still attached
Quercus	Gall wasps Powdery mildew Twig blight Wilt Scale Gypsy moth	Small galls on roots, shoots, and acorns White powdery coating on young leaves Twigs and small branches die. Spores are visible in spring Leaves droop, become curled, and turn brown. Trees may die Globular scales on new growth cause leaf distortion and may kill shoots Trees are rapidly defoliated by a gray caterpillar with blue and red dots
Rhododendron (inc. Azalea)	Lace bug (summer) Whitefly (summer) Powdery mildew (summer) Leaf spot and stem dieback Bud and twig blight (summer) Phytophthera dieback Black vine weevil Japanese weevil	1/8 in (4 mm) yellow-brown insects feed on foliage, causing yellow mottling White-winged insects 1/32 in (1 mm) long cause leaf discoloration White powdery coating on young leaves Silver-gray lesions on leaves, which form rings of dead tissue, causing dieback New buds turn brown and fail to open the next spring Buds and end leaves turn brown, leaves roll and droop Adults cut holes in leaf edges; grubs feed on roots, causing wilting New shoots stunted by small brown beetle's feeding
Rosa	Aphids (summer) Red spider mite (summer) Leafhopper (summer) Thrips (summer) Bristly rose-slug (summer) Capsid bugs (summer) Blackspot (summer-fall) Powdery mildew (summer) Rusts Japanese beetle Rose curculio Mossy rose gall Rose midge	Green or pink aphids cause reduced vigor and leaf and flower disfiguration Leaves become bronze, mottled yellow, and fall prematurely Pale yellow, 1/8 in (3 mm) insects cause loss of color to foliage 1/16 in (2 mm) long, yellow to brown insects cause brown mottling to upper leaf surface Sluglike insect larvae, white-green with brown heads, graze on leaves Pale green insects cause leaves to develop numerous small holes Fungus causes round, black spots to appear on the leaves White powdery fungal growths on new stems, leaves, and flowers Orange pimples appear on leaves, followed by brown ones in late season Metallic-green beetle devours flower and leaves (if no flowers open) Small red and black weevil feed on flower buds which fail to open Moss-like balls up to 2 in (5 cm) across occur on stems New growth and flower buds become deformed and turn brown
Salix	Scale (summer) Leaf blight (spring) Willow leaf beetle	Grayish white, pear-shaped scale insects 1/8 in (3 mm) long cover the bark A few leaves turn black and die, later remaining leaves wilt and die Small, metallic blue beetles eat foliage, leaving only main veins
Sorbus	Blister mite (summer) Fireblight (summer) Mountain ash sawfly (summer)	Microscopic mites cause pale green blotches on leaves, which slowly turn brown Entire branch dies, with brown shriveled leaves still attached Leaves eaten to main ribs by a green caterpillar with black dots
Syringa	Leaf mining moth (summer) Blight (spring-summer) Powdery mildew (late summer)	White larvae feed inside mines within the leaf, roll up the tips to pupate Brown spots develop on leaves, causing blackening and death of shoots Foliage is coated with gray felt and may fall early
Tilia	Aphids (summer) Borer Verticillium wilt	Infest underside of leaves, causing honeydew and sooty mold Adults feed on leaf veins and stems, causing wilting; larvae tunnel under bark, causing stunting Sudden wilting, withering, and dieback of stems. Wood stained greenish brown
Viburnum	Aphids (spring-summer) Viburnum beetle	Cause leaf curling in spring and summer 1/4 in (7 mm), gray-brown beetles and 1/4 in (7 mm), yellow larvae with black marking damage leaves

Control of Pests and Diseases

Pest/Disease	Chemical/Frequency	Mechanical	Biological
Adelgid	malathion, dimethoate, permethrin / every 7–14 days	remove infected foliage	
Anthracnose	Bordeaux mixture, ferbam / every 14 days	collect infected leaves and burn, reduce stress	
Aphids	malathion / every 7–14 days; insecticidal soap / every 2–3 days	remove or wash off	ladybugs, hoverflies
Beech scale	malathion, permethrin, dimethoate / every 14 days	wash off with pressurized water	
Black knot	ferbam / every 21 days	prune out in fall	
Blackspot	benomyl, Bordeaux mixture, captan / every 10–14 days	remove infected plants/leaves	
Borer	malathion, methoxychlor, injected into holes		
Budworm	malathion / every 14–21 days	remove infected shoots	*Bacillus thuringiensis*
Canker	benomyl, Bordeaux mixture / every 14–21 days	remove infected branches	
Capsid bugs	dimethoate, malathion / every 14–21 days	remove old foliage in winter	
Caterpillars	permethrin, carbaryl / every 7–14 days	remove, sticky bands	*Bacillus thuringiensis*
Clematis wilt	benomyl, Bordeaux mixture / every 14–21 days	plant deeper to protect stems	
Coral spot	spray infected plants with thiophanate–methyl / every 7 days	remove infected branches/plants	
Fireblight	remove infected branches 24 in (60 cm) below visual signs of infection	completely remove infected plants	
Galls		handpick	
Japanese beetle	methoxychlor / every 14 days; pyrethrum	handpick, traps	*Bacillus popilliae, Heterorhabditis*
Lace bug	dimethoate, malathion / every 14–21 days	remove eggs from young leaves	
Leafhopper	malathion / every 7 days; insecticidal soap / every 2–3 days	remove infected buds	parasitic wasps
Leaf miner	malathion, dimethoate (adults); insecticidal soap (eggs)	remove infested leaves	ladybugs
Leaf spots	benomyl, Bordeaux mixture / every 14 days	remove infected leaves	
Mealybug	malathion, acephate / every 14–21 days; insecticidal soap	wash off	
Midge	malathion, methoxychlor / every 14–21 days	remove damaged parts	
Mites	malathion / every 7–14 days; insecticidal soap / every 2–3 days	spray foliage with water	green lacewings, ladybugs
Needle blight	benomyl / every 14 days	remove infected plants	
Peach leaf curl	Bordeaux mixture / every 14 days	collect infected and fallen leaves	
Phytophthora root rot		remove infected plants, improve drainage	
Plant bugs	dimethoate, carbaryl, permethrin / every 14–21 days	remove or wash off	
Powdery mildew	benomyl, carbendazim, thiram / every 10–14 days	remove infected leaves	
Red spider mite	dimethoate / every 10–14 days; insecticidal soap / every 2–3 days	spray with water	predatory mites
Rusts	zineb, ferbam / every 10–14 days	remove infected leaves and alternate host	
Sawflies	malathion, permethrin / every 14–21 days; rotenone	remove infested leaves	
Scab	benomyl, captan / every 14 days	remove infected fruits	
Scale insect	dimethoate, diazinon / every 14–21 days; horticultural oil (larvae)	rub with swab dipped in alcohol	parasitic wasps
Shothole	Bordeaux mixture, benomyl, captan / every 14 days	collect infected leaves	
Stem diebacks/ twig blight	Bordeaux mixture, benomyl, captan / every 14 days	prune out infected parts	
Thrips	malathion, carbaryl / every 7–14 days; pyrethrum	blue sticky traps	predatory mites, green lacewings
Verticillium wilt	benomyl, thiram / every 10–14 days	remove infected plants	
Viburnum beetle	malathion, permethrin, dimethoate / every 14–21 days	remove infested leaves	
Vine weevil (adults)	chlorpyrifos, permethrin	sticky traps	
Vine weevil (larvae)	diazinon / every 14 days	remove dead leaves	*Heterorhabditis*
Webworm	dimethoate / every 21 days; insecticidal soap	handpick	
Whitefly	malathion, dimethoate / every 7–14 days; pyrethrum	remove leaves, yellow traps	*Encarsia formosa*
Woolly aphid	malathion, permethrin, dimethoate / every 14 days	remove infected leaves	
Yellow leaf blister	Bordeaux mixture / every 14 days	collect infected leaves and burn	

Plant Names

Shakespeare would have understood gardeners who shy away from botanical names. In Henry VI, a character exclaims, "Away with him! Away with him! He speaks Latin!" It is a sentiment you might harbor against botanists when the Latin names of plants seem to get longer and change constantly. Indeed, botanical Latin is regarded by many people as consisting of long, eminently forgettable words coined by cryptographers with a strong streak of sadism. Nothing, however, could be further from the truth.

There are exceptions of course. Even if you sympathized with the reasons for the change, you might find it hard to understand why the creeping dogwood *Cornus canadensis* has also been known as *Chamaepericlymenum canadense.* Nevertheless, the botanical names of plants are there to help everyone, and when changes occur they usually (but not quite always) do so in the interests of knowledge and understanding.

Why not use common names?

Our garden plants are gathered from all corners of the world, in relatively few of which is the English language traditional or even current. Those who demand "English" or "common" names for plants will find themselves up against more than one obstacle, not the least of which is the fact that botany and horticulture are international and other people have proper, legitimate common names in their own vernaculars. In Mexico, for example, there is a tree whose botanical name is *Cheirostemon platanoides.* There is no English equivalent for its Mexican common name, as there are for its relatives *cacahuatl* (cacao) and *xocoatl* (chocolate). This is not entirely surprising, as the only vernacular name it possesses is *macpalxochitlquahuitl.* Would you not agree that the Latin is a relief?

English itself should not be regarded as one gardening language. There are several variations, depending on the English-speaking country in question. In North America, wake robin is *Trillium grandiflorum*; in Britain it is *Arum maculatum.* In North America the sycamore is a plane tree, *Platanus occidentalis*; in Britain it is a maple, *Acer pseudoplatanus.* Even within America, one vernacular does not exist as far as common names are concerned. *Euonymus americanus*, for example, has several common names, including strawberry bush, bursting heart, wahoo, fish wood, brook euonymus, American spindle tree, and American burning bush.

Beyond mere names, you run into all sorts of complications when you try to be specific about plants. For instance, the blood-red geranium is a species of *Geranium* native to Europe. In one locality on the coast of Lancashire, England, the plant bears light pink instead of magenta-pink blossoms. The botanical name of this form is *Geranium sanguineum* var. *lancastriense.* Something of a mouthful, you might say. But then, how would you define the plant otherwise? Any attempt would produce a sentence like: "The light pink form of the blood-red geramium that grows almost exclusively on Walney Island, near Barrow-in-Furness, Lancashire, England" — because it is not the only light-colored form, but a specific one.

By using one word — *lancastriense* — we define not only the plant but its specific place of origin and also imply its color. Similarly, in using the botanical name of the birch *Betula albo-sinensis* var. *septentrionalis*, we define it as the northern form of this Chinese species, but also imply by definition that it is the form with matte instead of glossy leaves and bark that is more peachy-coppery-pink than just coppery-pink.

The binomial system

Before the great Swedish naturalist Carolus Linnaeus (1707–78) systematized plant names, botanists struggled to describe plants using Latin, the language of science since ancient times. They devised such names as *Tulipa globosa serotina aureo-colore punctata* and *Hyacinthus stellatus Aquitanicus coeruleo flore* — and those are mild examples.

The triumph of Linnaeus was to reduce plant names such as *Ranunculus seminibus aculeatis foliiss superioribus decompositis linearibus* to two basic components, in this case *Ranunculus arvensis.* These are perhaps analogous to first and last names. Provided that a recognized and authoritative description of the plant concerned was published in a proper manner, this "binomial," followed by the name of the author, would refer to that species and to that species only; moreover, it referred to the "type" the specific specimen described.

Family and genus Biological classification is a system of sorting organisms into related groups of ever decreasing size. The system starts with two kingdoms, animal and plant. But the largest grouping that concerns gardeners is family. The term *family* is often used mistakenly by nonbotanists. For example, you may often hear gardeners say something like, "It is a member of the cotoneaster family," when there is actually no such thing. In fact, cotoneasters belong to the rose family, which is properly called Rosaceae, but this does not mean that they are roses. The grouping really meant is the genus. Cotoneasters belong to the genus *Cotoneaster* and roses to the genus *Rosa*; both genera belong to the family Rosaceae, because in scientific terms their flowers, seeds, and so on are similar in composition.

In this book, you will find that the general entry for *Cotoneaster* begins with its generic name, followed by the name of the family. The first specific entry after this general one is for *Cotoneaster adpressus*. The generic name constitutes in effect the surname, while the specific epithet (in this case *adpressus*) plays the part of the first name (but comes second, as in Chinese usage) and closely defines the species, whose species name is *Cotoneaster adpressus*. Generic names are always spelled with capital initial letters and specific epithets with lowercase ones.

Species The concept of species is not always an easy one to grasp and is often misunderstood by gardeners. A species is an assemblage of individuals that have the same constant and distinctive characters. However, this is not to say that every member of a species is identical with any other: there is a degree of variation, be it ever so small. In the color blue, for example, there is a wide range of blueness, although blue as a definitive characteristic of the flowers of a species may always be present. Were there no variation of characteristics within a species, there would be no evolution and neither you nor I would be here.

Within a species, the grading of characteristics may be infinitesimal, but individuals at the extremes may seem so different as not to be the "same plant." "Educated" gardeners may be heard at shows murmuring that such-and-such is not "true to type" — a phrase that reveals a world of misapprehension. This is one of the main sources of friction between gardeners and botanists: gardeners, whose "common sense" tells them that two "species" are self-evidently distinct, cannot understand why the botanists declare that they are in fact one and the same. Unfortunately, they do not see the whole picture, and the expert on the genus (who does) is in a much better position to judge.

Subspecies, varietas, and forma If you stick strictly to binomials, you fail to take account of the minor classifications that can be bolted on, as it were, to the species. These subordinate divisions are, in descending order, subspecies, varietas, and forma. Thus, in the species *Cornus kousa*, there is an assemblage of individuals that are taller than the typical form and have somewhat larger leaves. The differences are within the range of variation within the species but are regarded as worth recognizing as distinct. These plants are given the rank of variety as *Cornus kousa* var. *chinensis*. As *Cornus kousa* covers both the typical form and var. *chinensis*, plants that do not belong to this variety should technically be referred to as *C. kousa* var. *kousa*, a practice that is rarely adopted in horticulture.

Subspecies is the next division down from species. Varietas (not to be confused with the loosely used term *variety*, which often does duty for *cultivar*) comes next, while forma is the last refuge into which botanists can place plants that they think are sufficiently distinct.

"Think" is the operative word. Subspecies, varietas, and forma are, ultimately, matters of opinion. However, we should by no means dismiss them, as the differences even at the level of forma, while relatively insignificant to a scientist, may be of considerable importance to a gardener, especially where such matters as habit and flower color are involved. For example, *Indigofera decora* f. *alba* has white flowers rather than the pink of the species but is not significantly different from it in other ways. *Stewartia pseudocamellia* var. *koreana* comes from a Korean population of the species characterized by better fall color and wider-opening flowers — sufficiently different from the Japanese population to warrant its rank. *Rhododendron fortunei* — the typical form of the species — has bell-shaped, lilac-pink flowers in trusses and flowers in late spring. *R. fortunei* subsp. *discolor* has funnel-shaped, pink flowers in much larger trusses and flowers in early to midsummer. These traits, along with differences in habit, have resulted in the plant's being classified, for now at any rate, in the rank of subspecies.

The addition of subdivisions to a species does not invalidate the binomial system. Species are designated by generic name and species epithet, but the minor categories are a little like the Welsh habit of defining people who have the same name with an additional reference, as in Thomas Jones Cefn Mawr and Thomas Jones Cefn Bach. Their Thomas-Jones-ness is not changed by the reference to their respective farms.

Ultimately, you are unlikely either to remember or care whether it is subspecies (subsp.), varietas (var.), or forma (f.) that is involved in a particular case, and we usually write *Cornus kousa chinensis* on our labels (which looks very much like a trinomial). The most important thing is simply to have a working understanding of the system.

Garden varieties, cultivars, and clones It does matter, however, that we should firmly distinguish between variety in the botanical sense and in its purely colloquial, gardening use. Perhaps it is better to stick to the formal Latin *varietas* for the former. Be that as it may, the word *variety* has another meaning entirely, but one that is not recognized by botanists, when applied to those plants that have a fancy name in a vernacular tongue added on to the species name.

For example, *Cornus kousa* 'Satomi' is a garden variety of the species we have been discussing. You will note that, whereas the Latin components of this and every other name are written in italics, and that everything below genus has a lowercase initial, this vernacular name is in Roman letters, has an uppercase initial, and is surrounded by single quotation marks. This convention should be followed closely by gardeners, as it avoids a great deal of unnecessary confusion. The correct term for a garden variety of this sort is *cultivar*.

A clone is an individual grown from a piece of a parent plant by means other than seed and is not only identical to its parent but also in reality the same plant. A tree or shrub cultivar does not actually have to be a clone but almost always is, and you can assume that if you purchase or are given a tree or shrub with a cultivar name it will have been propagated vegetatively — from cuttings, root cuttings, layering, budding, or grafting. It will therefore be identical to any other correctly labeled tree or shrub carrying the same cultivar (garden variety) name.

The difference between a botanical variety and a cultivar is that whereas a botanical variety is distinguished from the typical form by botanical characteristics that may or may not be relevant to gardeners, a cultivar has been selected by man, either from the wild or from a garden, for a feature or features that make that plant worth maintaining in cultivation by vegetative propagation. These features — for example, variegated foliage; larger, differently colored or double flowers; or a variation in habit giving a weeping, prostrate, or upright plant — distinguish the cultivar from the form or forms normally found in gardens. Here, though, personal taste comes into play, and many gardeners find that they prefer the simpler, wild forms to those that may be larger, more brightly colored, double, or "improved."

Hybrids

A hybrid is a cross between two species. A cross may produce many individual plants, all of which are different from one another. They are all indicated by one name, which is in Latin and contains the symbol "×." This name includes backcrosses. Thus, *Viburnum* × *burkwoodii* is the name for all hybrids between *V. carlesii* and *V. utile*. The plant that bears the name *V.* × *burkwoodii* 'Park Farm Hybrid' is a particular, rather more spreading form, while *V.* × *b.* 'Anne Russell' and 'Fulbrook' are backcrosses with *V. carlesii.*

Most hybrids are between plants in the same genus. Hybrids involving different genera occur infrequently in woody plants, but examples include × *Cupressocyparis (Chamaecyparis* × *Cupressus)* and × *Fatshedera (Fatsia* × *Hedera)*. These take the equivalent of specific epithets, as in × *Fatshedera lizei* and cultivar names, such as × *F.l.* 'Annemieke'.

Name changes

Nothing annoys gardeners more than name changes. They are not the currency of an amateur gardener's working life and are thus an unwanted complication of a leisure pursuit. However, most name changes result from a better understanding of the plants involved and give gardeners a better idea of their relationships. It was not that long ago that *Mahonia* was included in *Berberis*, but today most gardeners and botanists accept that, although closely related, they are quite distinct genera.

Of course, these changes do mean that we can occasionally lose a familiar name or gain an unfamiliar one. For example, William Fox-Strangways, fourth earl of Ilchester (1793–1865), was honored in the 19th century by having the shrub genus *Stranvaesia* named after him. In the late 20th century, the genus was absorbed into *Photinia*, and the Fox-Strangways family lost its foothold in botanical nomenclature for good and sufficient scientific reasons. It is most unlikely that *Stranvaesia* will ever be resurrected and with good reason, as there is really nothing to separate it as a genus from *Photinia.*

We can rest happy with the fact that the trend in both botany and horticulture is now very much away from unnecessary name changes and is focusing strongly on the stability of plant names. Although name changes will always be with us, they are likely to be less frequent than in the past.

Reasons for change There are several broad reasons for name changes, often based on new methods of diagnosis, such as chromosome analysis, but sometimes on pure academic research. Scientific advance may reveal that a plant simply can no longer be regarded as belonging to the genus or species in which it has been included. It may show that a genus is too varied and that it should be split into smaller ones — or, conversely, opinion may converge on the view that several others have hitherto been separated by considerations that are more nitpicking than scientific.

It happens more than occasionally that the laws governing the naming of plants have been breached in the case of a particular plant or plant grouping. In this case, as long as its naming was post-Linnaeus, the matter must be rectified. For example, if a name was published for plant X by John Doe, it would not matter that it had become universally accepted if it were later discovered that Richard Roe had published the same name for plant Y one year previously. A new name for X would have to be found.

Cultivar names cannot be changed frivolously. They have to be properly published in an article or a nursery catalog. Translation is permitted, as when 'Neige de Juillet' might become 'July Snow'; but you cannot change it to 'Summer White'. We are no longer allowed to use honorifics such as "Mrs.," "Madame," and "Professor-Doktor," and similar modesty should prevail whenever we imagine we have developed a new, improved cultivar. The chances are that there are better ones around already.

Pronunciation

The most self-confident people fall prey to all sorts of fears when faced with pronouncing botanical names. There is no need. The purpose of botanical names is to identify plants, not to impress others; as long as you get across what you mean, it does not matter how you do so — clarity and precision are what count.

Botanical Latin is not a classical language, nor is it a dead one. It is the living language of the herbalists and botanists and has been so continuously since classical Latin died after giving birth to the Romance languages. Besides, the Latin of ordinary people was as varied in its pronunciation as English is today.

Academic Latin has three systems of pronunciation. There is the English system (whereby "Julius Caesar" would be pronounced "Giulius Seezer"), the Reformed Academic ("Yewlius K-eye-sar"), and Church Latin, which is characterized by elements of modern Italian speech, such as the "ch" sound being used in some instances for the letter *c*. For example, the first two allow *caespitosa* (which means "growing in short tufts") to be pronounced either as "sea-spit-oh-sa" or "k-eye-spit-oh-sa," while a Roman Catholic cleric might say "chay-spit-oh-sa."

Plants that are apparently unrelated in practical gardening terms have botanical characteristics drawing them into the same family. For example, *Cotoneaster salicifolius* 'Pendulus' is in the rose family, Rosaceae.

Plant Selector

Many factors influence plant choice, but success in this field is strongly linked to the attention paid to location and soil characteristics. This chapter aims to provide a selection of recommended trees and shrubs for particular sites and specific effects. Neither is it comprehensive nor does it necessarily recommend that a particular specimen be planted only in the situation under which it is listed: a great many plants grow successfully in a wide range of locations.

Abies lasiocarpa 'Compacta', grown for its attractive gray-green leaves, is a conifer suitable for clay soils.

Plants for Clay Soils

Clay soils are sticky and unworkable when wet and can set as hard as concrete when dry. On the other hand, they tend to be fertile and, if worked properly, can be among the most satisfactory garden soils. If attention is given to providing the best drainage possible, a very wide range of trees and shrubs can be grown even in dense clays.

Trees

Acer (all)
Aesculus (all)
Alnus (all)
Betula (all)
Carpinus (all)
Crataegus (all)
Eucalyptus (all)
Fraxinus (all)
Ilex (all)
Laburnum (all)
Malus (all)
Platanus (all)
Populus (all)
Prunus (all)
Quercus (all)
Salix (all)
Sorbus (all)
Tilia (all)

Shrubs

Abelia (all)
Aralia elata and cvs
Aronia (all)
Aucuba japonica and cvs
Berberis (all)
Chaenomeles (all)
Choisya (all)
Colutea (all)
Cornus (all)
Corylus (all)
Cotinus (all)
Cotoneaster (all)
Cytisus (all)
Deutzia (all)
Escallonia (all)
Forsythia (all)
Genista (all)
Hamamelis (all)
Hibiscus syriacus and cvs
Hypericum (all)
Lonicera (all)
Magnolia (all)
Mahonia (all)
Osmanthus (all)
Philadelphus (all)
Potentilla (all)
Pyracantha (all)
Rhododendron Hardy hybrids
Ribes (all)
Rosa (all)
Senecio 'Sunshine'
Skimmia (all)
Spiraea (all)
Symphoricarpos (all)
Viburnum (all)
Weigela (all)

Conifers

Abies (all)
Chamaecyparis (all)
Juniperus (all)
Larix (all)
Pinus (all)
Taxodium (all)
Taxus (all)
Thuja (all)

Bamboos

Fargesia
Phyllostachys (all)
Pleioblastus (all)
Pseudosasa japonica
Sasa (all)
Sinarundinaria (all)
Thamnocalamus
Yushania (all)

Plants for Dry, Acid Soils

Dry, acid soils, such as those that occur in light, sandy heathland, can be greatly improved by the incorporation of organic material. They are, however, difficult to manage in drought and tend to be among the less fertile.

Many plants are perfectly adapted to dry, acid conditions, and some of the great nurseries were founded on them. Such soils are easy to work and warm up early in the year. Select plants from the following list to begin with and then expand to include other trees and shrubs after a few seasons of soil improvement. When planting, water in well and mulch heavily.

TREES

Acer negundo and cvs
Ailanthus altissima
Betula (all)
Castanea (all)
Cercis (all)
Gleditsia
Ilex aquifolium and cvs
Populus alba
tremula
Robinia (all)

SHRUBS

Acer ginnala
Berberis (all)
Calluna vulgaris and cvs
Caragana arborescens
Cistus (all)
Colutea arborescens
Cotoneaster (all)
Elaeagnus angustifolia
commutata
Erica (all)
Genista (all)
Halimodendron halodendron
Helianthemum (all)
Hibiscus (all)
Ilex crenata and cvs
Indigofera (all)
Kerria japonica and cvs
Lonicera (all)
Lycium barbarum
Pernettya mucronata and cvs
Physocarpus opulifolius and cvs
Rosa pimpinellifolia and cvs
Salix caprea
cinerea
repens var. *argentea*
Tamarix (all)
Ulex (all)

CONIFERS

Cupressus glabra and cvs
Juniperus (all)
Pinus (all)

This garden-worthy selection of plants includes, from the top: *Acer negundo* 'Flamingo', *Pinus mugo* 'Winter Gold', and *Hibiscus syriacus* 'Pink Giant'. All are suitable for dry, acid soils.

Plants for Shallow Alkaline Soils

Calcium and magnesium limestone support an extraordinarily rich flora in nature and form the bedrock in many parts of North America. Generally they are covered by a good depth of soil that is mostly alkaline. Sometimes, however, there is only a shallow layer of soil over the rock, and this is hard to work — more because of heat and dryness than the calcareous environment itself. Where many gardeners go wrong is to persist in trying to grow favorites such as rhododendrons and azaleas, which will not thrive in such soils. It is far better to garden using plants that will.

Incorporating organic matter will improve this kind of soil, although care must be taken for the first few years to ensure that plants receive adequate water. Most limestone rock is fissured, and trees and shrubs can push roots into these crevices for support and eventually for nutrition and water.

TREES

Acer campestre
negundo and cvs
platanoides and cvs
pseudoplatanus and cvs
Aesculus (all)
Carpinus betulus and cvs
Cercis siliquastrum
Crataegus laevigata and cvs
Fagus sylvatica and cvs
Fraxinus excelsior and cvs
ornus
Morus nigra
Populus alba
Prunus (Japanese cherries)
Sorbus aria and cvs
hybrida and cvs
intermedia

SHRUBS

Aucuba japonica and cvs
Berberis (all)
Buddleia davidii and cvs
Buxus sempervirens and cvs
Caragana arborescens and cvs
Ceanothus (all)
Cistus (all)
Colutea (all)
Cornus mas and cvs
Cotoneaster (all)
Cytisus nigricans
Deutzia (all)
Dipelta floribunda
Elaeagnus (deciduous spp.)
Euonymus (all)
Forsythia (all)
Fuchsia (all)
Hebe (all)
Hibiscus syriacus and cvs
Hypericum (all)
Laurus nobilis
Ligustrum (all)
Lonicera (all)
Mahonia aquifolium and hybrids
Olearia (all)
Paeonia delavayi
lutea
Philadelphus (all)
Phillyrea (all)
Photinia × *fraseri* cvs
serratifolia
Potentilla (most)
Rhus (most)
Rosa (most)
Rosmarinus (all)
Rubus tricolor
Sambucus (all)
Sarcococca (all)
Senecio (all)
Spartium junceum
Spiraea japonica and cvs
nipponica and forms
Stachyurus (all)
Symphoricarpos (all)
Syringa (all)
Vinca (all)
Weigela (all)
Yucca (all)

CONIFERS

Juniperus communis and cvs
× *media* and cvs
Pinus mugo and forms
nigra
Taxus baccata and cvs
Thuja occidentalis and cvs
Thuja plicata and cvs
Thujopsis dolabrata and cvs

BAMBOOS

Pseudosasa japonica
Sasa ramosa

Plants for Damp Sites

Generally speaking, trees and shrubs require good drainage and locations where soil is not waterlogged. Some, however, are adapted to living in conditions of permanent dampness or even wetness. In well-aerated soils oxygen levels rarely fall below 15 percent, whereas in wet sites they may be as low as 1 percent. Trees such as the swamp cypress *(Taxodium distichum)* can survive this for many months. On the other hand, trees and shrubs without special adaptations to such environmental conditions may live no longer than a few weeks if flooded during the growing season.

Where damp places are associated with water movement, they may be rich in oxygen. Plants that have evolved in such conditions thrive where the majority of trees and shrubs would fail.

TREES

Alnus (all)
Amelanchier (all)
Betula nigra
pendula and cvs
pubescens
Crataegus laevigata and cvs
Magnolia virginiana
Mespilus germanica cvs
Populus (all)
Pterocarya (all)
Pyrus betulifolia
communis cvs
Quercus palustris
Salix (all)
Sorbus aucuparia and cvs

SHRUBS

Amelanchier (all)
Aronia (all)
Calycanthus floridus
Clethra (all)
Cornus alba and cvs
stolonifera and cvs
Gaultheria shallon
Hippophae rhamnoides
Lindera benzoin
Myrica gale
Neillia thibetica
Photinia villosa
Physocarpus opulifolius and cvs
Prunus spinosa and cvs
Salix caprea
purpurea and cvs
repens and cvs
many other bush spp.
Sambucus (all)
Sorbaria (all)
Spiraea × *vanhouttei*
veitchii
Symphoricarpos (all)
Vaccinium (all)
Viburnum opulus and cvs

CONIFERS

Metasequoia glyptostroboides
Picea sitchensis
Taxodium ascendens and forms
distichum

BAMBOOS

Phyllostachys (all)
Pleioblastus (most)
Pseudosasa japonica
Sasa (all)
Sinarundinaria (all)
Thamnocalamus (all)
Yushania anceps

Plants for Industrial Areas

The air of industrial areas is cleaner now than it was during the first half of the 20th century, when soot and sulfuric acid, among other injurious substances, greatly reduced the range of plants that could be grown in cities and large towns. Although the situation has improved, pollution from industry still occurs and affects the growth of plants. In general, though, the range of trees and shrubs that can be grown in industrial areas is much more extensive than you might have thought; only relatively few, such as the Japanese maples, cannot tolerate modern levels of pollution.

TREES

Acer (many, but not Japanese maples)
Aesculus (all)
Ailanthus altissima
Alnus cordata
glutinosa and cvs
incana and cvs
Amelanchier (all)
Betula papyrifera and forms
pendula and cvs
pubescens
Carpinus betulus and cvs
Catalpa bignonioides and cvs
Crataegus (all)
Davidia (all)
Eucalyptus (most)
Fagus (all)
Fraxinus (all)
Ilex × *altaclerensis* and cvs
aquifolium and cvs
+ *Laburnocytisus adamii*
Laburnum (all)
Ligustrum lucidum and cvs
Liriodendron tulipifera and cvs
Magnolia denudata
kobus
× *loebneri* and cvs
× *soulangeana* and cvs
Malus (all)
Mespilus germanica cvs
Morus nigra
Platanus (all)
Populus (most)
Prunus × *amygado-persica* 'Pollardii'
avium
cerasifera and cvs
dulcis cvs
Japanese cherries
padus and cvs
Pterocarya (all)
Pyrus (all)
Quercus ilex
× *turneri*
Rhus (most)
Robinia pseudoacacia and cvs
Salix (most)
Sorbus aria and cvs
aucuparia and cvs
Tilia × *euchlora*
× *europaea* and cvs
platyphyllos and cvs

SHRUBS

Amelanchier (all)
Aralia elata
Arbutus unedo and cvs
Aucuba japonica and cvs
Berberis (all)
Buddleia davidii and cvs
Buxus sempervirens and cvs
Camellia japonica and cvs
× *williamsii* cvs
Ceratostigma willmottianum
Chaenomeles (all)
Cistus (all)
Clethra (all)
Colutea arborescens
Cornus alba and cvs
Cotoneaster (most)
Cytisus (most)
Daphne mezereum
Deutzia (many)
Elaeagnus × *ebbingei* and cvs
pungens and cvs
Escallonia (all)
Euonymus fortunei and cvs
japonicus and cvs
Fatsia japonica
Forsythia (all)
Garrya (all)
Genista (many)
Hibiscus sinosyriacus and cvs
syriacus and cvs
Hydrangea macrophylla and cvs
Hypericum (all)
Ilex aquifolium and cvs
cornuta and hybrids
Kerria japonica and cvs
Leycesteria formosa
Ligustrum japonicum
ovalifolium
Lonicera pileata
Lycium barbarum
Magnolia grandiflora and cvs
× *soulangeana* and cvs
stellata and cvs
Mahonia aquifolium and hybrids
japonica
lomariifolia
× *media* and cvs
pinnata
repens 'Rotundifolia'
Olearia × *haastii*
Osmanthus (all)
Pernettya mucronata and cvs
Philadelphus (all)
Phillyrea (all)
Photinia davidiana
Physocarpus (all)
Prunus laurocerasus and cvs
Pyracantha (all)
Rhododendron Hardy hybrids
Knap Hill azaleas
luteum
ponticum
Rhodotypos scandens
Rhus glabra
typhina
Ribes (all)
Rosa (most)
Salix (most)
Sambucus canadensis 'Maxima'
nigra and forms
Sarcococca (many)
Senecio monroi
'Sunshine'
Skimmia japonica and cvs
Sorbaria (all)
Spartium junceum
Spiraea (all)
Staphylea (all)
Symphoricarpos (all)
Syringa (all)
Tamarix tetranda
Ulex (all)
Viburnum (many)
Vinca major and cvs
minor and cvs
Weigela florida and cvs
hybrids

CLIMBERS

Ampelopsis (most)
Hedera (all)
Parthenocissus (all)

CONIFERS

Cephalotaxus fortunei and cvs
harringtonia and forms
Fitzroya cupressoides
Ginkgo biloba
Metasequoia glyptostroboides and cvs
Taxus baccata and cvs
× *media* and cvs
Torreya californica

Plants for Cold, Exposed Areas

Cold is one thing, but cold wind is quite another. Even though plants, not being warm blooded, do not experience windchill in the same way people do, they are still affected by wind exposure, especially in winter.

A plant in a windswept location is under greater stress than a similar plant in a sheltered site. Wind increases the rate of moisture evaporation from plant leaves and stems. When the soil is cold — or worse, frozen — plant roots are either almost dormant or unable to take up water from the soil. The plants therefore cannot replace the moisture lost from their foliage, and the result is wilting, browning, defoliation, and possible death. However, a number of conifers are adapted to windy conditions, and many deciduous trees and shrubs can tolerate blasts of winter wind.

TREES

Acer rubrum and cvs
Aesculus glabra
Betula (most)
Crataegus crus-galli and cvs
Fraxinus pennsylvanica and cvs
Malus baccata
Populus × *canadensis* 'Robusta'
  tremula
Quercus rubra
Salix pentandra
Sorbus aucuparia and cvs
Syringa reticulata
Tilia cordata and cvs

SHRUBS

Amelanchier × *grandiflora* and cvs
Amorpha fruticosa
Arctostaphylos uva-ursi
Aronia melanocarpa
Cornus alba and cvs
  stolonifera and cvs
Corylus colurna
Cotoneaster acutifolius
Daphne mezereum
Elaeagnus commutata
Euonymus nanus
Genista tinctoria and cvs
Halimodendron halodendron
Hippophae rhamnoides
Hydrangea paniculata 'Grandiflora'
Kalmia angustifolia and cvs
Ledum groenlandicum
Lonicera caerulea
Myrica gale
Philadelphus (many)
Physocarpus opulifolius and cvs
Potentilla cvs
Prunus × *cistena*
Rhus glabra
Ribes alpinum
Rosa foetida and cvs
Salix (most)
Spiraea (most)
Vaccinium vitis-idaea
Viburnum opulus and cvs
  trilobum

CONIFERS

Abies balsamea
  veitchii
Ginkgo biloba
Juniperus communis and cvs
  horizontalis and cvs
  × *media* and cvs
  scopulorum and cvs
Larix kaempferi
Picea abies and cvs
  omorika and cvs
  pungens and cvs
Pinus contorta subsp. *latifolia*
  mugo and cvs
  strobus and cvs
  sylvestris and cvs
Thuja occidentalis and cvs

From top: *Betula utilis* var. *jacquemontii* 'Doorenbos' is good for cold, exposed sites; *Pinus radiata* will flourish in seaside gardens; and *Skimmia japonica* subsp. *reevesiana* 'Robert Fortune' tolerates heavy shade.

Plants for Coastal Areas

Wind is a major factor in gardens near the sea, and temperatures often vary from those inland. What distinguishes coastal gardens is the prevalence of salt in the air, which can be carried 15 mi (24 km) inland during a storm. It can also accumulate in the soil. Salt makes it harder for plants to take up water, as there is insufficient difference between the concentration of salts in the soil water and those in the root cells. Plants with tough, waxy leaves and gray foliage often withstand coastal conditions well.

TREES

Acer pseudoplatanus
Arbutus unedo and cvs
Castanea sativa
Crataegus (all)
Eucalyptus (many)
Fraxinus angustifolia and cvs
excelsior and cvs
Griselinia littoralis
Ilex × *altaclerensis* and cvs
aquifolium and cvs
Laurus nobilis and cvs
Phillyrea latifolia
Populus alba
tremula
Quercus cerris
ilex
petraea
robur
× *turneri*
Salix (most)
Sorbus aria and cvs
aucuparia and cvs

SHRUBS

Atriplex halimus
Bupleurum fruticosum
Cassinia fulvida
Chamaerops humilis
Choisya (all)
Colutea (all)
Cordyline australis and cvs
Corokia cotoneaster
× *virgata* and cvs
Cotoneaster (many)
Cytisus (many)
Elaeagnus × *ebbingei* and cvs
pungens and cvs
Erica arborea var. *alpina*
lusitanica
× *veitchii*
Escallonia (most)
Euonymus fortunei and cvs
japonicus and cvs
Fabiana imbricata 'Prostrata'
Fuchsia magellanica and cvs
Garrya elliptica and cvs
Genista (most)
Halimium (all)
Halimodendron halodendron
Hebe (all)
Helianthemum (most)
Helichrysum (many)
Hippophae rhamnoides
Hydrangea macrophylla and cvs
Ilex aquifolium and cvs
Lavandula (all)
Lavatera thuringiaca cvs
Leycesteria formosa
Lonicera pileata
Lycium barbarum
Olearia (most)
Ozothamnus (many)
Parahebe (all)
Phlomis (most)
Phormium (all)
Pittosporum (most)
Prunus spinosa
Pyracantha (all)
Rhamnus alaternus and cvs
Rosa (many spp.)
Rosmarinus officinalis and cvs
Salix (many)
Sambucus racemosa and cvs
Santolina (all)
Senecio (most)
Spartium junceum
Spiraea (many)
Tamarix (all)
Ulex (all)
Viburnum (many, especially evergreen spp.)
Yucca (all)

CLIMBERS

Fallopia baldschuanica
Muehlenbeckia complexa

CONIFERS

× *Cupressocyparis leylandii*
Cupressus (many)
Juniperus (most)
Pinus contorta
mugo and forms
muricata
nigra
Pinus nigra subsp. *laricio*
pinaster
pinea
radiata
thunbergii
Podocarpus alpinus
nivalis

BAMBOOS

Pleioblastus (many)
Sasa (all)

Plants Tolerant of Heavy Shade

It is unnatural for most trees to tolerate shade, but some shrubs can tolerate the reduced light under dense tree canopies. In nature, shrubs usually appear toward the edges of the forest, either where it begins to give way to high moorland or, as with *Arbutus unedo*, on lakesides. Trees and shrubs that are adapted to dense shade are of great value in the garden. Many, such as *Fatsia japonica*, the hollies, and the mahonias, are notable for their foliage, while others, such as the camellias, are grown for their spectacular flowers.

TREES AND SHRUBS

Arctostaphylos uva-ursi
Aucuba japonica and cvs
Buxus sempervirens and cvs
Camellia japonica and cvs
× *williamsii* and cvs
Cornus canadensis
Daphne laureola
pontica
Elaeagnus (evergreen)
Euonymus fortunei and cvs
× *Fatshedera lizei*
Fatsia japonica
Gaultheria (all)
Hypericum androsaemum
calycinum
Ilex × *altaclerensis* and cvs
aquifolium and cvs
Leucothoë fontanesiana and cvs
Ligustrum (many)
Lonicera nitida cvs
pileata
Mahonia aquifolium and cvs
Osmanthus decorus
heterophyllus and cvs
Pachysandra terminalis
Prunus laurocerasus and cvs
lusitanica and cvs
Rhododendron Hardy hybrids
ponticum
Rhodotypos scandens
Ribes alpinum
Rubus odoratus
tricolor
Ruscus (all)
Sarcococca (all)
Skimmia (all)
Symphoricarpos (all)
Vaccinium vitis-idaea
Viburnum davidii
Vinca (all)

CONIFERS

Cephalotaxus (all)
Juniperus × *media* 'Pfitzeriana'
Podocarpus alpinus
andinus
nivalis
Taxus (all)

BAMBOOS

Fargesii (all)
Phyllostachys (most)
Pleioblastus (most)
Sasa (all)

Plants for Shady Walls

Plants that succeed on north-facing walls must be able to tolerate almost unbroken shade, while those facing east will receive sunshine only in the mornings. In addition, they may be further shaded from what sun there is by other plants that are farther to the east.

Another factor that comes into play is frost. If flower buds formed the previous fall become frozen, they will be killed by the rapid thawing when the sun's rays fall on them in the morning. This applies particularly to camellias.

Even in milder regions, easterly winds in the winter and spring are usually dry and often bitingly cold. Where the wall affords them no protection, care should be taken even with the following plants: *Azara* species, *Drimys winteri*, *Crinodendron* species, and *Osmanthus yunnanensis*.

SHRUBS

Azara microphylla
Berberis × *stenophylla*
Camellia (north walls only)
'Inspiration'
japonica and cvs
reticulata
sasanqua
× *williamsii* and cvs
Chaenomeles (most)
Choisya ternata
Crinodendron hookerianum
patagua
Daphne × *hybrida*
odora
Desfontainia spinosa
Drimys winteri
Eriobotrya japonica
Eucryphia cordifolia
× *intermedia* cvs
× *nymansensis* and cvs
Euonymus fortunei and cvs
Garrya elliptica and cvs
Grevillea rosmarinifolia
Ilex latifolia
Illicium anisatum
Jasminum humile and forms
nudiflorum
Kerria japonica 'Pleniflora'
Lomatia myricoides
Mahonia japonica
lomarifolia
× *media* and cvs
Mitraria coccinea
Osmanthus yunnanensis
Photinia × *fraseri* and cvs
serratifolia
Piptanthus nepalensis
Pyracantha (all)
Ribes laurifolium
Schima argentea
Viburnum foetens

CLIMBERS

Akebia quinata
Celastrus orbiculatus
Hedera colchica and cvs
helix and cvs
Hydrangea petiolaris
Muehlenbeckia complexa
Parthenocissus (all)
Pileostegia viburnoides
Rubus henryi var. *bambusarum*
Schizophragma hydrangeoides
integrifolium

Plants for Ground Cover

Gardeners have a saying that unless you cover the ground, nature will cover it for you. Bare soil soon becomes a mass of weeds. If you are a good gardener, you will want to prevent this from happening and also, perhaps, to make the site as attractive as possible without having to expend a great deal of time and energy.

"Ground-cover" plants have gained something of a bad name in the past because of a relatively unimaginative approach involving a fairly hackneyed selection of rapidly growing carpeters such as ivies *(Hedera)* and periwinkles *(Vinca)*. While these are of great value, they are only a few of the many interesting and exciting shrubs that can cover your ground in a way that is far from being merely utilitarian.

SHRUBS

Arctostaphylos uva-ursi
Artemisia 'Powis Castle'
Aucuba japonica 'Nana Rotundifolia'
Berberis tsangpoensis
wilsoniae
Buxus microphylla
Calluna vulgaris and cvs
Ceanothus prostratus
thyrsiflorus var. *repens*
Cornus canadensis
Cotoneaster: several, including
'Coral Beauty'
dammeri
'Gnom'
horizontalis and cvs
nanshan
'Skogholm'
Cytisus × *beanii*
scoparius subsp. *maritimus*
Daboecia cantabrica and cvs
Erica (most)
Euonymus fortunei and cvs
Gaultheria (most)
× *Gaulnettya* cvs
Halimiocistus 'Ingwersenii'
sahucii
Hebe: many, especially
albicans
pinguifolia 'Pagei'
rakaiensis
'Youngii'
Hedera (most)
Helianthemum (all)
Hypericum calycinum
moserianum
Jasminum nudiflorum
parkeri
Leptospermum humifusum
Leucothoë fontanesiana and cvs
Lonicera pileata
Mahonia aquifolium 'Apollo'
nervosa
Pachysandra terminalis
Pernettya mucronata cvs
Pimelea prostrata
Potentilla 'Abbotswood'
'Longacre'
Rhododendron: many, especially members of the subsections Lapponica and Saluenensia and most evergreen azaleas
Ribes laurifolium
Rosa 'Max Graf'
nitida
'Paulii'
wichuraiana
Rosmarinus officinalis 'Prostratus'
Rubus calycinoides
tricolor
Salix: several, including
× *cottetii*
repens and cvs
uva-ursi
Santolina (all)
Sarcococca hookeriana var. *humilis*
Stephanandra incisa 'Crispa'
Symphoricarpos × *chenaultii* 'Hancock'
Vaccinium: many, especially
delavayi
glauco-album
vitis-idaea
Viburnum davidii
Vinca (all)

CONIFERS

Cephalotaxus fortunei 'Prostrate Spreader'
Juniperus communis: several forms, including
'Hornibrookii'
'Repanda'
conferta
horizontalis and cvs
× *media* (several cvs)
sabina var. *tamariscifolia*

Podocarpus alpinus
nivalis
Taxus baccata 'Repandens'
'Repens Aurea'
Tsuga canadensis 'Bennett'

Bamboos
Indocalamus tessellatus
Sasa veitchii
Shibataea kumasaca

Plants of Pendulous Habit

Trees vary greatly in shape and habit, but most of them share the general configuration of a trunk topped by a head of branches. Garden design depends a great deal on contrasts, comparisons, and accents, and often just one or two trees that depart radically from the norm will make their neighbors look all the more interesting. Pendulous or weeping trees perhaps provide the strongest contrasting accents, with their downward sweeps often hiding their trunks and providing foliage where in other trees it is absent. Deciduous trees make strong architectural statements in winter, and there are many more available than the ubiquitous weeping willow.

Trees
Acer saccharinum f. *laciniatum*
Betula pendula 'Dalecarlica'
'Tristis'
'Youngii'
Cercidiphyllum japonicum
'Pendulum'
Fagus sylvatica 'Aurea Pendula'
'Pendula'
'Purpurea Pendula'
Fraxinus excelsior 'Pendula'
Malus 'Red Jade'
Populus tremula 'Pendula'
Prunus subhirtella 'Pendula Rubra'
× *yedoensis* 'Shidare Yoshino'
Pyrus salicifolia 'Pendula'
Robinia pseudoacacia
'Rozynskyana'
Salix babylonica 'Pendula'
× *sepulcralis* 'Chrysocoma'
'Erythroflexuosa'
Sophora japonica 'Pendula'
Tilia tomentosa 'Petiolaris'

The ultimate height of the following trees depends largely on the stem height at which they are grafted or to which they are trained.
Caragana arborescens 'Pendula'
'Walker'
Cotoneaster salicifolius
'Pendulus'
Ilex aquifolium 'Argentea
Marginata Pendula'
'Pendula'
Laburnum alpinum 'Pendulum'
Malus 'Royal Beauty'
Morus alba 'Pendula'
Prunus 'Cheal's Weeping'
× *yedoensis* 'Ivensii'
Salix caprea 'Kilmarnock'
purpurea 'Pendula'

Conifers
Cedrus atlantica 'Glauca Pendula'
'Pendula'
Chamaecyparis nootkatensis
'Pendula'
Cupressus lusitanica 'Glauca
Pendula'
Dacrydium franklinii
Fitzroya cupressoides
Larix kaempferi 'Pendula'
Picea abies 'Inversa'
breweriana
omorika 'Pendula'
smithiana
Taxus baccata 'Dovastoniana'
'Dovastonii Aurea'
Tsuga canadensis 'Pendula'
heterophylla 'Greenmantle'

Plants of Upright or Fastigiate Habit

Fastigiate means "having branches erect and close together." *Upright* is a nonbotanical term that covers trees and shrubs with ascending branches, such as several hollies and conifers, but, for design purposes, it also includes fastigiate trees and shrubs.

Single upright accents are not quite as strong as pendulous ones, but they become powerful design features when repeated or grouped. A group of strongly upright trees with broad crowns, such as *Fagus sylvatica* 'Dawyck', is highly effective. On a much smaller scale, a group of the diminutive *Juniperus communis* 'Compressa' can lend definitive character to a rock garden. A repeated vertical accent, such as that given by *Juniperus scopulorum* 'Skyrocket', can transform a large border that might otherwise lack focus because of its unbroken horizontal line. Trees such as fastigiate oaks, beeches, and Japanese cherries can be very useful at driveway entrances and on streets, providing height without too much width.

Trees and Shrubs
Acer × *lobelii*
platanoides 'Columnare'
pseudoplatanus 'Erectum'
rubrum 'Scanlon'
saccharinum 'Pyramidale'
Betula pendula 'Fastigiata'
Carpinus betulus 'Fastigiata'
Corylus colurna
Crataegus monogyna 'Stricta'
Fagus sylvatica 'Cockleshell'
'Dawyck'
'Dawyck Gold'
'Dawyck Purple'
Ilex aquifolium 'Green Pillar'
Liriodendron tulipifera 'Fastigiatum'
Malus tschonoskii
'Van Eseltine'
Populus alba 'Pyramidalis'
nigra 'Italica'
Prunus 'Amanogawa'
lusitanica 'Myrtifolia'
'Pandora'
× *schmittii*
'Snow Goose'
'Spire'
Pyrus calleryana 'Chanticleer'
Quercus castaneifolia 'Green Spire'
frainetto 'Hungarian Crown'
petraea 'Columna'
robur f. *fastigiata* 'Koster'
Robinia pseudoacacia 'Pyramidalis'
Sorbus aucuparia 'Fastigiata'
'Sheerwater Seedling'
commixta
Sorbus 'Joseph Rock'
× *thuringiaca* 'Fastigiata'
Tilia cordata 'Greenspire'
Ulmus × *hollandica* 'Dampieri
Aurea'

Conifers
Calocedrus decurrens
Cephalotaxus harringtonia
'Fastigiata'
Chamaecyparis lawsoniana
'Alumii'
'Columnaris'
'Ellwoodii'
'Erecta'
'Kilmacurragh'
'Pottenii'
'Wisselii'
'Witzeliana'
× *Cupressocyparis leylandii* and cvs
Cupressus glabra 'Pyramidalis'
sempervirens and cvs
Ginkgo biloba 'Tremonia'
Juniperus chinensis 'Pyramidalis'
communis 'Compressa'
'Hibernica'
'Sentinel'
scopulorum (several cvs)
Pinus sylvestris 'Fastigiata'
Taxus baccata 'Fastigiata'
'Standishii'
× *media* 'Hicksii'
Thuja occidentalis 'Malonyana'
plicata 'Fastigiata'

Plants with Ornamental Bark and Twigs

Many trees and shrubs have colored, patterned, or attractively peeling bark on their trunks and major branches. Others have colorful smaller branches and twiggy branchlets. An example of the former is the shining white trunk of *Betula utilis* var. *jacquemontii* 'Jermyns', while *Acer palmatum* 'Senkaki', with its branches of bright coral, typifies the latter.

In general, ornamental barks have their greatest effect among deciduous trees and shrubs, as they are prominent features in the garden in winter. However, many evergreens have strikingly beautiful bark and are outstanding throughout the year. Among these are *Eucalyptus*, *Arbutus* × *andrachnoides*, and *Myrtus luma*.

TREES

Acer capillipes
davidii 'George Forrest'
griseum
grosseri var. *hersii*
negundo var. *violaceum*
palmatum 'Senkaki'
pensylvanicum and cvs
Arbutus × *andrachnoides*
menziesii
Betula (most)
Carya ovata
Eucalyptus (most)
Fraxinus excelsior 'Jaspidea'
Myrtus luma
Parrotia persica
Platanus (all)
Prunus maackii 'Amber Beauty'
× *schmittii*
serrula
Salix acutifolia 'Blue Streak'
alba 'Britzensis'
var. *vitellina*
babylonica 'Tortuosa'
daphnoides and cvs
× *sepulcralis* 'Chrysocoma'
'Erythroflexuosa'
Stewartia (most)
Tilia platyphyllos 'Aurea'
'Rubra'

SHRUBS

Abelia triflora
Arctostaphylos (most)
Clethra barbinervis
Cornus alba and cvs
officinalis
stolonifera 'Flaviramea'
Corylus avellana 'Contorta'
Deutzia (several spp.)
Dipelta floribunda
Euonymus alatus
phellomanus
Hydrangea aspera and forms
heteromalla 'Bretschneideri'
Kerria japonica and cvs
Leycesteria formosa
Philadelphus (several)
Rhododendron barbatum
thomsonii
Rosa sericea f. *pteracantha*
virginiana
Rubus cockburnianus
phoenicolasius
thibetanus
Salix irrorata
moupinensis
Stephanandra tanakae
Vaccinium corymbosum

CONIFERS

Cryptomeria japonica
Pinus bungeana
sylvestris
Sequoia sempervirens
Sequoiadendron giganteum

Plants with Bold Foliage

Texture and contrast play a foremost role among design elements and can be richly provided by the foliage of trees and shrubs. Very large or interestingly shaped leaves draw the eye irresistibly and make strong and often exotic contrasts to the smaller, more tightly massed leaves of the majority of woody plants.

There is a great variety of types of bold leaves, each creating a different texture or accent. The spear-shaped clusters of the giant dracena *(Cordyline australis)*, for example, share a somewhat jungle-like character with the widely lobed *Fatsia japonica*, but each strikes a very different note. Bold or architectural foliage can have the greatest influence on the general atmosphere of your garden.

TREES

Ailanthus altissima
Aralia (all)
Catalpa (all)
Cordyline australis
Gymnocladus dioica
Idesia polycarpa
Kalopanax pictus
Magnolia hypoleuca
macrophylla
officinalis var. *biloba*
tripetala
Meliosma veitchiorum
Paulownia (all)
Platanus (all)
Populus lasiocarpa
szechuanica var. *tibetica*
Pterocarya (all)
Quercus frainetto 'Hungarian Crown'
velutina 'Rubrifolia'
Sorbus insignis
thibetica 'John Mitchell'
vestita
Toona sinensis
Trachycarpus fortunei

SHRUBS

Acer japonicum 'Vitifolium'
macrophyllum
Aralia (all)
Chamaerops humilis
Eriobotrya japonica
× *Fatshedera lizei*
Fatsia japonica
Hydrangea quercifolia and cvs
aspera subsp. *sargentiana*
Ilex latifolia
Magnolia delavayi
grandiflora and cvs
Mahonia japonica
lomariifolia
× *media* and cvs
Melianthus major
Osmanthus armatus
yunnanensis
Phormium (all)
Rhododendron: several, including
macabeanum
rex and forms
sinogrande
Sambucus canadensis 'Maxima'
Sorbaria (all)
Viburnum rhytidophyllum
Yucca gloriosa
recurvifolia

CLIMBERS

Actinidia chinensis
Ampelopsis megalophylla
Aristolochia macrophylla
Hedera algeriensis and cvs
Vitis 'Brant'
coignetiae

BAMBOOS

Indocalamus tessellatus

Plants for Fall Color

Fall foliage can be a truly spectacular sight in the garden. It varies from place to place, is better on some soils than others, and has good and bad years, but it is generally worth bearing in mind when you are planning the garden. The fiery combinations of glowing crimson, blazing scarlet and orange, and rich gold so typical of a picture-book fall are attainable if you choose carefully. Try to find room, even in a small garden, for one or two of these plants, particularly those that have interest in other seasons as well. With judicious planning, a larger garden can provide a succession of changing hues over several weeks.

TREES

Acer: many, including
  capillipes
  maximowiczianum
  rubrum and cvs
  saccharum
  triflorum
Aesculus: several, including
  glabra
Amelanchier (most)
Betula (most)
Carpinus (all)
Carya (all)
Cercidiphyllum japonicum
Cercis canadensis
Cladrastis (all)
Cornus controversa
Crataegus: many, especially
  crus-galli
  pinnatifida var. *major*
  prunifolia
Fagus (most)
Fraxinus angustifolia 'Raywood'
  excelsior 'Jaspidea'
  nigra 'Autumn Gold'
Gymnocladus dioica
Liquidambar (all)
Malus: several, including
  coronaria 'Charlottae'
  transitoria
  trilobata
  tschonoskii
Nothofagus antarctica
Nyssa (all)
Parrotia persica
Phellodendron (all)
Photinia beauverdiana
  villosa
Picrasma quassioides
Populus: several, including
Populus alba
  × *canadensis* 'Serotina Aurea'
  tremula
  trichocarpa
Prunus: many, including
  'Hillieri'
  sargentii
  verecunda 'Autumn Glory'
Quercus: many, including
  coccinea 'Splendens'
  palustris
  phellos
  rubra
Rhus trichocarpa
Sassafras albidum
Sorbus: many, including
  alnifolia
  commixta
  'Embley'
  'Joseph Rock'
  scalaris
Stewartia (all)
Toona sinensis

SHRUBS

Acer: many, especially
  ginnala
  japonicum and cvs
  palmatum and cvs
Aesculus parviflora
Amelanchier canadensis
Aronia (all)
Berberis: many, including
  dictyophylla
  × *media* 'Parkjuweel'
  thunbergii and cvs
  wilsoniae
Callicarpa (all)
Ceratostigma willmottianum
Clethra (all)
Cornus alba
  'Eddie's White Wonder'
  florida and cvs
  officinalis
Corylopsis (all)
Cotinus (all)
Cotoneaster: many, including
  bullatus
  divaricatus
  horizontalis
  nanshan
  splendens
Disanthus cercidifolius
Enkianthus (all)
Eucryphia glutinosa
Euonymus: many, including
  alatus and cvs
  europaeus and cvs
  latifolius
  oxyphyllus
  planipes
Fothergilla (all)
Hamamelis (all)
Hydrangea quercifolia
  serrata 'Preziosa'
Lindera (most)
Prunus: several, including
  glandulosa and cvs
  incisa
  pumila var. *depressa*
Ptelea trifoliata
Rhododendron: several, including
  arborescens
  calendulaceum
  'Coccineum Speciosum'
  'Corneille'
  luteum
  'Nancy Waterer'
  quinquefolium
Rhus: several, especially
  copallina
  glabra and cvs
  typhina and cvs
Ribes odoratum
Rosa nitida
  rugosa and cvs
  virginiana
Sorbaria aitchisonii
Spiraea thunbergii
Stephanandra (all)
Vaccinium: several, including
  corymbosum
  praestans
Viburnum: many, including
  carlesii and cvs
  furcatum
  × *hillieri* 'Winton'
  opulus and cvs
  plicatum cvs
Zanthoxylum piperitum

CLIMBERS

Ampelopsis (all)
Celastrus (all)
Parthenocissus (all)
Vitis (all)

CONIFERS

Ginkgo biloba
Larix (all)
Metasequoia glyptostroboides
  and cvs
Pseudolarix amabilis
Taxodium (all)

Plants with Red or Purple Foliage

Purple, in foliage terms, defines a group of plants with dark leaf tones from copper and mahogany to near-black. Trees and shrubs with such foliage provide very strong contrasts and should be used judiciously. Just one purple-leaved specimen is likely to be enough in a small garden, and it is easy to overdo dark foliage in gardens of any size.

These colored leaves are often at their most dramatic when backlit by the sun. It is worth finding a site for them where they will be between you and the sun as you walk along a path or relax in a sitting area.

TREES

Acer campestre 'Schwerinii'
platanoides 'Crimson King'
'Deborah'
'Schwedleri'
Betula pendula 'Purpurea'
Catalpa × *erubescens* 'Purpurea'
Fagus sylvatica 'Dawyck Purple'
Purpurea group:
'Purpurea Pendula'
'Riversii'
'Rohanii'
Malus 'Lemoinei'
'Liset'
'Profusion'
'Royal Beauty'
'Royalty'
Prunus × *blireana*
cerasifera 'Nigra'
'Pissardii'
'Rosea'
padus 'Colorata'
virginiana 'Shubert'
Quercus petraea
robur 'Atropurpurea'

SHRUBS

Acer palmatum: many, including
Atropurpureum group:
'Bloodgood'
'Crimson Queen'
'Dissectum Atropurpureum'
'Hessei'
'Red Pygmy'
Berberis × *ottawensis* 'Superba'
thunbergii: many, including
Atropurpurea group:
'Atropurpurea Nana'
'Red Chief'
'Rose Glow'
Cercis canadensis 'Forest Pansy'
Corylopsis willmottiae 'Spring Purple'
Corylus maxima 'Purpurea'
Cotinus coggygria 'Royal Purple'
'Velvet Cloak'
'Grace'
Phormium tenax 'Purpureum' and others
Pittosporum tenuifolium
'Purpureum'
'Tom Thumb'
Prunus cistena
Salvia officinalis 'Purpurascens'
Sambucus nigra 'Guincho Purple'
Weigela florida 'Foliis Purpureis'

CLIMBERS

Vitis vinifera 'Purpurea'

Plants with Golden or Yellow Foliage

Restraint with golden or yellow foliage is almost as important as it is with purple-leaved trees and shrubs. Too much brightly colored foliage is trying on the eyes in sunlight and can produce a rather tawdry effect. On the other hand, one or two well-placed, well-chosen subjects, especially in a dull corner, can have a wonderfully cheerful, lightening effect on the garden. It is advisable to avoid strong yellows, such as that of *Robinia pseudoacacia* 'Frisia', in smaller gardens or where there is a lot of red brick. It is highly attractive in a larger setting and among greens or set against gray stone, but where it is too strident, a greener, softer tone, such as that of *Gleditsia triacanthos* 'Sunburst', may be more fitting.

TREES

Acer cappadocicum 'Aureum'
negundo 'Auratum'
pseudoplatanus 'Worleei'
Alnus incana 'Aurea'
Catalpa bignonioides 'Aurea'
Fagus sylvatica 'Aurea Pendula'
'Zlatia'
Gleditsia triacanthos 'Sunburst'
Laurus nobilis 'Aurea'
Liquidambar styraciflua
'Moonbeam'
Populus alba 'Richardii'
× *canadensis* 'Serotina Aurea'
Quercus robur 'Concordia'
rubra 'Aurea'
Robinia pseudoacacia 'Frisia'
Sorbus aria 'Chrysophylla'
Tilia × *europaea* 'Wratislaviensis'
Ulmus × *hollandica* 'Dampieri Aurea'

SHRUBS

Acer shirasawanum 'Aureum'
Berberis thunbergii 'Aurea'
Calluna vulgaris 'Beoley Gold'
'Gold Haze'
'Joy Vanstone'
'Orange Queen'
'Robert Chapman'
'Sir John Charrington'
Choysia ternata 'Sundance'
Cornus alba 'Aurea'
mas 'Aurea'
'Aurea Elegantissima'
Corylus avellana 'Aurea'
Erica carnea 'Ann Sparkes'
'Aurea'
'Foxhollow'
Erica carnea 'Golden Drop'
'Golden Hue'
× *darleyensis* 'Jack H. Brummage'
vagans 'Valerie Proudley'
Euonymus japonicus 'Ovatus Aureus'
Ligustrum ovalifolium 'Aureum'
'Vicaryi'
Lonicera nitida 'Baggesen's Gold'
Philadelphus coronarius 'Aureus'
Physocarpus opulifolius 'Dart's Gold'
Pittosporum tenuifolium
'Warnham Gold'
Ptelea trifoliata 'Aurea'
Ribes alpinum 'Aureum'
sanguineum 'Brocklebankii'
Sambucus nigra 'Aurea'
racemosa 'Plumosa Aurea'
'Sutherland Gold'
Viburnum opulus 'Aureum'
Weigela 'Looymansii Aurea'
'Rubidor'

CLIMBERS

Hedera helix 'Buttercup'
Humulus lupulus 'Aureus'
Jasminum officinale 'Fiona Sunrise'

CONIFERS

Abies nordmanniana 'Golden Spreader'
Calocedrus decurrens 'Berrima Gold'
Cedrus atlantica 'Aurea'
deodara 'Aurea'

Chamaecyparis lawsoniana:
many cvs, including
'Aurea Densa'
'Lane'
'Minima Aurea'
'Stardust'
'Stewartii'
'Winston Churchill'
obtusa: several cvs, including
'Crippsii'
'Fernspray Gold'
'Nana Aurea'
'Tetragona Aurea'
pisifera: several cvs, including
'Filifera Aurea'
'Gold Spangle'
'Golden Mop'
'Plumosa Aurea'
Cryptomeria japonica 'Sekkan-sugi'
× *Cupressocyparis leylandii*
'Castlewellan Gold'
Cupressus macrocarpa: several
cvs, especially
'Donard Gold'
'Goldcrest'
sempervirens 'Swane's
Golden'
Juniperus chinensis 'Aurea'
communis 'Depressa Aurea'
× *media:* several, including
'Gold Coast'
'Old Gold'
'Pfitzeriana Aurea'
'Plumosa Aurea'
'Sulphur Spray'
Picea orientalis 'Aurea'
Pinus sylvestris 'Aurea'
Taxus baccata: several cvs,
including
'Adpressa Variegata'
'Dovastonii Aurea'
'Elegantissima'
'Standishii'
'Summergold'
Thuja occidentalis: several cvs,
especially
'Europe Gold'
'Rheingold'
orientalis: several cvs,
especially
'Aurea Nana'
plicata 'Aurea'
Thujopsis dolabrata 'Aurea'

From top: The deep red foliage of *Acer palmatum* 'Bloodgood' holds its color well; the featherlike leaves of *Sambucus racemosa* 'Plumosa Aurea' are graceful as well as colorful; and *Vitis vinifera* 'Purpurea' turns from claret red to vinous purple through the fall.

Plants with Gray or Silver Foliage

Gray, silver, and blue foliage does not have to be treated with quite the same degree of caution with which you should approach leaves of other colors. The subtle grading into shades of green makes for a much softer, quieter range of tones, and the contrasts are gentler.

Many woody plants with silver or gray foliage are adapted to withstand drought. The hairs or waxy coatings that give them their color are usually there to minimize water loss.

TREES

Eucalyptus: many, including
coccifera
gunnii
pauciflora subsp. *niphophila*
Populus alba
canescens
Pyrus: several, especially
nivalis
salicifolia 'Pendula'
Salix alba var. *sericea*
exigua
Sorbus aria 'Lutescens'

SHRUBS

Artemisia (all)
Atriplex halimus
Berberis dityophylla
temolaica
Buddleia: several, including
alternifolia 'Argentea'
fallowiana
Calluna vulgaris 'Silver Queen'
'Sister Anne'
Caryopteris × *clandonensis* cvs
Cassinia vauvilliersii var. *albida*
Cistus 'Peggy Sammons'
'Silver Pink'
Convolvulus cneorum
Cytisus battandieri
Elaeagnus: several, including
angustifolia
commutata
macrophylla
Erica tetralix 'Alba Mollis'
Euryops acraeus
pectinatus
Feijoa sellowiana
Halimiocistus wintonensis
Halimium lasianthum
ocymoides
Halimodendron halodendron
Hebe: several, including
albicans
pimeleoides 'Quicksilver'
pinguifolia 'Pagei'
Helianthemum: several cvs, including
'Rhodanthe Carneum'
'Wisley Pink'
'Wisley White'
Helichrysum (all)
Hippophae rhamnoides
Lavandula angustifolia: several cvs, including
'Grappenhall'
'Hidcote'
'Vera'
stoechas and forms
Leptospermum lanigerum
Olearia: several, including
× *mollis*
× *scilloniensis*
Perovskia atriplicifolia 'Blue Spire'
Potentilla arbuscula 'Beesii'
'Vilmoriniana'
Romneya (all)
Rosa glauca
Ruta graveolens and cvs
Salix elaeagnos
exigua
gracilistyla
lanata
repens var. *argentea*
Salvia officinalis
Santolina chamaecyparissus
pinnata subsp. *neapolitana*
Senecio: several, especially
'Sunshine'
Teucrium fruticans and cvs
Zauschneria cana

CLIMBERS

Lonicera caprifolium and cvs
Vitis vinifera 'Incana'

CONIFERS

Abies concolor 'Candicans'
'Compacta'
pinsapo 'Glauca'
Cedrus atlantica Glauca group
Chamaecyparis lawsoniana: many cvs, including
'Columnaris'
'Ellwoodii'
'Fletcheri'
'Pembury Blue'
'Triomf van Boskoop'
'Van Pelt'
pisifera 'Boulevard'
Cupressus cashmeriana
glabra 'Pyramidalis'
lusitanica 'Glauca Pendula'
Juniperus chinensis (several cvs)
'Grey Owl'
Juniperus horizontalis and cvs especially:
'Bar Harbor'
'Wiltonii'
× *media* 'Blaauw'
'Pfitzeriana Compacta'
procumbens
scopulorum: several cvs, including:
'Blue Heaven'
'Skyrocket'
'Springbank'
squamata 'Blue Carpet'
'Blue Star'
'Meyeri'
virginiana 'Glauca'
Picea pungens Glauca group
Pinus koraiensis 'Compacta Glauca'
sylvestris 'Edwin Hillier'
wallichiana

Plants with Variegated Foliage

Opinions on the value of variegated foliage vary. Some gardeners will not consider variegation in any form, while others actively collect plants with variegated leaves. There are so many kinds of variegation and individual tastes vary so greatly that it is impossible to generalize. What can be said is that colored foliage tends to be rewarding in direct proportion to the restraint applied to its use.

Trees with variegated foliage are at their most effective when grown apart from others so that their canopies are low and not too far from eye level. If they are overcrowded, their variegation may become all but invisible. Variegated shrubs are objects of contrast and accent and should be positioned with this in mind.

TREES

Acer negundo 'Elegans'
'Flamingo'
'Variegatum'
platanoides 'Drummondii'
pseudoplatanus 'Leopoldii'
'Nizetti'
Castanea sativa 'Albomarginata'
Cornus controversa 'Variegata'
Crataegus monogyna 'Variegata'
Fagus sylvatica 'Albovariegata'
Fraxinus pennsylvanica 'Variegata'
Ilex × *altaclerensis:* several cvs, including
Ilex altaclarensis × 'Belgica Aurea'
'Golden King'
Ligustrum lucidum 'Excelsum Superbum'
'Tricolor'
Liquidambar styraciflua 'Silver King'
'Variegata'
Liriodendron tulipifera
'Aureomarginatum'
Platanus × *hispanica* 'Suttneri'
Populus × *candicans* 'Aurora'
Quercus cerris 'Variegata'

SHRUBS

Acer palmatum: several cvs, especially
'Butterfly'
'Kagiri Nishiki'
'Ukigumo'
Aralia elata 'Aureovariegata'
'Variegata'
Aucuba japonica: several cvs, especially
'Crotonifolia'
'Gold Dust'
'Variegata'
Azara integrifolia 'Variegata'
microphylla 'Variegata'
Berberis thunbergii 'Pink Queen'
'Rose Glow'
Buddleia davidii 'Harlequin'
Buxus sempervirens 'Elegantissima'
Cleyera japonica 'Tricolor'
Cornus alba 'Elegantissima'
'Spaethii'
alternifolia 'Argentea'
florida 'Rainbow'
'Welchii'
mas 'Variegata'
stolonifera 'White Gold'
Coronilla valentina 'Variegatus'
Daphne × *burkwoodii* 'Carol Mackie' and similar cvs
cneorum 'Variegata'
longilobata 'Peter Moore'
odora 'Aureo-marginata'
Elaeagnus × *ebbingei* 'Gilt Edge'
'Limelight'
pungens 'Dicksonii'
'Frederici'
'Maculata'
'Variegata'
Euonymus fortunei 'Emerald Gaiety'
'Emerald 'n' Gold'
'Silver Pillar'
'Silver Queen'
'Variegatus'
japonicus: especially
'Aureus'
'Latifolius Albomarginatus'
'Microphyllus Pulchellus'
'Microphyllus Variegatus'
× *Fatshedera lizei* 'Annemieke'
'Variegata'
Fatsia japonica 'Variegata'
Feijoa sellowiana 'Variegata'
Fuchsia magellanica 'Sharpitor'
'Variegata'
'Versicolor'
Griselinia littoralis 'Dixon's Cream'
'Variegata'
Hebe × *andersonii* 'Variegata'
× *franciscana* 'Variegata'
glaucophylla 'Variegata'
'Purple Tips'
Hypericum × *moserianum* 'Tricolor'
Ilex aquifolium: many cvs, especially
'Argentea Marginata'
'Golden Milkboy'
'Golden Queen'
'Handsworth New Silver'
'Silver Milkmaid'
Kerria japonica 'Variegata'
Leucothoë fontanesiana 'Rainbow'
Ligustrum sinense 'Variegatum'
Myrtus communis 'Variegata'
luma 'Glanleam Gold'
Osmanthus heterophyllus 'Aureomarginatus'
'Goshiki'
'Variegatus'
Pachysandra terminalis 'Variegata'
Philadelphus coronarius 'Variegatus'
Phormium (many)
Photinia davidiana 'Palette'
Pieris japonica 'Little Heath'
'Variegata'
Pittosporum eugenioides 'Variegatum'
'Garnettii'
tenuifolium: several cvs, including
'Irene Paterson'
'Silver Queen'
tobira 'Variegatum'
Prunus laurocerasus 'Marbled White'
lusitanica 'Variegata'
Rhamnus alaternus 'Argenteovariegata'
Rhododendron ponticum 'Variegatum'
Rubus microphyllus 'Variegatus'
Salvia officinalis 'Icterina'
'Tricolor'
Sambucus nigra 'Aureomarginata'
'Pulverulenta'
Symphoricarpos orbiculatus 'Foliis Variegatis'
Viburnum tinus 'Variegatum'
Vinca major 'Variegata'
minor 'Argenteo-variegata'
Weigela florida 'Variegata'
praecox 'Variegata'
Yucca filamentosa 'Bright Edge'
'Variegata'
flaccida 'Golden Sword'
gloriosa 'Variegata'

CLIMBERS

Actinidia kolomikta
Ampelopsis brevipedunculata 'Elegans'
Hedera algeriensis 'Gloire de Marengo'
'Margino-maculata'
colchica 'Dentata Variegata'
'Sulphur Heart'
helix: several cvs, including
'Adam'
'Cavendishii'
'Glacier'
'Goldchild'
'Goldheart'
'Harald'
'Kolibri'
'Little Diamond'
'Sagittifolia Variegata'
'Sicilia'
Jasminum officinale 'Argenteovariegatum'
'Aureum'
Kadsura japonica 'Variegata'
Lonicera japonica 'Aureoreticulata'
Trachelospermum jasminoides 'Variegatum'

CONIFERS

Calocedrus decurrens 'Aureovariegata'
Chamaecyparis lawsoniana 'Pygmaea Argentea'
'White Spot'
Chamaecyparis pisifera 'Nana Aureo-variegata'
'Snow'
Thuja plicata 'Irish Gold'
'Zebrina'

BAMBOOS

Pleioblastus auricoma variegatus
Sasa veitchii

Plants with Ornamental Fruits

When botanists speak of fruits, they mean seed vessels in general, rather than just the fleshy, edible ones. There are many trees and shrubs whose fruits — in this broad sense — are highly ornamental and valuable in the fall garden.

If you have a small garden, it is important to choose from the quite wide selection of trees and shrubs whose fruits last well into winter or even as far as the following spring, as those of pyracanthas do. Yellow or amber berries often last longer then red ones, as they are not as attractive to birds. White fruits, such as those of *Sorbus hupehensis*, are often the longest lasting of all.

It helps to prolong the lives of fruits if the trees and shrubs bearing them are planted close to a frequently used area, as this tends to discourage birds. In contrast, trees and shrubs that attract wildlife have tasty, fleshy fruits or regularly attract insects that birds feed on.

TREES

Ailanthus altissima
Arbutus (all)
Catalpa bignonioides
Cercis siliquastrum
Crataegus: many, including
- *laciniata*
- *mollis*
- *prunifolia*

Diospyros kaki
Fraxinus ornus
Halesia (all)
Ilex: all females, including
- × *altaclerensis*
  - 'Camelliifolia'
  - 'Wilsonii'
- *aquifolium* 'J.C. van Tol'
- *latifolia*

Koelreuteria paniculata
Magnolia: several, including
- *campbellii* subsp. *mollicomata*
- *hypoleuca*
- *officinalis* var. *biloba*
- *tripetala*

Malus: many, including
- 'Crittenden'
- 'Golden Hornet'
- *hupehensis*
- 'John Downie'
- 'Red Jade'

Malus 'Red Sentinel'
- *transitoria*

Pterocarya (all)
Sorbus: most, including
- *aucuparia* and cvs
- *commixta*
- 'Joseph Rock'
- × *kewensis*
- *scalaris*
- *vilmorinii*
- 'Winter Cheer'

Tetradium daniellii

SHRUBS

Aucuba japonica (female cvs)
Berberis (most, especially deciduous)
Callicarpa (all)
Chaenomeles (most)
Citrus 'Meyer's Lemon'
Colutea (all)
Coriaria (all)
Cornus: many, especially
- *amomum*
- *mas*
  - 'Variegata'
- 'Porlock'

Cotinus (all)
Cotoneaster (all)

From top: Malus 'Golden Hornet' is a good example of a fruiting crab apple; *Rosa moyesii* 'Geranium' has the bonus of smooth scarlet fruits after flowering; and *Hamamelis mollis* 'Pallida' is known for its scent.

Daphne mezereum
tangutica
Decaisnea fargesii
Euonymus: many, including
europaeus 'Red Cascade'
hamiltonianus 'Coral Charm'
latifolius
oxyphyllus
planipes
× *Gaulnettya* cvs
Gaultheria: many, including
cuneata
miqueliana
procumbens
Hippophae rhamnoides
Ilex: females, including
aquifolium 'Amber'
'Bacciflava'
'Pyramidalis'
'Pyramidalis Fructu Luteo'
cornuta 'Burfordii'
Leycesteria formosa
Mahonia aquifolium
japonica
lomariifolia
Mespilus germanica cvs
Pernettya mucronata and cvs
Photinia davidiana and forms
Poncirus trifoliata
Prunus laurocerasus and cvs
Ptelea trifoliata
Pyracantha (all)
Rosa: many, including
'Arthur Hillier'
'Highdownensis'
macrophylla and cvs
moyesii and forms
rugosa and cvs
webbiana
Rubus phoenicolasius
Ruscus aculeatus
Sambucus (most)
Skimmia japonica (female forms)
subsp. *reevesiana*
Staphylea (all)
Symphoricarpos (most)
Symplocos paniculata
Vaccinium: several, including
corymbosum and cvs
cylindraceum
vitis-idaea
Viburnum: many, including
betulifolium
opulus and cvs
setigerum
wrightii 'Hessei'

CLIMBERS

Actinidia chinensis
Akebia quinata
trifoliata
Ampelopsis: several, especially
brevipedunculata
Billardiera longiflora
Celastrus (all)
Clematis: several, especially
tangutica
tibetana subsp. *vernayi*
Parthenocissus (several)
Passiflora caerulea
edulis
Schisandra
Stauntonia hexaphylla
Vitis: several, especially
'Brant'

CONIFERS

Abies: many, including
forrestii
koreana
procera
Picea: many, including
abies 'Acrocona'
likiangensis
purpurea
smithiana
Pinus: many, including
wallichiana
Taxus baccata 'Lutea'

Plants with Fragrant Flowers

Many trees and shrubs have fragrant flowers. In addition, it is worth noting that a high proportion of those that flower in winter in milder regions are scented, so if you plan to have flowers in winter, you are almost certain to enjoy scent as well.

It is possible to plant nothing but scented plants and have a diverse and interesting garden. In practice, however, you are more likely to select comparatively few, so it is important that they are sited to the best advantage. This means planting them near paths or sitting areas. It is also a good idea to put scented plants along the boundary of the garden from which the prevailing wind comes, otherwise their fragrance will be wafted into neighboring yards rather than your own. Alternatively, they may be located in a sheltered area near a kitchen window or walkway.

TREES

Acacia dealbata
Aesculus hippocastanum
Azara microphylla
Cladrastis lutea
sinensis
Crataegus monogyna
Drimys winteri
Eucryphia × *intermedia* 'Rostrevor'
lucida
Fraxinus mariesii
Laburnum alpinum
× *watereri* 'Vossii'
Magnolia hypoleuca
kobus
macrophylla
salicifolia
Malus baccata var. *mandshurica*
coronaria 'Charlottae'
floribunda
'Hillieri'
hupehensis
'Profusion'
× *robusta*
Michelia doltsopa
Myrtus luma
Prunus 'Amanogawa'
'Jo-nioi'
lusitanica and cvs
× *yedoensis* and cvs
Robinia pseudoacacia and cvs
Styrax japonica
Tilia × *euchlora*
oliveri
platyphyllos
tomentosa and cvs

SHRUBS

Abelia chinensis
× *grandiflora*
triflora
Abeliophyllum distichum
Berberis buxifolia
sargentiana
Brugmansia suaveolens
Buddleia: many, including
alternifolia
crispa
davidii and cvs
fallowiana
'Lochinch'
Buxus sempervirens and cvs
Camellia sasanqua cvs
Ceanothus 'Gloire de Versailles'
Chimonanthus praecox and cvs
Chionanthus virginicus
Choisya 'Aztec Pearl'
ternata
Citrus 'Meyer's Lemon'
Clerodendrum bungei
Clethra alnifolia and cvs
barbinervis
fargesii
Colletia hystrix 'Rosea'
paradoxa
Corokia cotoneaster
Coronilla valentina subsp. *glauca*
Corylopsis (all)
Cytisus battandieri
'Porlock'
× *praecox* and cvs
Daphne: many, including
bholua 'Jacqueline Postill'
blagayana

Plants with Fragrant Flowers (continued)

Daphne × *burkwoodii* and cvs
cneorum and forms
collina
× *hybrida*
× *mantensiana* 'Manten'
mezereum and cvs
× *napolitana*
odora and cvs
pontica
tangutica
Deutzia compacta and cvs
× *elegantissima* and cvs
Edgeworthia chrysantha
Elaeagnus (all)
Erica arborea var. *alpina*
× *darleyensis* and cvs
lusitanica
× *veitchii*
Eucryphia glutinosa
milliganii
Euonymus planipes
Fothergilla gardenii
major
Genista aetnensis
Hamamelis × *intermedia* cvs
mollis and cvs
Hoheria glabrata
lyallii
Itea ilicifolia
virginica
Jasminum humile 'Revolutum'
Ligustrum: all, including
quihoui
sinense
Lomatia myricoides
Lonicera fragrantissima
× *purpusii*
'Winter Beauty'
standishii
syringantha
Luculia gratissima
Lupinus arboreus
Magnolia denudata
grandiflora and cvs
× *loebneri* and cvs
sieboldii
sinensis
× *soulangeana* and cvs
stellata and cvs
× *thompsoniana*
Magnolia virginiana
× *wieseneri*
wilsonii
Mahonia japonica
Myrtus communis and cvs
Oemleria cerasiformis
Olearia × *haastii*
ilicifolia
macrodonta and cvs
Osmanthus (all)
Paeonia × *lemoinei* and cvs
Philadelphus: many, including
'Belle Etoile'
'Bouquet Blanc'
coronarius and cvs
'Erectus'
microphyllus
'Sybille'
'Virginal'
Pimelea prostrata
Pittosporum tenuifolium
tobira
Poncirus trifoliata
Prunus mume and cvs
Ptelea trifoliata
Pterostyrax hispida
Pyracantha (all)
Rhododendron: many, including
Albatross group
arborescens
auriculatum
calophytum
'Countess of Haddington'
decorum
fortunei
'Fragrantissimum'
loderi and cvs
luteum
'Polar Bear'
roseum
viscosum
deciduous azaleas: many, especially
'Daviesii'
'Exquisitum'
'Irene Koster'
Ribes alpinum
gayanum
odoratum
Romneya (all)
Rosa: many, including
'Albert Edwards'
'Andersonii'
Rosa 'Anemonoides'
banksiae (single forms)
bracteata
filipes 'Kiftsgate'
helenae
'Macrantha'
moschata
mulliganii
primula
rugosa and cvs
wichuraiana
Sarcococca (all)
Skimmia × *confusa* and cvs
japonica
'Rubella'
Spartium junceum
Syringa: many, including
× *chinensis* 'Saugeana'
× *josiflexa* 'Bellicent'
julianae
× *persica* and cvs
sweginzowii 'Superba'
vulgaris cvs
Ulex europaeus
Viburnum: many, including
× *bodnantense* cvs
× *burkwoodii* and cvs
× *carlcephalum*
carlesii and cvs
'Chesapeake'
farreri
Viburnum japonicum
× *juddii*
Yucca filamentosa
Zenobia pulverulenta

CLIMBERS

Actinidia chinensis
Akebia quinata
Clematis armandii and cvs
cirrhosa var. *balearica*
flammula
montana and forms
rehderiana
Decumaria sinensis
Dregea sinensis
Jasminum azoricum
beesianum
officinale and cvs
polyanthum
× *stephanense*
Lonicera × *americana*
caprifolium and cvs
etrusca
japonica and cvs
periclymenum and cvs
Mandevilla laxa
Stauntonia hexaphylla
Trachelospermum (all)
Wisteria (all)

Plants with Aromatic Foliage

Plants with scented foliage or wood may give off their aroma freely or as a result of gentle bruising. In both cases, they contribute much to the immediate environment. Again, it is advantageous to site such plants near paths or frequently used areas, but on a warm, still summer's day the air of the entire garden will be subtly but unmistakably aromatic.

TREES

Cercidiphyllum japonicum (in fall)
Clerodendrum (all)
Eucalyptus (all)
Juglans (all)
Laurus nobilis and cvs
Phellodendron amurense
Populus balsamifera
trichocarpa
Salix pentandra
Sassafras albidum

SHRUBS

Aloysia triphylla
Artemisia 'Powis Castle'
Caryopteris (all)
Cistus: many, including
× *cyprius*
ladanifer
× *loretii*
palinhae

Cistus × purpureus
Clerodendrum bungei
Comptonia peregrina
Elsholtzia stauntonii
Escallonia (many)
Gaultheria procumbens
Hebe cupressoides
Helichrysum italicum subsp.
  serotinum
Illicium (all)
Lavandula angustifolia and cvs
Lindera (all)
Myrica (all)
Myrtus communis and cvs
Olearia illicifolia
  mollis
Perovskia (all)
Prostanthera (all)
Ptelea trifoliata
Rhododendron: many, including
  augustinii
  cinnabarinum forms and
  hybrids
  Mollis azaleas
  'Pink Drift'
  saluenense
Ribes sanguineum and cvs
Rosmarinus officinalis and cvs
Ruta graveolens
Salvia (all)
Santolina (all)
Skimmia: all, particularly
  anquetilia
  × *confusa* and cvs

CONIFERS
Most conifers, particularly
Calocedrus decurrens
Chamaecyparis (all)
Cupressus (all)
Juniperus (all)
Pseudotsuga menziesii and forms
Thuja (all)

Flowering Plants for Every Season

It is possible to have woody plants in flower during every month of the year in many parts of the temperate world. It is all too easy when buying plants to be carried away by them when they are in flower, and as most people visit nurseries and garden centers during the warmer months, this tends to create a concentration of flowering in the summer.

In milder regions, the gardening year is much longer than many people realize, and the plants that flower in fall, winter, and early spring are often among the most interesting. There is nothing quite so cheering, for example, as the golden flowers of the Chinese witch hazel *Hamamelis mollis*, or the airy clouds of white blooms borne on leafless branches in the depths of winter by the cherry *Prunus subhirtella* 'Autumnalis'.

The following lists will allow most gardeners, depending on location and climate, to plan a balanced garden in which each month is given its due and each year merges seamlessly with the next.

Midwinter

TREES
Acacia dealbata

SHRUBS
Camellia sasanqua cvs
Chimonanthus praecox and cvs
Erica carnea and cvs
  × *darleyensis* and cvs
Garrya elliptica
Hamamelis (many)
Jasminum nudiflorum
Lonicera fragrantissima
  × *purpusii* and cvs
  standishii
Sarcococca (several)
Viburnum × *bodnantense* and cvs
  farreri
  tinus

Late Winter

TREES
Acacia dealbata
Magnolia campbellii and forms
Populus tremula
Prunus incisa 'Praecox'
  mume and cvs
Rhododendron arboreum & forms
Sorbus megalocarpa

SHRUBS
Camellia sasanqua cvs
Cornus mas
  officinalis
Daphne mezereum
  odora and cvs
Erica carnea and cvs
  × *darleyensis* and cvs
Garrya elliptica
Hamamelis (many)
Jasminum nudiflorum
Lonicera fragrantissima
  × *purpusii* and cvs
  setifera
  standishii
Mahonia japonica
Pachysandra terminalis
Rhododendron dauricum
  'Midwinter'
Sarcococca (several)
Ulex europaeus
Viburnum × *bodnantense* and cvs
  farreri
  tinus and cvs

Early Spring

TREES
Acer opalus
  rubrum
Magnolia (several)
Maytenus boaria
Prunus (several)
Rhododendron (several)
Salix (many)
Sorbus megalocarpa

SHRUBS
Camellia japonica (several cvs)
  sasanqua and cvs
Chaenomeles (several)
Corylopsis pauciflora
Daphne mezereum
Erica carnea and cvs
  × *darleyensis* cvs
  erigena and cvs
  lusitanica
  × *veitchii* cvs
Forsythia (several)
Lonicera setifera
Magnolia stellata
Mahonia aquifolium
  japonica
Osmanthus (several)
Pachysandra terminalis
Prunus (several)
Rhododendron (several)
Salix (many)
Stachyurus praecox
Ulex europaeus
Viburnum tinus and cvs

Midspring

TREES
Acer platanoides
Amelanchier (several)
Magnolia kobus
  × *loebneri* and cvs
  salicifolia
Malus (several)
Prunus (many)

SHRUBS
Amelanchier (several)
Berberis darwinii
Camellia japonica and cvs
  × *williamsii* and cvs
Chaenomeles (many)
Corylopsis (several)
Cytisus (several)
Daphne (several)
Erica (several)
Forsythia (many)
Kerria japonica and cvs
Magnolia × *soulangeana* and cvs
  stellata
Mahonia aquifolium
  pinnata
Osmanthus × *burkwoodii*
  decorus
  delavayi
Pieris (most)

Flowering Plants for Every Season (continued)

Prunus (many)
Rhododendron (many)
Ribes (many)
Spiraea 'Arguta'
thunbergii
Viburnum (many)

CLIMBERS
Clematis alpina
armandii
Holboellia coriacea

Late Spring

TREES
Aesculus (many)
Cercis (many)
Cornus nuttallii
Crataegus (many)
Davidia involucrata
Embothrium coccineum and cvs
Fraxinus ornus
Halesia (all)
Laburnum anagyroides
watereri 'Vossii'
Malus (many)
Paulownia tomentosa
Prunus (many)
Pyrus (all)
Sorbus (many)

SHRUBS
Camellia japonica cvs (several)
Ceanothus (several)
Chaenomeles (many)
Choisya (all)
Cornus florida and cvs
Cotoneaster (many)
Crinodendron hookerianum
Cytisus (many)
Daphne (many)
Dipelta floribunda
Enkianthus (all)
Erica (several)
Exochorda (all)
Genista (many)
Halesia (all)
Helianthemum (all)
Kerria japonica and cvs
Kolkwitzia amabilis
Ledum (all)
Lonicera (many)
Magnolia liliiflora
× *soulangeana* cvs
Menziesia (all)
Paeonia (many)
Piptanthus nepalensis
Potentilla (many)
Pyracantha (many)
Rhododendron (many)
Rosa (many)
Xanthoceras sorbifolium

CLIMBERS
Clematis (many)
Lonicera (many)
Schisandra (all)
Wisteria (all)

Early Summer

TREES
Aesculus (several)
Crataegus (many)
Embothrium coccineum and forms
Laburnum alpinum
× *watereri* 'Vossii'
Magnolia: several, including
hypoleuca
Malus trilobata
Robinia (several)
Styrax (several)

SHRUBS
Abelia (several)
Buddleia globosa
Cistus (many)
Colutea (all)
Cornus kousa
'Porlock'
Cotoneaster (many)
Cytisus (many)
Deutzia (most)

The pure pink flowers of *Viburnum* × *bodnantense* 'Charles Lamont' appear in late winter; *Jasminum nudiflorum* flowers in late winter; and *Pieris japonica* 'Blush' carries deep pink inflorescences in midspring.

Erica ciliaris and cvs
cinerea and cvs
tetralix and cvs
Escallonia (many)
Genista (many)
Halimiocistus (all)
Halimium (all)
Hebe (many)
Helianthemum (all)
Hydrangea (several)
Kalmia (all)
Kolkwitzia amabilis and cvs
Lonicera (several)
Magnolia: several, including
× *thompsoniana*
virginiana
Neillia (several)
Olearia (several)
Ozothamnus (all)
Paeonia (all)
Penstemon (several)
Philadelphus (many)
Potentilla (all)
Rhododendron (many)
Rosa (many)
Rubus (many)
Spartium junceum
Spiraea (many)
Staphylea (several)
Syringa (many)
Viburnum (many)
Weigela (all)
Zenobia pulverulenta

CLIMBERS
Clematis (many)
Jasminum (several)
Lonicera (many)
Schisandra (several)
Wisteria (all)

Midsummer

TREES
Aesculus indica
Castanea sativa
Catalpa (all)
Cladrastis sinensis
Eucryphia (several)
Koelreuteria paniculata
Liriodendron tulipifera
Magnolia delavayi
grandiflora and cvs
Stuartia (several)

SHRUBS
Aster albescens
Buddleia davidii and cvs
Calluna vulgaris and cvs
Cistus (many)
Colutea (all)
Daboecia cantabrica and cvs
Desfontainia spinosa
Deutzia setchuenensis
Erica ciliaris and cvs
cinerea and cvs
tetralix and cvs
vagans and cvs
Escallonia (many)
Fuchsia (many)
Grevillea juniperina 'Sulphurea'
Halimodendron halodendron
Hebe (many)
Hoheria (several)
Holodiscus discolor
Hydrangea (many)
Hypericum (many)
Indigofera (several)
Lavandula angustifolia and cvs
Magnolia virginiana
Olearia (several)
Penstemon (several)
Philadelphus (several)
Phygelius (all)
Potentilla (many)
Rhododendron (several)
Romneya (all)
Yucca (several)
Zenobia pulverulenta

CLIMBERS
Clematis (many)
Eccremocarpus scaber
Fallopia baldschuanica

From top: Kerria japonica 'Variegata' flowers in late spring; *Halesia monticola* var. *vestita* has large white flowers in late spring; and *Trachelospermum asiaticum* is an evergreen climber for midsummer flowering.

Flowering Plants for Every Season (continued)

Jasminum (several)
Lonicera (many)
Mutisia oligodon
Passiflora (several)
Schizophragma (all)
Solanum (all)
Trachelospermum (all)

Late Summer

TREES
Catalpa bignonioides
Eucryphia (several)
Koelreuteria paniculata
Ligustrum lucidum and cvs
Magnolia delavayi
  grandiflora and cvs
Oxydendrum arboreum
Stewartia (several)

SHRUBS
Buddleia (many)
Calluna vulgaris and cvs
Caryopteris (several)
Ceanothus (several)
Ceratostigma willmottianum
Clerodendrum (all)
Clethra (several)
Colutea (all)
Daboecia cantabrica and cvs
Desfontainia spinosa
Deutzia setchuenensis
Elsholtzia stauntonii
Erica ciliaris and cvs
  cinerea and cvs
  tetralix and cvs
  vagans and cvs
Fuchsia (many)
Genista tinctoria and cvs
Grevillea juniperina 'Sulphurea'
Hibiscus (several)
Hydrangea (many)
Hypericum (many)
Indigofera (several)
Itea ilicifolia
Lavandula angustifolia (several cvs)
Leycesteria formosa
Myrtus (several)
Olearia (several)
Perovskia (all)
Phygelius (all)
Potentilla (all)
Romneya (all)
Rosa (many)
Yucca (several)
Zenobia pulverulenta

CLIMBERS
Campsis (all)
Clematis (many)
Eccremocarpus scaber
Fallopia (all)
Jasminum (several)
Lapageria rosea cvs
Lonicera (many)
Mutisia oligodon
Passiflora (several)
Pileostegia viburnoides
Solanum (all)
Trachelospermum asiaticum

Early Fall

TREES
Eucryphia × nymanensis and cvs
Magnolia grandiflora and cvs
Oxydendrum arboreum

SHRUBS
Abelia chinensis
  × grandiflora
  schumannii
Aralia elata
Buddleia (several)
Calluna vulgaris and cvs
Caryopteris (several)
Ceratostigma griffithii
  willmottianum
Clerodendrum bungei
Colutea (several)
Daboecia cantabrica and cvs
Elsholtzia stauntonii
Erica ciliaris and cvs
  cinerea (several cvs)
  terminalis
  tetralix and cvs
  vagans and cvs
Fuchsia (several)
Genista tinctoria and cvs
Grevillea juniperina 'Sulphurea'
Hebe (several)
Hibiscus (several)
Hydrangea (several)
Hypericum (several)
Indigofera (several)
Lespedeza thunbergii
Leycesteria formosa
Perovskia (all)
Potentilla (most)
Romneya (all)
Vitex (all)
Yucca gloriosa
Zauschneria

CLIMBERS
Campsis (all)
Clematis (several)
Eccremocarpus scaber
Fallopia baldschuanica
Jasminum (several)
Lapageria rosea cvs
Mutisia oligodon
Passiflora (several)
Pileostegia viburnoides
Solanum crispum 'Glasnevin'

Midfall

TREES
Magnolia grandiflora and cvs

SHRUBS
Abelia × grandiflora
Calluna vulgaris (several cvs)
Ceratostigma griffithii
  willmottianum
Erica carnea 'Eileen Porter'
  vagans (several cvs)
Fatsia japonica
Fuchsia (several)
Hibiscus (several)
Hydrangea (several)
Hypericum (several)
Lespedeza thunbergii
Mahonia × media and cvs
Potentilla (several)
Vitex (all)
Zauschneria (all)

CLIMBERS
Clematis (several)
Eccremocarpus scaber
Lapageria rosea cvs

Late Fall

TREES
Prunus subhirtella 'Autumnalis'

SHRUBS
Erica carnea 'Eileen Porter'
Jasminum nudiflorum
Lonicera standishii
Mahonia × media and cvs
Viburnum × bodnantense cvs
  farreri

Early Winter

TREES
Prunus subhirtella 'Autumnalis'
  'Autumnalis Rosea'

SHRUBS
Erica carnea (several cvs)
  × darleyensis 'Silberschmelze'
Hamamelis × intermedia (some)
  mollis
Jasminum nudiflorum
Lonicera fragrantissima
  × purpusii and cvs
  standishii
Mahonia × media and cvs
Viburnum × bodnantense and cvs
  farreri
  foetens
  tinus and cvs

Plants for Hedges

Hedges are invaluable for screening unsightly areas beyond the property boundary and for reducing traffic noise. Inside the garden, they can be used to create "rooms," providing separate areas with a considerable degree of privacy or, if they are low, breaking up the eyeline and adding interest. A hedge gives an air of tradition to a garden, and topiary, employed selectively, adds grandeur. On the downside, hedges cast a good deal of shade and also absorb a lot of moisture from the soil, necessitating more frequent watering.

TREES

Acer campestre
Betula nigra
Carpinus betulus
Crataegus monogyna
Fagus sylvatica
Ilex (many)
Larix laricina
Laurus nobilis
Quercus ilex
imbricaria

SHRUBS

Berberis (several)
Buxus sempervirens
Caryopteris × *clandonensis* and cvs
Cotoneaster (several)
Deutzia scabra
Elaeagnus (several)
Escallonia
Euonymus japonicus
Griselinia littoralis
Hamamelis virginiana
Hebe (many)
Hippophae rhamnoides
Ilex verticillata
Lavandula (most)
Ligustrum ovalifolium
vulgare
Lonicera nitida
'Baggesen's Gold'
'Ernest Wilson'
pileata
Myrtus communis
Olearia haastii
Osmanthus × *burkwoodii*
delavayi
Phillyrea angustifolia
Pittosporum tenuifolium
Potentilla (many cvs)
Prunus cerasifera 'Nigra'
'Pissardii'
× *cistena*
laurocerasus and cvs
lusitanica
spinosa
tomentosa
Pyracantha (most)
Rhododendron ponticum
Ribes alpinum
Rosmarinus officinalis
'Miss Jessop's Upright'
Rosa (many)
Spiraea japonica and cvs
Symphoricarpos Doorenbos hybrids 'White Hedge'
Tamarix gallica
ramosissima

CONIFERS

Chamaecyparis lawsoniana and several cvs
× *Cupressocyparis leylandii* and cvs
Cupressus macrocarpa
sempervirens
Picea abies
Pinus cembra
strobus
Taxus (several)
Thuja occidentalis
plicata
'Fastigiata'
Tsuga heterophylla

From top: *Solanum crispum* 'Glasnevin' flowers from midsummer to early fall; *Oxydendrum arboreum* blooms in late summer; *Rosa* 'Canary Bird' can be trained to make an attractive, informal hedge.

Guide to Plant Characteristics

TREES

Key to symbols & abbreviations

☐ Suitable for conditions or has marked characteristics listed in column headings

■ Suitable for extreme conditions or has indicated characteristic to an intense degree

S Semievergreen

Flowering time is indicated as follows:
1 = midwinter, 2 = late winter, etc. (see box on p.107)

* Acid soil only

	CLAY	DRY	ALKALINE	MOIST/BOGGY	COLD EXPOSED INLAND	COASTAL	EVERGREEN (S=Semi)	DECIDUOUS	LARGE	MEDIUM	SMALL	WEEPING HABIT	UPRIGHT NARROW HABIT	RED OR PURPLE FOLIAGE	GOLD OR YELLOW FOLIAGE	GRAY OR SILVER FOLIAGE	VARIEGATED FOLIAGE	AUTUMN COLOR	BOLD ARCHITECTURAL FOLIAGE	AROMATIC FOLIAGE	ORNAMENTAL FRUIT	ORNAMENTAL BARK	FLOWERING TIME (in mild regions)	FRAGRANT FLOWERS	HEDGING/SCREENING	SOUTH/WEST WALLS	SHADE TOLERANT
ACER campestre & cvs (Hedge maple)	☐	☐	■		☐			☐		☐				☐	☐		☐	☐							☐		
ACER capillipes & other Snake-barks	☐		☐					☐			☐							☐			☐	☐					
ACER griseum (Paperbark maple)	☐		☐					☐			☐							■				☐					
ACER negundo & cvs (Box elder)	☐	☐	■		☐			☐		☐					☐		☐										
ACER platanoides & cvs (Norway maple)	☐		■		☐	☐		☐	☐	☐	☐		☐	☐			☐	☐					4				
ACER pseudoplatanus & cvs (Sycamore maple)	☐	☐	■	☐	☐	☐		☐	☐	☐	☐		☐	☐	☐		☐										
ACER rubrum & cvs (Red maple)	☐							☐	☐	☐			■					■									
ACER saccharinum & cvs (Silver maple)	☐	☐	☐					☐	☐				☐					☐									
AESCULUS (Horse chestnut)	☐		■					☐	☐		☐							☐					5/6	☐			
AILANTHUS altissima (Tree of heaven)	☐	☐	☐					☐	☐										☐		☐						
ALNUS (Alder)	■			■		☐		☐	☐	☐	☐	☐	☐		☐								3				
AMELANCHIER (Serviceberry)	☐			☐				☐			☐							■					4/5				
ARBUTUS (Manzanita)			☐			☐	☐				☐										☐	☐	10/11				
BETULA (Birch)	☐	☐	☐	☐	☐			☐	☐	☐	☐	☐	☐	☐				☐				☐					
CARAGANA (Pea tree)	☐	☐	☐		☐			☐			☐	☐											5/6				
CARPINUS (Hornbeam)	☐		■	☐	☐			☐	☐	☐			☐					☐			☐				☐		
CARYA (Hickory)	☐		☐					☐	☐									☐				☐					
CASTANEA (Chestnut)		☐				☐		☐	☐								☐						7				
CATALPA	☐		☐					☐		☐	☐			☐	☐				☐				7				
CELTIS (Hackberry)	☐	☐	☐					☐		☐																	
CERCIDIPHYLLUM (Katsura tree)		☐	☐					☐		☐		☐						☐		☐							
CERCIS (Redbud)		☐	■					☐			☐			☐							☐		5				
CLADRASTIS (Yellowwood)	☐		☐					☐		☐								☐					6/7	☐			
CORNUS (Dogwood)	☐		☐					☐		☐	☐						☐	☐			☐		5/6/7				
CORYLUS colurna (Turkish filbert)	☐		☐		☐			☐	☐													☐					
COTONEASTER	☐		☐			☐	S	☐			☐	☐									☐		6				
CRATAEGUS (Hawthorn)	■		■	■	☐	☐		☐		☐	☐	☐	☐				☐	■			☐		5	☐	☐		
DAVIDIA (Dovetree)			☐					☐		☐													5				
DIOSPYROS (Persimmon)		☐	☐					☐			☐							☐			☐		7				
EMBOTHRIUM (Chilean firebush) *				☐			☐				☐												5/6				
EUCALYPTUS	☐		☐			☐	☐		☐	☐	☐					☐						☐					
EUCRYPHIA *				☐			☐	☐		☐	☐							☐					7/8/9	☐			
FAGUS (Beech)			■		☐			☐	☐	☐	☐	☐	☐	☐	☐		☐	☐							☐		
FRAXINUS (Ash)	■	☐	■		☐	☐		☐	☐	☐	☐	☐					☐	☐				☐	5/6				
GLEDITSIA (Honey locust)		☐	☐		☐			☐		☐	☐	☐			☐						☐						
GYMNOCLADUS			☐					☐		☐								☐	☐		☐						
HALESIA (Silverbell) *				☐				☐	☐		☐												5				
IDESIA								☐		☐									☐		☐		6				
ILEX (Holly)	■	☐	☐			☐	☐			☐	☐	☐	☐		☐		☐				☐				☐		☐
JUGLANS (Walnut)			☐					☐	☐	☐								☐	☐								
KOELREUTERIA (Golden-rain tree)		☐	☐					☐		☐			☐								☐		7/8				
LABURNUM	☐		■		☐			☐			☐	☐			☐								6	☐			
LIGUSTRUM (Privet)	☐		☐				☐			☐	☐						☐						8	☐			
LIQUIDAMBAR (Sweet gum) *				☐				☐	☐								☐	■									
LIRIODENDRON (Tulip tree)	☐		☐					☐	☐	☐			☐				☐	☐	☐				6/7				

TREES

Key to symbols & abbreviations

□ Suitable for conditions or has marked characteristics listed in column headings

■ Suitable for extreme conditions or has indicated characteristic to an intense degree

S Semievergreen

Flowering time is indicated as follows:
1 = midwinter, 2 = late winter, etc. (see box below)

* Acid soil only

	CLAY	DRY	ALKALINE	MOIST/BOGGY	COLD EXPOSED INLAND	COASTAL	EVERGREEN (S=Semi)	DECIDUOUS	LARGE	MEDIUM	SMALL	WEEPING HABIT	UPRIGHT NARROW HABIT	RED OR PURPLE FOLIAGE	GOLD OR YELLOW FOLIAGE	GRAY OR SILVER FOLIAGE	VARIEGATED FOLIAGE	AUTUMN COLOR	BOLD ARCHITECTURAL FOLIAGE	AROMATIC FOLIAGE	ORNAMENTAL FRUIT	ORNAMENTAL BARK	FLOWERING TIME (in mild regions)	FRAGRANT FLOWERS	HEDGING/SCREENING	SOUTH/WEST WALLS	SHADE TOLERANT
MAACKIA			□					□			□								□				7/8				
MAGNOLIA [Some *]	□		□	□			□	□	□	□	□								□		□		8/9	□		□	
MALUS (Flowering crab apple)	□		■		□			□		□	□	□		□				□			□		4/5	□			
MORUS (Mulberry)			■					□		□	□	□									□						
NOTHOFAGUS (Southern beech) *				□			□	□	□	□								□									
NYSSA (Sour gum) *				□				□		□	□							■									
OSTRYA (Hop hornbeam)			□					□	□	□								□			□						
PARROTIA			□					□			□							■				□					
PAULOWNIA			□					□		□									□				5	□			
PHELLODENDRON (Amur cork tree)	□		□					□		□								□	□	□	□						
PHILLYREA	□		□			□	□		□		□												5	□			
PLATANUS (Plane tree)	□		□					□	□								□		□								
POPULUS (Poplar)	■	□	□	□	□	□		□	□			□	□		□	□	□	□	□	□							
PRUNUS (Almond, cherry, peach, etc.)	□		■				□	□		□	□	□	□									□	2 to 12	□	□		
PTEROCARYA (Wing nut)	□		□	□				□	□					□				□	□		□		6				
PYRUS (Pear)	□			□				□		□	□	□				□		■					4				
QUERCUS (Oak) [Some *]	□		□	□	□	□	□	□	□	□		□	□	□	□		□	□	□						□		
RHUS (Sumac)			□					□			□							□	□		□						
ROBINIA (False acacia)		□	□					□	□	□	□		□		□								6	□			
SALIX (Willow)	■		□	■		□		□	□	□	□	□				□						□	3				
SASSAFRAS *				□				□		□								□		□							
SOPHORA			□				□	□	□		□	□														□	
SORBUS (Mountain ash)	□		□	□	□	□		□	□	□	□		□		□	□		□			□	□	5/6	□			
STEWARTIA *				□				□			□							□				□	7/8				
STYRAX (Snowbell)				□				□			□												6	□			
TETRACENTRON			□					□		□								□	□				6	□			
TETRADIUM			■					□		□								□	□				6	□			
TILIA (Linden)			□					□			□												6				
TOONA	□		□		□			□	□	□	□	□	□		□				□				7/9	□			
TRACHYCARPUS	□	□	□			□	□				□								□				6				
ZELKOVA			□					□	□	□								□									

KEY TO FLOWERING TIMES IN MILD REGIONS

1 = midwinter	7 = midsummer
2 = late winter	8 = late summer
3 = early spring	9 = early fall
4 = midspring	10 = midfall
5 = late spring	11 = late fall
6 = early summer	12 = early winter

Guide to Plant Characteristics

CONIFERS AS TREES

Key to symbols & abbreviations

□ Suitable for conditions or has marked characteristics listed in column headings

■ Suitable for extreme conditions or has indicated characteristic to an intense degree

* Acid soil only

	CLAY	DRY	ALKALINE	MOIST/BOGGY	COLD EXPOSED INLAND	COASTAL	EVERGREEN	DECIDUOUS	LARGE	MEDIUM	SMALL	WEEPING	UPRIGHT NARROW HABIT	GOLD OR YELLOW FOLIAGE	GRAY OR SILVER FOLIAGE	VARIEGATED FOLIAGE	AUTUMN COLOR	AROMATIC FOLIAGE	ORNAMENTAL CONES	ORNAMENTAL BARK	HEDGING/SCREENING	SHADE TOLERANT
ABIES (Fir) [Some *]	□		□	□	□		□		□	□	□				□				□			
ARAUCARIA araucana (Monkey puzzle tree)	□		□	□			□			□												
CALOCEDRUS (Incense cedar)	□		■				□		□	□	□		□	□		□		□				
CEDRUS (Cedar)	□		□				□		□			□	□	□	□				□			
CHAMAECYPARIS lawsoniana & cvs (Lawson false cypress)	□	□	■	□			□		□	□	□	□	□	□	□	□		□			□	
CHAMAECYPARIS nootkatensis (Nootka false cypress)	□	□	□	□	□		□		□	□		□						□	□			
CHAMAECYPARIS obtusa & cvs (Hinoki false cypress)	□	□	□	□	□		□				□			□				□				
CHAMAECYPARIS pisifera & cvs (Sawara false cypress)	□	□	□	□	□		□			□	□			□				□				
CRYPTOMERIA (Japanese cedar)	□		□	□	□		□		□	□	□			□			□			□		
CUNNINGHAMIA (China fir)	□		□				□				□											
X CUPRESSOCYPARIS leylandii (Leyland cypress)	□	□	□	□	□	□	□		□					□							□	
CUPRESSUS (Cypress)	□	■	■			□	□			□	□	□	□	□	□			□				
GINKGO	□	□	□		□			□	□				□				□					
JUNIPERUS (Juniper)	□	■	■	□	□	□	□				□	□	□	□	□			□				
LARIX (Larch)	□	□	□		□			□	□	□		□			□		□		□			
METASEQUOIA (Dawn redwood)	□	□	□	■				□	□								□			□		
PICEA (Spruce)	□		□	□	□		□		□	□	□	□		□	□				□			
PINUS (Pine)	□		■		□	□	□		□	□	□	□	□	□	□		□		□	□		□
PSEUDOTSUGA (Douglas fir) *	□			□			□		□		□	□			□			□	□			
SEQUOIA (Redwood)	□	■	□	□			□		□											□		
SEQUOIADENDRON (Giant sequoia)	□		□				□		□			□							□			
TAXODIUM (Bald cypress) *	■			■				□	□	□							□			□		
TAXUS (Yew)	□	□	■		□		□			□			□	□					□		□	□
THUJA (Arborvitae)	□		■	□	□		□		□	□			□	□			□	□		□	□	
THUJOPSIS (False arborvitae)	□	□	■				□				□			□								
TORREYA	□	□	■				□			□	□											□
TSUGA (Hemlock)	□			□	□		□		□		□				□							□

SHRUBS

Key to symbols & abbreviations

□ Suitable for conditions or has marked characteristics listed in column headings

■ Suitable for extreme conditions or has indicated characteristic to an intense degree

S Semievergreen

Flowering time is indicated as follows:

1 = midwinter, 2 = late winter, etc. (see box on p.107)

* Acid soil only

	CLAY	DRY	ALKALINE	MOIST/BOGGY	COLD EXPOSED INLAND	COASTAL	EVERGREEN (S=Semi)	DECIDUOUS	LARGE	MEDIUM	SMALL	DWARF	GROUND COVER	RED OR PURPLE FOLIAGE	GOLD OR YELLOW FOLIAGE	GRAY OR SILVER FOLIAGE	VARIEGATED FOLIAGE	AUTUMN COLOR	BOLD ARCHITECTURAL FOLIAGE	AROMATIC FOLIAGE	ORNAMENTAL FRUIT	ORNAMENTAL BARK	FLOWERING TIME (in mild regions)	FRAGRANT FLOWERS	HEDGING/SCREENING	NORTH/EAST WALLS	SOUTH/WEST WALLS	SHADE TOLERANT
ABELIA	□		□				S	□	□		□												6/9	□			□	
ABELIOPHYLLUM			□					□			□							□					2	□			□	
ABUTILON		□	□					□	□	□						□	□						5/9				□	
ACACIA (Wattle)		□					□		□							□							1/2	□			□	
ACER japonicum, palmatum, & cvs (Japanese maples)	□							□	□	□	□			□	□			■			□	□						□
AESCULUS (Horse chestnut)	□		■					□	□									□	□				5/7					
ALOYSIA (Lemon verbena)		□	□					□		□										□			8				□	
AMELANCHIER (Serviceberry)	□			□				□	□									□					4/5					
ANDROMEDA *				□			□					□				□							5/6					□
ANTHYLLIS		□	□					□				□											6/7					
ARALIA	□		□	□				□	□								□	□	□				7/9					
ARBUTUS (Manzanita)			□		□	□		□													□	□	10/11					
ARCTOSTAPHYLOS *		□					□						□								□		4/5					□
ARONIA (Chokeberry)	□			□	□			□		□	□							□			□		4					
ARTEMISIA		□	□					□			□					□				□								
ATRIPLEX		□	□		□	□	S			□						□												
AUCUBA	□		■				□			□	□						□		□		□							□
AZARA							□		□														3	□		□		
BALLOTA		□	□									□				□							7					
BERBERIS (Barberry)	□	□	■		□		□	□	□	□	□	□	□	□	□			□			□		4		□			
BUDDLEIA	□	□	■	□	□			□	□	□						□	□						5/6 & 8/9	□				□
BUPLEURUM	□	□	□	□		□				□													7					
BUXUS (Boxwood)	□	□	□				□		□	□	□	□					□								□			□
CALLICARPA (Beautyberry)			□					□		□	□							□			□		8					
CALLISTEMON (Bottlebrush)		□				□	□			□										□			7				□	
CALLUNA (Heather) *		□		□	□	□	□					□	□			□	□						7/10					□
CALYCANTHUS (Sweet shrub)	□		□	□				□		□													7					
CAMELLIA *				□			□		□	□													2/5			□	□	□
CARAGANA (Pea tree)	□	□	□	□	□			□		□													5					
CARPENTERIA			□				□			□													7				□	
CARYOPTERIS		□	□					□			□					□				□			8					
CASSINIA		□	□			□	□				□			□	□								7					
CASSIOPE *				□			□					□											4					
CEANOTHUS		□	□			□	□	□	□	□		□	□										5 & 8			□		
CERATOSTIGMA (Plumbago)		□	□					□			□							□					8/10					
CERCIS (Redbud)		□	■					□	□												□		5					
CHAENOMELES (Flowering quince)	□	□	□		□					□	□	□									□		3/4			□	□	
CHAMAEROPS (Fan palm)		□	□			□	□				□								□									
CHIMONANTHUS (Wintersweet)			□					□		□													1	□			□	
CHIONANTHUS (Fringe tree)			□					□	□												□		6/7	□				
CHOISYA (Mexican orange)	□		□			□	□			□					□					□			5/6	□		□	□	□
CISTUS (Rock rose)		□	■			□	□				□	□				□							6/7					
CLERODENDRUM	□	□	□					□	□	□									□	□	□		8/9	□				
CLETHRA *				□				□		□								□				□	7/8	□				

Guide to Plant Characteristics

SHRUBS

Key to symbols & abbreviations

□ Suitable for conditions or has marked characteristics listed in column headings

■ Suitable for extreme conditions or has indicated characteristic to an intense degree

S Semi-evergreen

Flowering time is indicated as follows:

1 = midwinter, 2 = late winter, etc. (see box on p.107)

* Acid soil only

	CLAY	DRY	ALKALINE	MOIST/BOGGY	COLD EXPOSED INLAND	COASTAL	EVERGREEN (S=Semi)	DECIDUOUS	LARGE	MEDIUM	SMALL	DWARF	GROUND COVER	RED OR PURPLE FOLIAGE	GOLD OR YELLOW FOLIAGE	GRAY OR SILVER FOLIAGE	VARIEGATED FOLIAGE	AUTUMN COLOR	BOLD ARCHITECTURAL FOLIAGE	AROMATIC FOLIAGE	ORNAMENTAL FRUIT	ORNAMENTAL BARK	FLOWERING TIME (in mild regions)	FRAGRANT FLOWERS	HEDGING/SCREENING	NORTH/EAST WALLS	SOUTH/WEST WALLS	SHADE TOLERANT
CLIANTHUS		□	□					□			□												6				□	
COLLETIA		□	□																				7/8	□				
COLUTEA (Bladder senna)	□	□	■			□		□	□	□						□					□		6/8					
COMPTONIA (Sweet fern) *				□				□			□												3					
CONVOLVULUS		□	□				□					□				□							5					
CORNUS (Dogwood) [Some *]	□	□	□	□	□			□	□	□		□	□		□		□	□			□	□	2/5/6					□
COROKIA		□	□			□	□			□	□										□		5/6					
CORONILLA		□	□				□	□		□						□	□						5/7	□			□	
CORYLOPSIS (Winter hazel)	□		□					□	□	□	□			□									3/4	□				
CORYLUS (Filbert)	□	□	□	□	□			□	□					□	□			□				□	2		□			□
COTINUS (Smoke tree)			□		□			□	□	□				□				■					6/7					
COTONEASTER	□	□	□	□	□	□	□	□	□	□	□	□	□			□		□			□		6		□	□		□
CRINODENDRON *							□		□														5			□	□	
CYATHODES *							□					□				□					□		5					
CYTISUS (Broom)	□	□	□			□		□	□	□	□	□	□										5/7				□	
DABOECIA (Irish heath) *							□					□	□										6/8					
DANAE (Alexandrian laurel)	□		□				□				□																	□
DAPHNE			□				□	□			□	□					□				□		2/6	□		□		
DECAISNEA			□	□				□		□									□		□		5				□	
DESFONTAINIA *				□			□			□													7/9			□		
DEUTZIA	□	□	■		□			□		□	□												6/7					
DIERVILLA (Bush honeysuckle)	□	□	□		□			□										□					6/7					
DIPELTA			□					□	□														5	□				
DIPTERONIA	□		□					□	□										□		□							
DISANTHUS *	□			□					□	□								■					10					
DISTYLIUM	□						□		□														4					
DRIMYS							□		□	□													4/5	□		□		□
ELAEAGNUS	□	□	□		□	□	□	□	□	□						□	□				□	□	5/6 & 10	□	□			
ENKIANTHUS *				□				□	□	□								■					5					□
ERICA, tall forms (Heath) *		□				□	□			□													3/5	□				
ERICA carnea, mediterranea, terminalis, & x darleyensis		□	□		□		□			□	□	□	□		□								4/5 & 9	□				
ERICA, others *		□		□	□	□	□					□	□		□	□							6/10					
ERIOBOTRYA (Loquat)	□		□				□												□							□	□	
ESCALLONIA		□	□			□	□			□	□												6/7		□			
EUONYMUS	□	□	■		□	□	□	□	□	□	□	□	□				□	□			□	□	5/6		□	□		□
EXOCHORDA	□		□					□	□		□												5					
FABIANA				□			□			□	□												5/6					
X FATSHEDERA	□	□	□			□	□			□							□		□									□
FATSIA	□		□			□	□			□							□		□				10					
FORSYTHIA	□		■		□			□	□	□		□											3/4			□	□	□
FOTHERGILLA *	□							□		□		□						■					4	□				
FREMONTODENDRON (FREMONTIA)		□	□				□		□														6/8				□	
FUCHSIA			□			□				□	□	□											7/9			□		
GARRYA	□		□				□		□														1/2			□		□

SHRUBS

Key to symbols & abbreviations

□ Suitable for conditions or has marked characteristics listed in column headings

■ Suitable for extreme conditions or has indicated characteristic to an intense degree

S Semi-evergreen

Flowering time is indicated as follows:

1 = midwinter, 2 = late winter, etc. (see box on p.107)

* Acid soil only

	CLAY	DRY	ALKALINE	MOIST/BOGGY	COLD EXPOSED INLAND	COASTAL	EVERGREEN (S=Semi)	DECIDUOUS	LARGE	MEDIUM	SMALL	DWARF	GROUND COVER	RED OR PURPLE FOLIAGE	GOLD OR YELLOW FOLIAGE	GRAY OR SILVER FOLIAGE	VARIEGATED FOLIAGE	AUTUMN COLOR	BOLD ARCHITECTURAL FOLIAGE	AROMATIC FOLIAGE	ORNAMENTAL FRUIT	ORNAMENTAL BARK	FLOWERING TIME (in mild regions)	FRAGRANT FLOWERS	HEDGING/SCREENING	NORTH/EAST WALLS	SOUTH/WEST WALLS	SHADE TOLERANT
X GAULNETTYA *				□	□		□				□		□								□		5/6					□
GAULTHERIA *				□			□				□	□	□								□		5/6	□				□
GENISTA (Broom)	□	□	□					□	□		□	□	□										5/9					
GREVILLEA *		□					□			□		□											6/7				□	
GRISELINIA		□	□			□	□		□								□								□			
x HALIMIOCISTUS		□	■			□	□					□				□							5/9					
HALIMIUM		□	□			□	□				□	□	□			□							5/6					
HALIMODENDRON (Salt tree)		□	□			□		□			□					□							6/7					
HAMAMELIS (Witch hazel)	□				□			□	□									□					12/3	□				
HEBE		□	■			□	□			□	□	□	□			□	□						6/10					
HEDYSARUM		□	□					□			□												7/9					
HELIANTHEMUM (Sun rose)		□	■			□	□					□	□			□							5/9					
HELICHRYSUM		□	□			□	□				□	□				□				□			7					
HIBISCUS		□	■					□	□	□													7/10					
HIPPOPHAE (Sea buckthorn)	□	□	■	□	□	□		□	□							□					□							
HOHERIA		□	□				□	□	□								□						6/7	□			□	
HOLODISCUS	□	□	■					□	□							□							7					
HYDRANGEA	□		□	□		□		□	□	□	□	□					□	□	□				6/9					□
HYPERICUM (St-John's-wort)	□		■				□	□		□	□	□	□				□						6/10					□
ILEX (Holly)	□	□	□	□	□	□	□		□	□		□			□		□				□				□			
ILLICIUM				□			□			□										□			5/6					
INDIGOFERA	□	□	■					□		□	□												6/9				□	
ITEA ilicifolia	□		□				□			□													8	□			□	
JASMINUM (Jasmine)	□		□					□		□		□										□	11/12 & 6/7	□		□	□	
KALMIA *				□			□			□		□											4/6					
KERRIA	□		■		□			□		□	□						□					□	4/5				□	
KOLKWITZIA (Beautybush)	□	□	■		□			□		□													5/6					
LAURUS (Sweet bay)	□	□	■			□	□		□						□					□					□			
LAVANDULA (Lavender)		□	■			□	□				□	□	□			□				□			7	□	□			
LAVATERA (Mallow)	□	□	□			□		□		□	□												6/10					
LEDUM *				□			□				□	□											4/6					□
LEIOPHYLLUM *				□			□					□	□										5/6					□
LEPTOSPERMUM		□					□			□	□	□				□							5/6				□	
LESPEDEZA *	□	□	□					□		□	□												8/9					
LEUCOTHOË				□			□			□	□		□				□	□					5/8					□
LEYCESTERIA	□		□			□		□		□											□	□	6/9					
LIGUSTRUM (Privet)	□	□	■				□	□	□	□	□				□		□				□		6/9		□			□
LINDERA *				□				□		□								□										
LOMATIA *				□			□		□	□	□												7	□				
LONICERA (Honeysuckle)	□	□	■		□		□	□		□	□	□			□						□		1/3 & 5/6	□	□			□
MAGNOLIA (Some *)	□		□	□		□	□	□	□	□									□				7/9 & 3/4	□			□	
X MAHOBERBERIS	□	□	■		□	□	□				□										□		4					□
MAHONIA							□			□	□	□	□						□		□		11/4	□				□
MENZIESIA *	□	□	■	□				□			□												5					

Guide to Plant Characteristics

SHRUBS

Key to symbols & abbreviations

☐ Suitable for conditions or has marked characteristics listed in column headings

■ Suitable for extreme conditions or has indicated characteristic to an intense degree

S Semi-evergreen

Flowering time is indicated as follows:
1 = midwinter, 2 = late winter, etc. (see box on p.107)

∗ Acid soil only

	CLAY	DRY	ALKALINE	MOIST/BOGGY	COLD EXPOSED INLAND	COASTAL	EVERGREEN (S=Semi)	DECIDUOUS	LARGE	MEDIUM	SMALL	DWARF	GROUND COVER	RED OR PURPLE FOLIAGE	GOLD OR YELLOW FOLIAGE	GRAY OR SILVER FOLIAGE	VARIEGATED FOLIAGE	AUTUMN COLOR	BOLD ARCHITECTURAL FOLIAGE	AROMATIC FOLIAGE	ORNAMENTAL FRUIT	ORNAMENTAL BARK	FLOWERING TIME (in mild regions)	FRAGRANT FLOWERS	HEDGING/SCREENING	NORTH/EAST WALLS	SOUTH/WEST WALLS	SHADE TOLERANT
MYRICA		☐						☐		☐													6/7					
MYRTUS (Myrtle)		☐	☐			☐	☐		☐	☐	☐						☐		☐		☐		7/8				☐	
NANDINA (Heavenly bamboo)		☐	☐				☐			☐	☐			☐				☐					6/7					
NEILLIA	☐		■					☐		☐	☐												5/6					
OLEARIA (Daisy bush)	☐	☐	■			☐	☐		☐	☐	☐			☐					☐				5/8	☐	☐			
ONONIS		☐	■					☐			☐												6/7					
OSMANTHUS	☐	☐	☐				☐		☐	☐				☐			☐						4/5 & 9	☐				
X OSMAREA	☐	☐	☐				☐			☐													4/5					
OZOTHAMNUS		☐	☐				☐			☐	☐					☐							7	☐				
PACHYSANDRA	☐		☐	☐			☐					☐	☐				☐						2/3					☐
PAEONIA (Peony)			■							☐									☐				5/6					
PARAHEBE	☐	☐	☐									☐	☐										7/8					
PARROTIA	☐			☐				☐	☐									☐				☐	3					
PERNETTYA ∗	☐	☐	☐	☐	☐		☐					☐	☐								☐		5/6					☐
PEROVSKIA (Russian sage)		☐	☐			☐		☐			☐					☐				☐			8/9					
PHILADELPHUS (Mock orange)	☐	☐	■		☐			☐	☐	☐	☐	☐			☐		☐						6/7	☐				☐
PHILESIA ∗				☐			☐					☐											6/7					☐
PHILLYREA	☐	☐	☐				☐		☐														5	☐				☐
PHLOMIS		☐	☐			☐	☐				☐					☐				☐			6					
PHORMIUM		☐	☐			☐	☐			☐		☐		☐		☐	☐		☐				7/9					
PHOTINA	☐	☐	☐				☐	☐	☐	☐				☐					☐		☐		5/6					
PHYGELIUS (Cape fuchsia)		☐	☐				☐				☐												7/9				☐	
PHYLLODOCE ∗				☐	☐		☐					☐	☐										5/6					
PHYLLOSTACHYS (Bamboo)			☐				☐		☐	☐												☐						☐
PHYSOCARPUS (Ninebark)	☐	☐	☐	☐				☐		☐	☐				☐								6					
PIERIS ∗				☐			☐		☐	☐	☐			☐	☐		☐						3/5	☐				☐
PIPTANTHUS (Evergreen laburnum)		☐	☐				S			☐													5			☐		
PITTOSPORUM	☐	☐	☐			☐	☐		☐		☐			☐	☐	☐	☐						5/6	☐	☐		☐	
PLEIOBLASTUS (Bamboo)	☐		☐	☐		☐	☐		☐		☐		☐				☐											☐
POLYGALA ∗				☐			☐					☐	☐										4/6					
PONCIRUS (Hardy orange)	☐	☐	☐					☐		☐											☐	☐	5	☐				
POTENTILLA	☐	■	■		☐	☐		☐		☐	☐	☐	☐			☐							6/11		☐			☐
PRUNUS (Almond & cherry)	☐	☐	■	☐	☐		☐	☐	☐	☐	☐	☐		☐			☐	☐	☐		☐		3/6		☐			☐
PTELEA (Hop tree)	☐							☐	☐						☐						☐		6	☐				
PTEROSTYRAX	☐		☐					☐	☐												☐		6/7	☐				
PUNICA (Pomegranate)		☐	☐					☐	☐			☐						☐					9/10				☐	
PYRACANTHA (Firethorn)	☐	☐	■		☐	☐	☐		☐												☐		6	☐	☐	☐	☐	☐
RHAMNUS (Buckthorn)	☐	☐	■	☐	☐	☐	☐	☐	☐	☐		☐					☐				☐							☐
RHAPHIOLEPIS		☐	☐				☐				☐												6	☐		☐		
RHODODENDRON ∗	☐			☐			☐		☐	☐	☐	☐	☐						☐				1/8	☐	☐			☐
RHODODENDRON AZALEA, deciduous ∗	☐							☐		☐								☐					5/6	☐				
RHODODENDRON AZALEA, evergreen ∗	☐			☐			☐				☐	☐	☐										4/5					☐
RHODOTYPOS	☐	☐	■					☐			☐										☐		5/7					
RHUS (Sumac)	☐	☐	■					☐	☐	☐								■	☐					☐				
RIBES (Currants & gooseberries)	☐	☐	■		☐		☐	☐		☐	☐	☐			☐			☐					2/5					

SHRUBS

Key to symbols & abbreviations

□ Suitable for conditions or has marked characteristics listed in column headings

■ Suitable for extreme conditions or has indicated characteristic to an intense degree

S Semi-evergreen

Flowering time is indicated as follows:
1 = midwinter, 2 = late winter, etc. (see box on p.107)

∗ Acid soil only

	CLAY	DRY	ALKALINE	MOIST/BOGGY	COLD EXPOSED INLAND	COASTAL	EVERGREEN (S=Semi)	DECIDUOUS	LARGE	MEDIUM	SMALL	DWARF	GROUND COVER	RED OR PURPLE FOLIAGE	GOLD OR YELLOW FOLIAGE	GRAY OR SILVER FOLIAGE	VARIEGATED FOLIAGE	AUTUMN COLOR	BOLD ARCHITECTURAL FOLIAGE	AROMATIC FOLIAGE	ORNAMENTAL FRUIT	ORNAMENTAL BARK	FLOWERING TIME (in mild regions)	FRAGRANT FLOWERS	HEDGING/SCREENING	NORTH/EAST WALLS	SOUTH/WEST WALLS	SHADE TOLERANT
ROMNEYA (Tree poppy)		□	□			□				□							□						7/10	□				
ROSA (Rose species)	□	□	□			□		□	□	□	□		□	□							□		5/7	□	□			
ROSA (Shrub roses)	□		□					□		□	□										□		6/9	□	□		□	
ROSMARINUS (Rosemary)		□	■			□				□	□	□								□			5		□			
RUBUS (Brambles)	□	■	□	□	□	□	□	□		□	□	□	□				□					□	5/8					□
RUSCUS (Butcher's broom)	□	□	□	□			□				□	□									□							□
RUTA (Rue)		□	□				□				□					□				□			6/8					
SALIX (Willow)	■		□	■				□	□	□	□	□	□			□						□	2/3					
SALVIA		□	□				S	□			□	□	□	□		□	□			□			8/9				□	
SAMBUCUS (Elder)	□	□	■	□				□	□	□	□			□	□		□				□		6	□				□
SANTOLINA (Lavender cotton)		□	□			□	□					□	□			□				□			7					
SARCOCOCCA	□	□	■				□																2	□				□
SASA (Bamboo)	□		□	□			□			□	□	□	□				□											□
SENECIO	□	□	■			□	□			□	□		□			□							6/7					
SKIMMIA	□	□	□			□	□				□	□								□	□		4/5	□				□
SORBARIA	□	□	■	□	□	□		□	□	□									□				6/8					
SORBUS reducta (Dwarf mountain ash)	□	□	□									□						□			□		5					
SPARTIUM (Spanish broom)	□	□	■			□		□		□												□	6/8	□				
SPIRAEA (Spirea)	□	□	■	□	□	□		□		□	□	□	□		□			□					4/8					
STACHYURUS	□	□	□					□															3					
STAPHYLEA (Bladder nut)	□							□	□												□		5/6					
STEPHANANDRA	□	□	□					□		□	□	□	□					□				□	6					
SYCOPSIS	□		□				□			□													2/3					
SYMPHORICARPOS	□		■	□	□	□		□		□	□		□				□				□				□			□
SYRINGA (Lilac)	□		■					□	□	□	□												5/6	□				
TAMARIX (Tamarisk)	□	□	□		□	□		□	□														3&7/9					
TELOPEA (Waratah) ∗	□			□	□		□			□													6					
TEUCRIUM (Germander)		□	□				□				□					□							6/8				□	
TROCHODENDRON ∗	□						□		□														5/6					□
ULEX (Gorse)	□	■			□	□	□			□	□		□										3/5 &8/10					
VACCINIUM (Blueberry) ∗	□			□			□	□		□	□	□					□				□		5/6					□
VIBURNUM	□	□	□	□	□		□	□	□	□	□	□	□					□			□		11/3 &4/6	□	□			□
VINCA (Periwinkle)	□	□	□				□					□	□				□						4/6					
VITEX (Chaste tree)		□	□					□		□										□			9/10				□	
WEIGELA	□		■					□		□	□			□	□		□						5/6					
YUCCA		□	□			□	□		□		□					□	□		□				7/8					
ZENOBIA ∗				□				□			□					□							6/7					

Guide to Plant Characteristics

CONIFERS AS SHRUBS

Key to symbols & abbreviations

□ Suitable for conditions or has marked characteristics listed in column headings

■ Suitable for extreme conditions or has indicated characteristic to an intense degree

* Acid soil only

	CLAY	DRY	ALKALINE	MOIST/BOGGY	COLD EXPOSED INLAND	COASTAL	EVERGREEN	LARGE	MEDIUM	SMALL	DWARF	GROUND COVER	UPRIGHT, NARROW	GOLD OR YELLOW FOLIAGE	GRAY OR SILVER FOLIAGE	VARIEGATED FOLIAGE	AUTUMN COLOR	AROMATIC FOLIAGE	ORNAMENTAL CONES	SHADE TOLERANT
ABIES (Fir)	□		□		□		□			□	□			□	□					
CEDRUS (Cedar)	□	□	■				□		□	□	□									
CEPHALOTAXUS (Plum yew)	□		■				□	□	□		□	□	□							□
CHAMAECYPARIS lawsoniana & cvs (Lawson false cypress)	□	□	■	□			□	□	□	□	□			□	□			□		
CHAMAECYPARIS obtusa & cvs (Hinoki false cypress)	□	□	□	□	□		□	□		□	□			□		□		□		
CHAMAECYPARIS pisifera & cvs (Sawara false cypress)	□	□	□	□	□		□		□		□			□	□			□		
CHAMAECYPARIS thyoides & cvs (White cedar)	□	□	□	□			□			□	□						□	□		
CRYPTOMERIA (Japanese cedar)	□		□	□	□		□	□	□	□	□						□			
JUNIPERUS (Juniper)	□	□	■	□	□	□	□	□	□	□	□	□	□	□	□	□	□	□		□
PICEA (Spruce)	□		□	□	□		□	□	□	□	□				□					
PINUS (Pine)	□	□	■	□	□	□	□		□	□	□	□								
PODOCARPUS	□		□				□	□			□	□								□
PSEUDOTSUGA (Douglas fir) *	□			□			□			□					□			□		
TAXUS (Yew)	□	□	■		□		□	□	□		□	□	□	□						□
THUJA (Arborvitae)	□	□	■	□	□		□	□	□	□	□			□	□		□	□		
TSUGA (Hemlock)	□			□	□		□		□	□	□	□								

CLIMBERS

Key to symbols & abbreviations

□ Suitable for conditions or has marked characteristics listed in column headings

■ Suitable for extreme conditions or has indicated characteristic to an intense degree

S Semievergreen

Flowering time is indicated as follows:

1 = midwinter, 2 = late winter, etc. (see box on p.107)

* Acid soil only

	CLAY	DRY	ALKALINE	COASTAL	EVERGREEN (S=Semi)	DECIDUOUS	VIGOROUS	MEDIUM	GROUND COVER	TWINING	SELF-CLINGING	RED OR PURPLE FOLIAGE	GOLD OR YELLOW FOLIAGE	VARIEGATED FOLIAGE	AUTUMN COLOR	BOLD ARCHITECTURAL FOLIAGE	ORNAMENTAL FRUIT	FLOWERING TIME (in mild regions)	FRAGRANT FLOWERS	NORTH/EAST WALLS	SOUTH/WEST WALLS	SHADE TOLERANT
ACTINIDIA	□	□	□			□	□			□				□		□	□	7/8	□		□	
AKEBIA	□	□	□		S		□			□							□	4	□	□	□	
AMPELOPSIS	□	□	□			□	□	□			□			□	□						□	
ARISTOLOCHIA macrophylla (Dutchman's pipe)	□	□	□			□	□			□						□		6		□	□	
BERBERIDOPSIS			□		□													7/8			□	□
CAMPSIS (Trumpet creeper)			□			□	□				□							8/9			□	
CELASTRUS (Bittersweet)			□			□	□			□					□		□			□		
CLEMATIS	□		□		□	□	□	□		□								4/10	□	□	□	
FALLOPIA (Russian vine)	■	■	□			□	■			□								7/9		□		
HEDERA (Ivy)	■	□	□	□	□		□		□		□		□	□		□				□		■
HUMULUS (Hop)	□	□	□			□	□			□			□								□	
HYDRANGEA, climbing	□	□	□			□					□							6		□	□	□
JASMINUM (Jasmine)	□	□	□			□	□			□				□				8/9	□	□	□	
LONICERA (Honeysuckle)	□	□	□	□	□	□	□			□				□				5/10	□	□	□	□
PARTHENOCISSUS	□	□	□			□	■				□	□			■					□	□	
PASSIFLORA (Passion flower)	□	□	□			□	□			□							□	6/9			□	
PILEOSTEGIA	□	□	□		□			□										8/9		□		□
RUBUS (Bramble)	□	■	□		□		□		□											□		□
SCHISANDRA						□				□								5 & 8/9			□	
SCHIZOPHRAGMA	□	□	□			□	□				□							7		□	□	
SENECIO		□	□		S		□											9/11			□	
SOLANUM	□	□	■		S		□			□								7/10			□	
TRACHELOSPERMUM (Star jasmine)	□	□	□		□						□			□				7/8	□		□	
VITIS (Grape)	□	□	□			□	□			□		□			□	□	□				□	
WISTERIA	□	□	□			□	□			□								5/6	□		□	

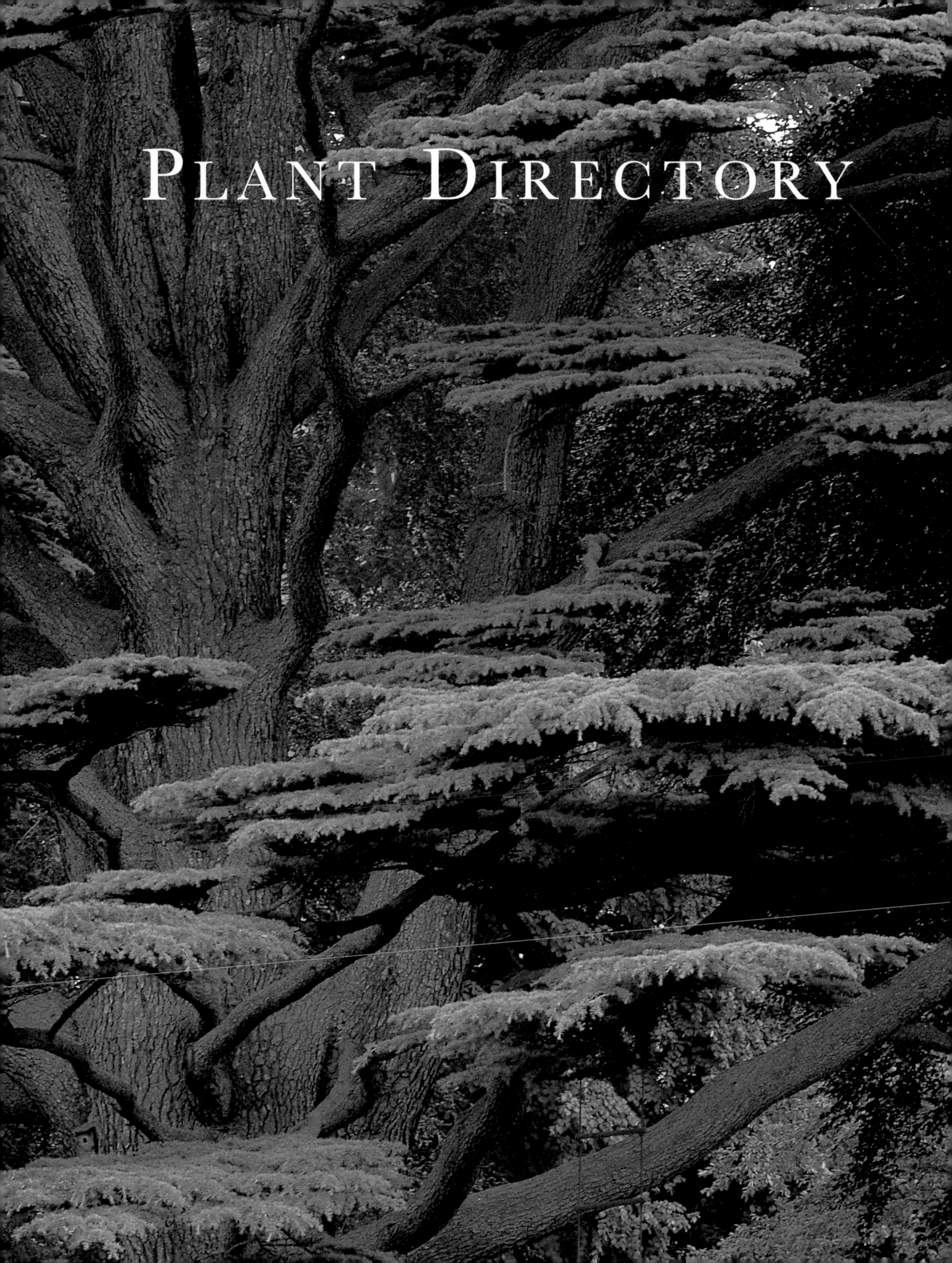

Plant Directory

Abelia *Caprifoliaceae*

A genus of about 30 species of evergreen and deciduous shrubs native to eastern Asia and Mexico. Their profusely borne, funnel-shaped or tubular flowers often have persistent calyxes that remain attractive long after the rest of the flower has fallen. They are easily grown in any average soil and perform best in full sun.

Abelia chinensis

A. chinensis A small deciduous shrub with fragrant, rose-tinted white flowers, usually borne in pairs and freely produced from midsummer to midfall. C and E China. In cultivation 1844.
Zone 6 US, 7 Can.

Abelia 'Edward Goucher'

***A.* 'Edward Goucher'** *(A. × grandiflora × A. schumannii)* A small, semievergreen shrub with glossy, bright green leaves that are bronze when young. The lilac-pink flowers are borne for a long period in summer and fall. A first-class shrub for the small garden. Raised 1911 in the United States.
Zone 6 US, 6 Can.

A. floribunda A medium-sized evergreen or semievergreen shrub producing an abundance of tubular, brilliantly cherry red flowers, each 2 in (5 cm) long, in early summer. Best against a warm wall. Mexico. Introduced 1841.
Zone 8 US, 9 Can.

Abelia × grandiflora

A. × grandiflora *(A. chinensis × A. uniflora)* A vigorous, arching, medium-sized, semievergreen shrub with glossy, dark green leaves. The slightly fragrant flowers appear from midsummer to midfall and may be borne singly or in clusters of up to four. They are white, tinged with pale pink, as are the persistent sepals. Raised before 1866 in Italy and possibly elsewhere.
Zone 5 US, 6 Can.

***A. × g.* 'Francis Mason'** A form with dark green leaves with a golden yellow margin, the best variegation being obtained in full sun and a dry soil. Originated early 1950s as a sport at Mason's Nurseries, New Zealand, and itself frequently sports to a form with all-gold leaves, which has been called 'Goldsport', 'Goldspot', and 'Goldstrike'.
Zone 5 US, 6 Can.

A. schumannii During late summer and well into fall, this small deciduous shrub gives a continuous display of slightly fragrant pink flowers, prettily blotched with orange. It may be semievergreen in warm climates. W China. Introduced 1910 by Ernest Wilson.
Zone 7 US, 8b Can.

Abelia schumannii

Abelia triflora

A. triflora A large, erect deciduous shrub of graceful habit with white, pink-tinged, exquisitely scented flowers produced in dense clusters in early summer. NW Himalaya. Introduced 1847.
Zone 6 US, 7a Can.

Abeliophyllum *Oleaceae*

A genus of one deciduous species. It is related to Forsythia *but has white flowers. Although quite hardy, it will not thrive unless it has hot sun, and it requires only ordinary soil. The flowers should be protected from late frost. It does best against a warm, sheltered wall.*

A. distichum A small, slow-growing shrub with fragrant white flowers tinged with

Abeliophyllum distichum

pink. They appear on the purplish, leafless stems in late winter. The leaves sometimes turn purple in fall. Korea. Introduced 1924.

Zone 5 US, 6a Can.

Abies *Pinaceae*

Fir

A genus of more than 50 species of evergreen conifers from the Northern Hemisphere, reaching as far south as Central America and Taiwan. Many of them attain great size, particularly in the wild. Most are conical when young. The linear leaves are usually flattened, with grayish or white lines on their lower surfaces and in some species on the upper surfaces as well. The cones are borne on the upper sides of the branchlets and are often an attractive blue-purple or violet when young.

Firs need a deep, moist, acidic soil for best development. Most of them dislike industrial atmospheres and shallow alkaline soils, the chief exceptions among those listed being A. cephalonica *and* A. pinsapo *'Glauca'.*

***A. alba* 'Pyramidalis'** A form of the silver fir, the common species of the mountains of France, Switzerland, and Germany, but an unsatisfactory garden tree. 'Pyramidalis' is a medium-sized, conical tree, narrow when young, with crowded, ascending branches with short, dark, shining green leaves. In cultivation 1851.

Zone 4 US, 4 Can.

A. balsamea* f. *hudsonia A dwarf shrub of dense and compact habit, with a flattish top and short leaves densely arranged on the branches. A specimen at the Hillier

Abies balsamea f. *hudsonia*

Gardens and Arboretum reached 2½ × 4 ft (0.75 × 1.2 m) in about 30 years. The typical form, the balsam fir of North America, is a medium-sized tree and will not tolerate alkaline soil, but this dwarf is more tolerant. Introduced before 1810.

Zone 3 US, 2 Can. 🏆

A. brachyphylla See *A. homolepis*.

A. cephalonica (Greek fir) A large, handsome tree to 100 ft (30 m) in the wild. The leaves are rigid, sharp-pointed, shining green, up to 1 in (2.5 cm) long, white beneath and spreading more or less around the branchlets. It is one of the best species for alkaline soils and is relatively free from disease, but it breaks into growth early and therefore should not be planted in frost pockets. Mountains of S Greece. Introduced 1824.

Zone 5 US, 6a Can.

Abies cephalonica 'Meyer's Dwarf'

***A. c.* 'Meyer's Dwarf'**, syn. *A. c.* 'Nana' A dwarf cultivar with horizontally spreading branches, rigid branchlets, and shorter leaves. In cultivation 1963.

Zone 5 US, 6a Can.

***A. c.* 'Nana'** See *A. c.* 'Meyer's Dwarf'.

A. concolor (White fir, Colorado fir) A very beautiful, large tree with smooth gray bark that is grooved and scaly on old trees. The leaves are up to 2½ in (6 cm) long, thick, attractively blue-green or gray-green, and arranged in two ranks. The cones are up to 5½ in (14 cm) long, pale green when young, and sometimes purplish bloomy. SW United States. Introduced 1873.

Zone 3 US, 4 Can. 🏆

Abies concolor 'Candicans'

***A. c.* 'Candicans'** A striking tree with vivid gray or silvery white leaves. Introduced before 1929.

Zone 3 US, 4 Can.

***A. c.* 'Compacta'**, syn. *A. c.* 'Glauca Compacta' A dwarf shrub of compact but irregular habit and attractive, grayish blue leaves. It is a wonderful plant, the most outstanding dwarf white fir, and is suitable for a large rock garden or as an isolated lawn

Abies concolor 'Compacta'

specimen. A specimen at the Hillier Gardens and Arboretum has exceeded 6 ft (2 m) in height and width. In cultivation 1891.
Zone 3 US, 4 Can.

***A. c.* 'Glauca Compacta'** See *A. c.* 'Compacta'.

***A. c.* 'Violacea'** A form with glaucous blue leaves. In cultivation 1875.
Zone 3 US, 4 Can.

A. fargesii A strong-growing, splendid, medium-sized tree with glossy, purple young shoots. The leaves are loosely two-ranked, up to 2 in (5 cm) long, notched, dark green above and with two whitish-bloomy bands beneath. In its native habitat it forms a conical tree to 130 ft (40 m). N China. Introduced 1901 by Ernest Wilson.
Zone 5 US, 6b Can.

A. fraseri (Fraser fir) A relatively fast-growing tree that will reach 65 ft (20 m) at maturity. The needles, ½–1 in (1.5–2.5 cm) long, are dark green above with two silvery bands beneath. Cones are short and wide, purple at first but becoming brown at maturity. This plant grows best in moist, well-drained soils. C United States. Introduced 1811.
Zone 4 US, 5 Can.

A. grandis (Giant fir) A remarkably fast-growing tree, rapidly attaining large size. The leaves are ¾–2½ in (2–6 cm) long, dark shining green above with two glaucous gray bands beneath, horizontally arranged on either side of the shoot. The cones are up to 4 in (10 cm) long and bright green when young. It grows best in areas with heavy rainfall and prefers a moist but well-

Abies grandis

drained soil. It is a good species for light shade and is moderately tolerant of alkaline soil. The leaves are delightfully aromatic when crushed. W North America. Introduced 1830 by David Douglas.
Zone 6 US, 7a Can.

A. homolepis, syn. *A. brachyphylla* (Nikko fir) A large, splendid tree, very tolerant of atmospheric pollution. The leaves are up to 1¼ in (3 cm) long, green above with two chalk white bands beneath, and are crowded on the upper sides of the branchlets. The cones are up to 4 in (10 cm) long, purple when young. Japan. Introduced 1861.
Zone 4 US, 5a Can.

A. koreana (Korean fir) A small, slow-growing, neat tree with leaves ½–¾ in (1–2 cm) long, dark green above, gleaming white beneath, radially arranged on strong shoots, loosely arranged on others. It produces violet-purple, cylindrical cones, which are 2–3 in (5–7.5 cm) long, even on specimens 20 in (50 cm) high. However, this description does not necessarily apply to

Abies koreana

a great many of the plants in cultivation, which are of a tall-growing but very poor form; plants of the more desirable kind are hard to find. S Korea. Introduced 1905.
Zone 4 US, 4 Can.

Abies koreana 'Silberlocke'

Abies lasiocarpa 'Compacta'

***A. k.* 'Silberlocke'** A slow-growing small tree with the leaves twisted upward to reveal their white undersides. Raised before 1979 in Germany.

Zone 4 US, 4b Can. 🏆

***A. lasiocarpa arizonica* 'Compacta'** See *A. l.* 'Compacta'.

***A. l.* 'Compacta'**, syn. *A. l. arizonica* 'Compacta' A slow-growing, compact form of the alpine fir, conical in habit and with leaves of an eye-catching silvery blue-gray and small purple cones. It is moderately alkaline tolerant. SW United States. In cultivation 1927.

Zone 2 US, 2b Can. 🏆

Abies nordmanniana

A. nordmanniana (Caucasian fir) A large to very large noble tree of great ornamental value, with tiered branches that sweep downward. The leaves are densely arranged on the branchlets, ³/₄–1¹/₄ in (2–3 cm) long, shining green above, and marked with two white bands beneath. The cones are 6–8 in (15–20 cm) long, greenish when young. It is a very satisfactory, generally disease-free species, now being used as a Christmas tree. W Caucasus. Introduced 1840.

Abies nordmanniana 'Golden Spreader'

Zone 4 US, 5b Can. 🏆

***A. n.* 'Golden Spreader'** A slow-growing dwarf shrub of compact habit. The leaves are ¹/₂–1 in (1–2.5 cm) long, light yellow above, pale yellowish white beneath. In cultivation 1960.

Zone 4 US, 5b Can. 🏆

***A. pinsapo* 'Glauca'** A form of the Spanish fir selected for its strikingly blue-gray rigid leaves, which are up to ³/₄ in (2 cm) long and radiate from all sides of the branchlets. It is a large tree. Good in alkaline soils. In cultivation 1863.

Zone 5 US, 5b Can. 🏆

Abies procera

A. procera (Noble fir) A very beautiful large to very large tree with leaves 1–1¹/₂ in (2.5–3.5 cm) long that are bluish green above with two narrow, bloomy bands beneath. They are crowded on the upper sides of the branchlets. The magnificent, cylindrical cones are 6–10 in (16–25 cm) long, green when young. W United States. Introduced 1830 by David Douglas.

Zone 4 US, 5b Can. 🏆

Abies procera 'Glauca'

***A. p.* 'Glauca'** A large tree with blue-gray leaves. In cultivation 1863.

Zone 4 US, 5b Can.

A. spectabilis (Himalayan fir) A magnificent large tree with reddish brown young shoots and densely two-ranked leaves, up to 2 in (5 cm) long or a little more, that are shining dark green above and gleaming silvery white beneath. The cones are cylindrical, 5¹/₂–7 in (14–18 cm) long, violet-purple when young. Unfortunately, this striking species is susceptible to spring frosts. Himalaya. Introduced 1822.

Zone 7 US, 8a Can.

A. veitchii A beautiful, large, fast-growing tree. The densely arranged, up-curved leaves, ¹/₂–1 in (1–2.5 cm) long, are glossy dark green above and silvery white beneath. The cones are 2–3 in (5–7.5 cm) long and bluish purple when young. It does not thrive in alkaline soils. Discovered 1860 by John Gould Veitch on Mt. Fuji and introduced 1879 by Charles Maries.

Zone 3 US, 4b Can. 🏆

Abutilon *Malvaceae*

There are more than 100 species of deciduous trees, shrubs, and herbaceous plants in this genus, occurring in the tropical and subtropical regions of both hemispheres. Those described below are small to large shrubs with conspicuous, brightly colored flowers borne over long periods: you can have abutilons in bloom from late spring to midfall. The flowers are large, bell- or open saucer-shaped, or in some species more like dainty paper lanterns. The plants are suitable mainly for a warm wall, cold greenhouse, or sunroom, although A. suntense, A. vitifolium, *and their forms will grow as freestanding specimens in sheltered, sunny sites. Abutilons do well in average, dry soil.*

Abutilon 'Ashford Red'

***A.* 'Ashford Red'** A medium-sized shrub with large, apple green leaves and bell-shaped flowers of good texture, size, and substance in a deep shade of crushed strawberry in summer and fall.
Zone 8 US, 9 Can. 🏆

Abutilon 'Canary Bird'

***A.* 'Canary Bird'** This medium-sized shrub is similar to 'Ashford Red' in form and size, has excellent lush green foliage, and is grown for its clear lemon yellow bell-shaped flowers, which it bears throughout the summer and into early fall.
Zone 8 US, 9 Can. 🏆

***A.* 'Cannington Carol'** A dwarf shrub with gold-variegated foliage. The bell-shaped flowers are a vivid, flaming orange in summer and early fall.
Zone 8 US, 9 Can. 🏆

Abutilon 'Cannington Peter'

***A.* 'Cannington Peter'** A medium-sized shrub with very dark red, bell-shaped flowers, which are carried throughout the summer and into early fall, and yellow-variegated foliage.
Zone 8 US, 9 Can. 🏆

Abutilon 'Kentish Belle'

***A.* 'Kentish Belle'** A small to medium-sized shrub with purplish stems and dark green, long-pointed, triangular leaves. The flowers are bell shaped, 1½ in (4 cm) long, with a red calyx and soft apricot petals faintly veined red, and make a spectacular display. They are borne through most of the summer season and into early fall. It does best supported against a warm wall.
Zone 8 US, 9 Can. 🏆

***A.* 'Louise Marignac'** A hybrid medium-sized shrub that is similar to 'Ashford Red' in form and size but with pale pink, bell-shaped flowers that are carried throughout the summer and into early fall.
Zone 8 US, 9 Can.

Abutilon megapotamicum

A. megapotamicum A small to medium-sized shrub with lantern-shaped flowers borne from summer into fall. They are pendulous and conspicuous, with a red calyx, bright yellow petals, and purple anthers. Best against a wall, for warmth and because the plant displays its flowers to best advantage when given support. Brazil. Introduced 1804.
Zone 8 US, 9 Can. 🏆

***A. m.* 'Variegatum'** This form differs from the above in having leaves with mottled yellow variegation.
Zone 8 US, 9 Can.

Abutilon × *milleri* 'Variegatum'

A.* × *milleri A medium-sized shrub with bell-shaped blooms in soft orange with crimson stamens. Again, it is best when supported against a warm wall, where it will flower continuously and generously throughout the summer and well into fall.

Zone 8 US, 9 Can. 🏆

***A.* × *m.* 'Variegatum'** A form differing from the above in having mottled yellow leaves.

Zone 8 US, 9 Can.

***A.* 'Nabob'** Similar in habit to 'Ashford Red', this medium-sized shrub is a sumptuous combination of dark green leaves and large burgundy flowers tinted plum-purple that are carried throughout the summer and into early fall.

Zone 8 US, 9 Can. 🏆

Abutilon 'Patrick Synge'

***A.* 'Patrick Synge'** A vigorous, medium-sized shrub similar to 'Ashford Red' in form and size but with flame red, bell-shaped flowers that are carried throughout the summer and into early fall.

Zone 8 US, 9 Can.

***A.* 'Souvenir de Bonn'** A tall, vigorous, upright shrub up to 11 ft (3.5 m). The leaves are maplelike and gray-green, with edgings and marblings in creamy white. The bell-shaped flowers, which are carried throughout the summer and into early fall, are large, salmon-orange, and veined in darker orange.

Zone 8 US, 9 Can. 🏆

A.* × *suntense *(A. ochsenii × A. vitifolium)* A large, fast-growing shrub that bears its saucer-shaped flowers between late spring and midsummer. Raised 1967 intentionally by the Hillier Nurseries' propagator Peter Dummer and also accidentally by Richard Gorer of Sunte House, after which it is named. The flower color varies. The following clones are available.

Zone 8 US, 9 Can.

Abutilon × *suntense*

Abutilon × *suntense* 'Jermyns'

***A.* × *s.* 'Jermyns'** A large shrub with saucer-shaped flowers of lavender to dark mauve selected from the cross made in the Hillier nursery. The pollen parent was *A. vitifolium* 'Veronica Tennant', which is described below.

Zone 8 US, 9 Can. 🏆

***A.* × *s.* 'Violetta'** A large shrub with deep violet-blue to indigo, saucer-shaped flowers. *(Photo on p.124.)*

Zone 8 US, 9 Can.

Abutilon vitifolium

Abutilon × suntense 'Violetta'

***A. × s.* 'White Charm'** A large shrub with pure white flowers and yellow stamens. A chance seedling, 1975. Zone 8 US, 9 Can.

A. vitifolium A large, handsome shrub with downy, gray-green, vine-shaped leaves and saucer-shaped flowers of pale violet to deep purple-blue. Flowering is from late spring to midsummer, and the shrub should be given a sheltered, sunny position to perform well. Two particularly recommended garden-worthy clones are described below. Chile. Introduced 1836.
Zone 7 US, 8 Can.

Abutilon vitifolium 'Tennant's White'

***A. v.* 'Tennant's White'** An especially free-flowering large shrub with very large blooms of pure white.
Zone 7 US, 8 Can. 🏆

***A. v.* 'Veronica Tennant'** This large shrub was selected for its abundant flowering and large lavender blooms. It is the pollen parent of *A.* × *s.* 'Jermyns'.
Zone 7 US, 8 Can. 🏆

Abutilon vitifolium 'Veronica Tennant'

Acacia *Leguminosae*
Wattle

This genus of evergreens should not be confused with the trees and shrubs commonly known as acacia, which belong to the genus Robinia. *These are entirely different and consist of some 1,000 species found throughout tropical and subtropical regions, particularly in Africa and Australia. Australian species are known as wattles because their timber was used by early settlers in the wattle-and-daub method of house building. The leaves are usually bipinnate, often filigree-feathery, but sometimes reduced to phyllodes — expanded, flattened leaf stalks that perform the functions of true leaves. Acacia species are mostly winter- or spring-flowering, cool greenhouse or sunroom shrubs, but some species grow rapidly to tree size outdoors in mild, sheltered areas. The flowers are typically yellow, borne in small rounded or bottlebrush heads, and made up mainly of stamens. Most species are unsuitable for shallow alkaline soils, in which their foliage becomes chlorotic yellow. Best grown in neutral or acid soil that is on the dry side.*

A. armata (Kangaroo thorn) A prickly large shrub with a dense, bushy habit and small, narrow, dark green phyllodes. In spring the branches are covered all along their length with masses of yellow flowers. Introduced 1803.
Zone 9 US, 9? Can.

A. baileyana (Cootamundra wattle) A large shrub or small tree with attractively

Acacia baileyana 'Purpurea'

Acacia armata

Acacia baileyana

feathery, very blue-green, bipinnate leaves and freely produced clusters of bright yellow flowers that are borne from late winter to early spring. New South Wales. Introduced 1888.

Zone 8 US, 9? Can.

***A. b.* 'Purpurea'** A spectacular large shrub or small tree whose young foliage is deep

Acacia dealbata

purple and contrasts well with the blue-green, older leaves.

Zone 8 US, 9? Can.

A. dealbata (Silver wattle) The florists' golden mimosa, this is a large shrub or small tree with silvery green, fernlike leaves and fluffy, golden, fragrant flowers from late winter to early spring. Suitable for a sheltered location in mild areas. SE Australia, Tasmania. Introduced 1820.

Zone 9 US, 9? Can.

A. longifolia (Sydney golden wattle, sallow wattle) A large shrub with long, lance-shaped, dark green phyllodes and bright yellow flowers in spikes 1½–3 in (4–8 cm) long that are borne in mid- or late winter. One of the hardier species and fairly tolerant of alkaline soil. Australia, Tasmania. Introduced 1792.

Zone 8 US, 9 Can.

Acacia mucronata

A. mucronata (Variable sallow wattle) A large shrub, related to and resembling *A. longifolia* but with much narrower, although variable, phyllodes carrying bright yellow flowers in spikes that are 1½–3 in (4–8 cm) long throughout their flowering period from mid- to late winter. SE Australia, Tasmania.

Zone 8 US, 9 Can.

A. pravissima (Oven's wattle) The phyllodes of this large shrub or small tree are quite distinctive, being triangular, two-veined, and blue-green on both sides and having a single spine on the lower side of the broad apex. The plant's beauty lies in its slender, arching shoots as well as its yellow flowers, which are borne in small

Acacia pravissima

Acacia retinodes

clusters in early spring. SE Australia.

Zone 9 US, 9? Can.

A. retinodes (Wirilda, four-seasons mimosa) A small tree with its main flowering season in summer, although it bears its conspicuous clusters of yellow pompoms freely for most of the year. The foliage consists of narrow, gray-green, willowlike, simple phyllodes. It is one of the most lime-tolerant species in the genus. SE Australia, Tasmania. Introduced 1871.

Zone 9 US, 9? Can.

A. riceana (Rice's wattle) A graceful large shrub or small tree with slender, weeping shoots and dark green, sharp-pointed phyllodes. The flowers are pale yellow and are borne in spring in drooping clusters. Tasmania.

Zone 9 US, 9? Can.

Acanthopanax

See ***Eleutherococcus.***

ACER

Aceraceae Maple

Maple trees have earned a prime place in the garden largely on account of their fall foliage.

FOR MANY PEOPLE, the word *maple* has come to mean merely the Japanese maples — the many beautiful forms of *Acer palmatum* and *A. japonicum* (particularly the former). Perhaps "merely" is the wrong word to use for a large and rapidly increasing group of shrubs and small trees that offer such a variety of foliage, but there is much more to the genus than just these two species, however distinguished they may be.

Acer is also the genus of the Amur maple *(A. ginnala)*, the box elder *(A. negundo)*, and many other sorts of maples, including the sugar *(A. saccharum)*, silver *(A. saccharinum)*, red *(A. rubrum)*, and Norway maples *(A. platanoides)*. Its species are found throughout the Northern Hemisphere, especially in eastern Asia and North America, and most of them are hardy, adaptable trees in cultivation.

The most recognizable characteristic of the maple is the leaf, which is usually lobed like the palm of a hand and either entire (all in one piece) or compound (consisting of several separate leaflets). The Norway and the hedge maple *(A. campestre)* are as immediately identifiable as maples as are the North American sugar maple — the source of maple syrup — or the snake-bark maple *A. grosseri* var. *hersii* from central China.

Beautiful bark is also found in many species, the most outstanding in this respect being *A. palmatum* 'Senkaki', the coral-bark maple, and the snake-bark maples. These last constitute a group of maples, occurring naturally in eastern North America as well as eastern Asia, whose bark is marked with a reticulate pattern or marbling of cream or white on a green or russet ground quite like the markings on the skin of a python.

However, the genus as a whole probably owes its prime position in the garden to its fall foliage color. Maples are magnificent in this respect, coloring well even in climates and conditions that generally inhibit the development of fall color. Nevertheless, it is a mistake to latch on to just one quality of any group of plants, and maples are among those that readily deserve their place in the front rank of trees and shrubs because of the many and varied ways in which they are beautiful.

SHAPES AND SIZES

Some maples are large, imposing trees, while others may take a century to attain a height and spread of 10 ft (3 m). In between are many small to medium-sized trees, and the genus offers a wide choice to owners of small gardens.

At the upper end are the Norway and sycamore maples. The latter, *A. pseudoplatanus*, is not a good garden tree in itself but comes into its own in a handful of forms with colored leaves, such as 'Atropurpureum' and 'Brilliantissimum'. The common species is dogged by disadvantages, including vulnerability to honeydew-producing aphids and a propensity for germinating its deep-rooted seedlings in the most inconvenient places.

The Norway maple also suffers from aphid attacks but not with such regularity as the sycamore maple. It is a fine, big tree with clear yellow, occasionally red, fall color. The purple-leaved form, *A. p.* 'Crimson King', is magnificent but should be used sparingly, while *A. p.* 'Drummondii' can be the best of all variegated trees in an open situation, although its leaves are inclined to revert to green. Any such growths should be cut back immediately.

The smallest maples are found among the varieties of *A. palmatum* (Japanese maple), some of which make mounds of foliage that, from a distance, look more like silky-haired animals than woody plants. Some of the Dissectum group are small enough for a large rock garden, while other forms of the species eventually grow into trees of 15 ft (4.5 m) or more.

Between the largest and the smallest is a wealth of trees and shrubs that share the distinction of never being coarse and always displaying elegance. They are aristocrats among the deciduous specimens in the garden, whether luxuriating in full leaf or displaying traceries of fine branches in winter.

Foliage

The typical palmate leaf of the maple can be bold in its effect or, in its smaller version, dainty. How it behaves in a breeze depends on the length of its stalk and the speed with which it twitches to turn its edge to the wind. It can be cut (dissected) to a greater or lesser degree so that the lobes, which may number as many as nine, are finely pinnate, making a soft pelt of foliage in green, bronze-red, or purple; or at the other extreme it can be three-lobed and striking in its simplicity, as in the Nikko maple, *A. maximowiczianum.*

The season for fall color among maples starts with the American *A. rubrum* 'October Glory', whose leaves turn to flame before any other tree, provided the soil is acid or reasonably neutral. The others follow with either canary yellow foliage, as in *A. pensylvanicum*, or brilliant red, such as *A. palmatum* 'Osakazuki'. The paperbark maple, *A. griseum*, whose leaves turn red and blackish crimson like dying embers, boasts a peeling, mahogany-orange bark that would warrant the tree's place in the garden even if its foliage never changed from green.

Cultivation

Maples as a whole are easily grown and most are very hardy. However, other than *A. campestre*, *A. negundo*, *A. platanoides*, and *A. pseudoplatanus*, it is advisable to plant them where they can be sheltered from wind. The reason for this is twofold. In the first place, trees that are valued for fall color should not be subjected to having their leaves stripped prematurely by wind, and in the second, several species are damaged by cold winds. This applies particularly to *A. palmatum* and its varieties and to *A. japonicum*, a species that also dislikes strong sunlight. It is advisable to avoid sites in which they may suffer from late frosts followed by early-morning sun.

A few species, including the hedge maple, positively thrive in a calcareous soil, while most will grow in nearly any soil — from stiff clay to sand and from limestone to acid strong enough for rhododendrons. The main requirement is that the soil should be rich and moisture retentive, but at the same time well drained.

A. buergerianum (Trident maple) A small, bushy deciduous tree with three-lobed, ivylike, persistent leaves that turn red or orange in fall. E China, Korea. In cultivation 1890.
Zone 4 US, 5b Can.

A. campestre (Hedge maple, field maple) A picturesque, medium-sized deciduous tree frequently used in informal hedges. In fall the foliage turns clear yellow and may sometimes be flushed with red. Europe, W Asia.
Zone 4 US, 5 Can. 🏆

***A. c.* 'Elsrijk'** A Dutch selection of dense, conical habit. A small tree good for streets. In cultivation 1953.
Zone 4 US, 5b Can.

***A. c.* 'Postelense'** A large shrub or mop-headed small tree with red-stalked leaves that are yellow when young and then turn yellow-green. In cultivation 1896.
Zone 4 US, 5 Can.

***A. c.* 'Pulverulentum'** The leaves of this medium-sized tree are thickly speckled and blotched with white. In cultivation 1859.
Zone 4 US, 5b Can.

***A. c.* 'Schwerinii'** A medium-sized tree with purple leaves. In cultivation 1897.
Zone 4 US, 5 Can.

A. capillipes A small deciduous tree with coral-red young shoots and green-brown bark striated with white. The bright green, three-lobed leaves turn attractive tints of orange and red in fall. Japan. Introduced 1892 by Charles Sargent, director of the Arnold Arboretum, Massachusetts, while collecting with James Veitch.
Zone 5b US, 7 Can. 🏆

A. cappadocicum (Caucasian maple) A medium-sized to large deciduous tree with broad, five- to seven-lobed, glossy leaves, turning rich butter yellow in fall. Caucasus, W Asia to the Himalaya. Introduced 1838.
Zone 5 US, 6b Can.

***A. c.* 'Aureum'** A striking small tree with red young leaves soon turning yellow and

Acer buergerianum

Acer campestre 'Pulverulentum'

Acer capillipes

Acer cappadocicum 'Aureum'

remaining so for many weeks into the summer, then becoming bright green by late summer, followed by yellow again in the fall. In cultivation 1914.
Zone 5 US, 6b Can. 🏆

***A. c.* 'Rubrum'** A very attractive medium-sized to large tree in which the young growths are blood red. The leaves are green in summer and yellow in fall. Introduced 1838.
Zone 5 US, 6b Can. 🏆

Acer carpinifolium

A. carpinifolium (Hornbeam maple) A small to medium-sized deciduous tree with leaves remarkably like those of the common hornbeam but opposite rather than alternately arranged. They turn gold and brown in fall. Japan. Introduced 1879 by Charles Maries.
Zone 5 US, 6a Can.

Acer circinatum

A. circinatum (Vine maple) A large deciduous shrub, or occasionally a small tree, with almost circular leaves that are tinted in summer and turn orange and crimson in fall. The contrast between the white petals and red bud scales makes for a lovely floral display in midspring. Grows well even in dry, shady locations. W North America. Introduced 1826 by David Douglas.
Zone 5 US, 6b Can. 🏆

Acer crataegifolium 'Veitchii'

***A. crataegifolium* 'Veitchii'** A large deciduous shrub or small tree with prettily marked bark and small leaves of variable shape, which are heavily mottled with white and pink and turn brilliant pink and purple in fall. The flowers are mustard yellow and borne in slender racemes in spring. In cultivation 1881.
Zone 6 US, 7b Can.

A. dasycarpum See *A. saccharinum*.

A. davidii A small deciduous tree with attractively striated, green and white "snake-bark" and shining, dark green, ovate leaves that color richly in fall. The green fruits are often brightly suffused with red and enhance the fall effect when hanging all along the branches. C China. Introduced 1879 by Charles Maries.
Zone 5 US, 6b Can.

***A. d.* 'Ernest Wilson'** A form that is rare in cultivation and a more compact tree, with a "snake-bark" trunk and branches that ascend and then arch over. The leaves, which are somewhat cup shaped at the base, have pink stalks and are pale green,

Acer davidii

turning orange-yellow in fall. This is the form originally introduced by Maries and later by Ernest Wilson and Frank Kingdon-Ward.
Zone 5 US, 6b Can.

Acer davidii 'George Forrest'

***A. d.* 'George Forrest'** The form most commonly seen in cultivation, this is a small, open, "snake-bark" tree of loose habit with vigorous, spreading branches and large, dark green leaves with rhubarb red stalks turning orange-red in fall. Introduced 1921–22 by George Forrest.
Zone 5 US, 6b Can. 🏆

***A. d.* 'Serpentine'** A small tree with an upright habit, smaller leaves, purple shoots, and very good striped bark.
Zone 5 US, 6b Can. 🏆

A. distylum A medium-sized deciduous tree with undivided, glossy green leaves, something like those of a linden, which are attractively tinted cream and pink when unfolding and provide rich fall colors. Japan. Introduced 1879 by Charles Maries.
Zone 6 US, 7b Can.

A. forrestii A beautiful small deciduous tree with striated "snake-bark" and young stems and leaf stalks of coral-red. It is not very tolerant of alkaline soil. China. Introduced 1906 by George Forrest.
Zone 6 US, 7 Can.

***A. f.* 'Alice'** A small tree with red young shoots and leaves tinged with red, pink, and white in summer.
Zone 6 US, 7 Can.

A. ginnala (Amur maple) A large deciduous shrub or small tree of vigorous, spreading but bushy habit with bright green, three-lobed leaves that turn orange and vivid crimson in fall. The yellowish white flowers, borne in late spring, are fragrant. Manchuria, China, Japan. Introduced 1860.
Zone 2 US, 2 Can. 🏆

Acer griseum

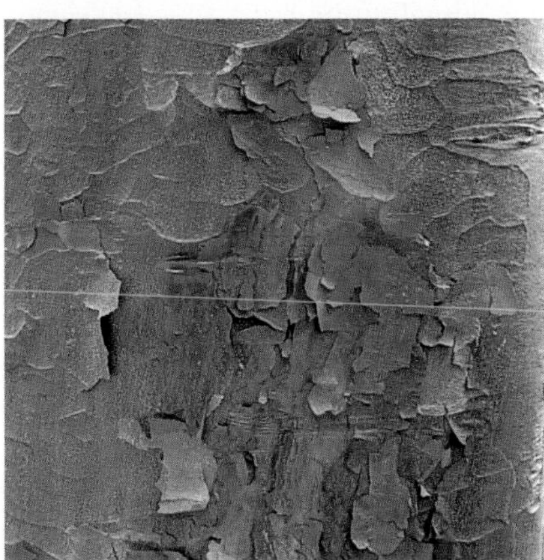

Bark of *Acer griseum*

A. griseum (Paperbark maple) This is one of the most beautiful of all small trees. The deciduous leaves are each made up of three leaflets and are dark green, turning intense shades of crimson and scarlet in fall. The bark is rich mahogany, and where it is older — on the trunk and primary branches — it peels in flakes that show orange in the sunlight and reveal the cinnamon-colored new bark underneath. C China. Introduced 1901 by Ernest Wilson.
Zone 4 US, 6 Can. 🏆

Acer grosseri var. *hersii*

***A. grosseri* var. *hersii*,** syn. *A. hersii* A superb small deciduous tree with wonderfully marbled bark. It bears fruits in long, conspicuous racemes and has rich fall color. C China. Introduced 1921.
Zone 5 US, 6b Can. 🏆

A. heldreichii A very handsome medium-sized deciduous tree, distinctive because of its deeply cleft, three-lobed leaves. SE Europe. Introduced 1879.
Zone 6 US, 7b Can.

A. henryi A small to medium-sized, spreading but quite slow-growing deciduous tree with stems marked with bluish striations. The young, beautifully tinted leaves

Acer henryi

have three leaflets, each drawn out into a slender point. As the leaves unfold, they coincide with the slender, drooping catkins of yellow flowers. This tree provides brilliant red fall color. C China. Introduced 1903 by Ernest Wilson.
Zone 6 US, 7 Can.

A. hersii See *A. grosseri* var. *hersii.*

Acer japonicum

A. japonicum (Full moon maple) A large shrub or small tree with soft green leaves on downy stalks that turn excellent fall colors of yellow-orange to red. The flowers are red with yellow anthers and appear in delicate, drooping clusters with the young leaves. This and the selected forms do best in moist, well-drained soil in a site sheltered from cold winds. Japan. Introduced 1864.
Zone 5 US, 6 Can.

Acer japonicum 'Aconitifolium'

***A. j.* 'Aconitifolium'**, syn. *A. j.* 'Filicifolium', *A. j.* 'Laciniatum' The leaves of this large shrub or small tree are deeply lobed and cut and turn a rich ruby-crimson in fall. In cultivation 1888.
Zone 5 US, 6 Can. 🏆

***A. j.* 'Aureum'** See *A. shirasawanum* 'Aureum'.

***A. j.* 'Filicifolium'** See *A. j.* 'Aconitifolium'.

***A. j.* 'Laciniatum'** See *A. j.* 'Aconitifolium'.

Acer japonicum 'Vitifolium'

***A. j.* 'Vitifolium'** This large shrub or small tree has broad, fan-shaped leaves with 10–12 lobes that change to a brilliant yellow-orange and red in fall. In cultivation 1882.
Zone 5 US, 6 Can. 🏆

Acer lobelii

A. lobelii A fast-growing, medium-sized to large deciduous tree, related to *A. cappadocicum.* It has bloomy young shoots and wavy-edged, dark green leaves with taper-pointed lobes. The branches ascend sharply to form a compact, columnar head that broadens with age. A good tree for growing in restricted spaces. S Italy. Introduced 1683.
Zone 6 US, 7b Can.

A. macrophyllum (Oregon maple) A large deciduous tree with very big, handsome, dark green, shining leaves that turn bright orange in fall. The drooping clusters of fragrant yellow flowers are also large, and the bristly fruits that follow are very ornamental. It is best planted where there is shelter from high wind. W North America.

Acer macrophyllum

Introduced 1826 by David Douglas.
Zone 5 US, 6b Can.

Acer maximowiczianum

A. maximowiczianum, syn. *A. nikoense* (Nikko maple) A very hardy and beautiful small to medium-sized deciduous tree. The hairy leaves, each consisting of three leaflets, are blue-green beneath and turn glorious orange and flame red in fall. It is now rare in its native ranges. Japan, C China. Introduced 1881.
Zone 6 US, 8 Can.

A. maximowiczii Any confusion between this and the last species will be dispelled if it becomes confirmed as a subspecies of *A. pectinatum.* It is an attractive small deciduous tree with purplish red stems that gradually take on the "snake-bark" striation. The leaves are tinted red throughout the growing season, a color that becomes richer as fall approaches. C China. Introduced 1910 by Ernest Wilson.
Zone 6 US, 7b Can.

Acer micranthum

A. micranthum The small, prettily cut, five-lobed leaves of this large deciduous shrub or small tree are beautifully tinted throughout the season and turn bright red in autumn. Japan. Introduced 1879.
Zone 6 US, 7b Can. 🏆

A. negundo (Box elder, Manitoba maple) A rather weedy, fast-growing, bushy-headed deciduous tree of medium to large size. The young shoots are bright green, and the leaves are pinnate, with 3–5 and sometimes 7–9 leaflets, which are bright green above and paler underneath. Variegated forms are inclined to revert, producing all-green shoots that should be removed. North America. In cultivation 1688.
Zone 2 US, 2 Can.

***A. n.* 'Argenteovariegatum'** See *A. n.* 'Variegatum'.

Acer negundo 'Auratum'

***A. n.* 'Auratum'** A small tree with leaves of bright golden yellow when young, which gradually pale to cream with age.
Zone 5 US, 7 Can.

***A. n.* 'Elegans'**, syn. *A. n.* 'Elegantissima' The young leaves of this small tree have bright yellow marginal variegation, paling with age, and the shoots are covered with a white bloom. In cultivation 1885.
Zone 5 US, 7 Can.

***A. n.* 'Elegantissima'** See *A. n.* 'Elegans'.

Acer negundo 'Flamingo'

***A. n.* 'Flamingo'** The young leaves of this attractive form have a broad, soft pink margin that changes to white, often green at first. The shoots have a glaucous bloom. Left to itself it will reach small tree size, but if pruned hard each winter it will make a bushy shrub and the color will be more effective.
Zone 4 US, 5 Can. 🏆

***A. n.* 'Variegatum'**, syn. *A. n.* 'Argenteovariegatum' A form whose leaves have broad, irregular, white margins. An effective small tree, but watch for reversion.
Zone 5 US, 7 Can.

Acer negundo var. violaceum

A. n.* var. *violaceum A medium-sized tree most attractive in spring, when it is draped with long, pendulous, reddish pink flower tassels, and also in winter, when its purple or violet shoots, covered with a white, powdery bloom, are at their most conspicuous. *(Photo on p.131.)* Zone 5 US, 7 Can. 🏆

A. nikoense See *A. maximowiczianum.*

A. oliverianum A handsome species, forming a large deciduous shrub or small tree. The leaves are deeply five-lobed and resemble those of *A. palmatum*, but they are more cleanly cut, taking on subtle shades of orange, red, and purple over a long period in fall. C China. Introduced 1901 by Ernest Wilson.

Zone 7 US, 8 Can.

A. opalus (Italian maple) A slow-growing deciduous tree, eventually of medium size. It has a rounded habit and shallowly five-lobed leaves that are glabrous above and downy beneath. The yellow flowers appear in conspicuous, crowded clusters on the leafless stems in early spring. S Europe. Introduced 1752.

Zone 5 US, 6 Can.

Acer palmatum

A. palmatum (Japanese maple) Generally a large deciduous shrub or small tree with a low, rounded head and five- or seven-lobed leaves that are bright green in spring, turning to lovely colors in fall. It is very variable and has given rise to many cultivars, which exhibit a wide range of habits and leaf shapes. Most of them grow to be large shrubs, while some are small trees. They are rightly renowned for their exquisite fall colors in red, orange, or yellow. Although the typical form and certain stronger ones will tolerate alkaline soils, the Japanese maples are at their best in a moist but well-drained loam, sheltered from cold winds. Japan, C China, Korea. Introduced 1820.

Zone 5 US, 6 Can.

Acer palmatum 'Asahi Zuru'

***A. p.* 'Asahi Zuru'** A large, fast-growing, spreading shrub with leaves variably blotched with white. When young they are sometimes nearly all white, or they may be pink. One of the best variegated forms.

Zone 5 US, 6 Can.

Atropurpureum group The most popular of the Japanese maples, these have leaves that are bronze-crimson throughout the summer and brilliant red in the fall. A number of selections have been named. In cultivation 1857.

Zone 4–5 US, 5b–6 Can.

Acer palmatum 'Beni Maiko'

***A. p.* 'Beni Maiko'** A small, bushy shrub with brilliant red young foliage that later turns pink and then greenish red.

Zone 5 US, 6 Can.

***A. p.* 'Beni Schichihenge'** A striking and rare small shrub whose blue-green leaves have 5–7 deep lobes that are margined with pinkish white or are almost entirely bright orange-pink.

Zone 5 US, 6 Can.

Acer palmatum 'Bloodgood'

***A. p.* 'Bloodgood'** (Atropurpureum group) The leaves of this large shrub are a very deep reddish purple and hold their color well. The foliage turns red in fall, when the red fruits are also attractive.

Zone 4 US, 5 Can. 🏆

***A. p.* 'Burgundy Lace'** A small, spreading tree with rich wine red leaves, divided to the base into narrow, sharply toothed lobes.

Zone 4 US, 5b Can. 🏆

Acer palmatum 'Butterfly'

***A. p.* 'Butterfly'** A medium-sized, upright shrub whose rather small, deeply cut leaves

are gray-green margined with cream, tinged with pink when young. The margins turn red in fall.
Zone 4 US, 5b Can.

***A. p.* 'Chitoseyama'** A superb clone with deeply cut, greenish bronze leaves that are richly colored in fall. A medium-sized shrub; old specimens form dense mounds with gracefully drooping branches.
Zone 5 US, 6 Can.

Acer palmatum 'Corallinum'

***A. p.* 'Corallinum'** A rarely seen, slow-growing, compact dwarf shrub. The young stems are soft coral-pink, and the five-lobed leaves, which are usually less than 2 in (5 cm) long, are bright shrimp pink when unfolding, turning a pale, mottled green by midsummer.
Zone 5 US, 6 Can.

Acer palmatum 'Crimson Queen'

***A. p.* 'Crimson Queen'** (Dissectum group) The leaves of this small shrub are a very long lasting, deep reddish purple and are divided into slender, finely cut lobes.
Zone 4 US, 5b Can.

***A. p.* 'Deshojo'** An upright shrub of medium size whose leaves have slenderly pointed lobes that are brilliant red when young and later turn bright green.
Zone 5 US, 6 Can.

Dissectum group A group of Japanese maples with leaves divided to the base into five, seven, or nine lobes. The individual lobes are themselves cut almost to their midribs and are thus pinnatifid, rather like the fronds of some ferns. Their general habit is shrubby, and they are somewhat mushroom-shaped when young, eventually making dense, rounded, small or medium-sized bushes with the branches falling from a high crown. They can be trained carefully when young to produce standards.
Zone 4–5 US, 5b–6 Can.

Acer palmatum 'Dissectum'

Acer palmatum 'Dissectum Atropurpureum'

***A. p.* 'Dissectum'** The leaves of this small to medium-sized shrub are green in spring and summer, turning red in fall.
Zone 4 US, 5b Can.

***A. p.* 'Dissectum Atropurpureum'** A small shrub with deep reddish purple foliage. For similar clones see 'Crimson Queen', 'Garnet', and 'Inaba Shidare'.
Zone 5 US, 6 Can.

Acer palmatum 'Dissectum Nigrum'

***A. p.* 'Dissectum Nigrum'**, syn. *A. p.* 'Ever Red' A small shrub with a dense habit and deep bronze-red leaves turning red in fall.
Zone 5 US, 6 Can.

Acer palmatum 'Dissectum Ornatum'

***A. p.* 'Dissectum Ornatum'** A small shrub with bronze-tinted leaves turning rich red in fall.
Zone 5 US, 6 Can.

Elegans group A group of Japanese maples previously known as the Heptalobum or Septemlobum group, consisting of shrubs that are large-leaved and usually seven-lobed, with the lobes finely double-

toothed and broadest about the middle.
Zone 4–5 US, 5b–6 Can.

***A. p.* 'Elegans Purpureum'** See *A. p.* 'Hessei'.

***A. p.* 'Ever Red'** See *A. p.* 'Dissectum Nigrum'.

Acer palmatum 'Garnet'

***A. p.* 'Garnet'** (Dissectum group) A strong-growing small shrub with large, deep garnet red leaves with finely cut lobes. Raised in Holland. In cultivation 1960.
Zone 5 US, 6 Can. 🏆

***A. p.* 'Hessei'**, syn. *A. p.* 'Elegans Purpureum' (Elegans group) A large shrub with dark bronze-crimson leaves.
Zone 5 US, 6 Can.

Acer palmatum 'Inaba Shidare'

***A. p.* 'Inaba Shidare'** (Dissectum group) A small, strong-growing shrub with large, red-stalked leaves that are deeply divided into finely pointed, deep purplish lobes and that turn crimson in fall. It retains its color well.
Zone 4 US, 5b Can. 🏆

***A. p.* 'Kagiri Nishiki'**, syn. *A. p.* 'Roseomarginatum' A charming medium-sized shrub with pale green leaves irregularly edged with coral-pink, but not constant in its variegation and liable to revert.
Zone 5 US, 6 Can.

***A. p.* 'Karasugawa'** The leaves of this medium-sized shrub are deeply five- to seven-lobed, pink when young and becoming streaked and speckled with white and pink.
Zone 5 US, 6 Can.

***A. p.* 'Koreanum'** The leaves of this medium-sized shrub or small tree become rich crimson in fall and last longer than most. As this plant has been raised for many years from seed, there is a small degree of variation.
Zone 5 US, 6 Can.

***A. p.* 'Linearilobum'** A medium-sized shrub with leaves that are divided to the base into long, narrow lobes that bear widely separated teeth.
Zone 5 US, 6 Can. 🏆

Acer palmatum 'Osakazuki'

***A. p.* 'Osakazuki'** (Elegans group) Probably the most brilliant of all the Japanese maples, this large shrub bears green leaves that become a vivid, fiery scarlet in autumn. There are some poor seedling forms available.
Zone 5 US, 6 Can. 🏆

***A. p.* 'Red Pygmy'** A slow-growing, small shrub resembling 'Linearilobum' but has reddish purple leaves and is less than 6 ft (2 m) tall. The color is held well, and the leaves are often divided to the base into very long, slender lobes, although in some the lobes are broader. Selected before 1969 in Holland.
Zone 5 US, 6 Can. 🏆

***A. p.* 'Reticulatum'** The leaves of this large shrub are soft yellow-green with green margins and dark veins.
Zone 5 US, 6 Can.

***A. p.* 'Ribesifolium'**, syn. *A. p.* 'Shishigashira' A slow-growing large shrub of distinctive, dense, upright habit. It is not quite fastigiate, as the crown is broad. The leaves are dark green and deeply cut and turn gold to orange-red in fall.
Zone 5 US, 6 Can.

***A. p.* 'Roseomarginatum'** See *A. p.* 'Kagiri Nishiki'.

***A. p.* 'Sango Kaku'** See *A. p.* 'Senkaki'.

Acer palmatum 'Seiryu'

***A. p.* 'Seiryu'** (Dissectum group) An unusual, upright form with bright green leaves, tinged red when young. The lobes are finely cut and the leaves turn orange-yellow splashed with crimson in fall. It becomes a large shrub.
Zone 5 US, 6 Can. 🏆

***A. p.* 'Senkaki',** syn. *A. p.* 'Sango Kaku' (Coral-bark maple) This large shrub or small tree is one of the most valuable and dramatic for winter effect. All the young branches are a conspicuous, highly attractive coral-red. The leaves turn soft canary yellow in fall. *(Photo on facing page.)*
Zone 5 US, 6 Can. 🏆

***A. p.* 'Shishigashira'** See *A. p.* 'Ribesifolium'.

***A. p.* 'Shishio Improved'** A bushy, medium-sized to large shrub with leaves that are small and brilliantly red when

Acer palmatum 'Senkaki'

young, turning green with maturity.
Zone 5 US, 6 Can.

***A. p.* 'Trompenburg'** A large shrub whose deep purplish red leaves become green and then red in fall. They are divided to the base and the lobes are narrow, with the margins rolled under. An outstanding plant. Raised in Holland.
Zone 5 US, 6 Can.

***A. p.* 'Ukigumo'** A striking variegated, small to medium-sized shrub with deeply five-lobed leaves, heavily mottled and edged with white and pink. The name means "passing cloud."
Zone 5 US, 6 Can.

Acer pensylvanicum

A. pensylvanicum (Striped maple, moosewood) A small understory tree with green young stems that are beautifully striped with white and pale jade green in "snake-bark" fashion. Its leaves are up to 7 in (18 cm) across, three-lobed, and turn an attractive bright, rich yellow in fall.

Acer pensylvanicum 'Erythrocladum'

E North America. Introduced 1755.
Zone 3 US, 2b Can. 🏆

***A. p.* 'Erythrocladum'** A lovely form in which the young shoots are brilliant candy pink, with white striations in winter. Attractive when young, it is best grown as a large shrub, although it will also make a small tree.
Zone 3 US, 2b Can. 🏆

A. platanoides (Norway maple) A handsome, fast-growing large tree. The large, five-lobed leaves turn yellow in fall but are seldom as brilliant as the native maples. The yellow flowers are borne in showy clusters on the bare stems in spring. Europe, Caucasus. Long cultivated.
Zone 4 US, 4b Can. 🏆

***A. p.* 'Cleveland'** A large tree with a strong, upright habit, making an oval head of branches with large, deep green leaves.
Zone 3b US, 4 Can.

Acer platanoides 'Columnare'

***A. p.* 'Columnare'** A large, erect tree of columnar habit. Raised 1855 in France.
Zone 4 US, 4b Can.

Acer platanoides 'Crimson King'

***A. p.* 'Crimson King'** A large, handsome tree with leaves of deep crimson-purple. The flowers are deep yellow, tinged with red. A seedling of *A. p.* 'Schwedleri'. In cultivation 1946.
Zone 4 US, 4b Can. 🏆

***A. p.* 'Crimson Sentry'** A dense, narrowly columnar, medium-sized tree with reddish purple leaves, not as dark as 'Crimson King'.
Zone 4 US, 5 Can.

***A. p.* 'Deborah'** A medium-sized tree that is a seedling of *A. p.* 'Schwedleri'. The young leaves are brilliant red, turning dark green, and have wavy margins. Raised in the United States.
Zone 4 US, 5 Can.

Acer platanoides 'Drummondii'

***A. p.* 'Drummondii'** A very striking medium-sized to large tree bearing leaves

with a broad marginal band of creamy white. Reverting shoots should be removed. In cultivation 1903.
Zone 4 US, 5 Can. 🏆

***A. p.* 'Emerald Queen'** A vigorous large tree with glossy, dark green leaves, upright when young and broadening with age. Raised 1959.
Zone 4 US, 5 Can.

Acer platanoides 'Globosum'

***A. p.* 'Globosum'** An eye-catching small tree with short branches forming a dense, mop-shaped head. In cultivation 1873.
Zone 4 US, 5 Can.

***A. p.* 'Schwedleri'** A large tree with rich crimson-purple young growths and leaves, at its most effective when pruned hard every other year.
Zone 4 US, 4b Can. 🏆

A. pseudoplatanus (Sycamore maple) Do not confuse this with the sycamore *(Platanus occidentalis)*. It is a picturesque tree and is suited to exposed locations in any soil. Europe, W Asia.
Zone 4 US, 5b Can.

***A. p.* 'Atropurpureum'**, syn. *A. p.* 'Purpureum Spaethii' A selected form reaching large tree size with leaves that are dark green above and purple beneath. In cultivation 1883.
Zone 4 US, 5b Can. 🏆

***A. p.* 'Brilliantissimum'** A distinctive small tree that is slow growing. The young spring leaves are a glorious shrimp pink when they first appear and later change to pale yellow-green before finally becoming green. In cultivation 1905.
Zone 4 US, 5b Can. 🏆

Acer pseudoplatanus 'Brilliantissimum'

***A. p.* 'Erectum'** A large tree with erect branches. In cultivation 1935.
Zone 4 US, 5b Can.

Acer pseudoplatanus 'Leopoldii'

***A. p.* 'Leopoldii'** The leaves of this large tree are yellowish pink at first, later becoming green, speckled and splashed with yellow and pink. Zone 4 US, 5b Can. 🏆

***A. p.* 'Purpureum Spaethii'** See *A. p.* 'Atropurpureum'.

***A. p.* 'Simon-Louis Frères'** The leaves of this large tree are pink when young and then become blotched and streaked with green and white, but are plain green beneath. In cultivation 1881.
Zone 4 US, 5b Can.

***A. p.* 'Worleei'** (Golden sycamore) A medium-sized tree with leaves that are soft yellow-green, becoming golden and then green. Raised before 1893 in Germany.
Zone 4 US, 5b Can. 🏆

A. rubrum (Red maple, swamp maple) A free-growing tree, of large size at maturity,

Acer pseudoplatanus 'Simon-Louis Frères'

whose palmate leaves are dark green above and bluish beneath. It is one of the earlier trees to show its fall color, becoming rich scarlet red. E North America. In culti-

Acer pseudoplatanus 'Worleei'

vation 1656.
Zone 3 US, 3b Can.

***A. r.* 'Autumn Flame'** Good, persistent fall color every year, usually turning before the species. Makes a dense, rounded tree.
Zone 4 US, 4b Can.

***A. r.* 'Morgan'** One of the brightest for fall color. Fast growing with an open shape. Selected 1971 by the Morgan Arboretum, Montreal.
Zone 3 US, 3b Can.

***A. r.* 'Northwood'** Leaves dark green in summer and orange-red in fall. Introduced 1980 by the University of Minnesota.
Zone 3 US, 3b Can.

***A. r.* 'October Glory'** The leaves of this medium-sized tree turn color quite early in the fall, becoming brilliant red and

Acer rubrum

Acer rubrum 'October Glory'

remaining so for a comparatively long time. In cultivation 1964.
Zone 3 US, 3b Can. 🏆

A. r. **'Red Sunset'** A medium-sized tree with upswept branches and particularly good orange-red to red fall color. In cultivation 1968.
Zone 3 US, 3b Can.

A. r. **'Scanlon'** A medium-sized, columnar tree that takes on rich fall color. In cultivation 1948.
Zone 3 US, 3b Can. 🏆

Acer rubrum 'Scanlon'

A. r. **'Schlesingeri'** A medium-sized tree notable for its outstanding, very early fall color, which is a rich, deep scarlet, but with an untidy habit. In cultivation 1888.
Zone 3 US, 3b Can.

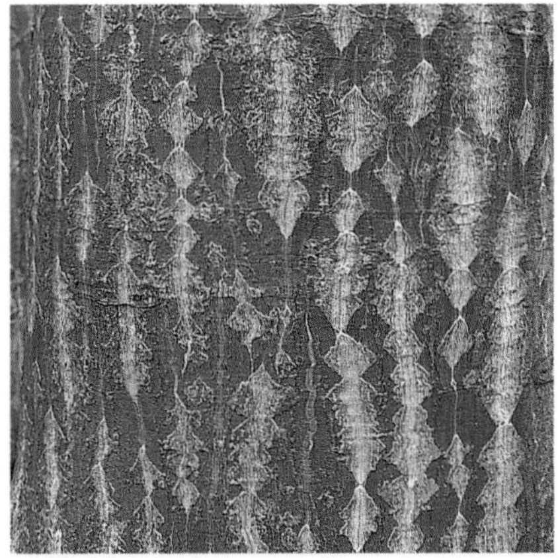
Acer rufinerve

A. rufinerve (Redvein maple) A medium-sized deciduous tree with bluish young stems, while the older ones and the trunk have "snake-bark" patterning of white striations on a green background. This is similar to the bark of *A. pensylvanicum*, and the three-lobed leaves also recall that species. It has bright red and yellow fall colors. Japan. Introduced 1879.
Zone 5 US, 6b Can. 🏆

Acer rufinerve f. *albolimbatum*

A. r.* f. *albolimbatum The leaves of this medium-sized tree are mottled and margined with white, turning brilliant red and purple in fall. In cultivation 1869.
Zone 5 US, 6b Can.

A. saccharinum, syn. *A. dasycarpum* (Silver maple) A large, fast-growing deciduous tree with deeply five-lobed leaves that are silvery white beneath. The foliage creates a delightful effect when it is ruffled by breezes. The wood is brittle and trees are often damaged by high winds. Fall color is not as good as

Acer saccharinum

that of sugar and red maples. E North America. Introduced 1725.

Zone 3 US, 2b Can. 🏆

***A. s.* 'Fastigiatum'** See *A. s.* 'Pyramidale'.

A. s.* f. *laciniatum See Laciniatum group.

Laciniatum group This name covers medium-sized or large trees with deeply cut leaves. See *A. s.* 'Wieri'.

Zone 3 US, 2b Can.

Acer saccharinum 'Lutescens'

***A. s.* 'Lutescens'** The leaves of this large tree are orange-yellow when young and yellow-green in summer. In cultivation 1881.

Zone 3 US, 3 Can.

***A. s.* 'Pyramidale'**, syn. *A. s.* 'Fastigiatum' A large tree with upright growth. In cultivation 1885.

Zone 3 US, 2b Can.

***A. s.* 'Wieri'** (Laciniatum group) A large tree with pendulous lower branches and leaves deeply divided into sharply cut lobes. Found in 1873.

Zone 3 US, 2b Can.

A. saccharum (Sugar maple) An ornamental, ultimately large deciduous tree, not to be confused with *A. saccharinum*. It resembles the Norway maple and is one of the finest trees for fall color, with different specimens displaying orange, gold, or scarlet tints. C and E North America. Introduced 1735.

Zone 3 US, 4 Can.

***A. s.* 'Green Mountain'** The dark green foliage is very heat resistant, and fall color is mostly yellow. Introduced 1964.

Zone 3 US, 4 Can.

Acer shirasawanum

Acer shirasawanum 'Aureum'

A. shirasawanum This relative of *A. japonicum* is an elegant large deciduous shrub or small tree. It has bloomy shoots, and the rounded, bright green leaves with smooth stalks usually have 11 sharply toothed lobes. The leaves turn a rich orange and red in the fall. The flowers, which have pink calyxes and cream petals, are held in spreading or almost upright clusters. Japan. In cultivation 1888.

Zone 5 US, 6b Can.

***A. s.* 'Aureum'**, syn. *A. japonicum* 'Aureum' A well-known, slow-growing large shrub or small tree with soft yellow leaves. It should be located in part shade, as the foliage is prone to scorching in hot sun.

Zone 4 US, 5b Can. 🏆

***A.* 'Silver Vein'** A strong-growing "snakebark" maple with arching branches conspicuously patterned and striated in green and white. The leaves of this small deciduous tree are large, three-lobed above the middle and tapered at the point. They are rich green on the upper sides, carried on long red stalks, and turn butter yellow in fall. Raised by Hillier Nurseries from a cross made in 1961.

Zone 4? US, 5? Can.

A. trautvetteri A small to medium-sized deciduous tree with large, deeply five-lobed leaves that turn golden yellow in fall. Its flowers are borne in upright panicles and are followed in late summer by fruits with showy, broad red wings. A handsome foliage tree, it is conspicuous when the bright red buds open in spring. Caucasus, SW Asia. Introduced 1866.

Zone 5 US, 6b Can.

A. triflorum A very rare, slow-growing, small tree related and similar to *A. maximowiczianum* but with characteristically pale gray-brown, flaking bark. The leaves have three leaflets and are bluish underneath. One of the most consistent trees for brilliant fall color. Manchuria, Korea. Introduced 1923.

Zone 5 US, 6 Can.

Acer × zoeschense

A. × zoeschense This hybrid between *A. campestre* and (probably) *A. cappadocicum* is of garden origin and is a medium-sized tree with five-lobed, dark green leaves, somewhat tinged with purple.
Zone 6 US, 7b Can.

Acradenia *Rutaceae*

There are just two species in this genus of evergreens, which will grow well in any average, well-drained soil. A. euodiiformis, *the second species in the genus, occurs in eastern Australia.*

Acradenia frankliniae

A. frankliniae This small to medium-sized shrub of upright habit succeeds well in mild areas. It is grown for its aromatic leaves, which are dark green, and for its flat clusters of white flowers in late spring. W Tasmania. Introduced 1845.
Zone 8 US, 9? Can.

Actinidia *Actinidiaceae*

A genus of about 30 species of deciduous climbers, natives of eastern Asia. They are vigorous, generally hardy, twining plants with simple leaves that sometimes bear edible, juicy fruits. (Those grown for fruits are best planted in pairs.) They are excellent for covering walls, trellises, or tall stumps and flourish in most fertile soils in sun or partial shade.

A. chinensis, syn. *A. deliciosa* (Kiwi, Chinese gooseberry) A large, vigorous climber reaching a height of 28 ft (9 m), with shoots densely covered with reddish hairs and large, heart-shaped leaves 6–9 in (15–

Actinidia chinensis

23 cm) long and up to 8 in (20 cm) wide. The 1½ in (4 cm) wide, fragrant flowers are cream turning buff-yellow and are produced in clusters in late summer. The edible fruits are green then brown, resembling large, elongated gooseberries and having a similar flavor. To obtain fruit it is necessary to plant both sexes. Worthwhile fruit is rarely produced in cool climates unless the plants are grown on a warm, sunny wall or in a greenhouse. Selected clones are cultivated for fruiting, notably 'Hayward' (female) and 'Tomuri' (male). The main commercial sources of the fruits are New Zealand, Kenya, and Israel. China. Introduced 1900 by Ernest Wilson.
Zone 7 US, 9? Can.

A. deliciosa See *A. chinensis.*

Actinidia kolomikta

A. kolomikta A striking, large, slender climber reaching 12–20 ft (4–6 m). It is remarkable for the tricolored variegation of many of its leaves, whereby the terminal half is cream, flushed with pink. Variegation seems to be best on male plants and in sun. There is no variegation on young plants. The flowers are small, white, and slightly fragrant, opening in early summer, and the round fruits are yellow, sweetish, and ¾ in (2 cm) in diameter. Japan, N China, Manchuria. Introduced c. 1855.
Zone 4 US, 4b Can. 🏆

Aesculus *Hippocastanaceae*

Horse chestnut, buckeye

This genus of about 13 deciduous species native to North America, southeastern Europe, and eastern Asia includes some of the most ornamental of the larger trees that flower in late spring and early summer. All of them have compound, palmate leaves and flowers borne in showy panicles. They are easily grown and thrive in slightly acidic, moist soil and sun or part shade. Care should be taken in siting these trees, however, as they are "dirty"—dropping the coarse, often spiny fruits along with leaves and twigs. The nuts are harmful if eaten.

Aesculus californica

A. californica (California buckeye) A low-growing, wide-spreading tree or large shrub whose leaves are relatively small, with 5–7 blue-green leaflets. The fragrant, white or pink-tinted flowers are borne in summer in dense, erect panicles up to 8 in (20 cm) long. California. Introduced c. 1850.
Zone 7 US, 9 Can.

A. × carnea *(A. hippocastanum × A. pavia)* (Red horse chestnut) A medium-sized to large tree often used for avenues and parks. The flowers are rose-pink and borne in panicles up to 8 in (20 cm) long in late spring.

Aesculus × *carnea*

It is similar to *A. hippocastanum* but generally smaller and more compact, with smaller, darker green leaflets. In cultivation 1820.
Zone 5 US, 6 Can.

Aesculus × *carnea* 'Briotii'

***A.* × *c.* 'Briotii'** A compact, medium-sized to large tree with deeper-colored pink to red flowers that have a yellow throat. Raised 1858.
Zone 4 US, 5b Can. 🏆

***A.* × *c.* 'Plantierensis'** *(A. × carnea × A. hippocastanum)* Perhaps the best form, this is a large tree resembling *A. hippocastanum* but with pale pink flowers that have a red or yellow throat. Raised c. 1894 in France.
Zone 5 US, 6b Can.

A.* × *dallimorei A graft hybrid that makes a medium-sized tree with dark green leaves that turn orange and red in fall. The flowers are cream with red flares and spots.
Zone 5 US, 6b Can.

A. flava, syn. *A. octandra* (Yellow buckeye) A medium-sized to large tree with flowers that are the nearest thing to yellow in the genus. They are borne from late spring to early summer. The leaves have 5–7 leaflets and color well in fall. SE United States. Introduced 1764.
Zone 3 US, 3b Can. 🏆

Aesculus flava

A. georgiana, syn. *A. × neglecta* var. *georgiana* A large shrub or small tree with dense panicles of orange-red flowers borne in late spring or early summer. SE United States. Introduced 1905.
Zone 4 US, 5 Can.

A. glabra (Ohio buckeye) A small to medium-sized tree with rough bark. Its leaves usually have five leaflets and turn orange-yellow in fall. The flowers, borne in late spring, are yellow-green; have protruding stamens; and are followed by prickly fruits. C and SE United States. In cultivation 1809.
Zone 7 US, 8b? Can.

A. hippocastanum (Common horse chestnut) One of the most beautiful large, flowering trees. It is exceptionally attractive when covered in late spring with its stout candles of flowers, which are white with a yellow blotch that later turns red. The fruits are not ornamental and are poisonous, as are the leaves. Greece, Albania, now rare in the wild. Introduced 1576.
Zone 3 US, 4b Can. 🏆

Aesculus hippocastanum

Aesculus hippocastanum 'Baumannii'

***A. h.* 'Baumannii'**, syn. *A. h.* 'Flore Pleno' In time becomes a large tree with double white flowers that does not set seed.
Zone 3 US, 4b Can. 🏆

***A. h.* 'Flore Pleno'** See *A. h.* 'Baumannii'.

A. indica (Indian horse chestnut) A magnificent large tree with panicles of pink-flushed flowers from early to midsummer that are as large as 16 in (40 cm) long and 5 in (13 cm) wide. The leaves have seven leaflets and are bronze when young; become glossy, dark green; and then eventually turn orange or yellow in fall. A splendid specimen grows in alkaline soil on the site of Hillier's West Hill Nursery in Winchester, where it was 50 ft (15 m) tall in

Aesculus indica

1994. NW Himalaya. Introduced 1851.
Zone 7 US, 9? Can. 🏆

***A. i.* 'Sydney Pearce'** A free-flowering large tree of upright habit with dark olive green leaves. Its flowers are borne in large panicles and individual blossoms are up to 1 in (2.5 cm) across, with white petals marked with yellow and prettily suffused with pink. Raised 1928 at Kew, England.
Zone 7 US, 9? Can.

***A.* × *mutabilis* 'Induta'**, syn. *A.* × *m.* 'Rosea Nana' A large shrub or small tree bearing apricot flowers with yellow markings in summer. In cultivation 1905.
Zone 5 US, 6b Can.

***A.* × *m.* 'Rosea Nana'** See *A.* × *m.* 'Induta'.

Aesculus × *neglecta* 'Erythroblastos'

***A.* × *neglecta* 'Erythroblastos'** A spectacular though rather slow-growing hybrid that eventually becomes a medium-sized tree. Its flowers, borne from late spring to early summer, are pale yellow, and the tree displays rich fall color. But the main attraction is the young leaves, which are brilliant shrimp pink, changing to a pale yellow-green later in the season. In cultivation 1935.
Zone 5 US, 6b Can. 🏆

A.* × *n.* var. *georgiana See *A. georgiana.*

A. octandra See *A. flava.*

Aesculus parviflora

A. parviflora (Bottlebrush buckeye) A suckering medium-sized to large shrub that flowers freely from mid- to late summer, bearing white flowers with protuberant red anthers in slender panicles 8–12 in (20–30 cm) long. The leaves are bronze when young and attractively colored yellow in fall. SE United States. Introduced 1785.
Zone 4 US, 4b Can. 🏆

A. pavia (Red buckeye) A beautiful and rewarding medium-sized to large shrub or small tree. Its leaves have five glossy green leaflets, and its striking crimson flowers, which are borne in panicles 6 in (15 cm) long, open in early to midsummer. SE

Aesculus pavia 'Atrosanguinea'

United States. Introduced 1711.
Zone 4 US, 5b Can. 🏆

***A. p.* 'Atrosanguinea'** A form with flowers of a little deeper red than those of the species.
Zone 4 US, 5b Can.

A. splendens This large shrub with long panicles of scarlet flowers in late spring is perhaps the most handsome of the buckeyes. Botanists now believe that it should be included in *A. pavia.*
Zone 5 US, 6b Can.

A. turbinata (Japanese horse chestnut) A large tree with outsize foliage — on young trees a leaf and its stalk may be more than 26 in (65 cm) long — attractively veined and tinted in fall. Its flowers are borne in long panicles, being yellowish white with a red spot, and appear in late spring or early summer, a little later than *A. hippocastanum.* The fruits are large, pear shaped, and not spiny. Japan. Introduced before 1880.
Zone 6 US, 8 Can.

Ailanthus *Simaroubaceae*

A genus of about five deciduous species from eastern Asia to Australia. Handsome, fast-growing trees with large, pinnate leaves, they are extremely tolerant of atmospheric pollution and grow well in most soils.

Ailanthus altissima

A. altissima (Tree of heaven) A large, imposing tree with distinct, ashlike leaves that can be up to 3 ft (1 m) long on young specimens. Female trees produce large, conspicuous bunches of reddish, winged fruits, rather like maple "keys," in mid- to

late summer. N China. Introduced 1751 by Peter Collinson.
Zone 5 US, 6 Can. 🏆

Akebia *Lardizabalaceae*

A genus of five species of vigorous, hardy, semievergreen, twining climbers with attractive foliage and flowers. They succeed in most soils in sun or shade and are excellent for growing over hedges, low trees, bushes, or stumps, though they can sometimes be a little overvigorous in mild climates. A mild spring is necessary for the flowers, and the conspicuous and unusual fruits are produced only after a long, hot summer.

Akebia quinata

A. quinata (Fiveleaf akebia) A large climber reaching up to 28–40 ft (9–12 m). The leaves have five notched leaflets, and the flowers are fragrant, red-purple, and borne on racemes in midspring. The male and female flowers are separate but carried on the same inflorescence, the females at the base and the males at the tip. The fruits are sausage shaped, 2–4 in (5–10 cm) long, and dark purple and contain black seeds embedded in a white pulp. Japan, Korea, China. Introduced 1845 by Robert Fortune.
Zone 4 US, 5b Can.

A. trifoliata (Threeleaf akebia) A large and elegant plant, climbing to 28 ft (9 m). The leaves have three shallowly lobed leaflets, and the flowers are dark purple, borne on racemes in midspring. The sausage-shaped fruits, 3–5 in (7.5–13 cm) long and often in groups of three, are pale violet. Japan, China. Introduced 1895.
Zone 5 US, 6b Can.

Akebia trifoliata

Alangium *Alangiaceae*

A genus of about 20 species of deciduous trees, shrubs, and climbers mainly from warm regions of the Old World. The following species is an attractive foliage plant. Plant it in full sun or partial shade and any type of well-drained, reasonably fertile soil.

A. platanifolium A large shrub with leaves that have 3–5 and sometimes 7 lobes and clusters of white flowers like miniature lilies in early to midsummer. Taiwan to Manchuria. Introduced 1879.
Zone 7 US, 8 Can.

Albizia *Leguminosae*

A genus of deciduous, mimosa-like shrubs or small trees with handsome foliage and attractive, fluffy flower clusters borne in early or midsummer. There are about 150 species, native mainly to the Old World tropics and South America and preferring any average, dryish soil.

***A. julibrissin* 'Rosea'** The hardiest form of the hardiest mimosa species, this is a small, spreading, graceful tree with dense plumes of bright pink flowers in late summer. To flower it requires a sheltered location in full sun. Korea. Introduced 1918 by Ernest Wilson.
Zone 6 US, 7 Can. 🏆

Alnus *Betulaceae*

Alder

A genus of about 35 species of fast-growing deciduous trees and shrubs native mainly to northern temperate regions. They will grow in most soils, even those that are infertile; but with very few exceptions, including A. cordata *and* A. glutinosa, *they do not thrive in shallow alkaline soils. They are especially valuable in damp or even wet situations, although* A. cordata *and* A. incana *will do well in drier soils.* A. glutinosa *can grow in very wet conditions, even where there is standing water. Male and female flowers are borne in spring on the same plant: the male catkins are long and drooping, while the females are short and become woody cones.*

Alnus cordata

A. cordata (Italian alder) A splendid, medium-sized to large, conical tree for all types of soil, including alkaline, in which it grows rapidly. It is notable for its bright green, glistening foliage and yellow catkins borne in late winter or early spring. Corsica, S Italy. Introduced 1820.
Zone 5 US, 6b Can. 🏆

A. glutinosa (European alder) A small to

Alnus glutinosa

Alnus glutinosa 'Imperialis'

medium-sized, bushy tree with sticky young growths and yellow catkins in early spring and dark green, toothed leaves. It can be grown as a multitrunked tree, like a birch. W Asia, N Africa, Europe.
Zone 3 US, 4 Can.

A. g. **'Imperialis'** An attractive and very graceful small tree with deeply and finely cut leaves. In cultivation 1859.
Zone 3 US, 4 Can. 🏆

A. g. **'Laciniata'** This medium-sized tree is similar to 'Imperialis' but stronger growing and with a stiffer habit. Its leaves are not as finely divided. Arose before 1819 in France.
Zone 3 US, 4 Can.

A. g. **'Pyramidalis'** The branches of this medium-sized tree grow at an acute angle, making a narrow, conical form.
Zone 3 US, 4 Can.

A. incana (Gray alder) An exceptionally hardy, large shrub or small tree with gray undersides to its leaves. Yellow or brown catkins are borne in late winter or early spring. Ideal for cold and wet situations. Europe, Caucasus. Introduced 1780.
Zone 2 US, 3 Can.

Alnus incana 'Aurea'

A. i. **'Aurea'** The young shoots and foliage of this small tree are yellow, and the catkins are conspicuously tinted red.
Zone 2 US, 3 Can.

A. i. **'Pendula'** A handsome, small, weeping tree forming a large mound of pendulous branches and gray-green leaves. Originated before 1900 in Holland.
Zone 2 US, 3 Can.

Alnus incana 'Pendula'

A. rubra (Red alder) This medium-sized, large-leaved tree is very fast growing. It has a graceful habit and in spring is festooned with male catkins 4–6 in (10–15 cm) long. W North America. Introduced before 1880.
Zone 6 US, 7 Can.

A. × ***spaethii*** A fast-growing tree of medium size, with large leaves that are purplish when young. An outstanding tree when bearing its 6 in (15 cm) long catkins in early spring. In cultivation c. 1908.
Zone 5 US, 6b Can. 🏆

Aloysia *Verbenaceae*

A genus of about 35 species of evergreen and deciduous aromatic shrubs, native to Central and South America and the southwestern United States, of which only one species is commonly grown. They will grow in any average, dry soil.

Aloysia triphylla

A. triphylla, syn. *Lippia citriodora* (Lemon verbena) A medium-sized to large deciduous shrub with lanceolate, lemon-scented leaves normally in whorls of three. The tiny, pale purple flowers are profusely borne in late summer in panicles at the ends of the branches. Best against a warm wall. Chile. Introduced 1784.

Zone 8 US, 9? Can.

Amelanchier *Rosaceae*

Serviceberry, Juneberry, shadbush

A genus of about 10 species of beautiful and very hardy, small, deciduous trees or shrubs, which are natives mainly of North America but are also found in Europe and Asia. The ones described below thrive in moist, well-drained soil and need irrigation during drought. The abundant white flowers are produced in racemes in spring before the leaves are fully developed. In fact, the common name "shadbush" pertains to the fact that the blooms usually appear when shad are running upstream to spawn in spring.

***A.* 'Ballerina'** A vigorous large shrub or small tree with finely toothed leaves that are bronze when young and color well in fall. The large white flowers are profusely borne. Probably a hybrid of *A. laevis*. Selected 1970 in Holland from plants sent from Hillier Nurseries.

Zone 4 US, 4b Can. 🏆

Amelanchier laevis

Amelanchier lamarckii in spring

A. canadensis (Shadbush, shadblow) The true species is rare. It is a medium-sized to large, suckering shrub with tall, erect stems and erect racemes of flowers. Unfortunately, its name is often attached to *A. laevis* and *A. lamarckii*, which are better garden plants and can be distinguished from it by their lax or pendulous racemes. It grows well in moist locations. North America.

Zone 3 US, 3b Can.

A. × grandiflora (Apple serviceberry) A large, spreading shrub with bronze young leaves and profuse clusters of large white flowers. This hybrid originated in the wild as well as in cultivation. The best clones are as follows. See also *A. lamarckii*.

Zone 4 US, 4b Can.

***A. × g.* 'Autumn Brilliance'** Possibly the brightest of all the serviceberries for fall color. It has showy white flowers in spring and edible fruit.

Zone 4 US, 4b Can.

***A. × g.* 'Robin Hill'** A large shrub or small tree of dense, upright habit with flowers that are pink in bud, open pale pink, and then become white.

Zone 4 US, 4b Can.

A. laevis (Allegheny serviceberry) A small tree, or occasionally a large shrub, that is often incorrectly named *A. canadensis*. It is a picture of striking beauty at the end of midspring, when the white flowers, profusely borne in pendulous racemes, contrast with the delicate pink young foliage. In fall the leaves take on orange and red tints. North America. In cultivation 1870.

Zone 3 US, 3b Can.

Amelanchier laevis in flower

A. lamarckii This is another plant often incorrectly known as *A. canadensis* and is the best species for general planting. It is a large shrub or small tree with a bushy, spreading habit and oval to oblong leaves, coppery red and silky when young and richly colored in fall. The flowers are borne in lax, ample racemes, scattered along the branches as the young leaves unfold, and a tree in full flower makes for a beautiful spectacle. The fruits that follow are black. Native to E North America; naturalized NW Europe, England.
Zone 4 US, 4b Can. 🏆

Amorpha *Leguminosae*

A genus of about 15 species of deciduous, sun-loving shrubs or subshrubs native to North America and Mexico, with pinnate leaves and dense, spiky heads of small flowers that are usually blue or violet. They are recognizably pea flowers but are unusual in having only one petal.

A. fruticosa (False indigo) A variable, medium-sized to large shrub with pinnate leaves and slender racemes of purplish blue flowers that are borne in midsummer. It will grow in any well-drained soil in sun. S United States. Introduced 1724.
Zone 4 US, 5 Can.

Ampelopsis *Vitaceae*

A genus of about 20 species of alternate-leaved, deciduous ornamental vines that climb by means of curling tendrils. They are natives mainly of North America and eastern Asia, excellent for covering walls and fences. Ampelopsis are vigorous and not suitable for small gardens. They are grown for their attractive foliage and for their fruits, which, however, need a long, hot summer and a mild fall if they are to develop. They will grow in any ordinary soil and in sun or part shade, but for those species with attractive fruits a warm, sunny, sheltered location is best. See also Vitis *and* Parthenocissus.

Amelanchier lamarckii in fall

Ampelopsis brevipedunculata

A. brevipedunculata A luxuriant large climber with three- or occasionally five-lobed, heart-shaped leaves up to 6 in (15 cm) wide, rather like those of the hop. As they ripen, the masses of small fruits vary in color between pale purple and verdigris (copper-rust blue), but they generally mature to a deep porcelain blue. NE Asia. In cultivation 1870.
Zone 4 US, 5 Can.

***A. b.* 'Elegans'**, syn. *A. b.* 'Tricolor' The leaves are densely mottled with white and tinged with pink. It is a weak grower and can be planted where space is restricted. It is sometimes seen in florists' shops as a houseplant.
Zone 4 US, 5 Can.

***A. b.* 'Tricolor'** See *A. b.* 'Elegans'.

A. megalophylla A large, strong but rather slow-growing climber of considerable quality, reaching to 28 ft (9 m) or more. The leaves are bipinnate, 1–2 ft (30–60 cm) long, with leaflets 2–6 in (5–15 cm) long. The loose bunches of top-shaped fruits are purple at first and finally black. W China. Introduced 1894.
Zone 5 US, 6 Can.

Andromeda *Ericaceae*

A genus of only two species of low-growing, slender-stemmed, evergreen shrubs for moist, humus-rich, acidic soils.

A. polifolia (Bog rosemary) A charming dwarf shrub. Its slender stems bear narrow, glaucous green leaves whose undersides are smooth and white. It carries clusters of soft

Andromeda polifolia

pink, bell-shaped flowers at the ends of the branches in late spring and early summer. Andromeda is widely distributed in N Hemisphere. In cultivation 1768.
Zone 2 US, 2 Can.

Andromeda polifolia 'Compacta'

***A. p.* 'Compacta'** A gem for a cool, peaty bed, which bears clusters of bright pink flowers from late spring onward. As its name suggests, it is of compact habit.
Zone 2 US, 2 Can. 🏆

***A. p.* 'Compacta Alba'** Another compact plant suitable for small gardens, this dwarf form has white flowers.
Zone 2 US, 2 Can. 🏆

***A. p.* 'Macrophylla'** A low-growing form with relatively broad leaves and deep pink flowers.
Zone 2 US, 2 Can. 🏆

***A. p.* 'Nikko'** Another neat, compact form, which some consider an improvement on 'Compacta'.
Zone 2 US, 2 Can.

Anthyllis *Leguminosae*

A genus of about 20 species of annual and perennial, evergreen and deciduous shrubs and herbaceous plants, which usually have pinnate leaves and clustered, pealike flowers. They are natives of Europe, western Asia, and North Africa and will grow in any average, well-drained soil.

A. hermanniae An attractive, deciduous, dwarf shrub for the rock garden with small, narrow leaves, all of which have three leaflets but sometimes appear to consist of one only, as the side leaflets are reduced practically to nothing. The flowers are freely borne in clusters of two to eight from early to midsummer and are small, pea shaped, and yellow, with orange markings on the standard petals. Mediterranean. Introduced early 1700s.
Zone 5 US, 6 Can.

Aralia *Araliaceae*

A genus of more than 35 species of perennials, deciduous shrubs, and one or two climbers native to parts of America and Asia, grown chiefly for the beauty of their large, compound leaves. They will grow in any average soil.

Aralia elata

A. elata (Japanese angelica tree) This species is usually seen as a large, suckering shrub but occasionally grows to a small, sparsely branched tree. The stems are often spiny. The huge leaves are doubly pinnate; in other words, they are divided, fernlike, into several leaflets on each side of the midrib, and then each leaflet is itself divided. They are gathered mainly in rufflike arrangements at the tips of the stems and often color well in fall. The flowers are white and borne in late summer in large panicles that are branched from the base. Japan. Introduced 1830.
Zone 4 US, 5 Can. 🏆

Aralia elata 'Aureovariegata'

***A. e.* 'Aureovariegata'** A large shrub with its leaflets irregularly margined and splashed with yellow. This is noticeable in spring, but later in summer the variegation becomes silvery white.
Zone 4 US, 5 Can.

Aralia elata 'Variegata'

***A. e.* 'Variegata'** A highly desirable large shrub with its leaves irregularly blotched and edged with creamy white, which changes to silvery white in summer. Both variegated forms are difficult to propagate, as they have to be grafted and produce little in the way of material for scions. Be prepared for prices that justifiably reflect this. Introduced 1865.
Zone 4 US, 5 Can. 🏆

Araucaria *Araucariaceae*

A genus of about 18 species of evergreen conifers from Oceania, Queensland, and South America. Apart from the following, the only nearly hardy species is A. heterophylla, *the Norfolk Island pine, which is a popular greenhouse plant, although it will attain heights of around 100 ft (30 m) in a favorable climate.*

Araucaria araucana detail

Araucaria araucana

A. araucana (Monkey puzzle tree) A medium-sized to large tree unique in appearance, with long, spidery branches and densely overlapping, rigid, spine-tipped, dark green leaves. The cones are globular, up to 7 in (18 cm) long, and take three years to mature. They break up while still on the tree, and the sharp scales can be hazardous on lawns. It makes an imposing specimen but does better in cooler, coastal regions than in hot southern states. It grows best in a moist, loamy soil. In industrial areas it loses its lower branches and becomes ragged. Chile, Argentina. Introduced first 1795 by Archibald Menzies and then 1844 by William Lobb.
Zone 7 US, 9 Can.

Arbutus *Ericaceae*

Manzanita, strawberry tree

A genus of about 15 species that are among the most ornamental and highly prized of small evergreen trees. They are found in both the New and Old Worlds and with few exceptions attain 10–20 ft (3–6 m) — but see A. unedo *below. The glossy, dark green leaves; panicles of white, urn-shaped flowers; and strawberry-like fruits are all very attractive. Apart from those mentioned below, species can also be found in the Canary Islands, southwestern United States, Mexico, and Central America.*

Arbutus × andrachnoides

A. × andrachnoides, syn. *A. × hybrida (A. unedo × A. andrachne)* This hybrid small tree has inherited its late-flowering tendency from the first parent and its beautiful cinnamon-red branches from the second. The flowers are white and borne in late fall and early winter. It thrives best in a maritime climate. Greece. In cultivation 1800.
Zone 8 US, 9? Can. 🏆

A. × hybrida See *A. × andrachnoides.*

Arbutus menziesii

A. menziesii (Madrone) This medium-sized tree occasionally reaches 60 ft (18 m) in cultivation. It has beautiful, smooth, reddish brown bark that peels in late summer to reveal the young, green bark beneath. The flowers are borne in conspicuous panicles in late spring and are followed by small, orange-yellow fruits. Hardiness depends to a large extent on how it is sited; it requires acid soil. W North America. Introduced 1827 by David Douglas.
Zone 6 US, 7 Can. 🏆

Arbutus unedo

A. unedo (Strawberry tree) A large shrub or small, gnarled tree in cultivation, but there is a specimen in the Killarney National Park that is well over 40 ft (12 m)

high, with the appearance of an old evergreen oak. The bark of this species is deep brown and shredding, and the white flowers and red fruits are produced simultaneously in fall. It is wind tolerant, withstanding gales in coastal areas, and is unusual among ericaceous plants for its lime tolerance, growing well in gardens with very alkaline soil. Mediterranean, SW Ireland.
Zone 6 US, 7 Can. 🏆

***A. u.* 'Elfin King'** A bushy form that eventually makes a medium-sized shrub. It is free flowering and fruits when small.
Zone 6 US, 7 Can.

Arbutus unedo 'Rubra'

***A. u.* 'Rubra'** A choice form with pink-flushed flowers and abundant fruits, still found wild in Ireland. It makes a large shrub or small tree. In cultivation 1835.
Zone 6 US, 7 Can. 🏆

Arctostaphylos *Ericaceae*

A genus of about 50 species native to western North America and Mexico. These distinctive evergreens vary from prostrate shrubs to small trees and in the larger species usually have attractive bark. The small, nodding flowers are white to pink, borne in clusters and followed by berrylike fruits. They are related to Rhododendron *and succeed in the same sorts of conditions, including acid soil, although they love the sun.*

A. uva-ursi (Common bearberry, kinnikinick) A creeping, alpine shrub with white, pink-tinged flowers borne in early or midsummer and red fruits. The foliage turns bronze in fall, becoming green again in spring. A good plant for sandy slopes. Cool-temperate regions of N Hemisphere.
Zone 3 US, 2 Can.

***A. u.* 'Vancouver Jade'** This selection, made at the University of British Columbia, makes an ideal ground cover. The foliage is a dark, lustrous green, turning red in winter, and the small flowers are pink.
Zone 3 US, 2 Can.

Aristolochia *Aristolochiaceae*

This is a genus of about 300 species of evergreen and deciduous shrubs, climbers, and herbaceous plants, mainly from warmer regions. They have more or less heart-shaped leaves and distinctive, oddly shaped flowers.

A. macrophylla (Dutchman's pipe) A large, vigorous, deciduous climbing species, reaching up to 28 ft (9 m). Its leaves are heart- to kidney-shaped and up to 1 ft (30 cm) long; they remain flat and overlap like shingles, making a dense screen. The flowers are tubular and bent in the lower half like a siphon or calabash pipe, and are 1–1½ in (2.5–4 cm) long and yellowish green with a brown-purple, flared mouth. They are produced in pairs in early summer. E United States. Introduced 1763.
Zone 4 US, 5 Can.

Aristotelia *Elaeocarpaceae*

A genus of about five species of mainly evergreen shrubs from Australasia and South America that need some protection even where hardy. Male and female flowers often occur on separate plants. They will grow in any average soil.

***A. chilensis* 'Variegata'** A graceful, medium-sized to large shrub whose leaves, 5 in (13 cm) long, are conspicuously variegated with yellow. It is an interesting evergreen for mild areas and does well in exposed places near the sea. Chile.
Zone 8 US, 9? Can.

Arctostaphylos uva-ursi

Aronia *Rosaceae*
Chokeberry

A genus of three species of attractive deciduous shrubs related to Pyrus *and* Sorbus. *They have white flowers in spring followed by conspicuous clusters of red or black fruits, and brilliant fall colors. They are not recommended for shallow alkaline soils.*

A. arbutifolia (Red chokeberry) A medium-sized shrub with narrow, dark green leaves, gray felted beneath. It is grown for its bright red fruits and exceptionally brilliant fall colors. E North America. In cultivation 1700.
Zone 4 US, 4b Can.
***A. a.* 'Brilliant'** This form was selected for its vivid red, long-lasting fruits, which are

Aronia arbutifolia 'Brilliant'

carried during the summer months. It has apparently been raised from seed, and several forms may be grown under this name or under 'Brilliantissima'.
Zone 4 US, 4b Can.
A. melanocarpa (Black chokeberry) A small shrub with glossy, dark green leaves that color brilliantly in fall. It bears white, hawthornlike flowers in spring that are followed by lustrous black fruits. E North America. Introduced 1700.
Zone 3 US, 4 Can.
***A. m.* 'Autumn Magic'** The brilliant fall colors of this shrub are unrivaled. The black fruits persist long after the leaves have fallen, birds allowing. Introduced 1988 by the University of British Columbia.
Zone 3 US, 4 Can.

Aronia melanocarpa

Artemisia *Compositae*

A genus of about 300 species of perennials and evergreen and deciduous shrubs and subshrubs with attractive, often aromatic, green or gray foliage and relatively insignificant yellow flowers. The shrubby species are suitable as wall shrubs and in mixed borders. They are natives mainly of the temperate Northern Hemisphere but are also found in South Africa and South America. They prefer a dry, well-drained soil in full sun.

A. abrotanum (Southernwood) A small, erect, deciduous shrub with a bushy habit and sweetly aromatic, downy, finely divided leaves. It is a traditional plant in cottage gardens. Dull yellow flowers are borne in panicles from midsummer to early fall.

Artemisia 'Powis Castle'

Artemisia abrotanum

Spain, S Europe. Now naturalized in E United States.
Zone 4 US, 5 Can.

A. filifolia (Sand sage, threadleaf sage) A small semievergreen shrub with aromatic, hairy, very fine foliage that is silver-blue in summer and turns silver-gray in winter. C and S United States, Mexico.
Zone 4 US, 5 Can.

***A.* 'Powis Castle'** A beautiful, small, deciduous shrub with deeply cut, silvery gray leaves. It is superior to other artemisias as a foliage shrub as it does not flower and thus retains its compact habit; it is also not as invasive as other types. The best one for general garden use and an excellent ground cover. Originated at the National Trust Garden at Powis Castle, Wales. *(Photo on p.149.)* Zone 4 US, 5b Can. 🏆

Arundinaria

Originally a genus of about 50 species of bamboo of tufted growth or with creeping underground stems that has now been reclassified under a variety of genera as listed below.

A. anceps See *Yushania anceps.*
A. auricoma See *Pleioblastus auricomus.*
***A.* 'Gauntlettii'** See *Pleioblastus humilis* 'Gauntlettii'.
A. fortunei See *Pleioblastus variegatus.*
A. hindsii See *Pleioblastus hindsii.*
A. japonica See *Pseudosasa japonica.*
A. murielae See *Thamnocalamus spathaceus.*
A. nitida See *Sinarundinaria nitida.*
A. pygmaea See *Pleioblastus pygmaeus.*
A. simonii See *Pleioblastus simonii.*
A. spathiflora See *Thamnocalamus spathiflorus.*
A. viridistriata See *Pleioblastus auricomus.*

Asimina *Annonaceae*

A genus of eight species of shrubs and small trees native to North America, where they tend to sucker and form thickets. Only one species is commonly grown. They need a deep, fertile, slightly acidic, well-drained soil in full sun.

A. triloba (Pawpaw) In the wild this will grow to a tree 40 ft (12 m) tall, but in gardens it is more commonly grown as a multistemmed shrub. The small purple flowers appear in early spring but are seldom noticed. They give rise to yellow, edible fruits that taste similar to a banana. The leaves are dark green above, paler beneath, and turn a good yellow color most falls. Named forms have been selected for their fruit, which may weigh almost 1 lb (0.5 kg) in some varieties. E United States. Introduced 1736.
Zone 5 US, 6 Can.

Astelia *Asteliaceae*

There are 25 species in this small genus of evergreen, clump-forming perennials that are native to the Pacific Islands, Australia, and New Zealand. They will grow in any average, well-drained soil.

A. nervosa (Kakaha) Technically not a shrub but a perennial with tufts of long, sword-shaped leaves that are similar to those of a *Phormium* species. They are sage green and conspicuously veined. The flowers are very small but sweetly scented and borne in dense, branching panicles in late summer. There are male and female plants, the latter bearing orange berries. New Zealand.
Zone 8 US, 9? Can.

Asteranthera *Gesneriaceae*

A genus of one evergreen species that climbs with aerial roots. It needs a cool soil, preferably neutral or acid, and grows well in milder areas in a sheltered site or against a north-facing wall.

A. ovata A beautiful, medium-sized, trailing creeper that will climb up wall surfaces or tree trunks. It can also make a charming ground cover, being more of a scrambler than a true climber. The leaves are small and more or less rounded. The flowers are tubular, two-lipped, and 2 in (5 cm) long and appear in early summer, arising in the leaf axils. They are red with a white throat and bear similarities to those of the closely related *Saintpaulia*. Chile. Introduced 1926 by Harold Comber.
Zone 8 US, 9? Can.

Athrotaxis *Cupressaceae*

A genus of three Tasmanian conifers needing warm, sheltered locations in cultivation, although the following species is hardy and long lived once established.

Athrotaxis laxifolia

A. laxifolia (Summit cedar) A small to medium-sized tree with a domed crown and brown, furrowed bark. The leaves are only ¼ in (5 mm) long, partly adpressed to the branchlets and partly spreading. Its small cones, often profusely borne, are bright green, changing to orange then brown. It is found in the wild in West Tasmania together with its two genus relatives, *A. cupressoides* and *A. selaginoides.* Introduced 1857.
Zone 8 US, 9? Can.

Atriplex *Chenopodiaceae*

There are more than 100 species of annuals,

perennials, and evergreen or semievergreen shrubs in this genus. They are widely distributed, especially in deserts and salt marshes. The flowers are inconspicuous.

A. halimus (Sea orach) A salt-marsh plant, making a medium-sized, semievergreen shrub with silvery gray leaves, ideal for seaside areas. Good in poor, dry soils. S Europe. In cultivation since the early 17th century.
Zone 8 US, 9? Can.

Aucuba *Cornaceae*

A genus of evergreen, shade-loving shrubs with the male and female flowers on separate plants. They form dense, rounded bushes 6–10 ft (2–3 m) tall and thrive in almost any soil or situation, however sunless. They are very handsome when well grown, especially the variegated forms (which retain their color best in open sites) and the berrying clones. There are three species, found in the Himalaya and eastern Asia.

A. japonica (Japanese aucuba) A medium-sized shrub with green leaves, often referred to as *A. concolor* or *A. viridis.* The small, reddish purple flowers, the males of which have conspicuous, creamy white anthers, are produced in midspring. The male plant is the more common in cultivation. The following forms are available. Japan. Introduced 1783.
Zone 6 US, 7 Can.

Aucuba japonica 'Crotonifolia'

***A. j.* 'Crotonifolia'** A medium-sized shrub with large leaves, boldly spotted and blotched with gold. The best of the gold-variegated aucubas. Female.
Zone 6 US, 7 Can. 🏆

Aucuba japonica 'Hillieri'

Aucuba japonica 'Gold Dust'

***A. j.* 'Gold Dust'** The leaves of this medium-sized shrub are brightly speckled and blotched with gold. Female.
Zone 6 US, 7 Can.

***A. j.* 'Golden King'** This medium-sized shrub is similar to 'Crotonifolia' but with a more striking variegation that displays bold blotches. Best in part shade. Male.
Zone 6 US, 7 Can.

***A. j.* 'Hillieri'** A noble medium-sized shrub with large, lustrous, dark green leaves and pointed fruits. Female.
Zone 6 US, 7 Can.

Aucuba japonica 'Lance Leaf'

***A. j.* 'Lance Leaf'** A striking, sculptural, medium-sized shrub with polished, deep

green, lance-shaped leaves. This is the male counterpart to 'Longifolia'.
Zone 6 US, 7 Can.

Aucuba japonica 'Longifolia'

A. j. **'Longifolia'** The leaves of this medium-sized shrub are long, lanceolate, and bright green. Female.
Zone 6 US, 7 Can. 🏆

A. j. **'Maculata'** See *A. j.* 'Variegata'.

A. j. **'Marmorata'** The leaves of this form are heavily spotted and blotched with yellow. Female.
Zone 6 US, 7 Can.

A. j. **'Nana Rotundifolia'** A small, free-berrying form whose small, rich green leaves have an occasional spot and are sharply toothed in the upper half. Its stems are an unusual shade of sea green. Female.
Zone 6 US, 7 Can.

Aucuba japonica 'Picturata'

A. j. **'Picturata'** The leaves of this form have a large central yellow blotch and are yellow spotted within the margin. However,

Aucuba japonica 'Variegata'

it reverts so readily that it is hardly worth growing. Male.
Zone 6 US, 7 Can.

A. j. **'Rozannie'** A medium-sized shrub with broad, dark green leaves, toothed above the middle. It is compact and bears its large red fruits freely and reliably. Female. In cultivation 1984.
Zone 6 US, 7 Can.

A. j. **'Salicifolia'** A free-berrying medium-sized shrub that differs from 'Longifolia' in its narrower leaves and sea green stems. Female.
Zone 6 US, 7 Can.

A. j. **'Sulphurea Marginata'** A distinct form with sea green stems and green leaves with a pale yellow margin. A medium-sized shrub, it is inclined to revert in shade. Usually grown under the name 'Sulphurea'. Female.
Zone 6 US, 7 Can.

A. j. **'Variegata'**, syn. *A. j.* 'Maculata' (Gold dust plant) A medium-sized shrub with yellow-speckled leaves, this is the

Aucuba japonica 'Sulphurea Marginata'

form that was introduced first. Japan. Introduced 1783.
Zone 6 US, 7 Can.

Austrocedrus *Cupressaceae*

A genus of one evergreen species of conifer with small, solitary cones. The leaves are scalelike and borne in unequal opposite pairs.

Austrocedrus chilensis

A. chilensis (Chilean cedar) A remarkably beautiful species. It is slow growing but hardy and makes a small columnar tree. The branchlets are flattened and divided so as to appear mosslike or ferny. The sea green leaves are borne in *V*-shaped pairs. This tree grew successfully at the Hillier Gardens and Arboretum for more than 40 years, but it is sensitive to cold, dry winds. It also dislikes dryness, and a moisture-retentive soil is necessary, although it must also be well drained. Chile, Argentina. Introduced 1847.
Zone 8 US, 9? Can.

Azara *Flacourtiaceae*

A genus of about 10 species of evergreen shrubs or small trees from Chile and Argentina. At the limit of their range, they must be grown in a sheltered location. They have accessory leaves at the bases of the true leaves, giving them an unusual "herringbone" appearance. The orange-yellow, fragrant flowers are made up mostly of stamens.

***A. integrifolia* 'Variegata'** The (nonvariegated) species is quite tall and has oval leaves; in this form the leaves are smaller and rounder and prettily variegated in pink and cream. Yellow spikes of flowers are borne in spring. Raised at Kew c. 1870.
Zone 8 US, 9? Can.

A. lanceolata A medium-sized or large shrub with attractive bright green leaves and small, fragrant, mustard yellow flowers from mid- to late spring. Chile, Argentina. Introduced 1926 by Harold Comber.
Zone 8 US, 9? Can.

A. microphylla An elegant small tree with large sprays of dainty foliage and yellow, vanilla-scented flowers that appear on the undersides of the twigs in early spring. The hardiest species. Chile, Argentina. Introduced 1861 by Richard Pearce.
Zone 8 US, 9? Can. 🏆

***A. m.* 'Variegata'** The leaves of this small tree are margined with cream. It is notably slow growing. In cultivation 1916.
Zone 8 US, 9 Can.

Azara serrata

A. serrata A large shrub of upright habit that is most suitable for a wall or sheltered site and has particularly distinctive oval, shiny, serrate leaves and conspicuous clusters of attractive orange-yellow flowers in midsummer. Small white berries are produced in hot summers. Hardier than most other species. Chile.
Zone 8 US, 9 Can.

Azara microphylla

B

Baccharis *Compositae*

A genus of 350 evergreen and deciduous species in all, consisting of small trees, shrubs, and herbaceous plants from North and South America. Their flowers are held in small heads, and the following is a fast-growing shrub for any soil. It is resistant to salt spray.

B. patagonica A medium-sized deciduous shrub with red shoots and short, stalkless, evergreen, glossy, dark green leaves. The flower heads are yellowish white and appear singly in the upper leaf axils in late spring. Patagonia.
Zone 8 US, 9? Can.

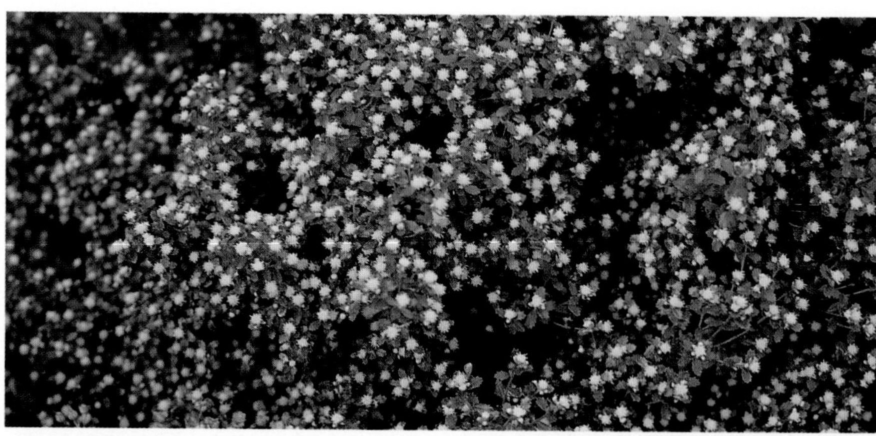

Baccharis patagonica

Ballota *Labiatae*

A genus of about 35 species of herbaceous perennials and deciduous subshrubs, mainly from the Mediterranean region and western Asia. The following requires a sunny, well-drained position but is otherwise tolerant of poor soils.

B. pseudodictamnus A dwarf subshrub for a sunny, well-drained position. The whole plant, including the rounded, slightly heart-shaped leaves, is covered with a dense, grayish white wool, and it is an effective foliage plant, particularly if pruned back each spring. An excellent addition to gray color schemes, with lilac-pink flowers in midsummer. Mediterranean region.
Zone 8 US, 9? Can. 🏆

Ballota pseudodictamnus

Berberidopsis *Flacourtiaceae*

A genus of one species that requires an open or sandy, loamy, preferably acid or neutral, moist soil and a sheltered position in shade. It may scorch badly in windy locations.

Berberidopsis corallina

B. corallina (Coral plant) A beautiful, medium-sized, evergreen plant with climbing stems. The leaves are thick and leathery, set with spiny teeth, and the flowers are deep crimson, quite small, but strikingly eye-catching. They are borne singly on slender stalks or in dangling clusters in late summer. Chile. Introduced 1862.
Zone 8 US, 9? Can.

Berberis

Berberidaceae Barberry

Berberis georgei

BERBERIS is a very large genus of shrubs — about 450 species and as many cultivars and hybrids — that are often referred to as barberries. The derivation of the name is uncertain but is probably related to the fact that most plants bear barblike spines, usually in threes.

It is not only the spines that make barberries highly distinctive plants but also their foliage, which is often spiny in a holly-like way and in many cases covered with a waxy, powdery bloom. Their flowers vary from pale yellow to orange and appear during spring.

There are evergreen and deciduous barberries; the latter contribute greatly to the fall color scene in the garden, while the former are a major asset during winter. Then, too, the conspicuous and often showy crops of berries help make these plants indispensable for anyone who wants to make the garden attractive year-round. The berries of deciduous plants are usually red, while those of the evergreens are predominantly blue-black.

Barberries vary from quite large shrubs, such as the 10 ft (3 m) tall *B. julianae,* to dwarf ones, such as the dense, compact *B.* × *stenophylla* 'Corallina Compacta', which is compact enough for a small rock garden or even a large trough. The majority, however, are of medium size, often building up to impenetrable barriers that can serve as hedges.

Once you have looked closely at the flowers of a barberry, you will always be able to recognize them again. They have a button-like appearance, with their parts in multiples of three — six stamens, six petals, and six or nine sepals. If the base of a stamen is touched with the point of a pin, it and its fellows will bend sharply inward toward the pistil — the reaction to the sharp proboscis of pollinating insects. The flowers are sometimes borne singly but are often carried in conspicuous clusters (racemes).

Care and cultivation

Barberries are not difficult to grow. The deciduous ones perform better in sun, where fall color in both leaf and berries is produced to best effect, while the evergreens prefer the dappled shade of trees. There is no hard-and-fast rule about this, but some shade is beneficial in areas with hot summers. In nature their role is as "pioneer" plants, and as a result they will thrive in most soils, even dry, thin ones. However, they will not tolerate soggy soil — good drainage is as important for them as it is for most shrubs.

Few shrubs are so little affected by atmospheric pollution as barberries are, and they are therefore sometimes used as barriers on highway medians. They will grow and flower successfully in the most heavily industrialized areas, and their spines provide some discouragement to intruders.

Some barberries are the alternate host of a rust disease that attacks wheat. In some areas of the United States and in Canada, it is illegal to grow them at all, or the available species are restricted to those that do not carry the disease.

Berberis *Berberidaceae*
Barberry

B.* × *antoniana *(B. buxifolia × B. darwinii)* The dark green leaves of this small, rounded, evergreen bush are almost spineless, and it is most attractive when bearing its single, long-stalked, deep yellow flowers and dark, purplish berries. Arose at Daisy Hill Nursery, Northern Ireland.
Zone 6 US, 7 Can.

Berberis 'Bountiful'

***B.* 'Bountiful'** A small, spreading, deciduous bush that is very decorative in fall, when it is laden with clusters of coral-red berries on arching branches. Pale yellow flowers are borne in late spring or early summer.
Zone 6 US, 7 Can.

B.* × *bristolensis *(B. calliantha × B. verruculosa)* A small, densely rounded, evergreen shrub with small prickly leaves that are glossy dark green on the upper sides and bloomy white beneath. Yellow flowers are borne in late spring. It makes an excellent dwarf hedge if clipped. Garden origin.
Zone 6 US, 7 Can.

Berberis 'Buccaneer'

***B.* 'Buccaneer'** An erect-branched, small, deciduous shrub notable for the large size of its deep red berries, which are carried in large clusters and last until early winter. It has good fall color.
Zone 6 US, 7 Can.

Berberis buxifolia 'Nana'

***B. buxifolia* 'Nana'** A slow-growing, dense, evergreen mound about 20 in (50 cm) high, with rounded leaves and virtually thornless. It rarely flowers. In cultivation 1867.
Zone 4 US, 5b Can.

B. cabrerae A large deciduous shrub remarkable for the large size of its flowers, which are yellow and pale orange. The berries are black. Some plants grown as *B. montana* really belong to this species. Argentinian Andes. Introduced 1925–27 by Harold Comber.
Zone 6 US, 7 Can.

B. calliantha A small evergreen shrub with crimson young stems and small holly-like leaves that are waxy-white beneath. It bears its pale yellow, comparatively large flowers either singly or in pairs in late spring, followed by blue-black fruits. SE Tibet. Introduced 1924 by Frank Kingdon-Ward.
Zone 7 US, 8b Can. 🏆

B. candidula A small, dense, dome-shaped, evergreen bush, with small, shining, dark green leaves that are silvery white beneath. The flowers are single and bright yellow. W China. Introduced 1895 by Père Farges.
Zone 5 US, 6b Can.

Berberis darwinii

B. darwinii This early-flowering, medium-sized, evergreen species is one of the finest of all flowering shrubs. Its leaves are three-pointed with shining, dark green upper sides, and its flowers are bright orange tinged with red, borne in drooping clusters over a long period in spring. Chile, Argentina. Discovered 1835 by Charles Darwin on the voyage of the *Beagle*. Introduced 1849 by William Lobb.
Zone 7 US, 7 Can. 🏆

Berberis dictyophylla

B. dictyophylla, syn. *B. dictyophylla* 'Albicaulis' A graceful deciduous shrub up to about 6 ft (2 m) with good fall color. The young stems are red and covered with a white bloom, and the leaves are chalk white underneath. Solitary pale yellow flowers are borne in late spring. The large, solitary, red berries are also covered with a white bloom. W China. Introduced 1916.
Zone 6 US, 6b Can. 🏆

***B. d.* 'Albicaulis'** See *B. dictyophylla.*

B.* ×*frikartii *(B. candidula × B. verruculosa)* A small evergreen shrub of dense habit with angled shoots and glossy, dark green, spiny leaves that are waxy white beneath. The relatively large, pale yellow flowers are borne singly or in pairs and are followed by blue-black berries. It is available in the following clones.
Zone 4 US, 5 Can.

Berberis × frikartii 'Amstelveen'

***B.* ×*f.* 'Amstelveen'** A small, dense, evergreen shrub with attractively drooping shoots and glossy green leaves that are white on their lower surfaces. Raised c. 1960 in Holland.
Zone 4 US, 5 Can. 🏆

Berberis × frikartii 'Telstar'

***B.* ×*f.* 'Telstar'** Similar to 'Amstelveen' but taller, growing up to 4 ft (1.2 m). At the same time, however, it is more compact in habit. Raised c. 1960 in Holland.
Zone 4 US, 5 Can. 🏆

B. gagnepainii (Black barberry) A small evergreen shrub that makes a dense thicket of erect stems, closely set with narrow leaves with undulating margins. The yellow flowers are borne in clusters of between 6 and 12 and are followed by black berries covered in a blue bloom. Suitable for making an impenetrable hedge. W China. Introduced c. 1904 by Ernest Wilson.
Zone 6 US, 7 Can.

Berberis georgei

B. georgei A rare and attractive deciduous shrub of medium height, with arching branches. It flowers in late spring, with yellow blooms borne in hanging, red-stalked clusters. The toothed leaves color well in fall, when the profusion of crimson berries in large, pendulous clusters are at their showiest. Origin uncertain.
Zone 6 US, 7 Can.

***B.* 'Goldilocks'** *(B. darwinii × B. valdiviana)* A large, vigorous, evergreen shrub with upright but arching branches and spiny, glossy, dark green leaves. The deep golden yellow flowers are profusely borne in hanging, red-stalked clusters over a long period in spring. Raised 1978 by the Hillier Nurseries' propagator Peter Dummer.
Zone 7 US, 7 Can. 🏆

B. hypokerina An outstanding small, evergreen shrub that forms a thicket of purple stems, with hollylike leaves as much as 4 in (10 cm) long with silvery white undersides. Yellow flowers are borne in clusters in midsummer. Its berries are dark blue and have a white bloom. This species does not thrive in shallow, alkaline soils. It is unfortunately not as hardy as most of the other barberries. Upper Burma. Discovered and introduced 1926 by the plant hunter Frank Kingdon-Ward.
Zone 8 US, 9? Can.

***B.* × *interposita* 'Wallich's Purple'** A small, dense, evergreen bush with arching shoots. Its leaves are bronze-red when young and turn glossy green later. Their undersides are tinted with blue.
Zone 6 US, 7 Can.

B.* × *irwinii See *B.* × *stenophylla* 'Irwinii'.

Berberis stenophylla 'Corallina Compacta'

***B.* × *i.* 'Corallina Compacta'** See *B.* × *stenophylla* 'Corallina Compacta'.

B. julianae (Wintergreen barberry) A dense, evergreen shrub growing up to 10 ft (3 m) tall with strong, spiny stems and clusters of stiff, narrow, spine-toothed leaves that are copper tinted when young. The yellow flowers, which are slightly scented, are borne in dense clusters of as many as 15. A good screening or hedge plant. China. Introduced 1900 by Ernest Wilson.
Zone 5 US, 6 Can.

Berberis linearifolia 'Jewel'

B. linearifolia An erect, medium-sized, evergreen shrub with a rather ungainly habit of growth and narrow, glossy, dark green, spine-tipped leaves. The orange-red flowers are produced early in spring and sometimes again in fall and are the most vividly colored in the genus. It is available in the following clones. Argentina, Chile. Introduced 1927 by Harold Comber.

Zone 6 US, 7 Can.

***B. l.* 'Jewel'** A splendid medium-sized shrub and possibly the best barberry of all for flowers, which are larger than average, scarlet in bud, and bright orange when open. In cultivation 1937. *(Photo on p.157.)*

Zone 6 US, 7 Can.

Berberis linearifolia 'Orange King'

***B. l.* 'Orange King'** A medium-sized shrub with bright orange flowers larger than those of the species.

Zone 6 US, 7 Can.

B.* × *lologensis *(B. darwinii × B. linearifolia)* A very beautiful, medium-sized, evergreen shrub that is the offspring of two superb species. Its leaves are variable in shape, with entire and spiny ones on the same bush. A natural hybrid found 1927 with the parents near Lake Lolog, Argentina, by Harold Comber. It is available in the following clones.

Zone 6 US, 7 Can.

Berberis × *lologensis* 'Apricot Queen'

Berberis × *lologensis*

***B.* × *l.* 'Apricot Queen'** This broadly upright shrub bears a profusion of pale orange flowers.

Zone 6 US, 7 Can. 🏆

***B.* × *l.* 'Mystery Fire'** A vigorous, upright shrub that bears a profusion of deep orange flowers.

Zone 6 US, 7 Can.

***B.* × *l.* 'Stapehill'** A free-flowering shrub with rich orange flowers.

Zone 6 US, 7 Can.

B.* × *media *(B. × chenaultii × B. thunbergii)* An evergreen hybrid, represented in gardens by the following forms.

Zone 5 US, 6b Can.

***B.* × *m.* 'Parkjuweel'** A small, dense, prickly shrub with leaves that are widest above the middle and almost spineless. They color richly in fall, occasionally remaining until the following spring. The yellow flowers are single or borne in clusters of 2–4 in late spring. Garden origin c. 1956 in Holland.

Berberis × *media* 'Parkjuweel'

Zone 5 US, 6b Can. 🏆

***B.* × *m.* 'Red Jewel'** A small, dense shrub

similar to 'Parkjuweel', of which it is a sport, but with somewhat broader leaves that become a deep, metallic purple.
Zone 5 US, 6b Can. 🏆

***B.* × *ottawensis* 'Purpurea'** See *B.* × *o.* 'Superba'.

Berberis × *ottawensis* 'Superba'

***B.* × *o.* 'Superba'**, syn. *B.* × *o.* 'Purpurea' A vigorous, medium-sized to large deciduous shrub and a first-class plant with rich wine-purple foliage, yellow flowers borne in late spring, and red berries.
Zone 4 US, 5 Can. 🏆

B. panlanensis See *B. sanguinea* 'Panlanensis'.

***B.* 'Pirate King'** A small, dense but vigorous shrub with yellow flowers and fiery orange-red berries.
Zone 6 US, 7 Can.

Berberis 'Rubrostilla'

***B.* 'Rubrostilla'** A beautiful, small, deciduous shrub that is very showy in late fall when it bears oblong, coral-red berries that are among the largest in the genus. Pale yellow flowers are borne in racemes $1^1/_2$ in (3 cm) long in late spring or early summer. Possibly a hybrid of *B. wilsoniae*. Garden origin.
Zone 6 US, 7 Can. 🏆

***B. sanguinea* 'Panlanensis'**, syn. *B. panlanensis* This is the form of the species that is usually grown. An excellent hedge plant, it is a charming, medium-sized, compact, evergreen shrub of very neat growth. Its leaves are linear, spine toothed, gray-green above, and olive green beneath. W China. Introduced 1908.
Zone 6 US, 7 Can.

B. sargentiana (Sargent barberry) This medium-sized species grows up to 6 ft (2 m) tall, with leathery, evergreen, net-veined leaves up to 5 in (13 cm) long. It has yellow flowers and blue-black berries. W China. Introduced 1907 by Ernest Wilson.
Zone 6 US, 7 Can.

B. sieboldii A small, compact, suckering, deciduous shrub with oval leaves that color richly in fall. The clusters of pale yellow flowers are followed by round, shiny, orange berries. Japan. Introduced 1892.
Zone 5 US, 6b Can.

B.* × *stenophylla *(B. darwinii* × *B. empetrifolia)* An indispensable evergreen bush that ultimately becomes a graceful, medium-sized shrub. In midspring its long, arching branches are wreathed with yellow flowers. In cultivation 1860.
Zone 5 US, 6b Can. 🏆

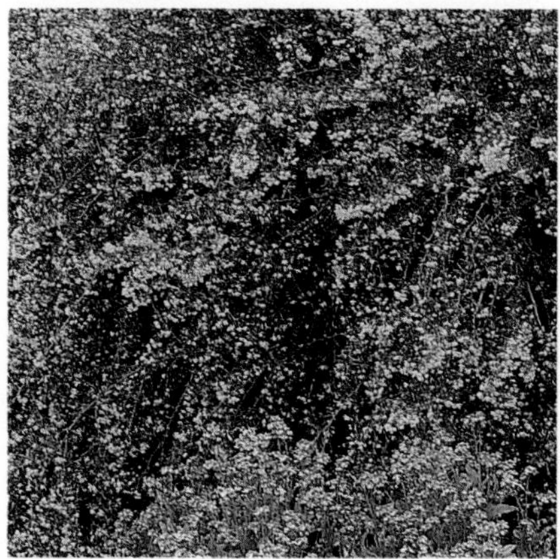

Berberis × *stenophylla* 'Claret Cascade'

***B.* × *s.* 'Claret Cascade'** A medium-sized shrub with rich orange flowers flushed with red on the outside and foliage tinged purple. It makes a striking display.
Zone 5 US, 6b Can.

***B.* × *s.* 'Corallina Compacta'**, syn. *B.* × *irwinii* 'Corallina Compacta' A dwarf shrub suitable for a rock garden and seldom exceeding 12 in (30 cm) in height. The buds are coral-red and open to yellow. In cultivation 1930. *(Photo on p.157.)*
Zone 5 US, 6b Can. 🏆

Berberis × *stenophylla* 'Crawley Gem'

***B.* × *s.* 'Crawley Gem'** A small shrub forming a dense mound of arching stems that are covered in spring with red-tipped buds that open to orange flowers. In cultivation 1930.
Zone 5 US, 6b Can.

***B.* × *s.* 'Cream Showers'** An unusual but garden-worthy medium-sized shrub with creamy white flowers.
Zone 5 US, 6b Can.

***B.* × *s.* 'Irwinii'**, syn. *B.* × *irwinii* A small, compact shrub with deep yellow flowers. In cultivation 1903.
Zone 5 US, 6b Can.

B. temolaica One of the most striking of the barberries, this is a vigorous deciduous shrub up to 10 ft (3 m) tall, with stout, erectly spreading branches. The young shoots and leaves are conspicuously glaucous, the shoots becoming a dark, bloomy purple-brown with age and the leaves having bloomy-green upper sides and strikingly white undersides. Pale yellow flowers are borne in late spring or early summer. The red berries are egg shaped and covered with bloom. SE Tibet. Introduced

Berberis thunbergii

1924 by Frank Kingdon-Ward.
Zone 5 US, 6b Can.

B. thunbergii (Japanese barberry) An invaluable small deciduous shrub of dense, compact habit, unsurpassed for its brilliant fall foliage and bright red berries. Small, pale yellow flowers tinged with red in mid- or late spring. Japan. Introduced c. 1864.
Zone 4 US, 4b Can. 🏆

***B. t.* 'Atropurpurea'** A small shrub that has rich reddish purple foliage in spring, summer, and fall; the color increases in intensity as winter approaches. In cultivation 1913.
Zone 4 US, 4b Can.

Berberis thunbergii 'Atropurpurea Nana'

***B. t.* 'Atropurpurea Nana'**, syn. *B. t.* 'Crimson Pygmy' A mounding dwarf form that is suitable for a rock garden and makes a fine, purple-foliaged hedge up to 2 ft (60 cm) tall. Raised 1942 in Holland.
Zone 4 US, 4b Can. 🏆

Berberis thunbergii 'Aurea'

***B. t.* 'Aurea'** A small shrub with bright yellow leaves that become pale green by late summer. It tends to burn in sun and does best in a moist atmosphere. In cultivation 1950.
Zone 4 US, 4b Can.

***B. t.* 'Bagatelle'** (*B. t.* 'Atropurpurea Nana' × *B. t.* 'Kobold') This cultivar is similar to *B. t.* 'Atropurpurea Nana' but is much more compact. Raised 1971 in Holland.
Zone 4 US, 4b Can. 🏆

***B. t.* 'Crimson Pygmy'** See *B. t.* 'Atropurpurea Nana'.

Berberis thunbergii 'Atropurpurea'

Berberis thunbergii 'Dart's Red Lady'

***B. t.* 'Dart's Red Lady'** A small shrub with very deep purple leaves that turn brilliant red in fall.
Zone 4 US, 4b Can.

Berberis thunbergii 'Golden Ring'

***B. t.* 'Erecta'** A small, compact, fastigiate shrub that forms a close clump and has superb fall colors. It is good as a low hedge but tends to fall open with age.

Zone 4 US, 4b Can.

***B. t.* 'Golden Ring'** The leaves of this small shrub are reddish purple with a narrow gold margin. Similar variegations can be produced by sowing seed of forms of *B. t.* 'Atropurpurea'. In cultivation 1950.

Zone 4 US, 4b Can.

***B. t.* 'Harlequin'** A small shrub similar to 'Rose Glow' but with smaller leaves heavily mottled with pink. In cultivation 1969.

Zone 4 US, 4b Can.

***B. t.* 'Helmond Pillar'** A narrow, upright, small shrub with rich purple foliage.

Zone 4 US, 4b Can.

Berberis thunbergii 'Harlequin'

Berberis thunbergii 'Helmond Pillar'

Berberis thunbergii 'Kelleriis'

***B. t.* 'Kelleriis'** A compact, spreading, small bush with leaves that are mottled with creamy white. In the fall the white portion of the leaf turns through shades of pink to a rich, deep crimson. Raised in Denmark.

Zone 4 US, 4b Can.

***B. t.* 'Kobold'** A free-fruiting, dwarf form with a very dense, rounded habit. Raised c. 1960 in Holland.

Zone 4 US, 4b Can.

***B. t.* 'Pink Queen'** A small shrub that is the best pink-variegated form, with reddish leaves heavily flecked with gray and white. Raised before 1958 in Holland.

Zone 4 US, 4b Can.

Berberis thunbergii 'Red Chief'

***B. t.* 'Red Chief'** A small, upright shrub with branches that arch as it gets older. Its stems are bright red and its narrow leaves deep red. Selected 1942 in Holland.

Zone 4 US, 4b Can. 🏆

***B. t.* 'Red Pillar'** A most attractive form of

Berberis thunbergii 'Red Pillar'

'Erecta'. It, too, falls open as it ages.
Zone 4 US, 4b Can.

Berberis thunbergii 'Rose Glow'

***B. t.* 'Rose Glow'** A small, very striking, colorful shrub. The leaves of the young shoots are purple, mottled with silver, pink, and bright rose, later becoming purple. Selected in Holland c. 1957.
Zone 4 US, 4b Can. 🏆

***B. t.* 'Silver Beauty'** This form is similar to *B. t.* 'Kelleriis', but it is somewhat less vigorous.
Zone 4 US, 4b Can.

B. tsangpoensis An interesting deciduous species that forms a dwarf, wide-spreading mound with slender, yellow stems often extending for a considerable distance along the ground. Deep yellow flowers are borne in clusters in late spring. It has attractive fall color and red berries. SE Tibet. Introduced 1925.
Zone 6 US, 7 Can.

B. valdiviana This large, stately, evergreen species is like a smooth-leaved holly and has distinctive large, leathery, polished, almost spineless leaves. Its flowers are saffron yellow and borne in long, drooping clusters. This is a first-class hardy shrub that deserves wider planting, but it is scarce because it is difficult to propagate. Chile. Introduced 1902.
Zone 8 US, 9? Can.

Berberis valdiviana

B. veitchii An evergreen shrub up to about $6\frac{1}{2}$ ft (2 m) tall with long, lance-shaped, spine-toothed leaves and red young shoots. The flowers are bronze-yellow, long stalked, and borne in axillary clusters of up to eight. The berries are black. C China. Introduced 1900 by Ernest Wilson.
Zone 6 US, 6b Can.

B. verruculosa (Warty barberry) A compact, slow-growing, evergreen shrub, about 5–$6\frac{1}{2}$ ft (1.5–2 m) tall, with rough, minutely warty, drooping stems densely covered with small, glossy, dark green leaves that are white beneath. The flowers are usually solitary and golden yellow. China. Introduced 1904 by Ernest Wilson.
Zone 6 US, 7 Can. 🏆

B. wilsoniae A splendid small deciduous shrub that forms dense mounds of thorny stems. The leaves are small and sea green and turn attractive shades in fall that blend with the coral of the fruit clusters. The true plant can be perpetuated only by seed obtained from the wild or by cuttings. W

Berberis wilsoniae

China. Introduced c. 1904 by Ernest Wilson and named after his wife.
Zone 6 US, 6b Can. 🏆

B. yunnanensis An attractive, medium-sized, rounded deciduous shrub with comparatively large, golden yellow flowers, brilliant fall colors, and bright red berries. W China. Introduced 1885 by Delavay.
Zone 6 US, 7 Can.

Beschorneria *Agavaceae*

A genus of about 10 evergreen shrubs and perennials that are related to Agave *and are natives of Mexico.*

Beschorneria yuccoides

B. yuccoides A striking, yuccalike plant that is not strictly a shrub but an evergreen perennial with a semiwoody stem. The flower stems reach about 6½ ft (2 m) in height and carry drooping racemes of bright green flowers with red bracts in mid- or late summer. This remarkable plant flourished in Hillier's Winchester nursery in alkaline soil at the foot of a south-facing wall for more than 20 years. Requires full sun and a well-drained location. Mexico. Introduced before 1859.
Zone 9 US 🏆

Betula *Betulaceae*
Birch

A genus of about 60 deciduous species, some of which are among the most beautiful garden trees. Birches are grown for their graceful habit, the lightness of their foliage, and their often singularly decorative bark, which can be stark white or may peel attractively. Their flowers consist of male and female catkins borne on the same tree; the males are pendulous and elongate in spring, while the females are shorter and erect. Many birches display bright yellow fall color. They perform best in moist, well-drained soil and are susceptible to insect pests, such as borers and miners, in exceptionally dry conditions.

B. alba See *B. pendula, B. pubescens.*

Betula albo-sinensis

B. albo-sinensis (Chinese red birch) A beautiful, medium-sized species with glossy, green leaves on slightly rough shoots. The attractive, peeling bark is pinkish to coppery red and cream when first exposed. W China. Introduced 1901 by Ernest Wilson.
Zone 5 US, 6b Can. 🏆

Betula albo-sinensis var. septentrionalis

B. a.* var. *septentrionalis This splendid medium-sized variety has strikingly gray-pink bark that is coppery pink on the main branches. Its leaves are matte rather than glossy. Introduced 1908 by Ernest Wilson.
Zone 5 US, 6b Can. 🏆

B. alleghaniensis, syn. *B. lutea* (Yellow birch) A medium-sized tree with smooth, shining, amber-colored or golden brown bark that peels attractively. Its downy leaves are oblong and broadest above the middle and turn rich yellow in fall. E North America. Introduced c. 1767.
Zone 3 US, 3b Can.

Betula costata

B. costata The true *B. costata* is rare in cultivation, and plants grown under this name are sometimes a form of *B. ermanii*, as described below.
Zone 6 US, 7 Can.

Betula ermanii

B. ermanii (Gold birch) A graceful, vigorous, large tree with rough shoots and bright green, often heart-shaped leaves with conspicuous veining. The bark is creamy white and pinkish, and fawn when first exposed

Bark of *Betula ermanii*

by peeling. It has many lenticels (raised pores on the surface) that are pale brown on the trunk and brown to red-brown on the branches. NE Asia.

Zone 4 US, 5 Can.

Betula ermanii 'Grayswood Hill'

***B. e.* 'Grayswood Hill'** A particularly fine form, and the tree usually offered as *B. costata.*

Zone 5 US, 6 Can. 🏆

***B.* 'Fetisowii'** A hybrid forming a graceful, medium-sized, narrow-headed tree notable for its peeling, chalk white bark that extends up the trunk to the branches. Plants grown under this name are probably seedlings of the original. C Asia.

Zone 6? US, 7? Can.

B. jacquemontii See *B. utilis* var. *jacquemontii.*

B. lenta (Sweet birch) This tree can grow to 80 ft (25 m) tall in native stands, but the tallest in cultivation tend to be around 46 ft (14 m). Its trunk is smooth, dark, and reddish brown or purple. The bark does not

Betula lenta

peel and, when young, is sweetly aromatic. The leaves turn rich yellow in fall. E North America. Introduced 1759.

Zone 3 US, 4 Can.

B. lutea See *B. alleghaniensis.*

B. mandshurica* var. *szechuanica See *B. szechuanica.*

Betula maximowicziana

B. maximowicziana (Monarch birch) This form has the largest leaves of all the birches and is a fast-growing, wide-headed tree of medium height except in its native habitat, where it is taller. Its trunk is orange-brown, becoming gray and pinkish but coppery on the branches and peeling in narrow strips. The leaves are heart shaped and up to 6 in (15 cm) long; they turn a lovely shade of butter yellow in fall. Japan. Introduced 1893.

Zone 5 US, 6b Can.

Betula medwedewii

B. medwedewii A large shrub or small, shrubby tree with stout, erect branches. It can be distinguished from other birches by its large terminal buds and particularly by its fine fall foliage, whereby the large, corrugated leaves turn bright yellow. Caucasus, NW Iran, NE Turkey. Introduced 1897.

Zone 5 US, 6 Can. 🏆

Betula nana

B. nana (Dwarf birch) A dwarf or small shrub, 20 in–3 ft (0.5–1 m) high, with tiny, rounded leaves. Subarctic Europe (includ-

ing some mountains of Scotland and N England), Asia, Greenland.
Zone 2 US, 1 Can.

Betula nigra

B. nigra (River birch, red birch) A beautiful, fast-growing, medium-sized tree, remarkable for its shaggy, pinkish orange bark that becomes brown and ridged on old trees. As its common name suggests, it is one of the finest trees for planting on damp sites. The soft green, diamond-shaped leaves are covered on their undersides with a bluish bloom. C and E United States. Introduced 1736 by Peter Collinson.
Zone 3 US, 3 Can. 🏆

Betula papyrifera

***B. n.* 'Heritage'** A form that is more tolerant of dry soil and shows resistance to leaf miners and borers.
Zone 3 US, 3 Can.

B. papyrifera (Paper birch, canoe birch) A striking large tree with white, papery bark and yellow fall foliage. North

Betula pendula

America. Introduced 1750.
Zone 2 US, 2 Can.

B. pendula, syn. *B. alba, B. verrucosa* (European white birch) Often described as "the lady of the woods," this is a medium-sized, white-stemmed tree that thrives on drier soils than *B. pubescens* (white birch), from which it is distinguished by its rough, warty shoots and sharply cut, diamond-shaped leaves. Its young twigs are generally pendulous, as opposed to those of *B. pubescens,* and unlike that species, old specimens develop rough, black bark at the base. N Asia, Europe.
Zone 2 US, 2 Can. 🏆

***B. p.* 'Dalecarlica'** (Swedish birch) A tall, slender, graceful tree with drooping branches and prettily cut leaves. The plant commonly grown under this name should correctly be known as 'Crispa' or 'Laciniata'. The true plant is rare and differs in that its leaves are more deeply cut and its branches are not as weeping. Discovered 1767 in Sweden.
Zone 2 US, 2 Can. 🏆

***B. p.* 'Fastigiata'** An erect form of medium size and rather stiff habit. 'Obelisk' is similar but perhaps does not become as wide. In cultivation 1870.
Zone 2 US, 2 Can.

***B. p.* 'Golden Cloud'** A small tree with yellow leaves that tends to burn badly and suffer from leaf miners, which cause premature leaf loss.
Zone 3 US, 3b Can.

***B. p.* 'Purpurea'** (European purple-leaf birch) A slow-growing small tree with purple leaves, drooping branches, and a rather

Betula pendula 'Tristis'

weak constitution. In cultivation 1872.
Zone 2 US, 2 Can.

***B. p.* 'Tristis'** A tall, graceful tree of outstanding merit, with slender, pendulous branches forming a symmetrical head. In cultivation 1867.
Zone 2 US, 2 Can. 🏆

***B. p.* 'Youngii'** (Young's weeping birch)

Betula pendula 'Youngii'

This form ultimately becomes a beautiful, small, dome- or mushroom-headed, weeping tree, as wide as it is tall.
Zone 2 US, 2 Can. 🏆

Betula pubescens

B. pubescens (White birch) A medium-sized tree that thrives in a variety of soils but prefers damp places. It is distinguished from *B. pendula* by its less weeping, more upright habit; smooth, downy shoots; more rounded leaves; and bark that is white to the base with dark lenticels. The twigs are generally a rich mahogany brown. N Europe, N Asia.
Zone 2 US, 2 Can.

Betula szechuanica

B. szechuanica A vigorous, medium-sized tree with glossy, blue-green leaves and chalk white, peeling bark. W China, SE Tibet. Introduced 1908 by Ernest Wilson.
Zone 6 US, 7b Can.

***B.* 'Trost's Dwarf'** A small shrub with slender, arching branches and small, finely cut leaves. Although superficially attractive, it is a weak grower and susceptible to birch leaf miner.
Zone 2 US, 3 Can.

Betula utilis var. *jacquemontii* in summer

B. utilis (Himalayan birch) In its typical form this is an attractive, medium-sized tree with orange-brown or dark, coppery brown, peeling bark, often bloomed gray-pink. However, the most-sought-after forms are those with white barks, which are among the most beautiful of all the birches. SW China to Nepal. Introduced 1849 by Sir Joseph Hooker.
Zone 3 US, 3b Can.

Betula utilis var. *jacquemontii* in winter

B. u.* var. *jacquemontii This medium-sized tree differs from the typical form in its

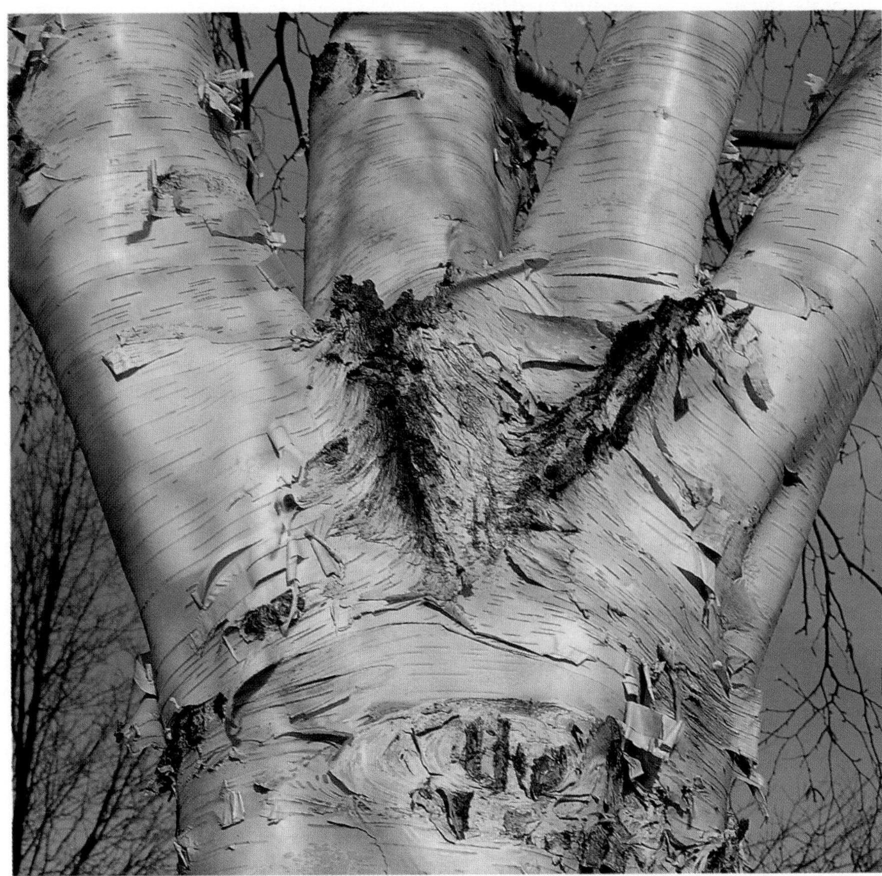
Betula utilis var. *jacquemontii* 'Jermyns'

white bark. However, contrary to popular belief, it is not the one that is most usually grown, although the best forms are too often grown under its name.
Zone 4 US, 4b Can.

***B. u.* var. *j.* 'Doorenbos'** The medium-sized Dutch clone that is readily available as *B. jacquemontii.* The striking white, peeling bark is pale orange when freshly exposed.
Zone 4? US, 4b? Can. 🏆

***B. u.* var. *j.* 'Jermyns'** A very vigorous form, making a medium-sized, broadly conical tree, whose very fine white bark is retained into maturity. Its catkins are showy and up to 7 in (17 cm) in length. Selected at Hillier Nurseries from plants received from Belgium, it had reached 46 ft (14 m) in the Hillier Gardens and Arboretum by 1990.
Zone 4? US, 4b? Can. 🏆

Betula utilis var. *jacquemontii* 'Silver Shadow'

***B. u.* var. *j.* 'Silver Shadow'** One of the loveliest birches, with dazzlingly white stems. It is a very distinct form of *B. utilis* var. *jacquemontii* and grows into a small to medium-sized tree whose large, drooping, dark green leaves contrast dramatically with its unmarked, pure white bark. The original tree grew for many years at Hillier West Hill Nurseries in Winchester, England and was previously distributed as *B. jacquemontii.*
Zone 4? US, 4b? Can. 🏆

B. verrucosa See *B. pendula.*

Bignonia *Bignoniaceae*

This is now a genus of one evergreen or semievergreen species.

B. capreolata (Crossvine) A large, vigorous plant that climbs with twining leaf tendrils. Each leaf consists of two fairly slender leaflets up to 5 in (13 cm) long. The tubular flowers, about 2 in (5 cm) long, are orange-red, paler within, and form in clusters in early summer. It is a rampant climber that will cover a fence or trellis or climb into a tree. The tendrils are tipped with small cups that can cling to masonry walls. SE United States. In cultivation 1653.
Zone 6 US, 7 Can.

Billardiera *Pittosporaceae*

A genus of about eight species of low-growing, evergreen, twining plants from Australia. The following is suitable for a warm, sunny location in milder areas and makes an unusual greenhouse plant.

Billardiera longiflora

B. longiflora A slender climber up to 6 ft (2 m) high. It has lance-shaped leaves and solitary, bell-shaped flowers that hang from slender stalks in summer and fall. Blossoms are greenish yellow, ¾ in (2 cm) long, and are followed by brilliantly deep blue, oblong fruits up to 1 in (2.5 cm) long. Tasmania. Introduced 1810.
Zone 8 US, 9? Can.

Broussonetia *Moraceae*

A genus of seven or eight species of deciduous shrubs and trees from eastern Asia and Polynesia. The male flowers are in catkinlike spikes, while the female ones are in round heads. They grow in any ordinary soil and withstand city pollution well.

B. papyrifera (Paper mulberry) A large shrub or small tree with unusually and variably lobed hairy leaves. The male and female flowers borne in early summer are on the same tree, the males in catkins and the females in round heads that give rise to the decorative, orange-red fruits. In Japan, paper is made from its bark. It will grow in soils that are quite poor but prefers a well-drained, warm, sunny site. E Asia, naturalized in the United States. Introduced early 18th century.
Zone 6 US, 7b Can.

Bruckenthalia *Ericaceae*

A genus of only one evergreen species, related to Erica *and requiring acid soil.*

B. spiculifolia (Spike heath) A dwarf, heathlike plant up to 10 in (25 cm) high, with terminal clusters of rose-pink, bell-shaped flowers in early summer. E Europe, Asia Minor. Introduced 1888.
Zone 4 US, 5 Can.

Brugmansia *Solanaceae*
Angel's trumpet

A genus of five species of highly attractive deciduous shrubs and trees native to South America, particularly the Andes. They have large, hanging, trumpet-shaped flowers and were previously included in Datura, *which is now restricted to annual species with upright flowers. They require a light, fertile soil that is moisture-retentive and can be grown outdoors only in regions that are virtually frost-free, but they are well suited*

Brugmansia × *candida* 'Grand Marnier'

to a greenhouse farther north. It is a useful container plant. Harmful if eaten.

B.* × *candida A splendid hybrid with yellow or pink flowers borne from early summer to early fall. The following forms are grown in gardens.
Zone 9 US

***B.* × *c.* 'Grand Marnier'** A large shrub with large, dangling, fragrant, trumpet-shaped flowers in a beautiful peach color, with the lobes ending in long, taillike points. *(Photo on p.167.)*
Zone 9 US

Brugmansia × *candida* 'Knightii'

***B.* × *c.* 'Knightii'** A large shrub with large, hanging, double white flowers.
Zone 9 US

Brugmansia sanguinea

B. sanguinea, syn. *Datura sanguinea* A tree-like shrub up to 10 ft (3 m) tall, or more when it is ideally sited. It has large, softly hairy leaves, toothed on young plants, and large, orange-red trumpets hanging from the branches in late spring and early summer. Colombia to N Chile.
Zone 9 US

Brugmansia suaveolens

B. suaveolens, syn. *Datura suaveolens* A large shrub or small tree whose untoothed leaves have something of the consistency of flannel. The very large, white flowers are pendulous, trumpet shaped, and highly fragrant and are borne from early to late summer. An excellent specimen for the greenhouse. Brazil.
Zone 9 US

Buddleia *Loganiaceae*

A genus of about 100 evergreen and deciduous species occurring in Africa, Asia, and both American continents, many of them being first-rate garden plants that thrive in almost any soil and revel in full sun. Most flower from midsummer to early fall, usually on the current year's wood.

Buddleia alternifolia

With the exception of B. alternifolia, *they are best grown in a shrub or mixed border, rather than as specimen plants. Buddleias are prized mainly for their massed clusters of tubular, nectar-rich, often fragrant flowers that in some species attract butterflies and day-flying moths from miles around. With the single exception of* B. alternifolia, *all have opposite leaves.*

B. alternifolia (Fountain buddleia) A large deciduous shrub or occasionally a small tree with arching branches and long, narrow, dark green leaves. In early summer the branches are wreathed all along their length with dense clusters of lighty fragrant, lilac flowers. China. Introduced 1915.
Zone 4 US, 5 Can.

Buddleia alternifolia 'Argentea'

***B. a.* 'Argentea'** An uncommon medium-sized shrub with leaves covered by closely laid, silky hairs that give them a silvery sheen.
Zone 4 US, 5b Can.

Buddleia asiatica

B. asiatica (Asian buddleia) A large deciduous shrub or small tree with long, lax stems; narrowly lance-shaped, evergreen leaves; and drooping, cylindrical panicles of scented white flowers in winter. E Asia from Nepal to the Philippines. Introduced 1876.
Zone 9 US 🏆

Buddleia auriculata

B. auriculata A medium-sized, open evergreen shrub with white felting on the undersides of the leaves. The strongly fragrant flowers are borne in long, cylindrical panicles and are creamy white with a yellow throat. It flowers in winter and is especially showy when in bloom. Southern Africa, from Zimbabwe to the Cape.
Zone 9 US

Buddleia colvilei 'Kewensis'

***B. colvilei* 'Kewensis'** A vigorous, large, deciduous shrub with outstandingly large, rich red flowers in terminal, drooping panicles in early summer. Although it is tender when young, mature specimens have withstood freezing temperatures at Hillier's West Hill Nursery, Winchester, Hampshire, and survived winters there since 1925. E Himalaya. Introduced 1849.
Zone 8 US, 9 Can.

Buddleia crispa

B. crispa A medium-sized to large deciduous shrub with deeply toothed leaves and stems covered with a dense, white felt. Its fragrant flowers are lilac with an orange throat and produced in terminal panicles in late summer. N India. Introduced 1850.
Zone 8 US, 9 Can.

B. davidii (Butterfly bush) This deciduous species is rather weedy and seeds itself abundantly, but its cultivars are superb medium-sized shrubs. Their fragrant flowers, borne in long racemes from mid- to late summer, are very attractive to but-

Buddleia davidii

Buddleia davidii 'Black Knight'

terflies. They do well in maritime areas and give the best results when pruned hard in early spring. The following are among the best garden selections. China, Japan. Introduced c. 1890.
Zone 4 US, 5b Can.

***B. d.* 'Black Knight'** A medium-sized shrub with long trusses of deep violet flowers. In cultivation 1959. *(Photo on p.169.)*
Zone 4 US, 5b Can. 🏆

***B. d.* 'Dartmoor'** A vigorous medium-sized to large shrub with drooping branches and large, dense, widely branched panicles up to 2 ft (60 cm) long of fragrant magenta flowers. Found 1957 near Yelverton on Dartmoor, Devon, England.
Zone 4 US, 5b Can. 🏆

Buddleia davidii 'Empire Blue'

***B. d.* 'Empire Blue'** A medium-sized shrub with rich violet-blue flowers that have an orange eye. In cultivation 1941.
Zone 4 US, 5b Can. 🏆

***B. d.* 'Fascinating'** A medium-sized shrub with wide, full panicles of vivid lilac-pink flowers. In cultivation 1940.
Zone 4 US, 5b Can.

***B. d.* 'Harlequin'** A sport of 'Royal Red' and lower growing than most. The leaves are brightly variegated with creamy white and the flowers are reddish purple. In cultivation 1964.
Zone 4 US, 5b Can.

***B. d.* 'Île de France'** A medium-sized shrub with long, elegant clusters of rich violet flowers. In cultivation 1930.
Zone 4 US, 5b Can.

***B. d.* 'Masquerade'** Large panicles of scented purple-red flowers. Broad, conspicuous leaves irregularly variegated with bright cream and yellow. Bred at East Malling Research Station, Kent, England.
Zone 4 US, 5b Can.

Buddleia davidii 'White Bouquet'

B. d.* var. *nanhoensis An elegant medium-sized shrub, growing half the size of the species, with slender branches, narrow leaves, and long, narrowly cylindrical panicles of mauve flowers. Found in Kansu Province, China, by Reginald Farrer. Introduced 1914.
Zone 4 US, 5b Can.

Buddleia davidii 'Peace'

***B. d.* 'Nanho Blue'** The pale blue flowers of this medium-sized form are very prone to reversion.
Zone 4 US, 5b Can.

***B. d.* 'Nanho Purple'** A medium-sized form with violet-purple flowers that have an orange center, but it too reverts. In cultivation 1980.
Zone 4 US, 5b Can.

***B. d.* 'Peace'** A form with large panicles of white, orange-eyed flowers. In cultivation 1945.
Zone 4 US, 5b Can.

***B. d.* 'Royal Red'** A medium-sized shrub with massive panicles of red-purple flowers. In cultivation 1941.
Zone 4 US, 5b Can. 🏆

***B. d.* 'White Bouquet'** A medium-sized shrub with large panicles of fragrant, white, yellow-eyed flowers. In cultivation 1942.
Zone 4 US, 5b Can.

Buddleia davidii 'White Cloud'

***B. d.* 'White Cloud'** A medium-sized shrub with pure white flowers borne in large panicles.
Zone 4 US, 5b Can.

***B. d.* 'White Profusion'** A very fine medium-sized shrub with large panicles of pure white, yellow-eyed flowers. In cultivation 1945.
Zone 4 US, 5b Can. 🏆

B. fallowiana A medium-sized to large deciduous shrub whose stems and leaves are white-woolly. Its flowers are very fragrant, pale lavender-blue, and borne in large panicles from mid- to late summer. Requires a sheltered position. N Burma and SW China. In cultivation 1921.
Zone 8 US, 9 Can.

B. f.* var. *alba The flowers of this medium-sized shrub are creamy white with an orange eye.
Zone 8 US, 9 Can. 🏆

B. globosa (Globe butterfly bush) A striking, medium-sized, erect, arching deciduous shrub with handsome foliage. In early summer it becomes laden with orange-yellow, globular flower clusters that make a bold statement. Andes of Chile, Peru, Argentina. Introduced 1774.
Zone 7 US, 8 Can. 🏆

Buddleia globosa

Buddleia lindleyana

B. lindleyana A medium-sized deciduous shrub with long, slender, curved racemes of violet-purple flowers, each one of which is strikingly beautiful. The flowers are borne from mid- to late summer. China, Japan. Introduced 1843 by Robert Fortune.
Zone 7 US, 8 Can.

***B.* 'Lochinch'** *(B. davidii × B. fallowiana)* A medium-sized, compact, bushy deciduous shrub with gray-pubescent young stems and leaves. Later the leaves become green and smooth above but retain a white woolliness beneath. The flowers are scented, violet-blue with a deep orange eye, and borne in dense, conical panicles from mid- to late summer.
Zone 8 US, 9 Can. 🏆

***B.* 'Pink Delight'** A recent hybrid making a medium-sized deciduous shrub with long panicles of bright pink flowers.
Zone 4 US, 5b Can. 🏆

B. salviifolia (South African sage wood) This medium-sized deciduous shrub is hardy only in mild, sheltered places. It has sagelike leaves and fragrant, white or pale lilac flowers with an orange eye that are borne from

Buddleia 'Pink Delight'

Buddleia × weyeriana

early to midspring. In cultivation 1783.
Zone 8 US, 9? Can.

B.* × *weyeriana (Weyer butterfly bush) A deciduous hybrid with orange-yellow flowers borne from mid- to late summer in long panicles of ball-shaped flower heads. The following are the most popular clones.
Zone 7 US, 8 Can.

***B.* × *w.* 'Golden Glow'** A medium-sized shrub with orange-yellow flowers flushed with lilac.
Zone 7 US, 8 Can.

***B.* × *w.* 'Sungold'** A beautiful sport of 'Golden Glow' that makes a medium-sized shrub with deep orange flowers. In cultivation 1966.
Zone 7 US, 8 Can. 🏆

Bupleurum *Umbelliferae*

A genus of about 75 evergreen and deciduous species, mostly herbs and subshrubs, from Europe, Asia, North Africa, and North America. The following is the only woody species normally cultivated in the open. It will grow in all types of soil.

Bupleurum fruticosum

B. fruticosum One of the best medium-sized evergreen shrubs for exposed coastal locations. It has sea green foliage and yellow flowers from early to late summer.
Zone 7 US, 8 Can.

Buxus *Buxaceae*
Boxwood

A genus of about 30 species of well-known evergreen shrubs and small trees with opposite, leathery leaves and inconspicuous male and female flowers on the same plant. Boxwoods grow well in a wide range of soils in sun or shade, although they prefer sun for at least part of the day. Often used for hedges and topiary specimens.

B. balearica (Balearic boxwood) A large shrub or small tree with comparatively large, leathery, bright green leaves, $1\frac{1}{2}$ in (4 cm) long by $\frac{3}{4}$ in (2 cm) wide. Balearics, SW Spain. Introduced before 1780.
Zone 8 US, 9? Can.

Buxus balearica

B. microphylla (Littleleaf boxwood) A dwarf to small, dense, rounded shrub with thinly textured, narrowly oblong leaves up to $\frac{1}{2}$ in (1.5 cm) long. Originated in Japan, but unknown in the wild. Introduced 1860.
Zone 6 US, 7 Can.

Buxus sempervirens 'Gold Tip'

B. sempervirens (Common boxwood) A large shrub or small tree with luxuriant masses of small, dark green leaves. It has given rise to many forms, several of which are suitable for hedges and topiary. S Europe, N Africa, W Asia; naturalized and possibly wild in England.
Zone 5 US, 6 Can. 🏆

***B. s.* 'Aurea Maculata'** See *B. s.* 'Aureovariegata'.

***B. s.* 'Aureovariegata'**, syn. *B. s.* 'Aurea Maculata' A medium-sized to large, dense, bushy shrub with green leaves that are variously striped, splashed, and mottled with creamy yellow.
Zone 5 US, 6 Can.

Buxus sempervirens 'Elegantissima'

***B. s.* 'Elegantissima'** A small to medium-sized, dense, compact, dome-shaped shrub. Its small leaves are often misshapen, but pleasantly so, and have irregular, creamy white margins. It makes an attractive specimen shrub and is the best silver-variegated boxwood.
Zone 4 US, 5b Can. 🏆

***B. s.* 'Gold Tip'** This small to medium-sized shrub is one of the most common forms of boxwood in commercial horticulture. The upper leaves of the terminal shoots are often tipped with yellow.
Zone 5 US, 6 Can.

***B. s.* 'Handsworthensis'** This form is erect at first but more spreading when mature. It is a large shrub with leathery, thick, dark green, rounded or oblong leaves and is excellent as a tall hedge or screen. In cultivation 1872.
Zone 5 US, 6 Can.

Buxus sempervirens 'Handsworthensis'

Buxus sempervirens 'Suffruticosa'

***B. s.* 'Japonica Aurea'** See *B. s.* 'Latifolia Maculata'.

***B. s.* 'Latifolia Maculata'**, syn. *B. s.* 'Japonica Aurea' Dense and compact when young, eventually forming a medium-sized shrub, this box has leaves that are irregularly blotched with yellow. When grown in the open, its bright yellow young growths are attractive in spring. Makes a slow-growing but otherwise excellent, dense hedge.
Zone 5 US, 6 Can. 🏆

***B. s.* 'Suffruticosa'** (Edging boxwood) A dwarf to small shrub commonly used as an edging for paths and flower beds, especially formal ones. The leaves are of medium size, broadest below the middle, and bright, shining green. In cultivation for centuries.
Zone 5 US, 6 Can. 🏆

Buxus sempervirens 'Latifolia Maculata'

C

Caesalpinia *Leguminosae*

A genus of about 100 species of evergreen and deciduous trees, shrubs, and climbers with showy flowers and leaves that are bipinnate (divided or cut into rows of leaflets that are themselves divided). They are spectacular shrubs for sunny, sheltered sites and are found throughout tropical and subtropical regions of the world.

Caesalpinia japonica

C. japonica A large, handsome deciduous shrub, but viciously armed with prominent spines. Its leaves are pinnate, acacia-like, and a refreshing shade of soft green. In midsummer it bears racemes of 20–30 bright yellow, pea-shaped flowers with scarlet stamens. Requires a sunny, sheltered position. Japan. Introduced 1881.
Zone 8 US, 9? Can.

Calceolaria *Scrophulariaceae*

A genus of about 300 species of shrubs and herbaceous perennials, including some popular greenhouse plants and alpines. The shrubby members are sun-loving evergreen plants with pouch-shaped flowers in terminal panicles. The following requires a well-drained position at the foot of a sunny wall.

C. integrifolia A small, shrubby member of the genus with clusters of large yellow flowers in late summer. Prefers a well-drained position at the foot of a sunny wall.

Calceolaria integrifolia

Chiloe area of Chile. Introduced 1822.
Zone 8 US, 9? Can. 🏆

C. i.* var. *angustifolia A small shrub with narrow leaves.
Zone 8 US, 9? Can. 🏆

Callicarpa *Verbenaceae*
Beautyberry

A genus of about 140 species of deciduous shrubs and small trees, found mainly in tropical and subtropical regions, among which are one or two that are particularly notable for their soft rose-madder fall color and conspicuous clusters of small, violet or lilac, berrylike fruits. They are freely produced, particularly where several specimens are grown together. The flowers are clustered and small.

Callicarpa bodinieri var. *giraldii*

C. bodinieri* var. *giraldii A medium-sized to large shrub with long-pointed leaves and lilac flowers that appear in late summer, followed by small fruits ranging from purple-red to dark lilac to pale violet. The best selection is described below. China. In cultivation 1900.
Zone 6 US, 6b Can.

Callicarpa bodinieri 'Profusion'

***C. b.* 'Profusion'** A medium-sized to large shrub on which the dense clusters of steely violet fruits are remarkably freely borne. It has bronze-purple young foliage.
Zone 6 US, 6b Can. 🏆

Callicarpa japonica 'Leucocarpa'

***C. japonica* 'Leucocarpa'** A small, compact shrub with oval leaves, white to pale pink flowers, and unusual white fruits.
Zone 6 US, 7 Can.

Callistemon *Myrtaceae*
Bottlebrush

A genus of about 25 species of shrubs and small trees that are found only in Australia and Tasmania. They are magnificent, sun-loving evergreens but suited only to the milder regions.

In summer, cylindrical spikes of flowers are formed, the most colorful parts being the tufts of long stamens. The branches continue to grow beyond the ends of the spikes. Bottlebrushes are not particular about soil type.

***C. citrinus* 'Splendens'** A graceful medium-sized shrub with dense spikes of brilliant scarlet flowers and narrow, rigid leaves that are lemon scented when crushed. It flowers throughout the summer and thrives in the open in mild areas. E Australia. Introduced 1788.
Zone 9 US 🏆

Callistemon linearis

C. linearis A species with small, narrow leaves and long, cylindrical spikes of scarlet flowers in summer. It grows best in sheltered, maritime locations. New South Wales. Introduced 1788.
Zone 9 US 🏆

Callistemon salignus

C. salignus One of the hardiest of the bottlebrushes. In a favorable spot it can grow to as much as 8 ft (2.5 m) high and wide. The leaves are narrow and willow-like, and the summer flowers are usually pale yellow. SE Australia. Introduced 1788.
Zone 8? US 🏆

Callistemon sieberi

C. sieberi (Alpine bottlebrush) A medium-sized shrub with small, narrow, densely arranged leaves and pale yellow flowers in short spikes in summer. This is the hardiest species and has survived many hard winters outdoors in the Hillier Gardens and Arboretum. SE Australia.
Zone 8 US, 9? Can. 🏆

***C. viminalis* 'Captain Cook'** A low-growing, spreading form of the weeping bottlebrush, with large clusters of deep crimson flowers in summer.
Zone 9 US 🏆

Calluna *Ericaceae*

A genus of just one species that is, however, of great importance to gardeners with poor, well-drained, acidic soil. See also Erica.

C. vulgaris (Heather) A dwarf to small shrub occurring widely on the mountains and moorland in the northern and western parts of the British Isles. It differs from *Erica* species in that the petals are concealed by the colored sepals. Its many cultivars are grown more frequently than the typical form is. Europe and Asia Minor.

Cultivars of *C. vulgaris* are all small shrubs, so the size of each is given below as an average for a mature plant that is well cultivated and trimmed back after flowering. They are all evergreen and hardy to zone 3 US and 3 Can. Flowering times are indicated as follows:

Early season	Mid- to late summer
Midseason	Late summer to early fall
Late season	Mid- to late fall

Calluna vulgaris 'Alba Plena'

***C. v.* 'Alba Plena'** A popular, free-flowering, midseason cultivar with double white flowers. 20 in (50 cm).

***C. v.* 'Alba Rigida'** An attractive plant with distinctive, horizontal branching and midseason white flowers. 6 in (15 cm).

***C. v.* 'Alexandra'** In this unusual and remarkable form, the profusely borne, deep dusky pink, pointed flower buds do not open fully but remain conspicuous for several months during late fall and early winter. 12 in (30 cm).

***C. v.* 'Allegro'** A neat heather with red flowers in mid- to late season. 20 in (50 cm). 🏆

***C. v.* 'Annemarie'** This excellent cultivar is an improvement on 'H. E. Beale'. Double flowers open light purple, deepening to carmine-rose. It has a compact habit and dark green foliage. 20 in (50 cm). 🏆

***C. v.* 'Anthony Davis'** An attractive plant with silvery gray foliage, which bears its midseason white flowers in profusion. 18 in (45 cm).

***C. v.* 'Battle of Arnhem'** Interesting over a long period, with light purple-red flowers in late season and dark green foliage, turn-

Calluna vulgaris 'Beoley Gold'

ing bronze in winter. 24 in (60 cm).

C. v. **'Beoley Gold'** A strong-growing form that is grown for its bright yellow foliage and short sprays of white flowers in midseason. 20 in (50 cm).

C. v. **'Blazeaway'** A startling plant with

Calluna vulgaris 'Blazeaway'

Calluna vulgaris 'Boskoop'

green foliage that changes to orange and rich red in winter. Its midseason flowers are lilac-mauve. 20 in (50 cm).

C. v. **'Boskoop'** A rewarding form grown for its rich gold foliage that turns orange-red in winter, and delicate lilac-pink flowers in midseason. 12 in (30 cm).

C. v. **'County Wicklow'** A dwarf but spreading plant with double, shell pink

Calluna vulgaris 'County Wicklow'

flowers in midseason. 10 in (25 cm).

C. v. **'Cuprea'** A cultivar with long shoots that are golden in summer and turn ruddy bronze in winter. Its midseason flowers are pale mauve. In cultivation before 1873. 12 in (30 cm).

C. v. **'Darkness'** A dense bush with bright green foliage and short, dense clusters of dark purplish pink flowers in midseason. 12 in (30 cm).

C. v. **'Dark Star'** A shrub of neat, dense habit and dark green foliage. The semi-double crimson flowers are borne from mid- to late season. 8 in (20 cm).

C. v. **'Drum-ra'** A pretty plant that bears white flowers in midseason. Raised 1960 in Scotland. 12–18 in (30–45 cm).

C. v. **'Elsie Purnell'** A sport from 'H. E. Beale' grown for its double flowers of lively silvery pink that are more deeply colored in the bud. It blooms from mid-

Calluna vulgaris 'Darkness'

Calluna vulgaris 'Elsie Purnell'

to late season. 24–32 in (60–80 cm).

C. v. 'Finale' A spreading plant with fresh green foliage and amethyst flowers from mid- to late season. 12 in (30 cm).

C. v. 'Firefly' The foliage of this cultivar is reddish brown, turning to deep orange-red in winter, and the midseason flowers are deep lilac. 18 in (45 cm).

Calluna vulgaris 'Gold Haze'

C. v. 'Gold Haze' A white-flowered, midseason cultivar with bright gold foliage. 20–24 in (50–60 cm).

C. v. 'Golden Carpet' A low-growing plant with orange-yellow foliage and short racemes of purplish pink flowers in midseason. 3 in (8 cm).

C. v. 'Golden Feather' A most attractive cultivar with feathery, golden foliage that changes to a gentle orange in winter. It bears mauve flowers in mid- to late season. 20 in (50 cm).

C. v. 'Hammondii Aureifolia' A dense-growing plant that carries white, midseason flowers, and the tips of its young shoots are colored golden yellow in spring. 20–24 in (50–60 cm).

Calluna vulgaris 'H. E. Beale'

C. v. 'H. E. Beale' A highly popular cultivar with long racemes of double, bright rose-pink flowers in mid- to late season. It is excellent for cutting but has nevertheless been improved upon (see 'Annemarie'). 24 in (60 cm).

C. v. 'J. H. Hamilton' A pretty, dwarf heather with large, double, clear fuchsia-pink flowers in early season. Perhaps the finest double. 10 in (25 cm).

C. v. 'Jimmy Dyce' A somewhat prostrate form with dark green foliage. Double lilac-pink flowers are borne from mid- to late season. 8 in (20 cm).

C. v. 'Joy Vanstone' This cultivar bears orchid-pink, midseason flowers over golden foliage, which deepens in winter to rich orange. 20 in (50 cm).

C. v. 'Kinlochruel' This sport of 'County Wicklow' is grown for its double white flowers, which it bears in midseason, and bright green foliage. 10 in (25 cm).

C. v. 'Mair's Variety' A tall heather with white flowers in midseason that are especially suitable for cutting. 32 in (80 cm).

Calluna vulgaris 'Kinlochruel'

C. v. 'Marleen' Similar to 'Alexandra' but with purple-pink buds that are white at the base in fall and early winter. 12 in (30 cm).

C. v. 'Melanie' A plant similar to 'Alexandra' but pure white. 12 in (30 cm).

Calluna vulgaris 'Mullion'

C. v. 'Mullion' A semiprostrate, well-branched heather with densely packed racemes of deep pink flowers in midseason. 6–10 in (15–25 cm).

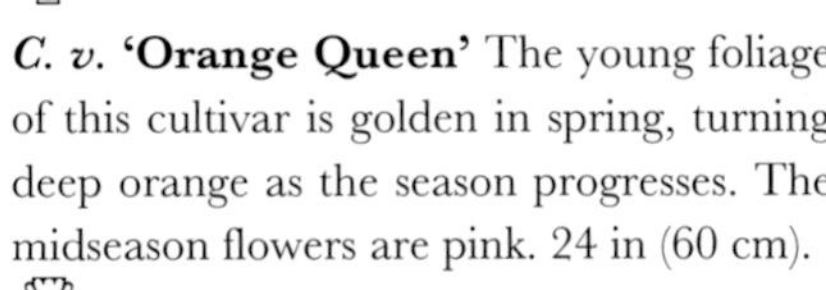

C. v. 'Orange Queen' The young foliage of this cultivar is golden in spring, turning deep orange as the season progresses. The midseason flowers are pink. 24 in (60 cm).

C. v. 'Peter Sparkes' A good heather for cutting because of its double, deep pink flowers, which are carried in long racemes from mid- to late season. 20 in (50 cm).

C. v. 'Radnor' A very compact plant, popular for its bright green foliage and midseason, double, pale lilac-pink flowers with

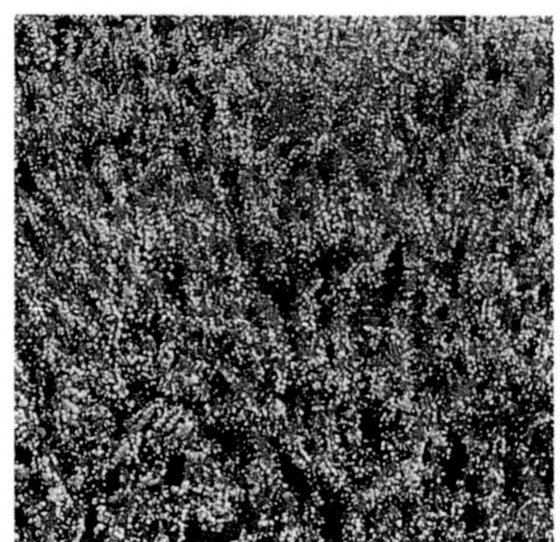

Calluna vulgaris 'Radnor'

white inner petals. 10 in (25 cm).

C. v. **'Red Star'** A shrub with an open habit that bears the reddest flowers of all the double-flowered red cultivars; blooms from mid- to late season. 16 in (40 cm).

C. v. **'Robert Chapman'** The foliage of this cultivar is golden in spring and changes during the winter months, first to orange and finally to red. The midseason flowers are soft purple. The heights of the individual growths vary from 12 to 24 in (30 to 60 cm), producing a pleasant effect.

C. v. **'Roland Haagess'** A bushy plant with pale purple flowers midseason and bronze-yellow foliage, turning orange- to bronze-red in winter. 12 in (30 cm).

C. v. **'Romina'** A plant similar to 'Alexandra' but of distinctly upright habit with white buds tipped deep pink. 14 in (35 cm).

Calluna vulgaris 'Serlei'

C. v. **'Serlei'** An erectly growing heather with late-season white flowers carried in long racemes and distinctive dark green foliage. 24 in (60 cm).

C. v. **'Serlei Aurea'** This cultivar is similar to 'Serlei' but has bright golden foliage. 24 in (60 cm).

Calluna vulgaris 'Silver Knight'

C. v. **'Silver Knight'** An upright heather with gray foliage and mauve-pink flowers in midseason. 12 in (30 cm).

C. v. **'Silver Queen'** A very beautiful plant with silvery gray foliage and pale mauve flowers in midseason. 24 in (60 cm).

C. v. **'Silver Rose'** A cultivar with bright rose-pink flowers in mid- to late season and silvery foliage on upright shoots. The combination of flower and foliage is delightful. 16 in (40 cm).

C. v. **'Sir John Charrington'** A vigorous, spreading heather with yellow leaves that are tinged with red in summer and become reddish all over in winter. Its early-season flowers are lilac-pink. 16 in (40 cm).

C. v. **'Sister Anne'** A dwarf plant that makes compact mounds of pretty, gray foliage. Its flowers borne during midseason are pink. 3–4 in (8–10 cm).

C. v. **'Spitfire'** The golden foliage of this cultivar turns bronze-red in winter. Its flowers are pink and borne in midseason.

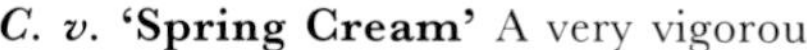

10–12 in (25–30 cm).

C. v. **'Spring Cream'** A very vigorous heather with dark green foliage tipped with cream in spring. The long spikes of white flowers are produced in abundance during midseason. 20 in (50 cm).

C. v. **'Sunrise'** A heather whose golden yellow foliage turns orange-red in winter. It has purple, midseason flowers. 12 in (30 cm).

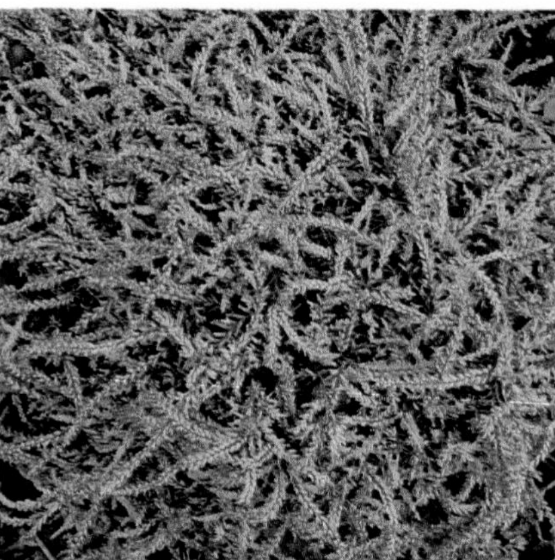

Calluna vulgaris 'Spitfire'

Calluna vulgaris 'Spring Cream'

Calluna vulgaris 'Sunrise'

Calluna vulgaris 'Sunset'

***C. v.* 'Sunset'** The foliage of this cultivar is variegated in yellow, gold, and orange and takes on deep orange-red tints in winter. The midseason flowers are pink. 10–12 in (25–30 cm).

***C. v.* 'Tib'** A lovely, floriferous plant,

Calluna vulgaris 'Tib'

blooming in early season with double flowers in rosy red. 12–24 in (30–60 cm).

***C. v.* 'Underwoodii'** The buds of this mid- to very-late-season cultivar do not open to form flowers but remain closed, and change from pale mauve to a silvery white color that lasts well into winter. 12 in (30 cm).

***C. v.* 'White Lawn'** A prostrate plant with deep green foliage and white flowers in midseason. 4 in (10 cm).

Calluna vulgaris 'Wickwar Flame'

***C. v.* 'Wickwar Flame'** This cultivar has bright orange and yellow summer foliage that turns copper and gold in winter. The midseason flowers are mauve-pink. Raised by the nurseryman George Osmond, of Avon, England. 12 in (30 cm).

Calluna vulgaris 'Winter Chocolate'

***C. v.* 'Winter Chocolate'** A cultivar with lilac-pink flowers midseason and greenish-yellow and orange summer foliage that turns brown and red in winter. 12 in (30 cm).

Calocedrus *Cupressaceae*

Incense cedar

A genus of three species of evergreen coniferous trees from Southeast Asia and North America. The

Calocedrus decurrens detail

branchlets are in broad, flattened sprays, and the leaves are scalelike, flattened, and densely borne in opposite pairs. Grows in ordinary soil.

Calocedrus decurrens

C. decurrens (California incense cedar) A large tree with a conical head of spreading branches in the wild. In cultivation, most trees belong to the form 'Columnaris' (syn. 'Fastigiata'); its characteristic columnar habit makes it unmistakable among cultivated trees. It is ideal for growing as a specimen or for adding height to a group of trees and shrubs. The dark green leaves are crowded into dense, fanlike sprays. W North America. Introduced 1853.
Zone 5 US, 6b Can. 🏆

C. d. 'Aureovariegata' Sprays of golden leaves occur irregularly spaced about the branches. This is an attractive, slow-growing, medium-sized tree.
Zone 5 US, 6b Can.

Calycanthus floridus

Calocedrus decurrens 'Berrima Gold'

C. d. 'Berrima Gold' A slow-growing form with orange bark and pale yellow-green foliage tipped with orange in winter. Introduced 1976 from an Australian nursery by Sir Harold Hillier. Its ultimate height is not yet known.
Zone 5? US, 6b? Can.

Calycanthus *Calycanthaceae*

Sweet shrub, allspice

Four species of deciduous, medium-sized North American shrubs with aromatic bark. They are easily grown and have striking, red-brown flowers consisting of numerous sepals and petals. The flowers are borne in summer and early fall.

C. floridus (Carolina allspice) A medium-sized shrub with aromatic, glossy, dark green leaves. The brownish red flowers, which consist of many strap-shaped petals, are borne over a long period in summer. SE United States. Introduced 1726.
Zone 4 US, 5 Can.

CAMELLIA

Theaceae

Camellia japonica 'Coquettii'

MORE THAN any other shrubs, camellias seem romantic and exotic. Their large yet delicate, ruffly flowers — ranging in color from pale ivory to shell pink to burnished crimson — are as exquisite as rose blossoms, and their dense, glossy, dark green foliage suggests the sultry tropics.

Camellias were introduced into Western gardens from China and Japan in the 18th century. At first they were thought to need warmth and were, therefore, grown in glasshouses in Europe and the United States. Eventually gardeners in mild areas, such as the American South and southwestern England, began experimenting with camellias in sheltered locations outdoors and discovered that the plants grew successfully with little attention. Camellias were soon established as suitable evergreen shrubs for gardens in temperate climates.

Today there is a wealth of camellias available; indeed, there are several thousand varieties. They are derived primarily from four species: *Camellia japonica, C. saluenensis, C. reticulata,* and *C. sasanqua.*

The mainstay of the garden is *C. japonica* and its hundreds of cultivars. The common camellia is widely grown throughout the southeastern United States and along the Pacific Coast. They are particularly valuable for their long bloom period and evergreen nature, which makes them suited for foundation plantings and borders, as well as for containers and espaliers.

C. sasanqua and its cultivars are smaller than the common camellia and are good for informal hedges or specimen plantings. They flower freely in fall and early winter, but the blooms shatter easily, making them better for landscaping than for cut blooms.

C. reticulata and its hybrids are becoming a more significant feature in the garden as time goes by and hardiness is better understood. Many of its cultivars and hybrids have withstood cold conditions better than had been anticipated, so the plant's large, beautifully proportioned blooms are now within the reach of gardeners who can grow other camellias.

Another promising camellia is the Williamsii, *C. × williamsii,* which is a cross between *C. japonica* and *C. saluenensis.* It has already achieved great popularity in England and is becoming more common in North America.

CAMELLIA FLOWERS

The size and form of camellia blossoms are subject to some variation in certain cultivars. Soil, site, and general cultivation can all play a part and can also occasionally cause some variation in color.

The flowers are classified according to shape and size, as indicated below.

Flower shapes:

Single One row of not more than eight regular, irregular, or loose petals and conspicuous stamens.

Semidouble Two or more rows of regular, irregular, or loose petals and conspicuous stamens.

Anemone form One or more rows of large outer petals lying flat or wavy; the center a convex mass of intermingled petaloids and stamens.
Peony form A deep, rounded flower consisting of a convex mass of petals, petaloids, and sometimes stamens.
Rose form double Imbricated petals (laid like roof tiles) showing stamens in a concave center when open.
Formal double Fully imbricated, with many rows of petals with no stamens.
Flower sizes:
Very large Over 5 in (12.5 cm) across.
Large 4–5 in (10–12.5 cm) across.
Medium 3–4 in (7.5–10 cm) across.
Small 2½–3 in (6–7.5 cm) across.
Miniature Up to 2½ in (6 cm) across.

CULTIVATION

Camellias require a temperate, humid climate for successful growth. In North America, the "camellia belt" runs from the northern limits of Washington, D.C., down along the Atlantic and Gulf coasts into Texas. It further extends along the Pacific coast of California up through coastal British Columbia.

Although camellias are generally easy to grow, and most of them are remarkably hardy, it is important to site the plants carefully, as their buds and flowers are vulnerable to a variety of conditions.

For camellia buds to form at all, which occurs in early summer, they need high temperatures and long days. Their opening, however, is triggered by cool temperatures and short days, when there is also the risk of frost. Buds that are tightly closed will usually not be damaged by freezing temperatures, but open flowers will turn brown if the thermometer dips much below freezing.

Flower buds can be severely damaged if they are allowed to thaw rapidly while frozen. This is most likely to happen if the plants are sited facing east, as the early-morning sun will strike them before the temperature has risen enough to thaw the ice in the tissues (the sun does not heat the air but does heat solid objects). The same conditions can also split the bark on the stems. Therefore, camellias should never be allowed to face the morning sun and are best located in filtered shade, where the tree canopy will reduce radiation frost and also provide shelter from drying wind. Partial shade also promotes the best bloom; the rule of thumb is the warmer the climate, the less direct sun is needed.

Once a proper site has been selected, the planting hole should be prepared well. Camellias prefer a moist but well-drained, crumbly soil with a pH of about 6.0 and with a generous amount of organic matter. They will not thrive in alkaline soil, where they will need constant treatment against chlorosis (yellowing of the leaves but with the veins remaining green) and will eventually die.

Camellias have shallow, fibrous roots that do not tolerate compaction. While the soil should be firmed, it should not be packed down. If the native soil is not suitable, or if the climate is too cold, camellias can be planted in containers in a loose potting mixture with a slightly acidic pH.

Mulching is beneficial, to limit weeding around shallow roots and to protect them from frost heaving. Mulch will also help keep the soil from freezing as long as possible, so that the roots will be able to draw up water and replenish the moisture that is continually lost by the evergreen leaves.

Camellias planted at the limits of their hardiness range should be placed in sheltered locations, where they will be protected from drying, chill winds. Camellias in containers are especially vulnerable to cold, as the soil ball can freeze solid quickly. If the pots are small enough, they can be plunged in soil or sand outdoors or moved indoors to a protected area for a short period. If not, the pots and plants should be covered with a material that insulates without absorbing water.

Pruning for shape and health should be done immediately after flowering, before the new buds form. Dead and spindly branches should be removed and interior growth should be thinned to allow air circulation. Although camellias are slow growing — it takes many years before they become more than medium-sized shrubs — it is important to prune them to promote vigorous growth.

Camellias are bothered by several insect and disease pests. Scale insects are the worst and cause the leaves to yellow and drop. In hot, dry weather, spider mites make foliage appear speckled and bronzy, especially along the main vein. Camellia canker and dieback is a serious fungal disease in the hot, humid Southeast and can kill entire plants. A flower blight causes brown spots on the petals, and while it can disfigure the blossoms, it does not affect the shrub itself. Camellias are also subject to root rot if the soil is not well drained.

Camellia hardiness is very complex; two winters, with identical minimum temperatures, may cause very different amounts of damage. While there is some variation between hybrids, camellias generally are hardy to zone 7 US, 8 Can.

Despite their exotic appearance, camellias flourish outdoors in cool climates if sited with care.

***C.* 'Barbara Hillier'** *(C. japonica × C. reticulata)* A first-class, large shrub with big, handsome, polished leaves and large, single, satin pink flowers. Originated at Embley Park, near Romsey, England.

***C.* 'Cornish Snow'** A delightful, free-growing, medium-sized to large hybrid that bears masses of small, single white flowers along the branchlets. Garden origin c. 1930. 🏆

***C.* 'Cornish Spring'** A medium-sized shrub of upright habit with small, single pink flowers. In cultivation 1972. 🏆

***C.* 'Dr. Clifford Parks'** A large, vigorous, upright camellia grown for its very large, semidouble to peony or anemone form flowers that are red with an orange cast. In cultivation 1971. 🏆

***C.* 'Forty-Niner'** A bushy, vigorous, upright plant with glossy foliage that may occasionally be flecked with white. Its flowers are peony form and rich red, measuring up to 6 in (15 cm) across. 🏆

***C.* 'Francie L'** A vigorous shrub grown for its very large, semidouble, rose-pink blooms with wavy petals. A good wall shrub, but the foliage is sparse, slender, and rather poor.

***C.* 'Harold L. Paige'** A vigorous plant with very large, rose form double to full peony blooms of bright red. Introduced 1972 in the United States.

***C.* 'Inspiration'** A medium-sized shrub with large, semidouble, deep pink flowers. An excellent, reliable hybrid. 🏆

C. japonica (Common camellia) A large shrub or small tree. The species is virtually never seen in cultivation except in its many cultivars, which are highly bred and very unlike the typical form. Japan, China. Introduced 1739.

***C. j.* 'Adolphe Audusson'** A first-class, well-proven, medium-sized shrub of vigorous but compact growth with large, semidouble, blood red flowers featuring a conspicuous central boss of yellow stamens. 🏆

***C. j.* 'Akashi-gata'** See *C. j.* 'Lady Clare'.

***C. j.* 'Alba Plena'** An erect, bushy, medium-sized shrub with medium, rose

Camellia 'Barbara Hillier'

Camellia 'Cornish Snow'

Camellia 'Dr. Clifford Parks'

Camellia 'Inspiration'

Camellia japonica 'Adolphe Audusson'

form double, white flowers.

Camellia japonica 'Alba Simplex'

C. j. **'Alba Simplex'** The most reliable white single, with large flowers with conspicuous stamens.

Camellia japonica 'Alexander Hunter'

C. j. **'Alexander Hunter'** A medium-sized shrub grown for its large, bright crimson, single to semidouble flowers with golden stamens.

C. j. **'Apollo'** A vigorous shrub with medium-sized blooms, semidouble and rose-red, occasionally blotched with white. It is often confused with 'Jupiter' but has a larger number of petals and a deeper color. The leaves are longer, too, and have characteristically twisted, pointed tips.

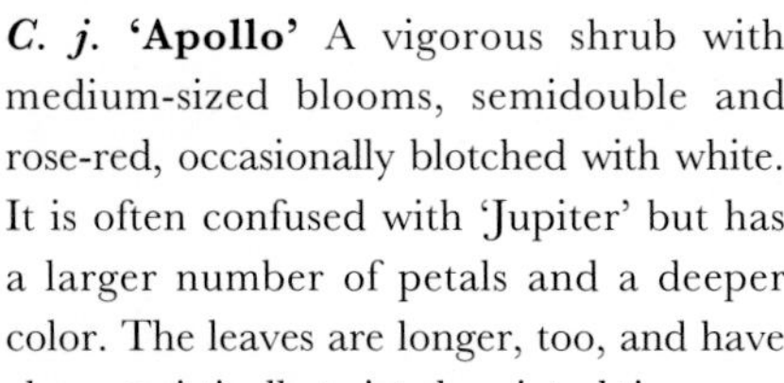

C. j. **'Apple Blossom',** syn. *C. j.* 'Joy Sander' A medium-sized shrub with medium-sized, semidouble, pale pink flowers, deepening at the margins.

Camellia japonica 'Ballet Dancer'

C. j. **'Ballet Dancer'** A compact, upright shrub with medium-sized, peony form, cream flowers shading to coral-pink at the margins. In cultivation 1960.

Camellia japonica 'Berenice Boddy'

C. j. **'Berenice Boddy'** A vigorous, erect shrub grown for its medium-sized, semidouble, light pink flowers that are deeper pink beneath the petals.

C. j. **'Betty Sheffield Supreme'** A medium-sized shrub with medium-sized to large, semidouble to loose peony form, white flowers, each petal bordered with deep pink to red. It is a lovely shrub but tends to sport badly.

C. j. **'Blood of China'** A vigorous, compact shrub with deep salmon-red, large, semidouble to loose peony form flowers.

Camellia japonica 'Blood of China'

C. j. **'Bob Hope'** Just about the darkest red camellia, approaching black-red. The large, semidouble blooms are borne on compact, medium-sized bushes. In cultivation 1972.

C. j. **'Bob's Tinsie'** A compact, medium-sized, upright shrub grown for its small, brilliant red flowers of anemone form. In cultivation 1962.

Camellia japonica 'Bob's Tinsie'

C. j. **'Carter's Sunburst'** A compact, medium-sized shrub with large to very large flowers, pale pink and striped and otherwise marked with pink of a deeper shade. They are semidouble to peony form, or even formal double. In cultivation 1958.

C. j. **'Chandleri Elegans'** See *C. j.* 'Elegans'.

C. j. **'Clarise Carlton'** A vigorous, upright, medium-sized bush with large to very large, semidouble red flowers. In cultivation 1955.

Camellia japonica 'C. M. Wilson'

***C. j.* 'C. M. Hovey'** A vigorous, compact, medium-sized plant with medium-sized, formal double, carmine flowers.

***C. j.* 'Contessa Lavinia Maggi'** See *C. j.* 'Lavinia Maggi'.

***C. j.* 'C. M. Wilson'** A slow-growing, spreading, medium-sized sport of *C. j.* 'Elegans' with very large, anemone form, light pink flowers.

***C. j.* 'Coquettii'** A slow-growing, erect, compact medium-sized shrub with flowers a bright rose, medium-sized and double.

***C. j.* 'Debutante'** A reliable midsized plant with light to medium green foliage. Blossoms are light pink, medium-full peony form. They bloom in early winter and are subject to frost damage.

***C. j.* 'Devonia'** A vigorous, erect shrub with medium-sized, white, rather cup-shaped single flowers. It blooms very early and is prone to frost damage.

Camellia japonica 'Donckelaeri'

***C. j.* 'Donckelaeri'** A slow-growing, medium-sized, bushy shrub with large, semidouble red flowers, often marbled with white. A first-class plant. Introduced before 1834.

***C. j.* 'Drama Girl'** A vigorous shrub of open growth with semi-pendulous branches and very large flowers that are easily damaged by weather. The blooms are semi-

Camellia japonica 'Drama Girl'

double and deep salmon-rose-pink.

***C. j.* 'Dr. Tinsley'** A compact, upright, medium-sized bush with medium-sized, semidouble flowers that are pale pink, shading to deep pink at the margins.

***C. j.* 'Elegans'**, syn. *C. j.* 'Chandleri Elegans' A medium-sized cultivar that has been well proven for general cultivation, with very large, deep pink flowers of anemone form. In cultivation 1822.

Camellia japonica 'Elegans'

***C. j.* 'Gloire de Nantes'** A splendid, early-flowering, well-proven cultivar with erect, compact growth and large, semidouble, rose-pink flowers.

***C. j.* 'Grand Prix'** A vigorous, upright, medium-sized shrub with very large, semi-double, brilliant red flowers with irregular petals. In cultivation 1968.

Camellia japonica 'Grand Prix'

***C. j.* 'Grand Slam'** A vigorous, open and upright, medium-sized bush with large, brilliant dark red, semidouble to anemone form blooms. In cultivation 1962.

Camellia japonica 'Grand Slam'

***C. j.* 'Guilio Nuccio'** A vigorous, erect, medium-sized shrub with pointed leaves. The flowers are very large, semidouble, and coral-pink.

Camellia japonica 'Guilio Nuccio'

***C. j.* 'Haku-rakuten'** A vigorous, erect camellia grown for its large, white, semi-double to peony form flowers, with curved, fluted petals and some petaloid stamens.

Camellia japonica 'Haku-rakuten'

***C. j.* 'Hawaii'** A sport of 'C. M. Wilson', this camellia is particularly useful for its late flowering. The blooms are medium to large, pale pink, peony form with fringed petals. In cultivation 1961.

***C. j.* 'Jingle Bells'** A vigorous, upright sport of 'Tinker Bell' with small red flowers of anemone form. In cultivation 1959.

***C. j.* 'Joy Sander'** See *C. j.* 'Apple Blossom'.

***C. j.* 'Jupiter'** One of the best camellias for general planting, this is a medium-sized bush with medium-sized, single to semi-double, bright scarlet flowers, sometimes blotched with white and with a conspicuous bunch of stamens.

***C. j.* 'Konron-koku'**, syn. *C. j.* 'Kouron-jura' A very reliable camellia producing exceptionally dark, almost black-red, medium-sized, formal double flowers; one of the darkest-colored of all camellias. The growth of this medium-sized bush is fairly vigorous and semierect.

***C. j.* 'Lady Clare'**, syn. *C. j.* 'Akashi-gata' A vigorous and spreading, medium-sized shrub that produces large, semidouble, deep, clear peach-pink flowers. It is still one of the best camellias. Introduced 1887.

***C. j.* 'Lady de Saumarez'** This is an excellent, vigorous, compact, medium-sized cultivar. A sport of 'Tricolor', it has medium-sized, semidouble, bright red flowers spotted with white.

Camellia japonica 'Lady Clare'

***C. j.* 'Lady Vansittart'** This is not the most reliable camellia, as its medium-sized, semidouble flowers, which are white striped with rose-pink, revert badly. It reaches medium height. Introduced 1887 from Japan.

***C. j.* 'Latifolia'** This is a broad-leaved, very hardy, medium-sized cultivar. It produces vigorous, bushy growth, which is known to succeed especially well in open situations. The flowers, which are are medium-sized, are rose-red in color, and semidouble.

***C. j.* 'Lavinia Maggi'**, syn. *C. j.* 'Contessa Lavinia Maggi' A medium-sized shrub with large, double flowers that are white or pale pink and have rose-cerise stripes.

Camellia japonica 'Latifolia'

***C. j.* 'Magnoliiflora'** A medium-sized, compact camellia with blush pink flowers that have forward-pointing petals, making them look rather like the expanding buds of *Magnolia stellata*. The blooms are medium-sized and semidouble.

***C. j.* 'Man Size'** This is an upright shrub with miniature, white, anemone form blossoms that are very consistent in shape and size. It was introduced 1961 in the United States.

Camellia japonica 'Magnoliiflora'

***C. j.* 'Margaret Davis'** A medium-sized shrub that is grown for its medium-sized, peony form, white flowers that are streaked rose-red and edged with deep vermilion. In cultivation 1961.

Camellia japonica 'Margaret Davis'

C. j. **'Mari Bracey'** A medium-sized shrub with an upright habit. Blooms are coral-rose, large, and semidouble to loose peony in form. Introduced 1953 in the United States.

Camellia japonica 'Mars'

C. j. **'Mars'** This camellia is often confused with both 'Apollo' and 'Mercury'. A medium-sized shrub, it has an open, loose habit, and the flowers are large, vivid red, and semidouble, with a conspicuous bunch of stamens.

C. j. **'Mathotiana Alba'** A first-class camellia, though not recommended for an exposed position, with large, formal double, white flowers, just occasionally with a pink spot.

C. j. **'Mercury'** A compact, medium-sized shrub with large, semidouble flowers in a deep, soft crimson with slightly darker veins.

C. j. **'Miss Charleston'** A neat, medium-sized, upright bush with very large, high-centered, deep red, semidouble to peony form flowers with golden stamens.

Camellia japonica 'Mercury'

C. j. **'Mrs. D. W. Davis'** The very large, semidouble, light blush-pink flowers of this medium-sized camellia are so big that they are easily damaged by weather. It needs shelter, but its vigorous though compact growth helps make it an excellent greenhouse plant.

C. j. **'Nagasaki'** A spreading, medium-sized shrub with large, semidouble, rose-pink flowers marbled with white.

Camellia japonica 'Nobilissima'

C. j. **'Nobilissima'** A fairly erect, medium-sized shrub with medium-sized, peony form, white flowers. Susceptible to frost damage.

C. j. **'Nuccio's Gem'** A compact and upright, medium-sized camellia grown for its pure white, medium-sized to large flowers of perfect formal double formation. In cultivation 1970.

C. j. **'Nuccio's Jewel'** A bushy medium-sized shrub with medium-sized, peony form flowers that are white, delicately and irregularly flushed with orchid-pink. In cultivation 1977.

C. j. **'Nuccio's Pearl'** A compact, upright, medium-sized bush that is grown for its medium-sized, formal double, white flowers that are washed with the palest pink and shaded orchid-pink on the outer petals. A beautiful, delicately colored camellia. In cultivation 1977.

C. j. **'Pink Perfection'** A lovely shrub with dark green foliage. Shell pink blossoms are small in size and formal double, never showing the stamens.

C. j. **'Preston Rose'** A vigorous shrub with medium-sized, peony form, salmon pink flowers.

Camellia japonica 'R. L. Wheeler'

C. j. **'Professor Charles S. Sargent'** A vigorous upright shrub with large, dark green leaves. The medium-sized blooms are dark red, peony form. Introduced 1925 in the United States.

C. j. **'R. L. Wheeler'** A beautiful, vigorous, large camellia with large to very large, rose-pink flowers of semidouble to anemone form. Raised by Wheeler's Nurseries, Georgia.

C. j. **'Rubescens Major'** An old, reliable cultivar with large, formal double, crimson flowers, veined in a darker tone. The plant is compact, medium-sized, and bushy. In cultivation 1886.

Camellia japonica 'Rubescens Major'

Camellia japonica 'Scentsation'

Camellia japonica 'Silver Anniversary'

***C. j.* 'Sawada's Dream'** A medium-sized plant with white flowers shading to flesh pink on the petal edges. The blooms are medium in size and formal double. Introduced 1958 in the United States.

***C. j.* 'Scentsation'** A compact, vigorous, upright bush with sweetly scented, medium to large pink, peony form flowers.

***C. j.* 'Silver Anniversary'** Vigorous shrub with large, white, semidouble flowers, irregular petals, and golden stamens.

***C. j.* 'Snowman'** A large, sprawling plant with semidouble white blossoms.

***C. j.* 'Tiffany'** A vigorous plant with upright growth and large pink flowers that are peony to anemone form. Introduced 1962 in the United States.

Camellia japonica 'Tricolor'

***C. j.* 'Tomorrow'** A vigorous, open shrub with slightly pendulous growth and large blooms that are red and semidouble to full peony form. Introduced 1953 in the United States.

***C. j.* 'Tricolor'** A compact, medium-sized camellia with distinctive crinkled leaves. The flowers are medium-sized, very variable single to semidouble, and striped with carmine and pink on a white ground.

***C. j.* 'Ville de Nantes'** A slow-growing plant with distinctive, striking flowers of red and white that are semidouble with upright, fringed petals.

***C.* 'Lasca Beauty'** A vigorous and beautiful shrub with very large, semidouble, soft pink flowers with yellow anthers. Introduced at Los Angeles State and County Arboretum (LASCA) by Dr. Clifford Parks.

***C.* 'Leonard Messel'** (*C. reticulata* × *C.* × *williamsii* 'Mary Christian') A very beautiful, large shrub. The flowers are large, semidouble, and clear pink, and the dark green leaves tend, like the flowers, toward *C. reticulata*. Originated in England.

Camellia 'Leonard Messel'

Camellia reticulata 'Arch of Triumph'

***C.* 'Mandalay Queen'** A *C. reticulata* seedling, probably a hybrid, with very large, rose-pink, semidouble flowers with yellow anthers and variegated petaloids. Its habit is vigorous and upright.

***C.* 'Michael'** A beautiful, medium-sized to large shrub, similar to 'Cornish Snow' but with larger, single, white flowers.

C. reticulata One of the most beautiful of all flowering shrubs. It makes a large, compact shrub of much better constitution than the more popular named cultivars. The forms described below will grow and flower outdoors in mild areas, but elsewhere they are magnificent plants for the greenhouse.

***C. r.* 'Arch of Triumph'** A seedling of

C. reticulata (wild type) with a vigorous, upright habit and very large, deep pink to wine red flowers of loose peony form. In cultivation 1970.

***C. r.* 'Captain Rawes'** A large, magnificent shrub of open, rather spreading habit with very large, semidouble, carmine-rose-pink flowers.

***C. r.* 'Curtain Call'** This is a vigorous plant with large leaves and very large, semidouble, coral-rose flowers with bright yellow stamens. Originated 1979 in the United States.

***C. r.* 'Hall's Pride'** This upright, open plant has very large semidouble blooms that are salmon pink with a center of golden yellow stamens. The blooms are among the largest of all camellias. Originated 1985 in the United States.

Camellia sasanqua 'Crimson King'

C. sasanqua (Sasanqua camellia) This species bears often fragrant flowers, generally from fall to early winter. The cultivars described are reliable and free-flowering.

***C. s.* 'Bonanza'** A spreading plant with dark green leaves and small, deep red blossoms of loose peony form.

***C. s.* 'Crimson King'** This medium-sized camellia is one of the most reliable and floriferous of all, with small, single, bright red flowers. Because of its color, frost damage is not very noticeable.

***C. s.* 'Narumi-gata'** This is a medium-sized bush with large, single, fragrant white flowers with pink edging.

***C. s.* 'Sparkling Burgundy'** A vigorous plant with small peony form blooms that are ruby-rose with a lavender sheen.

Camellia sasanqua 'Narumi-gata'

Camellia 'Spring Festival'

***C. s.* 'Yuletide'** A compact plant with distinctive small, single blooms of bright red with yellow stamens.

***C.* 'Satan's Robe'** A vigorous, upright shrub with large, semidouble, red flowers with a satin sheen to the petals.

***C.* 'Spring Festival'** The narrow, upright, fastigiate habit of this large shrub is unusual among camellias. The flowers are pink, fading to light pink, miniature and double. Raised before 1975 in California.

***C.* 'Tristram Carlyon'** A vigorous, upright, medium-sized bush with medium-sized, rose-pink flowers of peony form.

C. tsaii A tender, graceful, large shrub. The single white flowers are small but numerous. The young foliage is copper colored. W China, Burma, N Vietnam. Introduced 1924 by George Forrest.

***C.* 'Valentine Day'** A vigorous plant with large to very large, formal double, salmon pink blooms with a rosebud center. Introduced 1969 in the United States.

C. × williamsii This medium to large bush does not require as much warmth for the production of flower buds as *C. japonica* does. The cultivars tend toward *C. japonica* in their foliage and *C. saluenensis* in their flowers. They are exquisitely beautiful and flower freely over a long period from late fall to late spring. The following are among the best garden forms. Original cross made 1925 by J. C. Williams, Cornwall, England.

Camellia × williamsii 'Anticipation'

***C. × w.* 'Anticipation'** An upright, medium-sized shrub with large, lush, deep rose flowers of peony form. In cultivation 1962.

Camellia × williamsii 'Bowen Bryant'

***C. × w.* 'Bowen Bryant'** This is a vigorous, bush of upright habit that produces large, semidouble, deep pink flowers. In cultivation 1960.

***C. × w.* 'Brigadoon'** This camellia is compact, upright, and medium-sized. It pro-

Camellia × *williamsii* 'Brigadoon'

duces attractive medium-sized, semidouble flowers that are rose-pink with subtle veining in a slighly darker shade of pink. In cultivation 1960.

***C.* × *w.* 'China Clay'** An open, medium-sized shrub with white flowers that are

Camellia × *williamsii* 'Daintiness'

medium-sized and semidouble. In cultivation 1972.

🏆

***C.* × *w.* 'Daintiness'** The *C. japonica* parent of this open, medium-sized shrub was 'Magnoliiflora'. The salmon pink flowers are large and semidouble.

🏆

***C.* × *w.* 'Debbie'** One of the most popular of all camellias, this shrub produces large, peony form, clear pink flowers with a hint of blue.

🏆

***C.* × *w.* 'Donation'** This large camellia, has semidouble, orchid-pink flowers, with

Camellia × *williamsii* 'Debbie'

Camellia × *williamsii* 'Donation'

slightly darker veins. The growth is vigorous and erect. The *C. japonica* parent of 'Donation' was 'Donckelaeri'.

Camellia × *williamsii* 'Elsie Jury'

***C.* × *w.* 'Elsie Jury'** An open, spreading shrub with large, peony form flowers of clear pink, shaded to orchid-pink. In cultivation 1964.

Camellia 'E. T. R. Carlyon'

***C.* 'E. T. R. Carlyon'** (*C.* × *williamsii* 'J. C. Williams' × *C. japonica* 'Adolphe Audusson'). A vigorous, upright, medium-sized shrub with medium-sized, semidouble to double, white flowers. In cultivation 1972.

***C.* × *w.* 'Galaxie'** An open, upright bush with medium-sized to large, semidouble to rose form double flowers that are white striped with deep pink and have cupped and twisted, upright petals. The first striped Williamsii hybrid, it is slow growing.

***C.* × *w.* 'Glenn's Orbit'** A seedling of 'Donation' with large, deep orchid-pink, semidouble to loose peony form flowers on a vigorous, upright, medium-sized shrub.

🏆

Camellia × *williamsii* 'Glenn's Orbit'

C. × *w.* **'Golden Spangles'** A sport of 'Mary Christian' with unusually variegated foliage. The flowers are small, single, and phlox pink, and each leaf has a central yellow-green blotch. Found 1957 at RHS Wisley, England.

Camellia × *williamsii* 'Golden Spangles'

C. × *w.* **'Hiraethlyn'** A vigorous, erect, large shrub with narrow, matte leaves and perfect large, single, orchid-pink flowers. In cultivation 1950.

C. × *w.* **'J. C. Williams'** It has medium-sized, single, phlox pink flowers and is one of the most beautiful camellias. It makes a medium-sized bush.

C. × *w.* **'Jermyns'** A selection made at Hillier Nurseries that is grown for its broad-petaled, clear peach-pink flowers.

Camellia × *williamsii* 'Jermyns'

C. × *w.* **'Joan Trehane'** A shrub with a dense, spreading habit grown for its very large, rose form double to formal double, rose-pink flowers with 35 petals and a few petaloids among the cream stamens.

C. × *w.* **'Julia Hamiter'** A seedling of 'Donation' with medium-sized, semidouble to double, white flowers and a compact habit. In cultivation 1964.

C. × *w.* **'Jury's Yellow'** A compact, medium-sized, upright shrub grown for its medium-sized, anemone form, white flowers that have wavy petals and a distinctive central mass of creamy yellow petaloids. In cultivation 1976.

C. × *w.* **'Mary Christian'** This is a medium-sized shrub that is one of the earliest of the Williamsii hybrids to come into flower. It has small, single, clear pink flowers of fine quality.

C. × *w.* **'Muskoka'** This is a superb medium-sized to large shrub with medium-sized, semidouble, deep pink flowers with darker stripes.

Camellia × *williamsii* 'Muskoka'

C. × *w.* **'Rose Parade'** This is a vigorous, upright, yet compact shrub. It produces flowers that are medium-sized, deep rose-pink, and peony form to formal double. In cultivation 1969.

C. × *w.* **'St. Ewe'** Named for a Cornish saint of the early Celtic church, this medium-sized camellia has medium-sized, cup- to bell-shaped, single flowers of bright rose-pink.

Camellia × *williamsii* 'St. Ewe'

C. × *w.* **'Water Lily'** This is a graceful, vigorous, slender, and beautiful camellia with medium to large, formal double flowers. The pink petals are tinted with lavender and have a darker rim. In cultivation since 1967.

Camellia × *williamsii* 'Water Lily'

C. **'Winton'** This is a medium-sized to large shrub similar to 'Cornish Snow' but it produces large, single, soft almond-pink flowers.

Campsis *Bignoniaceae*

Trumpet creeper

A genus of two species of attractive, deciduous shrubs with long, climbing stems, related to Bignonia *and equally brilliant in flower. Both require a position in full sun to ripen growth and produce flowers. They are excellent when trained over tree stumps, walls, and roofs of outbuildings but can strangle living trees if allowed to climb into them. If they become too large, they can be pruned in late winter or early spring. They prefer a moist, well-drained soil.*

Campsis grandiflora

Campsis radicans

C. grandiflora (Chinese trumpet creeper) This large and beautiful climber will reach a height of 20 ft (6 m) or more. Its leaves are pinnate, with 7–9 leaflets; the deep orange and red flowers are trumpet shaped, up to 3½ in (9 cm) long, and carried in drooping panicles from the tips of the current year's growths in late summer and early fall. China. Introduced 1800.
Zone 7 US, 8 Can.

C. radicans (Trumpet vine) A tall, very vigorous species — rampant in the right conditions — that climbs by aerial roots but should still be given some support at first. The leaves have 9–11 leaflets, and the brilliant orange and scarlet flowers are trumpet shaped, up to 3 in (8 cm) long, and produced in clusters at the ends of the current year's growths in late summer and early fall. SE United States. In cultivation 1640.
Zone 4 US, 5b Can.

***C. r.* 'Flava'**, syn. *C. r.* 'Yellow Trumpet' An attractive large climber grown for its rich yellow flowers.
Zone 4 US, 5b Can. 🏆

***C. r.* 'Yellow Trumpet'** See *C. r.* 'Flava'.

***C.* × *tagliabuana* 'Madame Galen'** *(C. grandiflora × C. radicans)* A vigorous large climber with panicles of salmon red flowers that are borne in late summer. Provide the plant with support. In cultivation 1889.
Zone 5 US, 6 Can. 🏆

Campsis × tagliabuana 'Madame Galen'

Cantua *Polemoniaceae*

A genus of six species of shrubs and trees found in the northern Andes of South America. The genus as currently defined consists of semievergreen to evergreen, perennial shrubs and trees.

Cantua buxifolia

C. buxifolia (Magic flower) A little-known but very beautiful small shrub that bears graceful, drooping corymbs of bright cherry red, tubular flowers in midspring. It is semievergreen in mild areas and is best grown against a warm wall if it is to flower successfully. Bolivia, Peru, Chile. Introduced 1849.
Zone 9 US

Caragana *Leguminosae*
Pea tree

A genus of about 80 species of deciduous shrubs or small trees that are found mainly in Central Asia. The leaves are evenly pinnate, with the terminal leaflet reduced to a spine, although the reduction of one of the leaflets at the base of the spine can make them appear oddly pinnate. The pealike flowers are usually yellow and are borne in early summer. The trees do well in dry soils.

Caragana arborescens

C. arborescens (Siberian pea tree) A small, shrubby tree with yellow flowers. It is valuable as one of the toughest and most adaptable of all plants, succeeding in the most exposed areas and in all types of soil. Siberia, Manchuria. Introduced 1752.
Zone 2 US, 2 Can.

Caragana arborescens 'Lorbergii'

***C. a.* 'Lorbergii'** An extremely graceful, medium-sized shrub with narrow, almost grasslike leaflets and much smaller flowers. In cultivation from around 1906.
Zone 2 US, 2 Can. 🏆

Caragana arborescens 'Pendula'

***C. a.* 'Pendula'** A very attractive weeping form, making a medium-sized shrub. In cultivation 1856.
Zone 2 US, 2 Can.

***C. a.* 'Walker'** (*C. a.* 'Lorbergii' × *C. a.* 'Pendula') The foliage is similar to that of 'Lorbergii' but the growth is prostrate, and it is usually top-grafted to produce a small, narrow, weeping standard with hanging branches. Raised in Canada.
Zone 2 US, 2 Can.

Carpenteria *Philadelphaceae*

A genus of only one evergreen species, for warm, sunny sites.

Carpenteria californica

C. californica (Tree anemone) A beautiful medium-sized shrub whose large, white flowers with golden anthers are produced in midsummer. It needs a warm, sunny position and grows well against a wall. California. Introduced c. 1880.
Zone 8 US, 9? Can. 🏆

***C. c.* 'Bodnant'** A vigorous, large-flowered, medium-sized shrub. Selected during the 1960s at Bodnant, N Wales, by Charles Puddle.
Zone 8 US, 9? Can.

Carpinus *Carpinaceae*
Hornbeam

A genus of more than 30 species of picturesque, easily grown, deciduous trees, mainly from China but widely distributed in northern temperate regions as far as South America. They are suitable for all soils, including clay and limestone, and are especially attractive when laden with their hoplike fruit clusters.

Carpinus betulus

Carpinus betulus 'Fastigiata'

C. betulus (European hornbeam) A medium-sized to large tree with a charac-

teristically gray, fluted trunk and toothed, ribbed leaves. It is often used for hedges and will tolerate light shade. Europe, Asia Minor.
Zone 4 US, 4b Can. 🏆

***C. b.* 'Fastigiata'**, syn. *C. b.* 'Pyramidalis' A medium-sized tree of erect, conical habit. It is quite narrow as a young tree but broadens as it matures. In cultivation 1883. *(Photo on p.193.)* Zone 4 US, 4b Can. 🏆

***C. b.* 'Frans Fontaine'** A fastigiate medium-sized form that retains its habit with age. Selected from trees growing on a street in Eindhoven, Holland.
Zone 4 US, 5 Can.

***C. b.* 'Pyramidalis'** See *C. b.* 'Fastigiata'.

Carpinus caroliniana

C. caroliniana (American hornbeam, blue beech) A beautiful small tree with gray fluted bark among its many attractive features. It is not as tall as *C. betulus* and has spreading branches that arch at their tips. The leaves are a polished apple green and become red-orange in early fall. E North America. Introduced 1812.
Zone 3 US, 3b Can.

C. japonica (Japanese hornbeam) A beautiful, spreading, large shrub or small tree with corrugated leaves and conspicuous catkins in spring. Japan. Introduced 1895.
Zone 4 US, 5b Can.

C. laxiflora A medium-sized tree with rather drooping branches; ovate-oblong, slenderly pointed leaves; and loose clusters of bright green fruiting "keys" that are a particularly attractive feature in fall. Japan, Korea. Introduced 1914.
Zone 5 US, 6b Can. 🏆

Carpinus laxiflora

Carya *Juglandaceae*
Hickory

A genus of about 17 species of fast-growing, stately, large, deciduous trees allied to the walnuts (Juglans). *They are found mainly in eastern North America but also occur in Mexico and Southeast Asia. The large, compound leaves, often over 12 in (30 cm) long, turn clear yellow before falling, and the gray trunks become even more striking in winter. As they often have a long taproot, they are difficult to transplant; they should be sited carefully and planted when young. The nuts are contained in the four-valved fruit, but in moist climates with cool summers they are seldom if ever properly formed.*

C. cordiformis (Bitternut) Makes a large tree with thin, scaly, brown bark and characteristic yellow winter buds. The leaves usually have seven lanceolate leaflets but may occasionally have five or nine. Probably the best hickory for general planting. E North America. Introduced 1766.
Zone 4 US, 4 Can. 🏆

C. ovata (Shagbark hickory) The most valuable nut-producing species in the United States, with several cultivars grown for their heavy cropping. As an ornamental, it is a handsome tree of medium to large size with leaves consisting of five long-pointed leaflets, of which the two lower ones are rounder and shorter than the

Carya cordiformis

Carya ovata

other three. The foliage turns rich yellow in fall. The bark, which lifts off in long strips, makes it easy to identify. E North America. In cultivation 1629.
Zone 4 US, 4b Can. 🏆

Caryopteris *Verbenaceae*

A genus of about six species of small, showy deciduous shrubs with aromatic leaves, flowering in late summer. They grow best in well-drained soil and full sun and are excellent for alkaline soils. They may be found in the wild in an area stretching from the Himalaya to Japan.

C.* × *clandonensis (Bluebeard) A variable hybrid *(C. incana × C. mongholica)* that was raised by Arthur Simmonds, a noted secretary of the Royal Horticultural Society. It makes a small shrub to about 3 ft (1 m) tall and is especially valuable for its late season bloom. The plant usually seen in gardens under this name is *C.* × *c.* 'Arthur Simmonds'. Raised 1933.
Zone 5 US, 6 Can.

***C.* × *c.* 'Blue Mist'** This is an attractive hybrid that thrives almost anywhere, producing its bright blue flowers in late summer and early fall. It is an ideal subject for mass effect and can be kept to a height of about 24 in (60 cm) by pruning back in early spring. Rightly one of the most popular of all the bluebeards.
Zone 5 US, 6 Can.

***C.* × *c.* 'Heavenly Blue'** This is considered to be the best of the clones and certainly better than either 'Ferndown' or 'Kew Blue', which are hardly different from

Caryopteris × *clandonensis* 'Heavenly Blue'

'Arthur Simmonds'. It is a compact, free-flowering small shrub and has the deepest blue flowers.
Zone 5 US, 6 Can. 🏆

Caryopteris × *clandonensis* 'Worcester Gold'

***C.* × *c.* 'Worcester Gold'** Still rather difficult to find, this small shrub with leaves flushed golden yellow has a tendency, on occasion, to look somewhat chlorotic even when quite healthy.
Zone 5 US, 6 Can.

Cassinia *Compositae*

A genus of about 28 species of evergreen, heathlike shrubs found in Australia, New Zealand, and South Africa. Those listed below are from New Zealand and are grown mainly for their foliage, but they do bear numerous small heads of white flowers if conditions are right. They perform best when given full sun and good drainage.

C. fulvida (Golden cottonwood, golden heather) A small, erect, dense shrub with small, crowded leaves that give a golden effect. The flowers are white and are borne in dense terminal heads in midsummer. The young growths are sticky to the touch.
Zone 7 US, 8 Can.

C. vauvilliersii* var. *albida (Silver heather) This is similar to *C. fulvida* but taller and more upright and with larger leaves, which, along with the stems, are white and hoary.
Zone 8 US, 9? Can.

Cassiope *Ericaceae*

A genus of about 10 species of attractive dwarf shrublets, related to Calluna *and* Erica, *with tiny, densely overlapping leaves and solitary, bell-shaped flowers. They are natives of arctic and northern mountain regions and require a moist, peaty, acidic soil and conditions like those of open moorland. All are evergreen.*

Cassiope 'Edinburgh'

***C.* 'Edinburgh'** A hybrid with slender, dark green stems up to 7 in (18 cm) high, which in spring bear white flowers with a green calyx edged in red. It is perhaps the most easily grown of a fairly fussy genus. A chance seedling raised at the Royal Botanic Garden, Edinburgh.
Zone 3? US, 3b? Can. 🏆

C. lycopodioides This species forms a prostrate mat or shallow bun of threadlike branches, above which little white bells dangle from slender stalks in spring to summer. NE Asia, NW North America.
Zone 3 US, 3b Can. 🏆

***C.* 'Muirhead'** A tiny shrublet with char-

Cassiope 'Muirhead'

acteristically curved, repeatedly forked shoots and small, nodding, white flowers that are borne in spring.
Zone 3? US, 3b? Can. 🏆

***C.* 'Randle Cooke'** A mat-forming shrublet with stems up to 6 in (15 cm) tall. The white, bell-shaped flowers appear along the stems in midspring. Originated 1957 in a garden in Northumberland, England.
Zone 3? US, 3b? Can. 🏆

Castanea *Fagaceae*
Chestnut

A genus of about 12 species of deciduous trees and shrubs found in temperate parts of the Northern Hemisphere. They are long-lived, drought-resistant plants that thrive in well-drained, preferably light soils. Because it is susceptible to chestnut blight, which decimated stands of the native American chestnut (C. dentata), *the following species, a major ornamental tree in Europe, cannot be imported to North America.*

Castanea sativa

Castanea sativa 'Albomarginata'

C. sativa (Spanish chestnut, sweet chestnut) A fast-growing tree. A large specimen can be extremely ornamental, particularly at midsummer, when its large, sharply toothed leaves contrast with its yellowish male and female catkins. Hotter than average summers are generally required to produce good crops of nuts, although in sunnier areas with lower rainfall they occur more often. A valuable timber tree, useful for coppicing, that has been in cultivation for a long time. S Europe, N Africa, Asia Minor.
Zone 5 US, 6 Can. 🏆

***C. s.* 'Albomarginata'** A large tree bearing leaves with a creamy white margin.
Zone 5 US, 6 Can.

***C. s.* 'Marron de Lyon'** A cultivar selected for its large nuts, and the best fruiting clone, fruiting at an early age.
Zone 5 US, 6 Can.

Catalpa *Bignoniaceae*

A genus of about 11 species of midsummer-flowering deciduous trees, mostly of low, spreading habit. The foxglovelike flowers, which are not produced by young plants, are borne in showy panicles and are followed by slender beanlike seedpods. They should not be planted in exposed sites where their large, usually heart-shaped leaves might become tattered. Catalpas are suitable for all types of well-drained soil and tolerate pollution. They are natives of North America and China.

Catalpa bignonioides

Catalpa bignonioides flower detail

C. bignonioides (Southern catalpa, Indian bean tree) A round-headed tree with smaller leaves, up to 8 in (20 cm) long and wide, than those of the other species and dainty, scented white flowers with yellow and purple markings, borne in candelabras in midsummer. E United States. Introduced 1726. Zone 4 US, 5 Can. 🏆

Catalpa bignonioides 'Aurea'

***C. b.* 'Aurea'** An outstanding large shrub or small tree with large, velvety, soft yellow leaves that are almost green by the time the flowers open. In cultivation 1877.
Zone 4 US, 5b Can. 🏆

***C. b.* 'Variegata'** A large shrub or small tree with leaves that are variegated a cream-yellow.
Zone 4 US, 5b Can.

***C.* × *erubescens* 'Purpurea'** A medium-sized tree with broad leaves, some of which are entire and some three-lobed, and midsummer flowers like those of *C. bignonioides* but smaller and more numerous. The young leaves and shoots are dark purple, almost black, and gradually become dark green. In cultivation 1886.
Zone 5 US, 6 Can. 🏆

Catalpa speciosa

Catalpa bignonioides 'Variegata'

C. fargesii* f. *duclouxii A fine, midsummer-flowering, medium-sized tree with leaves smaller than those of *C. bignonioides.* The flowers are foxglovelike, lilac-pink with red-brown spots and stained with yellow, and are borne in clusters of 7–15. China. Introduced 1907 by Ernest Wilson.
Zone 5 US, 6 Can.

C. speciosa (Northern catalpa) A tall tree with large, heart-shaped leaves and purple-spotted flowers, slightly larger but with fewer in the cluster than those of *C. bignonioides.* C United States. Introduced 1880.
Zone 4 US, 5 Can.

Catalpa × *erubescens* 'Purpurea'

Ceanothus

Rhamnaceae

This mature ceanothus, with its exquisitely colored blooms and dense growth, is a superb choice for underplanting beneath elegant birches.

Ceanothus are sometimes called California lilacs — many of the species are native to that state and all bear fluffy panicles of blue, pink, or white blooms that are reminiscent of the lilac's conelike flower clusters. The genus includes some 55 species of evergreen and deciduous shrubs and trees that are widely distributed over the United States, southern Canada, and Mexico south to Guatemala.

Ceanothus range from the small-tree size of *C. arboreus* to prostrate, carpeting shrubs such as *C. prostratus* and *C. thyrsiflorus* var. *repens*. Most ceanothus are evergreen and require a warm climate, including the three species mentioned above. A few, however, are deciduous, such as 'Gloire de Versailles' and 'Topaz', which are hybrids between the very hardy East Coast native *C. americanus* and a Mexican species.

Ceanothus do well, perhaps surprisingly so, in areas outside their native habitat, and this is probably due to their origins in chaparral — bushy brushwood that grows at elevations where the climate is considerably cooler than on the coastal plain below. Most of the hybrids are not hardy enough to survive very far north, but they also do not thrive in summer heat and humidity and so are not good choices for the East or Midwest. They do grow successfully in the cooler conditions of the Pacific coastal area. However, their beauty is such that gardeners will find it worth every effort to make room in their yards for one or more of these spectacular shrubs.

The deciduous ceanothus are hardier than the evergreens, and among the latter those with smaller leaves (less than about 1 in/2.5 cm long) are usually, but not always, hardier than those with leaves on the large side. Although you might imagine that the deciduous plants would be more popular because of their greater hardiness, this is not the case, and the evergreens, which remain attractive even when not in flower, are much more sought after.

Care and cultivation

Ceanothus should be planted in a sunny location with light, well-drained soil and need to be sheltered from cold, drying winds; this is especially true of the evergreens. It is also advisable to site them carefully, as the evergreens resent being moved once they begin to get established; deciduous ceanothus tolerate transplanting somewhat better. At the limits of their range they benefit from being planted against or in the shelter of a warm wall, but failing that, the sunny side of a belt of evergreen shrubs can provide sufficient shelter.

Ceanothus are reasonably tolerant of lime, although they will not thrive in hot, shallow alkaline soils. Most are resistant to salty, coastal conditions.

Deciduous ceanothus should have their lateral branches pruned in early spring to within 3–4 in (8–10 cm) of the previous year's growth. Evergreens are best not pruned at all, if possible, except for removing dead wood in spring. This is another reason for selecting a permanent place for the plants with care, so that they can spread without interference. If they are adequately spaced from the start, there should be no need for pruning, which, if repeated regularly, shortens the lives of the shrubs. Any light trimming that may be necessary should be carried out immediately after flowering.

Ceanothus may be propagated by taking semihardwood cuttings in summer.

***C. arboreus* 'Trewithen Blue'** A vigorous, large, spreading evergreen shrub or small tree with large, ovate leaves. The big panicles of vivid, deep blue, slightly scented flowers are borne in spring. It is best grown against a wall, where it can be tied back if it becomes top-heavy.
Zone 8 US, 9? Can. 🏆

***C.* 'A. T. Johnson'** A vigorous and free-flowering evergreen hybrid with rich blue flowers in spring and again in fall. The leaves of this medium-sized shrub are ovate, glossy green, and gray-downy on their undersides.
Zone 8 US, 9 Can.

***C.* 'Autumnal Blue'** Of the evergreen hybrid ceanothus, this medium-sized shrub is possibly the hardiest. It bears abundant panicles of sky blue flowers in late summer, fall, and often spring as well. The leaves are broadly ovate, three-veined, and bright, glossy green.
Zone 8 US, 9 Can. 🏆

***C.* 'Blue Jeans'** A small to medium-sized evergreen shrub that makes a dense mound of arching branches with glossy dark green, hollylike, spine-toothed leaves. The massed clusters of deep lavender-blue flowers are so prolific that they almost completely hide the foliage in mid- to late spring.
Zone 7 US, 8 Can.

***C.* 'Blue Mound'** A dense, bushy, small to medium-sized, evergreen shrub with dense clusters of bright blue flowers in late spring, early summer, and usually again in late summer and fall. The leaves are glossy green and wavy edged. Raised at Hillier Nurseries.
Zone 7 US, 8 Can. 🏆

***C.* 'Burkwoodii'** A medium-sized, dense, rounded, evergreen shrub with rich dark blue flowers throughout summer and fall and oval, glossy leaves.
Zone 8 US, 9 Can. 🏆

***C.* 'Cascade'** A lovely hybrid of the evergreen, spring-flowering group, bearing its bright blue flowers in elongated clusters. It makes a medium-sized shrub.
Zone 8 US, 9? Can. 🏆

***C.* 'Concha'** A dense, medium-sized, evergreen shrub, broader than it is tall, with profuse clusters of deep blue flowers emerging from red buds in late spring to early

Ceanothus arboreus 'Trewithen Blue'

Ceanothus 'Blue Mound'

Ceanothus 'Burkwoodii'

Ceanothus 'Cascade'

Ceanothus 'Concha'

summer. It has arching branches and narrow, dark green leaves.
Zone 7 US, 8 Can.

C. **'Dark Star'** An arching, medium-sized, evergreen shrub bearing small ovate leaves up to 3/8 in (8 mm) long with deeply impressed veins. Deep purplish blue, honey-scented flowers are borne in clusters in early spring.
Zone 8 US, 9 Can.

Ceanothus 'Delight'

C. **'Delight'** A splendid evergreen hybrid, and one of the hardiest. It is a medium-sized shrub with rich blue flowers borne in long panicles in spring.
Zone 7 US, 8 Can. 🏆

Ceanothus 'Edinburgh'

C. **'Edinburgh'** A dense, medium-sized, evergreen shrub with large, olive green leaves and rich blue flowers in spring and early summer. Originated at the Royal Botanic Gardens, Edinburgh.
Zone 7 US, 8 Can. 🏆

Ceanothus 'Gloire de Versailles'

C. **'Gloire de Versailles'** This is the most popular deciduous ceanothus. It is a medium-sized shrub bearing large panicles of powder blue flowers in summer and fall.
Zone 7 US, 8 Can. 🏆

C. ***gloriosus*** **'Emily Brown'** A dwarf evergreen shrub making a low mound with arching shoots and hollylike leaves. Clusters of violet-blue flowers are borne in mid- to late spring.
Zone 7 US, 8 Can.

C. ***griseus*** **'Yankee Point'** This shrub makes a mound about 2 ft (60 cm) tall and 10 ft (3 m) wide. It is frequently grown for its very dark, evergreen leaves and deep blue flowers.
Zone 8 US, 9? Can.

Ceanothus impressus

C. ***impressus*** (Santa Barbara ceanothus) A small to medium-sized shrub with deep blue flowers in spring. It is very distinct in its small leaves, which have deeply impressed veins, and is among the hardiest of the evergreen ceanothus.
Zone 7 US, 8 Can.

Ceanothus 'Italian Skies'

C. **'Italian Skies'** A vigorous, medium-sized, densely branched, evergreen shrub with deep blue flowers in late spring and small, dark green leaves.
Zone 7 US, 8 Can. 🏆

Ceanothus 'Marie Simon'

C. **'Marie Simon'** A medium-sized, deciduous shrub with pink flowers borne in panicles on the young growths in summer.
Zone 8 US, 9 Can.

C. ***papillosus*** **subsp.** ***roweanus*** A narrow-leaved form of the species, this medium-sized to large, evergreen shrub gives a brilliant display of rich blue flowers in late spring. The leaves are notable for the slightly sticky, glandular papillae on their upper surfaces.
Zone 8 US, 9 Can.

C. **'Perle Rose'** A medium-sized, bushy, deciduous shrub with bright rose-carmine

to strawberry-pink flowers in summer.
Zone 7 US, 8 Can.

C. prostratus (Squaw carpet) A creeping evergreen, making a dense mat up to 5 ft (1.5 m) wide, with bright blue flowers in spring. Its leaves are opposite, leathery, dark green, and toothed.
Zone 7 US, 8 Can.

Ceanothus 'Puget Blue'

***C.* 'Puget Blue'** This magnificent dense, medium-sized, evergreen shrub is possibly a hybrid between *C. impressus* and *C. papillosus*. It bears deep blue flowers over a long period during late spring and early summer. Raised before 1945 at the Washington Arboretum, Seattle, Washington.
Zone 6 US, 7 Can. 🏆

***C.* 'Southmead'** A dense-growing, evergreen shrub of medium size with very dark, rich blue flowers in late spring and early summer. The small, oblong leaves are glossy, dark green on their upper sides.
Zone 8 US, 9 Can. 🏆

C. thyrsiflorus (Blueblossom) A large shrub and one of the hardiest evergreen species. It bears bright blue flowers in early summer and has broadly elliptic, dark green, three-veined leaves.
Zone 7 US, 8 Can.

***C. t.* 'Millerton Point'** A vigorous, medium-sized shrub with fresh green leaves and white flowers in late spring and early summer.
Zone 7 US, 8 Can.

C. t.* var. *repens (Creeping blueblossom) A vigorous, comparatively hardy, mound-forming variety, rather variable in habit, that produces generous quantities of blue flowers in spring and early summer.
Zone 7 US, 8 Can. 🏆

Ceanothus thyrsiflorus var. *repens*

***C. t.* 'Skylark'** A medium-sized evergreen shrub with glossy green leaves to 2 in (5 cm) long. Clusters of deep blue flowers are profusely borne over a long period during late spring and early summer.
Zone 8 US, 9 Can.

Ceanothus 'Topaz'

***C.* 'Topaz'** A medium-sized to large deciduous shrub renowned for its light indigo blue flowers borne in summer.
Zone 7 US, 8 Can. 🏆

C.* × *veitchianus A large evergreen shrub with deep blue flowers in late spring and early summer and small, glossy green, wedge-shaped leaves. It is deservedly popular, as it is free flowering, rich in color, and comparatively hardy. A naturally occurring hybrid discovered and introduced 1853 by William Lobb.
Zone 8 US, 9 Can.

Cedrela

C. sinensis See *Toona sinensis*.

Cedrus *Pinaceae*

Cedar

A genus of four species of evergreen coniferous trees — the true cedars. They are renowned for their grandeur and their longevity. Young trees are conical, often developing massive trunks and large, horizontal branches as they age. The narrow, needlelike leaves are in sparse spirals on terminal shoots and in rosettes on the spurlike side growths. Good drainage is essential, but cedars will grow in any soil from acid sand to clay and limestone.

C. atlantica (Atlas cedar) A large or very large tree that grows rapidly when it is young. The leaves are ¾–1½ in (2–3.5 cm) long, green or gray-green, and cover the young branches thickly. The species is very similar to *C. libani* and is now considered by some authorities to be one of its subspecies. N Africa. Introduced c. 1840.
Zone 5 US, 6 Can.

***C. a.* 'Aurea'** A medium-sized tree with shorter leaves that are distinctly golden yellow. It does not always grow satisfactorily. In cultivation 1900.
Zone 5 US, 6 Can.

Cedrus atlantica 'Fastigiata'

***C. a.* 'Fastigiata'** A large, densely branched, erect tree with sharply ascending branches and short, erect branchlets. The leaves are bluish green. In cultivation 1890.
Zone 5 US, 6 Can.

Glauca group (Blue cedar) Perhaps the

Cedrus atlantica Glauca group

most spectacular of all blue conifers and a very popular tree for specimen planting. The leaves are silvery blue and have a highly effective shimmering quality.
Zone 5 US, 6 Can.
🏆

***C. a.* 'Glauca Pendula'** A superb small tree with weeping branches and blue-bloomy leaves. In cultivation 1900.
Zone 5 US, 6 Can.

Cedrus deodara

***C. a.* 'Pendula'** A small, weeping tree distinguishable by its green or grayish green leaves. In cultivation 1875.
Zone 5 US, 6 Can.

C. brevifolia (Cyprus cedar) A rare, slow-growing tree, eventually reaching medium size. The leaves are much smaller than those of *C. libani*, of which some consider it to be a subspecies. Mountains of Cyprus. Introduced 1879. Zone 5 US, 6 Can. 🏆

C. deodara (Deodar cedar) A beautiful, large, somewhat pendent tree with leaves that are bluish bloomy when young but soon become deep green. It is readily distinguished from all other cedars by its drooping leader and its longer leaves, which are sometimes as long as 2 in (5 cm). W Himalaya. Introduced 1831.
Zone 6 US, 7 Can. 🏆

Cedrus deodara 'Aurea'

***C. d.* 'Aurea'** (Golden deodar cedar) The leaves of this large tree are golden yellow in spring, becoming greenish yellow later in the year. In cultivation 1866.
Zone 6 US, 6b Can. 🏆

***C. d.* 'Golden Horizon'** A large, spreading bush with golden yellow foliage. Raised in Holland.
Zone 6 US, 7 Can.

***C. d.* 'Karl Fuchs'** Very hardy, with good silvery blue foliage. Its ultimate height is as yet uncertain. Raised c. 1979 in Germany from seed collected in Afghanistan.
Zone 6 US, 6b Can.

C. libani (Cedar of Lebanon) A large, wide-spreading tree, slower growing than *C. atlantica* and also conical when young, gradually assuming the familiar, pic-

Cedrus libani

turesque, flat-topped and tiered structure of a mature tree. The leaves are green or grayish green, ³/₄–1¹/₂ in (2–3.5 cm) long. Asia Minor, Syria, Lebanon. Introduced c. 1645.
Zone 5 US, 6 Can. 🏆

***C. l.* 'Comte de Dijon'** A slow-growing, conical form of dense, compact growth, eventually a medium-sized shrub. In cultivation 1867.
Zone 5 US, 6 Can.

***C. l.* 'Sargentii'** A slow-growing, small

Cedrus libani 'Sargentii'

shrub with a short trunk and dense, weeping branches with blue-green leaves. It is ideal for a rock garden.
Zone 5 US, 6 Can.

Celastrus *Celastraceae*

Bittersweet

A genus of about 30 species of vigorous deciduous climbers whose main attraction is their seed capsules and fall color. The flowers have only one sex on each specimen, so unless a hermaphrodite form (which has flowers of both sexes) is grown, it is advisable to grow more than one plant for a display of capsules.

Celastrus orbiculatus

C. orbiculatus (Oriental bittersweet) A climber for sun or shade and reasonably fertile soil that can grow 40 ft (12 m) or more in a tree. The twining young shoots have a pair of spines at each bud and leaves up to 5 in (13 cm) long. In fall the capsules split open to reveal a yellow lining, against which the bright red seeds show brilliantly. NE Asia. Introduced 1860.
Zone 4 US, 4 Can. 🏆

C. scandens (American bittersweet) Similar to the previous species, but the capsules are orange inside. E North America.
Zone 3 US, 3 Can.

Celtis *Ulmaceae*

Hackberry, nettle tree

A genus of 60 or more species of medium-sized, deciduous trees related to the elms and occurring in northerly temperate regions and the tropics. They require consistently warm summers and are not at their best in cooler, maritime climates. They will grow in most soils and tolerate dryness.

C. australis (Mediterranean hackberry) A small to medium-sized tree with characteristically broad, lance-shaped leaves that are rough to the touch on their upper surfaces. S Europe, North Africa, Asia Minor. In cultivation since the 16th century.
Zone 5 US, 6 Can.

Celtis occidentalis

C. occidentalis (Common hackberry) A medium-sized tree; mature specimens have rough, warted, corky bark. Fruit is a small, black, edible berry with a large pit. North America. Introduced 1656.
Zone 2 US, 2b Can.

Cephalanthus *Rubiaceae*

A genus of about six species of evergreen and deciduous trees found in North and Central America, eastern Asia, and Africa.

Cephalanthus occidentalis

C. occidentalis (Buttonbush) An easily cultivated but rarely grown, medium-sized, deciduous shrub with ovate leaves 2–6 in (5–15 cm) long and creamy white, fragrant flowers produced in small, globular heads in late summer. It will grow in moist soils that are rich in organic matter and does best in an open site. E and S United States. Introduced 1735.
Zone 4 US, 5 Can.

Cephalotaxus *Cephalotaxaceae*

Plum yew

A genus of four species of evergreen coniferous shrubs or shrubby trees, in effect large-leaved yews, that are natives of the Himalaya and eastern Asia. Like yews, they grow well in shade and in the drip of other trees. The female plants produce large, olivelike fruits that ripen in their second year. The leaves have two broad, silvery bands beneath.

Cephalotaxus fortunei 'Prostrate Spreader'

***C. fortunei* 'Prostrate Spreader'** A low-growing shrub with wide-spreading branches and large, deep green, lanceolate leaves 2½–3½ in (6–9 cm) long, arranged spirally in two opposite rows along the branches. It is a superb, spreading groundcover plant that tolerates shade very well. It originated at Hillier Nurseries before World War I as a side cutting from the species, and the original plant reached 32 in (0.8 m) high by 15 ft (5 m) across.
Zone 6 US, 7 Can.

Cephalotaxus harringtonia 'Fastigiata'

C. harringtonia* var. *drupacea (Japanese plum yew) A dense, compact, medium-sized shrub rarely higher than 10 ft (3 m), with ascending leaves ¾–2 in (2–5 cm) long. Large plants make beautiful mounds with elegant, drooping branchlets. The olive green fruits are ¾–1¼ in (2–3 cm) long. C China, Japan.
Zone 5 US, 6b Can.

***C. h.* 'Fastigiata'** An erectly branched, medium to large shrub, resembling the Irish yew in habit. Its leaves are almost black-green and spread all around the shoots. Garden origin in Japan. Introduced 1861.
Zone 5 US, 6b Can.

***C. h.* 'Gnome'** A dwarf with ascending stems and radially arranged leaves, forming a flat-topped dome. A sport from 'Fastigiata'. Raised 1970 by Hillier Nurseries.
Zone 5 US, 6b Can.

Ceratostigma *Plumbaginaceae*

Plumbago

A genus of about eight deciduous species found in eastern Asia and eastern Africa. The cultivated species are small, ornamental shrubs that bear blue flowers over a long period in early fall and are suitable for dry, well-drained soil, preferably in full sun. For the best effect, the old flowering growths should be cut back in spring.

Ceratostigma griffithii

C. griffithii A beautiful, low-growing, semievergreen species with deep blue flowers and leaves that turn bright red in late fall, often persisting well into winter. After a severe winter, it is reluctant to flower well.
Zone 9 US

C. willmottianum (Chinese plumbago) A deciduous shrub about 3 ft (1 m) high with rich blue flowers appearing in mid-summer and continuing until fall, when the foliage becomes tinted with red. Ideal for either a shrub or herbaceous border. W China. Introduced 1908 by Ernest Wilson.
Zone 7 US, 8 Can. 🏆

Ceratostigma willmottianum

Cercidiphyllum *Cercidiphyllaceae*

A genus of one species of deciduous tree from eastern Asia, grown for the color and shape of its foliage. The inconspicuous red flowers emerge with the young leaves, with males and females on separate plants.

C. japonicum (Katsura tree) An attractive tree with leaves similar to those of the Judas tree *(Cercis siliquastrum)* but opposite and smaller. Pyramidal when young; mature shape varies and can become quite broad. New leaves are purplish pink, becoming blue-green, then turning pale yellow or apricot in fall and scenting the air with the aroma of burnt sugar, accentuated when crushed. It prefers a deep, moist, fertile soil and will not perform well in dry conditions. Can be grown as a multitrunked specimen. Japan, China. Introduced 1881.
Zone 4 US, 5 Can. 🏆

Cercidiphyllum japonicum

C. j.* var. *magnificum A rare, medium-sized tree with smoother bark and larger, more heart-shaped leaves with coarser serrations than the species. Its fall color is a lovely yellow. Japan.
Zone 4 US, 5 Can. 🏆

***C. j.* 'Pendulum'** An unusual form of medium height with long, pendulous branches. Japan.
Zone 4 US, 5 Can.

Cercis *Leguminosae*

Redbud

A genus of about six species of small, deciduous trees with broad, rounded, heart-shaped leaves and beautiful pea flowers in spring, widely distributed in temperate regions of the Northern Hemisphere. Their apparently simple leaves are in fact formed by fusion of the leaflets of pinnate leaves. They need full sun and good drainage. Pruning is rarely required.

C. canadensis (Eastern redbud) A small tree with a broad, round head. In its native range it flowers very freely, its branches covered with pale rose, pealike flowers before the foliage appears; the fall foliage is bright yellow. The following form is recom-

Cercis canadensis 'Forest Pansy'

mended. SE Canada, E United States, NE Mexico. Introduced 1730.
Zone 4 US, 6 Can.

***C. c.* 'Forest Pansy'** A splendid large shrub or small tree grown for its deep reddish purple leaves; it can be grown as a stooled specimen for a better foliage display. It flowers, but inconspicuously, in late spring and early summer.
Zone 4 US, 6 Can. 🏆

Cercis siliquastrum

C. siliquastrum (Judas tree) The branches and even the trunk of this medium-sized tree or large shrub are wreathed in rosy lilac flowers in late spring, making a unique display, often followed by purple-tinted seedpods from midsummer onward. Legend has it that this was the tree from which Judas Iscariot hanged himself, but the name may also derive from its having once been common in the hills of Judaea. E Mediterranean region.
Zone 6 US, 7 Can. 🏆

Cercis siliquastrum 'Bodnant'

***C. s.* 'Alba'** A large shrub (more usually in cooler climates) or medium-sized tree with pale green foliage and white flowers borne in late spring.
Zone 6 US, 7 Can.

***C. s.* 'Bodnant'** A clone that is grown primarily for its deep purple flowers borne in late spring.
Zone 6 US, 7 Can.

Cestrum *Solanaceae*

A large genus of about 200 species of evergreen and deciduous shrubs and small trees native to Central and South America and the West Indies. The cultivated species are showy, medium-sized, flowering shrubs suitable for a warm wall or greenhouse. They will grow in any well-drained, friable soil.

Cestrum elegans

C. elegans A small to medium-sized evergreen shrub with large, startling clusters of bright red flowers over a long period in summer and fall. It usually needs some support. Mexico. Introduced 1840.
Zone 8 US, 9? Can. 🏆

***C.* 'Newellii'** An evergreen seedling very much like *C. elegans* in habit but with large, orange-red flowers in midsummer. Requires support.
Zone 8 US, 9? Can. 🏆

C. parqui (Willow-leaved jessamine) A small to medium-sized shrub with yellowish green flowers, fragrant at night, borne from early to midsummer. It is hardy in sunny, sheltered places where frost is light and infrequent, and although it may be cut to the ground in such situations, it can quickly

Cestrum parqui

recover. Chile. Introduced 1787.
Zone 8 US, 9? Can. 🏆

Chaenomeles *Rosaceae*

Flowering quince

Old names for this genus of three species of deciduous shrubs from eastern Asia are still used sometimes, but are incorrect. While you may hear them called japonicas, "japonica" merely means "from Japan" and is applied to many plants. Cydonia *is now the genus name for the true quinces only, and the name has not applied to the flowering quinces for many years. Chaenomeles are among the most beautiful and easily grown of early-flowering spring shrubs and have saucer-shaped flowers in shades of red, pink, orange, and white followed by large, yellow, aromatic fruits. They will thrive in an open border or against a wall, even when shaded, although in general they flower better in sun. They will grow in any well-drained, friable soil. When grown as wall shrubs, they can be cut back immediately after flowering,*

Chaenomeles japonica

leaving a framework of main branches and reducing the shoots of the previous year's growth to two or three buds. Freestanding shrubs need not be pruned unless their branches become overcrowded.

C. japonica (Japanese quince) A small, thorny shrub with bright flame-orange flowers followed by rounded, yellow, fragrant fruits. Japan. Introduced c. 1869.
Zone 4 US, 5 Can.

C. speciosa (Flowering quince) This species is represented in gardens mainly by its cultivars, which are the well-known, early-flowering quinces. It is a much-branched, spreading, thorny, medium-sized shrub; seed-raised plants bear flowers in mixed colors, though predominantly red. The following forms are recommended. China. Introduced 1869 by Sir Joseph Banks.
Zone 4 US, 5b Can.

Chaenomeles speciosa 'Geisha Girl'

***C. s.* 'Geisha Girl'** A medium-sized shrub with double, deep apricot-peach flowers.
Zone 4 US, 5b Can.

***C. s.* 'Nivalis'** A medium-sized shrub grown for its large, pure white flowers. In cultivation 1881.
Zone 4 US, 5b Can.

***C. s.* 'Simonii'** An exceptionally beautiful, dwarf, spreading shrub with blood red, flat, semidouble flowers. In cultivation 1882.
Zone 4 US, 5b Can.

***C. s.* 'Toyo-Nishiki'** An upright shrub that bears flowers of white, pink, and red, all at the same time. A deservedly popular shrub.
Zone 4 US, 5b Can.

Chaenomeles speciosa 'Simonii'

C. × superba *(C. japonica × C. speciosa)* Small to medium-sized shrubs with slender thorns and a vigorous habit. The following are recommended.
Zone 4 US, 5b Can.

Chaenomeles × superba 'Crimson and Gold'

***C. × s.* 'Crimson and Gold'** A medium-sized shrub bearing flowers that have deep crimson petals and distinct golden anthers, a bold combination. In cultivation 1939.
Zone 4 US, 5 Can. 🏆

***C. × s.* 'Fire Dance'** *(C. speciosa* 'Simonii' × *C. × superba)* A backcross with striking red flowers and a spreading habit, making a medium-sized shrub. In cultivation 1953.
Zone 4 US, 5b Can.

***C. × s.* 'Jet Trail'** A medium-sized, spreading shrub with few thorns and profusely borne pure white flowers.
Zone 4 US, 5b Can.

***C. × s.* 'Knap Hill Scarlet'** This medium-sized hybrid bears its bright orange-scarlet flowers profusely throughout spring and

Chaenomeles × superba 'Knap Hill Scarlet'

early summer. In cultivation 1891.
Zone 4 US, 5 Can. 🏆

***C. × s.* 'Nicoline'** A medium-sized shrub with scarlet red flowers and a spreading habit. In cultivation 1954.
Zone 4 US, 5b Can. 🏆

Chaenomeles × superba 'Pink Lady'

***C. × s.* 'Pink Lady'** This spreading shrub has clear rose-pink flowers opening from darker buds, produced profusely and early. In cultivation 1946.
Zone 4 US, 5 Can. 🏆

***C. × s.* 'Texas Scarlet'** This spreading shrub has perhaps the brightest red blooms of all the flowering quinces.
Zone 4 US, 5b Can.

Chamaecyparis *Cupressaceae*
False cypress

A genus of about seven species of evergreen trees, native to North America, Japan, and Taiwan. They are distinguished from Cupressus *chiefly by their flattened, frondlike branches. Young trees are conical and broaden as they mature. The leaves are opposite, densely arranged, awl shaped in seedling plants and then becoming small and scalelike. They thrive best in moist, well-drained soils; in dry, limestone ones they are slower growing. Unlike* Cupressus, *they do not resent disturbance and may be moved even as small specimen trees. Although there are few species, they have given rise to an astonishing number of cultivars that cover a wide range of shapes and sizes, with foliage varying greatly in form and color. A few are really dwarf, others are merely slow growing, while many are as vigorous as their typical form.*

C. lawsoniana (Lawson false cypress) A large, conical tree with drooping branches and broad, fanlike sprays of foliage that are arranged in drooping horizontals. It is a very useful and ornamental tree and makes an excellent hedge or screen even in exposed locations and shade. Its numerous cultivars range from dwarf shrubs suitable for a rock garden to stately, columnar trees in many shades of green, gray, blue, and yellow, including a number of variegated forms. Native to SW Oregon and NW California, where trees 200 ft (60 m) tall have been recorded. In cultivation, however, 70 ft (20 m) is seldom exceeded. Introduced 1854.
Zone 5 US, 6 Can.

Chamaecyparis lawsoniana 'Albospica'

***C. l.* 'Albospica'** A slow-growing, small, conical tree with green foliage that is speckled white; the tips of scattered shoots are cream. In cultivation 1884.
Zone 5 US, 6 Can.

***C. l.* 'Allumii'** A medium-sized, columnar tree with dense, compact, and ascending branches. The foliage is blue-gray, soft, in large, flattened sprays. A popular and commonly planted conifer. In cultivation 1891.
Zone 5 US, 6 Can.

***C. l.* 'Alumigold'** A sport of 'Allumii' with more compact habit; the young foliage is tipped with golden yellow.
Zone 5 US, 6 Can.

Chamaecyparis lawsoniana 'Aurea Densa'

***C. l.* 'Aurea Densa'** A small, slow-growing, conical, compact bush, eventually up to 6 ft (2 m) high. The foliage is golden yellow and arranged in short, flattened, densely packed sprays that are stiff to the touch. It is one of the best golden conifers for the rock garden.
Zone 5 US, 6 Can. 🏆

***C. l.* 'Backhouse Silver'** See *C. l.* 'Pygmaea Argentea'.

***C. l.* 'Bleu Nantais'** A slow-growing, small, conical shrub with striking, silvery blue foliage; useful in a rock garden.
Zone 5 US, 5b Can.

***C. l.* 'Broomhill Gold'** A small, upright tree with golden yellow young foliage that later turns green.
Zone 5 US, 6 Can.

Chamaecyparis lawsoniana 'Chilworth Silver'

***C. l.* 'Chilworth Silver'** A slow-growing, broadly columnar, medium-sized bush with densely packed, silvery blue juvenile foliage. Until 1968 recognized as a sport of *C. l.* 'Ellwoodii'.
Zone 5 US, 5b Can. 🏆

Chamaecyparis lawsoniana 'Columnaris'

***C. l.* 'Columnaris'** A small, narrow, conical tree with densely packed, ascending branches and flattened sprays that are bluish beneath and at the tips. It is one of the best narrow conifers for the small garden, but see also *C. l.* 'Van Pelt'. Raised c. 1940 by Jan Spek of Boskoop, Holland.
Zone 5 US, 6 Can.

***C. l.* 'Elegantissima'** A beautiful, small,

broadly conical tree with pale yellow shoots and broad, flattened, drooping sprays of silvery gray or grayish cream foliage. Raised before 1920 in the Hillier Nurseries.
Zone 5 US, 6 Can.

Chamaecyparis lawsoniana 'Ellwoodii'

***C. l.* 'Ellwoodii'** A slow-growing, columnar bush of medium to large size. The short, feathery sprays of gray-green foliage are densely arranged and become steel blue in winter. It is a deservedly popular and commonly planted conifer. Raised before 1929 in Swanmore Park, Bishops Waltham, England.
Zone 5 US, 6 Can. 🏆

***C. l.* 'Ellwood's Gold'** A neat, compact, columnar, slow-growing, medium-sized bush. The tips of the sprays are tinged with yellow, which gives the whole bush a warm glow. In cultivation 1968.
Zone 5 US, 5b Can. 🏆

***C. l.* 'Ellwood's Pillar'** A narrow and compact medium-sized form of 'Ellwoodii' with attractive, feathery, blue-gray foliage.
Zone 5 US, 5b Can.

***C. l.* 'Ellwood's Silver'** A medium-sized shrub similar to 'Ellwoodii' but with intensely silvery gray foliage.
Zone 5 US, 6 Can.

Chamaecyparis lawsoniana 'Ellwood's White'

***C. l.* 'Ellwood's White'** A slow-growing medium-sized sport of 'Ellwoodii' with cream or pale yellow patches of foliage. In cultivation 1965.
Zone 5 US, 6 Can.

***C. l.* 'Erecta'**, syn. *C. l.* 'Erecta Viridis' A medium-sized to large tree of dense, compact growth, columnar when young and broadening in maturity. The foliage is bright, rich green, arranged in large, flattened, vertical sprays. It usually forms numerous, long, erect branches and should be given winter protection to prevent damage in heavy snowfalls.
Zone 5 US, 6 Can.

***C. l.* 'Fletcheri'** A well-known conifer, forming a dense column up to 15 ft (5 m) or taller. It is usually a broad, columnar bush with several main stems. The semijuvenile foliage, feathery like that of 'Ellwoodii', is grayish green and becomes bronzed in winter. It is slow growing but becomes much too large for a rock garden. Introduced in England.
Zone 5 US, 6 Can. 🏆

Chamaecyparis lawsoniana 'Fletcheri'

Chamaecyparis lawsoniana 'Forsteckensis'

***C. l.* 'Forsteckensis'** A dwarf, slow-growing, dense, globular bush with short branchlets in congested, fernlike sprays and grayish blue-green foliage. A specimen at Hillier Nurseries reached 3 × 4 ft (0.9 × 1.2 m) after 30 years. Raised before 1891 at Forsteck, near Kiel, Germany.
Zone 5 US, 6 Can.

***C. l.* 'Fraseri'** A medium-sized tree of narrowly conical or columnar habit. Its erect branches have gray-green foliage in flattened, vertically arranged sprays. It is similar to *C. l.* 'Alumii' but has greener foliage and a neater base.
Zone 5 US, 6 Can.

***C. l.* 'Gimbornii'** A dwarf, dense, globular bush of slow growth with bluish green foliage that is tipped with mauve. It is eminently suitable for a rock garden. In cultivation before 1938.
Zone 5 US, 5b Can. 🏆

***C. l.* 'Golden Pot'** A small, narrow, conical tree with soft, bright golden yellow foliage that retains its color well. Its name derives from its being a sport of 'Pottenii'.
Zone 5 US, 6 Can.

***C. l.* 'Golden Wonder'** A medium-sized, broadly conical tree with bright yellow

Chamaecyparis lawsoniana 'Gimbornii'

foliage. Raised c. 1955 in Holland.
Zone 5 US, 6 Can.

C. l. **'Grayswood Feather'** A small, slender, columnar tree with upright sprays of dark green foliage.
Zone 5 US, 6 Can.

C. l. **'Grayswood Pillar'** A medium-sized, narrowly columnar tree with tightly packed, ascending branches and gray foliage. The original tree reached about 28 ft × 20 in (9 × 0.5 m) after 16 years.
Zone 5 US, 6 Can. 🏆

C. l. **'Green Globe'** A very dense, dwarf, rounded bush that becomes more irregular with age. The foliage is deep, bright green in short, tightly congested sprays. It tends to revert, with larger, coarser branches emerging; these should be cut out. Raised before 1973 in New Zealand.
Zone 5 US, 6 Can.

C. l. **'Green Hedger'** An erect, medium-sized to large tree of dense, conical habit with branches from the base and rich green foliage. It is excellent for hedges and screens. Raised before 1949 by Jackman's.
Zone 5 US, 6 Can. 🏆

Chamaecyparis lawsoniana 'Green Hedger'

C. l. **'Green Pillar'** A conical, upright, medium-sized tree with ascending branches clothed in bright green foliage that is lightened even further with a tint of gold in early spring. In cultivation 1940.
Zone 5 US, 6 Can.

C. l. **'Intertexta'** A superb large, open tree of ascending habit. The branches are loosely borne, with widely spaced, drooping branchlets and large, thick, flattened, fan-like sprays of dark, bloomy, green foliage. An attractive conifer that resembles *Cedrus deodara* from a distance. Raised c. 1869 at Lawson's nursery, Edinburgh.
Zone 5 US, 6 Can. 🏆

C. l. **'Kilmacurragh'** A medium to large, dense, narrowly columnar tree. The short, ascending branches have irregular sprays of dark green foliage. It is a superb tree, similar in effect to the Italian cypress and perfectly hardy. It is remarkably resistant to snow damage because of the angle of branching. Raised before 1951 at Kilmacurragh, County Wicklow, Ireland.
Zone 5 US, 6 Can. 🏆

C. l. **'Lane'**, *syn. C. l.* 'Lanei' A medium-sized, columnar tree with thin, feathery sprays of golden yellow foliage. One of the best golden cypresses. In cultivation 1938.
Zone 5 US, 6 Can. 🏆

C. l. **'Little Spire'** A slow-growing, small, narrowly conical tree with the distinctive foliage of *C. l.* 'Wisselii'.
Zone 5 US, 6 Can.

C. l. **'Lutea'** A medium-sized, broadly columnar tree with a narrow, drooping top. The foliage is golden yellow and arranged in large, flattened, feathery sprays. This is a long-standing cultivar that has been well tried and is deservedly popular.
Zone 5 US, 6 Can. 🏆

Chamaecyparis lawsoniana 'Lutea'

C. l. **'Lutea Nana'** A small, slow-growing, narrowly conical bush, eventually 6 ft (2 m) high. Foliage is golden and arranged in flattened sprays. In cultivation 1930.
Zone 5 US, 6 Can. 🏆

Chamaecyparis lawsoniana 'Minima Aurea'

C. l. **'Minima Aurea'** A densely growing, dwarf, conical bush with vertically held sprays of golden yellow foliage that is soft to the touch. One of the best golden conifers for a rock garden. In cultivation 1929.
Zone 5 US, 6 Can. 🏆

C. l. **'Minima Glauca'** A dense, globular, dwarf bush of slow growth. The foliage is sea green, borne in short, densely packed, often vertically arranged sprays. A specimen at Hillier Nurseries reached 3 × 4 ft (1 × 1.2 m) in 25 years. In cultivation 1863.
(Photo on p.210.) Zone 5 US, 6 Can. 🏆

Chamaecyparis lawsoniana 'Minima Glauca'

***C. l.* 'Naberi'** A medium-sized, conical tree. The green foliage is distinctive because of its sulphur yellow tips that pale to a creamy blue during winter. In cultivation 1929.
Zone 5 US, 6 Can.

***C. l.* 'Pembury Blue'** A medium-sized, conical tree with sprays of silvery blue foliage. A very striking cultivar and perhaps the best blue Lawson false cypress.
Zone 5 US, 5b Can. 🏆

Chamaecyparis lawsoniana 'Pembury Blue'

***C. l.* 'Pottenii'** A medium-sized, columnar tree of dense, slow growth. The sea green foliage is partly juvenile and is in soft, crowded, feathery sprays. A very decorative conifer.
Zone 5 US, 6 Can.

***C. l.* 'Pygmaea Argentea'**, syn. *C. l.* 'Backhouse Silver' A dwarf, slow-growing, rounded bush with dark bluish green foliage tipped in silvery white. It is suitable for a rock garden and is perhaps the best dwarf, white-variegated conifer. Raised before 1891 by James Backhouse and Son of York.
Zone 5 US, 5b Can. 🏆

***C. l.* 'Silver Threads'** A large shrub or small tree with foliage marked in cream and silver. A sport of 'Ellwood's Gold'.
Zone 5 US, 6 Can.

***C. l.* 'Snow White'** A dwarf, compact shrub with juvenile foliage that is tipped with white.
Zone 5 US, 6 Can.

Chamaecyparis lawsoniana 'Stardust'

***C. l.* 'Stardust'** A superb columnar or narrowly conical, medium-sized tree with yellow foliage that is bronze at the tips.
Zone 5 US, 6 Can. 🏆

***C. l.* 'Stewartii'** A medium-sized to large, elegant, conical tree with slightly erect branches that have large, flattened sprays of golden yellow foliage that change to yellowish green in winter. A very hardy, popular conifer and one of the best golden Lawsons. In cultivation 1890.
Zone 5 US, 6 Can.

***C. l.* 'Summer Snow'** A small, bushy shrub with white young growth.
Zone 5 US, 5b Can.

***C. l.* 'Tamariscifolia'** A slow-growing, eventually medium to large bush with several ascending and spreading main stems. It is flat topped and spreading when young, becoming umbrella shaped. Foliage is sea green and arranged in horizontal, flattened, fanlike sprays. In cultivation 1923.
Zone 5 US, 6 Can.

Chamaecyparis lawsoniana 'Treasure'

***C. l.* 'Treasure'** A large, narrowly upright shrub with blue-green juvenile foliage heavily flecked with creamy yellow.
Zone 5 US, 6 Can.

***C. l.* 'Triomf van Boskoop'** This was once a very popular conifer, growing into a large, open, conical tree with bloomy blue foliage in large, flat sprays. It needs to be trimmed to keep it dense. Raised c. 1890 in Holland.
Zone 5 US, 6 Can.

***C. l.* 'Van Pelt'** A narrowly conical, small tree with deep blue-gray foliage that later becomes blue-green. An improvement on *C. l.* 'Columnaris', itself a fine conifer.
Zone 5 US, 6 Can. 🏆

***C. l.* 'Westermannii'** A medium-sized, broadly conical tree with loose, spreading branches. The foliage is in large sprays, light yellow when young and turning yellowish green. Raised c. 1880 in Holland.
Zone 5 US, 6 Can.

***C. l.* 'White Spot'** The foliage of this small tree is gray-green and the young growth is flecked with cream.
Zone 5 US, 6 Can.

Chamaecyparis lawsoniana 'Winston Churchill'

***C. l.* 'Winston Churchill'** A dense, broadly columnar, small to medium-sized tree with foliage that is rich yellow year-round. One of the best Lawson false cypresses, although it can be difficult to establish. Raised before 1945.
Zone 5 US, 6 Can.

Chamaecyparis lawsoniana 'Wisselii'

***C. l.* 'Wisselii'** A very distinct and attractive, fast-growing tree of medium to large size. It is slender and conical with widely spaced, ascending branches, and the stout, upright branchlets bear short, crowded, fernlike sprays of bluish green foliage. The rather numerous, red, male cones are most attractive in spring. In cultivation 1888. Raised by F. van der Wissel of Epe, Holland.
Zone 5 US, 6 Can. 🏆

***C. l.* 'Witzeliana'** A small, narrow, columnar tree with long, ascending branches and vivid green, crowded sprays. An effective conifer, like a slender green flame. In cultivation 1931.
Zone 5 US, 6 Can.

***C. l.* 'Yellow Transparent'** The young foliage is yellowish and in summer is transparent with the sun behind it. It turns bronze in winter. Slow growing. Raised c. 1955 at Boskoop, Holland.
Zone 5 US, 6 Can.

C. nootkatensis (Nootka false cypress) A large, conical tree with drooping branchlets and coarser, more aromatic, duller green foliage than *C. lawsoniana* that is rough to the touch due to sharp-pointed, scalelike leaves. The male cones are yellow. The following forms are recommended. W North America. Introduced c. 1853.
Zone 4 US, 5 Can.

***C. n.* 'Lutea'** A medium-sized, conical tree with foliage that is yellow when young and gradually becomes yellowish green as the tree matures. In cultivation 1891.
Zone 4 US, 5 Can.

Chamaecyparis nootkatensis 'Pendula'

***C. n.* 'Pendula'** A superb specimen tree of medium to large size with branchlets hanging vertically in long, graceful streamers. There are two forms of this tree in cultivation. In cultivation 1884.
Zone 4 US, 5 Can. 🏆

C. obtusa (Hinoki false cypress) A large, broad, conical tree with horizontally

spreading branches. The foliage is deep, shining green in thick, horizontally flattened sprays. The garden cultivars of this species, which include many of Japanese origin, are almost as numerous as those of *C. lawsoniana* and include several excellent dwarf or slow-growing forms. The following are recommended. Japan. Introduced 1861 by P. F. von Siebold and J. G. Veitch.
Zone 4 US, 5 Can.

Chamaecyparis obtusa 'Chabo-yadori'

***C. o.* 'Chabo-yadori'** A dwarf or small, dome-shaped or conical bush. Both juvenile and adult foliage is present in irregular, fanlike sprays. A most attractive conifer.
Zone 4 US, 5b Can.

***C. o.* 'Coralliformis'** A small to medium-sized bush with densely arranged, twisted, cordlike, brown branchlets. The foliage is dark green. A specimen in the Hillier Gardens and Arboretum in Hampshire, England, has reached 8 × 8 ft (2.5 × 2.5 m). In cultivation 1903.
Zone 4 US, 5b Can.

***C. o.* 'Crippsii'** A small, slow-growing, loosely conical tree with spreading branches and broad, frondlike sprays of rich golden yellow foliage. One of the loveliest and most elegant small golden conifers. Raised before 1899 by Thomas Cripps and Sons of Tunbridge Wells, England.
Zone 4 US, 5b Can. 🏆

***C. o.* 'Fernspray Gold'** A small to medium-sized shrub with golden yellow foliage in fernlike sprays.
Zone 4 US, 5b Can.

***C. o.* 'Kosteri'**, syn. *C. o.* 'Nana Kosteri' A dwarf bush that is intermediate in growth

Chamaecyparis obtusa 'Crippsii'

between 'Nana' and 'Pygmaea'. It is conical, with flattened and mossy sprays of bright green foliage that become bronze in winter. Suitable for the rock garden. In cultivation 1915.
Zone 4 US, 5b Can.

Chamaecyparis obtusa 'Mariesii'

***C. o.* 'Mariesii'** A small, slow-growing, cone-shaped bush of open growth. The foliage is in loose sprays, cream or pale yellow during summer and yellowish green in winter. In the Hillier Gardens and Arboretum it has reached 5½ ft (1.7 m) high and 5 ft (1.5 m) wide. In cultivation 1891.
Zone 4 US, 5b Can.

***C. o.* 'Nana'** A miniature, flat-topped

Chamaecyparis obtusa 'Nana'

Chamaecyparis obtusa 'Nana Aurea'

dome, consisting of tiers of densely packed, cup-shaped fans of black-green foliage. It is one of the best dwarf conifers for the rock garden. A specimen at Hillier's attained 30 in (0.75 m) high by 3 ft (1 m) wide at the base in 40 years. The stronger-growing plant found in many collections under this name is 'Nana Gracilis'. Japan. Introduced c. 1861 by Philip von Siebold.
Zone 4 US, 5b Can. 🏆

***C. o.* 'Nana Aurea'** A looser, slightly taller plant than 'Nana', with golden yellow foliage. It is perhaps the best dwarf golden conifer and is ideal for the rock garden. Japan. Introduced by J. G. Veitch. In cultivation 1867.
Zone 4 US, 5b Can. 🏆

Chamaecyparis obtusa 'Nana Gracilis'

***C. o.* 'Nana Gracilis'** A conical bush or eventually a small tree of dense, compact habit. The foliage is dark green, in short, shell-like sprays. It is one of the most commonly planted "dwarf" conifers but ultimately reaches a height of several yards. In cultivation 1874.
Zone 4 US, 5b Can. 🏆

Chamaecyparis obtusa 'Pygmaea'

***C. o.* 'Nana Kosteri'** See *C. o.* 'Kosteri'.

***C. o.* 'Pygmaea'** A small, wide-spreading bush with loose sprays of bronze-green foliage that is tinged with reddish bronze in winter and arranged in flattened tiers. Japan. Introduced 1861 by Robert Fortune.
Zone 4 US, 5b Can.

***C. o.* 'Tempelhof'** A dense, conical, small to medium-sized bush with deep green foliage in broad, dense, shell-like sprays.
Zone 4 US, 5 Can.

Chamaecyparis obtusa 'Tetragona Aurea'

***C. o.* 'Tetragona Aurea'** An unusual large shrub or small tree of distinctive angular appearance. The branches are sparse, usually wide spreading, and thickly covered with golden yellow, mosslike sprays of foliage. It is a very attractive conifer that combines well with heathers. Japan. Introduced around 1870.
Zone 4 US, 5b Can. 🏆

***C. o.* 'Tonia'** A dwarf sport of 'Nana Gracilis', making a dense, small bush of irregular habit with the shoots occasionally tipped with white. Raised c. 1928 in Holland.
Zone 4 US, 5b Can.

C. pisifera (Sawara false cypress) A large, broadly conical tree with spreading branches and horizontally flattened sprays of dark green foliage, which consists of sharply pointed, scalelike leaves that have white markings below. It has given rise to many cultivars, several of which have soft, juvenile foliage. The following are recommended. Japan. Introduced 1861 by Robert Fortune.
Zone 4 US, 4 Can.

***C. p.* 'Boulevard'** An outstanding medium-sized bush of dense, conical habit. The steel blue foliage is soft to the touch and becomes tinted with purple in winter. It is a juvenile form and one of the most popular of all the false cypresses. It tends to burn in full sun.
Zone 4 US, 4b Can. 🏆

Chamaecyparis pisifera 'Filifera Aurea'

***C. p.* 'Filifera Aurea'** A medium-sized to large bush with threadlike sprays of attractive, golden yellow foliage. It can burn in full sun. See also *C. p.* 'Sungold'. In cultivation 1889.
Zone 4 US, 4b Can. 🏆

***C. p.* 'Filifera Nana'** A dense, rounded, flat-topped, dwarf bush with long, threadlike branchlets. Suitable for the rock garden. In cultivation 1897.
Zone 4 US, 4b Can.

C. p. **'Filifera Nana Aurea'** See *C. p.* 'Golden Mop'.

Chamaecyparis pisifera 'Gold Spangle'

C. p. **'Gold Spangle'** Small and densely conical with sprays of golden yellow foliage. May be grown as a shrub by removing any strong-growing shoots. In cultivation 1900.
Zone 4 US, 4b Can.

Chamaecyparis pisifera 'Golden Mop'

C. p. **'Golden Mop'**, syn. *C. p.* 'Filifera Nana Aurea' A small, dense, bright golden form of 'Filifera Nana'.
Zone 4 US, 4b Can. 🏆

C. p. **'Nana'** A dwarf, slow-growing bush forming a flat-topped dome with crowded, flattened sprays of dark green foliage. Old specimens form a top tier, creating a tree with a two-tier shape somewhat like a figure 8. A specimen at Hillier Gardens and Arboretum in Hampshire reached 2 × 5 ft (0.6 × 1.5 m) after about 30 years. In cultivation 1891.
Zone 4 US, 4b Can.

C. p. **'Nana Aureovariegata'** Similar in habit to 'Nana', but the foliage has a golden tinge. It is excellent for the rock garden. In cultivation 1874.
Zone 4 US, 4b Can.

C. p. **'Plumosa Aurea'** A small to medium-sized, conical tree with feathery juvenile foliage, soft to the touch. The young growths are bright yellow and deepen with age to soft yellow-green, stained with bronze-yellow. Japan. Introduced 1861 by Robert Fortune.
Zone 4 US, 4b Can.

C. p. **'Plumosa Aurea Compacta'** A dwarf, dense, conical, slow-growing bush with soft yellow foliage, particularly colorful in spring. In cultivation 1891.
Zone 4 US, 4b Can.

C. p. **'Plumosa Compressa'** A dwarf, slow-growing bush shaped rather like a flat-topped bun, usually with both 'Plumosa' and 'Squarrosa' foliage, which on young plants is crisped and mosslike. Raised before 1929 in Holland.
Zone 4 US, 4b Can.

C. p. **'Plumosa Rogersii'** A small, upright bush with golden yellow foliage whose long needles are closer to those of 'Squarrosa'. Raised c. 1930 by Rogers.
Zone 4 US, 4b Can.

C. p. **'Snow'** A dwarf, bun-shaped bush with mossy, blue-gray foliage tipped with cream; green in winter. It tends to burn in full sun or cold wind. At the Hillier Gardens and Arboretum it has reached 2 ft (60 cm) high by 3 ft (1 m) across.
Zone 4 US, 4b Can.

C. p. **'Squarrosa Sulphurea'** A small to medium-sized, broadly conical tree with spreading branches and dense, billowy sprays of sulphur yellow foliage that is soft to the touch. Its color is especially good in spring. In cultivation before 1894.
Zone 4 US, 5 Can.

C. p. **'Sungold'** Similar to 'Filifera Aurea' but not as bright a yellow, although it withstands full sun.
Zone 4 US, 5 Can.

Chamaecyparis thyoides

C. thyoides (White cedar) A small to medium-sized, conical tree with erect, fan-shaped sprays of aromatic foliage. It is not suitable for shallow alkaline soils but will tolerate boggy conditions. The following forms are recommended. E United States. Introduced 1736 by Peter Collinson.
Zone 3 US, 4 Can.

C. t. **'Andelyensis'** A medium-sized, slow-growing, dense, narrowly columnar bush with short sprays of dark bluish green adult and juvenile foliage. It is attractive in late winter when peppered with color

from the bright red male cones. Raised c. 1850 at Les Andelys, France.
Zone 3 US, 4 Can. 🏆

Chamaecyparis thyoides 'Andelyensis Nana'

***C. t.* 'Andelyensis Nana'** A dwarf shrub of slow growth with mostly juvenile foliage, forming a dense, rather flat-topped bush. A specimen at Hillier Gardens and Arboretum was $3^1/_2 \times 3$ ft (1.1×0.9 m) after about 30 years. In cultivation 1939.
Zone 3 US, 4 Can. 🏆

***C. t.* 'Ericoides'** An attractive, small, conical form with sea green juvenile foliage, soft to the touch, that becomes bronze or plum-purple in winter. In cultivation 1897.
Zone 3 US, 4 Can. 🏆

***C. t.* 'Purple Heather'** A slow-growing, dwarf bush of bun-shaped habit. The gray-green juvenile foliage turns deep plum-purple in winter. 'Heatherbun', 'Red Star', and 'Rubicon' all appear to be the same or very similar.
Zone 4 US, 4b Can.

Chamaedaphne *Ericaceae*
Leatherleaf

A genus of one evergreen species requiring acid soil and related to Leucothoë.

C. calyculata A small, wiry shrub with white, heathlike flowers borne along the arching branches in spring. E North America, N Europe, N Asia. Introduced 1748.
Zone 2 US, 2b Can.

***C. c.* 'Nana'** A more compact and attractive form worthy of a place in the garden.
Zone 2 US, 2b Can.

Chamaedaphne calyculata 'Nana'

Chamaerops *Palmae*
Fan palm

A genus of one evergreen species that is native to Europe. While many other palms are commonly planted on that continent, the only other native palm is Phoenix theophrasti, *a date palm that is restricted to the coast of Crete.*

Chamaerops humilis

C. humilis (Dwarf fan palm) An interesting miniature palm, covering mountainsides in coastal areas in its native habitat. It rarely exceeds 5 ft (1.5 m) in height and is usually shrubby, forming a many-stemmed clump, although forms occasionally grow with a short trunk. Its leaves are large, deeply divided in the form of fans, and have very stiff segments. Makes a good container plant where not hardy. It will grow in any well-drained, friable soil. SW Europe, N Africa. Introduced 1731 by Philip Miller.
Zone 8 US, 9? Can. 🏆

Chiliotrichum *Compositae*

A genus of two species of evergreen shrubs related to Olearia *and native to South America. They will grow in any well-drained, friable soil.*

C. diffusum A small, variable shrub with linear leaves $^3/_4$–2 in (2–5 cm) long, which are white-woolly on their undersurfaces (eventually becoming brown) and green and leathery above. White, daisylike flowers are borne in summer. Some forms are hardier than others. A variable species found over a wide area in southern South America and the Falkland Islands. Introduced c. 1926 by Harold Comber.
Zone 8 US, 9? Can.

Chimonanthus *Calycanthaceae*
Wintersweet

A genus of six species of evergreen and deciduous shrubs found in China, with only one in general cultivation.

Chimonanthus praecox

C. praecox A medium-sized, easily grown, winter-flowering deciduous shrub that will thrive in any soil. Except in hot, sunny climates, the shrub is best planted against a warm wall to ripen the growth; if wall grown, the stems can be cut back immediately after flowering. The fragrant shrub is also suitable for lining walkways or sitting areas. The pale waxy-yellow, purple-centered flowers are not produced on young plants. The cultivars described below are both grafted and flower at an early age. China. Introduced 1766.
Zone 6 US, 7 Can.

Chimonanthus praecox 'Grandiflorus'

***C. p.* 'Grandiflorus'** A medium-sized form with deeper yellow flowers conspicuously stained with red.
Zone 6 US, 7 Can.

***C. p.* 'Luteus'** This medium-sized shrub is distinct from other forms because of its rather large flowers that do not have a purple stain but are a clear waxy-yellow and open rather later than the typical form.
Zone 6 US, 7 Can.

Chimonanthus praecox 'Luteus'

Chionanthus *Oleaceae*

Fringe tree

A genus of about 120 deciduous species, of which two are often grown. Both are easily grown in any good garden soil and perform best in full sun. They flower in midsummer, and the blooms are unusual in their 4–5 narrow, strap-shaped petals.

C. retusus (Chinese fringe tree) This is one of the most handsome large shrubs, with a profusion of snow white flowers borne in erect panicles in midsummer, followed by plumlike fruits. Leaves are light green with downy white undersides. China. Introduced 1845 by Robert Fortune.
Zone 5 US, 6b Can.

Chionanthus virginicus

C. virginicus (Fringe tree, old man's beard) Ultimately a large shrub with larger and more noteworthy leaves than its Chinese counterpart. The flowers are white, slightly fragrant, and held in pendent panicles. Bright yellow fall foliage. E North America.
Zone 4 US, 5 Can.

Choisya *Rutaceae*

A genus of seven species of evergreen, aromatic flowering shrubs, natives of Mexico and the southwestern United States. They will grow in any well-drained, friable soil.

***C.* 'Aztec Pearl'** (*C. arizonica* × *C. ternata*)

Choisya 'Aztec Pearl'

The first hybrid in the genus and an elegant, small shrub whose aromatic leaves are attractively divided into 3–5 slender, bright green leaflets. The almond-scented flowers are like those of *C. ternata* but larger and pink-flushed in the bud, opening white with a pink flush on the backs of the petals. They are profusely borne in late spring and again in summer and appear in clusters of 3–5 in the leaf axils. Raised 1982 by the Hillier Nurseries' propagator Peter Moore.
Zone 8? US, 9? Can.

Choisya ternata

C. ternata (Mexican orange) A medium-sized shrub of rounded habit with shining, dark green leaves, aromatic when crushed. The flowers are white, sweetly scented, and borne in clusters of up to six from the leaf axils during late spring and early summer, and usually again in fall. Thrives in sun or shade. Mountains of SW Mexico. Introduced 1825.
Zone 7 US, 8 Can.

Choisya ternata 'Sundance'

***C. t.* 'Sundance'** A striking small to medium-sized shrub, whose young foliage is bright yellow.
Zone 7 US, 8 Can. 🏆

Chordospartium *Leguminosae*

A genus of only one deciduous species, related to Carmichaelia.

Chordospartium stevensonii

C. stevensonii (Weeping broom) A medium-sized, broomlike, leafless shrub, bearing racemes of white, lavender-pink-tinged flowers in summer and looking very much like a miniature weeping willow in habit. The stems of young plants appear brown and lifeless for the first three or four years. It is scarce in cultivation and rare in the wild. It will grow in any well-drained, friable soil. South Island of New Zealand. Introduced 1923.
Zone 8 US, 9? Can.

Chusquea *Gramineae*

A genus of graceful, mainly South American, evergreen bamboos, distinct in their numerous, densely clustered branches and solid stems. They are useful for cutting, as their leaves do not wilt as easily as those of hollow-stemmed bamboos.

C. culeou A shrubby species, forming broad, dense clumps. The deep olive green canes, 8–11 ft (2.5–3.5 m) high or occasionally up

Chusquea culeou

to 28 ft (9 m), produce dense clusters of slender, short, leafy branches along their whole length, giving them a characteristic bottle-brush effect. The first-year canes have conspicuous white sheaths at each node. The graceful leaves are 1–3 in (2.5–7.5 cm) long and $^1/_4$–$^1/_2$ in (6–10 mm) wide and have a slenderly pointed shape. Chile. Introduced 1926 by Harold Comber.
Zone 7 US, 8 Can.

Cistus *Cistaceae*
Rock rose

A genus of about 20 species of evergreen, usually small shrubs found in the wild from the Canary Islands throughout the Mediterranean region to the Caucasus. There are many hybrids that have originated either in the wild or in cultivation. They thrive in full sun and are ideal for dry banks, rock gardens, and similar locations. Although the flowers are individually short lived, they are very freely produced. From early to midsummer, and sometimes for longer, there is a succession of bloom, so much so that the short life of the individual, papery flowers hardly matters. Most rock roses are killed by severe frost but are remarkably wind tolerant and are ideal shrubs for gardens near the sea or in alkaline, shallow, or poor soils. They are usually about 3 ft (1 m) tall and exceptions are noted in the individual descriptions.

Rock roses resent pruning, which should be confined to cutting away any dead wood, although young plants can be pinched back to promote bushiness. The locations for the plants should be chosen carefully, as rock roses are very difficult to transplant once established.

Cistus × *aguilari* 'Maculatus'

***C.* × *aguilari* 'Maculatus'** The white flowers of this handsome small shrub have a central ring of crimson blotches.
Zone 8 US, 9 Can. 🏆

Cistus 'Chelsea Bonnet'

***C.* 'Chelsea Bonnet'** A small shrub with narrow, dark green leaves. Pure white, lightly scented flowers with five notched petals and a yellow center are profusely borne in early summer.
Zone 7? US, 8? Can.

Cistus × *cyprius*

C.* × *corbariensis See *C.* × *hybridus*.

C.* × *cyprius *(C. ladanifer* × *C. laurifolius)* Vigorous hybrid about 6 ft (2 m) tall, bearing white flowers 3 in (8 cm) wide with crimson blotches at the petal base. France, Spain.
Zone 6 US, 7 Can. 🏆

Cistus 'Elma'

***C.* × *dansereaui* 'Decumbens'** A small shrub growing to 4 ft (1.2 m) or more wide and 2 ft (0.6 m) tall, with lance-shaped, dark green, sticky, wavy-edged leaves and large white flowers with crimson basal blotches.
Zone 7 US, 8 Can. 🏆

***C.* 'Elma'** *(C. laurifolius* × *C. palhinhae)* The beautifully formed, extra-large, pure white flowers of this hybrid contrast well with the deep green, polished, lanceolate leaves that are bloomy beneath. The shrub is sturdy, bushy, and grows to 6 ft (2 m).
Zone 6 US, 7 Can. 🏆

***C.* 'Grayswood Pink'** A dwarf shrub with soft gray-green leaves complemented by clear pink flowers.
Zone 7? US, 8? Can.

C.* × *hybridus, syn. *C.* × *corbariensis* A dense, spreading, small shrub and one of the hardiest, with crimson-tinted buds that open to pure white.
Zone 6 US, 7 Can. 🏆

C. ladanifer (Gum rock rose) A tall, erect shrub growing to over 6 ft (2 m) with lance-

Cistus laurifolius

Cistus ladanifer

shaped, dark green leaves. The flowers are up to 4 in (10 cm) across and white with a distinctive chocolate basal blotch and rumpled petals. SW Europe and North Africa. In cultivation 1629.
Zone 6 US, 7 Can. 🏆

C. laurifolius (Laurel rock rose) This is the hardiest species of all, sometimes exceeding 6 ft (2 m) in height, and has leathery, bloomy dark green leaves and white flowers with yellow centers. SW Europe to C Italy. Introduced 1731.
Zone 5 US, 6 Can. 🏆

Cistus × *loretii*

C.* × *loretii A dwarf hybrid with large white flowers that have crimson basal blotches. It occurs naturally in the wild. S Europe and North Africa.
Zone 8 US, 9 Can.

C. palhinhae This strikingly handsome and distinct species is low growing and compact and has glossy leaves and pure white flowers that are nearly 4 in (10 cm) across. SW Portugal. Introduced 1939 by Captain Collingwood Ingram.
Zone 7 US, 8 Can.

Cistus 'Peggy Sammons'

***C.* 'Peggy Sammons'** A small to medium-sized hybrid shrub of erect habit, with gray-green, downy stems and leaves and flowers in a delicate shade of pink. Raised 1955 by J. E. Sammons.
Zone 7? US, 8? Can. 🏆

Cistus populifolius var. *lasiocalyx*

C. populifolius* var. *lasiocalyx An erect shrub up to 6 ft (2 m) tall with smallish, hairy, poplarlike leaves and large, wavy, white flowers with a conspicuously inflated calyx. A rewarding cistus and one of the hardiest. S Spain, S Portugal, Morocco.
Zone 6 US, 7 Can. 🏆

C.* × *pulverulentus, syn. *C.* 'Sunset' A dwarf shrub of compact habit, with sage green, wavy leaves and vivid cerise flowers. SW Europe. In cultivation 1929.
Zone 6 US, 7 Can. 🏆

Cistus × *pulverulentus*

Cistus × *purpureus*

C.* × *purpureus A small shrub with reddish stems and narrow, rather wavy-edged, dark green leaves. The flowers are large and rosy crimson, with a dark maroon blotch at the base of each petal, contrasting with the central cluster of yellow stamens. Occurs naturally in the wild. S Europe. Introduced 1790.
Zone 6 US, 7 Can. 🏆

Cistus 'Silver Pink'

C. 'Silver Pink' An exceptionally hardy small cistus with flowers in a lovely shade of silver-pink carried in long clusters. Originated as a chance hybrid of *C. laurifolius* at Hillier Nurseries c. 1910. *(Photo on p.219.)*
Zone 5? US, 6? Can.

Cistus × *skanberghii*

C. × ***skanberghii*** A small shrub, one of the most beautiful of all cistus, with silky-petaled, clear pink flowers and stems whitened by down. Occurs naturally in the wild. Greece.
Zone 8 US, 9 Can. 🏆
C. 'Sunset' See *C.* × *pulverulentus.*

Citrus *Rutaceae*

A genus of about 15 species of semievergreen trees and shrubs from Southeast Asia, encompassing oranges, lemons, grapefruits, limes, and other citrus fruits. They will grow in any well-drained soil and make good container plants where they are not hardy.

Citrus × *meyeri* 'Meyer'

Cladrastis lutea

C. × ***meyeri*** **'Meyer'** The hardiest lemon is a medium-sized to large shrub with short-stalked, large, dark green leaves and clusters of fragrant white flowers that are followed by freely produced, large, yellow lemons. Makes a good houseplant.
Zone 9 US

Cladrastis *Leguminosae*
Yellowwood

A genus of about six species of deciduous trees with pinnate leaves, native to eastern Asia but with one species from the southeastern United States. The flowers are not produced by young trees. They will grow in any well-drained, friable soil.

C. lutea (American yellowwood) A very handsome, medium-sized tree producing long, drooping, wisteria-like panicles of fragrant white flowers in early summer. The leaves turn clear yellow before falling. SE United States. Introduced 1812.
Zone 4 US, 4b Can. 🏆

Cladrastis sinensis

C. sinensis (Chinese yellowwood) A remarkably beautiful medium-sized tree, flowering in midsummer. The compound leaves are soft green above and bloomy beneath, and the pink-tinged, white, slightly fragrant flowers are borne in large panicles. The plant is scarce and not easily obtained. China. Introduced 1901 by Ernest Wilson.
Zone 5 US, 6 Can.

CLEMATIS

Ranunculaceae

Clematis 'Dawn'

CLEMATIS ARE AMONG the most popular of all climbers — and with good reason. They are unsurpassed for variety of color and flower shape, for the length of their flowering season, and in many cases for the sheer power of their display. Clematis can be modest and understated or flamboyant and dramatic — or somewhere in between. There are clematis for spring, summer, autumn, and even winter. They can climb a tree or trellis, sprawl elegantly over shrubs, allow themselves to be trained neatly against a wall, drape themselves nonchalantly over a porch, and always look as if they belong.

Clematis are divided into two main groups. The first consists of species clematis and their primary hybrids (that is, hybrids that are a cross between two species or very few, rather than the product of complex breeding). These are generally more modest than the other group — the large-flowered clematis — and are also more varied in habit, flower shape, size, and general impact. A few species, including *C. flammula*, are also pleasantly scented. Interestingly, the species are for the most part easier to establish than their large-flowered counterparts. And a few are sometimes a little overwhelming in their ability to cover anything in their path with tangles of stems that can in time become heavy and unstable and need to be pruned simply to keep them in bounds.

Among the species are the renowned *C. montana*, the most beautiful of the spring clematis, and its forms; *C. alpina*, which is never too large even for the smallest garden; and the utterly delightful small-flowered forms of *C. viticella*, which are thought by many gardeners to be the most desirable of all. If you are looking for an evergreen climber to flower in winter, look no further than *C. cirrhosa* var. *balearica*, and if you want a beautiful display in autumn, the informal drapery of *C. tangutica* 'Aureolin', studded with yellow lanterns and silky-mop seed heads, is irresistible and entirely reliable.

The large-flowered clematis offer such a wide choice that it can be difficult to know where to begin. Perhaps the best way is to select plants that will provide the longest possible succession of flowers. Many come into flower in late spring and early summer, after *C. montana* and alongside *C. macropetala*, and several of them flower again in early fall. Sometimes the flowers produced in the different seasons by the same plant are of different kinds. 'Vyvyan Pennell', for example, has double flowers from late spring to midsummer and single blooms in autumn. Others occupy the mid- to late season; 'Ascotiensis', for instance, flowers from midsummer to early autumn, while 'Daniel Deronda' starts a month or so earlier. October is the end of the season for these wonderful flowers, but a full six months of color is easy to obtain with just a few well-chosen cultivars.

CARE AND CULTIVATION

Clematis require fertile, moist, but well-drained soil for best growth. They are usually long-lived plants that will remain in the garden for many years, so proper soil preparation is essential. The planting hole should be at least 18 in (45 cm) in diameter and as deep as the depth of topsoil will

Clematis 'Ville de Lyon'

allow. The bottom of the hole should be loosened well, and a mixture of equal parts good topsoil and well-rotted manure or leaf mold should be used as backfill. A handful or two of bonemeal can be added as well.

Large-flowered clematis should be planted deep enough so that the crown (the point where the leaves or stems of the plant meet the roots) is 1–3 in (2.5–7.5 cm) below soil level. This encourages growth buds at the base and also helps prevent an outbreak of clematis wilt, a disease that often afflicts the plant.

The planting hole should be located well away from the feeder roots of any tree or shrub up which the clematis is to grow, but it also should not be so close to the trunk as to make planting difficult. A cane can be placed at a slant between the clematis and its eventual support so that the vines can be trained toward the trunk.

For clematis that are to be grown against a wall, the planting hole should not be too close to the structure, as the soil at the base of a wall is often sheltered from rain, and clematis cannot tolerate dry conditions. The plants should be watered while they are still in their containers, then watered well again as soon as they are in the ground. Clematis planted in spring must be monitored carefully until fall and watered well whenever they seem dry.

While clematis flowers and leaves generally need full sun, their roots prefer cool shade. The plants should be mulched well and underplanted with a low-growing, shallow-rooted ground cover. Some pale-colored large-flowered cultivars, however, such as 'Nelly Moser', are best sited with the top growth in some shade; otherwise their flowers fade badly.

The large-flowered clematis are listed with a letter after their names as follows: F = Florida, J = Jackmanii, L = Lanuginosa, P = Patens, T = Texensis, and V = Viticella. The letter indicates the group to which the cultivar belongs. This information is helpful when it comes time to prune.

There are two divisions of these groups for pruning purposes. The first — the Florida, Lanuginosa, and Patens groups — flower on the previous year's wood, usually in late spring and early summer. The only pruning required is to trim back the old flowering growths immediately after flowering. Old, dense plants can also be pruned hard in late winter, but the first crop of flowers will be lost. The second — the Jackmanii, Texensis, and Viticella groups — flower on the current year's shoots, usually in late summer and fall. They can be pruned hard to within 12 in (30 cm) of the ground in late winter or early spring. Old, unpruned plants will become bare at the base.

SPECIES AND PRIMARY HYBRIDS

C. aethusifolia A slender-stemmed climber about 6½ ft (2 m) high, with deeply divided leaves. The fragrant, nodding, pale primrose flowers appear in late summer and are bell shaped, ¾ in (2 cm) long with turned-back lobes. N China. Introduced c. 1875.

Zone 5 US, 6 Can.

C. akebioides A relative of *C. tibetana* that grows up to 12 ft (4 m). It has pinnate leaves with up to seven leaflets and bell-shaped, yellow flowers that may be tinged green or purple on the outside and are borne on long stalks in summer and early fall. W China.

Zone 5 US, 6 Can.

C. alpina A lovely species with slender stems to 8 ft (2.5m) long and leaves with nine leaflets. The flowers are solitary, blue or violet-blue with a central tuft of white, petaloid stamens (staminodes). They open in mid- to late spring and are followed by silky seed heads. It looks especially good growing over a low wall, large rock, or small bush. Europe, C Asia. Introduced 1792.

Zone 4 US, 4 Can.

***C. a.* 'Columbine'** A medium-sized clematis with pale lavender, bell-shaped flowers with taper-pointed sepals and white staminodes.

Zone 4 US, 3 Can.

Clematis alpina 'Frances Rivis'

***C. a.* 'Frances Rivis'** A vigorous, free-flowering, medium-sized form with larger flowers and a contrasting sheaf of white stamens and staminodes in the center.

Zone 2 US, 2 Can. 🏆

***C. a.* 'Frankie'** A medium-sized form with a profusion of rich blue flowers, similar to but an improvement upon 'Frances Rivis'.
Zone 2 US, 2 Can.

***C. a.* 'Helsingborg'** A medium-sized form with deep blue flowers.
Zone 4 US, 4 Can. 🏆

***C. a.* 'Pamela Jackman'** A medium-sized clematis with large, rich blue flowers. The outer staminodes are tinged with blue and the inner ones are tinged with white. In cultivation 1960.
Zone 2 US, 2 Can.

Clematis alpina 'Ruby'

***C. a.* 'Ruby'** A medium-sized clematis bearing rose-red flowers with creamy staminodes. Raised 1935 by Ernest Markham.
Zone 4 US, 4 Can.

***C. a.* 'White Columbine'** A medium-sized clematis grown for its white flowers on upright shoots.
Zone 4 US, 4 Can. 🏆

***C. a.* 'White Moth'** See *C. macropetala* 'White Moth'.

***C. a.* 'Willy'** A medium-sized form bearing mauve-pink flowers that have a distinctive deep pink blotch at the base of each sepal. In cultivation 1971.
Zone 2 US, 2 Can.

C. armandii (Armand clematis) A vigorous, evergreen climber with stems 13–20 ft (4–6 m) long. The leaves have three long, leathery, glossy, dark green leaflets, and the creamy flowers, 2–2¾ in (5–7 cm) across, are borne in clusters in mid- or late spring. It is a beautiful species but subject to injury in exposed locations and is best planted against a warm, sunny wall. Seedling plants are occasionally available, but these usually produce smaller, inferior flowers. China. Introduced 1900 by Ernest Wilson.
Zone 5 US, 6 Can.

Clematis armandii 'Apple Blossom'

***C. a.* 'Apple Blossom'** The true plant is a superb medium-sized clematis with broad sepals that are white and shaded with pink, especially on the reverse. It is scarce, and a poor form that is easy to propagate has appeared on the market.
Zone 5 US, 6 Can.

Clematis armandii 'Snowdrift'

***C. a.* 'Snowdrift'** A medium-sized form with pure white flowers. Though beautiful, this plant is rare in cultivation.
Zone 5 US, 6 Can.

***C.* 'Bill MacKenzie'** *(C. tangutica × C. tibetana* subsp. *vernayi)* A vigorous, free-flowering, medium-sized climber with bright green leaves made up of sharply toothed leaflets. The flowers are held on long stalks, are up to 2½ in (6 cm) across, and have four widely spreading, thick, bright yellow sepals with purple filaments. Make sure to obtain the true plant, as there are many seedlings available that are less desirable. Introduced before 1976.
Zone 4 US, 4 Can.

***C.* 'Blue Bird'** *(C. alpina × C. macropetala)* A vigorous small hybrid between two popular species, both of which it resembles. The flowers are 3 in (7.5 cm) wide, purple-blue, and semidouble. In cultivation 1965.
Zone 4 US, 3 Can.

C. campaniflora A vigorous climber up to 20 ft (6 m) with pinnate leaves and leaflets in groups of three. Its small, bowl-shaped, blue-tinted flowers, borne profusely from midsummer to early autumn, are most effective in mass plantings. Portugal, S Spain. Introduced 1810.
Zone 5 US, 6 Can.

C. chrysocoma This very beautiful plant, whose name is in doubt, resembles *C. montana*, though it is less rampant. The trifoliate leaves, shoots, and flower stalks are covered with a thick yellowish down. The soft pink flowers, 1½–2½ in (4–6 cm) across, are borne in profusion in early summer and periodically into late summer on young growths. The true plant has recently been rediscovered in China.
Zone 5 US, 6 Can.

C. c.* var. *sericea A very attractive variety with white flowers produced singly or in pairs on older growths in late spring.
Zone 5 US, 6 Can. 🏆

C. cirrhosa* var. *balearica (Fern-leaved clematis) An elegant, evergreen climber

Clematis cirrhosa var. *balearica*

with slender stems up to 12 ft (4 m) long. The leaves are attractively divided into several segments and are tinged with bronze in winter. The flowers are pale yellow, spotted with reddish purple on the inside. They reach up to 2 in (5 cm) across and are produced freely throughout the winter. Balearic Isles. Introduced before 1783.
Zone 5 US, 6 Can. 🏆

Clematis cirrhosa 'Freckles'

***C. c.* 'Freckles'** A medium-sized evergreen climber bearing flowers very heavily spotted and streaked with red.
Zone 5 US, 6 Can. 🏆

***C. c.* 'Wisley Cream'** A medium-sized evergreen climber with large, creamy white, unspotted flowers.
Zone 5 US, 6 Can.

C.* × *durandii A lovely hybrid up to 10 ft (3 m). The leaves are simple and up to 6 in (15 cm) long, and the dark blue, four-sepaled flowers are sometimes more than 4 in (10 cm) across. They have a central cluster of yellow stamens and appear from early summer to early fall. Garden origin c. 1870.
Zone 4 US, 5 Can. 🏆

***C.* × *eriostemon* 'Hendersonii'** A beautiful, semiherbaceous clematis. Each year it sends up slender stems 6½–8 ft (2–2.5 m) in length with simple or pinnate leaves. The flowers are deep bluish purple, widely bell shaped, slightly fragrant, up to 2¾ in (7 cm) across, nodding, and borne singly on slender stalks from midsummer to early autumn. It is best given some support. Raised c. 1830 by the Hendersons of St. John's Wood, London.
Zone 4 US, 5 Can.

Clematis × *eriostemon* 'Hendersonii'

Clematis flammula

C. flammula (Plume clematis) A vigorous climber, 13–16 ft (4–5 m) high, that forms a dense tangle of stems, covered with bright green, bipinnate leaves. From late summer to midautumn, the loose panicles of small, white, sweetly scented flowers are abundantly scattered over the whole plant and are followed by silky seed heads. It is an ideal climber for covering unsightly walls and fences. S Europe. In cultivation since the late 16th century.
Zone 6 US, 7 Can.

C. florida An elegant species with wiry stems 10–16 ft (3–5 m) long and glossy, compound leaves. The flowers are creamy white, up to 4 in (10 cm) across, and open in early to midsummer. A parent of many hybrids. The following forms are recommended. China, Japan. Introduced 1776.
Zone 5 US, 6 Can.

***C. f.* 'Alba Plena'** In this striking medium-sized form, each flower is fully double, creating a dense mass of greenish white sepals.

Clematis florida 'Alba Plena'

These flamboyant flowers are long lasting and borne over a long period.
Zone 5 US, 6 Can.

Clematis florida 'Sieboldii'

***C. f.* 'Sieboldii'** A beautiful medium-sized form reminiscent of a passionflower. The flowers are white, 3 in (8 cm) wide, with a central boss of violet-purple petaloid stamens. Japan. Introduced before 1836.
Zone 5 US, 6 Can.

C. forsteri A scrambling species of clematis with bright apple-green leaves composed of three leaflets, each of which is lobed or prettily cut. The flowers are verbena scented and starlike. The males are up to 1½ in (4 cm) across, with 5–8 white to creamy yellow sepals; the females are smaller. New Zealand.
Zone 6 US, 7 Can.

C.* ×*jackmanii (Jackman clematis) A spectacular hybrid, 10–13 ft (3–4 m) high, with pinnate leaves and flowers 4–5 in (10–13 cm) across that have four rich purple-

Clematis forsteri

Clematis × jackmanii

violet sepals. They are borne in great profusion either singly or in threes from midsummer to midfall, on the current year's growth. Many clones have been named, and some are listed among the large-flowered clematis on pp.228–233. Raised 1858 by the Jackmans of Woking, England.
Zone 3 US, 2 Can. 🏆

Clematis × jouiniana

C.* × *jouiniana (Jouin clematis) A somewhat shrubby climber that reaches up to 11 ft (3.5 m) high. Its leaves have 3–5 coarsely toothed leaflets, and its small, white, lilac-tinted flowers are borne very freely in fall. The following forms are recommended. Garden origin before 1900.
Zone 3 US, 3 Can.

***C.* × *j.* 'Côte d'Azur'** A charming medium-sized form with azure blue flowers, excellent for covering low walls, mounds, or tree stumps.
Zone 3 US, 4 Can.

***C.* ×*j.* 'Praecox'** A vigorous, early flowering, medium-sized form with slightly larger, pale blue flowers.
Zone 3 US, 4 Can. 🏆

C. macropetala (Big petal clematis) A slender-stemmed climber up to 8 ft (2.5 m) with divided leaves. The flowers are up to 3 in (7.5 cm) across, violet-blue, with conspicuously paler petaloid stamens that give the effect of doubling. Flowering is from late spring or early summer onward. The seed heads are silky and become fluffy and gray with age. A beautiful species for a low wall or fence. N China, Siberia. Introduced 1910 by William Purdom.
Zone 2 US, 1 Can.

Clematis macropetala 'Jan Lindmark'

***C. m.* 'Jan Lindmark'** This clematis is a small to medium-sized form with pale purple flowers.
Zone 2 US, 1 Can.

***C. m.* 'Lagoon'**, syn. *C. m.* 'Blue Lagoon' A small to medium-sized climber similar to 'Maidwell Hall' but with slightly deeper blue flowers. It is considered to be the best clone. In cultivation 1959.
Zone 3 US, 3 Can. 🏆

***C. m.* 'Maidwell Hall'** A small to medium-sized climber with deep lavender-blue flowers. In cultivation 1956.
Zone 2 US, 1 Can.

Clematis macropetala 'Markham's Pink'

***C. m.* 'Markham's Pink'** A lovely small to medium-sized form with flowers the shade of crushed strawberries.
Zone 2 US, 1 Can. 🏆

***C. m.* 'White Moth'**, syn. *C. alpina* 'White Moth' A small to medium-sized climber grown for its pure white flowers. In cultivation 1955.
Zone 3 US, 3 Can.

***C. m.* 'White Swan'** See *C.* 'White Swan'.

C. montana (Anemone clematis) A popular species, usually grown in one of the forms listed below. Their stems are 20–30 ft (6–9 m) long, and the leaves consist of three leaflets. The flowers are borne profusely in late spring. They are rampant climbers in any location and are excellent for growing into trees and over walls, especially where there is some shade. Root-hardy to zone 4 US, 5 Can., but flowers only in the zones given. Himalaya. Introduced 1831.
Zone 5 US, 6b Can.

***C. m.* 'Alexander'** A lovely large form with creamy white, scented flowers. N India. Introduced by Col. R. D. Alexander.
Zone 5 US, 6b Can.

***C. m.* 'Elizabeth'** A very beautiful large form with large, lightly vanilla-scented, soft pink flowers in late spring and early summer.
Zone 5 US, 6b Can 🏆

Clematis montana 'Elizabeth'

***C. m.* 'Freda'** A large climber bearing deep cherry-pink flowers with darker edges and bronze young foliage.
Zone 5 US, 6b Can. 🏆

C. m.* f. *grandiflora A vigorous variety, occasionally up to 40 ft (12 m), with an abundance of white flowers in late spring and early summer. A particularly valuable characteristic of this clematis is its ability to flourish on a north-facing wall.
Zone 5 US, 6b Can. 🏆

***C. m.* 'Marjorie'** A large plant with semi-double, creamy pink flowers with a salmon-pink center.
Zone 5 US, 6b Can.

Clematis montana 'Pink Perfection'

***C. m.* 'Pink Perfection'** A large climber with fragrant flowers, similar to 'Elizabeth' but slightly more deeply colored.
Zone 5 US, 6b Can.

C. m.* var. *rubens A beautiful large variety with bronze-purple shoots and leaves and rose-pink flowers up to 3 in (7.5 cm) across in late spring and early summer. Hillier Nurseries' clone of this plant was selected best in trials in 1990. China. Introduced 1900 by Ernest Wilson.
Zone 5 US, 6b Can. 🏆

Clematis montana var. *rubens*

Clematis montana 'Tetrarose'

***C. m.* 'Tetrarose'** An excellent large form with bronze foliage and lilac-rose flowers up to 3 in (7.5 cm) across that are borne in late spring and early summer.
Zone 5 US, 6b Can. 🏆

C. m.* var. *wilsonii A large form with masses of rather small, white, chocolate-scented flowers in early summer.
Zone 5 US, 6b Can.

C. orientalis The true species is rare in cultivation. For the plant commonly grown under this name see *C. tibetana* subsp. *vernayi*.

C. pitcheri A climber of about 10–13 ft (3–4 m) with leaves that have up to nine leaflets. The flowers are pitcher shaped and purplish blue, deeper inside. The sepals are curved backward and the flowers are solitary on long stalks. The species name refers to its discoverer, Zina Pitcher, and not to the shape of the flowers. C United States. Introduced 1878.
Zone 4 US, 5b Can.

C. rehderiana A charming species that reaches 26 ft (8 m). The leaves are pinnate or bipinnate, and the nodding, bell-shaped flowers are soft primrose yellow and have a delicious scent. They are in erect panicles

Clematis rehderiana

up to 9 in (23 cm) long in late summer and fall. Introduced 1898.
Zone 5 US, 6 Can. 🏆

***C.* 'Rosy O'Grady'** *(C. alpina × C. macropetala)* A successful small hybrid with large, rose-pink, semidouble flowers. Introduced 1967 in Canada.
Zone 3 US, 3 Can.

C. serratifolia A slender species up to 10 ft (3 m) with prettily divided green leaves. The flowers are 1 in (2.5 cm) long and yellow with purple stamens. They are borne most profusely in late summer and early fall and followed by silky seed heads. Korea, China, C Asia. Introduced c. 1918.
Zone 4 US, 5 Can.

Clematis tangutica

C. tangutica (Golden clematis) A dense climber up to 16 ft (5 m) with divided, sea green leaves and yellow flowers that are usually lanternlike. It is probably the best species with yellow flowers, ideal for low walls, fences, trellises, and slopes, but it is very variable when grown from seed. The following form is recommended. China. Introduced 1908 by Ernest Wilson.
Zone 2 US, 1b Can.

Clematis tangutica 'Aureolin'

***C. t.* 'Aureolin'** A medium-sized form specially selected for its large, nodding, bright yellow flowers with sepals to $1\frac{1}{2}$ in (4 cm) long, often opening widely.
Zone 2 US, 1b Can. 🏆

C. terniflora A vigorous species up to 33 ft (10 m), often forming a dense tangle of growth. The leaves have 3–5 long-stalked leaflets, and the hawthorn-scented white flowers are borne in panicles on the current year's growth in fall. It needs a long, hot summer to induce flowering. Korea, China, Japan. Introduced c. 1864.
Zone 2 US, 2 Can.

Clematis tibetana subsp. *vernayi*

C. tibetana* subsp. *vernayi This is the form of the species that is grown in gardens: the type is not in cultivation. It is a vigorous and graceful medium-sized climber with finely divided, blue-bloomy leaves. The flowers are nodding, yellow to greenish yellow or purple-flushed, with purple stamens. It is remarkable for its thick, spongy sepals, which have earned it the nickname "orange-peel clematis." Nepal, Tibet. Introduced 1947 by Ludlow & Sherriff.
Zone 3 US, 3 Can. 🏆

***C.* × *triternata* 'Rubromarginata'** A vigorous climber to 16 ft (5 m) with pinnate or bipinnate leaves and terminal panicles of fragrant flowers that are white, edged with reddish violet, and borne in such masses in late summer that they give the effect of dark, billowing clouds.
Zone 5 US, 6 Can. 🏆

C. vitalba (Traveler's joy, old man's beard). An extremely rampant, European native whose ropelike stems will provide dense coverage over a fence or pergola. The small, white, lightly scented flowers appear in late summer, followed by fluffy seed heads.
Zone 2 US, 2 Can.

C. viticella A slender climber up to 11 ft (3.5 m) with pinnate leaves. Some truly delightful, small-flowered hybrids are recommended below.

Clematis viticella 'Abundance'

***C. v.* 'Abundance'** Delicately veined, soft purple to red flowers.
Zone 3 US, 3 Can.

***C. v.* 'Alba Luxurians'** White flowers, tinted mauve.
Zone 3 US, 3 Can. 🏆

***C. v.* 'Kermesina'** Wine-red flowers.
Zone 3 US, 3 Can.

Clematis viticella 'Alba Luxurians'

***C. v.* 'Minuet'** Flowers are erect and cream, with a broad band of purple at the end of each sepal.
Zone 3 US, 3 Can. 🏆

Clematis viticella 'Purpurea Plena Elegans'

***C. v.* 'Purpurea Plena Elegans'** Double flowers up to $2^1/_2$in (6 cm) across, with many sepals. Lilac-purple, paler in the center.
Zone 3 US, 3 Can. 🏆

***C. v.* 'Royal Velours'** Deep velvety purple.
Zone 3 US, 3 Can. 🏆

***C.* 'White Swan'**, syn. *C. macropetala* 'White Swan' A small hybrid with pure white, double flowers up to $4^3/_4$in (12 cm) across. Raised 1961 in Canada.
Zone 2 US, 1 Can.

LARGE-FLOWERED CLEMATIS

All the following are medium-sized climbers hardy to zone 3 US, 4 Can. The letters in parentheses after the names indicate the groups to which the cultivars belong (see p.222).

Clematis 'Asao'

***C.* 'Asao'** (P) Large flowers with 6–7 broad, rose-carmine sepals.

***C.* 'Ascotiensis'** (V) Azure blue flowers up to 5 in (13 cm) across. Very free flowering, midsummer to early fall. In cultivation 1871.
🏆

***C.* 'Barbara Dibley'** (P) Pansy violet flowers 8 in (20 cm) or more across, with a deep carmine stripe along each sepal. They appear in late spring to early summer and again in early fall.

Clematis 'Barbara Jackman'

***C.* 'Barbara Jackman'** (P) Deep violet flowers striped with magenta, up to 6 in (15 cm) wide. They have cream stamens and are borne from late spring to early summer. In cultivation 1952.

***C.* 'Beauty of Worcester'** (L) Blue-violet flowers, occasionally double, with contrasting creamy white stamens, up to 6 in (15 cm) across. They are borne from late spring to late summer. In cultivation 1900.

Clematis 'Bees Jubilee'

***C.* 'Bees Jubilee'** (P) Renowned for its blush pink flowers banded with carmine, up to 7 in (18 cm) across. Makes a striking display. In cultivation 1958.
🏆

***C.* 'Belle of Woking'** (F) Pale mauve, double flowers, 4 in (10 cm) across, borne in late spring and early summer.

***C.* 'Carnaby'** (L) Deep raspberry pink flowers with a deeper bar. Good in shade. In cultivation 1983.

Clematis 'Comtesse de Bouchaud'

***C.* 'Comtesse de Bouchaud'** (J) Beautiful, soft rose-pink flowers with yellow stamens, up to 6 in (15 cm) across. Vigorous and free flowering. Early to late summer. In cultivation 1903.
🏆

***C.* 'Countess of Lovelace'** (P) Double and single flowers, bluish lilac with cream anthers, 6 in (15 cm) wide, borne in late spring to midsummer. In cultivation 1876.

***C.* 'Daniel Deronda'** (P) Large, violet-

Clematis 'Daniel Deronda'

blue flowers, paler at the center, up to 8 in (20 cm) across, with creamy stamens. The flowers are often double and appear in early summer to early fall.

C. **'Dawn'** (L/P) Pale pink flowers shading to white toward the base, 6 in (15 cm) across, with conspicuous red anthers. Best in shade. Late spring to early summer. In cultivation 1969.

Clematis 'Dr. Ruppel'

C. **'Dr. Ruppel'** (P) Deep pink flowers with a carmine bar and yellow stamens, up to 8 in (20 cm) across. In cultivation 1975.

C. **'Duchess of Albany'** (T) Tubular, nodding flowers, bright pink, shading to lilac-pink at the margins. Midsummer to frost.

C. **'Duchess of Edinburgh'** (F) Large, double, rosette-like, scented, white flowers with green shading, up to 4 in (10 cm)

Clematis 'Duchess of Edinburgh'

across. Late spring to early summer. In cultivation 1875.

C. **'Duchess of Sutherland'** (V) Red flowers with a darker bar on each tapered sepal, up to 6 in (15 cm) across, often double. Mid- and late summer.

C. **'Edith'** (L) Similar to 'Mrs. Cholmondeley', of which it is a seedling, but the flowers are white with red anthers.

Clematis 'Elsa Späth'

C. **'Elsa Späth'** (P) Popular for its large, lavender-blue flowers with red stamens, up to 8 in (20 cm) wide. Late spring or early summer and again in early fall.

C. **'Ernest Markham'** (V) Glowing red flowers with a velvety sheen and rounded sepals, up to 6 in (15 cm) across. Early summer to early fall. Best in a sunny location. In cultivation 1938.

C. **'Etoile Rose'** (T) A semiherbaceous plant whose flowers are nodding, bell-shaped, 2 in (5 cm) long, and deep cherry-purple with a silvery pink margin. Summer.

Clematis 'Etoile Violette'

C. **'Etoile Violette'** (V) A vigorous and free-flowering clematis with deep purple flowers, up to 4 in (10 cm) across with 4–6 sepals. Midsummer to early fall. In cultivation 1885.

C. **'Fair Rosamond'** (L/P) Fragrant flowers up to 6 in (15 cm) across, pale blush pink with a carmine bar, fading to white. The anthers are purple. Late spring and early summer. In cultivation 1871.

C. **'Fireworks'** (L) Violet flowers, striped with red; long, slender, twisted sepals.

Clematis 'Fujimu-Sumi'

C. **'Fujimu-Sumi'** (L) Deep lavender-blue flowers that have six pointed sepals with a white bar on the reverse and a center composed of green-white stamens.

C. **'General Sikorski'** (L) Midblue flowers, reddish at the bases of the sepals, up to 6 in (15 cm) across. Early to midsummer.

C. **'Gillian Blades'** (J) Very large, pure white flowers, up to 8¾ in (22 cm) across, with frilled edges appear in midsummer. Little or no pruning is required.

C. **'Gipsy Queen'** (J) Rich, velvety violet-purple flowers, up to 4¾ in (12 cm) across, with broad, rounded sepals. Vigorous and free flowering. Midsummer to early fall. In cultivation 1871.

Clematis 'Gravetye Beauty'

C. **'Gravetye Beauty'** (T) The cherry red flowers of this clematis are bell shaped at first, but the sepals eventually spread. Midsummer to early fall.

C. **'Hagley Hybrid'** (J) Shell pink flowers with contrasting, chocolate brown anthers, up to 6 in (15 cm) across. Free flowering, early summer to early fall. Also listed as 'Pink Chiffon'. In cultivation 1956.

Clematis 'Hagley Hybrid'

C. **'Henryi'** (L) Large, creamy white flowers, up to 7 in (18 cm) across, with pointed sepals and dark stamens. Late spring or early summer and again in late summer or early fall. In cultivation 1858.

Clematis 'Henryi'

C. **'H. F. Young'** (P) Deep blue flowers, up to 8 in (20 cm) across, with broad, overlapping sepals and creamy white stamens. Late spring or early summer and early fall. In cultivation 1962.

C. **'Horn of Plenty'** (L) Cup-shaped, rose-purple flowers with darker stripes and a center of plum stamens in early summer.

C. **'Huldine'** (V) Pearly white flowers with a mauve bar on the reverse. Requires full sun. Midsummer to midfall.

C. **'Jackmanii Alba'** (J) White flowers veined with blue, up to 5 in (13 cm) wide. Early flowers are double, later ones single. Very vigorous. In cultivation 1878.

Clematis 'Jackmanii Alba'

Clematis 'Jackmanii Superba'

C. **'Jackmanii Superba'** (J) Large, rich violet-purple flowers with broad sepals; vigorous and free flowering, midsummer to early fall.

C. **'John Huxtable'** (J) An excellent, late-flowering white clematis, a seedling of 'Comtesse de Bouchaud', which it resembles in all but color. Mid- to late summer.

C. **'John Warren'** (L) Pinkish lilac flowers with a deeper bar and margins and red stamens, the bar fading as the flower opens to 10 in (25 cm) across.

C. **'Kathleen Wheeler'** (P) Deep mauve-blue flowers up to 7 in (18 cm) across. The prominent stamens have lilac filaments. Late spring and early summer, with smaller flowers in fall. In cultivation 1967.

C. **'Ken Donson'** (P) Blue flowers with golden anthers in late summer.

C. **'Lady Betty Balfour'** (V) Deep, velvety purple flowers, 4¾ in (12 cm) across, with golden stamens. Very vigorous and best in full sun. Late summer to midfall. In cultivation 1910.

C. **'Lady Londesborough'** (P) Flowers pale mauve at first, becoming silvery gray. To 6 in (15 cm) wide, with dark stamens and broad, overlapping sepals. Free flowering, late spring and early summer.

C. **'Lady Northcliffe'** (L) Rich violet-blue flowers with broad, wavy sepals and cream stamens, up to 6 in (15 cm) wide. Early summer through fall.

Clematis 'Lasurstern'

C. **'Lasurstern'** (P) Deep lavender-blue flowers, up to 7 in (18 cm) wide, with white stamens and broad, tapering, wavy-margined sepals. Late spring or early summer and again in early fall.

Clematis 'Lincoln Star'

C. **'Lincoln Star'** (P) Brilliant raspberry-pink flowers, 6 in (15 cm) across, with dark red stamens. Late spring and early summer. Flowers borne during a second flush in early fall are paler and have a deep pink bar. In cultivation 1954.

C. **'Lord Nevill'** (P) A vigorous plant with bronze young foliage. The flowers are deep purplish blue, up to 7 in (18 cm) across, and have darker veins. Early summer and early fall. In cultivation 1878.

C. **'Madame Baron Veillard'** (J) A vigorous plant with pale lilac-pink flowers, 5 in (13 cm) wide, with six sepals. Midsummer to early fall. In cultivation 1885.

Clematis 'Madame Baron Veillard'

C. **'Madame Edouard André'** (J) Rich crimson flowers, up to 4¾ in (12 cm) wide, with yellow stamens. Very free flowering, early to late summer. In cultivation 1893.

Clematis 'Madame Grangé'

Clematis 'Madame Julia Correvon'

C. **'Madame Grangé'** (J) Grown for its velvety, deep purplish red flowers, up to 4¾ in (12 cm) wide. Midsummer to early fall. In cultivation 1873.

C. **'Madame Julia Correvon'** (V) Rose-red flowers, up to 5 in (13 cm) across, with cream stamens. Free flowering, midsummer to early fall. In cultivation 1900.

C. **'Margot Koster'** (V) Deep rose-pink flowers, to 4 in (10 cm) across, with up to 6 reflexed sepals. Midsummer to early fall.

C. **'Marie Boisselot'** (P) Large flowers, up to 8 in (20 cm) wide, pure white, with cream stamens and broad, rounded, overlapping sepals. Vigorous and free flowering. Late spring to midfall. Also sold as 'Madame le Coultre'. In cultivation 1900.

Clematis 'Miss Bateman'

C. **'Miss Bateman'** (P) White flowers, 6 in (15 cm) wide, banded with pale green when first open. Late spring to early summer. In cultivation 1869.

C. **'Mrs. Cholmondeley'** (J) Pale blue flowers, up to 8 in (20 cm) wide, with long-pointed sepals. Vigorous and free flowering, late spring to late summer.

C. **'Mrs. George Jackman'** (P) White flowers, up to 7 in (18 cm) wide, with broad, overlapping petals. It is similar to 'Marie Boisselot', but the sepals have a cream bar and the darker anthers are more prominent. Late spring or early summer and early fall. In cultivation 1873.

C. **'Mrs. N. Thompson'** (P) Violet flowers,

up to 4¾ in (12 cm) across, with a scarlet bar. Late spring or early summer and early fall. In cultivation 1961.

C. **'Multi-Blue'** (P/L) Deep violet-blue, fully double flowers with a center of blue and white staminodes. Late spring or early summer and again in fall.

Clematis 'Nelly Moser'

C. **'Nelly Moser'** (L) One of the most popular clematis of all. Large, pale mauve-pink flowers, up to 8 in (20 cm) across, each sepal with a carmine central bar. Very free flowering but best on a north-facing wall or in another shady location, to prevent flowers from fading. Late spring or early summer and again in late summer or early fall. In cultivation 1897.

Clematis 'Niobe'

C. **'Niobe'** (J) The best red clematis. Deep red flowers, up to 6 in (15 cm) wide, with yellow anthers. In cultivation 1975.

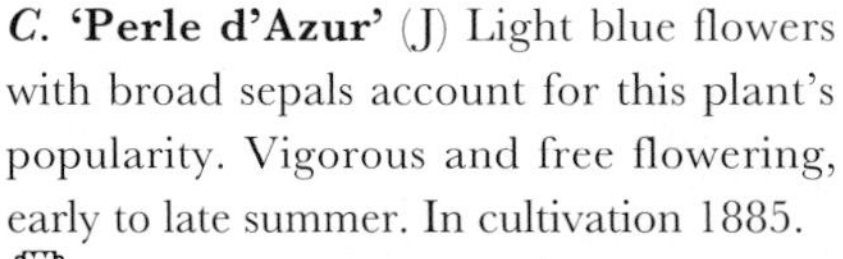

C. **'Perle d'Azur'** (J) Light blue flowers with broad sepals account for this plant's popularity. Vigorous and free flowering, early to late summer. In cultivation 1885.

C. **'Pink Champagne'** (P) Large, rich pink flowers in early summer.

C. **'Polish Spirit'** (V) A fast-growing clematis bearing rich purple flowers with deep red stamens from July to November. It requires hard pruning.

C. **'Proteus'** (F) Deep mauve-pink, double flowers, up to 6 in (15 cm) wide, with many sepals. The later flowers are single. Early summer and early fall.

C. **'Richard Pennell'** (P) Lavender flowers flushed with white, up to 8 in (20 cm) across, with wavy-margined sepals, red stamen filaments, and cream anthers. Late spring or early summer and again in early fall. In cultivation 1974.

Clematis 'Rouge Cardinal'

C. **'Rouge Cardinal'** (J) Velvety crimson flowers, up to 6 in (15 cm) wide, with brown anthers. Early to late summer. In cultivation 1968.

C. **'Royalty'** (P) A vigorous and compact plant with double flowers, single in fall. Similar to 'Vyvyan Pennell' but darker blue-purple.

C. **'Silver Moon'** (L) A vigorous and bushy plant with large, pale lavender flowers borne over a long period. Good on a north-facing wall.

C. **'Star of India'** (J) Red-purple flowers, becoming violet-purple with a redder central bar, up to 6¼ in (16 cm) across, with broad sepals. Early summer to early fall.

C. **'Sylvia Denny'** (F) Pure white, semi-double, rosette-like flowers with pink stamens in late spring and summer.

Clematis 'The President'

C. **'The President'** (P) A popular clematis with deep purple-blue flowers that are silver on the reverse and measure 7 in (18 cm) across. Free flowering from early summer to early fall.

C. **'Venosa Violacea'** (V) A very distinct hybrid of *C. viticella* that develops flowers up to 4 in (10 cm) wide. They have 5–6 boat-shaped sepals and a white center, and they are veined and edged with purple. The anthers are blackish purple. Early summer to early fall. In cultivation 1910.

Clematis 'Victoria'

***C.* 'Victoria'** (J) Rose-purple flowers with three darker ribs on each sepal, up to 6 in (15 cm) wide, with white stamens. Vigorous and free flowering. Blooms are borne from early summer to early fall.

***C.* 'Ville de Lyon'** (V) Bright carmine red flowers, deeper at the margins, with golden stamens. Midsummer to midfall.

***C.* 'Vyvyan Pennell'** (P) Considered to be one of the best double clematis. The flowers are deep violet-blue, suffused with purple and carmine in the center, to 6 in (15 cm) wide, fully double, and produced from late spring to midsummer. Single, lavender-blue flowers are produced in fall. In cultivation 1959.
🏆

***C.* 'Wada's Primrose'** (P) Pale creamy yellow flowers, best in shade. Late spring and early summer. In cultivation 1979.

***C.* 'Will Goodwin'** (P) Large, pale lavender flowers with broad, overlapping, wavy-edged sepals and a center of golden stamens. Late spring to early fall.
🏆

***C.* 'William Kennet'** (L) Lavender-blue flowers with dark stamens, and sepals with crimped margins. Early to late summer.

Clerodendrum *Verbenaceae*

A large genus of about 400 species of deciduous trees, shrubs, and climbers with opposite leaves and showy flowers. They are found mainly in tropical regions, and, apart from the hardy species, many are grown for greenhouse decoration. They will grow in sun or shade and in any well-drained, friable soil.

Clerodendrum bungei

C. bungei A remarkable, suckering shrub of medium height that makes a thicket of dark-colored, erect stems that bear large, heart-shaped leaves and large, terminal flower heads. These are borne from late summer to early fall and consist of fragrant, rosy red flowers that, superficially, look somewhat like those of a mophead hydrangea. The plant grows and flowers well in the shade of large shrubs or trees. In contrast to the sweet scent of the flowers, the leaves are fetid when disturbed, so the plant requires careful siting. China. Introduced 1844 by Robert Fortune.
Zone 7 US, 8 Can. 🏆

Clerodendrum trichotomum var. *fargesii*

C. trichotomum* var. *fargesii A vigorous, large shrub that comes into its own in late summer and early autumn with very fragrant white flowers, enclosed in maroon calyxes, which are followed by bright blue berries that look like jewels in the contrasting setting of the persistent calyxes. This variety flowers more freely than the species but shares its tendency to succumb to unusually cold winters and so requires careful siting. W China. Introduced 1898 by Père Farges.
Zone 5 US, 6 Can. 🏆

Clethra *Clethraceae*

This genus is now considered to include around 60 species of evergreen and deciduous shrubs and trees native to the southern United States, Central and South America, Southeast Asia, and Madeira. Their flowers are small, white, and fragrant and are produced in long clusters from mid- to late summer. Several of them have attractive, peeling bark, and all require a lime-free soil. Although routine pruning is not required, the older wood of established shrubs can be thinned out to improve their shape, and, particularly with C. alnifolia, *any growths from the base can be removed in the winter. Really old specimens can be renewed by cutting them back hard in spring and then feeding.*

Clethra alnifolia

C. alnifolia (Summersweet) A deciduous shrub seldom more than 6½ ft (2 m) tall with white or nearly white flowers borne in erect, terminal panicles in late summer. The fall foliage is yellow to orange. The following forms are recommended. E North America. Introduced 1731.
Zone 4 US, 4b Can.

***C. a.* 'Paniculata'** A superior small to medium-sized form, recommended for planting instead of the species.
Zone 4 US, 4b Can. 🏆

***C. a.* 'Rosea'** Also recommended over the species, this lovely small to medium-sized

Clethra barbinervis

clone has glossy leaves and buds and flowers tinged with pink. 'Pink Spire' is similar. Introduced 1906.
Zone 4 US, 5b Can.

C. barbinervis (Japanese clethra) A handsome, medium-sized deciduous species with long racemes of fragrant white flowers and leaves that turn red and yellow in fall. Japan. Introduced 1870.
Zone 5 US, 6 Can. 🏆

C. delavayi A magnificent, very beautiful, large, deciduous shrub that requires a sheltered location and protection from late-spring frosts. It has long, broad, many-flowered racemes of white, lily-of-the-valley-like flowers that are borne at the ends of branchlets and are held more or less horizontally. W China. Introduced 1913.
Zone 7 US, 8 Can. 🏆

C. fargesii A very beautiful deciduous species about 8 ft (2.5 m) tall that produces pure white, fragrant flowers in panicles up to 10 in (25 cm) long in midsummer. Its leaves turn rich yellow in fall. C China. Introduced 1900 by Ernest Wilson.
Zone 6 US, 7 Can.

Cleyera *Theaceae*

A genus of about 18 species of evergreen trees and shrubs, mostly from Mexico and Central America but with one species native to eastern Asia.

Cleyera japonica 'Tricolor'

***C. japonica* 'Tricolor'** A slow-growing shrub, eventually about 10 ft (3 m) tall, with rigidly spreading and densely leaved branches. The foliage is shining dark green, marbled gray, and has a cream margin that is flushed deep rose when the leaves are young. A very attractive shrub if carefully sited. Japan. Introduced 1861.
Zone 8 US, 9? Can.

Clianthus *Leguminosae*

A genus of two species of semievergreen shrubs; the species described below requires a hot, sunny location in well-drained soil. Pruning can be done in early summer after the flowers are past and is mainly a matter of removing any dead wood and preventing the plant from shading itself too much, which will inhibit flowering.

C. puniceus (Glory pea, parrot's beak) A vigorous semievergreen shrub with climbing stems. It is medium-sized and has attractive pinnate leaves 3–6 in (8–15 cm) long, composed of 11–25 oblong leaflets. The clawlike flowers — which are really very large, long, pointed pea flowers — are brilliant red and carried in bright, showy clusters in early summer. When grown outdoors it performs best against a warm, sunny wall, but this is possible only in the mildest climates; elsewhere, it is ideal as a dramatic greenhouse shrub. Extremely rare in the wild. North Island of New Zealand. Introduced 1831.
Zone 8 US, 9? Can. 🏆

***C. p.* 'Albus'** This medium-sized form has

Clianthus puniceus 'Albus'

Clianthus puniceus

white flowers with a slight green tint.
Zone 8 US, 9? Can. 🏆

***C. p.* 'Flamingo'** A medium-sized shrub with deep rose-pink flowers.
Zone 8 US, 9? Can.

***C. p.* 'White Heron'** This medium-sized cultivar has pure white flowers, delicately flushed with green.
Zone 8 US, 9? Can.

Colletia *Rhamnaceae*

A genus of five species of deciduous shrubs native to southern South America. Those described below are very distinct among cultivated plants in that they are entirely or almost leafless and bear very prominent spines. The attractive, small, honey-scented flowers are usually produced in late summer and fall. Pruning can be difficult but is fortunately seldom necessary, except for tip-pinching young plants to promote bushiness. Up to a point, the poorer the soil, the hardier the plants are, and the sunnier their location, the more profusely they flower.

C. armata See *C. hystrix*.
C. cruciata See *C. paradoxa*.

Colletia hystrix

C. hystrix, syn. *C. armata* This robust shrub, up to 8 ft (2.5 m), has strong, stout, rounded spines. In late summer and fall the branches are crowded with small, fragrant, pitcher-shaped white flowers. Chile, N Argentina. Introduced c. 1882.
Zone 7 US, 9 Can.

***C. h.* 'Rosea'** A pretty medium-sized shrub with white flowers that are pink in bud.
Zone 7 US, 9 Can.

Colletia hystrix 'Rosea'

C. paradoxa, syn. *C. cruciata* A remarkable, rather slow-growing, medium-sized shrub with branchlets transformed into formidable, flat, triangular spines, making it a suitable boundary plant. It is covered with small, white, pitcher-shaped flowers in late summer and early fall. E Argentina, Uruguay, S Brazil. Introduced 1824.
Zone 7 US, 9 Can.

Colquhounia *Labiatae*

A genus of three species of evergreen subshrubs from the Himalaya and Southeast Asia. They will grow in any well-drained, friable soil.

Colquhounia coccinea

C. coccinea A showy, medium-sized shrub with large, downy leaves and scarlet, tubular flowers borne in fall. It needs a sunny site, preferably against a wall, where it will reach a height of 8 ft (2.5 m). It is occasionally killed back by frost but usually sends up shoots again in early summer. Himalaya. Introduced before 1850.
Zone 7 US, 9 Can. 🏆

Colutea *Leguminosae*
Bladder senna

A genus of about 25 species of deciduous shrubs, ranging from southern Europe to North Africa and the western Himalaya. They are easily grown shrubs with pinnate leaves and very striking pea flowers throughout the summer, and they are made even more distinct by their inflated seedpods. They should be pruned hard in early spring if they are getting in the way of other plants or growing out of bounds, although this is unlikely to happen in poorer soils.

Colutea arborescens

C. arborescens A vigorous shrub, up to 13 ft (4 m) tall, with yellow flowers and puffy, pink seedpods that are quite eye-catching. Mediterranean region. Introduced in the 16th century.
Zone 4 US, 5 Can.

***C. × media* 'Copper Beauty'** A vigorous, medium-sized shrub with blue-green leaves and an abundance of bright orange flowers.
Zone 5 US, 6b Can.

Comptonia *Myricaceae*

A genus of one deciduous species, related to and once included in Myrica.

C. peregrina (Sweet fern) A small, suckering, aromatic shrub with downy stems, rather like the fronds of a small spleenwort fern, and small, glistening, brown catkins

in spring. It requires moist, peaty, acid soil and part shade to full sun. It is difficult to transplant E North America. Introduced 1714.
Zone 2 US, 2 Can.

Convolvulus *Convolvulaceae*

This genus is widely distributed, mostly in temperate regions and with many of the 200 species occurring in the Mediterranean area. It is probably best known for its many trailing perennials, but there are also several evergreen and deciduous shrubby species.

Convolvulus cneorum

C. cneorum (Silverbush) A very beautiful, evergreen, rock-garden shrub with silvery, silky leaves and large, pale pink and white, funnel-shaped flowers borne mainly in late spring, although they may be produced sporadically for several months. Flowering and hardiness are greatly enhanced in a gritty, very well drained soil and in a site that gets full sun. SE Europe. In cultivation 1640.
Zone 8 US, 9? Can. 🏆

Coprosma *Rubiaceae*

A genus of about 90 species of evergreen shrubs or small trees, primarily from New Zealand. Flowers are small and fruits are attractive.

***C. × kirkii* 'Variegata'** A pretty, dwarf, spreading shrub. The small, narrow leaves are pale green with white margins. It makes a good ground cover in mild areas.
Zone 8 US, 9? Can.

Cordyline *Agavaceae*

A genus of 15 species of evergreen trees and shrubs native to New Zealand, Australia, India, South America, and Polynesia.

Cordyline australis

C. australis (Giant dracena) A small to medium-sized tree, usually forming a single trunk, and bearing several stout, ascending branches, each one crowned with a large, dense mass of long, swordlike leaves. The flowers are small, creamy white, and fragrant and are produced in large terminal panicles in early summer. It makes a striking foliage feature in gardens in mild areas and is also commonly grown as a houseplant or specimen for a warm greenhouse. New Zealand. Introduced 1823.
Zone 8 US, 9 Can. 🏆

***C. a.* 'Purpurea'** A small to medium-sized tree with purple leaves.
Zone 8 US, 9 Can.

***C. a.* 'Red Star'** A selected purple-leaved form with deeply colored foliage.
Zone 8 US, 9 Can.

***C. a.* 'Sundance'** A small tree bearing yellow leaves with midribs and bases attractively flushed with deep pink.
Zone 8 US, 9 Can.

***C. a.* 'Torbay Dazzler'** A small form whose leaves are edged with creamy white.
Zone 8 US, 9 Can.

Coriaria *Coriariaceae*

An interesting genus, of which about 80 species in all are now recognized, including some deciduous, shrubby plants suitable for cool-temperate gardens. Their foliage is frondlike, and the flower petals, borne in late spring, persist, becoming thick and fleshy and enclosing the fruits in fall. They will grow in any well-drained, friable soil.

Coriaria japonica

C. japonica A pleasing, small, low-growing shrub with arching stems that makes a good ground cover. It has eye-catching red fruits and good fall foliage that is attractively tinted. Japan. Introduced before 1893.
Zone 6 US, 7 Can.

C. myrtifolia A graceful shrub up to 5 ft (1.5 m) tall that has four-angled, curving branches and glistening black fruits. Both the leaves and fruits are poisonous. Mediterranean region. Introduced 1629.
Zone 7 US, 8b Can.

C. terminalis* var. *xanthocarpa An attractive, small subshrub with frondlike leaves that turn rich colors in fall. Its fruits are translucent yellow. Sikkim, E Nepal.
Zone 6 US, 7 Can.

Cornus

Cornaceae Dogwood, cornel

Cornus alba 'Sibirica'

This is a genus of some 50 mainly deciduous species, ranging from creeping ground covers to beautiful trees and shrubs — many of which are of great value in the garden. They are relatively easy to grow, are not troubled by many pests, and will thrive in nearly every region of North America, except where it is exceptionally hot and dry. Dogwoods also offer an enormous range of seasonal interest — from delicate spring and summer flowers, to colorful fall foliage and fruits, to dramatic winter bark. The branch structure of some plants is so handsome that even the bare trees are ornamental. No wonder they have been put to so many uses, including as ground covers, screens and windbreaks, hedges, foundation and woodland plantings, borders, and striking lawn specimens.

Because the genus includes species with great differences in structure and appearance, botanists have from time to time advocated that *Cornus* be divided into up to four new genera. One of them would have included just *C. mas* and its close relative *C. officinalis*, which are shrubs that bear flowers on their bare branches in winter and red, cherrylike fruits. Another proposed reclassification would create a genus to comprise shrubs that form clumps of brilliantly colored, often osier-like stems that generally prefer moist sites and sometimes bear handsomely variegated foliage. Included in this genus would have been the magnificent *C. controversa*, which has a slow-growing, variegated form that is a good choice for small gardens.

Flowering dogwoods

Perhaps the showiest and most captivating dogwoods are the species that some botanists would distinguish on the basis of their beautiful floral bracts, which surround and support the otherwise inconspicuous, tight heads of minute flowers. These, and their hybrids and cultivars, are among the loveliest of all garden shrubs and trees.

These flowering dogwoods are native to North America and the Far East, and they vary considerably in their suitability to different climates. *C. florida*, for example, prefers the cool conditions of the eastern United States, whereas *C. nuttallii* thrives in the milder, moister climate of the Pacific Northwest. The hardy *C. kousa* cannot stand summer heat, while *C. mas* is extremely drought tolerant.

Breeders have produced a large number of spectacular hybrids and cultivars. 'Eddie's White Wonder', for instance, is a cross between *C. florida* and *C. nuttallii* and is one of a superb series raised by the Eddie nursery in British Columbia. There is also a wide range of *C. florida* varieties available with many ornamental features. While some have yellow, instead of red, fruits, others offer colored foliage, from red and reddish green tints to pink and cream variegations. Perhaps the greatest range is in bract color, which runs from snowy white to pale pink and soft rose to deep ruby.

Cornus capitata

Cornus alba

C. alba (Tartarian dogwood) This well-known deciduous species forms clumps of stems up to 10 ft (3 m) tall, with the young branches glowing blood red in winter and the leaves coloring well in fall. The fruits, when borne, are white to very light blue. Siberia to Manchuria, N Korea. Introduced 1741.

Zone 2 US, 2 Can.

Care and cultivation

Dogwoods are not fussy plants, and will generally grow in any good, well-drained garden soil, but different types do have different requirements.

The clump-forming species — including *C. alba*, *C. sanguinea*, *C. stolonifera* — are the most adaptable. They tolerate poor, thin, shallow, dry, or wet soils and full sun to shade. While *C. stolonifera*, which is native to swampy areas, prefers moist soil, it will also grow well in average conditions. *C. mas* and *C. officinalis* are nearly as tolerant as those above, drawing the line only at very wet soil and deep shade.

Dogwoods grown for their colorful stems give the best displays when they are pruned back hard every year, or at least every other year, to within a few inches of the ground in early spring. If this is not done, the plants tend to become somewhat straggly, with the old stems showing indeterminate color and the new branchlets bearing bright color that appears to be an anomaly. Proper pruning will produce a fairly dense clump of upright, whiplike stems that are uniformly and brilliantly colored.

The remainder of the genus will grow in average conditions but perform best in a neutral to acid, organic, slightly moist but well-drained soil. While they are not lime hating, they become less vigorous as the soil becomes more alkaline or shallow.

Since much of their beauty is in their branch structure — with some having a graceful weeping form and others boasting handsomely tiered branches — dogwoods should always be sited with care. They do not need to be shaped by pruning, except in the very early years, and should never be cut back like the clump-forming types.

Dogwoods with colorful stems will be even more colorful in bright light, although they do tolerate shade. Other dogwoods not only take shade, but some require it to prevent the leaves from burning or to keep them cool in warm climates. Dogwoods are rare among woody plants in that those with variegated foliage will not revert when grown in shade. The one caution is with *C. florida*, which is subject to anthracnose; trees grown in shade, where the foliage remains wet after rain, are more vulnerable to this devastating fungal disease.

Cornus alba 'Aurea'

C. a. **'Aurea'** A medium-sized form whose leaves are suffused with soft yellow.

Zone 2 US, 2 Can.

C. a. **'Elegantissima'** The leaves of this medium-sized shrub are broadly margined and mottled with white. 'Sibirica Variegata' is similar. In cultivation 1900.

Zone 2 US, 2 Can. 🏆

C. a. **'Gouchaltii'** Although this medium-sized shrub is often confused with 'Spaethii', the leaves are duller in comparison, with a pink tinge. In cultivation 1888.

Zone 2 US, 2 Can.

Cornus alba 'Elegantissima'

***C. a.* 'Kesselringii'** The stems of this striking medium-sized shrub are almost black-purple, making the plant a suitable focal point in winter. The leaves open brown. In cultivation 1907.

Zone 2 US, 2 Can.

***C. a.* 'Sibirica'**, syn. *C. a.* 'Westonbirt' (Siberian dogwood) This is less robust than some other forms but is nevertheless an excellent medium-sized shrub with brilliant coral-crimson winter shoots.

Zone 2 US, 2 Can.

Cornus alba 'Sibirica Variegata'

***C. a.* 'Sibirica Variegata'** A medium-sized shrub whose leaves have a broad, creamy white margin that turn interesting shades in fall. The winter shoots are deep red. It is similar to 'Elegantissima' but

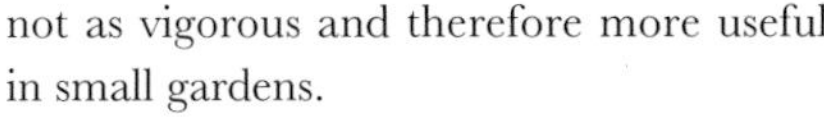

not as vigorous and therefore more useful in small gardens.

Zone 2 US, 2 Can.

***C. a.* 'Spaethii'** A superb medium-sized shrub with conspicuously gold-variegated leaves.

Zone 2 US, 2 Can.

***C. a.* 'Westonbirt'** See *C. a.* 'Sibirica'.

C. alternifolia (Pagoda dogwood) A large deciduous shrub, or occasionally a small tree, with horizontally spreading branches. Leaves are alternate and tinted red in fall; the berries are bluish black. The following form is recommended. E North America. Introduced 1760.

Zone 3 US, 3b Can.

Cornus alternifolia 'Argentea'

***C. a.* 'Argentea'**, syn. *C. a.* 'Variegata' This is one of the best silver-variegated shrubs, forming a bush about 8–10 ft (2.5–3 m) tall. Its leaves are small and have a regular, creamy white margin.

Zone 3 US, 3b Can.

***C. a.* 'Variegata'** See *C. a.* 'Argentea'.

C. amomum (Silky dogwood) A medium-sized shrub notable for its blue fruits and purple winter shoots. The leaves turn red in fall. E North America. Introduced 1683.

Zone 4 US, 4b Can.

***C.* 'Ascona'** *(C. florida × C. nuttallii)* A wide-spreading, large deciduous shrub. The flower heads are freely borne in midspring even when the shrub is young and measure, with their four-pointed white bracts, up to 3 in (7.5 cm) across. The leaves color beautifully in fall.

Zone 6 US, 7 Can.

C. canadensis (Bunchberry) This is,

Cornus alba 'Gouchaltii'

strictly speaking, not a shrub but an herbaceous perennial with a creeping, woody rootstock. Its 6 in (15 cm) shoots, with whorled leaves, form attractive mats that are covered in early summer with white flowers, followed by bunches of vivid red fruits. It prefers moist, peaty soil and light shade. North America. Introduced 1774.
Zone 2 US, 2 Can. 🏆

C. capitata (Evergreen dogwood) In mild areas this beautiful evergreen species is a small tree. From early to midsummer, the buttonlike flower heads are surrounded by lovely, sulphur yellow bracts, which are followed in autumn by large, raspberry-like fruits. The leathery leaves turn bronze in winter. Himalaya, China. Introduced 1825.
Zone 8 US, 9 Can.

Cornus controversa

Cornus controversa 'Variegata'

C. controversa (Giant dogwood) A magnificent medium-sized or large deciduous tree with alternate leaves and sweeping, layered branches covered in late spring with broad, flat clusters of cream-colored flowers. In autumn, small bluish black fruits are produced and the foliage often turns purple-red. Japan, China, Taiwan. Introduced before 1880.
Zone 4 US, 5b Can.

***C. c.* 'Variegata'** One of the best and most ornamental small trees. It has the same horizontal, tiered branching as the species but is considerably slower growing and has narrower, more pointed leaves, variegated with silver margins. In cultivation 1890.
Zone 4 US, 5b Can. 🏆

***C.* 'Eddie's White Wonder'** *(C. florida × C. nuttallii)* A superb large deciduous shrub or small tree of compact, upright habit. It flowers in spring, and the rounded bracts that surround the flower heads give the appearance of perfectly round, white flowers wreathing the branches. The leaves turn brilliant orange in fall. The expectations of its Canadian breeder have been more than fulfilled, and it is reliable as well as highly ornamental.
Zone 6 US, 7 Can. 🏆

C. florida (Flowering dogwood, Eastern dogwood) This large deciduous shrub or small tree is often represented in gardens by its cultivars. Its flower buds are enclosed in winter by bracts that enlarge and turn white, so that each buttonlike flower head has four showy, petallike bracts in late spring. The leaves turn scarlet in fall, sometimes with a violet flush, and the fruits are bright red berries held in clusters. The following forms are recommended. E United States. In cultivation 1730.
Zone 5 US, 6 Can.

Cornus florida 'Cherokee Chief'

***C. f.* 'Cherokee Chief'** A large shrub or small tree with bracts of a bright, deep rose-red. In cultivation 1958.
Zone 6 US, 7 Can. 🏆

***C. f.* 'Cloud Nine'** A cultivar with large, showy white bracts, free flowering even when young.
Zone 5 US, 6 Can.

***C. f.* 'First Lady'** This plant is considered by many to be an improvement on 'Rainbow', with leaves that are variegated with yellow.
Zone 6 US, 7 Can.

Cornus florida 'Rainbow'

***C. f.* 'Rainbow'** A large shrub or small tree with a dense, upright habit and leaves margined with deep yellow that turn red-purple margined with scarlet in autumn. The bracts are large and white. In cultivation 1967.
Zone 6 US, 7 Can.

***C. f.* Rubra group** These are large shrubs or small trees with bracts that are pink

Cornus florida Rubra group

to red; they may be offered for sale as *C. f.* 'Rubra'. The best and most beautiful forms have full rosy pink — not washed-out pink — bracts, and the young leaves are usually reddish. Buds are not as hardy as those of the species In cultivation 1889.
Zone 5 US, 6 Can.

***C. f.* 'Tricolor'** See *C. f.* 'Welchii'.

***C. f.* 'Welchii'**, syn. *C. f.* 'Tricolor' A superb but slow-growing, medium-sized variegated shrub whose green leaves have an irregular, creamy white margin, flushed rose, and turn to bronze-purple edged with rosy red in fall.
Zone 6 US, 7 Can.

***C. f.* 'White Cloud'** This large shrub or small tree has bronze young foliage in the spring and is notable for the exceptional number and the whiteness of its large floral clusters. In cultivation 1946.
Zone 6 US, 7 Can.

C. kousa (Kousa dogwood, Japanese dogwood) A large, elegant, deciduous shrub or small tree. The abundant flowers, which have showy, pointy, white bracts, are poised on slender, erect stalks that cover the spreading branches in early summer and are followed by fruits that resemble small strawberries dangling on long stems. The leaves turn bronze and crimson in fall. Japan, Korea. Introduced 1875.
Zone 5 US, 6 Can.

Cornus kousa var. *chinensis*

C. k.* var. *chinensis (Chinese dogwood) This beautiful form is taller, more open, and hardier, with slightly larger leaves and flower bracts. China. Introduced 1907.
Zone 4 US, 5b Can. 🏆

Cornus mas

***C. k.* 'Gold Star'** The leaves of this large shrub or small tree have a large central blotch of golden yellow. In fall the leaf centers turn red and the margins turn purple. Introduced 1977.
Zone 5 US, 6 Can.

***C. k.* 'Satomi'** A recently introduced Japanese selection with pink bracts and leaves that turn deep purple-red in fall. It makes a large shrub or small tree.
Zone 5 US, 6 Can. 🏆

***C. k.* 'Snowboy'** Young plants have pretty gray-green leaves, each with a wide margin of creamy white and sometimes a blotch of pale yellow. It can make a large shrub or small tree but is quite slow growing. It tends to revert, and these shoots must be pruned out. In cultivation before 1977.
Zone 5 US, 6 Can.

C. mas (Cornelian cherry) A large shrub or small, densely branched deciduous tree that produces an abundance of small yellow flowers on the bare twigs in late winter. These are followed by bright red, cherry-like, edible fruits. The leaves turn reddish purple in fall. C and S Europe. Long cultivated.
Zone 4 US, 4b Can. 🏆

Cornus mas flower detail

***C. m.* 'Aurea'** A large shrub with leaves suffused with yellow. In cultivation 1895.
Zone 4 US, 5 Can.

***C. m.* 'Aurea Elegantissima'**, syn. *C. m.* 'Tricolor' A notably slow-growing,

medium-sized shrub with leaves variegated yellow and flushed with pink. Needs shelter from strong sun. Originated c. 1869.
Zone 4 US, 5 Can.

***C. m.* 'Tricolor'** See *C. m.* 'Aurea Elegantissima'.

Cornus mas 'Variegata'

***C. m.* 'Variegata'** An outstanding, variegated, free-fruiting large shrub or small tree with leaves brightly margined with white. In cultivation 1838.
Zone 4 US, 5 Can. 🏆

Cornus 'Norman Hadden'

***C.* 'Norman Hadden'** *(C. kousa × C. capitata)* A beautiful, graceful, spreading, small deciduous tree that develops peeling bark with age. The small flower heads have four taper-pointed, creamy white bracts that open in early summer and turn deep pink about a month later. Large crops of long-lasting, strawberry-like fruits are borne in fall. In mild areas the foliage persists until spring; where it is colder, some leaves may last through the winter while others turn red and drop. It is a seedling that arose in the garden of Norman Hadden near Porlock, Somerset, England, in the late 1960s. See also *C.* 'Porlock'.
Zone 7? US, 8? Can. 🏆

Cornus nuttallii

C. nuttallii (Pacific dogwood, Western dogwood) A medium-sized deciduous tree. Its flowers appear in late spring, and occasionally again in late summer, and the heads are usually furnished with six large, white floral bracts that sometimes become flushed with pink. The flower heads are not enclosed by bracts in winter; the foliage turns yellow or red in autumn. Orange-red fruits are visible in summer and fall. Be sure to obtain the true species from the nursery, as many plants have turned out to be hybrids with *C. florida*. W North America. Introduced 1835.
Zone 6 US, 7 Can.

***C. n.* 'Colrigo Giant'** A vigorous large shrub or medium-sized tree with large leaves and very large flower heads, up to 6 in (15 cm) across the bracts, and an upright habit. It was found in the Columbia River gorge, after which it is named.
Zone 7 US, 8 Can.

Cornus nuttallii 'Colrigo Giant'

***C. n.* 'Gold Spot'** A large shrub with leaves splashed, spotted, and mottled with yellow; perhaps the same as *C. n.* 'Eddiei'. This plant sometimes produces many of its flowers in fall.
Zone 7 US, 8 Can.

***C. n.* 'North Star'** A large shrub or medium-sized tree with strong, vigorous growth; dark purple young shoots; and large flower heads.
Zone 7 US, 8 Can.

Cornus nuttallii 'Portlemouth'

***C. n.* 'Portlemouth'** A large shrub or medium-sized tree selected for its large bracts and good fall color.
Zone 7 US, 8 Can.

C. officinalis (Japanese cornelian cherry)

Cornus officinalis

A large deciduous shrub or small tree with attractive, peeling bark and clusters of yellow flowers on the bare twigs in late winter. It bears red fruits and colorful fall foliage. Related to *C. mas*, it is coarser and earlier flowering, and the flowers have longer stalks. Japan, Korea. Introduced c. 1870.
Zone 5 US, 6 Can.

Cornus 'Ormonde'

C. 'Ormonde' *(C. florida × C. nuttallii)* A large deciduous shrub similar to 'Eddie's White Wonder' but with a spreading habit. The large white bracts have pink tips. It flowers in midspring. Its origin is unknown, but it grew at Kew Gardens for many years as *C. nuttallii.*
Zone 6 US, 7 Can.

C. 'Porlock' A small, spreading, beautiful deciduous tree similar, if not nearly identical, to 'Norman Hadden'. It, too, occurred as a seedling in Norman Hadden's Somerset garden, but in 1958.
Zone 7? US, 8? Can. 🏆

Cornus sanguinea 'Winter Beauty'

***C. sanguinea* 'Winter Beauty'**, syn. *C. s.* 'Winter Flame' A striking Dutch selection that makes a small, rounded shrub. It is grown mainly for the fall and winter twig color. Stems have a yellow base, becoming bright orange and then red toward the tips. The stems must be cut back almost to the ground in spring for the best display. The deciduous foliage is green in summer, turning yellow and orange in fall.
Zone 4 US, 4b Can.

C. s. 'Winter Flame' See *C. s.* 'Winter Beauty'.

Cornus stolonifera 'White Gold'

C. stolonifera (Red-twig dogwood) A rampant, suckering, deciduous shrub with vigorous shoots up to 8 ft (2.5 m) that form a dense clump of dark red stems. The flowers and fruits are white. The following forms are recommended. North America. Introduced 1656.
Zone 2 US, 1b Can.

C. s. 'Flaviramea' (Yellow-twig dogwood) A medium-sized winter shrub with ocher yellow to olive green young shoots. It is particularly dramatic when planted with the red-stemmed dogwoods and is ideal for moist or wet places. In cultivation 1899.
Zone 2 US, 1b Can. 🏆

Cornus stolonifera 'Flaviramea'

C. s. 'Kelsey Dwarf' See *C. s.* 'Kelseyi'.

Cornus stolonifera 'Kelseyi'

C. s. 'Kelseyi', syn. *C. s.* 'Kelsey Dwarf' A dwarf, dense form often used as ground cover. It has small, crowded leaves and yellowish green winter shoots with red tips.
Zone 2 US, 1b Can.

C. s. 'White Gold', syn. *C. s.* 'White Spot' The leaves of this medium-sized shrub have a white margin, resembling those of *C. alba* 'Elegantissima'. *(See photo at left.)*
Zone 2 US, 2 Can.

C. s. 'White Spot' See *C. s.* 'White Gold'.

Corokia *Cornaceae*

A genus of three species of interesting evergreen shrubs or small trees native to New Zealand. In mild areas, the cultivated species make medium-sized to large shrubs with small, starry, yellow flowers and often very showy red or orange fruits. They will grow in any well-drained, friable soil. Pruning is not necessary.

C. cotoneaster A curiously attractive, small to medium-sized shrub with a tangled tracery of wiry stems that resembles crumpled wire netting. It has sparse foliage, tiny yellow flowers in late spring, and orange fruits. Introduced 1875. North and South Islands.
Zone 7 US, 8 Can.

Corokia × *virgata*

C.* × *virgata A medium-sized, erect shrub with sparse leaves that are white beneath and broadest above the middle. It bears midspring yellow flowers and bright orange fruits freely. The following popular forms make excellent and unusual hedges in mild climates. Introduced 1907.
Zone 8 US, 9 Can.

Corokia × *virgata* 'Red Wonder'

***C.* × *v.* 'Red Wonder'** A medium-sized shrub with masses of deep red berries.
Zone 8 US, 9 Can.

***C.* × *v.* 'Yellow Wonder'** This cultivar is similar to 'Red Wonder' but is more vigorous, with larger leaves and equally profuse, bright yellow fruits.
Zone 8 US, 9 Can.

Coronilla *Leguminosae*

A genus of about 55 species of evergreen and deciduous shrubs and herbaceous plants with pinnate leaves, native to central and southern Europe, the Mediterranean, Africa, northern Asia, and China. Those described here are free-flowering shrubs, grown for their umbels of bright yellow, fragrant pea flowers that are often produced through the growing season. Light, well-drained soil in full sun is preferred. In late winter, dead or weak growth can be pruned away, and old specimens whose flowering is declining can be renewed by cutting back to near ground level.

Coronilla emerus

C. emerus (Scorpion senna) A hardy, medium-sized, elegant deciduous shrub with clusters of yellow flowers in the leaf axils and seedpods that are like a scorpion's tail. C and S Europe. Long cultivated.
Zone 6 US, 7 Can.

Coronilla valentina

C. valentina A small evergreen shrub with slightly bloomy leaves and rich yellow, scented flowers. The forms described below are the ones grown most often. Mediterranean region. In cultivation 1596.
Zone 9 US

Coronilla valentina subsp. *glauca*

C. v.* subsp. *glauca A small to medium-sized shrub suitable for growing against a warm wall or in a sheltered position. It has bloomy leaves and masses of yellow flowers that smell like peaches. Its main flowering is in midspring, but it continues to bloom intermittently throughout most of the year. S Europe. Introduced 1722.
Zone 9 US 🏆

Coronilla valentina 'Citrina'

***C. v.* 'Citrina'** A small to medium-sized form with lemon yellow flowers.
Zone 9 US 🏆

***C. v.* 'Variegata'** A small form of subsp. *glauca* with leaves prettily variegated with creamy white.
Zone 9 US

Correa *Rutaceae*

A small genus of about 10 species of evergreen shrubs, native to Australia and Tasmania and suitable only for mild climates or greenhouse cultivation. The attractive, showy, usually bell-shaped flowers are regularly and abundantly produced in late winter. They need a well-drained, preferably sandy soil and can be pruned after flowering to keep them neat.

C. backhousiana Capable of becoming a medium-sized shrub, this species bears clusters of drooping, tubular, greenish white flowers. Tasmania.
Zone 8 US, 9? Can. 🏆

***C.* 'Harrisii'** See *C.* 'Mannii'.

***C.* 'Mannii'**, syn. *C.* 'Harrisii' A beautiful, early-flowering, small hybrid shrub with rose-scarlet flowers about 1 in (2.5 cm) long.
Zone 8 US, 9? Can. 🏆

Corylopsis *Hamamelidaceae*

Winter hazel

A genus of seven species of deciduous shrubs from the eastern Himalaya, China, and Japan. They are easy to grow and exquisitely beautiful. Just before the leaves appear in spring, the plants are covered with drooping racemes of fragrant, primrose yellow, cup-shaped flowers. They thrive in acid or neutral, sandy soil and, with the exception of C. pauciflora, *will also grow in limestone soil as long as there is a minimum depth of 2 ft (60 cm). At the limit of their hardiness range, they may need protection from cold, drying winds that can cause dieback. Prune only to remove dead wood.*

Corylopsis glabrescens

C. glabrescens (Fragrant winter hazel) A wide-spreading, medium-sized to large shrub with rounded leaves that are slightly bloomy on the undersides. The primrose yellow flowers are freely borne in slender tassels. Japan. Introduced 1905.
Zone 5 US, 6 Can.

C. gotoana For the plant previously named *C. gotoana*, see *C. sinensis* var. *calvescens*.

Corylopsis pauciflora

C. pauciflora (Buttercup winter hazel) A densely branched shrub with slender stems, slowly growing to 6½ ft (2 m) high and wide. The rounded, bristle-toothed leaves, 1½–2½ in (4–6 cm) long, are the smallest in the genus and are pink when young. The flowers are primrose yellow, scented, and borne in short tassels of 2–3 blooms each, opening in early spring, usually before the other species. Japan, Taiwan. Introduced c. 1860 by Robert Fortune.
Zone 6 US, 7 Can. 🏆

Corylopsis sinensis

C. sinensis (Chinese winter hazel) A large shrub or small tree 13–16 ft (4–5 m) tall with slightly bloomy leaves that are downy on the undersides and lemon yellow flowers. C and W China. Introduced c. 1901.
Zone 5 US, 6 Can.

C.s.* var. *calvescens This large shrub differs from the species mainly in the characteristics of its leaves, which may be considerably larger and more rounded, smooth and sometimes chalk white on the undersides, and pink-flushed when young. W China. Introduced 1907.
Zone 5 US, 6 Can.

Corylopsis spicata

C. spicata (Spike winter hazel) A spreading, medium-sized shrub with soft down on the young shoots and the undersides of the leaves. The flowers, borne in spring, are in rather narrow clusters about 6 in (15 cm) long, with long, bright yellow petals and dark purple anthers. Japan. Introduced c. 1860 by Robert Fortune.
Zone 5 US, 6 Can.

Corylopsis veitchiana

C. veitchiana A very distinct, large, erect-

growing shrub with characteristically elongated, bright green leaves, edged with incurved teeth and tinted purplish when young. The primrose yellow flowers have conspicuous, brick red anthers and are borne in large racemes. W China. Introduced 1900 by Ernest Wilson.
Zone 6 US, 7 Can. 🏆

Corylopsis willmottiae

C. willmottiae A medium-sized to large shrub with variable leaves, generally purple or reddish purple when young. The flowers are soft yellow and borne in dense, showy racemes. Fruits are glabrous. W China. Introduced 1909 by Ernest Wilson.
Zone 6 US, 7 Can. 🏆

Corylopsis willmottiae 'Spring Purple'

***C. w.* 'Spring Purple'** This gardenworthy plant is a medium-sized to large shrub with very attractive, plum-purple young growths. Raised at Hillier Nurseries before 1969.
Zone 6 US, 7 Can.

Corylus avellana 'Contorta'

Corylus *Betulaceae*
Filbert, hazel

A genus of about 10 species of deciduous large shrubs or small trees from temperate regions of the Northern Hemisphere. Their flowers are borne in catkins, the males of which are pendulous and elongate to make an attractive feature in late winter and early spring. The female catkins are little tufts of bright red stigmas. Many filberts are grown for their edible nuts, while others are purely ornamental. They do well in almost any garden soil, especially well-drained loams, and are excellent in alkaline soils. Most can be pruned regularly to maintain shape and size.

Corylus avellana

C. avellana (European filbert) A large shrub or small, multistemmed tree, impressive when draped in late winter with its long, yellow flowers, which resemble lamb's tails. It is useful in large gardens as a tall screening shrub. The leaves turn yellow in fall. Europe, W Asia, N Africa.
Zone 4 US, 5 Can.

***C. a.* 'Aurea'** A large shrub or small tree with soft yellow leaves, excellent when used to contrast with *C. maxima* 'Purpurea'. In cultivation 1864.
Zone 4 US, 5 Can.

***C. a.* 'Contorta'** (Harry Lauder's walking stick) The branches of this shrub are curiously twisted in spirals, and it is slow growing, eventually reaching about 10 ft (3 m).

For it to develop into a strong garden feature, rather than an unattractive tangle, it should be pruned to a few main stems so that their sinuous twists are clearly defined and create an interesting architectural focal point. Its winter catkins also contribute to its beauty. Discovered c. 1863 in a hedgerow in Gloucestershire, England.
Zone 4 US, 5 Can. 🏆

Corylus colurna

C. colurna (Turkish filbert) A remarkable, large tree of very symmetrical, pyramidal form, with striking, corky furrows in the bark that make an attractive feature. It is the only commonly grown hazel with a straight, single trunk. SE Europe, W Asia. Introduced 1582.
Zone 4 US, 5 Can. 🏆

***C. maxima* 'Purpurea'** (Purple-leaved filbert) A large shrub grown for its large, rounded, purple leaves that rival those of the purple beech in their intense color.
Zone 4 US, 5 Can. 🏆

Cotinus *Anacardiaceae*

Smoke tree

A genus of three species that used to be included in Rhus *and are among the most attractive of the large summer-flowering shrubs. They are deciduous and come from a wide range of habitats in the temperate parts of the Northern Hemisphere. Grown mainly for their fine fall effects, they thrive in any well-drained soil in full sun — too rich a diet can inhibit the development of fall colors and make the shrubs too coarse and sappy. Prune only to remove dead wood or, in spring, to shorten any growths that have become too long.*

Cotinus coggygria

C. coggygria (Smoke tree, smokebush) This species grows to 8–12 ft (2.5–4 m) and has smooth, rounded, green leaves that color well in fall. The fawn-colored, plumelike inflorescences, 6–8 in (15–20 cm) long, which are borne in profusion from early to midsummer, are persistent and by late summer will have turned smoky gray. Europe to the Himalaya, China. In cultivation 1656.
Zone 4 US, 4b Can. 🏆

***C. c.* 'Atropurpureus'** See *C. c.* f. *purpureus.*

Cotinus coggygria 'Foliis Purpureis'

***C. c.* 'Foliis Purpureis'**, syn. *C. c.* 'Rubrifolius' The leaves of this medium-sized shrub, especially when young, are rich plum-purple, changing to light red shades in fall.
Zone 4 US, 5 Can.

C. c.* f. *purpureus, syn. *C. c.* 'Atropurpureus' This medium-sized shrub bears large panicles of purplish gray flowers, which from a distance resemble puffs of pink smoke, as the plant's common name suggests. The leaves are greenish purple and are colorful in fall.
Zone 4 US, 5 Can.

Cotinus coggygria 'Royal Purple'

***C. c.* 'Royal Purple'** A selected form with deep wine-purple leaves that are translucent in the sun and turn reddish as fall approaches. It makes a medium-sized shrub. *C. c.* 'Notcutt's Variety' is similar.
Zone 4 US, 5 Can. 🏆

***C. c.* 'Rubrifolius'** See *C. c.* 'Foliis Purpureis'.

Cotinus coggygria 'Velvet Cloak'

***C. c.* 'Velvet Cloak'** The leaves of this medium-sized shrub are deep red-purple, almost black in some light, and retain their color well into autumn, when they eventually turn red. Found as a seedling in the United States before 1962.
Zone 4 US, 5 Can.

***C.* 'Flame'** A large shrub resembling

Cotinus 'Flame'

C. coggygria but more vigorous and treelike, with larger leaves on younger plants or strongly growing shoots. Its fall color is truly extraordinary, with the leaves turning brilliant orange-red before they drop. Large, pink flower clusters are borne in summer. Almost certainly a hybrid between *C. coggygria* and *C. obovatus*.
Zone 4 US, 5 Can. 🏆

Cotinus 'Grace'

***C.* 'Grace'** (*C. obovatus* × *C. coggygria* 'Velvet Cloak', Dummer hybrids) A vigorous, tall shrub with large, soft purplish red leaves that turn scarlet in autumn, and large, conical, purplish pink flower clusters in summer. Raised late 1970s by the Hillier Nurseries' propagator Peter Dummer as part of the series from the same cross known as Dummer hybrids.
Zone 4 US, 4b Can. 🏆

C. obovatus (American smoke tree) A rare large shrub or small tree that, in favorable seasons and situations, is one of the most brilliantly colored fall shrubs. Its leaves are much larger than those of *C. coggygria* and turn to shades of orange, red, and purple. SE United States. Introduced 1882.
Zone 4 US, 5 Can. 🏆

Cotinus obovatus

Cotoneaster *Rosaceae*

Botanical authorities vary in their estimate of how many species there are in this far-flung and indispensable genus of ornamental shrubs. Some say there are about 200, others say twice that many, while still others reduce the genus to just 70 species. Whatever the case may be, cotoneasters range from prostrate mats to small trees, most of which are deciduous, though some are evergreen. Their great variety of habits makes them suitable for many purposes in the garden, from hedges and ground covers to specimen and wall shrubs. They are grown chiefly for their brilliant fall color and bright, showy berries, although the white or pink-tinged flowers that often smother the branches in early summer are beautiful as well as attractive to bees.

Cotoneasters will grow in almost any soil but prefer a moist, well-drained site. They can be grown in sun or part shade, though the best ornamental results are often obtained in full sun. They are hardy shrubs and tolerate air pollution.

Pruning requirements vary, but pruning is essentially a matter of removing dead wood and any shoots that are growing in unwanted directions. Old, overgrown shrubs can be renewed by cutting them back hard in late winter. This is also the time for trimming informal cotoneaster hedges.

Cotoneasters are, unfortunately, highly susceptible to fireblight and spider mites.

C. adpressus (Creeping cotoneaster) A dwarf, wide-spreading deciduous shrub, good for large rock gardens, with white flowers, bright red fruits, and small, wavy-edged leaves that turn scarlet in fall. W China. Introduced 1896.
Zone 4 US, 4b Can. 🏆

C. a.* var. *praecox See *C. nanshan*.

Cotoneaster amoenus

C. amoenus A pretty, semievergreen shrub resembling *C. franchetii* but with smaller leaves and a more compact, bushy habit. The fruits are bright red and the flowers white. Yunnan Province, China. Introduced 1899 by Ernest Wilson.
Zone 6 US, 7 Can.

Cotoneaster bullatus

C. bullatus A large deciduous shrub with broad, handsome, noticeably corrugated leaves that color well in fall; white flowers; and clusters of large, bright red fruits early in the season. One of the finest species in cultivation. See also *C. rehderi*.

W China. Introduced 1898.

Zone 5 US, 6 Can. 🏆

C. cashmiriensis A prostrate evergreen shrub that forms a low mound and has small, glossy, dark green leaves. White flowers are followed by small, bright red berries. It makes a good ground cover and will cascade over a rock or low wall. This plant is also sometimes grown as *C. microphyllus* var. *cochleatus*. Kashmir.

Zone 6 US, 7 Can. 🏆

C. cavei A small, semievergreen, clump-forming shrub with red shoots and rounded, glossy, dark green leaves. White flowers tinged with pink are followed by bright red berries that persist for a long period throughout fall and winter. Himalaya, W China.

Zone 6? US, 7? Can.

Cotoneaster cochleatus

Cotoneaster congestus

C. cochleatus This charming, slow-growing, prostrate evergreen shrub is related to *C. microphyllus* but has paler, duller green, broader leaves. It bears small, bright red berries and white flowers. W China, SE Tibet, E Nepal.

Zone 4 US, 5 Can.

C. congestus A creeping evergreen shrub with a dense habit that forms a series of molehill-like mounds of small, bluish green leaves. Unfortunately, this species does not bear its red fruits freely. The form described here is often sold in the trade as 'Nanus'. Introduced 1868.

Zone 4 US, 5b Can.

Cotoneaster conspicuus in flower

Cotoneaster conspicuus in fruit

***C. conspicuus* 'Decorus'** (Necklace cotoneaster) A free-fruiting, low-growing but wide-spreading evergreen shrub that is ideal for covering slopes. Its white flowers blanket the plant in early summer and are followed by large numbers of bright red berries that persist for many months. Although the name is not botanically accurate, this is the cultivar used in gardens.

Zone 6 US, 7 Can. 🏆

***C.* 'Coral Beauty'** A very dense, small evergreen shrub with arching branches. The leaves are glossy, green, ovate-elliptic, and up to 3/4 in (2 cm) long. White flowers are followed in autumn by abundant, bright orange-red berries. It makes an excellent ground cover and is sometimes available as a small, topworked, weeping tree. In cultivation 1967.

Zone 4 US, 4b Can.

Cotoneaster 'Cornubia'

***C.* 'Cornubia'** A vigorous semievergreen shrub growing to 20 ft (6 m) or more. Its red fruits are probably the largest among the tall-growing cotoneasters, and they are borne so profusely after the white flowers that they weigh down the branches. It is often available as a standard tree. Raised 1930 at Exbury, Hampshire, England.

Zone 5 US, 6 Can. 🏆

C. dammeri (Bearberry cotoneaster) A prostrate evergreen shrub with long, trailing shoots that bear white flowers with purple anthers in spring; in fall they are studded with red fruits. The leaves are oval or obovate, prominently veined, and 1–1 1/2 in (2.5–4 cm) long. It is an ideal shrub for covering slopes and as a ground cover beneath other shrubs. See also *C. radicans*. China. Introduced 1900 by Ernest Wilson.

Zone 4 US, 4 Can. 🏆

C. divaricatus (Spreading cotoneaster) A medium-sized deciduous shrub, one of the most reliable for fall fruits and foliage. The berries are dark red and the flowers a bright, rosy red. Excellent for hedges. W China. Introduced 1904 by Ernest Wilson.

Zone 4 US, 5 Can.

***C.* 'Exburiensis'** A large deciduous shrub with white flowers followed by apricot-yellow fruits that become tinged with pink in winter. Almost identical to 'Rothschildianus'. Raised 1930 at Exbury in England.
Zone 7 US, 8 Can.

Cotoneaster franchetii

C. franchetii A very graceful, medium-sized, semievergreen shrub with sage green foliage. The flowers are white, with erect petals that become flushed with pink and are succeeded by ovoid, orange-scarlet fruits. One of the most popular species. China. Introduced 1895.
Zone 6 US, 6b Can.

C. frigidus (Himalayan cotoneaster) The true plant is a variable, fast-growing, large deciduous shrub or small spreading tree with large, broad elliptic, magnolia-like leaves and large, heavy clusters of orange to crimson fruits in fall and winter. However, it is now seldom seen; *C. frigidus* in the trade is a form of the Watereri group of hybrids. Himalaya. Introduced 1824.
Zone 7 US, 8 Can.

C. glabratus A medium-sized evergreen shrub with arching purple shoots and glossy, dark green leaves, blue-white beneath, becoming purple-tinged in winter. The white flowers are followed by small, bright red fruits in broad clusters. W China. Introduced 1906 by Ernest Wilson.
Zone 6 US, 7 Can.

***C.* 'Gnom'** A dwarf evergreen shrub with slender, purplish, arching shoots that make a low, wide mound. The glossy leaves are lance shaped, up to about 1 × 1/2 in (about 2.5 × 1 cm), dark green, and bronze-tinged in winter. It makes an excellent ground cover despite the fact that the small, bright red berries that ripen in late fall following the white flowers are not abundant. Raised c. 1938 in Germany.
Zone 4 US, 5b Can.

C. hjelmqvistii This recently described deciduous species is in effect a large version of *C. horizontalis*, with which it has been confused. It makes a small, spreading shrub with arching branches and glossy green leaves that turn red in fall. White flowers tinged with pink are followed by red berries. W China.
Zone 4? US, 5? Can.

Cotoneaster horizontalis

C. horizontalis (Rockspray cotoneaster) A low-growing deciduous shrub of spreading habit, with branches in a herringbone pattern; it is invaluable for shady walls or slopes. Flowers are red with white stamens, fruits are orange-red, and the foliage is richly colored in fall. W China. Introduced c. 1870 by Père David.
Zone 4 US, 5 Can.

Cotoneaster horizontalis 'Variegatus'

***C. h.* 'Variegatus'** This prostrate form is especially pleasing in fall, when the small, cream-margined leaves are suffused with red. In cultivation 1922.
Zone 4 US, 5 Can.

***C.* 'Hybridus Pendulus'** A very striking evergreen or semievergreen with glossy leaves, white flowers, and long, prostrate branches that carry an abundance of brilliant red fruits in fall and winter. When trained as a standard, it makes a small weeping tree. Bush specimens are very prone to fireblight, standards less so. Garden origin.
Zone 7 US, 8 Can.

Cotoneaster hylmoei

C. hylmoei A medium-sized evergreen shrub with arching branches, related to *C. salicifolius* but with broader, darker leaves that are deeply veined above and white-woolly beneath. The white flowers are large and pink in the bud, and the fruits persist for a long time. One of the most ornamental species.
Zone 7? US, 8? Can.

C. integrifolius A dwarf, mound-forming evergreen shrub with small, glossy, dark green leaves. The small white flowers are followed by relatively large, deep reddish pink fruits. It is commonly grown as *C. microphyllus* and is useful as a ground cover and for growing over low walls. Himalaya, W China. Introduced 1824.
Zone 4 US, 5 Can.

C. lacteus (Parney cotoneaster) A medium-sized evergreen shrub with large, oval,

Cotoneaster lacteus

leathery leaves that are gray-woolly beneath and quite unlike any other species. The flowers are milky white and followed by red fruits that are rather small but carried in broad clusters, ripening late in the year and lasting well into midwinter. China. Introduced 1913 by George Forrest.
Zone 7 US, 8 Can. 🏆

C. lucidus (Hedge cotoneaster) An upright species that makes a good hedge or screen. It will grow up to 10 ft (3 m) tall but can be kept to one-third of this height as a hedge. The foliage is shiny, dark green, turning red in fall, while the black fruits last well into winter.
Zone 3 US, 2 Can.

Cotoneaster microphyllus

C. microphyllus (Small-leaved cotoneaster) A dwarf, stiffly branched, spreading evergreen shrub forming a low mound. The leaves are more or less elliptic, usually less than 1/2 in (1 cm) long, and rounded or notched at the apex. Tiny white flowers are followed by reddish pink berries. Several other plants are grown under this name (see *C. cashmiriensis* and *C. integrifolius*). Himalaya.
Zone 5 US, 6 Can. 🏆

C. nanshan A vigorous, dwarf to small deciduous shrub with arching branches, related to *C. adpressus* but growing up to 3 ft (1 m) high and 6 1/2 ft (2 m) across and with larger leaves. The flowers are pink, the fruits extra large and orange-red, and the fall color red. It was previously known as *C. adpressus* var. *praecox*. W China. Introduced 1905.
Zone 3 US, 3 Can.

Cotoneaster nanshan

Cotoneaster 'Pink Champagne'

***C.* 'Pink Champagne'** A large, vigorous, dense-growing deciduous shrub with slender, arching branches and narrow leaves. The pink-tinged white flowers are insignificant. The fruits are small but plentifully produced, at first creamy yellow and then becoming tinged with pink.
Zone 7 US, 8 Can.

C. radicans A prostrate evergreen shrub related to *C. dammeri*, with which it is sometimes confused. Its leaves, however, are smaller, have longer stalks, and lack the deep veins of *C. dammeri*, and its white flowers are usually in pairs instead of solitary. The berries are bright red. *C. dammeri* 'Oakwood' and 'Eichholz' are very similar if not identical. China.
Zone 4 US, 4 Can.

C. rehderi A very handsome, medium-

Cotoneaster rehderi

sized to large deciduous shrub of open habit, with large, dark green, deeply veined leaves. White flowers with a rosy flush are followed by a profusion of deep red berries. It is often listed as a form of *C. bullatus*. W China.

Zone 4 US, 5 Can.

***C.* 'Rothschildianus'** A large deciduous shrub with a distinctive, spreading habit

Cotoneaster 'Rothschildianus'

Cotoneaster salicifolius

when young. Large, creamy yellow fruits follow the white flowers, and a mature shrub fully laden with the almost luminescent berries is a pretty sight. Similar to 'Exburiensis', both being raised at Exbury, Hampshire, England.

Zone 7 US, 8 Can. 🏆

C. salicifolius (Willowleaf cotoneaster) A tall, variable, evergreen shrub, bearing heavy crops of red fruits in fall, and the parent of many hybrids. Unfortunately, it is very susceptible to fireblight. See *C. hymoei*. China. Introduced 1908.

Zone 4 US, 5 Can.

Cotoneaster serotinus

C. serotinus A vigorous deciduous shrub up to 16 ft (5 m) tall or more, with blue-green, oval to elliptic leaves that are woolly on the undersides. It bears its white flowers abundantly in midsummer, and the berries take on their red color in early winter. W China. Introduced 1907 by George Forrest.

Zone 5 US, 6b Can.

C. simonsii (Simon's cotoneaster) A well-known, erectly growing, semievergreen, medium-sized shrub, frequently used for hedges and given to self-seeding. The flowers are white with pink stamens, and the fruits are large and scarlet. Himalaya. Introduced 1865.

Zone 6 US, 7 Can. 🏆

***C.* 'Skogholm'** A dwarf evergreen shrub of wide, spreading habit, with small leaves and teardrop-shaped, coral-red berries in fall that are not abundant. The white flowers with a pink tinge borne in spring are insignificant. A hybrid of *C. dammeri*, selected 1941.

Zone 4 US, 4b Can.

C. splendens A deciduous species up to 6½ ft (2 m) tall. The arching shoots, with small, grayish green, rounded leaves, are covered with pink flowers with red margins. These are followed by large, bright orange fruits in fall. The seedling 'Sabrina' appears identical. Introduced 1934.

Zone 5 US, 6 Can. 🏆

Cotoneaster sternianus

C. sternianus An excellent medium-sized shrub with spreading branches and an arching habit that is more or less evergreen. It has sage green leaves with silvery white undersides, pink flowers, and large, round but slightly flattened, bright orange-red berries produced in large numbers. A rewarding garden plant. S Tibet, N Burma. Introduced 1913.

Zone 6 US, 6b Can. 🏆

C.* × *watereri A group of variable, semi-evergreen, complex hybrids. All of them are hardy, medium-sized to large shrubs or occasionally small trees of strong, vigorous growth, with long leaves and heavy crops of fruits that are normally red or orange-red. The white flowers with a pink tinge are insignificant. In the trade they tend to stand in for *C. frigidus*, which was only one of the several parents of the cross. There are many named clones.

Zone 7 US, 8 Can.

***C.* × *w.* 'John Waterer'** A large, semi-evergreen shrub with long, spreading branches laden with bunches of red fruits in fall. In cultivation 1928.

Zone 7 US, 8 Can. 🏆

Crataegus *Rosaceae*
Hawthorn

These are among the most adaptable deciduous trees and are found throughout the temperate parts of the Northern Hemisphere. Although until quite recently there were thought to be as many as 1,000 species from North America alone, many of them are now regarded as hybrids or forms of variable species, and the true number in the genus may now be between 100 and 200.

With their dense habit and thorns, they make superb hedges and barriers. They are also grown for their flowers, which are usually white but may be pink or red, and for their berries, which are typically red but can also be yellow or occasionally blue or black. The flowers are intensely fragrant, but it is a scent that not everyone finds pleasant. They prefer full sun and will grow in any good garden soil, especially a sandy loam. Many will also tolerate industrial pollution, salt spray, wind, drought, and even waterlogged soil.

Any pruning should be done after flowering. Hedges that are intended to bear flowers and fruits should also be trimmed after flowering, but only then; an annual trim is sufficient.

Crataegus crus-galli

C. crus-galli (Cockspur thorn) This wide-spreading small tree, with thorns up to 3 in (8 cm) long, has attractive leaves; white, pink-tinged flowers in late spring; and long-lasting berries. It is often confused with *C. prunifolia*. E and C North America. Introduced 1691.
Zone 3 US, 2b Can.

C. durobrivensis A large shrub, and one of the most ornamental of the North American hawthorns, with white flowers that are

Crataegus durobrivensis

probably the largest in the genus and open from late spring to early summer, followed by large red fruits that remain until mid-winter. New York State. Introduced 1901.
Zone 5 US, 6 Can.

C.* × *grignonensis A small tree, late in bearing its white flowers and ripening its large, bright red, gray-speckled fruits. The leaves remain green until winter. Introduced c. 1873.
Zone 4 US, 5 Can.

Crataegus laciniata

C. laciniata, syn. *C. orientalis* A beautiful, small, not very thorny tree with deeply cut, downy leaves that are dark green above and gray beneath. The flowers are white and borne in clusters of 12 or more in late spring, and the fruits are large and coral-red or yellowish red. SE Europe to SW Asia. Introduced 1810.
Zone 6 US, 6b Can.

C. laevigata, syn. *C. oxyacantha* (English hawthorn) The clones described below, often listed under this species, are more probably hybrids between it and *C. monogyna*. They are all large shrubs or small trees and are very showy when covered with white, pink, or red flowers in late spring. The small fruits are scarlet. Europe.
Zone 5 US, 6 Can.

Crataegus laevigata 'Paul's Scarlet'

***C. l.* 'Paul's Scarlet'** A sport of 'Rosea Flore Pleno' with double scarlet flowers and deep red fruits. Introduced 1858.
Zone 5 US, 6 Can. 🏆

***C. l.* 'Plena'** A form with double white flowers and deep red fruits. In cultivation 1770.
Zone 5 US, 6 Can.

***C. l.* 'Punicea'** This form has single scarlet flowers with a pronounced white eye and deep red fruits. This is the same plant as 'Crimson Cloud'. In cultivation 1828. *(See photo on p.254.)* Zone 5 US, 5b Can.

Crataegus laevigata 'Rosea Flore Pleno'

***C. l.* 'Rosea Flore Pleno'** An attractive

Crataegus laevigata 'Punicea'

form with double pink flowers.
Zone 5 US, 6 Can. 🏆

***C.* × *lavallei* 'Carrièrei'** A small, dense-headed tree, distinguished by its long, glossy, dark green leaves that often remain until midwinter. The flowers are white with pink anthers, and the berries are orange-red, persist throughout the winter, and are very colorful against the dark foliage. Garden origin c. 1870.
Zone 4 US, 5 Can. 🏆

C. mollis (Downy hawthorn) One of the best American species, forming a wide-spreading tree 33–40 ft (10–12 m) tall, with downy leaves, white flowers, and showy fruits like red cherries carried in large clusters. C United States. Long cultivated.
Zone 3 US, 4 Can.

Crataegus monogyna

C. monogyna (English hawthorn) This is a popular native in Britain, grown for hedges throughout the country and often called may because of its spectacular flowering in late spring, when the densely branched plant is laden with white, strongly scented blossoms. In fall it bears small red fruits, also called haws. It makes a large shrub or small tree with a rounded head. It is a bad fireblight host, but if hedges are kept trimmed, whereby flowering wood is removed, the disease should not occur. Europe, North Africa, W Asia.
Zone 4 US, 4b Can.

***C. m.* 'Stricta'** An excellent, tough, small tree with erect branches that is particularly suited to exposed sites.
Zone 4 US, 4b Can.

***C.* × *mordenensis* 'Snowbird'** This is a seedling from *C.* × *m.* 'Toba'. It makes a small tree with only a few thorns. The flowers are double white and turn pale pink with age. The fruits are red but are not freely produced. Fall color is a copper-red.
Zone 3 US, 3 Can.

***C.* × *m.* 'Toba'** This hybrid originated in Morden, Manitoba, and has the more tender *C. laevigata* 'Paul's Scarlet' as one parent. The double, fragrant, rose flowers are similar to those of 'Paul's Scarlet'.
Zone 3 US, 3 Can.

C. orientalis See *C. laciniata.*

C. oxyacantha See *C. laevigata.*

Crataegus phaenopyrum

C. phaenopyrum (Washington hawthorn) A striking, round-headed, slender tree, to 33 ft (10 m). It has glossy, maplelike leaves that turn bright orange in fall. White flowers with pink anthers precede a profusion of small, dark crimson, long-lasting fruits. SE United States. Introduced 1738.
Zone 4 US, 5 Can.

C. pinnatifida* var. *major (Large Chinese hawthorn) One of the most ornamental hawthorns, with large, conspicuously lobed leaves; white flowers with pink anthers; and glossy, crimson fruits almost 1 in (2.5 cm) across. It is among the best small trees for red fall color. N China. In cultivation 1880.
Zone 6 US, 6b Can.

Crataegus prunifolia

C. prunifolia An excellent small, compact, broad-headed tree notable for its persistent, showy fruits, which are green flushed with purple and then become dark red and glossy. The flowers are white with red anthers, and the tree provides good fall color. Origin unknown; possibly a hybrid between two North American species. In cultivation 1797.
Zone 4 US, 4b Can. 🏆

***C. viridis* 'Winter King'** With its large, persistent red fruits and peeling, silvery bark, this tree adds greatly to the winter garden. In summer, the leaves are dark green, turning scarlet to purple in the fall. Introduced 1955.
Zone 3 US, 4 Can.

Crinodendron *Elaeocarpaceae*

Both species of this evergreen genus come from Chile, and one in particular is of great value to gardens in the South. Crinodendrons require lime-free soil, partial shade, and protection from wind. No pruning is necessary.

C. hookerianum (Chilean lantern tree) This shrub is an asset in mild-winter gardens. The scarlet red flowers hang thickly

Crinodendron hookerianum

from the branches on long stalks in late spring to early summer and resemble miniature lanterns; they contrast beautifully with the glossy, dark green foliage. It is a large, dense shrub that can sometimes withstand surprisingly low temperatures. Chile. Introduced 1848 by William Lobb.
Zone 8 US, 9? Can. 🏆

C. patagua (White lilytree) A large shrub or small tree with white, slightly fragrant, fringed, bell-shaped flowers in late summer and red-tinged cream seedpods. It is not as resilient as the above species and requires wall protection or a greenhouse. Chile. Introduced 1901.
Zone 8 US, 9? Can.

Cryptomeria *Taxodiaceae*

A genus of one evergreen coniferous species.

C. japonica (Japanese cedar). A large, fast-growing, broadly columnar tree with reddish, shredding bark and spreading or decurved branches. The leaves are awl shaped and densely crowded on the long, slender branchlets. In some ways it resembles the giant sequoia *(Sequoiadendron giganteum)*, but its leaves are longer and the bark does not have the spongy thickness of the sequoia. It is easily cultivated and thrives in moist soil. Japan, China. Introduced 1842.
Zone 5 US, 6 Can. 🏆

***C. j.* 'Bandai-Sugi'** A small, slow-growing, compact bush that becomes more irregular in old age. The foliage is in congested, mosslike clusters with intermittent

Cryptomeria japonica

Cryptomeria japonica 'Bandai-Sugi'

normal growth, turning bronze in very cold weather. In cultivation 1939.
Zone 5 US, 6 Can. 🏆

***C. j.* 'Compressa'** This is a very slow-growing, dwarf bush and is similar to 'Vilmoriniana', forming a compact, rather flat-topped globe. The foliage, which is densely crowded, turns reddish purple in

Cryptomeria japonica 'Compressa'

winter. It is very suitable for a rock garden or scree.
Zone 5 US, 6 Can.

Cryptomeria japonica 'Elegans'

***C. j.* 'Elegans'** A beautiful, tall, bushy form that eventually makes a small tree. The soft, feathery, juvenile foliage is retained throughout life and turns to an attractive red-bronze in autumn and winter. Introduced 1854 by Thomas Lobb.
Zone 5 US, 6 Can.

***C. j.* 'Elegans Compacta'** A slower-growing, smaller shrub than 'Elegans', with even softer, more feathery foliage, forming a medium-sized, billowy bush. The leaves turn an attractive purple in winter. In cultivation 1881.
Zone 5 US, 6 Can. 🏆

***C. j.* 'Elegans Nana'** A very dense, slow-growing, small shrub with juvenile foliage that turns bronze in winter. The foliage is fairly stiff to the touch. In cultivation 1923.
(See photo on p.256.) Zone 5 US, 6 Can.

Cryptomeria japonica 'Elegans Nana'

***C. j.* 'Lobbii'** A desirable, medium-sized to large, conical tree, differing from the type in its longer branchlets that are more clustered at the ends of the shorter branches. The leaves are deep, rich green and more adpressed to the shoots. Introduced c. 1850 by Thomas Lobb.
Zone 5 US, 6 Can.

***C. j.* 'Nana'** A small, slow-growing, compact bush with slender branchlets that end in recurved tips. In cultivation 1850.
Zone 4 US, 5b Can.

Cryptomeria japonica 'Sekkan-Sugi'

***C. j.* 'Sekkan-Sugi'** A small tree with pale creamy yellow young foliage. It is liable to burn in full sun. Introduced 1930.
Zone 5 US, 6 Can.

***C. j.* 'Spiralis'** Although this plant can occasionally grow to be a large tree, it is usually a small to medium-sized, slow-growing bush of dense, spreading habit with the leaves spirally twisted around the stems. The foliage is a pleasant bright green. Introduced 1860.
Zone 5 US, 6b Can.

Cryptomeria japonica 'Vilmoriniana'

***C. j.* 'Vilmoriniana'** An exceedingly slow-growing, dwarf bush with very small, crowded branchlets and leaves, forming a dense globe that turns reddish purple in winter. It is one of the most popular dwarf conifers for the rock garden, very similar to 'Compressa' but with leaves a little shorter and more congested on the branchlets. A specimen at the Hillier Gardens and Arboretum reached 2 × 3 ft (60 × 90 cm) in about 30 years. Raised 1890 in France by M. de Vilmorin.
Zone 4 US, 5b Can. 🏆

Cunninghamia *Taxodiaceae*
China fir

A small genus of probably just two species of distinct, evergreen, coniferous trees that resemble Araucaria. *They are fairly hardy but do best in a sheltered site in a mild area. The whorled branches are densely covered with spirally arranged leaves that are twisted and so seem to be organized in two ranks.*

Cunninghamia lanceolata

C. lanceolata (Common China fir) A small to medium-sized, exotic-looking tree. The lance-shaped leaves, 1–2¾ in (3–7 cm) long, are irregularly arranged, emerald to blue-green above with two white bands beneath. They become dark and bronze by fall. China. Introduced 1804 by William Kerr.
Zone 7 US, 7b Can.

× Cupressocyparis *Cupressaceae*

These interesting hybrids between Cupressus *and* Chamaecyparis *have all arisen in cultivation. They are extremely fast-growing evergreen trees with many uses and are by far the most commonly planted conifers. They need much the same conditions as* Chamaecyparis.

× *C. leylandii* *(Cupressus macrocarpa × Chamaecyparis nootkatensis)* (Leyland cypress) A large, noble, extremely vigorous, densely columnar tree. The foliage is in flattened or irregular, slightly drooping sprays, and in general the tree looks more like its *Chamaecyparis* parent. It is probably the fastest-growing conifer and, with the exception of some eucalyptus, the fastest-growing evergreen. Even in poor sites plants have reached a height of 50 ft (15 m) in 16 years from cuttings. It is unsurpassed for tall screens but is generally too vigorous for hedges in small gardens. Only young growths should be trimmed. It is tolerant

× *Cupressocyparis leylandii* 'Castlewellan Gold'

of a wide range of conditions, except waterlogged, very dry, or very alkaline soil. May cause skin allergy.
Zone 6 US, 7 Can.

× ***C. l.*** **'Castlewellan Gold'** The young foliage is golden yellow on small plants and tends to become bronze-green with age. It can make a large tree but is slower growing and more suitable for hedges than the green forms. Raised 1962 at Castlewellan, County Down, Northern Ireland.
Zone 6 US, 7 Can.

× *Cupressocyparis leylandii*

× ***C. l.*** **'Gold Rider'** A large tree with yellow foliage. This is one of the best forms.
Zone 6 US, 7 Can.

× ***C. l.*** **'Haggerston Grey'** A large and common clone in cultivation, whose foliage is green, often with a slight gray cast, and is arranged in dense, irregular sprays. Raised 1888 at Leighton Hall, Powys, Wales.
Zone 6 US, 7 Can.

× ***C. l.*** **'Naylor's Blue'** A columnar cultivar with feathery foliage that is gray-blue above and gray-green beneath.
Zone 6 US, 7 Can.

× ***C. l.*** **'Robinson's Gold'** Similar to 'Castlewellan Gold' but has better color. Raised c. 1962 at Belvoir Castle, County Down.
Zone 6 US, 7 Can.

× ***C. l.*** **'Silver Dust'** The foliage of this large tree is conspicuously blotched with cream. Introduced 1966.
Zone 6 US, 7 Can.

× *Cupressocyparis notabilis*

× ***C. notabilis*** *(Chamaecyparis nootkatensis × Cupressus glabra)* An attractive, medium-sized tree with sinuous, upswept branches draped with flattened sprays of dark gray-green foliage. The crown is broader and more open than that of × *C. leylandii.* Raised 1956 by the Forestry Commission, Britain.
Zone 6? US, 7? Can.

Cupressus *Cupressaceae*
Cypress

A genus of around 20 species of evergreen coniferous trees, mostly of conical or columnar habit. The globular cones become woody and often remain on the trees for several years. Cypresses do not tolerate clipping and thus do not make good hedges. They are on the whole less hardy than Chamaecyparis. *They do not transplant easily, which is why young trees are always pot-grown. They tolerate a wide range of soils, with the exception of wet ones, and several species will grow well even in shallow alkaline soils.*

Cupressus cashmeriana

C. cashmeriana (Kashmir cypress) One of the most graceful and beautiful conifers, making a small to medium-sized tree with a conical habit. The branches are ascending and draped with long, pendulous branchlets. The foliage is blue-gray and arranged in flattened sprays. This conifer will grow out-of-doors in the warmest areas and elsewhere is a fine specimen for a large greenhouse. Its exact origin is unknown, but some authorities consider it a form of *C. torulosa*, a species from the Himalaya. It is quite possible that it does not come from Kashmir at all. Introduced 1862.
Zone 9 US

Cupressus glabra

Cupressus glabra

C. glabra (Smooth Arizona cypress) A small to medium-sized tree with attractive, peeling, red bark and grayish green or gray foliage. It is common in cultivation but usually grown under the name *C. arizonica*, which is a rarer species with green foliage and less attractive bark. Some authorities now classify it as *C. arizonica* var. *glabra*.

Cupressus glabra 'Aurea'

The following forms are recommended. Introduced 1907. *(See photo on p.257.)*
Zone 7 US, 8 Can.

***C. g.* 'Aurea'** A broadly conical, small to medium-sized tree with leaves suffused with yellow in summer, getting paler toward winter. Raised 1957 in Australia.
Zone 7 US, 8 Can.

***C. g.* 'Blue Ice'** A small, slow-growing, conical tree with striking blue-gray foliage. Originated c. 1984 in New Zealand.
Zone 7 US, 8 Can.

***C. g.* 'Pyramidalis'** A dense, compact, conical tree of medium size, with blue-gray foliage. In late winter the branches are dotted with yellow male cones. It is one of the best formal blue conifers in cultivation. In cultivation 1928.
Zone 7 US, 8 Can. 🏆

C. lusitanica (Mexican cypress) A medium to large, graceful tree with rich brown, peeling bark. The branches are spreading, with pendulous branchlets and grayish green foliage. Both the branchlets and the cones are somewhat spiny. NE Mexico, Guatemala, Honduras. In cultivation 1682.
Zone 9 US

***C. l.* 'Glauca Pendula'** A beautiful form, selected by Edwin Hillier, with a spreading crown and graceful, drooping, glaucous blue branchlets. It makes a small, wide-spreading tree. In cultivation 1925.
Zone 9 US

Cupressus macrocarpa

C. macrocarpa (Monterey cypress) A popular, very fast-growing tree of medium to large size, conical or broadly columnar when young, becoming broad-crowned with age and resembling a cedar of Lebanon. The foliage is bright green, in densely packed sprays. It is a valuable shelter tree in coastal regions, but young plants are subject to damage in cold areas. The forms with yellow foliage color best in open sites and become green in shade. California. Introduced c. 1838.
Zone 7 US, 8 Can.

***C. m.* 'Donard Gold'** A conical or broadly columnar tree of medium size. The foliage is deep golden yellow and is an improvement on 'Lutea'. Raised 1935 in the Slieve Donard Nursery, Northern Ireland.
Zone 7 US, 8 Can. 🏆

Cupressus macrocarpa 'Goldcrest'

***C. m.* 'Goldcrest'** This is a medium-sized, narrowly columnar, dense, compact tree and has rich yellow, feathery juvenile foliage. It is one of the best of its color. Raised c. 1948 by the Treseders of Truro, Cornwall, England.
Zone 7 US, 8 Can. 🏆

***C. m.* 'Golden Pillar'** A small, narrow tree with golden yellow foliage. Raised before 1955 in Holland.
Zone 7 US, 8 Can.

***C. m.* 'Gold Spread'** A distinct and ornamental, compact, wide-spreading form about 3 ft (1 m) tall, with bright golden yellow foliage. It is an excellent ground cover on the West Coast.
Zone 7 US, 8 Can. 🏆

***C. m.* 'Lutea'** A tall tree with yellow foliage that turns green. Now superseded by 'Donard Gold'. In cultivation before 1893.
Zone 7 US, 8 Can.

Cupressus sempervirens 'Green Pencil'

***C. m.* 'Wilma'** A small, narrow tree with bright yellow spring and summer foliage.
Zone 7 US, 8 Can.

C. sempervirens (Italian cypress) A medium-sized, narrowly columnar tree with steeply ascending branches and dark green foliage. It is familiar in the Mediterranean region, and young plants are susceptible to injury in cold areas. The form sometimes known as 'Fastigiata' or 'Stricta' is unknown in the wild.
Zone 7 US, 8 Can.

***C. s.* 'Green Pencil'** A very slender, medium-sized form with bright green foliage. Hardier than most *C. sempervirens* forms. It was selected at Hillier Nurseries. The original plant in the Hillier Gardens and Arboretum was 34½ ft (10.5 m) tall and only 32 in (80 cm) wide in 1990.
Zone 7 US, 8 Can.

Cupressus sempervirens 'Swane's Golden'

***C. s.* 'Swane's Golden'** A compact, columnar form with gold-tinted foliage. It is one of the best medium-sized golden conifers for the small garden.
Zone 7 US, 8 Can.

Cyathodes *Epacridaceae*

A genus of about 15 species of heatherlike evergreen shrubs from New Zealand and Australia that have tiny, white, pitcher-shaped flowers in spring and very attractive foliage. These shrubs require a lime-free soil with some shelter and are especially suited to rock gardens.

C. colensoi A small, decumbent, sometimes prostrate shrub with narrow, unstalked, glaucous leaves and white or red fruits. It is a beautiful small shrub and is proving quite hardy. New Zealand.
Zone 8 US, 9? Can.

Cydonia *Rosaceae*

Quince

A genus of one deciduous species that is a small to medium-sized tree with attractive fruits and is related to Chaenomeles.

Cydonia oblonga

Cydonia oblonga fruits

C. oblonga (Common quince) A tree up to 20 ft (6 m) high, with white or pink flowers, grown for its fruits.
Zone 5 US, 6 Can.

***C. oblonga* 'Vranja'** A named clone that forms a small, picturesque lawn tree and was selected for its flavorful, fragrant, large golden fruits. The flowers are white.
Zone 5 US, 6 Can.

Cytisus & Genista

Leguminosae Broom

MOST GARDENERS know a broom when they see one. They expect a shrub with whiplike branches that apparently have few leaves and with branchlets that are so green they give an evergreen appearance even to deciduous species. Gardeners would also expect the plants to bear pealike flowers, usually but not always yellow, and to have a range of forms, from prostrate mats to stiffly erect shrubs.

Botanists, however, distinguish between two main broom genera: *Cytisus* (usually pronounced "sigh-ti-sus") and *Genista*. The difference between the two — a minute but constant difference in the seed and in the notching of the calyx — may seem trifling but is enough for botanists to separate them. On the other hand, the genera are alike enough for gardeners to think of them as one.

There are about 50 species of *Cytisus* and 80 of *Genista*, and their distribution in the wild is roughly the same: brooms of both genera are found in Europe, western Asia, and North Africa. While what a gardener might recognize as the "typical" broom characteristics are found throughout the range, a shrub occasionally occurs with such idiosyncratic appearance that it is hard to believe it is a broom.

One example is the stunning *Cytisus battandieri*, a native of North Africa. It has broad, trifoliate, lustrous leaves that are intensely silver and large, packed heads of brilliant yellow flowers whose deliciously fruity scent has given rise to the common name of pineapple broom. Another example is *Genista aetnensis*, which is an entirely leafless small tree with cordlike branches and masses of yellow flowers in summer. Because it occurs on the slopes of Sicily's famous volcano (among other places), it is called Mount Etna broom.

Cytisus × beanii

Their wide range of sizes and forms means that brooms are highly versatile. There are several that are compact enough for a small rock garden and a few that will never become too large for a container. There are other brooms, however, that need to be kept in bounds even in large gardens, and still others that grow and bloom so rapidly that they are ideal for planting in a new garden, where height and color are particularly welcome.

Care and Cultivation

Members of both genera are relatively tolerant of a range of soils, although they prefer a site that is dry and infertile. Both will tolerate slightly acid or alkaline soil but cannot stand the extremes, and *Cytisus* will not succeed in poor, shallow soil over limestone. Brooms can also take considerable heat.

Pruning is somewhat tricky. For those *Genista* species *(see p.317)* whose beauty depends largely on their shape or a general characteristic such as elegance (*G. aetnensis* is a good example), pruning should be avoided. However, it is sometimes necessary to train them to establish a good stem. Other *Genista* species and cultivars can be pinched back each year to preserve bushiness, but cutting into the old wood should never be done.

The rules for *Cytisus* are roughly the same, although those plants that flower on the previous year's wood — and most of them do — should have that wood cut back by a little more than half after flowering. The major exception is *C. battandieri*, which benefits greatly if it is pruned hard every few years. This means cutting back deeply into the old wood, where there are buds that will rapidly renew the shrub, reducing legginess and instability and substantially increasing the spectacle. This treatment would destroy most other brooms.

Perhaps the two most important points to remember when growing brooms are to plant them in the right place from the beginning and to make certain that the drainage is as good as possible. They resent root disturbance — this applies especially to *Cytisus* — and cannot safely be moved once planted. Their natural habitats dictate their preference for sun and well-drained soil, and they also benefit when sheltered from the wind.

Beyond its value in the garden, broom is also of historical interest. In the early 12th century, Geoffrey, count of Anjou, who would become the father of King Henry II of England, took a sprig of broom as his emblem. In Plantagenet, the surname that he adopted and that was applied to a succession of 14 kings, Geoffrey's *planta genista* has been immortalized.

C. ardoinii (Ardoin broom) A miniature, mat-forming, deciduous alpine shrub with bright yellow flowers from mid- to late spring. Maritime Alps of France. Introduced 1866.

Zone 7? US, 8? Can. 🏆

C. battandieri (Pineapple broom) A tall deciduous shrub with silvery gray, silky, laburnum-like leaves and cone-shaped clusters of bright yellow, pineapple-scented flowers in midsummer. An excellent shrub for a high wall, and it is surprisingly hardy for a plant from its native range, capable of surviving in exposed locations. Morocco. Introduced c. 1922.

Zone 6 US, 7b Can. 🏆

***C. b.* 'Yellow Tail'** A form with flower clusters 6 in (15 cm) long or more. Selected before 1975 at Hillier Nurseries.

Zone 6 US, 7b Can. 🏆

C.* × *beanii (Bean's broom) A charming, dwarf, deciduous shrub up to 14 in (35 cm) in height, with golden yellow flowers in late spring. Garden origin 1900.

Zone 4 US, 5 Can. 🏆

***C.* × *b.* 'Golden Carpet'** This form was raised from seed at the Dominion Arboretum in Ottawa, Ontario. It is more upright than the species.

Zone 5 US, 5 Can.

***C.* 'Boskoop Ruby'** A small, rounded deciduous shrub with deep crimson flowers borne very profusely in mid- to late spring. One of the most striking red hybrids. Raised in Holland.

Zone 4 US, 5b Can. 🏆

***C.* 'Burkwoodii'** A vigorous, medium-sized deciduous hybrid with long sprays of cerise flowers, whose wings are deep crimson edged with yellow; it blooms from late spring to early summer.

Zone 4 US, 5b Can. 🏆

C. decumbens (Prostrate broom) A prostrate, deciduous rock-garden shrublet with bright yellow flowers in late spring and early summer. S Europe. Introduced 1775.

Zone 3 US, 2b Can.

C. demissus A prostrate deciduous shrub no more than 4 in (10 cm) high. It is a good choice for the rock garden and has exceptionally large yellow flowers with brown keels in late spring. Found on Mount Olympus, Greece, at about 7,500 ft (2,500 m).

Zone 6 US, 7 Can. 🏆

Cytisus battandieri

Cytisus battandieri 'Yellow Tail'

Cytisus 'La Coquette'

Cytisus 'Burkwoodii'

Cytisus 'Hollandia'

C. **'Dukaat'** A small, deciduous, erectly branched shrub of dense habit, with silky-hairy young shoots and small, narrow leaves. The small, golden yellow flowers are borne in late spring. In cultivation 1965.
Zone 5 US, 6 Can.

C. **'Goldfinch'** A compact, medium-sized deciduous shrub grown for its creamy yellow flowers flushed with pink and red in mid- to late spring.
Zone 5 US, 6 Can.

C. **'Hollandia'** A medium-sized deciduous shrub, similar to *C.* × *praecox*. The flowers appear from late spring to early summer and are pale cream, with the back of the standard petal cerise and the wings dark cerise.
Zone 4 US, 5 Can. 🏆

Cytisus 'Johnson's Crimson'

C. **'Johnson's Crimson'** A fine medium-sized deciduous hybrid, resembling *C. multiflorus* in habit, with clear crimson flowers in mid- to late spring.
Zone 5 US, 6 Can.

Cytisus × *kewensis*

C. × ***kewensis*** (Kew broom) Sheets of cream-colored flowers are borne in late spring on this semi-prostrate, deciduous shrub. Raised 1891 at Kew, England.
Zone 6 US, 7 Can. 🏆

C. × *k.* **'Niki'** A prostrate form grown for its golden yellow flowers. Found 1984 as a sport in Holland.
Zone 6 US, 7 Can.

C. **'Killiney Red'** A medium-sized deciduous broom of the *C. scoparius* type, with flowers produced from late spring to early summer. These are rich red, with darker red, velvety wings.
Zone 5 US, 6 Can.

C. **'La Coquette'** A medium-sized deciduous hybrid in which the standard of the late-spring flowers is rose-red but yellow inside, and the wings are a deep orange-yellow, veined with brick red. The keel is pale yellow, faintly marked with rose-red.
Zone 5 US, 6 Can.

Cytisus 'Lena'

C. **'Lena'** A vigorous, compact, medium-sized deciduous shrub that flowers freely in mid- to late spring. The standard is deep red, the wings red margined with yellow, and the keel pale yellow. Raised at Kew.
Zone 5 US, 6 Can. 🏆

C. **'Luna'** A medium-sized deciduous hybrid with large, late-spring flowers whose broad standard petal is pale creamy yellow and is tinged red on the back and inside; the wings are rich yellow and the keel pale yellow. In cultivation 1959.
Zone 4 US, 5b Can. 🏆

C. **'Maria Burkwood'** A vigorous, medium-sized deciduous shrub. Large red flowers with coppery wings are an attractive spectacle in late spring.
Zone 5 US, 6 Can.

Cytisus 'Minstead'

C. **'Minstead'** A charming medium-sized deciduous hybrid derived from *C. multiflorus*. It produces multitudes of small flowers from late spring to early summer that are white flushed with lilac and are darker on the wings and in bud.
Zone 6 US, 7 Can. 🏆

Cytisus multiflorus

C. ***multiflorus*** (White Spanish broom) An erect deciduous shrub of medium size whose stems are studded with small white flowers in late spring and early summer. This species is a parent of many hybrids. It should be given a slightly acidic soil. Spain, Portugal, N Africa.
Zone 7 US, 8 Can. 🏆

C. ***nigricans*** (Spike broom) A useful and elegant small, late-flowering, deciduous shrub that produces its long, terminal clus-

Cytisus 'Porlock'

Cytisus × *praecox* 'Allgold'

ters of clear yellow flowers continuously during late summer. C and SE Europe to C Russia. Introduced 1730.
Zone 4 US, 3b Can.

***C.* 'Palette'** A vigorous medium-sized shrub with large flowers in late spring. The standard shades from cerise-pink at the tip to orange-yellow at the base, with rich vermilion wings and pale yellow tips to the pink keel. In cultivation 1959.
Zone 5 US, 6 Can.

***C.* 'Porlock'** A hybrid that quickly forms a large, semievergreen bush. The flowers are golden yellow, very fragrant, and borne in racemes, and they appear in mild weather between autumn and spring. It is hardy in the West, especially against a sunny wall, and is also a lovely greenhouse shrub. Raised c. 1922.
Zone 7 US, 8 Can. 🏆

C.* ×*praecox A group of small or medium-sized deciduous hybrids. The following cultivars are recommended, and the original form that was previously listed under this name and known as Warminster broom has been given the cultivar name 'Warminster' *(see below)*.

Cytisus × *praecox* 'Albus'

***C.* ×*p.* 'Albus'** A small or medium-sized, white-flowered selection with the compact habit and profuse flowering that are typical of the group. It flowers in mid- to late spring.
Zone 5 US, 6 Can.

***C.* ×*p.* 'Allgold'** An outstanding small shrub with arching sprays of long-lasting yellow flowers in mid- to late spring.
Zone 4 US, 5b Can. 🏆

Detail of *Cytisus* × *praecox* 'Warminster'

***C.* ×*p.* 'Warminster'** A spectacular, smallish shrub, forming a tumbling mass of rich cream flowers in late spring. Garden origin c. 1867. *(See also photo on p.264.)*
Zone 5 US, 6 Can. 🏆

C. procumbens (Ground broom) A dwarf deciduous shrub with prostrate branches. The flowers are formed in the leaf axils in late spring and early summer. SE Europe.
Zone 4 US, 4b Can.

***C. purpureus* 'Albus'** A pretty, low-growing, deciduous shrub about 18 in (45 cm) high with white flowers produced in late spring. In cultivation 1838.
Zone 4 US, 5 Can.

***C. p.* 'Atropurpureus'** A superb dwarf shrub with deep purple flowers.
Zone 4 US, 5 Can. 🏆

Cytisus × *praecox* 'Warminster'

***C.* 'Red Wings'** A vigorous but compact deciduous shrub. The flowers, profusely borne in mid- to late spring, are deep, velvety red with a yellow keel flushed with bright red.
Zone 5 US, 6 Can.

Cytisus scoparius

C. scoparius (Scotch broom) A medium-sized deciduous shrub as conspicuous as gorse *(Ulex europaeus)* but spineless. It has rich butter yellow flowers in late spring. The following forms are recommended. Europe.
Zone 6 US, 6b Can.

***C. s.* 'Andreanus'** A medium-sized form in which the flowers are attractively marked with brown-crimson. Found wild c. 1884 in Normandy.
Zone 6 US, 6b Can. 🏆

***C. s.* 'Cornish Cream'** A very attractive medium-sized form with cream flowers.
Zone 6 US, 6b Can. 🏆

***C. s.* 'Fulgens'** A late-flowering small to medium-sized clone with a dense, compact habit. The flowers are brownish red in bud and open to orange-yellow with deep crimson wings. Raised c. 1906.
Zone 6 US, 6b Can.

***C. s.* 'Golden Sunlight'** A vigorous medium-sized form with rich yellow flowers. In cultivation 1929.
Zone 6 US, 6b Can.

Cytisus × *spachianus*

C. s.* subsp. *maritimus A nearly prostrate, spreading shrub with large yellow flowers. Found in the wild on sea cliffs in a few places in Cornwall and Channel Isles.
Zone 6 US, 6b Can.

C.* × *spachianus A medium-sized evergreen shrub with arching shoots and long clusters of fragrant yellow flowers in late winter and early spring. It is frost sensitive and is often grown under protection in a greenhouse or as a houseplant.
Zone 9 US 🏆

***C.* 'Windlesham Ruby'** A medium-sized deciduous form of upright habit grown for its strikingly colored flowers of rich mahogany-crimson.
Zone 4 US, 5b Can.

***C.* 'Zeelandia'** This medium-sized deciduous hybrid produces its flowers from late spring to early summer. The standard petal is lilac outside and cream inside; the wings are pinkish and the keel cream. An elegant plant deserving a place in the garden.
Zone 5 US, 6 Can. 🏆

Cytisus 'Zeelandia'

D

Daboecia *Ericaceae*
Irish heath

There are only two species in this genus of low-growing, acid-loving, evergreen shrubs that are related to Erica *but are distinct in their large flowers and broader, elliptic leaves. They do best in a peaty, moist, but well-drained soil; sandy soil to which quantities of organic matter have been added is close to ideal. As with other heaths, a sunny location is preferred, but Irish heath grows and flowers well in part shade, where there is less danger of damage from drought.*

In shady sites, however, Irish heath tend to be less compact. This is not the drawback it might be with most other heaths, which cannot safely be cut back into the old wood. Plants that have become leggy can be pruned back drastically.

D. cantabrica (Irish heath) This species is one of the most charming dwarf shrubs, producing long racemes of very showy, rose-purple, bell-shaped flowers from early summer to late fall. The following forms are recommended. Coastal strip of Portugal and NW Spain, Connemara (a mountainous, boggy area NW of Galway, Ireland). In cultivation 1800.
Zone 5 US, 6 Can.

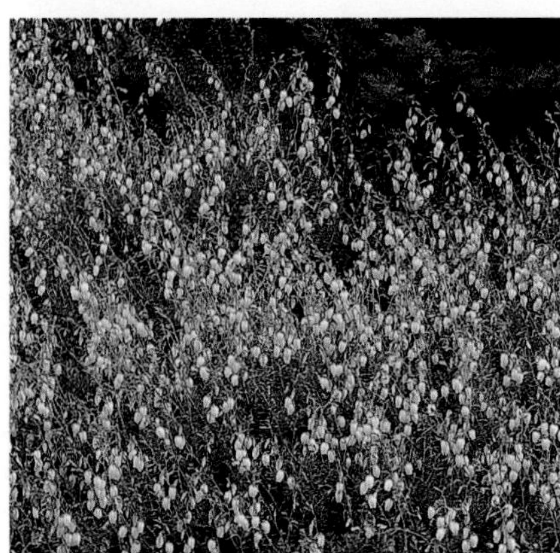

Daboecia cantabrica 'Alba'

D. c. **'Alba'** A dwarf shrub with long racemes of white flowers.
Zone 5 US, 6 Can.

D. c. **'Atropurpurea'** The bell-shaped flowers of this dwarf shrub are rose-purple, darker than the type.
Zone 5 US, 6 Can.

Daboecia cantabrica 'Bicolor'

D. c. **'Bicolor'** A dwarf cultivar with white, rose-purple, and striped flowers, often in the same cluster.
Zone 5 US, 6 Can.

D. c. **'David Moss'** A dwarf shrub with white, freely borne flowers and glossy, dark green foliage.
Zone 5 US, 6 Can.

Daboecia cantabrica 'Praegerae'

D. c. **'Praegerae'** A dwarf, spreading shrub with rich pink flowers, curiously narrowed. Connemara. Found wild c. 1932.
Zone 5 US, 6 Can.

D. c. **'Waley's Red'** A form with deep, glowing magenta-colored flowers with a bluish tinge.
Zone 5 US, 6 Can.

Daboecia cantabrica 'Waley's Red'

D. × ***scotica*** A group of hybrids between *D. cantabrica* and *D. azorica*, the other species in the genus. Like *D. cantabrica*, they flower from early summer to late fall. The following forms are recommended. Garden origin, Glasgow, Scotland, c. 1953.

D. × ***s.*** **'Jack Drake'** A dwarf shrub 10 in (25 cm) high with ruby red flowers.
Zone 5 US, 6 Can.

D. × ***s.*** **'Silverwells'** A dwarf shrub up to about 6 in (15 cm) with white flowers.
Zone 5 US, 6 Can.

D. × ***s.*** **'William Buchanan'** A form with deep purple flowers on a dwarf shrub 18 in (45 cm) high. Zone 5 US, 6 Can.

Dacrydium *Podocarpaceae*

A genus of about 25 species of evergreen coniferous trees and shrubs, related to Podocarpus.

Dacrydium franklinii

D. franklinii (Huon pine) In warm areas this forms a large, graceful shrub or small,

conical tree. The slender, drooping branches are covered in bright green, scalelike leaves. It is subject to frost injury. Tasmania.
Zone 9 US

Danaë *Ruscaceae*

A genus of one species of evergreen shrub, which is related to Ruscus *(butcher's broom) but has hermaphrodite flowers in short, terminal panicles as opposed to male and female flowers on separate plants. As in* Ruscus, *the leaves are in fact flattened stems.*

D. racemosa (Alexandrian laurel) A charming small shrub with arching sprays of narrow, polished, green "leaves" and cream flowers in early summer followed by orange-red fruits if the summer has been hot. Suitable for growing in moisture-retentive soil in sun or part shade and excellent for cutting. SW Asia to N Iran. Introduced 1713.
Zone 8 US, 9 Can. 🏆

Daphne *Thymelaeaceae*

A genus of about 50 species of evergreen and deciduous shrubs from Europe, Asia, and North Africa, a remarkably high proportion of which are desirable garden plants. Daphnes are justifiably renowned for their beauty and particularly for their scent, which can often be detected from several yards away, and it is well worth planting them where you are likely to pass by frequently.

Daphnes are mostly small but vary from prostrate plants suitable for the rock garden to quite large shrubs. Their flowers are cylindrical tubes that suddenly flare outward into four lobes, so that the bloom looks flat when viewed head-on. Blossom colors vary from mauve or purple to white and greenish yellow and are enhanced by a luminescent, frost-sprinkled appearance. Attractive but poisonous seeds sometimes follow.

The best growing medium is loose, loamy, fertile soil that is moist but well drained. Some alpine species, including D. cneorum *and* D. retusa, *will also grow in a rich scree.*

Daphnes are excellent for cutting, but you should be careful, as the exquisite daphne fragrance can become overwhelming in a confined space. Also be careful to keep children and animals away from daphne, which is toxic if eaten.

D. alpina (Alpine daphne) A dwarf deciduous species, suitable for a rock garden, with gray-green leaves and terminal clusters of fragrant white flowers from late spring to early summer, followed by orange-red fruits. Mountains of S and C Europe. In cultivation 1759.
Zone 4 US, 5 Can.

Daphne arbuscula

D. arbuscula A dwarf, rounded, evergreen alpine shrublet with crowded, narrow leaves and rose-pink, scented flowers in late spring to early summer, followed by brownish yellow fruits. Carpathian Mountains of C Europe.
Zone 5 US, 6 Can. 🏆

D. bholua A deciduous or semievergreen shrub up to 6½ ft (2 m) high with stout, erect branches and oblanceolate leaves. The large, sweetly scented flowers are deep reddish mauve in bud and open white, with a reddish mauve reverse. They are borne in terminal clusters from mid- to late winter.

Daphne bholua

The fruits are black. The following forms are recommended. Himalaya. In cultivation 1938.
Zone 8 US, 9 Can.

Daphne bholua 'Gurkha'

***D. b.* 'Gurkha'** A deciduous form of this highly variable medium-sized shrub that, in its best forms, is stunning and has greatly increased the popularity of the species. It reaches a height of up to 6½ ft (2 m) and bears a long succession of large, richly scented, purplish pink flowers with white insides. The blossoms are produced in clusters of up to 20 from mid- to late winter. E Nepal. Introduced 1962.
Zone 8 US, 9 Can. 🏆

Daphne bholua 'Jacqueline Postill'

***D. b.* 'Jacqueline Postill'** An evergreen or semievergreen, medium-sized form that bears its flowers when in full leaf. The flowers, produced from mid- to late winter, are larger and showier than those of 'Gurkha' and have an equally powerful

fragrance. Raised 1982 as a seedling of the latter by the Hillier Nurseries' propagator Alan Postill.
Zone 8 US, 9 Can.

D. blagayana (Balkan daphne) A dwarf deciduous shrub with prostrate branches, at the ends of which are bunches of oval leaves and clusters of richly scented, creamy white flowers from early to midspring. The fruits are whitish. It is not one of the easiest plants to grow, succeeding best in deep leaf mold and semishade. Mountain forests of SE Europe. Introduced c. 1875.
Zone 6 US, 7 Can.

Daphne × *burkwoodii*

D. **×** ***burkwoodii*** (Burkwood daphne) A group of deciduous or semievergreen hybrids, including some of the most popular and easily grown plants in the genus. The plants listed under this name are usually the seedlings 'Albert Burkwood' and 'Somerset'.
Zone 4 US, 5 Can.

Daphne × *burkwoodii* 'Albert Burkwood'

***D.* × *b.* 'Albert Burkwood'** A fast-growing semievergreen shrub up to 3 ft (1 m) high with pale pink, deliciously fragrant flowers borne in clusters on short, leafy shoots from late spring to early summer and often again in fall. Raised 1931.
Zone 4 US, 5 Can.

***D.* × *b.* 'Carol Mackie'** A small semievergreen form whose leaves have a yellow margin that becomes creamy white. Named for the breeder, in whose garden in New Jersey it originated as a sport. Previously distributed as 'Variegata'. Introduced 1962.
Zone 4 US, 5 Can.

Daphne × *burkwoodii* 'Somerset'

***D.* × *b.* 'Somerset'** A sister seedling to 'Albert Burkwood', but slightly larger and more upright, with paler flowers.
Zone 4 US, 5 Can.

Daphne cneorum

D. cneorum (Rose daphne, garland flower) A prostrate deciduous shrub that is a favorite because of its fragrant clusters of rose-pink flowers borne from mid- to late spring. The occasional fruits are brownish yellow. Most gardeners find it difficult to establish, although it usually grows well at first. For good rooting and a long life, the plant needs cool, moist growing conditions, with soil rich in peat moss or leaf mold spread over and among the branches. C and S Europe.
Zone 3 US, 2b Can.

***D. c.* 'Eximia'** An even more prostrate form with larger leaves and flowers. The buds are crimson and open to rich pink.
Zone 3 US, 2b Can.

Daphne cneorum 'Ruby Glow'

***D. c.* 'Ruby Glow'** A prostrate form with very deep pink flowers.
Zone 3 US, 2b Can.

Daphne cneorum 'Variegata'

***D. c.* 'Variegata'** A vigorous prostrate form with dark green leaves attractively margined with cream.
Zone 3 US, 2b Can.

Daphne collina

D. collina A first-rate evergreen dwarf shrub for the rock garden, forming a shapely bush only 10–14 in (25–35 cm) high. Each shoot is covered with blunt, deep green leaves and bears a cluster of fragrant, rose-purple flowers at the end in late spring. This rewarding daphne is now considered synonymous with or a form of *D. sericea*. S Italy. In cultivation 1752.
Zone 8 US, 7b Can. 🏆

D. genkwa (Lilac daphne) This is one of the loveliest species, but it is difficult to grow and establish. It is a small deciduous shrub with lilaclike and lilac-colored flowers all along the leafless branches from mid- to late spring. The fruits are small white berries. For the best chances of success, the plant needs maximum summer warmth, perfect drainage, and summer watering. It is a rare plant and can be difficult to obtain. China, Taiwan. Introduced 1843 by Robert Fortune.
Zone 5 US, 6 Can.

D.* × *houtteana A small, semievergreen, erect shrub with more or less oblong, pointed, purplish leaves and dark red-purple flowers in midspring. Stocks were subject to virus, but new, clean material has been obtained through micropropagation. In cultivation 1850.
Zone 6 US, 7 Can.

D.* × *hybrida This charming small evergreen shrub with dark, glossy leaves has the beauty and fragrance of *D. odora* and is hardier. Reddish purple, highly scented flowers are produced from late fall through winter. Raised c. 1820.
Zone 6 US, 7 Can.

Daphne retusa

D. jasminea A dwarf, cushion-forming shrublet with small, narrow, glaucous, evergreen leaves. The flowers are rose-pink in bud, opening white in spring, and deliciously fragrant. It is a rare alpine gem and requires winter protection, preferably in an alpine house or cold greenhouse. Cliffs and rocks in Greece (notably at Delphi). Introduced 1954. There is also an upright form that stands about 18 in (45 cm) high and is from other Greek locations.
Zone 9 US

D. jezoensis A dwarf shrub with pale green young leaves that emerge in autumn. They are dark blue-green when mature and drop in early summer (summer-deciduous). In winter it bears dense clusters of fragrant, golden yellow, green-tinged flowers with protruding stamens. Best in a moist but well-drained, peaty soil in a bright but not exposed position. Japan. Introduced c. 1960.
Zone 6 US, 7 Can.

D. laureola* subsp. *philippi A dwarf form of the spurge laurel, this is an evergreen shrub ideal for a shady site in a rock garden. It has fragrant, yellow-green flowers in dense clusters beneath the leathery, glossy, green leaves in late winter to early spring. May cause skin allergy. Pyrenees. In cultivation 1894.
Zone 7 US, 8 Can.

Daphne laureola subsp. *philippi*

***D. longilobata* 'Peter Moore'** A strikingly variegated, small to medium-sized, erect, deciduous or semievergreen shrub with gray-green leaves margined with creamy white. White flowers in summer are followed by red berries. A seedling found 1980 by the Hillier Nurseries' propagator Peter Moore.
Zone 6 US, 7 Can.

Daphne × *mantensiana* 'Manten'

***D.* × *mantensiana* 'Manten'** A dwarf evergreen shrub of dense, rounded habit with glossy dark green leaves up to $1^1/_4$ in (3.5 cm) long. The strongly scented flowers are deep rose-purple outside, deep lilac within, and borne in dense clusters at the ends of the branches from mid- to late spring, usually with a second flush in summer. Introduced 1953 in British Columbia.
Zone 5 US, 6b Can.

D. mezereum (February daphne, mezereon) The best-known, sweet-scented daphne. A small, twiggy deciduous shrub, it flowers in late winter and early spring; the purple-red flowers, which cover the previous year's shoots, are followed by scarlet, poisonous fruits. It thrives in limestone soils. Unfortunately, virus is common in this species and causes poor, yellowish foliage. May cause skin allergy. Europe, Asia

Daphne mezereum

Minor, Siberia; naturalized in E United States. In cultivation 1561.
Zone 3 US, 3 Can.

D. m.* f. *alba A form with more upright branches. The flowers are white and the fruits translucent amber.
Zone 3 US, 3 Can.

D.* × *napolitana This, not *neapolitana,* is the correct spelling for a beautiful, dwarf, evergreen shrub that is rarely more than 3 ft (1 m) high, with blunt, ash green leaves. Clusters of fragrant, rose-pink flowers are borne profusely from midspring to very early summer. In cultivation 1823.
Zone 8 US, 9? Can. 🏆

Daphne × *napolitana*

Daphne odora

D. odora (Winter daphne) This small evergreen shrub flowers in winter and early spring. It should be given some protection from drying winter winds, especially at the limits of its range. It makes a bush 4–6½ ft (1.2–2 m) tall with dark green leaves and highly fragrant, reddish purple and white flowers. It and its forms are prone to viral infection. China, Japan. Introduced 1771.
Zone 7 US, 8 Can.

D. o.* f. *alba A form with white flowers.
Zone 7 US, 8 Can.

Daphne odora 'Aureo-Marginata'

***D. o.* 'Aureo-Marginata'** The leaves of this form have a narrow yellow margin that becomes creamy white with age. It is hardier than the typical species.
Zone 7 US, 8 Can.

***D. petraea* 'Grandiflora'** A tiny, gnarled, evergreen, alpine shrublet only 2–3 in (5–7.5 cm) high with small, linear leaves and rosy pink, fragrant flowers produced in clusters at the ends of the branches in early summer. Best grown in an alpine house or cold greenhouse but also possible on a well-made scree. Not easily obtained. N Italy. Collected 1914 from the wild.
Zone 6 US, 7 Can.

D. pontica (Twin-flowered daphne) A small, wide-spreading evergreen shrub that will thrive under the drip of trees and in

Daphne pontica

heavy soil. It has glossy, bright green leaves and loose clusters of fragrant, spidery, yellow-green flowers from mid- to late spring. The fruits are black. SE Bulgaria, N Iran, N Turkey. Introduced 1752.
Zone 6 US, 7 Can. 🏆

D. retusa A slow-growing, dwarf evergreen shrub with stout, stiff branches. It bears clusters of fragrant, deep rose-purple flowers from late spring to early summer and often again in fall. Some authorities include it in *D. tangutica;* both are variable and could be extremes within the same species. In gardens, *D. retusa* has shorter, glossier leaves and is even slower growing. W China, Himalaya. Introduced 1901 by Ernest Wilson. *(See photo on p.268.)*
Zone 6 US, 7 Can. 🏆

Daphne tangutica

D. tangutica A dwarf evergreen shrub bearing clusters of fragrant flowers from early to midspring. These are white with a purple tinge on the inside and rose-purple

on the outside. China. Introduced early 1900s by Ernest Wilson.
Zone 5 US, 6 Can. 🏆

Daphne 'Valerie Hillier'

***D.* 'Valerie Hillier'** A dwarf, spreading, evergreen shrub with downy shoots and narrowly oblong, glossy, green leaves up to 2 in (5 cm) long. Its fragrant flowers are borne in terminal clusters on the young growths continuously from late spring to fall. They are purplish pink in bud, opening to pale pink and fading nearly to white with pink-edged lobes; the tube of the flower is pale pink, shading to green at the base. A splendid hybrid. Raised 1984 by the Hillier Nurseries' propagator Alan Postill and named after the wife of John Hillier, the elder son of Sir Harold Hillier.
Zone 6? US, 7? Can.

Daphniphyllum *Daphniphyllaceae*

A genus of 10 species of evergreen trees and shrubs from East and Southeast Asia to Australia. These aristocratic-looking shrubs have leaves similar to those of Rhododendron decorum, *but the flowers are not conspicuous. They thrive in part shade and a neutral, loamy soil but are nevertheless lime tolerant.*

Daphniphyllum macropodum

D. macropodum A large, striking shrub with large leaves that are pale green above, with bloomy undersides. The flowers are borne in late spring in clusters beneath the leaves and have no petals, but they contribute a pungent scent. The fruits are blue-black and shaped like peas. It is surprisingly hardy but should be sheltered from cold, drying winds. Prune to open up the center of the shrub or cut back old specimens really hard. China, Japan. Introduced 1879 by Charles Maries.
Zone 7 US, 8 Can.

Datura

D. sanguinea See *Brugmansia sanguinea.*
D. suaveolens See *Brugmansia suaveolens.*

Davidia *Davidiaceae*

A genus of medium-sized deciduous trees that somewhat resemble lindens. Authorities differ as to whether there are two species or just one, but gardeners agree that whatever their botanical status, davidias are extremely beautiful in a haunting way when in flower. A deep, moist but well-drained, loamy soil is best, although they tolerate alkaline soil. They should be planted with some shelter from wind. As broad-headed trees, and because their beauty is best appreciated from a distance, they should always be given enough room. No pruning is required.

Davidia involucrata

D. involucrata (Dovetree, ghost tree, pocket handkerchief tree) This sublimely beautiful tree is outstanding in late spring, when it is draped with large white bracts, which give the impression of a flight of doves or a scattering of pure white pocket handkerchiefs. The leaves are smooth on young plants but become densely hairy on their undersides. C and W China. Introduced 1869 by Père David, reintroduced 1904 by Ernest Wilson.
Zone 6 US, 7 Can. 🏆

Davidia involucrata var. *vilmoriniana*

D. i.* var. *vilmoriniana This form is very similar to *D. involucrata*, but its leaves are smooth underneath. For garden purposes this and the typical form are both of equal merit, and most plants that are grown as *Davidia involucrata* belong in fact to this variety. China. Introduced 1897.
Zone 5 US, 6b Can. 🏆

Decaisnea *Lardizabalaceae*

A genus of two species of deciduous shrubs from western China and the Himalaya.

D. fargesii A most interesting shrub, up to 10 ft (3 m) high, with large, bold, pinnate leaves 2–3 ft (60–90 cm) long, blue-tinged when young. The yellow-green flowers, in clusters up to 18 in (45 cm) long, are borne in late spring and are followed by remarkable, metallic blue pods much like those of broad beans. It will grow in sun or partial

Decaisnea fargesii

shade and in a moist but well-drained soil. W China. Introduced 1895.
Zone 6 US, 7 Can.

Decumeria *Hydrangeaceae*

A genus of two semievergreen or evergreen species of shrubs that climb by means of aerial roots. They are related to Hydrangea, *but their flowers are fertile. Like the climbing hydrangeas, they grow in sun or shade in any soil.*

D. barbara A semievergreen climber up to 30 ft (9 m). The small, sweetly scented white flowers are borne in small clusters from early to midsummer. In the wild it climbs the trunks of trees. SE United States. Introduced 1785.
Zone 7 US, 8 Can.

D. sinensis A rare evergreen species up to 16 ft (5 m) with a profusion of small green and white flowers in clusters in late spring. They are deliciously honey scented. China. Introduced 1908 by Ernest Wilson.
Zone 8 US, 9? Can.

Dendromecon *Papaveraceae*
Bush poppy, tree poppy

A genus of two species of evergreen shrubs, native to California and related to Romneya, *but with entire leaves and smaller, yellow flowers.*

D. rigida A large, tender shrub, worth trying in mild areas against a warm, sunny wall and in extremely well drained, loamy soil. The leaves are narrow, rigid, and bloomy, and the flowers are poppylike,

Dendromecon rigida

four-petaled, bright buttercup yellow, and produced over a long period in summer. Prune out weak branches. It has now become scarce. California. Introduced c. 1854 by William Lobb.
Zone 8 US

Desfontainia *Loganiaceae*

A genus of one, somewhat variable evergreen species, found in South America, mainly in the Andes but always in cool, moist places. It prefers acid soil and will not thrive in alkaline or shallow soil over limestone. Requires a sheltered location.

D. spinosa A beautiful shrub, slowly growing to 6–6½ ft (1.8–2 m). The leaves are small and easily mistaken for those of a holly. The tubular flowers, borne in late summer, are scarlet with a bright yellow mouth. Prune for shape only if necessary. Costa Rica to Cape Horn. Introduced c. 1843 by William Lobb.
Zone 8 US, 9b? Can. 🏆

Desfontainia spinosa

Desmodium *Leguminosae*
Tick trefoil

A genus of about 300 species of herbaceous perennials and deciduous shrubs, related to Lespedeza *and widely distributed in tropical and subtropical regions.*

D. tiliifolium A small to medium-sized,

Desmodium tiliifolium

semiwoody shrub with erect stems and leaves with three leaflets. Massed, large panicles of pale lilac pea flowers appear in summer, followed by flattened and lobed pods. It will grow in any good, well-drained soil in sun. Himalaya. Introduced 1879.
Zone 6 US, 7 Can.

Deutzia *Philadelphaceae*

A genus of about 70 species of deciduous shrubs native to the Himalaya and South and East Asia. They are generally easy to grow in all types of fertile soil, usually reaching 4–6½ ft (1.2–2 m). Flowering is in early summer. Thin out the shoots that have finished flowering and cut them back to within a short distance of the old wood. Flowering is prolonged and color better preserved if there is a little shade during the hottest part of the day.

D. chunii A beautiful medium-sized shrub, blooming in midsummer. The flowers are 1/2 in (12 mm) across with white or pink petals, reflexed to expose the yellow anthers, and are borne all along the branches in panicles up to 4 in (10 cm) long. This plant, in both its pink and white forms, is sometimes seen under the name *D. ningpoensis*. E China. Introduced 1935.
Zone 6 US, 7 Can.

***D. c.* 'Pink Charm'** A pink-flowered form selected at Hillier Nurseries.
Zone 6 US, 7 Can.

***D. compacta* 'Lavender Time'** A medium-sized shrub with flowers that are lilac at first, turning to pale lavender in midsummer. A very distinct shrub collected from the wild by Frank Kingdon-Ward that, in fact, may be a new species.
Zone 6 US, 7 Can.

Deutzia × elegantissima

D. × elegantissima A medium-sized hybrid with clusters of fragrant flowers, tinted with rose-pink. Garden origin 1909.
Zone 6 US, 7 Can.

***D. × e.* 'Rosalind'** A lovely clone with clusters of flowers in deep carmine-pink. In cultivation 1962.
Zone 6 US, 7 Can. 🏆

Deutzia × elegantissima 'Rosalind'

Deutzia gracilis

D. gracilis (Slender deutzia) An elegant, white-flowered species, parent of many good hybrids. It was previously used for forcing and needs protection from late-spring frosts. Japan. Introduced c. 1840.
Zone 4 US, 5b Can.

D. × hybrida A group of hybrids of identical parentage, all of which are extremely free flowering. The following are recommended.
Zone 6 US, 7 Can.

Deutzia × hybrida 'Magician'

***D. × h.* 'Magician'** This medium-sized form has large flowers, mauve-pink edged with white and tinted purple on the reverse.
Zone 6 US, 7 Can.

Deutzia × hybrida 'Mont Rose'

***D. × h.* 'Mont Rose'** A very free-flowering, medium-sized form that has rose-pink flowers with darker-colored tints borne in

large clusters. Raised c. 1925.
Zone 5 US, 6b Can. 🏆

***D.* × *h.* 'Pink Pompon'** A medium-sized shrub with dense heads of double flowers, pink at first and then becoming white.
Zone 6 US, 7 Can.

***D.* × *h.* 'Strawberry Fields'**, syn. *D.* × *magnifica* 'Rubra' A medium-sized shrub with large flowers that are deep crimson outside and white flushed with pink within.
Zone 6 US, 7 Can.

Deutzia × *kalmiiflora*

D.* × *kalmiiflora (Kalmia deutzia) A medium-sized, free-flowering shrub with large, white, carmine-flushed flowers. The fall leaves are purple. Garden origin 1900.
Zone 4 US, 5b Can.

Deutzia longifolia 'Veitchii'

D.* × *lemoinei (Lemoine deutzia) One of the hardiest deutzias, this forms a rounded shrub up to 6½ ft (2 m) tall and wide. The white flowers are in upright corymbs and appear in late spring. Raised 1891.
Zone 4 US, 5 Can.

***D. longifolia* 'Veitchii'** A handsome, medium-sized shrub with long, narrowly lance-shaped leaves and large clusters of flowers tinted a rich lilac-pink from early to midsummer. The most aristocratic of this genus. The species introduced from W China 1905 by Ernest Wilson.
Zone 6 US, 7 Can. 🏆

D.* × *magnifica (Showy deutzia) A vigorous, medium-sized shrub with panicles of double white flowers. Garden origin 1909.
Zone 5 US, 6 Can.

***D.* × *m.* 'Rubra'** See *D.* × *hybrida* 'Strawberry Fields'.

***D.* 'Nikko'** This shrub, welcomed for its dwarf, compact habit, has proved less than worthy of its reception. Its small white flowers are not as freely produced as anticipated. It needs summer heat to bloom well. In cultivation 1975.
Zone 4 US, 5b Can.

D. pulchra A magnificent shrub of medium size. The clusters of white flowers resemble the nodding spikes of lily-of-the-valley. Philippines, Taiwan. Introduced 1918 by Ernest Wilson.
Zone 6 US, 7 Can.

Deutzia × *rosea* 'Campanulata'

***D.* × *rosea* 'Campanulata'** An erect medium-sized shrub bearing bell-shaped flowers whose white petals contrast with the purple calyx. In cultivation 1899.
Zone 5 US, 6 Can

***D.* × *r.* 'Carminea'** A very attractive small to medium-sized shrub with flowers flushed with rose-carmine. In cultivation 1900.
Zone 5 US, 6 Can. 🏆

Deutzia × *rosea* 'Carminea'

Deutzia scabra 'Candidissima'

***D. scabra* 'Candidissima'** A medium-sized to large shrub with large clusters of double pure white flowers from early to midsummer. In cultivation 1867.
Zone 5 US, 6 Can.

***D. s.* 'Plena'** The double white flowers of this medium-sized to large shrub are suffused with rose-purple on the outside.

Deutzia scabra 'Punctata'

Introduced 1861 by Robert Fortune.
Zone 5 US, 6 Can.

***D. s.* 'Punctata'** A form whose leaves are dotted with white. *(See photo on p.273.)*
Zone 5 US, 6 Can.

Deutzia setchuenensis var. corymbiflora

D. setchuenensis* var. *corymbiflora A charming, slow-growing shrub up to 6½ ft (2 m) high, producing dome-shaped heads of small, white, starlike flowers very freely from mid- to late summer. One of the best summer-blooming shrubs. Some shelter from cold winds is advisable.
Zone 6 US, 7 Can. 🏆

Diervilla *Caprifoliaceae*

Bush honeysuckle

A genus of three species of easily grown, small, summer-flowering deciduous shrubs from North America; they are related to Lonicera. *They have small, yellow, two-lipped flowers and will grow in any well-drained, friable soil.*

Diervilla sessilifolia

D. sessilifolia (Southern bush honeysuckle) A small shrub with narrow, pointed leaves that are often copper-tinted when young and sulphur yellow flowers borne in short panicles from early to late summer. SE United States. Introduced 1844.
Zone 3 US, 4 Can

D. × splendens A small hybrid shrub with short-stalked leaves and sulphur yellow flowers in summer. Introduced c. 1850.
Zone 3 US, 3 Can.

Diospyros *Ebenaceae*

Persimmon

There are almost 500 species of evergreen and deciduous trees and shrubs in this genus, which is best known as the source for ebony (D. ebenum) *and other decorative woods, as well as for fruits such as date plums and persimmons. Most are native to tropical regions, and very few are hardy.*

Diospyros kaki

D. kaki (Kaki, Japanese persimmon) A large deciduous shrub or small tree long cultivated in the Far East for its edible fruits and in gardens chiefly for the orange-yellow to orange-red and plum-purple fall color of its large, lustrous leaves. The orange-yellow, tomato-like fruits are borne in most summers in temperate regions. They are edible but unless fully ripe are bitter due to high concentrations of tannin. China. Introduced 1796.
Zone 7 US, 8b Can.

Dipelta *Caprifoliaceae*

A small genus of four species of tall shrubs, bearing a general resemblance to Weigela. *The difference is mainly in their showy, winged fruits.*

D. floribunda A first-class large shrub with fragrant, weigela-like flowers produced in great quantities in late spring. They are pink, with throats flushed in yellow. Propagation is extremely difficult, so the plant is somewhat rare. It is an adaptable shrub, tolerant of alkaline and poor soils, and should be pruned after flowering to remove old and crowded branches. C and W China. Introduced 1902 by Ernest Wilson.
Zone 6 US, 7 Can.

Dipteronia *Aceraceae*

A genus of two species of large deciduous shrubs from central and southern China, related to Acer, *and the only other member of the family. They differ from the maples, however, in that the fruits are winged all around instead of down one side.*

Dipteronia sinensis

D. sinensis A large shrub with bold, pinnate leaves. The insignificant flowers are followed in fall by large clusters of pale green seeds, later red, that resemble those of the wych elm *(Ulmus glabra)* but are more eye-catching. China. Introduced c. 1900.
Zone 7 US, 8 Can.

Disanthus *Hamamelidaceae*

A genus of one deciduous species related to Liquidambar.

D. cercidifolius A medium-sized shrub that is like a witch hazel *(Hamamelis)* in

Disanthus cercidifolius

habit and a Judas tree *(Cercis siliquastrum)* in leaf, highly valued for its beautiful, soft crimson and claret-red fall colors. The tiny purplish flowers are produced in midfall. It requires a moist but well-drained, acid soil in part shade and protection from wind. Japan, SE China. Introduced 1893.
Zone 6 US, 7 Can. 🏆

Distylium *Hamamelidaceae*

A genus of about 12 species of evergreen shrubs and trees native to East and Southeast Asia and Central America. They do best in conditions suitable for Hamamelis.

D. racemosum (Isu tree) A wide-spreading but slow-growing, medium-sized to large shrub that reaches tree size in the wild. It has glossy, leathery leaves, and its flowers, which have no petals, consist of bright red stamens and are produced in clusters from mid- to late spring. The plant is similar to *Sycopsis*, to which it is related.

Distylum racemosum

It prefers an acid soil in part shade. S Japan, Taiwan, Korea, China. Introduced 1876.
Zone 7 US, 8 Can.

Dorycnium *Leguminosae*

A genus of about 12 species of deciduous subshrubs and herbaceous perennials from the Mediterranean region and the Canary Islands. The leaves usually have five leaflets, and the flowers are borne in tight, cloverlike heads.

Dorycnium hirsutum

D. hirsutum (Canary clover) A charming, dwarf subshrub with erect annual stems and terminal heads of pink-tinged, white pea flowers from late summer into autumn. The foliage is silvery-hairy and makes a pleasant foil for the red-tinted fruit pods. It is suitable for a dry site in full sun that is as well drained as possible, perhaps in a rock garden. Mediterranean region, S Portugal. In cultivation 1683.
Zone 8 US, 9? Can.

Dregea *Asclepiadaceae*

A genus of three species of deciduous climbers from warm regions of the Old World. The following one can be grown out-of-doors in warm regions against a warm, sheltered wall or in a greenhouse.

Dregea sinensis

D. sinensis The hardiest species, with

slender stems up to 10 ft (3 m) long that need some support. The ovate leaves are gray-felted beneath, and the deliciously scented flowers, very much like those of a hoya, are white with a central zone of red spots. They are borne in long-stalked, downy umbels in summer. China. Introduced 1907 by Ernest Wilson.
Zone 9? US

Drimys *Winteraceae*

The estimates of species in this genus of evergreen trees and shrubs vary from around 10 to about 30. They are native to Malaysia, eastern Australia, New Guinea, and Central and South America. The cultivated species are fine, handsome plants for milder places.

D. lanceolata (Pepper tree) A medium-sized to large, aromatic, slender, upright shrub with purplish red shoots and dark green leaves that are light green beneath. It has copper-tinted young growths and bears numerous small, creamy white flowers from mid- to late spring. Male and female flowers are on separate plants. Tasmania, SE Australia. Introduced 1843.
Zone 8 US, 9? Can.

Drimys winteri

D. winteri (Winter's bark) A large shrub or small tree with large, leathery leaves with bloomy undersides. The ivory white flowers are fragrant and borne in loose umbels in late spring. It can be encouraged to form a tree by training when it is young. It does well against a wall. C Chile. Introduced 1827.
Zone 9 US

Dryas *Rosaceae*

A genus of two species of creeping plants with small, evergreen, oaklike leaves that are shiny dark green above and startlingly white beneath. They are natives of northern temperate and arctic regions and are suitable for screes, the top of stone walls, paving, or the rock garden. Flowering is at its best and the plants are more compact if they are grown in a poor, gravelly, but moist soil.

Dryas octopetala

D. octopetala (Mountain avens, Mount Washington dryad) The white flowers of this prostrate, mat-forming species are like little dog roses *(Rosa canina)*, with a mass of golden yellow stamens in the center. Each flower is carried separately on a 3 in (7.5 cm) stalk that rises above the fans of distinctive oaklike leaves, which are dark green on top and gray-green beneath. The flower is clasped by long, green sepals. In ideal conditions the flowers cover the whole plant during late spring and early summer and are followed by silky tassels of seed heads that change to balls of down. A good plant for rock gardens. Scotland, Ireland, the Rocky Mountains, Canada, and other circumpolar regions. In cultivation 1750.
Zone 1 US, 1 Can.

D. × suendermannii (Suendermann dryad) This is a rather uncommon hybrid that is very similar to *D. octopetala* but with larger, more erect leaves and creamy white flowers, which are ivory in bud and nodding when open. They appear in late spring or early summer. In cultivation 1750.
Zone 2 US, 2 Can.

E

Eccremocarpus *Bignoniaceae*

A genus of about five species of evergreen or nearly evergreen plants that climb by means of coiling leaf tendrils. The following is hardy in mild-climate gardens and can be grown in colder areas in the greenhouse; as it is easy to raise from seed and grows quickly to flowering in the same year, it can also be treated as a half-hardy annual. It will grow in any soil.

Eccremocarpus scaber

E. scaber (Chilean glory flower) A vigorous, fast-growing climber that quickly covers a support with angular stems that are up to 16 ft (5 m) long. The leaves are bipinnate and end in a slender tendril. The scarlet to orange or yellow, tubular flowers, 1 in (2.5 cm) long, are in clusters that are continually produced throughout summer and autumn. Chile. Introduced 1824.
Zone 8 US, 9 Can. 🏆

Edgeworthia *Thymelaeaceae*

A genus of two species of semievergreen or deciduous shrubs, related to Daphne *and native to the Himalaya and China.*

E. chrysantha This deciduous species grows to 4–5 ft (1.2–1.5 m) and in late winter bears dense, nodding, terminal clusters of fragrant yellow flowers covered on the outside with silky hairs. It requires a sheltered spot in a mild area and will not

Edgeworthia chrysantha

tolerate hot, dry summers. The soil should be well drained and high in organic matter. It is used in Japan to make high-grade banknote paper. China. Introduced 1845.
Zone 8 US, 9? Can.

Elaeagnus *Elaeagnaceae*

There are about 40 evergreen and deciduous species in this genus. Some of the plants are called oleaster, which means "lesser olive" or almost "tries hard to be an olive." These plants are not olives at all but are evergreen or deciduous, fast-growing shrubs or small trees that may have little egg-shaped fruits. They are native to southern Europe and Asia, with one species in North America. They are grown chiefly for their lustrous foliage, which can tolerate wind, even in coastal and other exposed locations. The white or off-white flowers, though small, are pleasantly scented and abundantly produced, although on evergreen species they are often hidden by the leaves. They will thrive in any fertile soil except very shallow, alkaline ones.

E. angustifolia (Russian olive) This species, to which the term *oleaster* properly applies, is a large, spiny deciduous shrub or small tree with silvery gray, willowlike leaves and fragrant flowers in early summer. The fruits are silvery amber, oval, and $^{1}/_{2}$ in (12 mm) long. It is easily mistaken for the willow-leaved pear, *Pyrus salicifolia*. Temperate W Asia. Widely naturalized. In cultivation in the 16th century.
Zone 2 US, 2 Can.

E. a.* var. *caspica See *E.* 'Quicksilver'.

E. commutata (Silverberry) A medium-sized deciduous shrub, spreading by underground shoots, with intensely silver leaves and fragrant flowers in late spring. The fruits are small, egg shaped, and silvery. Good in poor soils. North America. Introduced 1813.
Zone 2 US, 2 Can.

Elaeagnus × *ebbingei*

Elaeagnus × *ebbingei* 'Gilt Edge'

E.* × *ebbingei A large, hardy, fast-growing, evergreen shrub, ideal for creating shelter, even in coastal areas. The large, glossy, dark green leaves are silvery beneath, and the silvery-scaly, fragrant flowers are borne in fall, followed by silver-speckled orange fruits in spring. Garden origin 1929.
Zone 6 US, 7 Can.

***E.* × *e.* 'Gilt Edge'** The leaves of this large shrub are margined with golden yellow. In cultivation 1961.
Zone 6 US, 7 Can. 🏆

Elaeagnus × *ebbingei* 'Limelight'

***E.* × *e.* 'Limelight'** A large shrub whose leaves are green above at first with silvery scales, then develop a broad blotch of deep yellow and pale green, silvery beneath. Liable to revert.
Zone 6 US, 7 Can.

Elaeagnus macrophylla

E. macrophylla The broad, rounded leaves of this evergreen species are silvery on both surfaces, becoming glossy, dark green above as the season progresses. It eventually forms a large, spreading shrub. The fragrant

flowers are borne in fall. Korea, Japan. Introduced 1879 by Charles Maries.
Zone 8 US, 9? Can.

E. parvifolia A large deciduous shrub with arching branches and bronze-scaly shoots that are silvery when young. The leaves are elliptic-lanceolate, scaly above when young and then becoming glossy, bright green. Fragrant, creamy white flowers in spring and early fall are followed by red fruits. Himalaya, W China.
Zone 7 US, 8 Can. 🏆

E. pungens (Thorny elaeagnus) A large, vigorous, spreading evergreen shrub reaching 16 ft (5 m) in height and excellent for creating shelter. The leaves are shiny dark green above and dull white, speckled with brown, beneath. Its fragrant flowers are borne in fall. The following forms are recommended. Japan. Introduced 1830.
Zone 6 US, 7 Can.

***E. p.* 'Dicksonii'** A rather slow-growing, medium-sized shrub. The upper sides of the leaves are green with a wide, irregular margin of golden yellow.
Zone 6 US, 7 Can.

Elaeagnus pungens 'Frederici'

***E. p.* 'Frederici'** A slow-growing medium-sized shrub with narrow leaves, mainly pale, creamy yellow with a narrow, bright green border. In cultivation 1888.
Zone 6 US, 7 Can.

***E. p.* 'Goldrim'** A large, striking shrub with glossy, deep green leaves edged in bright yellow. The margin is brighter than that of 'Variegata' and narrower than that of 'Dicksonii'. A sport of 'Maculata'.
Zone 6 US, 7 Can.

Elaeagnus pungens 'Goldrim'

Elaeagnus pungens 'Maculata'

***E. p.* 'Maculata'** The leaves of this large shrub have a central blotch of gold, creating a very bright effect. This is a handsome shrub of moderate growth, but it tends to revert.
Zone 6 US, 7 Can. 🏆

***E. p.* 'Variegata'** A large shrub on which the dark green leaves are brightened with a thin, creamy yellow margin.
Zone 6 US, 7 Can.

***E.* 'Quicksilver'** An outstanding large deciduous shrub or small tree with narrowish leaves that are exceptionally silvery, especially when young. Until fairly recently it was grown under the name *E. angustifolia* var. *caspica*. Caucasus.
Zone 3? US, 2b? Can. 🏆

Eleutherococcus *Araliaceae*

A genus of about 50 species of deciduous trees and shrubs, sometimes climbing, related to Fatsia *and* Aralia *and native to East and Southeast Asia. Until recently this genus was known as* Acanthopanax.

***E. sieboldianus* 'Variegatus'** A medium-sized shrub with numerous erect, canelike stems and clusters of large leaves parted into three or five leaflets and edged with creamy white, each cluster with a small curved thorn at its base. The small, greenish white, late-spring flowers form in umbels and are followed by clusters of black fruits. It tolerates poor soil but should be sheltered from cold winds.
Zone 4 US, 5 Can.

Elsholtzia *Labiatae*

A genus of about 30 species of aromatic herbs and deciduous subshrubs from Asia, Europe, and Ethiopia. The following species is valued for its late flowering.

E. stauntonii (Staunton elsholtzia) A small subshrub with rounded stems and lance-shaped leaves that are mint scented when crushed. Lilac-purple flowers are borne freely from late summer to midfall and provide a welcome splash of late color. The stems may be killed back to the ground by frost, especially at the limit of its range, but they usually regrow the following spring. It is easy to grow in any fertile soil in an open site in full sun. N China. Introduced 1909.
Zone 5 US, 6 Can.

Embothrium *Proteaceae*
Chilean firebush

A genus of eight species of evergreen trees or shrubs, native to the Andes of South America. Their preferred location is in a sheltered border or woodland clearing in a deep, moist but well-drained, acidic soil. They are particularly suitable for cool, moist, equable climates.

E. coccineum (Chilean firebush) This beautiful species, with its profusion of brilliant orange-scarlet flowers in late spring and early summer, is one of the most desirable garden specimens. The blooms are long, tubular, and borne in clusters. Usually it is an erect, slender, semiever-

Embothrium coccineum

green tall shrub or small tree, but it is capable of extremely rapid growth and a long life. It grows well in southern California and along the Pacific coast. Chile. Introduced 1846.
Zone 8 US, 9 Can.

Embothrium coccineum Lanceolatum group

***E. c.* Lanceolatum group** These forms are the least evergreen and by far the hardiest, with linear-lanceolate leaves rather than broad, paddle-shaped ones. The best is 'Norquinco', whose flower clusters touch one another so that each whole branch is covered in scarlet in late spring to early summer.
Zone 8 US, 9 Can. 🏆

Empetrum *Empetraceae*
Crowberry

A genus of about five species of dwarf, trailing, heathlike, evergreen shrubs that are natives of moors and mountains and other wild, windswept places in the Northern Hemisphere, southern Andes, and Falkland Islands.

Empetrum nigrum

E. nigrum (Black crowberry) A very widely distributed, procumbent shrub that forms wide-spreading, dense carpets. The purple-red flowers, borne in spring, are not very significant, but they are followed by glossy black fruits. Requires a moist, peaty, acidic soil. High northern latitudes of Europe, Asia, and America.
Zone 2 US, 2 Can.

Enkianthus *Ericaceae*

A genus of about 10 species of outstanding deciduous shrubs ranging in the wild from the Himalaya to Japan. They all require acidic soil and flower in late spring, producing clusters of drooping, cup- or urn-shaped, prettily veined blooms. Their fall foliage is almost unrivaled.

E. campanulatus (Redvein enkianthus) A species with erect branches, growing to 8–10 ft (2.5–3 m). It is a somewhat variable shrub with subtle qualities and is one of the easiest to grow. Flowers are cup shaped, sulphur yellow to pale bronze with reddish veins, and carried in great profusion for about three weeks. They last well when cut. Fall foliage varies from yellow to scarlet. Japan. Introduced 1880 by Charles Maries.
Zone 4 US, 5b Can. 🏆

Enkianthus campanulatus

***E. c.* Albiflorus group** The flowers of this group are creamy white.
Zone 4 US, 5b Can.

***E. c.* 'Red Bells'** A medium-sized shrub of compact, upright habit, with flowers richly streaked with red.
Zone 4 US, 5b Can.

Enkianthus cernuus f. *rubens*

E. cernuus* f. *rubens A very choice, small to medium-sized shrub noteworthy for its deep red, fringed flowers and brilliant, reddish purple fall color. Japan.
Zone 5 US, 6 Can. 🏆

Enkianthus chinensis

E. chinensis A beautiful small tree or tall, narrow shrub that reaches 20 ft (6 m) under favorable conditions. The flowers are yellow and red with darker veins and are borne in many-flowered umbels. The leaves are comparatively large, usually with red stalks, and are attractively tinted in fall. W China, Upper Burma. Introduced 1900.
Zone 7 US, 8 Can.

Enkianthus perulatus

E. perulatus A densely leaved, slow-growing, compact shrub up to 6½ ft (2 m) high. Masses of urn-shaped white flowers appear with the leaves in spring. It is one of the most consistent shrubs for the intensity of its scarlet leaves in fall. Japan. Introduced c. 1870.
Zone 5 US, 6 Can. 🏆

Epigaea *Ericaceae*

A genus of two creeping ground covers found in woodlands, generally in well-drained, acidic soils. They have alternate leaves and flowers in terminal racemes. Native to Japan and eastern North America.

E. repens (Trailing arbutus, Mayflower) A beautiful, small subshrub growing about 4 in (10 cm) high that makes a good addition to the woodland garden. The white to pink, bell-shaped flowers in spring are very fragrant. It is difficult to transplant and should always be purchased container-grown. Given the right conditions — shade and a sandy, acidic soil with plenty of humus — it will form a thick mat that smothers weeds. E North America.
Zone 3 US, 2 Can.

Ercilla *Phytolaccaceae*

This is a genus of two species of evergreen climbers that support themselves with aerial roots and are grown particularly for their neat, green leaves, which densely cover the stems. These plants will not tolerate frost but may be successfully grown on a wall in either sun or shade, and they also make an attractive ground cover in any ordinary well-drained soil.

E. volubilis This self-clinging, medium-sized climber has rounded, leathery leaves and bears dense spikes of small, purplish white flowers in spring. Plant it where it will be sheltered from cold winds. Chile. Introduced 1840.
Zone 9 US

ERICA

Ericaceae Heaths and heathers

Erica arborea 'Albert's Gold' is a vigorous treelike shrub with bright yellow foliage.

HEATHS AND HEATHERS comprise *Erica* and several other genera of related shrubs and small trees that have become very popular. Few other groups of plants are so large and varied or offer such a long succession of flowering. Indeed, gardeners can arrange their plantings so that there is a heath or heather blooming every week of the year, providing dainty bells of color from icy white to lilac to crimson. Even more important is their incredible variety of foliage, with which gardeners can create undulating carpets of gold, silver, gray, red, and an almost infinite range of greens, from burnished olive to bright lime.

While heaths and heathers are dramatic enough to stand alone, they mix well with conifers, although the design must be planned carefully so that the conifers complement, rather than overwhelm, the more delicate heaths and heathers. They are also good companions for small azaleas and brooms, rugosa roses, and Japanese maples — providing the scale is compatible — as well as for evergreen ground covers such as wintergreen and bearberry.

Heath and *heather* are neither scientific nor truly horticultural terms, but they are used somewhat loosely to refer to a number of genera. In general, the genus *Calluna* is called heather, while *Erica* is known as heath, as is *Daboecia* (Irish heath) and *Bruckenthalia* (spike heath). Originally, all these plants that grow wild on the heaths — tracts of land considered useless for agriculture — were called heathers, but gardeners have come to distinguish them with different names. They are also distinguished botanically in that *Erica* has needlelike foliage held away from the stems and flowers whose corolla (petals), not the calyx (sepals), bears the color; *Calluna* foliage is smaller, scalelike, and overlapping along the stems.

Erica is a genus of more than 500 evergreen species, from dwarf shrubs to small trees, native to Europe, Turkey, and Africa, with the largest number of species occurring in South Africa. While these last can be grown only in a very warm climate — they are popular in California — there are also heaths that tolerate extreme cold and will survive winters in the Northeast and Midwest.

Erica show a wide range of heights. At the upper end of the scale are the treelike heaths. They can be magnificent shrubs,

Erica carnea 'Aurea' with a purple-flowered heather

fully 16 ft (5 m) high and wide, and often grow to great age in the wild. In gardens they are imposing year-round features and ideal architectural accents among the ground-hugging heaths and heathers.

In the lower range are the true dwarf shrubs, under 12 in (30 cm) high, that form dense mounds of weed-suppressing ground cover; these are ideal specimens for the rock garden and also for lining paths. Not only is their foliage often extremely ornamental, but they bear flowers prolifically and generously over long periods.

Heath and heathers bloom throughout the year. In winter and early spring, cultivars of *E. carnea* provide drifts of bright flowers and are complemented by those of *E.* × *darleyensis*, which begins blooming in fall. At the same time comes the taller *E. erigena*, and, in mild climates, they may be joined by the magnificent treelike heath *E. lusitanica*. This early pageant is joined by the tree heath *E. arborea*, which also needs warm weather and which blooms until early summer.

In early summer *E. cinerea* and *E. tetralix* begin their display as well, to be joined later by *E. vagans* and a few other species; they all continue into fall. Irish heath adds its relatively large flowers and distinct appearance at the same time.

Calluna vulgaris and its many cultivars *(see p.175)* offer a succession of bloom from midsummer into late fall, just in time for the first flowers of *E.* × *darleyensis*. The heathers provide one of the great spectacles in cool-temperate gardens, and those who can offer these plants the right conditions will be rewarded with quite a show.

Care and cultivation

Heaths and heathers have a reputation as finicky, demanding plants and are sometimes avoided for that reason. While they do have particular cultural requirements, they are not, however, as difficult to grow as is often believed.

The majority of heaths and heathers need acidic, sandy, peaty soil that is poor — much like the moors they inhabit in the wild. The most important consideration is that the soil be moisture retentive but very well drained, because the fibrous roots of the plants never run very deep. Generous amounts of peat moss or well-rotted organic matter should be incorporated to achieve these conditions. In general, the plants are unsuccessful in shallow alkaline soils.

They perform best in full sun, as shade makes the plants more open and leggy. While the plants prefer cool, moist weather, they are relatively drought tolerant once established. The foliage is vulnerable to drying winds and needs protection in winter with a fence or hedge or a covering of evergreen boughs.

Heaths and heathers look spectacular in large drifts and should never be planted in dribs and drabs. This applies equally to just a few plants and to a great quantity. Proper spacing is important, so that the plants spread into mats, and depends on the mature sizes of the plants. In general, heaths and heathers should be spaced 18 in (45 cm) on center. With dwarf plants, such as the forms of *E. mackaiana*, 14 in (35 cm) is enough. Most *C. vulgaris* cultivars need to be spaced 36 in (90 cm) on center, with the exception of dwarf forms, which can be planted 18 in (45 cm) apart.

The plants require a little pampering until well established. They require watering the first few months, especially in hot weather, as the porous soil will dry out rapidly; they will also need moisture before the ground freezes. Until they form a continuous ground cover, the soil should be kept free of weeds. A good mulch of chopped oak leaves, pine needles, or shredded pine bark is recommended to suppress weeds, retain moisture, regulate soil temperature, and protect the shallow roots. The mulch will also provide nutrients as it decomposes, and the plants should not need any additional fertilizer. In fact, a rich soil will encourage lush growth susceptible to fungal disease and winter damage.

Calluna should be clipped back in early spring to below the previous year's flowers to keep them tidy. *Erica* need pruning less frequently, although pruning them after flowering helps them remain bushy. In either case, the plants should not be trimmed into neat mounds but should be allowed to retain their wild, "spiky" look. Old plants can be cut back hard, and new shoots will form from their bases.

E. arborea (Tree heath) The cultivars of this species are medium-sized to large shrubs with fragrant white flowers that are produced very profusely in early spring. The following forms are recommended. S Europe, Caucasus, N and E Africa. Introduced 1658.
Zone 8 US, 8 Can.

***E. a.* 'Albert's Gold'** A vigorous form with bright yellow foliage.
Zone 8 US, 8 Can. 🏆

E. a.* var. *alpina A hardier form that is shorter but more erect and has brighter green foliage. Mountains of Spain. Introduced 1899.
Zone 8 US, 8 Can. 🏆

***E. a.* 'Estrella Gold'** A slow-growing form with bright yellow young foliage. Portugal. Found wild 1972.
Zone 8 US, 8 Can. 🏆

E. australis (Spanish heath) A medium-sized shrub with fragrant rose-purple flowers from mid- to late spring. It is one of the showiest of the treelike heaths. Spain, Portugal. Introduced 1769.
Zone 8 US, 8 Can. 🏆

***E. a.* 'Mr. Robert'** A beautiful white-flowered form. Found 1912 in Spain.
Zone 8 US, 8 Can. 🏆

***E. a.* 'Riverslea'** A lovely cultivar with flowers of fuchsia-purple.
Zone 8 US, 8 Can. 🏆

E. canaliculata This beautiful treelike heath can reach a height of 6 ft (2 m) in the mildest regions, but elsewhere it is best grown in a greenhouse. The fragrant flowers are white or tinged with purple-pink and have protruding brown anthers; they appear from midwinter to early spring. S Africa. In cultivation c. 1802.
Zone 9 US

E. carnea (Spring heath, winter heath) One of the hardiest and most widely planted heaths in cultivation, forming dense hummocks and mats. The cultivars bear flowers in a wide selection of shades in the white-purple-pink range. They are all lime tolerant but are nevertheless not recommended for shallow soils. All are hardy to zone 4 US, 4b Can. and grow 6–9 in (15–23 cm) tall and 12–18 in (30–45 cm) wide. Flowering times are indicated as follows:
Early season: late fall to midwinter

Erica arborea

Erica australis 'Riverslea'

Erica arborea var. *alpina*

Erica australis

Erica canaliculata

Midseason: midwinter to early spring
Late season: midspring

E. c. 'Adrienne Duncan' A form with dark bronze-green foliage and carmine red flowers at midseason.

Erica carnea 'Ann Sparkes'

E. c. 'Ann Sparkes' A slow-growing, spreading form with golden foliage and rich purple flowers in late season.

E. c. 'Aurea' A form with bright gold foliage in spring and early summer. Deep pink flowers that pale almost to white are produced from mid- to late season.

E. c. 'Challenger' A form with dark green foliage and midseason magenta flowers with crimson sepals.

E. c. 'December Red' This form has deep green foliage and strong spikes of rose-red flowers from mid- to late season.

E. c. 'Eileen Porter' A low-growing form with rich carmine red flowers from midfall to midspring. The dark corollas and pale calyxes give a delightful effect. In cultivation 1934.

Erica carnea 'Eileen Porter'

E. c. 'Foxhollow' The yellowish green foliage of this form becomes rich yellow tinged with red in winter. Pale pink flowers appear in late season. In cultivation 1970.

Erica carnea 'Golden Starlet'

E. c. 'Golden Starlet' The foliage of this form is bright yellow in winter, becoming lime green in summer. White flowers appear in midseason.

E. c. 'Heathwood' A form with dark green foliage that turns bronze in winter. Bright rose-purple flowers appear in late season.

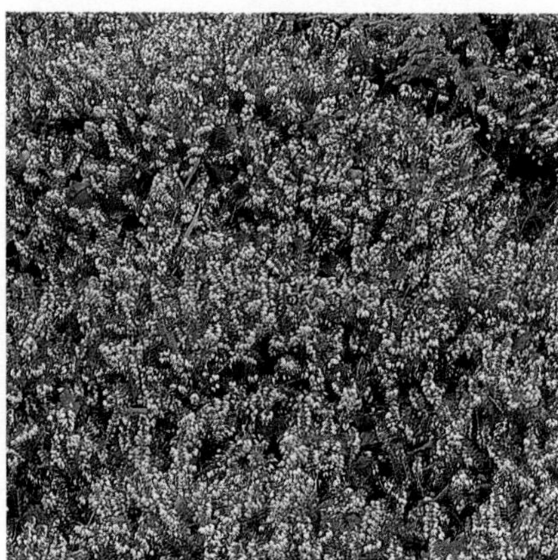

Erica carnea 'King George'

E. c. 'King George' There is very little difference between this plant and 'Winter Beauty'. In bud, however, the sepals are pale green and the corolla pale mauve. Flowering begins in early winter.

Erica carnea 'Loughrigg'

E. c. 'Loughrigg' A form with dark green foliage and rose-purple flowers appearing at midseason.

E. c. 'March Seedling' A spreading form with dark green foliage and rich red-purple flowers in late season.

Erica carnea 'Myretoun Ruby'

E. c. 'Myretoun Ruby' An excellent plant with deep green foliage and masses of deep rose-pink flowers in late season. Raised 1965 at Myretoun House, Scotland.

E. c. 'Pink Spangles' An improvement on 'Springwood Pink', with pink flowers profusely produced in midseason.

E. c. 'Praecox Rubra' A form with deep rose-red flowers in early to midseason.

Erica carnea 'Pink Spangles'

Erica carnea 'R. B. Cooke'

***E. c.* 'R. B. Cooke'** The clear pink flowers of this form are produced over a long period from mid- to late season.

***E. c.* 'Ruby Glow'** A form with large dark red flowers produced in late season and bronzed foliage.

***E. c.* 'Snow Queen'** In this form the large, pure white, midseason flowers are held well above the foliage. In cultivation 1934.

Erica carnea 'Snow Queen'

***E. c.* 'Springwood Pink'** This form has clear rose-pink, midseason flowers, plus a good habit and foliage, but has now been superseded by 'Pink Spangles'.

Erica carnea 'Springwood White'

***E. c.* 'Springwood White'** Still one of the finest white cultivars. Its strong, trailing growths are packed with long, urn-shaped flowers in midseason.

***E. c.* 'Sunshine Rambler'** A form with clear yellow foliage, becoming bronze-yellow in winter. Pink flowers appear in late season. In cultivation 1971.

Erica carnea 'Vivellii'

***E. c.* 'Vivellii'** A superb cultivar with deep, vivid carmine flowers in midseason. It develops bronze-red foliage in winter. In cultivation 1919.

Erica carnea 'Westwood Yellow'

***E. c.* 'Westwood Yellow'** A compact form with golden yellow foliage and deep pink flowers in late season.

***E. c.* 'Whitehall'** A compact, bushy form with bright green foliage and large, pure white flowers, profusely borne in midseason. Some experts believe it to be an improvement on 'Springwood White'.

***E. c.* 'Winter Beauty'** This cultivar has been confused with 'King George'. It has bright rose-pink flowers with the sepals and corolla tinged red in the bud. Flowering starts in early winter.

E. ciliaris (Fringed heath) A low, spreading species up to 18 in (45 cm) high. The flowers are comparatively large, rosy red, and borne in short, terminal clusters from midsummer to midautumn. The foliage is gray-green and slightly hairy. The following forms are recommended. SW Europe, including SW England.

Zone 5 US, 6 Can.

***E. c.* 'Corfe Castle'** This dwarf form has leaves that turn bronze in winter and salmon-pink flowers. 12 in (30 cm).

Zone 5 US, 6 Can.

***E. c.* 'David McClintock'** A dwarf form with gray foliage and white flowers that are tipped with mauve-pink. Found wild in Brittany. 16 in (40 cm).

Zone 5 US, 6 Can.

***E. c.* 'Mrs. C. H. Gill'** A dwarf cultivar with dark green foliage and freely produced, clear red flowers. 12 in (30 cm).

Zone 5 US, 6 Can.

***E. c.* 'Stoborough'** A dwarf form with long racemes of white flowers. Found in

Dorset, England. 20–24 in (50–60 cm). Zone 5 US, 6 Can.

E. cinerea (Twisted heath, Scotch heath) This common European species forms mats of wiry stems and produces its red-purple flowers from early summer to early fall. The green foliage turns orange-bronze in fall. The species and cultivars are hardy to zone 5 US, 6 Can. and unless otherwise stated grow to 10–12 in (25–30 cm) tall. The following are recommended. W Europe.

Erica cinerea 'Alba Minor'

***E. c.* 'Alba Minor'** A compact, white-flowered form. 6 in (15 cm).

Erica cinerea 'C. D. Eason'

***E. c.* 'C. D. Eason'** A form with glowing, deep pink flowers. In cultivation 1931.

***E. c.* 'Cevennes'** This cultivar produces lavender-rose flowers over a long period.

Erica cinerea 'C. G. Best'

***E. c.* 'C. G. Best'** A form with soft salmon-pink flowers. In cultivation 1931.

***E. c.* 'Cindy'** A cultivar with large, pure pink flowers and bronze-green foliage.

Erica cinerea 'Domino'

***E. c.* 'Domino'** A charming form with white flowers with ebony calyxes.

***E. c.* 'Eden Valley'** A cultivar with soft lilac-pink flowers that are paler at the base. 6 in (15 cm). In cultivation 1926.

***E. c.* 'Fiddler's Gold'** A compact, vigorous form with pale green foliage, flushed with yellow and red when young. The flowers are deep mauve.

***E. c.* 'Foxhollow Mahogany'** This form has dark green foliage and bears its deep wine red flowers profusely.

***E. c.* 'Golden Drop'** The summer foliage of this form is golden copper, turning to

Erica cinerea 'Golden Drop'

rusty red in winter. The pink flowers are rarely produced. 6 in (15 cm).

***E. c.* 'Golden Hue'** A most effective plant, with golden foliage turning red in winter. 20 in (50 cm).

***E. c.* 'Hookstone White'** A form with bright green foliage and large white flowers borne in long clusters. 14 in (35 cm).

***E. c.* 'Knap Hill Pink'** A vigorous form, producing long trusses of pure carmine-pink flowers.

***E. c.* 'My Love'** The striking, mauve-blue flowers of this cultivar contrast beautifully with the foliage.

***E. c.* 'Pentreath'** A delightful form with rich purple flowers.

Erica cinerea 'Pink Ice'

***E. c.* 'Pink Ice'** A compact, vigorous form with distinctively bright, deep green leaves, bronze in winter and when young. The

flowers are clear, pale pink.

Erica cinerea 'P. S. Patrick'

***E. c.* 'P. S. Patrick'** This form produces long sprays of bright purple flowers. In cultivation 1928.

Erica cinerea 'Purple Beauty'

***E. c.* 'Purple Beauty'** A form with deep rose-purple flowers and dark green foliage.
***E. c.* 'Sherry'** This form has glossy, green foliage and produces its clear, dark red flowers in abundance.
***E. c.* 'Stephen Davis'** A compact form with dark green foliage and vivid, deep pink flowers. 8 in (20 cm). 🏆
***E. c.* 'Velvet Night'** A form with flowers in an unusual shade of blackish purple.
🏆
***E. c.* 'Windlebrooke'** A vigorous cultivar with golden yellow foliage that turns orange-red in winter. The flowers are a pretty shade of mauve. 🏆

Erica cinerea 'Stephen Davis'

E. × darleyensis (Darley heath) A useful hybrid in its various forms and a natural companion for *E. carnea*. The following recommended cultivars average 20–24 in (50–60 cm) in height unless otherwise stated, and they flower from fall until spring. They are all hardy to zone 4 US, 5 Can. and are lime tolerant, but they are not recommended for shallow soils. See also 'Darley Dale' below.
***E. × d.* 'Ada S. Collins'** The white flowers of this form contrast well with the attractive, dark green foliage. 8 in (20 cm).
***E. × d.* 'Arthur Johnson'** This form produces long, dense sprays of magenta flowers, which are good for cutting.

***E. × d.* 'Darley Dale'** This form produces pale pink flowers over a long period and is one of the most popular of all heaths. Originally cataloged as *E. × darleyensis*, it is the original of the hybrid, which arose in the Darley Dale Nurseries, Derbyshire, England, c. 1890.
***E. × d.* 'Furzey'** A vigorous, compact form with dark green foliage. The flowers, borne over a long period, are deep rose-pink. Also known as 'Cherry Stevens'.

***E. × d.* 'George Rendall'** A superb form with rich pink flowers over a long period.
***E. × d.* 'Ghost Hills'** A sport of 'Darley Dale' with bright green foliage, tipped with cream in spring, and pink flowers with deeper pink tips.

***E. × d.* 'Jack H. Brummage'** The pale yellow foliage of this form turns gold with a red tinge in winter. The flowers are deep pink and borne in short spikes.
***E. × d.* 'Jenny Porter'** A vigorous, upright form with soft pink flowers.

***E. × d.* 'J. W. Porter'** A form with mauve-pink flowers and shoots that are reddish when young in spring.

***E. × d.* 'Kramer's Rote'** A cultivar with deep magenta flowers and bronze-green foliage. 14 in (35 cm).

***E. × d.* 'Margaret Porter'** This form has glossy green foliage, tipped with cream when young. The flowers are clear rose and borne in short, curving racemes.

Erica × darleyensis 'Silberschmelze'

***E. × d.* 'Silberschmelze'** Until recently, this was considered the best white form, but it has now been superseded by 'White Perfection'. Its sweetly scented flowers are produced over a long period.
***E. × d.* 'White Perfection'** A form with bright green foliage and white flowers.

E. erigena, syn. *E. mediterranea* This species is a dense, small to medium-sized shrub, covered from early to late spring with particularly fragrant, rose-red flowers. It and its cultivars are lime tolerant but are not recommended for shallow soils. The following are recommended. S France, Spain, W Ireland.
Zone 6 US, 7 Can.
***E. e.* 'Brian Proudley'** A vigorous,

upright form growing up to 3 ft (90 cm) tall, with bright green foliage and long racemes of white flowers.
Zone 6 US, 7 Can. 🏆

Erica erigena 'Brightness'

***E. e.* 'Brightness'** A form with bronze-red buds that open to rose-pink. 2–3 ft (60–90 cm). In cultivation 1925.
Zone 6 US, 7 Can.

Erica erigena 'Golden Lady'

***E. e.* 'Golden Lady'** A compact form with golden yellow foliage and white flowers. 12 in (30 cm).
Zone 6 US, 7 Can. 🏆

***E. e.* 'Irish Dusk'** A compact form with dark green foliage and salmon-pink flowers. 18 in (45 cm).
Zone 6 US, 7 Can. 🏆

***E. e.* 'Superba'** This is a fine pink-flowered form, growing to a height of $6\frac{1}{2}$ ft (2 m) or more.
Zone 6 US, 7 Can.

***E. e.* 'W. T. Rackliff'** A charming, dense, compact plant with dark green foliage and pure white flowers with prominent brown anthers. 3–4 ft (90–120 cm).
Zone 6 US, 7 Can. 🏆

Erica erigena 'Superba'

Erica erigena 'W. T. Rackliff'

Erica lusitanica

E. lusitanica (Spanish heath) A fine tree-like heath, resembling *E. arborea* but earlier flowering. The large, pale green, feathery stems are crowded with tubular, fragrant white flowers that are pink in bud and borne over a long period from late fall to early spring. Spain, Portugal.
Zone 7 US, 8 Can. 🏆

Erica lusitanica 'George Hunt'

***E. l.* 'George Hunt'** A form with golden yellow foliage.
Zone 7 US, 8 Can.

Erica mackaiana

E. mackaiana A rare, dwarf species, up to about 6 in (15 cm). Flowers are rose-crimson, in umbels, and appear from mid-summer to early fall. The following are recommended. N and W Ireland, Spain.
Zone 4 US, 5 Can.

***E. m.* 'Dr. Ronald Gray'** A form with white flowers.
Zone 4 US, 5 Can.

***E. m.* 'Maura'** An upright form growing to 10 in (25 cm). Gray-green foliage and profuse semidouble, purple flowers.
Zone 4 US, 5 Can. 🏆

***E. m.* 'Plena'** A form with double, rose-crimson flowers. Found in W Galway.
Zone 4 US, 5 Can.

***E. m.* 'Shining Light'** A form with a profusion of large, white, freely borne flowers and dark green foliage.
Zone 4 US, 5 Can.

***E. manipulifera* 'Heaven Scent'** A vigorous, small, upright shrub up to 3 ft (1 m) tall, with dark gray-green foliage. It has long sprays of fragrant, lilac-pink flowers over a long period from summer to fall. Needs acidic soil.
Zone 8 US, 9 Can.

E. mediterranea See *E. erigena*.

E.* × *stuartii A group of hybrids requiring lime-free soil. They flower over a very long period from late spring to early fall. The following are recommended.
Zone 4 US, 5 Can.

***E.* × *s.* 'Irish Lemon'** A form with bright pink flowers. The young foliage is lemon yellow in spring. 12 in (30 cm).
Zone 4 US, 5 Can.

Erica × *stuartii* 'Irish Orange'

***E.* × *s.* 'Irish Orange'** The flowers of this form are deep pink, and the young foliage is orange-tipped. 12 in (30 cm).
Zone 4 US, 5 Can.

E. terminalis (Corsican heath) A bushy, medium-sized shrub with erect branches. The rose-colored flowers, borne in late summer in terminal heads, fade to a warm brown and remain throughout the winter. It is excellent in limestone soils. W Mediterranean. Introduced 1765.
Zone 8 US, 8 Can.

E. tetralix (Cross-leaved heath) This hardy species grows 8–20 in (20–50 cm) tall and usually produces its rosy flowers in terminal clusters from early summer to midfall. It and its cultivars require a moist, peaty soil. The following are recommended. N and W Europe.
Zone 4 US, 5 Can.

Erica tetralix 'Alba Mollis'

***E. t.* 'Alba Mollis'** A form that reaches 12 in (30 cm) in height and has pretty gray foliage and white flowers.
Zone 4 US, 5 Can.

***E. t.* 'Con Underwood'** A form that makes mounds of gray-green foliage studded with crimson flower clusters. 8 in (20 cm). In cultivation 1938.
Zone 4 US, 5 Can.

Erica tetralix 'Hookstone Pink'

***E. t.* 'Hookstone Pink'** A vigorous form with silvery gray foliage and pale pink flowers. 12 in (30 cm). In cultivation 1953.
Zone 4 US, 5 Can.

***E. t.* 'L. E. Underwood'** A cultivar that forms 8 in (20 cm) high mounds of silver-gray foliage with pale pink flowers, strikingly terra-cotta in bud. In cultivation 1937.
Zone 4 US, 5 Can.

Erica tetralix 'Pink Star'

***E. t.* 'Pink Star'** An interesting and unusual form which produces lilac-pink flowers that are held erect in starlike patterns on the stems. The foliage is gray-green, and the plant is only 8 in (20 cm) high and spreading in habit. Found in the wild in Cornwall, England.
Zone 4 US, 5 Can.

E. vagans (Cornish heath) A vigorous, dwarf, spreading shrub with midgreen foliage and long sprays of pink or purple-pink flowers from midsummer to midfall. It and its cultivars are hardy to zone 4 US, 5 Can. The following are recommended. SW Europe, England, N Ireland; naturalized on Nantucket Island.

***E. v.* 'Birch Glow'** A form with bright green foliage and glowing rose-pink flowers.

Erica vagans 'Fiddlestone'

Grows to a height of 18 in (45 cm).
🏆

E. v. 'Cornish Cream' The creamy white flowers are borne in slender racemes. Found in Cornwall, England. 20 in (50 cm).
🏆

E. v. 'Diana Hornibrooke' A compact form with red flowers and dark green foliage. 12 in (30 cm).

E. v. 'Fiddlestone' A superb form that sends up long racemes of rose-cerise flowers over a long period. 20–24 in (50–60 cm). *(See photo on p.289.)* 🏆

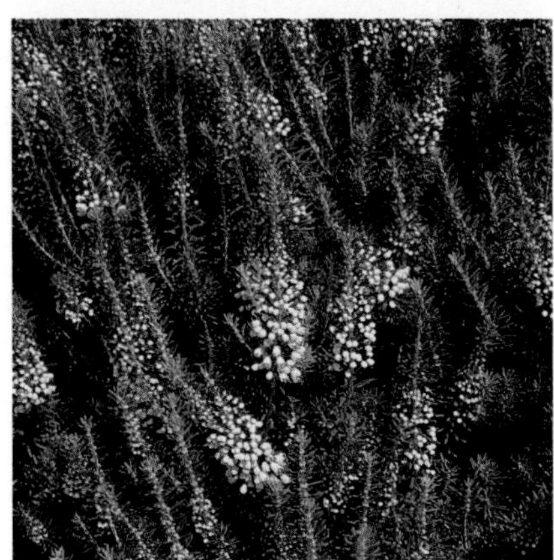

Erica vagans 'Holden Pink'

E. v. 'Holden Pink' A compact, mound-forming plant with dark green foliage. The flowers are white, flushed with mallow-purple at the tips. 14 in (35 cm).

E. v. 'Kevernensis Alba' A compact form with small racemes of white flowers. 12 in (30 cm).
🏆

E. v. 'Lyonesse' A form with pure white flowers with protruding brown anthers. 20–36 in (50–90 cm). In cultivation 1925.
🏆

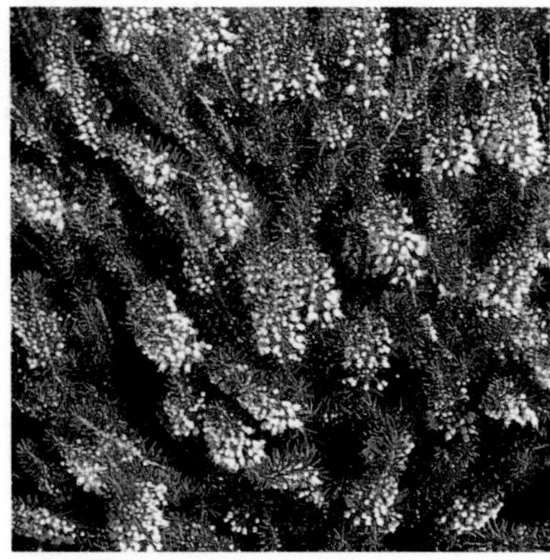

Erica vagans 'Lyonesse'

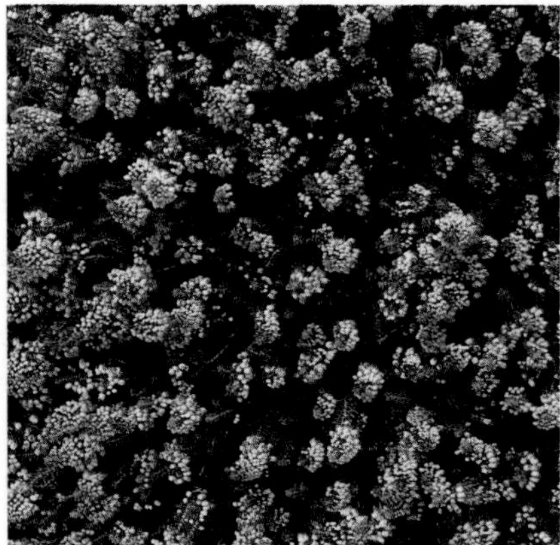

Erica vagans 'Mrs. D. F. Maxwell'

E. v. 'Mrs. D. F. Maxwell' A superb cultivar with deep cerise flowers. 20 in (50 cm).
🏆

E. v. 'Pyrenees Pink' This form bears long clusters of pink flowers. 20 in (50 cm).

E. v. 'St. Keverne' A form with clear, rose-pink flowers but unfortunately tends to revert to the usual wild form. Found in Cornwall, England. 20 in (50 cm).

Erica vagans 'Valerie Proudley'

E. v. 'Valerie Proudley' A dwarf bush 8 in (20 cm) high with bright yellow foliage and white flowers. It has won RHS awards for both summer and winter foliage.
🏆

E. × *veitchii* Tree heath hybrids reaching 7 ft (2.2 m) and requiring acidic soil. The following are recommended.
Zone 7 US, 8 Can.

E. × v. 'Exeter' A beautiful medium-sized shrub with attractive, bright green foliage and great plumes of fragrant white flowers in spring. Not recommended for the coldest areas. Raised before 1900 by Veitch in Exeter, England.
Zone 7 US, 8 Can.

E. × v. 'Gold Tips' The young foliage of this medium-sized shrub is bright yellow, becoming dark green.
Zone 7 US, 8 Can. 🏆

Erica × *watsonii* 'Dawn'

E. × *watsonii* 'Dawn' A spreading plant with young foliage that is yellow in spring and terminal clusters of large, rose-pink flowers from midsummer to mid- or even late fall. 9 in (23 cm). It requires a lime-free soil. Found 1923 in Dorset, England.
Zone 4 US, 5 Can. 🏆

E. × *williamsii* 'P. D. Williams' A pretty, late-flowering heath. The young growths are tipped with yellow in spring and turn bronze in winter. The rose-pink flowers are borne in umbels from midsummer to early fall, and the plant grows to 12–24 in (30–60 cm). It requires a lime-free soil. This is the original clone found 1910 in the wild in Cornwall, England.
Zone 4 US, 5 Can. 🏆

Erinacea *Leguminosae*

A genus of one species of deciduous shrubs related to Genista *and* Spartium.

E. anthyllis (Hedgehog broom, blue broom) A dwarf, slow-growing, spiny shrub that makes a very dense, rigid mound. It

Erinacea anthyllis

requires a well-drained location in full sun and a gritty soil. The flowers, borne from late spring to early summer, are slate blue. SW Europe, N Africa. Introduced 1759.
Zone 10 US 🏆

Eriobotrya *Rosaceae*
Loquat

A genus of about 27 species of evergreen trees and shrubs native to the Himalaya and East Asia. They will grow in any well-drained, friable soil. No pruning is required.

Eriobotrya japonica

E. japonica (Loquat, Japanese medlar) This is an architectural plant grown as a large shrub or a small tree; in cold climates it can be grown in a container. It is a striking evergreen thanks to its firm, leathery, corrugated leaves, which are up to 12 in (30 cm) long. The clusters of white, strongly fragrant, hawthornlike flowers open intermittently from late fall to midspring and are largely hidden by the foliage. The fruits are globular or pear-shaped, orange-yellow, and 1 1/2–2 in (4–5 cm) across. They are edible and usually begin to appear after 2–3 years. It requires good drainage but is otherwise not particular about soil. Introduced 1787.
Zone 8 US, 9? Can. 🏆

Erythrina *Leguminosae*
Coral tree

A genus of more than 100 species of mainly tropical deciduous trees and shrubs with trifoliate leaves and often prickly stems. They are natives of tropical and subtropical regions of the world and grow in any well-drained, friable soil.

Erythrina crista-galli

E. crista-galli (Cockspur coral tree) A beautiful, semiwoody plant whose leaves have three leaflets. The flowers resemble waxy, scarlet sweet peas and are borne in large, terminal clusters in late summer. It will survive outdoors only in the warmest regions; otherwise it can be used as a greenhouse plant and moved outside in summer. Brazil. Introduced 1771.
Zone 9 US 🏆

Escallonia *Grossulariaceae*

A genus of about 40 species of shrubs and small trees, mainly evergreen, all natives of South America and mostly from the Andes. They are valued among flowering evergreens, especially because they put on their display in summer, fall, and even early winter. They require a warm climate, although they are very tolerant of wind and salt spray; they are often used in coastal areas as hedges and windbreaks. They average 5–8 ft (1.5–2.5 m) in height but can grow even taller in mild, maritime areas. With rare exceptions, escallonias are not particular about soil, as long as it is well drained, and are drought resistant. None of them have large leaves or large flowers; reference to size below is merely comparative within the genus itself. Immediately after flowering, the old flowering growths should be cut back and large, unwieldy plants can be pruned hard at the same time.

Escallonia 'Apple Blossom'

***E.* 'Apple Blossom'** A very attractive, slow-growing, evergreen, small to medium-sized shrub with pink and white flowers.
Zone 7 US, 8 Can. 🏆

Escallonia 'C. F. Ball'

***E.* 'C. F. Ball'** A vigorous evergreen shrub up to 10 ft (3 m) tall, excellent for coastal sites. It has large leaves that are aromatic when bruised and crimson flowers. Raised

1912 at Glasnevin, Scotland.
Zone 7 US, 8 Can.

E. **'Donard Beauty'** A graceful evergreen shrub, to about 5 ft (1.5 m), with large leaves that are aromatic when bruised and rich rose-red, freely borne flowers.
Zone 7 US, 8 Can.

E. **'Donard Radiance'** A magnificent, vigorous but compact evergreen shrub of medium size. It has large, brilliant, soft rose-red, chalice-shaped flowers and large, shining, deep green leaves.
Zone 7 US, 8 Can. 🏆

Escallonia 'Donard Radiance'

E. **'Donard Seedling'** A vigorous evergreen hybrid up to 10 ft (3 m) tall. The flowers are flesh pink in bud and open white, and the leaves are large.
Zone 7 US, 8 Can.

E. **'Donard Star'** A medium-sized, compact, upright evergreen shrub with large leaves and lovely rose-pink, large flowers.
Zone 7 US, 8 Can.

E. **'Edinensis'** A neat, bushy evergreen shrub that grows to 6½–8 ft (2–2.5 m) tall, with small, bright green leaves. The flowers are carmine in bud, opening to clear shell pink. Raised before 1914 at the Royal Botanic Garden Edinburgh, Scotland.
Zone 7 US, 8 Can. 🏆

E. **'Gwendolyn Anley'** A small, robust, bushy evergreen shrub with small leaves and flesh pink flowers.
Zone 7 US, 8 Can.

Escallonia 'Donard Star'

Escallonia 'Iveyi'

E. **'Iveyi'** A large, vigorous, evergreen hybrid with large, handsome, glossy leaves that are aromatic when bruised, and large panicles of fragrant flowers that are pink in bud and open white in fall.
Zone 7 US, 8 Can. 🏆

E. **'Langleyensis'** A hardy, graceful, evergreen shrub, up to 8 ft (2.5 m) tall, with small leaves and rose-pink flowers that cover the arching branches.
Zone 7 US, 8 Can. 🏆

E. macrantha See *E. rubra* var. *macrantha*.

Escallonia 'Peach Blossom'

E. **'Peach Blossom'** An attractive, medium-sized evergreen shrub, similar in growing habit to 'Apple Blossom' but with flowers of clear peach-pink.
Zone 7 US, 8 Can. 🏆

E. **'Pride of Donard'** The flowers of this medium-sized evergreen shrub are large, brilliant rose, somewhat bell shaped, and carried in terminal clusters from early summer on. The leaves are large and have

Escallonia 'Pride of Donard'

polished, dark green upper surfaces.
Zone 7 US, 8 Can. 🏆

***E.* 'Red Dream'** A compact, small shrub with reddish young shoots and small, glossy, green leaves. The relatively large, clear pinkish red flowers open over a long period during summer. An excellent plant for a container or garden with limited space.
Zone 7 US, 8 Can.

***E.* 'Red Elf'** A vigorous, medium-sized, evergreen shrub with glossy, dark green leaves and freely borne, deep crimson flowers. In cultivation 1970.
Zone 7 US, 8 Can.

***E.* 'Red Hedge'** A vigorous, erect, medium-sized to large shrub with dark, glossy leaves and vivid crimson flowers.
Zone 7 US, 8 Can.

***E. rubra* 'Crimson Spire'** A vigorous evergreen shrub of erect growth up to 6½ ft (2 m) tall. The leaves are large and glistening dark green, and the flowers are bright crimson, appearing throughout the summer. An excellent hedge shrub.
Zone 7 US, 8 Can. 🏆

Escallonia rubra 'Woodside'

Escallonia × *virgata*

***E. r.* var. *macrantha*,** syn. *E. macrantha* A vigorous shrub up to 13 ft (4 m) tall, and one of the best hedge plants for withstanding coastal winds. It has rose-crimson flowers set among large, glossy, aromatic leaves. Chile. Introduced 1848.
Zone 7 US, 8 Can.

Escallonia rubra 'Slieve Donard'

***E. r.* 'Woodside'** A small, neat shrub, the product of a witches'-broom that occurred in Ireland. It is small enough for a large rock garden, although its branches spread over a considerable area. The flowers are small and crimson.
Zone 7 US, 8 Can.

***E.* 'Slieve Donard'** A medium-sized, compact, evergreen shrub with small leaves and large panicles of apple-blossom-pink flowers. Very hardy.
Zone 7 US, 8 Can.

***E.* × *stricta* 'Harold Comber'** A clone of a natural hybrid and one of the hardiest of the family. This is a dense shrub that grows up to 5 ft (1.5 m) tall. The slender stems become crowded with small leaves and small white flowers.
Zone 7 US, 8 Can.

E.* × *virgata A graceful, small-leaved, deciduous shrub with arching branches and white flowers. Not suitable for alkaline soils. Chile. Introduced 1866.
Zone 7 US, 8 Can.

EUCALYPTUS

Myrtaceae

EUCALYPTUS IS A GENUS of more than 400 species of fast-growing, evergreen trees that can reach enormous size and resemble no other plants seen in temperate gardens. The species are native to Australia and Tasmania and often have very wide distribution in the wild. By selecting seed from trees that live in the more southerly parts of their ranges and at the greatest altitudes, it has become possible to have a wider range of species for our gardens.

Eucalyptus are usually pest free, aromatic, and attractive to bees. They are also highly ornamental, with lush foliage, multi-stamened flowers, and attractive stems and trunks. The leaves of adult trees are usually narrow and somewhat lance shaped, and they hang edge-downward to minimize exposure to the hot sun of their native habitat. Juvenile leaves, by contrast, are typically rounded. Either type, when cut, provides wonderful foliage for flower arrangements. Eucalyptus flowers are often shaped like feathery puffballs and can be vividly colored in red and orange, while the bark may be mottled in gray, russet, or cream and peel in sheets.

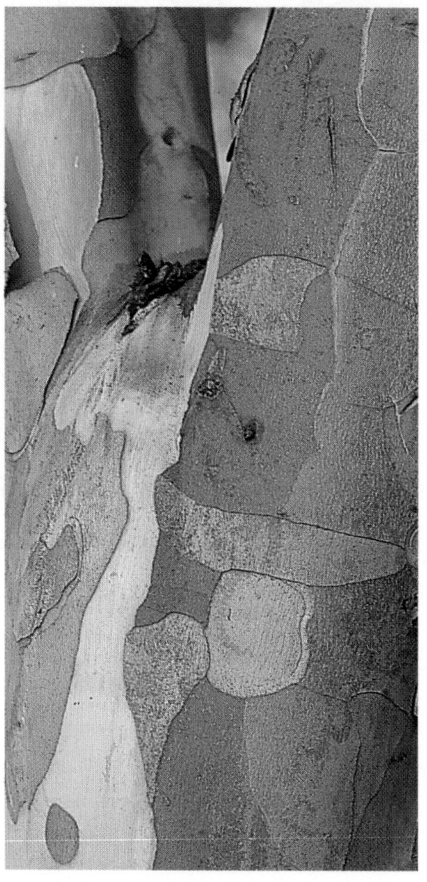

Eucalyptus parvifolia

CARE AND CULTIVATION

Eucalyptus will grow in a variety of soils and are generally tolerant of wet sites and drought. With the exception of *E. parvifolia,* most species tend to suffer from chlorosis (yellowing of the leaves, followed by death) in shallow, alkaline soil.

Because eucalyptus can grow to such great heights — some tower more than 300 ft (90 m) in their native environment and up to 200 ft (60 m) in California — careful siting is essential. They are best raised from small, pot-grown plants and not staked. They should be pruned for shape one year after being planted and annually thereafter in spring or late summer.

Cold, strong winds and frost can endanger eucalyptus, and they should be provided with shelter when necessary. Plants that appear dead after a severe cold spell should be left alone until at least the end of early summer, when new shoots may grow from any part of the tree, including from ground level. Shoots higher up will soon establish a new branch structure, and the dead wood can then be cut back; with ground-level shoots, the strongest one can be trained as a new main stem or several can be trained to create a bushy plant.

E. camaldulensis (Red gum) A large tree with a spreading, weeping habit and smooth, mottled tan bark. The twigs and young shoots are reddish. Australia.
Zone 8 US, 9 Can.

E. citriodora (Lemon-scented gum) A large, slender, fast-growing tree with smooth, bright white bark and lance-shaped, lemon-scented leaves. Queensland.
Zone 8 US, 9 Can.

Eucalyptus coccifera

E. coccifera (Tasmanian snow gum) A large tree with strikingly bloomy leaves and stems, not apparent in young plants. The bark peels to reveal a white trunk. Tasmania. Introduced 1840.
Zone 7 US, 8 Can. 🏆

E. dalrympleana (Mountain gum) A fast-growing, medium-sized to large tree with bark mottled white, gray, and pink. The gray-green leaves are bronze when young. New South Wales, Tasmania, Victoria.
Zone 7 US, 8 Can. 🏆

E. ficifolia (Red flowering gum) A medium-sized tree with very showy clusters of feathery red flowers up to 12 in (30 cm) long. Australia.
Zone 9 US

Eucalyptus dalrympleana

Eucalyptus pauciflora subsp. *niphophila*

E. globulus (Tasmanian blue gum) This species can grow to a large tree, up to 200 ft (60 m). The large leaves are almost silvery when young, turning blue-green with age. The trunk is bluish white. Tasmania, Victoria. In cultivation 1829.

Zone 8 US, 9 Can. 🏆

E. gunnii (Cider gum) The best-known species in cultivation and one of the hardiest. The juvenile leaves are rounded and silver-blue, becoming lance shaped with maturity. It can reach large tree size or remain as an attractive shrub if pruned regularly. Tasmania. In cultivation 1853.

Zone 7 US, 8 Can. 🏆

E. johnstonii (Yellow gum) A large, relatively hardy tree with reddish peeling bark and bright, glossy, apple green leaves. Tasmania. In cultivation 1886.

Zone 7 US, 8b Can.

E. leucoxylon (White ironbark) A medium-sized tree with bark mottled white and bluish gray that shreds in irregular sheets. Performs well in humid coastal sites. New South Wales, Victoria.

Zone 9 US

E. parvifolia A handsome, medium-

Eucalyptus gunnii

Eucalyptus johnstonii

Eucalyptus parvifolia

sized tree with attractively peeling bark. It tolerates alkaline soil. The mature leaves are small, narrow, and blue-green. New South Wales. *(See photo on p.294.)*
Zone 8 US, 9 Can. 🏆

E. pauciflora* subsp. *niphophila (Snow gum) This beautiful small tree of comparatively slow growth has large, leathery, gray-green leaves. The trunk is mottled green, gray, and cream and has been compared to the skin of a python. Queensland to S Australia and Tasmania. *(See photo on p.295.)* Zone 7 US, 8 Can. 🏆

E. perriniana (Spinning gum) A small tree that has silver leaves and white, dark-blotched stems. The juvenile leaves are round (perfoliate); the mature leaves are oblanceolate and bloomy. New South Wales, Tasmania, Victoria.
Zone 9 US

E. sideroxylon (Red ironbark) A medium-sized tree with a weeping habit and rough reddish to blackish brown bark. The narrow, blue-green leaves turn bronze in winter, and the flowers are clusters of dainty white, pink, or red puffs. New South Wales, Victoria.
Zone 9 US

Eucalyptus perriniana

Eucalyptus urnigera

Eucryphia cordifolia

E. urnigera (Urn gum) A small to medium-sized tree with grayish, peeling bark and dark green leaves. The distinctive fruits are urn shaped. In cultivation 1860.
Zone 8 US, 9? Can.

Eucommia *Eucommiaceae*

A genus of one deciduous species, which is quite hardy and thrives in all types of fertile soil.

E. ulmoides (Hardy rubber tree) The only hardy tree known to produce rubber. It is a vigorous and ornamental tree up to 60 ft (18 m), with rather large, leathery, glossy leaves, which, when torn, display fine strands of latex. Introduced 1896 from cultivation in China but not known in the wild.
Zone 4 US, 5b Can.

Eucryphia *Eucryphiaceae*

A genus of five species of highly ornamental evergreen and deciduous shrubs and trees that flower from midsummer to early fall once they are a few years old. They all have white flowers with conspicuous stamens. They thrive in sheltered locations and moist loam, preferably acidic, but they can be grown in slightly alkaline soil if large amounts of organic matter are added. The roots should be shaded from hot sun, and this can be done by underplanting with a shallow-rooted, noncompetitive ground cover such as Erica carnea. *Pruning is generally unnecessary.*

E. cordifolia A beautiful, large, evergreen shrub or, in favorable conditions, a broad columnar tree 30–40 ft (9–12 m) tall. Its leaves are oblong, wavy edged, and often heart shaped at the base. The flower is like a white rose-of-Sharon (*Hypericum calycinum*). This species is reasonably alkaline tolerant. Chile. Introduced 1851.
Zone 8 US, 9? Can.

Eucryphia glutinosa

E. glutinosa A good choice for southern gardens, this species is a deciduous large shrub or small tree (although evergreen in the wild) with erect branches. It has pinnate leaves and white flowers 2½ ft (6 m) across, borne profusely in mid- to late summer. The leaves have beautiful tints of orange and red in fall. Chile. Introduced 1859.
Zone 9 US 🏆

***E.* × *hillieri* 'Winton'** A medium-sized evergreen shrub bearing pinnate leaves with 3–7 leaflets and pretty, cup-shaped, white flowers like those of *E. lucida*. This interesting hybrid originated as a self-sown seedling at one of the Hillier Nurseries.
Zone 9 US

Eucryphia × intermedia 'Rostrevor'

***E.* × *intermedia* 'Rostrevor'** A lovely, fast-growing, small evergreen tree of compact, broadly columnar habit. On the same plant there will be simple leaves and others with three leaflets. The fragrant white flowers are each 1–2 in (2.5–5 cm) across and smother the branches in late summer and early fall. Raised at Rostrevor, County Down, Northern Ireland.
Zone 9 US 🏆

Eucryphia lucida

E. lucida (Leatherwood) A delightful, densely leaved, large evergreen shrub or small tree with simple, oblong leaves that are bloomy on the undersides. The charming, fragrant, pendulous flowers, up to 2 in (5 cm) across, appear in early to midsummer. Tasmania. Introduced 1820.
Zone 9 US

***E. l.* 'Pink Cloud'** The margins of the petals on this form are pale pink shading to white, and the petals are red at the base. Found as a single 65 ft (20 m) tree in a remote area of NW Tasmania.
Zone 9 US

E. milliganii A delightful, relatively slow-growing species that eventually forms a small, usually slender, shrubby deciduous tree. The tiny, neat leaves are shining dark green and bloomy beneath, and the buds are very sticky. The flowers are cup shaped and similar to those of *E. lucida* but somewhat smaller. This species flowers freely, even as a small shrub. Tasmania. Introduced 1929 by Harold Comber.
Zone 9 US

Eucryphia × nymansensis 'Nymansay'

***E.* × *nymansensis* 'Nymansay'** A magnificent, small to medium-sized, densely columnar evergreen tree of rapid growth, with both simple and compound leaves on the same plant. The flowers are fully 2½ in (6 cm) across, covering the branches in white in late summer and early fall. It tolerates alkalinity if large quantities of organic matter are present. Raised 1915 at Nymans, Sussex, England.
Zone 9 US 🏆

Euodia

E. daniellii See *Tetradium daniellii.*

Euonymus

Celastraceae

THE 170 SPECIES of evergreen and deciduous shrubs that make up the genus *Euonymus* are an extremely versatile group of plants and are widely distributed; they are found in North and Central America, Europe, Asia, Africa, and Australia. The genus encompasses dwarf shrubs, creepers, climbers, and small trees, which play a number of roles in the garden. Euonymus are used as ground cover, hedges, edging, screens, and specimens. The evergreens are all resistant to salt spray and wind and are therefore particularly valuable in coastal areas.

Among the deciduous species, some are grown for their attractive shape. Most, however, have won a place in the garden for their brilliant fall color and dangling, brightly colored fruits, which make every branch look as if it has been adorned with jewelry. The evergreen species are grown for their foliage, which is often variegated and contributes bright color to the landscape that is especially welcome in winter. Even in summer many euonymus stand out from the competition.

Euonymus bear their flowers in spring or early summer; the blooms are usually green or purplish and are not significant. The fruits emerge in midsummer and last until frost; unlike the flowers, they are very colorful and open to reveal equally showy seeds. Sometimes the fruit, seeds, and aril (a fleshy attachment to the seeds) will all be different colors, in red, pink, or orange.

The best way to ensure heavy fruiting for most euonymus is to plant more than one specimen, so there will be cross-pollination. *Euonymus alatus* is something of an exception, but even so it is better to grow them in a small group. With a single specimen, the fruits tend to ripen in twos instead of fours. With a group, however, there is a much better chance of all four fruits in each cluster being fertilized and eventually displaying their orange seeds against the vivid red color of the opened fruit.

Euonymus phellomanus has attractive pink fruits.

Care and cultivation

Euonymus are remarkably unfussy when it comes to soil. They will grow in poor locations and are tolerant of shallow, dry, alkaline soils, where the value of the deciduous species for fall color is exceptional. Euonymus will even succeed in dry shade, which is an environment that supports very few plants. *E. fortunei* and *E. japonicus*, especially their brightly variegated forms, should be among the first shrubs considered for such a site. They are also unusually tolerant of compacted soil and grow well near paths and other high-traffic areas. While euonymus can take shade, and are often used as tough ground cover under trees, where little else will grow, the deciduous species put on their best fall show in sun.

Euonymus generally do not need pruning. Cutting away any dead, diseased, or damaged branches is enough. Variegated evergreen shoots that have reverted to green should also be removed immediately.

Although this is a genus of plants that are on the whole easy to grow, it is vulnerable to various insect pests, including spider mites, thrips, and especially scale. There are several different scales that attack euonymus, but the worst is the euonymus scale. This can cause severe stunting and, in extreme cases, may even kill plants. The whitish males cluster on the leaves and new shoots, while the brown females, which look similar to oyster scale, are found on the more mature wood. Scales can prove fatal to varieties of *E. fortunei*, as well as *E. europaeus* and *E. hamiltonianus*.

E. alatus (Winged euonymus, burning bush) A many-branched, vase-shaped, medium-sized shrub, distinguished by the broad, corky wings that develop on the branchlets in favorable conditions. It is one of the finest and most reliable deciduous shrubs for fall color, with the leaves turning brilliant crimson-pink. The fruits are reddish purple, opening to reveal bright orange-coated seeds. China, Japan. Introduced 1860.
Zone 3 US, 3 Can. 🏆

***E. a.* 'Compactus'** A dense, small, compact, globe-shaped form that colors equally well; ideal for a low hedge. Raised before 1928 in Springfield, Mass.
Zone 3 US, 3 Can. 🏆

E. europaeus (European spindletree) A vigorous deciduous shrub with abundant brilliant red capsules that open to show vivid orange seeds; it grows especially well in alkaline soils. It is usually grown as one of its forms or cultivars. The wood was once used to make spindles. Europe, W Asia.
Zone 3 US, 4 Can.

E. e.* f. *albus A white-fruited form, showy in winter. At 10 ft (3 m), it is about half the height of the usual wild form.
Zone 3 US, 4 Can.

***E. e.* 'Red Cascade'** A selected form that eventually becomes a small tree with arching branches made pendulous by the weight of the rosy red fruits. The leaves turn rich scarlet in fall.
Zone 3 US, 4 Can. 🏆

E. fortunei (Winter creeper) A very hardy, trailing or climbing evergreen species good for shade or sun. It makes an excellent ground cover, and it will also climb without assistance. It seldom flowers or fruits and then only on adult stems. Many cultivars have arisen from *E. f.* var. *radicans.* The following forms are recommended.
Zone 4 US, 5 Can.

***E. f.* 'Canadale Gold'** This cultivar is a small shrub with green leaves broadly edged with deep yellow.
Zone 4 US, 4b Can.

***E. f.* 'Coloratus'** A trailing or climbing form reaching 26 ft (8 m) with support. Its leaves are beautifully colored a deep red-purple throughout the winter, especially when the roots are starved or controlled.

Euonymus alatus

Euonymus alatus 'Compactus'

Euonymus europaeus

Euonymus europaeus 'Red Cascade'

Euonymus fortunei 'Canadale Gold'

An interesting feature is that the leaves may resume their green color in spring.
Zone 4 US, 5 Can.

***E. f.* 'Dart's Blanket'** An improvement on 'Coloratus', selected in Holland, where it is widely planted as a ground cover. The leaves are deep green and turn bronze-red in autumn. In cultivation 1969.
Zone 4 US, 5 Can.

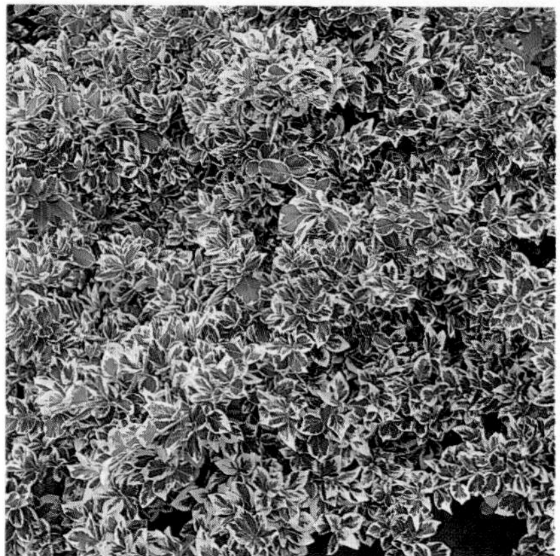

Euonymus fortunei 'Emerald Gaiety'

***E. f.* 'Emerald Gaiety'** A small, compact, bushy shrub that has deep green leaves with an irregular white margin that becomes attractively tinged with pink in winter. Raised in the United States.
Zone 4 US, 5 Can.

Euonymus fortunei 'Emerald 'n' Gold'

***E. f.* 'Emerald 'n' Gold'** A very striking, dense, dwarf bush with deep green leaves that are broadly margined in bright gold. The margin becomes cream flushed with pink in winter. This cultivar will also climb if it is provided with support. Raised before 1967 in the United States.
Zone 4 US, 5 Can.

***E. f.* 'Gold Tip'** A small, compact shrub of broadly upright habit whose leaves are edged in golden yellow.
Zone 4 US, 5 Can.

Euonymus fortunei 'Harlequin'

***E. f.* 'Harlequin'** A recently introduced dwarf shrub with leaves heavily mottled with white. Its value as a garden plant has not yet been proven.
Zone 4 US, 5 Can.

***E. f.* 'Kewensis'** A dainty form with slender, prostrate stems and minute, whitish-veined leaves no larger than $1/4$ in (6 mm) long. It is suitable for a rock garden and will climb if given support. Introduced 1893.
Zone 4 US, 5 Can.

Euonymus fortunei 'Kewensis'

***E. f.* 'Silver Pillar'** A shrub of erect habit with narrow leaves that have a broad marginal white variegation.
Zone 4 US, 5 Can.

Euonymus fortunei 'Silver Queen'

***E. f.* 'Silver Queen'** A small, compact shrub, although it can reach 8–10 ft (2.5–3 m) against a wall. The unfolding leaves in spring are rich creamy yellow, later becoming green with a broad, creamy white margin. It is one of the loveliest variegated shrubs and has the added bonus of occasionally producing pale green flowers that are followed by pink fruits. In cultivation 1914.
Zone 4 US, 5 Can.

Euonymus fortunei 'Sunspot'

***E. f.* 'Sunspot'** A compact shrub with deep green leaves with a central golden blotch, tinged red beneath in winter. The stems are yellowish. In cultivation 1980 in Canada.
Zone 4 US, 5 Can.

***E. f.* 'Variegatus'** This medium-sized trailing or climbing form has grayish green leaves edged in white and often tinged with pink. It has now been superseded by other selections.
Zone 4 US, 5 Can.

Euonymus grandiflorus

E. grandiflorus An erect, slow-growing semievergreen shrub reaching 13 ft (4 m) high. It bears conspicuous, comparatively large, straw yellow flowers and yellow capsules with scarlet seeds. The leaves turn a wine-purple color in fall. Himalaya, W China. Introduced 1824.

Zone 9 US

E. hamiltonianus A large semievergreen or deciduous shrub or small tree bearing pink fruits with orange or red seeds. This is a particularly variable species, the typical form of which is thought not to be in cultivation. The following forms are recommended. Himalaya.

Zone 4 US, 5 Can.

Euonymus hamiltonianus 'Coral Charm'

***E. h.* 'Coral Charm'** This large shrub or small tree of spreading habit has pale yellow leaves that are green in fall; the freely borne fruits are pale pink and the seeds have red arils. A Hillier selection.

Zone 4 US, 5b Can.

***E. h.* 'Coral Chief'** This cultivar is similar to 'Coral Charm' but upright, with pink fruits showing red arils. A Hillier selection.

Zone 4 US, 5b Can.

Euonymus hamiltonianus subsp. *sieboldianus*

E. h.* subsp. *sieboldianus This large shrub or small tree has dull green leaves that turn yellow, pink, or red in fall. The showy fruits are rose-pink and often abundantly borne. Japan, E China, Korea. Introduced 1865.

Zone 4 US, 5 Can.

E. japonicus (Japanese euonymus) A large, densely branched, evergreen shrub with glossy, dark green, leathery leaves. It is one of the best evergreens for coastal or urban planting and succeeds in sun or shade. China, Japan, Korea.

Zone 5 US, 6 Can.

***E. j.* 'Aureopictus'** See *E. j.* 'Aureus'.

***E. j.* 'Aureovariegatus'** See *E. j.* 'Ovatus Aureus'.

***E. j.* 'Aureus'**, syn. *E. j.* 'Aureopictus' A large shrub whose leaves have a gold center and broad green margin. It tends to revert.

Zone 5 US, 6 Can.

Euonymus japonicus 'Aureus'

Euonymus japonicus 'Duc d'Anjou'

***E. j.* 'Duc d'Anjou'** A large shrub with dark green leaves with a central blotch of pale or yellowish green.

Zone 5 US, 6 Can.

Euonymus japonicus 'Latifolius Albomarginatus'

***E. j.* 'Latifolius Albomarginatus'**, syn. *E. j.* 'Macrophyllus Albus' The leaves of this large shrub have an eye-catching broad white margin. One of the showiest of the variegated forms.

Zone 5 US, 6 Can.

***E. j.* 'Macrophyllus Albus'** See *E. j.* 'Latifolius Albomarginatus'.

***E. j.* 'Marieke'** With its creamy-yellow-margined foliage, this is similar to *E. j.* 'Ovatus Aureus' but has smaller leaves.

Zone 5 US, 6 Can. *(See photo on p.302.)*

***E. j.* 'Microphyllus Aureus'** See *E. j.* 'Microphyllus Pulchellus'.

Euonymus japonicus 'Marieke'

***E. j.* 'Microphyllus Pulchellus'**, syn. *E. j.* 'Microphyllus Aureus' A small, slow-growing form of dense, compact habit with small, narrow green leaves suffused with gold. It somewhat resembles boxwood *(Buxus)* in appearance.
Zone 5 US, 6 Can.

***E. j.* 'Microphyllus Variegatus'** A similar plant to the above with green leaves edged in white.
Zone 5 US, 6 Can.

Euonymus japonicus 'Ovatus Aureus'

***E. j.* 'Ovatus Aureus'**, syn. *E. j.* 'Aureo-variegatus' The leaves of this medium-sized shrub are margined and suffused with creamy yellow, particularly when young; growth is rather slow and compact. It requires a sunny site to retain its color but is one of the most popular golden euonymus.
Zone 5 US, 6 Can.

E. latifolius (Broadleaf euonymus) Growing to 11–16 ft (3.5–5 m) tall, this deciduous species has larger scarlet fruits and more

Euonymus latifolius

brilliant fall foliage than the European spindletree. It is similar to, and has been confused with, *E. planipes* but differs in the sharp-edged wings of the fruit. Europe. Introduced 1730.
Zone 6 US, 7 Can.

E. nanus A useful, procumbent, semievergreen shrub with narrow leaves and tiny, brown-purple flowers. Ideal as a ground cover and for slopes. Caucasus to China. Introduced 1830.
Zone 3 US, 2b Can.

E. n.* var. *turkestanicus A semierect variety, up to 3 ft (1 m), with longer leaves. It is the most common form in cultivation and has bright pink fruits with orange seeds. C Asia. In cultivation 1883.
Zone 3 US, 3 Can.

Euonymus oxyphyllus

E. oxyphyllus A slow-growing, medium-sized to large deciduous shrub with leaves that turn red and purple-red in the fall, when the branches are strung with carmine red capsules. Japan, Korea, China. Introduced 1892.
Zone 5 US, 6 Can.

E. phellomanus A large shrub with conspicuously corky-winged shoots, oval to obovate leaves, and four-lobed pink fruits.
Zone 5 US, 6 Can.

Euonymus planipes

E. planipes A large, handsome deciduous shrub, similar to *E. latifolius* and equally colorful in fall. The large and showy scarlet fruits are freely borne. NE Asia.
Zone 4 US, 5 Can.

Eupatorium *Compositae*

A genus of around 500 species of evergreen and deciduous trees, shrubs, and herbaceous perennials, widely distributed for the most part in tropical America.

Eupatorium ligustrinum

E. ligustrinum An evergreen shrub producing large, flat heads of small, white, fra-

grant flowers in late summer and fall. It can grow to 8 ft (2.5 m) and thrives in most soils but needs shelter from wind. No pruning is necessary.
Zone 10 US

Euphorbia *Euphorbiaceae*
Spurge

The spurges make up a very large genus of more than 1,500 species. There are many excellent herbaceous perennials and a large number of spiny, cactuslike succulents, sometimes growing to be large trees. Among these mainly subtropical and tropical plants are some hardy, evergreen subshrubs with flowers that, while not very showy individually, are highly effective in the typical euphorbia clusters. They grow in any ordinary garden soil and do not require pruning. Of those below, the first is the hardiest. They are harmful if eaten and are skin and eye irritants.

***E. amygdaloides* var. *robbiae*,** syn. *E. robbiae* A dwarf evergreen subshrub that spreads rapidly by underground stems. Its glossy, green leaves are arranged in dense rosettes at the stem tips. Eye-catching greenish yellow flower heads are borne in late winter and early spring. Turkey. Introduced early 1890s.
Zone 5 US, 6 Can. 🏆

Euphorbia characias

E. caput-medusae (Medusa's head) A dwarf spineless succulent with numerous snakelike branches that can form clumps up to 3 ft (1 m) wide. South Africa.
Zone 10 US

E. characias A small evergreen subshrub that displays erect, unbranched stems, each living for two years; the downy, bluish green, linear leaves are held in dense clusters at the ends of the shoots. The flowers are in terminal panicles with yellowish green bracts and reddish purple glands and are attractive for several months in spring and summer. Mediterranean region.
Zone 7 US, 8 Can. 🏆

Euphorbia characias subsp. *wulfenii*

Euphorbia characias 'John Tomlinson'

***E. c.* 'John Tomlinson'** The flowers of this form are borne in large heads, with long upper rays that make the inflorescence almost rounded. The bracts are yellow-green. Found 1966 in the wild in the former Yugoslavia.
Zone 7 US, 8 Can. 🏆

***E. c.* 'Lambrook Gold'** A form with columnar inflorescence and bright golden-green bracts.
Zone 7 US, 8 Can. 🏆

Euphorbia characias 'Lambrook Gold'

E. c.* subsp. *wulfenii This differs from the typical form in the yellowish green glands of the flower cluster.
Zone 7 US, 8 Can. 🏆

Euphorbia × *martinii*

E.* × *martinii *(E. amygdaloides × E. characias)* A clump-forming evergreen subshrub producing tufts of dark green leaves flushed purple when young. Green flowers, tinged purple, appear over a long period in spring.
Zone 5 US, 6 Can. 🏆

E. pulcherrima (Poinsettia) A slender, medium-sized, winter-flowering shrub most often grown in the greenhouse for Christmas decoration but also planted outdoors in warm climates. The stiff, upright branches bear coarse evergreen leaves and bright red bracts that surround the tiny yellow flowers. Many cultivars are available with bracts in white, pink, or various reds. Mexico, Central America.
Zone 9 US

E. robbiae See *E. amygdaloides* var. *robbiae.*

Euptelea *Eupteleaceae*

A genus of two or perhaps three species of deciduous large shrubs or small trees with petalless flowers made up of dense bunches of red-anthered stamens, borne in dense clusters all along the bare branches in spring. It does well in full sun in any reasonably moisture-retentive soil, and pruning is not necessary.

E. polyandra (Japanese euptelea) This is a large shrub or small tree that attracts attention in spring when it is crowded with flowers consisting of clusters of red anthers. The young growths are tinted copper, and the narrow, oval, long-stalked, coarsely and irregularly toothed leaves turn red and yellow in fall. Japan. In cultivation 1887.
Zone 6 US, 7 Can.

Euryops *Compositae*

A genus of about 100 species of evergreen shrubs with bright yellow, daisy flower heads. They are natives mainly of South Africa but extend north into Arabia. The following need a warm, sunny position and a well-drained soil.

Euryops acraeus

E. acraeus A dwarf shrub of neat, domed habit when well grown, forming a compact mound of gray stems and narrow, silver-gray leaves. The canary yellow flowers (strictly flower heads), 1 in (2.5 cm) across, cover the plant entirely during late spring and early summer. It is ideal for a rock garden or scree, but the drainage must be near perfect. It is subject to unaccountable failures and periodic attacks of rust, but these experiences should be balanced against those of the many growers for whom this is one of the best shrubs of its size. Drakensberg Mountains of South Africa.
Zone 9 US 🏆

E. chrysanthemoides A small, tender shrub with purplish stems and leaves deeply divided into oblong lobes that become linear toward the base. The solitary, yellow, daisy flower heads are deeper colored in the center and 2½ in (6 cm) across. They are borne on long, erect stalks from midsummer onward. South Africa.
Zone 10 US

Euryops pectinatus

E. pectinatus (Gray-leaved euryops) A small shrub, up to 3 ft (1 m), with erect, grayish, downy shoots. The leaves are 2–3 in (5–7.5 cm) long, deeply lobed like the teeth of a comb (pectinate), and gray-downy. The flower heads are yellow, 1½ in (4 cm) across, and carried on long, slender, erect stalks in late spring and early summer. If it is cut back by about 6 in (15 cm) after the main flush of flowers, it may flower again almost as freely and continue through the winter. It flowers best in fairly poor soil in full sun. It will survive and flower through frosty winters in mild areas and is good for the greenhouse. South Africa.
Zone 8 US, 9 Can. 🏆

Exochorda *Rosaceae*

There are four or five species of beautiful and showy deciduous shrubs in this genus. Their long, arching branches are festooned in late spring with impressive racemes of comparatively large, paper-white flowers. Preferring full sun, they grow in almost all garden soils but are inclined to become chlorotic in very shallow alkaline ones. Pruning, where necessary to reduce overcrowding and remove weak stems, can be done after flowering has finished.

Exochorda giraldii var. *wilsonii*

E. giraldii* var. *wilsonii (Wilson pearlbush) A large, free-flowering shrub with the largest flowers in the genus at 2 in (5 cm)

Exochorda × *macrantha* 'The Bride'

across. C China. Introduced 1907.
Zone 5 US, 6 Can.

Exochorda korolkowii

E. korolkowii A vigorous species exceeding 14½ ft (4.5 m) in height and one of the best for growing in alkaline soils. Turkestan. Introduced 1881.
Zone 5 US, 6 Can.

***E. × macrantha* 'The Bride'** This is a small to medium-sized, dense bush with an elegant weeping habit. It is highly attractive when the arching branches are covered with large white flowers in mid- or late spring. In cultivation 1938.
Zone 4 US, 5 Can. 🏆

Exochorda racemosa

E. racemosa (Common pearlbush) This is the best-known species. It is a large, rather spreading shrub with upright clusters of white flowers in late spring and oblong, deep blue-green leaves. It grows best in acidic soils. China. Introduced 1849.
Zone 4 US, 5 Can.

F

Fabiana *Solanaceae*

A genus of about 25 species of evergreen, heathlike shrubs, belonging to the potato family and most closely related to Cestrum *among hardy plants. For the most part they are natives of temperate regions of South America. Just one species is in general cultivation, and it performs best in a sunny location and in moist, well-drained, neutral or acidic soil. However, it is lime-tolerant enough that it can be grown in all but very shallow limestone soils. Prune leggy older plants for shape in spring.*

Fabiana imbricata

Fabiana imbricata f. violacea

F. imbricata The branches of this charming, medium-sized shrub are transformed in early summer with plumes of white, tubular flowers. Chile. Introduced 1838.
Zone 8 US, 9? Can.

***F. i.* 'Prostrata'** A small shrub, somewhat hardier than the typical form, making a dense, rounded mound of feathery branchlets that are usually covered with small, pale, mauve-tinted flowers in late spring and early summer. Ideal for large rock gardens or the top of walls.
Zone 8 US, 9 Can.

F. i.* f. *violacea A medium-sized shrub that is similar to the typical form but with lavender-mauve flowers.
Zone 8 US, 9? Can. 🏆

Fagus *Fagaceae*
Beech

There are only about 10 species of beeches, which are majestic, trouble-free, deciduous trees of the north temperate regions. They are best grown in a deep, well-drained soil and a sunny location.

F. grandiflora (American beech) This species will thrive in regions with hot summers. It forms an impressive tree that can reach 65 ft (20 m) in height with a similar spread. The bark is smooth, pale gray, and very attractive. E to C North America.
Zone 3 US, 4 Can.

Fagus sylvatica

F. sylvatica (European beech) This is undoubtedly one of the most graceful large specimen trees, forming a broad, round top. The lustrous, finely toothed leaves are delicately veined and turn golden copper in fall. It is ideal for hedges and tolerates extremes of acidity and alkalinity. There are many named cultivars. Europe.
Zone 4 US, 5b Can. 🏆

F. s. **'Albovariegata'** A large tree with leaves margined and streaked with white. In cultivation 1770.
Zone 5 US, 6 Can.

F. s. **'Aspleniifolia'** (Cut-leaf beech, fern-leaf beech) The leaves of this large tree are relatively narrow and deeply cut into slender lobes.

Fagus sylvatica 'Aspleniifolia'

Zone 4 US, 5 Can. 🏆

F. s. **'Atropunicea'** (Copper beech) A large, stately form with purplish or reddish bronze leaves. Also known as *F. s.* 'Cuprea'.
Zone 4 US, 5b Can.

F. s. **'Aurea Pendula'** An tall, slender form with branches hanging almost parallel to the main stem. The golden yellow leaves can scorch in full sun, but lose their color in deep shade. Originated 1900 as a sport.
Zone 4 US, 5b Can.

F. s. **'Dawyck'** (Dawyck beech) A stately, tall, columnar tree with erect branches that broadens in maturity. This species is sometimes incorrectly known by the name 'Fastigiata'. Originated before 1850 at Dawyck, Scotland.

Fagus sylvatica 'Dawyck'

Zone 5 US, 6 Can. 🏆

F. s. **'Dawyck Gold'** A dense, tall, columnar tree with bright yellow young foliage that turns pale green in summer. A seedling of 'Dawyck'. Raised 1969 by J. R. P. van Hoey-Smith.

Fagus sylvatica 'Dawyck Gold'

Zone 5 US, 6 Can. 🏆

F. s. **'Dawyck Purple'** A tall, splendid, narrowly columnar tree with deep purple foliage. It is narrower than 'Dawyck Gold' and not as dense.
Zone 5 US, 6 Can. 🏆

F. s. **Heterophylla group** The plant previously grown under this name is *F. s.* 'Aspleniifolia'.

F. s. **'Pendula'** (Weeping beech) A spectacular, large, weeping tree that takes on various forms. Sometimes the enormous branches hang close and perpendicular to the main stem like elephants' trunks, while in other specimens some primary branches are almost horizontal and draped with long, hanging branchlets. In cultivation 1836.

Fagus sylvatica 'Pendula'

Zone 5 US, 6 Can. 🏆

F. s. **'Purple Fountain'** A seedling of 'Purpurea Pendula', this is a large, narrowly upright tree with purple leaves and weeping

Fagus sylvatica 'Riversii'

branches. Raised 1975 in Holland.
Zone 4 US, 5b Can. 🏆

***F. s.* Purpurea group** This name refers to purplish-leaved forms normally selected from among plants raised from seed. They are best used for hedges.

***F. s.* 'Purpurea Pendula'** (Weeping purple beech) A superb, small, weeping tree with dark leaves. It is usually grafted high to make a small, mushroom-headed tree. In cultivation 1865.
Zone 5 US, 6 Can.

Fagus sylvatica 'Purpurea Pendula'

***F. s.* 'Purpurea Tricolor'** See *F. s.* 'Roseomarginata'.

***F. s.* 'Riversii'** A large tree with large, dark purple leaves. In cultivation 1880.
Zone 5 US, 6 Can. 🏆

***F. s.* 'Rohanii'** A beautiful, slow-growing, medium-sized to large tree that is a purple-leaved form of *F. s.* 'Aspleniifolia'. In cultivation 1894.
Zone 5 US, 6 Can.

Fagus sylvatica 'Rohanii'

***F. s.* 'Roseomarginata'** syn. *F. s.* 'Purpurea Tricolor' A large, attractive, but not very constant cultivar whose purple leaves are edged with an irregular pale pink border. In cultivation 1888.
Zone 5 US, 6 Can.

***F. s.* 'Rotundifolia'** (Round-leaf beech) A large tree with small, rounded leaves, up to 1 in (2.5 cm) in diameter, and horizontal branches that turn up at the ends. Originated about 1872.
Zone 5 US, 6 Can.

Fagus sylvatica 'Zlatia'

***F. s.* 'Zlatia'** (Golden beech) A slow-growing, medium-sized tree. The leaves are soft yellow at first, becoming green in late summer. Originally a wild form from the former Yugoslavia. In cultivation 1890.
Zone 5 US, 6 Can.

Fallopia *Polygonaceae*

A genus of nine species of herbaceous perennials and deciduous woody climbers, native to north temperate regions.

F. baldschuanica, syn. *Polygonum baldschuanicum* (Russian vine) A rampant climber with stems up to 40 ft (12 m) long and more or less heart-shaped, pale green leaves. The pinkish flowers are individually small but are borne in large, crowded panicles throughout summer and fall. It is not a plant for a small garden, as it is very fast growing and large, but it can be kept within bounds with severe pruning in late winter, after which new growth will arise from the old wood. It will grow in any soil. Tajikistan. In cultivation 1883.
Zone 4 US, 5b Can. 🏆

Fascicularia *Bromeliaceae*

A genus of about five species of stemless plants that form dense clumps of evergreen, strap-shaped, spiny leaves similar to many of the tropical bromeliads. They are all natives of Chile. They require a warm, sunny, sheltered location in a well-drained soil or rock fissure and are hardy only in the warmest climates.

Fascicularia bicolor

F. bicolor The leaves of this evergreen perennial are long, narrow, and spine toothed, sage green above and bloomy beneath. They are produced in dense, tufted rosettes. The shorter, central leaves are rich crimson, giving a delightful effect. The sky blue, tubular flowers are gathered into a dense, sessile head in the center of the rosette. While in bud, the flower head is concealed by showy, ivory-colored bracts. It is hardy only in the mildest climates and may need winter protection. It also makes a striking specimen for a container, which can be put outside in summer.
Zone 10 US

× Fatshedera *Araliaceae*

This splendid, shade-bearing evergreen plant is a hybrid between the two genera Fatsia *and* Hedera. *It is an excellent ground cover where it is hardy as long as it is sheltered from wind. It tolerates maritime exposure and pollution, grows in all types of soil, and does well even in dry shade. It is also popular as a houseplant.*

× *Fatshedera lizei* 'Variegata'

× ***F. lizei*** A small to medium-sized shrub of loose or sprawling habit, forming a mound of branches clothed with large, leathery, palmate leaves. Spherical heads of white flowers are borne in autumn. Garden origin 1910.
Zone 7 US, 7b Can. 🏆

× ***F. l.* 'Annemieke'** The leaves of this small to medium-sized shrub have a central blotch of bright yellow-green.
Zone 7 US, 8 Can. 🏆

× ***F. l.* 'Variegata'** A small to medium-sized shrub, the gray-green leaves of which have an irregular, creamy white margin.
Zone 7 US, 8 Can. 🏆

Fatsia *Araliaceae*

A genus of just one evergreen species. It thrives in any well-drained soil.

F. japonica (Japanese fatsia) A bold, handsome, medium-sized to large, dense shrub, tending to be wider than it is high. The very large, polished, dark green, palmate leaves produced on stout shoots give a subtropical effect and are an admirable foil to the panicles of milk white, globular flower heads that appear at the ends of the branches in midfall. It grows in sun or part shade and is suitable for coastal gardens. It is proving much hardier than had been believed. Japan. Introduced 1838.
Zone 7 US, 7b Can. 🏆

Fatsia japonica

Fatsia japonica 'Variegata'

***F. j.* 'Variegata'** A very attractive and eye-catching, medium-sized to large shrub. The lobed leaves are white at the tips.
Zone 7 US, 7b Can. 🏆

Feijoa *Myrtaceae*

A genus of two species of evergreen shrubs with opposite leaves and solitary flowers in the leaf joints. They are natives of South America and closely related to guavas.

Feijoa sellowiana

F. sellowiana (Pineapple guava) A large shrub, grown commercially for its fruit in warm countries and as an ornamental in temperate ones. It requires a warm and sheltered location and soil that is on the light side. Its leaves are gray-green, white-felted on the undersides, and the fleshily textured flowers are crimson and white, with a central bunch of long, crimson stamens. The large, egg-shaped fruits are sometimes produced after a long, hot summer. The petals and fruits are both edible and have a rich, aromatic flavor. Brazil, Uruguay. Introduced 1898.
Zone 8 US, 9? Can.

Feijoa sellowiana 'Variegata'

***F. s.* 'Variegata'** The leaves of this large shrub are edged with cream and white.
Zone 9 US

Ficus *Moraceae*
Fig

The fig genus is very large and includes more than 800 species of evergreen and deciduous trees, shrubs, and woody vines from all over the tropical and subtropical regions of the world. Only a few can be grown outside in cool-temperate gardens, but many are popular as greenhouse plants.

***F. carica* 'Brown Turkey'** The most popular fruit-producing form of the common fig, making a large deciduous shrub, or a small tree where the climate is mild. Its handsome, lobed leaves and delicious fruits provide interest year-round, especially when the plant is grown against a warm, sunny wall. It is remarkably resistant to salt

Ficus carica 'Brown Turkey'

spray. Skin irritant in sunlight. The species, from W Asia, has been in cultivation in Europe since the early 16th century.
Zone 5 US, 6b Can.

Ficus pumila

F. pumila (Creeping fig) In its native habitat, this species scrambles up the trunks of trees much as ivy does. The juvenile growths have small, neat, ovate or heart-shaped leaves, and in time growths are formed that produce much larger leaves, up to 4 in (10 cm) long, and bear flowers and fruits if conditions are suitable. It is a tender plant for the greenhouse, where it can cover walls or be used in hanging baskets. In the very mildest climates it can be grown out-of-doors in a sheltered location. Far East. Introduced 1721.
Zone 10 US 🏆

Fitzroya *Cupressaceae*

A genus of one evergreen coniferous species.

F. cupressoides (Patagonian cypress) A graceful, cypresslike, large shrub or small dense tree shaped like a vase with scalelike, white-lined, dark green leaves on drooping branchlets. Chile, Argentina. Introduced 1849 by William Lobb.
Zone 6 US, 7 Can.

Forsythia *Oleaceae*

These very colorful, spring-flowering deciduous shrubs are easy to grow. There are seven species, six native to East Asia and one to southeast Europe. The star-shaped flowers that cover the branches are golden yellow in most cases. Any ordinary garden soil suits them. As soon as flowering is finished, thin out and cut back the old flowering shoots, making sure to cut back to within a short distance of the old wood.

Forsythia 'Beatrix Farrand'

***F.* 'Arnold Dwarf'** A low, spreading plant that makes a good ground cover, inasmuch as the branches root where they touch the soil. It often does not flower until it is mature. Raised 1941 in the United States.
Zone 5 US, 6 Can.

***F.* 'Beatrix Farrand'** The nodding, deep canary yellow flowers of this dense, upright bush are exceptionally large — well over 1 in (2.5 cm) wide when fully expanded. It is named after the renowned American garden designer.
Zone 4 US, 5b Can.

F. × intermedia (Border forsythia) There are several named clones of this vigorous, medium-sized to large hybrid, which flower in late winter and spring.
Zone 5 US, 6 Can.

***F. × i.* 'Lynwood'** A lovely medium-sized to large shrub with large, broad-petaled, yellow flowers profusely borne all along the branches in midspring. This is one of the most spectacular forsythias, considered to

Forsythia × intermedia 'Lynwood'

be an improvement over *F. × i.* 'Spectabilis'. Introduced 1953 into the United States.
Zone 5 US, 6 Can. 🏆

***F. × i.* 'Spectabilis'** One of the most popular of the many shrubs that flower in early spring. The large blooms on this medium-sized to large, upright shrub are borne so generously that they create a mass of deep yellow that verges on being brassy. Garden origin 1906.
Zone 5 US, 6b Can.

Forsythia × intermedia 'Spectabilis'

***F. × i.* 'Spring Glory'** A floriferous medium-sized to large shrub that blooms in midspring. The flowers, up to 2 in (5 cm) in diameter, are light yellow without the greenish tinge found in some other for-

sythia. Found c. 1930 in a garden in Ohio.
Zone 5 US, 6 Can.

Forsythia × *intermedia* 'Spring Glory'

***F.* 'Meadowlark'** A selection from the University of North Dakota that has expanded the range where forsythia can be grown: the buds are hardy to −35°F (−37°C). The plant will grow up to 10 ft (3 m) tall.
Zone 3 US, 4 Can.

***F.* 'Northern Gold'** Another very hardy selection, developed by Agriculture Canada in Ottawa to extend the range where forsythia will bloom reliably — and not just below the snow line. It grows a little over 6½ ft (2 m) high.
Zone 3 US, 3b Can.

Forsythia ovata 'Tetragold'

***F.* 'Northern Sun'** This introduction from the Minnesota Landscape Arboretum grows over 10 ft (3 m) tall and will flower to the top in extremely low temperatures.
Zone 4 US, 4b Can.

***F. ovata* 'Ottawa'** This arose as a chance seedling in a row of *F. ovata* (Korean forsythia) at the Central Experimental Farm in Ottawa, Canada. It was chosen for its bud hardiness and has been widely used in breeding other hardy forsythias. Introduced c. 1970.
Zone 3 US, 3 Can.

***F. o.* 'Tetragold'** A small, dense shrub with amber-yellow flowers produced in late winter. In cultivation 1963.
Zone 4 US, 5 Can.

F. suspensa (Weeping forsythia) A shrub to about 10 ft (3 m) with slender, arching branches. The deep yellow flowers appear from early to midspring, and the leaves may have three lobes. It is good on north- and east-facing walls. China. Introduced 1833.
Zone 4 US, 5b Can. 🏆

Forsythia viridissima 'Bronxensis'

***F. viridissima* 'Bronxensis'** (Bronx greenstem forsythia) A compact, slow-growing shrub only about 12 in (30 cm) high with masses of tiny leaves and abundant bright yellow, slightly green-tinged flowers. Originated 1939 at the New York Botanical Garden.
Zone 4 US, 5b Can.

Fothergilla *Hamamelidaceae*

There are two species in this genus, both deciduous and native to the southeastern United States; they are related to Hamamelis. *They are especially outstanding in spring, when they bear fragrant, white, bottlebrush flower spikes, and in fall, when their foliage turns a beautiful spectrum of gold, orange, and red. They need an acidic, sandy loam that is well drained. No pruning is necessary.*

Fothergilla gardenii

F. gardenii (Dwarf fothergilla) A pretty, small shrub, usually less than 3 ft (1 m) high, notable for its erect spikes of clusters of white stamens in mid- to late spring and its crimson fall leaf color. 'Blue Mist' is a form with intensely blue-green leaves. North Carolina to S Alabama. Introduced 1765.
Zone 4 US, 5b Can.

Fothergilla major

F. major, syn. *F. monticola* (Large fothergilla) A slow-growing, medium-sized shrub with fragrant white flower clusters, up to 4 in (10 cm) long, borne before the leaves emerge. The leaves are bloomy beneath and change to yellow and scarlet in fall. Allegheny Mountains. Introduced 1780.
Zone 4 US, 5b Can. 🏆

F. monticola See *F. major.*

Franklinia *Theaceae*

A genus of one deciduous species. This is a lovely fall-flowering plant usually grown as a small tree in the South and as a shrub at the northern limits of its range. It needs full sun for best fall color but will tolerate part shade and acidic, fertile soil rich in organic matter; provide winter protection.

F. alatamaha A beautiful specimen with large, lustrous, oblong, green leaves that turn crimson in fall. The fragrant, frilly, white flowers with golden stamens resemble those of a camellia and spread open to 3 in (8 cm) wide. Georgia, USA; extinct in the wild since 1803. Introduced 1770 by the botanists John and William Bartram and named after Benjamin Franklin.
Zone 5 US, 6 Can.

Fraxinus *Oleaceae*
Ash

There are 65 deciduous species of ash — mainly hardy, fast-growing trees that thrive in almost any soil. They are tolerant of windswept and coastal sites and of industrial pollution. Their leaves are pinnate. Those of the section Ornus are attractive flowering trees.

Fraxinus americana 'Autumn Purple'

***F. americana* 'Autumn Purple'** A selection of the white ash that makes a broadly conical tree with dark green leaves that are reddish purple in fall. E North America.
Zone 3 US, 3b Can.

Fraxinus angustifolia 'Raywood'

***F. angustifolia* 'Raywood'**, syn. *F. oxycarpa* 'Raywood' A large, fast-growing, dense, fairly upright tree that is especially attractive in autumn, when its long, narrow, dark green leaves turn plum-purple. An excellent tree of relatively compact habit. In cultivation 1928.
Zone 5 US, 6 Can. 🏆

Fraxinus chinensis

F. chinensis (Section Ornus) (Chinese ash) A freely growing, medium-sized tree with attractive leaves that sometimes turn wine-purple in fall. The winter buds are conspicuously gray and the off-white flowers, borne in spring, are sweetly scented. China. Introduced 1891.
Zone 6 US, 7 Can.

Fraxinus excelsior

F. excelsior (European ash) A large, magnificent tree with black winter buds. Its shiny, dark green leaves do not change color in fall. Very adaptable and pest resistant. Europe, Caucasus.
Zone 4 US, 5 Can. 🏆

Fraxinus excelsior 'Jaspidea'

***F. e.* 'Jaspidea'** A large, vigorous clone with golden yellow young shoots and yellowish branches, making a fine show in winter. The leaves are clear yellow in fall. It is often mislabeled 'Aurea', which is a dwarf, slow-growing tree. In cultivation 1873.
Zone 4 US, 5 Can. 🏆

***F. e.* 'Pendula'** (Weeping ash) A large, vigorous tree, forming an attractive, wide-spreading, umbrella-shaped mound of divergent, weeping branches. *(See photo on p.312.)* Zone 4 US, 5 Can. 🏆

Fraxinus excelsior 'Pendula'

***F. e.* 'Westhof's Glorie'** A vigorous, medium-sized to large tree, narrowly upright when young and later developing a more spreading habit. The leaves are dark green and open late. Often used as a street tree because it does not set seed. In cultivation 1947.
Zone 4 US, 5 Can. 🏆

***F. nigra* 'Fallgold'** This form of black ash makes an upright tree that grows well in wet soils. It will reach about 33 ft (10 m) at maturity and is virtually seedless. The bright yellow fall color is long lasting. Introduced by Agriculture Canada in Morden, Manitoba.
Zone 3 US, 2b Can.

Fraxinus ornus

F. ornus (Section Ornus) (Manna ash) A pretty, round-topped tree of medium size with scented, off-white flowers abundantly borne in late spring. This is the type species of the section Ornus, popularly known as the flowering ashes. S Europe, SW Asia. Introduced before 1700.
Zone 5 US, 6 Can. 🏆

***F. oxycarpa* 'Raywood'** See *F. angustifolia* 'Raywood'.

***F. pennsylvanica* 'Summit'** A broadly conical form of the native green ash (also known as the red ash). It is a medium-sized, fast-growing tree with large, glossy leaves that turn golden yellow in fall. Selected in the United States.
Zone 3 US, 2b Can.

Fraxinus pennsylvanica 'Summit'

Fraxinus sieboldiana

***F. p.* 'Variegata'** A medium-sized tree with silver-gray leaves, brightly margined and mottled with creamy white.
Zone 3 US, 2b Can.

F. sieboldiana (Section Ornus) A medium-sized tree whose leaves have five or sometimes seven leaflets that often color beautifully in fall. The white flowers are borne in panicles at the ends of the branchlets in late spring. Japan, Korea. Introduced 1894.
Zone 6 US, 7 Can.

F. velutina (Velvet ash) A neat, pretty tree of 30–40 ft (9–12 m), remarkable for its leaves and shoots, which are densely covered in gray, velvety down. Winter buds are brown. A good street and shade tree. Arizona, New Mexico. Introduced 1891.
Zone 6 US, 7 Can.

Fremontodendron *Sterculiaceae*

A genus (formerly Fremontia*) of two species of tall, evergreen shrubs or small trees native to California, Arizona, and Mexico. The flowers have no petals but have large, colored calyxes. They require full sun and good drainage and grow well in alkaline soil. Too rich a soil may encourage growth at the expense of flowers. Pruning is unnecessary. Skin and eye irritant.*

Fremontodendron 'California Glory'

***F.* 'California Glory'** A floriferous, vigorous, large shrub or small tree that is a hybrid between the two species that make up the genus. The yellow flowers are up to

2½ in (6 cm) across and are borne over a long period from summer to fall.
Zone 9 US 🏆

Fremontodendron californicum

F. californicum (Common flannel bush) A beautiful large shrub or small tree bearing yellow flowers throughout summer and fall. It is still widely grown but has been superseded by 'California Glory', which is even more spectacular and a little hardier. California, Arizona. Introduced 1851.
Zone 9 US

Fuchsia *Onagraceae*

There are about 100 species of Fuchsia, *including shrubs, small trees, and climbers. All deciduous, they are natives primarily of Central and South America, but there are outlying species in Tahiti and New Zealand. The flowers are usually pendulous and showy and have often been likened to earrings.*

The fuchsias listed here are those that have passed successfully through many winters at the Hillier Nurseries in the south of England. Although the tender forms, and even the hardiest, may be killed back to ground level by winter cold, they normally shoot up again rapidly in spring to flower freely throughout summer and fall. They are remarkably adaptable to sun or shade and grow in any well-drained soil.

The pruning of outdoor fuchsias depends on the climate. Where outdoor specimens are subject to frost damage, they can be pruned back to good wood in spring; a reduction of top growth by about one-third preserves their bushiness after mild winters. F. magellanica *and its forms and cultivars can be allowed to grow large and unconfined in mild areas, where they will flower from midspring until late fall, or they can be controlled by pruning and clipping, especially if used for hedges.*

***F.* 'Alice Hoffman'** A small shrub with small, purple-tinged leaves in dense clusters. The diminutive flowers have scarlet calyxes and white petals.
Zone 8 US, 8b Can.

***F.* 'Blue Gown'** A dwarf, free-flowering, compact shrub. The flowers are double, with a deep purple corolla and scarlet calyx.
Zone 8 US, 8b Can.

***F.* 'Chillerton Beauty'** A beautiful small shrub with medium-sized flowers. The calyx is white, flushed rose; the petals are a soft, clear violet.
Zone 8 US, 8b Can. 🏆

***F.* 'Corallina'** A strong, robust small shrub with large, deep green leaves and scarlet and violet flowers. Raised 1914.
Zone 8 US, 8b Can. 🏆

Fuchsia 'Corallina'

Fuchsia 'Garden News'

***F.* 'Garden News'** A vigorous, hardy, upright small shrub with large double flowers; the calyx and tube are pale pink, the corolla magenta-rose. In cultivation 1978.
Zone 8 US, 8b Can.

Fuchsia 'Genii'

***F.* 'Genii'** A dwarf, upright shrub with red shoots and attractive, lime-yellow leaves, richer yellow in sun. The small flowers have a corolla that is violet and then reddish purple, and the calyx is cerise.
Zone 8 US, 8b Can.

***F.* 'Hawkshead'** A very hardy (for a fuchsia) small shrub with small leaves and an upright habit. The slender flowers have pure white petals, and the calyx is white tinged with green.
Zone 7 US, 8 Can.

Fuchsia 'Lady Thumb'

***F.* 'Lady Thumb'** A dwarf shrub. Semi-double flowers with light red calyx and red-veined white corolla. In cultivation 1966.
Zone 8 US, 8b Can. 🏆

Fuchsia 'Lena'

***F.* 'Lena'** The flowers of this small cultivar are semidouble, with pale pink calyxes and corollas of rosy magenta flushed with pink. This is a lax shrub but is a good fuchsia for training as a standard.
Zone 8 US, 8b Can. 🏆

***F.* 'Madame Cornelissen'** A small hybrid of *F. magellanica* bearing large flowers with red calyxes and white petals.
Zone 7 US, 8 Can. 🏆

Fuchsia 'Madame Cornelissen'

Fuchsia magellanica var. *gracilis*

F. magellanica (Magellan fuchsia) A graceful shrub of medium size, with long, slender flowers with scarlet calyxes and violet petals. The leaves are generally held in whorls of three. The following forms are recommended. South America.
Zone 6 US, 7 Can.

F. m.* var. *gracilis A slender, medium-sized shrub with a trailing habit and leaves generally held in pairs. The small, freely borne flowers are scarlet and violet.
Zone 6 US, 7 Can. 🏆

F. m.* var. *molinae The flowers of this medium-sized form are shorter and white, faintly blushed with mauve.
Zone 6 US, 7 Can.

***F. m.* 'Riccartonii'** See *F.* 'Riccartonii'.

***F. m.* 'Sharpitor'** A small form of var. *molinae* with gray-green leaves margined with white. In cultivation 1973.
Zone 6 US, 7 Can.

Fuchsia magellanica 'Thompsonii'

Fuchsia magellanica 'Variegata'

***F. m.* 'Thompsonii'** A small to medium-sized form with flowers smaller and more profusely borne than on the typical species.
Zone 6 US, 7 Can. 🏆

***F. m.* 'Variegata'** A striking medium-sized form with green leaves edged in creamy yellow flushed pink, against which the small scarlet and purple flowers are most effective. It is less hardy, however, than the green form.
Zone 7 US, 8 Can. 🏆

Fuchsia magellanica 'Versicolor'

***F. m.* 'Versicolor'** A small, spreading shrub with slender stems sporting strikingly gray-green leaves that are rose-flushed when young and irregularly variegated with cream and white when mature. A lovely foliage shrub.
Zone 6 US, 7 Can. 🏆

***F.* 'Margaret'** A vigorous small shrub with an abundance of crimson and violet-purple semidouble flowers.
Zone 8 US, 8b Can.

Fuchsia 'Mrs. Popple'

***F.* 'Margaret Brown'** A dwarf, erect, compact plant with attractive large flowers; the calyxes are rich crimson and the petals magenta.
Zone 8 US, 8b Can.

***F.* 'Mrs. Popple'** A small, large-flowered hybrid with spreading, scarlet sepals, violet petals, and long, protruding stamens and style.
Zone 8 US, 8b Can. 🏆

***F.* 'Mrs. W. P. Wood'** The single flowers of this small shrub are very freely borne; they have a pale pink calyx with slender, upturned petals, and a white corolla.
Zone 8 US, 8b Can. 🏆

Fuchsia 'Pixie'

***F.* 'Pixie'** An upright, bushy shrub, to about 3 ft (90 cm), with yellowish green foliage. The single flowers have a carmine tube and sepals and have a mauve-purple, carmine-veined corolla.
Zone 8 US, 8b Can.

F. procumbens (Trailing fuchsia) A trailing, small-leaved species with small, erect flowers. The calyx tube is yellow, the sepals violet and green, and the stamens red and blue; petals are absent. It has large magenta fruits. New Zealand. Introduced c. 1854.
Zone 6 US, 7 Can.

Fuchsia 'Prosperity'

Fuchsia 'Tennessee Waltz'

***F.* 'Prosperity'** A beautiful, small, upright shrub of vigorous growth. The large flowers are double and have a white corolla veined with pink and a deep rose-pink calyx. It is one of the more spectacular fuchsias.
Zone 8 US, 8b Can. 🏆

***F.* 'Riccartonii'**, syn. *F. magellanica* 'Riccartonii' This common, hardy shrub can attain 13 ft (4 m) and is often used as a hedge plant in mild areas. It has a deeper-colored calyx and broader sepals than *F. magellanica*.
Zone 6 US, 7 Can. 🏆

***F.* 'Snowcap'** A dwarf shrub with flowers 2 in (5 cm) long. The sepals and tube are red and the petals white, veined with red.
Zone 8 US, 8b Can.

***F.* 'Tennessee Waltz'** A low, elegantly arching shrub. The bold corolla is violet and the calyx deep glossy rose-scarlet. In cultivation 1950.
Zone 8 US, 8b Can.

Fuchsia 'Tom Thumb'

***F.* 'Tom Thumb'** The profusely borne flowers of this dwarf shrub have rose-scarlet calyxes and violet petals.
Zone 6 US, 7 Can. 🏆

G

Garrya *Garryaceae*

A genus of about 13 species of evergreen shrubs, native to Central and South America, with leathery leaves and long, slender, silky catkins. The male and female flowers are on separate plants. Garryas are excellent for growing in coastal sites and do well on north- or east-facing walls. They tolerate air pollution and thrive in all types of well-drained soil but need protection from cold winds. Prune only to remove dead wood.

Garrya elliptica

G. elliptica (Silk tassel) The male plant of this species is a magnificent evergreen large shrub or small tree, draped during the end of winter with long, grayish green catkins. The female plant is also effective, bearing long clusters of attractive deep purple-brown fruits in summer. California, Oregon. Introduced 1828 by David Douglas.
Zone 7 US, 8 Can.

***G. e.* 'James Roof'** A strong, vigorous male plant making a large shrub or small tree with large, leathery leaves and catkins as much as 8 in (20 cm) long.
Zone 7 US, 8 Can. 🏆

Garrya elliptica 'James Roof'

× Gaulnettya *Ericaceae*

The following are evergreen hybrids between the closely related Gaultheria shallon *and* Pernettya mucronata *and are of garden origin. Other hybrids between the two genera have occurred in the wild in New Zealand and the United States. According to some authorities,* Pernettya *is now merged into* Gaultheria, *and the following two plants should be* Gaultheria × wisleyensis *'Pink Pixie' and 'Wisley Pearl', respectively. They require an acidic soil, preferably amended with a large quantity of organic matter, and some shade. These plants are popular for their foliage, flowers, and fruits.*

× *Gaulnettya* 'Pink Pixie'

× *Gaulnettya* 'Wisley Pearl'

× *G.* 'Pink Pixie' A dwarf, suckering shrub, blooming in late spring with white flowers tinged with pink that are followed by purplish red fruits. Raised 1965 by the Hillier Nurseries' propagator Peter Dummer through backcrossing 'Wisley Pearl' with *Gaultheria shallon.*
Zone 6 US, 7 Can.

× *G.* 'Wisley Pearl' A small shrub with dull, dark green leaves. Branches become laden in fall and winter with short but crowded bunches of large, red fruits.
Zone 6 US, 7 Can.

Gaultheria *Ericaceae*

A genus of 150 evergreen species in all, thriving in moist, acidic, preferably peaty soil and a shady location. They occur mainly in the Andes but also in North America, eastern Asia, and Australasia. They are mostly tufted shrubs, spreading by underground stems. The white, bell-shaped flowers are generally borne in late spring or early summer and are followed by fleshy, colored fruits.

G. adenothrix A dainty, dwarf, creeping shrub, forming a low carpet of zigzag, red-brown, hairy stems with small, leathery, dark green leaves. The flowers are white, blushed pink, and are borne from late spring to midsummer. They are followed by crimson fruits. Japan. Introduced 1915.
Zone 9 US

Gaultheria cuneata

G. cuneata A dwarf, compact shrub with narrow leaves and white flowers from late spring to early summer. The white fruits have an antiseptic odor when crushed. A

delightful species. China. Introduced 1909 by Ernest Wilson.
Zone 6 US, 7 Can.

G. hispidula (Creeping pearlberry) A dwarf, prostrate, creeping shrub that is only 2–3 in (5–8 cm) high and is suitable as ground cover in naturalistic or bog gardens. The minute white flowers appear in late spring, followed by pearl white berries, 1/4 in (6 mm) across, in fall. North America.
Zone 3 US, 2b Can.

G. hookeri A dwarf, densely spreading shrub with bristly, arching stems. The leathery, glandular-toothed leaves are more or less elliptic and 2–3 in (5–7.5 cm) long. The white flowers are in dense clusters in the axils of the leaves and at the ends of the branches and are borne in late spring; the fruits are an exquisite shade of blue. Himalaya, W China. Introduced 1907 by Ernest Wilson.
Zone 6 US, 7 Can.

G. itoana A rare, creeping species, forming close mats of bright green, pernettya-like foliage. The flowers, borne from late spring to early summer, are white or pink and the fruits white. Taiwan. Introduced shortly before 1936.
Zone 6 US, 7 Can.

Gaultheria miqueliana

G. miqueliana (Miquel wintergreen) A neat, dwarf shrub, usually not over 1 ft (30 cm) high, with shining green, oblong leaves. The short racemes of white flowers are borne in early summer and are followed by white or pink, edible fruits. Japan. Introduced 1892.
Zone 6 US, 7 Can.

Gaultheria procumbens

G. procumbens (Wintergreen) A creeping shrub, making carpets of dark green leaves that turn purplish in fall, when the tiny, bright red, aromatic fruits emerge. The small flowers are white to pinkish. E North America. Introduced before 1762.
Zone 4 US, 4 Can.

G. pyroloides A dwarf, creeping shrub, forming mats of short stems and bright green, more or less rounded, net-veined (reticulate) leaves 1 in (2.5cm) long. The pinkish flowers are in short, leafy racemes from late spring until midsummer, and the fruits are blue-black. Himalaya. In cultivation 1933.
Zone 6 US, 7 Can.

G. shallon (Salal) A vigorous species, forming dense, ground-covering thickets up to 5½ ft (1.7 m) tall in favorable conditions. In poor soil and sun it creates a low, spreading mat. The leaves are broad and leathery, and the flowers, which bloom from late spring to early summer, are pinkish white. The dark purple fruits are borne in large clusters. W North America. Introduced 1826.
Zone 5 US, 6 Can.

Gaultheria shallon

G. tricophylla A charming, tufted shrublet with tiny leaves. The pink flowers are produced from late spring to early summer and are followed by large, pale blue fruits. Himalaya, W China. Introduced 1897.
Zone 8 US, 9 Can.

***G. × wisleyensis* 'Pink Pixie'** See × *Gaulnettya* 'Pink Pixie'.

***G. × w.* 'Wisley Pearl'** See × *Gaulnettya* 'Wisley Pearl'.

Gelsemium *Loganiaceae*

Carolina jessamine, yellow jessamine

A genus of two or three species of tender, evergreen, twining shrubs with attractive flowers. The following is useful for a trellis or as ground cover. It grows in any reasonably fertile soil.

G. sempervirens (Carolina jessamine, evening trumpet flower) A species with stems up to 20 ft (6 m) long, bearing glossy green leaves and fragrant, yellow, funnel-shaped flowers 1 in (2.5 cm) long in spring and early summer. S United States.
Zone 6 US, 7 Can.

Genista *Leguminosae*

Broom

For genus information see Cytisus, *p.260.*

G. aetnensis (Mount Etna broom) An ele-

Genista aetnensis

gant, deciduous, large shrub or small tree with slender, green, leafless shoots. The fragrant yellow flowers are borne in abundance in mid- to late summer. Sardinia, Sicily.
Zone 6 US, 7 Can. 🏆

G. delphinensis This tiny, decumbent deciduous shrub is one of the best species for the rock garden. It has deep yellow flowers in terminal or axillary clusters in mid- to late summer. It is like a miniature *G. sagittalis*. S France.
Zone 7 US, 8 Can. 🏆

Genista hispanica

G. hispanica (Spanish gorse) One of the best plants for sunny sites, dry slopes, and poor soils, this deciduous shrub makes dense, prickly mounds 2 ft (60 cm) tall that are covered in late spring and early summer with masses of yellow, pealike flowers. SW Europe. Introduced 1759.
Zone 7 US, 8 Can.

Genista lydia

G. lydia An outstanding deciduous dwarf shrub. Its elegantly slender, pendulous branches are smothered in a mass of golden flowers in late spring and early summer. E Balkans. Introduced 1926.
Zone 3 US, 3b Can. 🏆

Genista pilosa

G. pilosa (Silky-leaf broom) A deciduous dwarf shrub, up to 18 in (45 cm), producing cascades of golden yellow flowers in late spring. The flowers and leaves have silky hairs. The forms 'Lemon Spreader' and 'Vancouver Gold' are hardly different from the typical plant. W and C Europe.
Zone 4 US, 5 Can.

***G. p.* 'Goldilocks'** A vigorous selection with ascending branches, reaching up to 2 ft (60 cm) tall. It bears golden yellow flowers on short stalks profusely over a long period. In cultivation 1970.
Zone 4 US, 5 Can.

Genista sagittalis

G. sagittalis (Arrow broom) A deciduous, dwarf shrub with broadly winged, prostrate branches, giving an evergreen appearance. It has yellow flowers in early summer and is a good plant for dry walls. C and S Europe. In cultivation 1588.
Zone 4 US, 5 Can.

Genista tenera 'Golden Shower'

***G. tenera* 'Golden Shower'** A vigorous, large, arching, deciduous shrub with masses of brilliant yellow, fragrant flowers in early summer. Grows to a height of 10 ft (3 m). Long grown incorrectly as *G. cinerea*.
Zone 9? US 🏆

Genista tinctoria

***G. tinctoria* 'Plena'** A free-flowering, dwarf, semiprostrate deciduous form of the native European dyer's broom with double yellow flowers from early to midsummer. It is an ideal dwarf shrub for use in the rock garden.
Zone 3 US, 3 Can. 🏆

***G. t.* 'Royal Gold'** A small, free-flowering, deciduous shrub with stems that become thickly covered with rich yellow flowers

Genista tinctoria 'Royal Gold'

throughout the summer.
Zone 3 US, 3 Can. 🏆

Gingko *Ginkgoaceae*

A genus of one remarkable deciduous coniferous species. It is the sole survivor of an ancient family of plants whose ancestors were widespread about 160 million years ago. It is of great botanical and geological interest. After several decades, it bears fruits that consist of a nut inside an offensive-smelling pulp, but the beauty of the tree far outweighs this; and male trees are usually planted for this reason. It was once thought to have been extinct. The tree is held sacred by Buddhists and is often found planted near Buddhist temples.

Gingko biloba

G. biloba (Ginkgo, maidenhair tree) A medium-sized to large tree of conical habit when young. It is easily recognized by its peculiar, fan-shaped, undivided leaves that turn a beautiful clear yellow before dropping. It is magnificent either as a single specimen or in a group. A hardy tree, it is suitable for most soils and tolerant of air pollution. China. Introduced about 1727.
Zone 3 US, 3 Can. 🏆

***G. b.* 'Princeton Sentry'** A narrow columnar form introduced by Princeton Nurseries, New Jersey.
Zone 3 US, 3 Can.

***G. b.* 'Saratoga'** A fast-growing, medium-sized, broadly conical male tree with excellent yellow fall color.
Zone 3 US, 3 Can.

***G. b.* 'Variegata'** The leaves of this form are streaked creamy white. Slow growing and prone to reversion. In cultivation 1855.
Zone 4 US, 4 Can.

Gleditsia *Leguminosae*
Honey locust

A genus of about 12 species of deciduous, spiny trees, native mostly to North America and Asia, with one species in Argentina. Their foliage is extremely beautiful and the mature trunks often bear formidable thorns. They succeed in all types of well-drained soil and tolerate air pollution. No pruning is required.

Gleditsia triacanthos detail

G. triacanthos (Common honey locust) This elegant large tree with frondlike leaves is very tolerant of air pollution. The thornless var. *inermis* was the source of the cultivars listed below. C and E United States. Introduced 1700.
Zone 3 US, 4 Can.

Gleditsia triacanthos 'Elegantissima'

***G. t.* 'Elegantissima'** A slow-growing, dense, bushy shrub with fernlike foliage. It can grow to 11–14½ ft (3.5–4.5 m) tall.
Zone 3 US, 4 Can.

Gleditsia triacanthos detail

***G. t.* 'Ruby Lace'** A medium-sized tree selected in America for its deep bronze-red young foliage. In cultivation 1961.
Zone 3 US, 4 Can.

***G. t.* 'Shademaster'** A large, vigorous, thornless tree with ascending branches and dark green leaves that persist well into fall. In cultivation 1961.
Zone 3 US, 4 Can.

Gleditsia triacanthos 'Sunburst'

***G. t.* 'Sunburst'** A striking medium-sized tree with thornless stems and fernlike, bright yellow-green young leaves that contrast delightfully with the older, dark green foliage. In cultivation 1953.
Zone 3 US, 4 Can. 🏆

Grevillea *Proteaceae*

A genus of about 250 species of beautiful evergreen trees and shrubs, almost all of which are native to Australia or Tasmania. The flowers, which are a little like those of honeysuckle but smaller and with showy, protruding styles, are produced over a long period. Good drainage is essential, and shade and alkaline soil should be avoided; they are drought tolerant. Pruning is not required.

***G.* 'Canberra Gem'** A vigorous, rounded, medium-sized shrub that grows up to about 8 ft (2.5 m) tall and potentially as wide. It has aromatic foliage and clusters of waxy, bright pink flowers.
Zone 10 US

Grevillea juniperina 'Sulphurea'

***G. juniperina* 'Sulphurea'** A beautiful small to medium-sized shrub for mild areas. It has terminal clusters of bright yellow flowers in summer and bright green, needlelike leaves.
Zone 9 US 🏆

Grevillea rosmarinifolia

G. rosmarinifolia This is a lovely medium-sized shrub for mild areas, where it can grow as tall as 6 ft (1.8 m). The eye-catching crimson flowers are borne in long terminal clusters from spring to summer, and the needlelike leaves are dark green with silky hairs. SE Australia. Introduced c. 1822.
Zone 9 US 🏆

Grindelia *Compositae*

A genus of about 60 species of evergreen and deciduous subshrubs and herbaceous plants, natives of western North America and South America.

Grindelia chiloensis

G. chiloensis A handsome, small evergreen subshrub. It has hoary, narrow leaves, toothed at the margin, and large, cornflower-like yellow flowers borne singly on tall, stout stems from early summer to midautumn. It requires full sun and very well drained soil. Argentina. Introduced c. 1850.
Zone 9 US

Griselinia *Cornaceae*

A small genus of about six species of evergreen trees and shrubs that are natives of New Zealand, Chile, and southern Brazil.

G. littoralis This densely leafy large shrub,

Griselinia littoralis 'Dixon's Cream'

which is treelike in mild places, is an excellent hedge plant for coastal locations. The leaves are leathery and bright apple green, the flowers are insignificant, and the fruit is a berry. It succeeds in all types of fertile soil but is susceptible to frost damage. New Zealand. Introduced c. 1850.
Zone 9 US 🏆

***G. l.* 'Dixon's Cream'** A medium-sized shrub, one of several forms with leaves splashed and otherwise marked with creamy white. Others include 'Luscombe's Gold' and 'Bantry Bay', and similar sports have occurred in New Zealand. They are all prone to reversion.
Zone 9 US

***G. l.* 'Variegata'** A medium-sized shrub with conspicuous white-variegated foliage.
Zone 9 US

Gymnocladus *Leguminosae*

A genus of deciduous trees with a single species in North America and three in eastern Asia. They are related to Gleditsia *and have bipinnate leaves, inconspicuous flowers, and seeds in long, flat pods. They will grow in any well-drained soil.*

Gymnocladus dioica

G. dioica (Kentucky coffee tree) This medium-sized, slow-growing tree is one of the handsomest of all hardy trees. The young twigs are such a light gray that they are almost white and are especially noticeable in winter. The large, compound leaves are tinted pink when unfolding and turn a clear yellow before dropping. E and C United States. Introduced before 1748.
Zone 4 US, 5 Can.

H

Hakea *Proteaceae*

A remarkable genus of about 100 species of evergreen shrubs or small trees native to Australia and Tasmania. A few make excellent specimens for sunny, dry locations in warm climates. They are not good in alkaline soils.

Hakea lissosperma

H. lissosperma, syn. *H. sericea* A tall, erectly branched, columnar shrub, somewhat like a young Scotch pine. The rigid, gray-green, needlelike, sharply pointed leaves are 1–3 in (2.5–7.5 cm) long, narrowed at the base, and held more or less erect on the shoots. Showy white flowers are produced in clusters in the leaf axils from mid- to late spring. A specimen at the Hillier Gardens and Arboretum was 18 ft (5.5 m) high in 1990. SE Australia and Tasmania.
Zone 10 US

Halesia *Styracaceae*

Silverbell, snowdrop tree

A genus of five species of very beautiful deciduous shrubs or small trees, related to Styrax *and native to the southeastern United States, with one species in eastern China. The silvery white, bell-shaped flowers hang in clusters along the bare stems in late spring and resemble little drops of snow. The blooms are followed by small, green, winged fruits. They thrive in a moist but well-drained, acidic soil in sun or part shade; they are particularly suited to the edge of a woodland. Pruning is seldom necessary for species of* Halesia *but can be done after flowering.*

Halesia tetraptera

H. carolina See *H. tetraptera.*

H. diptera* var. *magniflora A large, wide-spreading shrub with broad leaves, two-winged fruits, and relatively large flowers. SE United States.
Zone 5 US, 6 Can.

H. monticola (Mountain silverbell) A small, spreading tree, larger than *H. tetraptera* and with larger flowers and fruits, the latter up to 2 in (5 cm) long. Mountains of SE United States. Introduced c. 1897.
Zone 5 US, 6 Can.

Halesia monticola

H. m.* var. *vestita A superb variety with even larger flowers, up to 1 in (3 cm) across, that are white but sometimes blushed with rose. The leaves are more or less downy beneath at first and then become smooth.
Zone 5 US, 6 Can. 🏆

H. tetraptera, syn. *H. carolina* (Carolina sil-

verbell) A large shrub, very beautiful in spring when the branches are covered with white, nodding, bell-shaped flowers in clusters of three or five. The fruits are pear shaped. SE United States. Introduced 1756.
Zone 4 US, 5b Can.

× Halimiocistus *Cistaceae*

These are pretty and interesting evergreen hybrids between Halimium *and* Cistus. *Given a location with full sun and good drainage, they can survive temperatures around freezing.*

× *Halimiocistus* 'Ingwersenii'

× ***H.*** **'Ingwersenii'** A freely growing, dwarf, spreading shrub with pure white flowers borne over a long period in summer and linear, dark green, hairy leaves. Portugal. Introduced 1929.
Zone 9 US

× *Halimiocistus sahucii*

× ***H. sahucii*** A dwarf, spreading shrub with linear leaves and pure white, cuplike flowers, borne from late spring to early fall. S France. Introduced 1929.
Zone 9 US 🏆

× ***H. wintonensis*** A beautiful dwarf shrub with gray leaves. The saucer-shaped flowers, borne from late spring to early summer, are 2 in (5 cm) across and are pearly white with a feathered and penciled zone of crimson-maroon, contrasting with yellow stains at the base of the petals. Originated 1910 at Hillier Nurseries, England.
Zone 9 US 🏆

× ***H. w.*** **'Merrist Wood Cream'** In this beautiful dwarf form the base color of the flowers is creamy yellow. A sport found 1978 at Merrist Wood Agricultural College, England.
Zone 9 US 🏆

Halimium *Cistaceae*

The seven evergreen species in this genus are from the Mediterranean region and western Asia. They are mostly low, spreading, evergreen shrubs, akin to Helianthemum. *They require full sun and good drainage and are subject to injury by severe frost. Pruning is not usually necessary.*

Halimium commutatum

H. commutatum A dwarf, semierect shrub with linear leaves and golden yellow flowers 1 in (2.5 cm) across, produced in early summer. Mediterranean region.
Zone 9 US

H. lasianthum A low, spreading shrub, ultimately growing up to 2–3 ft (60 cm–1 m) high, with grayish leaves and golden yellow flowers that have a dark blotch at the base of each petal and are borne in late spring.

Halimium lasianthum

S Portugal, S Spain. Introduced 1780.
Zone 9 US 🏆

H. ocymoides A charming, compact shrub, 2–3 ft (60 cm–1 m) tall, with small gray leaves and bright yellow flowers with blackish brown basal markings in summer. Portugal, Spain. In cultivation 1800.
Zone 9 US 🏆

H. o. **'Susan'** A more compact form with relatively broad leaves.
Zone 9 US 🏆

Halimodendron *Leguminosae*

A genus of one deciduous species, related to Caragana, *which will succeed in any well-drained soil and an open location.*

H. halodendron (Salt tree) An attractive, spiny, silvery-leaved shrub up to $5^1/_2$ ft (1.7 m). The leaves have 2–3 pairs of slender, gray-woolly leaflets and a terminal spine. In early to midsummer it bears masses of purplish pink pea flowers. It is an excellent plant for the seashore and for alkaline soil. Siberia, SE Russia, SW Asia. Introduced 1779.
Zone 4 US, 5 Can.

Hamamelis *Hamamelidaceae*
Witch hazel

The witch hazels are a distinct and beautiful genus of deciduous shrubs or small trees that flower mainly in the winter. There are five or six species in eastern North America and Asia. In most cases the spiderlike, yellow or reddish flowers appear on the leafless branches from early winter to early spring. The curious, strap-shaped petals withstand severe weather without injury, and the hazellike foliage often turns beautiful colors in fall. On the whole they prefer moisture-retentive, neutral or slightly acid soil, but they can grow on limestone as long as the soil is deep. Pruning is simply a matter of removing any dead wood.

H.* × *intermedia *(H. japonica* × *H. mollis)* These are large shrubs of variable nature, often with large leaves and occasionally strong-scented flowers, usually grown as one of the following cultivars.

Hamamelis × *intermedia* 'Advent'

***H.* × *i.* 'Advent'** A large shrub with ascending branches and medium-sized, fragrant, bright yellow flowers 3/4–1 in (2–3 cm) across. The petals are tinged with red at the base and the calyxes are purplish. Flowers are abundantly produced from the beginning of winter.
Zone 5 US, 6b Can.

Hamamelis × *intermedia* 'Arnold Promise'

***H.* × *i.* 'Arnold Promise'** A vigorous, large, wide-spreading bush with freely borne, medium-sized, bright yellow flowers. Raised 1928 at the Arnold Arboretum, Boston, Mass.
Zone 5 US, 6b Can. 🏆

Hamamelis × *intermedia* 'Barmstedt Gold'

***H.* × *i.* 'Barmstedt Gold'** A vigorous and upright large shrub with faintly scented, deep golden yellow flowers over 1 in (3 cm) across.
Zone 5 US, 6b Can.

Hamamelis × *intermedia* 'Carmine Red'

***H.* × *i.* 'Carmine Red'** A large, strong-growing shrub with a spreading habit. The large, almost round leaves are dark, shining green on their upper surfaces, turning yellow in fall. The flowers are over 1 in (3 cm) across, pale bronze, and suffused at their tips with copper, making them appear red. Raised at Hillier Nurseries.
Zone 5 US, 6b Can.

***H.* × *i.* 'Diane'** One of the best red-

Hamamelis × *intermedia* 'Diane'

flowered seedlings ever raised, and superior in this respect to 'Ruby Glow'. The flowers are of medium size. The large leaves turn a rich red in fall.
Zone 5 US, 6b Can. 🏆

***H.* × *i.* 'Hiltingbury'** A large, spreading shrub whose large leaves give a brilliant display of orange, scarlet, and red in fall. The flowers are medium to large, pale copper, and suffused with red. Raised at Hillier Nurseries, England.
Zone 5 US, 6b Can.

Hamamelis × *intermedia* 'Jelena'

***H.* × *i.* 'Jelena'** A superb large witch hazel of vigorous, spreading habit, with large, broad, softly hairy leaves that turn orange, red, and scarlet in fall. The flowers appear in dense clusters, are over 1 in (3 cm) across, and are yellow suffused with a rich coppery red, making them look orange.
Zone 5 US, 6b Can. 🏆

***H.* × *i.* 'Moonlight'** A large shrub with ascending branches. The flowers are

Hamamelis × *intermedia* 'Moonlight'

medium to large and have folded and crimped petals. They are pale sulphur yellow with a claret tinge at the base and give off a strong, sweet scent. It is as effective a shrub as *H. mollis* 'Pallida', but its narrower, paler, more crimped petals distinguish it. The fall color is yellow.
Zone 5 US, 6b Can.

Hamamelis × *intermedia* 'Orange Beauty'

Hamamelis × *intermedia* 'Primavera'

H. **×** ***i.*** **'Orange Beauty'** A large shrub of broad, spreading habit, bearing orange-yellow, early flowers over 1 in (3 cm) across.
Zone 5 US, 6b Can.

H. **×** ***i.*** **'Primavera'** A broadly upright, large shrub. It produces its medium-sized, bright yellow flowers with purplish red bases later than most other witch hazels.
Zone 5 US, 6b Can.

H. **×** ***i.*** **'Ruby Glow'** A vigorous, erect shrub with medium-sized, coppery red flowers and rich fall color.
Zone 5 US, 6b Can.

H. **×** ***i.*** **'Sunburst'** An upright shrub with yellow fall foliage. The pale yellow, faintly scented flowers are over 1 in (3 cm) across. In many ways this is an improvement over 'Moonlight', but unfortunately it is spoiled by poor foliage.
Zone 5 US, 6b Can.

Hamamelis × *intermedia* 'Vesna'

H. **×** ***i.*** **'Vesna'** A vigorous and upright large shrub with strongly fragrant, deep orange-yellow flowers well over 1 in (3 cm) across. The hanging petals are flushed red at the base and the calyx is deep red.
Zone 5 US, 6b Can.

H. **×** ***i.*** **'Westerstede'** A vigorous, upright large shrub with large, light yellow, faintly scented flowers over 1 in (3 cm) across.
Zone 5 US, 6b Can.

H. mollis (Chinese witch hazel) Perhaps the handsomest of all the witch hazels, and certainly the most popular. It is a large shrub with softly hairy, rounded leaves and clusters of sweetly fragrant, golden yellow, broad-petaled flowers over 1 in (3 cm) across from early winter to early spring.

Hamamelis mollis

The fall color is yellow. This species must be grown as a named, vegetatively propagated clone, otherwise you are likely to obtain a hybrid. Hillier Nurseries' clone is now called 'Jermyns Gold'. China. Introduced 1879 by Maries and early 20th century by Ernest Wilson.
Zone 4 US, 5b Can. 🏆

Hamamelis mollis 'Brevipetala'

H. m. **'Brevipetala'** A large, upright form with yellow color in fall and thick clusters of deep yellow, short-petaled flowers that appear orange from a distance. They have a heavy, sweet perfume. This form has poor foliage.
Zone 4 US, 5b Can.

H. m. **'Goldcrest'** A large shrub selected for its strongly and sweetly scented flowers of rich golden yellow, suffused with claret at their bases. The red blush is also on the backs of the rolled petals in the buds and creates a characteristic orange-cluster effect. The flowers are over 1 in (3 cm)

Hamamelis mollis 'Goldcrest'

across and generally appear later than in the other forms of the species. The fall foliage color is yellow.
Zone 5 US, 6 Can.

***H. m.* 'Pallida'** Deservedly one of the most popular witch hazels, this large shrub has sulphur yellow flowers over 1 in (3 cm) across held in densely crowded clusters

Hamamelis mollis 'Pallida'

Hamamelis vernalis 'Sandra'

along the bare stems. The scent, although strong and sweet, is nevertheless delicate. The fall foliage color is yellow.
Zone 5 US, 6 Can. 🏆

***H. vernalis* 'Sandra'** A form of the vernal witch hazel whose young, unfolding leaves are suffused with plum-purple, becoming green and purple-flushed on the undersides. In fall, the whole bush turns orange, scarlet, and red. The very small flowers are cadmium yellow. Originated 1962 at Hillier Nurseries.
Zone 4 US, 5b Can. 🏆

H. virginiana (Common witch hazel) This is the commercial source of the astringent witch hazel and is a large shrub, occasionally a broad-crowned small tree. Its main use is as an understock for witch hazels with larger, more ornamental flowers. E North America. Introduced 1736.
Zone 4 US, 4b Can.

Hebe *Scrophulariaceae*

A genus of 100 or more species of evergreen shrubs, or occasionally trees, formerly included in Veronica. *Most are natives of New Zealand, with a few from Australia and South America. Their flowering period is spring to fall, and they are invaluable for seashore gardens. Most of those that would not thrive inland can safely be planted in coastal areas, where temperatures are slightly warmer. In cold climates, they make good container plants for the greenhouse. They grow well in all types of well-drained soil. Many hebes benefit from a light clipping in spring, and leggy specimens can be cut back hard, although this should not be done to* H. salicifolia *or the whipcord hebes.*

Hebe albicans

H. albicans A splendid dwarf shrub that has a dense, rounded habit and produces bloomy foliage. The white flowers are borne in dense spikes during summer and are very ornamental. New Zealand. Introduced c. 1880.
Zone 9 US 🏆

Hebe 'Alicia Amherst'

***H.* 'Alicia Amherst'** A magnificent hybrid of *H. speciosa* with long racemes of deep purple-blue flowers in late summer. Raised 1911.
Zone 10 US 🏆

Hebe 'Amy'

***H.* 'Amy'** A small, rounded but upright, compact shrub with leaves tinted purple when young and holding the color for a long period before becoming glossy dark green. Clusters of violet-purple flowers are borne in summer.
Zone 9 US

***H. andersonii* 'Variegata'** A highly attractive medium-sized shrub with 4 in

(10 cm) leaves broadly margined and splashed with creamy white. Vigorous and fast-growing, it is well worth overwintering as cuttings where there is a danger of frost.
Zone 9 US

Hebe ochracea

H. armstrongii A dwarf "whipcord" species that is commonly grown under the name of *H. ochracea.*

Hebe 'Autumn Glory'

***H.* 'Autumn Glory'** A small shrub with a loose habit that has short, dense racemes of intensely violet flowers throughout late summer and autumn. The small round leaves are deep green and tinted purple. In cultivation 1900.
Zone 9 US

***H.* 'Baby Marie'** A very dainty shrub reaching only 12 × 18 in (30 × 45 cm) that makes an excellent ground cover. During mid- to late spring its fresh green foliage is almost completely hidden by masses of tiny white flowers. For best results, it should be planted in free-draining soil in a sunny site.
Zone 9 US

***H.* 'Blue Clouds'** A small shrub with glossy, dark green leaves, purplish in winter. Long spikes of wisteria blue flowers are borne over a long period in summer and fall. A seedling of 'Mrs. Winder'.
Zone 9 US 🏆

Hebe 'Bowles' Hybrid'

***H.* 'Bowles' Hybrid'** A charming, dwarf shrub that is suited to the rock garden. The flowers, both in spring and again in summer, crowd the short branches in a pretty display of mauve racemes.
Zone 9 US

Hebe brachysiphon

H. brachysiphon A popular shrub, growing to 5 ft (1.5 m) or more and producing white flowers profusely in early or midsummer. New Zealand. Introduced 1868.
Zone 7 US, 8 Can.

***H.* 'Caledonia'** A small, compact, and rounded shrub with red-tinted young leaves. Spikes of violet flowers are borne from spring to fall.
Zone 8 US, 9? Can.

***H.* 'Carl Teschner'** See *H.* 'Youngii'.

***H.* 'Carnea Variegata'** An attractive shrub to 4 ft (1.2 m) high. From late spring to late summer, it bears masses of long racemes of rose-pink flowers that fade to white. The leaves are gray-green, margined with creamy white. In cultivation 1945.
Zone 9 US

H. carnosula A dwarf to prostrate shrub with small, bloomy, shell-like leaves and white flowers in mid- to late summer. It is suitable for rock gardens and makes an excellent ground cover. New Zealand.
Zone 9 US

***H.* 'County Park'** A dwarf, spreading shrub suitable for ground cover. The leaves are gray-green, margined with red and flushed pink in winter. The violet flowers are borne in short racemes in summer.
Zone 9 US

***H.* 'Cranleighensis'** A small shrub with glossy leaves that are red-purple beneath when young. Long spikes of pink flowers are borne in summer.
Zone 9 US

Hebe cupressoides

H. cupressoides Usually a small shrub, but occasionally reaching as tall as 6½ ft (2 m), this species has a very distinctive appearance. The long, slender, green or gray branches are remarkably like those of a cypress *(Cupressus)*. The flowers are small, pale blue, and freely produced in early to midsummer. New Zealand.
Zone 8 US, 9 Can.

***H. c.* 'Boughton Dome'** A dense, dwarf, compact, rounded bush with white flowers.
Zone 8 US, 9? Can.

***H.* 'Emerald Green'**, syn. *H.* 'Green Globe' A bun-shaped, compact shrub, to 1 ft (30 cm) high, with upright green shoots and tiny, densely arranged, glossy leaves. Small white flowers are borne in summer. Found 1970 in the wild in New Zealand and possibly a hybrid.
Zone 9 US

Hebe × franciscana 'Blue Gem'

***H. ×franciscana* 'Blue Gem'** A small, compact, dome-shaped shrub with dense racemes of bright blue flowers. This commonly planted species is one of the hardiest hebes, excellent as a low hedge, and is highly resistant to salt spray. Raised 1868.
Zone 9 US

Hebe × franciscana 'Variegata'

***H. ×f.* 'Variegata'** An impressive small shrub with abundant leaves broadly edged with creamy white. It is sometimes seen in window boxes.
Zone 10 US

***H. glaucophylla* 'Variegata'** A small, neat shrub with slender, wiry shoots and white flowers in mid- to late summer. The leaves are grayish green, margined with creamy white.
Zone 9 US

***H.* 'Gloriosa'** A very attractive *H. speciosa* hybrid. It is a small, compact shrub with bright pink flowers in conspicuous, long racemes from midsummer onward.
Zone 10 US

Hebe 'Great Orme'

***H.* 'Great Orme'** A compact bush to 3 ft (1 m) high. The leaves are lance shaped and 2–3 in (5–7.5 cm) long, and the bright pink flowers are borne in long, tapering racemes from midsummer.
Zone 9 US

***H.* 'Green Globe'** See *H.* 'Emerald Green'.

***H.* 'Hagley Park'** A dwarf, upright shrub with glossy green, red-margined, bluntly toothed leaves. The rose-purple flowers are borne in large panicles in early summer. Raised in the Christchurch Botanic Gardens, New Zealand.
Zone 9 US

***H.* 'Highdownensis'** A small, spreading, tender shrub with glossy leaves and dark stems. Slender spikes of deep purple-blue flowers open in summer.
Zone 9 US

H. hulkeana Perhaps the most beautiful hebe species in cultivation. It is a small shrub of loose habit, occasionally reaching 5½ ft (1.7 m) tall. It has glossy, green, toothed, ovate leaves and large clusters of delicate lavender-blue flowers in late spring and early summer. Deadhead by pruning lightly after flowering. New Zealand. In cultivation c. 1860.
Zone 9 US

Hebe hulkeana

Hebe 'La Seduisante'

***H.* 'La Seduisante'** A very lovely hybrid of *H. speciosa.* It is a small shrub with large racemes of bright crimson flowers from midsummer onward and glossy, dark green leaves that are flushed with purple when they are young.
Zone 10 US

***H.* 'Lindsayi'** A hardy shrub that grows to about 3 ft (1 m) high and wide. The green leaves are rather rotund, and the pink flowers are held in short but showy racemes from early summer.
Zone 7 US, 8 Can.

H. lycopodioides A dwarf shrub with slender, erect, four-sided, yellow-green stems. The leaves are scalelike, each with a sharp,

hornlike point, and cover the branches densely. The white flowers are borne in midsummer. New Zealand.
Zone 7 US, 8 Can.

Hebe macrantha

H. macrantha A very valuable dwarf shrub, notable for its leathery, toothed leaves and pure white flowers, which are as much as 3/4 in (2 cm) across. Mountains of New Zealand.
Zone 8 US, 9? Can. 🏆

***H.* 'Margaret'** A compact, hardy shrub with bright green leaves. It bears an abundance of sky blue flowers on short spikes in late spring or early summer and tends to repeat several times in late summer and autumn. As the flowers age they fade to pale blue and then white, producing a bicolor effect.
Zone 6 US, 7 Can.

Hebe 'Marjorie'

***H.* 'Marjorie'** A moderately hardy hebe that forms a neat bush about 3 ft (1 m) tall with racemes 2–2 3/4 in (5–7 cm) long of light violet and white flowers from midsummer to early fall.
Zone 7 US, 8 Can.

***H.* 'Midsummer Beauty'** A handsome, small to medium-sized shrub whose leaves have reddish undersides. The flowers are in long, lavender racemes throughout summer. It is moderately hardy.
Zone 8 US, 9? Can. 🏆

Hebe 'Mrs. Winder'

***H.* 'Mrs. Winder'** A small to medium-sized, moderately hardy hybrid with purple foliage whose color becomes deeper in winter. The late-summer bright blue flowers also occur sometimes in winter.
Zone 7 US, 8 Can. 🏆

***H.* 'Nicola's Blush'** A dwarf shrub, flowering profusely over a long period from summer to fall. The pale pink flowers fade to white.
Zone 9 US

H. ochracea A dwarf, densely branched shrub with erect, glossy, whipcordlike stems of a characteristic ocher or mellow gold color. The white flowers appear in mid- to late summer. This plant is found under the name *H. armstrongii*, but that species has greener branches and sharply keeled and pointed leaves. New Zealand.
Zone 7 US, 8 Can.

Hebe ochracea 'James Stirling'

***H. o.* 'James Stirling'** A dwarf form with stouter branches and bright ocher-gold foliage. It lacks the grace of the typical form.
Zone 6 US, 7 Can. 🏆

***H.* 'Pewter Dome'** A low-growing shrub, making a dense, dome-shaped bush that is covered with gray-green leaves and short spikes of white flowers in early summer. A hybrid of *H. albicans*.
Zone 7 US, 8 Can. 🏆

Hebe pimeleoides 'Glauco-caerulea'

***H. pimeleoides* 'Glauco-caerulea'** A dwarf with small, glaucous blue leaves and violet-blue flowers in early to midsummer.
Zone 8 US, 9 Can.

Hebe pinguifolia 'Pagei'

***H. p.* 'Quicksilver'** A dwarf, spreading shrub with tiny, silvery blue leaves that contrast with the dark shoots and pale lilac flowers.
Zone 8 US, 9 Can. 🏆

***H. pinguifolia* 'Pagei'** This is a prostrate shrub with wide mats of small, bloomy gray leaves that remain attractive throughout the year. The short spikes of small, pure white flowers are borne freely in late spring. It makes an excellent ground-cover or rock-garden plant.
Zone 6 US, 7 Can. 🏆

Hebe pinguifolia 'Sutherlandii'

***H. p.* 'Sutherlandii'** This form differs from 'Pagei' in its much denser, more upright habit, making a compact, rounded, dwarf bush with gray-green foliage.
Zone 6 US, 7 Can.

***H.* 'Purple Pixie'** A dense bush reaching up to 20 in (50 cm) across and 28 in (70 cm) high. The dark green leaves are narrowly oval, 1 in (2.5 cm) long and ½ in (1 cm) wide. The flowers are similar in color to those of 'Autumn Glory' and are borne in racemes 1–2 in (3–5 cm) long from June to August and sometimes until frost. A chance seedling; the parent may be 'Great Orme'.
Zone 7 US, 8 Can.

***H.* 'Purple Queen'** This outstanding *H. speciosa* hybrid is a small shrub with large racemes of purple flowers in summer. There seems to be little difference between it and 'Amy'.
Zone 9 US

***H.* 'Purple Tips'**, syn. *H. speciosa* 'Tricolor' A small shrub that is a sport of 'La Seduisante'. Its leaves are rose-purple on the back when young and open to gray-green with deep green veins, broadly margined with creamy white and becoming rose-tinted in winter. Flowers are magenta-purple, fading to white, and are carried in long clusters. They are borne from late summer onward. In cultivation 1926.
Zone 9 US

Hebe rakaiensis

H. rakaiensis A dwarf shrub forming dense, compact mounds of crowded stems with small, neat, pale green leaves. The white flowers are borne in short racemes in early to midsummer. A splendid ground-cover plant in full sun. Sometimes found wrongly labeled in gardens as *H. subalpina.* New Zealand.
Zone 8 US, 9 Can. 🏆

H. recurva A small, slender-branched, open, rounded shrub up to 3 ft (1 m). The leaves are narrow, lance shaped, and bloomy on the upper sides, and the white flowers are borne in slender racemes in late summer. The clone in general cultivation is known as 'Aoira'. New Zealand. Introduced 1923.
Zone 8 US, 9 Can.

Hebe recurva 'Boughton Silver'

***H. r.* 'Boughton Silver'** A compact small shrub with silvery blue leaves.
Zone 9 US 🏆

Hebe 'Red Edge'

***H.* 'Red Edge'** A dwarf shrub with blue-gray leaves densely arranged and narrowly margined with red, particularly in winter. The flowers, borne in summer, are lilac, becoming white.
Zone 9 US 🏆

***H.* 'Rosie'** A dwarf shrub with profuse spikes of clear pink flowers with purple anthers, borne over a long period in summer and autumn. The best dwarf pink hebe.
Zone 6 US, 7 Can.

H. salicifolia A medium-sized shrub for coastal areas. The leaves are lance shaped and bright green, and the flowers, borne in long, slender racemes from early to late

Hebe 'Simon Delaux'

summer, are white or blushed with lilac. A parent of many hybrids. New Zealand, S Chile.
Zone 7 US, 8 Can.
***H.* 'Sapphire'** A small, upright shrub with slender, red-tinged leaves and long spikes of rose-purple flowers during summer and autumn.
Zone 7 US, 8 Can.

Hebe 'Spender's Seedling'

***H.* 'Simon Delaux'** A small, rounded shrub with rich crimson flowers in large racemes from late summer onward. One of the best of the *H. speciosa* hybrids.
Zone 9 US 🏆
***H. speciosa* 'Tricolor'** See *H.* 'Purple Tips'.
***H.* 'Spender's Seedling'** A small, very hardy, free-flowering shrub with fragrant white flowers produced over a long period during summer.
Zone 6 US, 7 Can. 🏆

Hebe topiaria

Hebe vernicosa

***H.* 'Spring Glory'** An attractive, small, spreading shrub bearing deep purple flowers in summer. It does best in full sun and well-drained soil.
Zone 6 US, 7 Can.
H. subalpina A small, dense, very hardy shrub with a rounded outline. It is similar to *H. rakaiensis* and often confused with it, but it is distinguished by having larger leaves and glabrous seed capsules. White flowers are borne in early to midsummer.
Zone 6 US, 7 Can.
H. topiaria A small shrub to 3 ft (1 m) with yellow-green leaves and short clusters of white flowers in summer. New Zealand.
Zone 7 US, 8 Can.
H. vernicosa A dwarf shrub with a spreading habit that has small, bright, glossy green leaves. The flowers are white but may be pale lilac at first and are borne in slender spikes up to 2 in (5 cm) long in late spring. New Zealand.
Zone 7 US, 8 Can.
***H.* 'Watson's Pink'** A small, tender shrub with slender leaves and spikes of bright pink flowers throughout summer.
Zone 8 US, 9? Can.
***H.* 'White Gem'** A dwarf, compact, hardy shrub rarely over 18 in (45 cm), producing a profusion of white flowers in early summer. It is a hybrid of *H. brachysiphon*, from which it differs in that it is smaller overall and has smaller, paler leaves; it also flowers earlier, on shorter racemes.
Zone 7 US, 8 Can.
***H.* 'Wingletye'** A prostrate shrub of compact habit, suitable for the rock garden. The leaves are small and glaucous. Ascending shoots bear racemes of deep mauve flowers in early summer.
Zone 6 US, 7 Can.
***H.* 'Youngii',** syn. *H.* 'Carl Teschner' A hardy, dwarf, compact shrub, prostrate at first but becoming more dome shaped, with small dark green leaves and abundantly produced short racemes of violet flowers with white throats in early to midsummer. A free-growing plant that works well as a ground cover.
Zone 6 US, 6b Can. 🏆

HEDERA

Araliaceae Ivy

Hedera hibernica

THE IVIES are a very widely grown group of evergreen, woody, creeping or climbing vines and are valued for their ability to quickly cover tree stumps, sheds, walls, chain-link fences, and large expanses of bare ground. They also provide a habitat for wildlife, and their deep roots help stabilize soil on slopes. Although the genus comprises only 11 species, there are many distinctive ivies from which gardeners can choose, offering a variety of leaf size, shape, and color.

Some ivies grow to great lengths — reaching up to 50 ft (15 m) — while others, such as *H. helix* 'Conglomerata', are compact enough for the rock garden. Some, such as *H. h.* 'Baltica' and 'Thorndale', are very hardy, while others are relatively tender and are also suitable as houseplants. The leaves may be glossy, rich green or bright gold, glistening silver or soft cream. Many varieties have prominent veining or are mottled, marbled, or splashed with a combination of colors. Leaf edges may be wavy, crimped, curled under, deeply lobed, or coarsely toothed.

The plants have two distinct stages of growth. In the initial, climbing phase, the leaves are markedly different from those on the flowering shoots that develop in the arborescent phase. These juvenile leaves are the "typical" ivy shape, with up to seven lobes, whereas the adult foliage is often unlobed and heart shaped at the base. Likewise, young stems are flexible and bear rootlets, while older growths are stiffer and rootless.The greenish flowers on adult stems are small and inconspicuous, borne in umbels and replaced by small, berrylike fruits that are usually black.

Ivies are easily grown in rich, moist soil high in organic matter and are generally carefree once established. They need part shade, as full sun will scorch the leaves on some varieties. Indeed, many ivies thrive in the dense shade beneath trees and shrubs where little else, including grass, will grow.

The stems climb by aerial rootlets that cling easily to any rough surface, such as tree bark, brick, or stone. Although they can spread very rapidly, it is not difficult to keep them in bounds: ivies can be clipped back hard without harm and will send out vigorous new growth. Even shoots damaged by extreme cold will produce new leaves once the weather warms.

Unfortunately, ivy can become too vigorous and invasive. While it is not parasitic and does not interfere with the systems of trees on which it climbs, it can overwhelm a host tree and hasten the demise of a plant that is struggling. It is best to keep ivy clipped back at least 6 in (15 cm) from the base of a tree. It can also find its way into crevices in a masonry wall and cause damage. One further caution: ivies are harmful if eaten and may cause skin allergy.

H. algeriensis, syn. *H. canariensis* (Algerian ivy) A large, vigorous species with large, leathery, dark green leaves that grow up to

Hedera algeriensis

6–8 in (15–20 cm) across and have 5–7 lobes. The leaves on the climbing shoots are kidney shaped, while those on the flowering shoots are rounded and heart shaped at the base. They are bright green in summer, often turning bronze with green veins in winter. Related to *H. helix* but distinguished by its deep red stems and larger black fruits. Makes an excellent ground cover. N Africa and Canary Islands. In cultivation 1833.
Zone 7 US, 8 Can.

Hedera algeriensis 'Gloire de Marengo'

***H. a.* 'Gloire de Marengo'** An attractive and colorful large form perfect for walls. The large leaves are deep green in the center, flecked with silvery gray and margined with white. Less hardy than green-leaved forms and popular as a houseplant.
Zone 7 US, 8 Can. 🏆

Hedera algeriensis 'Margino-maculata'

***H. a.* 'Margino-maculata'** The leaves of this large climber are a mixture of both deep green and pale green mottled with cream. The shoots often bear leaves that are similar to those of 'Gloire de Marengo' but with a mottled margin. In the open the leaves become even more heavily spattered with cream. It is often grown as a houseplant. In cultivation 1942.
Zone 6 US, 7 Can. 🏆

Hedera azorica

H. azorica A distinct and hardy large species with broad, matte, light green leaves. Those on the climbing shoots have 5–7 blunt lobes. Azores.
Zone 6 US, 7 Can.

H. canariensis See *H. algeriensis.*

H. colchica (Persian ivy) A large, handsome, vigorous species with the largest leaves in the genus. They are ovate or elliptic and 6–8 in (15–20 cm) long or more on the climbing shoots, somewhat smaller and more oblong in shape on the flowering shoots; all are dark green and leathery. Caucasus. In cultivation 1850.
Zone 6 US, 7 Can. 🏆

***H. c.* 'Dentata'** A spectacular large climber with leaves even larger and more irregularly shaped than those of the typical species. They are slightly softer in outline and are somewhat toothed.
Zone 6 US, 7 Can. 🏆

Hedera colchica 'Dentata-variegata'

***H. c.* 'Dentata-variegata'** An ornamental large ivy with large, broad, often elongated leaves that are bright green shading to gray; they are notably margined with creamy yellow when young and with cream when mature. It is hardier than *H. algeriensis* 'Gloire de Marengo' and just as effective.
Zone 6 US, 7 Can. 🏆

***H. c.* 'Paddy's Pride'** See *H. c.* 'Sulphur Heart'.

***H. c.* 'Sulphur Heart'**, syn. *H. c.* 'Paddy's Pride' A large, impressive variegated ivy with large, broad leaves that are boldly

Hedera colchica 'Sulphur Heart'

marked with an irregular central blotch of yellow, merging into pale green and finally deep green. Occasionally almost the entire leaf is yellow. On old leaves the yellow blotch becomes pale yellow-green.
Zone 6 US, 7 Can. 🏆

H. helix (English ivy) One of the most adaptable and variable of all plants, English ivy makes an excellent ground cover and is useful in situations where little else will grow. The leaves on the climbing shoots are variable and may be three- to five-lobed, while the leaves borne on the flowering shoots are entire and ovate to rhomboidal. The following forms have green leaves and are hardy to zone 4 US, 5b Can. unless otherwise stated. Europe, Asia Minor to N Iran.

Hedera helix 'Adam'

***H. h.* 'Adam'** The leaves of this large climber are rather small, shallowly three-lobed, green and gray-green in the center, and narrowly margined with cream. In cultivation 1968.

***H. h.* 'Angularis Aurea'** A large climber with broad, glossy leaves flushed with bright yellow. Not suitable for ground cover.
🏆

***H. h.* 'Atropurpurea'** The leaves of this large form are entire or have two short lateral lobes. They are dark purplish green, darker in winter, often with bright green veins. In cultivation 1884.
🏆

***H. h.* 'Baltica'** The most commonly available form. It has small, dark green leaves and increased hardiness. Introduced by the Missouri Botanical Garden.

Hedera helix 'Buttercup'

***H. h.* 'Bulgaria'** This is the hardiest of all the ivy varieties and is the best choice for the limits of the range. It is also very tolerant of drought.

Hedera helix 'Cavendishii'

***H. h.* 'Buttercup'** A slow-growing, medium-sized form with rich yellow leaves that become yellowish green or pale green with age. In cultivation 1925.
🏆

***H. h.* 'Caenwoodiana'** See *H. h.* 'Pedata'.

***H. h.* 'Cavendishii'** A pretty, medium-sized form with small, angular, green leaves mottled with gray and broadly margined with cream. In cultivation 1867.
🏆

***H. h.* 'Congesta'** An upright, small, non-climbing form similar to 'Erecta' but more congested in habit and with smaller leaves. In cultivation 1887.
🏆

***H. h.* 'Conglomerata'** A dense, slow-growing form with stiffly erect stems that

Hedera helix 'Erecta'

makes a low mound. The leaves are with or without lobes and have wavy margins. It is excellent for the rock garden.

***H. h.* 'Erecta'** A slow-growing dwarf form with stiffly erect shoots. The leaves are three-lobed and arrow shaped. It is good in a rock garden. In cultivation 1898.
🏆

Hedera helix 'Glacier'

Hedera helix 'Goldchild'

***H. h.* 'Glacier'** The leaves of this medium-sized climber are silvery gray with narrow white margins. In cultivation 1950.

***H. h.* 'Goldchild'** When young, leaves are bright green, shading to pale green in the center, and have a broad gold margin. Later they are blue-green and gray-green with a margin of creamy yellow.

Hedera helix 'Goldheart'

***H. h.* 'Goldheart'** This is a striking medium-sized ivy of neat growth. The leaf has a large, bright, central splash of yellow. Although this is a very popular ivy, it can revert badly after a few years.
Zone 5 US, 6 Can.

Hedera helix 'Green Ripple'

***H. h.* 'Green Ripple'** An attractive medium-sized form with small, pale-veined, jaggedly lobed leaves; the central lobe is long and tapering.

***H. h.* 'Harald'** A medium-sized form with leaves shallowly five-lobed, green and gray-green in the center and margined with cream. In cultivation 1958.

***H. h.* 'Ivalace'** A small, compact ivy with bright green, shallowly five-lobed leaves, stiffly curled at the margins. It makes a good

Hedera helix 'Ivalace'

ground cover. In cultivation 1955.

***H. h.* 'Kolibri'** A striking medium-sized ivy with dark green leaves that are broadly and brightly blotched and streaked with

Hedera helix 'Kolibri'

cream. The primary veins are tinged pink.

***H. h.* 'Little Diamond'** A dwarf, bushy, dense plant. The diamond-shaped leaves can be entire or three-lobed. They are green mottled with gray and have a cream margin. In cultivation 1976.

***H. h.* 'Manda's Crested'** An attractive medium-sized ivy, suitable for ground cover. The leaves have five pointed lobes

Hedera helix 'Little Diamond'

Hedera helix 'Manda's Crested'

that point upward while the sinuses point down, creating a wavy-edged effect. They turn bronze in winter. In cultivation 1940.

***H. h.* 'Midas Touch'** A medium-sized climber with golden yellow leaves splashed with lime green and dark green; some are edged with bright green.

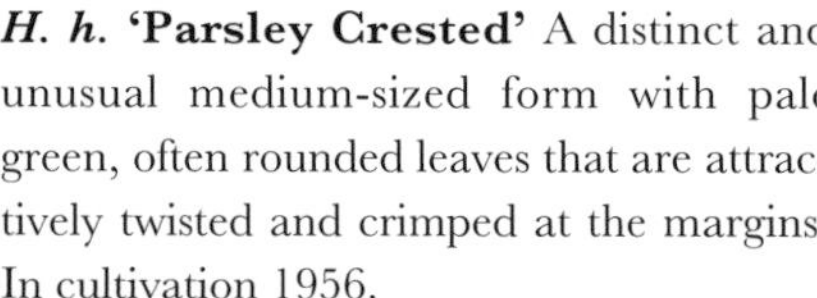

***H. h.* 'Parsley Crested'** A distinct and unusual medium-sized form with pale green, often rounded leaves that are attractively twisted and crimped at the margins. In cultivation 1956.

***H. h.* 'Pedata'**, syn. *H. h.* 'Caenwoodiana' (Bird's foot ivy) A medium-sized form with small gray-green leaves that have white veins. They are deeply divided into five narrow lobes, with the middle one being the longest, and resemble the foot of a bird. In cultivation 1863.

***H. h.* 'Persian Carpet'** A large, vigorous

Hedera helix 'Parsley Crested'

form good for ground cover or a wall, with green shoots and light green, shallowly lobed leaves.

H. h. **'Sagittifolia'** The leaves of this large form are bluntly three-lobed and arrow shaped. *H. h.* 'Königer's Auslese' is often sold under this name. In cultivation 1872.

H. h. **'Sagittifolia Variegata'** A large form with gray-green leaves margined with white. In cultivation 1965.

Hedera helix 'Sagittifolia Variegata'

H. h. **'Shamrock'** (Cloverleaf ivy) A very distinct medium-sized form with small, bright green leaves that are entire to deeply three-lobed and flushed with purple at the base. The leaves turn bronze in winter. In cultivation 1954.
🏆

H. h. **'Sicilla'** A form with crisped leaf margins similar to 'Parsley Crested' but with the edges colored creamy white.

H. h. **'Spetchley'** A dense, prostrate, and congested form with very small leaves. It is good for a rock garden, low wall, or tub.
🏆

H. h. **'Thorndale'** Another slightly hardier form that has large, dark green leaves with the veins bordered in white. It makes a good ground cover.

H. h. **'Tricolor'** A medium-sized form with small, grayish green leaves, margined with white and edged in rose-red in winter.

H. hibernica (Irish ivy, Atlantic ivy) This species is closely related to *H. helix* but often produces large leaves, which in the commonly grown forms are dark green, usually five-lobed, 3–6 in (7.5–15 cm) wide, and veined with gray at the base. Young stems and leaves are slightly downy. It is a large, vigorous ivy, particularly suited to being grown as a ground cover. Atlantic coasts of Spain, Portugal, W France, and Ireland.
Zone 5 US, 6 Can. 🏆

H. h. **'Deltoidea'** (Sweetheart ivy, shield ivy) A small form with a neat, close growth habit. The green leaves have two shallow

Hedera hibernica 'Deltoidea'

Hedera nepalensis

basal lobes that lend a heartlike shape. They turn a purplish bronze in winter. In cultivation 1872.
Zone 5 US, 6 Can.

H. nepalensis (Nepal ivy) A large, vigorous species with grayish green, taper-pointed leaves up to 5 in (13 cm) long.
Zone 8 US, 9? Can.

H. pastuchowii A large, vigorous species with leaves that may be entire, heart shaped, or shallowly lobed or toothed. They are blackish green with pale green veins, and the midrib is red beneath. Best grown against a wall. N Iran. Introduced 1972 to Hillier Nurseries.
Zone 7? US, 8? Can.

H. rhombea (Japanese ivy) The Japanese equivalent of *H. helix*, differing from the

Hedera rhombea

common species in its ovate or triangular-ovate leaves that sometimes have two shallow lobes.
Zone 4? US, 5b? Can.

Hedysarum *Leguminosae*

A large genus of about 100 species of perennials and deciduous shrubs found throughout northern temperate regions. The following is easily grown in full sun and any average, well-drained soil. It can become leggy, in which case the old stems can be completely removed and the strong, younger ones cut back by half in spring.

H. multijugum (Mongolian sweetvetch) This is a small shrub with a lax habit, with sea green, pinnate leaves and long racemes of rose-purple pea flowers throughout the

summer and occasionally into autumn. Mongolia. Introduced 1883.
Zone 5 US, 6 Can.

Heimia *Lythraceae*

A genus of three species of deciduous shrubs related to loosestrife (Lythrum). *They are natives of the Americas. The following succeeds in any well-drained soil in sun, and pruning is a matter of removing crowded growths at the base in spring.*

H. salicifolia An interesting shrub of 4 ft (1.2 m), with narrow leaves and small yellow flowers ½ in (1.5 cm) across, which are produced in the leaf axils from midsummer to early fall. Central and South America. Introduced in 1821.
Zone 9 US

Helianthemum *Cistaceae*

Sun rose

There are more than 100 species of these usually dwarf, trailing, evergreen or semievergreen shrubs, which have a wide distribution in temperate areas. Those in cultivation are mainly hybrids and produce multitudes of brilliantly colored flowers that resemble roses throughout the summer. They are excellent plants for dry, sunny locations and prefer sandy, very well drained soil. They should be cut back after their first flush of flowers to encourage bushiness and repeat flowering in the same season.

Helianthemum lunulatum

H. lunulatum A dainty, cushionlike alpine with yellow flowers, each petal of which has a small orange spot at its base, borne in early to midsummer. NW Italy.
Zone 7 US, 8 Can.

H. nummularium (Common sun rose) This is a compact, dwarf shrub with green foliage that is silvery beneath and yellow, white, or pink flowers. The flowers can be single or double. Prefers limestone soil.
Zone 5 US, 6 Can. 🏆

Hybrids

The colorful plants generally seen in cultivation are mainly hybrids developed from three species: *H. appeninum*, *H. nummularium*, and *H. croceum*. Between them they have produced a great variety of attractive silver- and green-leaved plants with flowers ranging in color from orange, yellow, or white to rose, red, and scarlet, both single and double. All of the following are low growing, are more or less prostrate, and spread to 12–18 in (30–45 cm) across. All are hardy to zone 5 US, 6 Can. The 'Ben' cultivars are named after Scottish mountains.

***H.* 'Afflick'** Bright, deep orange-bronze flowers with a bronze-copper center; green foliage.
***H.* 'Ben Dearg'** Deep copper-orange flowers with a darker center; green foliage.
***H.* 'Ben Fhada'** Golden yellow flowers with an orange center; gray-green foliage.
***H.* 'Ben Hope'** Carmine flowers with a deep orange center; green foliage.

Helianthemum 'Ben Ledi'

***H.* 'Ben Ledi'** Bright, deep rose flowers; dark green foliage.
***H.* 'Ben More'** Bright, rich orange flowers with a darker center; dark green foliage.

Helianthemum 'Ben More'

***H.* 'Ben Nevis'** Deep buttercup yellow flowers with a bronze-crimson center; green foliage.

Helianthemum 'Cerise Queen'

***H.* 'Cerise Queen'** Scarlet double flowers and green foliage.

Helianthemum 'Fire Dragon'

***H.* 'Fire Dragon'**, syn. *H.* 'Mrs. Clay'

Bright orange-scarlet flowers and gray-green foliage.

H. 'Henfield Brilliant' Bright orange flowers and green foliage.

H. 'Jubilee' Drooping, primrose yellow, double flowers and green foliage.

H. 'Mrs. Clay' See *H.* 'Fire Dragon'.

Helianthemum 'Mrs. C. W. Earle'

H. 'Mrs. C. W. Earle' Scarlet double flowers with a yellow basal flush set off by dark green foliage.

H. 'Praecox' Lemon yellow flowers; a dense habit with gray foliage.

Helianthemum 'Raspberry Ripple'

H. 'Raspberry Ripple' Deep reddish pink flowers with white-tipped petals; dark green foliage.

H. 'Red Orient' See *H.* 'Supreme'.

H. 'Rhodanthe Carneum' Pale, showy pink flowers with an orange center; silver-gray foliage.

Helianthemum 'Rose of Leeswood'

H. 'Rose of Leeswood' Rose-pink double flowers; green foliage.

H. 'Sudbury Gem' Deep pink flowers with a flame center; gray-green foliage.

H. 'Supreme', syn. *H.* 'Red Orient' Crimson flowers and gray-green foliage.

Helianthemum 'Sudbury Gem'

Helianthemum 'The Bride'

H. 'The Bride' Creamy white flowers with a bright yellow center; silver-gray foliage.

H. 'Wisley Pink' Soft pink flowers and gray foliage.

Helianthemum 'Wisley Primrose'

H. 'Wisley Primrose' Primrose yellow flowers with a deeper center; light gray-green foliage. An unusually vigorous form.

H. 'Wisley White' Pure white single flowers with a center composed of golden anthers; narrow gray leaves.

Helichrysum *Compositae*

A genus of about 500 species of perennials and evergreen shrubs, widely distributed in the Old World, particularly in South Africa and Australia. Among the shrubby members are some interesting, mainly low-growing, often aromatic plants with attractive foliage. Most are reasonably hardy in full sun and a well-drained, poorish soil.

H. italicum A dwarf shrub with long, narrow, gray leaves and terminal long-stalked clusters of bright yellow flower heads in summer. It is one of the best silvery gray shrubs. Mediterranean region.
Zone 8 US, 9? Can.

H. i. subsp. serotinum (Curry plant) A dense, dwarf shrub with narrow, sage green leaves that smell strongly like curry powder. It bears heads of yellow flowers in midsummer. S Europe.
Zone 8 US, 9? Can.

Helichrysum petiolare

H. petiolare A dwarf, often trailing shrublet forming mounds of white-woolly stems and long-stalked, ovate, gray-woolly leaves. The yellow flowers are borne in late summer. It is a tender species, usually grown as an annual, but may overwinter in mild areas if given good drainage and protection. South Africa.

Zone 9 US 🏆

H. selago See *Ozothamnus selago*.

H. splendidum A small, globular shrub of about 3 ft (1 m), producing white-woolly shoots densely covered with silvery gray leaves. Clusters of small, yellow, everlasting flowers appear from midsummer to autumn and may remain into the middle of winter. South Africa.

Zone 9 US 🏆

Heptacodium jasminoides

Helichrysum splendidum

Heptacodium *Caprifoliaceae*

A genus of two species of deciduous Chinese shrubs, related to Abelia.

H. jasminoides (Seven Son Flower of Zhejiang) A vigorous and large deciduous shrub of upright habit, with peeling bark. Bold, three-veined leaves are retained until late autumn or early winter, and small, fragrant, white flowers are borne in whorls at the ends of the shoots in late summer and fall. In the right conditions, the calyx enlarges and turns bright red after flowering. E China (Zhejiang). Introduced 1981 to the Hillier Gardens and Arboretum.

Zone 4? US, 5? Can.

Hibiscus *Malvaceae*

A large genus of about 200 species of perennials and deciduous shrubs and trees, widely distributed in tropical and subtropical regions. Just a few species are hardy in cool-temperate climates, but they include some of the most effective shrubs for late summer and early autumn, as long as they are planted in full sun. They should have a rich, fertile soil, and in colder areas, it is necessary to grow the plants in the shelter of a warm wall and to mulch the roots to protect them from freezing. Any shoots that grow too long can be cut back lightly in spring, and old specimens can be cut back hard at the same time.

H. sinosyriacus A handsome, vigorous species, more spreading than *H. syriacus* and with larger, sage green leaves, but requiring the same conditions. The single flowers are

Hibiscus sinosyriacus 'Lilac Queen'

similar but a little larger. It is grown exclusively as named clones, which include the following:

***H. s.* 'Autumn Surprise'** A medium-sized shrub. The flower petals are white with an attractively feathered cerise base.
Zone 8 US, 9? Can.

***H. s.* 'Lilac Queen'** A medium-sized shrub whose flowers have lilac petals with a garnet red base.
Zone 8 US, 9? Can.

H. syriacus (Rose-of-Sharon, shrub althea) No late-flowering shrub is more beautiful than the cultivars of this shrubby "mallow." The large, usually single, trumpet-shaped flowers open in succession between midsummer and midfall. They are displayed on medium to large-sized shrubs of upright habit that may occasionally reach the size of small trees. The following are recommended. E Asia.
Zone 5 US, 6 Can.

***H. s.* 'Blue Bird'** A medium-sized shrub with violet-blue single flowers with a darker eye. The best single blue.
Zone 4 US, 5b Can. 🏆

Hibiscus syriacus 'Blue Bird'

Hibiscus syriacus 'Diana'

***H. s.* 'Diana'** A medium-sized shrub with large, pure white, single flowers with crimped petals, occasionally with a few petaloids in the center. The best white. Raised 1963 at the U.S. National Arboretum, Washington, D.C.
Zone 4 US, 5b Can. 🏆

Hibiscus syriacus 'Hamabo'

***H. s.* 'Hamabo'** A medium-sized shrub with large, pale blush pink, single flowers, each with a crimson eye. One of the best cultivars and not to be confused with *H. hamabo*, which is a tender species with yellow, red-centered flowers.
Zone 4 US, 5b Can. 🏆

***H. s.* 'Helene'** The large flowers of this medium-sized shrub are 3½ in (9 cm) across, often semidouble, and white that is flushed pink when opening; the outer petals are streaked with deep pink. They also have attractively feathered, deep maroon blotches at the base and white petaloid stamens at the center. A sister seedling of 'Diana'.
Zone 5 US, 6 Can.

***H. s.* 'Lady Stanley'** A medium-sized shrub with white, almost double flowers shaded blush pink, with a maroon base. In cultivation 1875.
Zone 4 US, 5b Can.

***H. s.* 'Pink Giant'** A medium-sized shrub bearing clear pink, single flowers with a deep red eye. It was raised by crossing 'Red Heart' and 'Woodbridge' and has larger flowers than the latter. They have a dark band near the apex of each basal blotch and are distinctly feathered.
Zone 4 US, 5b Can. 🏆

Hibiscus syriacus 'Pink Giant'

Hibiscus syriacus 'Red Heart'

***H. s.* 'Red Heart'** A medium-sized shrub with large white single flowers with a bright red eye.
Zone 5 US, 6 Can. 🏆

***H. s.* 'Russian Violet'** The single flowers

Hibiscus syriacus 'Woodbridge'

of this medium-sized shrub are large and luminous lilac-pink with a deep red center.
Zone 5 US, 6 Can.

***H. s.* 'William R. Smith'** A medium-sized shrub with large, pure white, single flowers. In cultivation 1916.
Zone 5 US, 6 Can.

***H. s.* 'Woodbridge'** A medium-sized shrub bearing large, single, rich rose-pink flowers with a carmine center. *(Photo on p.339.)*
Zone 4 US, 5b Can. 🏆

Hippophaë *Elaeagnaceae*

Sea buckthorn

A genus of three species of hardy deciduous shrubs or small trees, native to Eurasia, with attractive orange berries on female plants.

Hippophaë rhamnoides

H. rhamnoides A tall shrub or small tree that succeeds in almost any soil and is often planted in coastal areas, as it is very resistant to salt spray and wind. The attractive, narrow, willowlike leaves are gray-green above and silvery green beneath. The fruits are fleshy, egg-shaped, orange-yellow berries that are borne profusely through the winter and contain an acrid juice that repels birds. Plants of both sexes must be present to obtain fruits. Because it is difficult to transplant, it should be planted when small and sited carefully. E Asia, Europe.
Zone 3 US, 2b Can. 🏆

Hoheria *Malvaceae*

A genus of five species of beautiful evergreen and deciduous shrubs or small trees belonging to the mallow family. They all have honey-scented white flowers, which are borne freely in mid- to late summer. The evergreen species need a sheltered location or protection except in mild areas, and the same applies to the deciduous ones at the limits of their hardiness range; they grow well in California and the South. The leaves of juvenile plants are often deeply toothed and lobed and smaller than those of adult plants. Hoherias do best in a deep soil rich in humus and in sun or dappled shade, but the more nutritious the soil, the more likely it is that growth may be soft and susceptible to frost. Dead or damaged wood can be pruned out in spring. All the species are from New Zealand.

H. angustifolia An elegant, small, evergreen, columnar tree with roundish to narrowly lance-shaped leaves up to 2 in (5 cm) long. Juvenile plants are dense and bushy with slender, interlacing branches and minute, shallowly toothed leaves. Masses of small white flowers cover the plant in the middle of summer.
Zone 9 US

Hoheria glabrata

H. glabrata (Mountain ribbonwood) A magnificent deciduous large shrub or small tree, possibly a little hardier than *H. lyallii*. In early to midsummer its branches are festooned with fragrant, almost translucent, white flowers. In cultivation 1871.
Zone 9 US 🏆

***H.* 'Glory of Amlwch'** A large shrub or small to medium-sized deciduous tree that retains its leaves in mild winters. The flowers are pure white, over 1¼ in (3.5 cm) across, and densely crowded on the stems.
Zone 9 US 🏆

Hoheria 'Glory of Amlwch'

Hoheria lyallii

H. lyallii (Lacebark) A beautiful but variable large shrub or small tree. Juvenile leaves are green, adult ones gray. Clusters of cherry-blossom-like white flowers crowd the branches in midsummer, usually later than those of *H. glabrata*.
Zone 9 US 🏆

H. sexstylosa (Ribbonwood) This splendid, tall, free-flowering, vigorous evergreen

Hoheria sexstylosa

shrub or small tree blooms in late summer or autumn and has narrow, glossy green leaves. The fragrant flowers are over 1 in (2.5 cm) across. In young trees the leaves are extremely variable.
Zone 9 US 🏆

***H. s.* 'Stardust'** A form with a compact and upright habit, glossy leaves, and very profusely borne flowers.
Zone 9 US

Holboellia *Lardizabalaceae*

A genus of about five species of luxuriant, evergreen, twining plants with attractive foliage, native to the Himalaya and China. They will grow in any fertile soil in sun or shade but need sun if they are to flower and fruit. Weak growths can be removed in spring.

H. coriacea A vigorous, reasonably hardy species up to 20 ft (6 m) or more. The leaves consist of three glossy green leaflets, and the flowers, which appear in mid- to late spring, are separately male and female. The males are purplish, borne in terminal clusters, and the females are greenish white in axillary clusters. The fruit is a purplish, fleshy pod up to 3 in (7.5 cm) long, filled with rows of black seeds. C China. Introduced 1907 by Ernest Wilson.
Zone 7 US, 8 Can.

Holodiscus *Rosaceae*

A genus of about eight species of hardy, spirea-like deciduous shrubs from western North America to Colombia. The following can be grown in sun or light shade in any average soil, provided it is not likely to dry out. Prune in spring only to remove dead or overcrowded branches.

Holodiscus discolor

H. discolor (Ocean spray) A handsome and elegant shrub to 11 ft (3.5 m) high that blooms in the middle of summer, when its long, drooping, feathery panicles of creamy white flowers are most prominent. The leaves are grayish white and woolly beneath. W North America. Introduced 1827 by David Douglas.
Zone 5 US, 6b Can.

Humulus *Cannabidaceae*
Hop

A genus of three species of perennial climbers from Europe and Asia. The following species is herbaceous and grows in any fertile soil.

H. lupulus (Common hop) The fruit of this large climber is used for making beer. The twining stems may reach 10–20 ft (3–6 m) long and produce rough, hairy, deeply three- to five-lobed and coarsely toothed leaves. The cone-shaped fruit is borne in clusters in late summer and early fall.
Zone 3 US, 4 Can.

Fruit of *Humulus lupulus*

***H. l.* 'Aureus'** A magnificent medium-sized form with yellow leaves, best grown in full sun on a pergola, trellis, or arch.
Zone 3 US, 3b Can. 🏆

Humulus lupulus 'Aureus'

HYDRANGEA

Hydrangeaceae

HYDRANGEAS OFFER the gardener a range of beautiful flower forms — from the large, voluptuous globes of the "mopheads" to the delicate, frothy discs of the "lacecaps" to the dense, nodding cones of panicle and oakleaf hydrangeas. Equally striking are the range of colors, from chalk white to bright crimson, soft lilac to vivid blue. Some varieties, such as *H. macrophylla* 'Lanarth White', even provide two-toned blooms — in this case, blue or pink with white. Even single-color flowers may have contrasting eyes, with white flowers dotted with blue or magenta marked with green.

Hydrangeas are all the more outstanding because they flower late, from midsummer until frost, when there is often little else in bloom. Further, they change color in fall, with white blooms turning, say, to light lime green and pale blue becoming a deep greenish blue. Others may adopt russet red, pale rose, or purple shades. Their texture changes as well, taking on the appearance of fine, velvety kid leather, particularly when the blooms are cut and dried. They make lovely, long-lasting material for floral arrangements.

The flower heads of hydrangeas consist of two kinds of florets. The fertile or "perfect" florets are usually tiny and bear male and female flower parts; they are less conspicuous and are found in the center of the flower cluster. The sterile or "ray" florets are male and form the large, colorful sepals on the outside of the cluster. The flower heads of mophead hydrangeas consist almost entirely of sterile florets, while lacecaps have fertile florets in the inner part of the inflorescence surrounded by an outer ring of sterile ones.

While the flowers are the main attraction, hydrangeas also have other commendable features. The oakleaf hydrangea, for example, bears deeply lobed leaves much like those of its namesake, and they turn a brilliant crimson in fall. Stems of *H. aspera* have peeling bark that may be colored a rich cinammon brown.

Hydrangea arborescens **has large flower heads up to 6 in (15 cm) across.**

There are hydrangeas sized for every garden. Plants range from dwarfs, such as *H. involucrata* 'Hortensis', which is about 3 ft (1 m) high, to *H. aspera* subsp. *sargentiana*, whose bristly stems can rise to over 10 ft (3 m). There are also climbing hydrangeas, such as *H. anomala* subsp. *petiolaris*, whose aerial rootlets can bring the stems up to 80 ft (25 m).

CARE AND CULTIVATION

Hydrangeas are not difficult to grow. They prefer loamy, well-drained, acidic soil (pH 6.5 to 4.5) amended generously with organic matter. *H. macrophylla* and *H. serrata* will take a good deal of sun but also thrive in dappled shade for part of the day. Many other hydrangeas, including *H. aspera*, require somewhat more shade, which helps preserve blossom color. With all hydrangeas, especially those planted near trees, it is important to keep the roots moist and well fed and covered with mulch. The plants may also need protection from spring frosts, which can kill the buds.

H. macrophylla, which includes the mopheads and lacecaps, is remarkable in that the flowers can change color depending on the amount of aluminum and level of acidity in the soil. In acidic soil, where more aluminum is available, the plants produce blue flowers — the lower the pH, the bluer the blooms. In neutral soils, hydrangeas take up less aluminum and the flowers turn pink. On white flowers, only the color of the eyes on the male flowers change. Some, such as *H. m.* 'Ami Pasquier', lack the ability to absorb aluminum and remain pink.

To produce blue blooms in neutral or alkaline soil, aluminum sulfate or sulfur can be added to increase acidity. Hydrangeas grown in soil with a pH higher than 7 can also become chlorotic, due mainly to a lack of iron, and must be treated to correct the nutrient deficiency.

Deadheading and pruning should be done in late winter or early spring. Old flower heads should be cut back to just above the first leaf node that has buds, and dead, weak, and crowded stems, as well as two or three of the oldest stems, should be removed by cutting them out at the base.

SHRUBS

H. arborescens (Smooth hydrangea) A small deciduous shrub of loose, bushy growth, with ovate, slender-pointed, serrated leaves. The flowers are in corymbs up to 6 in (15 cm) across, bearing several long-stalked, creamy white marginal ray florets. They appear in succession from midsummer to early fall. Introduced 1736.
Zone 2 US, 2b Can.

***H. a.* 'Annabelle'** A small, loose, bushy shrub that is the most commonly cultivated form and has ovate, slender-pointed, serrated leaves. The flowers are huge, spectacular, rounded heads of white, sterile florets and are up to 8 in (20 cm) across.
Zone 2 US, 2b Can. 🏆

***H. a.* 'Grandiflora'** A small shrub with large, globular heads of creamy white, sterile florets borne from midsummer to early fall. Introduced 1907.
Zone 2 US, 2b Can. 🏆

H. aspera A magnificent but variable, large-leaved, deciduous species of medium size that bears large heads of pale porcelain blue flowers in early and midsummer. Himalaya, W and C China, Taiwan.
Zone 6 US, 7 Can.

***H. a.* Kawakamii group** A small to medium-sized shrub that flowers very late. The deep violet flower heads with white sterile florets open in fall.
Zone 5 US, 6 Can.

***H. a.* 'Macrophylla'** A striking medium-sized form of this variable species, in which the leaves and flower heads are even larger than usual. The latter are pale porcelain blue with a ring of lilac-pink or white ray florets.
Zone 5 US, 6 Can. 🏆

H. a.* subsp. *sargentiana (Sargent hydrangea) A medium-sized to large shrub. Its shoots have a curious, mosslike covering of stiff hairs and bristles, and the leaves are very large and velvety. The huge, flat flower heads are borne in mid- to late summer and are bluish with white ray florets. It is suitable for a sheltered shrub border or woodland but requires shade and wind protection. China. Introduced 1908 by Ernest Wilson.
Zone 5 US, 6 Can. 🏆

Hydrangea arborescens 'Annabelle'

Hydrangea arborescens 'Grandiflora'

Hydrangea aspera subsp. *sargentiana*

Hydrangea aspera Villosa group

Hydrangea heteromalla

***H. a.* Villosa group** Close to the typical form but less coarse and with smaller leaves and flower heads. It is one of the loveliest of the later-flowering hydrangeas and is a medium-sized shrub of spreading habit, with stems, leaves, and flower stalks densely covered in long, soft hairs. The large flower heads are lilac-blue with toothed margins to the sepals. It requires part shade. W China. Introduced 1908.
Zone 5 US, 6 Can. 🏆

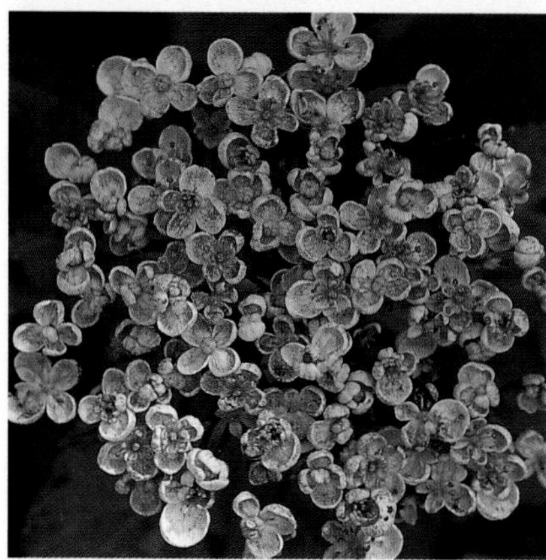

Hydrangea 'Ayesha'

***H.* 'Ayesha'**, syn. *H. m.* 'Silver Slipper' A distinctive and unusual deciduous hydrangea of puzzling origin but great beauty. It is often included in the hortensias but is quite different from the typical mophead. The leaves are bold and glossy green above. The rather flattened, dense, faintly fragrant flower heads, borne in late summer, are composed of thick-petaled, cup-shaped florets resembling those of a large lilac. They are grayish lilac or pink, depending on the soil, and eventually fade to a stunning shade that is somewhere between greenish blue and turquoise.
Zone 6 US, 7 Can. 🏆

H. heteromalla A very variable medium-sized to large deciduous shrub or small tree. The leaves are dark green above and white beneath. The flowers, borne in broad corymbs in midsummer, are white with conspicuous marginal ray florets, which age to deep pink. Himalaya, N and W China. Introduced 1821.
Zone 3 US, 3b Can.

***H. h.* 'Bretschneideri'** A medium-sized shrub with broad, flattened, white lacecap flower heads. It has dark brown peeling bark and the leaves are white beneath. China. Introduced 1882.
Zone 3 US, 4 Can. 🏆

Hydrangea heteromalla 'Jermyns Lace'

***H. h.* 'Jermyns Lace'** A vigorous, large shrub with broad, lacecap heads whose white outer florets turn to pink.
Zone 3 US, 4 Can.

***H. h.* 'Snowcap'** A superb, large, stately shrub with big, heart-shaped leaves and white flowers in large, flattened corymbs 8–10 in (20–25 cm) across. It is tolerant of wind, sun, and drought.
Zone 3 US, 4 Can.

H. involucrata A pretty, deciduous dwarf species with blue or rosy lilac flowers surrounded by white or variously tinted ray florets, borne in mid- to late summer. Japan, Taiwan. In cultivation 1864.
Zone 7 US, 8 Can.

Hydrangea involucrata 'Hortensis'

***H. i.* 'Hortensis'** A remarkable and attractive hydrangea that grows about 3–4 ft (1–1.2 m) tall. Its double, creamy white florets become rose-tinted in open locations.
Zone 7 US, 8 Can. 🏆

H. macrophylla (Bigleaf hydrangea) The hortensias and lacecaps that follow are all considered to be cultivars of this species, although some may be of hybrid origin. The hortensias, or mopheads, have globe-shaped flower heads up to 1 ft (30 cm) in diameter. The lacecaps' disclike heads are about 6 in (15 cm) across. Flower color varies from blue to pink depending on soil. Unless otherwise stated, all are small shrubs. All are deciduous and hardy to zone 5 US, 6 Can.

Hortensias

***H. m.* 'Altona'** Rose-colored, large florets; blues well when treated. Best in shade.

Hydrangea macrophylla 'Ami Pasquier'

***H. m.* 'Ami Pasquier'** A dwarf shrub with deep red flower heads that age to rose.
🏆

Hydrangea m. 'Generale Vicomtesse de Vibraye'

***H. m.* 'Ayesha'** See *H.* 'Ayesha'.

***H. m.* 'Europa'** Deep pink flower heads with large florets.

***H. m.* 'Generale Vicomtesse de Vibraye'** Vivid rose-purple flower heads; light blue in acid soils or when treated.

***H. m.* 'Hamburg'** Large, deep rose or purplish florets.

***H. m.* 'King George'** Large, rose-pink florets with serrated sepals.

Hydrangea m. 'Madame Emile Mouillère'

***H. m.* 'Madame Emile Mouillère'** Large florets with serrated sepals, white with a pink or blue eye. Perhaps the best white-flowered cultivar.

***H. m.* 'Masja'** A shrub with a compact habit and red flower heads.

***H. m.* 'Miss Belgium'** A dwarf shrub with rosy red flowers.

***H. m.* 'Nigra'** A distinctive cultivar with stems black or almost so; the florets are rose or occasionally blue. In cultivation 1870.

Hydrangea macrophylla 'Westfalen'

***H. m.* 'Nikko Blue'** The most readily available form. It is a good blue in acid soils but becomes a grayish blue in alkaline ones.

***H. m.* 'Silver Slipper'** See *H.* 'Ayesha'.

***H. m.* 'Westfalen'** Vivid crimson to violet flower heads.

Lacecaps

***H. m.* 'Blue Wave',** syn. *H. m.* 'Mariesii Perfecta' A vigorous shrub of medium size, bearing beautifully shaped heads of blue fertile flowers surrounded by numerous large ray florets, varying in color from pink to blue. In suitable acid soils the color is a vivid gentian blue. The sepals are noticeably wavy-edged. Best in part shade.

***H. m.* 'Geoffrey Chadbund'** The flowers of this medium-sized shrub are brick red in alkaline or neutral soils, purple in acid ones.

***H. m.* 'Lanarth White'** A medium-sized shrub of compact growth, with large, flattened heads of bright blue or pink fertile flowers surrounded by a ring of large white ray florets that have blue or pink eyes. This is a superb cultivar.

***H. m.* 'Libelle'** A very beautiful medium-sized hydrangea with heads of blue fertile flowers surrounded by pure white sterile florets. In cultivation 1964.

Hydrangea macrophylla 'Libelle'

***H. m.* 'Maculata',** syn. *H. m.* 'Variegata' A medium-sized, erect shrub. The flower heads have a few small, white ray florets, but this hydrangea is grown mainly for its attractive leaves, which have a broad, creamy white margin.

***H. m.* 'Mariesii'** A medium-sized shrub with wide, flat heads of rosy pink flowers with very large ray florets. When grown in a suitable acid soil, the flowers turn a very rich blue. Japan. Introduced 1879.

Hydrangea macrophylla 'Mariesii'

***H. m.* 'Mariesii Perfecta'** See 'Blue Wave'.

***H. m.* 'Tricolor'** A choice, vigorous, medium-sized cultivar with leaves that are attractively variegated green, gray, and pale yellow. The flowers are pale pink to white, large, and freely produced.

***H. m.* 'Variegata'** See *H. m.* 'Maculata'.

***H. m.* 'Veitchii'** A medium-sized shrub with rich dark green leaves, growing best in part shade. The flowers are in flattened

Hydrangea macrophylla 'White Wave'

corymbs, the sterile outer florets white, fading to pink. It is a very hardy plant and is lime tolerant.

***H. m.* 'White Wave'** A small but vigorous shrub with flattened heads of bluish or pinkish fertile flowers, surrounded by large, beautifully formed, pearly white ray florets. It is free-flowering when grown in an open location. *(Photo on p.345.)*

H. paniculata (Panicle hydrangea) A medium-sized to large deciduous shrub with both fertile and large, creamy white, sterile florets in dense, terminal panicles in late summer to fall. To obtain really large panicles, the laterals should be cut back to within 2–3 in (5–7.5 cm) of the previous year's growth in early spring. This does not apply to 'Praecox', and some gardeners prefer to prune only every other year or every third year for the sake of a shapelier bush, although smaller panicles will result. Best in part shade and a well-fed soil. The following forms are recommended. Japan, China, Taiwan. Introduced 1861.
Zone 3 US, 3b Can.

Hydrangea paniculata 'Floribunda'

***H. p.* 'Floribunda'** A medium-sized to large shrub producing long, narrow panicles with numerous white ray florets, flowering from just after the middle of summer. In cultivation 1867.
Zone 3 US, 3b Can.

***H. p.* 'Grandiflora'** (Peegee hydrangea) One of the showiest large, hardy shrubs. The massive panicles of large numbers of small, white, sterile florets, appearing in

Hydrangea paniculata 'Grandiflora'

summer to fall, become deep pink. They are excellent decoration when dried. Japan. Introduced c. 1867.
Zone 3 US, 3b Can.

Hydrangea paniculata 'Greenspire'

***H. p.* 'Greenspire'** Similar to 'Kyushu' but with green sterile flowers that become tinged with pink.
Zone 3 US, 3b Can.

***H. p.* 'Kyushu'** An upright, medium-sized to large shrub with glossy, dark green, taper-pointed leaves and panicles liberally sprinkled with sterile flowers.
Zone 3 US, 4 Can.

***H. p.* 'Pink Diamond'** A medium-sized to large shrub with large heads of sterile, white florets that become pink. They are similar to but larger than those of 'Unique'.
Zone 3 US, 3b Can.

***H. p.* 'Praecox'** This is the earliest-flowering form and has smaller panicles of toothed ray florets. Flowering generally occurs just before the middle of summer. This medium-sized to large cultivar will not flower if pruned hard in the early part of the year.
Zone 3 US, 3b Can.

Hydrangea paniculata 'Tardiva'

***H. p.* 'Tardiva'** A medium-sized to large shrub that flowers late, from the end of summer or early fall. The large heads have numerous ray florets.
Zone 3 US, 4 Can.

Hydrangea paniculata 'Unique'

***H. p.* 'Unique'** Similar to 'Grandiflora' but with even larger flower heads.
Zone 3 US, 4 Can.

H. quercifolia (Oakleaf hydrangea) A medium-sized deciduous shrub valued for its magnificent fall color. The leaves are large and strongly lobed much like those of a white oak. Large, white, sterile flowers are carried in conical heads in late summer. SE United States. Introduced 1803.
Zone 4 US, 5b Can.

***H. q.* 'Snowflake'** A striking medium-

Hydrangea quercifolia

sized form in which several series of bracts are produced in each flower, creating a double appearance.
Zone 5 US, 6 Can.

***H. q.* 'Snow Queen'** A medium-sized shrub bearing upright panicles of large, white florets that turn pink. The dark green leaves are bronze-red in autumn.
Zone 5 US, 6 Can.

H. serrata A charming deciduous shrub that rarely exceeds 3 ft (1 m). The flattened flower heads consist of blue or white fertile flowers, surrounded by a circle of white, pink, or bluish ray florets that often deepen to crimson in fall. Flowering begins in mid- to late summer. A variable species. The following forms are recommended. Japan, Korea. Introduced 1843.
Zone 5 US, 6 Can.

***H. s.* 'Blue Deckle'** A small, compact, and slow-growing lacecap type with clear blue to pink, toothed ray florets.
Zone 5 US, 6 Can.

Hydrangea serrata 'Bluebird'

***H. s.* 'Bluebird'** A small, robust shrub with stout shoots and abruptly pointed leaves. The blue fertile flowers are borne in slightly dome-shaped heads, surrounded by large ray florets that are reddish purple in alkaline soils and sea blue in acid ones.
Zone 4 US, 5b Can. 🏆

***H. s.* 'Diadem'** A hardy, compact small shrub with vivid blue or pink flowers. The leaves redden in full sun.
Zone 5 US, 6 Can.

***H. s.* 'Grayswood'** A small shrub with flattened heads of blue fertile flowers, surrounded by a ring of white ray florets, changing to rose and then deep crimson.
Zone 5 US, 6 Can. 🏆

***H. s.* 'Preziosa'** A handsome small shrub with purplish red stems up to 5 ft (1.5 m) high and leaves that are purple-tinged when young. Attractive, globular heads of large, rose-pink florets deepen to reddish purple in fall.
Zone 4 US, 5b Can. 🏆

Hydrangea serrata 'Preziosa'

Hydrangea serrata 'Rosalba'

***H. s.* 'Rosalba'** A small shrub that has larger leaves than the other cultivars. The violet-blue flowers are surrounded by ray florets that are white or pale pink at first, quickly turning to crimson.
Zone 5 US, 6 Can. 🏆

CLIMBERS

Hydrangea anomala subsp. *petiolaris*

H. anomala* subsp. *petiolaris (Climbing hydrangea) A vigorous deciduous species that reaches 60–80 ft (18–25 m) and is excellent on a shady wall. It can also be grown as a shrub. The flowers are in flattened clusters 6–10 in (15–25 cm) wide and are dull greenish white with several large, white, sterile florets along the margin of the cluster; they are produced in early summer. The brown bark peels prettily. It may need support at first until the aerial roots become active. Japan, Korea. Introduced 1865.
Zone 4 US, 5 Can. 🏆

H. seemanii A large, vigorous, evergreen climber that supports itself by aerial roots. It has leathery leaves and bears rounded heads of white flowers with white marginal florets in late summer. A tender species suitable for a wall or tree trunk in a sheltered location in mild climates.
Zone 9 US

H. serratifolia A large evergreen species with leathery leaves and small, cream flowers in crowded, columnar panicles up to 6 in (15 cm) long in late summer. Best against a wall in sun or shade. Chile. Introduced 1925/27 by Harold Comber.
Zone 9 US

Hypericum *Guttiferae*
St.-John's-wort

A genus of about 370 species of perennials and evergreen and deciduous shrubs and trees. The shrubby plants thrive in almost any well-drained soil and are very desirable, producing their prominent, bright yellow flowers in great abundance in summer and fall. They require full sun or part shade. Many of the Asiatic species have been misnamed in cultivation, and those described below are in accordance with research carried out by Dr. Robson of the Natural History Museum, London. Some species, particularly H. calycinum *and* H. × inodorum, *are increasingly susceptible to rust.* H. calycinum *is best cut to ground level every other spring; a tool such as a brushcutter or string trimmer can be used. Apart from that, most shrubby plants require little or no pruning.*

H. androsaemum (Tutsan) A good deciduous or semievergreen shrub, seldom more than 30 in (75 cm) high, flowering freely in summer. The flowers are rather small but have conspicuous anthers and are held in clusters of 3–9 at the stem ends. The leaves grow up to 4 in (10 cm) long, and the fall fruits are erect, red, berrylike capsules that turn black. W and S Europe, N Africa, W Asia. In cultivation before 1600.
Zone 3 US, 4 Can.

Hypericum calycinum

H. calycinum (Aaronsbeard St.-John's-wort) A dwarf evergreen shrub with large leaves and large golden flowers. It is an excellent ground cover in dry and shaded locations, but if left unchecked it can become a weed. It is occasionally naturalized. It suffers badly from rust. Bulgaria, N Turkey. Introduced 1676.
Zone 4 US, 5b Can.

Hypericum coris

H. coris A dwarf or prostrate evergreen shrublet, rarely more than 6 in (15 cm) in cultivation. It has slender stems and slender, linear leaves arranged in whorls of 3–6. The golden yellow flowers, $^{1}/_{2}$–$^{3}/_{4}$ in (1–2 cm) across, are borne in terminal panicles up to 5 in (13 cm) long in summer. It is ideal for a rock garden, scree, or dry wall. C and S Europe. In cultivation 1640.
Zone 7 US, 8 Can.

***H. × cyathiflorum* 'Gold Cup'** A graceful, small, deciduous shrub with lanceolate leaves arranged along the branches in two opposite rows. The flowers are deep yellow, cup shaped, and 2$^{1}/_{2}$ in (6 cm) across.
Zone 4 US, 5 Can.

Hypericum forrestii

H. forrestii A neat, hardy, deciduous shrub, that usually grows to 3–4 ft (1–1.2 m) tall. The leaves provide rich color in fall and persist into early winter. The saucer-shaped, golden yellow flowers, 2–2$^{1}/_{2}$ in (5–6 cm) across and rounded in bud, are profusely borne throughout summer and fall. SW China, NE Burma. Introduced 1906 by George Forrest.
Zone 5 US, 6 Can. 🏆

Hypericum 'Hidcote'

***H.* 'Hidcote'** A superb, small to medium-sized semievergreen shrub of compact habit, about 5 ft (1.5 m) high and wide. The golden yellow, saucer-shaped flowers, which are among the largest of any hardy St.-John's-wort, are produced freely from midsummer to midfall. At the limits of its range, the plant will regrow from the roots if cold kills the top growth. Origin is uncertain, but it probably arose at Hidcote Manor, Gloucestershire, England.
Zone 6 US, 6b Can. 🏆

H. × inodorum This erect, smallish decid-

Hypericum × inodorum 'Elstead'

uous shrub with small yellow flowers and red fruits is variable and is usually grown as one of its named clones. However, 'Albury Purple' is subject to mildew, 'Elstead' suffers badly from rust, and 'Summergold', which has yellow foliage, burns badly in sun. SW Europe, naturalized in Britain. In cultivation 1850.
Zone 6 US, 7 Can.

Hypericum kouytchense

H. kouytchense A small, deciduous or semievergreen, rounded, compact shrub with ovate leaves. The golden yellow flowers are up to $2^1/_2$ in (6 cm) across and have conspicuously long stamens. They are freely borne from early summer until midfall and are followed by bright red seed capsules. China.
Zone 5 US, 6 Can.

Hypericum × *moserianum*

H.* × *moserianum (Goldflower) A first-rate dwarf to small deciduous shrub, usually not more than 20 in (50 cm) high, making an excellent ground cover. The arching stems are reddish, and the flowers are 2–$2^1/_2$ in (5–6 cm) across with reddish anthers contrasting with the gold petals from the middle of summer to midfall.
Zone 4 US, 5b Can.

Hypericum × *moserianum* 'Tricolor'

***H.* × *m.* 'Tricolor'** A dwarf to small deciduous shrub with leaves prettily variegated with white, pink, and green. It succeeds best when growing fast in a sheltered location or in a greenhouse.
Zone 4 US, 5b Can.

H. olympicum (Olympic St.-John's-wort) A dwarf, erect or mound-forming, deciduous subshrub with small, bloomy green leaves. The bright yellow flowers are borne in clusters at the ends of the slender, radiating shoots in summer. A good rock-garden plant. Balkans, Turkey. Introduced 1675.
Zone 4 US, 5 Can.

***H. o.* 'Citrinum'** A dwarf shrub with stems bearing terminal clusters of pale sulphur

Hypericum olympicum 'Citrinum'

Hypericum 'Rowallane'

yellow flowers $1^1/_4$ in (3.5 cm) across.
Zone 4 US, 5 Can.

***H.* 'Rowallane'** This magnificent small to medium-sized semievergreen shrub is the finest of the genus but needs a warm location. The firm-textured, beautifully molded flowers are widely bowl shaped, 2–3 in (5–7.5 cm) across, and colored rich golden yellow. It has a graceful habit and grows up to $6^1/_2$ ft (2 m) high. It has been wrongly labeled *H. rogersii*.
Zone 9 US

Idesia *Flacourtiaceae*

A genus of one deciduous species, related to Azara.

I. polycarpa A medium-sized tree with large, ovate, long-stalked leaves that are bloomy on their undersides. The tiny, fragrant, yellowish green flowers are borne in large panicles at the ends of the shoots in summer, but not on young trees, so it is not a tree for a small garden. Large bunches of bright red berries resembling peas are borne on female trees in fall. It grows best in a deep, neutral or somewhat acid soil but does quite well over limestone as long as there is about 30 in (75 cm) of good soil. It is hardiest where summers are long and hot. The only pruning needed is the removal of dead or diseased wood. Japan, China. Introduced c. 1864 by Richard Oldham.
Zone 6 US, 6b Can.

Ilex

Aquifoliaceae Holly

Ilex is a large genus with about 400 species of evergreen and, surprisingly, deciduous trees and shrubs, along with numerous cultivars and hybrids. Not surprisingly, there is enormous variation among hollies, with one suited to every type of garden.

Hollies, especially the evergreens, are landscape features with strong presence, so it is important to consider the whole plant when selecting specimens. They range in size and habit from dense, compact dwarfs, such as *I. crenata* 'Helleri', to imposingly large, majestic trees, such as the pyramidal *I. opaca,* which can reach 50 ft (15 m).

Hollies are valued foremost for their foliage, which might be a lustrous green, gold, blue-green, or reddish purple. Many varieties are rimmed or splotched with cream, yellow, or silvery white. Some leaves are typically prickly, although others are smooth and do not have even a single spine. *I. pernyi* has dainty, boxwoodlike leaves no more than 1 in (2.5 cm) long, while *I. latifolia* boasts prominent leaves up to 6 in (15 cm) long.

The genus is also noted for its showy berries, which can be colored red, yellow, orange, or black. Because most hollies are dioecious, both male and female plants need to be grown for the female to bear fruit. One male for every dozen females is a good ratio to ensure a berry crop, and the plants can be as far apart as 100 ft (30 m), since they are pollinated by bees. There are some exceptions: *I. cornuta,* for one, can produce berries without pollination.

A little extra care is often needed when choosing varieties, as some male hollies have feminine names, and some females sound masculine. *I. aquifolium* 'Golden Queen', for example, is a male, while *I.* × *altaclarensis* 'Golden King' is a female.

Although hollies are generally vigorous, resilient plants, able to bounce back from a severe winter or a hot, dry summer, there are of course limits to their hardiness. The native European *I. aquifolium* does best in cool, moist climates, as in the Pacific Northwest. *I. cornuta* and *I. latifolia* are excellent choices for the warm South. The hardier forms of *I. opaca* can tolerate the conditions of the Midwest and Central Plains. And gardeners in the North and other cold regions can grow *I.* × *meserveae, I. glabra,* and *I. verticillata,* a lovely deciduous holly that fruits profusely.

Ilex × *altaclarensis* 'Camelliifolia'

Care and cultivation

Most hollies are adaptable and will grow in any good garden soil; they perform best, however, in moist but well-drained loam. The native North American hollies, including *I. glabra, opaca,* and *verticillata,* all prefer moist, acidic soil and can generally withstand even wet conditions. *I. cornuta* is tolerant of heat and drought. All hollies can be grown in sun or part shade.

Hollies should be planted in early spring, after the ground has thawed completely, as the roots need the whole summer to become well established. While they do not require much fertilization, and should not be fed during the first year, hollies should be kept moist after planting.

Pruning is seldom necessary, except for hollies being trained as hedges, which should be pruned early to promote dense growth. Variegated hollies, especially when young, need to be watched carefully for reverting shoots. These should be cut out as soon as possible, since reverted branches can quickly take over if missed.

The most serious holly pest is leaf miners, which can utterly destroy the foliage. They must be treated at the first sign of damage.

I.* × *altaclarensis (Altaclara holly, highclere holly) A number of similar but nevertheless variable hybrid evergreen hollies, mostly large shrubs or small to medium-sized, vigorous trees with handsome, usually large leaves. Most make excellent tall hedges or screens and are tolerant of air pollution and coastal conditions. The name derives from *Alta Clera* (Highclere), the home of the earls of Carnarvon.
Zone 7 US, 8 Can.

***I.* × *a.* 'Belgica Aurea'**, syn. *I.* × *a.* 'Silver Sentinel' One of the handsomest variegated hollies, this is a vigorous, erect, female large shrub or medium-sized tree with firm, flat, sparsely spiny leaves that are often 3–4 in (8–10 cm) long. The leaves are attractive deep green with pale green and gray mottling and have irregular but prominent creamy white or creamy yellow margins.
Zone 7 US, 8 Can. 🏆

***I.* × *a.* 'Camelliifolia'** A beautiful, pyramidal, large-fruiting female holly with purple stems. The long, large, mainly spineless, and camellia-like leaves of this large shrub or medium-sized tree are reddish purple when young and a lovely shining dark green in maturity. In cultivation 1865.
Zone 7 US, 8 Can. 🏆

***I.* × *a.* 'Golden King'** This large shrub or medium-sized tree is one of the best hollies with gold variegation. The broad, almost spineless leaves are green with a bright yellow margin. Despite its name, it is female. Found 1884 in Edinburgh.
Zone 6 US, 7 Can. 🏆

***I.* × *a.* 'Hodginsii'** A strong, vigorous clone with purple stems. Some of the large, dark green, rounded or oval leaves are boldly spiny, while others have few spines, the latter being more prevalent on older plants. It makes a large shrub or a medium-sized specimen tree and is especially suitable for coastal and industrial areas. Although usually male, there is a female form.
Zone 7 US, 8 Can. 🏆

***I.* × *a.* 'Lawsoniana'** A very colorful female holly with large, generally spineless leaves, splashed with yellow in the center. Reverting shoots may occur and should be removed. It makes a large shrub or medium-sized tree.
Zone 7 US, 8 Can. 🏆

Ilex × *altaclarensis*

Ilex × *altaclarensis* 'Belgica Aurea'

Ilex × *altaclarensis* 'Camelliifolia'

Ilex × *altaclarensis* 'Golden King'

Ilex × *altaclarensis* 'Lawsoniana'

***I.* × *a.* 'Silver Sentinel'** See *I.* × *a.* 'Belgica Aurea'.

Ilex × *altaclarensis* 'Wilsonii'

***I.* × *a.* 'Wilsonii'** A compact, dome-shaped female clone with green stems and large, evenly spiny, prominently veined leaves. It makes a large shrub or medium-sized tree with large scarlet fruits and is deservedly popular. Raised early 1890s by Fisher, Son and Sibray.
Zone 7 US, 8 Can. 🏆

Ilex aquifolium

I. aquifolium (English holly) Although capable of reaching 60–70 ft (18–21 m) in favorable conditions, it is usually a large shrub or small tree. There are innumerable evergreen cultivars with different habits and varying leaf shapes and colorings. The color of the berries is also variable, but in the forms listed below it is red unless otherwise stated. The sex of seed-raised plants cannot be ascertained for a number of years. The typical form and many of the cultivars make good hedges and are excellent in industrial and coastal areas but will not tolerate extreme heat and drought. W and S Europe, N Africa, W Asia. In cultivation since ancient times.
Zone 6 US, 7 Can. 🏆

***I. a.* 'Amber'** A female large shrub or small tree with green leaves and attractive, large, bronze-yellow fruits. Selected before 1955 at Hillier Nurseries.
Zone 6 US, 7 Can.

***I. a.* 'Argentea Marginata'** A handsome, free-fruiting female large shrub or small tree with green stems and white-margined leaves. The young growth is shrimp pink.
Zone 6 US, 7 Can. 🏆

Ilex aquifolium 'Argentea Marginata Pendula'

***I. a.* 'Argentea Marginata Pendula'** (Perry's weeping silver holly) A small, graceful female tree with weeping branches, forming a compact mushroom of leaves with white margins. It fruits freely.
Zone 6 US, 7 Can.

***I. a.* 'Bacciflava'** (Yellow-fruited holly) A green-leaved female large shrub or small tree bearing heavy crops of bright yellow fruits. 'Fructu-Luteo' is similar.
Zone 5 US, 6 Can.

***I. a.* 'Ferox'** (Hedgehog holly) A male cultivar, lower- and slower-growing than most, that makes an excellent hedge. The upper surfaces of the small leaves are puckered and almost covered with short, sharp spines. In cultivation since at least the 17th century.
Zone 6 US, 7 Can.

***I. a.* 'Ferox Argentea'** (Silver hedgehog holly) A medium-sized male shrub with a very effective combination of rich purple twigs and leaves with creamy white margins and spines. In cultivation 1662.
Zone 6 US, 7 Can. 🏆

Ilex aquifolium 'Ferox Argentea'

***I. a.* 'Ferox Aurea'** (Gold hedgehog holly) The leaves of this medium-sized male shrub have a distinguishing central, deep gold or yellow-green blotch.
Zone 6 US, 7 Can.

***I. a.* 'Flavescens'** A female holly whose leaves are suffused with canary yellow and shade to gold. It is especially effective on a dull winter afternoon or in spring when the young leaves appear. It does best in full sun.
Zone 6 US, 7 Can.

***I. a.* 'Fructu-Luteo'** See *I. a.* 'Bacciflava'.

Ilex aquifolium 'Golden Milkboy'

***I. a.* 'Golden Milkboy'** A striking male holly with large, spine-edged leaves that are green with a large splash of gold in the center. Reverting shoots should be removed. It makes a large shrub or a small tree.
Zone 6 US, 7 Can. 🏆

***I. a.* 'Golden Queen'** An eye-catching large shrub or small tree with green young shoots and broad, spiny, dark green leaves with pale green and gray shading and a broad yellow margin. As noted in the introduction to this genus, the plant is male despite its name.
Zone 6 US, 7 Can. 🏆

***I. a.* 'Golden van Tol'** A female large shrub or small tree with particularly attractive gold-margined leaves. It is a sport of 'J.C. van Tol'.
Zone 5 US, 6 Can.

Ilex aquifolium 'Green Pillar'

***I. a.* 'Green Pillar'** An erect, narrow female form with upright branches and dark green, spiny leaves. Excellent as a specimen tree and suitable for growing in containers. It is also good for hedges, requiring very little pruning.
Zone 6 US, 7 Can. 🏆

***I. a.* 'Handsworth New Silver'** An attractive, purple-stemmed, free-fruiting female holly, distinguished by its comparatively long, deep green leaves, which have a gray mottle and a broad, creamy margin. It makes a large shrub or small tree.
Zone 6 US, 7 Can. 🏆

Ilex aquifolium 'Handsworth New Silver'

Ilex aquifolium 'J.C. van Tol'

***I. a.* 'J.C. van Tol'** A superb female cultivar with dark, shining, almost spineless green leaves and large, regular crops of red fruits. A large shrub or small tree, it is self-pollinating and does not need a male for berry production.
Zone 5 US, 6 Can. 🏆

Ilex aquifolium 'Madame Briot'

***I. a.* 'Madame Briot'** An attractive purple-stemmed female holly with large, strongly spiny green leaves mottled and margined with dark yellow. It makes a large shrub or small tree.
Zone 6 US, 7 Can. 🏆

***I. a.* 'Myrtifolia'** A neat male large shrub or small tree with purple shoots and small, dark green leaves that are variably edged with sharp spines and may even be spineless.
Zone 6 US, 7 Can.

Ilex aquifolium 'Myrtifolia Aureomaculata'

***I. a.* 'Myrtifolia Aureomaculata'** A dense, compact, male large shrub or small tree with small, evenly spined, dark green leaves with pale green shading and an irregular splash of gold in the center.
Zone 6 US, 7 Can. 🏆

***I. a.* 'Pendula'** An elegant, free-fruiting, small female tree, forming a dense mound of weeping stems thickly covered with dark green, spiny leaves.
Zone 6 US, 7 Can.

Ilex aquifolium 'Pyramidalis'

***I. a.* 'Pyramidalis'** A free-fruiting female form with green stems and bright green, slightly spiny leaves. It is conical when young and broadens as it matures into a large shrub or small tree.
Zone 6 US, 7 Can. 🏆

***I. a.* 'Pyramidalis Fructu-Luteo'** A female form similar to 'Pyramidalis' but with profusely borne, bright yellow berries. Zone 6 US, 7 Can. 🏆

Ilex aquifolium 'Silver Milkmaid'

***I. a.* 'Silver Milkmaid'** An attractive large shrub or small tree with strongly spiny, dark green leaves with a central blotch of creamy white. It is female, and so are plants previously grown as 'Silver Milkboy'. Reverting shoots should be removed.
Zone 6 US, 7 Can. 🏆

***I. a.* 'Silver Queen'** A striking male holly with blackish purple young shoots and broadly ovate, dark green leaves faintly marbled with gray and bordered with cream. The young leaves are pink. It makes a large shrub or small tree.
Zone 6 US, 7 Can. 🏆

I. cornuta (Chinese holly) A dense, slow-growing evergreen species, rarely reaching 8 ft (2.5 m) high, with peculiar rectangular, mainly five-spined leaves. It produces large red fruits freely. A tough holly that survives both heat and drought. The following form is the most popular. China, Korea. Introduced 1846.
Zone 7 US, 8 Can.

***I. c.* 'Burfordii'** A free-fruiting, compact, small to medium-sized female form with glossy, green, leathery leaves, which are entire except for a short terminal spine. Excellent for planting in the South, where it can reach 13 ft (4 m). Originated 1930s in Atlanta, Ga.
Zone 7 US, 8 Can.

I. crenata (Japanese holly) A tiny-leaved, slow-growing evergreen, reaching 13–20 ft (4–6 m), with small, shiny, black berries. It is variable, especially in cultivation, so cultivars are more reliable. Good for hedges, as it tolerates shearing well. The following forms are recommended. Korea, Japan. Introduced 1864 into the United States.
Zone 6 US, 7 Can.

Ilex crenata 'Convexa'

***I. c.* 'Convexa'** A free-fruiting, small, bushy female shrub with glossy, puckered or convex leaves. It makes a superb low hedge. Introduced 1919.
Zone 6 US, 7 Can. 🏆

Ilex crenata 'Golden Gem'

***I. c.* 'Golden Gem'** A small, compact shrub with a flattened top and yellow leaves. It is particularly attractive in winter and spring. It is female but flowers sparsely, so does not bear many berries.
Zone 6 US, 7 Can. 🏆

***I. c.* 'Helleri'** (Heller's holly) Perhaps the most attractive dwarf, small-leaved form, making a low, dense, flattened mound. It is female. Originated 1925 in Newport, R.I.
Zone 6 US, 7 Can. 🏆

Ilex crenata 'Mariesii'

***I. c.* 'Mariesii'** A dwarf, almost unholly-like female shrub of very slow growth, with crowded, tiny, round leaves. It is ideal for container or bonsai culture. It eventually makes a stiffly upright shrub of about 6½ ft (2 m) and is attractive when bearing black berries in winter. A male plant with larger leaves and faster growth has also been grown under this name. Introduced 1879.
Zone 6 US, 6b Can.

I. glabra (Inkberry) A medium-sized evergreen shrub with small, glossy, oblong leaves and tiny, pealike, black fruits. Excellent for coastal areas and tolerant of wet soil. E North America.
Zone 5 US, 6 Can.

I. latifolia (Lusterleaf holly) A small evergreen tree or large shrub, usually about 23 ft (7 m) in cultivation. It is a magnificent species with leaves that rival those of *Magnolia grandiflora* in size; they are glossy, dark green, leathery, and oblong and have short spines. It succeeds best in a sheltered loca-

Ilex latifolia

tion, as it is tender when young. Its orange-red fruits are often abundantly produced. Japan, China. Introduced 1840.
Zone 7 US, 8 Can.

I.* × *meserveae (Meserve holly, blue holly) A group of hybrid evergreens that are bushy, small to medium-sized shrubs up to 6½ ft (2 m) with angled, purplish shoots and softly spiny, dark, glossy, blue-green leaves. Raised 1960s in New York to produce a hardier ornamental holly than *I. aquifolium*.

***I.* × *m.* 'Blue Angel'** A slow-growing, compact, small to medium-sized female shrub with dark purple stems and red berries.
Zone 4 US, 5b Can. 🏆

***I.* × *m.* 'Blue Prince'** A small to medium-sized male shrub with purple-tinged stems.
Zone 4 US, 5b Can.

***I.* × *m.* 'Blue Princess'** A small to medium-sized female form with glossy foliage and numerous red berries.
Zone 4 US, 5b Can. 🏆

***I.* × *m.* 'China Boy'** This has a slightly different parentage than the previous selections and is a little hardier. It makes a rounded shrub up to 10 ft (3 m) tall.
Zone 4 US, 5 Can.

Ilex × meserveae 'Blue Angel'

***I.* × *m.* 'China Girl'** The female counterpart of 'China Boy', with shiny, green foliage and copious fruits.
Zone 4 US, 5 Can.

I. opaca (American holly) A pyramidal tree that can grow to 50 ft (15 m) in its native range. Foliage is dark green and the persistent fruits a dull red. E and S North America. Introduced 1744.
Zone 5 US, 6 Can.

***I. o.* 'Greenleaf'** A medium-sized form with glossy green foliage and red berries.
Zone 5 US, 6 Can.

Ilex pernyi

***I. o.* 'Merry Christmas'** A fast-growing, large selection with shiny red fruits.
Zone 5 US, 6 Can.

I. pernyi (Perny holly) A distinguished large evergreen shrub or small tree with small, peculiarly spined, almost triangular-shaped leaves. The small fruits are bright red. C and W China. Introduced 1912.
Zone 6 US, 7 Can.

I. verticillata (Winterberry) A large deciduous shrub whose leaves turn yellow in autumn. The fruits are bright red and persist for a long time. It grows best in moist, acid conditions. E North America. Introduced 1736.
Zone 4 US, 5b Can.

Illicium *Illiciaceae*

The genus consists of about 40 species of aromatic evergreen trees and shrubs native to East and Southeast Asia and warmer parts of the United States. It is the only genus in the family and is related to Magnolia. *It requires conditions similar to those for rhododendrons, although it is tolerant of a slightly higher pH.*

I. anisatum (Japanese anise tree) A medium-sized to large, slow-growing, aromatic shrub. The leaves are more or less oval, pointed, fleshy, and glossy, deep green. The pale yellow, many-petaled flowers are about 1 in (2.5 cm) across and borne, even on young plants, in spring. Japan, China. Introduced 1790.
Zone 8 US, 9 Can.

Illicium floridanum

I. floridanum (Florida anise tree) A medium-sized, aromatic shrub with glossy leaves and maroon-purple, many-petaled flowers in late spring and early summer. S United States. Introduced 1771.
Zone 7 US, 8 Can.

Indigofera *Leguminosae*

This is a very large genus of about 700 species of deciduous shrubs and perennials, found mainly in tropical and subtropical regions. The following are very attractive shrubs whose flower clusters are produced from the leaf axils of growing shoots, which means that they flower continuously throughout summer and autumn. All of them have elegant pinnate leaves and prefer full sun. They thrive in all types of soil and are especially good in dry locations. If the top growth is killed back by cold in a severe winter, the plant will send up a clump of strong shoots the following spring. Old

Indigofera amblyantha

or poorly shaped specimens can be pruned hard to produce the same effect.

I. amblyantha (Pink indigo) A splendid medium-sized shrub with 5–8 in (13–20 cm) racemes of shrimp pink flowers. China. Introduced 1908.
Zone 6 US, 7 Can.

I. decora A pretty and rare dwarf shrub with long racemes of pink pea flowers. China, Japan. Introduced 1846.
Zone 8 US, 9 Can.

I. d.* f. *alba An attractive dwarf form with white flowers. Introduced c. 1878.
Zone 8 US, 9 Can.

Indigofera heterantha

I. heterantha A small to medium-sized shrub with bright purplish rose flowers and particularly elegant foliage. It grows to 3–4 ft (1–1.2 m) in the open but much higher against a wall. Plants that are named *I. divaricata* are probably just geographical variants of this species. NW Himalaya. In cultivation 1840.
Zone 7 US, 8 Can.

I. potaninii (Potanin indigo) A medium-sized shrub similar in many ways to *I. amblyantha* but slightly smaller in size and with slightly shorter racemes of clear pink flowers. In cultivation 1925.
Zone 6 US, 7 Can.

I. pseudotinctoria A vigorous species reaching about 5 ft (1.5 m) in height and bearing pink flowers in dense clusters up to 4 in (10 cm) long. This plant is related to *I. amblyantha*. China. Introduced 1897 by Augustine Henry.
Zone 6 US, 7 Can.

Indocalamus *Gramineae*

A genus of about 15 evergreen species of bamboo, natives of China, of which only the following is generally grown. It prefers moist soil and is good in shade. It will grow in good soil over limestone.

I. tessellatus This remarkable species forms dense clumps of slender, bright green canes up to 6½ ft (2 m) tall. The shining green leaves, up to 2 ft (60 cm) long by 2–4 in (5–10 cm) wide, are the largest of all found on hardy bamboos; their collective weight will eventually cause the canes to bend down, giving the clump an almost dwarf habit. China. Introduced 1845.
Zone 8? US, 9? Can.

Itea *Grossulariaceae*

A genus of about 10 species of evergreen and deciduous shrubs and small trees native to eastern Asia from the Himalaya to the Philippines, with one species in eastern North America. The following are attractive, unusual, summer-flowering shrubs that thrive in part shade, although the evergreen species will take full sun against a south- or west-facing wall if the soil is not too dry.

Itea ilicifolia

I. ilicifolia A lax, evergreen, hollylike shrub to 10 ft (3 m) or more in height. It is particularly charming in late summer, when it is laden with long, drooping, catkin-like clusters of pleasantly fragrant, greenish white flowers. C China. Introduced before 1895 by Augustine Henry.
Zone 6 US, 7 Can.

Itea virginica

I. virginica (Sweetspire) A small, attractive, erectly branched, deciduous shrub with upright, cylindrical clusters of fragrant cream flowers in midsummer. The foliage often turns rich red in fall. It prefers a moist, acid soil. E United States. Introduced 1744.
Zone 5 US, 6 Can.

Jasminum *Oleaceae*
Jasmine

There are more than 200 species of Jasminum, *including evergreen and deciduous shrubs and climbers found in the tropical and temperate regions of the Old World. The plants are very popular, valued especially for their attractive, intensely fragrant flowers in early spring. Jasmines are excellent greenhouse plants in cold climates.*

CLIMBERS

The climbing jasmines are easily grown in most fertile soils in a sunny location and are excellent for training up walls or pergolas. The hardy species withstand air pollution well. Except for *J. officinale* and *J. polyanthum*, which need thinning after flowering, no pruning is necessary.

J. angulare A choice medium-sized evergreen species with thickish, dark green leaves with three leaflets. The sweetly scented white flowers, 2 in (5 cm) long, are borne in large panicles in late summer. Suitable for mild climates only. S Africa.
Zone 9 US

J. azoricum A beautiful, medium-sized, evergreen species with attractive clusters of sweetly scented white flowers that are flushed purple in bud and open in summer and winter. Suitable only for mild climates or a greenhouse. Madeira, where it is very rare. Introduced in the 17th century.
Zone 9 US

J. beesianum (Bees jasmine) A vigorous deciduous plant up to 11 ft (3.5 m), with fragrant, rather small flowers of an unusual deep velvet red but sometimes pinkish crimson. They appear in late spring and early summer and are followed by shiny black berries that persist into winter. SW China. Introduced 1907.
Zone 8 US, 9 Can.

Jasminum beesianum

Jasminum mesnyi

Jasminum officinale

J. mesnyi (Primrose jasmine) A beautiful evergreen species with bright yellow flowers $1^1/_2$ in (4 cm) long. They are semidouble and produced in succession from early to late spring. It is best grown against a sunny wall in mild areas, where it can reach 13 ft (4 m); alternatively, it can be grown in a greenhouse. China. Introduced 1900 by Ernest Wilson.
Zone 8 US, 9 Can. 🏆

J. officinale (Common white jasmine) A vigorous deciduous or semievergreen climber reaching 20–30 ft (6–9 m). The leaves are pinnate and have 5–9 leaflets; the deliciously fragrant white flowers are borne in terminal clusters from early summer to early autumn. It should be thinned out after flowering. It is widely grown in the South and is ideal for trellises and arbors. Caucasus to China. Introduced 1548.
Zone 7 US, 8 Can. 🏆

J. o.* f. *affine A superior medium-sized to large form with slightly larger flowers that are usually tinged with pink on the outside. Sometimes known as *J. o.* 'Grandiflorum', which leads to confusion with *J. grandiflorum*, a tender species for the greenhouse.
Zone 7 US, 8 Can.

Jasminum officinale 'Argenteovariegatum'

***J. o.* 'Argenteovariegatum'** A very striking medium-sized form with gray-green leaves edged with creamy white margins that complement the flowers.
Zone 7 US, 8 Can. 🏆

***J. o.* 'Aureum'** The leaves of this medium-sized form are variegated and suffused with yellow. Effective and free-flowering.
Zone 7 US, 8 Can.

***J. o.* 'Fiona Sunrise'** A striking new form whose fragrant white flowers are produced in summer and resemble those of the species, but it has bright golden yellow foliage.
Zone 7 US, 8 Can.

Jasminum polyanthum

J. polyanthum A beautiful, vigorous, twining evergreen species up to 23 ft (7 m), related to the common jasmine but tender. The intensely fragrant white flowers, flushed rose on the outside, are borne in panicles from late spring to late summer and earlier in the greenhouse. It grows best on a warm wall or trellis and is excellent in the greenhouse as long as it is pruned regularly. The shoots should be thinned but not shortened. China. Introduced 1891.
Zone 8 US, 9 Can. 🏆

J. sambac (Arabian jasmine) The evergreen leaves of this attractive medium-sized climber are glossy and undivided, and the very fragrant white flowers, which flush with pink as they age, are continuously produced from early spring to late summer or year-round when grown in a greenhouse. For a warm, sheltered, sunny location in the mildest areas or in the greenhouse. Possibly originally from India.
Zone 10 US

Jasminum × *stephanense*

J.* × *stephanense (Stephan jasmine) A vigorous deciduous climber up to 23 ft (7 m), with fragrant pale pink flowers in early and midsummer and slender green angular shoots. The leaves on young shoots are often flushed with creamy yellow. It is the only known hybrid jasmine and is very beautiful where there is enough space for it to develop fully. China. Found 1887.
Zone 7 US, 8b Can. 🏆

J. suavissimum A tall-growing, deciduous species with slender twining stems and sweetly fragrant white flowers in loose panicles in late summer that will perfume the whole garden or greenhouse. Australia.
Zone 9 US

SHRUBS

All the hardy shrubby species have yellow flowers and are more or less deciduous in winter, though their green stems create an evergreen effect. They will grow in any good garden soil and full sun.

Jasminum humile 'Revolutum'

***J. humile* 'Revolutum'** A remarkable and very beautiful medium-sized shrub with deep green, persistent leaves usually made up of 5–7 leaflets. These create a splendid setting for the comparatively large, deep yellow, slightly fragrant flowers that are borne in domed heads during summer. China. Introduced 1814.
Zone 8 US, 9? Can. 🏆

Jasminum nudiflorum

J. nudiflorum (Winter jasmine) One of the most beautiful winter-flowering shrubs, with bright yellow flowers on the bare green branches from late fall to late winter. It makes strong, angular growths up to 13 ft (4 m) long and is excellent for covering walls and banks. Although hardy, it requires winter protection or a warm wall at the limits of its range. The long growths can be cut back immediately after flowering. It is deciduous. W China. Introduced 1844.
Zone 6 US, 7b Can. 🏆

***J. n.* 'Aureum'** A medium-sized shrub bearing leaves that are blotched with, or almost entirely, yellow. In cultivation 1889.
Zone 6 US, 7b Can.

Jasminum parkeri

J. parkeri (Parker jasmine) A dwarf or prostrate deciduous shrub, usually forming

a low, 1 ft (30 cm) mound of densely crowded, greenish stems. It bears small pinnate leaves and, in summer, tiny yellow flowers. It is particularly suited to the rock garden. W Himalaya. Introduced 1923.
Zone 8 US, 9 Can.

Jovellana *Scrophulariaceae*

A genus of about six species of perennials and evergreen and deciduous subshrubs related to Calceolaria *and native to New Zealand and Chile. They can be grown outdoors in warmer climates in sun or part shade and any good soil. They make small clumps, and any dead stems should be cut back at ground level.*

J. sinclairii A dwarf deciduous species with white or pale lavender, purple-spotted flowers in early summer. Good for rock gardens. New Zealand. Introduced 1881.
Zone 9 US

J. violacea A small evergreen shrub with erect branches and small, neat leaves. The pale violet flowers with yellow throats and darker markings are produced in early to midsummer. Chile. Introduced 1853.
Zone 9 US 🏆

Jovellana violacea

Juglans *Juglandaceae*
Walnut

The walnuts are a genus of around 20 species of deciduous trees from North and South America and from southeastern Europe to Southeast Asia. They are mostly fast-growing ornamental trees and are not particular about the soil, although they should not be planted where they may be hit by late frosts. The pinnate, ashlike leaves are large and beautiful in some species. The edible fruits can be messy if they fall in undesirable locations, so the trees should be sited carefully.

Juglans ailanthifolia

J. ailanthifolia (Japanese walnut) An erect, medium-sized tree with large, handsome leaves often as long as 3 ft (1 m). Japan. Introduced 1860.
Zone 4 US, 4b Can.

J. cineria (Butternut) A large tree with furrowed bark. The roots emit a toxic substance that inhibits growth of other species. E North America. Introduced 1633.
Zone 3 US, 3 Can.

Juglans nigra

J. nigra (Black walnut) A large, fast-growing tree with deeply furrowed bark and large leaves. The fruits, generally in pairs, are large and round. E and C United States. In cultivation 1686.
Zone 3 US, 3 Can. 🏆

Juglans regia

J. regia (English walnut) A slow-growing, medium-sized to large tree with a characteristically rounded head, silvery gray bark, and dense foliage. It has been cultivated in Europe for many centuries, and the timber is highly prized and very valuable. Where fruit is the main consideration, plant clones such as 'Broadview' and 'Buccaneer' that have been selected for their early and good-quality fruits and have to be propagated vegetatively. SE Europe, Himalaya, China.
Zone 5 US, 6 Can. 🏆

***J. r.* 'Laciniata'** (Cut-leaved walnut) A form with rather pendulous branches and deeply cut leaflets. One of the best ornamental walnuts.
Zone 5 US, 6 Can.

Juniperus *Cupressaceae*
Juniper

A genus of about 60 species of evergreen coniferous trees and shrubs, from prostrate alpines to dense, bushy shrubs and conical or columnar trees. They are native to most of the Northern Hemisphere and extend from inside the Arctic Circle to Mount Kenya on the equator; they are probably the most widely distributed of all trees and shrubs in nature. The leaves of juvenile plants are awl shaped and usually pointed, while those of adult plants are normally scalelike and crowded, although in some species they retain their juvenile form. Juniper fruits are typically rounded or egg shaped, becoming fleshy and berrylike.

Junipers are very versatile and include plants for most soils and situations. They are among the most suitable conifers for alkaline soils. Their foliage color ranges from green and yellow to gray and steel blue. The prostrate forms make excellent ground covers.

J. chinensis (Chinese juniper) An extremely variable species. In cultivation it is typically a tall, dense, grayish tree with both adult and juvenile foliage. Its many cultivars are far more frequently grown. The following are recommended. China, Japan. Introduced before 1767.
Zone 3 US, 4 Can.

Juniperus chinensis 'Aurea'

***J. c.* 'Aurea'** (Young's golden juniper) A tall, slow-growing, conical or columnar tree with golden foliage that can burn in full sun. It has both adult and juvenile foliage. Raised c. 1855 as a sport in Surrey, England.
Zone 4 US, 5 Can.

***J. c.* 'Fairview'** A fast-growing, narrow form that has bright green branchlets and produces silvery berries in late summer.

Juniperus chinensis 'Kaizuka'

Introduced c. 1930 by Evergreen Nurseries, Fairview, Pa. Zone 4 US, 5 Can.

***J. c.* 'Kaizuka'** A large, erect shrub, eventually becoming a small tree, with long, spreading branches covered with characteristic dense clusters of scalelike bright green foliage. It is a very distinct form, ideal in a large garden as a lawn specimen. Japan. Introduced c. 1920.
Zone 4 US, 5 Can.

***J. c.* 'Mountbatten'** A narrow gray-green column with needlelike leaves. Introduced 1948 by Sheridan Nurseries, Toronto.
Zone 3 US, 4 Can.

***J. c.* 'Pyramidalis'** A dense and slow-growing, medium-sized columnar bush with almost entirely juvenile, prickly, bloomy leaves on ascending branches. Japan. Introduced 1843.
Zone 4 US, 5 Can.

***J. c.* 'San Jose'** A prostrate shrub with blue-green branchlets. The leaves are mostly awllike but not prickly. Originated 1935 in San Jose, Calif.
Zone 3 US, 4 Can.

***J. c.* 'Spartan'** Another slender, conical form with densely packed, midgreen branches. Introduced 1961 by Monrovia Nursery, Monrovia, Calif.
Zone 4 US, 5 Can.

J. communis (Common juniper) A variable species that may be prostrate or dwarf but usually makes a medium-sized to large shrub. It has silver-backed leaves that are awl shaped, prickly, and arranged in whorls of three. The fruits are rounded, berrylike, black, and covered with a bluish bloom; they are sometimes used to flavor gin. The foliage may turn brown in winter if the weather is severe. The species is very widely distributed. The following forms are recommended. North America, Europe, Asia, Korea, Japan.
Zone 3 US, 3 Can.

***J. c.* 'Compressa'** Ideal for a rock garden or scree. It is a dwarf, compact, slow-growing column something like a miniature Irish juniper and almost never exceeds 3 ft (1 m) in height. It is more effective when planted in a group. In cultivation 1855.
Zone 3 US, 4 Can.

Juniperus communis 'Depressa Aurea'

***J. c.* 'Depressa Aurea'** A dwarf, wide-spreading form about 2 ft (60 cm) high. The leaves and young shoots are golden yellow in early summer, paling to green. It is unfortunately very prone to the disease needle blight. In cultivation 1887.
Zone 3 US, 3 Can.

***J. c.* 'Gold Cone'**, syn. *J. c.* 'Suecica Aurea' An erect, slow-growing, medium-sized shrub with steeply ascending branches and golden yellow foliage in summer that fades to green in winter.
Zone 3 US, 4 Can.

***J. c.* 'Green Carpet'** A dense, low-growing and wide-spreading shrub with bright green foliage. Norway. Found before 1975.
Zone 3 US, 4 Can.

***J. c.* 'Hibernica'** (Irish juniper) A compact, slender, columnar form 10–16 ft (3–5 m) tall, with densely arranged leaves. It is excellent for formal gardens and can be considered a hardier, shorter counterpart of the Italian cypress. In cultivation 1838.
Zone 3 US, 4 Can.

Juniperus communis 'Hibernica'

***J. c.* 'Hornibrookii'** This is a dwarf, creeping ground cover. The leaves are quite small, loosely spreading, sharply pointed, and silvery white beneath. Ireland. In cultivation 1923.
Zone 3 US, 4 Can.

***J. c.* 'Pencil Point'** See *J. c.* 'Sentinel'.

***J. c.* 'Repanda'** A dwarf, carpeting shrub with densely packed, semiprostrate stems and foliage that becomes slightly bronze in winter. It makes an excellent ground cover in full sun. Ireland. In cultivation 1934.
Zone 3 US, 3 Can. 🏆

Juniperus communis 'Hornibrookii'

Juniperus communis 'Repanda'

***J. c.* 'Sentinel'**, syn. *J. c.* 'Pencil Point' A very narrowly columnar form with densely packed, erect branches. The deep bluish green leaves contrast well with the reddish purple shoots. It reaches 13 ft (4 m) tall and 20 in (50 cm) wide in 30 years. Raised before 1961 in Canada.
Zone 3 US, 3 Can.

***J. c.* 'Suecica Aurea'** See *J. c.* 'Gold Cone'.

J. conferta (Shore juniper) A prostrate species, making large patches of bright green, prickly leaves with a white band on the upper surface. It has round, purplish black, bloomy berries. It is a first-class ground-cover conifer, although it is vulnerable to needle blight. Japan. Introduced 1915 by Ernest Wilson.
Zone 4 US, 5 Can.

Juniperus conferta

***J. c.* 'Blue Pacific'** The blue-green leaves of this prostrate form are broader and less prickly than the species.
Zone 4 US, 5b Can.

***J. davurica* 'Expansa Aureospicata'** A slow-growing dwarf shrub with rigid, almost horizontal branches and juvenile foliage that is grayish green with scattered splashes of yellow. In cultivation 1940.
Zone 3 US, 4 Can.

***J. d.* 'Expansa Variegata'** Similar in habit and foliage but with scattered sprays of cream. It is sometimes listed as a form of *J. chinensis*. In cultivation 1933.
Zone 3 US, 4 Can.

Juniperus davurica 'Expansa Variegata'

J. drupacea (Syrian juniper) A striking and distinctive, narrowly columnar small tree whose short branches are densely crowded with sharply pointed, awl-shaped leaves. SW Asia, Greece. Introduced c. 1854.
Zone 7 US, 8 Can.

***J.* 'Grey Owl'** A splendid, vigorous, medium-sized shrub with widely spreading branches held out like arms and soft, silvery gray foliage. It is probably a hybrid of *J. virginiana*. Originated 1938.
Zone 2 US, 2b Can. 🏆

***J.* 'Holger'** A small, spreading hybrid of *J. squamala* with bloomy blue foliage that is creamy yellow when young. See also *J.* 'Hunnetorp'. Raised 1946 in Sweden.
Zone 4 US, 5 Can. 🏆

Juniperus 'Holger'

J. horizontalis (Creeping juniper) A dwarf or prostrate shrub with long, sometimes procumbent branches, forming carpets

6 ft (2 m) or more across. The leaves on cultivated plants are mostly juvenile and cover

Juniperus horizontalis

the branchlets densely with glaucous green, gray-green, or blue, often turning plum-purple in winter. It is one of the best species for ground cover. The following forms are recommended. North America. In cultivation 1830.

Zone 2 US, 2 Can.

***J. h.* 'Andorra Compact'** Similar to but an improvement over 'Plumosa', with a denser habit. It has bronze-purple foliage in winter. In cultivation 1955.

Zone 2 US, 2 Can.

***J. h.* 'Bar Harbor'** A prostrate form that has widespread, closely ground-hugging branches. The foliage is an attractive glaucous gray-green. In cultivation 1930.

Zone 2 US, 2 Can.

***J. h.* 'Blue Chip'** A prostrate form with foliage that is bright blue throughout the year. Raised 1940 in Denmark.

Zone 2 US, 2 Can.

***J. h.* 'Blue Rug'** See *J. h.* 'Wiltonii'.

***J. h.* 'Douglasii'** A trailing plant with steel-blue foliage. Introduced before 1855 by the Douglas Nurseries, Waukegan, Ill.

Zone 2 US, 2 Can.

***J. h.* 'Emerald Spreader'** A very low-growing plant, forming dense mats of bright green foliage. In cultivation 1973.

Zone 2 US, 2 Can.

***J. h.* 'Hughes'** A vigorous form with ascending branches and gray-green foliage. Raised 1979 in the United States.

Zone 3 US, 2b Can.

***J. h.* 'Plumosa'** (Andorra juniper) A dense, procumbent, compact form with ascending, feathery branches up to 2 ft (60 cm) high. The awl-shaped leaves are usually gray-green, turning purplish in winter. In cultivation 1916; named by the Andorra Nurseries, Philadelphia, Pa.

Zone 2 US, 2 Can. 🏆

***J. h.* 'Prince of Wales'** A low-growing, dense form that makes mats up to 6 in (15 cm) high. The foliage is bright green tinged with blue and flushed with purple in winter. Found 1931 in Alberta, Canada.

Zone 2 US, 2 Can.

***J. h.* 'Wiltonii'**, syn. *J. h.* 'Blue Rug' One of the best forms, with long, prostrate branches that form flattened, glaucous blue carpets. In cultivation 1914.

Zone 2 US, 2 Can. 🏆

***J.* 'Hunnetorp'** A sister seedling of 'Holger', under which name it has been distributed. It differs in its foliage, which is glaucous blue throughout its life.

Zone 4 US, 5 Can.

Juniperus × media 'Blaauw'

J. × media These hybrids are very variable, and the following examples are among the best cultivars available.

***J. × m.* 'Blaauw'** A vigorous shrub up to 5 ft (1.5 m), with strongly ascending main branches and shorter outer ones, all densely covered with feathery sprays of mainly scalelike, grayish blue leaves. In cultivation 1924. It is possibly a form of *J. chinensis*.

Zone 3 US, 4 Can. 🏆

Juniperus × media 'Carberry Gold'

***J. × m.* 'Carberry Gold'** A prostrate shrub with striking foliage that remains bright creamy yellow year-round.

Zone 3 US, 3 Can.

Juniperus × media 'Gold Coast'

***J. × m.* 'Gold Coast'** A flat-topped, low-growing, and wide-spreading form with golden foliage.

Zone 4 US, 5 Can.

***J. × m.* 'Hetzii'** A medium-sized to large, wide-spreading shrub similar to 'Pfitzeriana' but with stems that are more ascend-

ing. The glaucous, mainly adult foliage is also softer to the touch. In cultivation 1920.
Zone 3 US, 2b Can.

***J.* × *m.* 'Kallays Compact'** A flat-topped form with dark green foliage. Originated at Kallay Nursery, Painesville, Ohio.
Zone 3 US, 3 Can.

Juniperus × *media* 'Mint Julep'

***J.* × *m.* 'Mint Julep'** A spreading, flat-topped bush with arching shoots. It resembles 'Pfitzeriana' but has bright green foliage. In cultivation 1960.
Zone 3 US, 3 Can.

Juniperus × *media* 'Old Gold'

***J.* × *m.* 'Old Gold'** A sport of 'Pfitzeriana Aurea', from which it differs in its more compact habit and darker gold foliage that does not fade in winter. In cultivation 1958.
Zone 4 US, 5 Can. 🏆

***J.* × *m.* 'Pfitzeriana'** (Pfitzer juniper) One of the most popular and commonly planted of all conifers. It is eventually a medium-sized, wide-spreading shrub with stout, ascending branches that are held out like arms and droop at the tips. The leaves are mainly green and scalelike, but there are scattered sprays of juvenile leaves with glaucous upper surfaces, particularly in the center of the bush. An excellent conifer either as a lawn specimen or as a design element to vary the outline of a bed or border. Also ideal for covering unsightly structures. Origin uncertain. In cultivation 1896.
Zone 3 US, 2b Can. 🏆

Juniperus × *media* 'Pfitzeriana Aurea'

***J.* × *m.* 'Pfitzeriana Aurea'** The terminal shoots and foliage of this medium-sized shrub are suffused with golden yellow in summer and become yellowish green in winter. A sport of 'Pfitzeriana' that originated 1923 in the United States.
Zone 2 US, 2 Can.

***J.* × *m.* 'Pfitzeriana Compacta'** A sport of 'Pfitzeriana' but denser and more compact and with a preponderance of juvenile awl-shaped leaves. In cultivation 1930.
Zone 3 US, 4 Can. 🏆

***J.* × *m.* 'Pfitzeriana Glauca'** A little denser than 'Pfitzeriana', with mainly awl-shaped, glaucous gray leaves. In cultivation 1940 in the United States.
Zone 3 US, 2b Can.

***J.* × *m.* 'Plumosa Aurea'** A most attractive medium-sized shrub with ascending branches that arch at their tips and are densely covered with feathery sprays of yellow, scalelike leaves that ripen to bronze-gold in winter. In cultivation 1885.
Zone 3 US, 3 Can. 🏆

***J.* × *m.* 'Sulphur Spray'** A sport of 'Hetzii', which it resembles in habit but is slower

Juniperus × *media* 'Sulphur Spray'

growing. It eventually reaches about 6 ft (2 m) high and an equal size wide. The foliage is a striking pale sulphur yellow. In cultivation 1962.
Zone 3 US, 4 Can. 🏆

J. procumbens (Japgarden juniper) A dwarf, procumbent species with long, stiff branches that form carpets up to 1 ft (30 cm) high in the center and 6 ft (2 m) or more across. The tightly packed branches are crowded with awl-shaped, glaucous green, sharply pointed leaves. It is an excellent ground cover for an open, sunny location in well-drained soil. Japan. Introduced 1843.
Zone 4 US, 4b Can.

Juniperus procumbens 'Nana'

***J. p.* 'Nana'** A more compact plant with shorter branches. Japan. Introduced c. 1900.
Zone 3 US, 4 Can. 🏆

J. recurva (Drooping juniper) A large shrub or small tree, broadly conical, with stringy, shaggy bark and drooping branchlets. The leaves are awl shaped, held in threes; they are green or grayish green, usually with white bands above. It is an extremely variable species. The following forms are recommended. Himalaya. Introduced 1825.

Zone 7 US, 8 Can.

***J. r.* 'Castlewellan'** A small, loose, open tree with lax branches like fishing rods. The branchlets droop in long, slender sprays of soft, threadlike foliage.

Zone 7 US, 8 Can.

J. r.* var. *coxii (Cox juniper) An elegant small tree with gracefully drooping branchlets that are longer and more pendulous than those of the typical form. The leaves are also more loosely arranged and are sage green. Upper Burma. Introduced 1920 by E. H. M. Cox and Reginald Farrer.

Zone 6 US, 7 Can.

***J. r.* 'Embley Park'** See *J. squamata* 'Embley Park'.

J. sabina (Savin juniper) An extremely variable juniper that in its typical form is a low, spreading shrub. It has a pungent, disagreeable, catty odor and is more attractive when young. Mountains of S and C Europe to the Caucasus.

Zone 2 US, 2 Can.

Juniperus sabina 'Tamariscifolia'

***J. s.* 'Arcadia'** A low shrub with slightly arching, bright green branches. This and the following two varieties were selected 1933 by the D. Hill Nursery, Dundee, Ill., from seedlings received from a Russian forestry station. All are resistant to juniper blight.

Zone 3 US, 4 Can.

***J. s.* 'Broadmoor'** One of the most prostrate forms. It is similar to 'Tamariscifolia' but has finer gray-green foliage.

Zone 3 US, 4 Can.

***J. s.* 'Skandia'** A flat-growing shrub with blue-gray, needlelike foliage.

Zone 3 US, 4 Can.

***J. s.* 'Tamariscifolia'** A wide-spreading, flat-topped bush with horizontal branches and light green leaves that are mainly awl shaped. A popular landscape specimen and good ground cover. In cultivation c. 1750.

Zone 2 US, 2 Can.

J. scopulorum (Rocky Mountain juniper, Western red cedar) A small, conical, cypresslike tree, often with several main stems. The bark is red-brown and shredding. It has given rise to many forms that are commonly grown in gardens. The following are recommended. Rocky Mountains from British Columbia to Arizona, Texas, and New Mexico. Introduced 1839.

Zone 2 US, 2 Can.

Juniperus scopulorum 'Springbank'

***J. s.* 'Blue Heaven'** A small conical tree with striking blue foliage.

Zone 2 US, 2 Can. 🏆

***J. s.* 'Moonglow'** A small, compact, conical tree with blue-gray foliage.

Zone 3 US, 3 Can.

***J. s.* 'Skyrocket'**, syn. *J. virginiana* 'Skyrocket' A spectacular, very narrowly columnar tree with blue-gray foliage. It is one of the narrowest of all conifers and an excellent plant for adding height to a horizontal landscape design. In cultivation 1949 in the United States.

Zone 3 US, 3 Can.

***J. s.* 'Springbank'** A small, erect tree of columnar habit with ascending and spreading branches, slender branchlets, and silvery gray-green foliage.

Zone 3 US, 3 Can.

J. squamata (Singleseed juniper) An extremely variable species whose forms range from prostrate shrubs to small trees. All forms have shoots with nodding tips and short, awl-shaped, channeled leaves that are white or pale green above. In gardens it is always seen as one of its forms or cultivars. The following are recommended. Wide distribution throughout Asia. Introduced 1824.

Juniperus squamata 'Blue Carpet'

***J. s.* 'Blue Carpet'** A low-growing form with spreading branches, a depressed center, and blue-gray foliage.

Zone 4 US, 5 Can. 🏆

***J. s.* 'Blue Spider'** A dwarf shrub, similar to 'Blue Carpet' but highest in the center and with silvery blue foliage. In cultivation 1980.

Zone 4 US, 5 Can.

Juniperus squamata 'Blue Star'

***J. s.* 'Blue Star'** A low-growing, dense, dwarf shrub that makes a compact, dwarf bun with comparatively large, silvery blue, awl-shaped leaves. Introduced 1964.
Zone 3 US, 3 Can.

Juniperus squamata 'Chinese Silver'

***J. s.* 'Chinese Silver'** A beautiful, medium-sized to large, multistemmed, dense but somewhat shapeless shrub with down-turning terminal shoots. The awl-shaped leaves are an intense, silvery blue-green.
Zone 3 US, 4 Can.

***J. s.* 'Embley Park'**, syn. *J. recurva* 'Embley Park' A distinctive, small, spreading shrub with reddish brown, ascending branches covered with rich grass green, awl-shaped leaves.
Zone 4 US, 4b Can.

***J. s.* 'Loderi'** A slow-growing, dense, usually conical shrub, eventually reaching 10 ft (3 m). The branchlets nod at their tips and are densely set with short, awl-shaped leaves marked with two white bands above. Raised 1925 by Sir Edmund Loder at Leonardslee, Sussex, England.
Zone 3 US, 4 Can.

Juniperus squamata 'Loderi'

***J. s.* 'Meyeri'** A popular and easily recognized juniper of semierect habit, with stout, ascending, angular branches and densely packed, glaucous blue, awl-shaped leaves. Although regarded as a small to medium-sized shrub, it will eventually become large. The characteristic tendency of the species to retain its old, brown leaves is pronounced in this form and can create an untidy appearance. It is the parent of several superior forms, including 'Blue Carpet' and 'Blue Star'. China. Introduced 1914 by Frank N. Meyer.
Zone 4 US, 5 Can.

J. virginiana (Eastern red cedar) One of the hardier conifers, forming a medium-sized tree but grown mostly as one of its cultivars.
Zone 3 US, 3 Can.

***J. v.* 'Burkii'** An excellent, dense, columnar, medium-sized form with ascending branches and both scalelike and awl-shaped, steel blue leaves that are bronze-purple in winter. In cultivation 1932.
Zone 3 US, 4 Can.

***J. v.* 'Canaertii'** A small, conical, fairly dense tree with bright green foliage. It is very attractive when dotted with small, cobalt blue to purple-bloomed, violet fruits.
Zone 3 US, 2b Can.

***J. v.* 'Glauca'** A dense, columnar form with spreading branches covered with silvery gray, mainly scalelike leaves. A very attractive small to medium-sized tree.
Zone 3 US, 3 Can.

Juniperus virginiana 'Burkii'

***J. v.* 'Skyrocket'** See *J. scopulorum* 'Skyrocket'.

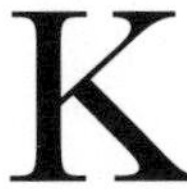

K

Kadsura *Schisandraceae*

A genus of about 20 species of evergreen twining plants from East and Southeast Asia.

K. japonica (Scarlet kadsura) A slender climber up to 11 ft (3.5 m), with dark green leaves that often turn an attractive red in autumn. The fragrant flowers are solitary, cream, and 3/4 in (2 cm) across and appear in summer and early fall. The berries are scarlet and borne in clusters. It needs a location sheltered from cold winds. Japan, China, Taiwan. Introduced 1860.
Zone 9 US

***K. j.* 'Variegata'** The leaves of this small

to medium-sized form have a broad margin of creamy yellow.
Zone 9 US

Kalmia *Ericaceae*

A genus of seven species of mainly evergreen shrubs, natives of North America except for one from Cuba. They are charming shrubs that flower in spring and early summer and thrive under conditions similar to those required by rhododendrons. The flowers are saucer shaped. For maximum flowering, plant in full sun or dappled shade and moist, acid soil. Pruning is generally unnecessary, but old specimens of K. angustifolia *can be cut back hard and will regenerate if fed. Harmful if eaten.*

***K. angustifolia* 'Rubra'** A cultivar of sheep laurel with deep rosy red flowers in summer. It is an evergreen shrub that grows to 3 ft (1 m) high and slowly spreads to form clumps. The deep green leaves, with lighter undersides, are variable in shape. The species and its forms are highly poisonous. E North America. Introduced 1736.
Zone 3 US, 3 Can. 🏆

Kalmia latifolia

K. latifolia (Mountain laurel) A magnificent, rhododendron-like, evergreen shrub of medium size. Along with roses and rhododendrons, it is one of the best early-summer shrubs for acid soils. The glossy leaves are 2–5 in (5–13 cm) long and create a pleasing setting for the clusters of bright pink, saucer-shaped flowers that are a rich sugar pink in bud. A large number of cultivars have been selected in the United States and offer a range of flower colors from white to pink to red. E North America. Introduced 1734.
Zone 4 US, 5b Can. 🏆

Kalmia latifolia 'Ostbo Red'

***K. l.* 'Ostbo Red'** A large shrub with flowers that are bright red in bud and open to pale pink. The first red-budded mountain laurel. Selected 1940s in the United States.
Zone 4 US, 5b Can. 🏆

K. polifolia (Bog laurel) A dwarf, wiry evergreen shrub up to about 2 ft (60 cm) high, with narrow leaves that are dark, shining green above and glaucous beneath, borne in pairs or threes. The bright rose-purple flowers are in large, terminal clusters in midspring. In the wild it is found in swamps and bogs. E North America. Introduced 1767.
Zone 2 US, 2 Can.

Kalmiopsis *Ericaceae*

A genus of one evergreen spring-flowering species that is related to Rhodothamnus *and most frequently grown for its flowers.*

K. leachiana A choice, rare, beautiful, dwarf shrub with pink, kalmia-like flowers that are borne in terminal leafy clusters from early to late spring. It is best grown in a moist, peaty soil in the rock garden or in an alpine house or frame. It can be grown in full sun if the soil is moist enough; if not, it should be given part shade. From rocky ledges in the mountains of Oregon. Introduced 1931.
Zone 7 US, 8 Can. 🏆

Kalmiopsis leachiana

Kalopanax *Araliaceae*

A genus of one species of deciduous tree.

Kalopanax pictus

K. pictus (Castor aralia) A small to medium-sized tree in cultivation, superficially like a maple. The branches and sucker growths have scattered, stout spines; the leaves, over 1 ft (30 cm) across in young plants, have 5–7 lobes. Small clusters of white flowers are borne in large, flattish heads, 1–2 ft (30–60 cm) across, in fall. It prefers a deep, moisture-retentive soil in sun or part shade. Japan, E Russia, Korea, China. Introduced 1865.
Zone 4 US, 5 Can.

Kerria *Roseaceae*

A genus of one deciduous species, related to Rhodotypos.

K. japonica (Japanese kerria) A graceful suckering shrub reaching 6 ft (1.8 m) high.

Kerria japonica

In mid- to late spring, or earlier in a mild season, its branches are wreathed with rich yellow flowers. Its green stems are effective in winter. It does best in a moist, well-drained soil with enough shade to prevent the flowers from bleaching. Pruning is seldom necessary. China. Introduced 1834.
Zone 4 US, 5 Can.

Kerria japonica 'Golden Guinea'

Kerria japonica 'Pleniflora'

***K. j.* 'Flore Pleno'** See *K. j.* 'Pleniflora'.

***K. j.* 'Golden Guinea'** A medium-sized shrub with very large, single yellow flowers.
Zone 4 US, 5b Can. 🏆

***K. j.* 'Picta'**, syn. *K. j.* 'Variegata' A pleasing and elegant form with a lower, spreading habit; the leaves are variegated in creamy white. It grows to about 5 ft (1.5 m). In cultivation 1844.
Zone 4 US, 5b Can.

***K. j.* 'Pleniflora'**, syn. *K. j.* 'Flore Pleno' The double yellow-flowered form, taller and more vigorous and erect than the single-flowered form. Green shoots and bright green leaves. China. Introduced 1804.
Zone 4 US, 5b Can. 🏆

***K. j.* 'Variegata'** See *K. j.* 'Picta'.

Koelreuteria *Sapindaceae*
Golden-rain tree

A genus of three species of deciduous trees, natives of China and Taiwan, only one of which is widely cultivated. It is easily grown in all soils and flowers and fruits best in hot summers. It is tolerant of drought, poor conditions, and wind, but not salt. Pruning is best avoided.

Koelreuteria paniculata

K. paniculata (Varnish tree, golden-rain tree) This is the best-known species and is an attractive, broad-headed tree 30–40 ft (9–12 m) tall, with pinnate leaves. Each leaf has 9–15 leaflets that are broadest below the middle. Large panicles of small yellow flowers in mid- to late summer are followed by bladderlike fruits. Leaves turn yellow in autumn. China. Introduced 1763.
Zone 5 US, 6 Can. 🏆

***K. p.* 'Fastigiata'** A rare and remarkable, slow-growing form with a narrowly columnar habit, eventually reaching 26 ft (8 m) high by 3 ft (1 m) wide.
Zone 5 US, 6 Can.

Kolkwitzia *Caprifoliaceae*

A genus of a single deciduous species, related to Abelia. *It grows in all kinds of soils.*

Kolkwitzia amabilis

K. amabilis (Beautybush) A medium-sized, dense, twiggy shrub. In late spring and early summer its drooping branches are draped with bell-shaped flowers that are soft pink with a yellow throat. China. Introduced 1901 by Ernest Wilson.
Zone 4 US, 5 Can.

***K. a.* 'Pink Cloud'** A beautiful medium-sized shrub. Flowers are a deeper pink than the type. Selected 1946 at the Royal Horticultural Society's garden, Wisley.
Zone 4 US, 5 Can. 🏆

Kolkwitzia amabilis 'Pink Cloud'

L

+ Laburnocytisus *Leguminosae*

A graft hybrid (chimera) between Cytisus *and* Laburnum, *of which only the following form is known. It is usually grown for its flowers.*

+ *L. adamii* A small deciduous tree with laburnum forming the core and broom the outer envelope. It is better described as odd rather than beautiful. Some branches bear the yellow flowers of *Laburnum anagyroides,* while other branches have the dense, congested clusters of the purple-flowered broom, *Cytisus purpureus.* In addition, most branches produce intermediate flowers of a striking coppery pink. Cultivation is as for *Laburnum.* Originated 1825 in the nurseries of M. Adam near Paris.
Zone 5 US, 6 Can.

Laburnum *Leguminosae*

A genus of two species of small, ornamental deciduous trees that are easily grown in almost all kinds of soil. The yellow pea flowers are produced in drooping racemes in late spring and early summer. If pruning is necessary (and it seldom is), it should be done in late summer. Spur-pruning of laburnums grown in arches is best carried out in early winter. The plants are toxic if eaten.

Laburnum alpinum

L. alpinum (Scotch laburnum) A small, broad-headed tree with long, drooping clusters of fragrant yellow flowers in early summer. The leaves have three leaflets and are deep, shining green above, paler and with a few hairs beneath. The seedpods are flattened and shining. C and S Europe. In cultivation 1596.
Zone 4 US, 5b Can.

***L. a.* 'Pendulum'** A slow-growing form developing a low, dome-shaped head of stiffly weeping branches.
Zone 4 US, 5b Can.

***L.* × *watereri* 'Vossii'** A lovely, very free-flowering small tree with glossy leaves and long racemes of yellow flowers in early summer; it does not, however, produce a heavy seed crop.
Zone 5 US, 6 Can. 🏆

Laburnum × *watereri* 'Vossii'

Lapageria *Philesiaceae*

A genus of one evergreen climbing species.

L. rosea (Chilean bellflower) One of the most beautiful of all climbers and the national flower of Chile. It has twining stems that reach 10–16 ft (3–5 m). The leaves are leathery, and the rose-crimson, fleshy, bell-shaped flowers, 3 in (7.5 cm) long by 2 in (5 cm) wide, are single or in pendulous clusters during most of the summer and fall. It needs a neutral to slightly acidic, cool, moist soil in full or part shade. It performs best on a sheltered wall and is an excellent greenhouse plant but does not

Lapageria rosea

tolerate long exposure to strong sunlight. Chile, Argentina. Introduced 1847.
Zone 9 US 🏆

L. r.* var. *albiflora A small to medium-sized climber with white flowers.
Zone 9 US

***L. r.* 'Flesh Pink'** A small to medium-sized form with flesh pink flowers.
Zone 9 US 🏆

***L. r.* 'Nash Court'** A small to medium-sized climber with soft pink flowers marbled with deeper pink.
Zone 9 US 🏆

Larix *Pinaceae*
Larch

A small genus of generally fast-growing, deciduous coniferous trees. The branches are set in irregular whorls that end in long, slender, flexible branchlets, which on older trees tend to droop or hang gracefully. The leaves are arranged spirally on younger wood, while they are in dense rosettes of short spurs on older wood. They are generally bright green or occasionally blue-green in spring and summer and turn butter yellow or mellow gold in autumn. The cones remain intact for a long time after shedding their seed and are often cut for indoor decoration. Larches are adaptable to most soils, except shallow ones over limestone. However, they generally prefer a moist, somewhat acidic soil, and the American larch needs moist, even wet conditions. All need full sun.

Larix decidua

L. decidua (European larch) A large tree with a slender, conical crown when young. The branches and branchlets droop in old specimens. The rosette leaves are up to 1¼ in (3.5 cm) long and light green, and the egg-shaped, red-brown cones are about the same length. European Alps, Carpathians. Introduced 1620.
Zone 2 US, 2b Can. 🏆

L. × eurolepis *(L. decidua × L. kaempferi)* (Dunkeld larch, hybrid larch) A vigorous large tree, more important commercially than horticulturally, as it produces high-grade timber and is disease resistant. Originated 1904 in Perthshire, Scotland.
Zone 2 US, 2b Can.

Larix kaempferi

L. kaempferi (Japanese larch) A vigorous larch making a large tree with reddish shoots and sea green leaves up to 1¼ in (3.5 cm) long and broader than those of *L. decidua.* Japan. Introduced 1861.
Zone 2 US, 2b Can. 🏆

***L. k.* 'Pendula'** A beautiful, tall, elegant tree with long, weeping branchlets. In cultivation 1896.
Zone 2 US, 2b Can.

Larix kaempferi 'Pendula'

***L. k.* 'Wolterdingen'** A dense, dwarf, bun-shaped bush with blue-gray foliage. Found 1970 in Germany.
Zone 2 US, 2b Can.

Larix kaempferi 'Wolterdingen'

L. laricina (American larch, tamarack) Similar to the European larch but with brighter yellow fall color. E North America.
Zone 1 US, 1 Can.

Laurelia *Atherospermataceae*

A genus of three species of evergreen trees from Chile, Argentina, and New Zealand.

Laurelia sempervirens

L. sempervirens (Chilean laurel) A large shrub or small to medium-sized, lime-tolerant tree. The leathery leaves are bright matte green and have an aroma very similar to that of *Laurus nobilis.* It grows best in a location sheltered from strong wind. Chile. Introduced before 1868.
Zone 9 US

Laurus *Lauraceae*

Sweet bay, laurel, bay laurel

There are only two species in this genus. They are evergreen shrubs or small trees with small, yellowish green flowers clustered on the branches in midspring, or earlier in a mild season. On female trees they are followed by shiny black fruits.

Laurus nobilis

L. nobilis (Bay laurel, sweet bay) The tree that produces the bay leaves used in cooking. Not only is the foliage highly aromatic, but the plant is very tolerant of being clipped and makes fine-shaped small to medium-sized specimen trees, topiary, and hedges. It is salt resistant and valuable for planting in mild coastal areas. A good, moisture-retentive, fertile soil is best, and clipping should be done in summer. Susceptible to frost but, given shelter, is not as tender as commonly supposed. Mediterranean region. In cultivation 1562.
Zone 8 US, 9 Can. 🏆

Laurus nobilis 'Aurea'

***L. n.* 'Angustifolia'** A form with long, narrow, pale green, wavy, leathery leaves. It may be slightly hardier than the species.
Zone 8 US, 9 Can.

***L. n.* 'Aurea'** A large shrub or small tree with golden yellow leaves that are particularly attractive in winter and spring.
Zone 8 US, 9 Can. 🏆

Lavandula *Labiatae*

Lavender

A genus of about 20 species of aromatic evergreen shrubs and herbaceous perennials, native to the Mediterranean region. Lavender is perhaps the most highly prized of all aromatic shrubs and is a favorite for dwarf hedges, mixing well with stonework or formal rose beds and providing an attractive element in gray or blue borders. It succeeds in all types of well-drained soil, is best grown in full sun, and is excellent in coastal areas. The flowers can be dried and used to fill sachets. The heights given include the flower spike.

Lavandula angustifolia

L. angustifolia (English lavender) The garden forms are usually listed under the name of this species, but they are in fact hybrids between *L. angustifolia* and *L. latifolia* and include backcrosses. Flowers are borne in dense spikes on long, slender stems and retain their scent for years when dried. Plants are not generally long lived and so need to be replaced after about a decade, as they become over-woody and unattractive. They should be trimmed back yearly after flowering to retain bushiness. In cultivation since the mid-16th century.
Zone 5 US, 6 Can.

***L. a.* 'Alba'** A robust form with long, narrow, gray-green leaves and erect stems 3–4 ft (1–1.2 m) high. The white flowers open in the latter half of summer.
Zone 5 US, 6 Can.

***L. a.* 'Folgate'** A compact lavender with narrow, gray-green leaves and stems 24–32 in (60–80 cm) high. The lavender-blue flowers open around midsummer. In cultivation 1933.
Zone 5 US, 6 Can.

Lavandula angustifolia 'Grappenhall'

***L. a.* 'Grappenhall'** A robust form with comparatively broad, gray-green leaves and strong stems that are 3–4 ft (1–1.2 m) high. The flowers are lavender-blue, opening in the latter half of summer.
Zone 5 US, 6 Can.

Lavandula angustifolia 'Hidcote'

***L. a.* 'Hidcote'** A compact lavender with narrow, gray-green leaves and stems that are 24–32 in (60–80 cm) high. The violet flowers are in dense spikes and open toward

the end of the first half of summer. It is one of the best and most popular lavenders, but it has to be grown from cuttings from the true plant; seed from named clones such as this does not come true.
Zone 5 US, 6 Can. 🏆

***L. a.* 'Hidcote Pink'** A compact shrub, growing to 2 ft (60 cm). It is similar to 'Hidcote' but has pale pink flowers. In cultivation 1962.
Zone 5 US, 6 Can.

***L. a.* 'Munstead'** A compact form with narrow, gray-green leaves and stems that are 24–30 in (60–75 cm) high. The dense spikes of tiny, tubular flowers are bluer than most and open toward the end of the first half of summer. In cultivation 1916.
Zone 4 US, 5 Can.

Lavandula angustifolia 'Nana Alba'

***L. a.* 'Nana Alba'** A dwarf, compact form with comparatively broad, gray-green leaves and stems up to 1 ft (30 cm). The flowers are white and open toward the end of the first half of summer.
Zone 5 US, 6 Can.

***L. a.* 'Rosea'** A compact lavender with narrow leaves, more green than gray, and stems that are 24–30 in (60–75 cm) high. The lavender-pink flowers open in midsummer. It is used in making eau de cologne. In cultivation 1949.
Zone 5 US, 6 Can.

***L. a.* 'Twickel Purple'** A compact form with comparatively broad gray leaves and stems that are 24–30 in (60–75 cm) high. The flowers are lavender-blue and open toward the end of the first half of summer.
Zone 5 US, 6 Can. 🏆

Lavandula angustifolia 'Rosea'

Lavandula angustifolia 'Vera'

***L. a.* 'Vera'** (Dutch lavender) A robust form with comparatively broad gray leaves and stems 3–4 ft (1–1.2 m) high. The lavender-blue flowers open in the latter half of summer.
Zone 5 US, 6 Can. 🏆

L. lanata (Woolly lavender) A small, white-woolly shrub that produces long-stalked

Lavandula stoechas

spikes of fragrant, bright violet flowers from midsummer to early fall. Spain.
Zone 8 US, 9 Can.

L. stoechas (Spanish lavender) A dwarf, intensely aromatic shrublet with narrow, grayish leaves. The dark purple flowers are borne in dense, congested, terminal heads in summer and are topped by prominent purple bracts. It requires a warm, dry, sunny site. Mediterranean region. In cultivation since the mid-16th century.
Zone 8 US, 9 Can. 🏆

L. s.* var. *leucantha A dwarf shrub with white flowers and bracts.
Zone 8 US, 9 Can.

Lavandula stoechas subsp. *pedunculata*

L. s.* subsp. *pedunculata The flower spikes of this gray-leaved dwarf form are shorter and borne on long stalks. The ear-like purple bracts, 2 in (5 cm) long, have earned it the common name "papillon" (French for "butterfly"). Spain, Portugal.
Zone 8 US, 9 Can. 🏆

Lavatera *Malvaceae*
Mallow

A genus of some 25 species of herbaceous plants and deciduous shrubs, native to Europe, western Asia, Australia, and California. The shrubby mallows have typical mallow flowers and palmate leaves. They are excellent for seashore gardens and do well in all types of soil, preferably in full sun.

L. maritima An elegant species, growing to 5–6½ ft (1.5–2 m). The stems and palmate leaves are grayish and downy; the large, saucer-shaped flowers, which are

pale lilac with purple veins and eye, are produced continuously from midsummer to late fall. It needs a warm, sheltered location with every possible protection from cold wind. N Africa.
Zone 9 US 🏆

***L. olbia* 'Rosea'** See *L. thuringiaca* 'Rosea'.

L. thuringiaca An elegant species growing to 5–6 ft (1.5–1.8 m) high. Both stems and leaves are grayish and downy. Large saucer-shaped flowers are produced in summer. Plants become herbaceous in cold climates. C and S Europe to W Himalaya.
Zone 4 US, 5 Can.

Lavatera thuringiaca 'Barnsley'

***L. t.* 'Barnsley'** A splendid medium-sized shrub that originated as a sport of *L. t.* 'Rosea'. The flowers are very pale pink, almost white, with a red eye. It is now one of the most popular of all garden shrubs. Any reversions must be removed.
Zone 4 US, 5 Can. 🏆

***L. t.* 'Blushing Bride'** A form with all the good qualities of 'Barnsley' but without its tendency to revert. The very pale pink to white flowers with a red center are borne over a long period in summer.
Zone 4 US, 5 Can.

Lavatera thuringiaca 'Burgundy Wine'

***L. t.* 'Burgundy Wine'** A medium-sized shrub with deep purplish pink flowers.
Zone 4 US, 5 Can.

***L. t.* 'Candy Floss'** A medium-sized shrub with very pale pink flowers.
Zone 4 US, 5 Can.

Lavatera thuringiaca 'Ice Cool'

***L. t.* 'Ice Cool'** A small shrub with a weaker constitution than others. It bears white flowers with a slight green cast.
Zone 4 US, 5 Can.

***L. t.* 'Pink Frills'** A beautiful form with small, semidouble, pink flowers on slender spikes. It is compact and upright in habit, with a mature size of approximately 4 × 4 ft (1.2 × 1.2 m).
Zone 4 US, 5 Can.

***L. t.* 'Kew Rose'** A medium-sized shrub, more vigorous than 'Rosea', with darker, purplish stems and large, bright pink flowers. Previously grown as *L. olbia*.
Zone 4 US, 5 Can.

Lavatera thuringiaca 'Rosea'

***L. t.* 'Rosea'**, syn. *L. olbia* 'Rosea' A medium-sized shrub with deep pink flowers.
Zone 4 US, 5 Can. 🏆

Ledum *Ericaceae*

A genus of about four species of low-growing, evergreen shrubs from swampy moors in northern latitudes. All have neat foliage, usually covered below with a white or rust-colored woolly felt, and terminal clusters of white flowers. They need a moist, acidic soil.

Ledum groenlandicum

L. groenlandicum (Labrador tea) A dwarf, upright shrub occasionally as tall as 3 ft (1 m). The white flowers are produced from midspring to early summer. Best-known species of the genus. North America, Greenland. Introduced 1763.
Zone 2 US, 2 Can.

***L. g.* 'Compactum'** A compact form, developing into a neat shrub 12–18 in (30–45 cm) high, with broader leaves on shorter branches and smaller flower clusters than the typical form.
Zone 2 US, 2 Can.

Leiophyllum *Ericaceae*

A genus of only one evergreen species.

L. buxifolium (Sand myrtle) A neat, compact, rounded, dwarf shrub with boxwood-like leaves that are smooth on both surfaces.

Leiophyllum buxifolium

The clusters of white flowers are pink in bud and emerge in late spring and early summer. It is an attractive species needing slightly acidic, moist soil. E North America. Introduced 1736 by Peter Collinson.
Zone 5 US, 6 Can. 🏆

Leonotis *Labiatae*

There are about 15 species of Leonotis, *including annuals, perennials, and deciduous shrubs, native to tropical and southern Africa. The following is an easily grown shrub in all types of soil but is suitable for outdoor cultivation only in the very mildest regions. In cooler climates it is an excellent plant for the greenhouse.*

Leonotis leonurus

L. leonurus (Lion's ear) A small, square-stemmed shrub with downy, lance-shaped leaves and bright orange-scarlet, two-lipped flowers 2 in (5 cm) long in fall. South Africa. Introduced 1712.
Zone 10 US

Leptospermum *Myrtaceae*

A genus of some 30 species of attractive, small-leaved evergreen shrubs or small trees, mainly natives of Australia, with a few found in New Zealand, New Caledonia, and Malaysia. They are related to the myrtles. In warm coastal areas and mild climates, many form large shrubs up to 13 ft (4 m) high or more, but elsewhere they need to be grown in a greenhouse. They flower in late spring and early summer and do best in full sun in well-drained acid or neutral soil. Bushiness can be maintained by pinching out the shoot tips after the plant has flowered.

L. humifusum An extremely prostrate shrub, forming an extensive carpet of reddish stems and small, blunt, leathery, aromatic leaves that turn bronze-purple in cold weather. Small white flowers stud the branches of mature specimens in early summer; branch bark is somewhat flaky. Tasmania. Introduced 1930.
Zone 9 US 🏆

Leptospermum lanigerum

L. lanigerum A beautiful medium-sized shrub with long, silvery leaves that often turn bronze in fall. It bears its white flowers in early summer. Australia, Tasmania. Introduced 1774.
Zone 9 US 🏆

***L. l.* 'Silver Sheen'** A medium-sized shrub selected from plants previously grown as *L. cunninghamii*, with attractive, silvery gray leaves and reddish stems. It flowers in midsummer, several weeks later than the typical *L. lanigerum*.
Zone 9 US

Leptospermum scoparium

Leptospermum scoparium 'Keatleyi'

L. scoparium (Manuka, tea tree) A variable, white-flowered species ranging from a medium-sized to large shrub. It has given rise to many forms. Australia, Tasmania, New Zealand. Introduced 1772.
Zone 9 US

***L. s.* 'Keatleyi'** An outstanding medium-sized shrub with large, waxy-petaled, soft pink flowers and silky, crimson young foliage. New Zealand. Introduced before 1926 by Captain Keatley.
Zone 9 US 🏆

***L. s.* 'Kiwi'** A dwarf, dense form with freely produced, deep pink flowers and bronze foliage. A seedling of 'Nanum'. Raised in New Zealand.
Zone 9 US 🏆

***L. s.* 'Nanum'** A charming dwarf form reaching about 1 ft (30 cm), with rose-pink flowers that are produced profusely. An excellent alpine-house shrub. Raised before 1940 in New Zealand.
Zone 9 US

***L. s.* 'Nicholsii'** The flowers of this medium-sized shrub are carmine and the foliage is dark, purplish bronze. In cultivation 1904.
Zone 9 US 🏆

***L. s.* 'Red Damask'** A small shrub with very double, deep red, long-lasting flowers like tiny roses all along the shoots. Raised 1944 in California.
Zone 9 US 🏆

Lespedeza *Leguminoseae*
Bush clover

A genus of about 40 species of perennials and deciduous shrubs from North America, eastern Asia, and Australia. The cultivated species are useful, late-flowering shrubs with profusely borne racemes of small pea flowers along the shoots, which are bowed by their weight. The leaves of all of them have three leaflets. They are easy to grow and thrive in all types of soil.

L. bicolor (Shrub bush clover) A medium-sized, semierect shrub with bright rose-purple flowers borne in racemes in late summer. Korea, Manchuria, China, Japan. Introduced 1856 by Maximowicz.
Zone 4 US, 5 Can.

L. thunbergii One of the best fall-flowering shrubs, with arching stems 4–5 ft (1.2–1.5 m) long that are bowed to the ground in early fall by the weight of the huge terminal panicles of rose-purple pea flowers. Japan, China. Introduced 1837.
Zone 6 US, 7 Can. 🏆

Leucothoë *Ericaceae*

A genus of more than 40 species of evergreen and deciduous shade-bearing shrubs native to North America and Japan. They require an acidic, peaty, or otherwise moisture-retentive organic soil. Old or weak growth or shoots that are too vigorous can be pruned after flowering.

L. davisiae (Sierra laurel) A pretty evergreen shrub, usually less than 3 ft (1 m) high, with dark green, glossy leaves and erect clusters of white flowers in early summer. California. Introduced 1853 by William Lobb.
Zone 8 US, 9 Can.

L. racemosa (Sweetbells) A slowly suckering shrub that will form a dense clump. The bright green foliage turns scarlet in fall, and the fragrant white flowers emerge in spring. Massachusetts to Florida. Introduced 1736.
Zone 5 US, 6 Can.

Leucothoë *walteri* 'Scarletta'

Leucothoë *davisiae*

L. walteri (Drooping leucothoë) An elegant, small to medium-sized, deciduous shrub that grows as tall as $6^1/_2$ ft (2 m) and provides excellent ground cover. The gracefully arching stems carry lance-shaped, leathery, green leaves, which in fall and winter become flushed with beet red or bronze-purple, especially in exposed locations. The short, drooping clusters of urn-shaped white flowers appear all along the stems in late spring. For many years this plant has been grown as *L. fontanesiana*, the name by which it is probably still known in

Leucothoë *walteri* 'Rainbow'

most nurseries. SE United States. Introduced 1793.

Zone 5 US, 6 Can. 🏆

***L. w.* 'Rainbow'** The leaves of this small to medium-sized shrub are variegated with cream, yellow, and pink. It arose as a seedling at one of the Hillier Nurseries.

Zone 5 US, 6 Can.

***L. w.* 'Rollisonii'** A selection with narrower leaves, making the flower clusters appear even more prominent.

Zone 5 US, 6 Can. 🏆

***L. w.* 'Scarletta'** A form with glossy red young foliage, turning dark green, then red-purple in autumn and winter.

Zone 5 US, 6 Can.

Leycesteria *Caprifoliaceae*

A genus of six species of hollow-stemmed deciduous shrubs, native to the Himalaya and China.

Leycesteria formosa

L. formosa (Himalaya honeysuckle) A medium-sized, erect shrub with stout, hollow, sea green shoots covered at first with a bluish bloom. The white flowers have claret-colored bracts and are carried in dense, terminal, drooping clusters from early summer to early fall. They are followed by large, shining, reddish purple berries that are attractive to birds. It is suitable for any type of soil, including poor ones, and tolerates lime, coastal conditions, and air pollution. The stems can be cut almost to the ground in fall to protect against winter injury; new shoots will emerge from the base the next spring.

Zone 7 US, 8 Can.

Ligustrum *Oleaceae*
Privet

A genus of about 50 species of evergreen and deciduous shrubs native to the Himalaya, East and Southeast Asia, and Australia, with one species in Europe and North Africa. They are mostly fast growing and tolerant of almost any soil and can be grown in sun or shade. Many produce attractive, often fragrant, white flowers, and the evergreens are commonly used for hedges. Specimens grown particularly for their flowers should be fed if soil is poor. Hedges should be clipped 2–3 times a year, and old, untidy hedges can be cut back hard, provided they are fed and watered. Harmful if eaten.

L. amurense (Amur privet) A good hedge plant that stands up to city conditions well. When it is not sheared as a hedge, it bears white flowers in 2 in (5 cm) panicles that are unpleasantly scented. The resulting black fruits last well into winter. N China. Introduced 1860.

Zone 5 US, 6 Can.

L. japonicum (Japanese privet) A compact, medium-sized, dense, evergreen shrub with shining, olive green, camellia-like foliage and large panicles of attractive white flowers in late summer. Not as vigorous as *L. lucidum*. An excellent plant for use as a screen or hedge; widely grown in the South. N China, Korea, Taiwan, Japan. Introduced 1845 by Siebold.

Zone 8 US, 9 Can.

Ligustrum japonicum 'Rotundifolium'

***L. j.* 'Rotundifolium'** A very slow-growing, rigid, compact small form with round, leathery, black-green leaves. Japan. Introduced 1860 by Robert Fortune.

Zone 8 US, 9 Can.

Ligustrum lucidum

L. lucidum (Glossy privet) A large evergreen shrub or small to medium-sized tree with large, glossy green, long-pointed leaves and handsome panicles of white flowers in late summer. It occasionally makes a symmetrical tree, 40 ft (12 m) tall or more, with a fluted trunk. China. Introduced 1794.

Zone 8 US, 9 Can. 🏆

Ligustrum lucidum 'Excelsum Superbum'

***L. l.* 'Excelsum Superbum'** A strikingly variegated large shrub or small to medium-sized tree with bright green leaves marked with pale green and edged with yellow or greenish yellow.

Zone 8 US, 9 Can. 🏆

***L. l.* 'Latifolium'** An effective large shrub or small to medium-sized tree with large, camellia-like leaves.

Zone 8 US, 9 Can.

Ligustrum lucidum 'Tricolor'

***L. l.* 'Tricolor'** The leaves of this large shrub or small to medium-sized tree are narrow, deep green and prominently marked with gray-green, edged with creamy yellow or nearly white, and tinged with pink when young. In cultivation 1895.
Zone 8 US, 9 Can.

L. ovalifolium (California privet) This is the ubiquitous evergreen hedge privet, one of the most common shrubs in cultivation. If left unpruned it will reach a large size, but the resultant flowers, borne in summer, have an unpleasant smell. It tolerates most soils and exposures and loses its leaves only where winters are cold. Japan. In cultivation 1885.
Zone 6 US, 7 Can.

***L. o.* 'Argenteum'** A medium-sized shrub, the leaves of which have a creamy margin.
Zone 6 US, 7 Can.

Ligustrum ovalifolium 'Aureum'

***L. o.* 'Aureum'** (Golden privet) A brightly colored medium-sized shrub with rich yellow, green-centered leaves that are often completely yellow. In cultivation 1862.
Zone 6 US, 7 Can. 🏆

Ligustrum quihoui

L. quihoui One of the best privets for producing attractive blooms, this is an elegant, medium-sized, deciduous shrub whose very fragrant, white flowers are held in trusses up to 20 in (50 cm). It blooms late among the privets, in late summer and early fall. China. Introduced 1862.
Zone 7 US, 8 Can. 🏆

Ligustrum sinense

L. sinense (Chinese privet) This large shrub is perhaps the most free-flowering of the deciduous privets. It is a large, spreading shrub or small tree with downy stems, oval leaves, and white flowers produced in long, dense sprays in midsummer, followed by large numbers of rich black-purple fruits. Introduced 1852 by Robert Fortune.
Zone 7 US, 8 Can.

***L. s.* 'Variegatum'** A large, attractive shrub that will light the darkest corner with its softly gray-green, white-margined leaves and white flowers.
Zone 7 US, 8 Can.

Ligustrum 'Vicaryi'

***L.* 'Vicaryi'** (Vicary golden privet) A medium-sized semievergreen shrub with leaves suffused with golden yellow, turning bronze-purple in winter. It is said to be a hybrid between *L. ovalifolium* 'Aureum' and *L. vulgare*. In cultivation c. 1920.
Zone 5 US, 6 Can.

L. vulgare (Common privet) Despite its common name, this is not the almost universal hedge plant, although it has now become naturalized in parts of the eastern United States. The leaves are lance-shaped and dark green, and the off-white, strongly scented, tubular summer flowers are followed by long clusters of particularly conspicuous, round, black fruits in fall. It makes a vigorous, medium-sized semievergreen shrub. Europe, N Africa, SW Asia. In cultivation 1884.
Zone 4 US, 5b Can.

Lindera *Lauraceae*

There are about 80 species of evergreen and deciduous aromatic trees and shrubs in this genus, related to the Laurus nobilis. *They are natives mainly of South and East Asia, with two species in North America. They require acidic soil and part shade. Prune out dead wood in spring.*

L. benzoin (Spicebush) A medium-sized to large deciduous shrub with large, ovate leaves that turn yellow in fall. The small, fragrant, greenish yellow flowers in spring are followed by red berries. The leaves and stems are spicily aromatic when crushed. SE United States. Introduced 1683.
Zone 4 US, 5b Can.

Lindera obtusiloba

L. obtusiloba (Japanese spicebush) A medium-sized to large deciduous shrub of erect or compact habit. The large, three-nerved, broad leaves are sometimes three-lobed at the tip, and in fall the foliage turns from bright green to butter yellow with pink tints. The flowers, borne in early spring, are mustard yellow. Japan, China, Korea. Introduced 1880.
Zone 6 US, 7 Can. 🏆

Linnaea *Caprifoliaceae*

A genus of one evergreen species, named in honor of Carolus Linnaeus (1707–78), the botanist and father of the binomial system of plant names.

L. borealis (Twinflower) A charming shrublet with slender stems that carpet the ground and form extensive colonies in moist, acid soil; it can be difficult to establish. The small, nodding, pinkish, bell-like flowers are carried in pairs on threadlike stems from early to late summer. Found throughout the Northern Hemisphere.
Zone 2 US, 2 Can.

Linum *Linaceae*

A genus of about 200 species of annuals, perennials, and small evergreen and deciduous shrubs with a wide distribution. They are attractive plants with uniquely silky flowers, and the following requires full sun and good drainage.

L. arboreum (Tree flax) A spreading evergreen shrub, 9–24 in (23–60 cm) high, suitable for a large rock garden. It has narrow, bloomy leaves and golden yellow flowers in loose terminal clusters in summer. E Mediterranean region. In cultivation 1788.
Zone 10 US 🏆

Linum arboreum

Lippia

L. citriodora See *Aloysia triphylla.*

Liquidambar *Hamamelidaceae*
Sweet gum

A genus of four species of deciduous trees with maplelike, alternate leaves that usually color well in fall, their foliage changing to brilliant colors. Sweet gums do best in moist, acidic soil; they do not tolerate dryness and need to be watered well and mulched during drought. Site carefully, as their prickly, round fruits can be messy.

Liquidambar formosana

L. formosana (Formosan sweet gum) A beautiful large tree with large, usually three-lobed leaves that color well in fall. China. Introduced 1908 by Ernest Wilson.
Zone 6 US, 7 Can.

L. orientalis A slow-growing large bush or small bushy tree. The small, hairless leaves are deeply five-lobed and attractively tinted in fall. In warm, dry climates it will reach the size of a large tree. Asia Minor. Introduced c. 1750.
Zone 7 US, 8 Can.

Liquidambar styraciflua

L. styraciflua (Sweet gum) A beautiful, symmetrical, large tree, especially valued for its deeply lobed, shining green, starlike leaves that turn crimson, yellow, or purplish in fall. The pendent fruits are small globes of spiny seed capsules and persist in winter. Twigs sometimes have corky bark, which is ornamental in winter. A fragrant resin is exuded from crevices in the trunk, particularly in the Southeast. It can be difficult to

transplant. E United States. Introduced 17th century.
Zone 5 US, 6 Can.

***L. s.* 'Lane Roberts'** A selected clone and one of the most reliable for its fall color, which is rich, black-crimson-red, like the embers of a coal fire. The bark of this large tree is comparatively smooth.
Zone 5 US, 6 Can. 🏆

Liquidambar styraciflua 'Lane Roberts'

Liquidambar styraciflua 'Silver King'

***L. s.* 'Moonbeam'** The leaves of this tree are creamy yellow, eventually green, turning red, yellow, and purple in autumn.
Zone 5 US, 6 Can.

***L. s.* 'Silver King'** A large tree with leaves attractively margined with cream and flushed rose in late summer and fall. Previously listed as 'Variegata'.
Zone 5 US, 6 Can.

Liquidambar styraciflua 'Worplesdon'

***L. s.* 'Variegata'** A large tree with leaves that are striped and mottled yellow. Previously listed as 'Aurea'.
Zone 5 US, 6 Can.

***L. s.* 'Worplesdon'** The leaves of this large tree are divided into long, narrow lobes that turn an attractive orange and yellow in fall.
Zone 5 US, 6 Can. 🏆

Liriodendron *Magnoliaceae*

Tulip tree

There are two species in this genus, one in China and one in North America. They are large, fast-growing deciduous trees, succeeding in all types of fertile soil and bearing large, curiously shaped leaves with three lobes, the central one of which is blunted and looks as if it has been cut in half. The foliage turns clear yellow in fall.

L. tulipifera (Tulip tree) A beautiful large tree whose odd-looking leaves turn a rich butter yellow in autumn. The strange

Liriodendron tulipifera

Liriodendron tulipifera 'Fastigiatum'

flowers, appearing in early and midsummer, are like very short-stemmed tulips, yellow-green and banded with orange at the base of the petals. They are not produced on young trees. E North America. In cultivation 1688.
Zone 4 US, 5b Can. 🏆

Liriodendron tulipifera 'Aureomarginatum'

***L. t.* 'Aureomarginatum'** A striking large tree with leaves bordered with bright yellow, turning greenish yellow by late summer. In cultivation 1903.
Zone 4 US, 5b Can. 🏆

***L. t.* 'Fastigiatum'** An erect, broadly columnar, medium-sized tree; a good choice for planting in a confined space when height is required.
Zone 4 US, 5b Can. 🏆

Lithodora *Boraginaceae*

A genus of seven species of dwarf evergreen shrubs, natives of Europe and Southwest Asia. The following are low-growing, blue-flowered shrubs, especially delightful in the rock garden but not exclusive to it. They need excellent drainage, and L. diffusa *requires an acidic soil and part shade.*

L. diffusa A prostrate shrub that forms large mats to 3 ft (1 m) wide or more, covered with lovely blue blooms in late spring and early summer. S and W Europe.
Zone 5 US, 6 Can.

***L. d.* 'Grace Ward'** A cultivar with masses of large deep blue flowers. This is now the most common form in cultivation.
Zone 5 US, 6 Can. 🏆

***L. d.* 'Heavenly Blue'** Once very popular, this variety has been superseded by the dwarfer 'Grace Ward'.
Zone 5 US, 6 Can. 🏆

Lithodora oleifolia

L. oleifolia A choice and rare semi-prostrate subshrub for a sheltered rock garden or alpine house. It has rich sky blue, bell-shaped flowers from early summer to early fall. The corolla and the leaf undersides have silky hairs. E Pyrenees. Introduced 1900.
Zone 6 US, 7 Can. 🏆

Lomatia *Proteaceae*

A genus of about 12 species of striking Australian and South American evergreen trees and shrubs. They are attractive in both foliage and flower and deserve to be better known and more widely planted. They perform best in part shade; should be given a peaty, acid soil; and are not suitable for planting where the soil is very alkaline. Old growth may be removed at the base to allow room for new shoots.

L. ferruginea A magnificent foliage plant, this species makes a large shrub or small tree with large, deep green, much divided, fernlike leaves and red-brown, velvety stems. The buff and scarlet flowers are borne in short clusters in midsummer. Chile, Argentina. Introduced 1846 by William Lobb.
Zone 9 US

L. myricoides A long-lived species, making a wide-spreading shrub 6½–8 ft (2–2.5 m) high. The leaves are long, narrow, and toothed toward the tips, and the attractive, white, very fragrant flowers are similar to those of a grevillea; they open in midsummer. It is an excellent evergreen for flower arrangements. SE Australia. Introduced 1816.
Zone 9 US

Lomatia silaifolia

L. silaifolia A small, spreading shrub with ascending stems, finely divided deep green leaves, and large panicles of cream flowers in midsummer, each with four narrow, twisted petals. The leaves are less finely divided than those of the very similar *L. tinctoria*. Both species have been successfully grown for many years. E Australia. Introduced 1792.
Zone 9 US

L. tinctoria A small, suckering shrub that forms a dense clump. Leaves are pinnate or doubly pinnate, with long, narrow segments. Flowers, borne in long, spreading clusters at the ends of the shoots in midsummer, are sulphur yellow in bud, turning cream. Tasmania. Introduced 1822.
Zone 9 US

LONICERA

Caprifoliaceae Honeysuckle

Lonicera japonica 'Halliana'

ALTOGETHER THERE ARE some 180 species of evergreen and deciduous shrubs and woody climbers in this genus, distributed throughout the Northern Hemisphere. They are valued for their very showy flowers, which are sometimes fragrant, as well as their ornamental fruits, which are attractive to birds.

The shrub honeysuckles are useful in borders and rock gardens and as hedges, while the climbers, which are twining plants, can quickly cover a trellis, arch, or pergola. Some honeysuckles, such as *L. japonica,* are so vigorous, even rampant, that they can be used to stabilize a steep slope or hide a chain-link fence. The less vigorous types can be allowed to scramble over a shrub, particularly an evergreen that will provide a handsome green backdrop but will not compete with its own floral display. Climbing honeysuckles also make good companions for fellow climbers and wall shrubs; they will readily twine around the stems of a climbing rose, for example, or winter jasmine.

The characteristically trumpetlike blossoms range in color from cream and pale yellow to brilliant scarlet and purplish rose. Some varieties of *L. tatarica* even have striped flowers, in deep pink and white. The bloom season begins in late winter or early spring with *L. fragrantissima* and *L. standishii* and concludes in late summer with *L.* × *heckrottii* and *L. sempervirens.*

The flowers are complemented by colorful, fleshy fruits, in white, yellow, orange, red, blue, and black. While most honeysuckles bear fruits in summer, some produce in late spring and others retain their berries well into fall.

CARE AND CULTIVATION

Honeysuckles are sturdy plants that will thrive with very little care. Although they can adapt to most soils, they prefer a moist loam amended with organic matter. They benefit from being mulched, except with manure, which promotes foliage at the expense of flowers. Some honeysuckles bloom best with their heads in full sun, but most enjoy part or even full shade, and all prefer their roots to be in shade.

It is a good idea to shorten the stems of young plants to stimulate early branching and ultimately ensure a generous framework for the maximum possible floral display. Once this is achieved, pruning is needed only to keep the plants within the desired bounds and to thin them out once there is an excessive amount of old wood. For most honeysuckles, pruning should be done immediately after flowering; honeysuckles that flower in late summer should be pruned in early spring.

Honeysuckles are affected by leaf curl, crown gall, and powdery mildew. Several species, but especially *L. tatarica,* are attacked by the Russian aphid, which causes new growth to become distorted and tassellike. *L. tatarica* is also susceptible to sawflies and a leaf roller.

CLIMBERS

L.* × *americana A magnificent, very free-flowering deciduous climber that reaches a height of 30 ft (9 m). The 2 in (5 cm) long, fragrant, white flowers soon turn to pale and finally deep yellow, heavily tinged with pink-purple outside. They are in whorls at the ends of the shoots and provide one of the most spectacular floral displays of midsummer. In cultivation before 1730.
Zone 6 US, 7 Can. 🏆

L.* × *brownii (Scarlet trumpet honeysuckle) A deciduous or semievergreen, medium-sized climber. It is moderately vigorous and has attractive orange-scarlet flowers in whorls at the ends of the branches in late spring and again in late summer. The following forms are recommended. Garden origin before 1850.
Zone 3 US, 3 Can.

***L.* × *b.* 'Dropmore Scarlet'** A taller-growing form with clusters of bright scarlet, tubular flowers from midsummer to midfall. This is the most common form of the hybrid in cultivation, but like its parent, *L. sempervirens*, it is very susceptible to aphid attack. Developed c. 1950 in Dropmore, Manitoba.
Zone 2 US, 3 Can.

***L.* × *b.* 'Fuchsioides'** This variety is hardly distinguishable from the typical form.
Zone 3 US, 3 Can.

L. caprifolium (Italian honeysuckle, sweet honeysuckle) A fairly vigorous deciduous climber up to 20 ft (6 m). The upper pairs of leaflets are fused, so the stem appears to perforate a single, round leaf (perfoliate). The flowers are $1^{1}/_{2}$–2 in (4–5 cm) long, fragrant, cream, and occasionally tinged with pink on the outside. They are in whorls at the ends of the shoots in early and midsummer and are followed by orange-red berries. Europe, Asia Minor. Long in cultivation.
Zone 6 US, 7 Can. 🏆

***L. c.* 'Pauciflora'** The flowers of this medium-sized variety are rose-flushed on the outside.
Zone 6 US, 7 Can.

L. etrusca (Cream honeysucke) A large and very vigorous deciduous honeysuckle with fragrant flowers that open cream,

Lonicera × *americana*

Lonicera × *brownii* 'Dropmore Scarlet'

Lonicera × *brownii* 'Fuchsioides'

Lonicera caprifolium

Lonicera etrusca

Lonicera henryi

often flushed with red, and deepen to yellow. They are in whorls at the ends of the shoots in early to midsummer, though not on young plants. The uppermost leaves are perfoliate. It is a superb species and is at its best where the climate is not too wet. Mediterranean region. Introduced 1750.
Zone 8 US, 9 Can.

***L. e.* 'Donald Waterer'** The young shoots of this large climber are red instead of purplish, and the flowers are red outside and white inside, becoming orange-yellow. French Pyrenees. Found 1973 by Donald Waterer.
Zone 8 US, 9 Can.

***L. e.* 'Superba'** A large, vigorous variety with red young shoots and red flowers that are white inside and turn orange-yellow.
Zone 8 US, 9 Can.

L. giraldii An evergreen species forming a dense tangle of slender, hairy stems to 6½ ft (2 m). The leaves, heart shaped at the base, are densely velvety. The flowers are purplish red with yellow stamens and are yellowish downy on the outside; they are held in terminal clusters in early to midsummer. The berries are purplish black. NW China.
Zone 6 US, 7 Can.

L.* × *heckrottii (Everblooming honeysuckle) A large, shrubby deciduous plant with some climbing branches. The fragrant flowers are yellow, heavily flushed with purple, and are abundantly borne at the ends of the shoots from midsummer to late summer. The name 'American Beauty' has been proposed for it.
Zone 4 US, 4 Can.

***L.* × *h.* 'Gold Flame'** Regarded by some as the only clone of the cross and by others as a separate one. The latter opinion is based on several differences, the more important ones from the gardener's point of view being that it is more of a climber and has brighter flowers. The typical form.
Zone 4 US, 4 Can.

L. henryi (Henry honeysuckle) A vigorous, more or less evergreen, medium-sized species with yellow flowers stained with red, borne in terminal clusters in early to midsummer. Fruits are black berries. W China. Introduced 1908 by Ernest Wilson.
Zone 5 US, 6 Can.

L. japonica (Japanese honeysuckle) A rampant evergreen or semievergreen species reaching 20–30 ft (6–9 m). The ovate to oblong leaves are often lobed on young or vigorous shoots. The fragrant flowers, 1–1½ in (2.5–4 cm) long, are white, changing to yellow with age. They are produced from early summer onward. The fruits are eaten by birds, and the plant has become an invasive weed in many states. Japan, Korea, Manchuria, China. Introduced 1806.
Zone 5 US, 6 Can.

Lonicera japonica 'Aureoreticulata'

***L. j.* 'Aureoreticulata'** (Yellow-net honeysuckle) A delightful form whose small, neat, bright green leaves have a conspicuous pattern of golden net veining. Introduced before 1862 by Robert Fortune.
Zone 5 US, 6 Can.

Lonicera japonica 'Halliana'

***L. j.* 'Halliana'** (Hall's honeysuckle) A very vigorous climber with white flowers changing to yellow and bright green leaves. Considered by some authorities to be the typical form. It is particularly valuable for covering a fence or slope but can become invasive and weedy if not kept under control.
Zone 5 US, 6 Can. 🏆

***L. j.* 'Hall's Prolific'** A vigorous climber that flowers profusely even when young. Selected in Holland from plants grown as 'Halliana'.
Zone 5 US, 6 Can.

L. j.* var. *repens A distinct variety whose leaves and shoots are flushed with purple and whose flowers are flushed with purple on the outside. It is very fragrant. Japan, China. Introduced early 19th century.
Zone 5 US, 6 Can.

L. periclymenum (Woodbine honeysuckle) A vigorous, medium-sized, deciduous species common in Europe. The sweetly fragrant flowers are up to 2 in (5 cm) long, purplish or yellowish outside and cream inside, darkening with age. It flowers throughout summer, and red berries follow in early fall. The following forms are recommended. Europe, Morocco.
Zone 4 US, 4b Can.

***L. p.* 'Belgica'** (Early Dutch honeysuckle) The flowers of this medium-sized climber are reddish purple on the outside, fading to yellowish, and are produced in late spring and early summer and again in late summer. In cultivation since the 17th century.
Zone 4 US, 4b Can. 🏆

***L. p.* 'Graham Thomas'** A medium-sized form whose flowers are white in bud and become yellow when open. They are borne over a long period, particularly if the plant is pruned hard in spring. Found 1960 in Warwickshire, England, by Graham Thomas when he was garden adviser to the National Trust.
Zone 4 US, 5 Can. 🏆

Lonicera periclymenum 'Harlequin'

***L. p.* 'Harlequin'** A medium-sized form whose leaves have bright cream margins.
Zone 4 US, 5 Can.

***L. p.* 'Munster'** A medium-sized form whose flowers are deep pink in bud, open to white streaked with pink, and fade to cream.
Zone 4 US, 5 Can.

Lonicera periclymenum 'Serotina'

***L. p.* 'Serotina'** (Late Dutch honeysuckle) A medium-sized form with flowers rich reddish purple outside, appearing from midsummer to midfall.
Zone 4 US, 5 Can. 🏆

L. sempervirens (Trumpet honeysuckle) A high-climbing, semievergreen species with flowers to 2 in (5 cm) long, orange-scarlet outside, yellow within, in whorls toward the ends of the shoots in summer. A striking species that attracts hummingbirds. E and S United States. Introduced 1656.
Zone 4 US, 4b Can. 🏆

L. s.* f. *sulphurea A large climber with clear yellow flowers.
Zone 4 US, 4b Can.

L. splendida A rather fastidious evergreen or sometimes semievergreen species with blue-bloomy leaves and fragrant flowers up to 2 in (5 cm) long. They are reddish purple outside and yellowish white within, borne in dense terminal clusters in summer. It needs to be grown in a mild area. Spain. Introduced 1880.
Zone 9 US

Lonicera splendida

L.* × *tellmanniana (Tellman honeysuckle) A superb medium-sized deciduous hybrid with flowers 2 in (5 cm) long, rich coppery yellow, flushed red in bud. They are borne in large terminal clusters in early to midsummer. It grows best in part to full shade.

Lonicera × *tellmanniana*

Lonicera tragophylla

Raised before 1927 at the Royal Hungarian Horticultural School, Budapest.

Zone 5 US, 6 Can. 🏆

L. tragophylla (Chinese honeysuckle) A very beautiful and showy, medium-sized deciduous climber with flowers 2½–3½ in (6–9 cm) long. They are bright golden yellow and in large terminal clusters of 10–20 flowers in early to midsummer. It needs almost complete shade. W China. Introduced 1900 by Ernest Wilson.

Zone 6 US, 7 Can. 🏆

SHRUBS

The shrubby honeysuckles are very different in appearance from the climbing ones. Their flowers emerge in pairs and are followed by berries. They are all easy to grow in any ordinary soil. Old flowering shoots can be thinned out and cut back immediately after flowering to within a few inches of the old wood.

L. chaetocarpa A pretty, erect deciduous

Lonicera chaetocarpa

shrub about 6½ ft (2 m) high, with bristly stems and leaves. The comparatively large, primrose yellow flowers are accompanied by large, eye-catching bracts and appear in late spring and early summer. It has bright red berries. W China. Introduced 1904 by Ernest Wilson.

Zone 5 US, 6 Can.

L. fragrantissima (Winter honeysuckle) A partially evergreen, medium-sized shrub with sweetly fragrant cream flowers in late winter and spring. Red berries follow in late

Lonicera fragrantissima

spring. China. Introduced 1845.

Zone 4 US, 5 Can.

L. involucrata (Twinberry) A vigorous, spreading, distinctive deciduous shrub of medium size, flowering in early summer. The yellow flowers are each accompanied by two prominent red bracts that persist while the shiny black berries form. It is robust and adaptable and grows well in coastal gardens and industrial areas. W North America. Introduced 1824.

Lonicera involucrata

Lonicera involucrata var. *ledebourii*

Zone 6 US, 7 Can.

L. i.* var. *ledebourii The flowers of this medium-sized shrub are orange-yellow, tinged with red. California coast. Introduced 1838.

Zone 6 US, 7 Can.

L. korolkowii (Blueleaf honeysuckle) A very attractive, vigorous, large deciduous shrub with a graceful, arching habit. It is given a striking gray-blue appearance by the down on the shoots and leaves and has pink flowers in early summer, followed by red berries. Turkestan. In cultivation 1880.

Zone 3 US, 4 Can.

L. nitida (Boxleaf honeysuckle) A dense, small-leaved evergreen species reaching 5–6 ft (1.5–1.8 m) in height. It is fast-growing and responds well to clipping, making it suitable for a hedge. The fragrant cream flowers are not significant. W China. Introduced 1908 by Ernest Wilson.

Zone 6 US, 7 Can.

Lonicera nitida 'Baggesen's Gold'

***L. n.* 'Baggesen's Gold'** A first-class medium-sized hedge shrub with a dense habit and small leaves that are yellow in summer and turn yellow-green in fall.

Zone 6 US, 7 Can. 🏆

***L. n.* 'Ernest Wilson'** This is the most common honeysuckle for hedges. It has a spreading, slightly arching habit and tiny, almost oval leaves. The flowers and fruits are not often produced, especially when the plant is clipped.

Zone 6 US, 7 Can.

L. pileata (Privet honeysuckle) A small to medium-sized, semievergreen, horizontally branched shrub, suitable for underplanting and ground cover, particularly in shade. The leaves are small, long-elliptic, and bright green, and the young, light green leaves contrast with the older, darker ones in spring. It bears clusters of translucent violet berries. China. Introduced 1900.
Zone 6 US, 7 Can.

Lonicera pileata

L. ×purpusii *(L. fragrantissima × L. standishii)* A vigorous, medium-sized deciduous hybrid with fragrant cream flowers in winter.
Zone 6 US, 7 Can.

L. pyrenaica (Pyrenees honeysuckle) A choice deciduous species, about 3 ft (1 m) high, with small, sea green leaves and nodding, relatively large, funnel-shaped, cream and pink flowers in late spring and early summer. Orange-red berries follow. Pyrenees and Balearic Islands. Introduced 1739.
Zone 7 US, 8 Can.

Lonicera × purpusii

L. setifera A rare and beautiful, medium-sized deciduous shrub with erect, bristly stems. The tubular, sweetly scented, daphnelike white and pink flowers appear in short clusters on the bare stems during the late winter and early spring. The berries are red and bristly. Himalaya, China. Introduced 1924.
Zone 7 US, 8 Can.

L. standishii A deciduous or semievergreen, medium-sized, winter-flowering species, resembling *L. fragrantissima.* The fragrant flowers are white blushed with pink and have noticeable yellow anthers. The red berries are borne in early summer. Introduced 1845 by Robert Fortune.
Zone 6 US, 7 Can.

Lonicera setifera

L. tatarica (Tartarian honeysuckle) A vigorous, variable deciduous shrub up to 10 ft (3 m) high, with masses of fragrant pink flowers in late spring and early summer, followed by red or yellow berries. It is very hardy. C Asia to Russia. Introduced 1752.
Zone 2 US, 3 Can.

***L. t.* 'Arnold Red'** A form with dark red flowers and larger red berries than the typical species. Originated 1945 at the Arnold Arboretum, Boston, Mass.
Zone 2 US, 3 Can.

***L. t.* 'Hack's Red'** A first-class medium-sized selection with purple-pink flowers.
Zone 2 US, 3 Can.

***L. t.* 'Zabelli'** A popular variety that grows to 6 ft (1.8 m) with dark red flowers similar in color to those of 'Arnold Red'. Unfortunately, it is susceptible to Russian aphid.
Zone 2 US, 3 Can.

Lonicera standishii

***L. × xylosteoides* 'Clavey's Dwarf'** A quick-growing shrub that may reach 8 ft (2.5 m) at maturity but it is generally half this size and can easily be kept dwarf with pruning. The flowers are greenish yellow. Introduced c. 1950 by Clavey's Nurseries, Deerfield, Ill.
Zone 3 US, 3 Can.

***L. × x.* 'Miniglobe'** A dwarf form with dense foliage. Introduced 1981 by Morden Research Station, Manitoba, Canada.
Zone 2 US, 2 Can.

***L. × xylosteum* 'Emerald Mound'** (European fly honeysuckle) This handsome dwarf shrub is one of the smallest honeysuckles. It makes a good ground cover or low hedge. The blue-green foliage is attractive all summer long, while the creamy flowers produce bright red fruits. Introduced into North America by the Morton Arboretum, Lisle, Ill., but this may be identical to a form grown in Poland since 1931.
Zone 3 US, 4 Can.

Lophomyrtus

L. bullata See *Myrtus bullata.*

Luculia *Rubiaceae*

A genus of five species of evergreen shrubs or small trees from the temperate Himalaya and western China. They are suitable primarily as winter-flowering shrubs for the greenhouse or for outdoor culture in very mild climates.

L. gratissima (Fragrant luculia) A semievergreen, free-flowering shrub with sweetly

Luculia gratissima

fragrant, rich pink flowers in many-flowered trusses in winter. It can potentially reach about 16 ft (5 m) but this height is seldom attained. Himalaya. Introduced 1816.
Zone 10 US 🏆

Luma

L. apiculata See *Myrtus luma*.
L. chequen See *Myrtus chequen*.

Lupinus *Leguminosae*
Tree lupine

Most lupines, of which there are more than 200 species in the Americas and the Mediterranean region, are herbaceous perennials, but some are deciduous shrubs.

Lupinus arboreus

L. arboreus (Yellow tree lupine) A fairly short-lived, more or less evergreen, fast-growing shrub to about $6\frac{1}{2}$ ft (2 m). The flowers are usually yellow, but from seed they may be blue or lavender. They are delicately scented and are produced in dense clusters continuously through the summer. It thrives in full sun in any well-drained location and naturalizes in sandy or pebbly soils, particularly in coastal areas. California. In cultivation 1793.
Zone 8 US, 9 Can. 🏆

Lycium *Solanaceae*

A genus of about 100 species of rambling, often spiny deciduous shrubs widely distributed throughout the world. They require full sun and will grow in any dry, poor soil.

Lycium barbarum

L. barbarum (Matrimony vine) A vigorous, medium-sized shrub with long, usually spiny, scrambling, arching stems. The purple, funnel-shaped flowers are borne in clusters in the leaf axils from early summer to early fall, followed by small, egg-shaped, orange or scarlet berries. Good for seashore plantings. China. Introduced 1700.
Zone 6 US, 7 Can.

Lyonia *Ericaceae*

A genus of about 35 species of attractive evergreen and deciduous shrubs or occasionally small trees, closely related to Pieris *and requiring a moist, acidic soil. They have a wide range of distribution, from the United States to the Himalaya.*

L. ligustrina (Male berry) A deciduous, small to medium-sized shrub with more or less oval leaves that turn red in fall and panicles of urn-shaped white flowers in mid- to late summer. It thrives in a moist, peaty or sandy loam. E North America. Introduced 1748.
Zone 4 US, 5 Can.

Lyonothamnus *Rosaceae*

A genus of one evergreen species.

L. floribunda* subsp. *asplenifolius A small, graceful, fast-growing tree, soon forming a remarkable slender trunk like a miniature redwood, with handsome, predominantly chestnut bark that shreds and peels attractively. The leaves are fernily pinnate, with the leaflets divided into oblong lobes that are glossy green above and hairy-gray below. The creamy white flowers are borne in early summer in slender, spirea-like panicles. It needs the shelter of a warm wall even in the mildest areas. Santa Catalina and other offshore islands of California. Introduced 1900.
Zone 9 US

M

Maackia *Leguminosae*

A genus of about eight species of hardy, attractive, slow-growing, small deciduous trees related to Cladrastis *but differing in the solitary, exposed leaf buds; opposite leaflets; and densely packed, more or less erect clusters of flowers. They are natives of East Asia. They succeed in most soils, including deep soil over limestone, and require a sunny location.*

M. amurensis (Amur maackia) A small tree with pinnate leaves and white, pea-shaped flowers, tinged pale slate blue, in erect racemes in early and midsummer, even on young plants. Manchuria. Introduced 1864.
Zone 3 US, 3b Can.
M. chinensis A small, broad-headed tree that produces dull white pea flowers in summer. The dark bluish young shoots are particularly outstanding in late spring. China. Introduced 1908.
Zone 4 US, 5b Can.

Magnolia

Magnoliaceae

Magnolia is an ancient genus, and its 125 species of evergreen and deciduous trees and shrubs are found in the wild from the Himalaya and East and Southeast Asia to North and Central America. Due to their exquisite flowers, handsome foliage, and oft statuesque proportions, magnolias have come to be appreciated by gardeners throughout the temperate regions of the world. They are, simply, among the most beautiful plants in cultivation.

Magnolia campbellii 'Charles Raffill'

Forms and flowers

Magnolias vary in size from noble trees that reach 80 ft (25 m) to multistemmed shrubs that spread more than 15 ft (4.5 m) wide to plants compact enough to be grown as hedges. While some are broadly triangular or round headed in silhouette, others are columnar or decidedly bushy.

The leaves on magnolias are usually large, glossy, and paddle shaped, somewhat similar to rhododendron foliage. A leaf can grow more than 2 ft (60 cm) long and 12 in (30 cm) wide, as those on *M. macrophylla* do. Many leaves are covered with a rusty brown or gray-blue wool or felt on the undersides that contrasts attractively with the lustrous green of the top surface.

Although magnolia foliage does not offer fall color, the plants do bear brown or red, sometimes woolly, conelike fruits beginning in late summer. When ripe, these cones split to reveal bright scarlet or orange seeds that dangle from threadlike follicles.

But the true glory of the magnolias is the flowers, which are often deliciously fragrant. The majority bear large chalice- or cup-shaped blooms up to 8 in (20 cm) tall. While the flowers may be a solid color in white, yellow, pink, or magenta-purple, the most dramatic ones are "stained" with a second hue. The flowers of *M.* × *soulangeana,* for example, are generally white with a pink, rose, or purple blush along the outside, especially around the base. Other magnolias, notably *M. stellata* and its hybrid *M.* × *loebneri,* have open, starlike flower forms comprising 12–18 petals.

In general, deciduous magnolias flower on bare branches in spring before the leaves appear, and the evergreens come into bloom in summer. This is only a guide, as some deciduous plants, such as a few cultivars of *M.* × *soulangeana,* flower at the same time that the leaves unfold. In some parts of the Southeast, magnolias begin blooming as early as February, and some remain in flower in late summer.

The large tree magnolias usually do not flower until they have attained considerable size, but again this varies. When grown from seed, the magnificent *M. campbellii* is likely to be 30 years old before it begins blooming, although grafted clones will flower in about half that time. *M. c.* subsp. *mollicomata,* however, will flower when it is 7–8 years old. With seedlings of the evergreen *M. grandiflora,* flowering is again long delayed, but vegetatively propagated cultivars such as *M. g.* 'Goliath' and 'Exmouth' produce their beautifully scented flowers early in their lives.

Among the smaller magnolias, *M. kobus* can take up to 15 years to bloom, while its hybrid *M.* × *loebneri* 'Merrill' will flower in about five years.

Soil and planting

Magnolias perform best in deep, moist, acidic to neutral soil that is well drained.

and heavily amended with organic matter, such as leaf mold, compost, or peat moss; they need supplemental watering in dry spells. Some prefer higher acidity, including *M. dawsoniana, macrophylla,* and *salicifolia.* And while they generally dislike alkaline soil, *M. acuminata, delavayi, grandiflora, kobus,* × *loebneri, stellata,* and *wilsonii* are somewhat lime tolerant, depending on soil depth and moisture retention. Magnolias will also tolerate clay soil.

The plants have thick, fleshy, shallow roots, which are easily damaged and should not be disturbed; root damage at an early stage in a magnolia's life is usually fatal in the long term. A good layer of mulch around the root zone provides sufficient protection, as well as retains moisture. If a magnolia is planted in a lawn, the grass around it should be replaced with mulch. Magnolias also should not be transplanted; when it is necessary to do so, they can be moved in spring, not fall, and the root ball should be wrapped in burlap.

Hardiness and Shelter

While some magnolias, including *M. acuminata* and *M. denudata,* are quite hardy, others will survive only in warm climates and can not tolerate frost. Frost destroys the flowers of early spring-flowering species, such as *M. denudata, salicifolia,* and *stellata,* and these can be grown only in mild areas or in sites sheltered from cold winds and away from pockets where frost may settle. The main enemy of flowering is a mild early spring followed by sudden late frost.

Large-leaved deciduous magnolias, including *M. macrophylla, officinalis* var. *biloba,* and *tripetala,* along with the evergreen specimens, need shelter from winds to prevent such damage to the foliage as burning or shredding. *M. macrophylla* in particular requires a protected spot, lest its enormous leaves tear, detracting from the otherwise impressive appearance of this tree.

Magnolia leaves and branches are also vulnerable to damage from the weight of snow. For this reason, snow should be shaken or gently brushed from the branches as soon as possible.

Magnolias are generally grown in full sun, but some will tolerate part shade.

M. acuminata (Cucumber tree) A fast-growing, large, deciduous tree with a spreading habit with age. The yellow-green flowers, not produced on young trees, open at the same time as the greenish blue leaves in early summer but are insignificant. Its fruits are cucumber shaped. E United States and SE Canada. Introduced 1736.
Zone 4 US, 5 Can.

Magnolia 'Ann'

***M.* 'Ann'** A medium-sized to large, upright, deciduous shrub. The flowers appear in midspring before the leaves and have eight upright, deep reddish pink tepals, paler on the inside. It requires an acid soil.
Zone 4 US, 5 Can. 🏆

Magnolia 'Betty'

***M.* 'Betty'** A vigorous, medium-sized, deciduous shrub with large flowers to 8 in (20 cm) across that have up to 19 tepals, purplish red outside, white within, and are borne in midspring. It requires an acid soil.
Zone 4 US, 5 Can. 🏆

M. campbellii This is regarded by many as one of the most beautiful trees in the world. It becomes a large tree in acid soils in mild, sheltered locations and bears enormous, goblet-shaped flowers on leafless branches, rose-pink outside and pale within, that eventually spread wide like water lilies. Unfortunately, flowers are not usually produced until the tree is 20–30 years old or even more in some cases (records show that one planted in 1864 eventually flowered in 1900, but it now blooms magnificently every year). It is better to acquire young plants of vegetatively propagated forms that flower at an earlier age, at around 12 years old. The flowers are produced in late winter or early spring and may be destroyed by spring frost. It is a deciduous species. Himalaya, SW China. Introduced 1864.
Zone 9 US

***M. c.* 'Charles Raffill'** A large, vigorous hybrid between the typical form and *M. c.* subsp. *mollicomata,* inheriting the latter's habit of flowering early in life, between 10 and 15 years old. The large flowers are deep rose-pink in bud and open to rose-purple on the outside and white with a pinkish purple flush on the inside.
Zone 9 US 🏆

Magnolia campbellii 'Darjeeling'

***M. c.* 'Darjeeling'** A superb clone with flowers that are dark, rich rose. The original tree grows in the Darjeeling Botanic Gardens, India.
Zone 9 US

***M. c.* 'Kew's Surprise'** The flowers of this large tree are larger than those of

'Charles Raffill', and the outside of the petals is a richer pink. Raised at Caerhays Castle, Cornwall, England.

Zone 9 US

M. c.* subsp. *mollicomata This is similar in many ways to the typical form but is

Magnolia campbellii subsp. *mollicomata*

hardier and flowers at an earlier age, sometimes at 7–8 years. It usually flowers about two weeks later and thus stands a better chance of escaping frost damage. The pink to rose-purple blooms resemble large water lilies and can reach 6–7 in (15–18 cm) across. The twigs and flower stalks are downy and bronze colored. SE Tibet, N Burma, Yunnan. Introduced 1924 by George Forrest.

Zone 7 US, 8 Can.

***M. c.* 'Werrington'** A form of *M. c.* subsp. *mollicomata*. Like 'Lanarth', it has very large purple flowers with even darker stamens but has a better constitution.

Zone 7 US, 8 Can.

Magnolia cylindrica

M. cylindrica A very rare, large deciduous shrub or small tree. The white flowers are similar to those of *M. denudata* but are more elegant, appearing on the bare stems in midspring. It requires an acid soil. E China. In cultivation before 1936.

Zone 6 US, 7 Can. 🏆

Magnolia dawsoniana

M. dawsoniana (Dawson magnolia) A large evergreen shrub or small tree with leathery, bright green leaves almost 6 in (15 cm) long. Its large, pale rose flowers, suffused with purple on the outside and held horizontally, are borne in early spring but not on young trees. It requires an acid soil. China. Introduced 1908 by Ernest Wilson.

Zone 9 US

Magnolia delavayi

M. delavayi With the exception of *Rhododendron sinogrande* and its relatives and *Trachycarpus fortunei*, this species probably has the largest leaves of any evergreen tree or shrub grown in cool-temperate areas. It is a large shrub or bushy tree (eventually a medium-sized, broad-headed tree) up to 46 ft (14 m), with paddle-shaped leaves that are matte sea green above and gray-green beneath. The parchment-colored, slightly fragrant flowers appear a few at a time in late summer, each one lasting for about two days. Except in the mildest areas, it needs a sheltered location or the protection of a wall. It will tolerate alkaline soil. China. Introduced 1899 by Ernest Wilson.

Zone 9 US

Magnolia denudata

M. denudata (Yulan magnolia) A large shrub or small, rounded, deciduous tree, usually under 30 ft (9 m) in height. The fragrant, pure white, cup-shaped flowers are abundant, open in early spring, and have thick, fleshy tepals. It requires an acid soil. E China. Introduced 1789.

Zone 4 US, 5b Can. 🏆

***M.* 'Elizabeth'** A small, conical, deciduous tree. The fragrant, clear pale primrose yel-

Magnolia 'Elizabeth'

low, cup-shaped flowers open before the leaves in mid- or late spring. It requires an acid soil. Raised at the Brooklyn Botanic Garden by Eva Maria Sperber and selected 1978.
Zone 6 US, 6b Can. 🏆

***M.* 'Eric Savill'** A small, upright, deciduous tree with large, cup-shaped flowers, rich pink outside and nearly white inside, borne in midspring before the leaves appear. It requires an acid soil.
Zone 5 US, 6 Can.

Magnolia 'Galaxy'

***M.* 'Galaxy'** A vigorous, small, conical, deciduous tree with striking purple-pink to red, tulip-shaped flowers in mid- to late spring. It flowers when 3–4 years old. It requires an acid soil.
Zone 5 US, 6 Can. 🏆

Magnolia grandiflora

M. grandiflora (Southern magnolia, bull bay) This exquisite evergreen tree can reach 80 ft (25 m) tall and is widely grown from North Carolina to Florida and Texas. The large, oblong leaves, about 5–8 in (13–20 cm) long, are glossy above and covered with a rusty brown felt on the undersides; they are often dried and used in floral arrangements. The young branches and buds are also woolly. The very fragrant, creamy white flowers are waxy and cup shaped, emerging from silky buds and growing up to 10 in (25 cm) across; blooming begins in early summer and continues sporadically. The species can take years to flower, though some cultivars bloom earlier in their lives. Woolly fruits open to reveal red seeds in fall. It will tolerate alkaline soil. SE United States. Introduced 1734.
Zone 6 US, 7 Can.

***M. g.* 'Exmouth'** A splendid clone with large, polished leaves that are soft green above and felted with reddish brown on the undersides; the felt gradually disappears. The flowers, appearing at an early age, are about 10 in (25 cm) across and richly fragrant. In cultivation 1768.
Zone 7 US, 8 Can. 🏆

Magnolia grandiflora 'Exmouth'

Magnolia grandiflora 'Goliath'

***M. g.* 'Goliath'** A large shrub or small tree whose leaves are shorter and broader than the type and are rounded or blunt at the ends. They are glossy dark green above and have no felting on the lower surfaces. The long-lasting, globular flowers can reach up to 12 in (30 cm) in diameter and are produced when the plant is young. Selected before 1910 in Guernsey, Channel Islands.
Zone 7 US, 8 Can. 🏆

***M. g.* 'Little Gem'** A form of American origin that makes a compact large shrub or small tree with a narrowly columnar habit. The flowers and leaves are smaller than usual, the latter being glossy, dark green above with a deep brown felt beneath. Often grown as a hedge plant in the Southeast. Selected 1952.
Zone 7 US, 8 Can.

Magnolia grandiflora 'Samuel Sommer'

***M. g.* 'Samuel Sommer'** A hardy, wind-resistant large shrub or small tree, good for an open location. Dark green, glossy leaves have deep brown felty undersides. The large flowers, up to 14 in (35 cm) across, are borne early in the plant's life.
Zone 6 US, 7 Can.

***M. g.* 'Victoria'** One of the hardiest selections, from Victoria, British Columbia, this small tree with typical white flowers is widely grown on the West Coast. The foliage is shiny green with a cinnamon brown underside.
Zone 6 US, 7 Can.

***M.* 'Heaven Scent'** A magnificent small to medium-sized deciduous tree. The flowers,

borne in mid- to late spring, are richly scented and narrowly cup shaped. They have pale pink tepals heavily flushed with deep pink at the base and a magenta-pink stripe on the back. It requires an acid soil.
Zone 4 US, 5 Can. 🏆

***M.* 'Iolanthe'** A vigorous, upright, deciduous hybrid, forming a small to medium-sized tree. The very large, cup-shaped, rose-pink flowers are cream inside and are borne in spring when the tree is still young. It requires an acid soil. Raised 1974 in New Zealand by Felix Jury.
Zone 5 US, 6 Can. 🏆

***M.* 'Jane'** A medium-sized, compact, upright, deciduous shrub suitable for gardens with limited space. The fragrant, cup-shaped flowers open in mid- to late spring from narrow, erect, red-purple buds, and the tepals are red-purple outside and white within. It requires an acid soil.
Zone 4 US, 5 Can. 🏆

***M.* 'Judy'** A medium-sized, upright deciduous shrub with small, slender, candlelike flowers that are red-purple outside and creamy white inside. They are borne in mid- to late spring. It requires an acid soil.
Zone 4 US, 5b Can. 🏆

Magnolia 'Judy'

***M.* 'Kewensis'** A small, slender, broadly conical, deciduous tree with fragrant white flowers 2 1/2 in (6 cm) long, very freely borne in midspring before the leaves appear. It is slightly lime tolerant. Originated 1938 at Kew Gardens, England.
Zone 5 US, 6 Can.

M. kobus (Kobus magnolia) A hardy, deciduous, large shrub or small tree that does

Magnolia 'Kewensis'

not produce slightly fragrant, white flowers until it is about 12–15 years old. They are borne in spring. Japan. Introduced 1865.
Zone 4 US, 5b Can.

M. k.* var. *borealis A more upright form, often multistemmed, that will grow up to 70 ft (21 m). Cream white flowers appear in midspring; blooms at an early age.
Zone 4 US, 5 Can.

***M. liliiflora* 'Nigra'** A wide-spreading but compact, medium-sized, deciduous shrub with broad, shining green leaves and erect flowers that resemble slender tulips and gradually open wide. They are deep

Magnolia liliiflora 'Nigra'

wine-purple outside, creamy white stained with purple inside, and are borne freely over a long period in late spring and summer. It requires an acid soil. Japan. Introduced 1861 by J. G. Veitch.
Zone 5 US, 6 Can. 🏆

M.* × *loebneri *(M. kobus × M. stellata)* Excellent variable deciduous hybrids having the best features of both parents. They are large shrubs or small trees with fragrant, straplike tepals in midspring. They flower profusely even when young and grow in any good soil. Originated before 1910 in Germany.
Zone 4 US, 5 Can.

***M.* × *l.* 'Ballerina'** One of the most popular forms, this eventually grows into a small tree. The flowers are fragrant and white with a pink flush at the base of the many tepals and emerge in early spring. Introduced 1960 by the University of Illinois.
Zone 4 US, 4b Can.

Magnolia × *loebneri* 'Leonard Messel'

***M.* × *l.* 'Leonard Messel'** A magnificent tall shrub or small tree with fragrant lilac-pink flowers, deeper in bud.
Zone 4 US, 5 Can. 🏆

Magnolia × *loebneri* 'Merrill'

***M.* × *l.* 'Merrill'** A hardy, vigorous, small tree that blooms when as young as 5 years. The flowers are large, white, and fragrant, with about 12 wide petals. Originated 1939

at the Arnold Arboretum, Boston, Mass.
Zone 4 US, 5 Can. 🏆

M. macrophylla (Bigleaf magnolia) A small to medium-sized tree with larger leaves than any other deciduous tree or shrub hardy in cool-temperate areas. The leaves are thin, blue-gray-bloomy beneath and sometimes more than 2 ft (60 cm) long. The large (12 in/30 cm), fragrant flowers are creamy white with purple markings in the center and appear in summer. It requires an acid soil and protection from wind. SE United States. Introduced 1800.
Zone 5 US, 6 Can.

***M.* 'Manchu Fan'** A small to medium-sized deciduous tree with large, goblet-shaped flowers that have nine broad, creamy tepals; the inner ones are flushed purplish pink at the base. They are borne in spring. It is similar to 'Sayonara', but the flowers are less goblet shaped and less flushed with green at the base. It requires an acid soil.
Zone 6 US, 6b Can.

***M.* 'Maryland'** *(M. grandiflora × M. virginiana)* (Freeman hybrids) A large evergreen shrub or small tree with rich glossy green leaves that are thinly felted beneath. It produces large, white, lemon-scented, globular flowers in summer that open wide. It tolerates lime.
Zone 7 US, 8 Can. 🏆

Magnolia officinalis var. *biloba*

M. officinalis* var. *biloba A rare and distinctive small to medium-sized deciduous tree. It has large leaves, broadest above the middle and as much as 20 in (50 cm) long; they are pale green above, bloomy and finely downy beneath, and deeply notched at the apex. The parchment-colored flowers, borne in early summer, have maroon centers and are fragrant. It requires an acid soil. Introduced 1936 from the Botanic Garden, Lushan, China.
Zone 8 US, 9? Can. 🏆

***M.* 'Peppermint Stick'** A vigorous, medium-sized, conical, deciduous tree with narrowly columnar flower buds up to 4 1/2 in (11 cm) long. There are nine cream tepals, flushed with pink at the base and with a central deep pink line; the outer ones spread with age, while the inner ones, heavily flushed with deep pink toward the base, remain erect. They appear in spring. It requires an acid soil.
Zone 6 US, 7 Can. 🏆

***M.* 'Pinkie'** A medium-sized deciduous shrub with cup-shaped flowers up to 7 in (18 cm) across that have 9–12 tepals, pale red-purple becoming pink outside, white within. They appear in mid- to late spring.

Magnolia 'Pinkie'

Magnolia × *proctoriana*

It requires an acid soil.
Zone 6 US, 6b Can. 🏆

M.* ×*proctoriana *(M. salicifolia × M. stellata)* A large, very free-flowering, deciduous shrub with white flowers. These have 6–12 tepals and appear in spring. It requires an acid soil. Garden origin 1928.
Zone 4 US, 5 Can. 🏆

***M.* 'Randy'** A medium-sized, upright,

Magnolia 'Randy'

deciduous shrub with large, pink flowers that open wide from slender, red-purple buds in mid- to late spring. It requires an acid soil.
Zone 5 US, 6 Can. 🏆

***M.* 'Ricki'** A medium-sized deciduous shrub with large flowers, deep purplish pink in bud, up to 6 in (15 cm) across when open. There are 15 rather narrow tepals, shading from pink to deep rose-purple at the bases of the outside surfaces. They are borne in mid- to late spring. It requires an acid soil.
Zone 4 US, 5b Can. 🏆

Magnolia 'Royal Crown'

M. **'Royal Crown'** A small deciduous tree with large, 12-tepaled flowers that are purplish pink in bud and open before the leaves to white inside, shading to white at the tips outside. They appear in mid- to late spring. It requires an acid soil.
Zone 4 US, 5 Can.

Magnolia salicifolia

M. salicifolia (Anise magnolia) A large deciduous shrub or small, broadly conical tree with slender branches. The leaves are usually narrow and willowlike, and the flowers, often produced on young plants, are white and fragrant and generally have six narrow tepals. They are produced on the leafless stems in early to midspring. The leaves, bark, and wood are pleasantly lemon scented if bruised. It requires an acid soil. Japan. Introduced 1892.
Zone 5 US, 6 Can. 🏆

***M. s.* 'Jermyns'** A slow-growing, shrubby form with broader leaves and larger flowers that appear later than those of the typical species. It is one of the best flowering clones of this beautiful magnolia.
Zone 5 US, 6 Can.

Magnolia sargentiana var. *robusta*

M. sargentiana* var. *robusta A medium-sized deciduous tree with flowers up to 12 in (30 cm) in diameter, produced in early to midspring before the leaves appear but not until tree size is reached. They are rosy crimson outside and paler inside. It requires an acid soil. China. Introduced 1908 by Ernest Wilson.
Zone 9 US

Magnolia 'Sayonara'

M. **'Sayonara'** A small deciduous tree with a profusion of white, goblet-shaped, nine-tepaled flowers 4 in (10 cm) across in midspring. They are lightly flushed with pink and cool green at the base, while the inner tepals are heavily blushed with pink above the middle. It requires an acid soil.
Zone 6 US, 6b Can. 🏆

Magnolia sieboldii

M. sieboldii (Oyama magnolia) A large, wide-spreading, deciduous shrub with fragrant, waxy, white flowers that are nodding and egg shaped in bud but then turn horizontal and open to a wide dish shape. They appear intermittently from late spring to late summer. The crimson fruit clusters are eye-catching. It requires an acid soil. Japan, Korea. Introduced 1865.
Zone 6 US, 6b Can. 🏆

Magnolia sinensis

M. sinensis A large, wide-spreading deciduous shrub resembling *M. wilsonii* but easily distinguished by its broader leaves and wider, more strongly lemon-scented, white, nodding flowers, 4–5 in (10–13 cm) wide with a contrasting central cone of red stamens. They appear with the leaves in early summer. It is lime tolerant. W China. Introduced 1908 by Ernest Wilson.
Zone 8 US, 9 Can. 🏆

M.* × *soulangeana (*M. denudata* × *M. liliiflora*) (Saucer magnolia) The most popular and best known of the larger magnolias, this hybrid is grown as a multistemmed large shrub or small tree that averages about 15 ft (4.5 m) tall and wide but can reach twice that size. The deciduous leaves are oval with slightly hairy undersides. It blooms in midspring before the leaves emerge and will flower when still young. The flowers are cup shaped and range in color from white to pink to lavender. It tolerates clay soil and air pollution and is moderately tolerant of lime. The plant usually grown under this name is in fact 'Etienne Soulange-Bodin'. Originated about 1820.
Zone 4 US, 5b Can.

***M.* × *s.* 'Alexandrina'** One of the most

Magnolia × *soulangeana* 'Alexandrina'

Magnolia × *soulangeana* 'Brozzonii'

popular clones, this vigorous, erect, and free-flowering large shrub or small tree has large, erect, white flowers heavily flushed pink-purple at the base. In cultivation 1831.
Zone 4 US, 5 Can. 🏆

M. × ***s.*** **'Brozzonii'** An aristocratic plant with large, elongated, white flowers, shaded purple at the base. One of the largest-flowered and the latest of the group to bloom. In cultivation 1873.
Zone 4 US, 5b Can. 🏆

Magnolia × *soulangeana* 'Lennei'

M. × ***s.*** **'Etienne Soulange-Bodin'** The typical form, usually grown as *M.* × *soulangeana.* It has large, tulip-shaped, white flowers, stained purple at the base.
Zone 4 US, 5b Can. 🏆

M. × ***s.*** **'Lennei'** A vigorous, spreading, multistemmed shrub with large leaves and large, goblet-shaped flowers that are deep rosy purple outside and creamy white stained with soft purple inside. The flowers appear from late midspring to late spring, and there is sometimes a second flush of bloom in fall. Introduced 1852.
Zone 4 US, 5 Can. 🏆

M. × ***s.*** **'Lennei Alba'** A form with ivory white, cup-shaped flowers, similar to *M. denudata.* In cultivation 1905.
Zone 4 US, 5 Can. 🏆

M. × ***s.*** **'Picture'** A vigorous, erectly branched large shrub or small tree with large leaves and long, erect flowers that are wine-purple outside and white inside. It flowers when young. Found 1930 in Japan.
Zone 4 US, 5b Can.

Magnolia × *soulangeana* 'Rustica Rubra'

M. × ***s.*** **'Rustica Rubra'** A vigorous large shrub with oval leaves and cup-shaped flowers of rich rosy red outside and white inside. Introduced c. 1893.
Zone 4 US, 5b Can. 🏆

Magnolia × *soulangeana* 'Lennei Alba'

***M.* × *s.* 'San Jose'** A vigorous large shrub with large, fragrant flowers that are deep pink-purple outside and cream inside. Raised c. 1938 in San Jose, California.
Zone 5 US, 6 Can. 🏆

***M.* × *s.* 'Sundew'** A large shrub with large, creamy flowers flushed with pink at the base. In cultivation 1966.
Zone 4 US, 5b Can.

***M. sprengeri* 'Claret Cup'** A small to medium-sized deciduous tree, up to 43 ft (13 m), with fragrant, purplish pink flowers that are white flushed with pink inside. They appear in early to midspring. The leaves are up to 7 in (18 cm) long.
Zone 9 US

M. stellata (Star magnolia) A slow-growing, spreading, rounded, deciduous shrub, usually about 10 ft (3 m) tall and wide. The abundant, silky, hairy buds open to fragrant, white, many-tepaled, starlike flowers borne in early spring. It will tolerate some alkalinity and needs protection from late frosts. Japan. Introduced 1862.
Zone 4 US, 5 Can. 🏆

***M. s.* 'Centennial'** A fast-growing form that has pure white flowers with up to 32 tepals. Introduced 1972 by the Arnold Arboretum, Boston, Mass., to commemorate its centennial.
Zone 4 US, 5 Can.

***M. s.* 'Royal Star'** A shrub with very large flowers that are pink-tinged in bud and open white, with up to 30 tepals. Raised 1947 on Long Island, New York.
Zone 4 US, 5 Can.

***M. s.* 'Waterlily'** An outstanding shrub with large white flowers that are pink in bud. It is bushier and more upright than the species. Originated c. 1939.
Zone 4 US, 5 Can. 🏆

Magnolia stellata

Magnolia 'Susan'

***M.* 'Susan'** A medium-sized, upright, deciduous shrub with six-tepaled flowers, deep red-purple in bud, paler inside when open. They are borne in mid- to late spring. It requires an acid soil.
Zone 4 US, 5b Can. 🏆

Magnolia × *thompsoniana*

M.* × *thompsoniana (Thompson magnolia) A large, wide-spreading, deciduous shrub like *M. virginiana* but with larger leaves, up to 10 in (25 cm) long, that persist into early winter. The large, fragrant, creamy white flowers are carried intermittently in summer even on young plants. It requires an acid soil. Garden origin 1808.
Zone 5 US, 6 Can.

M. tripetala (Umbrella magnolia) A hardy deciduous tree, sometimes as tall as 40 ft (12 m), with an open head of branches. The leaves are 12–24 in (30–60 cm) long and 6–10 in (15–25 cm) wide. The cream flowers, 7–10 in (18–25 cm) across, are strongly and pungently scented and are borne in late spring and early summer. They are followed by attractive, cone-shaped, red fruit clusters. It requires an acid soil. E United States. Introduced 1752.
Zone 4 US, 5 Can.

Magnolia tripetala

Magnolia × *veitchii* 'Peter Veitch'

***M.* × *veitchii* 'Peter Veitch'** As soon as this first-class, potentially medium-sized to large deciduous tree reaches small tree size, it begins to bear lovely, white, goblet-shaped flowers flushed with purple-pink on the bare branches in midspring. It requires an acid soil.
Zone 7 US, 8 Can.

M. virginiana (Sweet bay magnolia) A deciduous or semievergreen large shrub or small to medium-sized tree with small, very fragrant, globular, cream flowers from early to late summer. The leaves are up to 5 in

Magnolia 'Wada's Memory'

(13 cm) long, glossy green above and blue-white beneath. It requires an acid soil and tolerates wet soil and shade. E and S United States. In cultivation late 17th century.
Zone 5 US, 6 Can.

***M.* 'Wada's Memory'** This deciduous magnolia probably had the same parents as 'Kewensis'. Its attractively floppy white flowers are larger than those of *M. kobus* and are borne profusely in midspring, even while the plant is still young. It is a large shrub or small to medium-sized conical tree requiring an acid soil.
Zone 5 US, 6 Can.

M. watsonsii See *M.* × *wieseneri*.

M.* × *wieseneri, syn. *M. watsonsii* A splendid deciduous shrub or small bushy tree with leathery leaves. The upward-facing flowers open from early to midsummer from attractive, rounded, white buds and are creamy white with prominent, rosy crimson anthers and pink sepals. They are saucer shaped, 5 in (13 cm) wide, and have a very powerful fragrance. Japan. Garden origin c. 1889. Zone 6 US, 7 Can.

Magnolia × *wieseneri*

M. wilsonii (Wilson magnolia) A large, wide-spreading deciduous shrub with fairly slim, pointed leaves and pendulous, saucer-shaped, fragrant, white flowers with crimson stamens in summer. It is a lovely species, differing from *M. sinensis* in its narrower leaves and smaller flowers. It is easy to grow, does best in part shade, and is moderately lime tolerant. W China. Introduced 1908 by Ernest Wilson.
Zone 7 US, 8 Can. 🏆

Magnolia wilsonii

***M.* 'Yellow Lantern'** This hybrid between *M. acuminata* and *M.* × *soulangeana* 'Alexandrina' forms a medium-sized upright tree with lemon yellow flowers up to 8 in (20 cm) in early spring, just before the leaves unfurl. Introduced c. 1980 in the United States.
Zone 4 US, 5b Can.

× Mahoberberis *Berberidaceae*

These tough evergreen to semievergreen shrubs are hybrids between Mahonia *and* Berberis. *They will grow in any soil and any exposure.*

× ***M. aquisargentii*** A vigorous, dense, upright, medium-sized shrub. The leaves are either slender-stalked, up to 8¼ in (21 cm) long and regularly spine-toothed, or short-stalked and edged with spines ¾ in (2 cm) long. Some leaves are compound, with two leaflets at their base. All are shining dark green above and paler underneath. They turn bronze in winter, and the plant requires some shade if the leaves are to persist. The soft yellow flowers, in clusters at the ends of the shoots, are borne in spring and followed by black berries. Of garden origin before 1948 in Sweden.
Zone 6 US, 7 Can.

× ***M. a.* 'Magic'** A medium-sized upright shrub with spiny foliage and dense clusters of bright yellow flowers in spring.
Zone 6 US, 7 Can.

MAHONIA

Berberidaceae

Mahonia × *media* 'Charity'

MAHONIAS HAVE BECOME more widely recognized in recent decades as great assets to the garden — particularly in winter and spring, when many members of the genus are in flower. These broadleaf evergreen shrubs, which can reach heights of 10–16 ft (3–5 m) or more and boast handsome foliage, are also magnificent architectural specimens, ideal for foundation plantings, borders, and ground cover.

Mahonias are related to *Berberis* but are easily differentiated from them by the lack of thorns on their stems and by their thick, leathery, spiny leaves, which are usually pinnate but sometimes trifoliolate (having three leaflets). The "typical" mahonia leaf has between 13 leaflets (the average for *M. japonica*) and 41 (the maximum for *M. lomariifolia*); a leaf can be 10–24 in (25–60 cm) long. Foliage color ranges from deep, dark green to bluish green and may be purplish, reddish, or bronze in winter.

The shrubs bear conspicuous racemes or panicles of blossoms, which are usually yellow and fragrant. The flower clusters may be stiffly erect, as with *M.* × *media* 'Winter Sun', or elegantly pendent, as with *M. japonica*. The flowers are followed by showy fruits — a usually purple, blue, or blue-black grapelike berry that is often bloomy. The edible fruits taste something like currants.

Mahonia can be divided roughly into two groups: the taller, more vigorous species are from Asia, and the shorter, more spreading ones are native to North America. The former do better in partial shade, preferably provided by trees or large shrubs, while the North American mahonias can tolerate dry soil and more sun.

These cultural distinctions are only a guideline, however, as mahonias will generally grow in any well-drained soil and any degree of shade. Some are very tough and adaptable: the native North American *M. aquifolium* can take full sun except in very hot climates and will also tolerate dry shade. All mahonias benefit from protection from wind and sun in winter.

Mahonias vary widely in hardiness, but most of those listed below will tolerate considerable exposure to temperatures of 5° F (–15° C), provided they receive shelter from wind. The main exception is *M. lomariifolia*, which is hardy only to zone 9 US and does best in coastal areas; its hybrids with *M. japonica* — collectively *M.* × *media* — will take a bit more cold than their parent.

The larger mahonias do not require regular pruning, although weak stems should be removed to make room for stronger ones. After a particularly severe winter, it may be necessary to prune away any stems with windburned foliage or those that are showing signs of dieback.

The North American species, such as *M. wagneri*, *M. repens*, and *M. aquifolium*, spread by suckers, which makes them almost impenetrable ground covers. But they do not become invasive, as any superfluous suckers are easily removed.

Some mahonias serve as the alternate host for a wheat rust; only those species that are resistant to the disease should be grown.

Mahonia aquifolium

M. aquifolium (Mahonia, Oregon grape holly) A small shrub, valuable for underplanting in sun or shade. The polished green leaves are pinnate, with 5–13 leaflets (the odd one is at the end); they often turn bronze in winter. The small yellow flowers, opening in early spring, are borne in erect racemes, which in turn are in clusters. The decorative, edible berries are blue-black. W North America. Introduced 1823.
Zone 4 US, 4b Can.

Mahonia aquifolium 'Apollo'

***M. a.* 'Apollo'** A vigorous form that makes a dense, low-growing, spreading bush. The leaves are deep green with reddish stalks, and the bright yellow flowers are in large, dense clusters.
Zone 4 US, 4b Can. 🏆

***M. a.* 'Atropurpurea'** A shrub whose leaves turn a rich reddish purple in winter and early spring. In cultivation 1915.
Zone 4 US, 4b Can.

***M. a.* 'Moseri'** A form with attractive

Mahonia aquifolium 'Moseri'

bronze-red leaves that turn apple green and finally dark green. It has a rather weak constitution. In cultivation 1895.
Zone 4 US, 5 Can.

***M. a.* 'Smaragd'** A spreading shrub with dark green, glossy leaves that are bronze when young. The bright yellow flowers are borne in large clusters. In cultivation 1979.
Zone 4 US, 4b Can.

Mahonia fremontii

M. fremontii A beautiful small to medium-sized shrub for a well-drained site in full sun. The blue-green pinnate leaves are composed of small, bloomy, curled, and spiny leaflets. Small clusters of yellow flowers in late spring and early summer are followed by inflated, dry, yellowish or red berries. SW United States.
Zone 9 US

M. japonica (Japanese mahonia) This beautiful medium-sized species has deep green leaves made up of 7–19 leaflets and terminal clusters of long, pendulous racemes of fragrant, lemon yellow flowers from midwinter to early spring. The small fruits are purple. The form 'Bealei' has now become more popular. China.
Zone 6 US, 7 Can. 🏆

Mahonia japonica

***M. j.* 'Bealei'** (Leatherleaf mahonia) This form differs mainly in having shorter, stiffer, more or less erect racemes and broad-based, often overlapping leaflets. It is deservedly the most popular of the non-native mahonias. May need pruning to restrain growth. Some authorities place it in a species of its own *(M. bealei)*. W China. Introduced c. 1849 by Robert Fortune.
Zone 6 US, 7 Can.

Mahonia lomariifolia

M. lomariifolia An imposing species but suitable only for milder areas with adequate protection. It is a large shrub with stout, erect branches that are closely set with long leaves made up of 15–19 pairs of rigid, narrow leaflets. The rich yellow flowers are

borne during winter in dense clusters of erect racemes, each being 6–10 in (15–25 cm) long and carrying as many as 250 small flowers on each blossom. W China, Burma. Introduced 1931.
Zone 9 US 🏆

M.* × *media *(M. japonica × M. lomariifolia)* This cross is represented in gardens by several named clones. They are magnificent shrubs with yellow flowers from late fall to midwinter that are usually slightly fragrant. The following are recommended.
Zone 9 US

Mahonia × media 'Buckland'

***M.* × *m.* 'Buckland'** A handsome medium-sized shrub with leaves like those of *M. japonica*, tinted in autumn, and long, spreading racemes of flowers.
Zone 9 US 🏆

***M.* × *m.* 'Charity'** A superb, medium-sized to large, upright, stately shrub with leaves 20–24 in (50–60 cm) long, bearing two ranks of long, spiny leaflets. The slightly fragrant, deep yellow flowers are in long, spreading, and ascending racemes that are in large terminal clusters in fall and early winter.
Zone 9 US 🏆

Mahonia × media 'Lionel Fortescue'

***M.* × *m.* 'Lionel Fortescue'** A medium-sized shrub with large numbers of upright racemes of bright yellow, fragrant flowers.
Zone 9 US 🏆

***M.* × *m.* 'Underway'** A relatively compact medium-sized shrub whose leaves are composed of 17–21 leaflets. The bright yellow flowers are in long, upright racemes.
Zone 9 US 🏆

Mahonia × media 'Winter Sun'

***M.* × *m.* 'Winter Sun'** A medium-sized shrub bearing erect racemes densely packed with fragrant yellow flowers.
Zone 9 US 🏆

M. nervosa (Cascades mahonia) A relatively dwarf, suckering species with lustrous leaves in 11–19 leaflets that often turn red in winter. The bright yellow flowers are borne in racemes 6–8 in (15–20 cm) long in late spring, and the berries are blackish blue. It prefers a slightly acid soil. W North America. Introduced 1822.
Zone 5 US, 6 Can.

M. pinnata See *M. × wagneri* 'Pinnacle'.

***M. repens* 'Rotundifolia'** A small, distinctive shrub form of creeping mahonia with oval or rounded, sea green, spineless leaves and large plumes of rich yellow flowers in late spring, followed by bloomy black berries. It is suitable as ground cover. In cultivation 1875.
Zone 3 US, 3 Can.

M. trifoliolata* var. *glauca An attractive medium-sized shrub that will grow to 13–16 ft (4–5 m). The leaves have three spiny, conspicuously veined, bloomy leaflets. The clusters of yellow flowers, appearing in spring, are followed by berries resembling red currants. SW United States. Introduced 1839.
Zone 9 US

Mahonia trifoliolata var. *glauca*

Mahonia × wagneri 'Pinnacle'

***M.* × *wagneri* 'Pinnacle'** A vigorous, upright, small to medium-sized shrub with bright green leaves that are bronze when young and showy clusters of yellow flowers in late spring. It is a selection from plants previously grown as *M. pinnata*, the true plant of which is rare in cultivation.
Zone 8 US 🏆

***M.* × *w.* 'Undulata'** A small to medium-sized shrub, taller than *M. aquifolium*, with lustrous, dark green leaves and undulate margins to the leaflets. The deep yellow flowers are borne in spring.
Zone 8 US 🏆

MALUS

Rosaceae Crab apple

Malus 'Eleyi'

THE GENUS *Malus* includes about 35 species of deciduous trees and shrubs that produce edible fruits. While the much-loved fruits of the orchard apple run 2–4 in (5–10 cm) in diameter, those of the crab apple are generally 2 in (5 cm) and smaller. The crab apple, however, is grown less for food production than for beauty. It numbers among the best of the small landscape trees, offering handsome silhouettes, prolific flowers in spring, conspicuous and oft persistent ornamental fruits, and even attractive fall foliage.

Befitting the family heritage, crab apples bear flowers that resemble roses, with single, semidouble, and double blooms that run from white to rose to deep burgundy. The buds are sometimes of a different color than the blooms, which makes a lovely contrast while the flowers are opening, and many blossoms are also fragrant.

Crab apple fruits can be as small as ¼ in (6 mm) in diameter, but on the whole they are large enough and colorful enough to contribute to the plant's presence in late summer and fall. They range in color from yellow and orange to bright crimson and maroon; some are prettily flushed with a second color. Most fruits are round, although some are egg or pear shaped.

While crab apple fruits are edible, they can be somewhat sour and are used primarily to make jelly. The best for this purpose are *M.* 'Crittenden', 'Dartmouth', 'Dolgo', 'Golden Hornet', and the most popular, 'John Downie'.

Crab apples whose fruits persist well into winter are of greater ornamental value and are especially welcome in small gardens. Good choices include *M.* 'Candied Apple', 'Crittenden', 'Red Jade', 'Rudolph', and 'Wintergold'. And for gardeners who do not want to bother cleaning up dropped fruits, there is even a "clean" crab apple: *M.* 'Spring Snow', which sets little fruit.

CARE AND CULTIVATION

Crab apples are easy to grow in any reasonably fertile, well-drained soil; in too rich a soil, they are likely to produce growth at the expense of flowers. While established plants can tolerate drought, excess soil moisture can be fatal. Crabs generally need full sun, but they can take dappled shade for part of the day.

Young trees must be pruned early to train the shape. Thereafter, dead and diseased wood or any crossing, crowded, or damaged branches should be pruned in winter. Water sprouts must also be removed regularly in early summer.

Unfortunately, crab apples suffer from a number of pests and diseases, including aphids, scale, and borers, along with scab, canker, fireblight, and rust.

***M.* 'Adams'** A small, round-headed tree with bright red buds that open to pink flowers 1½ (4 cm) across. The red fruits are ⅝ in (16 mm) and last well into winter.
Zone 2 US, 2b Can.

***M.* 'American Beauty'** A vigorous small to medium-sized tree with bronze-tinged leaves. It has double, deep red flowers and few fruits. Resists scab. In cultivation 1978.
Zone 4 US, 5 Can.

M. baccata* var. *mandshurica A hardy, round-headed, medium-sized tree with fragrant white flowers in early spring. The small, berrylike fruits are red or yellow. NE Asia. Introduced 1824.
Zone 2 US, 2b Can.

***M.* 'Butterball'** A small, spreading tree with slightly drooping branches and pink-budded flowers that open blush-white. The fruits are yellow with an orange flush and reach about 1 in (2.5 cm) across. In cultivation 1961.
Zone 4 US, 4b Can.

***M.* 'Candied Apple'** A weeping form to 15 ft (4.5 m) with single pink flowers 1 in (2.5 cm) across and persistent, bright red, ⅝ in (16 mm) apples. The foliage has a reddish tint. Somewhat susceptible to scab.
Zone 4 US, 5 Can.

***M.* 'Centurion'** An upright tree when young, becoming rounded with age and reaching 20 ft (6 m). Flowers are dark pink, and the fruits are cherry red and last well. Introduced by Lake County Nursery, Ohio.
Zone 4 US, 5 Can.

***M.* 'Crittenden'** A small, compact tree with attractive pale pink flowers. It has particularly heavy crops of bright scarlet fruits that persist throughout fall and winter.
Zone 4 US, 5 Can.

***M.* 'Dartmouth'** An attractive small tree with abundant white flowers and equally plentiful reddish purple, bloomy fruits. Raised before 1883.
Zone 2 US, 2b Can.

***M.* 'Dolgo'** A good choice for jelly because the red fruits are 1¼ in (3.5 cm) across and tasty but fall every early. The flowers are white and fragrant, and the small to medium-sized tree is disease resistant. Introduced 1917 by the South Dakota Experimental Station.
Zone 2 US, 2b Can.

Malus 'American Beauty'

Malus baccata var. *mandshurica*

Malus 'Butterball'

Malus 'Crittenden'

Malus 'Dartmouth'

***M.* 'Donald Wyman'** A small, spreading tree with red buds, opening to white flowers 1¾ in (4.5 cm) across. The ⅜ in (9 mm), bright red fruits persist well.
Zone 4 US, 5 Can.

***M.* 'Eleyi'** A small tree with rosy crimson flowers, dark purplish shoots and leaves, and very ornamental purple-red fall fruits.
Zone 4 US, 5 Can.

Malus 'Evereste'

***M.* 'Evereste'** A conical small tree with dark green leaves that are sometimes slightly lobed. The flowers, 2 in (5 cm) across, are red in bud and later become white. The fruits are up to 1 in (2.5 cm) across and are orange or orange-yellow. In cultivation 1980.
Zone 3 US, 3 Can. 🏆

Malus floribunda

M. floribunda (Japanese crab apple) A popular large shrub or small tree with long, arching branches. It is particularly beautiful when the crimson buds open to white or pale blush. The fruits are small and yellow. This is one of the earliest-flowering crab apples. Japan. Introduced 1862.
Zone 4 US, 5b Can. 🏆

Malus 'Golden Hornet'

***M.* 'Golden Hornet'** A small tree with white flowers followed by numerous bright yellow fruits that persist until late in the year. It is one of the best fruiting crab apples. In cultivation before 1949.
Zone 4 US, 4b Can. 🏆

M. hupehensis (Tea crab apple) A small tree with stiff, ascending branches. The fragrant flowers are pink in bud, open white, and are borne abundantly in late spring and early summer. The small fruits are usually deep red. China, Japan. Introduced 1900.
Zone 4 US, 4b Can. 🏆

***M.* 'Indian Magic'** A rounded tree that grows to about 20 ft (6 m) tall and wide. The 1½ in (4 cm) flowers open deep pink, and the ½ in (13 mm) fruits are red.
Zone 4 US, 5 Can.

Malus 'John Downie'

***M.* 'Indian Summer'** Unlike most crab apples, this small variety has good fall color. The flowers are rose-pink, and the bright red fruits are ⅝ in (16 mm) in diameter.
Zone 4 US, 5 Can.

***M.* 'John Downie'** Perhaps the best fruiting crab apple. The late-spring flowers are white, and the fruits are large, conical, and bright orange and red. It makes a small tree. Raised 1875.
Zone 3 US, 3 Can. 🏆

Malus 'Katherine'

***M.* 'Katherine'** A small tree with a regular, densely branched, globular head. Deep pink buds open to double pink flowers that are over 2 in (5 cm) in diameter and gradually fade to white. The small fruits are red flushed with yellow. In cultivation c. 1928.
Zone 4 US, 5b Can. 🏆

***M.* 'Liset'** A small, dense, rounded tree with purplish young foliage and rose-red flowers that open from deep crimson buds and are followed by glossy crimson fruits.

Raised before 1935 in Holland.
Zone 4 US, 5 Can.

***M.* 'Molten Lava'** A small, wide-spreading, weeping form that has 1½ in (4 cm) white flowers, followed by ⅜ in (9 mm) orange fruits. It is very resistant to the common problems that affect crab apples. Introduced by Lake County Nursery, Ohio.
Zone 4 US, 5b Can.

Malus 'Neville Copeman'

***M.* 'Neville Copeman'** A seedling of *M.* 'Eleyi' that develops into a small tree with green leaves that are shaded with purple throughout the summer. The flowers are light purple and followed by somewhat conical, orange-red fruits.
Zone 4 US, 4b Can.

***M.* 'Pink Spires'** This is a small, upright selection that has red-tinged foliage in early spring. The flowers are light mauve, and the ¾ in (2 cm) fruits are dark red.
Zone 4 US, 5 Can.

***M.* 'Prairiefire'** Upright when young, this forms a rounded, 20 ft (6 m) tree with age. The flowers are a dark pink, and the ⅝ in (16 mm) fruits are dark red.
Zone 4 US, 5 Can.

***M.* 'Profusion'** Like 'Liset', this is one of the crab apples with wine-red flowers and purplish leaves that are prone to apple canker and mildew. This is the best of them, bearing its flowers in great profusion in fragrant clusters of 6–7 blooms, each of which is about 1½ in (4 cm) across. The fruits are small and dark red, and the young leaves are coppery crimson. In cultivation 1938.
Zone 3 US, 4 Can.

***M.* 'Red Jade'** A small shrub or tree with

Malus 'Red Jade'

weeping branches and bright green young leaves. The flowers are white and pink; the persistent fruit is red and grows to the size of cherries. Introduced 1953 by the Brooklyn Botanic Garden.
Zone 4 US, 5 Can.

***M.* 'Red Jewel'** This 15 ft (4.5 m) variety gets its name from the ½ in (1 cm) bright red fruits that hold their color well into winter. The white flowers are freely produced. It is somewhat prone to scab and fireblight. Introduced by Cole Nursery, Ohio.
Zone 4 US, 5 Can.

***M.* 'Robinson'** A very disease-resistant tree, up to 25 ft (7.5 m), with dark pink flowers followed by ⅜ in (9 mm) dark red fruits.
Zone 4 US, 4 Can.

***M.* × *robusta* 'Red Siberian'** An attractive small hybrid tree with masses of more

Malus × *robusta* 'Red Siberian'

or less globular, cherrylike, red fruits without calyxes, and white or pinkish flowers.
Zone 3 US, 3 Can.

***M.* × *r.* 'Yellow Siberian'** A form similar to 'Red Siberian' but with yellow fruits.
Zone 3 US, 3 Can.

***M.* 'Royalty'** A small, fairly upright tree with tapered, glossy, dark purple leaves that turn red in autumn. The large, purplish crimson flowers are somewhat hidden in the foliage; the fruits are dark red. Raised 1953 in Canada.
Zone 2 US, 2b Can.

***M.* 'Rudolph'** A small, upright tree with bronze-red leaves that change to dark bronze-green. The flowers are rose-red, deeper in bud, and almost 1½ in (4 cm) across. The fruits are orange-yellow and remain on the tree for a long time. Raised 1954 in Canada.
Zone 2 US, 2b Can.

M. sargentii (Sargent crab apple) This species makes a dense, rounded large shrub or small tree seldom higher than 12 ft (3.5 m), but can be twice as wide as it is tall. In spring pink buds open to fragrant, pure white flowers with golden anthers. The small, bright red, pealike fruits appear abundantly in late summer and persist into early winter. Japan. Introduced 1892.
Zone 4 US, 5 Can.

Malus sargentii

***M.* 'Selkirk'** A small tree that reaches up to 25 ft (7.5 m) tall with single to semidouble, rose-colored flowers 1½ in (4 cm) across. The fruits are almost 1 in (2.5 cm) in diameter and very shiny. Moderately susceptible to disease. Introduced 1962 by Morden Experimental Station. Manitoba.
Zone 2 US, 2b Can.

***M.* 'Snowdrift'** A free-flowering, wide-

spreading, densely rounded tree with snow white flowers 1¼ in (3.5 cm) across. The fruits, borne from fall to winter, are orange-red and ⅜ in (9 mm) in diameter. Somewhat prone to apple scab and fireblight.
Zone 4 US, 4 Can.

Malus toringoides

***M.* 'Spring Snow'** A good choice for those who want a "clean" tree, as this sets very little fruit. It makes an upright tree about 25 ft (7.5 m) tall with pure white flowers.
Zone 4 US, 4 Can.

***M.* 'Sugar Tyme'** A small, fast-growing, upright tree with sugar white, fragrant flowers and copious, long-lasting, red fruits ½ in (1 cm) in diameter. Very disease resistant. Introduced by Lake County Nursery, Ohio.
Zone 4 US, 4 Can.

***M.* 'Thunderchild'** This small, upright tree, to 15 ft (4.5 m), has pale pink flowers and dark purplish red fruits. Good disease resistance. Introduced by P. Wright of Saskatoon, Saskatchewan.
Zone 2 US, 2b Can.

M. toringoides (Cutleaf crab apple) A beautiful, small, shrubby tree with graceful, slender, wide-spreading branches and lobed leaves. The slightly fragrant, creamy white flowers are borne in late spring and are followed by rounded or pear-shaped, red and yellow fruits that last into late fall. It also has attractive fall color. W China. Introduced 1904 by Ernest Wilson.
Zone 4 US, 5 Can.

M. tschonoskii An attractive, vigorous, erect, conical tree up to 40 ft (12 m) high. In spring the leaves appear silvery, becoming grey-green in summer. The flowers are white tinged with pink, and the round fruits are yellowish green, tinged with reddish purple. It is one of the best trees for fall color, with bold foliage in yellow, orange, purple, and scarlet. Japan. Introduced 1897 by Siebold.
Zone 5 US, 6 Can.

Malus 'Van Eseltine'

***M.* 'Van Eseltine'** A small, distinctively columnar tree with erect branches. The double flowers, up to 2 in (5 cm) across, are rose-scarlet in bud and open shell pink with white on the inner petals. The fruits are yellow. A good choice for a small garden. Introduced 1938 by the N.Y. State Experiment Station, Geneva, N.Y.
Zone 2 US, 2b Can.

***M.* 'Wintergold'** A shapely, small, round-headed tree with carmine-budded, white flowers and abundant clear yellow fruits that persist into winter. In cultivation 1946.
Zone 3 US, 3 Can.

***M.* 'Wisley'** A vigorous small tree with

Malus 'Wisley'

bronze-red leaves and large, wine-red, slightly scented flowers, followed by large, purple-red fruits.
Zone 4 US, 5 Can.

Mandevilla *Apocynaceae*

A genus of about 100 evergreen and deciduous species, most of which are twining climbers. They are members of the periwinkle family from tropical America.

Mandevilla × *amoena* 'Alice du Pont'

***M.* × *amabilis* 'Alice du Pont'** See *M.* × *amoena* 'Alice du Pont'.

***M.* × *amoena* 'Alice du Pont'**, syn. *M.* × *amabilis* 'Alice du Pont' A vigorous evergreen climber with glossy, dark green, deeply veined leaves and racemes of large, funnel-shaped, pink flowers that deepen in color as they age. They are borne over a long period from spring to fall.
Zone 10 US

M. laxa, syn. *M. suaveolens* (Chilean jasmine) An elegant, sun-loving deciduous climber with long, slender stems 10–14½ ft (3–4.5 m) or more and a loose, open habit. The leaves are heart shaped and slender-pointed. The fragrant, funnel-shaped, white or pinkish flowers, 2 in (5 cm) across, are borne in clusters from the leaf joints throughout summer. Its flowers are so attractive that it is well worth trying to grow this plant on a sunny wall outdoors in mild areas; otherwise it is best grown in a greenhouse. Bolivia, N Argentina. Introduced 1837 by H. J. Mandeville.
Zone 9 US

M. suaveolens See *M. laxa.*

Margyricarpus *Rosaceae*

A genus of one evergreen species, related to Acaena *and* Alchemilla.

M. pinnatus (Pearlberry) A charming, prostrate or slightly erect shrub with finely cut, deep green leaves. The flowers are insignificant. The small, round berries are pearl white tinted with purple. It will grow in any well-drained soil and is suitable for the rock garden. Chilean Andes. Introduced 1829.
Zone 9 US

Maytenus *Celastraceae*

This is a large genus of more than 200 evergreen trees and shrubs from tropical and subtropical regions. Only one or two species are hardy in temperate gardens.

M. boaria (Chile mayten tree) A large evergreen shrub or small tree with slender branches and narrow, elliptic, finely toothed leaves. The flowers are small and insignificant, but the plant is grown for its foliage and gently weeping habit. It will grow in any well-drained soil. Chile. Introduced 1829.
Zone 8 US, 9? Can.

Maytenus boaria

Medicago *Leguminosae*

A genus of more than 50 evergreen and deciduous species, mainly of annual and perennial cloverlike plants. They are native to Europe, western Asia, and Africa and require well-drained soil and sun.

M. arborea (Moon trefoil, tree medick) A small semievergreen shrub with clusters of yellow pea flowers produced continuously, though often sparsely, from late spring to early fall. The seedpods resemble snail shells. It is a good choice for seashore gardens in mild climates. Mediterranean region. Introduced 1596.
Zone 9 US

Melaleuca *Myrtaceae*

Honey myrtle, bottlebrush, tea tree

A genus of about 150 species of broadleaf evergreen trees and shrubs that are related to and resemble Callistemon. *They are tender natives of Australia and Southeast Asia and can be grown out-of-doors only in very warm areas. In parts of the southeastern United States, some of the large species have become invasive pests. Those described here require full sun and will not tolerate alkaline soil.*

Melaleuca hypericifolia

M. hypericifolia A large, graceful shrub that grows to about 6 ft (2 m), with small leaves like those of a St.-John's-wort. The flowers, borne in summer, are red. Australia. Introduced 1792.
Zone 10 US

M. linariifolia (Flaxleaf paperbark) A small, rounded to vase-shaped tree, up to 30 ft (9 m), with white bark that flakes in thin shreds. The fluffy white flowers are borne in 2 in (5 cm) spikes in late spring and resemble puffs of snow. It is very drought tolerant. Australia.
Zone 10 US

Melia *Meliaceae*

A genus of three species of sun-loving, deciduous or semievergreen, large shrubs or small trees from Asia and Australia; only one is commonly grown in the United States. They will grow in any well-drained, friable soil and tolerate drought, pests, and wet soil.

M. azedarach (Chinaberry, bead tree) A fast-growing, round-headed small to medium-sized tree that can grow to 50 ft (15 m) tall. It has large, elegant, doubly pinnate leaves and small, fragrant, lilac flowers borne in loose panicles in summer. Clusters of yellow, beadlike, poisonous fruits are produced in fall and remain on the plant long after the leaves have dropped. It is popular in the South and suitable as a shade tree, although it is weak wooded and short lived. China, Himalaya. In cultivation since the 16th century.
Zone 8 US

Melianthus *Melianthaceae*

A genus of about six species of sun-loving evergreen subshrubs from South Africa. The following can be grown in the mildest areas but even so may be herbaceous in cold winters. It will grow in any well-drained, friable soil.

M. major (Large honey bush) A handsome foliage plant with spreading, hollow stems covered in blue-gray, deeply toothed, pinnate leaves up to 18 in (45 cm) long and having 9–11 leaflets. It can grow to 10 ft (3 m). The tubular flowers are brownish

Melianthus major

crimson and borne in dense, erect terminal panicles up to 6 in (15 cm) long in summer. It is popular in southern California gardens. S Africa. Introduced 1688.
Zone 10 US 🏆

Meliosma *Sabiaceae*

A genus of about 25 species of evergreen and deciduous trees and shrubs native to Asia and Central and South America. The following species will grow in any well-drained, friable soil.

Meliosma veitchiorum

M. veitchiorum A small deciduous tree distinguished by its very large, pinnate, red-stalked leaves; stout, rigid branches; and prominent winter buds. The creamy white, fragrant flowers are borne in panicles 12–18 in (30–45 cm) long in late spring. The fruits are violet. It is extremely rare. W and C China. Introduced 1901 by Ernest Wilson.
Zone 8 US, 9? Can.

Menziesia *Ericaceae*

A genus of about seven species from North America and eastern Asia. They are small, slow-growing, deciduous shrubs resembling Enkianthus *and need an acidic soil and protection from late frosts. The flowers are borne at the ends of the shoots, similar to those of* Daboecia *but waxy.*

M. ciliicalyx A small shrub with oval leaves and nodding, urn-shaped, cream to soft purple flowers borne in clusters in late spring. Japan. Introduced 1915.
Zone 6 US, 7 Can.

M. pilosa (Allegany menziesia) A small to medium-sized shrub with oblong, pointy, bristly leaves. The drooping, yellow or pink, bell-shaped flowers are borne in late spring and early summer. E United States.
Zone 4 US, 5 Can.

Mespilus *Rosaceae*
Medlar

A genus of one deciduous species.

Mespilus germanica

M. germanica The medlar is grown for its ornamental qualities as well as its fruits, which make a delicious jelly. It is a wide-spreading small tree and makes a fine architectural specimen. The large white or pinkish flowers are produced in late spring and early summer and are followed by large, brown, apple-shaped fruits. The fruits are eaten when overripe and have a tart taste. Native from SE Europe to C Asia but long cultivated.
Zone 5 US, 6 Can.

Mespilus germanica 'Nottingham'

***M. g.* 'Nottingham'** The most widely grown of the medlars selected for their fruit-bearing potential. They are less thorny than the wild trees and have larger leaves.
Zone 5 US, 6 Can.

Metasequoia *Taxodiaceae*

A genus of one deciduous species, thought to have been long extinct until found in a Chinese village in 1944; until that time it had been known only from fossils. It is similar in general appearance to Taxodium *species and is related to the* Sequoia *and* Sequoiadendron *genera.*

Metasequoia glyptostroboides

M. glyptostroboides (Dawn redwood) A strong, vigorous, fast-growing tree, narrowly conical to pyramidal in shape, with shaggy, cinnamon-brown bark. It can reach 100 ft (30 m) and is suitable only for large gardens. The leaves are linear, flattened, and borne in two opposite ranks on short, deciduous branchlets, somewhat like nee-

dles. They are bright green in summer and become tawny pink and gold in fall. It performs best in moist but well-drained soil that is slightly acidic. It is fairly hardy and tolerates pollution, but young shoots may be burned in pockets where late frost occurs. China. Introduced 1948 to the Arnold Arboretum, Boston, Mass. Seed sent from China during the early 1980s has produced trees that are now about 15–18 ft (5–5.5 m). Seedling trees develop the buttressed trunks characteristic of the species, but buttresses are not made by trees that have been vegetatively propagated.
Zone 4 US, 5b Can. 🏆

***M. g.* 'Emerald Feathers'** A fine tree of regular, conical habit with lush green foliage that colors well in fall.
Zone 4 US, 5b Can.

Metasequoia glyptostroboides 'Emerald Feathers'

***M. g.* 'National'** An upright selection from the U. S. National Arboretum that seems to be slightly hardier.
Zone 4 US, 5 Can.

Metrosideros *Myrtaceae*

A genus of about 50 species of handsome evergreen trees, shrubs, and aerial-rooted climbers. They are related to Callistemon *and are native to Australasia, Malaysia, and southern Africa. The brilliant bottlebrush flowers are spectacular. The following species requires very well-drained soil and a hot climate, although it can also be grown in a container and overwintered indoors.*

M. excelsa (New Zealand Christmas tree, ironwood) This is a noble and picturesque tree native to the North Island. It has dark green, leathery leaves with white undersides and large, crimson, bottlebrush flowers in summer. It can become a large tree and is useful in coastal areas, as it tolerates salt spray. Introduced 1840.
Zone 9 US

Metrosideros excelsa

***M. e.* 'Variegata'** The leaves of this form have broad creamy margins.
Zone 9 US

Michelia *Magnoliaceae*

A genus of about 45 species of evergreen trees or shrubs closely related to Magnolia *but with the flowers borne mainly in the axils of the leaves. They are natives of tropical and subtropical Southeast Asia and suitable only for mild climates.*

Michelia doltsopa

M. doltsopa A small to medium-sized, semievergreen tree with leathery leaves, 6–7 in (15–18 cm) long, glaucous beneath. The multipetaled, white, scented flowers are formed in fall and open in spring. Himalayan region. Introduced c. 1918.
Zone 9 US

M. figo (Banana shrub) A medium-sized to large shrub with carmine-edged yellow flowers that smell like bananas. China.
Zone 9 US

Microbiota *Cupressaceae*

A genus of one evergreen species.

Microbiota decussata

M. decussata (Siberian carpet cypress) A densely branched, prostrate, very hardy shrub with wide-spreading branches bearing small, almost scalelike leaves, although awl-shaped leaves are present on some branches. They are pale green in summer, turning bronze-red or purple in winter. It has very small, berrylike fruits in autumn. It is an excellent ground-covering conifer that grows to 1 ft (30 cm) tall and 15 ft (4.5 m) wide. E Siberia. Found 1921.
Zone 3 US, 3 Can. 🏆

Microcachrys *Podocarpaceae*

A genus of one evergreen species, related to Podocarpus.

M. tetragona A dwarf bush with snakelike, four-angled, arching branches covered with minute, scalelike leaves arranged in four ranks. The fruits are egg shaped, bright red, fleshy, and translucent. It is rare in the wild. Tasmania. Introduced 1857.
Zone 9 US

Mimulus *Scrophulariaceae*

A large genus of about 150 species, mainly annuals and herbaceous perennials, but including one or two woody evergreen plants that can be grown in sunny locations. They are mostly from North America.

M. aurantiacus (Bush monkey flower) A pretty, multistemmed, small shrub with downy hairs that grows to about 4 ft (1.2 m) high. The bell-like flowers are orange or yellow shot with salmon and are borne throughout summer and fall. Especially good for coastal areas. California, Oregon. Introduced late 18th century.
Zone 9 US 🏆

M. a.* var. *puniceus A form that differs mainly in its smaller, brick red or orange-red flowers. California.
Zone 9 US

Mitraria *Gesneriaceae*

A genus of one evergreen species.

Mitraria coccinea

M. coccinea A low, spreading or scrambling shrub with small, oval and toothed, glossy leaves and comparatively large, bright orange-scarlet, tubular flowers borne singly in the leaf axils from late spring throughout the summer. It is a charming plant for a partially shaded, sheltered location in a mild area and will not tolerate shallow alkaline soils. Given suitable support, it will climb for a short distance. Chile. Introduced 1846 by William Lobb.
Zone 7 US, 8 Can.

Moltkia *Boraginaceae*

A genus of six species of herbaceous perennials and evergreen and deciduous subshrubs native to southern Europe and Southwest Asia. They will grow in any fertile, well-drained soil in full sun.

M.* × *intermedia A dwarf evergreen subshrub, domed in habit and reaching 12 × 20 in (30 × 50 cm). The leaves are dark green and very narrow; the bright blue, open funnel-shaped flowers are profusely borne on spikes in summer.
Zone 7 US, 8 Can. 🏆

M. petraea A deciduous subshrub that forms a neat dwarf bush up to 18 in (45 cm) high. The tubular flowers are pink in bud, opening violet-blue in midsummer. Balkan peninsula. Introduced c. 1840.
Zone 7 US, 8 Can.

Morus *Moraceae*
Mulberry

A genus of seven species of deciduous trees and shrubs from the Americas, Africa, and Asia, generally forming small, picturesque trees. They will grow in any well-drained soil but respond well to richer soils that have been mulched. They tolerate salt spray, drought, and pollution. Special care should be taken at planting time, as their fleshy roots are brittle.

M. alba (White mulberry) A small to medium-sized, rugged tree with heart- or lance-shaped leaves, often up to 6 in (15 cm) wide, which are the traditional food of silkworms. The whitish fruits change to reddish pink or nearly black in some forms and are sweetly edible; often used for preserves. C Asia to China. In cultivation c. 1596.
Zone 3 US, 3 Can.

Morus alba 'Pendula'

***M. a.* 'Pendula'** A striking, small, weeping tree with closely packed, pendulous branches. Ornamental when in full fruit.
Zone 3 US, 3 Can.

Morus nigra

M. nigra (Black mulberry) A small, very long-lived, architectural tree with a wide-spreading head, becoming interestingly gnarled as it ages. The leaves are heart shaped, and the fruits are a dark, almost black red and have a pleasant taste. W Asia. In cultivation for centuries.
Zone 7 US, 8 Can. 🏆

Muehlenbeckia *Polygonaceae*

A genus of about 15 species of creeping or climbing deciduous plants from Australasia and South America. They are not very ornamental in flower but provide dense cover. They grow in any soil in sun or light shade.

M. axillaris (Creeping wire vine) A slow-growing, prostrate species forming dense carpets of intertwining, threadlike stems with small, almost round leaves barely 1/4 in (5 mm) long. It has tiny, yellow-green flowers in summer and white fruits. Useful as a ground cover in rock gardens and on screes. New Zealand, Australia, Tasmania.
Zone 8 US, 9? Can.

M. complexa (Wire vine) A twining species with slender, dark, interlacing stems occasionally up to 20 ft (6 m) or more, form-

ing dense, tangled curtains or carpets. The rounded leaves are $^1/_8$–$^3/_4$ in (3–20 mm) long. The minute greenish flowers in fall are followed in female plants by small, white, fleshy fruits. Very salt tolerant. New Zealand. Introduced 1842.
Zone 9 US

Mutisia *Compositae*
Climbing gazania

A genus of about 60 species of erect or climbing South American evergreens. They climb by means of leaf tendrils and can be grown on a wall, pergola, or arch, but they are perhaps best planted near a small bushy tree so that their stems can grow into and be supported by it. They need a warm, sunny location in a rich but well-drained soil. The colorful gazania-like flower heads are produced singly on long stalks.

M. decurrens A rare climbing species up to 10 ft (3 m), with narrow, oblong, stalkless leaves 3–5 in (7.5–13 cm) long. The daisy-like flowers, 4–5 in (10–13 cm) wide, have brilliant orange or vermilion petals and are borne continuously throughout the summer. It is a superb species but difficult to establish and performs best in a warm, sheltered location such as a partially shaded, west-facing wall and in a rich, friable, sandy loam. Chile. Introduced 1859.
Zone 8 US, 9? Can.

M. ilicifolia A vigorous species with stems 10–16 ft (3–5 m) long. The stalkless leaves are strongly toothed, dark green above and pale woolly beneath. The lilac-pink flowers are 2–3 in (5–7.5 cm) wide and are borne in summer and early fall. Chile. Introduced 1832.
Zone 8 US, 9? Can.

M. oligodon A beautiful, suckering species with straggling stems that are not too difficult to establish if grown into a sparsely branched shrub, but they barely reach 5 ft (1.5 m). The leaves are coarsely toothed and heart shaped at the base, and the flowers, which are 2–3 in (5–7.5 cm) across, have salmon pink petals and appear throughout the summer and intermittently into fall. It needs a sunny site and can look quite dead in winter. Chile. Introduced 1927.
Zone 7 US, 8 Can.

Myrica *Myricacaceae*

A genus of about 50 species of interesting aromatic evergreen and deciduous shrubs widely distributed throughout the world.

Myrica gale

M. gale (Sweet gale) A small, dense, deciduous shrub with golden brown male and female catkins on separate plants in mid- to late spring. The whole plant is strongly aromatic. It can be grown in wet, acid, boggy locations. Weak growth should be cut back to ground level in spring. Europe, NE Asia, North America. In cultivation 1750.
Zone 1 US, 1 Can.

M. pensylvanica (Bayberry) A medium-sized, semievergreen, aromatic shrub with showy, profuse, waxy gray berries used to make candles. Excellent for coastal sites, as it is very tolerant of salt spray and poor, sandy soil. E North America.
Zone 3 US, 4 Can.

Myrsine *Myrsinaceae*

A genus of five species of evergreen trees and shrubs that have fairly inconspicuous flowers and are grown for their foliage and decorative fruit. They are moderately lime tolerant but not suitable for shallow soils. They require a sunny location.

M. africana (Cape myrtle) A small shrub with aromatic, myrtlelike, evergreen leaves. It bears axillary clusters of tiny, reddish brown flowers in late spring, after which the female plants produce blue-black, pealike berries. This a very slow-growing plant. Azores, Himalaya, Far East, and parts of Africa. Introduced 1691.
Zone 9 US

Myrteola

M. nummularia See *Myrtus nummularia*.

Myrtus *Myrtaceae*
Myrtle

An easily cultivated and effective group of evergreen shrubs or trees grown for their handsome foliage. They are primarily for mild climates and perform best in full sun in any well-drained soil, although one or two can tolerate part shade. They are excellent for exposed, coastal sites.

Myrtus communis

Myrtus communis 'Variegata'

M. bullata, syn. *Lophomyrtus bullata* A large bush or small tree with distinctive, round, leathery, coppery green or reddish brown, puckered leaves. The late-summer white flowers are followed by blackish red berries. Suitable only for mild climates. New

Zealand. In cultivation 1854.
Zone 9 US

M. chequen, syn. *Luma chequen* A small, densely leafy tree with white flowers in summer and fall. The leaves are aromatic, bright green, and undulate. Chile. Introduced 1847 by William Lobb.
Zone 9 US

M. communis (Common myrtle) A tender plant suitable for mild climates or the greenhouse, growing well in coastal areas. It is an aromatic, densely leafy shrub that will reach 10–13 ft (3–4 m). The leaves are shining green, oval, and 1–2 in (2.5–5 cm) long. The white or pinkish flowers are borne profusely in mid- to late summer and are followed by blue-black berries. It tolerates shearing and can be used for hedges and topiary. Mediterranean region. In cultivation since the 16th century.
Zone 8 US, 9 Can.
🏆

***M. c.* 'Flore Pleno'** An uncommon form with double flowers. Zone 8 US, 9 Can.

***M. c.* 'Jenny Reitenbach'** See *M. c.* subsp. *tarentina.*

M. c.* subsp. *tarentina, syn. *M. c.* 'Jenny Reitenbach' A very pretty, compact, small to medium-sized shrub with small, narrow leaves and white berries. The pink-tinged flowers are profusely borne in autumn. Mediterranean region.
Zone 8 US, 9 Can. 🏆

***M. c.* 'Variegata'** The leaves of this medium-sized shrub are mainly gray-green, narrowly margined with cream. A variegated form of *M. c.* subsp. *tarentina* is also in cultivation.
Zone 8 US, 9 Can.

M. luma, syn. *Luma apiculata* A lovely species reaching the size of a small tree in mild areas but often with multiple trunks. The cinnamon-colored outer bark of even young trees peels off in patches, exposing the beautiful, cream-colored inner surface. The oval, sharply pointed leaves are dark green, and the delicate white flowers cover the branches in late summer and fall. The red and black fruits, produced only after a warm summer and fall, are edible and sweet. It may self-sow abundantly in favorable locations, becoming naturalized. Chile. Introduced 1843.
Zone 9 US 🏆

***M. l.* 'Glanleam Gold'** The leaves of this large shrub or small tree have a bright creamy yellow margin and are pink-tinged when young.
Zone 9 US

M. nummularia, syn. *Myrteola nummularia* This tiny, prostrate shrublet, the hardiest myrtle, has wiry, reddish stems and neat, rounded leaves borne in two opposite ranks. White flowers appear at the ends of the stems in late spring or early summer, followed by pink berries. Argentina, Chile, Falklands. Introduced before 1927.
Zone 7? US, 8? Can.

M. ugni, syn. *Ugni molinae* (Chilean guava) A slow-growing, small to medium-sized, leathery leaved, rather stiffly erect shrub, with nodding, waxy, pink bell-shaped flowers in late summer and deliciously edible, aromatic, mahogany berries. Chile. Introduced 1844 by William Lobb.
Zone 9 US

Nandina *Berberidaceae*

A genus of just one deciduous species that looks a little like bamboo but is related to Berberis. *It is grown for its foliage and flowers.*

Myrtus luma

Nandina domestica

N. domestica (Heavenly bamboo) A decorative, bamboolike, medium-sized shrub with long, erect, unbranched stems. The large, compound, green leaves are tinged with purplish red in spring and fall. The small white flowers are borne in large terminal clusters in summer. Red berries are produced only after very hot summers. It should be given a sheltered location in any well-drained soil. It grows equally well in full sun or dense shade. C China, Japan. Introduced 1804.
Zone 6 US, 7 Can.

Nandina domestica 'Firepower'

***N. d.* 'Firepower'** A small shrub similar to 'Nana Purpurea' but with yellow-green foliage in summer that turns brilliant orange-red in winter.
Zone 6 US, 7 Can.

Nandina domestica 'Nana Purpurea'

***N. d.* 'Nana Purpurea'** A small shrub with a more compact habit than the species and with simpler leaves and broader leaflets. The young foliage is reddish purple throughout the season.
Zone 6 US, 7 Can.

***N. d.* 'Richmond'** A vigorous medium-sized form with an abundance of red fruits in winter.
Zone 6 US, 7 Can.

Neillia *Rosaceae*

A genus of about 10 species of deciduous shrubs related to Spiraea. *They are very easily grown in all types of soil, except very dry ones.*

Neillia thibetica

N. thibetica (Tibet neillia) An attractive medium-sized shrub with erect, downy stems; slenderly pointed, often three-lobed leaves; and slender terminal clusters of tubular pink flowers in late spring and early summer. After flowering, the old flowering stems should be cut to ground level to promote new growth. W China. Introduced 1904 by Ernest Wilson.
Zone 5 US, 6 Can.

Nerium *Apocynaceae*
Oleander

A genus of two species of tender, ornamental, sun-loving evergreen shrubs that need heat and well-drained soil and tolerate salt and drought. All parts of the plants are poisonous and should not be eaten or burned.

N. oleander (Oleander, rose bay) This is a well-known medium-sized to large shrub or small tree that can reach 20 ft (6 m) tall. It has erect branches; long, lance-shaped,

Nerium oleander

dark green leaves; and flowers like large periwinkles. There are now many named forms with single to double or semidouble flowers in colors ranging from white and yellow to scarlet and purple; flowering is from early summer to midfall. Some plants are fragrant and a few have variegated leaves. Often grown as a container plant in the greenhouse in cold climates. Mediterranean region, SW Asia. Introduced 1596.
Zone 8 US

Nothofagus *Fagaceae*
Southern beech

A genus of about 20 species of ornamental, fast-growing evergreen and deciduous trees or large shrubs from South America and Australasia, valued for their shape and foliage. They are related to Fagus *but usually have small leaves closely spaced along the branchlets. They vary in hardiness and many are easily damaged by wind. They will not tolerate very alkaline soils.*

Nothofagus antarctica

Nothofagus dombeyi

N. antarctica (Antarctic beech) An elegant, fast-growing, medium-sized deciduous tree broadly conical in shape. The small, rounded, and heart-shaped leaves are irregularly toothed and glossy dark green and turn yellow in fall. The trunk and main branches are often curiously twisted. Chile. Introduced 1830. *(Photo on p.411.)*
Zone 6 US, 7 Can.

Nothofagus betuloides

N. betuloides A medium-sized to large, densely leafy evergreen tree, columnar when young. The shining dark green leaves are rounded, usually less than 1 in (2.5 cm) long, and closely arranged on the branchlets. Chile, Argentina. Introduced 1830.
Zone 8 US, 9? Can.

N. dombeyi A medium-sized to large, vigorous evergreen tree. The leaves are 1–1½ in (2.5–4 cm) long, doubly toothed, and shining dark green. It may lose its leaves during cold winters. Chile, Argentina. Introduced 1916.
Zone 9 US

N. fusca (Red beech) This species is tender when young but develops into a beautiful, small to medium-sized evergreen tree. The rounded or oval, coarsely toothed leaves, 1–1½ in (2.5–4 cm) long, often turn copper in fall. The bark on old trees becomes flaky. New Zealand.
Zone 9 US

N. menziesii (Silver beech) A graceful, small to medium-sized evergreen tree with dark green, doubly toothed, roundish leaves only ½ in (12 mm) long. The bark of the young wood is like that of a cherry tree. New Zealand.
Zone 9 US

N. nervosa, syn. *N. procera* A fast-growing, large deciduous tree with large, prominently veined leaves about 1½–4 in (4–10 cm) long, rather like those of a hornbeam. It is often very colorful in fall. Chile, Argentina. Introduced 1913.
Zone 8 US, 9? Can.

N. obliqua (Roblé beech) A large, elegant, very fast-growing deciduous tree, making a handsome specimen in a few years. Its leaves are broad, 2–3 in (5–7.5 cm) long, and irregularly toothed. Chile, Argentina. Introduced 1902.
Zone 7 US, 8 Can.

N. procera See *N. nervosa.*

N. solanderi* var. *cliffortioides (Mountain beech) An elegant, small to medium-sized, fast-growing evergreen tree with very

Nothofagus solanderi var. *cliffortioides*

small leaves that have curled edges and a raised tip. New Zealand.
Zone 9 US

Notospartium *Leguminosae*

A genus of three species of leafless broomlike shrubs from New Zealand. They need full sun in any well-drained soil and are susceptible to injury from frost.

N. carmichaeliae (Pink broom, Southern broom) A charming, medium-sized, graceful shrub with arching, leafless stems wreathed in lilac-pink pea flowers in the middle of summer. This is a rare plant.
Zone 9 US

Nyssa *Nyssaceae*
Sour gum, tupelo

A genus of about five species of deciduous trees, natives of eastern North America and eastern Asia, noted for their rich autumn colors. They need moist, acidic soil and are best planted when small, as they resent disturbance.

Nyssa sinensis

N. sinensis (Chinese sour gum) A magnificent large shrub or small tree with fairly narrow leaves up to 6 in (15 cm) long. The young growths are red throughout the growing season, and in fall the leaves change to many shades of red and yellow. China. In cultivation 1902.
Zone 7 US, 8 Can.

N. sylvatica (Black gum, black tupelo) A handsome, slow-growing, dense-headed, medium-sized to large tree with a broadly

Nyssa sylvatica

pyramidal outline. The leaves are variable in shape but more or less oval, pointed, up to 6 in (15 cm) long, and glossy, dark green, occasionally dull green above. The foliage turns scarlet, orange, and yellow in fall. S Canada to S Mexico. Introduced 1750.
Zone 4 US, 5b Can.

***N. s.* 'Jermyns Flame'** A form bearing relatively large leaves with striking autumn colors of red, yellow, and orange. Selected 1985 by John Hillier.
Zone 4 US, 5b Can.

Oemleria *Rosaceae*

A genus of only one deciduous species, related to Prunus *but quite different. It produces suckers, and growth can be restricted if desired by removing these and cutting back old shoots in late winter.*

O. cerasiformis (Osoberry) A suckering shrub, making a clump of erect stems 6½–8 ft (2–2.5 m) tall, with hanging racemes of fragrant, white, currantlike flowers in late winter and early spring. The fruits are plumlike, brown at first and then purple when ripe; since male and female flowers are borne on separate plants, fruits can be obtained only if plants of both sexes are grown. The leaves are sea green and emerge early, with the flowers. It grows in all kinds of fertile soil but may suffer from chlorosis in very poor, alkaline ones. California. Introduced 1848.
Zone 7 US, 8 Can.

Olea *Oleaceae*
Olive

A genus of about 20 species of tender evergreen trees and shrubs with opposite, leathery leaves; one species has been grown for centuries for its edible fruits. They are native to warm regions of the Old World, and require fertile, deep, well-drained soil and full sun. They are prone to suckers at the base, which should be removed regularly in early summer to maintain a tree shape.

Olea europaea

O. europaea (Common olive) A large shrub or small tree with gray-green leaves, silver-bloomy beneath, and clusters of small, fragrant, white flowers in late summer. Culinary olives and olive oils are obtained from named cultivars; for landscape use there are also cultivars with few fruits, which can stain paving. Mediterranean region.
Zone 9 US

Olearia *Compositae*
Daisy bush, tree aster

A genus of about 130 species of attractive, easily grown, wind-resistant, sun-loving, evergreen shrubs. They are excellent for planting in coastal areas. They all have daisylike flower heads, and their average height range is 4–8 ft (1.2–2.5 m). Straggly specimens can be pruned hard in mid-spring; any further pruning should be done after flowering. Olearia *succeed in any well-drained soil and are highly recommended for alkaline ones. An individual daisy "flower" is technically a flower head, and the flower heads are usually in clusters called corymbs.*

Olearia avicennifolia 'White Confusion'

***O. avicennifolia* 'White Confusion'** A medium-sized to large shrub with pointed leaves that are whitish or buff underneath and slightly wavy. The wide corymbs of sweetly scented, white flower heads are borne profusely in summer. It makes a fine, dense hedge.
Zone 9 US

O. chathamica A beautiful small shrub up to 4 ft (1.2 m), similar to 'Henry Travers' but with broader green leaves. The flower heads, up to 2 in (5 cm) across, are solitary and borne on long stalks in early summer. They are pale violet with purple centers. Chatham Islands. Introduced 1910.
Zone 9 US

Olearia × *haastii*

O.* × *haastii (New Zealand daisy bush) A rounded, medium-sized bush with small leaves that are white-felted beneath. It becomes smothered with fragrant, white flower heads in mid- to late summer. It tolerates urban pollution and is a well-proven hedge plant. Popular in southern California, as it tolerates heat and full sun. New Zealand. Introduced 1858.
Zone 9 US

***O.* 'Henry Travers'**, syn. *O. semidentata* This is one of the loveliest shrubs for seashore gardens. It is a medium-sized shrub with slender, gray-green leaves that are silvery beneath. The large, pendent, asterlike flower heads are lilac with purple centers and appear in early summer. Introduced 1908 into Ireland.
Zone 9 US 🏆

Olearia ilicifolia

O. ilicifolia A dense, medium-sized shrub with thick, leathery, gray-green leaves that are sharply toothed and whitish-felted beneath. The fragrant, white flower heads are borne in early summer, and the whole plant has a musky aroma. It is one of the best species. New Zealand.
Zone 9 US

O. lacunosa A medium-sized to large but slow-growing shrub with stout, white-woolly stems. The leaves are rigid, long and narrow, up to 6½ in (17 cm) long by ½ in (1 cm) across, and are covered with loose white flock on the upper surfaces at first, before becoming dark green with a pale midrib. The undersides are persistently silver. The white flower heads are small and rarely produced in gardens. New Zealand.
Zone 9 US

O. macrodonta (New Zealand holly) A vigorous and handsome shrub reaching 10 ft (3 m) or more, with sage green, holly-like leaves 2½–3½ in (6–9 cm) long and silvery white beneath. The fragrant, white

Olearia macrodonta

flower heads are borne in broad corymbs in early summer. It is one of the best screening or hedge plants for exposed coastal gardens. The whole plant has a slight musky aroma. New Zealand.
Zone 9 US 🏆

***O. m.* 'Major'** A form with larger leaves and flower clusters.
Zone 9 US

O.* × *mollis A small, rounded, compact shrub with wavy-edged, silvery gray, slightly toothed leaves up to 1½ in (4 cm) long. White flower heads are borne in large corymbs in late spring. It is one of the hardier *Olearia*.
Zone 9 US

Olearia nummulariifolia

O. nummulariifolia This is a medium-sized, stiffly branching, unusual-looking shrub, with small, thick, yellow-green leaves crowding the stems. The small, fragrant, white flower heads are borne in the angles of the leaves in midsummer. Some plants

grown under this name are hybrids. New Zealand.
Zone 9 US

***O.* × *oleifolia* 'Waikariensis'** A small, attractive shrub with lance-shaped leaves measuring about 2 × ½ in (5 × 1.5 cm). They are glossy green above and white beneath with a buff midrib. The white flowers are in clusters in the angles of the leaves in mid- to late summer. New Zealand. Introduced early 1930s.
Zone 9 US

O. paniculata A large shrub or small tree with distinctive, bright olive green, wavy leaves, reminiscent of *Pittosporum tenuifolium*. Although the flower heads are not very conspicuous, they are borne in late fall and early winter and are fragrant. In mild coastal areas it is used as a hedge. New Zealand. Introduced 1816.
Zone 9 US

O. phlogopappa (Tasmanian daisy bush) A very variable species that grows into an erect, medium-sized shrub with aromatic, toothed leaves thickly crowding the stems; leaf undersides are hairy. The flower heads can be blue, lavender, or rose and are ¾ in (2 cm) across in late spring. Introduced 1930.
Zone 9 US

Olearia paniculata

Olearia phlogopappa

O. ramulosa A small, twiggy shrub with slender, arching stems and small, linear leaves. The small white flower heads crowd the stems in late summer. Tasmania, S Australia. In cultivation 1872.
Zone 10 US

O.* × *scilloniensis A compact, rounded, gray-leaved shrub, sometimes reaching 8 ft (2.5 m) but usually considerably smaller. It is a very free-flowering hybrid, literally covering itself with froths of white bloom in late spring. Garden origin 1910 at Tresco Abbey, Isles of Scilly.
Zone 9 US 🏆

O. semidentata See *O.* 'Henry Travers'.

Olearia solanderi

O. solanderi A dense, heathlike shrub of medium size that gives a yellowish effect, rather like *Cassinia fulvida*. Its leaves are needlelike, ¼ in (6 mm) long, and in clusters. The small, white, sweetly scented flower heads are borne in late summer. Unless grown in a mild place, it needs the protection of a wall. New Zealand.
Zone 9 US

O. stellulata A variable, rather lax, small to medium-sized shrub a little like *O. phlogopappa* but taller, longer leaved, and not as compact. The white flower heads are borne in panicles in late spring. Tasmania.
Zone 9 US

Olearia stellulata

O. traversii This is considered one of the best and fastest-growing evergreens for windbreaks in mild coastal areas, growing to 20 ft (6 m) even in exposed locations in sandy soils. The shoots are four-angled and white-felted. The leaves are broad, leathery, and polished green above, silvery white beneath. The flower heads, produced in summer, are insignificant. Chatham Islands. Introduced 1887.
Zone 9 US

O. virgata* var. *lineata A large, very graceful, loose shrub with slender, pendulous branches and narrow leaves. The summer flowers are insignificant. New Zealand.
Zone 7 US, 8 Can.

O. viscosa A small to medium-sized shrub up to 6½ ft (2 m), with sticky young shoots and shiny green, lance-shaped leaves that are silvery white and densely woolly beneath. It has broad corymbs of attractive white flower heads in mid- and late summer. A very free-flowering form introduced

Olearia 'Zennorensis'

by Sir Harold Hillier in 1977. Tasmania, SE Australia.
Zone 9 US

***O.* 'Zennorensis'** A form of *O.* × *mollis*, this is a striking foliage plant up to 6½ ft (2 m), with narrow, pointed, sharply toothed leaves about 4 in (10 cm) long and ½ in (12 mm) wide, dark olive green above and white beneath. The young stems and leaf stalks are heavily coated with pale brown wool. An excellent shrub for warm climates, especially in coastal areas, but do not expect flowers. Garden origin at Zennor, Cornwall, England. *(Photo on p.415.)*
Zone 9 US

Ononis *Leguminosae*

A genus of about 75 species of deciduous shrubs and herbaceous plants that are often spiny. They have a wide distribution from Europe to North Africa and western Asia and are good dwarf plants for the border or rock garden. All have leaves with three leaflets and pea-shaped flowers. They need full sun and do well on any well-drained soil, including shallow alkaline ones.

Ononis fruticosa

O. fruticosa A splendid small shrub forming a compact mound up to 3 ft (1 m) high, long grown for its display of bright rose-pink flowers in small clusters throughout summer. W Mediterranean region. In cultivation 1680.
Zone 8 US, 9 Can.

Orixa *Rutaceae*

A genus of one deciduous species.

O. japonica (Japanese orixa) A pungently aromatic, dioecious, medium-sized shrub with lustrous, bright green leaves that change to pale lemon or white in fall, contrasting with the more prevalent reds and purples. It thrives in any well-drained soil. Japan, China, Korea. Introduced 1870.
Zone 6 US, 7 Can.

Osmanthus *Oleaceae*

A genus of about 14 species of evergreen shrubs and trees, native to the United States, Asia, and the Pacific Islands. The following are attractive, frequently hollylike shrubs that do well in almost all soils, but especially acidic ones. Their flowers are small and white or cream and usually have a sweet fragrance. They will grow in sun or part shade, and only leggy or damaged shoots need to be pruned.

O. armatus (Chinese osmanthus) A large, handsome shrub of dense habit, with thick, leathery, rigid leaves up to 6 in (15 cm) long that have stout, spiny, coarse teeth. Its tiny, ¼ in (6 mm), sweetly scented white blooms emerge in fall, followed by violet egglike fruits. W China. Introduced 1902 by Ernest Wilson.
Zone 9 US

Osmanthus × burkwoodii

O.* × *burkwoodii This is an excellent, hardy, compact shrub that slowly grows to about 8–10 ft (2.5–3 m). Its oval leaves are 1–2 in (2.5–5 cm) long, shining dark green, leathery, and toothed. They contrast nicely with the highly fragrant white flowers, which are profusely borne in midspring.

Osmanthus decorus

Raised 1930 in England. Zone 6 US, 7 Can.

O. decorus, syn. *Phillyrea decora* A very distinctive, dome-shaped bush up to 10 ft (3 m), usually wider than high, with comparatively large, glossy green, leathery leaves. The clusters of small, fragrant, white flowers are borne freely in spring and followed by purplish black fruits resembling miniature plums. W Asia. Introduced 1866.
Zone 7 US, 8 Can.

Osmanthus delavayi

O. delavayi One of the most beautiful small evergreen shrubs. It has small leaves and slowly grows to 6½ ft (2 m) high and more in width. Its fragrant, white, jasmine-like flowers are borne very freely in early spring, followed by blue-black berries in summer. China. Introduced 1890 by the Abbé Delavay.
Zone 8 US, 9? Can.

O.* × *fortunei (Fortune's osmanthus) A large, vigorous shrub of dense habit, with

Osmanthus × *fortunei*

large, broad, polished, dark green leaves with prominently veined upper sides and a spiny edge; on mature plants, the leaves often become spineless. The white, fall-borne flowers are sweetly scented and are followed by blue-black berries. Japan. Introduced 1862 by Robert Fortune.
Zone 8 US, 9? Can.

O. heterophyllus (Holly osmanthus) A fairly slow-growing, hollylike shrub, occasionally a small tree, with entire or coarsely spine-toothed leaves of dark, shining green. The fragrant white flowers appear in fall. It can be distinguished from a holly by its leaves, which are opposite rather than alternate. Good for hedges. The following are recommended. Japan. Introduced 1856.
Zone 6 US, 7 Can.

Osmanthus heterophyllus 'Aureomarginatus'

***O. h.* 'Aureomarginatus'** A medium-sized shrub whose leaves are margined with deep yellow. In cultivation 1877.
Zone 6 US, 7 Can.

***O. h.* 'Goshiki'** A striking medium-sized form whose leaves are mottled with yellow and tinged with bronze when young. The name means "five-colored".
Zone 6 US, 7 Can.

Osmanthus heterophyllus 'Gulftide'

***O. h.* 'Gulftide'** A dense, medium-sized bush with leaves somewhat lobed or twisted and strongly spiny. It is a remarkable and worthwhile shrub.
Zone 6 US, 7 Can. 🏆

Osmanthus heterophyllus 'Purpureus'

Osmanthus heterophyllus 'Variegatus'

***O. h.* 'Purpureus'** The growths of this form are at first purple, later turning green with a purple tinge. Raised 1860 at Kew.
Zone 6 US, 7 Can.

***O. h.* 'Variegatus'** A medium-sized shrub bearing leaves bordered with cream.
Zone 6 US, 7 Can. 🏆

Osmanthus serrulatus

O. serrulatus A medium-sized, slow-growing, compact, rounded shrub with large, fairly slender, glossy, dark green leaves that are sharply toothed or smooth, purple-red when young. Clusters of fragrant white flowers are borne in the leaf axils in spring. Himalaya. Introduced 1910.
Zone 9 US

O. suavis An erect shrub up to 13 ft (4 m), related to *O. delavayi* but with sharply toothed, shining green leaves 3 in (8 cm) long. Its white flowers, borne in spring, are fragrant. It grows best in a location sheltered from strong winds. Himalaya.
Zone 9 US

O. yunnanensis (Forrest's osmanthus) A remarkable large shrub or small tree with lance-shaped, dark olive green leaves up to 6 in (15 cm) long, varying from wavy and toothed to flat and smooth, both on the same plant. The ivory-cream flowers are intensely fragrant and appear in late winter. It has grown well at the Hillier Arboretum in a sheltered spot for many years and survived a number of cold winters. China. Introduced 1923 by George Forrest.
Zone 9 US

Ostrya *Carpinaceae*
Hop hornbeam

A small genus of medium to large deciduous trees resembling hornbeams, with hoplike fruits in late summer. They are easily grown in any fertile soil.

Ostrya carpinifolia

O. carpinifolia (European hop hornbeam) A round-headed, medium-sized tree with double-toothed leaves 3–5 in (8–13 cm) long that turn clear yellow in autumn. The fruits are 1¼–2 in (3.5–5 cm) long, with each nutlet contained in a flat, bladderlike husk. It is lovely in spring, when the many branches are strung with numerous long, drooping male catkins. S Europe, W Asia. Introduced 1724.
Zone 5 US, 6 Can.

Ostrya virginiana

O. virginiana (American hop hornbeam) An attractive, slow-growing, small tree of elegant, rounded or conical habit with rich, warm, yellow autumn color. Difficult to transplant. E North America. Introduced 1692.
Zone 3 US, 3 Can.

Othonna *Compositae*

A genus of about 150 species of evergreen and deciduous shrubs and herbaceous plants that are native primarily to tropical and southern Africa. The following species needs a warm location in full sun and well-drained soil.

Othonna cheirifolia

O. cheirifolia A dwarf evergreen shrub with spreading stems and short, ascending branches, covered with distinctive, paddle-shaped, gray-green leaves. The golden yellow flower heads are borne singly at the ends of the shoots in spring and summer and intermittently through fall and winter. Algeria, Tunisia. Introduced 1752.
Zone 9 US

Oxydendrum *Ericaceae*

A genus of one deciduous species.

O. arboreum (Sourwood) A beautiful large shrub or small tree grown for its exquisite crimson and yellow fall color. White flowers are borne in slender, drooping racemes produced in clusters from the tips of the shoots in mid- to late summer. The leaves are pleasantly, if acidly, flavored. It thrives under conditions suitable for rhododendrons, doing well in part shade or sun in acidic soil. E and SE United States. Introduced 1752.
Zone 5 US, 6 Can.

Oxydendrum arboreum

Oxypetalum *Asclepiadaceae*

There is only one species of interest to gardeners in this genus of about 100 species of herbaceous twining climbers, and even this is placed by most authorities in the genus Tweedia. *It can be grown outdoors only in warm climates. It can also be treated as an annual, if seed is sown early, or raised in a greenhouse. It will grow in any well-drained soil.*

Oxypetalum caeruleum

O. caeruleum, syn. *Tweedia caerulea* A beautiful deciduous subshrub with twining stems and oblong or heart-shaped, sage green leaves. The flowers are powder blue at first and slightly tinged with green, turning purplish and finally lilac. They are freely borne in erect clusters with a few flowers each in summer. The tips of the young shoots should be pinched out to encourage branching. South America. Introduced 1832.
Zone 10 US 🏆

Ozothamnus *Compositae*

A genus of 50 evergreen, summer-flowering shrubs related to Helichrysum. *They are woody perennial herbs, requiring full sun and a well-drained location.*

Ozothamnus ledifolius

O. ledifolius A small, dense, globular, aromatic shrub with yellow-backed, incurved leaves and comparatively large flowers with inner bracts that have notably white, spreading tips and are reddish in bud. The seed heads are honey scented. Tasmania. Introduced 1930
Zone 9 US

Ozothamnus rosmarinifolius

O. rosmarinifolius A medium-sized shrub with white-woolly stems and slender, dark green, warty leaves. The dense corymbs of red buds are spectacular for 10 days or more before they open to white, scented flowers. Given sun and a well-drained soil, it blooms freely. Tasmania, E Australia. Introduced 1827.
Zone 9 US

***O. r.* 'Silver Jubilee'** A form with silvery gray leaves.
Zone 9 US

O. selago, syn. *Helichrysum selago* A dwarf shrublet with slender, erect or ascending stems that are rather stiffly held and much branched. The tiny, green, scalelike leaves are closely adpressed to the stems, and they are smooth on the outside but coated with white on the inside, giving the stems a checkered appearance. The small, creamy flower heads are borne at the tips of the shoots in early spring. It may be grown in a rock garden, container, or alpine house for best effect. New Zealand.
Zone 9 US

Pachysandra *Buxaceae*

A genus of four or five evergreen and deciduous species of dwarf shrubs or subshrubs, native to North America and eastern Asia. They are suitable for ground cover in moist, shaded sites and do not tolerate shallow alkaline soils.

Pachysandra terminalis

P. terminalis (Japanese pachysandra) A dwarf, evergreen, carpeting shrublet that is excellent for planting under trees. The leaves are clustered at the ends of the stems and are somewhat diamond-shaped and toothed in the upper half. Spikes of greenish white flowers are produced at the ends of the previous year's shoots in late winter and early spring. Japan. Introduced 1882.
Zone 3 US, 3 Can.

Pachysandra terminalis 'Variegata'

***P. t.* 'Variegata'** The leaves of this form are attractively variegated white.
Zone 3 US, 3 Can.

Paeonia *Paeoniaceae*

Peony

There are 30 or so species in this genus, mainly herbaceous perennials that are natives of temperate regions of Europe, Asia, and North America. The deciduous shrubby members, known as tree peonies, come from western China and southeastern Tibet and are represented in gardens by just a few species and their varieties and hybrids. However, the term "tree peony" is most frequently applied to those that have originated from P. suffruticosa, *which have been bred and cultivated for many centuries in China and then in the West. Among the most beautifully colored of all shrubs, they are not injured by severe winters, though spring frosts may damage their early young growths. This can be prevented to a large extent by erecting a burlap or close-mesh netting screen on a framework of bamboos and positioning it over the plants during frosty spring nights. The protection can be removed once the frost has dispersed in the morning. Some species, including* P. delavayi *and* P. lutea, *have splendid architectural foliage. Given full sun and a sheltered location, tree peonies will thrive in any well-drained soil.*

P. delavayi A handsome, suckering shrub up to 6½ ft (2 m) high. Its flowers, borne in late spring, are deep crimson with golden

Paeonia delavayi

anthers and are followed by large, black-seeded fruits surrounded by brightly colored, persistent sepals. The large, deeply cut leaves make this a notable foliage shrub, and it is tolerant of alkaline soil. W China. Introduced 1908.
Zone 5 US, 6 Can. 🏆

***P.* × *lemoinii* 'Chromatella'** A hybrid between *P. lutea* and *P. suffruticosa* with large, double, sulphur yellow flowers in late spring and early summer. It grows to about 5–6½ ft (1.5–2 m) high, appreciates a rich loam, and does well in alkaline soil.
Zone 5? US, 6? Can.

***P.* × *l.* 'Souvenir de Maxime Cornu'** A medium-sized shrub with very large, fragrant, double flowers that are bright yellow with carmine edges.
Zone 5? US, 6? Can.

Paeonia lutea

P. lutea A bold shrub reaching about 6½ ft (2 m) in height, with foliage similar to that of *P. delavayi* but with bright yellow, cup-shaped flowers 2½ in (6 cm) across in early to midsummer. It does not flower prolifically. China. Introduced 1886.
Zone 6 US, 7 Can.

Paeonia lutea var. *ludlowii*

P. l.* var. *ludlowii This splendid, free-flowering, medium-sized shrub has large, beautiful, golden yellow, saucer-shaped flowers. First collected in Tibet.
Zone 6 US, 7 Can. 🏆

Paeonia suffruticosa

P. suffruticosa (Tree peony) A branching shrub up to 6½ ft (2 m) high, with large flowers as wide as 6 in (15 cm) or more in late spring. There are now many tree peonies available that range in color from white to pink to red and usually have semi-double or double flowers. Among the best are 'Banksii', with deep flesh-pink double flowers; 'Godaishu', with very large, white, semidouble flowers; 'Reine Elizabeth', with large, red-tinged, salmon-pink double flowers that have ruffled edges; 'Kintei', with lemon yellow flowers streaked with a darker yellow; and 'Souvenir de Ducher', whose double flowers are deep violet with a reddish tinge. NW China, Bhutan, Tibet.
Zone 4 US, 5b Can.

Pandorea *Bignoniaceae*

A genus of about six species of evergreen twining plants, natives of Southeast Asia and Australia. The following require a warm, sheltered location in a very mild climate or can be grown in the greenhouse.

P. jasminoides (Bower plant) A beautiful climber that has pinnate leaves with 5–9 slender-pointed leaflets. The funnel-shaped flowers, 1½–2 in (4–5 cm) long, are white stained with crimson in the throat and are borne in panicles in summer. E Australia.
Zone 10 US

***P. j.* 'Rosea Superba'** A form with large, bell-shaped, pink flowers, darker in the throat and with purple spots, produced from spring to summer.
Zone 10 US 🏆

Parahebe *Scrophulariaceae*

A genus of about 30 species of semiwoody, dwarf, deciduous plants that are native to New Zealand and were formerly included in Veronica. *They are good rock-garden plants and grow in all types of soil.*

P. catarractae A small-leaved dwarf plant that forms low, spreading mounds and is a good ground cover for full sun. The oval

Parahebe catarractae 'Diffusa'

leaves are sharply toothed. The flowers are white to rose-purple with a central zone of crimson and are borne in erect clusters in late summer. Blue-flowered forms are also grown. New Zealand.
Zone 9 US 🏆

***P. c.* 'Delight'** The flowers of this form are white with reddish purple veining; they are borne profusely over a long period.
Zone 9 US 🏆

***P. c.* 'Diffusa'** A form with smaller leaves and white flowers that are veined with rose-pink. It forms a dense mat.
Zone 9 US

***P. c.* 'Miss Willmott'** A shrub bearing rose-lilac flowers veined with mauve.
Zone 9 US

P. decora A creeping subshrub that forms low mounds. It has tiny, rounded leaves with one or two pairs of teeth, and the flowers are white or pink in long-stalked clusters in summer. New Zealand.
Zone 9 US

Parahebe lyallii

P. lyallii A low, prostrate shrublet with small, rounded or ovate, leathery leaves. The flowers are white, prettily veined with pink, and have blue anthers; they are borne in slender racemes from mid- to late summer. New Zealand. Introduced 1870.
Zone 9 US

***P. l.* 'Mervyn'** A dwarf, spreading shrub with small, red-edged leaves and clusters of lilac-blue flowers in summer. It is probably a hybrid of *P. lyallii.*
Zone 9 US

P. perfoliata (Digger's speedwell) A dwarf subshrub, usually herbaceous, with erect

Parahebe perfoliata

stems to about 12–18 in (30–45 cm) high. The leaves are perfoliate, with the stem appearing to pass through a pair of fused leaves, and are an attractive gray-green. The violet-blue flowers are borne in long racemes in late summer. It is an unusual plant for sunny, well-drained sites in mild areas. Australia. Introduced 1834.
Zone 9 US 🏆

Parasyringa *Oleaceae*

A genus of one evergreen species, related to Ligustrum *and* Syringa.

P. sempervirens A striking, small to medium-sized evergreen shrub with dark green, leathery, rounded leaves. The small white flowers are produced in dense, broad clusters in late summer and early fall. It will grow in any good garden soil. W China. Introduced 1913.
Zone 8 US, 9? Can.

Parrotia *Hamamelidaceae*

A genus of one deciduous species.

P. persica (Persian parrotia) A large shrub or small tree with a wide-spreading habit. The mottled gray-and-white bark of older trees flakes beautifully, much like that of plane trees. The leaves turn crimson, orange, and gold in fall, often starting in

Parrotia persica

late summer before almost any other tree or shrub. The flowers consist of clusters of crimson stamens like tiny paintbrushes and appear in winter and early spring. It is one of the finest trees for fall color and is remarkably lime tolerant for a member of the witch hazel family. N Iran to the Caucasus. In cultivation 1840.
Zone 5 US, 6 Can. 🏆

Parrotiopsis *Hamamelidaceae*

A genus of one deciduous species.

P. jaquemontiana A large, erect shrub with rounded leaves that usually turn yellow in autumn. The flower clusters have conspicuous creamy white bracts, rather like those of *Cornus florida*, and are seen in mid- to late spring and intermittently throughout the summer. It grows best in a deep, well-drained, acidic or neutral soil, but it will tolerate some lime. W Himalaya. Introduced 1879.
Zone 5 US, 6 Can.

Parthenocissus *Vitaceae*

A genus of about 10 deciduous species of high-climbing vines, related to Vitis *and attaching themselves by means of leaf tendrils that twine or bear adhesive pads. The self-clinging species are excellent on masonry walls and tree trunks. The leaves are often richly colored in autumn. The attractive fruits are produced only after a hot, dry summer. Plant in a moisture-retentive soil enriched with well-rotted organic matter. Prune away from windows and roof eaves in early winter.*

Parthenocissus henryana

P. henryana (Silver-vein creeper) A beautiful self-clinging species with 3–5 narrow leaflets originating from a central point. They are dark green or bronze, with silvery white veining that shows up better when the plant is grown in part shade, and turn red in fall. The fruits are dark blue. It is best grown on a wall. Discovered 1885. C China. Introduced 1900 by Ernest Wilson.
Zone 7 US, 8 Can. 🏆

Parthenocissus quinquefolia

P. quinquefolia (Virginia creeper) A tall-growing, more or less self-clinging vine, excellent for high walls and trees. The leaves usually have five stalked leaflets that are dull green but turn brilliant orange and scarlet in autumn. The fruits are blue-black. A small flea beetle feeds on the foliage, often reducing it to tatters and spoiling the full effect. E United States.
Zone 3 US, 2b Can. 🏆

P. tricuspidata (Boston ivy) A vigorous, self-clinging vine with extremely variable leaves that are conspicuously three-lobed on old plants. They turn rich crimson and scarlet in autumn. The fruits are dark blue, bloomy, and attractive to birds. It is very beautiful on the walls of buildings. Japan. Introduced 1862 by J. G. Veitch.
Zone 4 US, 5b Can. 🏆

Parthenocissus tricuspidata

***P. t.* 'Veitchii'** A selected form with slightly smaller, ovate or trifoliate leaves that are purple when young.
Zone 4 US, 5b Can.

Passiflora *Passifloraceae*
Passion flower

There are about 350 evergreen and deciduous species in this fascinating genus. They are mainly climbers that attach themselves to supports by twining tendrils, and most are natives of tropical South America. The majority are too tender to be planted out-of-doors in cool-temperate gardens, but those that are hardy enough can be ranked among the most beautiful and exotic of all flowering creepers and perform best on a sunny, sheltered, south-facing wall.

The exquisite and intriguing flowers are usually borne singly on long stalks. Each has a tubular calyx with five lobes or sepals, and these are often the same size and shape as the petals. Sepals and petals are collectively referred to as tepals. Inside the tepals are rings of threadlike colored filaments, and these are collectively referred to as the corona. The five stamens are on a long central column and are topped by the ovary and its three naillike stigmas.

The flower was used by Spanish missionaries in South America to illustrate the story of the Passion of Christ. The three stigmas represented the three nails, the five anthers the five wounds, the corona the crown of thorns or the halo of glory, the 10 tepals the 10 apostles (Peter and Judas were not present during the Passion), and the lobed leaves and whiplike tendrils the hands and scourges of Christ's persecutors.

Passion fruits vary in size and shape and contain many seeds in an edible, jellylike pulp. Out-of-doors they are produced only where the summertime temperature is a minimum of 60°F (16°C) during flowering. Commercial passion-fruit production is possible only in hot regions.

Pruning is usually unnecessary in the open, at the northern limits of its range. In the greenhouse or farther south, a framework of branches should be established, to which the plant is pruned back in spring. This main pruning should be supplemented by pinching back during the growing season.

P. alata A large, vigorous, deciduous climber with stout, four-angled shoots and ovate leaves up to 6 in (15 cm) long. The fragrant flowers, borne from spring to summer, are 4¾ in (12 cm) across. The sepals are green to white beneath and pale crimson above, the petals brilliant crimson, and the filaments have purple, red, and white bands. NE Peru, E Brazil.
Zone 10 US

P.* × *allardii A strong-growing, very free-flowering deciduous climber with large, three-lobed leaves. The flowers are 3½–4½ in (9–11.5 cm) across, with white tepals that are shaded with pink and a white and deep cobalt blue corona. They appear through summer and fall. Raised 1907 at the University Botanic Garden, Cambridge, England.
Zone 9 US

***P.* 'Amethyst'** See *P. amethystina.*

Passiflora amethystina

P. amethystina, syn. *P.* 'Amethyst', *P.* 'Lavender Lady' A large, vigorous, deciduous climber with three-lobed leaves. The flowers are 3 in (8 cm) across, with a green bell-shaped calyx and pointed sepals that are blue inside, deeper blue petals and dark purple filaments. They are produced from spring to summer.
Zone 10 US

P. antioquiensis A beautiful, medium-sized, deciduous climber with some leaves

Passiflora antioquiensis

lance shaped and others deeply three-lobed. The flowers are pendulous, 4–5 in (10–13 cm) across, rich rose-red with a small violet corona, and borne in late summer and autumn. It can be grown outside in the mildest, most sheltered places but is otherwise a plant for the greenhouse. Colombia. Introduced 1858.
Zone 9 US 🏆

Passiflora caerulea

P. caerulea (Blue passion flower) A vigorous, even rampant climber that can reach 20 ft (6 m). It is evergreen outdoors in mild areas and is a good greenhouse plant. The leaves have 5–7 narrow lobes, and the slightly fragrant flowers are 3–4 in (7.5–10 cm) across, with white or pink-tinged tepals; the corona's outer filaments are blue at the tips, white in the middle, and purple at the base. Flowering is continuous throughout summer and fall. The ovoid fruits are orange-red and remain on the plant for a long time. It grows well on a warm, sunny wall and is very resistant to pests. S Brazil, Argentina. Introduced 1609.
Zone 8 US, 9? Can. 🏆

Passiflora caerulea 'Constance Elliott'

***P. c.* 'Constance Elliott'** A superb clone with ivory white flowers.
Zone 8 US, 9? Can. 🏆

Passiflora × *caeruleoracemosa*

P.* × *caeruleoracemosa A rampant, free-flowering climber once it is established. It has deeply five-lobed, deciduous leaves and singly borne flowers with the tepals flushed deep violet, the corona deep violet-purple, the column apple green, and the stigmas purple and green. It is suitable only for the mildest climates or a large greenhouse.
Zone 9 US 🏆

P. edulis (Purple granadilla) A vigorous deciduous climber with ovate, deeply three-lobed leaves. The flowers are 2½ in (6 cm) across, with white tepals, green without; the corona has curly white filaments, banded with purple. They are produced through-

out summer. The yellow or dull purple fruits are edible. Brazil. Introduced 1810.
Zone 9 US

P. 'Exoniensis' A deciduous hybrid with downy stems and three-lobed, downy leaves. The pendulous flowers are 4–5 in (10–13 cm) across and have a 2½ in (6 cm) tube, with rose-pink tepals and a small, whitish corona in summer. Raised c. 1870.
Zone 10 US 🏆

P. incarnata (Maypop) The hardiest species, whose 2 in (5 cm) wide flowers have five white petals with a crown of purple filaments in summer. SE United States.
Zone 7 US, 8 Can.

Passiflora 'Incense'

P. 'Incense' A large, vigorous, deciduous climber with violet-mauve, lacelike flowers 4¾ in (12 cm) across, gathered in the center to produce a banding effect of alternate white and deep purple. They have an exquisite sweet-pea fragrance and are borne in early to midsummer. The fruits are edible but slightly acid.
Zone 10 US 🏆

P. 'Lavender Lady' See *P. amethystina*.

P. mollissima (Softleaf passion flower) A vigorous deciduous climber with downy shoots and deeply three-lobed leaves that are densely hairy beneath. The pendulous flowers are up to 3 in (7.5 cm) across, with a tube 2¾–3 in (7–8 cm) long. The petals and sepals are pink and the corona purple. The yellow fruits are edible. South America. In cultivation 1843.
Zone 10 US 🏆

P. quadrangularis (Giant granadilla) A vigorous deciduous climber with four-angled stems and unlobed leaves up to 8 in (20 cm) long. The fragrant flowers are 3 in (8 cm) across, greenish outside and white, pink, or red within, the corona banded with reddish purple, blue, and white. The edible yellow fruits are 8–12 in (20–30 cm) long.
Zone 10 US

P. 'Star of Bristol' A large, slender, vigorous, deciduous climber with three- to five-lobed leaves. The summer flowers have green sepals that are purple above and mauve petals; the filaments are mauve banded with lilac.
Zone 10 US 🏆

Passiflora racemosa

P. racemosa (Red passion flower) A medium-sized deciduous climber with three-lobed leaves and vivid scarlet flowers with purple, white-tipped outer filaments, borne in terminal, drooping clusters in midsummer. It is a magnificent species but will survive outdoors only in the mildest regions. Brazil. Introduced 1815.
Zone 10 US 🏆

P. umbilicata A fast-growing, medium-sized, deciduous species with small violet flowers and round, yellow fruits. It is one of the hardiest and thrives in the open in mild areas. Bolivia, Paraguay, N Argentina. Introduced 1954.
Zone 10 US

Paulownia *Scrophulariaceae*

A genus of about six species of deciduous trees from eastern Asia. The cultivated species are among the grandest of ornamental flowering trees and are notable for their foxglovelike flowers, which do not appear on very young trees, and for their large, velvety leaves, which on vigorous plants are enormous. The flowers are in erect panicles, up to 10 in (25 cm) long, formed in fall but opening the following spring. Frost can destroy the flower buds, and the plants need shelter from strong winds. Paulownias need rich, well-drained soil, either neutral or acidic, and tolerate wet and dry locations. They will grow in part shade.

P. fargesii This species is a magnificent tree of 60–70 ft (18–21 m) that seems better adapted to the variable conditions of early spring than the better-known *P. tomentosa*. It also flowers when comparatively young. The fragrant violet flowers are speckled with dark purple in the throat and have a creamy basal stain. It should not be confused with a lilac-flowered form of *P. tomentosa*, which is sometimes mistakenly given the same name. W China. Introduced c. 1896.
Zone 7 US, 8 Can.

Paulownia tomentosa

P. tomentosa (Empress tree, paulownia) A round-topped tree sometimes reaching 30–50 ft (9–15 m). The flowers are pale violet striped with yellow inside and provide a spectacular display in late spring. Winter-damaged plants can be pruned to the ground in spring, and the resulting suckers thinned to a single shoot. If well fed, the shoot can reach 8–10 ft (2.5–3 m) in a single season and bear large leaves up to 2 ft (60 cm) across. China; escaped from cultivation in the E United States. Introduced 1834 via Japan.
Zone 5 US, 6b Can. 🏆

Paxistima *Celastraceae*

A genus of two species of interesting, dwarf evergreen shrubs with tiny leaves and quadrangular stems. They do best in a moist, shady location and do not tolerate shallow, alkaline soil.

P. canbyi A dwarf shrub with narrow leaves and small, greenish flowers appearing in summer, followed by white fruits. It makes an unusual hedge or ground cover. E United States. In cultivation 1800.
Zone 3 US, 2b Can.

Penstemon *Scrophulariaceae*

A large genus of about 250 species of evergreen and deciduous subshrubs, herbaceous plants, and a few small shrubs, mainly from northwestern North America and from Mexico. The hardy, woody ones are excellent rock-garden plants in full sun and well-drained soil.

Penstemon davidsonii

P. davidsonii (Davidson penstemon) A dwarf or prostrate, evergreen shrublet for the rock garden. It has short-stalked, shallowly toothed leaves and plentiful erect clusters of large, tubular, red-purple flowers in late spring and early summer. NW North America. In cultivation 1902.
Zone 5 US, 6 Can. 🏆

***P. fruticosus* 'Albus'** A form of bush penstemon with white flowers.
Zone 4 US, 5 Can. 🏆

P. f.* var. *scouleri A dwarf deciduous subshrub with narrow, lance-shaped leaves and large, lilac-colored flowers in erect racemes in early summer. A good rock-garden plant.

Penstemon fruticosus var. *scouleri*

W North America. Introduced 1828.
Zone 4 US, 5 Can. 🏆

Penstemon heterophyllus 'Blue Gem'

***P. heterophyllus* 'Blue Gem'** A dwarf, erect deciduous shrublet with long, narrow leaves and lovely, azure-blue flowers in long racemes in summer. California.
Zone 6 US, 7 Can.

Penstemon newberryi

P. newberryi Plants under this name are usually f. *humilior*, a deciduous dwarf shrub for the rock garden, similar to *P. davidsonii* but with longer, pointed leaves and scarlet to deep rose-pink flowers in profusion in early summer. W United States.
Zone 5 US, 6 Can. 🏆

P. pinifolius A dwarf evergreen shrub with very slender, needlelike, pointed leaves. The bright scarlet, tubular flowers end in five-pointed lobes and are borne in terminal spikes throughout summer. A first-class rock-garden plant. SW North America.
Zone 4 US, 5 Can.

P. rupicola A dwarf, mat-forming deciduous shrub with small blue-green leaves and dense racemes of deep pink flowers in late spring to summer. W North America.
Zone 4 US, 5 Can. 🏆

Pernettya *Ericaceae*

A genus of about 20 species of evergreen shrubs, closely related to and by many authorities now included in Gaultheria, *although they are likely to be found for sale under* Pernettya *for some years to come. Their native range extends from Mexico to the Strait of Magellan, and there are a few species in Tasmania and New Zealand. They are tolerant of shade but fruit best in sun and should be provided with an acidic soil. Pruning is unnecessary.*

P. mucronata (Chilean pernettya) The showiest in fruit of all dwarf evergreens and one of the hardiest South American shrubs. It forms dense clumps of wiry stems about 2–3 ft (60–90 cm) high and bears a profusion of small, white, heatherlike flowers in late spring and early summer, followed by dense clusters of long-persistent, marblelike berries that range from pure white to mulberry-purple. It is best to plant it in groups of three or more, which should include a proven male form such as 'Thymifolia'; otherwise you may not see many berries. It is tolerant of shade but fruits best in sun and should be provided with a slightly acidic soil. In large gardens it makes an excellent ground cover. Pruning is unnecessary. The following forms are recommended. Chile to Strait of Magellan. Introduced 1828.
Zone 6 US, 7 Can.

Pernettya mucronata 'Bell's Seedling'

P. m. **'Bell's Seedling'** A hermaphrodite form with attractive reddish young stems and dark, shining leaves. The berries are large and dark red.
Zone 6 US, 7 Can. 🏆

P. m. **'Cherry Ripe'** Similar to 'Bell's Seedling' but with medium-sized to large, bright cherry red berries.
Zone 6 US, 7 Can.

Pernettya mucronata 'Crimsonia'

P. m. **'Crimsonia'** A selection with white flowers and very large crimson fruits. In cultivation 1968.
Zone 6 US, 7 Can. 🏆

P. m. **'Lilian'** This selection has white flowers and very large, lilac-pink berries. In cultivation1968.
Zone 6 US, 7 Can.

P. m. **'Mulberry Wine'** The young stems of this shrub are green rather than reddish. The large berries are magenta, ripening to deep purple.
Zone 6 US, 7 Can. 🏆

Pernettya mucronata 'Mulberry Wine'

Pernettya mucronata 'Pink Pearl'

P. m. **'Pink Pearl'** A selection with medium-sized, lilac-pink berries.
Zone 6 US, 7 Can. 🏆

Pernettya mucronata 'Sea Shell'

P. m. **'Sea Shell'** A selection with medium-sized to large berries that are shell pink, deepening to rose.
Zone 6 US, 7 Can. 🏆

P. m. **'Thymifolia'** A charming, neat male form with small leaves. It is covered in white flowers in early summer.
Zone 6 US, 7 Can.

P. m. **'White Pearl'** A selection that develops medium-sized to large berries that are gleaming white.
Zone 6 US, 7 Can.

P. m. **'Wintertime'** A selection with large, pure white berries.
Zone 6 US, 7 Can. 🏆

Perovskia *Labiatae*

Russian sage

A genus of seven species of late-flowering, aromatic evergreen and deciduous subshrubs with deeply toothed or finely cut aromatic leaves, native from central Asia to the Himalaya. They combine well with lavender and other blue and gray plants in the border and grow in sun in all types of well-drained soil. For the most striking foliage effects, they can be cut down close to ground level in spring.

Perovskia atriplicifolia 'Blue Spire'

P. atriplicifolia **'Blue Spire'** A deciduous shrub, to about 5 ft (1.5 m) high, with deeply cut, gray foliage, whitish stems, and abundant large panicles of lavender-blue flowers in late summer.
Zone 4 US, 5 Can. 🏆

Persicaria *Polygonaceae*

A genus consisting mainly of herbaceous perennials, containing several garden favorites previously listed under Polygonum. *The following is the best known of the shrubby deciduous species. They will grow in any reasonably moisture-retentive soil but do not like one that is very fertile. They prefer sun and require pruning only if they are becoming too invasive.*

P. vacciniifolia, syn. *Polygonum vacciniifolium* A prostrate, mat-forming shrub with slender stems and small, glossy green leaves that are bluish bloomy beneath. The bright rose-pink flowers are borne in slender, erect spikes in late summer and autumn. It is a good rock-garden plant for a sunny location. Himalaya. Introduced 1845.
Zone 6 US, 7 Can. 🏆

Petteria *Leguminosae*

A genus of one deciduous species.

Petteria ramentacea

P. ramentacea (Dalmatian laburnum) An unusual, upright shrub with laburnum-like leaves. It reaches 5½–8 ft (1.7–2.5 m) in height and bears erect racemes of scented yellow flowers, also laburnum-like, at the ends of the current season's growth in early summer. The seeds are poisonous. It requires full sun in any well-drained soil. W former Yugoslavia, N Albania. Introduced 1838.
Zone 5 US, 6 Can.

Phellodendron *Rutaceae*
Cork tree

A genus of about 10 species of small to medium-sized, wide-spreading deciduous trees from East Asia, resembling Ailanthus *in their large, handsome, pinnate leaves and graceful habit. They grow well on all types of garden soil, and their attractive, aromatic leaves turn clear yellow before falling. The small, yellow-green flowers, which are very attractive to bees, are followed by small, black, resin-scented fruits.*

P. amurense (Amur cork tree) A small to medium-sized tree with corky bark in maturity and 9½–15 in (24–38 cm) long, bright green leaves with 5–11 leaflets. The winter buds are silvery and silky. NE Asia. Introduced 1885.
Zone 3 US, 3 Can.

Philadelphus *Hydrangeaceae*
Mock orange

A genus of about 65 deciduous species of shrubs from north-temperate regions. They provide a good floral display even in poor soil, and their flowers, appearing in early to midsummer, are usually fragrant and white. The "orange" scent is redolent of orange blossoms rather than of orange fruits, as is sometimes expected. Old flowering shoots should be thinned and cut back to within a short distance of the old wood immediately after flowering. They typically reach 5–8 ft (1.5–2.5 m) tall and resist most pests and diseases.

***P.* 'Avalanche'** A small, semierect shrub with small leaves and masses of small, single, richly fragrant flowers in summer, borne so plentifully that they weigh down the branches. In cultivation 1896.
Zone 3 US, 4 Can.

Philadelphus 'Beauclerk'

***P.* 'Beauclerk'** A medium-sized shrub with single, broad-petaled flowers 2½ in (6 cm) across. They are milk white with a zone of light cerise around the stamens and are very fragrant.
Zone 3 US, 3 Can. 🏆

Philadelphus 'Belle Etoile'

***P.* 'Belle Etoile'** A beautiful, compact shrub up to 6½ ft (2 m) high. It has single white flowers, 2 in (5 cm) wide, with a maroon flush at the center. They are delightfully fragrant. In cultivation 1930.
Zone 4 US, 5 Can. 🏆

***P.* 'Boule d'Argent'** A small shrub with large, double, pure white flowers that are freely produced in dense clusters. They are slightly fragrant. In cultivation 1893.
Zone 3 US, 4 Can.

***P.* 'Bouquet Blanc'** A small shrub with double, scented flowers in large, crowded clusters. In cultivation 1903.
Zone 3 US, 4 Can.

***P.* 'Buckley's Quill'** A broadly upright, medium-sized shrub with big, double flowers with quill-like petals. Raised in Canada.
Zone 3 US, 4 Can.

Philadelphus 'Burfordensis'

P. 'Burfordensis' A magnificent and particularly attractive, erect, medium-sized shrub raised by Sir William Lawrence. It bears large, single, white, cup-shaped flowers with bright yellow stamens. Originated 1920 as a sport of 'Virginal'.
Zone 3 US, 3b Can.

Philadelphus coronarius

P. coronarius (Common mock orange) A vigorous, medium-sized shrub with creamy white, richly scented, single flowers. It is the most commonly grown species and is suitable for very dry soils.
Zone 3 US, 3 Can.

Philadelphus coronarius 'Aureus'

***P. c.* 'Aureus'** The most effective mock orange when not in flower, with bright yellow leaves that become greenish yellow as they age.
Zone 3 US, 3 Can.

***P. c.* 'Variegatus'** The leaves have a creamy white margin. In cultivation 1770.
Zone 3 US, 4 Can.

Philadelphus coronarius 'Variegatus'

P. 'Dwarf Snowflake' A small form of 'Minnesota Snowflake' that grows only 4 ft (1.2 m) tall. The fragrant, double flowers smother the branches in late spring. Originated in the United States.
Zone 4 US, 4b Can.

P. 'Frosty Morn' A small shrub with fragrant double flowers. In cultivation 1953.
Zone 3 US, 4 Can.

P. 'Galahad' A very popular shrub that grows up to 5 ft (1.5 m) and has a rounded silhouette. The pure white flowers are single but very fragrant. Originated at Skinners Nursery, Dropmore, Manitoba.
Zone 3 US, 3 Can.

Philadelphus 'Innocence'

P. 'Innocence' A medium-sized shrub with single, white, fragrant flowers that are very freely borne. The leaves often have a cream variegation. In cultivation 1927.
Zone 4 US, 4b Can.

***P. lewisii* 'Waterton'** A small, bushy plant with reddish brown young shoots and profuse single, starlike, white flowers. Selected in Waterton National Park on the Alberta-Montana border.
Zone 2 US, 2b Can.

Philadelphus 'Manteau d'Hermine'

P. 'Manteau d'Hermine' A popular, compact, almost dwarf shrub that reaches about 2$\frac{1}{2}$–4 ft (0.75–1.2 m), with fragrant, creamy, double flowers.
Zone 3 US, 4 Can.

P. microphyllus (Littleleaf mock orange) A dainty, small-leaved species, making a twiggy bush about 3–4 ft (1–1.2 m) high. The very small single flowers are richly fragrant. SW United States. Introduced 1883.
Zone 5 US, 6 Can.

P. 'Silberregen', syn. 'Silver Showers' A dense small shrub with small, pointed leaves and profusely borne, single, white, fragrant flowers.
Zone 4 US, 5 Can.

P. 'Silver Showers' See *P.* 'Silberregen'.

P. 'Snowbelle' A Canadian introduction

Philadelphus 'Virginal'

that grows into a medium-sized shrub with fragrant, double flowers borne in clusters.

Zone 3 US, 3 Can.

***P.* 'Virginal'** A vigorous, erectly branched shrub reaching 10 ft (3 m) tall, with white, strongly scented flowers, 1–1¼ in (2.5–3.5 cm) across. It is probably the best double-flowered cultivar.

Zone 3 US, 3b Can. 🏆

Philesia *Liliaceae*

A genus of one evergreen species of shrubs, related to Lapageria.

P. magellanica (Magellan box lily) One of the choicest and most beautiful dwarf shrubs. It is suckering and forms wide clumps of wiry stems with narrow, rigid leaves and tubular, crimson flowers 2 in (5 cm) long in summer and fall. It needs a moist, peaty, partly shady site in well-drained soil and a sheltered location. S Chile. Introduced 1847 by William Lobb.

Zone 9 US

Phillyrea *Oleaceae*

A genus of four species of handsome evergreen shrubs or small trees, related to Osmanthus. *They succeed in all types of soil and in sun or part shade. Little pruning is required.*

Phillyrea angustifolia

P. angustifolia (Narrowleaf phillyrea) A compact, rounded, medium-sized bush with narrow, dark green leaves. The flowers are small, fragrant, creamy yellow, and borne in clusters in late spring and early summer. It is good for coastal sites. N Africa, S Europe. In cultivation before 1597.

Zone 9 US

P. a.* f. *rosmarinifolia An attractive, neat, compact form with even narrower leaves than the species.

Zone 9 US

P. decora See *Osmanthus decorus.*

Phillyrea latifolia

P. latifolia (Tree phillyrea) An elegant, olivelike large shrub or small tree that grows to 30 ft (9 m) and resembles the holly oak *(Quercus ilex)*. Its branches are bowed by the weight of luxuriant masses of small, glossy, dark green leaves. Dull white flowers appear in late spring, followed by tiny black fruits that are produced only in a continental-type climate. S Europe, Asia Minor. In cultivation 1597.

Zone 9 US

Phlomis *Labiatae*

A genus of about 100 species of low-growing evergreen shrubs, subshrubs, and herbaceous perennials, usually densely hairy or woolly and bearing attractive flowers in whorls. They are widely distributed in Europe and Asia and require full sun and good drainage.

P. chrysophylla An attractive small shrub with sagelike foliage that takes on a yellow tinge after midsummer. The golden yellow flowers are borne in early summer. Flowering is best where summers are particularly hot. Lebanon.

Zone 9 US 🏆

Phlomis chrysophylla

***P.* 'Edward Bowles'** A small to medium-sized hybrid subshrub with large, hoary, heart-shaped leaves and whorls of sulphur yellow flowers with a distinctly paler upper lip in late summer and autumn.

Zone 9 US

Phlomis fruticosa

P. fruticosa (Jerusalem sage) A small gray-green shrub with mostly horizontal branches. Its whorls of bright yellow flowers are attractive in summer, and it is a good plant for a sunny slope. Mediterranean region. In cultivation 1596.

Zone 8 US, 9 Can. 🏆

P. italica A desirable dwarf shrub, not much more than 12 in (30 cm) high, with white-hairy stems and leaves and terminal spikes of pale lilac flowers in summer. Balearic Islands. In cultivation 1750.

Zone 9 US

P. lanata A dense, dwarf, mound-forming shrub with yellow-woolly shoots and small, sage green, ovate leaves up to 1¼ in (3 cm)

Phlomis lanata

long, with the veins on the upper surfaces deeply impressed. The flowers are golden yellow with brownish hairs and are borne in whorls in summer. Crete.
Zone 9 US

P. longifolia An attractive small shrub with white-woolly young stems and bright green, deeply veined, almost triangular leaves that are heart shaped at the base. The terminal clusters of deep golden yellow flowers are borne in summer. SW Asia.
Zone 9? US

Phormium *Phormiaceae/Agavaceae*

A genus of two species of evergreens from New Zealand with long, handsome, swordlike leaves; strictly speaking, they are not shrubs but perennials. They play the same architectural role in the garden as yuccas and ornamental grasses do and combine well with them. They thrive in a wide variety of soils and are among the best plants for coastal sites and industrial areas. They are best in mild climates, and many of the newer hybrids are relatively tender.

***P.* 'Apricot Queen'** A shrub of low, weeping habit, with soft yellow leaves that are flushed with apricot and margined with dark green and bronze.
Zone 7 US, 8 Can.

***P.* 'Bronze Baby'** The leaves of this small shrub are bronze and droop at the tips.
Zone 7 US, 8 Can.

P. colensoi See *P. cookianum.*

P. cookianum, syn. *P. colensoi* A smaller species than *P. tenax* and with thinner, greener leaves that are more lax and flexible. The yellowish flowers are borne in panicles up to 3 ft (1 m) long in summer. Introduced 1848.
Zone 7 US, 8 Can. 🏆

Phormium cookianum 'Cream Delight'

***P. c.* 'Cream Delight'** The leaves of this form have a broad cream central band and narrower stripes of cream toward the margin. Raised before 1978 in New Zealand.
Zone 7 US, 8 Can. 🏆

***P. c.* 'Tricolor'** Leaves are brightly edged with creamy yellow and narrowly margined with red. Found 1880s in New Zealand.
Zone 8 US, 9 Can. 🏆

***P.* 'Dark Delight'** A form up to 3 ft (1 m) high, with broad, upright, dark purple-bronze leaves with reddish midribs.
Zone 8 US, 9 Can.

Phormium 'Dazzler'

***P.* 'Dazzler'** A striking plant up to 3 ft (1 m) high, with deep red-purple leaves striped with rose-red in the center.
Zone 7 US, 8 Can.

Phormium 'Maori Chief'

***P.* 'Maori Chief'** The leaves of this small shrub are upright, drooping at the tips and variegated with attractive shades of scarlet, crimson, and bronze.
Zone 8 US, 9 Can.

***P.* 'Maori Maiden'** A small shrub with leaves to 3 ft (90 cm) long, drooping at the tips. They are bronze-green striped with rose-red.
Zone 8 US, 9 Can.

***P.* 'Maori Queen'** A small shrub bearing upright leaves with drooping tips that appear with an attractive combination of bronze-green and rose-red stripes.
Zone 8 US, 9 Can.

Phormium 'Maori Sunrise'

***P.* 'Maori Sunrise'** A low-growing form with slender, arching leaves that are pale red to pink, margined with bronze.
Zone 8 US, 9 Can.

P. tenax (New Zealand flax) A striking large evergreen shrub with dramatic foliage. It forms clumps of rigid, leathery,

Phormium tenax

swordlike leaves 3–10 ft (1–3 m) long and bears bronze-red flowers, 2 in (5 cm) long, in panicles up to 13 ft (4 m) or more in summer. It is a superb architectural plant and can be grown in all types of fertile soil. It is very resistant to wind, salt spray, and industrial pollution, and its leaves contain one of the toughest and finest fibers known. In parts of Europe it has become naturalized and is sometimes used as a highly effective coastal windbreak where few other plants will grow. It is equally good as a specimen plant or in groups. New Zealand. Introduced 1789.

Zone 7 US, 8 Can. 🏆

***P. t.* 'Duet'** A small shrub with upright or slightly spreading leaves up to 3 ft (1 m) in length, margined with creamy white.

Zone 8 US, 9 Can. 🏆

***P. t.* 'Nanum Purpureum'** A compact dwarf shrub with slender, red-purple leaves up to 18 in (45 cm) long.

Zone 7 US, 8 Can. 🏆

Phormium tenax 'Purpureum'

***P. t.* 'Purpureum'** A large shrub with bronze-purple leaves up to 6½ ft (2 m) long; a striking plant that contrasts well with plants with gray foliage.

Zone 7 US, 8 Can. 🏆

Phormium tenax 'Sundowner'

***P. t.* 'Sundowner'** A medium-sized shrub with bronze-green leaves up to 5 ft (1.5 m) long with a deep rose-red margin.

Zone 8 US, 9 Can. 🏆

***P. t.* 'Variegatum'** A medium-sized shrub with creamy-margined leaves.

Zone 8 US, 9 Can. 🏆

***P. t.* 'Veitchii'** Similar to 'Variegatum' but with creamy yellow stripes in the center of the leaves.

Zone 8 US, 9 Can.

Phormium 'Yellow Wave'

***P.* 'Yellow Wave'** A small shrub with drooping leaves to 3 ft (1 m) long with a greenish yellow band variously striped with green. Raised c. 1967 in New Zealand.

Zone 7 US, 8 Can. 🏆

Photinia *Rosaceae*

A genus of about 40 species of evergreen and deciduous large shrubs or trees from East and Southeast Asia and the Himalaya. The genus Stranvaesia *is now included in* Photinia. *The white flowers are borne in clusters, usually in spring, and are followed in autumn by bright red fruits. The foliage of some deciduous species turn vivid colors before dropping, and the unfolding leaves of some evergreens are very showy. The deciduous species generally dislike alkaline soil, while the evergreens are more lime tolerant. With the exception of* P. davidiana, *the evergreen species do not flower or fruit prolifically and require sun and warmth. They are somewhat susceptible to fireblight.*

P. beauverdiana A desirable small deciduous tree up to 20 ft (6 m) high. As spring passes into summer it becomes covered with wide clusters of hawthornlike flowers, and in fall it bears dark red fruits and richly tinted leaves. It is moderately lime tolerant. C and W China. Introduced 1908 by Ernest Wilson.

Zone 6 US, 7 Can. 🏆

P. davidiana, syn. *Stranvaesia davidiana* A very vigorous evergreen large shrub or small tree with erect branches and dark green, lance-shaped, leathery, untoothed leaves. The round, brilliant crimson fruits are borne in pendent bunches. The oldest leaves turn bright red in fall in contrast to the younger ones, which are still green. This species is susceptible to fireblight. W China. Introduced 1917.

Zone 6 US, 7 Can.

Photinia davidiana 'Palette'

***P. d.* 'Fructuluteo'** A selected tree with bright yellow fruits.
Zone 6 US, 7 Can.

***P. d.* 'Palette'** A slow-growing form with leaves blotched and streaked with cream and tinged with pink when young. Raised before 1980 in Holland. *(See photo on p.431.)*
Zone 6 US, 7 Can.

***P. d.* 'Prostrata'** A low-growing, more or less prostrate form.
Zone 6 US, 7 Can.

***P. d.* 'Salicifolia'** The most commonly cultivated form, differing from the typical one only in its slightly narrower leaves with more veins. W China. Introduced 1907 by Ernest Wilson.
Zone 6 US, 7 Can.

P.* ×*fraseri (Fraser photinia, red tip) A variable hybrid that makes a large, vigorous evergreen shrub with dark glossy green, leathery leaves that are bright coppery red when young. Often planted as a hedge.
Zone 6 US, 7 Can.

Photinia × *fraseri* 'Birmingham'

Photinia × *fraseri* 'Red Robin'

***P.* ×*f.* 'Birmingham'** A clone with generally obovate, abruptly pointed leaves that are bright coppery red when young. Tends toward the *P. glabra* parent. Raised 1940 in the United States.
Zone 7 US, 8 Can.

***P.* ×*f.* 'Red Robin'** A spectacular shrub with sharply toothed leaves and brilliant red young growths, equal to the best forms of *Pieris formosa*. Raised in New Zealand.
Zone 7 US, 8 Can. 🏆

***P.* ×*f.* 'Robusta'** A strong-growing shrub, tending toward the *P. serratifolia* parent, with thick, leathery leaves and coppery red young growths. It is the hardiest of the three. Raised in Australia.
Zone 6 US, 7 Can. 🏆

***P. glabra* 'Parfait'** A small to medium-sized evergreen shrub whose bronze young leaves are margined with pink and become green flecked with gray-green, with a narrow creamy margin. It is a weak grower.
Zone 7 US, 8 Can.

Photinia glabra 'Rubens'

***P. g.* 'Rubens'** A choice medium-sized shrub whose young leaves are a brilliant waxy red.
Zone 7 US, 8 Can.

***P.* 'Redstart'**, syn. × *Stranvinia* 'Redstart' A vigorous, evergreen large shrub or small tree with bright red young foliage. The leaves are dark green, and the white flowers are borne in early summer in dense, domed clusters with reddish purple stalks. The fruits are orange-red, flushed with yellow. Raised 1969 by Hillier Nurseries' propagator Peter Dummer.
Zone 7 US, 8 Can. 🏆

P. serratifolia (Chinese photinia) A very handsome evergreen large shrub or small tree with oblong, dark green, leathery, and coarsely toothed leaves up to 6 in (15 cm) long. The young leaves are bright coppery red throughout the growing season. The white flowers are borne in large clusters in the second half of spring, and the profuse, red, hawthornlike fruits are effective in fall and early winter. It prefers well-drained soil and dry summers. It is very popular in the South. China.
Zone 6 US, 7 Can.

P. villosa (Oriental photinia) A deciduous species that forms a large shrub or small, broad-headed tree. It has hawthornlike flowers in late spring, followed by small, egg-shaped, bright red fruits, and is effective in fall, when its foliage turns scarlet and gold. Not for shallow, alkaline soil. Japan, Korea, China. Introduced 1865.
Zone 4 US, 5b Can. 🏆

Phygelius *Scrophulariaceae*
Cape fuchsia

A genus of two species of attractive, evergreen or semievergreen, penstemon-like subshrubs from South Africa. P. capensis *is one of the very few South African shrubs that are relatively hardy in the cooler temperate climates. Cape fuchsias reach their greatest height against a sunny wall but look good almost anywhere in a shrub or herbaceous border. They are best in full sun and grow well in any type of well-drained soil as long as it is not too dry. In colder areas it is best to mulch the root area heavily in fall. The old, soft top growth can be cut back in spring, as can any dead wood.*

Phygelius aequalis

P. aequalis A small subshrub, growing to about 3 ft (1 m), with four-angled stems. The tubular flowers, 1–1½ in (2.5–4 cm) long, are slightly down-curved and evenly lobed at the mouth. They are pale dusky pink to red with a yellow throat and are produced in late summer and early fall on one side of the stem. It is not as hardy as the other species and needs the protection of a wall to survive.
Zone 8 US, 9 Can.

Phygelius aequalis 'Yellow Trumpet'

***P. a.* 'Yellow Trumpet'** A striking form with pale creamy yellow flowers and broad, light green leaves. South Africa. Introduced 1973 by B. L. Butt and Sir Harold Hillier.
Zone 8 US, 9 Can.

P. capensis (Cape fuchsia) A small shrub, occasionally growing to 6½ ft (2 m) in mild areas. The flowers are tubular, nodding and turning back toward the stem when open, and unevenly lobed at the mouth. They are orange-red to deep red with a yellow throat, elegantly borne on all sides of the stems in tall, open panicles in summer and fall. In cultivation 1855.
Zone 7 US, 8 Can. 🏆

***P. c.* 'Coccineus'** The plants that were originally given this name had rich red flowers, but the ones that are grown now have large, rich orange-red flowers.
Zone 7 US, 8 Can.

P. × rectus A group of hybrids between *P. aequalis* and *P. capensis*. The F_1 hybrids have pendulous flowers with a more or less straight tube, while backcrosses tend more toward one or other of the parents. Several forms have been raised in various colors and are about 3–5 ft (1–1.5 m) tall.
Zone 7 US, 8 Can.

Phygelius × rectus 'African Queen'

***P. × r.* 'African Queen'**, syn. *P. × r.* 'Indian Chief' An F_1 hybrid, this is a small shrub with pale red flowers. It was the first hybrid. See *P. × r.* 'Winchester Fanfare'.
Zone 7 US, 8 Can.

***P. × r.* 'Devil's Tears'** A small shrub that is a backcross between *P. × r.* 'Winchester Fanfare' and *P. capensis* 'Coccineus'. The tall and open flowers are deep reddish pink, deeper in bud, and have orange-red lobes. Raised 1985 by the Hillier Nurseries' propagator Peter Dummer.
Zone 7 US, 8 Can.

***P. × r.* 'Indian Chief'** See *P. × r.* 'African Queen'.

***P. × r.* 'Moonraker'** A backcross between *P. × r.* 'Winchester Fanfare' and *P. aequalis* 'Yellow Trumpet'. It is like 'Yellow Trumpet' but has almost straight flowers on all sides of the stems. It makes a small shrub. Raised 1985 by Peter Dummer.
Zone 7 US, 8 Can.

Phygelius × rectus 'Moonraker'

Phygelius × rectus 'Salmon Leap'

***P. × r.* 'Salmon Leap'** From the same backcross as 'Devil's Tears', this small shrub is distinguished from it in that it has orange flowers with deeper lobes. Raised 1985 by Peter Dummer at Hillier Nurseries, England.
Zone 7 US, 8 Can.

Phygelius × rectus 'Winchester Fanfare'

***P. × r.* 'Winchester Fanfare'** A cross between *P. aequalis* 'Yellow Trumpet' and *P. capensis* 'Coccineus'. It has straight, tubular but pendulous flowers and is a dusky reddish pink color with scarlet lobes. It is similar to 'African Queen' but has a different flower color, and its broader triangular leaves are inherited from 'Yellow Trumpet'. Raised 1974 by Peter Dummer at Hillier Nurseries, England.
Zone 7 US, 8 Can.

× Phylliopsis *Ericaceae*

An evergreen hybrid that occurred at Hillier Nurseries between two genera of dwarf shrubs (Kalmiopsis × Phyllodoce). *It needs a peaty, acidic soil in part shade.*

× ***P. hillieri* 'Pinocchio'** A delightful dwarf shrub with small, glossy green leaves and deep pink, bell-shaped flowers about 1/2 in (1 cm) across, freely borne in long, slender racemes over a long period in spring and again in fall.
Zone 6 US, 7 Can.

Phyllodoce *Ericaceae*

A genus of about six species of dainty, dwarf, heathlike evergreen shrubs from north-temperate and Arctic regions. Flowering is from midspring to midsummer. They thrive in cool, moist, fairly open locations and acidic soil.

P. aleutica A dwarf, mat-forming shrublet, 6–9 in (15–23 cm) high. It has pitcher-shaped, creamy or pale yellow flowers in flat terminal clusters in late spring and early summer. Arctic. Introduced 1915.
Zone 2 US, 2 Can.

Phyllodoce caerulea

P. caerulea (Blue mountain heath) A dwarf, cushion-forming shrublet up to 6 in (15 cm), with pitcher-shaped, bluish purple flowers in terminal clusters in late spring and early summer. Arctic and sub-Arctic regions. In cultivation 1800.
Zone 2 US, 2 Can.

***P.* × *intermedia* 'Fred Stoker'** A vigorous dwarf hybrid, forming mats up to 12 in (30 cm) high and as much as four times wide. Its pitcher-shaped flowers are light purple and puckered at the mouth. A form of the wild hybrid from W North America.
Zone 3 US, 3 Can.

P. nipponica One of the best rock-garden shrublets for peaty soil. It is a dwarf, erect, neat, compact species 6–9 in (15–23 cm) high, with bell-shaped white or pinkish flowers that appear in terminal clusters in late spring. N Japan. Introduced 1915.
Zone 3 US, 3 Can.

Phyllostachys *Gramineae*
Bamboo

A genus of 60 tall, graceful evergreen bamboos that are less invasive than many in Pleioblastus, *from which they differ most markedly in their zigzag stems, which are flattened or shallowly grooved on alternate sides between the joints. The branches are usually in pairs at each joint. They are moisture lovers but will grow in good soil over limestone. They are natives of China.*

Phyllostachys aurea

P. aurea (Fishpole bamboo) A graceful species, forming large clumps 8–11 ft (2.5–3.5 m) high. The canes are bright green at first, maturing to pale creamy yellow, dull yellow in full sun. The leaves are 3–7 in (7.5–18 cm) long. Can be invasive. China. Introduced before 1870.
Zone 6 US, 7 Can. 🏆

P. bambusoides (Giant timber bamboo) An ornamental species that eventually forms large clumps. The canes are 10–14 1/2 ft (3–4.5 m) tall, deep green at first,

Phyllostachys bambusoides

turning brown at maturity. The leaves are 2–7 1/2 in (5–19 cm) long and up to 1 1/4 in (3 cm) wide. China. Introduced 1866.
Zone 9 US

***P. b.* 'Castillonis'** A form with golden yellow stems striped horizontally with a distinctive green.
Zone 9 US 🏆

P. edulis (Moso bamboo) A vigorous bamboo with bright green canes up to 14 1/2 ft (4.5 m) high that turn dull yellow in late summer and fall. The young shoots are edible. The leaves are 3 × 4 in (7.5 × 10 cm) long and 3/4 in (2 cm) wide. It is best grown in a sheltered location. China.
Zone 7 US, 8 Can.

Phyllostachys flexuosa

P. flexuosa A graceful bamboo, 8–10 ft (2.5–3 m) high, with slender, somewhat wavy canes that are bright green at first and become darker at maturity. It forms large clumps over time. The leaves are 2–5 in (5–13 cm) long and 1/2–3/4 in (1–2 cm) wide.

The shoots are noticeably zigzag at the bases. It is excellent as a screening plant. N China. Introduced 1864.
Zone 7 US, 8 Can.

P. nigra (Black bamboo) A beautiful, clump-forming, gracefully arching plant. The canes are normally 8–11 ft (2.5–3.5 m), green in the first year, becoming mottled with dark brown or black and finally an even jet black. In cooler regions the canes often remain a mottled, brownish green. The leaves are 2–5 in (5–13 cm) long and ¼–½ in (6–12 mm) wide. This distinctive and attractive species needs a sunny location. China. Introduced 1827.
Zone 6 US, 7 Can.

***P. n.* 'Boryana'** An elegant bamboo with luxuriant masses of arching, leafy stems. The canes are 8–13 ft (2.5–4 m) high, green at first, changing to yellow and splashed with purple. The leaves are 2–3½ in (5–9 cm) long by ¼–½ in (6–12 mm) wide. Originated in Japan.
Zone 6 US, 7 Can.

Phyllostachys nigra var. *henonis*

P. n.* var. *henonis A handsome plant with tall, graceful canes to 13 ft (4 m) high, swathed in dark green clouds of shiny leaves. The canes are bright green at first, maturing to brownish yellow. The leaves are 3–4½ in (7.5–11 cm) long by ½–¾ in (1–2 cm) wide. It is one of the best bamboos for planting in a lawn or similar prominent location. In cultivation c. 1890.
Zone 6 US, 7 Can.

P. viridi-glaucescens A graceful, clump-forming species with canes 13–20 ft (4–6 m) high, green at first, changing to dull yellowish green in late summer and fall. Leaves are 3–6 in (7.5–15 cm) long, ½–¾ in (1–2 cm) wide, brilliant green above and blue-bloomy beneath. In ideal locations it forms a clump, but it is otherwise a fine specimen. E China. Introduced 1846.
Zone 7 US, 8 Can.

Phyllostachys viridi-glaucescens

× Phyllothamnus *Ericaceae*

An evergreen hybrid between Phyllodoce *and* Rhodothamnus *suitable for an acidic, moist, peaty soil.*

×*P. erectus* A dwarf shrublet 12–18 in (30–45 cm) high, with stems crowded with narrow leaves and shallowly funnel-shaped, delicate rose flowers, produced in flat clusters in mid- to late spring.
Zone 4? US, 5? Can.

Physocarpus *Rosaceae*
Ninebark

A genus of about 10 species of tall deciduous shrubs that grow well in open, moist locations but tend to become chlorotic on dry, shallow, alkaline soils. They are natives of North America, Mexico, and northeastern Asia.

P. opulifolius (Eastern ninebark) A vigorous, medium-sized shrub that will grow well in most locations. The bark peels in attractive curls, and the leaves are three-lobed. The flowers are white tinged with pink and are held in dense clusters along the stems in early summer. E North America.
Zone 2 US, 2b Can.

Physocarpus opulifolius 'Dart's Gold'

***P. o.* 'Dart's Gold'** A small, compact shrub, an improvement over 'Luteus' because it has brighter yellow foliage and especially because it retains its attractive color much longer.
Zone 2 US, 2b Can.

Physocarpus opulifolius 'Luteus'

***P. o.* 'Luteus'** The young growths of this medium-sized shrub are clear yellow and very effective when the shrub is used as a contrast among plants with purple leaves. In cultivation 1969.
Zone 2 US, 2b Can.

Picea *Pinaceae*
Spruce

A genus of about 35 species of conifers, found throughout the north-temperate regions. They are evergreen trees, usually conical, with branches borne in whorls. The leaves are short and needlelike, flattened or square in section, and arranged spirally or in two ranks. This is an extremely ornamental group of trees that thrive in a variety of soils but cannot be recommended for really poor, shallow, or dry soils, or for planting in exposed sites. The principal foliage colors range from green to gray and there are many dwarf forms.

P. abies (Norway spruce) A fast-growing, very common large tree with orange or reddish brown shoots and shining dark green leaves up to 1 in (2.5 cm) long that cover the upper sides of the branchlets densely. It has given rise to many dwarf forms, most of which are extremely slow growing and ideal for the rock garden. Often used as a Christmas tree, it grows well in a variety of soils but needs an annual shearing for shape. Bears cones fall to winter. Widely distributed in N and C Europe. Introduced 1500.
Zone 2 US, 2b Can.

***P. a.* 'Acrocona'** A large, spreading bush or small tree with semipendulous branches that usually end in a distorted cone, even when the tree is young. In cultivation 1890.
Zone 2 US, 2 Can.

Picea abies 'Gregoryana'

***P. a.* 'Gregoryana'** A dense, dwarf bush that develops into a somewhat billowy, rounded, flat-topped dome. Its radially arranged, sea green leaves are eye-catching. A specimen at the Hillier Gardens and Arboretum was 20 in × 4 ft (0.5 × 1.2 m) after 30 years. In cultivation 1862.
Zone 3 US, 3 Can.

***P. a.* 'Inversa'** An unusual form, sometimes seen as a large shrub with weeping branches. In cultivation 1855.
Zone 2 US, 2b Can.

Picea abies 'Inversa'

Picea abies 'Little Gem'

***P. a.* 'Little Gem'** A dwarf, slow-growing, globular bun-shaped shrub with tiny, densely crowded leaves.
Zone 3 US, 3 Can.

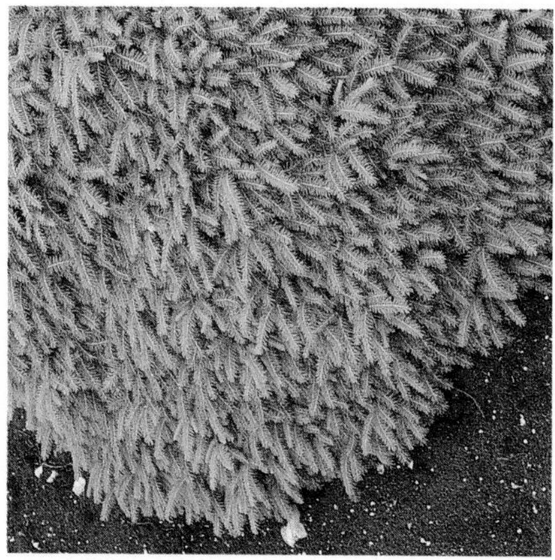

Picea abies 'Nidiformis'

***P. a.* 'Nidiformis'** (Bird's nest spruce) A very popular form, making a dwarf, dense, flat-topped bush with the branches that form a series of tight, horizontal layers with a depressed center, likened to a bird's nest. It will reach 2 × 6 ft (0.6 × 1.8 m) after 30 years. In cultivation 1907.
Zone 2 US, 2b Can.

***P. a.* 'Ohlenforffii'** A small, conical, dense shrub with yellow-green, rather small leaves similar to those of *P. orientalis*. It will reach 5½ × 4 ft (1.7 × 1.2 m) after 30 years. In cultivation 1845.
Zone 2 US, 2b Can.

***P. a.* 'Repens'** A slow-growing, dwarf, flat-topped bush with arching branches in layers. It is a low, wide-spreading form suitable for a large rock garden. In cultivation 1898.
Zone 2 US, 2b Can.

Picea breweriana

P. breweriana (Brewer spruce) Perhaps the most beautiful spruce. It is a small to medium-sized, broadly conical tree with spreading or decurved branches hung with slender, taillike branchlets 5½–8 ft (1.7–2.5 m) long. The leaves are up to 1¼ in (3 cm) long, shining dark blue-green above and marked with two white bands beneath. The cones are up to 4 in (10 cm) long, green at first, turning purple later. Best at cool, high elevations. NW California, SW Oregon. Introduced 1897.
Zone 4 US, 5b Can.

P. glauca (White spruce) A large tree of dense, conical habit with gray-white bark and decurved branches ascending at the tips. The densely arranged, four-angled leaves, up to ¾ in (2 cm) long, emit a fetid aroma when bruised. The cones are up to 2½ in (6 cm) long. It is very tolerant of heat, wind, and drought. Canada, NE United

States. Introduced 1700.
Zone 1 US, 1 Can.

***P. g.* var. *albertiana* 'Conica'** (Dwarf Alberta spruce) An extremely popular, perfectly cone-shaped bush with bright grass green leaves. In 30 years it will be a symmetrical, pointed cone 6½ ft (2 m) high and 4 ft (1.2 m) at the base. Found 1904 in the wild in Alberta.
Zone 3 US, 3 Can. 🏆

***P. g.* 'Densata'** (Black Hills spruce) A very slow growing form with dense needles and a conical shape. It will ultimately reach about 35 ft (10.5 m).
Zone 2 US, 2 Can.

***P. g.* 'Echiniformis'** A dwarf, slow-growing, globular, dense bush with glaucous gray-green leaves that point forward, making it feel prickly to the touch. A first-class miniature conifer for the rock garden. In cultivation 1855.
Zone 2 US, 2 Can. 🏆

Picea likiangensis

P. likiangensis (Lijiang spruce) An ornamental, vigorous, medium-sized tree. The upper branches have ascending terminal shoots; the leaves are flattened, ½–¾ in (1–2 cm) long, green or bluish green above, bloomy beneath, and loosely packed on the upper surfaces of the branchlets. The cones are 4 in (10 cm) long, reddish pink when young, and freely produced. It is beautiful in mid- to late spring when laden with male flowers and red young cones. W China. In cultivation 1910.
Zone 6 US, 7 Can.

P. mariana (Black spruce) A medium-sized, narrowly conical tree with dark bluish green leaves densely crowding the upper surfaces of the branchlets. The following form is recommended. NW North America. In cultivation 1700.
Zone 3 US, 3 Can.

Picea mariana 'Nana'

***P. m.* 'Nana'** A slow-growing, dwarf, dense, mound-forming bush with gray-green leaves. It is ideal for the rock garden. In cultivation 1884.
Zone 2 US, 2b Can. 🏆

P. omorika (Serbian spruce) One of the most beautiful and adaptable spruces. It quickly forms a tall, graceful, slender, medium-sized to large tree with relatively short, drooping branches that curve upward at the tips. The leaves are dark green above, bloomy beneath, and densely arranged on the upper surfaces of the branchlets; on young plants they are narrower, sharply pointed, and more spreading on the shoots. The cones are up to 2½ in (6 cm) long and bluish black when young. It is good for

Picea omorika 'Pendula'

Picea omorika

industrial areas and alkaline soils. Grows well in the East. Balkans. Introduced 1889.
Zone 3 US, 3b Can. 🏆

***P. o.* 'Nana'** A small to medium-sized, densely conical, compact bush with conspicuous white bands on the leaves. At the Hillier Gardens and Arboretum a specimen was 4 × 4 ft (1.2 × 1.2 m) after 15 years. In cultivation 1930.
Zone 3 US, 3 Can.

***P. o.* 'Pendula'** A beautiful, medium-sized, slender tree with drooping, slightly twisted branches and bloomy upper leaf surfaces. In cultivation 1920.
Zone 3 US, 4 Can. 🏆

P. orientalis (Oriental spruce) A large, densely branched, broadly conical tree with branches to the ground. Dark green leaves with blunt tips are pressed to the upper surfaces of the branchlets. Cones are up to 3½ in (9 cm) long and purple when young. Asia Minor, Caucasus. Introduced c. 1839.
Zone 4 US, 5 Can. 🏆

***P. o.* 'Aurea'** The young shoots of this medium-sized tree are creamy yellow, becoming golden yellow and then green. Spectacular in spring. In cultivation 1873.
Zone 4 US, 5 Can. 🏆

***P. o.* 'Skylands'** A beautiful, slow-growing small tree similar to 'Aurea' but golden yellow throughout the year.
Zone 4 US, 5 Can.

P. pungens (Colorado spruce) A medium-sized to large conical tree with rigid, sharply pointed, green to gray leaves up to $1^1/_4$ in (3 cm) long that spread all around the branchlets but are denser on top. The typical form is grown mostly for windbreaks and screens, while the blue forms are commonly planted in parks and gardens. SW United States. Introduced 1862.
Zone 2 US, 2 Can.

P. p.* var. *glauca (Colorado blue spruce) A medium-sized to large tree with stiffly horizontal, whorled branches. The glaucous leaves tend to lose intensity with age, those at the base of the branches being grayish green or green. It is variable. The most glaucous cultivated forms are usually small to medium-sized trees.
Zone 2 US, 2 Can.

Picea pungens 'Globosa'

***P. p.* 'Globosa'** A dwarf, flat-topped, globular, dense bush with glaucous blue leaves. In cultivation 1937.
Zone 2 US, 2 Can. 🏆

***P. p.* 'Hoopsii'** An excellent small to medium-sized tree with a densely conical habit and vividly glaucous blue leaves. In cultivation 1958.
Zone 2 US, 2 Can. 🏆

Picea pungens 'Koster'

***P. p.* 'Koster'** Once the most popular form of blue spruce for growing in the garden but now superseded by bluer and narrower forms. A small to medium-sized, dense, conical tree with intensely silver-blue leaves. In cultivation 1885.
Zone 2 US, 2 Can. 🏆

***P. p.* 'Moerheim'** A small to medium-sized tree of dense, conical habit with intensely glaucous blue leaves. In cultivation 1912.
Zone 2 US, 2 Can.

***P. p.* 'Montgomery'** A dwarf selection that eventually forms a broad, silver-blue cone. Originated in Cos Cob, Conn.
Zone 2 US, 2 Can.

***P. p.* 'Procumbens'** A dwarf shrub with low, spreading branches and pendulous branchlets. Glaucous blue leaves. Reversions should be removed. In cultivation 1910.
Zone 3 US, 3 Can. 🏆

***P. p.* 'Thomsen'** A beautiful small to medium-sized, conical tree that displays strikingly silver-blue leaves. In cultivation 1928.
Zone 2 US, 2 Can.

P. purpurea (Purple-coned spruce) A small to medium-sized tree previously regarded as a variety of *P. likiangensis*. It has a narrower, more pointed upper crown, and the upper branches have erect terminal shoots. The leaves are also darker green, smaller, and more closely pressed to the upper surfaces of the branchlets. The cones are smaller and violet-purple. China. Introduced 1910.
Zone 3 US, 3 Can. 🏆

Picea purpurea

P. sitchensis (Sitka spruce) A fast-growing, large to very large, broadly conical tree of economic importance. This prickly-leaved spruce thrives in moist climates, but grows best where summers are cool. A timber tree in the Pacific Northwest. California to Alaska. Introduced 1831 by David Douglas.
Zone 2 US, 2 Can.

P. smithiana (Himalayan spruce) A large, extremely beautiful tree with a broadly pyramidal habit and branches that are upwardly curved at the tips and bear long, pendulous branchlets. The leaves are up to $1^1/_2$ in (4 cm) long, dark green, needlelike, and flexible, spreading all around the branchlets. The young green cones, up to 7 in (18 cm) long, become purplish. Young plants are occasionally subject to injury by late-spring frost, but established trees are fairly hardy and develop into specimens second in elegance only to *P. breweriana*. W Himalaya. Introduced 1818.
Zone 8 US, 9 Can. 🏆

Picrasma *Simaroubaceae*

A genus of six species of deciduous trees and shrubs related to Ailanthus *and native for the most part to tropical areas.*

P. quassioides A surprisingly hardy small tree, grown mainly for its brilliant orange and scarlet autumn foliage. The tiny yellow-green flowers in late spring and early summer are followed by small red fruits. It is lime tolerant but does best in neutral or acid soils in sun or part shade. Japan, Korea, China, Himalaya.
Zone 5 US, 6 Can.

PIERIS

Ericaceae

THE GENUS *PIERIS* comprises about seven species of evergreen trees and shrubs closely related to the rhododendrons and native to North America and eastern Asia. It offers a wide range of attractive attributes that make the plants valuable in the landscape year-round. They are superb specimens for shrub borders, foundation plantings, rock gardens, and accents at entryways.

One of their most outstanding characteristics is the brilliant coloring — ranging from lustrous chestnut to flaming scarlet — of the new spring growth on many forms. *P.* 'Forest Flame' and *P. japonica* 'Red Mill', for instance, have bright red young shoots that are particularly distinctive. *P.* 'Bert Chandler' has such spectacular foliage color — turning from pink to yellow to white to green — that gardeners hardly notice or care that it seldom flowers.

The foliage is complemented in spring by the abundant, usually nodding clusters of small bell-shaped flowers that are reminiscent of lily-of-the-valley blooms. Often lightly and sweetly fragrant, the flowers are generally waxy, creamy white to bright snow-white, although some forms bear light pink or rose-pink blossoms. *P. japonica* 'Flamingo' is noteworthy in that the deep red buds open to pink flowers that eventually become striped with white.

Once the flowers fade, the foliage forms a wonderful backdrop of glossy, dark green foliage. Some cultivars, such as *P.* 'Flaming Silver', have white-variegated leaves, while the leaves of others turn color in fall. *P. japonica* 'Dorothy Wyckoff', for instance, bears reddish-bronze fall foliage.

The flower buds are formed in autumn. Some cultivars of *P. japonica* have inflorescences borne on dark reddish brown stems, making these plants very ornamental throughout the winter.

CARE AND CULTIVATION

Like other members of the heath family, pieris prefer a sandy, peaty, well-drained, acidic soil. They benefit from a mulch of well-rotted oak-leaf mold, pine needles, or shredded pine bark, which not only protects the roots from frost heaves but also feeds the soil. While most like sun, many will tolerate or prefer light shade. Pieris are generally slow growing and do not require much pruning, although the fruit clusters should be removed.

P. floribunda and *P. formosa* benefit from shelter from winter wind and sun, and the young spring growth on all pieris may need protection from late frosts. Even if the new shoots are damaged, all is not lost: they may be renewed from dormant buds along the stems after a short recovery period. While these shoots will also be colorful, they may be shorter than the original growths.

If your garden does not have suitable soil for pieris, they can be grown in containers. At the northern limits of their range, it will be necessary to insulate their roots over winter, either by surrounding the containers with bales of straw or by plunging the containers in the garden.

Pieris are generally resilient plants, but they do suffer from lacebug infestations in the eastern United States from late spring to early fall. Their presence is noticeable by the silvery spots on the leaf surface and the reddish "rust," along with the bugs themselves, clinging to the undersides. Lacebugs can be easily treated with insecticidal soap.

Pieris 'Firecrest'

P. 'Bert Chandler' An unusual small shrub reaching about 5 ft (1.5 m) high, with bright salmon pink young foliage that changes to creamy yellow, then white, and finally to green. It rarely flowers. Raised 1936 in Australia.
Zone 4 US, 5b Can.

Pieris 'Bert Chandler'

P. 'Firecrest' A vigorous large shrub with bright red young foliage similar to that of 'Forest Flame' but with broader, more deeply veined leaves. Large white flowers are borne in dense panicles in spring.
Zone 4 US, 5b Can. 🏆

P. 'Flaming Silver' A small shrub with bright red young leaves that show no variegation at first but soon develop pink margins that turn striking silvery white. The flowers are creamy white. It is a sport of 'Forest Flame'. Raised in Holland.
Zone 4 US, 5b Can. 🏆

P. floribunda (Mountain pieris) A small to medium-sized shrub valued for its upright clusters of fragrant, nodding, small white flowers in early spring. The leaves are 1–3 in (2.5–7.5 cm) long and slightly toothed. SE United States.
Zone 4 US, 5b Can.

P. 'Forest Flame' A large shrub whose leaves turn from red to pink and creamy white before becoming green. The white flowers are massed in large, drooping panicles at the ends of the shoots.
Zone 4 US, 5b Can. 🏆

Pieris 'Flaming Silver'

Pieris 'Forest Flame'

Pieris formosa 'Jermyns'

***P. formosa* 'Jermyns'** A superb shrub whose young leaves turn from deep wine-red to glossy green. The long, pendulous flower panicles are present over a long winter period and are an attractive red except for the white flowers themselves, which open in spring.
Zone 7 US, 8 Can. 🏆

***P. f.* 'Wakehurst'** A strong and vigorous shrub with relatively short, broad leaves. The vivid red young foliage contrasts with the glistening white flowers.
Zone 7 US, 8 Can. 🏆

P. japonica (Japanese pieris) A medium-sized shrub with attractive, glossy green foliage that is coppery when young and white, waxy, slightly fragrant flowers borne in drooping panicles. Japan, E China, Taiwan. In cultivation 1870.
Zone 4 US, 5b Can.

Pieris formosa 'Wakehurst'

Pieris japonica 'Blush'

P. j. **'Blush'** A form with attractive, dark, glossy green foliage that is coppery when young. The white, waxy flowers open from rose-pink buds in a deep purplish pink inflorescence.
Zone 4 US, 5b Can. 🏆

P. j. **'Christmas Cheer'** A very attractive shrub with white flowers flushed deep rose at the tips, creating a delightfully bicolored effect. The flowers have a crimped appearance and are abundantly produced even on young plants, often appearing in winter. The flower stalks are deep rose.
Zone 4 US, 5b Can.

P. j. **'Daisen'** From Mount Daisen in Japan. The pink flowers are deeper pink in bud. In cultivation 1967.
Zone 4 US, 5b Can.

P. j. **'Debutante'** A unusual low-growing form, making a compact mound. The white flowers are in dense, strictly upright panicles. Yaku-shima Island.
Zone 4 US, 5b Can. 🏆

P. j. **'Dorothy Wyckoff'** The leaves of this compact form are dark green and deeply veined, turning bronze in cold weather. The inflorescence is purplish red in winter, and the flowers open white from pale pink buds and contrast with the deep red calyxes. Raised 1960 in the United States.
Zone 4 US, 5b Can.

Pieris japonica 'Flamingo'

P. j. **'Flamingo'** A form whose flowers are deep red in bud, borne in large panicles, and open deep pink before fading to rose-pink and eventually becoming striped with white. Raised 1961 in the United States.
Zone 4 US, 5b Can.

Pieris japonica 'Grayswood'

P. j. **'Grayswood'** A compact small shrub with narrow, dark green leaves and panicles with long, spreading, and drooping branches bearing many densely packed small white flowers.
Zone 4 US, 5b Can. 🏆

P. j. **'Little Heath'** Similar to 'White Rim' but more dwarf and compact and with smaller leaves. It usually flowers sparsely but can be free-flowering if grown in a location with enough light. The buds are pink. It occasionally sports to 'Little Heath Green'.
Zone 4 US, 5b Can. 🏆

Pieris japonica 'Little Heath'

Pieris japonica 'Little Heath Green'

P. j. **'Little Heath Green'** A compact, dwarf shrub that forms a mound and has small green leaves that are bronze-red when young. It rarely if ever flowers.
Zone 4 US, 5b Can. 🏆

P. j. **'Mountain Fire'** The young leaves of this small to medium-sized shrub are red, turning to deep, glossy, chestnut brown. The flowers are white.
Zone 4 US, 5b Can. 🏆

P. j. **'Pink Delight'** A small to medium-sized shrub with long, drooping panicles of pale pink flowers, white at the base and fading to white overall.
Zone 4 US, 5b Can. 🏆

Pieris japonica 'Pink Delight'

Pieris japonica 'Purity'

***P. j.* 'Purity'** A small, compact shrub with fairly upright trusses of relatively large, snow-white flowers. The young foliage is pale green.

Zone 4 US, 5b Can. 🏆

***P. j.* 'Red Mill'** A very hardy small to medium-sized shrub with dark green leaves that are a brilliant bronze-red when young, gradually fading to green. The white flowers are carried in drooping panicles.

Zone 4 US, 5b Can.

Pieris japonica 'Red Mill'

Pieris japonica 'Scarlett O'Hara'

***P. j.* 'Scarlett O'Hara'** A small to medium-sized shrub with an abundance of dense, hanging clusters of pure white flowers that open early. The young growths are bronze.

Zone 4 US, 5b Can.

***P. j.* Taiwanensis group** There is no absolute distinction between the plants from Japan and Taiwan, but the latter tend to have matte green, more leathery leaves with fewer teeth and the panicles are less drooping. The young growths are bronze or bronze-red. Taiwan. Introduced 1918 by Ernest Wilson.

Zone 5 US, 6 Can.

***P. j.* 'Valley Rose'** The flowers of this small to medium-sized shrub are deep pink in bud, open rose-pink streaked with white at the base, and then fade to white. They are freely borne in large, hanging clusters. This form is somewhat like 'Blush' when in flower but without the attractively colored young inflorescence. The young foliage is a pale green.

Zone 4 US, 5b Can.

***P. j.* 'Valley Valentine'** A small to medium-sized shrub with deep dusky red

Pieris japonica Taiwanensis group

Pieris japonica 'Valley Rose'

Pieris japonica 'Valley Valentine'

flowers, hardly fading at all, and white at the base. They are borne in large, drooping clusters and tend to be lost among the dark foliage.
Zone 4 US, 5b Can. 🏆

Pieris japonica 'White Rim'

***P. j.* 'White Rim'** A slow-growing shrub with leaves prettily variegated with creamy white and flushed with pink when young. This is one of the most attractive of all silver-variegated shrubs and has been mistakenly known in the nursery trade as 'Variegata' for some time.
Zone 4 US, 5 Can. 🏆

Pileostegia *Hydrangeaceae*

A genus of three species of East Asian evergreen shrubs that climb by aerial roots. The following species, the only one in general cultivation, needs a wall for support and will grow in all types of fertile soil, in sun or shade. Prune woody stems in spring if required.

Pileostegia viburnoides

P. viburnoides (Tanglehead) A slow-growing plant, reaching 20 ft (6 m). Its leaves are leathery, slender, and strongly veined, and the creamy white flowers are borne in crowded terminal clusters in late summer and fall. It is one of the best evergreen climbers for growing in shade, including on north-facing walls. Himalaya. Introduced 1908 by Ernest Wilson.
Zone 9 US 🏆

Pimelea *Thymelaeaceae*

A genus of about 80 species of shrubs from Australasia. They are small-leaved evergreens, closely related to Daphne *and needing much the same conditions. They are not recommended for shallow, alkaline soils.*

P. prostrata A pretty, interesting, spreading species with prostrate or nearly prostrate branches that are covered with small, gray-green leaves. The fragrant white flowers are borne in clusters in summer and followed by fleshy, white berries. It is a good plant for a scree. New Zealand.
Zone 9 US

Pimelea prostrata

Pinus *Pinaceae*
Pine

A genus of more than 100 species of evergreen trees, widely distributed in the temperate regions of the Northern Hemisphere, South to Central America, and Indonesia. Young trees are usually conical and broaden as they age, becoming bushy or flat-topped. The leaves are long and needlelike, in bundles of 2–5. Cones vary from rounded and conical to banana shaped and ripen at the end of the second year. In most species the seeds are released as soon as they ripen, but in some they are retained in closed cones for many years until, in nature, the cones are acted upon by the heat of forest fires, which causes them to open and release their seeds. This mechanism ensures the maximum chance for the forest to renew itself.

Some pines succeed in the poorest soils, whether alkaline or acid, but as a rule those with needles in bundles of five will not thrive in shallow, alkaline soils. Some species make excellent windbreaks, especially in coastal areas. All of them dislike shade, and very few will tolerate smoke-polluted air. Several dwarf or slow-growing forms have appeared in cultivation, many of them suitable for the rock garden.

P. aristata (Bristlecone pine) A large shrub or small tree with bluish green leaves in fives, up to 1½ in (4 cm) long, flecked with white resin and closely pressed to the branchlets. The cones are up to 3½ in (9 cm) long, and their scales have slender-spined, bristlelike bosses. Trees up to 2,000 years old have been recorded in the wild. (See also *P. longaeva.*) Rocky Mountains of the United States. Introduced 1863.
Zone 3 US, 3 Can.

P. armandii (Chinese white pine) A medium-sized tree with leaves in fives and 4–6 in (10–15 cm) long. The cones are in twos and threes, barrel shaped, and up to 7½ in (19 cm) long, becoming pendulous. Himalayan region, Taiwan.
Zone 7 US, 8 Can.

P. bungeana (Lacebark pine) A small to medium-sized tree or large shrub, typically

Pinus armandii

Pinus bungeana

branching from or near the base. The smooth gray-green bark flakes irregularly, creating a beautiful patchwork of white, yellow, purple, brown, and green. The leaves are in threes, 2–4 in (5–10 cm) long, and rigid; the cones are up to 2¾ in (7 cm) long. Discovered 1831 by Dr. Bunge in a temple garden near Beijing and introduced 1846 by Robert Fortune.
Zone 5 US, 6 Can.

P. cembra (Swiss stone pine) A small to medium-sized tree with a characteristically dense, conical or columnar habit. The leaves are in fives, 2–3 in (5–8 cm) long, densely crowded, and dark blue-green with blue-white inner surfaces. The cones are deep blue, up to 3 in (8 cm) long; they never open and the edible seeds are released only when attacked by rot, squirrels, or birds. A formal-looking tree good for small gardens. Mountains of C Europe and N Asia. In cultivation 1746.
Zone 2 US, 2 Can. 🏆

Pinus contorta

P. contorta (Shore pine, beach pine) A medium-sized to large tree, occasionally a large bush, with short branches. The leaves are in pairs, up to 2 in (5 cm) long, twisted, and yellowish green. The cones are paired or in clusters, 2 in (5 cm) long, and spiny and open when mature. It will not grow in alkaline soils but thrives in light, stony or sandy soil and is used for stabilizing dunes on the seashore. W North America. Introduced 1831 by David Douglas.
Zone 3 US, 4 Can.

Pinus contorta subsp. *latifolia*

P. c.* subsp. *latifolia (Lodgepole pine) A medium-sized tree, less vigorous than the type and with slightly broader leaves and larger cones, which open in the wild only as a result of forest fire. Native Americans often used it for the central pole of their tepees. W North America. Introduced 1853 by John Jeffrey.
Zone 1 US, 1 Can.

***P. c.* 'Spaan's Dwarf'** A small, slow-growing form with numerous upright, spreading shoots densely covered with short, dark green leaves.
Zone 4 US, 5 Can.

P. coulteri (Big-cone pine, Coulter pine) A remarkable, striking, medium-sized to large tree with very stout shoots. The leaves are in threes, up to 1 ft (30 cm) long, stiff and curved, and pale bluish gray-green. The cones are very large, up to 14 in (35 cm) long, and remain a long time on the tree. They weigh up to 6½ lb (3 kg) when fresh and are among the largest of any conifer. S California, N Mexico. Discovered 1832 by Dr. Coulter and introduced the same year by David Douglas.
Zone 8 US, 9 Can. 🏆

P. densiflora (Japanese red pine) A medium-sized to large, flat-topped tree with twisted, bluish green leaves in pairs, up to 4¾ in (12 cm) long. The cones are in twos or threes and 2 in (5 cm) long. Its bark is similar to that of the Scotch pine (*P. sylvestris*). It needs acid soil. Introduced 1852.
Zone 4 US, 4b Can.

***P. d.* 'Oculus-draconis'** (Dragon's-eye pine) A curious form whose branchlets, when viewed from above, show alternate yellow and green rings of needles, hence the common name. In cultivation 1890.
Zone 4 US, 5b Can.

***P. d.* 'Umbraculifera'** (Tanyosho pine) A miniature tree of extremely slow growth. It has an umbrella-like head of branches and bears tiny cones; the older branches turn reddish. It seldom reaches over 12 feet (3.5 m) tall. In cultivation 1890.
Zone 4 US, 5 Can.

Pinus densiflora 'Umbraculifera'

Pinus jeffreyi

P. jeffreyi (Jeffrey pine) A large, imposing tree with a conical or pyramidal crown. The leaves are in threes, up to $8\frac{3}{4}$ in (22 cm) long, dull bluish green or pale gray, and crowded toward the ends of the branchlets. The cones are 5–8 in (13–20 cm) long and spiny. It differs from *P. ponderosa* in its black or purple-gray bark and stouter, longer, bluish leaves. SW United States. Introduced c. 1852.

Zone 5 US, 6 Can.

P. koraiensis (Korean pine) A slow-growing, medium-sized, loose, conical tree. The blue-green leaves are usually in fives, up to $4\frac{3}{4}$ in (12 cm) long, and stiff and rough to the touch. The cones are up to $5\frac{1}{2}$ in (14 cm) long. E Asia. Introduced 1861.

Zone 3 US, 3 Can.

***P. k.* 'Compacta Glauca'** A vigorous, compact form with short, stout branches and attractive, densely packed, blue-bloomy leaves. In cultivation 1949.

Zone 4 US, 4b Can.

P. lambertiana (Sugar pine) An enormous, narrowly columnar tree, reaching up to 200 ft (60 m) tall. The leaves are in fives, 3–4 in (7.5–10 cm) long, and bluish green with silvery lines. The cones are 10–20 in (25–50 cm) long. Oregon to California.

Zone 6 US, 7 Can.

P. leucodermis (Bosnian pine) A medium-sized tree with smooth, greenish gray bark, an egg-shaped outline, and a dense habit. The leaves are in pairs, up to $3\frac{1}{2}$ in (9 cm) long, rigid and erect, and almost black-green. The cones are up to 3 in (7.5 cm) long and bright blue in the first year. Good for dry or shallow, alkaline soil. Italy,

Pinus leucodermis 'Schmidtii'

Balkans. Introduced 1864.

Zone 4 US, 5 Can.

***P. l.* 'Satellit'** A narrowly conical form with leaves densely clustered and pressed against the shoots on the young growths. In later life it is more spreading.

Zone 4 US, 5 Can.

***P. l.* 'Schmidtii'** A slow-growing, dwarf or small form that develops into a dense, compact mound. Previously listed as 'Pygmy'.

Zone 4 US, 5 Can.

P. longaeva (Ancient pine) This species, first described in 1970, is closely related to *P. aristata* but does not have the white specks of resin on its leaves. It is also a bristlecone pine, and specimens in the White Mountains of California have been proved to be up to 5,000 years old.

Zone 3 US, 3 Can.

P. montezumae (Montezuma pine) A medium-sized to large tree with rough, deeply fissured bark and a large, domed crown. The leaves are usually in fives but

Pinus montezumae

vary from three to eight on some trees. They are 7–10 in (18–25 cm) long, bluish gray, spreading and drooping. The cones are 3–10 in (7.5–25 cm) long. It is a bold, imposing, and beautiful tree. Mountains of Mexico. Introduced 1839.

Zone 9 US

Pinus mugo

P. mugo (Swiss mountain pine) A very hardy, small to large shrub or small tree with leaves in pairs. It is very variable in the wild and has given rise to several dwarf forms that will grow in almost any soil. C Europe.

Zone 2 US, 2b Can.

***P. m.* 'Gnom'** A small, compact selection that forms a dense, dark green, globular mound. In cultivation 1937.

Zone 2 US, 2 Can.

***P. m.* 'Mops'** A dwarf, globular, dense, slow-growing bush. It is ideal for a rock garden or scree. In cultivation 1951.

Zone 2 US, 2b Can.

Pinus mugo 'Gnom'

Pinus mugo 'Mops'

Pinus mugo 'Ophir'

***P. m.* 'Ophir'** A compact, bun-shaped dwarf shrub with golden yellow winter foliage.
Zone 3 US, 3 Can.

P. m.* var. *pumilio A dwarf form that is often prostrate but occasionally reaches a height of 6½ ft (2 m). Alps of C Europe.
Zone 2 US, 2b Can.

Pinus mugo var. *pumilio*

Pinus mugo 'Winter Gold'

Pinus muricata

***P. m.* 'Winter Gold'** A dwarf, spreading bush with an open habit. The foliage is golden yellow in winter.
Zone 3 US, 3 Can.

P. muricata (Bishop pine) A picturesque medium-sized to large tree with a dense, rather flat head of branches. The leaves are in pairs, up to 6 in (15 cm) long, stiff and curved or twisted, and dark bluish gray or yellowish gray-green. The cones are up to 3½ in (9 cm) long and often remain unopened on the branches for many years. In the wild the cones have been known to stay intact for 30–40 years until liberated by forest fires. This pine is suitable for exposed sites but requires an acid soil. California. Introduced 1848.
Zone 8 US, 9 Can.

Pinus nigra

P. nigra (Austrian pine) A commonly planted, broadly conical, large tree with dark, rough bark and a dense head of large branches. The dark green leaves are in pairs, 3–4¾ in (8–12 cm) long, and densely crowded on the branches. The cones are egg shaped and 3 in (7.5 cm) long. It and all its forms are excellent for coastal sites and do well in most soils. It makes an excellent windbreak or screen. SE Europe. Introduced 1835.
Zone 3 US, 4 Can.

Pinus nigra 'Hornibrookiana'

P. n. 'Hornibrookiana' A dwarf, very slow growing form that makes a round, low mound. Originated before 1932 in Rochester, N.Y.
Zone 4 US, 4b Can.

P. n. subsp. *laricio*, syn. *P. nigra* var. *maritima* (Corsican pine) A large tree with a straight main stem to the top. It is more open than the Austrian pine and has fewer, shorter, and more level branches. Its gray-green needles are not as stiff and are less densely arranged. S Italy and Corsica. Introduced 1759.
Zone 4 US, 4b Can. 🏆

P. nigra var. *maritima* See *P. n.* subsp. *laricio.*

Pinus parviflora

P. *parviflora* (Japanese white pine) A small to medium-sized tree, conical when young, flat-topped in maturity. The leaves are in fives, 2–3 in (5–7.5 cm) long, slightly curved, and deep blue-green with blue-white inner surfaces. The cones are 2–3 in (5–8 cm) long. Japan. Introduced 1861 by J. G. Veitch.
Zone 4 US, 5b Can. 🏆

P. p. 'Adcock's Dwarf' A slow-growing, eventually medium-sized shrub of rather compact, upright habit. The leaves are up to 1 in (2.5 cm) long, grayish green, and produced in congested bunches at the tips of the shoots. Raised 1961 at Hillier Nurseries by Graham Adcock and in 1990 was 8 ft (2.5 m) high and 4 ft (1.3 m) across.
Zone 4 US, 5b Can. 🏆

P. p. 'Tempelhof' A vigorous form with glaucous blue foliage.
Zone 4 US, 5 Can.

Pinus parviflora 'Adcock's Dwarf'

Pinus parviflora 'Tempelhof'

Pinus patula

P. *patula* (Jelecote pine) A beautiful, small to medium-sized, graceful tree with reddish bark; long, spreading branches; and pendulous, glaucous green young shoots. The leaves are bright green, usually in threes but occasionally in fours or fives, and up to 1 ft (30 cm) long. This lovely tree requires an acid soil and is of use primarily in southern California. Mexico. Zone 9 US 🏆

P. *pinaster* (Maritime pine, cluster pine) A sparsely branched, pyramidal, medium-sized or occasionally large tree with a bare stem and thick, reddish brown or deep purple bark furrowed into small squares. The leaves are in pairs, up to 10 in (25 cm) long, rigid, curved, and dull gray. The cones are up to 7 in (18 cm) long and glossy brown, often remaining on the tree for several years. It is an excellent species for sandy soil and coastal areas. Young trees need to be sited carefully as mature specimens are difficult to transplant. Mediterranean region. In cultivation since the 16th century.
Zone 8 US, 9 Can. 🏆

P. *pinea* (Italian stone pine) A very distinctive, small to medium-sized tree with a characteristically dense, asymmetrical, flat-topped or umbrella-shaped head. The leaves are in pairs, up to 6 in (15 cm) long, stiff and slightly twisted, and sharply pointed. The stalked cones are up to 6 in (15 cm) long, and the seeds are large and edible. It is particularly good in sandy soil and coastal areas. Mediterranean region.
Zone 8 US, 9 Can. 🏆

Pinus pinea

P. *ponderosa* (Ponderosa pine, Western yellow pine) This is a large, fast-growing tree that produces a tall, clear trunk with scaly cinnamon bark and spreading or drooping branches. The yellowish green leaves, in threes and up to 10 in (25 cm) long, are stiff and curved, and are crowded at the ends of the branchlets. The cones have spines and are up to 6 in (15 cm) long. It is a variable species. W North America.

Pinus ponderosa

Introduced 1826 by David Douglas.
Zone 4 US, 4b Can. 🏆

P. p.* var. *scopulorum (Rocky Mountain yellow pine) A variety that is more compact and hardier than the species, and is almost columnar in habit. Rocky Mountains.
Zone 3 US, 3 Can.

***P. pumila* 'Glauca'** A form of the very variable dwarf Siberian pine that grows to a bushy, small to medium-sized shrub with

Pinus pumila 'Glauca'

bright gray-blue foliage. The leaves are in fives. It should be grown in an acidic soil.
Zone 2 US, 2 Can. 🏆

P. radiata (Monterey pine) A large, fast-growing tree with deeply fissured bark and a dense head of branches. The leaves are in threes, up to 6 in (15 cm) long, bright green, and densely crowded on the branchlets. The cones are up to 6 in (15 cm) long and borne in whorls, often persisting for years. It needs acid soil and is good for coastal locations, as it withstands wind. In an open

Pinus radiata

site it tends to bear branches almost to ground level; if grown among other trees it forms a long, fairly straight trunk. California. Introduced 1833 by David Douglas.
Zone 8 US, 9 Can. 🏆

Pinus strobus

P. strobus (Eastern white pine) A fast-growing large tree, conical when young and rounded when older. The leaves are in fives, up to 6 in (15 cm) long, and somewhat bloomy green. The cones are up to 8 in (20 cm) long, pendent, on slender stalks liberally flecked with resin. One of the most useful ornamental pines. E North America. In cultivation since the mid-16th century.
Zone 3 US, 3 Can.

***P. s.* 'Nana'** (Dwarf Eastern white pine) A small form that develops into a dense, rounded or conical bush. There are several slight variations of this form.
Zone 3 US, 3b Can. 🏆

***P. s.* 'Nivea'** An attractive medium-sized form whose glaucous leaves are tipped with

Pinus strobus 'Nana'

milky white, giving the whole tree an unusual silvery appearance.
Zone 3 US, 3 Can.

P. sylvestris (Scotch pine) A large, tall-stemmed tree that may sometimes be low, picturesque, and spreading. It is easily recognized by its characteristic and attractive reddish young bark. The leaves are in pairs, up to 4 in (10 cm) long, twisted, and gray-green or blue-green. The cones are up to 3 in (7.5 cm) long on short stalks. It can be grown in all kinds of soil but does not reach its maximum size or age in damp, acid or shallow soil. It is drought tolerant. Siberia to Scotland.
Zone 2 US, 2 Can. 🏆

Pinus sylvestris

***P. s.* 'Aurea'** A slow-growing small tree with leaves that are a striking golden yellow in winter.
Zone 3 US, 3 Can. 🏆

***P. s.* 'Beuvronensis'** A miniature Scotch pine that forms a small, compact, dome-

Pinus sylvestris 'Aurea'

Pinus sylvestris 'Beuvronensis'

shaped shrublet. It is an excellent specimen for the rock garden. In cultivation 1891.
Zone 2 US, 2 Can. 🏆

***P. s.* 'Edwin Hillier'** A beautiful form with silvery blue-green leaves and reddish stems. It is occasionally referred to as 'Argentea' but is not related to *P. s.* f. *argentea*, which is from the Caucasus. Selected 1926 by Edwin Hillier.
Zone 3 US, 3 Can.

***P. s.* 'Fastigiata'** (Pyramidal Scotch pine) A remarkable form with a distinctive narrow columnar shape. In cultivation 1856.
Zone 3 US, 3 Can.

***P. s.* 'Gold Coin'** A slow-growing small tree similar to 'Aurea' but with deep yellow foliage in winter.
Zone 3 US, 3 Can.

***P. s.* 'Moseri'** A very slow growing, dense, globular or ovoid, miniature tree with leaves that turn yellow or yellow-green in winter. In cultivation 1900.
Zone 3 US, 3 Can. 🏆

Pinus sylvestris 'Fastigiata'

Pinus sylvestris 'Moseri'

***P. s.* 'Watereri'** (Waterer Scotch pine) A slow-growing, medium-sized bush or rarely a small tree with steely blue leaves, conical at first, later becoming rounded. The original plant, which dates from about 1865, is about 26 ft (8 m) high.
Zone 3 US, 3 Can.

P. thunbergii (Japanese black pine) A

Pinus sylvestris 'Watereri'

distinctive large tree with stout, twisted branches. The rigid, twisted needles, 2¾–7 in (7–18 cm) long, are in pairs, and the cones, up to 2½ in (6 cm) long, are borne singly or in clusters. It is extremely tolerant of salt spray, makes a good windbreak in coastal areas, and grows well in poor, sandy soil. This pine is an important timber tree in Japan. Japan, Korea. Introduced 1852.
Zone 4 US, 4b Can.

Pinus thunbergii

P. wallichiana (Himalayan pine) An elegant, large, broad-headed tree that retains its lower branches when grown in an open location. The needles are in fives, up to 8 in (20 cm) long, blue-green, slender, and drooping with age. The stalked cones are solitary or in bunches, banana shaped, and 6–10 in (15–25 cm) long. This graceful species is moderately lime tolerant but will not grow in shallow soils. Himalaya. Introduced c. 1823. *(See photo on p.450.)*
Zone 5 US, 6 Can.

Pinus wallichiana

***P. w.* 'Umbraculifera'** A small, dome-shaped, glaucous, slow-growing, dense bush. It has long needles that are often kinked.
Zone 5 US, 6 Can.

Piptanthus *Leguminosae*
Evergreen laburnum

A genus of two species of large evergreen shrubs with leaves made up of three leaflets and with showy yellow pea flowers. They grow well in any well-drained soil.

P. laburnifolius See *P. nepalensis.*

Piptanthus nepalensis

P. nepalensis, syn. *P. laburnifolius* An attractive shrub 8–11 ft (2.5–3.5 m) tall, with large, bright yellow, laburnum-like flowers in late spring. It may lose its leaves at the colder limits of its range. It can be grown in the open as a specimen shrub but is also suitable against a wall. An earlier-flowering, more silky-leaved form from Bhutan is slightly more tender. Himalaya. Introduced 1821.
Zone 9 US

Pistacia *Anacardiaceae*
Pistachio

A genus of nine species of evergreen and deciduous shrubs or trees, related to Rhus *and found in warm-temperate regions of the Northern Hemisphere. The following is the most commonly grown species; it is sometimes used as a street tree. It needs sun and will grow in all types of soil.*

Pistacia chinensis

P. chinensis (Chinese pistachio) A medium-sized deciduous tree with glossy green, pinnate leaves that turn beautiful colors in fall. The inconspicuous, greenish, unisexual flowers are held in dense clusters, and the fruits are small, reddish at first and then blue. China. Introduced 1897.
Zone 9 US

Pittosporum *Pittosporaceae*

A large genus of some 200 species of evergreen shrubs or trees, most of which are suitable only for mild climates, where they will grow well, especially in coastal areas. They come from Australasia, South and Southeast Asia, and tropical and South Africa. Several have small, five-petaled, scented flowers, but they are grown primarily for their very attractive, unusual, and distinctive foliage, which is excellent for cutting. They will grow in all types of well-drained soil, take sun or part shade, and benefit if given shelter from wind. They are tolerant of hot, dry climates.

***P. crassifolium* 'Variegatum'** Leaves are 2–3 in (5–7.5 cm) long, more or less oval, thick, and leathery. They are gray-green and attractively margined with light cream. The flowers, borne in terminal clusters, are deep purple. A large shrub or small tree, it makes an excellent dense screen or shelterbelt.
Zone 9 US

P. dallii A large, spreading shrub or occasionally a rounded, small tree. The shoots and leaf stalks are dark reddish purple, and the elliptic to lance-shaped leaves are leathery and usually jagged-toothed (occasionally entire) and matte green. The fragrant cream flowers with protruding stamens are borne in small clusters in summer. New Zealand, rare in the wild.
Zone 9 US

Pittosporum dallii

***P. eugenioides* 'Variegatum'** A pretty and elegant medium-sized shrub for mild climates. Its undulating leaves, 2–4 in (5–10 cm) long, are margined with cream and pleasantly aromatic. In cultivation 1882.
Zone 9 US 🏆

***P.* 'Garnettii'** A medium to large, conical to broadly columnar shrub with gray-green leaves irregularly margined with cream and marked, flushed, or spotted with pink to red from late summer through winter.
Zone 9 US 🏆

P. rhombifolium (Diamondleaf pittosporum) A large tree with glossy, diamond-shaped leaves up to 4 in (10 cm) long and bright orange berries in midwinter. It is popular in southern California. E Australia.
Zone 9 US

Pittosporum 'Garnettii'

Pittosporum tenuifolium

P. tenuifolium (Tawhiwhi) A charming large shrub or small tree of columnar habit, with bright, pale green, oblong, wavy leaves contrasting with the black twigs. The small, chocolate-purple, honey-scented flowers appear either singly or in clusters in the leaf axils in late spring to summer. It is used for cut greens by florists and is a good edging plant. New Zealand.
Zone 9 US 🏆

***P. t.* 'Abbotsbury Gold'** A form similar to 'Eila Keightley' but with the variegation most apparent on young foliage and becoming indistinct with age. Reputed to have arisen 1970 as a sport at Abbotsbury, England, but this is doubtful.
Zone 9 US

***P. t.* 'Eila Keightley'** syn. *P. t.* 'Sunburst' The leaves of this form are blotched in the center with bright greenish yellow, and this variegation is most noticeable on older foliage. Discovered 1964 as a sport.
Zone 9 US

***P. t.* 'Gold Star'** A compact form making a medium-sized shrub. The leaves have a conspicuous blotch of bright yellow-green in the center, becoming dark green.
Zone 9 US

Pittosporum tenuifolium 'Irene Paterson'

***P. t.* 'Irene Paterson'** An attractive, slow-growing form reaching about 8 ft (2.5 m) high. Its young leaves emerge cream, become deep green marbled with white, and develop a pink tinge in winter. Later summer growth is pale green. New Zealand. In cultivation 1970.
Zone 9 US 🏆

***P. t.* 'Purpureum'** A medium-sized shrub with pale green leaves that turn deep bronze-purple.
Zone 9 US

Pittosporum tenuifolium 'Silver Queen'

***P. t.* 'Silver Queen'** A neat and handsome specimen shrub with leaves suffused with silvery gray, narrowly margined with white.
Zone 9 US 🏆

Pittosporum tenuifolium 'Purpureum'

***P. t.* 'Sunburst'** See *P. t.* 'Eila Keightley'.

***P. t.* 'Tom Thumb'** A dense, rounded dwarf shrub with leaves that are green and become deep reddish purple. The color is brighter and redder than that of 'Purpureum'. Raised c. 1960 in New Zealand.
Zone 9 US 🏆

***P. t.* 'Warnham Gold'** The young leaves of this medium-sized shrub are greenish yellow, maturing to golden yellow, particularly attractive in fall and winter. Raised 1959 in Sussex, England.
Zone 9 US 🏆

P. tobira (Japanese pittosporum) A rather slow growing species, eventually making a large shrub with leaves broadest toward the ends, bright glossy green and growing in whorls. The orange-scented flowers emerge in summer and are creamy white at first, then turn yellow. It is a good wall shrub or hedge and is very drought resistant. China, Taiwan, Japan. Introduced 1804.
Zone 8 US, 9? Can. 🏆

Pittosporum tenuifolium 'Tom Thumb'

Pittosporum tenuifolium 'Warnham Gold'

Pittosporum tobira

***P. t.* 'Variegatum'** A medium-sized shrub bearing gray-green leaves with an irregular bright cream margin. It is more compact than the species and is grown in the South as a low, clipped hedge.
Zone 8 US, 9? Can.

***P. t.* 'Wheeler's Dwarf'** A compact form that makes a dark green mound good for ground cover. Not as hardy as the species.
Zone 9 US

Plagianthus *Malvaceae*

A genus of two species of graceful deciduous trees or shrubs native to New Zealand. They grow in mild areas in all types of fertile soil.

P. regius (Ribbon wood) A graceful, slender, small to medium-sized tree with toothed leaves. The individual white flowers are inconspicuous but are borne in large panicles in late spring. Juvenile plants form dense bushes of slender, interlacing branches with toothed or lobed leaves. It is a curious tree that passes through several distinct stages of growth. Introduced 1870.
Zone 9 US

Platanus *Platanaceae*
Plane tree

A genus of about six species of magnificent, maplelike deciduous trees with attractive flaking bark. Apart from P. orientalis *and one species from Southeast Asia, they are North American. They can be grown in all types of fertile soil but may become chlorotic in shallow, alkaline ones.*

Platanus × *hispanica*

P.* × *acerifolia See *P.* × *hispanica.*

P.* × *hispanica, syn. *P.* × *acerifolia* (London plane tree) A large, noble tree with attractive mottled, flaking bark and large palmate leaves. The rounded, burrlike fruit clusters are in strings of 2–6 and persist from early summer to the following spring. It is very tolerant of urban growing conditions and is an excellent street tree.
Zone 4 US, 5b Can. 🏆

***P.* × *h.* 'Bloodgood'** This variety has greater resistance to anthracnose and poor growing conditions than does the species. Dark green leaves turn yellow in fall.
Zone 5 US, 6 Can.

P. occidentalis (American plane tree, sycamore, buttonwood) An impressive tree

Platanus orientalis

with flaking bark and an irregular branch structure. It can be distinguished from *P.* × *hispanica* by its single fruits. United States.
Zone 4 US, 5 Can.

P. orientalis (Oriental plane tree) A large, stately, long-lived tree that develops a wide-spreading head of branches. The bark is attractively dappled and flaking, and the five-lobed leaves are deeply cut, to the middle of the leaf or more. The bristly fruit clusters are 2–6 on a stalk. SE Europe. In cultivation early 16th century.
Zone 7 US, 8 Can. 🏆

P. racemosa (California sycamore) The western counterpart of *P. occidentalis,* this large tree has a gnarled, asymmetrical habit and fruits in clusters of 3–7. California.
Zone 7 US, 8 Can.

Platycarya *Juglandaceae*

A genus of one deciduous species, related to Pterocarya.

P. strobilacea A small tree with pinnate leaves made up of 7–15 stalkless, lance-shaped, toothed leaflets. The flowers are small, with the males in cylindrical catkins and the females in erect, green, conelike clusters at the ends of the current year's growth in late summer. It has distinctive, conelike fruits. It will grow in any good,

Platycarya strobilacea

preferably deep soil. China. Introduced 1845 by Robert Fortune.
Zone 6 US, 7 Can.

Pleioblastus *Gramineae*

Bamboo

A genus of mostly smaller to medium-sized evergreen bamboos with underground running stems. Many species form extensive clumps and should be planted only where there is enough space. They are moisture lovers but will grow in good soil over limestone. The genus includes many species previously in Arundinaria.

Pleioblastus auricoma

P. auricoma, syn. *Arundinaria viridistriata, A. auricoma* A hardy species with erect, purplish green canes up to 3–6½ ft (1–2 m) high, forming small clumps. The leaves are variable in size, up to 8 in (20 cm) long and 1½ in (4 cm) wide, and dark green striped with yellow, often more yellow than green. It is the best of the variegated bamboos, smaller when grown in shade and an excellent container plant. Old canes can be cut to ground level in fall to encourage bright young foliage. Japan. Introduced c. 1870.
Zone 7 US, 8 Can. 🏆

P. hindsii, syn. *Arundinaria hindsii* A vigorous species that forms dense clumps of erect, olive green canes 8–11 ft (2.5–3.5 m) high. The leaves are variable in size, up to 9 in (23 cm) long and 1 in (2.5 cm) wide, rich sea green, and thickly clustered toward the tops of the canes. It thrives in sun or dense shade and makes an excellent hedge or small screen. Japan. Introduced 1875.
Zone 8 US, 9 Can.

***P. humilis* 'Gauntlettii'**, syn. *Arundinaria* 'Gauntlettii' A small, clump-forming bamboo with bright green, later dull purple canes up to 32 in (80 cm) high. The leaves are 3–7 in (7.5–18 cm) long by ½–¾ in (1–2 cm) wide. It is an uncommon bamboo of obscure, possibly Japanese, origin.
Zone 7 US, 8 Can.

P. pumilus, syn. *Arundinaria pumila* A dwarf bamboo forming dense stands of slender, dull purple canes 12–32 in (30–80 cm) high, with conspicuously hairy joints. The leaves are 2–7 in (5–18 cm) long by ½–¾ in (1–2 cm) wide. It is a far-creeping plant, useful as a ground cover but only where there is plenty of space. Japan. Introduced late 19th century.
Zone 8 US, 9 Can.

P. pygmaeus, syn. *Arundinaria pygmaea* A dwarf species forming carpets of slender stems up to 10 in (25 cm) long, taller in shade. The leaves are up to 5 in (13 cm) long by ¾ in (2 cm) wide. An excellent ground-cover plant where there is enough space. Japan. Introduced c. 1870.
Zone 8 US, 9 Can.

P. simonii, syn. *Arundinaria simonii* (Simon bamboo) A vigorous bamboo of erect habit, forming dense clumps of tall, olive green canes up to 14½ ft (4.5 m) or more. The first-year canes are covered with a white bloom. The leaves are 3–12 in (7.5–30 cm) long by ½–1¼ in (1–3 cm) wide. The leaf underside is green on one side and grayish green on the other. It is useful as a hedge or screen. China. Introduced 1862.
Zone 7 US, 8 Can.

P. variegatus, syn. *Arundinaria fortunei* A low, tufted species forming dense clumps of erect, zigzag, pale green canes 32 in–4 ft (0.8–1.2 m) high. The leaves are 2–8 in (5–20 cm) long by ½–1 in (1–2.5 cm) wide, dark green with white stripes that fade to pale green. It is the best of the white-variegated bamboos and good for a rock garden or container. Japan. Introduced 1863.
Zone 7 US, 8 Can.

Pleioblastus variegatus

Plumbago *Plumbaginaceae*

A genus of about 15 species of deciduous shrubs, annuals, and herbaceous plants from warm-temperate and tropical regions. The following is valued as a greenhouse plant, where it makes a superb display when given support.

P. auriculata, syn. *P. capensis* (Cape plumbago) A beautiful deciduous shrub, best treated as if it were a climber. It bears an extraordinary profusion of sky blue, somewhat phloxlike flowers on the current season's growth throughout summer and fall and sometimes into early winter. It should be given a sunny location in a rich, well-drained soil and be watered freely during the growing season. It is important to keep it cool and dry in winter and early spring. S Africa, naturalized in S Europe.
Zone 10 US

P. capensis See *P. auriculata.*

Podocarpus *Podocarpaceae*

A genus of about 90 species of evergreen coniferous trees and shrubs, confined in the wild mainly to the Southern Hemisphere in warm-temperate and tropical countries. Their leaves are variable in shape and they are typically spirally arranged. The fruits are usually red, fleshy, and berrylike. The flowers are insignificant. Several species are suitable for growing in milder areas. They succeed in most types of soil, whether acid or alkaline, and tolerate shade.

P. alpinus (Tasmania podocarpus) A dwarf species that forms a low, densely branched mound or creeping mat. Sometimes it is a small bush of upright or pendulous habit. The leaves are yewlike, narrow, and blue-green or gray-green and crowd the stems. It can be grown in the rock garden or as a ground cover. SE Australia, Tasmania. Zone 8 US, 9 Can.

Podocarpus alpinus

P. andinus (Andes podocarpus) A large shrub or small to medium-sized tree resembling a yew. The leaves are linear, up to 1 in (2.5 cm) long, bright green above, and twisted to show the bloomy green undersurfaces. The egg-shaped fruits are pale yellowish green and turn bloomy black, like small damson plums. It grows in good alkaline soil. Andes of S Chile. Introduced 1860 by Robert Pearce.
Zone 8 US, 9 Can.

Podocarpus macrophyllus

P. macrophyllus (Yew podocarpus) This species forms a distinctive large shrub or small tree. The leaves are similar to yew needles and are 4–7 in (10–18 cm) long and ½ in (12 mm) wide. They are bright green above and arranged in dense spirals on the stems. It is not suitable for calcareous soils. Popular in the South. China, Japan.
Zone 9 US

Podocarpus nivalis

P. nivalis (Alpine totara) One of the hardier species, this shrub is tolerant both of cold and of alkaline soil. It makes a spreading mound of prostrate and short, upright stems that are densely branched and covered with small, narrow, leathery, olive green leaves up to 3/4 in (2 cm) long. It makes an excellent ground cover. S New Zealand.
Zone 7 US, 8 Can.

Podocarpus salignus

P. salignus (Willowleaf podocarpus) An attractive, elegant, large shrub or small tree with drooping branches and long, narrow, shiny green leaves, 2–6 in (5–15 cm) long and curved. A well-grown specimen creates an almost tropical effect with its lush piles of glossy, evergreen, willowlike foliage. At the limits of its range it should be given the protection of other evergreens. Thrives in sun or shade and in most friable, well-drained soils. Chile.
Zone 9 US

Poliothyrsis *Flacourtiaceae*

A genus of one deciduous species grown for its foliage and flowers, related to Idesia.

P. sinensis An interesting large shrub or small tree with slender-pointed leaves 4–6 in (10–15 cm) long. They are red-tinged and downy on both sides when young and become dark green, smooth, and red-stalked. The unisexual flowers are fragrant, whitish in bud but opening to creamy yellow in panicles up to 10 in (25 cm) long in mid- to late summer. It flowers best in hot summers. It thrives in all types of fertile soil, preferring a sunny location but tolerating part shade. Introduced 1908 by Ernest Wilson.
Zone 7 US, 8 Can.

Polygala *Polygalaceae*

A very large genus of annuals, perennials, and evergreen and deciduous shrubs with colorful pea-type flowers. They are found in many parts of the world. The shrubby species thrive in most kinds of soil except shallow, alkaline ones.

Polygala chamaebuxus

P. chamaebuxus (Groundbox polygala) A dwarf evergreen shrublet that forms large tufts rarely more than 6 in (15 cm) high. The flowers are cream with bright yellow at the tips and are freely borne from mid-spring to early summer. It thrives in a cool, moist site in deep, acid soil. It is common in the European alps. In cultivation 1658.
Zone 7 US, 8 Can. 🏆

P. c.* var. *grandiflora A beautiful form, strikingly colored with purple wing petals and yellow keel.
Zone 7 US, 8 Can. 🏆

P. × dalmaisiana (Sweet pea shrub) A small, almost continuously flowering deciduous shrub with bright purple or rosy red pea flowers. Its parents are from South Africa. It requires a minimum temperature of 36°F (2°C).
Zone 10 US 🏆

Polygala myrtifolia

P. myrtifolia One of the parents of the above, this is an erect deciduous shrub of about 1.5m (5ft) high with greenish white flowers veined with purple. *P. m.* var. *grandiflora* has larger flowers of rich purple in summer. For the greenhouse or a very sheltered spot in a mild area. South Africa.
Zone 9 US

Polygonum

P. baldschuanicum See *Fallopia baldschuanica.*

P. vacciniifolium See *Persicaria vacciniifolia.*

Poncirus *Rutaceae*

A genus of one deciduous species related to Citrus.

P. trifoliata (Hardy orange, trifoliate orange) A slow-growing, medium-sized shrub with green, thorny stems. The leaves are made up of three leaflets. It is very beautiful in spring, when it is covered with flattish white flowers that smell like orange blossoms and are about 2 in (5 cm) wide;

Poncirus trifoliata in autumn

Populus alba

it is exquisite when in late bud. The fruits are green and ripen to yellow, resembling miniature oranges; the flesh is aromatic but very bitter and inedible. It grows well in all types of well-drained soil, preferably in full sun, and makes an impenetrable hedge. N China. Introduced 1850.

Zone 7 US, 8 Can.

Populus *Salicaceae*
Poplar

A genus of about 35 deciduous species, found wild throughout the northern temperate regions of the world. Poplars should be treated with caution, as they are very fast growing and their roots rapidly invade drains and disturb foundations if they are planted near houses. The problems can be especially severe in clay soil. In large gardens they are perfectly safe and make dramatic, if not extremely long-lived, additions to the landscape. Few poplars will grow in alkaline or very wet soils, but they are otherwise not fussy; many are tolerant of air pollution, and several are excellent for coastal locations. The balsam poplars have pleasantly aromatic young leaves, and many of the black poplars have copper-colored growths in spring. Long catkins drape the branches of many of these attractive trees. Some species and their hybrids, however, especially the balsam poplars, are susceptible to canker, a disease that causes branches to die back and crack, oozing a bacterial slime. Black poplars, including the Lombardy poplar (Populus nigra *'Italica'*), *are very prone to this.*

P. alba (White poplar) A large, suckering tree whose leaves have white-woolly undersides, particularly noticeable in breezy weather. The leaves are variable in shape, some irregularly lobed and others larger and distinctly three- to five-lobed like a maple; they turn yellow or reddish in fall. The smooth, grayish white bark is also attractive. It is an excellent tree for exposed locations, especially in coastal areas. Europe and Asia.

Zone 3 US, 3 Can.

***P. a.* 'Pyramidalis'** (Bolleana poplar) A large tree with erect branches. It resembles *P. nigra* 'Italica', but it is slightly broader and more resistant to canker. In cultivation 1841.

Zone 3 US, 3 Can.

Populus alba 'Richardii'

***P. a.* 'Raket'** A very narrow tree with upright branches. Raised before 1956 in Holland.
Zone 3 US, 3 Can.

***P. a.* 'Richardii'** (Richard's white poplar) A smaller-growing, less vigorous tree or large shrub with bright golden yellow leaves that are white on their undersides. A delightful form and very effective from a distance. In cultivation 1910.
Zone 3 US, 3 Can.

***P.* 'Balsam Spire'** A large, narrow, female poplar, extremely fast growing, with white-backed leaves and pleasantly aromatic buds in spring.
Zone 4 US, 4 Can. 🏆

Populus balsamifera

P. balsamifera (Balsam poplar) A very hardy large tree with erect branches, grown mainly for the balsam aroma of its unfolding leaves. Its buds are large and sticky. North America. Introduced before 1689.
Zone 1 US, 1 Can.

P.* × *canadensis (Canada poplar) A large group of vigorous hybrids, also known collectively as the hybrid black poplars. The following are recommended.
Zone 3 US, 2b Can.

***P.* × *c.* 'Eugenei'** (Carolina poplar) A large, narrow, male tree with short, ascending branches and coppery young leaves.
Zone 3 US, 2b Can.

Populus x canadensis 'Robusta'

***P.* × *c.* 'Robusta'** A large, vigorous, male tree with an open crown and a straight bole all the way up. The young leaves are an attractive coppery red. Raised 1895 in France.
Zone 3 US, 2b Can.

***P.* × *c.* 'Serotina Aurea'** (Golden poplar) A large tree with leaves clear golden yellow in spring and early summer, becoming yellowish green and then golden yellow in autumn.
Zone 3 US, 2b Can. 🏆

***P.* × *candicans* 'Aurora'** A highly variegated form of the Ontario poplar. It is a medium-sized tree with broad, ovate leaves that are cream well into late summer and often pink-tinged before turning green. It should be pruned back hard in late winter. *(See photo on p.458.)* Zone 4 US, 4 Can.

Populus × *canadensis* 'Serotina Aurea'

P.* × *canescens (Gray poplar) A medium-sized to large suckering tree that sometimes forms clumps. Mature specimens develop an attractive creamy gray trunk. The leaves are variable in shape, being rounded or triangular, and may turn yellow and sometimes red in fall. It bears woolly, crimson male catkins up to 4 in (10 cm). Europe.
Zone 2 US, 2 Can.

***P.* × *c.* 'Tower'** As its name suggests, this is a very narrow form. It is resistant to canker, does not sucker, and is almost seedless.
Zone 2 US, 2 Can.

P. deltoides (Eastern poplar, cottonwood) This large tree has an open, spreading form when mature. It tends to shed twigs freely in storms, and the cottony seeds cover the ground in white. E North America.
Zone 3 US, 3 Can.

***P. d.* 'Siouxland'** A fast-growing male selection that is cotton-free. It is more upright than the species but subject to canker once well established. Introduced by South Dakota State University.
Zone 3 US, 3 Can.

P. nigra (Black poplar) A large, heavy-branched tree with a characteristically burred trunk. The leaves are slender-pointed and bright shining green. Europe and W Asia.
Zone 3 US, 3 Can.

***P. n.* 'Italica'** (Lombardy poplar) A fast-

Populus × *candicans* 'Aurora'

growing but short-lived tree that makes a tall, narrow column with close, erect branches. Because older trees are so prone to canker, it should be grown only as a temporary screen and removed when still young. Introduced 1758.
Zone 4 US, 4 Can. 🏆

***P. n.* 'Lombardy Gold'** A striking tree

Populus nigra 'Italica'

with golden yellow foliage, discovered as a sport on a mature Lombardy poplar in 1974. By 1990 it had reached more than 40 ft (12 m) at RHS Wisley, England.
Zone 4 US, 4 Can.

***P. n.* 'Thevestina'** A hardier form that is not quite as narrow in shape. The bark becomes almost white as it matures. Introduced 1903.
Zone 3 US, 2b Can.

***P.* 'Northwest'** A hybrid poplar that was selected for its rapid growth and disease resistance. It makes a large tree at maturity.
Zone 2 US, 2 Can.

***P. tremula* 'Erecta'** (Swedish aspen) A good upright tree with a narrow growth habit that should be used instead of the disease-prone Lombardy poplar. Discovered 1911 in a Swedish forest.
Zone 2 US, 2 Can.

***P. t.* 'Pendula'** (Weeping aspen) This is one of the most effective small weeping trees. It is especially attractive in late winter, when it bears an abundance of long, purplish gray, male catkins.
Zone 2 US, 2 Can

Populus tremula 'Pendula'

P. tremuloides (Quaking aspen) Fast growing, this species reaches a height of 40 ft (12 m) but is relatively short lived. The small leaves move in the slightest breeze and turn yellow in fall. North America from Labrador to Alaska and south to Mexico.
Zone 1 US, 1 Can.

P. trichocarpa (Black cottonwood) The fastest- and tallest-growing balsam poplar, reaching a height of over 100 ft (30 m) and up to twice that in the wild. The bark of young trees peels. The buds are large and sticky, and the leathery, dark green leaves are paler and net-veined beneath. They are strongly balsam scented as they unfold and turn a rich yellow in fall. W North America. Introduced 1892.
Zone 6 US, 7 Can.

Potentilla *Rosaceae*

A large genus consisting of about 500 species, most of which are herbaceous and natives of north-temperate regions. The shrubby potentillas are very hardy, dwarf to medium-sized deciduous shrubs that thrive in any soil (although soil that is too rich will tend to promote growth at the expense of flowers). The flowers are like small single roses and are displayed over a long season that begins in late spring and early summer and in some forms lasts well into late fall. Although they are shade tolerant, they should be grown in full sun for the best results, with the exception of those with red, pink, or orange flowers, which tend to fade, sometimes badly, in hot sun. Species with flowers of these colors are much better when shaded during the hottest part of the day.

Pruning consists of removing weak or very old growth at soil level and cutting back the strongest growths by about one-third. Really old bushes can be pruned for renewal by being cut back hard, and all pruning should be done in spring.

All the cultivars are now considered to belong to one species, P. fruticosa.

***P.* 'Abbotswood'** A dwarf, spreading shrub with dark foliage and white flowers that are plentifully and continuously produced.
Zone 1 US, 1 Can. 🏆

Potentilla 'Abbotswood'

***P.* 'Abbotswood Silver'** A sport of the above with the leaflets narrowly margined with cream. Nonvariegated shoots should be pruned to prevent reversion to green.
Zone 3 US, 2b Can.

***P.* 'Beesii'** A delightful dwarf shrub that displays its golden flowers in mounds of silvery, hairy foliage.
Zone 3 US, 2b Can. 🏆

***P.* 'Coronation Triumph'** A neat bush with light yellow flowers that have narrow petals. Originated 1950 at Indian Head, Saskatchewan.
Zone 3 US, 2b Can.

***P.* 'Dart's Golddigger'** A dense, compact, dwarf shrub with light gray-green foliage and large, butter yellow flowers. In cultivation 1970.
Zone 3 US, 3 Can.

***P.* 'Daydawn'** A small shrub with flowers of an unusual shade of peach-pink suffused with cream. A sport of 'Tangerine' and best in a little shade.
Zone 3 US, 3 Can. 🏆

***P.* 'Eastleigh Cream'** A small, dense shrub that spreads to form a low mound. The leaves are green and the flowers cream and 1 in (2.5 cm) across. Raised 1969 at Hillier Nurseries at Eastleigh, England.
Zone 3 US, 3 Can.

***P.* 'Elizabeth'** A hybrid that makes a dome-shaped bush 3 × 4 ft (1 × 1.2 m), studded from late spring to early fall with large, rich canary yellow flowers. Raised 1950 at Hillier Nurseries.
Zone 3 US, 3 Can. 🏆

***P.* 'Farreri'** See *P.* 'Gold Drop'.

***P.* 'Floppy Disc'** A small shrub with semi-double pink flowers. Introduced by Liss Forest Nurseries.
Zone 3 US, 3 Can.

***P.* 'Gold Drop'** A dwarf, compact shrub with small, neat leaves and small, bright golden yellow flowers. It is often grown wrongly under the name *P.* 'Farreri'. In cultivation 1953.
Zone 2 US, 2 Can.

***P.* 'Goldfinger'** A dwarf, compact shrub with pinkish shoots and blue-green leaves, usually with five leaflets. It has an abundance of large, richly golden yellow flowers. Raised c. 1970 in Holland.
Zone 3 US, 2b Can. 🏆

***P.* 'Goldstar'** An upright shrub, to 32 in (80 cm), with very large, deep yellow flowers up to 2 in (5 cm) across, borne over a long period. In cultivation 1976.
Zone 3 US, 3 Can.

***P.* 'Hopley's Orange'** A dwarf, spreading shrub with bright orange flowers.
Zone 3 US, 3 Can.

***P.* 'Jackman's Variety'** A shrub of up to 5 ft (1.5 m). It has strong, erect growth; sage green leaves; and dense clusters of large, canary yellow flowers.
Zone 3 US, 3 Can.

***P.* 'Katherine Dykes'** A shrub up to 6½ ft (2 m), with silvery foliage and primrose yellow flowers in summer. In cultivation 1925.
Zone 2 US, 2 Can. 🏆

***P.* 'Klondike'** A first-rate dwarf shrub, similar to 'Gold Drop' but with larger flowers. In culitvation 1950.
Zone 3 US, 2b Can. 🏆

***P.* 'Longacre'** This is a dense, dwarf, mat-forming shrub that bears large, bright, almost sulphur yellow flowers. In cultivation 1956.
Zone 3 US, 3 Can. 🏆

Potentilla 'Katherine Dykes'

***P.* 'Maanelys'**, syn. *P.* 'Moonlight' A small shrub with a continuous succession of soft yellow flowers from late spring to late fall. Raised 1950 in Scandinavia.
Zone 3 US, 3 Can. 🏆

***P.* 'McKay's White'** A more upright shrub to 4 ft (1.2 m), with creamy white flowers freely produced. Introduced by McKay Nursery, Wisconsin.
Zone 3 US, 3 Can.

***P.* 'Moonlight'** See *P.* 'Maanelys'.

***P.* 'Pretty Polly'** A low, spreading shrub with medium-sized, pale pink flowers.
Zone 3 US, 3 Can.

***P.* 'Primrose Beauty'** A small, spreading, free-flowering shrub with arching branches, gray-green foliage, and primrose yellow flowers with deeper yellow centers.
Zone 3 US, 3 Can. 🏆

***P.* 'Princess'** A compact, dwarf shrub of spreading habit, bearing flowers of a delicate pale pink with yellow centers and on some occasions a few extra petals.
Zone 3 US, 3 Can.

***P.* 'Red Ace'** A compact, dwarf shrub forming a dense mound of bright green foliage, the leaves usually having five narrow leaflets. The flowers are bright orange-red with cream on the backs of the petals. Unless it is grown in partial shade, the flowers revert to yellow. In cultivation 1973.
Zone 3 US, 3 Can.

P. 'Red Robin' A low, spreading shrub with red flowers, slightly deeper than those of 'Red Ace'.
Zone 2 US, 2 Can.

P. 'Royal Flush' A seedling of 'Red Ace' with deep pink flowers. In cultivation 1980.
Zone 3 US, 3 Can.

P. 'Snowbird' A fairly new introduction, growing 4 ft (1.2 m) tall, that has rapidly become popular because of its free-flowering habit. The double white flowers are produced from early summer well into fall. Introduced by the University of Manitoba.
Zone 3 US, 2b Can.

P. 'Sunset' A small shrub with flowers that vary between deep orange and brick red. It is a sport of 'Tangerine' and is best grown in part shade.
Zone 3 US, 2b Can.

P. 'Tangerine' A dwarf, wide-spreading shrub that forms a dense mound. The color of the flowers is a pale coppery yellow, which is developed best on plants growing in part shade.
Zone 3 US, 3 Can. 🏆

P. 'Tilford Cream' A dense, dwarf bush, broader than it is tall, with rich green foliage and large, creamy flowers about 1¼ in (3.5 cm) across.
Zone 3 US, 3 Can. 🏆

Potentilla 'Sunset'

P. 'Vilmoriniana' A splendid shrub with erect branches, growing to 6½ ft (2 m). It has very silvery leaves and cream flowers and is the best tall, erect potentilla.
Zone 3 US, 3 Can.

P. 'Yellow Bird' An upright shrub that reaches about 4 ft (1.2 m) and bears a profusion of double, bright yellow flowers with 10–12 petals. Introduced by the University of Manitoba.
Zone 3 US, 2b Can.

Potentilla 'Tilford Cream'

P. 'Yellow Gem' A smaller shrub that forms a low mound of soft yellow flowers.
Zone 2 US, 2 Can.

Prosopis *Leguminosae*
Mesquite

A genus of more than 40 spiny deciduous trees or shrubs native to North America, Southwest Asia, and Africa. The drought-tolerant plants make good screens, windbreaks, and shade trees in arid areas. They need deep soil and irrigation when young to develop into trees; otherwise they remain shrubs.

P. glandulosa (Honey mesquite) A tough-wooded large shrub or small tree with a wide-spreading crown. It has feathery, bright green leaves and tiny, fragrant, yellow-green flowers in spring and summer that are very attractive to bees. SW United States, Mexico.
Zone 7 US, 8 Can.

Prostanthera *Labiatae*
Mint bush

A genus of about 50 species of small to medium-sized, free-flowering, aromatic evergreen shrubs native to Australasia. Established specimens are best pruned back hard immediately after flowering.

P. 'Chelsea Pink' A small shrub, similar to *P. rotundifolia*. It has aromatic, gray-green leaves that are wedge shaped at the base and pale pink flowers with purple anthers.
Zone 9 US

Prostanthera cuneata

P. cuneata A dwarf spreading shrub with small, dark, glossy green leaves. The late spring flowers are white, flushed with lilac. Australia, Tasmania. In cultivation 1886.
Zone 9 US 🏆

P. lasianthos An erect, medium-sized to large shrub with lanceolate leaves and purple-tinted white flowers in spring. Australia, Tasmania. In cultivation 1808.
Zone 9 US

P. melissifolia* var. *parvifolia A small shrub with lilac flowers almost 1 in (2.5 cm) across, borne freely in early summer.
Zone 9 US

Prostanthera rotundifolia

P. rotundifolia A beautiful, small to medium-sized, dense shrub with tiny, rounded leaves. The attractive pink-purple flowers cover the branches in summer, and their massed effect is stunning.
Zone 9 US 🏆

PRUNUS

Rosaceae

THIS LARGE GENUS, with more than 400 species, is of enormous agricultural and economic value for its fruits, providing us with cherries, plums, peaches, nectarines, apricots, and almonds. It is also the source of some of the most beautiful trees and shrubs for the garden, both evergreen and deciduous. Among the most prominent and best-known plants are the Japanese cherries, although many other members of the genus are equally ornamental and deserving of attention.

Not surprisingly, the genus is extremely diverse. It comprises handsome foliage shrubs, such as *P. laurocerasus,* and exquisite flowering trees, including *P.* 'Kanzan' and *P.* × *yedoensis*. There are erect dwarf shrubs, such as *P. tenella* 'Fire Hill', as well as gracefully weeping trees, among them *P. subhirtella* 'Pendula Rosea'. There are prostrate ground covers — like *P. pumila* var. *depressa* — and towering trees, such as *P. serotina.*

While many of the genus are appreciated for their dainty white or pink blossoms, some *Prunus* are valued more for their colorful foliage. *P. cerasifera* 'Pissardii' has dark red young foliage that soon colors to a deep purple, while *P. sargentii* bears bronze young leaves that turn orange and bright red in the fall. There are also *Prunus* with ornamental bark: the main attraction of *P. serrula,* for instance, is not its white flowers but its red-brown bark, which gleams like polished mahogany.

Even within a species there is remarkable variation. *P. laurocerasus* 'Otto Luyken', for instance, has a low, compact profile and narrow, glossy leaves, while *P. l.* 'Magnolifolia' is a tall, wide-spreading bush with leaves up to 12 in (30 cm) long.

CARE AND CULTIVATION

The deciduous *Prunus* tend to prefer a sunny location, and, indeed, the purple-leaved varieties need full sun to develop their foliage color. The evergreens, however, can take part shade, and some, like *P. l.* 'Otto Luyken' even tolerates the dry, deep shade under trees. They will generally grow in all types of moist, well-drained soil, and *P. lusitanica* can tolerate alkaline and shallow soils better than the others. *Prunus* benefit from deep, regular watering during dry spells and should be provided with an organic mulch year-round.

While *Prunus* are exceptionally beautiful and tempting to grow, it should be noted that these fast-growing plants are short-lived, usually lasting only about 20–30 years, even when well maintained. They are subject to a variety of disease and insect problems, including root rot, borers, and cankers. The problems can be especially serious or even fatal if the plants are under stress from poor cultural conditions, such as soil compaction, root disturbance, or drought.

Prunus spinosa

THE ORNAMENTAL CHERRIES

"Cherry blossom time" is one of the most beautiful periods of the year, wherever the flowering cherries are planted. The most celebrated of these are the Japanese Sato Zakura, the garden cherries that have been developed and cultivated for more than a thousand years. Extremely ornamental in appearance, varied in character, and easily grown, they are widely planted and are a major tourist attraction in many places. In Washington, D.C., for instance, the hundreds of flowering cherries around the Potomac Tidal Basin are among the capital's most celebrated features.

The Sato Zakura trees demonstrate a wide range of habits and characteristics. *P.* 'Amanogawa', for one, is as erect and columnar as a small Lombardy poplar, while 'Mount Fuji' has a flat head of horizontal branches. Flowers may be single, as with 'Tai Haku', the great white cherry whose blooms are noteworthy for their size and dazzling whiteness, or fully double and frilled, as with 'Ichiyo'. And between the two lies a variety of floral forms that contribute to the appeal of Japanese cherries.

As far as blossom color goes, the palette is not very diverse. But centuries of careful breeding has brought the subtle variations on a theme of white, pink, and soft rose to perfection. In many cases, the softly hued flowers are enhanced by the bronze, copper, or buff tones of the emerging young foliage. Later, when their spring performance is only a memory, the trees' fine autumn foliage color of yellow and tawny orange creates continuing interest.

The flowering season for Japanese cherries, which never seems to last long enough, spans roughly an eight-week period around midspring. Each cultivar occupies part of the season and can therefore be described as early, mid, or late.

The Sato Zakura, like other cherries, will grow in all types of well-drained soils. During the dormant season the buds may be damaged by squirrels, in which case it is advisable to use a repellent. They can also be nipped by frost, which may destroy the buds and ruin the spring show.

Pruning of any kind is seldom necessary. But if it is unavoidable, it should be done in late spring, after flowering, so that the cuts heal before winter.

Damage to the trees and their roots provides an entry point for diseases, and care should be taken with gardening chores, like mowing and raking, around the trees. They are vulnerable to canker, although not as much as the edible cherries are.

***P.* 'Accolade'** *(P. sargentii × P. subhirtella)* An outstanding cherry that grows to a small deciduous tree with spreading branches and semidouble pink flowers 1½ in (4 cm) across in pendulous clusters. It is very free-flowering in early to midspring.
Zone 6 US, 7 Can. 🏆

Prunus 'Accolade'

***P.* × *amygdalo-persica* 'Pollardii'** A hybrid between the peach and the almond. It is a beautiful small deciduous tree with larger, more richly pink flowers than the almond. They are single and borne in midspring. It is susceptible to peach leaf curl.
Zone 5 US, 6 Can.

Prunus × *amygdalo-persica* 'Pollardii'

***P. armeniaca* 'Ansu'** An ornamental form of the apricot that makes a small tree with purplish shoots and flowers that are flushed pink.
Zone 6 US, 7 Can.

***P. a.* 'Charles Abraham'** A form with red buds and long-lasting, deep pink, double flowers. Raised in China.
Zone 6 US, 7 Can.

Prunus avium 'Plena'

P. avium (Mazzard cherry) A medium-sized to large deciduous tree with smooth gray bark that turns mahogany-red, peels, and becomes fissured with age. The white, cup-shaped, single flowers are in clusters, open with the leaves in mid- to late spring, and last only a few days. The fruits are small, reddish purple, and shiny, and the fall foliage is crimson. Most of the sweet cherries are derived from this species. Europe, W Asia.
Zone 4 US, 4b Can. 🏆

***P. a.* 'Plena'** (Double mazzard cherry) One of the loveliest flowering trees, with branches covered in masses of drooping, white, double flowers. In cultivation 1700.
Zone 4 US, 4b Can.

P. besseyi (Western sand cherry) A small deciduous shrub with grayish green leaves that turn rusty purple in autumn. Clusters of tiny white single flowers are massed along the branches in late spring. The fruits, rounded and black with a purplish bloom, need warm summers to develop fully. C United States. Introduced 1892.
Zone 3 US, 2b Can.

P.* × *blireana (Blireana plum) A beautiful large deciduous shrub or small tree with metallic-coppery purple leaves and slightly fragrant, rose-pink, double flowers, over 1 in (2.5 cm) across, opening just before the leaves in midspring. Garden origin 1895.
Zone 5 US, 6 Can. 🏆

Prunus cerasifera

P. cerasifera (Cherry plum, myrobalan plum) A small deciduous tree with greenish young shoots. The myriad small single flowers crowd the twigs in early spring, occasionally earlier or later. Mature trees sometimes bear red cherry-plums. It is an excellent shrub for a dense hedge. In cultivation during the 16th century.
Zone 4 US, 4b Can.

***P. c.* 'Hessei'** A medium-sized, shrubby form with leaves that are pale green at first and then become bronze-purple with irregular creamy to yellowish or pink edges. The

Prunus cerasifera 'Hessei'

snow-white flowers crowd the branches toward midspring.
Zone 4 US, 4b Can.

Prunus cerasifera 'Nigra'

***P. c.* 'Newport'** The very early, pale pink flowers make this small tree distinctive. New foliage opens a light purple and darkens as summer progresses. The fruits are dull purple and thus are hard to find among the leaves. This is considered by many to be the hardiest form and is probably the best to try at the limits of its hardiness. Introduced 1923 by the University of Minnesota.
Zone 4 US, 4b Can.

***P. c.* 'Nigra'** (Black myrobalan plum) An effective small tree, flowering prolifically in early to midspring with pink blossoms that fade to blush. The leaves and stems are blackish purple. It is an excellent hedge plant. In cultivation 1916.
Zone 4 US, 4b Can. 🏆

***P. c.* 'Pissardii'** (Purple-leaved plum) A form with dark red young foliage that turns

Prunus cerasifera 'Pissardii'

deep purple. It flowers profusely in midspring, with blossoms that open white from pink buds. The purple fruits are produced only occasionally. An excellent hedge plant.
Zone 4 US, 4b Can.

Prunus cerasus 'Rhexii'

***P. c.* 'Thundercloud'** This variety and 'Newport' are by far the most popular forms. The small tree has fragrant, single, midpink flowers that open before the leaves, which are purple and hold their color until late summer. Introduced 1937.
Zone 4 US, 4b Can.

***P. cerasus* 'Rhexii'** A popular form of the sour cherry, this small, bushy deciduous tree has double white flowers 1–1½ in (2.5–4 cm) across in mid- to late spring. In cultivation since the 16th century.
Zone 4 US, 4b Can.

P. × cistena (Purple-leaf sand cherry) A beautiful deciduous shrub up to 6½ ft (2 m) high, with red leaves and single white flowers in midspring and black-purple fruits. An excellent hedge plant. Garden origin before 1910 in South Dakota.
Zone 3 US, 3 Can.

Prunus dulcis

P. dulcis (Common almond) One of the best spring-flowering trees. It is small and has lance-shaped, long-pointed, finely toothed deciduous leaves and single pink flowers, 1–2 in (2.5–5 cm) across, in early to midspring. Native from N Africa to W Asia but extensively grown and naturalized in the Mediterranean region. In cultivation since the 16th century or earlier.
Zone 7 US, 8 Can.

***P. d.* 'Macrocarpa'** A small tree with very pale pink or white flowers up to 2 in (5 cm) across. It is one of the best of the edible forms and has large fruits.
Zone 7 US, 8 Can.

***P. glandulosa* 'Alba Plena'** (White dwarf flowering almond) A very beautiful small deciduous shrub. Each shoot is weighed down in midspring with a wealth of double

Prunus glandulosa 'Alba Plena'

white flowers up to $1^{1}/_{2}$ in (4 cm) in diameter. It grows best in a warm, sunny location. In cultivation 1852.
Zone 4 US, 5 Can. 🏆

***P. g.* 'Sinensis'** (Pink dwarf flowering almond) A form with double, bright pink flowers. In cultivation 1774.
Zone 4 US, 5 Can. 🏆

***P.* 'Hally Jolivette'** A large deciduous shrub or small, graceful tree. Its slender, willowy stems are covered in spring with small, semidouble, blush-white flowers that persist over a long period. Raised by Dr. Karl Sax at the Arnold Arboretum, Boston, Mass., and named after his wife.
Zone 5 US, 6 Can.

***P.* 'Hillieri'** A hybrid of *P. sargentii* raised before 1928 at the Hillier Nurseries. The original is now a broad-crowned deciduous tree more than 33 ft (10 m) high, and in spring its single flowers give the impression of a soft pink cloud. In favorable locations the fall color is beautiful.
Zone 6 US, 7 Can.

***P.* × *hillieri* 'Spire'** See *P.* 'Spire'.

P. incisa (Fuji cherry) A lovely deciduous species, generally shrubby but occasionally a small tree, blooming very profusely in early spring. The leaves are small and are beautifully colored in autumn, and the single flowers are small and white, tinged with pink in bud and appearing pink at a distance. The small purple-black fruits are seldom produced. Japan. In cultivation 1910.
Zone 6 US, 7 Can.

***P. i.* 'Kojo Nomai'** A slow-growing small shrub with pale pink flowers.
Zone 6 US, 7 Can.

Prunus incisa

***P. i.* 'Praecox'** A winter-flowering shrub or small tree with white flowers, opening from pale pink buds.
Zone 6 US, 7 Can. 🏆

Prunus incisa 'Praecox'

P. jamasakura, syn. *P. serrulata* var. *spontanea* (Hill cherry) A medium-sized, spreading deciduous tree with bronze young foliage and single white or pink flowers borne in mid- to late spring. It is extremely variable, with the best forms having coppery red young foliage and pure white flowers. The fruits are dark purplish crimson, and the leaves have good fall color. Japan. Introduced c. 1914.
Zone 5 US, 6 Can.

P. japonica (Chinese bush cherry) A small, very hardy shrub that has small, white or pale pink, single flowers and dark red fruits. C China to Korea, Japan.
Zone 2 US, 2 Can.

***P.* 'Kursar'** A beautiful small deciduous tree. The single flowers, though small, are

Prunus 'Kursar'

rich deep pink and are produced in great profusion toward midspring with or just before the appearance of the reddish bronze young leaves. Raised by Capt. Collingwood Ingram in England.
Zone 6 US, 7 Can. 🏆

P. laurocerasus (Cherry laurel) A vigorous, wide-spreading evergreen shrub or

Prunus laurocerasus

small tree to about 20 ft (6 m) or more high and wide. The leaves are large, leathery, and dark, lustrous green. It is often grown as a screen or hedge, but it is also attractive in midspring, when it has erect clusters of small, single white flowers that are followed by cherrylike fruits, red at first and finally purple-black. It is very tolerant of shade and of water dripping from overhanging trees. Pruning can be done in either spring or late summer, and old specimens or hedges that have grown too large can be cut back hard into the old wood in spring. Harmful if eaten. E Europe, Asia Minor.

Introduced 1576. Zone 6 US, 7 Can.

P. l. 'Castlewellan' See *P. l.* 'Marbled White'.

P. l. 'Cherry Brandy' A dense small shrub that makes a low mound only 2 ft (60 cm) high. The bronze young foliage later turns green.
Zone 6 US, 7 Can.

P. l. 'Green Carpet' A dwarf form that grows wide and flat and has narrow, dark green leaves. It is excellent for growing as a ground cover. The correct name is probably 'Grüner Teppich'.
Zone 6 US, 7 Can.

P. l. 'Magnoliifolia' This is an imposing evergreen with glossy leaves that are as much as 12 in (30 cm) long and 4 in (10 cm) wide, making it the largest-leaved laurel. In cultivation 1869.
Zone 6 US, 7 Can.

P. l. 'Marbled White', syn. *P. l.* 'Castlewellan' A slow-growing, dense, broadly conical bush that eventually becomes quite large. The leaves are green and gray-green, marbled with white or gray, and variable in shape. It was originally grown as 'Variegata'. In cultivation 1811.
Zone 6 US, 7 Can.

Prunus laurocerasus 'Marbled White'

P. l. 'Mischeana' A very ornamental plant, slowly forming a dense, rather flat-topped mound of dark, lustrous green, oblong leaves. It makes a fine medium-sized lawn specimen and is attractive when the short racemes of white flowers cover the stems in spring. In cultivation 1898.
Zone 6 US, 7 Can.

P. l. 'Mount Vernon' A slow-growing, dwarf, shrubby laurel that makes a dense mound about 12 in (30 cm) high covered with glossy, dark green leaves.
Zone 6 US, 7 Can.

P. l. 'Otto Luyken' A low, compact shrub with erect stems and narrow, shining green leaves. It is outstanding for both its foliage and its white flowers and is tolerant of deep shade. Raised 1940. Zone 6 US, 7 Can.
🏆

Prunus laurocerasus 'Mount Vernon'

P. l. 'Reynvaanii' A small, slow-growing, compact form with stiff branches and white flowers. In cultivation 1913.
Zone 6 US, 7 Can.

P. l. 'Rotundifolia' A bushy form, excellent for hedges. The leaves are half as broad as long. In cultivation 1865.
Zone 6 US, 7 Can.

P. l. 'Schipkaensis' (Shipka cherry laurel) A free-flowering, narrow-leaved form with a spreading habit. It is hardier than the species and has smaller leaves. Bulgaria. Introduced 1888.
Zone 6 US, 7 Can.

P. l. 'Zabeliana' A low, horizontally branched form with long, narrow, willow-like leaves and profusely borne flowers. It reaches 4–5 ft (1.2–1.5 m) high and twice as wide and is an excellent ground cover, even in shade. In cultivation 1898.
Zone 6 US, 7 Can.

Prunus laurocerasus 'Otto Luyken'

Prunus laurocerasus 'Zabeliana'

Prunus lusitanica

P. lusitanica (Portugual cherry laurel) A large evergreen shrub or small to medium-sized tree that becomes a beautiful specimen when allowed to develop naturally. It can also be clipped as a hedge. The ovate leaves are dark green with reddish stalks, and the small, white, hawthorn-scented single flowers are borne in long racemes in early summer. The fruits are small and red, gradually turning dark purple. It is not as hardy as *P. laurocerasus* but is a better choice for planting in alkaline or very shallow soil. Spain, Portugal. Introduced 1648.
Zone 7 US, 8 Can. 🏆

P. l.* subsp. *azorica (Azores cherry laurel) A magnificent, evergreen large shrub or small tree. The bright green leaves are thicker and larger than those of the species. They are reddish when unfolding and have reddish stalks. Azores. Introduced 1860.
Zone 7 US, 8 Can. 🏆

***P. l.* 'Myrtifolia'** A dense cone up to 16 ft (5 m) tall, with polished, dark green leaves

Prunus lusitanica subsp. *azorica*

that are smaller and neater than those of the type. In cultivation 1892.
Zone 7 US, 8 Can.

***P. l.* 'Variegata'** An attractive medium-sized to large shrub with leaves margined with white, sometimes pink-flushed in winter. In cultivation 1865.
Zone 7 US, 8 Can.

Prunus lusitanica 'Myrtifolia'

Prunus lusitanica 'Variegata'

P. maackii (Amur chokecherry) A popular small deciduous tree with amber-colored, flaking bark. It is pyramidal when young, becoming more rounded with age. The small, single white flowers are borne in clusters on the previous year's shoots in mid-spring. Korea, Manchuria.
Zone 3 US, 2b Can.

P. mume (Japanese apricot) A delightful small deciduous tree with green young shoots and single, almond-scented, pink flowers that pale as they age. They appear in early spring. China, Korea, extensively cultivated in Japan. Introduced 1844.
Zone 4 US, 5b Can.

***P. m.* 'Alboplena'** A form with semidouble white flowers.
Zone 4 US, 5b Can.

***P. m.* 'Alphandii'**, syn. *P. m.* 'Flore Pleno' A beautiful form with double pink flowers. In cultivation 1902.
Zone 4 US, 5b Can.

***P. m.* 'Beni-shidare'** A striking form with fragrant, double, cup-shaped, rose-pink flowers, darker in bud and paling with age.
Zone 4 US, 5b Can.

Prunus mume 'Beni-shidare'

***P. m.* 'Flore Pleno'** See *P. m.* 'Alphandii'.

***P. m.* 'Omoi-no-mama'** A charming small tree with semidouble, cup-shaped, usually white flowers. Occasionally petals and sometimes whole flowers are pink.
Zone 4 US, 5b Can.

***P. nipponica* var. *kurilensis* 'Ruby'** A bushy, slow-growing, deciduous large shrub or small tree with erect branches that bear a mass of pale pink, single flowers with noticeably purplish red calyxes toward mid-

spring. In cultivation 1958.
Zone 4 US, 5 Can.

P. 'Okame' A lovely small deciduous tree with masses of carmine-rose single flowers opening throughout early spring. The foliage is attractively colored in fall.
Zone 7 US, 8 Can. 🏆

Prunus 'Okame'

P. padus (European bird cherry) A deciduous small to medium-sized tree, widely distributed in the Northern Hemisphere. It bears abundant white, almond-scented, single flowers in 3–6 in (7.5–15 cm) drooping racemes in late spring after the leaves; the leaves are among the first to emerge in

Prunus padus

spring. The small black fruits in summer are bitter. Europe, N Asia to Japan.
Zone 2 US, 2 Can.

P. p. 'Albertii' A vigorous, very free-flowering form. In cultivation 1902.
Zone 2 US, 2 Can.

P. p. 'Colorata' A remarkable tree with

Prunus padus 'Albertii'

dark purplish shoots, coppery purple young foliage, and pale pink flowers. The leaves in summer are somber green with purple-

Prunus padus 'Colorata'

tinged veins and undersurfaces. 'Purple Queen' is very similar. Sweden.
Zone 2 US, 2 Can. 🏆

P. p. var. commutata (Mayday tree) While similar in habit to the species, this variety flowers and leafs out about three weeks earlier. E Asia. In cultivation c. 1880.
Zone 2 US, 2 Can.

P. p. 'Grandiflora' See *P. p.* 'Watereri'.

P. p. 'Plena' (Double European bird cherry) A form with large, long-lasting, double flowers.
Zone 2 US, 2 Can. 🏆

P. p. 'Watereri', syn. *P. p.* 'Grandiflora' A form with flower clusters up to 8 in (20 cm) long. In cultivation 1914.
Zone 2 US, 2 Can. 🏆

P. 'Pandora' A small deciduous tree with ascending branches generously covered

Prunus padus 'Watereri'

with pale shell pink, single flowers 1 in (2.5 cm) across in early spring or later. The leaves are bronze-red when unfolding and often richly colored in fall.
Zone 6 US, 7 Can. 🏆

P. pensylvanica (Pin cherry) A comparatively small tree with small spikes of white flowers in spring and clusters of sour, bright

Prunus 'Pandora'

red fruits in summer. Fall foliage is red. E and C North America.
Zone 1 US, 1 Can.

Prunus persica 'Klara Mayer'

***P. persica* 'Klara Mayer'** A large shrub or small tree with double, peach-pink flowers; the best double peach for general planting. In cultivation 1890.
Zone 5 US, 6 Can.

***P. p.* 'Peppermint Stick'** A form with double, white flowers striped with pink. Introduced 1933 in San Jose, California.
Zone 5 US, 6 Can.

***P.* 'Pink Shell'** One of the loveliest cherries in the genus. It is a small, elegant deciduous tree whose slender, spreading branches droop beneath a profusion of cup-shaped, shell pink, single blossoms that blend beautifully with the pale green emerging leaves in midspring.
Zone 6? US, 7? Can. 🏆

P. prostrata (Rock cherry) A dwarf, spreading deciduous shrub that usually forms a low, gnarled mound up to 28 in (70 cm) high by 6½ ft (2 m) wide in 25 years. The bright pink, single flowers are borne all along the wiry stems in midspring. SE Europe, Mediterranean region, W Asia. Introduced 1802.
Zone 6 US, 7 Can.

P. pumila* var. *depressa A prostrate deciduous form of the sand cherry (see also *P. besseyi*), less than 6 in (15 cm) high. It is a good ground cover and is studded with white single flowers in late spring. United States. Introduced 1864.
Zone 4 US, 5 Can.

P. sargentii (Sargent cherry) Considered by many people to be the loveliest cherry, this is a round-headed, small deciduous tree with chestnut brown bark and bronze-red young foliage. The single pink flowers open in early spring, and the small, almost black fruits ripen in midsummer. It is one of the first trees to color in fall, when its leaves turn orange and crimson. Japan, Korea. Introduced 1890. Zone 4 US, 5b Can.
🏆

Prunus pumila var. *depressa*

Prunus sargentii

Prunus sargentii 'Rancho'

***P. s.* 'Rancho'** A small to medium-sized tree with a narrowly upright habit. Raised before 1962 in the United States.
Zone 4 US, 5 Can.

P. serotina (Black cherry) A large deciduous tree with gracefully drooping branches and lustrous green leaves. It bears small white flowers in late spring and red cherries that turn black. E and C North America.
Zone 4 US, 5 Can.

Prunus serrula

P. serrula A small but vigorous deciduous tree whose main attraction is its polished, red-brown, mahogany-like new bark. The leaves are narrow and willowlike, and the small, white, single flowers are produced at the same time as the leaves toward late spring. The small, egg-shaped fruits are bright red. W China. Introduced 1908 by Ernest Wilson.
Zone 6 US, 7 Can. 🏆

Prunus serrulata var. *hupehensis*

P. serrulata* var. *hupehensis (Chinese hill cherry) This is considered to be the prototype of the cultivated double white cherry. It is a medium-sized deciduous tree with ascending branches and clusters of white or blush flowers in mid- to late spring. The young leaves are bronze, and the fall foliage is attractively colored. C China. Introduced 1900 by Ernest Wilson.
Zone 6 US, 7 Can.

P. s.* var. *spontanea See *P. jamasakura*.

Prunus 'Shosar'

***P.* 'Shosar'** A vigorous, somewhat fastigiate, medium-sized deciduous tree with single, clear pink flowers early in the season. It usually has good fall color.
Zone 8 US, 9 Can.

***P.* 'Snow Fountains'®** A very versatile plant that is available in forms ranging from a prostrate ground cover to a weeping tree. The single white flowers are produced freely, and the foliage turns orange to red in fall. Introduced by Lake County Nursery, Ohio.
Zone 4 US, 5 Can.

***P.* 'Snow Goose'** A small deciduous tree with ascending branches covered densely in midspring with pure white, single flowers.
Zone 5 US, 6 Can.

P. spinosa (Blackthorn, sloe) A deciduous large, dense shrub or small, bushy tree with dark spiny branches, crowded in early spring with small, white, single flowers. The fruits are like small damson plums, blue-bloomy at first and shiny black later. Its fruits are used in preserves and for making sloe gin. Europe, N Africa, W Asia.
Zone 4 US, 5b Can.

Prunus 'Snow Goose'

Prunus spinosa

***P. s.* 'Purpurea'** A neat, compact bush with rich purple leaves.
Zone 4 US, 5b Can.

***P.* 'Spire'**, syn. *P.* × *hillieri* 'Spire' A vase-shaped tree reaching a height of 33 ft (10 m) and, eventually, a width of 23 ft (7 m). The single flowers, borne in midspring, are soft pink, and the leaves have rich red fall color.
Zone 6 US, 7 Can.

P. subhirtella (Higan cherry) A small to medium-sized deciduous tree with a profusion of small, pale pink, single flowers in early spring. It includes among its forms some of the most delightful early-spring-flowering trees, and in a good year most of these also produce attractive fall color. Unknown in the wild and probably of hybrid origin. Introduced 1894.
Zone 5 US, 6 Can.

***P. s.* 'Autumnalis'** (Autumn cherry) A small tree up to 24 ft (7.5 m), with semidouble white flowers at intervals from late fall to early spring. It may bloom in winter if the weather is mild; in cold winters, it may not bloom until spring. The flowers are effective over a long period. In cultivation 1900.
Zone 6 US, 7 Can.

***P. s.* 'Autumnalis Rosea'** A small tree similar in many ways to 'Autumnalis' but with blush pink flowers. *(See photo on p.470.)*
Zone 6 US, 7 Can.

Prunus 'Spire' in autumn

Prunus subhirtella 'Autumnalis Rosea'

P. s. **'Fukubana'** This very striking small tree, with its profusion of semidouble rose-pink flowers, is the most colorful of this group, collectively known as the spring cherries. Introduced 1927 from California by Capt. Collingwood Ingram.

Zone 6 US, 7 Can. 🏆

P. s. **'Pendula'** A lovely, slender, very showy, weeping tree of medium size. It bears numerous small blush flowers on gracefully pendent branches in midspring. Introduced 1862.

Zone 6 US, 7 Can.

P. s. **'Pendula Plena Rosea'** A weeping shrub or small tree with semidouble flowers like rosettes. They are rose colored and similar to those of 'Fukubana' but slightly paler. Introduced 1928 by Capt. Collingwood Ingram.

Zone 6 US, 7 Can.

P. s. **'Pendula Rosea'** (Weeping spring cherry) A small, weeping, mushroom-shaped tree. The flowers are rich pink in

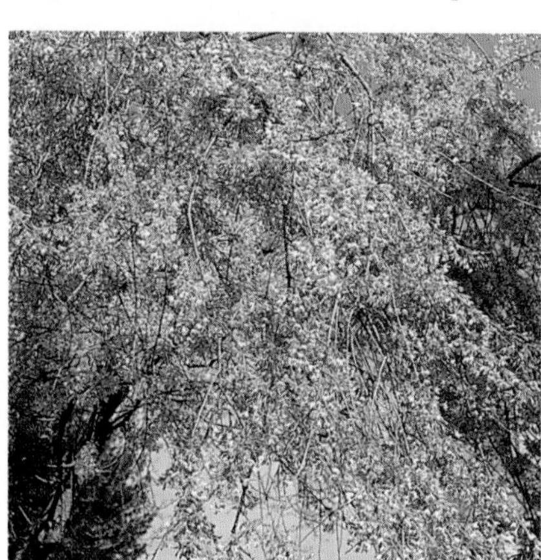

Prunus subhirtella 'Pendula Rosea'

bud and become pale blush, covering the graceful, drooping branches. It is often grown as *P. subhirtella* 'Pendula', a name that properly applies to the form with less conspicuous flowers.

Zone 6 US, 7 Can. 🏆

Prunus subhirtella 'Pendula Rubra'

P. s. **'Pendula Rubra'** A small tree with deep rose flowers, carmine in bud, borne all along the long, pendulous branches.

Zone 6 US, 7 Can. 🏆

Prunus subhirtella 'Stellata'

P. s. **'Stellata'** A very beautiful form with larger, clear pink, star-shaped spring flowers in crowded clusters along the branches. Introduced c. 1955.

Zone 6 US, 7 Can.

P. tenella **'Fire Hill'** (Dwarf Russian almond) An outstanding small deciduous shrub with erect stems covered in brilliant rose-red, single flowers in midspring; perhaps the best dwarf almond.

Zone 2 US, 2 Can. 🏆

Prunus tenella 'Fire Hill'

Prunus triloba 'Multiplex'

P. tomentosa (Nanking cherry, Manchu cherry) A tall shrub with reddish brown, exfoliating bark. The pink flowers appear in spring, and the red fruits are edible. It makes a good specimen plant 10 ft (3 m) tall but can also be clipped to a 3 ft (90 cm) hedge. China, Japan. Introduced 1870.

Zone 2 US, 2 Can.

P. triloba **'Multiplex'** A medium-sized to large deciduous shrub with small, coarsely toothed, three-lobed leaves. The flowers are large, double, rosette shaped, and clear rose-pink and are produced freely toward midspring. It makes a splendid wall shrub if the old flowering shoots are pruned back immediately after flowering. China. Introduced 1855 by Robert Fortune.

Zone 3 US, 2b Can. 🏆

P. **'Umineko'** A narrowly growing, upright, small deciduous tree with single white flowers that are produced with the leaves, which color beautifully in fall.

Zone 5 US, 6 Can.

Prunus 'Umineko'

***P. virginiana* 'Shubert'** A small, conical deciduous tree, a form of the chokecherry, with green young foliage that changes to reddish purple. It bears small, white, single flowers in late spring. In cultivation 1950.
Zone 2 US, 2 Can.

Prunus yedoensis

P. × yedoensis (Yoshino cherry, Tokyo cherry) A graceful, small to medium-sized, deciduous tree with arching branches. It bears a profusion of almond-scented, blushed, single flowers in spring. In 1912 about 900 of these trees were planted around the Tidal Basin in Washington, D.C. Japan, unknown in the wild. Introduced 1902.
Zone 6 US, 7 Can.

***P. × y.* 'Ivensii'** A small, vigorous, weeping tree with long, tortuous branches and long, slender, drooping branchlets that bear delicately fragrant, white blossoms in early to midspring. Raised 1925.
Zone 6 US, 7 Can.

Prunus × yedoensis 'Ivensii'

***P. × y.* 'Shidare Yoshino'** A small tree with long, elegant, arching branches that often weep to the ground and carry pale pink flowers in midspring.
Zone 6 US, 7 Can.

***P. × y.* 'Tsubame'** A small tree with slightly weeping, spreading branches and white flowers.
Zone 6 US, 7 Can.

The Sato Zakura — Japanese Cherries of Garden Origin

The flowering season of the Sato Zakura lasts from the latter part of early spring to the middle of late spring. The cherries are early, mid, or late within that season.

Prunus 'Amanogawa'

***P.* 'Amanogawa'** A small, narrowly columnar deciduous tree with strongly erect branches and dense, upright clusters of fragrant, semidouble, shell pink flowers. Mid to late.
Zone 5 US, 6 Can.

Prunus 'Asano'

***P.* 'Asano'** A small deciduous tree with ascending branches and dense clusters of deep pink, very double flowers. The young leaves are greenish bronze. It is in effect an upright form of 'Cheal's Weeping'. Mid. Introduced 1929 by Capt. Collingwood Ingram.
Zone 5 US, 6 Can.

***P.* 'Cheal's Weeping'** A small deciduous tree with arching or drooping branches, very attractive when covered with the clear deep pink, very double flowers. The young leaves are bronze-green and later become green and glossy. It is often wrongly referred to as 'Kiku-shidare Sakura'. Mid. *(See photo on p.472.)* Zone 5 US, 6 Can.

***P.* 'Choshu-hizakura'** A beautiful small deciduous tree with single, deep pink flowers and attractive purplish brown calyxes. The young leaves are reddish brown or coppery red. Mid. Often listed as 'Hisakura'.
Zone 5 US, 6 Can.

***P.* 'Fugenzo'** In some respects this small deciduous tree resembles 'Kanzan', but it is smaller and has a broader, flat-topped head. The flowers are large, double, rose-pink, and borne in drooping clusters, and the young leaves are coppery red. Very late.
Zone 5 US, 6 Can.

***P.* 'Hisakura'** See under 'Choshu-hizakura' and 'Kanzan'.

***P.* 'Hokusai'** A vigorous, wide-spreading, small deciduous tree. Its branches are hidden in spring by the generous clusters of large, semidouble, pale pink flowers. The leaves are brownish bronze when young, dark green when mature, and orange-red in fall. Mid.
Zone 5 US, 6 Can.

***P.* 'Ichiyo'** A beautiful small deciduous tree with ascending branches and double, shell pink flowers with a circular, frilled appearance, borne in long-stalked corymbs. The young leaves are bronze-green. Mid.
Zone 5 US, 6 Can. 🏆

Prunus 'Cheal's Weeping'

***P.* 'Jo-nioi'** A vigorous, spreading, small deciduous tree with single, white, deliciously scented blossoms covering the branches in spring, their white petals contrasting with the purple-brown sepals. The young leaves are pale golden brown. Mid. Introduced c. 1910.
Zone 5 US, 6 Can.

***P.* 'Kanzan'** The most popular and most commonly planted ornamental cherry; it is also known as 'Kwanzan'. It is a vigorous, medium-sized, deciduous tree with stiffly ascending branches at first, spreading when the tree is older. The flowers are large, showy, double, and purplish pink. The young leaves are coppery red or reddish brown. It is often wrongly grown as 'Hisakura' (see under 'Choshu-hizakura'), but it is taller and has double flowers that appear a week later. Mid.
Zone 5 US, 6 Can. 🏆

***P.* 'Kiku-shidare Sakura'** See under *P.* 'Cheal's Weeping'.

Prunus 'Ichiyo'

Prunus 'Jo-nioi'

***P.* 'Mikuruma-gaeshi'** A distinctive small deciduous tree with long, ascending, rather gaunt, short-spurred branches. The mostly single, blush pink flowers are densely packed on the branches. The young leaves are bronze-green. Mid.
Zone 5 US, 6 Can.

***P.* 'Mount Fuji'** This beautiful cherry is one of the most distinctive. It is a small, vigorous deciduous tree with widely spreading, horizontal or slightly drooping branches that often reach to the ground. The flowers are very large, single or semidouble, fragrant, and snow-white and burst from the soft green young foliage in long, drooping clusters. The leaves are distinctively fringed. It has long been grown as 'Shirotae', which is similar. Mid. Introduced c. 1905.
Zone 5 US, 6 Can. 🏆

***P.* 'Ojochin'** A striking small deciduous tree, easily distinguished by its large leaves and single flowers 2 in (5 cm) across, which are pink in bud and open blush. They are profusely borne in long-stalked clusters of as many as seven or eight. The young leaves are bronze-brown, becoming rather tough and leathery when mature. Mid. Introduced before 1905.
Zone 5 US, 6 Can.

***P.* 'Pink Perfection'** A striking small deciduous tree with a habit intermediate between 'Shogetsu', its seed parent, and 'Kanzan', which was probably its pollen parent. Its flowers are bright rosy pink in bud and open double, paler pink; they are carried in drooping clusters. The young leaves are bronze. It is less showy than 'Kanzan'. Mid to late. Introduced 1935.
Zone 5 US, 6 Can. 🏆

***P.* 'Shimidsu'** See *P.* 'Shogetsu'.

***P.* 'Shirofugen'** A vigorous, wide-spreading deciduous tree up to 33 ft (10 m). The flowers are large, double, and dull purplish pink in bud, opening white then fading to purplish pink. They are in long-stalked clusters and contrast superbly with the copper young leaves. Blossoms are very late and long-lasting. Introduced 1900.
Zone 5 US, 6 Can. 🏆

***P.* 'Shirotae'** See under *P.* 'Mount Fuji'.

***P.* 'Shogetsu'**, syn. *P.* 'Shimidsu' One of the loveliest Japanese cherries. It is a small deciduous tree with spreading branches that form a broad, flattened crown. The large, slightly frilled, double flowers are pink in bud and open to pure white, hanging all along the branches in long-stalked clusters. The young leaves are green. Mid to late.

Zone 5 US, 6 Can.

***P.* 'Tai Haku'** (Great white cherry) A superb, robust deciduous tree up to 40 ft (12 m). The flowers are very large, single, and dazzling white, the color accented by the coppery red young leaves. It is one of the finest cherries and perhaps the best of the whites. Mid. Introduced 1900.

Zone 5 US, 6 Can.

***P.* 'Taki-nioi'** A strong, vigorous, medium-sized deciduous tree with spreading branches. The honey-scented, single white flowers are rather small but are profusely borne and contrast effectively with the reddish bronze young leaves. Late.

Zone 5 US, 6 Can.

***P.* 'Ukon'** A robust, spreading, small to medium-sized deciduous tree with semidouble, pale yellowish flowers, tinged green and occasionally pink-flushed, freely borne and very effective against the brownish bronze young leaves. Mature leaves turn rusty red or purplish brown in fall. Mid. Introduced 1905.

Zone 5 US, 6 Can.

***P.* 'Yedo-Zakura'** A small, upright deciduous tree with semidouble flowers, carmine in bud and almond-pink when open. The young leaves are coppery gold. Mid. Introduced 1905.

Zone 5 US, 6 Can.

Pseudolarix *Pinaceae*

A genus of one deciduous coniferous species.

P. amabilis (Golden larch) A beautiful, hardy, slow-growing, medium-sized tree of broadly conical habit. The long, larchlike, light green leaves, up to 2½ in (6 cm) long, turn clear golden yellow in autumn. On a mature tree the cones stud the long, slender branches and are reddish brown when ripe; the cones shatter and fall in autumn. It requires a moist, acidic soil. China. Introduced 1852 by Robert Fortune.

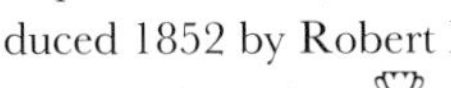

Pseudolarix amabilis

Pseudopanax *Araliaceae*

A genus of about six species of evergreens, mainly from New Zealand. They have remarkable variable leaves that are often sword shaped but are of different shapes according to the age of the plant, with distinct foliage stages punctuating its life. The flowers are small, greenish, and insignificant, and these plants are therefore valued primarily for their foliage. They are hardy only in very mild climates and grow in all types of well-drained soil. Some make good houseplants.

P. crassifolius (Lancewood) A small evergreen tree with leaves that vary remarkably with the age of the plant. There are four distinct phases: first, they are 1–2 in (2.5–5 cm) long and more or less diamond shaped; next, unbranched young trees have sword-shaped, sharply toothed leaves, usually 2 ft (60 cm) long but sometimes more; in stage three (when branching starts), many leaves have 3–5 leaflets with no stalks, while some have the second-stage shape but are shorter; in the fourth stage, rarely seen in cultivation, the leaves are around 6 in (15 cm) long and simple. Stage two leaves have red midribs and purple undersurfaces. New Zealand. Introduced 1846.

Zone 9 US

P. ferox (Toothed lancewood) A small, slender-stemmed tree like *P. crassifolius* but with the leaves simple at all stages though varying from 6 in (15 cm) to 2 ft (60 cm) in length. The leaves on young plants are pendent and grayish green and have strongly hooked teeth. New Zealand.

Zone 9 US

Pseudopanax ferox

***P. lessonii* 'Gold Splash'** Usually a large shrub, sometimes a small tree, with bright green leaves vividly blotched with yellow. They are made up of 3–5 leathery leaflets that can be either toothed or entire. New Zealand.

Zone 9 US

Pseudopanax lessonii 'Gold Splash'

Pseudosasa *Gramineae*

A small genus of evergreen bamboos from eastern Asia that tolerate damp, even wet conditions.

Pseudosasa japonica

P. japonica, syn. *Arundinaria japonica* An adaptable bamboo that forms dense clumps of olive green canes. It grows up to 20 ft (6 m) high, arching at the summit and bearing lush masses of dark, glossy green leaves 7–12 in (18–30 cm) long by 1 in (2.5 cm) wide. The grayish undersurface of the leaf has a greenish marginal strip. Branches are borne singly from each of the upper joints. Japan, S Korea. Introduced 1850.
Zone 7 US, 8 Can.

Pseudotsuga *Pinaceae*
Douglas fir

This genus includes eight coniferous species of broadly conical, evergreen trees with whorled branches. The leaves are linear, soft to the touch, and marked with two bloomy bands on their lower sides. The cones are pendulous. Most of the species require moist, well-drained soil that is neutral to acidic and full sun. They will not tolerate poor, dry soil or high wind, and young growth can be killed by late spring frost.

P. menziesii (Douglas fir) A fast-growing, stately tree that reaches about 80 ft (24 m) tall in cultivation and is popular as a Christmas tree. The lower branches of large specimens are downswept, and the bark is corky, thick, and deeply furrowed. The leaves are up to 1¼ in (3 cm) long, in two horizontal ranks, and are fragrant when crushed. The cones are up to 4 in (10 cm) long. W North America. Introduced 1827 by David Douglas.
Zone 6 US, 7 Can.

***P. m.* 'Fletcheri'** A slow-growing, shrubby form that eventually reaches 5–6½ ft (1.5–2 m) in height. The needlelike leaves are blue-green, ¾–1 in (2–2.5 cm) in length, and loosely arranged. Originated 1906.
Zone 6 US, 7 Can.

P. m.* var. *glauca (Blue Douglas fir, Colorado Douglas fir) This slower-growing form with bluish green needles comes from higher elevations and is hardier and denser than the species. C and S United States. Introduced 1863.
Zone 4 US, 5 Can.

***P. m.* 'Glauca Pendula'** A small, graceful, weeping tree with branchlets covered in bluish green leaves. In cultivation 1891.
Zone 4 US, 5 Can.

Pseudowintera *Winteraceae*

A New Zealand genus of three evergreen species related to Drimys.

P. colorata (Pepper tree) A small to medium-sized shrub with aromatic, oval, leathery leaves that are pale yellow-green above, flushed pink and marked with dark crimson-purple, and blue-bloomy beneath. The small, greenish yellow flowers are occasionally followed by dark red to black fruits. New Zealand.
Zone 9 US

Ptelea *Rutaceae*
Hop tree

A genus of 11 North American aromatic deciduous shrubs or small trees, of which the following is the best known. They are suitable for all types of fertile soil and require full sun or light shade.

P. trifoliata (Hop tree, water ash) A large shrub or low, spreading tree. It produces domed clusters of small, star-shaped, yellowish flowers that open in early summer and are probably the most fragrant among hardy trees. They are followed by dense green clusters of persistent, winged, elmlike fruits. E North America, Mexico. Introduced 1704.
Zone 3 US, 4 Can.

Ptelea trifoliata

Ptelea trifoliata 'Aurea'

***P. t.* 'Aurea'** A form with soft yellow leaves that eventually turn lime green.
Zone 3 US, 4 Can.

Pterocarya *Juglandaceae*
Wing nut

A genus of about 10 species of fast-growing, wide-crowned deciduous trees of the walnut family, with handsome, pinnate, ashlike leaves and catkinlike flower clusters. They come primarily from China. Wing nuts will grow in all types of fertile soil. The trees send out suckers, which can grow over 3 ft (1 m) in a season and must be removed.

P. fraxinifolia (Caucasian wing nut) A large, wide-spreading tree that occasionally forms clumps of suckering stems and usually has a short trunk and deeply furrowed bark. The leaves are 1–2 ft (30–60 cm) long and composed of many oblong, toothed leaflets.

The pendulous catkins of flowers are lime green and drape the branches in summer; the females are up to 20 in (50 cm) long. It is hardy and fast growing, and does best in a moist, loamy soil; it is particularly suitable for planting near a pond or stream. Caucasus to N Iran. Introduced 1782.
Zone 5 US, 6 Can. 🏆

Pterocarya × rehderiana

P.* × *rehderiana *(P. fraxinifolia × P. stenoptera)* A large suckering tree that is intermediate in character between its parents and bears its long catkins for several months. A tree at the Hillier Gardens and Arboretum reached 52 ft (16 m) in less than 40 years. Raised 1879 at the Arnold Arboretum, Boston, Mass.
Zone 6 US, 7 Can.

P. stenoptera A large, vigorous tree with leaves 10–16 in (25–40 cm) long. The female catkins are 8 in (20 cm) long. China. Introduced 1860.
Zone 6 US, 7 Can.

Pterostyrax *Styracaceae*

A genus of four species of interesting Asiatic deciduous large shrubs or small trees with silverbell-like leaves and long panicles of small flowers. They succeed in any good, deep soil, although they will not do well in shallow, alkaline ones. Pruning for shape can be done after flowering if necessary.

P. corymbosa A rare, spreading, large shrub or small tree with bristle-toothed, ovate leaves and broad, nodding clusters of fragrant white flowers in late spring and early summer. It bears winged fruits. China, Japan. Introduced 1850.
Zone 6 US, 7 Can.

Pterostyrax hispida

P. hispida (Epaulette tree) A large shrub or small tree with more or less oval leaves and fragrant white flowers in early to midsummer. They are borne in drooping panicles up to 9 in (23 cm) long and are followed by spindle-shaped, ribbed fruits. Japan, China. Introduced 1875.
Zone 5 US, 6 Can. 🏆

Punica *Punicaceae*
Pomegranate

A genus of two deciduous species, only one of which is in general cultivation.

***P. granatum* 'Flore Pleno'** This is a showy form of the pomegranate, with double orange-red flowers in late summer to early fall. It is a medium-sized shrub or small, bushy tree and needs a warm location with good drainage. The shining green, oblong leaves are coppery when young and yellow in fall. The fruits are borne only after a long, hot summer.
Zone 9 US 🏆

Punica granatum

***P. g.* 'Nana'** A charming dwarf form 6–9 in (15–23 cm) high. It has narrow leaves and profusions of orange-scarlet flowers. It is suitable for a sunny site in a rock garden. In cultivation 1806.
Zone 9 US

Pyracantha *Rosaceae*
Firethorn

These evergreens are relatives of Cotoneaster *but are easily distinguished from them by their thorny branches and toothed leaves. Their masses of white hawthornlike flowers open in early summer and are followed by red, orange, or yellow berries in fall and winter. All hardy, firethorns are often grown as wall shrubs and include some of the best evergreen flowering and berrying shrubs for north-*

and east-facing walls. On a wall they will reach a height of 16 ft (5 m) or more and their long growths should be cut back immediately after flowering. They are shorter but equally effective when grown as freestanding shrubs. They are tolerant of all exposures and pollution and grow well in all fertile soils. Pyracantha *are, unfortunately, very susceptible to fireblight and canker, one or the other of which will eventually affect them, even if the young, fast-growing plants brought from the nursery or garden center are extremely healthy. Some varieties are more resistant to these diseases than others, and a number of resistant forms have been bred in recent years at the U.S. National Arboretum in Washington, D.C.*

***P.* 'Apache'** A compact shrub with fruits that are bright red, ripen early, and persist well into winter. Introduced by the U.S. National Arboretum, Washington, D.C.
Zone 6 US, 7 Can.

Pyracantha atalantoides

P. atalantoides (Gibbs firethorn) A robust large shrub, or occasionally a small tree, with large, oval, glossy dark green leaves. Very susceptible to fireblight.
Zone 7 US, 8 Can.

***P. coccinea* 'Lalandei'** Once a popular form of the scarlet firethorn, this is very susceptible to canker and fireblight and is not as widely grown now.
Zone 5 US, 6 Can.

***P. crenatoserrata* 'Graberi'** A handsome, vigorous form of the Chinese firethorn, with reddish brown, downy shoots and wavy-margined leaves. The large clusters of brick-red fruits last through winter.
Zone 7 US, 8 Can.

Pyracantha coccinea 'Lalandei'

Pyracantha 'Golden Charmer'

***P.* 'Golden Charmer'** A vigorous medium-sized to large shrub with long, arching branches and finely toothed, bright glossy leaves. Large, round, orange-yellow berries ripen early. In cultivation 1960.
Zone 6 US, 7 Can.

***P.* 'Golden Dome'** A small shrub that makes a dense mound of arching branches and dark green leaves. An abundance of white flowers in early summer are followed by an equally abundant crop of small, deep yellow berries. Selected before 1973 at Hillier Nurseries.
Zone 6 US, 7 Can.

Pyracantha 'Golden Dome'

***P.* 'Mohave'** A popular, dense, medium-sized to large shrub with bright orange-red berries. Highly prone to scab. It makes a

Pyracantha 'Mohave'

Pyracantha 'Navaho'

Pyracantha 'Orange Glow'

good low hedge or can be trained against a wall as an espalier. 'Mohave Silver' is a variable variegated form. Introduced 1963 by the U.S. National Arboretum, Washington, D.C.

Zone 6 US, 7 Can.

***P.* 'Navaho'** A small to medium-sized, dense, spreading shrub with narrow, almost untoothed leaves up to $2^1/_2 \times {}^1/_2$ in (6 × 1 cm). The small but firm, distinctly flattened berries are orange, becoming orange-red, and are borne in dense clusters. Raised 1966 at the U.S. National Arboretum, Washington, D.C.

Zone 6 US, 7 Can.

***P.* 'Orange Charmer'** A large shrub resembling 'Orange Glow' but with deeper orange, more flattened berries. In cultivation 1962.

Zone 6 US, 7 Can.

***P.* 'Orange Glow'** A vigorous, dense, medium-sized shrub. The branches are covered in autumn with bright orange-red berries that last well into winter and beyond.

Zone 6 US, 7 Can. 🏆

***P.* 'Red Column'** A dense, bushy, medium-sized upright shrub with reddish shoots and ovate to elliptical, sharply toothed, glossy leaves. The dense clusters of scarlet berries ripen early.

Zone 5 US, 6 Can.

P. rogersiana A large, dense, free-fruiting shrub with small, lanceolate, bright green leaves and bright reddish orange berries. W China. Introduced 1911.

Zone 7 US, 8 Can. 🏆

***P. r.* 'Flava'** A form that produces bright yellow berries.

Zone 7 US, 8 Can. 🏆

***P.* 'Sappho Orange'** A medium-sized upright shrub with dark green leaves and an abundance of deep orange berries. It is resistant to scab and canker and is suitable for a container.

Zone 6 US, 7 Can.

***P.* 'Sappho Red'** A medium-sized upright shrub with glossy dark green leaves and profuse, flattened, carmine-red berries that ripen to orange. It is good for hedges and resistant to scab and fireblight.

Zone 6 US, 7 Can.

***P.* 'Sappho Yellow'** A form of the two previous plants that bears attractive yellow

Pyracantha 'Sappho Yellow'

Pyracantha 'Soleil d'Or'

berries.
Zone 6 US, 7 Can.

***P.* 'Soleil d'Or'** A medium-sized upright shrub with reddish stems and dark green, broadly elliptical leaves. Golden yellow berries ½ in (1 cm) across are borne in large clusters. The flowers are white. Raised 1970 in France.
Zone 6 US, 7 Can.

***P.* 'Sparkler'** A beautifully variegated form whose leaves are heavily mottled with white and tinged with pink in fall and winter. Unfortunately, it is particularly tender and suitable only for warm regions.
Zone 7 US, 8 Can.

***P.* 'Teton'** A large, vigorous, upright shrub with reddish shoots and small, bright glossy green, wavy-edged leaves. The profusely borne berries are small and yellow-orange. It is highly resistant to fireblight. Raised 1963 at the U.S. National Arboretum, Washington, D.C.
Zone 5 US, 6 Can.

Pyracantha 'Watereri'

***P.* 'Watereri'** A very free-berrying, compact, medium-sized shrub with clusters of white flowers followed by bright red fruits.
Zone 6 US, 7 Can. 🏆

Pyrus *Rosaceae*
Pear

A genus of about 20 species of deciduous trees and shrubs that are natives of the temperate regions of the Old World. The ornamental pears are small to medium-sized, deep-rooted trees with green to silvery gray leaves and white flowers in midspring. They are tolerant of drought, cold, and air pollution and succeed in all types of fertile soil, especially a good loam, in full sun. They cannot take extremely wet, dry, or alkaline soil. Diseases such as fireblight and scab are more of a problem with culinary pears than with ornamental ones.

P. betulifolia A graceful, small, fast-growing tree. The leaves are rounded, slenderly pointed, toothed, and grayish green, becoming green and glossy. N China. Introduced 1882.
Zone 5 US, 6 Can.

***P. calleryana* 'Bradford'** (Bradford pear) An extremely popular, pyramidal small tree with profuse white flowers in spring and glossy green leaves all summer that turn red or purple in fall. Selected 1918 and introduced 1963 by the USDA, Glen Dale, Md.
Zone 4 US, 5b Can.

***P. c.* 'Chanticleer'** (Chanticleer pear) A vigorous, dense, narrow, medium-sized cultivar. It flowers profusely in spring and has yellow foliage in fall.
Zone 4 US, 5b Can. 🏆

***P. c.* 'Red Spire'** This seedling of 'Bradford' has a more pyramidal habit and the foliage changes color earlier in the fall.
Zone 4 US, 5b Can.

***P. c.* 'Whitehouse'** A small tree with a compact, narrow columnar habit and snow-white flowers. The leaves turn bright scarlet in fall. Introduced by the USDA.
Zone 4 US, 5b Can.

P. nivalis A small tree with stout ascending branches. The profuse pure white flowers appear in spring with the white-woolly young leaves. The fruits are small, rounded, and yellowish green and become sweet

Pyrus nivalis

when overripe. S Europe. Introduced 1800.
Zone 6 US, 7 Can.

P. ussuriensis (Ussurian pear, Chinese pear) A vigorous, dense, medium-sized tree with shiny green leaves that are paler beneath and turn purple-red in fall. The white flowers are sometimes tinged with pink in bud. NE Asia.
Zone 4 US, 5 Can. 🏆

QUERCUS

Fagaceae Oak

THE OAKS are a genus of roughly 600 species of trees and, occasionally, shrubs native to the Northern Hemisphere. Most are evergreen, and even some of the deciduous species retain their withered and brown leaves well into the winter. Oaks are much more diverse in form and habit than might be supposed: along with some of the largest, noblest trees in the world, the genus also includes a number of more compact specimens suitable for a small garden.

Oaks have two easily identified features common to almost all species. The leaf is generally deeply lobed, although some, such as *Q. imbricaria,* have unlobed, simple leaves, and others, like *Q. variabilis,* have leaves that are toothed. And the oak fruit is a nut — the acorn — nestled in a cup that varies in size and may be hairy. The acorn cup of *Q. macrocarpa,* for instance, is so fringed that the species is sometimes called the mossy cup oak.

In general, the warmer the summer, the better oaks will grow. The species tend to thin out further north in the Northern Hemisphere, and a given species tends to perform less reliably the farther north you attempt to grow it. There is an east-west factor, too, as is evident by the fact that the native ranges of eastern and western oaks in North America do not overlap. Several Asian and European species grow very well in the eastern United States: *Q. petraea* and *Q. robur,* for example, can tolerate the cold winters of the Great Lakes region.

The native North American oaks are generally the best for fall foliage color, although the bright reds displayed by some of them become muted when the plants are grown in cooler areas. The European oaks do not have fall color.

Quercus coccinea 'Splendens'

CARE AND CULTIVATION

Oaks need full sun, but will sometimes take part shade. They grow in almost any soil, but the genus as a whole prefers a deep, rich soil that is well drained but moisture retentive. *Q. alba* and *Q. palustris* prefer a wet, heavy clay. Many oaks do not tolerate lime, but others, such as *Q. shumardii,* will; some require an acidic soil.

Oaks benefit from year-round mulch, and the roots — which can extend three times beyond the dripline — should not be disturbed. Some oaks are particularly sensitive and difficult to transplant, including *Q. alba* and *Q. velutina.*

They do best in open locations and some are remarkably wind tolerant. *Q. ilex,* for example, can take salt spray off the ocean, and *Q. macrocarpa* thrives in the open, windswept prairies of the Midwest.

There are many pests and quite a few diseases that attack oaks, but on the whole the trees are capable of tolerating almost all of them and shrugging them off. Nevertheless, it is important to prevent or repair wind and other damage. It is also essential to watch for attacks of gypsy moths, which can rapidly defoliate a tree and, in time, cause death.

Q. acutissima (Sawtooth oak) A medium-sized deciduous tree with narrowly oblong leaves like those of a chestnut. They are bright, glossy green, are margined with bristly-tipped teeth, and persist into winter. Japan, Korea, China. Introduced 1862 by Richard Oldham.

Zone 5 US, 6 Can.

Q. agrifolia (California live oak) This large, fast-growing, rounded evergreen tree can reach 80 ft (24 m). The dark gray bark is broken into plates, and the hollylike leaves are wavy and slightly toothed. California. Introduced 1849.

Zone 8 US, 9 Can.

Q. alba (White oak) For sheer mass, this round-headed deciduous tree with open branching is hard to beat. It is slow growing and generally reaches 80 ft (24 m). The leaves are dark green above, paler beneath, with 5–9 deeply divided, rounded lobes and turn a ruddy brown-purple in fall. E North America. Introduced 1724.

Zone 2 US, 2b Can.

Q. bicolor (Swamp white oak) This large deciduous tree forms a rounded head with a spread equal to its height. The leaves are almost entire to shallowly lobed, and the mature bark has deep vertical furrows. Prefers moist soil. North America. Introduced 1800.

Zone 4 US, 4b Can.

Q. cerris (Turkish oak) A large, broadly pyramidal tree and one of the fastest growing. The oval or oblong deciduous leaves are coarsely toothed or shallowly lobed and slightly rough to the touch. It tolerates lime. S Europe, Asia Minor. Introduced 1735.

Zone 5 US, 6 Can. 🏆

***Q. c.* 'Variegata'** A variegated tree bearing leaves with a cream margin.

Zone 5 US, 6 Can.

Q. chrysolepsis (Canyon live oak) A large evergreen tree with a wide-spreading, open head and branchlets that are often pendulous. The leaves are toothed and white-felted beneath. W United States.

Zone 8 US, 9? Can.

Q. coccinea (Scarlet oak) A large deciduous tree with attractive, broad, dark green, deeply lobed leaves, each lobe having several bristle-tipped teeth. The leaves turn a glowing scarlet in fall. It requires a well-drained, acidic soil. SE Canada, E United States. Introduced 1691.

Quercus cerris

Quercus cerris 'Variegata'

Quercus coccinea

Zone 4 US, 4b Can.

***Q. coccinea* 'Splendens'** A form selected for its rich scarlet fall foliage.

Zone 4 US, 4b Can.

Q. ellipsoidalis (Northern pin oak) A medium-sized to large deciduous tree, related to *Q. coccinea*, usually with a short trunk and spreading head. The deeply lobed leaves on slender stalks turn deep crimson-purple in fall. It requires a well-drained, acidic soil. N and C North America. Introduced 1902.

Zone 3 US, 3 Can.

Q. emoryi (Emory oak) A medium-sized evergreen tree that grows wider than tall and has deeply furrowed bark on old trees. SW United States, Mexico.

Zone 9 US

Q. falcata (Southern red oak) A large tree with a spreading crown. The leaves have two prominent lobes and a slender tapered tip and turn orange in fall. SE United States. Introduced 1763.

Zone 7 US, 8 Can.

Quercus frainetto 'Hungarian Crown'

***Q. frainetto* 'Hungarian Crown'** This was the name proposed by Hillier for the tree widely grown in Europe as *Q. frainetto*, the Hungarian oak. It is a large deciduous tree with a broadly oval head. The leaves are deeply and regularly lobed and are up to 8 in (20 cm) long. The species was from SE Europe, introduced 1838.

Zone 5 US, 6 Can. 🏆

Q. gambelii (Rocky Mountain oak) In its native habitat this deciduous oak often forms a low, stunted tree, but in good growing conditions it will reach to 25 ft (8 m) tall. Rocky Mountains of the United States. Introduced 1894.

Zone 4 US, 5 Can.

Q. garryana (Oregon white oak) A deciduous oak that can grow to 90 ft (27.5 m) in rich soil. The bark is pale, almost white, and

Quercus coccinea 'Splendens'

Quercus libani

Quercus × *ludoviciana*

the leaves are similar to those of *Q. alba.* It is an important timber tree on the Pacific Coast. North America. Introduced 1873.

Zone 6 US, 7 Can.

Q. ilex (Holly oak, holm oak) A medium-sized evergreen tree with attractive corrugated bark and a rounded head of branches. The hollylike leaves are leathery, glossy dark green, and variable in shape and size depending on age and growing conditions. It thrives in all kinds of well-drained soil and is valuable in warm coastal areas, as it withstands wind and benefits from the moist air. It responds well to clipping and tolerates shade. Mediterranean region and SW Europe. In cultivation since the 16th century.

Quercus ilex

Zone 7 US, 8 Can. 🏆

Q. imbricaria (Shingle oak, laurel oak) This deciduous species forms an upright tree when young, later becoming more rounded and reaching 75 ft (22.5 m). The dark green, entire leaves turn rusty brown in fall but persist well into winter, making an effective screen or windbreak. E United States. Introduced 1890.

Zone 4 US, 4b Can.

Q. kelloggii (California black oak) A large, dense, broad-spreading deciduous tree with very dark bark. The leaves are pinkish when young, become glossy green when mature, and turn yellow and orange in fall. Tolerates dry, sandy soil. Oregon to California. Introduced 1878.

Zone 8 US, 9? Can.

Q. libani (Lebanon oak) A small, elegant deciduous tree with slender branches and long-persistent, slender, glossy green leaves that are margined with bristle-tipped teeth. Syria, Asia Minor. Introduced c. 1855.

Zone 6 US, 7 Can.

Q. lobata (Valley oak, California white oak) This could be considered the western counterpart of *Q. alba.* It has the same magnificent crown, wide-spreading branches, and lobed leaves, although the lobes are not bristle-tipped. The acorns, however, are long and pointed instead of short and round. California. Introduced 1874.

Zone 8 US, 9? Can.

Q.* × *ludoviciana An attractive, large, vigorous semievergreen tree with deeply and irregularly lobed, shining green leaves that have rich fall color. It requires an acidic

soil. SE United States. Introduced 1880.
Zone 6 US, 7 Can.

Q. macrocarpa (Bur oak, mossy cup oak) One of the easiest oaks to identify when in fruit because of the fringe of hairs on the cup. The leaves are lobed on the bottom half only; the top half is entire. It makes a large, broad-crowned tree. E and C North America. Introduced before 1873.
Zone 2 US, 2 Can.

Quercus myrsinifolia

Q. marilandica (Blackjack oak) A small, slow-growing deciduous tree with a low, spreading habit. The leaves are broadest above the middle, sometimes triangular, tapered to the base, and more or less three-lobed at the broad end. They are up to 7 in (18 cm) long and often as wide, are glossy green above and tawny yellow beneath, and turn yellow or brown in fall. It requires an acidic soil. E United States. In cultivation 1739.
Zone 5 US, 6 Can.

Quercus palustris

Q. montana, syn. *Q. prinus* (Chestnut oak) Native to dry, rocky sites, this forms a large, stately tree with entire, toothed leaves, resembling those of the chestnut. North America. Introduced 1688.
Zone 4 US, 5 Can.

Q. muehlenbergii (Chinquapin oak, yellow chestnut oak) The leaves are similar to those of *Q. montana*, but this species prefers rich, moist soil. It will survive in drier soils but will not reach its mature size of 100 ft (30 m). United States. Introduced 1822.
Zone 5 US, 6 Can.

Quercus petraea

Quercus petraea 'Columna'

Q. myrsinifolia (Chinese evergreen oak) A small, densely branched evergreen tree with a compact habit. The smooth, shiny leaves are lance shaped with tapered points. They are purple-red when unfolding and become dark green above, paler beneath. It requires an acidic soil. China, Japan. Introduced 1854 by Robert Fortune.
Zone 7 US, 8 Can.

Q. nigra (Water oak) This large, semievergreen oak grows in swamps with bald cypress *(Taxodium distichum)*. In cultivation, it grows well in dry soils and has a rounded form. The leaves are broadest toward the tip. SE United States. Introduced 1723.
Zone 6 US, 7 Can.

Quercus phillyreoides

Q. palustris (Pin oak) A large, dense-headed deciduous tree with a broadly pyramidal habit and drooping lower branches. The leaves are deeply and sharply lobed, shining green on both surfaces, and smaller than those of *Q. coccinea;* they turn scarlet in fall. Tolerates wet soil and city conditions. It requires an acidic soil. SE Canada, E and C United States. Introduced 1800.
Zone 3 US, 4 Can. 🏆

Q. petraea (Sessile oak) This native European species forms a large deciduous tree with rather large, long-stalked leaves, not auricled at the base, and stalkless fruits. W, C, and SE Europe; Asia Minor.
Zone 4 US, 4b Can. 🏆

Quercus phellos

Quercus robur 'Fastigiata'

***Q. p.* 'Columna'** A densely branched, columnar tree of medium size.
Zone 4 US, 4b Can.

Q. phellos (Willow oak) A large deciduous tree with slender branches and narrow, willowlike leaves that are glossy green above and turn yellow and orange in fall. It requires acidic soil and is a good street tree. E United States. Introduced 1723.
Zone 7 US, 8 Can. 🏆

Q. phillyreoides A rare, large evergreen shrub resembling *Phillyrea latifolia*, generally a dense, rounded bush to 16 ft (5 m) or more but occasionally a small tree. It has more or less oval, leathery, glossy green leaves with small, sharp teeth that are usually bronze when unfolding. China, Japan. Introduced 1861.
Zone 7 US, 8 Can.

Q. prinus See *Q. montana.*

Q. robur (English oak) This is a large, long-lived deciduous tree that develops a broad head of rugged branches atop a short trunk. The leaves are stalkless or nearly so, auricled at the base, and shallowly lobed. The acorns are one to several on a slender stalk. Europe, Caucasus, Asia Minor, N Africa.
Zone 4 US, 5 Can. 🏆

***Q. r.* 'Fastigiata'** (Upright English oak) A large, imposing, columnar tree that is useful where space is restricted and that makes a beautiful formal specimen.
Zone 4 US, 5 Can. 🏆

Quercus robur

Q. rubra (Red oak) A large, fast-growing deciduous tree that develops from broadly conical to rounded with age. It has large, more or less oval, markedly lobed leaves that generally turn red or yellow-brown and finally russet-brown before falling. Its branches are stouter than those of *Q. coccinea,* and its leaves are less deeply lobed and are matte rather than glossy. It prefers a light, sandy soil. E and C North America. Introduced 1724. *(See photo on p.484.)*
Zone 3 US, 3 Can. 🏆

***Q. r.* 'Limelight'** This name has been proposed for the tree grown as 'Aurea', but unlike the true 'Aurea', it does not scorch in full sun. It requires an acidic soil. *(See photo on p.484.)* Zone 4 US, 4b Can.

Q. rysophylla A vigorous, large-leaved, evergreen tree with elliptical leaves that are glossy green above and wrinkled beneath. They are up to 10 in (25 cm) long and 3 in

Quercus rubra

Quercus rubra 'Limelight'

(8 cm) wide, auricled at the base, and entire or shallowly toothed. It is proving hardy in the South, but its ultimate height is not yet known. Introduced 1979 from the Horsetail Falls above Monterrey, Mexico.
Zone 7 US, 8 Can.

Q. shumardii (Shumard oak) A large deciduous tree with particularly attractive, deeply cut leaves that turn a beautiful red in fall. It will tolerate alkaline soil. S and C United States. Introduced 1897.
Zone 4 US, 5 Can.

Q. stellata (Post oak) A medium-sized, spreading, deciduous tree whose leaves are red when young, dark green at maturity, and reddish brown in fall. The central lobes are wider than the rest of the leaf, giving it a cruciform appearance. Tolerates poor, sandy soil. United States. Introduced 1819.
Zone 5 US, 6 Can.

Quercus shumardii

Q. suber (Cork oak) Usually a short-stemmed, wide-spreading evergreen tree that will occasionally reach 65 ft (20 m) tall. Its bark is thick, rugged, and deeply corky and is the source of cork, harvested mostly in Spain and Portugal. It needs dry soil and can withstand only brief periods of frost. S Europe, N Africa. In cultivation 1699.
Zone 7 US, 8 Can.

Q.* × *turneri (Turner's oak) A distinctive, small to medium-sized semievergreen tree with a compact, rounded head of dark green leaves with 4–6 broad teeth on each margin. In fall the leaves on the inner parts of the branches are shed, while those toward the ends are retained, making the tree appear to have an outer "shell" of foliage in winter. It tolerates alkaline soil.
Zone 7 US, 8 Can.

Quercus suber

Quercus × *turneri*

Q. variabilis (Oriental oak, Chinese cork oak) A large deciduous tree with ornamental gray, corky bark that is up to 4 in (10 cm) thick. The oblong, glossy green leaves are silvery-downy beneath and toothed. China, Japan, Korea.
Zone 4 US, 5 Can.

Q. velutina (Black oak) A large deciduous tree that is one of the most striking oaks. Its glossy leaves are deeply and irregularly lobed, dark green above, pale and downy beneath. In fall the foliage is reddish brown and yellow. It requires acid soil and is difficult to transplant. E and C United States.
Zone 4 US, 5 Can.

Q. virginiana (Live oak) A magnificent large tree that spreads twice as wide as its height. The simple, dark, evergreen leaves are deciduous at the northern limits of its range. SE United States. Introduced 1739.
Zone 7 US, 8 Can.

Q. wislizeni (Interior live oak) A slow-growing, rounded evergreen tree. The glossy, leathery leaves are hollylike and oblong to ovate with slender spiny teeth at the margins; they are almost stalkless. California, Mexico. Introduced 1874.
Zone 8 US, 9 Can.

R

Rehderodendron *Styraceae*

A genus of 9 or 10 species of deciduous trees from southwestern China, known only since 1930. They require an acid soil.

R. macrocarpum A small tree with reddish branches and more or less elliptical, finely toothed leaves, 3–4 in (7.5–10 cm) long, that color well before falling. The cup-shaped, slightly fragrant flowers are white tinged with pink, have prominent yellow anthers, and are produced in hanging clusters as the leaves emerge. Fruits are oblong, ribbed, and bright red. China (Mount Omei). Introduced 1934.
Zone 8 US, 9? Can.

Rhamnus *Rhamnaceae*
Buckthorn

A large genus of about 125 species of evergreen and deciduous trees and shrubs. Widely distributed, mainly in north-temperate regions, the species are grown mainly for their foliage. The inconspicuous flowers are small but numerous and borne in axillary clusters. Buckthorns will grow in all types of well-drained soil in sun or part shade.

Rhamnus alaternus 'Argenteovariegata'

***R. alaternus* 'Argenteovariegata'** An evergreen plant that is one of the best variegated shrubs, with green and marbled gray leaves that have an irregular, creamy margin. It thrives in dry shade but needs shelter from winter wind. It is a good choice for coastal sites. The species was introduced in the early 17th century from the Mediterranean region and Portugal.
Zone 7 US, 8 Can. 🏆

R. cathartica (Common buckthorn) A large deciduous shrub or small tree with spiny branches that are attractive in fall when laden with shining, dark fruits. A weedy species whose seeds are spread by birds. It is starting to become invasive and should not be planted. Europe.
Zone 2 US, 2 Can.

Rhamnus cathartica

R. frangula (Alder buckthorn) A large deciduous shrub or small tree with ovate green leaves that turn yellow in fall. The fruits are red, changing to black, and make the plant ornamental. Europe, N Africa.
Zone 3 US, 3b Can.

***R. f.* 'Asplenifolia'** (Feathery buckthorn) A form with very narrow, fine-textured, wavy leaves that create a feathery effect.
Zone 3 US, 3b Can.

***R. f.* 'Columnaris'** (Tallhedge buckthorn) A dense, narrow, columnar shrub for hedges and screens that seldom requires pruning. It has oval leaves that turn bright yellow in fall and red fruits that turn black. Raised before 1955 in Painesville, Ohio.
Zone 3 US, 3b Can.

Rhaphiolepis *Rosaceae*

A genus of about 15 species from eastern Asia. They are rather slow growing, evergreen shrubs with firm, leathery leaves and require a warm, sunny location in a well-drained, fertile soil.

***R. × delacourii* 'Coates' Crimson'** A rounded shrub, usually less than 6½ ft (2 m) high, with rose-crimson flowers in erect terminal clusters from late spring to summer. It makes an attractive wall shrub. Raised 1952 in California.
Zone 9 US

Rhaphiolepis × delacourii 'Spring Song'

***R. × d.* 'Spring Song'** A small to medium-sized form bearing apple-blossom pink flowers from late spring to summer.
Zone 9 US

Rhaphiolepis umbellata

R. umbellata (Yeddo raphiolepis, yeddo hawthorn) A dense, slow-growing, rounded shrub, to 4 ft (1.2 m) in the open and higher against a wall. The leaves are thick, leathery, and dark green. Terminal clusters of fragrant white flowers in late spring are followed by pear-shaped black-bronze fruits. It is drought tolerant. Japan, Korea. Introduced 1862.
Zone 9 US 🏆

Rhododendron

Ericaceae

The genus *Rhododendron* is a very large one, with some 800 species and thousands of hybrids that are considered among the most beautiful, valuable landscape plants. It comprises both deciduous and evergreen shrubs, and occasionally trees, that are found primarily in the north-temperate zone, particularly in the Himalayan region; about 30 species are native to North America. While some members of the genus have been in cultivation for more than a millennium — since at least the 8th century — new hybrids are constantly being developed and introduced.

Rhododendron includes both rhododendrons and azaleas. And while gardeners readily distinguish between the two types of plants, botanists do not; that is, there are not enough technical differences between them to warrant their being classified in two separate genera. (In this guide, *"Rhododendron"* refers to the genus; "rhododendron" and "azalea" are the common names.

It is possible, however, to make some general distinctions. Usually, rhododendrons are evergreen and azaleas are deciduous, although there are a few evergreen azalea species and many hybrids. Rhododendrons have 10 or more stamens, while azaleas have five. Rhododendrons have large, paddle-shaped leaves often covered with scales on the undersides and relatively large, bell-shaped or widely funnelform flowers held in terminal trusses. Azaleas have small, elliptical, sometimes hairy leaves and tubular or trumpet-shaped, comparatively smaller flowers borne along the sides and at the ends of the shoots. And although both rhododendrons and azaleas can be dwarf, azaleas are twiggy, spreading shrubs that generally reach no more than 8 ft (2.5 m) tall, while rhododendrons are upright and can grow to 80 ft (25 m).

Rhododendron luteum **growing with bluebells**

Both groups of plants offer gardeners a range of features. Foremost are the flowers, which can be sweetly or spicily fragrant. They come in an astounding range of colors — from ice-white and palest pastels to fiery orange and gold to jewellike amethyst and ruby. Blooms on many of the plants open from deeper-colored buds, giving a striking two-tone effect. There are also flowers that change color over time or are marked with a blotch or streak of a second color.

Rhododendrons are noted for their large, heavy spheres or cones of flowers, which often seem to float above the leaves. Azalea flowers are diverse in shape, with some resembling ruffled, double roses and others opening wide into a simple star shape.

Even when not in bloom, rhododendrons make handsome landscape specimens thanks to their prominent, bold, leathery leaves. Many rhododendrons feature scales or felt on the leaf undersides, which may be rusty red, fawn, or silvery white. While most rhododendron leaves are green, *R. lepidostylum* is among those that have blue-green foliage. Some leaves even change color in cold weather — most notably those of *R.* 'P.J.M.', which turn from very dark green to a wonderful purplish color.

The deciduous azaleas also make a valuable contribution when not in flower. In fall the leaves of some varieties turn as colorful as those of a maple, taking on vivid yellow, orange, and red tones. The stems also may take on a red or copper color in winter, and a few produce red new growth in spring.

Rhododendron is easy to use in the landscape; because the genus is so large and diverse, there is a species or hybrid to suit almost any need. Both rhododendrons and azaleas are valuable as specimens and can be readily showcased in a lawn or used as an accent around paved areas. They are also at home in foundation plantings — where the house provides welcome shade and shelter — and in beds and borders, either alone or in combination with other plants. A variety of azaleas, for instance, can be massed on a slope for a spectacular splash of color, or a group of dwarf rhododendrons can be grouped around a tree that provides dappled shade, such as a dogwood. The only caution is to choose varieties wisely, as a mix of brightly hued blossoms can clash. *Rhododendron* works very well with other members of the Ericaceae family, such as pieris and mountain laurel, and with other acid-lovers, including holly.

They are indispensable in informal, woodland gardens, where their flowers provide bright color in shade. But they can also be formal elements: large rhododendrons look stately lining a driveway, for example, and azaleas can be sheared into hedges. Rhododendrons and azaleas can be used for informal hedges or screens, but are not suitable for windbreaks, as they do not tolerate exposed sites. Low-growing specimens are ideal for rock gardens, which mimic the mountain habitat where many species live in the wild, and slow-growing dwarfs are suitable for containers.

Care and Cultivation

While rhododendrons and azaleas vary in their tolerance to light and cold, they uniformly require acidic soil (pH 4.5–6) and prefer a cool, moist climate. This means that it is difficult to grow *Rhododendron* successfully in certain parts of North America, particularly in the Midwest. They thrive, however, in the Pacific Northwest and the East, and some azaleas do well in the South.

Additionally the soil should also be moist but well-drained and amended with generous amounts of organic matter. Heavy soil can be amended with gypsum (calcium sulfate) to promote drainage. A permanent mulch of an acid-forming organic material, such as pine needles, oak leaf mold, or shredded pine bark, is highly recommended, as rhododendrons and azaleas have shallow roots. Mulch keeps the soil cool and moist, protects roots from injury and insulates them from temperature fluctuations, and suppresses weeds. Because the roots grow close to the surface, the soil should not be cultivated and weeds must be removed carefully by hand.

Rhododendron grows best in dappled shade, especially in hot climates, where intense sun can burn the foliage, fade the blooms, and dry the soil. Small-leaved rhododendrons can take relatively more sun and drier conditions than larger-leaved types, but they still appreciate relief from heat. Too much shade, however, can result in leggy growth and poor flowering.

The plants should be watered in prolonged dry spells with a deep soaking. With a large bed, the most efficient method is to use a soaker hose that will deliver moisture directly to the roots. Watering is critical after flowering, when the new growth is developing, and in late fall, so that evergreens will have sufficient moisture before the ground freezes and winter wind increases moisture loss from the leaves.

Rhododendron benefits from an annual spring feeding of an acid-forming, balanced fertilizer and a topping of compost. Acidic fertilizer is especially important if the plants are grown around concrete walkways or masonry foundations, where alkaline materials may leach into the soil.

Deadheading is a good practice to promote blooming, although it is impractical with large rhododendrons and most azaleas. To deadhead a rhododendron, snap or

Rhododendron 'Blue Peter'

cut the spent flower head from the stem — but be very careful not to damage the buds growing just below the head on either side of the stem.

If plants become leggy or too large for their site, they can be pruned after flowering. Azaleas can be pruned anywhere along the stem, and older stems can be removed at the base; branch tips can also be pinched out to promote bushiness. Rhododendrons should be pruned just above a leaf cluster or above a growth bud along the stem (it will be difficult to detect, but it looks like a slight ring or swelling, indicating where a leaf cluster once grew).

Rhododendrons and azaleas vary vastly in their hardiness. Ironclad hybrid rhododendrons and Northern Lights hybrid azaleas are quite tough, hardy to −30°F (−34°C) and −40°F (−40°C) respectively. Indian hybrid azaleas, however, tolerate temperatures only to 10°F (−12°C). Nursery tags sometimes show a hardiness rating devised by the American Rhododendron Society. This runs from H1 to H7 in 10° increments, with H1 plants hardy to −25°F (−32°C), which is roughly equivalent to zone 4 US, 5 Can., and H7 plants not tolerating temperatures below freezing, about zone 10 US. The regular hardiness zone ratings *(see pp.14–15)* are used in this book and are based on bud hardiness.

Rhododendron fulvum

Even hardy plants may need winter protection, as the evergreens resent the drying effect of cold wind, which can burn their foliage. Plants should be sited out of the prevailing wind or sheltered with a windbreak. Particularly vulnerable specimens, such as those at the limits of their hardiness or in exposed locations, should be protected with burlap screens or other barriers.

A number of pests and diseases affect *Rhododendron*, although the plants are generally easy to care for. The most common pests are lacebugs and spider mites, both of which suck sap from the leaves. The first are insects with lacy wings that cause the leaves to become speckled with yellow and leave black droplets on the undersides; the second are tiny insects whose webs on the leaf undersides are usually visible. Both can be controlled by spraying the leaves with a strong jet of water or with insecticidal soap.

Rhododendrons can suffer from root rot in poorly drained soil; it causes the leaves to wilt and the bark to discolor and will eventually kill the plant. The soil can be treated with fungicide and drainage should be improved by amending the soil or planting in a raised bed. Some rhododendrons and deciduous azaleas are prone to powdery mildew, which can be controlled with improved air circulation and fungicide.

RHODODENDRON AND AZALEA SPECIES

Rhododendron and azalea species are enormously diverse, ranging from ground-covering dwarfs to trees. They may be evergreen or deciduous and generally flower between spring and early summer.

In the entries that follow, common names are given when available; otherwise each species is designated simply as a rhododendron or an azalea.

R. aberconwayi (Rhododendron) A small evergreen shrub with narrow leaves that are slightly hairy beneath. The saucer-shaped flowers are white to pale pink and are spotted with dark purplish red; they appear in late spring. China. Introduced 1937.
Zone 7 US, 8 Can.

Rhododendron albrechtii

R. albrechtii (Albrecht azalea) A beautiful, medium-sized, deciduous shrub with leaves that turn yellow in fall. Deep rose-pink to red flowers, 2 in (5 cm) across, appear with or before the leaves in mid- to late spring. Japan. Introduced 1914.
Zone 5 US, 6 Can. 🏆

R. amagianum (Mt. Amagi azalea) An outstanding medium-sized to large deciduous shrub with broad leaves in clusters of three at the ends of the branches. The funnel-shaped flowers are orange-red with a red blotch and borne in late spring. Japan.
Zone 6 US, 7 Can.

Rhododendron atlanticum

R. ambiguum (Rhododendron) A medium-sized to large evergreen shrub with leaves 2–3 in (5–7.5 cm) long and clusters of 3–6, funnel-shaped, greenish yellow flowers with green spots in mid- to late spring. China. Introduced 1904 by Ernest Wilson.
Zone 7 US, 8 Can.

R. anthopogon (Sulfur rhododendron) A dwarf, compact, evergreen shrub with narrowly tubular flowers in tight, terminal clusters in midspring. They vary from cream to pink and fade to yellow. Himalayan region. Introduced 1820.
Zone 7 US, 8 Can.

R. arborescens (Sweet azalea) A large deciduous shrub with more or less oval, glossy green leaves that usually turn red in fall. The fragrant, funnel-shaped flowers are white, occasionally flushed with pink, and the red style is long and protruding. They are borne in early and midsummer. E North America. Introduced 1818.
Zone 4 US, 5b Can.

Rhododendron augustinii 'Electra'

R. arboreum (Tree rhododendron) A magnificent, evergreen, large shrub or small to medium-sized tree. The leaves, up to 8 in (20 cm) long, are silvery white to russet-brown beneath. The bell-shaped flowers, 2 in (5 cm) long, vary from white to blood red and are borne 12–20 in a truss up to 6 in (15 cm) across. It flowers in late winter to early spring and may be damaged by frost at the limits of its hardiness. Himalayan region. Introduced c. 1810.
Zone 9 US

R. a.* subsp. *cinnamomeum A form whose leaves have a thick cinnamon or rust-colored woolly covering underneath. The flowers range from red or pink to white.
Zone 8 US, 9? Can.

***R. a.* 'Sir Charles Lemon'** See *R.* 'Sir Charles Lemon' under Rhododendron Hybrids.

***R. a.* 'Tony Schilling'** A form with deep pink flowers that have darker spots.
Zone 9 US 🏆

Rhododendron auriculatum

Rhododendron augustinii

***R. argyrophyllum* 'Chinese Silver'** (Rhododendron) A beautiful, large, densely leafy evergreen shrub with long, very glossy leaves that are intensely silver beneath. It has pink flowers, slightly darker on the lobes and 2 in (5 cm) across, in late spring.
Zone 6 US, 7 Can. 🏆

R. atlanticum (Coast azalea) A charming, small, deciduous shrub with bright green leaves. It has fragrant, funnel-shaped flowers, white or white flushed with pink and occasionally with a white blotch, in late spring. E United States. Introduced 1916.
Zone 5 US, 6 Can.

R. augustinii (Augustine rhododendron) A large, small-leaved evergreen shrub whose flowers are blue to rosy lavender. It flowers in mid- to late spring and is somewhat leggy. China. Introduced 1899.
Zone 7 US, 8 Can.

***R. a.* 'Electra'** A magnificent form with violet-blue flowers with greenish yellow blotches. Raised 1937 at Exbury, England.
Zone 7 US, 8 Can. 🏆

R. aureum (Rhododendron) A small evergreen shrub, only 1 ft (30 cm) tall, with dark green leaves that are pale green or brown beneath. The yellow flowers are in clusters in late spring. It needs good snow cover. Mountains of Manchuria and Japan.
Zone 2 US, 2 Can.

R. auriculatum (Earleaf rhododendron) An evergreen large shrub or sometimes a small tree that flowers late, usually in mid- to late summer or later. The large, white to pinkish, funnel-shaped flowers are richly scented and borne in trusses up to 4 in (10 cm) across. China. Introduced 1901 by Ernest Wilson.
Zone 6 US, 7 Can.

R. austrinum (Florida flame azalea) A small to medium-sized deciduous shrub with funnel-shaped, creamy yellow to orange flowers up to $1\frac{1}{4}$ in (3.5 cm) long, often tinged or striped with purple. They open with or before the leaves in spring. S United States.
Zone 6 US, 7 Can. 🏆

R. baileyi (Rhododendron) A small to medium-sized evergreen shrub, to $6\frac{1}{2}$ ft (2 m) high, with saucer-shaped, red-purple flowers, usually with darker markings, in late spring. The young shoots and the

undersides of the small leaves are covered with reddish brown scales. Himalaya. Introduced 1913.
Zone 7 US, 8 Can.

R. bakeri (Cumberland azalea) A dwarf to medium-sized deciduous shrub with terminal clusters of funnel-shaped flowers from orange to yellow or red in early summer. SE United States.
Zone 5 US, 6 Can.

R. balfourianum (Rhododendron) A medium-sized evergreen shrub with narrow, dark green leaves that are silvery beneath when young and become brownish at maturity. The pale pink, bell-shaped flowers open in spring. China. Introduced 1906.
Zone 6 US, 7 Can.

R. barbatum (Giantblood rhododendron) An evergreen large shrub or small tree with peeling bark and bell-shaped, blood red flowers in globular heads in early spring. Himalayan region. In cultivation 1829.
Zone 8 US, 9? Can.

R. beanianum (Rhododendron) An open, medium-sized, evergreen shrub with chestnut brown wool on the undersides of the leaves. The loose trusses of bell-shaped, waxy flowers are usually red but are sometimes pink and are borne in early to late spring. N India, Upper Burma.
Zone 8 US, 9 Can.

R. brachycarpum (Fujiyama rhododendron) An attractive medium-sized evergreen shrub whose leaves are covered with fawn or brownish wool on the undersides. The funnel-shaped flowers are cream flushed with pink and are borne in early to midsummer. Japan, Korea.
Zone 6 US, 7 Can.

R. bureaui (Rhododendron) A medium-sized evergreen shrub with glossy dark green leaves covered beneath with a rich red wool. The bell-shaped flowers are rose with crimson markings, borne in a tight truss of 10–15 in mid- to late spring. The young growths vary in color from pale fawn to rusty red. China. Introduced 1904.
Zone 5 US, 6 Can. 🏆

Rhododendron bureaui

Rhododendron burmanicum

R. burmanicum (Rhododendron) A small evergreen shrub with densely scaly, dark green leaves. It bears funnel-shaped, greenish yellow, fragrant flowers, to 2 in (5 cm) long, that age to white in early to mid-spring. Mt. Victoria, C Burma.
Zone 9 US 🏆

R. calendulaceum (Flame azalea) A medium-sized to large deciduous shrub with leaves that turn orange or red in fall. The funnel-shaped flowers, 2 in (5 cm) across, vary from yellow to orange in early summer. E North America. Introduced 1806.
Zone 4 US, 5 Can.

Rhododendron calophytum

R. calophytum (Bigleaf rhododendron) One of the hardiest large-leaved species, this is an evergreen large shrub or small tree with rosettes of narrow leaves up to 12 in (30 cm) long. It bears large trusses of white or pink bell-shaped flowers, each with a

maroon basal blotch, in early to midspring. It needs plenty of moisture. China. Introduced 1904 by Ernest Wilson.
Zone 5 US, 6 Can.

R. calostrotum (Purple-elf rhododendron) A dwarf evergreen shrub with gray-green foliage and relatively large, flat, magenta-purple flowers in late spring and early summer. The following forms are recommended. China, Burma. Introduced 1919.
Zone 6 US, 7 Can.

***R. c.* 'Gigha'** A beautiful selection with deep claret flowers that contrast with the gray-green young leaves.
Zone 6 US, 7 Can.

R. c.* subsp. *keleticum A dwarf shrub that forms mats or mounds of small leaves from which the saucer-shaped, purple-crimson flowers arise singly or in pairs. Himalayan region. Introduced 1919 by George Forrest.
Zone 5 US, 6 Can.

R. campanulatum (Bellflower rhododendron) A large evergreen shrub whose unfolding leaves are covered with a fawn or rust-colored, suedelike indumentum. The bell-shaped flowers vary from pale rose to lavender-blue and are borne in mid- to late spring. The following forms are recommended. Himalaya. Introduced 1825.
Zone 6 US, 7 Can.

R. c.* subsp. *aeruginosum A slow-growing, compact shrub with striking, metallic blue-green young growths. Himalayan region.
Zone 6 US, 7 Can.

Rhododendron campylocarpum subsp. *caloxanthum*

***R. c.* 'Knap Hill'** A form that bears lavender-blue flowers. Zone 6 US, 7 Can.

R. campylocarpum* subsp. *caloxanthum (Rhododendron) A small to medium-sized, free-flowering, evergreen shrub with small, rounded leaves and clusters of citron yellow flowers tipped with orange-scarlet in the bud. Himalayan region. Introduced 1919 by Reginald Farrer.
Zone 7 US, 8 Can.

R. campylogynum (Rhododendron) A dwarf evergreen shrub with small leaves that are glaucous beneath and long-stalked, nodding, bell-shaped, rose-purple to almost mahogany flowers, produced when the plant is still only a few inches high. It flowers in late spring and early summer. Himalayan region. Introduced 1912 by George Forrest.
Zone 7 US, 8 Can.

***R. c.* 'Bodnant Red'** A form that produces red flowers.
Zone 7 US, 8 Can.

***R. c.* 'Crushed Strawberry'** A form with strawberry-red flowers. Selected c. 1955.
Zone 7 US, 8 Can.

R. camtschaticum (Azalea) A dwarf, spreading, twiggy, deciduous shrublet up to 12 in (30 cm) high with relatively large, saucer-shaped, rose-purple flowers in late spring. The lower side of the flower is split almost to the base. The leaves are 2 in (5 cm) long and turn color in fall. Alaska, Kamchatka, Japan. Introduced 1799.
Zone 5 US, 6 Can.

R. canadense (Rhodora azalea) A small deciduous shrub with upright twiggy shoots bearing gray-green leaves. The narrow-petaled, rose-pink flowers appear before the leaves in early to midspring. NE North America. Introduced 1767.
Zone 3 US, 3 Can.

R. canescens (Woolly azalea, Florida pinxter) A large, upright, deciduous shrub with dark green leaves that are gray-woolly beneath. White to pink flowers with a long tube open with the leaves in spring. North Carolina to Texas. Introduced 1810.
Zone 7 US, 8 Can.

R. carolinianum (Carolina rhododendron) A medium-sized, compact, evergreen shrub with pale rose-purple flowers in midspring. The leaves are 3 in (7.5 cm) long and scaly-brown beneath. North Carolina.
Zone 6 US, 7 Can.

R. c.* var. *album A form with pure white flowers that have a yellow-green blotch.
Zone 6 US, 7 Can.

Rhododendron cerasinum

Rhododendron chamaethomsonii

R. catawbiense (Catawba rhododendron) A large, spreading evergreen shrub that is one parent of many of the Ironclad hybrid rhododendrons. The shiny green leaves are widest toward the base, and the lilac-purple flowers open in late spring. E North America. Introduced 1799 by John Fraser.
Zone 4 US, 5 Can.

R. cerasinum (Rhododendron) A medium-sized to large evergreen shrub with elliptical leaves 2–4 in (5–10 cm) long. It has drooping trusses of long, bell-shaped flowers from white with a red marginal band to crimson in late spring. Himalaya.
Zone 7 US, 8 Can.

R. chamaethomsonii (Rhododendron) A dwarf, more or less prostrate, evergreen

shrub displaying trusses of 5–6 bell-shaped, crimson or rose-crimson flowers in early to midspring. W China, E Tibet.
Zone 7 US, 8 Can.

Rhododendron ciliatum

R. ciliatum (Fringed rhododendron) A dome-shaped evergreen shrub 4–5 ft (1.2–1.5 m) high with peeling bark and bristle-edged leaves. The fragrant, bell-shaped flowers are white to rose-lilac, borne in early to midspring. Himalaya. Introduced 1850 by Sir Joseph Hooker.
Zone 5 US, 6b Can. 🏆

Rhododendron cinnabarinum

R. cinnabarinum (Cinnabar rhododendron) A beautiful medium-sized to large evergreen shrub with tubular or bell-shaped flowers that are usually cinnabar red but can also be orange, yellow, pink, or purple; it blooms in late spring to early summer. The leaves are obovate-elliptic and scaly beneath and are very susceptible to powdery mildew. Himalayan region. Introduced 1849 by Sir Joseph Hooker.
Zone 5 US, 6 Can.

R. c.* subsp. *xanthocodon A form with waxy, yellow, bell-shaped to funnel-shaped flowers in late spring and early summer. It flowers best with some shelter and is less prone to powdery mildew than the species. Himalayan region. Introduced 1924.
Zone 5 US, 6b Can. 🏆

R. citriniflorum (Rhododendron) A small evergreen shrub with shiny green leaves, covered beneath with a dense brown fur. The clusters of 6–8 flowers are a pure lemon yellow. China.
Zone 8 US, 9 Can.

R. concinnum (Rhododendron) A lovely medium-sized to large evergreen shrub with elliptical leaves and clusters of funnel-shaped, deep ruby-red or purple-red flowers in mid- to late spring. W China.
Zone 8 US, 9? Can.

R. dalhousiae* var. *rhabdotum (Rhododendron) A medium-sized to large evergreen shrub with bristly shoots and veined leaves. The very fragrant, lilylike, creamy white flowers, streaked outside with crimson, are borne in late spring. Himalaya.
Zone 9 US 🏆

R. dauricum (Azalea) A charming, medium-sized, deciduous or semievergreen

Rhododendron dauricum

shrub that has leathery, elliptical leaves about 1 in (2–3 cm) long and funnel-shaped, bright rose-purple flowers from late winter to early spring. NE Asia. In cultivation 1870.
Zone 4 US, 4b Can.

***R. d.* 'Hiltingbury'** A compact form with leaves that turn bronze in cold weather.
Zone 4 US, 4b Can.

***R. d.* 'Midwinter'** A form with bright purple flowers that open earlier than those of the species.
Zone 4 US, 4b Can. 🏆

Rhododendron davidsonianum

R. davidsonianum (Davidson rhododendron) A medium-sized to large evergreen shrub with lance-shaped leaves. The funnel-shaped flowers are borne in clusters at the ends of the shoots and in the joints of the leaves in mid- to late spring. They vary in color from white to purplish rose and are sometimes spotted. China. Introduced 1904 by Ernest Wilson.
Zone 5 US, 6 Can. 🏆

R. decorum (Sweetshell rhododendron) A beautiful, large, evergreen shrub with glabrous, more or less oblong leaves up to 6 in (15 cm) long and large, fragrant, funnel-shaped flowers in lax trusses in late spring to early summer. They are white or shell pink

Rhododendron decorum

and sometimes spotted. China, NE Burma. Introduced 1901 by Ernest Wilson.
Zone 7 US, 8 Can.

R. d.* subsp. *diaprepes A form with larger flowers and leaves up to 1 ft (30 cm) long.
Zone 7 US, 8 Can.

R. degronianum (Rhododendron) A leafy, small to medium-sized, mounding, evergreen shrub with leaves that are fawn-felted beneath and deep green above. The flowers are soft pink to rose with deeper lines on the throat and are borne in clusters of 12–15 in late spring. Introduced 1894 from Japan by F. Doleshy.
Zone 7 US, 8 Can.

Rhododendron edgeworthii

R. dichroanthum (Rhododendron) A slow-growing, dome-shaped evergreen shrub 4–6½ ft (1.2–2 m) high with leaves that are 2–4 in (5–10 cm) long and have a white to gray wool beneath. The bell-shaped flowers vary in color but are usually deep orange and are borne in loose trusses in late spring and early summer. The calyx is large and fleshy and the same color as the corolla. It is a parent of many hybrids. China. Found 1906 by George Forrest.
Zone 5 US, 6b Can.

R. edgeworthii (Edgeworth rhododendron) A medium-sized evergreen shrub with soft fawn or brown indumentum on the branches and undersides of the dark green, bullate leaves. The fragrant flowers are funnel shaped and white or slightly pink in spring. It forms a rather straggly shrub. China, Tibet, Upper Burma. Introduced 1904 by George Forrest.
Zone 10 US 🏆

R. falconeri (Rhododendron) This magnificent evergreen large shrub or small tree has very large, broadly obovate leaves with deeply impressed veins and a rusty indumentum beneath. It has huge, dome-shaped trusses of waxy, creamy yellow, purple-blotched, bell-shaped flowers in mid- to late spring. Himalayan region. Introduced 1850 by Sir Joseph Hooker.
Zone 9 US 🏆

Rhododendron falconeri

R. f.* subsp. *eximium A large shrub or small tree whose young growths and leaves are covered with orange-brown felt. The leaves are up to 12 in (30 cm) long and 3 in (7.5 cm) wide; the pink or rose, bell-shaped flowers are 2 in (5 cm) long. NE India.
Zone 9 US

R. fastigiatum (Rhododendron) A dense, small, dome-shaped, evergreen shrub 2–3 ft (60–90 cm) high with small, scaly leaves that are sea green when young. The funnel-shaped, lavender-purple flowers are borne in mid- to late spring. China. Introduced 1906 by George Forrest.
Zone 6 US, 7 Can. 🏆

R. ferrugineum (Rock rhododendron, alpine rose) A small, spreading, evergreen shrub with a flattish dome shape and leaves that are reddish beneath. The flowers are rose-crimson, tubular, and borne in small trusses in early summer. Pyrenees, Alps. In

Rhododendron ferrugineum

cultivation 1740.
Zone 4 US, 5 Can.

R. flavidum (Amberbloom rhododendron) A pretty, erect, evergreen shrub 2–3 ft (60–90 cm) high with small, glossy, aromatic leaves and funnel-shaped, pale yellow flowers in early spring. China. Introduced 1905 by Ernest Wilson.
Zone 6 US, 7 Can.

R. formosum (Rhododendron) A medium-sized evergreen shrub with glossy green, pointed leaves that are margined when young with long bristles. The fragrant, broadly funnel-shaped flowers are more than 2 in (5 cm) long and are white or slightly pink with a yellow throat in late spring and early summer. Himalaya.
Zone 8 US, 9? Can. 🏆

***R. forrestii* Repens group** (Rhododendron) Choice, creeping, prostrate, evergreen shrubs forming mats of dark green leaves that are pale or glaucous green below. The surprisingly large, bell-shaped, bright scarlet flowers are borne singly or in pairs in mid- to late spring. Tibet.
Zone 8 US, 9? Can.

R. fortunei (Fortune rhododendron) A large evergreen shrub with leaves up to 8 in (20 cm) long and funnel-shaped, fragrant, pink or rose-lilac flowers borne in large trusses in late spring to early summer. China. Introduced 1859.
Zone 5 US, 6 Can.

R. f.* subsp. *discolor (Mandarin rhododendron) A form with white to pale pink flowers in early summer. China. Introduced 1900 by Ernest Wilson.
Zone 5 US, 6 Can.

Rhododendron fulgens

R. fulgens (Rhododendron) A medium-sized evergreen shrub with broad leaves, felted reddish brown beneath, and peeling bark. The rounded trusses have 10–12 bell-shaped, scarlet flowers. Himalayan region. Introduced 1850 by Sir Joseph Hooker.
Zone 7 US, 8 Can.

Rhododendron fulvum

R. fulvum (Rhododendron) An evergreen large shrub or small tree with large, glossy, dark green leaves that are cinnamon-felted beneath. The bell-shaped flowers, borne in early to midspring, are blush to deep rose and may have a crimson blotch. Himalaya. Introduced 1912 by George Forrest.
Zone 7 US, 8 Can. 🏆

R. giganteum (Giant rhododendron) The largest rhododendron, forming an evergreen tree to 80 ft (25 m) tall. It bears trusses of 20–25 crimson, funnel-shaped flowers in late winter, but not on young plants. China.
Zone 9 US

R. glaucophyllum (Rhododendron) A small, aromatic, evergreen shrub with lance-shaped leaves, white beneath. The pale rose to lilac, bell-shaped flowers open in mid- to late spring. Himalayan region. Introduced 1850 by Sir Joseph Hooker.
Zone 8 US, 9? Can.

R. griersonianum (Grierson rhododendron) A striking, medium-sized, evergreen shrub with long, lance-shaped leaves, matte green above and buff-woolly beneath. The bright scarlet, narrowly bell-shaped flowers appear in early summer. China, N Burma. Introduced 1917 by George Forrest.
Zone 8 US, 9 Can.

R. griffithianum (Griffith rhododendron) A large evergreen shrub with lightly scented, white to pink flowers that have frilled edges, blooming in late spring. The leaves are up to 1 ft (30 cm) long. Himalaya.
Zone 8 US, 9 Can.

R. haematodes (Royalblood rhododendron) A compact, small to medium-sized, slow-growing, evergreen shrub with dark green leaves that are thickly rufous-felted beneath. The flowers are bell shaped and brilliant scarlet, appearing in late spring and early summer. China. Introduced 1911 by George Forrest.
Zone 7 US, 8 Can.

***R. hanceanum* Nanum group** (Rhododendron) Slow-growing, dainty, dwarf, evergreen shrubs that make neat mounds up to 14 in (35 cm) high. They bear funnel-shaped, cream or pale yellow flowers 1 in (2.5 cm) long. China.
Zone 5 US, 6 Can.

R. hippophaeoides (Sea buckthorn rhododendron) A small, erect, evergreen shrub that resembles sea buckthorn. It has pale green leaves and light blue-lavender to pale rose flowers in early to midspring. Tolerates boggy conditions.
Zone 5 US, 6 Can. 🏆

Rhododendron impeditum

R. hirsutum (Garland rhododendron) A small evergreen shrub with small leaves that are golden-scaly beneath and bristled at the margins. It has rose-pink flowers in summer. Tolerates alkaline soil. C Europe.
Zone 4 US, 5 Can.

R. hodgsonii (Rhododendron) An evergreen large shrub or small tree with handsome leaves that are up to 12 in (30 cm)

long and 5 in (13 cm) wide and are dark green above and gray or fawn beneath. The bell-shaped, dark magenta flowers are carried in large trusses in midspring. Himalaya. Introduced 1850 by Sir Joseph Hooker.
Zone 9 US

R. impeditum (Cloudland rhododendron) A dwarf alpine evergreen shrub, usually about 18 in (45 cm) high. It has tiny leaves and makes a low, tangled mound of scaly branches. The flowers are funnel shaped, light purplish blue to violet, and borne in mid- to late spring. Good for the rock garden and not tolerant of hot, dry summers. China. Introduced 1911 by George Forrest.
Zone 4 US, 5 Can.

***R. indicum* 'Balsaminiflorum'** (Balsam azalea) A dwarf, dense, semievergreen shrub with leaves that often turn crimson or purple in fall. The double, salmon pink flowers are single or in pairs and appear in early summer. It is a form of the Indica azalea and should not be confused with the Indian hybrid azaleas. Japan.
Zone 6 US, 7 Can.

R. insigne (Rhododendron) A slow-growing evergreen that eventually becomes a large shrub. It has leathery, glossy green leaves that are silvery beneath when young and take on a metallic luster. The bell-shaped flowers are soft pink with dark markings and borne in late spring to early summer in large trusses. China. Introduced 1908 by Ernest Wilson.
Zone 6 US, 7 Can.

R. japonicum (Japanese azalea) A vigorous, deciduous, medium-sized shrub whose large flowers vary from orange-red to brick red, blooming in late spring. The flowers have a very unpleasant scent. Introduced 1861. Japan.
Zone 5 US, 6 Can.

R. johnstoneanum (Rhododendron) A large evergreen shrub with rounded leaves that have bristly margins. The large, fragrant, funnel-shaped flowers are borne in late spring in clusters of 3–4 and are cream or pale yellow with red spots and a yellow blotch. Manipur. Introduced 1882.
Zone 7 US, 8 Can.

R. kaempferi (Torch azalea) A beautiful, medium-sized, deciduous or semievergreen shrub. The funnel-shaped flowers are in clusters of 2–4 and vary from pink to scarlet, salmon-red, and orange-red. They open in late spring to early summer. Leaves have reddish fall color. It is a parent of many of the Kurume hybrid azaleas. Japan. Introduced 1892 by Professor Sargent.
Zone 5 US, 6 Can.

***R. k.* 'Mikado'** A form with dark red flowers in midsummer and wine red fall color.
Zone 5 US, 6 Can.

R. keiskii (Keisk rhododendron) A free-flowering, semievergreen, dwarf shrub. The lance-shaped leaves are 1–3 in (2.5–7.5 cm) long, and the flowers are pale yellow, widely funnel shaped, and borne in trusses of 3–5 in late spring. Japan. Introduced 1908.
Zone 4 US, 5b Can.

***R. k.* 'Yaku Fairy'** A very dwarf or prostrate form. Yakushima.
Zone 4 US, 5b Can.

R. kiusianum (Kyushu azalea) A dense, dwarf, evergreen or semievergreen shrub, up to 3 ft (1 m), with small, oval leaves. The

Rhododendron kaempferi

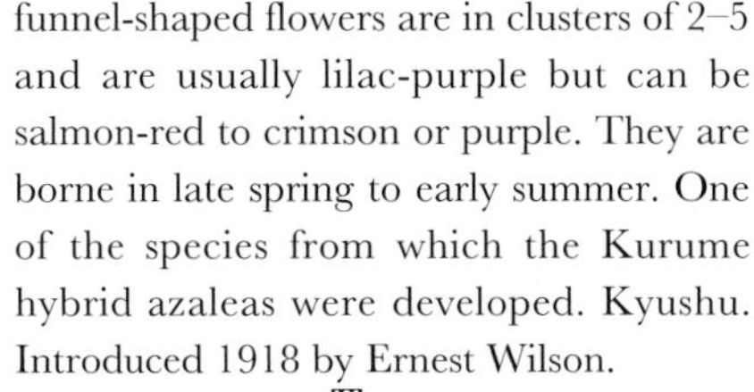

funnel-shaped flowers are in clusters of 2–5 and are usually lilac-purple but can be salmon-red to crimson or purple. They are borne in late spring to early summer. One of the species from which the Kurume hybrid azaleas were developed. Kyushu. Introduced 1918 by Ernest Wilson.
Zone 5 US, 6 Can.

***R. k.* 'Hillier's Pink'** A lovely form with clear lilac-pink flowers. Raised 1957 by Hillier Nurseries.
Zone 5 US, 6 Can.

Rhododendron leucaspis

R. lapponicum (Lapland rhododendron) A dwarf, prostrate, evergreen shrub with small, fine-textured leaves that are scaly beneath and small, purple to violet-rose, broadly bell-shaped flowers in early summer. N North America, N Europe, N Asia.
Zone 2 US, 2 Can.

R. lepidostylum (Rhododendron) A dwarf evergreen or semievergreen shrub, occasionally as much as 3 ft (1 m) high. The small, bristly, ovate leaves are steely blue-green on their upper surfaces until winter. The flowers are funnel shaped, pale yellow, single or in pairs, appearing in late spring and early summer. It is a good choice for a shady rock garden and has the bluest leaves of the dwarf rhododendrons. China. Introduced 1924 by George Forrest.
Zone 6 US, 7 Can.

R. leucaspis (Whiteshield rhododendron) A dwarf evergreen shrub, up to 3 ft (1 m) high, with hairy leaves. The saucer-shaped flowers, in clusters of 2–3, are 2 in (5 cm) wide and milky white with contrasting chocolate brown anthers. It flowers in late

Rhododendron lutescens 'Bagshot Sands'

Rhododendron luteum

winter and early spring and needs protection from frost. Burma-Tibet frontier. Introduced 1925 by Frank Kingdon-Ward.
Zone 8 US, 9? Can. 🏆

R. lindleyi (Rhododendron) A large, open, evergreen shrub with bluish leaves. The very fragrant, widely funnel-shaped flowers, 4 in (10 cm) across, are cream blotched with orange or yellow at the base and sometimes edged with pink. They are borne in mid- to late spring. Himalayan region.
Zone 9 US 🏆

***R. lutescens* 'Bagshot Sands'** A medium-sized to large, free-flowering form of the evergreen canary rhododendron with bronze-red young growths. The large, funnel-shaped, primrose yellow flowers bloom in late winter to early spring and need protection from frost.
Zone 7 US, 8 Can. 🏆

R. luteum (Pontic azalea) A medium-sized deciduous shrub, occasionally growing up to 11 ft (3.5 m) high and wide. The fragrant, funnel-shaped, yellow flowers are borne in late spring. The leaves turn crimson, purple, and orange in fall. Caucasus, E Europe. Introduced 1793.
Zone 3 US, 4 Can. 🏆

R. macabeanum (Rhododendron) A rounded, evergreen, large shrub or small tree with leaves up to 12 in (30 cm) long that are shiny above and gray-white-woolly beneath. The large trusses of bell-shaped, purple-blotched, pale yellow or canary yellow flowers are borne in early to midspring, but not on young plants. NE India. Introduced c. 1928 by Frank Kingdon-Ward.
Zone 8 US, 9? Can. 🏆

R. macrophyllum (California rhododendron, California rosebay) A medium-sized to large evergreen shrub with leaves up to 8 in (20 cm) long and pale rosy purple flowers in early summer. W North America.
Zone 7 US, 8 Can.

R. maculiferum* subsp. *anwheiense (Rhododendron) A medium-sized evergreen shrub with oval lance-shaped leaves 2–3 in (5–7.5 cm) long and rounded heads of bell-shaped white flowers, usually with a pink flush and reddish purple spots. They are borne in mid- to late spring. China.
Zone 9 US 🏆

Rhododendron maddenii

R. maddenii (Madden rhododendron) A large evergreen shrub or small tree with fra-

grant white or pink flowers. Himalaya. Introduced 1850 by Sir Joseph Hooker.
Zone 10 US 🏆

Rhododendron makinoi

R. m.* subsp. *crassum (Sweetbay rhododendron) A medium-sized to large shrub with rigid leaves that are rusty-scaly below. The fragrant, funnel-shaped flowers are 2–3 in (5–7.5 cm) long and white to pink, sometimes with a yellow blotch; they appear in early to midsummer. Himalayan region. Introduced 1906 by George Forrest.
Zone 9 US 🏆

Rhododendron minus

R. makinoi (Rhododendron) A medium-sized evergreen shrub with young growth appearing in late summer covered in white or tawny, woolly indumentum. The leaves are narrowly lance shaped, wrinkled above and tawny-woolly beneath. The bell-shaped pink flowers, borne in early summer, sometimes have crimson spots. Japan.
Zone 7 US, 8 Can. 🏆

R. maximum (Rosebay rhododendron) A spreading, evergreen, large shrub or small tree with leathery leaves with rolled edges. The heads of rose-purple or pink-purple flowers open in summer but are often hidden by the foliage. E North America. Introduced 1736 by John Bartram.
Zone 3 US, 3 Can.

R. minus (Piedmont rhododendron) A very attractive, free-flowering, evergreen shrub up to 15 ft (4.5 m) high with tubular, soft rose-purple flowers in late spring and early summer. SE United States. Introduced 1812.
Zone 6 US, 7 Can.

R. moupinense (Moupin rhododendron) A delightful, early-flowering, medium-sized, evergreen shrub with bristly branchlets. The sweetly scented flowers are funnel shaped and white, pink, or deep rose, sometimes spotted red. It flowers in late winter and early spring and needs protection from frost. China.
Zone 6 US, 7 Can. 🏆

R. mucronatum (Snow azalea) A medium-sized evergreen or semievergreen shrub with a spreading, dome-shaped habit and gray-green leaves. The fragrant, funnel-shaped, pure white flowers are borne in late spring. Long cultivated in Japan but unknown in the wild and possibly of hybrid origin. Introduced 1819.
Zone 6 US, 7 Can.

R. mucronulatum (Korean rhododendron) A slender, medium-sized, deciduous shrub with elliptic-lanceolate leaves up to 2 in (5 cm) long that turn yellow to bronze-red in fall. The large, funnel-shaped, rose-purple flowers are borne from late winter to early spring and need protection from frost. E Russia to Japan. Introduced 1882.
Zone 3 US, 4 Can.

***R. m.* 'Cornell Pink'** A form that produces clear pink flowers.
Zone 4 US, 4b Can. 🏆

***R. m.* 'Winter Brightness'** The flowers of this form are a deeper purple-rose than those of the species.
Zone 4 US, 4b Can. 🏆

R. nakaharai (Azalea) An attractive, rare, dwarf, creeping evergreen shrub with small, lance-shaped leaves. The funnel-shaped flowers, up to 1 in (2.5 cm) long, are an

Rhododendron neriiflorum Euchaites group

Rhododendron niveum

unusual dark brick red and are borne in clusters in early to midsummer. Taiwan.
Zone 4 US, 5 Can.

***R. neriiflorum* Euchaites group** (Rhododendron) Medium-sized evergreen shrubs with narrow leaves that are glaucous white beneath. Trusses of bell-shaped, fleshy, crimson-scarlet flowers open in mid-

Rhododendron nuttallii

Rhododendron oreotrephes

spring; the calyx is large and the same color as the corolla. China. Introduced 1913.
Zone 7 US, 8 Can.

R. niveum (Rhododendron) An attractive large evergreen shrub whose leaves, up to 6 in (15 cm) long, are lance shaped and covered with a persistent white, suedelike indumentum that turns pale brown on the undersurfaces. The flowers are bell shaped, smoky blue to rich purple, and borne in tight, globular heads in mid- to late spring. Himalayan region. Introduced 1849 by Sir Joseph Hooker. *(See photo on p.497.)*
Zone 7 US, 8 Can. 🏆

***R. n.* 'Clyne Castle'** A large evergreen shrub with larger leaves than the species and rich purple flowers.
Zone 7 US, 8 Can.

R. nudiflorum See *R. periclymenoides.*

R. nuttallii (Rhododendron) A medium-sized to large evergreen shrub with leaves up to 8 in (20 cm) long, wrinkled above and metallic purple when unfolding. The fragrant, funnel-shaped, lilylike flowers are 5 in (13 cm) or more long and are borne in loose trusses of 3–9 in mid- to late spring; they are yellow or white flushed with yellow within and are tinged with pink on the lobes. Himalayan region. Introduced 1850.
Zone 10 US 🏆

R. occidentale (Western azalea) A medium-sized deciduous shrub with more or less oval, glossy green leaves that turn yellow, scarlet, or crimson in fall. The flowers usually appear with the leaves in early summer and are widely funnel shaped, fragrant, and cream to pale pink with pale yellow or orange-yellow basal stains. It is a parent of many hybrids. W North America. Introduced 1851 by William Lobb.
Zone 5 US, 6 Can. 🏆

R. orbiculare (Globe rhododendron) An outstanding evergreen species that forms a symmetrical, dome-shaped shrub up to 10 ft (3 m) high and wide. The leaves are rounded and heart shaped at the base, and the flowers are bell shaped, seven-lobed, and rose-pink, sometimes with a bluish tinge. They are borne in early to midspring. China. Introduced 1904 by Ernest Wilson.
Zone 6 US, 7 Can.

R. oreodoxa* var. *fargesii (Pere Farges rhododendron) A medium-sized to large, free-flowering, evergreen shrub with

Rhododendron orbiculare

oblong-elliptic leaves and funnel-shaped flowers that are 2 in (5 cm) long, deep rose-pink on the outside, and paler within. They are borne about eight in a truss in early to midspring. China. Introduced c. 1901 by Ernest Wilson.
Zone 6 US, 7 Can. 🏆

R. oreotrephes (Oread rhododendron) A free-flowering, large, semievergreen shrub with glaucous young growths and leaves that are usually oblong-elliptic and glaucous beneath. The flowers, borne in mid- to late spring, are generally funnel shaped and vary from mauve to rosy red, with or without crimson spots. China. Introduced 1910 by George Forrest.
Zone 6 US, 7 Can.

R. pachysanthum (Rhododendron) A medium-sized evergreen shrub that produces oblong leaves up to 3½ in (9 cm) long, with silvery or brownish tomentum on their upper surfaces when young and densely so beneath. The broadly bell-shaped flowers appear in early to midspring in large trusses of up to 20 and are white to pale pink, sometimes spotted inside. Taiwan. Introduced 1972 by John Patrick.
Zone 9? US 🏆

R. pemakoense (Pemako rhododendron) A beautiful, dwarf, suckering, evergreen shrub with small leaves and relatively large, funnel-shaped, silvery lilac-pink flowers in early to midspring. It flowers freely as long as the buds escape frost damage. Himalayan region. Introduced 1924 by Frank Kingdon-Ward.
Zone 6 US, 7 Can.

R. periclymenoides, syn. *R. nudiflorum* (Pinxterbloom azalea) A medium-sized deciduous shrub with dull green leaves and pink, lightly scented flowers that appear with the foliage. E United States. Introduced 1735.
Zone 3 US, 3 Can.

R. polycladum (Rhododendron) A small, upright evergreen shrub with funnel-shaped, lavender-blue flowers in mid- to late spring. This plant has been known until recently as *R. scintillans*. China. Introduced 1913 by George Forrest.
Zone 6 US, 7 Can. 🏆

Rhododendron ponticum

Rhododendron ponticum 'Variegatum'

R. ponticum (Ponticum rhododendron) A large, vigorous, densely branched, evergreen shrub with glossy, pointed leaves. The mauve to lilac-pink flowers appear in summer. It is one of the few shrubs that will grow well under dense shade trees. Portugal to Caucasus. Introduced 1763.
Zone 7 US, 8 Can.

Rhododendron pseudochrysanthum

***R. p.* 'Variegatum'** A rare variegated form, with leaves margined with cream.
Zone 7 US, 8 Can.

R. prinophyllum See *R. roseum.*

R. prunifolium (Plumleaf azalea) A large deciduous shrub with elliptical leaves up to 5 in (13 cm) long. The flowers, which appear in mid- to late summer, are funnel shaped and bright orange-red or scarlet.

Georgia-Alabama border. Introduced 1918 by Professor Sargent.
Zone 5 US, 6 Can.

R. pseudochrysanthum (Rhododendron) A slow-growing, compact, medium-sized, dome-shaped, evergreen shrub. The leaves, 2–3 in (5–7.5 cm) long, have a woolly covering when young. The bell-shaped flowers are pale pink or white, with darker lines and spots, and are borne in midspring. Taiwan. Introduced 1918 by Ernest Wilson. *(See photo on p.499.)* Zone 8 US, 9? Can. 🏆

Rhododendron racemosum

R. quinquefolium (Cork azalea) A medium-sized to large deciduous shrub with ovate to diamond-shaped leaves in whorls of 4–5 at the ends of the shoots. They are green, bordered with reddish brown when young, and turn color in fall. The pendulous, saucer-shaped flowers, 2 in (4–5 cm) wide, are white with green spots and appear in small clusters after the leaves in mid- to late spring. Japan. Introduced 1896.
Zone 8 US, 9? Can. 🏆

R. racemosum (Mayflower rhododendron) A variable species, usually a dense, small to medium-sized, evergreen shrub with oblong-elliptical, leathery leaves that are glaucous beneath. The funnel-shaped, pale to bright pink flowers arise in racemes from the leaf axils in early to midspring. Introduced c. 1889.
Zone 6 US, 7 Can.

***R. r.* 'Forrest's Dwarf'** A dwarf form with red branchlets and bright pink flowers. China. Collected 1921 by George Forrest.
Zone 6 US, 7 Can.

***R. r.* 'Rock Rose'** A free-flowering, small, compact form with bright pink flowers.
Zone 6 US, 7 Can. 🏆

R. reticulatum (Azalea) A medium-sized to large deciduous shrub with leaves somewhat diamond shaped, notably net veined beneath; they are purplish when young and turn wine-purple in fall. The funnel-shaped, bright purple flowers appear alone or in pairs before the leaves in mid- to late spring. Japan. Introduced 1865.
Zone 6 US, 7 Can. 🏆

R. rex (Rhododendron) An evergreen large shrub or small tree with large, shiny, dark green leaves covered with gray to pale buff felt beneath. Bell-shaped flowers, borne in large trusses in mid- to late spring, are rose or white, with a crimson basal stain and spots. China.
Zone 7 US, 8 Can.

Rhododendron rex subsp. *fictolacteum*

R. r.* subsp. *arizelum A form with large leaves covered beneath with a cinnamon indumentum. The flowers are borne in midspring in compact heads of creamy yellow bells, sometimes rose-tinted, with a dark crimson blotch. It does best in moist, woodland conditions. Himalayan region.
Zone 7 US, 8 Can.

R. r.* subsp. *fictolacteum A form whose shoots are covered with cinnamon felting. The leaves, which are as long as 12 in (30 cm), are brown-felted on the undersides. The bell-shaped flowers, cream or pink with a crimson blotch, are borne in large trusses. Himalaya. Introduced 1885 by the Abbé Delavay.
Zone 7 US, 8 Can.

***R. r.* 'Quartz'** A form with pale pink flowers that are blotched and speckled with crimson.
Zone 7 US, 8 Can. 🏆

Rhododendron roxieanum Oreonastes group

R. roseum, syn. *R. prinophyllum* (Roseshell azalea, piedmont azalea) A lovely medium-sized to large deciduous shrub with more or less oval leaves. The clove-scented, funnel-shaped, pale to deep pink flowers appear with the leaves in late spring. E North America. Introduced 1812 or earlier.
Zone 3 US, 4 Can. 🏆

***R. roxieanum* Oreonastes group** (Rhododendron) Small to medium-sized evergreen shrubs with very narrow leaves 2–4 in (5–10 cm) long, coated beneath with a fawn or rust-red indumentum. The bell-shaped flowers are cream, usually flushed with rose, and borne 10–15 in a tight truss in mid- to late spring. Himalayan region.
Zone 7 US, 8 Can. 🏆

R. rubiginosum (Rusty rhododendron) A free-flowering, large, evergreen shrub with

Rhododendron russatum

aromatic leaves 1½–2½ in (4–6 cm) long, covered with rust-colored scales beneath. The flowers, borne in mid- to late spring, are funnel shaped and pink or rosy lilac, with brown spots. Himalaya, China. Introduced 1889 by the Abbé Delavay.
Zone 6 US, 7 Can.

R. russatum (Royal alp rhododendron) A small evergreen shrub up to 4 ft (1.2 m) tall. The leaves are about 1 in (2.5 cm) long, and the funnel-shaped flowers are deep blue-purple and borne in mid- to late spring. It needs cool summers and moist air to thrive. China. Introduced 1917 by George Forrest.
Zone 4 US, 5 Can. 🏆

R. saluenense (Rhododendron) A small, densely matted, evergreen shrub of variable habit. The small, ovate-elliptic, aromatic leaves are hidden in mid- to late spring by clusters of funnel-shaped, rose-purple or purplish crimson flowers. SE Himalaya. Introduced 1914 by George Forrest.
Zone 6 US, 7 Can.

R. s.* subsp. *chameunum A dwarf evergreen shrub with erect stems and bristle-clad branchlets. The flowers are saucer shaped with wavy margins, rose-purple with crimson spots, and borne in loose clusters of up to six in mid- to late spring. SE Himalaya.
Zone 6 US, 7 Can. 🏆

R. sanctum (Azalea) A large deciduous shrub with reddish shoots and glossy green leaves that have long red hairs on their upper surfaces. The dark pink, bell-shaped flowers open in late spring. Japan.
Zone 7 US, 8 Can.

R. schlippenbachii (Royal azalea) A medium-sized to large deciduous shrub of rounded habit with large leaves in whorls of five at the ends of the branches; they are suffused with purplish red when young and

Rhododendron schlippenbachii

turn orange, yellow, and crimson in fall. The fragrant flowers, which appear with or before the leaves in mid- to late spring, are saucer shaped, 3 in (7.5 cm) across, and pale pink to rose-pink, occasionally white. They are subject to frost damage in mild areas where growth starts early. Korea, Manchuria. Introduced 1893 by James Veitch.
Zone 4 US, 5 Can. 🏆

R. serpyllifolium (Wildthyme azalea) A small, dense, spreading, deciduous shrub with tiny, elliptic, slightly hairy leaves. The small rose-pink flowers are funnel shaped and bloom in spring. C and S Japan.
Zone 6 US, 7 Can. 🏆

R. simsii (Sim's azalea) A medium-sized evergreen or semievergreen shrub with small, elliptic, hairy leaves. The broadly funnel-shaped flowers are rosy red to crimson, held 2–6 in a truss, and appear in mid-spring to late spring. It is a parent of the Indian hybrid azaleas. China, Taiwan.
Zone 7 US, 8 Can. 🏆

R. sinogrande (Rhododendron) A large evergreen shrub or small tree for woodland locations with shiny, dark green leaves as large as 32 in (80 cm) long and 12 in (30 cm) wide. The lower surface has a silvery or silvery fawn indumentum. The flowers, creamy white with a crimson blotch, are borne in huge trusses in midspring as the plant reaches maturity. Himalayan region. Introduced 1913 by George Forrest.
Zone 8 US, 9? Can. 🏆

R. smirnowii (Smirnow rhododendron) A hardy, compact, slow-growing, medium-sized to large evergreen shrub with leaves up to 6 in (15 cm) long, felted gray or pale brown beneath. The bell-shaped, rose-purple or rose-pink flowers are borne in late spring to early summer. NE Turkey, Republic of Georgia. Introduced 1886. *(See photo on p.502.)* Zone 4 US, 5b Can.

R. souliei (Soulie rhododendron) A beautiful medium-sized evergreen shrub with leaves that are almost round and 2–3 in (5–7.5 cm) long. The saucer-shaped, white or soft pink flowers are borne in late spring to early summer. China. Introduced 1903 by Ernest Wilson.
Zone 8 US, 9? Can.

Rhododendron sutchuenense

R. sutchuenense (Szechwan rhododendron) A large evergreen shrub with stout shoots and drooping leaves up to 12 in (30 cm) long. It blooms in late winter to

Rhododendron smirnowii

early spring with loose trusses of bell-shaped flowers 2¾ in (7 cm) long that vary from pale pink to rosy lilac, with purple spots. It needs protection from late frost. China. Introduced 1900 by Ernest Wilson.
Zone 6 US, 7 Can.

R. taliense (Rhododendron) A medium-sized evergreen shrub with dark green leaves, densely brown-felted beneath. The flowers are bell shaped, cream to yellow but sometimes flushed pink with red spots, and borne in trusses of up to 20 in mid- to late spring. China. Introduced c. 1910 by George Forrest.
Zone 6 US, 7 Can.

Rhododendron taliense

R. tephropeplum (Ashrobe rhododendron) A dwarf or small evergreen shrub, occasionally growing up to 5 ft (1.5 m), with narrow, lance-shaped leaves that are an attractive plum-purple beneath when young. The bell-shaped flowers vary in color from pinkish white to carmine-rose and are profusely borne in mid- to late spring. Himalaya. Introduced 1921 by George Forrest.
Zone 8 US, 9? Can. 🏆

Rhododendron tephropeplum

R. thomsonii (Thomson rhododendron) An evergreen large shrub or small tree with smooth plum- or cinnamon-colored bark and rounded or oval leaves. The bell-shaped flowers are held in loose trusses and are deep blood red with large, cup-shaped, apple green calyxes that are attractive when flowering has finished. It flowers consistently and freely in early to midspring. It is prone to powdery mildew. Himalaya. Introduced 1850 by Sir Joseph Hooker.
Zone 8 US, 9? Can.

Rhododendron trichanthum

R. trichanthum (Rhododendron) A large evergreen shrub with bristly branches and funnel-shaped flowers that are dark violet-purple, or sometimes paler, and held 3–5 in a truss in late spring to early summer. China. Introduced 1908 by Ernest Wilson.
Zone 7 US, 8 Can.

R. trichostomum (Rhododendron) A small, twiggy, aromatic, evergreen shrub with small, narrow leaves 1 in (2.5 cm) long. The tight, terminal heads of tubular, daphnelike flowers may be white, pink, or rose and appear in late spring to early summer. China. Introduced 1908 by Ernest Wilson.
Zone 7 US, 8 Can.

Rhododendron trichostomum

R. triflorum (Triflorum rhododendron) A slender, medium-sized to large, evergreen shrub with peeling bark. The flowers are funnel shaped, lemon yellow with a ray of green spots, and borne in trusses of three in late spring to early summer. Himalaya. Introduced 1850 by Sir Joseph Hooker.
Zone 7 US, 8 Can.

Rhododendron vaseyi

R. vaseyi (Pinkshell azalea) A beautiful, medium-sized to large, deciduous shrub with narrowly oval leaves up to 5 in (13 cm) long, often turning fiery red in fall. The flowers appear before the leaves in mid- to late spring and are widely funnel shaped, up to 2 in (5 cm) across, and pale pink, rose-pink, or white with orange-red spots. North Carolina. Introduced c. 1880.
Zone 4 US, 5 Can. 🏆

R. veitchianum (Rhododendron) A small to medium-sized evergreen shrub. It bears relatively large, widely funnel-shaped, fragrant, five-cleft white flowers with a faint green cast and crinkled petals in late spring to early summer. Myanmar, Laos, Thailand. Introduced 1850 by Thomas Lobb.
Zone 9 US 🏆

***R. v.* Cubittii group** Medium-sized to large shrubs with a spreading habit whose leaves are margined with bristles and are scaly beneath. The flowers, borne in early to midspring, are broadly funnel shaped, fragrant, and deep pink, sometimes blotched with orange-yellow.
Zone 9 US 🏆

R. viscosum (Swamp azalea) A medium-sized, deciduous, bushy shrub with small leaves that are dark green above and glaucous green beneath; they turn orange-bronze in fall. The spicily fragrant white flowers appear after the leaves in early to midsummer and are 1–1¼ in (2.5–3.5 cm) across, sticky on the outside, and sometimes stained with pink. E North America. Introduced 1734.
Zone 3 US, 4 Can.

Rhododendron wardii

R. wardii (Ward rhododendron) A compact large evergreen shrub with glossy, dark green, rather rounded leaves 2–4 in (5–10 cm) long. The flowers, borne in late spring in loose trusses, are saucer shaped and clear yellow, sometimes with a crimson basal blotch. It is prone to powdery mildew. China, Tibet. Introduced 1913 by Frank Kingdon-Ward.
Zone 7 US, 8 Can.

R. williamsianum (Williams rhododendron) A charming dwarf to small evergreen shrub with a maximum height of about 5 ft (1.5 m). It has small, round, heart-shaped leaves that are bronze when young and bluish when mature. The young growth is also bronze. The bell-shaped, shell pink flowers are borne in midspring. China. Introduced 1908 by Ernest Wilson.
Zone 7 US, 8 Can. 🏆

Rhododendron williamsianum

R. yakushimanum (Yako rhododendron) A small, compact, rounded, evergreen shrub with bell-shaped white or pale pink flowers that open from pink buds in late spring. Yakushima. Introduced 1934.
Zone 4 US, 5 Can.

Rhododendron yakushimanum 'Koichiro Wada'

***R. y.* 'Koichiro Wada'** A dome-shaped, dense bush up to 4 ft (1.2 m) high and more wide. The young growth is silvery, and the leathery leaves, recurved at the margins, are glossy, dark green above and densely fawn-felted beneath. The bell-shaped flowers are borne in late spring in a compact truss; they are rose in bud, open to apple-blossom pink, and turn white.
Zone 4 US, 5 Can. 🏆

R. yedoense (Yodogawa azalea) A small, dense, deciduous shrub whose leaves turn purplish in fall. The double, deep purple flowers appear in midspring. Korea, Japan.
Zone 5 US, 6 Can.

R. yunnanense (Yunnan rhododendron) A leggy but very free-flowering shrub up to 10 ft (3 m) high that is evergreen or semideciduous. The funnel-shaped flowers, borne in late spring, are white, mauve-lavender, or pink, speckled with red. China.
Zone 7 US, 8 Can. 🏆

RHODODENDRON HYBRIDS

Like the species, the hybrids vary greatly in size, from prostrate ground covers to large, imposing specimens; they are evergreen except as noted. They usually bear large, globular or conical trusses of blooms on the branch tips and flower early in the year. The flowering seasons are given as follows:

Early	Midspring
Mid	Late spring to early summer
Late	The latter part of early summer onward

***R.* 'A. Bedford'** A beautiful, large, vigorous, free-flowering shrub with compact, conical trusses of up to 16 funnel-shaped, pale mauve to light purple flowers. They are marked inside with a dark rose-purple blotch and have lightly ruffled petals. It is possibly a hybrid of *R. ponticum*. Mid. Introduced 1936.
Zone 5 US, 6 Can.

***R.* 'Aglo'** This is a small shrub, related to *R.* 'P.J.M.', with small leaves that turn a mahogany color in winter. The funnel-shaped flowers are light pink with a darker blotch and borne in early spring.
Zone 4 US, 5 Can.

Rhododendron 'Alice'

***R.* 'Aladdin'** A very beautiful, medium-sized shrub with large, widely expanded, bright salmon-cerise flowers held in loose trusses. Late.
Zone 6 US, 7 Can.

***R.* 'Album Elegans'** (Ironclad) An older variety developed from *R. catawbiense* that makes a large shrub with an open habit. The flowers are pale lilac fading to white with a yellowish blotch at the throat and held in tight trusses. Late. Introduced 1847.
Zone 4 US, 4b Can.

***R.* 'Alice'** A large, vigorous, upright shrub that has funnel-shaped, rose-pink flowers with lighter centers held in tall, conical trusses. Mid. Introduced 1910.
Zone 5 US, 6 Can. 🏆

***R.* 'Alison Johnstone'** A dainty medium-sized shrub with oval leaves and trusses of slender-tubed flowers that are greenish in bud and open to pale yellow, flushed with orange or pink. It is prone to powdery mildew. Mid. Introduced 1945.
Zone 7 US, 8 Can.

Rhododendron 'Anna Baldsiefen'

***R.* 'Alpine Glow'** A large, handsome shrub with long, rich green leaves and widely funnel-shaped, sweetly scented flowers, 4 in (10 cm) across, in large trusses. They are delicate pink with a deep crimson blotch at the base. Early. Introduced 1933.
Zone 6 US, 7 Can. 🏆

***R.* 'America'** (Ironclad) A *R. catawbiense* hybrid that makes a medium-sized, straggly shrub with dark green, veined leaves and is covered with ball-shaped clusters of dark red blooms. Mid. Introduced 1920.
Zone 4 US, 5 Can.

Rhododendron 'Anna Rose Whitney'

***R.* 'Anah Kruschke'** A dense, compact, bushy shrub that has shiny leaves and is very tolerant of heat and sun. The flowers are reddish purple to deep purple and carried in compact conical trusses. Mid to late. Introduced 1955.
Zone 5 US, 6 Can.

***R.* Angelo group** A group of excellent hybrids, including 'Exbury Angelo', a large shrub or small tree. It produces handsome foliage and huge, shapely trusses of large, fragrant, trumpet-shaped, white flowers, $5^1/_2$ in (14 cm) across, with green markings. Late. Introduced 1933.
Zone 6 US, 7 Can.

***R.* 'Anna Baldsiefen'** A dwarf, compact, upright shrub with light green leaves that become bronze-red in winter and are up to 1 in (2.5 cm) long. The vivid pink, funnel-shaped flowers, $1^1/_4$ in (3 cm) across, are borne profusely and have deeper-colored, wavy margins. Early. Introduced 1964.
Zone 4 US, 5b Can. 🏆

***R.* 'Anna H. Hall'** This *R. yakushimanum* hybrid has a conspicuous brown indumentum on the new leaves. It makes a small, bushy plant with pink buds that open white. Mid.
Zone 4 US, 5 Can.

***R.* 'Anna Rose Whitney'** A vigorous, medium-sized shrub with leaves up to $4^1/_2$ in (11 cm) long and dense, rounded trusses of widely funnel-shaped flowers, 4 in (10 cm) across; they are deep rose-pink,

spotted with brown on the upper lobes. Mid. Introduced 1954 by Van Veen.
Zone 5 US, 6 Can. 🏆

R. 'Arctic Tern' A vigorous, compact, free-flowering, upright, dwarf shrub up to 2 ft (60 cm) high with leaves $1^1/_4$ in (3.5 cm) long. The flowers are $^1/_2$ in (1 cm) long, white tinged with green, and borne in compact, globular trusses. It has been suggested that a species of the genus *Ledum* may have been involved in the parentage. Mid. Introduced 1982.
Zone 6 US, 7 Can. 🏆

Rhododendron Augfast group

R. Augfast group Small, dense, rounded shrubs with small, scattered leaves and small, funnel-shaped flowers in terminal clusters that vary from dark lavender-blue to reddish purple. Early. Introduced 1921.
Zone 6 US, 7 Can.

R. 'Autumn Gold' A medium-sized shrub with narrow, light green, slightly twisted leaves. The flowers are apricot-salmon with a pink tinge at the tips and an orange eye; they are held in small trusses of 10 blooms. Mid to late. Introduced 1956 by Van Veen.
Zone 6 US, 7 Can.

Rhododendron Avalanche group

R. Avalanche group Large shrubs with bold leaves on red stalks and large trusses of enormous, fragrant, widely funnel-shaped, snow-white flowers that are flushed pink in bud and have a red basal stain within. Early. Introduced 1933.
Zone 6 US, 7 Can. 🏆

Rhododendron 'Baden-Baden'

R. 'Baden-Baden' A dwarf shrub with small, glossy, dark green leaves and waxy, deep red flowers. Mid. Introduced before 1972.
Zone 6 US, 7 Can.

R. 'Bambi' A small *R. yakushimanum* hybrid with a compact habit that produces dark green, deeply veined leaves that are felted with pale brown when young. The flowers are red in bud and open pale pink flushed with yellow. Mid. Introduced c. 1964.
Zone 4 US, 5 Can.

R. 'Bashful' A medium-sized *R. yakushimanum* hybrid of wide-spreading habit, with narrow, red-tinged leaves that are silvery when young. The flowers are light pink with a rust-red blotch and fade to white. Mid. Introduced 1971.
Zone 5 US, 6 Can. 🏆

R. 'Beatrice Keir' A large shrub with handsome foliage and large trusses of funnel-shaped, lemon yellow flowers. Early. Introduced 1974.
Zone 6 US, 7 Can. 🏆

R. 'Beauty of Littleworth' A striking large shrub with immense conical trusses of white, crimson-spotted flowers. It has been considered one of the best hybrid rhododendrons for many decades. Mid. Introduced c. 1900.
Zone 6 US, 7 Can. 🏆

R. 'Belle Heller' A large, vigorous shrub with dark green leaves and large, dense, conical trusses of white flowers with a gold

Rhododendron 'Bashful'

Rhododendron 'Beatrice Keir'

Rhododendron 'Beauty of Littleworth'

flare. It tolerates sun well. Mid; it may flower in the fall in warm climates. Introduced 1958 by Shammarello.
Zone 5 US, 6 Can.

Rhododendron 'Belle Heller'

***R.* 'Besse Howells'** A compact, medium-sized shrub with dark green leaves and ruffled, red flowers in globular trusses. Early to mid. Introduced 1961 by Shammarello.
Zone 4 US, 5 Can.

Rhododendron 'Betty Wormald'

***R.* 'Betty Wormald'** A vigorous, upright, spreading, medium-sized to large shrub that bears immense trusses of large, widely funnel-shaped, wavy-edged flowers. They are crimson in bud and open to deep rose-pink, lighter in the center, with a broad pattern of blackish crimson markings within. Mid. Introduced before 1922.
Zone 6 US, 7 Can. 🏆

***R.* 'Blewbury'** A small, compact shrub with narrow, pointed leaves that have loose, pale brown felt underneath. The flowers are bell shaped and white with reddish purple spots. Mid. Introduced 1968.
Zone 6 US, 7 Can. 🏆

Rhododendron 'Blewbury'

***R.* 'Blue Bird'** A neat, dwarf, small-leaved shrub that is suitable for the rock garden. The lovely violet-blue flowers are borne in small, compact trusses. Early. Introduced 1930.
Zone 6 US, 7 Can. 🏆

Rhododendron 'Blue Bird'

***R.* 'Blue Diamond'** A slow-growing, compact shrub about 3 ft (1 m) high, with terminal clusters of rich lavender-blue, saucer-shaped flowers in tight clusters. It is now being superseded by other cultivars. Early to mid. Introduced 1935.
Zone 5 US, 6 Can.

***R.* 'Blue Ensign'** A medium-sized shrub with dark green leaves and lavender-blue flowers that have a dark blotch. Mid. Introduced 1959.
Zone 5 US, 6 Can.

***R.* 'Blue Peter'** A vigorous, upright, very free-flowering, medium-sized shrub with flowers in compact, conical trusses. They are funnel shaped, frilled, and cobalt-purple, paling to white at the throat, with a ray of maroon spots. Mid. Introduced 1930.
Zone 4 US, 5 Can. 🏆

Rhododendron 'Blue Peter'

***R.* 'Blue Tit'** A dense shrub up to 3 ft (1 m) high and wide. The small, widely funnel-shaped flowers are in clusters at the tips of the branchlets and are a lovely lavender-blue that intensifies with age. It is a good shrub for the rock garden. Early. Introduced 1933.
Zone 5 US, 6 Can.

***R.* 'Bo-Peep'** A small, slender shrub with widely funnel-shaped, primrose yellow flowers that have two broad bands of pale orange spots and streaks. They are $1^1/_2$ in (4 cm) across and are borne singly or in pairs in early spring. It is a very free-flowering shrub and a beautiful sight when in full flower. Introduced 1934.
Zone 7 US, 8 Can. 🏆

***R.* 'Boule de Neige'** (Ironclad) A vigorous, rounded, medium-sized shrub with pale green foliage. The white flowers are in compact trusses and are freely produced. It is a very popular variety but is susceptible to lacebug attacks. Mid. Introduced 1878.
Zone 4 US, 4b Can.

***R.* 'Boursault'** One of the hardiest and most popular *R. catawbiense* hybrids, this forms a dense, medium-sized to large shrub with dull green leaves. The lavender-purple flowers are in rounded trusses. Mid to late.
Zone 4 US, 4b Can.

***R.* 'Bow Bells'** A charming, compact, bushy medium-sized shrub with bright coppery young growth. The widely bell shaped flowers are deep cerise in bud and open to soft pink on the inside and rich pink on the outside. They are borne in loose trusses. Early to mid. Introduced 1934 by Lord Rothschild.
Zone 5 US, 6 Can.

Rhododendron 'Bow Bells'

***R.* 'Bric-a-brac'** A small, neat, free-flowering shrub bearing open flowers, 2½ in (6 cm) across, that are white with chocolate-colored anthers. It needs a sheltered location to protect the flowers, which appear in early spring or even earlier in a mild season. Introduced 1934.
Zone 7 US, 8 Can.

Rhododendron 'Bric-a-brac'

***R.* 'Britannia'** (Ironclad) A superb, slow-growing, medium-sized shrub forming a compact, rounded bush that is generally broader than it is high. The pretty, glowing red flowers are trumpet shaped and carried in compact trusses backed by bold, handsome foliage. It resists wind well. Mid. Introduced 1921.
Zone 4 US, 5 Can.

Rhododendron 'Britannia'

***R.* 'Brocade'** A small, dome-shaped shrub whose young foliage has a coppery tint. Its bell-shaped, frilly-margined flowers are borne in loose trusses and are vivid carmine in bud, opening to peach-pink. Early to mid. Introduced 1934.
Zone 6 US, 7 Can.

***R.* 'Bruce Brechtbill'** A medium-sized shrub that is a sport of 'Unique', which it closely resembles, except that the flowers are rich pink with a yellow throat. Early to mid. Introduced 1970.
Zone 6 US, 7 Can.

***R.* 'Buttermint'** A compact dwarf shrub with glossy dark green leaves that are bronze when young. Bright yellow, bell-shaped flowers edged with deep pink open from orange-red buds. It is a beautiful rhododendron but the buds are tender. Mid. Introduced 1979.
Zone 6 US, 7 Can.

***R.* 'C.I.S'** A vigorous, free-flowering, medium-sized shrub with flowers in compact globular trusses. They are widely funnel-shaped with wavy margins and are 2½ in (6 cm) across. The buds are red and open orange-yellow, flushed and veined with red and speckled with orange-brown in the throat. The initials stand for Claude I. Sersanous, who was formerly president of the American Rhododendron Society. Mid. Introduced 1952.
Zone 7 US, 8 Can.

***R.* Carita group** Beautiful hybrids raised by Lord Rothschild that form medium-sized shrubs bearing well-filled trusses of large, bell-shaped flowers; they are very pale lemon yellow, with a small basal blotch of cerise within. Mid.
Zone 7 US, 8 Can.

***R.* 'Carita Golden Dream'** A form whose flowers are cream flushed and shaded with pink; they become ivory white at maturity. Early. Introduced 1935.
Zone 7 US, 8 Can.

***R.* 'Carita Inchmery'** A form whose flowers are red in bud and open to pink with a fawn-yellow center, usually with six lobes. Mid. Introduced 1935. *(See photo on p.508.)*
Zone 7 US, 8 Can.

***R.* 'Carmen'** A dwarf or prostrate shrub with waxy, bell-shaped, glistening dark crimson flowers. Mid. Introduced 1935. *(See photo on p.508.)* Zone 5 US, 6b Can.

***R.* 'Caroline'** A medium-sized shrub with

Rhododendron 'Bruce Brechtbill'

Rhododendron 'Carita Inchmery'

glossy dark green leaves that have wavy margins. The lightly fragrant flowers are pale orchid-pink and held in large trusses. Mid to late. Introduced 1956.

Zone 5 US, 6 Can.

Rhododendron 'Carmen'

***R.* 'Caroline Allbrook'** A vigorous *R. yakushimanum* hybrid that makes a small, compact, spreading shrub with dark green leaves up to 4½ in (11 cm) long and widely funnel-shaped flowers with very wavy margins borne in compact globular trusses. They are lavender-pink with a paler center and fade with age. Mid. Introduced 1975.

Zone 6 US, 7 Can. 🏆

***R.* 'Cary Ann'** A compact, small shrub with dark green leaves and dense, rounded trusses of coral-pink flowers. Mid. Introduced 1962.

Zone 7 US, 8 Can.

***R.* 'Charlotte de Rothschild'** A large shrub that has long leaves and large, compact, rounded trusses of clear pink flowers

Rhododendron 'Caroline Allbrook'

spotted with chocolate brown. Mid. Introduced 1935.

Zone 5 US, 6 Can. 🏆

***R.* 'Cheer'** This dense, compact, rounded shrub has glossy foliage and cone-shaped trusses of shell pink flowers with a conspicuous red blotch. Early. Introduced before 1958 by Shammarello.

Zone 5 US, 6 Can.

Rhododendron 'Charlotte de Rothschild'

***R.* 'Chevalier Felix de Sauvage'** A very old hybrid and still considered among the best. It is a medium-sized to large shrub of dense habit with trusses of deep rose-pink, dark-blotched flowers that are 2½ in (6 cm) across and wavy at the margins. Mid. Introduced 1870.

Zone 6 US, 7 Can. 🏆

***R.* 'Chikor'** A choice dwarf shrub with small leaves and clusters of yellow flowers. Mid.

Zone 7 US, 8 Can.

***R.* 'Chionoides'** A wide-spreading, medium-sized shrub with narrow foliage and a dense habit of growth. The flowers are white with a yellow eye. Mid. Introduced before 1883.

Zone 6 US, 7 Can.

***R.* 'Christmas Cheer'** A medium-sized shrub of rather dense, compact habit with flowers that are pink in bud and fade to pale pink or white after opening. It usually flowers in early spring and occasionally in late winter; its name refers to the traditional

Rhododendron 'Christmas Cheer'

English practice of forcing this variety for holiday decoration. It will sometimes flower outdoors around Christmastime if the weather is very mild. Introduced 1908.

Zone 6 US, 7 Can.

***R.* 'Chrysomanicum'** A small, compact, spreading shrub with glossy dark green leaves and primrose yellow flowers. Early. Introduced 1947.

Zone 8 US, 9 Can. 🏆

***R.* Cilpinense group** Beautiful, free-flowering, neat, rounded shrubs up to 3 ft (1 m) high, with glossy green, bristle-margined leaves. The flowers are in loose trusses, shallowly bell shaped, and sparkling white, flushed with pink but deeper in bud. They

Rhododendron Cilpinense group

open in early spring. Introduced 1927.
Zone 7 US, 8 Can. 🏆

***R.* Cinnkeys group** Choice shrubs of upright habit with oval, glossy green leaves. The tubular flowers are bright orange-red, shading to pale apricot on the lobes, and are produced in dense, drooping clusters. Mid. Introduced 1926.
Zone 7 US, 8 Can.

Rhododendron Cinnkeys group

***R.* 'Corona'** A medium-sized shrub that forms a charming, slow-growing, compact mound with funnel-shaped, rich coral-pink flowers, 2 in (5 cm) across, in rather elongated trusses. Mid. Introduced before 1911.
Zone 5 US, 6 Can. 🏆

***R.* 'Cotton Candy'** A vigorous medium-sized shrub with glossy dark green leaves to 6 in (15 cm) long. The dark pink buds open to light pink and fade to pale pink in the center; they are carried in large trusses. A good choice for the Pacific Northwest. Mid.
Zone 8 US, 9 Can. 🏆

***R.* 'Countess of Haddington'** A small to medium-sized shrub with a somewhat straggly habit. The leaves are usually in terminal clusters of five and are glaucous green and dotted with glands beneath. The fragrant, trumpet-shaped flowers are in umbels of 2–4 and are white, flushed with pale rose. Early. Introduced 1862.
Zone 8 US, 9 Can. 🏆

***R.* 'County of York'** A large, vigorous shrub with long, glossy leaves and large trusses of white flowers marked with a showy olive blotch at the throat. Mid.
Zone 6 US, 7 Can.

Rhododendron 'Cowslip'

***R.* 'Cowslip'** A small, neat, rounded shrub with bell-shaped flowers 2–2½ in (5–6 cm) across that open from pink buds to cream or pale primrose with a pale pink flush when young. They are carried in loose trusses. Mid. Introduced 1937.
Zone 6 US, 7 Can.

***R.* 'Creeping Jenny'** See *R.* 'Jenny'.

***R.* 'Crest'** A vigorous, medium-sized shrub with a very open habit and reddish purple shoots. The bell-shaped, primrose yellow flowers with a slight darkening in the throat are orange in bud, open to 4 in (10 cm) across, and are held in large trusses. Mid. Introduced 1953 by Lord Rothschild.
Zone 6 US, 7 Can. 🏆

***R.* 'Cunningham's White'** A small, compact shrub with dark green foliage. The pale pink buds open to white flowers that

Rhododendron 'Curlew'

have a pale yellow-green blotch and are held in upright trusses. It is more tolerant of alkaline soil than most rhododendrons. Mid to late. Introduced 1830.
Zone 5 US, 6 Can.

***R.* 'Curlew'** An attractive dwarf, spreading shrub with small, dark green leaves. The widely funnel-shaped flowers, 2 in

Rhododendron 'Cynthia'

(5 cm) across, are pale yellow marked with greenish brown and are borne profusely. It grows best in a cool location. Mid. Introduced 1970.
Zone 6 US, 7 Can. 🏆

Rhododendron 'David'

***R.* 'Cynthia'** One of the best rhododendrons for general planting, this large, vigorous, dome-shaped shrub thrives in a variety of conditions. It bears conical trusses of widely funnel-shaped, rose-crimson flowers that have a ray of blackish crimson markings within. Mid. Introduced before 1870. *(See photo on p.509.)* Zone 5 US, 6 Can. 🏆

***R.* 'David'** A medium-sized shrub that produces compact trusses of funnel-shaped, frilly-margined, deep blood red flowers that are slightly spotted within. Mid. Introduced 1939.
Zone 7 US, 8 Can. 🏆

***R.* 'Doc'** A small, compact *R. yakushimanum* hybrid that is a free-flowering shrub with dull green leaves and funnel-shaped, wavy-margined flowers 1½ in (4 cm) across, borne in globular trusses. They are rose-pink with deeper edges and spots and fade to cream. Mid. Introduced 1972.
Zone 4 US, 5b Can. 🏆

***R.* 'Doncaster'** A small shrub, broadly dome shaped in habit, with somewhat glossy, leathery, very dark green leaves that are held stiffly on the shoots. The funnel-shaped flowers are in a dense truss and are brilliant red with a ray of black markings within. Unfortunately, this once popular hybrid is prone to bud blast and is now seldom grown. Mid.
Zone 6 US, 7 Can.

Rhododendron 'Doncaster'

Rhododendron 'Dopey'

***R.* 'Dopey'** A small to medium-sized *R. yakushimanum* hybrid that makes a compact shrub with bell-shaped, wavy-edged, bright orange-red flowers that are paler toward the margins and spotted with orange-brown. They are freely borne in globular trusses. Mid. Introduced 1970.
Zone 4 US, 5b Can. 🏆

Rhododendron 'Dora Amateis'

***R.* 'Dora Amateis'** A mound-forming, medium-sized shrub with flowers freely produced in open clusters. They are funnel shaped, 2 in (5 cm) across, and pale pink in bud, opening to white and faintly spotted with yellow. Early. Introduced 1955.
Zone 4 US, 5 Can. 🏆

***R.* 'Dusky Maid'** A tall, erect, robust shrub with tight, rounded trusses of dark, dusky red flowers. Mid to late. Introduced 1936.
Zone 6 US, 7 Can.

Rhododendron 'Earl of Donoughmore'

***R.* 'Earl of Donoughmore'** A medium-sized hybrid of *R. griersonianum* that bears bright red flowers with an orange glow. Mid. Introduced 1953.
Zone 6 US, 7 Can. 🏆

***R.* 'Egret'** A compact and free-flowering dwarf shrub of neat habit with widely funnel-shaped flowers that are ¾ in (2 cm) across and white with a green cast. They are borne in open trusses 2¾ in (7 cm) across. Mid. Introduced 1982.
Zone 6 US, 7 Can. 🏆

***R.* 'El Camino'** A vigorous large shrub with dark green leaves and very large, wavy-edged, glowing red flowers with darker spots. Mid. Introduced 1976.
Zone 6 US, 7 Can.

***R.* 'Elisabeth Hobbie'** A dwarf shrub with loose umbels of 6–10 translucent, scarlet, bell-shaped flowers. Early. Introduced 1945.
Zone 6 US, 7 Can. 🏆

***R.* 'Elizabeth'** A dwarf or small spreading shrub with dark red, trumpet-shaped flowers, 3 in (7.5 cm) across, carried in profuse

Rhododendron 'Elisabeth Hobbie'

clusters of 6–9. It is prone to powdery mildew and may be damaged by late frost. A good choice for the West. Early. Introduced 1939.

Zone 5 US, 6 Can.

Rhododendron 'Elizabeth'

***R.* 'Elizabeth Lockhart'** A small, mound-forming shrub with deep bronze-purple, oval to oblong leaves and loose clusters of bell-shaped, deep red flowers. Early. Introduced 1965.

Zone 7 US, 8 Can.

***R.* 'English Roseum'** (Ironclad) This *R. catawbiense* hybrid makes a vigorous, upright, fast-growing, medium-sized to large shrub with glossy, dark green leaves. The flowers are a light rose-lavender in rounded trusses. It is tolerant of heat and humidity. Mid to late.

Zone 4 US, 4b Can.

***R.* 'Everestianum'** A vigorous, medium-sized shrub with oval, dark green leaves and frilled, lilac-pink flowers with darker spots in the throat. It grows equally well in sun or light shade. Mid to late. Introduced before 1850.

Zone 4 US, 5b Can.

Rhododendron 'Fabia'

***R.* 'Fabia'** A beautiful, widely dome-shaped shrub bearing loose, flat trusses of funnel-shaped scarlet flowers that are shaded with orange in the tube and freely speckled with brown markings. Mid. Introduced 1934.

Zone 7 US, 8 Can. 🏆

Rhododendron 'Faggetter's Favourite'

***R.* 'Faggetter's Favourite'** A tall shrub with fine foliage and large trusses of sweetly scented, shell pink flowers with white shading. Mid. Introduced 1933.

Zone 6 US, 7 Can. 🏆

***R.* 'Fastuosum Flore Pleno'** A large, dome-shaped shrub with lax trusses of semi-double flowers that have wavy margins. They are pale bluish mauve with a ray of brown-crimson markings within. Mid. Introduced before 1846.

Rhododendron 'Fastuosum Flore Pleno'

Zone 4 US, 5b Can. 🏆

***R.* Flava group** *R. yakushimanum* hybrids that make small, compact shrubs with glossy dark green leaves and bell-shaped, pale yellow flowers that are blotched with red and borne in dense, dome-shaped trusses. There are several cultivars; one of the best of them is 'Volker'. Mid.

Zone 7 US, 8 Can.

Rhododendron 'Fragrantissimum'

***R.* 'Fragrantissimum'** A beautiful medium-sized hybrid with attractive, dark green, corrugated leaves. The extremely fragrant, widely funnel-shaped flowers are in terminal umbels of four and are up to 3 in (7.5 cm) long; they are white flushed with pale rose outside and greenish inside at the base. The stamens have brown anthers. It makes a good greenhouse specimen in cold climates. Early. Introduced 1868.

Zone 8 US, 9 Can. 🏆

***R.* 'Frank Galsworthy'** A medium-sized

shrub with narrow, slightly twisted leaves. The funnel-shaped flowers are deep purple with a large blotch of yellow and white and have white anthers. They are borne in dense, rounded trusses. Late.
Zone 5 US, 6 Can. 🏆

***R.* 'Fred Wynniatt'** A large shrub with large, maize yellow flowers flushed with pink, borne in flat-topped trusses. Mid. Introduced 1964.
Zone 6 US, 7 Can. 🏆

***R.* 'Furnivall's Daughter'** Similar to *R.* 'Mrs. Furnivall' but more vigorous and with larger leaves and flowers. The flowers are widely funnel shaped and light rose-pink with a bold splash of dark markings. Mid to late. Introduced 1957.
Zone 5 US, 6 Can. 🏆

***R.* 'Fusilier'** A beautiful, dense, medium-sized shrub. The long, narrow leaves are brown-felted beneath; the large trusses of brilliant red, funnel-shaped flowers are 3 in (8 cm) wide and have darker spots on all the lobes. Mid. Introduced 1938.
Zone 8 US, 9 Can. 🏆

***R.* 'Gartendirektor Glocker'** A compact, small, domed shrub with rounded leaves that are blue-green when young. The deep rose-red, funnel-shaped flowers are in loose trusses. Mid. Introduced 1952.
Zone 6 US, 7 Can.

***R.* 'George Johnstone'** A medium-sized shrub with aromatic leaves and loose trusses of bright orange, bell-shaped flowers. Early to mid. Introduced 1968.
Zone 7 US, 8 Can. 🏆

***R.* 'GiGi'** A medium-sized shrub with glossy leaves and trusses of 18 deep pink flowers marked with dark red spots. Early.
Zone 5 US, 6b Can.

Rhododendron 'Ginny Gee'

***R.* 'Ginny Gee'** An excellent dwarf, free-flowering shrub with a compact habit. The widely funnel-shaped, pale pink flowers are deeper in bud and fade to near-white, edged with pink. Early to mid. Introduced 1979.
Zone 5 US, 6b Can. 🏆

***R.* 'Golden Gala'** A dwarf, bushy, spreading plant with olive green leaves, suitable for smaller gardens. The flowers are bell shaped and yellow-ivory. Mid to late. Introduced 1983.
Zone 4 US, 5b Can.

***R.* 'Golden Orfe'** A medium-sized to large shrub resembling *R. cinnabarinum,* with tubular orange-yellow flowers 2 in (5 cm) long. Mid. Introduced 1965.
Zone 7 US, 8 Can. 🏆

***R.* 'Golden Torch'** A small, compact shrub with leaves up to 2½ in (6 cm) long and bell-shaped flowers 2 in (5 cm) wide. They are salmon pink in bud, opening to pale yellow, and are borne in compact trusses. Mid. Introduced 1972.
Zone 6 US, 7 Can. 🏆

Rhododendron 'Golden Torch'

***R.* 'Goldflimmer'** This forms a medium-sized, dense shrub and is grown chiefly for the foliage, which is variegated with an irregular yellow stripe down the center of each leaf. The ruffled flowers are mauve, similar to those of *R. ponticum.* Late.
Zone 5 US, 6 Can.

***R.* 'Goldkrone'** A small, compact shrub that forms a mound and has large trusses of golden yellow, funnel-shaped flowers, profusely borne over a long period. Mid. Introduced 1983.
Zone 5 US, 6 Can.

***R.* 'Goldsworth Orange'** A small, low-growing shrub with large trusses of pale orange flowers, tinged with apricot-pink. Although it is popular, its color is somewhat muddy and there are better rhododendrons in its range. Late. Introduced 1938.
Zone 6 US, 7 Can.

Rhododendron 'Gomer Waterer'

***R.* 'Gomer Waterer'** (Ironclad) A very beautiful, medium-sized, dense shrub with large, leathery leaves and fragrant flowers in large, dense, rounded trusses. They are 3 in (8 cm) wide, funnel shaped but deeply divided, and white flushed with pale mauve toward the edges, with a mustard-green basal blotch. It tolerates heat and sun. Mid to late. Introduced before 1900.
Zone 5 US, 6 Can. 🏆

***R.* 'Grace Seabrook'** A vigorous, tough, medium-sized shrub with dark green, pointed leaves. It has deep red flowers with paler margins carried in compact, broadly conical trusses. Early to mid. Introduced 1965.
Zone 6 US, 7 Can.

***R.* 'Gristede'** A compact, dwarf shrub resembling 'Blue Diamond', with glossy green leaves and clusters of funnel-shaped, violet-blue flowers. Early to mid. Introduced 1977.
Zone 6 US, 7 Can.

***R.* 'Grosclaude'** A neat, compact shrub producing lax trusses of bell-shaped, waxy, blood red flowers that have wavy margins and darker spots inside. The calyx is the

Rhododendron 'Grosclaude'

same color as the petals. Mid. Introduced 1941.
Zone 7 US, 8 Can.

Rhododendron 'Grumpy'

***R.* 'Grumpy'** A small, compact *R. yakushimanum* hybrid that makes a spreading shrub with funnel-shaped flowers, 2 in (5 cm) wide, borne in rounded trusses. They are cream tinged with pale pink at the margins and spotted with orange-yellow. It does not flower profusely. Mid. Introduced 1971.
Zone 4 US, 4b Can.

***R.* 'Hachmann's Polaris'** A small *R. yakushimanum* hybrid that makes a compact mound with hairy leaves. The light rosy pink flowers are carmine in bud and edged with fuchsia-purple. Mid. Introduced 1963.
Zone 5 US, 6 Can.

***R.* 'Halfdan Lem'** A vigorous, medium-sized shrub that has broad, dark green, somewhat twisted leaves. Its bright red flowers are marked with a darker blotch and are borne in large, tight trusses. Mid. Introduced 1974. Zone 6 US, 7 Can.

***R.* 'Hallelujah'** This medium-sized shrub has distinctive large leaves that are dark green and fold downward about halfway along. The rose-colored flowers are in large trusses. Mid. Introduced 1976.
Zone 5 US, 6 Can.

***R.* 'Harvest Moon'** A lovely medium-sized hybrid with bell-shaped cream flowers marked with a broad ray of carmine spots inside. Mid. Introduced 1938.
Zone 6 US, 7 Can.

***R.* 'Hélène Schiffner'** A small, dense, rounded shrub that bears rounded trusses of widely funnel-shaped flowers. They are mauve in bud and open to pure white, occasionally with an inconspicuous ray of greenish or yellow markings inside. Mid. Introduced 1893.
Zone 6 US, 7 Can.

Rhododendron 'Halfdan Lem'

***R.* 'Hello Dolly'** A small, rounded shrub whose leaves have fawn indumentum beneath. The flowers are yellow-pink fading to yellow at the throat, which is marked with green spots. Mid.
Zone 5 US, 6 Can.

***R.* 'Holden'** A dwarf shrub that grows wider than it is tall and has shiny, dark green foliage. The flowers are rose-red with darker spots and held in conical trusses. Early. Introduced 1958 by Shammarello.
Zone 5 US, 6 Can.

***R.* 'Hoppy'** A vigorous, compact *R. yakushimanum* hybrid that makes a free-flowering small shrub. The funnel-shaped flowers, 2 in (5 cm) across, are pale lilac that fades to white spotted with yellow. They are borne in compact trusses up to 7 in (18 cm) wide. Mid. Introduced 1972.
Zone 5 US, 6 Can.

Rhododendron 'Hotei'

Rhododendron 'Hugh Koster'

***R.* 'Hotei'** A compact, medium-sized shrub with deep yellow, widely bell-shaped flowers. Mid. Introduced 1964.
Zone 7 US, 8 Can.

***R.* 'Hugh Koster'** A sturdy, leafy, medium-sized shrub with stiff, erect branches. Its funnel-shaped flowers are borne in well-formed trusses and are glowing red with black markings within. It is similar to *R.* 'Doncaster', except that the flowers are slightly lighter and the leaves are a little wavy at the margins. Mid. Introduced 1915.
Zone 7 US, 8 Can.

***R.* 'Humming Bird'** A small, compact, dome-shaped shrub with a distinctive appearance. The half-nodding, widely bell-shaped, carmine flowers are shaded with

Rhododendron 'Humming Bird'

Rhododendron 'Hydon Dawn'

glowing scarlet inside the tube. Early. Introduced 1955.
Zone 6 US, 7 Can.

***R.* 'Hurricane'** A medium-sized, well-branched shrub that is covered with dark green foliage. The cotton-candy-pink flowers are liberally marked with darker lines in their throat and are in ball-shaped clusters. Mid. Introduced 1976.
Zone 7 US, 8 Can.

***R.* 'Hydon Dawn'** A compact *R. yakushimanum* hybrid that makes a dwarf shrub with leaves that are cream-felted beneath when young. The flowers are 2 in (5 cm) across, funnel shaped with wavy margins, and borne in compact trusses. They are light pink with paler margins and reddish brown spots. Mid. Introduced 1969.
Zone 7 US, 8 Can. 🏆

***R.* 'Idealist'** A very free-flowering, large shrub or small tree with flowers in large, compact trusses. They are widely funnel shaped with 5–7 lobes, up to 3 in (8 cm)

Rhododendron 'Idealist'

across, and coral-pink in bud, opening to pale creamy yellow with reddish markings at the base. Early to mid. Introduced 1941.
Zone 7 US, 8 Can. 🏆

Rhododendron 'Ilam Violet'

***R.* 'Ilam Violet'** A very free-flowering, small, upright shrub with deep violet-blue, widely funnel-shaped flowers with wavy margins. They are $1^1/_2$ in (4 cm) wide and borne in globular trusses. Early to mid. Introduced 1947.
Zone 7 US, 8 Can.

***R.* 'Impi'** A medium-sized, upright shrub. The funnel-shaped flowers are borne in small trusses and are 2 in (5 cm) across; they are nearly black in bud and open to a very deep wine-crimson, faintly spotted with black within. The color seems even more vivid when the plant is seen lit from behind. Late. Introduced 1945.
Zone 7 US, 8 Can. 🏆

***R.* Intrifast group** Dwarf, dense shrubs with innumerable clusters of small, violet-

Rhododendron Intrifast group

blue flowers. Mid.
Zone 5 US, 6 Can.

***R.* 'Isabel Pierce'** A stiffly branched, large shrub with long, narrow leaves and rose-red flowers that fade to pink with deeper margins and are noticeably blotched and spotted. They are borne in large trusses. Mid. Introduced 1975.
Zone 7 US, 8 Can. 🏆

Rhododendron 'Jacksonii'

***R.* 'Ivory Coast'** A very early flowering, small, rounded shrub with small, scaly, oval leaves. The flowers open a pale yellowish green and gradually fade to almost white. Introduced 1985.
Zone 4 US, 5b Can.

***R.* 'Jacksonii'** A broadly dome-shaped, slow-growing, medium-sized shrub. The flowers, borne in well-formed trusses, are widely funnel shaped and bright rose-pink, with maroon markings and paler spotting within. It tolerates air pollution and often succeeds where other rhododendrons fail.

Early. Introduced 1835.
Zone 5 US, 6 Can.

R. 'Jalisco Elect' A medium-sized shrub with primrose yellow flowers that have paler lobes and slightly frilled margins. They are marked with brownish red spots within, and the calyx is yellow. Late. Introduced 1942.
Zone 7 US, 8 Can. 🏆

R. 'Janet Blair' A vigorous, well-branched, medium-sized shrub that grows wider than tall. The leaves are dark green, and the fringed, pale pink blossoms have tan to light gold rays inside. Mid. Introduced 1962 by Leach.
Zone 4 US, 5b Can.

R. 'Jean Marie de Montague' See *R.* 'The Honourable Jean Marie de Montague'.

R. 'Jenny', syn. *R.* 'Creeping Jenny' A prostrate shrub with large, deep red, bell-shaped flowers. Mid. Introduced 1939.
Zone 6 US, 7 Can. 🏆

Rhododendron 'Jenny'

R. 'Jervis Bay' A rounded, medium-sized shrub with dark green leaves and widely funnel-shaped flowers borne in firm, round trusses. They are golden yellow tinged with orange in bud and open to primrose yellow with a maroon basal blotch and maroon markings inside. Mid. Introduced 1951.
Zone 7 US, 8 Can. 🏆

R. 'Jonathan Shaw' This dwarf form makes a dense shrub with leaves that have wavy edges. The flowers, in ball-shaped trusses, are violet-purple with a reddish center. Late. Introduced 1988.
Zone 5 US, 6 Can.

Rhododendron 'Kate Waterer'

R. 'Kate Waterer' A dense, medium-sized to large shrub with funnel-shaped flowers up to 2½ in (6 cm) wide. They open rose-crimson, become clear rose, and have a ray of greenish yellow spots on a white background on the upper lobe. Mid. Introduced before 1876.
Zone 5 US, 6 Can. 🏆

Rhododendron 'Kilimanjaro'

R. 'Kilimanjaro' A superb shrub with compact, globular trusses of funnel-shaped, currant red, wavy-edged flowers that are spotted with chocolate inside. Mid to late. Introduced 1943.
Zone 6 US, 7 Can. 🏆

R. 'King of Shrubs' A medium-sized shrub with narrow, pointed leaves and open trusses of large apricot flowers banded in pink. Mid.
Zone 7 US, 8 Can. 🏆

R. 'Lady Alice Fitzwilliam' A beautiful medium-sized shrub with dark green, deeply veined leaves. The very fragrant, funnel-shaped flowers, 4 in (10 cm) across, are white flushed with pink and have yellow markings in the throat. Mid. Introduced 1881.
Zone 8 US, 9 Can. 🏆

Rhododendron Lady Chamberlain group

Rhododendron Lady Rosebery group

R. Lady Chamberlain and Lady Rosebery groups These lovely shrubs have clusters of long, drooping, waxy, narrowly bell-shaped flowers in shades of red, pink, and buff-orange. Unfortunately, they are prone to mildew, so they must be sited in locations with good air circulation. Mid to late. Introduced 1930.
Zone 8 US, 9 Can.

R. 'Lady Clementine Mitford' A large shrub with its widely funnel-shaped flowers held in firm trusses. They are peach-pink shading to white in the center and have a V-shaped pattern of pink, olive green, and brown markings within. Mid to late. Introduced 1870.
Zone 6 US, 7 Can. 🏆

R. **'Lady de Rothschild'** See *R.* 'Mrs. Lionel de Rothschild'.

R. **'Lady Eleanor Cathcart'** A dome-shaped large shrub or small tree with handsome and distinctive long, dark gray-green leaves that are rusty beneath and point downward; they are felted when young. The widely funnel-shaped flowers, which are borne in rounded trusses, are bright clear rose with slightly darker veins and a maroon basal blotch within. Mid to late. Introduced before 1844.
Zone 5 US, 6 Can. 🏆

Rhododendron 'Lamplighter'

R. **'Lamplighter'** A vigorous large shrub of open habit with narrow, pointed, dark green leaves and bright red flowers borne in large trusses. Mid. Introduced 1955.
Zone 6 US, 7 Can. 🏆

R. **'Lavender Girl'** A vigorous, free-flowering, small, compact shrub with dome-shaped trusses of fragrant, funnel-shaped flowers. They are lilac-mauve in bud and open pale lavender, darker at the margins, with a pinkish yellow throat. Mid. Introduced 1950.
Zone 6 US, 7 Can. 🏆

Rhododendron 'Lavender Girl'

R. **'Lee's Dark Purple'** (Ironclad) A large, compact, rounded shrub with widely funnel-shaped flowers borne in dense, rounded trusses. They are royal purple with a ray of greenish brown to ocher markings within. It may bloom in fall in warm climates. Mid. Introduced before 1851.
Zone 4 US, 5 Can.

Rhododendron 'Lee's Dark Purple'

R. **'Lem's Cameo'** A medium-sized, upright shrub with matte, dark green leaves up to 6¼ in (16 cm) long that are bronze when young. It bears funnel-shaped flowers up to 3½ in (9 cm) wide that are red in bud and open to cream and apricot flushed with red and spotted with pink. They are borne in rounded trusses. Mid. Introduced 1962.
Zone 7 US, 8 Can. 🏆

R. **'Lem's Monarch'** A vigorous, large shrub with thick-textured, pointed, dark green leaves. The flowers are pale pink at first, fading to white edged with deep pink, and are held in very large, conical trusses. Mid. Introduced 1971.
Zone 7 US, 8 Can. 🏆

R. **'Lionel's Triumph'** An outstanding medium-sized shrub with large trusses of bell-shaped yellow flowers, spotted and blotched with crimson at the base within. The flowers are 4 in (10 cm) across. Mid. Introduced 1954.
Zone 6 US, 7 Can.

R. **'Lodauric Iceberg'** A large shrub or small tree with nodding trusses of richly scented, trumpet-shaped, pure white flowers 5 in (13 cm) across, with two streaks of brownish-crimson at the base within. Late. Introduced 1936.
Zone 6 US, 7 Can. 🏆

Rhododendron 'Lionel's Triumph'

R. **'Loderi King George'** Probably the best of the Loderi group and among the best hybrid rhododendrons. It is a vigorous, rounded, large shrub or small tree with enormous trusses of large, lilylike, trumpet-shaped, very fragrant flowers 5–6 in (13–15 cm) across. They are soft pink in bud and open to pure white with a green basal flare inside. Early to mid. Introduced 1901.
Zone 6 US, 7 Can. 🏆

Rhododendron 'Loderi King George'

R. **'Loderi Pink Diamond'** A large shrub or small tree with flowers similar to those of *R.* 'Loderi King George' but a bit smaller and delicate pink with a basal flare of crimson that changes to green flushed with brown. Early to mid. Introduced 1901.
Zone 6 US, 7 Can. 🏆

Rhododendron 'Loderi Pink Diamond'

***R.* 'Loderi Venus'** A large shrub or small tree with flowers that are deep pink in bud, open to strong rose-pink, and fade to pale pink with a very faint greenish flare at the base within. Early to mid. Introduced 1901.
Zone 5 US, 6b Can. 🏆

***R.* 'Loder's White'** A large, dome-shaped shrub covered with handsome foliage (it is not related to the Loderi group). Its widely funnel-shaped flowers, borne in conical

Rhododendron 'Loder's White'

trusses, are mauve-pink in bud and open to pure white edged with pink and marked with a few scattered crimson spots. Mid. Introduced before 1884.
Zone 6 US, 7 Can. 🏆

***R.* 'Lodestar'** A wide-spreading, medium-sized to large shrub with long, oval, pointed leaves. The flowers open pale lilac with darker spots and fade to white. Mid to late. Introduced 1964.
Zone 4 US, 5b Can.

***R.* 'Lord Roberts'** A large shrub of erect growth with flowers borne in dense, round trusses. They are funnel shaped and dark crimson with an extensive V-shaped pattern of black markings. Mid to late.
Zone 4 US, 5 Can.

Rhododendron 'Madame de Bruin'

***R.* 'Madame de Bruin'** A vigorous, leafy, medium-sized shrub that produces conical trusses of cerise red flowers. Mid. Introduced 1904.
Zone 5 US, 6 Can.

Rhododendron 'Madame Masson'

***R.* 'Madame Masson'** A medium-sized shrub with trusses of white flowers, deeply cut into five lobes, with a striking yellow basal blotch within. Mid. Introduced 1849.
Zone 4 US, 5b Can.

***R.* 'Mariloo'** A large, handsome shrub with bold leaves and large trusses of lemon yellow flowers that are flushed green. Early to mid. Introduced 1941.
Zone 8 US, 9 Can.

***R.* 'Marinus Koster'** A shrub whose flowers, 4 in (10 cm) wide, are borne profusely in large trusses. They are deep pink in bud, gradually fade to white on opening, and shade to pink at the margins, with a purple blotch within. Mid. Introduced 1937.
Zone 6 US, 7 Can. 🏆

Rhododendron 'Mariloo'

Rhododendron 'Marinus Koster'

***R.* 'Marion Street'** A vigorous, small *R. yakushimanum* hybrid with dark green leaves up to 4 in (10 cm) long, brown-felted beneath. The widely funnel-shaped flowers, up to 2¾ in (7 cm) across, are pale pink, edged with flushed white, and fade to white. Mid. Introduced 1965. *(See photo on p.518.)*
Zone 5 US, 6 Can. 🏆

***R.* 'Markeeta's Prize'** A medium-sized to large shrub with scarlet flowers that have darker spots. They are freely borne in large, flat-topped trusses. Mid. Introduced 1967.
Zone 6 US, 7 Can. 🏆

***R.* 'Mars'** A compact, medium-sized shrub with waxy, dark green leaves and deep red flowers that have lighter-colored stamens

Rhododendron 'Marion Street'

and are held in compact trusses. Mid.
Zone 6 US, 7 Can.

***R.* 'Mary Belle'** A medium-sized, bushy shrub with bright green, pointed leaves and salmon pink flowers that fade to a peach color and have a crimson throat. Mid. Introduced 1964.
Zone 5 US, 6 Can.

***R.* 'Mary Fleming'** A compact, dwarf shrub whose foliage turns bronze in cold weather. The flowers, borne in small clusters, are buff-yellow and flushed pink at the margins. Early to mid. Introduced 1967.
Zone 5 US, 6 Can.

***R.* 'Matador'** A large, spreading shrub whose leaves are densely covered with rusty hairs beneath. The flowers, borne in large, loose trusses, are 2 in (5 cm) across and vibrant, dark orange-red. Early to mid. Introduced 1945.
Zone 6 US, 7 Can. 🏆

***R.* 'May Day'** A magnificent, comparatively low, wide-spreading shrub with loose

Rhododendron 'May Day'

trusses of slightly drooping, funnel-shaped flowers that are bright red or orange-red, with large calyxes of the same color. The leaves are felted with fawn beneath. Mid. Introduced 1937.
Zone 7 US, 8 Can. 🏆

***R.* 'Mission Bells'** A small, compact shrub with small, glossy green leaves and open trusses of lightly scented, pale pink, bell-shaped flowers. It tolerates sun and is well suited to the West. Mid.
Zone 6 US, 7 Can.

***R.* 'Moerheim'** A dwarf, compact shrub with glossy green leaves that turn maroon in winter. The clusters of small, violet flowers are freely borne. Mid. Introduced 1966.
Zone 5 US, 6 Can. 🏆

***R.* 'Moerheim's Pink'** A small, dome-shaped, dense shrub with funnel-shaped flowers that are deep pink in bud. They open to pale lilac, are spotted rose inside, and have slightly frilled lobes. Mid. Introduced 1973.
Zone 6 US, 7 Can.

***R.* 'Molly Ann'** A dwarf, rounded shrub, as wide as it is tall, with dark green, rounded leaves. The many trusses of bright red flowers are long lasting. Early to mid. Introduced 1974.
Zone 5 US, 6 Can.

Rhododendron 'Moerheim's Pink'

***R.* 'Molly Fordham'** A small to medium-sized, compact shrub with scaly stems and glossy dark green, somewhat warty leaves that curve downward. The individual white flowers are small but are carried in large trusses. Early.
Zone 4 US, 5b Can.

Rhododendron 'Moonshine Crescent'

***R.* 'Moonshine Crescent'** A medium-sized shrub that produces clear yellow flowers. They are borne in compact, dome-shaped trusses. Early to mid. Introduced 1962.
Zone 6 US, 7 Can.

Rhododendron 'Morning Cloud'

***R.* 'Morgenrot'**, syn. *R.* 'Morning Red' A small *R. yakushimanum* hybrid with a compact habit. This is a rounded shrub with dark green leaves and flowers that are deep red in bud, open rose-red, and are borne in large trusses. Mid. Introduced 1983.
Zone 5 US, 6 Can.

***R.* 'Morning Cloud'** A dwarf, compact shrub. The leaves have a woolly felting beneath, and the flowers are white, heavily flushed with a rich pink that fades to cream. They are borne in rounded trusses. Mid to late. Introduced 1970.
Zone 6 US, 7 Can. 🏆

***R.* 'Morning Red'** See *R.* 'Morgenrot'.

***R.* 'Mother of Pearl'** A medium-sized to

Rhododendron 'Mother of Pearl'

large shrub that is a sport of *R.* 'Pink Pearl'. The flowers are rich pink in bud, open to a delicate blush, and fade to white with a few external pink streaks. Mid. Introduced before 1914.

Zone 6 US, 7 Can.

***R.* 'Mount Everest'** A large, vigorous

Rhododendron 'Mount Everest'

shrub that is very free-flowering. It has conical trusses of narrow, bell-shaped, pure white flowers with red speckling in the throat. Early. Introduced 1930.

Zone 5 US, 6 Can.

***R.* 'Mrs. A. T. de la Mare'** A vigorous, upright, medium-sized shrub of compact habit, with dome-shaped trusses of funnel-shaped, frilly-margined flowers that are borne profusely. They are pink-tinged in bud and open to white with greenish yellow spotting in the throat. Mid.

Zone 5 US, 6 Can. 🏆

***R.* 'Mrs. Charles E. Pearson'** A robust, erect, medium-sized shrub that has erect

Rhododendron 'Mrs. Charles E. Pearson'

branches and bears conical trusses of widely funnel-shaped flowers 4 in (10 cm) across. They are mauve-pink in bud and open to pale pinkish mauve that fades eventually to near-white. There is also a ray of brown markings within. Mid. Introduced 1909.

Zone 6 US, 7 Can. 🏆

***R.* 'Mrs. E.C. Stirling'** A medium-sized

Rhododendron 'Mrs. A.T. de la Mare'

to large shrub that is upright when young but becomes more spreading with age. The ruffled, rose-pink flowers have a slightly darker picotee and prominent up-curved stamens and are freely produced. Mid. Introduced c. 1900.

Zone 5 US, 6 Can.

***R.* 'Mrs. Furnivall'** A magnificent, large, densely growing shrub that produces compact, dome-shaped trusses of widely funnel-shaped, light rose-pink flowers marked with a blotch of brown and crimson inside. It is considered to be one of the finest rhododendron hybrids ever produced. Mid to late. Introduced 1920. *(See photo on p.520.)*

Zone 5 US, 6 Can. 🏆

***R.* 'Mrs. G.W. Leak'** A splendid, large, dense shrub with somewhat lax trusses of widely funnel-shaped flowers 3 in (8 cm) wide. They are mottled light rose-pink, darker in the tube, and have a splash of blackish brown and crimson markings inside; the nectaries are blood red. Although

Rhododendron 'Mrs. Furnivall'

Rhododendron 'Mrs. G.W. Leak'

the flowers are beautiful, this rhododendron is prone to foliage diseases. Mid. Introduced 1916.

Zone 6 US, 7 Can.

***R.* 'Mrs. Lionel de Rothschild'**, syn. *R.* 'Lady de Rothschild' A compact, erect, medium-sized shrub with large, firm trusses of fleshy, widely funnel-shaped flowers that are white, edged with apple-blossom pink and marked with a ray of dark crimson. Mid. Introduced 1931.

Rhododendron 'Mrs. Lionel de Rothschild'

Zone 6 US, 7 Can. 🏆

***R.* 'Mrs. P.D. Williams'** A medium-sized, free-flowering shrub with flowers in compact, flattened trusses. They are ivory white with a large brown blotch on the upper lobe. Mid to late.

Zone 6 US, 7 Can. 🏆

***R.* 'Mrs. R.S. Holford'** A vigorous, medium-sized to large shrub that tends to become leggy with age. Its widely funnel-shaped flowers, borne in large trusses, are salmon-rose with a small pattern of crimson spots within. Mid to late. Introduced 1866.

Zone 5 US, 6 Can. 🏆

***R.* 'Mrs. T.H. Lowinsky'** A vigorous, large shrub with open funnel-shaped flowers 3 in (7.5 cm) across. They are lilac, whitish toward the center, and heavily spotted with orange-brown. Mid. Introduced before 1917.

Rhododendron 'Mrs. P. D. Williams'

Zone 5 US, 6 Can. 🏆

***R.* 'Naomi Astarte'** A large shrub or small tree with large, shapely trusses of fragrant, widely expanded, pink flowers that are shaded with yellow and have a yellow throat. It is prone to powdery mildew. Early to mid.

Zone 6 US, 7 Can.

***R.* 'Naomi Exbury'** A large shrub or small tree with lilac flowers tinged with yellow. It is prone to powdery mildew. Early to mid. Introduced 1926.

Zone 6 US, 7 Can.

***R.* 'Nobleanum Coccineum'** A large, conical shrub with trusses of bell-shaped, deep rose flowers, marked with a few dark crimson spots at the base within. They are borne in midwinter to early spring. Introduced 1832.

Zone 6 US, 7 Can.

***R.* 'Nobleanum Venustum'** A densely leafy, broadly dome-shaped shrub up to $6^1/_2$ ft (2 m) high and 10 ft (3 m) wide. The funnel-shaped flowers, borne in neat trusses, are pink shading to white at the center and have a small pattern of dark crimson markings at the base within and crimson nectaries. They usually appear in late winter but may open in early winter in mild weather. Introduced 1829.

Zone 6 US, 7 Can.

***R.* 'Normandy'** A broadly rounded, small shrub that bears an abundance of funnel-shaped, rose-pink flowers with darker, wavy edges and tangerine spots on the upper petals. It is a popular variety that blooms well in sun or dappled shade. Mid.

Zone 4 US, 5b Can.

***R.* 'Nova Zembla'** (Ironclad) An excellent and hardy medium-sized shrub that is also heat tolerant. It has deeply veined leaves and rich red flowers with a darker blotch, borne in compact trusses. Mid. Introduced 1902.

Zone 4 US, 5 Can.

Rhododendron 'Nova Zembla'

***R.* 'Noyo Brave'** A small shrub that produces rounded trusses of 20 or more flowers, which are pink with a red blotch. Early.

Zone 7 US, 8 Can.

***R.* 'Odee Wright'** A neat, small to medium-sized shrub with glossy, wavy, dark

green leaves. The flowers are widely funnel-shaped and have frilled lobes; they open from reddish orange buds and are pale yellow tinged with pink and spotted with red. Mid. Introduced 1964.
Zone 6 US, 7 Can. 🏆

***R.* 'Old Copper'** A medium-sized to large, upright shrub with large, bell-shaped flowers in loose trusses. They are an unusual coppery color and open from red buds. Mid to late. Introduced 1958.
Zone 6 US, 7 Can.

***R.* 'Old Port'** A vigorous, leafy, dome-shaped shrub with very glossy foliage. The flowers, up to 2½ in (6 cm) wide and borne in dense trusses, are widely funnel shaped with frilled lobes. They are a rich plum color with a well-defined pattern of blackish crimson markings. Mid to late. Introduced 1865.
Zone 5 US, 6 Can.

***R.* 'Olive'** A free-flowering, small to medium-sized, upright shrub whose flowers are in twos and threes. They are funnel shaped, mauve-pink with deeper spots, and up to 1½ in (4 cm) wide. It blooms in early spring. Introduced 1936.
Zone 5 US, 6 Can.

***R.* 'Oudjik's Sensation'** A small shrub that produces bronze-tinged foliage and bell-shaped flowers. They are strikingly bright pink with a few spots in the upper lobe and borne in open, flat-topped trusses. Mid. Introduced 1965.
Zone 6 US, 7 Can.

***R.* 'P.J.M.'**, syn. *R.* 'Peter John Mezitt' A small to medium-sized, free-flowering shrub with broad, elliptical leaves up to 2 in (5 cm) long, blackish green above, with a bronze luster beneath; they turn purplish in winter. The saucer-shaped flowers are carried in small, dense clusters and are vivid lavender-pink, with two patches of pink spots. It is among the hardiest rhododendron hybrids. Early. Introduced 1943.
Zone 4 US, 4b Can. 🏆

Rhododendron 'Oudjik's Sensation'

Rhododendron 'P.J.M.'

Rhododendron 'Olive'

***R.* 'Parker's Pink'** This makes a well-branched, medium-sized shrub that grows as wide as it is tall and has glossy dark green leaves. The lightly fragrant flowers are medium pink marked heavily with red spots and have a white throat. Mid to late. Introduced 1973.
Zone 4 US, 5 Can.

Rhododendron 'Percy Wiseman'

***R.* 'Parson's Gloriosum'** (Ironclad) An old but popular variety that makes a medium-sized, upright bush with dense, dark green foliage. The flowers are a pinkish lavender and borne in conical trusses. Mid to late. Introduced 1850.
Zone 4 US, 5 Can.

***R.* 'Patty Bee'** A compact and vigorous dwarf shrub with dark green leaves 1¾ in (4.5 cm) long that turn bronze in winter. It produces funnel-shaped, pale yellow flowers with wavy margins that are borne in compact trusses. Early. Introduced 1977.
Zone 6 US, 7 Can. 🏆

***R.* 'Percy Wiseman'** A small, compact *R. yakushimanum* hybrid that has glossy dark green leaves and funnel-shaped flowers 2 in (5 cm) wide. They are cream flushed with pink, fading to creamy white, and are borne in globular trusses. Mid. Introduced 1971.
Zone 7 US, 8 Can. 🏆

***R.* 'Peter John Mezitt'** See *R.* 'P.J.M.'

***R.* 'Pink Cherub'** A vigorous but compact *R. yakushimanum* hybrid that makes a small shrub with flowers that are very freely borne in large, rounded trusses. They are funnel shaped, with wavy margins, and salmon pink in bud, opening to whitish pink with a fuschia-purple flush. The petal

Rhododendron 'Pink Cherub'

reverses are rich rose. Introduced 1969.
Zone 6 US, 7 Can. 🏆

***R.* 'Pink Drift'** A neat, dwarf shrub, resembling an evergreen azalea, with small, aromatic leaves and clusters of soft lavender-rose flowers. It is suitable for a rock garden. Mid. Introduced 1955.
Zone 6 US, 7 Can.

***R.* 'Pink Pearl'** A vigorous shrub that eventually becomes tall and bare at the base. The flowers, borne in magnificent

Rhododendron 'Pink Pearl'

large, conical trusses, are widely funnel shaped, rose in bud, opening to deep lilac-pink. They fade to white at the margins and have a well-defined ray of crimson-brown markings. This old variety is a parent of many modern cultivars. Mid. Introduced before 1897.
Zone 5 US, 6 Can.

***R.* 'Pink Pebble'** A free-flowering, dense, small shrub with loose trusses of widely bell-shaped, rose-pink flowers opening from red

Rhododendron 'Pink Pebble'

buds. Mid. Introduced 1954.
Zone 6 US, 7 Can. 🏆

***R.* 'Pioneer'** A medium-sized semideciduous shrub (especially at the limit of its hardiness zone) with an upright habit and small leaves. It is very free flowering, bears trusses of mauvish pink blooms, and is one of the first of the hardier rhododendrons to bloom. Introduced 1952.
Zone 4 US, 5b Can.

***R.* 'Polar Bear'** A superb large shrub or small tree. The richly fragrant flowers, borne in large trusses, are trumpet shaped, like pure white lilies, with a green flash within. It does not flower when young and requires woodland conditions. Late. Introduced 1926.
Zone 6 US, 7 Can. 🏆

***R.* Praecox group** Small, compact, semideciduous shrubs with leaves that are aromatic when crushed. The widely funnel-shaped flowers are in twos and threes at the tips of the shoots and are rosy purple but slightly darker on the outside. They are borne in late winter to early spring. Introduced c. 1855.
Zone 5 US, 6 Can. 🏆

***R.* 'Princess Anne'** An attractive dwarf shrub with a dense habit that has matte, light green leaves and greenish buds that open to pale yellow, funnel-shaped flowers $1^1/_4$ in (3 cm) wide. Early to mid. Introduced 1974.
Zone 6 US, 7 Can. 🏆

***R.* 'Professor Hugo de Vries'** A large shrub with widely funnel-shaped flowers in large, conical trusses. They are rich rose in bud and open to lilac-rose with a ray of red-

Rhododendron 'Princess Anne'

Rhododendron 'Professor Hugo de Vries'

dish brown markings on a light ground. Mid. Zone 6 US, 7 Can.
🏆

***R.* 'Ptarmigan'** A free-flowering, very dwarf, spreading shrub with flowers usually in threes, saucer shaped, $1^1/_4$ in (3 cm) wide, and pure white. Early. Introduced 1966.
Zone 6 US, 7 Can. 🏆

Rhododendron 'Ptarmigan'

***R.* 'Purple Lace'** A medium-sized shrub with slender, pointed, glossy green leaves and dense clusters of dark pink to purplish, fringed flowers. Mid to late.
Zone 5 US, 6 Can.

Rhododendron 'Purple Splendour'

***R.* 'Purple Splendour'** A sturdy shrub with widely funnel-shaped flowers in neat trusses, rich purplish blue, with a distinct ray of black embossed markings on a purplish brown background. Mid to late. Introduced before 1900.
Zone 6 US, 7 Can. 🏆

Rhododendron 'Queen Elizabeth II'

***R.* 'Queen Elizabeth II'** A medium-sized shrub with slender leaves and seven-lobed, widely funnel-shaped, pale greenish yellow flowers that are $4\frac{1}{2}$ in (11 cm) wide and borne in trusses of up to 12. Mid. Introduced 1968.
Zone 6 US, 7 Can. 🏆

***R.* 'Queen of Hearts'** A medium-sized shrub that produces dome-shaped trusses of deep crimson flowers speckled white within. Early to mid. Introduced 1949.
Zone 6 US, 7 Can. 🏆

Rhododendron 'Queen of Hearts'

***R.* 'Ramapo'** A dwarf, compact shrub with attractive blue-gray young foliage. The clusters of small, violet-purple flowers are borne freely. It does best in sun. Early to mid. Introduced 1940.
Zone 4 US, 5 Can. 🏆

***R.* 'Razorbill'** A dwarf shrub, reaching 2 ft (60 cm) high, with tubular flowers that are deep pink in bud and open to rose-pink outside, paler inside. They are carried upright in dense trusses. Early to mid. Introduced 1976.
Zone 6 US, 7 Can. 🏆

Rhododendron 'Razorbill'

***R.* 'Red Carpet'** A dwarf shrub with striking, bright red, bell-shaped flowers $2\frac{1}{4}$ in (5.5 cm) wide with wavy margins. They are borne in lax trusses. Mid. Introduced 1967.
Zone 8 US, 9 Can. 🏆

Rhododendron 'Red Carpet'

***R.* 'Renoir'** A compact, upright, small shrub with rounded trusses of rich rose flowers that are spotted crimson and fade to nearly white. Mid to late. Introduced 1963.
Zone 6 US, 7 Can. 🏆

Rhododendron 'Renoir'

***R.* 'Ring of Fire'** A striking small shrub with dense foliage and yellow flowers edged in orange. Mid. Introduced 1984.
Zone 7 US, 8 Can.

***R.* Riplet group** Small shrubs with

rounded trusses of bell-shaped, rose flowers that are white in the throat with crimson spots. Early to mid. Introduced 1963.
Zone 6 US, 7 Can.

R. 'Robert Keir' A large shrub with dark green foliage and dense, rounded trusses of pale yellow flowers flushed with pink. Mid. Introduced 1951.
Zone 6 US, 7 Can.

R. 'Rocket' A medium-sized, rounded shrub that has glossy, veined leaves and very frilled, coral-pink flowers with a bright red blotch. Early. Introduced 1955.
Zone 5 US, 6 Can.

Rhododendron 'Robert Keir'

R. 'Romany Chai' A lovely medium-sized shrub with large, compact trusses of rich terra-cotta flowers that have a dark maroon basal blotch. Mid to late. Introduced 1912.
Zone 7 US, 8 Can.

R. 'Rosy Dream' A small, spreading shrub whose green leaves have silvery wool beneath that changes to red-brown. It bears domed trusses of funnel-shaped, rose-pink flowers with a paler throat. Mid.
Zone 6 US, 7 Can.

R. 'Roseum Elegans' (Ironclad) A very popular, fast-growing, large shrub grown for its tolerance to heat and humidity and its reliable blooming. Its flowers are purplish rose-pink and carried in dome-shaped trusses. Mid. Introduced 1851.
Zone 4 US, 5 Can.

R. 'Saffron Queen' A beautiful medium-sized shrub with glossy green leaves and tubular, sulphur yellow flowers that are spotted with a darker tone on the upper lobes. Mid. Introduced 1948.
Zone 9 US

Rhododendron 'Saffron Queen'

R. 'Saint Breward' A small, rounded shrub with full, globular trusses of shallowly bell-shaped, soft lavender flowers that are darker at the margins and have pale blue anthers. Early to mid. Introduced 1963.
Zone 5 US, 6 Can.

Rhododendron 'Saint Breward'

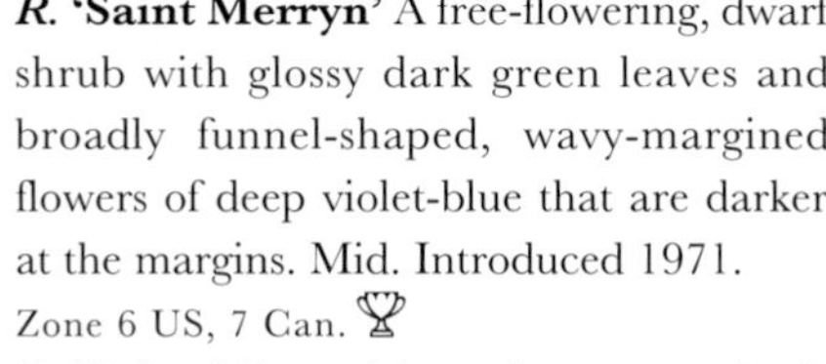

R. 'Saint Merryn' A free-flowering, dwarf shrub with glossy dark green leaves and broadly funnel-shaped, wavy-margined flowers of deep violet-blue that are darker at the margins. Mid. Introduced 1971.
Zone 6 US, 7 Can.

R. 'Saint Minver' A small, compact shrub with clusters of violet-blue flowers. Early to mid. Introduced 1973.
Zone 6 US, 7 Can.

R. 'Saint Tudy' A small, dense shrub with dense trusses of shallowly bell-shaped, blue flowers. Early to mid. Introduced 1962.
Zone 6 US, 7 Can.

R. 'Sapphire' A dwarf, small-leaved shrub of open habit with pale lavender-blue flowers. Early. Introduced 1969.
Zone 6 US, 7 Can.

R. 'Sappho' A large, rounded or dome-shaped shrub with glossy, dark olive-green leaves and conical trusses of widely funnel-shaped flowers. They are mauve in bud and open to pure white with a conspicuous

Rhododendron 'Sapphire'

Rhododendron 'Sappho'

blotch of deep purple overlaid with black. Mid. Introduced before 1867.
Zone 6 US, 7 Can. 🏆

***R.* 'Scarlet Wonder'** A compact, dwarf shrub that forms a neat mound of dense foliage. The ruby red flowers are trumpet shaped with frilly margins and are borne in loose trusses. Mid. Introduced 1965.
Zone 5 US, 6 Can. 🏆

***R.* 'Scintillation'** A medium-sized to large shrub, broader than it is tall, with shiny, waxy, deep green leaves 6 in (15 cm) long or more. The lightly scented, pale pink flowers are in large trusses of 12–15 and have a blotch of bronze markings in the throat. It is a very popular variety and a reliable bloomer. Mid. Introduced c. 1930.
Zone 5 US, 6 Can.

Rhododendron 'Scarlet Wonder'

***R.* 'Seta'** A distinctive, medium-sized shrub of erect habit with umbels of unspotted, narrowly bell-shaped flowers that are white at the base, shading to vivid pink in the lobes. It is one of the first rhododendron hybrids to flower, in early to midspring. Introduced 1933.
Zone 7 US, 8 Can. 🏆

***R.* 'Seven Stars'** A large, vigorous *R. yakushimanum* hybrid forming a free-flowering shrub. It bears reddish buds that open to bell-shaped, wavy-margined white flowers flushed with pink. Mid. Introduced 1966.
Zone 6 US, 7 Can. 🏆

***R.* 'Shamrock'** A compact, dwarf shrub that bears a profusion of pale yellow flowers opening from yellow-green buds. Early to mid. It tolerates drought. Introduced 1978.
Zone 6 US, 7 Can.

Rhododendron 'Seta'

Rhododendron 'Seven Stars'

***R.* 'Sham's Candy'** A vigorous medium-sized shrub with yellow-green leaves and conical trusses of dark pink flowers that have yellow-green markings. Mid to late. Introduced by Shammarello.
Zone 5 US, 6 Can.

***R.* 'Sham's Juliet'** A small to medium-sized shrub that has dark green leaves. The flowers are light pink with darker pink at the edges and brownish spots in the throat. Mid. Introduced by Shammarello.
Zone 5 US, 6 Can.

Rhododendron 'Shamrock'

***R.* 'Silver Cloud'** A dwarf *R. yakushimanum* hybrid that makes a dense, rounded shrub with dark green leaves and pale purple, frilly-margined flowers that are darker outside and spotted with yellow-green. Mid. Introduced 1963.
Zone 6 US, 7 Can.

***R.* 'Silver Sixpence'** An upright, small shrub with cream flowers spotted with yellow. The buds are green, tinged with mauve. Mid. Introduced 1975.
Zone 6 US, 7 Can. 🏆

Rhododendron 'Sir Charles Lemon'

***R.* 'Sir Charles Lemon'**, syn. *R. arboreum* 'Sir Charles Lemon' A magnificent large shrub or small tree with leaves that are rusty brown beneath. The white flowers are borne in dense trusses. Early.
Zone 7 US, 8 Can. 🏆

***R.* 'Snipe'** A dwarf, dense shrub with pale green leaves and pale pink to white flowers that are flushed with violet and purple and have deeper spots. Early to mid. Introduced 1978.
Zone 6 US, 7 Can. 🏆

***R.* 'Snow Lady'** A compact, small shrub of spreading habit with bristly leaves up to 3 in (7.5 cm) long and fragrant white flowers borne in lax trusses. Mid. Introduced 1955.
Zone 7 US, 8 Can. 🏆

***R.* 'Snow Queen'** A lovely large shrub with profusely borne, dome-shaped trusses of large, funnel-shaped, pure white flowers that open from dark pink buds and have a

Rhododendron 'Snow Queen'

small basal blotch within. Mid. Introduced 1926. Zone 7 US, 8 Can. 🏆

***R.* 'Songbird'** A small shrub with clusters of violet bell-shaped flowers. Early. Introduced 1954.
Zone 6 US, 7 Can.

***R.* 'Souvenir d'Anthony Waterer'** A vigorous, upright, large shrub with dark rose-red flowers with a prominent yellow eye, borne in domed trusses. Mid. Introduced before 1924.
Zone 6 US, 7 Can. 🏆

***R.* 'Souvenir de Dr. S. Endtz'** A compact, medium-sized shrub with widely funnel-shaped flowers in dome-shaped trusses.

Rhododendron 'Souvenir de Dr. S. Endtz'

Rhododendron 'Songbird'

They are rich rose in bud, opening to a mottled pink that is paler in the center and marked with a ray of crimson; the nectaries are crimson. Mid. Introduced 1927.
Zone 6 US, 7 Can. 🏆

***R.* 'Spring Glory'** Another popular variety from the same cross as 'Cheer', 'Holden', and 'Rocket'. It is a medium-sized shrub that produces pink flowers with a purple blotch. It grows well in sun or shade. Early to mid.
Zone 4 US, 5b Can.

Rhododendron 'Surrey Heath'

***R.* 'Surrey Heath'** A small *R. yakushimanum* hybrid that makes a bushy, spreading shrub with narrow leaves that are slightly woolly above when young. The funnel-shaped flowers, borne in globular trusses, are 1 3/4 in (4.5 cm) wide and pale rose-pink, deeper at the margins. Mid. Introduced 1975.
Zone 7 US, 8 Can. 🏆

***R.* 'Susan'** A tall, bushy shrub with large

Rhododendron 'Susan'

trusses of bluish mauve flowers, darker at the margins and spotted with purple. Early to mid. Introduced 1930.
Zone 6 US, 7 Can. 🏆

Rhododendron 'Sweet Simplicity'

***R.* 'Sweet Simplicity'** A medium-sized, bushy shrub with large, glossy leaves. It bears ruffled white flowers with pink edges and olive spots carried in rounded trusses. Mid to late. Introduced before 1922.
Zone 6 US, 7 Can. 🏆

***R.* 'Taurus'** A stout-branched, large shrub with prominently veined leaves. The vivid red, widely funnel-shaped flowers, with frilled margins, are borne in large, rounded trusses. Early to mid. Introduced 1972.
Zone 6 US, 7 Can. 🏆

***R.* 'Teal'** A dwarf, rather upright shrub with pale green leaves more than 2 in (5 cm) long and bark that peels with age. The flowers, up to 1¼ in (3.5 cm) wide, are broadly bell shaped and primrose yellow. Mid. Introduced 1977.
Zone 7 US, 8 Can. 🏆

***R.* 'Teddy Bear'** A small, compact shrub with shiny dark green leaves that have a brown indumentum. Flowers are pink in tight trusses. It is a *R. yakushimanum* hybrid. Early to mid. Introduced 1991.
Zone 5 US, 6 Can.

***R.* 'Temple Belle'** A neat, rounded shrub that is similar to *R. orbiculare*, one of its parents. It bears rounded leaves that are attractively glaucous on the undersides. The bell-shaped flowers are held in a loose cluster and are of a uniform rose-pink without markings. Early to mid. Introduced 1916.
Zone 6 US, 7 Can. 🏆

Rhododendron 'Temple Belle'

***R.* 'The General'** A *R. catawbiense* hybrid that forms a medium-sized to large, upright shrub with shiny dark green leaves and crimson flowers, each with a darker blotch, held in upright trusses. It is a reliable performer, even at the limits of its hardiness. Mid to late. Introduced 1955.
Zone 4 US, 5 Can.

***R.* 'The Honourable Jean Marie de Montague'**, syn. *R.* 'Jean Marie de Montague' A vigorous, medium-sized shrub with dark green leaves and bell-shaped flowers with wavy margins. They are 3 in (8 cm) across, vivid deep red with darker spots in the throat, and borne in neat, domed trusses up to 6 in (15 cm) wide. Mid. Introduced 1921 from Holland.
Zone 6 US, 7 Can. 🏆

***R.* 'Thunderstorm'** A medium-sized shrub with glossy dark green leaves. It produces dark red, wavy-edged flowers that have darker spots and white stamens and are borne in neat, dome-shaped trusses. Mid to late. The cross was made 1930.
Zone 6 US, 7 Can. 🏆

***R.* 'Tidbit'** A small, dense, spreading shrub with bell-shaped, wavy-margined flowers that are straw yellow, with red in the throat. They are borne in compact, domed trusses. Mid. Introduced 1957.
Zone 7 US, 8 Can.

***R.* 'Titian Beauty'** A small, compact, fairly upright *R. yakushimanum* hybrid shrub with dark green leaves lightly covered with thin, brown felt beneath. The flowers are waxy red. Mid. Introduced 1971.
Zone 7 US, 8 Can. 🏆

***R.* 'Todmorton'** A spreading, medium-sized shrub with globe-shaped trusses of frilled-edged flowers that open a rosy pink and then fade to almost white, giving a two-tone effect. Mid. Introduced 1983.
Zone 6 US, 7 Can.

Rhododendron 'Tortoiseshell Champagne'

***R.* 'Tortoiseshell Champagne'** A medium-sized shrub with funnel-shaped, yellow flowers that fade to pale yellow tinged with pink at the margins of the lobes. Mid to late. Introduced 1945.
Zone 7 US, 8 Can. 🏆

***R.* 'Tortoiseshell Wonder'** A medium-sized shrub with salmon pink flowers. Mid to late. Introduced 1945. *(See photo on p.528.)*
Zone 7 US, 8 Can. 🏆

***R.* 'Trude Webster'** A vigorous medium-sized to large shrub. The flowers are clear pink, fading to pale pink or white on the lobes, and have reddish spots; they are borne in very large, conical trusses. Mid to late. Introduced 1961.
Zone 6 US, 7 Can.

***R.* 'Tyermannii'** An upright medium-

Rhododendron 'Tortoiseshell Wonder'

Rhododendron 'Tyermannii'

sized shrub with glossy leaves and fragrant lilylike flowers that are cream fading to white inside and tinged green and brown outside. Mid. Introduced 1925.
Zone 9 US 🏆

***R.* 'Unique'** A leafy, dense, medium-sized shrub with dome-shaped trusses of funnel-shaped flowers. They are cream with a faint

Rhododendron 'Unique'

blush and are marked with scattered, faint crimson spots. Early to mid. Introduced 1934.
Zone 5 US, 6 Can. 🏆

***R.* 'Vanessa Pastel'** A spreading, shapely, medium-sized shrub with loose trusses of soft rose-pink flowers that are flushed with buff and have a deep crimson eye. Mid to late. Introduced 1946.
Zone 7 US, 8 Can. 🏆

***R.* 'Van Ness Sensation'** A small, compact shrub with dense, shiny, midgreen leaves and fragrant, funnel-shaped, blush pink flowers held in domed clusters. Mid.
Zone 6 US, 7 Can.

***R.* 'Venetian Chimes'** A vigorous, small *R. yakushimanum* hybrid with bell-shaped flowers, 2 in (5 cm) wide, carried in compact, globular trusses. They are brick red, flushed with scarlet toward the base and spotted with blackish-red. Mid to late. Introduced 1971.
Zone 7 US, 8 Can.

***R.* 'Vintage Rosé'** A small *R. yakushimanum* hybrid that has leaves up to 4 in (10 cm) long with a thick felting beneath. The flowers are funnel shaped with wavy margins, 2½ in (6 cm) wide, and rose pink, deeper in the center. They are borne in large, conical trusses. Mid to late. Introduced 1974.
Zone 7 US, 8 Can. 🏆

***R.* 'Virginia Richards'** A small to medium-sized, vigorous shrub of upright habit with funnel-shaped, wavy-margined flowers in large, globular trusses up to 6 in (15 cm) wide. The flowers open from pink buds to light pink, then turn yellow-pink with a pale orange cast in the center; they are flushed with rose-pink at the margins and have red spots inside. It is a popular rhododendron and lovely when in flower but is prone to powdery mildew. Mid. Introduced 1962.
Zone 7 US, 8 Can.

Rhododendron 'Virginia Richards'

Rhododendron 'Vulcan'

***R.* 'Vulcan'** A compact, medium-sized shrub with funnel-shaped, wavy-margined, bright red flowers in dome-shaped trusses. Mid. Introduced 1938.
Zone 4 US, 5 Can. 🏆

***R.* 'Weston's Pink Diamond'** A medium-sized, upright, well-branched semi-evergreen shrub with glossy yellow-green leaves and trusses of flat, frilled, pinkish purple flowers. Early. Introduced 1977.
Zone 5 US, 6 Can.

***R.* 'Wheatley'** A medium-sized to large shrub with dark green leaves up to 7 in (17.5 cm) long. The large trusses have up to 16 frilled, fragrant, rose-pink flowers with

greenish markings. Mid. Introduced 1970.
Zone 5 US, 6 Can.

R. 'White Swan' A large, upright shrub with gray-green leaves. The flowers, borne in large trusses, are pale pink, fading to white marked with green. Mid to late. Introduced 1937.
Zone 6 US, 7 Can. 🏆

R. 'Wigeon' A free-flowering dwarf shrub with funnel-shaped, wavy-margined flowers 1½ in (4 cm) across. They are deep lavender-pink with dark spots, borne in dome-shaped trusses. Mid. Introduced 1982.
Zone 6 US, 7 Can.

R. 'Wilgen's Ruby' A medium-sized shrub with large, rounded trusses of deep red, funnel-shaped flowers with darker spots. Mid to late. Introduced 1951.
Zone 5 US, 6 Can. 🏆

R. 'Willbrit' A small shrub with dark green leaves that are reddish when young. The deep pink, bell-shaped flowers, paler at the margin, are borne in open trusses. Mid to late. Introduced 1960.
Zone 7 US, 8 Can.

R. 'Windbeam' A small, compact shrub whose dark green leaves turn red-brown in winter. The apricot buds open to pale pink flowers that fade to near-white. Early.
Zone 5 US, 6 Can.

R. 'Windsor Lad' A medium-sized *R. ponticum* hybrid. It bears widely funnel-shaped flowers that open from purple buds to lilac-purple with a prominent green patch. Mid to late. Introduced 1958.
Zone 6 US, 7 Can.

R. 'Winsome' A small shrub with coppery young growth and leaves thinly covered with rusty felt beneath. The funnel-shaped flowers, in loose, pendent clusters, are scarlet in bud and open rose-pink, reddish toward the base. Mid. Introduced 1939.
Zone 5 US, 6 Can. 🏆

R. 'Wishmoor' A neat, small *R. yakushimanum* hybrid that bears seven-lobed flowers, 3 in (8 cm) wide, that are orange-red in bud and open to pale yellow, deeper in the throat. Mid. Introduced 1972.
Zone 6 US, 7 Can. 🏆

Rhododendron 'Woodcock'

R. 'Wissahickon' A popular medium-sized to large shrub with an open habit. The flowers, in large trusses, are a deep pink that does not fade in the sun. Mid.
Zone 5 US, 6 Can.

R. 'Woodcock' A small, rounded shrub with rich green, deeply veined leaves up to 4 in (10 cm) long with recurved margins. The funnel-shaped, clear pale pink flowers have red spots and are borne in flat-topped trusses of about 10. The buds are deep strawberry-pink. Mid. Introduced 1972.
Zone 6 US, 7 Can. 🏆

Rhododendron 'Winsome'

R. 'Wren' A prostrate, mound-forming, dwarf shrub with glossy leaves, reddish young growth, and clear yellow flowers. Early to mid. Introduced 1983.
Zone 7 US, 8 Can.

R. 'Yaku Prince' A dwarf *R. yakushimanum* hybrid whose purple-pink flowers have a pink blotch spotted with red-orange. Mid.
Zone 5 US, 6 Can.

Rhododendron 'Yellow Hammer'

R. 'Yaku Princess' A small, dense, rounded *R. yakushimanum* hybrid whose leaves have a pale brown felt beneath. The flowers are apple-blossom pink with greenish spots and are borne in dense, rounded trusses. Mid to late. Introduced 1977.
Zone 4 US, 5 Can.

R. 'Yellow Hammer' A charming, somewhat slender, small to medium-sized shrub with pairs of bright yellow flowers at the ends of the shoots and in the axils of the leaves. They are very narrowly bell shaped. Early. Introduced before 1931.
Zone 7 US, 8 Can. 🏆

AZALEODENDRONS

Azaleodendrons are hybrids between deciduous azaleas and evergreen rhododendrons. They are very small to medium-sized evergreen or semievergreen shrubs that flower in late spring and early summer.

R. 'Galloper Light' A leafy semievergreen shrub with loose trusses of funnel-shaped flowers that are cream in the tube

Rhododendron 'Glory of Littleworth'

and shade to soft salmon pink in the lobes. A chrome yellow blotch adds to the general effect of creamy pink.

Zone 6 US, 7 Can.

***R.* 'Glory of Littleworth'** A superb small, semievergreen shrub with a stiff, erect habit. The more or less oblong leaves, 3–4½ in (7.5–11 cm) long, are often curled and wavy. The fragrant, funnel-shaped flowers are cream at first and become milk white with a conspicuous coppery blotch.

Zone 6 US, 7 Can.

***R.* 'Hardijzer Beauty'** A small, compact evergreen shrub with dense trusses of purple flowers in late spring.

Zone 6 US, 7 Can. 🏆

***R.* 'Martha Isaacson'** A medium-sized evergreen shrub with tubular-funnel-shaped, slightly fragrant, white flowers striped with pink.

Zone 6 US, 7 Can.

***R.* 'Martine'** A small, densely branched evergreen shrub with bright glossy green leaves and funnel-shaped, shell pink flowers that are produced abundantly.

Zone 6 US, 7 Can.

***R.* 'Ria Hardijzer'** A small evergreen shrub with rich purple flowers, spotted inside, in trusses of 5–10.

Zone 6 US, 7 Can.

DECIDUOUS AZALEA HYBRIDS

These are fairly twiggy shrubs, up to 8 ft (2.5 m) tall, and usually have large, trumpet-shaped single flowers, although a few are double. Colors range from soft pastels to vibrant red and orange. Some are fragrant, and many have colorful fall foliage.

The hybrids are classified in groups, which are given below. Hybrids that do not fall into any of the groups are listed with (-). **Ghent hybrids** (Gh) originated in Ghent, Belgium, in the early 19th century. They reach 6–8 ft (1.8–2.5 m) tall and are very hardy. The fragrant, tubular flowers, like those of a honeysuckle, open in late spring; most are single, but some are double.

Knap Hill hybrids (Kn) were developed in 1870 at the Knap Hill Nursery in England and have trumpet-shaped, brightly colored, usually scentless flowers in late spring. Knap Hill hybrids bred beginning in 1922 by Lionel de Rothschild at Exbury, England, are called Exbury azaleas (Kn-Ex). They reach 6–8 ft (1.8–2.5 m) tall.

Mollis hybrids (M) have large, scentless, beautifully colored flowers generally ranging from yellow to red. They are borne in handsome trusses, usually in midspring, before the leaves emerge. Their average height is 3–6 ft (1–1.8 m).

Northern Lights hybrids (N) originated at the University of Minnesota in 1957 and have small trusses of blooms in a range of colors. They are very hardy and their average size is 6–7 ft (1.8–2.2 m) tall and wide.

Occidentale hybrids (O) have delicate, pastel-colored, fragrant flowers in late spring, about two weeks after the Mollis hybrids bloom. Their average height is 6–8 ft (1.8–2.5 m).

Rustica hybrids (R) have sweetly scented, double flowers that bloom in late spring and early summer. Their average height is 4–5 ft (1.2–1.5 m).

Rhododendron 'Annabella'

***R.* 'Aida'** (R) Fragrant, double flowers of deep peach-pink with a deeper flush. Introduced 1888.

Zone 5 US, 6 Can.

***R.* 'Annabella'** (Kn) Orange and yellow buds open to golden yellow, flushed with orange-rose. Introduced 1947.

Zone 5 US, 6 Can. 🏆

***R.* 'Apricot Surprise'** (N) Apricot flowers have a shading of yellow at the throat.

Zone 3 US, 4 Can.

***R.* 'Ballerina'** (Kn-Ex) Large, white, frilly-edged flowers with an orange flush; they are flesh pink in bud.

Zone 5 US, 6 Can.

***R.* 'Balzac'** (Kn-Ex) Fragrant, star-shaped, vivid red flowers with an orange flare.

Zone 5 US, 6 Can.

Rhododendron 'Cecile'

***R.* 'Berryrose'** (Kn-Ex) Fragrant, red-orange flowers flushed with rose-pink and marked with a yellow flare. Young leaves are coppery red.

Zone 5 US, 6 Can. 🏆

***R.* 'Cannon's Double'** (Kn-Ex) Bright pink, double flowers shaded with orange.

Zone 4 US, 5b Can.

***R.* 'Cecile'** (Kn-Ex) Dark salmon pink buds open to large flowers that are salmon pink with a yellow flare. Introduced 1947.

Zone 4 US, 5 Can. 🏆

***R.* 'Coccineum Speciosum'** (Gh) One of the best old azaleas, with fragrant, brilliant orange-red flowers with a yellow blotch. Introduced 1846.

Zone 4 US, 5 Can. 🏆

***R.* 'Corneille'** (Gh) Pink buds open to fragant, cream, double flowers that are flushed

Rhododendron 'Daviesii'

Rhododendron 'Delicatissimum'

deep pink on the outside. Good fall color. Zone 4 US, 5b Can. 🏆

R. **'Corringe'** (Kn-Ex) Flame-colored flowers.
Zone 5 US, 6 Can. 🏆

R. **'Daviesii'** (Gh) Fragrant, pale yellow flowers fade to white with a yellow flare. Good fall color. Introduced c. 1840.
Zone 5 US, 6 Can. 🏆

R. **'Delicatissimum'** (O) Fragrant, pale yellowish white flowers that are flushed pink and have a yellow blotch.
Zone 5 US, 6 Can. 🏆

R. **'Diorama'** (M-Kn) Fragrant, deep red flowers.
Zone 5 US, 6 Can.

R. **'Dr. M. Oosthoek'** (M) Deep orange-red flowers. Introduced 1920.
Zone 5 US, 6 Can. 🏆

R. **'Exquisitum'** (O) Fragrant, frilly, pink flowers are flushed deep pink on the outside and have an orange flare. Introduced 1901.
Zone 5 US, 6 Can. 🏆

Rhododendron 'Exquisitum'

R. **'Fanny'** (Gh) Fragrant, rose-magenta flowers with a darker tube and orange flare.
Zone 4 US, 5 Can. 🏆

R. **'Fireball'** (Kn-Ex) Deep orange-red flowers and deep copper-red young foliage. Introduced 1951.
Zone 5 US, 6 Can.

Rhododendron 'Freya'

R. **'Fireglow'** (Kn) Rich reddish orange flowers.
Zone 5 US, 6 Can.

R. **'Freya'** (R) Fragrant, pale pink, double flowers, tinted a rich orange-salmon. Introduced 1888.
Zone 5 US, 6 Can.

R. **'Gibraltar'** (Kn-Ex) Large, flame-orange flowers with a warm yellow flare and frilled petals; they are deep crimson-orange in bud. Introduced 1947.
Zone 4 US, 5 Can.
🏆

R. **'Ginger'** (Kn-Ex) The flowers are orange-carmine in bud, opening to bright

Rhododendron 'Gibraltar'

orange with a warm golden upper petal. Introduced 1947. Zone 5 US, 6 Can.

R. **'Girard's Mount Saint Helens'** (-) An American hybrid that has wavy-edged, pink to salmon flowers with a red-orange blotch, borne in large trusses.
Zone 5 US, 6 Can.

R. **'Glowing Embers'** (Kn-Ex) Vivid reddish orange flowers with an orange blotch.
Zone 5 US, 6 Can.

R. **'Golden Lights'** (N) Bright yellow to gold, fragrant flowers in midspring on an upright plant.
Zone 3 US, 4 Can.

R. **'Golden Sunset'** (Kn) Vivid sunset yellow flowers with an orange blotch.
Zone 5 US, 6 Can.

R. **'Homebush'** (Kn) Rose-pink, semi-double flowers with paler shading, borne in tight, rounded heads. Introduced 1926.
Zone 4 US, 5b Can. 🏆

R. **'Hotspur'** (Kn-Ex) Large, dazzling, flame-red flowers with darker markings on the upper petals and a yellow blotch.
Zone 4 US, 5 Can. 🏆

R. **'Irene Koster'** (O) Fragrant, rose-pink flowers with a small yellow blotch inside, opening late.
Zone 5 US, 6 Can. 🏆

R. **'King's Red'** (Kn-Ex) Ruffled, bright red blooms in rounded trusses.
Zone 4 US, 5b Can.

R. **'Klondyke'** (Kn-Ex) Large flowers that are glowing orange-gold, tinted red on the back. Buds are flushed red, and the young foliage is coppery red. Introduced 1947. *(See photo on p.532.)* Zone 5 US, 6 Can. 🏆

R. **'Nancy Waterer'** (Gh) Large, fragrant,

Rhododendron 'Klondyke'

Rhododendron 'Nancy Waterer'

bright golden yellow flowers. Introduced before 1876.
Zone 4 US, 5 Can. 🏆

***R.* 'Narcissiflorum'** (Gh) Double, sweetly scented, pale yellow flowers, darker in the center and on the outside. Introduced before 1871.
Zone 4 US, 5 Can. 🏆

Rhododendron 'Norma'

***R.* 'Norma'** (R) Rose-red double flowers with a salmon glow. Introduced 1888.
Zone 5 US, 6 Can. 🏆

***R.* 'Northern Hi-lights'** (N) Lightly fragrant, pale yellow flowers that age to white.
Zone 3 US, 4 Can.

***R.* 'Orchid Lights'** (N) Orchid-pink to lilac flowers on a somewhat smaller bush than most of the hybrids in this group.
Zone 3 US, 4 Can.

Rhododendron 'Persil'

***R.* 'Oxydol'** (Kn-Ex) Large white flowers with a distinctive yellow blotch. In cultivation 1947.
Zone 5 US, 6 Can. 🏆

***R.* 'Persil'** (Kn) White flowers with an orange-yellow flare.
Zone 5 US, 6 Can. 🏆

***R.* 'Pink Delight'** (Kn) Deep pink flowers.
Zone 5 US, 6 Can.

***R.* 'Pink Lights'** (N) Fragrant, pale pink flowers with orange spots in trusses of about 12 blooms.
Zone 3 US, 4 Can.

Rhododendron 'Pink Delight'

***R.* 'Rosy Lights'** (N) A spreading shrub with fragrant flowers that are rose-pink with darker shading.
Zone 3 US, 4 Can.

***R.* 'Royal Command'** (Kn-Ex) Vivid reddish orange flowers.
Zone 5 US, 6 Can.

Rhododendron 'Satan'

***R.* 'Royal Lodge'** (Kn-Ex) Deep vermilion red flowers, becoming crimson with age. Introduced 1947.
Zone 5 US, 6 Can. 🏆

***R.* 'Satan'** (Kn) Deep red flowers that are darker in bud. Introduced 1926.
Zone 4 US, 5 Can. 🏆

***R.* 'Silver Slipper'** (Kn-Ex) White flowers that are flushed with pink and have an orange flare. Young foliage is tinted copper. Introduced 1948.
Zone 5 US, 6 Can. 🏆

***R.* 'Spicy Lights'** (N) Dark orange flowers with a pleasing, spicy fragrance.
Zone 3 US, 4 Can.

Rhododendron 'Strawberry Ice'

***R.* 'Strawberry Ice'** (Kn-Ex) Flesh pink flowers that are mottled deeper pink at the margins and have a gold flare. They are deep pink in bud. Introduced 1947.
Zone 4 US, 5 Can. 🏆

***R.* 'Sugared Almond'** (Kn-Ex) Pale pink flowers. In cultivation 1951.
Zone 5 US, 6 Can. 🏆

***R.* 'Sun Chariot'** (Kn-Ex) Vivid yellow flowers with an orange-yellow blotch.
Zone 5 US, 6 Can. 🏆

***R.* 'Tunis'** (Kn) Deep crimson flowers with an orange flare, opening from darker buds. Introduced 1926.
Zone 4 US, 5 Can.

***R.* 'Westminster'** (O) Fragrant, rich pink flowers with a faint orange flare.
Zone 5 US, 6 Can.

***R.* 'White Lights'** (N) Large, fragrant, pale pink to white flowers have a yellow center and are freely produced. The buds are rose-pink.
Zone 3 US, 4 Can.

Rhododendron 'Westminster'

Rhododendron 'Whitethroat'

***R.* 'Whitethroat'** (Kn) A compact shrub with pure white flowers that have frilly margins. Introduced 1941.
Zone 5 US, 6 Can. 🏆

Rhododendron 'Wryneck'

***R.* 'Wryneck'** (Kn) Straw yellow flowers, darker at the margins, with a deeper yellow flare. They are pinkish in bud.
Zone 5 US, 6 Can. 🏆

EVERGREEN AZALEA HYBRIDS

There are numerous evergreen azalea hybrids, varying considerably in size and hardiness. They generally flower between spring and early summer, and they bloom so profusely that their foliage is often hidden. The majority have single flowers, although some are hose-in-hose doubles, whereby the calyx is the same color as the petals — giving the appearance of one flower sitting inside another.

The hybrids are classified in groups, the most popular of which are listed below. Hybrids that do not fall into any of these groups are designated with (-).

Gable hybrids (G) were developed by Joseph Gable of Pennsylvania and include some of the first hardy evergreen azaleas available in the United States. The flowers are up to $2^1/_2$ in (6 cm) wide and are usually red or purple.

Glenn Dale hybrids (GD) were developed at Glenn Dale, Md., in a large breeding program aimed at producing hardy hybrids for the Mid-Atlantic region. Their flowers vary from 2–4 in (5–10 cm) across and bloom in a range of colors.

Indian hybrids (I) are large plants with large single or double flowers, ranging from white to rose-red. These tender shrubs are grown in greenhouses in cold areas for forcing but are popular outdoors in the South.

Kaempferi hybrids (Kf) are vigorous plants that can reach 8 ft (2.5 m) tall and have flowers up to 2 in (5 cm) across.

Kurume hybrids (K) originated in Japan in the 19th century and were introduced into the United States in the early 1900s. The plants range from dwarfs to 5 ft (1.5 m) tall and bear their small flowers very freely.

Satsuki hybrids (S) were introduced from Japan into the United States in the 1930s. They are compact, small or medium-sized plants with medium to large flowers.

Vuyk hybrids (V) usually have large flowers, 2–3 in (5–7.5 cm) wide.

Wada hybrids (W) were raised by the nurseryman Koichiro Wada of Yokohama, Japan, before 1940. The flowers are medium to large.

***R.* 'Addy Wery'** (K) Deep vermilion red flowers. Introduced 1940.
Zone 6 US, 7 Can. 🏆

***R.* 'Aladdin'** (K) Intense red flowers that fade to salmon.
Zone 6 US, 7 Can.

***R.* 'Alexander'** (-) Deep reddish orange, medium-sized flowers with a darker blotch.
Zone 7 US, 8 Can.

***R.* 'Atalanta'** (Kf) Soft lilac flowers. *(See photo on p.534.)* Zone 7 US, 8 Can.

***R.* 'Azuma Kagami'** (K) Pink hose-in-hose flowers with darker shading.
Zone 6 US, 7 Can. 🏆

Rhododendron 'Atalanta'

Rhododendron 'Beethoven'

***R.* 'Beethoven'** (V) Orchid-purple flowers with a deeper blotch and fringed petals. Introduced 1941.
Zone 7 US, 8 Can.

***R.* 'Betty'** (Kf) Vivid purple-pink flowers with a deeper center. Introduced 1922.
Zone 7 US, 8 Can.

***R.* 'Blaauw's Pink'** (K) Salmon pink flowers with paler shading, borne early.
Zone 6 US, 7 Can.

Rhododendron 'Blaauw's Pink'

***R.* 'Blue Danube'** (Kf) Striking bluish violet flowers.
Zone 7 US, 8 Can.

***R.* 'Buccaneer'** (GD) A vigorous shrub with vivid reddish orange flowers.
Zone 6 US, 7 Can.

***R.* 'Caroline Gable'** (G) A low, spreading shrub with vivid red flowers.
Zone 5 US, 6 Can.

***R.* 'Chippewa'** (-) Purplish red medium-sized flowers with a darker blotch.
Zone 7 US, 8 Can.

***R.* 'Coral Bells'** See *R.* 'Kirin'.

***R.* 'Delaware Valley White'** (-) Single white flowers up to 3 in (7.5 cm) across that are freely produced. A very popular variety.
Zone 6 US, 7 Can.

***R.* 'Double Beauty'** (-) A low, compact shrub with large, purplish red, hose-in-hose flowers. In cultivation 1966.
Zone 7 US, 8 Can.

***R.* 'Fedora'** (Kf) Pale pink flowers with a darker flare. Introduced 1922.
Zone 7 US, 8 Can.

***R.* 'Flame Creeper'** (-) A low, spreading, *R. indicum* hybrid that makes a good ground cover. Flowers are a bright orange-red.
Zone 6 US, 7 Can.

***R.* 'Formosa'** (I) Large, deep purple-rose flowers with a darker blotch inside.
Zone 8 US, 9? Can.

***R.* 'Gaiety'** (GD) Large, purplish pink flowers with a darker blotch.
Zone 6 US, 7 Can.

***R.* 'Hardy Gardenia'** (-) A dwarf, spreading shrub with double white flowers that are 2½ in (6 cm) wide. Zone 7 US, 8 Can.

Rhododendron 'Hatsugiri'

Rhododendron 'Hino Crimson'

***R.* 'Hatsugiri'** (K) A dwarf shrub with magenta-purple flowers.
Zone 6 US, 7 Can.

Rhododendron 'Hinomayo'

***R.* 'Herbert'** (G) The hose-in-hose flowers are bright purple with a darker blotch. A popular variety.
Zone 5 US, 6 Can.

***R.* 'Hershey's Red'** (K) One of the most popular varieties, with bright red, hose-in-hose flowers that hide the foliage.
Zone 6 US, 7 Can.

***R.* 'Higasa'** (S) Large, deep rose-pink flowers with paler edges and a dark blotch.
Zone 6 US, 7 Can.

***R.* 'Hino Crimson'** (K) Freely borne bright red flowers and red winter foliage.
Zone 6 US, 7 Can.

***R.* 'Hinode Giri'** (K) A popular variety with bright purplish red flowers.
Zone 6 US, 7 Can.

Rhododendron 'Iroha Yama'

Rhododendron 'Johanna'

***R.* 'Hinomayo'** (K) An upright shrub with clear pink flowers. Introduced c. 1910.
Zone 6 US, 7 Can. 🏆

***R.* 'Iroha Yama'** (K) White flowers with a pink flush that fade to a lavender margin and have a faint chestnut brown eye.
Zone 6 US, 7 Can. 🏆

***R.* 'Johanna'** (-) Small to medium-sized, deep red flowers.
Zone 7 US, 8 Can.

***R.* 'John Cairns'** (Kf) Dark orange-red flowers.
Zone 7 US, 8 Can. 🏆

***R.* 'Joseph Hill'** (-) A dwarf, spreading plant with bright red, wavy-edged flowers.
Zone 6 US, 7 Can.

***R.* 'Kermesina'** (-) A small, compact shrub with small, vivid purplish red flowers.
Zone 7 US, 8 Can.

***R.* 'Kirin'**, syn. *R.* 'Coral Bells' (K) Rose-pink, hose-in-hose flowers that are shaded silvery rose and are freely borne.
Zone 6 US, 7 Can. 🏆

***R.* 'Kure-no-Yuki'** (K) A dwarf shrub with white, hose-in-hose flowers.
Zone 6 US, 7 Can.

***R.* 'Lemur'** (-) A dwarf, prostrate shrub with deep pink, medium-sized flowers and red winter buds.
Zone 7 US, 8 Can.

***R.* 'Louise Dowdle'** (GD) Large, brilliant rose-pink flowers with a deep rose blotch.
Zone 7 US, 8 Can.

***R.* 'Macrantha'** (-) A small *R. indicum* hybrid with numerous double red flowers.
Zone 7 US, 8 Can.

***R.* 'Martha Hitchcock'** (GD) White flowers with an edging of magenta-purple.
Zone 7 US, 8 Can.

***R.* 'Mother's Day'** (S) Bright red, hose-in-hose to semidouble flowers.
Zone 6 US, 7 Can. 🏆

***R.* 'Naomi'** (Kf) A medium-sized shrub with salmon pink flowers borne very late. Introduced 1933.
Zone 7 US, 8 Can.

Rhododendron 'Kirin

Rhododendron 'Mother's Day'

***R.* 'Niagara'** (GD) White flowers with a frilly margin and yellow-green blotch.
Zone 7 US, 8 Can. 🏆

***R.* 'Obtusum Amoenum'** (-) A small, densely branched, spreading, evergreen or semievergreen shrub. The small, bright magenta or rose-purple, hose-in-hose flowers are profusely borne. Introduced 1845 from Japan.
Zone 7 US, 8 Can.

***R.* 'Orange Beauty'** (Kf) Salmon-orange flowers that fade badly in sun; it is best grown in part shade. Introduced 1920.
Zone 7 US, 8 Can. 🏆

***R.* 'Palestrina'** (V) Distinctive and attractive white flowers with a faint ray of yellow-green. Introduced 1926.
Zone 7 US, 8 Can. 🏆

***R.* 'Pearl Bradford'** (-) A vigorous low shrub, wider than tall, with white flowers that have a purple blotch.
Zone 7 US, 8 Can.

***R.* 'Pride of Mobile'** (I) Rich watermelon-

Rhododendron 'Palestrina'

pink flowers with a darker blotch.
Zone 8 US, 9? Can.

***R.* 'Purple Splendor'** (-) Medium-sized, frilled, reddish purple, hose-in-hose flowers.
Zone 7 US, 8 Can.

***R.* 'Purple Triumph'** (V) Deep purple flowers.
Zone 7 US, 8 Can.

***R.* 'Rosebud'** (G) A small, spreading shrub with rose-pink, hose-in-hose flowers.
Zone 6 US, 7 Can.

***R.* 'Rose Greeley'** (G) A small, compact, spreading shrub with fragrant, medium-sized, hose-in-hose flowers that are white with a green blotch.
Zone 7 US, 8 Can.

***R.* 'Salmon Leap'** (-) Large, clear salmon pink flowers. The leaves have a striking, silver-white margin.
Zone 7 US, 8 Can.

***R.* 'Sherwood Orchid'** (K) Dark orchid-pink to violet flowers with a darker blotch.
Zone 6 US, 7 Can.

***R.* 'Silvester'** (K) Purplish red flowers that have paler margins, borne early. In cultivation 1969.
Zone 6 US, 7 Can.

***R.* 'Squirrel'** (-) A dwarf, compact shrub with small, deep reddish orange flowers.
Zone 7 US, 8 Can.

***R.* 'Stewartsonianum'** (G) Vivid red flowers. The foliage is reddish in winter.
Zone 7 US, 8 Can. 🏆

***R.* 'Surprise'** (GD) Large, light coral-pink flowers. Introduced 1939.
Zone 6 US, 7 Can.

***R.* 'Treasure'** (GD) A vigorous, spreading shrub with white flowers edged in pale pink.
Zone 7 US, 8 Can.

***R.* 'Vuyk's Rosyred'** (V) Deep satiny rose flowers with a darker flare inside. Introduced 1954.
Zone 7 US, 8 Can. 🏆

***R.* 'Vuyk's Scarlet'** (V) Bright red flowers with wavy petals. Introduced 1954.
Zone 7 US, 8 Can. 🏆

***R.* 'White Rosebud'** (GD) A small, horizontal shrub with creamy white double flowers shaped like rosebuds.
Zone 7 US, 8 Can.

***R.* 'Wombat'** (-) A prostrate shrub with profuse, medium-sized, pink flowers.
Zone 7 US, 8 Can.

Rhododendron 'Vuyk's Rosyred'

Rhododendron 'Vuyk's Scarlet'

Rhodotypos *Rosaceae*

A genus of one deciduous species related to Kerria *but with white flowers and black berries.*

R. scandens (Jetbead, white kerria) A free-flowering, erect shrub up to 4 ft (1.2 m). The roselike white flowers, $1^3/_4$–2 in (4–5 cm) across, appear from late spring to midsummer and are followed by shiny black fruits. It can be grown in all types of soil and in sun or part shade. China, Korea, Japan. Introduced 1866.
Zone 4 US, 5b Can.

Rhus *Anacardiaceae*

Sumac

A genus of about 200 species of deciduous shrubs and trees that do well in any fertile soil. They are grown mainly for their striking foliage and vivid fall colors. The individual flowers are small but in several species are followed by persistent fruits that are colorful en masse. The genus includes a number of species whose sap is a severe skin irritant, such as poison ivy (R. radicans) *and poison oak* (R. toxicodendron). R. glabra *and* R. typhina *make handsome foliage plants if pruned to the ground each or every other year in late winter. They can tolerate poor, dry soil and rocky slopes.*

R. aromatica (Fragrant sumac) A small shrub whose leaves have three leaflets and small yellow flowers in spring, before the leaves. The foliage turns red in early summer, then bright scarlet and orange in fall. E North America.
Zone 3 US, 3 Can.

Rhus copallina

R. copallina (Shining sumac, dwarf sumac) A small to medium-sized, downy shrub with dense, erect clusters of small, greenish yellow flowers. The leaves, with 9–21 leaflets, are lustrous dark green and turn red or purple in fall, combining well with the red fruit clusters. E North America. Introduced 1688.
Zone 2 US, 2b Can.

R. glabra (Smooth sumac) A wide-spreading, medium-sized shrub with attractive pinnate leaves that are bloomy beneath and usually turn an intense red or orange-yellow in fall. The erect, scarlet, hairy, plume-like fruit clusters on the female plants are eye-catching in fall. E North America. In cultivation 1620.
Zone 2 US, 2b Can.

***R. g.* 'Laciniata'** The true plant has become quite rare in cultivation, and most plants that are grown under this name are

Rhus glabra

in fact the hybrid *R.* × *pulvinata* 'Red Autumn Lace'.

Zone 2 US, 2b Can.

***R.* × *pulvinata* 'Red Autumn Lace'** A foliage plant with fernlike leaves with deeply cut leaflets that turn orange, yellow, and red in fall.

Zone 2 US, 2b Can. 🏆

Rhus trichocarpa

R. trichocarpa A large shrub or small tree with large, pinnate, downy leaves that are coppery pink when young and turn deep orange in autumn. The yellow, bristly fruits are borne in drooping clusters on female plants in fall. Japan, Korea, China. Introduced 1894.

Zone 8 US, 9 Can.

Rhus typhina

R. typhina (Staghorn sumac) A wide-spreading, sparsely branched, irregular large shrub or small tree that develops a gaunt, flat-topped appearance, particularly noticeable in winter. When young, the branchlets are covered with a dense coat of reddish brown hairs. The large, pinnate leaves turn rich orange, yellow, red, or purple in fall. The dense, conical clusters of crimson, hairy fruits are most decorative at the end of the year on female plants. It forms clumps of suckering stems. E North America. In cultivation 1629.

Zone 3 US, 3 Can. 🏆

***R. t.* 'Dissecta'** A striking female form with leaflets deeply cut into narrow segments that create a fernlike effect. It has orange and yellow fall color.

Zone 3 US, 3 Can. 🏆

Rhus typhina 'Dissecta'

Ribes *Grossulariaceae*

Currant and gooseberry

A genus of about 150 evergreen and deciduous species from temperate regions of the Northern Hemisphere and South America. They are primarily spring-flowering shrubs and are easily cultivated in all kinds of soil in sun or shade. The leaves usually have 3–5 lobes, and the flowers vary from being inconspicuous to very showy. Straggly or untidy specimens can be pruned hard immediately after flowering.

R. alpinum (Alpine currant) A small to medium-sized, fairly erect, neat and densely twiggy deciduous shrub that makes a good hedge. The lobed leaves are toothed, the small flowers are greenish yel-

low, and the berries are red. It is very shade tolerant. N and C Europe.
Zone 2 US, 2 Can.

***R. a.* 'Aureum'** A small, wide shrub with leaves that are yellow when young.
Zone 2 US, 2 Can.

Ribes gayanum

R. gayanum A small, suckering evergreen shrub with soft green, velvety leaves. The bell-shaped, yellow flowers are honey scented and densely packed into erect, cylindrical clusters in early summer. The berries are black. Mountains of Chile. In cultivation 1858.
Zone 8 US, 9? Can.

R.* × *gordonianum *(R. odoratum × R. sanguineum)* A vigorous deciduous shrub, intermediate between its parents. The lobed leaves are toothed and the flowers are in drooping clusters, bronze-red on the outside and yellow within. The berries are black. Garden origin 1837.
Zone 6 US, 7 Can.

Ribes laurifolium

R. laurifolium An excellent dwarf evergreen shrub with large, leathery leaves and drooping clusters of greenish white flowers in late winter and early spring. The berries are red and then blackish. It creates early interest in the rock garden. China. Introduced 1908 by Ernest Wilson.
Zone 9 US

Ribes odoratum

R. odoratum (Clove currant) A small to medium-sized, loose, erect deciduous shrub with shiny green leaves that turn scarlet in fall. It has lax clusters of clove-scented, golden yellow flowers in midspring. The berries are black. C United States. Introduced 1812.
Zone 2 US, 2 Can.

R. sanguineum (Flowering currant, winter currant) This popular medium-sized deciduous shrub has a characteristic pungent smell. The flowers vary from white to deep red and appear in midspring in racemes that droop at first, later becoming more upright. The berries are black and bloomy. The following forms are recommended. NW North America. Introduced 1817.
Zone 5 US, 6b Can.

***R. s.* 'Albescens'** A form with whitish flowers, tinged with pink.
Zone 5 US, 6b Can.

***R. s.* 'Brocklebankii'** A small, slower-growing shrub with attractive golden yellow leaves and pink flowers. It tends to burn in full sun.
Zone 5 US, 6b Can. 🏆

***R. s.* 'King Edward VII'** A small to medium-sized shrub, rather slower growing

Ribes sanguineum 'Albescens'

Ribes sanguineum 'Brocklebankii'

than the typical form, that produces intensely crimson flowers and blue-black berries.
Zone 5 US, 6 Can.

***R. s.* 'Pulborough Scarlet'** A form with deep red flowers.
Zone 5 US, 6 Can. 🏆

***R. s.* 'Tydeman's White'** This medium-

Ribes sanguineum 'Pulborough Scarlet'

Ribes sanguineum 'Tydeman's White'

Ribes speciosum

sized shrub is the best white-flowered form. Zone 5 US, 6b Can. 🏆

R. speciosum (Fuchsia-flowered gooseberry) An attractive, medium-sized semievergreen shrub with reddish bristly stems and fruits, and shiny leaves. The fuchsia-like, rich red flowers are borne in pendulous clusters in mid- to late spring. California. Introduced 1828. Zone 7 US, 8 Can. 🏆

Richea *Epacridaceae*

A genus of some 10 species of subtly attractive evergreen shrubs, natives mainly of Tasmania but with one species in southeast Australia.

R. scoparia An unusual, small, spreading shrub resembling a dwarf, shrubby monkey puzzle tree. The stems are covered with stiff, sharply pointed leaves, and the pink flowers are in erect terminal clusters 2–4 in (5–10 cm) long in late spring. It requires a moist, acid soil. Tasmania.
Zone 9 US

Robinia *Leguminosae*
False acacia, locust

A genus of about eight species of fast-growing deciduous trees and shrubs, confined in the wild to the United States and Mexico. Although some are commonly referred to as acacias, they should not be confused with members of the genus Acacia, *which are mainly from Africa and Australia.* Robinia *have attractive pinnate leaves, stems that are often spiny, and hanging racemes of pea flowers. They will grow in ordinary soil and are especially good for dry, sunny locations. They are also tolerant of air pollution. While they are small it is a good idea to prune them fairly hard after flowering.*

***R. × ambigua* 'Bella-rosea'** An elegant small tree with rather sticky shoots and racemes of large pink flowers in early summer. Raised c. 1860.
Zone 3 US, 3b Can.

Robinia hispida

R. hispida (Rose acacia) A medium-sized suckering shrub with short, pendulous racemes of large, deep rose flowers in late spring and early summer. It is an excellent small tree when grafted onto *R. pseudoacacia* but is a bit brittle and needs a sheltered site. It tolerates poor soil and can be grown on slopes. SE United States. Introduced 1743.
Zone 4 US, 5 Can. 🏆

***R. h.* 'Macrophylla'** A medium-sized shrub or small tree with larger leaflets and flowers than the typical species, resembling a pink wisteria.
Zone 4 US, 5 Can.

R. × holdtii In habit and vigor this plant resembles *R. pseudoacacia.* It bears long, loose racemes of pale pink flowers from early to midsummer that often continue almost into fall. They are followed by red, bristly seedpods. Garden origin c. 1890.
Zone 4 US, 5 Can.

R. kelseyi (Alleghany moss locust) A medium-sized shrub or small tree with slender branches and elegant foliage, producing slightly fragrant, lilac-pink flowers in early summer. E United States. Introduced 1901.
Zone 5 US, 6 Can.

***R. × margaretta* 'Casque Rouge'** A suckering large shrub or small tree with profusely borne, large, purplish pink flowers. Raised c. 1934 in the United States.
Zone 5 US, 6 Can.

R. pseudoacacia (Black locust) A large, suckering tree with rugged, furrowed bark and slightly fragrant white flowers with a yellow stain at the base of the standard

Robinia pseudoacacia

petal. They appear in early summer and are attractive to bees. E United States.
Zone 3 US, 4 Can. 🏆

***R. p.* 'Bessoniana'** A small to medium-sized, round-headed tree, usually spineless. In cultivation 1871.
Zone 4 US, 4b Can.

Robinia pseudoacacia 'Frisia'

***R. p.* 'Frisia'** A dramatic small to medium-sized tree with golden leaves from spring to fall, creating a brilliant splash of color. It can be cut back hard each spring and grown as a shrub where space is limited. Raised 1935 in Holland.
Zone 3 US, 4 Can. 🏆

R. p.* var. *inermis A form that produces thornless shoots. For the mop-head acacia often grown under this name, see *R. p.* 'Umbraculifera'.
Zone 3 US, 4 Can.

***R. p.* 'Monophylla'** See *R. p.* 'Unifoliola'.

***R. p.* 'Pyramidalis'** A slender, columnar, medium-sized tree with spineless, closely erect branches. In cultivation 1843.
Zone 4 US, 4b Can.

***R. p.* 'Rozynskyana'** An elegant, beautiful, large shrub or small spreading tree. The branches droop at the tips and bear large drooping leaves. In cultivation 1903.
Zone 4 US, 4b Can.

***R. p.* 'Tortuosa'** A picturesque, slow-growing, small to medium-sized tree with somewhat contorted branches.
Zone 4 US, 4b Can.

***R. p.* 'Umbraculifera'** (Mop-head acacia) A small tree with a dense, globe-shaped head and spineless branches. It needs protection from strong wind and snow and ice.

Robinia pseudoacacia 'Tortuosa'

Robinia pseudoacacia 'Umbraculifera'

It rarely flowers. This tree is often grown under the name *R. p.* var. *inermis*.
Zone 3 US, 4 Can.

***R. p.* 'Unifoliola'**, syn. *R. p.* 'Monophylla' A curious form with the leaves reduced to a single large leaflet, which may be accompanied by one or two normal-sized leaflets. It makes a medium-sized to large tree. Raised c. 1855.
Zone 3 US, 4 Can.

***R.* × *slavinii* 'Hillieri'** An elegant small tree with delicate foliage produced on a rounded head of branches. The lilac-pink flowers, borne in early summer, are slightly fragrant. It is an excellent tree for a small garden.
Zone 4 US, 5 Can. 🏆

Romneya *Papaveraceae*

Tree poppy

A genus of two species of subshrubby perennials from California and Mexico with deeply cut, gray to gray-green leaves and large, white, papery, poppylike flowers with a central mass of golden yellow stamens. They are sometimes difficult to establish but once settled spread by underground stems. They need full sun and will grow in any well-drained soil, even dry, poor ones. They should not be disturbed once planted.

Romneya coulteri

R. coulteri A small to medium-sized perennial with large, solitary, fragrant flowers 4–6 in (10–15 cm) wide, opening from slightly conical buds from midsummer to midfall. Introduced 1875.
Zone 6 US, 7 Can. 🏆

R. trichocalyx This plant closely resembles *R. coulteri*, but the stems are more slender and the buds more rounded.
Zone 7 US, 8 Can.

Romneya 'White Cloud'

***R.* 'White Cloud'** A vigorous small to medium-sized perennial with extra-large white flowers.
Zone 6 US, 7 Can.

Rosa

Rosaceae Rose

Many gardeners who consider shrubs that flower for a month or more to be very desirable nonetheless turn their backs on species and primary hybrid roses, fearing that they will be too demanding or not as rewarding as the popular modern roses. These "simple" old roses, however, are not only easy to grow, but they are among the most elegant and charming of all shrubs. And they have many more features to recommend them besides their flowers.

The "wild" roses offer a variety of forms. There are species that climb and ramble, covering slopes and decorating pergolas, arches, and trellises. There are shrubs that stand tall and others that arch gracefully, while still others are low, dense, and bushy. Some also have colorful foliage and stems, which contribute greatly to the landscape when the plants are not in bloom. *R. glauca,* for instance, has reddish violet canes and purplish leaves. The green leaves of *R. virginiana* turn purple, then orange, red, and yellow in fall.

The majority of the wild roses remain in flower as long as and even longer than any mock orange, deutzia, or lilac. They also begin blooming at a fortunate time — in early to midsummer, when the transition from shrubs that flower on old wood to those that flower on new means that there are few shrubs in bloom.

Rosa nutkana 'Plena'

Their flowers are not as luxurious and "perfect" as those of many modern roses and have instead a refreshing simplicity and natural beauty in their color and shape. The flowers range from vivid jewel tones to soft pastels and are sometimes bicolored, but they are seldom strident. They may be formed like dainty, open saucers, usually with five petal, or be gathered into deeply ruffled pompons.

They also have another trait that many modern roses lack and that makes them especially welcome: fragrance. The leaves and blooms of these roses emit wonderful perfumes, from an earthy tea aroma to the tangy scent of cloves to the sweet spiciness of apples.

And then there are the fruits. The intense breeding of modern roses for flowers reduces their ability to set seed. But the wild roses and their near hybrids produce brightly colored hips, which evolved naturally to be as eye-catching as possible. Usually red or orange-red, they may be round or flasklike and persist on the shrubs well into fall and sometimes into winter.

Care and cultivation

Species roses need full sun, but will tolerate a little shade, and any well-drained soil, except one that is highly acidic. The more ornamental species respond well to an annual or biannual application of well-rotted manure.

Pruning is a matter of common sense. Once the plants are established, remove the oldest canes each year and also prune out any dead wood. Prune immediately after flowering except those roses that produce ornamental hips; these should be pruned in late winter. Older specimens that have become tangled and overcrowded should be thinned back to form a good framework.

R. 'Agnes' A medium-sized deciduous hybrid of *R. rugosa* with arching branches and dull, dark green leaves densely arranged on very thorny canes. The amber-tinted, butter yellow, fully double flowers are deliciously scented and borne in late spring; they are sometimes recurrent. Originated 1922 in Ottawa, Ontario.
Zone 3 US, 3 Can.

Rosa × *alba* 'Alba Maxima'

R. × *alba* 'Alba Maxima' (Jacobite rose) A small deciduous shrub with gray-green foliage; pure white, very double flowers in upright clusters; and occasional red hips.
Zone 5 US, 6 Can. 🏆

R. × *a.* 'Alba Semiplena' (White rose of York) A medium-sized deciduous shrub with grayish green leaves and white, usually semidouble, richly scented flowers 3 in (7.5 cm) wide. The hips are oblong and red. In cultivation before 1600.
Zone 3 US, 3 Can. 🏆

R. 'Alexander Mackenzie' A medium-sized upright shrub with clusters of deep red, double, cup-shaped flowers produced all summer long. It is resistant to the major rose diseases. Introduced 1985 as part of the Explorer series of hardy roses by Agriculture Canada, Ottawa, Ontario.
Zone 3 US, 3 Can.

R. 'Andersonii' A medium-sized, strong deciduous shrub with arching, prickly stems and scented single flowers 2–3 in (5–7.5 cm) across. They are a rich, clear rose-pink and are freely produced over a long period. The scarlet, urn-shaped hips resemble those of *R. canina*. In cultivation 1912.
Zone 5 US, 6 Can.

Rosa 'Anemonoides'

R. 'Anemonoides' A lovely deciduous shrub rose with single flowers 4 in (10 cm) wide, produced over several weeks. They are silver-pink and shaded with rose-pink. It is a hybrid of *R. laevigata* and requires, as does its parent, a warm, sheltered location. Garden origin c. 1895.
Zone 8 US, 9 Can.

Rosa 'Arthur Hillier'

R. 'Arthur Hillier' A large, vigorous, deciduous shrub with a multitude of large, rose-crimson single flowers in early to midsummer. They are followed in fall by bright red, flask-shaped fruits. Occurred c. 1938 at Hillier Nurseries.
Zone 6? US, 7? Can.

R. *banksiae* (Banks rose) A beautiful, tall-growing semievergreen climber, reaching 20–30 ft (6–9 m) in a suitable location. It prefers a warm wall in full sun, and plants growing at the limit of its hardiness tend to suffer frost damage that reduces or prevents flowering. The single, white or yellow flowers are borne on nearly thornless canes in late spring and early summer and have a delicate scent of violets; it does not flower when young. China.
Zone 7 US, 8 Can.

R. *b.* 'Alba Plena' This form, which is the one that was originally named in honor of Lady Banks, has very fragrant, double white flowers in densely packed umbels. Introduced 1807 from a garden in Canton, China, by William Kerr.
Zone 7 US, 8 Can.

Rosa banksiae 'Lutea'

R. *b.* 'Lutea' (Yellow Banks rose) A beautiful rose bearing double yellow flowers with a delicate fragrance. Introduced before 1824.
Zone 7 US, 8 Can. 🏆

R. *b.* 'Lutescens' A form with single, yellow, sweetly fragrant flowers. Introduced before 1807.
Zone 7 US, 8 Can.

R. *b.* 'Normalis' This, the wild form, has single, cream, sweetly fragrant flowers. China. Said to have been introduced 1796 by Robert Drummond.
Zone 7 US, 8 Can.

R. 'Blanc Double de Coubert' An upright, medium-sized, deciduous hybrid of *R. rugosa*. The fragrant, semidouble white flowers are blush-tinted in bud. The leaves turn yellow in fall. Garden origin 1892.
Zone 2 US, 2b Can. 🏆

R. *bracteata* (Macartney rose) A medium-sized to large evergreen shrub with prickly, rambling stems and leaves composed of 5–11 leaflets. The white, lemon-scented, single flowers are 3–4 in (7.5–10 cm) wide

and have golden anthers; each head is surrounded by large, downy bracts. The fruits are spherical and orange-red. It is highly ornamental but needs a warm, sunny, sheltered location. SE China, Taiwan. Introduced 1795 by Lord Macartney.
Zone 7 US, 8 Can.

R. brunonii **'La Mortola'** A fine selection of the Himalayan musk rose, with large, richly fragrant, single white flowers in tight clusters in early to midsummer. It is a rampant deciduous climber reaching 30–40 ft (9–12 m) high but needs a sheltered location and full sun to ripen its growth.
Zone 7 US, 8 Can.

R. californica **'Plena'** See *R. nutkana* 'Plena'.

Rosa 'Canary Bird'

R. **'Canary Bird'** A beautiful medium-sized deciduous shrub with arching stems, small fernlike leaves, and bright canary yellow, single flowers that wreathe the branches in late spring and early summer.
Zone 4 US, 4b Can. 🏆

R. canina (Dog rose) A rose familiar in Europe, where it is native, that has become naturalized in North America. It is a medium-sized to large deciduous shrub with strong prickly stems, leaves with 5–7 leaflets, and white to pink, fragrant single flowers, followed by bright red, egg-shaped hips. It is highly variable.
Zone 3 US, 4 Can.

R. **'Cantabrigiensis'** A medium-sized, deciduous, arching shrub with fragrant, fernlike leaves. The single flowers, 2 in (5 cm) wide, are soft yellow fading to cream.
Zone 5 US, 6 Can.

Rosa canina

Rosa 'Cantabrigiensis'

R. centifolia (Cabbage rose, Provence rose) A complex hybrid, once thought to be one of the oldest roses but now known to have appeared in its present form in the 18th century. It is a small deciduous shrub with aromatic leaves and large, double, rose-pink, very fragrant flowers. There are several cultivars, and it is the parent of many hybrids.
Zone 3 US, 4 Can.

R. c. **'Cristata'** (Crested cabbage rose) A small shrub whose sepals are crested to such an extent that the flower buds are completely enveloped. The flowers are large, fully double, and rosy pink. Possibly discovered 1820 in Fribourg, Switzerland.
Zone 3 US, 4 Can. 🏆

R. c. **'Muscosa'** (Common moss rose) The archetypal moss rose, with a dense, moss-like, glandular-bristly covering on the upper stems, leaf stalks, flower stalks, and calyxes. This unusual and characteristic covering is sticky to the touch and gives off

Rosa centifolia 'Muscosa'

a balsam-like scent when bruised. The clear pink, globular, flat-topped, very double flowers later open much wider and are very fragrant. In cultivation 1720.
Zone 3 US, 4 Can. 🏆

R. chinensis (China rose) A small to medium-sized deciduous shrub with stout branches and leaves with 3–5 leaflets. The single flowers are 2 in (5 cm) across; crimson, pink, or white; produced from early summer; and followed by scarlet fruits. C China.
Zone 6 US, 7 Can.

R. **'Champlain'** This dwarf rose grows only 3 ft (90 cm) tall and makes a good informal hedge. Blooms are bright red and freely produced. Introduced 1982.
Zone 3 US, 3 Can.

Rosa chinensis 'Old Blush'

R. c. **'Mutabilis'** See *R.* × *odorata* 'Mutabilis'.

R. c. **'Old Blush'** (Monthly rose) An important rose because it introduced re-

montant flowering into garden roses. It is compact and generally small and has pink double flowers that smell like sweet peas and are produced over a long period.
Zone 6 US, 7 Can.

Rosa chinensis 'Viridiflora'

***R. c.* 'Viridiflora'** (Green rose) A curious small shrub with double flowers consisting of crowded, greenish, petallike scales.
Zone 6 US, 7 Can.

***R.* 'Complicata'** A beautiful medium-sized deciduous shrub with vigorous, arching, nearly smooth canes. It has many very large, rose-pink, white-eyed single flowers that have golden stamens and a rich fragrance. It is a hybrid of *R. gallica*.
Zone 3 US, 4 Can. 🏆

***R.* × *damascena* 'Versicolor'** (York and Lancaster rose) An unusual form of the damask rose with loosely double flowers, some of which are completely white, while others may be completely pink, and still others have some pink petals and some white ones; no two flowers are quite the same. It makes a small deciduous shrub. In cultivation before 1629.
Zone 5 US, 6 Can.

***R.* 'Dupontii'** A strong-growing, medium-sized deciduous shrub with large, fragrant single flowers 3 in (7.5 cm) wide. They are blush, fading to creamy white, and are borne in domed clusters in midsummer. It has a loose habit and may need a little support. In cultivation 1817.
Zone 6 US, 7 Can.

R. ecae A small, dainty deciduous shrub with prickly, slender, arching, chestnut brown branches. The buttercup yellow, single flowers, 1 in (2.5 cm) wide, are borne in very early summer. The hips are round and red. Afghanistan. Introduced 1880 by Dr. Aitchison.
Zone 7 US, 8 Can.

Rosa 'Dupontii'

Rosa ecae

R. eglanteria, syn. *R. rubiginosa* (Eglantine, sweetbrier) A medium-sized deciduous shrub with apple-scented leaves and clear pink, fragrant, beautifully formed single flowers $1^1/_4$–$1^1/_2$ in (3–4 cm) wide that stud the arching branches in summer. The oval, bright red hips last well into winter. It is the parent of many hybrids. Europe.
Zone 5 US, 6 Can. 🏆

Rosa eglanteria

***R. elegantula* 'Persetosa'** (Threepenny-bit rose) A charming deciduous rose up to $6^1/_2$ ft (2 m) high, with dainty, fernlike leaves that contrast with the coral-red buds, which open to soft pink, single flowers less than 1 in (2.5 cm) across.
Zone 3 US, 4 Can.

R. fedtschenkoana An erect, medium-sized deciduous shrub with sea green leaves and white single flowers, 2 in (5 cm) wide, produced continuously throughout the summer and followed by orange-red, bristly, pear-shaped fruits. Turkestan.
Zone 4 US, 5 Can.

Rosa filipes 'Kiftsgate'

***R. filipes* 'Kiftsgate'** An extremely vigorous, deciduous rambling species that creates the effect of a waterfall when in bloom. In midsummer each panicle, up to 18 in (45 cm) across, may have as many as 100 or more sweetly scented, white, single flowers, each 1 in (2.5 cm) wide. The display of myriad fruits, small and bright red, is almost as spectacular. Grows too large for the average garden. In cultivation 1938.
Zone 5 US, 6 Can. 🏆

R. foetida (Austrian brier rose) A small deciduous shrub with erect, slender stems and rich yellow, single flowers 2–$2^1/_2$ in (5–6 cm) across. The blooms have an unpleasant odor. It has been extremely important in the development of many of

the modern garden roses. SW Asia, naturalized in Europe. In cultivation since the 16th century.
Zone 3 US, 3 Can.

***R. f.* 'Bicolor'** (Austrian copper rose) A remarkably beautiful shrub whose flowers are brilliant coppery red with a bright yellow reverse. Its scent is not as strong as the species'. It is also important in the history of the modern rose.
Zone 3 US, 3 Can.

Rosa foetida 'Bicolor'

Rosa foetida 'Persiana'

***R. f.* 'Persiana'** (Persian yellow rose) A beautiful shrub with golden yellow, double flowers. It is the parent of numerous garden hybrid roses. Iran. Introduced 1837.
Zone 2 US, 2 Can.

R. forrestiana A vigorous, medium-sized, deciduous shrub with arching stems to $6^{1}/_{2}$ ft (2 m). The rose-crimson, strongly fragrant single flowers, $1^{1}/_{4}$–$1^{1}/_{2}$ in (3–4 cm) wide, are in clusters surrounded by leafy bracts and are followed by bright red, bottle-shaped hips. W China. Introduced 1918 by George Forrest.
Zone 5 US, 6 Can.

***R.* 'Frau Dagmar Hastrup'** A hybrid of *R. rugosa* that makes a dense deciduous shrub up to $6^{1}/_{2}$ ft (2 m), with dark green, etched leaves. The single, clove-scented flowers are pale rose-pink with cream stamens, and it bears large crops of crimson hips. Good for hedges. Garden origin 1914.
Zone 4 US, 4b Can. 🏆

Rosa 'Frau Dagmar Hastrup'

R. gallica (French rose) A small, suckering deciduous shrub with erect, slender, thorny stems and leaves composed of 5–7 leaflets. The deep pink to red, single flowers, 2–$2^{3}/_{4}$ in (5–7 cm) across, are followed by rounded or top-shaped, red fruits. C and S Europe. In cultivation for centuries.
Zone 3 US, 4 Can.

R. g.* var. *officinalis (Apothecary rose, red rose of Lancaster) A shrub with richly fragrant, semidouble, rosy crimson flowers with prominent yellow anthers in early to midsummer. Its petals retain their fragrance even when dried and powdered. In cultivation since at least 1310.
Zone 3 US, 4 Can. 🏆

Rosa gallica var. *officinalis*

***R. g.* 'Rosa Mundi'** See *R. g.* 'Versicolor'.

Rosa gallica 'Versicolor'

***R. g.* 'Versicolor'**, syn. *R. g.* 'Rosa Mundi' An old, much-loved rose with semidouble flowers, usually rose-red striped with white, but with a few entirely red blooms. In some seasons all the flowers may be "self" red. It should not be confused with *R.* × *damascena* 'Versicolor'.
Zone 3 US, 4 Can. 🏆

Rosa glauca

R. glauca, syn. *R. rubrifolia* (Redleaf rose) A medium-sized deciduous shrub with reddish violet, almost thornless stems and attractive foliage that is bloomy purple in sun and grayish green with a burgundy tinge in shade. The small, clear pink, single flowers are followed by ovoid, dark red, shiny hips. C and S Europe. In cultivation before 1830.

Zone 2 US, 2b Can. 🏆

***R.* 'Hansa'** This popular *R. rugosa* hybrid forms a small upright mound covered with fragrant purplish flowers all summer. The red hips are plentiful, and the foliage turns yellow and orange in fall. Introduced 1905.

Zone 2 US, 2b Can.

Rosa × *harisonii* 'Harison's Yellow'

***R.* × *harisonii* 'Harison's Yellow'** (Yellow rose of Texas) A small, free-flowering deciduous shrub, occasionally reaching 6½ ft (2 m). It has brilliant yellow, double flowers with a slightly unpleasant odor. The fruits are small and almost black.

Zone 2 US, 2 Can. 🏆

Rosa 'Helen Knight'

***R.* 'Helen Knight'** A small deciduous shrub similar to *R. ecae* but larger and with larger flowers. Raised 1966 at RHS Wisley, England.

Zone 6? US, 7? Can.

***R.* 'Henry Hudson'** One of the Explorer series, this dwarf *R. rugosa* hybrid can be used as a ground cover. The red flowers open in early summer and then occasionally until fall. Introduced 1982.

Zone 2 US, 2b Can.

***R.* 'Henry Kelsey'** A climber with bright red flowers that have prominent bright yellow stamens. They have a spicy scent and are produced all summer. Introduced 1984.

Zone 3 US, 3 Can.

Rosa 'Highdownensis'

***R.* 'Highdownensis'** A medium-sized deciduous shrub, something like *R. moyesii*, of which it is a seedling. It has dainty leaves and light velvety crimson, single flowers 2½ in (6 cm) across. The large hips are flagon shaped and orange-scarlet. Raised before 1925 by Sir Frederick Stern.

Zone 5 US, 6 Can.

***R.* 'Hillieri'** A beautiful deciduous seedling of *R. moyesii*. Its flowers are like those of the species but so dark a crimson that it

Rosa 'Hillieri'

is the darkest of all single roses. Raised c. 1924 at Hillier Nurseries.

Zone 5? US, 6? Can.

R. hugonis (Father Hugo rose) A graceful deciduous shrub reaching 6½ ft (2 m), with long, arching branches covered with neat, fernlike leaves. It blooms in late spring with hundreds of soft yellow, single flowers, 2 in (5 cm) wide, which are followed by small, rounded, dark red hips. It performs best in poor soil and makes a good informal hedge. C China. Introduced 1899.

Zone 4 US, 5 Can. 🏆

Rosa hugonis

***R.* 'John Cabot'** One of the most popular Explorer roses, this climber produces several flushes of bright red flowers in summer. In harsh climates it makes a shrub rather than a climber. Introduced 1978.

Zone 2 US, 2b Can.

***R.* 'John Davis'** The bright pink buds, which look like miniature hybrid teas, open to form semidouble pale pink blooms with a spicy perfume. Introduced 1986.

Zone 3 US, 3 Can.

***R.* 'John Franklin'** A medium-sized Explorer rose with large clusters of red flowers that have fringed petals. Introduced 1980.

Zone 3 US, 4 Can.

***R.* 'Lady Penzance'** A medium-sized deciduous shrub with arching branches, fragrant leaves, and single, copper-tinted flowers with bright yellow centers.

Zone 4 US, 5b Can.

***R.* 'Macrantha'** A small, variable deciduous shrub with large single flowers that are pink in bud and open to clear almond-pink, changing to near-white. They are deli-

Rosa 'Macrantha'

ciously fragrant and measure 3–4 in (7.5–10 cm) across. The hips are rounded and red. It is a magnificent rose that has a mounding habit and loose, trailing stems that are ideal for covering slopes. In cultivation 1888.

Zone 5 US, 6 Can.

***R.* 'Martin Frobisher'** Very pale pink flowers are carried all summer on an upright shrub. The fragrant blossoms have about 40 petals, and the foliage is disease resistant. This was the first of the Explorer roses. Introduced 1968.

Zone 2 US, 2b Can.

***R.* 'Max Graf'** A superb deciduous rose

Rosa 'Max Graf'

with long, trailing stems that makes an excellent ground cover. The fragrant, rose-pink, golden-centered single flowers, 2 in (5 cm) wide, are borne over a long period. Originated 1919.

Zone 2 US, 2b Can.

***R.* 'Mermaid'** An evergreen rambling rose

Rosa 'Mermaid'

with long stems. It has glossy, dark green leaves and single, yellow flowers, 5–6 in (13–15 cm) wide, with amber stamens. It blooms for a long period. Introduced 1918.

Zone 5 US, 6 Can. 🏆

***R.* 'Morden Amorette'** A very compact rose, growing only 1–1½ ft (30–45 cm) tall and bearing carmine red flowers. Deadheading promotes continuous flowering. A Parkland rose from Morden Research Station, Manitoba. Introduced 1977.

Zone 3 US, 3b Can.

***R.* 'Morden Centennial'** Small clusters of scented pink flowers appear in early and late summer. Shrubs grow to 3 ft (90 cm) tall. A Parkland rose. Introduced 1980.

Zone 2 US, 2 Can.

***R.* 'Morden Fireglow'** This dwarf shrub produces orange-red flowers, which are distinctive in such a hardy rose. Flowers are semidouble and recurrent. A Parkland rose. Introduced 1989.

Zone 2 US, 2b Can.

R. moschata (Musk rose) A strong, rather lax deciduous shrub reaching 11 ft (3.5 m) tall. The sweetly musk-scented, creamy single flowers, 2 in (5 cm) across, are borne in large heads in late summer and fall.

Zone 5 US, 6 Can.

R. m.* var. *nastarana (Persian musk rose) A more vigorous variety than the species, with a sturdier habit. The single, pink-tinged cream flowers are over 2 in (5 cm) in diameter and produced profusely.

Zone 6 US, 7 Can.

R. moyesii (Moyes rose) A medium-sized to large, erect, deciduous shrub with a loose, open habit. The single flowers are

Rosa moyesii 'Geranium'

blood red and up to 3 in (7.5 cm) across, with either one or two terminating each short spur in early and midsummer. They are followed by large, flask-shaped, orange-red hips. W China. Introduced 1894 and reintroduced 1903 by Ernest Wilson.

Zone 3 US, 4 Can.

***R. m.* 'Geranium'** A slightly more compact plant than the species, with bright geranium-red flowers. The fruits are smoother and a little larger. Raised 1938.

Zone 5 US, 6 Can. 🏆

Rosa multiflora

R. multiflora (Japanese rose) A vigorous, invasive deciduous shrub or rambler. The single, honey-scented, white flowers are about 1 in (2.5 cm) across, abundantly borne in large conical heads, and followed by small, bright red hips eaten by birds. Japan, Korea. Introduced 1804.

Zone 5 US, 6 Can.

R. nitida (Shining rose) A dwarf suckering shrub with slender, reddish stems and

glossy, deciduous leaves that turn crimson and purple in fall. The rose-red single flowers are 2 in (5 cm) wide and are followed by slightly bristly, scarlet fruits. An excellent creeping shrub. NE North America. Introduced 1807.
Zone 3 US, 4 Can.

Rosa nutkana 'Plena'

R. nutkana **'Plena'**, syn. *R. californica* 'Plena' A medium-sized, free-flowering deciduous shrub with thorny stems and corymbs of semidouble, rich dark pink flowers that fade to rose and purple. Alaska to California.
Zone 3 US, 3 Can. 🏆

R. × odorata (Tea rose) A group of old and variable evergreen or semievergreen hybrids from China with white, pink, or yellow flowers that have a tealike fragrance. Among them are the following forms.
Zone 7 US, 8 Can.

R. × o. **'Fortune's Double Yellow'**, syn. *R. × o.* 'Pseudindica' An old rose up to 10 ft (3 m) high with semidouble flowers. They are salmon-yellow or coppery yellow, flushed with coppery scarlet, and strongly scented. It flowers on second-year wood and as a result should not be pruned like an ordinary climber. Introduced 1845 by Robert Fortune.
Zone 5 US, 6 Can.

R. × o. **'Mutabilis'**, syn. *R. chinensis* 'Mutabilis' A vigorous, small to medium-sized, slender shrub with few thorns, deep purplish young shoots, and coppery young foliage. The slender-pointed, vivid orange buds open to buff single flowers that are shaded with carmine and that change to rose and finally to crimson. They are borne over a very long period, are strongly tea scented, and expand to 3–4 in (7.5–10 cm) in diameter.
Zone 5 US, 6 Can. 🏆

R. × o. **'Pseudindica'** See *R. × o.* 'Fortune's Double Yellow'.

Rosa 'Parvifolia'

R. **'Parvifolia'** (Burgundian rose) A slow-growing, small, almost thornless deciduous rose with flat pompon flowers in deep rose suffused with claret. In cultivation since at least 1764.
Zone 4 US, 5 Can.

R. **'Paulii'** A mound-forming deciduous shrub with extremely thorny stems 10–13 ft (3–4 m) long. The leaves and flowers are like those of *R. rugosa*. The blooms are white and slightly clove scented. It is a good ground cover and can be grown beneath larger shrubs. Garden origin before 1903.
Zone 2 US, 2 Can.

R. pendulina (Alpine rose) A small, semi-erect deciduous shrub with magenta single flowers up to 2 in (5 cm) across in early summer and red, pear-shaped hips. Mountains of S and C Europe. Introduced 1683.
Zone 2 US, 2 Can.

R. pimpinellifolia (Scotch rose, Burnet rose) A small, suckering deciduous shrub that makes dense, low mounds of thorny canes. The small, white or pale pink, single flowers, up to 2 in (5 cm) wide, are profusely borne in late spring and early summer and are followed by rounded, black fruits. Parent of many hybrids. Europe and N Asia. In cultivation before 1600.
Zone 3 US, 3 Can.

Rosa pimpinellifolia

R. p. **var.** ***altaica*** See *R. p.* 'Grandiflora'.

R. p. **'Andrewsii'** A form with deep pinkish red and cream, semidouble flowers with yellow stamens. Occasionally repeats in fall.
Zone 3 US, 3 Can. 🏆

R. p. **'Double White'** A shrub with a profusion of pure white, double flowers.
Zone 3 US, 3 Can.

R. p. **'Glory of Edzell'** A beautiful, early-flowering shrub reaching $6^1/_2$ ft (2 m), with pink, lemon-centered flowers covering the slender branches in late spring.
Zone 3 US, 3 Can.

R. p. **'Grandiflora'**, syn. *R. p.* var. *altaica* A more vigorous form to $6^1/_2$ ft (2 m) high and more across. The creamy white flowers are up to $2^1/_2$ in (6 cm) wide and are followed by maroon-black hips. It makes a good hedge. Siberia. In cultivation 1820.
Zone 2 US, 2 Can.

R. p. **'William III'** A dwarf, suckering, densely bushy shrub with grayish green leaves and magenta-crimson, semidouble flowers that change to plum, paler on the reverse. The fruits are black.
Zone 3 US, 3 Can.

R. primula (Primrose rose) A medium-sized deciduous shrub with arching stems and leaves of 7–13 dark, glossy leaflets with an incenselike aroma. The single, fragrant flowers are $1^1/_2$ in (4 cm) across and primrose yellow fading to white; they are among the earliest to open. The round hips are red. Turkestan to N China. Introduced 1910.
Zone 5 US, 6 Can. 🏆

R. **'Red Max Graf'** A shrub similar to 'Max Graf' but with scarlet flowers.
Zone 2 US, 2b Can.

Rosa primula

Rosa 'Red Max Graf'

***R.* 'Rose d'Amour'** (St. Mark's rose) A medium-sized deciduous shrub up to 6½ ft (2 m) high. The double, fragrant flowers are deep pink with paler outer petals, continuing for several weeks from mid- to late summer. A vigorous, free-flowering rose. Garden origin before 1820.
Zone 5? US, 6? Can. 🏆

Rosa 'Roseraie de l'Haÿ'

***R.* 'Roseraie de l'Haÿ'** A deciduous hybrid of *R. rugosa* with long, pointed, purplish red buds that open to rich crimson-purple flowers 4–4¾ in (10–12 cm) across with cream stamens. The double flowers are very fragrant. A superb, vigorous rose and an excellent hedge. Garden origin 1901.
Zone 2 US, 2 Can. 🏆

R. roxburghii (Chestnut rose, Roxburgh rose) A medium-sized to large deciduous shrub with peeling bark, 9–15 leaflets, and fragrant, shell pink, single flowers up to 3 in (7.5 cm) wide. They are followed by tomato-shaped, orange-yellow hips covered with stiff spines. China. Introduced 1908 by Ernest Wilson.
Zone 6 US, 7 Can.

R. rubiginosa See *R. eglanteria.*

R. rubrifolia See *R. glauca.*

Rosa rugosa

R. rugosa (Rugosa rose) A vigorous, perpetual-flowering deciduous shrub with very thorny canes up to 6½ ft (2 m) high. The leaflets are conspicuously veined and etched (rugose). The purplish rose, fragrant single flowers are up to 3½ in (9 cm) wide and are followed by bright red, tomato-shaped hips 1 in (2.5 cm) across. It forms dense clumps and makes a good hedge, especially in coastal areas, as it is very tolerant of salt spray. NE Asia; naturalized NE United States. Introduced 1796.
Zone 2 US, 2b Can.

***R. r.* 'Alba'** A form with white flowers, tinted blush in bud. It is very vigorous and exceptionally free-fruiting.
Zone 2 US, 2b Can. 🏆

***R. r.* 'Rubra'** A shrub with wine-crimson, fragrant flowers. Conspicuous large hips.
Zone 2 US, 2b Can. 🏆

Rosa rugosa 'Alba'

Rosa rugosa 'Rubra'

Rosa 'Scabrosa'

***R.* 'Scabrosa'** A vigorous medium-sized deciduous hybrid of *R. rugosa* valued for its foliage. The flowers are deep crimson, single, and up to 5½ in (14 cm) wide. The fruits are large, like cherry tomatoes.
Zone 2 US, 2b Can. 🏆

Rosa sericea f. pteracantha

R. sericea f. pteracantha A distinctive deciduous rose whose canes have flat, translucent, crimson thorns. The flowers are single, four-petaled, yellowish white, and borne in late spring and early summer. Himalaya and W China. Introduced 1890.
Zone 5 US, 6 Can.

R. setigera (Prairie rose) A medium-sized deciduous shrub that spreads to form a clump and is valued for its late-season blooming. It has rose-pink, single flowers that fade to pale pink, red fruits, and reddish fall foliage. E and C North America.
Zone 6 US, 7 Can.

R. setipoda A medium-sized deciduous shrub with fragrant foliage and clear pink, single flowers, more than 2 in (5 cm) across, on contrasting purplish stalks all along the branches. They are followed by large, flask-shaped, crimson hips. W China. Introduced 1901 by Ernest Wilson.
Zone 6 US, 7 Can.

R. 'Silver Moon' A vigorous deciduous rambler up to 30 ft (9 m) high, with large, creamy, richly scented single flowers that are butter yellow in bud.
Zone 5 US, 6 Can.

R. soulieana A large deciduous shrub with long, climbing stems making large mounds. The leaves are gray-green, and the single white flowers are up to 1½ in (4 cm) wide in large, domed clusters, but only on well-established, mature plants. The fruits are small, orange-red, and egg shaped. W China. Introduced 1896.
Zone 6 US, 7 Can. 🏆

R. sweginzowii A strong deciduous shrub 10–13 ft (3–4 m) high, resembling *R. moyesii*. The bright rose-pink, single flowers are 1½ in (4 cm) wide, are usually in clusters, and precede flask-shaped, bright red hips about the same size and color as those of *R. moyesii* but ripening earlier. NW China. Introduced 1903 by Ernest Wilson.
Zone 5 US, 6 Can.

Rosa soulieana

Rosa sweginzowii

R. 'Thérèse Bugnet' A complex hybrid with some *R. rugosa* blood, this is a very popular rose. The large, fragrant, double, pale pink flowers appear from June to frost, while the deep red canes are a winter attraction. Introduced 1950 in Alberta, Canada.
Zone 2 US, 2b Can.

R. villosa (Apple rose) A vigorous, medium-sized deciduous shrub with aromatic leaves and single flowers 2 in (5 cm) wide that are carmine in bud and open clear pink. In early fall it has large, bristly, apple-shaped, crimson hips. C and S Europe, W Asia. Introduced 1771.
Zone 4 US, 4b Can.

Rosa virginiana

R. virginiana (Virginia rose) A small, suckering deciduous shrub with leaflets that are glossy green and turn in fall first to purple, then to orange-red, crimson, and yellow. The single flowers are 2–2½ in (5–6 cm) wide, bright pink but deeper in bud, and appear continuously from early to late summer. The hips are small, bright red,

Rosa webbiana

and slightly flattened. It is excellent in sandy soils, especially in coastal sites. E North America. Introduced before 1807.
Zone 3 US, 3 Can. 🏆

R. webbiana A graceful, slender deciduous shrub up to 6½ ft (2 m). The single flowers are clear almond-pink, up to 2 in (5 cm) wide, and are borne all along the arching canes in early summer. Bottle-shaped, red fruits follow in late summer. W Himalaya. Introduced 1879.
Zone 6 US, 7 Can.

Rosa 'Wedding Day'

***R.* 'Wedding Day'** A vigorous, deciduous climbing or rambling shrub reaching 33 ft (10 m) with support. The richly scented single flowers are deep yellow in bud, opening to creamy white and fading to pink; the stamens are vivid yellow. They are borne in large trusses.
Zone 6 US, 7 Can.

***R.* 'White Max Graf'** A shrub resembling 'Max Graf' but with large, single, pure white flowers. It is prostrate or climbing to 6½ ft (2 m).
Zone 2 US, 2b Can.

R. wichuraiana (Memorial rose) A vigorous semievergreen rambler. It has fragrant, white, single flowers up to 2 in (5 cm) across, borne in small conical clusters in late summer and followed by tiny, oval, red hips. The stems root as they grow, making a good ground cover, especially for slopes. Parent of the wichuraiana hybrids, including 'Albéric Barbier', 'Albertine', and 'Dorothy Perkins'. E Asia. Introduced 1891 from Japan.
Zone 3 US, 4 Can.

Rosa wichuraiana

***R.* 'William's Double Yellow'** A small deciduous hybrid of *R. pimpinellifolia* bearing fragrant double yellow flowers with a central cluster of green carpels.
Zone 3 US, 4 Can.

R. willmottiae A medium-sized deciduous shrub with gracefully arching branches and small, sea green, fernlike leaves that are aromatic when crushed. The single flowers are up to 1½ in (4 cm) wide and lilac-pink with cream anthers, and the fruits are pear shaped and orange-red. W China. Introduced 1904 by Ernest Wilson.
Zone 6 US, 7 Can.

R. woodsii* var. *fendleri A dense, leafy deciduous bush about 5 ft (1.5 m) high with bright lilac-pink, single flowers and red hips that persist well into winter. W North America. In cultivation 1888.
Zone 4 US, 5 Can.

R. xanthina (Manchu rose) A beautiful, medium-sized deciduous shrub with small, dainty, fernlike leaves and semidouble, golden yellow flowers 1½ in (4 cm) wide. A garden form, cultivated in China and Korea for more than 100 years.
Zone 4 US, 5 Can.

Rosmarinus *Labiatae*
Rosemary

A genus of two species of evergreen, aromatic shrubs, thriving in all well-drained soils in sun.

R. officinalis (Rosemary) A dense shrub up to 6½ ft (2 m) high and wide, with gray-green, lance-shaped leaves and, in early spring, blue flowers held in many upright

Rosmarinus officinalis

spikes along branches made the previous year. It makes an informal hedge that can be lightly pruned immediately after flowering. S Europe, Asia Minor.
Zone 6 US, 7 Can.

***R. o.* 'Albus'** A white-flowered form.
Zone 6 US, 7 Can.

***R. o.* 'Benenden Blue'** A smaller form with very narrow, dark green leaves and bright blue flowers.
Zone 6 US, 7 Can.

***R. o.* 'Fastigiatus'** See *R. o.* 'Miss Jessop's Upright'.

***R. o.* 'Miss Jessop's Upright'**, syn. *R. o.* 'Fastigiatus' A strong, erect, small to medium-sized shrub.
Zone 6 US, 7 Can. 🏆

Rosmarinus officinalis 'Prostratus'

***R. o.* 'Prostratus'** A low-growing form making large, dense, prostrate mats with clusters of blue flowers in late spring and early summer.
Zone 6 US, 7 Can. 🏆

***R. o.* 'Roseus'** A small shrub with lilac-pink flowers.
Zone 6 US, 7 Can.

***R. o.* 'Severn Sea'** A dwarf shrub with arching branches and brilliant blue flowers.
Zone 6 US, 7 Can. 🏆

Rosmarinus officinalis 'Sissinghurst Blue'

***R. o.* 'Sissinghurst Blue'** Upright dwarf form with blue flowers. Introduced c. 1958.
Zone 6 US, 7 Can. 🏆

Rosmarinus officinalis 'Tuscan Blue'

***R. o.* 'Tuscan Blue'** A small shrub with broader leaves and brighter-colored, deep blue flowers that often appear in winter.
Zone 6 US, 7 Can.

Rubus *Rosaceae*
Bramble

A large genus of 250 evergreen and deciduous species. The ornamental brambles vary greatly but share a tendency to grow well in poor soils and in all kinds of adverse conditions. Several have attractive flowers and foliage, others have striking white stems in winter, and the great majority have thorns. Those with ornamental stems should have the old flowering stems cut down to ground level each year immediately after flowering. The climbing members of the genus are fairly vigorous and have long, prickly stems. They can be trained up supports or into hedges. They are grown mainly for their ornamental foliage and thrive in all types of well-drained soil.

Rubus 'Benenden'

***R.* 'Benenden'** A beautiful deciduous hybrid, producing erect, peeling, thornless shoots up to 10 ft (3 m) high with three- to five-lobed leaves. The flowers are 2 in (5 cm) wide, glistening white with a central boss of golden yellow stamens, and produced singly all along the branches in late spring. Raised 1950 by Capt. Collingwood Ingram.
Zone 7? US, 8? Can. 🏆

***R.* 'Betty Ashburner'** A prostrate evergreen shrub with glossy green, rounded, more or less three-lobed leaves with wavy margins. It makes a good ground cover where *R. tricolor* may be too invasive.
Zone 4 US, 5 Can.

Rubus 'Betty Ashburner'

R. biflorus A vigorous, medium-sized deciduous shrub with green stems covered with a vivid white, waxy bloom. The leaves have five (or occasionally three) leaflets and are white-felted beneath. The small white flowers are borne in terminal clusters in summer and followed by edible, yellow fruits. Himalaya. Introduced 1818.
Zone 9 US

Rubus calycinoides

R. calycinoides A creeping alpine evergreen that forms dense mats. The leaves are small, three- to five-lobed and mallowlike, glossy green and puckered above, gray-felted below. White flowers appear in summer. It is a good plant for ground cover, even in shade. The true species is possibly not in cultivation, and the plant generally grown is probably *R. pentalobus*. Taiwan.
Zone 4 US, 5b Can.

Rubus cockburnianus

R. cockburnianus A medium-sized deciduous species with purple, arching stems overlaid with a vivid white bloom, which is outstanding in winter. The attractive, fern-like leaves have 7–9 leaflets and are white or gray beneath. The flowers are of little merit but are followed by bloomy black fruits. China. Introduced 1907 by Ernest Wilson.
Zone 6 US, 7 Can. 🏆

***R. c.* 'Goldenvale'** A form with equally striking white shoots in winter, but it also offers the added bonus of yellow foliage in summer.
Zone 6? US, 7? Can.

Rubus crataegifolius

R. crataegifolius A dwarf deciduous shrub with arching shoots that are red-purple in winter. The deeply lobed leaves turn striking orange, red, and purple in fall.
Zone 5 US, 6 Can.

R. deliciosus (Boulder raspberry, Rocky Mountain raspberry) The gracefully arching branches of this medium-sized, thornless deciduous shrub have peeling bark. The leaves have 3–5 lobes, and the white flowers, 2 in (5 cm) wide, are like those of *R. canina.* They open in late spring and early summer. Colorado. Introduced 1870.
Zone 5 US, 6 Can.

R. flagelliflorus An evergreen climber with long, white-felted, minutely prickly stems. The leaves are broadly egg shaped to more or less lance shaped, up to 7 in (18 cm) long, shallowly lobed and toothed, and felted beneath. The small white flowers are borne in clusters in early summer and are followed by black, edible fruits. It is most often grown for its striking foliage. China.

Rubus flagelliflorus

Introduced 1901 by Ernest Wilson.
Zone 7 US, 8 Can.

R. × fraseri A medium-sized, suckering deciduous shrub with palmate leaves and fragrant, rose-colored flowers from early to late summer. It is good for shady areas under trees. Garden origin 1918.
Zone 5 US, 6 Can.

Rubus fruticosus

R. fruticosus (Blackberry, bramble) A ferocious, invasive weed of horticulture and agriculture, occurring in one form or another in most of the temperate world. However, the species also includes the blackberries, fruiting clones of which are nonweedy and of ornamental value. They include 'Black Satin', 'Darrow', 'Navajo',

Rubus × fraseri

and 'Thornfree', all of which are restrained enough for the average garden. It is a deciduous species.

Zone 4 US, 5 Can.

R. henryi* var. *bambusarum An evergreen climbing species with long stems, up to 20 ft (6 m) on a suitable support. The leaves are composed of three distinct, lance-shaped leaflets and are 4–6 in (10–15 cm) long, glossy dark green above, white-felted beneath. The pink flowers are borne in slender racemes in summer, followed by black fruits. China. Introduced 1900.

Zone 7 US, 8 Can.

***R.* 'Kenneth Ashburner'** A prostrate, vigorous evergreen shrub with glossy green, pointed leaves. It is good for ground cover.

Zone 4? US, 5? Can.

R. lineatus A deciduous or semi-evergreen shrub with rambling, silky-hairy stems, usually less than 4 ft (1.2 m). The leaves, which have five leaflets, are unique and beautiful; they are dark green above and covered with a shining, silvery, silky down beneath, and spines are almost entirely absent. The white flowers are in small clusters, and the small fruits are red or yellow. It needs a warm, sheltered location. E Himalaya to Malaya. Introduced 1905 by George Forrest.

Zone 9 US

***R. microphyllus* 'Variegatus'** A small, deciduous suckering shrub, forming dense mounds of prickly stems and prettily three-lobed leaves that are green, mottled with cream and pink.

Zone 9 US

R. nepalensis A dwarf, evergreen, creeping shrub with softly bristly stems and leaves with three leaflets. The attractive, nodding, white flowers, 1–1½ in (2.5–4 cm) wide, are on erect, leafy shoots in early summer and are followed by edible fruits. A charming shrub for a shady border or slope. Himalaya. Introduced 1850.

Zone 7? US, 8? Can.

R. odoratus (Flowering raspberry) A vigorous, suckering deciduous shrub with erect, peeling, thornless stems up to 8 ft (2.5 m) high. The leaves are large, velvety, and palmate, and the fragrant, purplish rose flowers are in branched clusters, up to 2 in (5 cm) wide, opening from early summer to early fall. The red fruits are edible. It is an excellent, very ornamental shrub for dappled shade beneath trees. E North America. Introduced 1770.

Rubus odoratus

Zone 3 US, 3 Can.

R. phoenicolasius (Japanese wineberry) The reddish, glandular-bristly stems of this arching deciduous shrub are 8–10 ft (2.5–3 m) high, and the leaves are large, with three leaflets that are white-felted beneath. The small, pale pink flowers are in clusters in midsummer, and the fruits are bright orange-red and sweetly edible. It can spread rapidly in good soil and form a dense barrier. Japan, China, Korea. Introduced c. 1876.

Zone 6 US, 7 Can.

R. spectabilis (Salmonberry) A vigorous, suckering deciduous shrub with erect stems 4–6 ft (1.2–1.8 m) high and leaves with three leaflets. The fragrant flowers are solitary or in small clusters, up to 1½ in (4 cm) across, bright magenta-rose, and borne in midspring. The edible fruits are large, egg shaped, and orange-yellow. Makes a good ground cover under trees. W North America. Introduced 1827 by David Douglas.

Zone 4 US, 5 Can.

***R. s.* 'Olympic Double'** A striking, double-flowered form.

Zone 4 US, 5 Can.

Rubus thibetanus 'Silver Fern'

Rubus phoenicolasius

***R. thibetanus* 'Silver Fern'** An attractive deciduous plant with semierect, purplish brown stems covered with a blue-white bloom. They are up to 6½ ft (2 m) high and bear small, fernlike leaves with 7–13 coarsely toothed leaflets that are silvery-silky-hairy above and white or gray-felted beneath. The flowers are small and purple, and the fruits are black or red. W China. Introduced 1904 by Ernest Wilson.

Zone 4 US, 4b Can. 🏆

R. tricolor A vigorous, evergreen ground cover with long, trailing stems and dark, glossy leaves with white undersides. The white, 1 in (2.5 cm) wide flowers are borne in midsummer and are sometimes followed by large, bright red, edible fruits. It will form a mat even under dense trees but can become 3 ft (1 m) high with age. W China. Introduced 1908 by Ernest Wilson.

Zone 7 US, 8 Can.

***R. ulmifolius* 'Bellidiflorus'** A rambling deciduous shrub with plum-colored stems and large panicles of double pink flowers in mid- to late summer. It is too vigorous for the average garden.

Zone 7 US, 8 Can.

Rubus ulmifolius 'Bellidiflorus'

Ruscus *Ruscaceae*

Butcher's broom

A genus of about six species of evergreen subshrubs occurring from Madeira to Iran and spreading by underground stems. What appear to be leaves are really flattened stems (cladodes), and the minute flowers are borne on the surfaces of these in spring, with male and female on separate plants. The females bear attractive fruits. These are good plants for dry shade in all kinds of soil.

Ruscus aculeatus

R. aculeatus (Butcher's broom, box holly) A small, erect shrub with thick clumps of green stems, 1½–3 ft (0.5–1 m) high, that are sturdy but flexible. The cladodes are small, sharply spine-tipped, and densely arranged on the upper parts of the stems. The berries resemble bright red cherries and are sometimes abundantly borne where both sexes are grown. It grows in dense shade. Cut stems are used in floral arrangements. S and W Europe.

Zone 7 US, 8 Can.

R. hypoglossum A dwarf shrub with broad clumps of green, "leafy" stems. The comparatively large, leaflike cladodes have tiny green flowers on the upper surface and, on female plants, large, cherrylike fruits. It can provide excellent ground cover in shade. S Europe. In cultivation since the 16th century.

Zone 8 US, 9? Can.

Ruta *Rutaceae*

Rue

A genus of about seven species of evergreen and deciduous shrubs and perennials with aromatic, deeply divided leaves, grown for both flowers and foliage, sometimes for medical purposes. Native to Europe and Southwest Asia, they thrive in sun in almost any well-drained soil.

Ruta graveolens 'Jackman's Blue'

***R. graveolens* 'Jackman's Blue'** This strikingly glaucous blue form of rue, the one most commonly grown, is a compact and bushy deciduous shrub. Less than 3 ft (1 m) high, it has leaves something like the fronds of a maidenhair fern and clusters of small, mustard yellow flowers in summer. It is a popular herb, but it can cause a skin rash on people who are sensitive to it; this can be severe if the plant is handled in sunlight. S Europe. In cultivation for several centuries.

Zone 4 US, 5 Can. 🏆

Salix

Salicaceae Willow

Willows are a large and diverse group of deciduous plants, all easily grown in the garden, that offer a variety of ornamental characteristics throughout the year. Some varieties have gracefully weeping branches that are perfect for planting beside a stream or pond and seem refreshing when stirred by a summer's breeze. Others have brightly colored stems that bring beauty to the oft-stark winter landscape. And still others are favorite harbingers of spring, sprouting silky, furry catkins early in the season.

There are some 300 species of willows, ranging from lofty, noble trees to small, gnarled, alpine bushes and prostrate shrubs of the tundra. Most are native to the north temperate zone, and some are remarkably hardy and tough, tolerating temperatures to −50°F (−46°C).

A number of them are grown for their interesting habits: besides the well-known weeping willows, there are *S. babylonica* var. *pekinensis* 'Tortuosa' and *S. udensis* 'Sekka', which have twisted branches. Among the delightful dwarf willows are *S.* × *boydii* and *S.* 'Stuarti', which are gnarled little shrublets. Other willows have particularly attractive foliage, including *S. elaeagnos, exigua, lanata,* and *pentandra.*

Salix alba 'Britzensis'

Some of the most striking willows have colorful stems. *S. alba* 'Britzensis' and *S.* × *rubens* 'Basfordiana' bear brilliant orange-red stems, and *S. acutifolia* 'Blue Streak', *S. daphnoides,* and *S. irrorata* all have purple wands covered with white bloom. Several have shimmery golden stems, including *S. alba* 'Tristis', *S. a.* var. *vitellina,* and *S.* × *sepulcralis* 'Chrysocoma'.

There are four willows grown primarily for their showy, downy catkins, which are among the most welcome flowers early in the garden year and are even more beautiful when positioned so that they are backlit by the sun. *S. caprea* and *S. discolor* have gray or silvery gray catkins. The catkins of *S. gracilistyla* are gray with a distinctive reddish, then gold tint, and, most dramatic of all, those of *S. gracilistyla* 'Melanostachys' are blackish with red and yellow highlights.

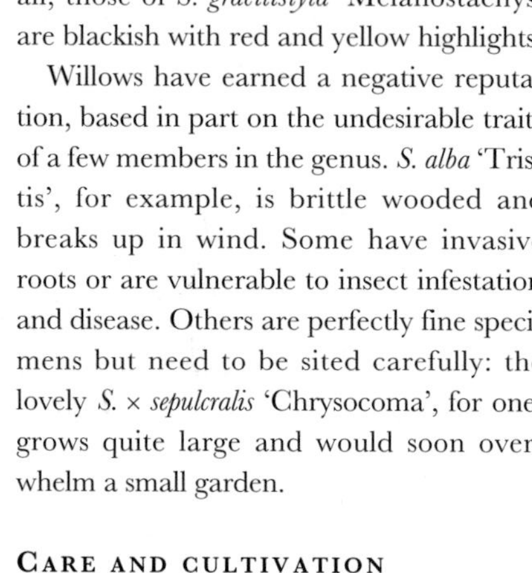

Willows have earned a negative reputation, based in part on the undesirable traits of a few members in the genus. *S. alba* 'Tristis', for example, is brittle wooded and breaks up in wind. Some have invasive roots or are vulnerable to insect infestation and disease. Others are perfectly fine specimens but need to be sited carefully: the lovely *S.* × *sepulcralis* 'Chrysocoma', for one, grows quite large and would soon overwhelm a small garden.

Care and cultivation

Willows can grow in ordinary garden soil, although there are some that require a moist or even wet site and others that tolerate poor, sandy soil. They will not thrive in shallow, alkaline soil or one that becomes hot and dry. They need full sun.

The willows with colored stems put on

the best display if they are pruned hard in early spring every other year. Except for this, pruning is seldom necessary but, if needed, can be done any time of year.

More than 100 insects prey on willows, but the most destructive are various beetles that feed on the leaves. Willows are also prone to blight and scab.

***S. acutifolia* 'Blue Streak'** A graceful large shrub or small tree with lance-shaped, long-pointed leaves and slender, polished, black-purple stems covered with a vivid, blue-white bloom. The male catkins appear before the leaves.
Zone 3 US, 3 Can.

S. aegyptiaca (Musk willow) A large shrub, or occasionally a small tree, with densely gray-downy twigs and lance-shaped leaves that are downy beneath. Its large, bright yellow male catkins appear in late winter and early spring, making this a very beautiful, early-flowering tree. SW to S Asia. In cultivation 1820.
Zone 6 US, 7 Can.

S. alba (White willow) A species for wet soil, this is a large, elegant, conical tree with an open habit and slender branches that droop at the tips. The lance-shaped, silky-hairy leaves emerge in great, billowy masses and give the tree its characteristically silver appearance from a distance. The slender catkins appear with the young leaves in spring. A vigorous, fast-growing tree. Europe, W Asia.
Zone 2 US, 2 Can.

***S. a.* 'Britzensis'** (Scarlet willow) A remarkable small to medium-sized tree with brilliant orange-scarlet branches in winter, especially if it is pruned severely every second year.
Zone 2 US, 2 Can.

***S. a.* var. *caerulea*,** syn. *S.* 'Caerula' (Cricket-bat willow) A large tree with leaves that are sea green above and slightly bloomy beneath. Discovered c. 1700 in Norfolk, England.
Zone 2 US, 2 Can.

***S. a.* 'Tristis'** (Golden weeping willow) This is often confused with *S.* × *sepulcralis* 'Chrysocoma', but it is much hardier. It is a large tree, growing to 70 ft (21 m) high and wide, whose young branches are golden yellow. It is common in the North and sheds twigs and small branches readily.
Zone 2 US, 2 Can.

S. a.* var. *vitellina (Golden willow) A smaller tree than the type with brilliant, yolk yellow shoots that are made showier by severe pruning every second year.
Zone 2 US, 2 Can.

S. apoda A dwarf species with ground-hugging stems and glossy green leaves. The erect, silver-furry male catkins appear all along the branches in early spring, before the leaves. They gradually become more than 1 in (2.5 cm) long and turn bright yellow. A good plant for the rock garden. Caucasus, Turkey. In cultivation before 1939.
Zone 6 US, 7 Can.

S. arbuscula A dwarf, creeping shrub forming dense mats of green leaves that are glaucous beneath. It produces long, slender catkins as the leaves appear in spring. Scandinavia, N Russia, Scotland.
Zone 3 US, 3 Can.

Salix alba var. *vitellina*

Salix apoda

S. babylonica (Babylon weeping willow) A medium-sized tree with a wide-spreading head of long, pendulous, brown branches. The leaves are long and narrow, green above and bluish gray beneath. The slender catkins appear with the young leaves in spring. It is now largely superseded by *S.* × *sepulcralis* 'Chrysocoma' and similar hybrids. China. Introduced c. 1730.
Zone 5 US, 6 Can.

***S. b.* var. *pekinensis* 'Pendula'**, syn. *S. matsudana* 'Pendula' A very graceful tree and one of the best weeping willows, showing resistance to scab and canker.
Zone 4 US, 5 Can.

***S. b.* var. *pekinensis* 'Tortuosa'**, syn. *S. matsudana* 'Tortuosa' (Corkscrew willow, dragon's claw willow) A curious small to medium-sized tree with branches and twigs that are very twisted and contorted.
Zone 4 US, 5 Can.

S.* × *balfourii A splendid, vigorous, medium-sized to large shrub with gray-

Salix babylonica

Salix babylonica var. *pekinensis* 'Tortuosa'

woolly leaves that later become green and downy. The yellowish, silky-hairy catkins with tiny red bracts appear before the leaves in midspring. It is good for growing in moist soil.

Zone 4? US, 5? Can.

S. bockii A small to medium-sized shrub, making a neat, spreading bush 3–4 ft (1–1.2 m) high. It has slender, reddish twigs and many small, grayish catkins that appear in late summer and fall along the current year's growth. It is the only willow to flower at this time of year. W China. Introduced 1908 by Ernest Wilson.

Zone 6 US, 7 Can.

S.* × *boydii A dwarf, erect, extremely slow growing, gnarled shrub with round, gray-downy leaves that become gray-green above. It rarely produces catkins but is good for a container or a rock garden. Discovered in the 1870s in Scotland.

Zone 6 US, 7 Can. 🏆

***S.* 'Caerulea'** See *S. alba* var. *caerulea.*

S. caprea (Goat willow, French pussy willow) A common European species that makes a large shrub or small tree. It is particularly noticeable in spring for its yellow

Salix caprea

male catkins and silvery pink female ones. Cut stems can be brought indoors in late winter and forced. Europe, W Asia.

Zone 4 US, 4b Can.

S. c.* var. *pendula (Weeping goat willow) A small, umbrella-like, male tree with stiffly weeping branches that rarely grows to 10 ft (3 m) tall. It has silver catkins studded with golden anthers in late winter.

Zone 4 US, 5 Can. 🏆

Salix caprea var. *pendula*

***S. cinerea* 'Tricolor'** A variegated form of the gray willow and the only form with garden merit. It is a large shrub with leaves variegated with yellow and cream.

Zone 2 US, 2 Can.

S.* × *cottetii A vigorous, low-growing shrub with long, trailing stems making mats several yards (meters) across. The leaves are dark, shiny green, and the catkins appear before the leaves in early spring. It makes a good ground cover. European Alps. In cultivation 1905.

Zone 5 US, 6 Can.

S. daphnoides (Violet willow) A fast-growing small tree with long, purple-violet shoots covered with a white bloom. The catkins appear before the leaves in spring. It is very effective if pruned hard every year or two in midspring. N Europe, C Asia, Himalaya. In cultivation 1829.

Zone 2 US, 2b Can.

***S. d.* 'Aglaia'** A male clone with large, handsome catkins, silvery at first and then bright yellow, in early spring. The stems are red in winter and not bloomed.

Zone 3 US, 3 Can. 🏆

S. discolor (Common pussy willow) A large shrub or small tree that is hardier than *S. caprea* but not as showy. The stems can be cut and forced indoors. E North America.

Zone 3 US, 3 Can. 🏆

S. elaeagnos (Rosemary willow) A graceful, medium-sized to large, dense shrub with leaves that resemble those of rosemary but are elongated. They are grayish and hoary at first, then become green above and white beneath. They are thickly arranged along the slender, reddish brown stems and

Salix daphnoides 'Aglaia'

turn yellow in fall. The slender catkins appear with the leaves in spring. This is one of the prettiest willows for planting near water. Europe, Asia Minor. Introduced c. 1820.

Zone 4 US, 5 Can. 🏆

Salix exigua

S. exigua (Coyote willow) A beautiful, large, erect shrub or small tree with linear, silvery-silky, minutely toothed leaves. The catkins are slender and appear with the leaves. W North America, N Mexico. Introduced 1921.

Zone 3 US, 3b Can.

S. fargesii A medium-sized to large, rather open shrub with polished, reddish brown shoots and elliptical, deep glossy green leaves up to 7 in (18 cm) long, with impressed veins. The catkins appear with or after the leaves, and the females are 4–6 in (10–15 cm) long. C China. Introduced 1911 by Ernest Wilson.

Zone 5 US, 6 Can.

Salix fargesii

S.* × *finnmarchica A dwarf shrub that forms a low, wide-spreading patch with slender, ascending shoots and small leaves. The small catkins crowd the stems before the leaves in early spring, and female clones are the more attractive. It is excellent for a rock garden or as a ground cover. N and C Europe.

Zone 4 US, 5 Can.

Salix fragilis

S. fragilis (Crack willow, brittle willow) A large tree with widely spreading branches, often seen by rivers and streams. It has rugged bark, lance-shaped green leaves, and slender catkins that appear with the leaves in spring. The twigs are brittle at their joints. Europe, N Asia.

Zone 3 US, 3b Can.

S. glaucosericea (Alpine gray willow) An attractive gray dwarf shrub suitable for the rock garden. The leaves are narrowly elliptic to elliptic-lanceolate and are densely gray-hairy at first, becoming less so by fall. European Alps, Pyrenees.

Zone 6 US, 7 Can.

Salix gracilistyla

S. gracilistyla (Rosegold pussy willow) A vigorous, medium-sized shrub with silky gray-downy leaves that gradually become green and smooth and persist late into fall. The catkins appear before the leaves in early spring. The young males are covered with gray silk, through which the reddish, unopened anthers can be seen. Later they develop to become bright yellow. NE Asia. Introduced 1895.

Zone 4 US, 4b Can.

***S. g.* 'Melanostachys'** (Black pussy willow) A form outstanding for its catkins, which are very dark, with blackish scales and brick red anthers that open to yellow. They appear before the leaves. The winter stems are purple-black. It is a male clone and known only in cultivation. Japan.

Zone 4 US, 4b Can. 🏆

***S.* × *grahamii* 'Moorei'** A dwarf shrub, ideal for the rock garden, forming a low, wide-spreading mound of slender stems. The leaves are small and shiny green, and the catkins appear before the leaves in spring. Discovered 1886 in County Donegal, Ireland by Douglas Moore.

Zone 4 US, 5b Can.

Salix hastata 'Wehrhahnii'

***S. hastata* 'Wehrhahnii'** A slow-growing, small to medium-sized shrub. In spring the stout twigs become alive with pretty, silvery gray, male catkins that later turn yellow. Switzerland. Found c. 1930.

Zone 6 US, 7 Can. 🏆

Salix helvetica

S. helvetica (Swiss willow) A small, bushy shrub with its leaves and catkins covered in soft, downy hairs. The small leaves are gray-green above and white beneath, and the catkins appear with the young leaves in spring. An attractive shrub for the rock garden. European Alps. In cultivation 1872.

Zone 5 US, 6 Can. 🏆

S. herbacea (Dwarf willow) A tiny, alpine species that forms mats of creeping, often

underground stems. The rounded, very small leaves are glossy green and net-veined, and borne in pairs or threes at the tips of the shoots. Catkins up to $^{3}/_{4}$ in (2 cm) long appear with the leaves in spring. It is an interesting and unusual dwarf shrub for a moist location in the rock garden. Europe, North America.
Zone 2 US, 2 Can.

S. hookeriana A medium-sized to large shrub or small tree with glossy, reddish brown branches and oblong leaves that are densely felted beneath. The catkins appear with the leaves. W North America. In cultivation 1891.
Zone 6 US, 7 Can.

Salix integra 'Hakuru Nishiki'

***S. integra* 'Hakuru Nishiki'** An elegant large shrub or small tree with slightly drooping branches and slender catkins on the polished stems before the leaves, which are prettily blotched with white. It is ideal for waterside planting but tends to burn in full sun. Japan. Introduced 1979 by Harry van de Laar.
Zone 6 US, 7 Can.

S. irrorata A vigorous medium-sized shrub with long shoots that are green at first and then purple, covered with a striking white bloom that is particularly eye-catching in winter. The catkins appear before the leaves, the males having brick red anthers that turn yellow. SW United States. Introduced 1898.
Zone 5 US, 6 Can.

S. lanata (Woolly willow) An attractive, slow-growing shrub up to 4 ft (1.2 m) or occasionally more, with rounded, silvery

Salix irrorata

Salix lanata

gray, downy leaves and erect, yellowish gray, woolly catkins in spring. The female catkins elongate considerably when seeding, sometimes becoming up to 4 in (10 cm) long. N Europe.
Zone 4 US, 5 Can. 🏆

S. lucida (Shining willow) A large shrub or small tree with glossy yellow-brown twigs and lustrous, lance-shaped green leaves up to 5 in (12.5 cm) long. North America.
Zone 2 US, 2 Can. 🏆

S. magnifica A large, sparse shrub or small tree with large, magnolia-like leaves up to 8 in (20 cm) long and 5 in (13 cm) wide. Catkins are produced with the leaves in spring, and the females are often 6–10 in (15–25 cm) long. W China. Introduced 1909 by Ernest Wilson.
Zone 5 US, 6 Can. 🏆

***S.* 'Mark Postill'** A dwarf, spreading shrub with purplish brown winter shoots and stout catkins that are silvery at first and are produced over a long period with and after the leaves. Raised 1967 by the Hillier Nurseries' propagator Alan Postill.
Zone 5? US, 6? Can.

***S. matsudana* 'Pendula'** See *S. babylonica* var. *pekinensis* 'Pendula'.

***S. matsudana* 'Tortuosa'** See *S. babylonica* var. *pekinensis* 'Tortuosa'.

S. moupinensis A medium-sized shrub related to and generally resembling *S. fargesii*. It has red-brown shoots and slender, erect, green catkins. Its leaves are slightly smaller and usually smooth. China. Introduced 1869 by Armand David and 1910 by Ernest Wilson.
Zone 6 US, 7 Can.

S. ×pendulina (Wisconsin weeping willow, Niobe willow) A small to medium-sized, usually female, weeping tree similar to *S. babylonica* but with a better constitution. Originated early 19th century in Germany.
Zone 3 US, 4 Can.

***S. ×p.* 'Elegantissima'** (Thurlow weeping willow) A form with a wide-spreading head of long, weeping branches. The catkins are produced with the leaves. It is a hybrid of *S. babylonica*.
Zone 3 US, 4 Can.

S. pentandra (Laurel willow) A beautiful

Salix pentandra

small to medium-sized tree with glossy twigs and attractive, lustrous leaves that resemble those of the bay laurel and are pleasantly aromatic when unfolding or crushed. The catkins are produced with the leaves in spring, and the males are bright yellow. Europe to Caucasus.
Zone 1 US, 1b Can.

***S.* 'Prairie Cascade'** This hybrid, devel-

oped at Morden, Manitoba, combines the hardiness and good foliage of *S. pentandra* with the weeping habit of *S.* × *pendulina*.
Zone 3 US, 3 Can.

S. purpurea (Purple osier, basket willow) A graceful, medium-sized to large shrub with long, arching, often purplish shoots. The narrowly oblong leaves are dull green above, paler or glaucous beneath. Slender catkins are produced all along the shoots in spring before the leaves. Europe, C Asia.
Zone 4 US, 4b Can.

Salix purpurea 'Pendula'

***S. p.* 'Nana'** A dwarf, compact, slender-branched shrub with narrow leaves that makes a good hedge for a damp site.
Zone 4 US, 4b Can.

***S. p.* 'Pendula'** An attractive form with long, pendulous branches. When trained as a standard it forms a charming, small, weeping tree.
Zone 4 US, 5 Can. 🏆

S. repens* var. *argentea A pretty form of the creeping willow that is a prostrate shrub with silvery-silky leaves. When trained as a standard it makes an effective miniature weeping tree. W coast of Europe.
Zone 2 US, 2 Can. 🏆

Salix repens var. *argentea*

S. reticulata (Neatleaf willow) A dwarf shrub with prostrate stems forming dense mats. The small, rounded, dark green leaves are attractively net-veined, and the erect, magenta-red catkins appear very early in spring. Arctic and mountain areas of North America, Europe, N Asia. In cultivation 1789.
Zone 3 US, 4 Can. 🏆

Salix retusa

S. retusa A prostrate species forming extensive carpets of creeping stems and small, notched, shiny green leaves. Catkins are erect and very small and appear with the leaves. Europe. Introduced 1763.
Zone 1 US, 1 Can.

***S.* × *rubens* 'Basfordiana'** A medium-sized to large tree with long, narrow leaves and bright orange-red twigs in winter. It is male and has long, slender, yellow catkins that appear with the leaves in spring. Ardennes. Introduced c. 1863.
Zone 6 US, 7 Can. 🏆

Salix × *rubens* 'Basfordiana'

***S.* × *rubra* 'Eugenei'** A slender, conical, small tree with erect branches and subtly attractive, gray-pink male catkins.
Zone 6 US, 7 Can.

***S.* × *sepulcralis* 'Chrysocoma'** Possibly the most beautiful weeping willow. It is a medium-sized, wide-spreading tree with vigorous, arching branches that end in slender, golden yellow, weeping branchlets, ultimately of great length. The leaves are slender, and the catkins, which are both male and female, appear with the leaves in midspring. It is not suitable, however, for small gardens, and it is subject to scab and canker, though these can be controlled by spraying. In cultivation 1888.
Zone 4 US, 4b Can. 🏆

***S.* × *s.* 'Erythroflexuosa'** An unusual ornamental small tree. The vigorous, orange-yellow, pendulous shoots are contorted and twisted, as are the narrow leaves. Argentina.
Zone 4 US, 5 Can.

***S.* 'Stuartii'** A dwarf, gnarled shrublet with yellow shoots and orange buds that are outstanding in winter. It is a hybrid of *S. lanata* and has smaller leaves and larger catkins than that species.
Zone 4? US, 5? Can.

S. subopposita A rare and distinct dwarf shrub with slender, erect stems and small leaves that are almost opposite (rather than spirally arranged, as in the genus as a whole). The catkins come before the leaves in early spring, and the males have brick red anthers that turn yellow. This unusual willow resembles a hebe. Japan, Korea.
Zone 5 US, 6 Can.

***S. udensis* 'Sekka'** (Japanese fantail willow) A large shrub or small tree with curiously recurved and flattened stems and slender, pointed leaves. It is a male clone, with large catkins that appear before the leaves. The stems can be encouraged by hard pruning and are often used in floral arrangements.
Zone 4 US, 4b Can.

S. uva-ursi (Bearberry willow) A prostrate

Salix uva-ursi

shrub forming dense mats of creeping stems covered with small, glossy leaves that are glaucous on the undersides. The small, red catkins appear with the young leaves and are held close on the stems. It is a good plant for a rock garden. Canada, NE United States. Introduced 1880.

Zone 1 US, 1 Can.

S. viminalis (Common osier) A large shrub or small tree with long, straight shoots and long, finely tapering leaves with a covering of silky hairs beneath. The catkins appear before the leaves. It is often found beside rivers, streams, and lakes and has been long cultivated for basket making. Europe, NE Asia, Himalaya.

Zone 3 US, 3b Can.

S. yezoalpina A prostrate shrub with long, trailing stems and attractive, long-stalked, rounded or obovate, glossy green leaves with veins in a conspicuous net pattern. The catkins appear with the leaves in spring. It is a rare alpine species suitable for a rock garden or scree and is now considered to be a variety of *S. nakamurana.* Japan.

Zone 5 US, 6 Can.

Salvia *Labiatae*

A large genus of about 900 semievergreen and deciduous species of aromatic, flowering plants, consisting primarily of herbs and subshrubs; except for S. officinalis, *all are more or less tender. They need a warm, dry, well-drained location in full sun, and a surprising number will survive cold spells as long as these conditions are met and they have shelter from winds. The two-lipped flowers are often brightly, even dramatically colored, and the more tender salvia are excellent greenhouse specimens as long as they are not allowed to become lanky. Flowering is usually in late summer and fall and can continue for several weeks; in mild areas some species will flower right through into early winter. Old plants can be pruned severely if required. It is a good idea to take a few cuttings of the more tender salvias; taken in late summer, they will produce flowering plants the following year.*

Salvia elegans

S. elegans (Pineapple sage) A small deciduous species up to 3 ft (1 m). It has softly downy, heart-shaped leaves that smell strongly of pineapple and loose panicles of brilliant scarlet, tubelike flowers throughout the summer. Mexico. In cultivation before 1873.

Zone 8 US, 9? Can.

Salvia fulgens

S. fulgens (Mexican red sage) A small, upright deciduous species up to 3 ft (1 m) tall with heart-shaped leaves and long clusters of showy, densely hairy, scarlet flowers, 2 in (5 cm) long, in late summer. Mexico. Introduced 1829.

Zone 9 US 🏆

S. greggii (Autum sage) A beautiful, small, semievergreen shrubby species with fragrant leaves and rosy-red or purple-red flowers in fall. Texas, Mexico.

Zone 9 US

Salvia guaranitica

S. guaranitica A small deciduous subshrub with erect stems up to 5 ft (1.5 m). It has softly downy, heart-shaped leaves and long racemes of deep azure-blue flowers about 2 in (5 cm) long in summer and fall. South America. Introduced 1925.

Zone 9 US 🏆

S. involucrata A small deciduous species with ovate, long-pointed leaves and spikelike racemes of rose-magenta flowers that are sticky to the touch. Late summer to fall. Mexico. Introduced 1824.

Zone 9 US 🏆

S. lavandulifolia (Spanish sage) A dwarf deciduous species with narrow, downy, gray, leaves and spikelike racemes of blue-violet flowers in early summer. Spain.

Zone 5 US, 6 Can.

S. leucantha (Mexican bush sage) A small subshrub that spreads into wide clumps. The arching stems are covered with narrow gray-green leaves and bear spikes of purple-rose bracts and white flowers at the tips. It blooms from midsummer to late fall and should be cut back in early spring. Mexico.

Zone 8 US, 9? Can.

S. microphylla* var. *neurepia A deciduous subshrub reaching 4 ft (1.2 m) high,

Salvia involucrata

Salvia lavandulifolia

Salvia microphylla var. neurepia

with showy, bright rosy red flowers in late summer and autumn. Mexico.
Zone 9 US

S. officinalis (Common sage) The well-known, dwarf semievergreen species long cultivated as a herb. The leaves are gray-green, wrinkled, and strongly aromatic. The flowers are bluish purple and borne in

Salvia officinalis

summer. Europe. Cultivated since 1597 and probably before.
Zone 4 US, 5 Can.

***S. o.* 'Icterina'** A low, spreading form with leaves variegated with green and gold.
Zone 5 US, 6 Can. 🏆

***S. o.* 'Purpurascens'** (Purple-leaved sage) The stems and young foliage of this form

Salvia officinalis 'Icterina'

Salvia officinalis 'Tricolor'

are suffused with purple. It is particularly effective in colored-foliage groups.
Zone 4 US, 5b Can. 🏆

***S. o.* 'Tricolor'** A distinctive, compact form with gray-green leaves splashed with cream and suffused with purple and pink. It is slightly more tender than the species, but it is well worth planting each year.
Zone 5 US, 6 Can.

Sambucus *Caprifoliaceae*
Elder

A genus of about 20 species of deciduous shrubs, small trees, and perennial herbs, widely distributed in temperate and subtropical regions. The cultivated species will grow in almost all soils and locations. The flowers are not showy, but many elders have very ornamental foliage and fruits. They all have pinnate leaves and serrated leaflets. Production of large flower heads or lush foliage can be encouraged by cutting back the lateral branches to within a short distance of the previous year's growth in early spring. These are ideal specimens for informal gardens.

Sambucus canadensis 'Maxima'

***S. canadensis* 'Maxima'** A handsome form of the American elder, this is a strong shrub of medium to large size. The leaves have 5–11 (usually 7) leaflets and are 12–18 in (30–45 cm) long. The large flower heads are 12 in (30 cm) or more across, and the rose-purple flower stalks, which remain after the flowers have fallen, are an added attraction. It is a bold shrub that should be pruned each spring to encourage production of new shoots.
Zone 3 US, 3 Can.

Sambucus nigra

S. nigra (European elder) A large shrub or small tree with rugged bark and leaves with 5–7 leaflets. The flattened heads of cream, heavily fragrant flowers are borne in early summer and are followed by heavy bunches of shining black fruits. The flowers and fruits can be used for making wines. It grows well in most soils but is too large for most gardens and can become weedy. Europe, North Africa and W Asia. Long in cultivation.
Zone 3 US, 4 Can.

Sambucus nigra 'Aurea'

***S. n.* 'Aurea'** (Golden elder) The leaves of this form are an attractive golden yellow, turning greenish with age. It is one of the hardiest and best golden-foliaged shrubs available. In cultivation 1883.
Zone 3 US, 4 Can. 🏆

***S. n.* 'Aureomarginata'** The leaflets of this form have an irregular, bright yellow margin.
Zone 4 US, 4b Can.

Sambucus nigra 'Guincho Purple'

***S. n.* 'Guincho Purple'** In this form the leaves are green when young and become deep blackish purple then red in fall. The flowers are pink in bud, opening to white flushed with pink, and the stalks are stained with purple.
Zone 3 US, 4 Can. 🏆

Sambucus nigra f. laciniata

S. n.* f. *laciniata (Fern-leaved elder) An attractive large shrub with finely divided, fernlike leaves.
Zone 3 US, 3b Can. 🏆

***S. n.* 'Marginata'** The leaflets of this large shrub have an irregular cream margin.
Zone 3 US, 4 Can.

***S. n.* 'Pulverulenta'** A slow-growing but effective medium-sized shrub whose leaves are striped and mottled with white.
Zone 4 US, 4b Can.

***S. n.* 'Pyramidalis'** A stiff, erect, medium-sized to large shrub, wider above than below, with densely clustered leaves.
Zone 3 US, 4 Can.

Sambucus nigra 'Pulverulenta'

Sambucus nigra 'Pyramidalis'

S. racemosa (European red elder) A medium-sized to large shrub with leaves that have 5–7 coarsely toothed leaflets. The yellowish white flowers are in conical heads and crowd the branches in midspring; they are followed by dense clusters of bright scarlet berries that ripen in summer. Europe, W Asia. In cultivation since the 16th century. The following are recommended.
Zone 3 US, 3 Can.

***S. r.* 'Plumosa Aurea'** A medium-sized shrub with feathery, deeply cut, golden foliage that contrasts beautifully with the red berries. It is among the finest golden-leaved shrubs, fairly slow growing and best in light shade to avoid sunscorch. The flowers are a rich yellow.
Zone 3 US, 3 Can.

***S. r.* 'Sutherland Gold'** An excellent plant, like 'Plumosa Aurea' but less liable to scorch in the sun. Introduced 1971 by W. L. Kerr of Sutherland, Saskatchewan.
Zone 3 US, 3 Can. 🏆

Sambucus racemosa 'Plumosa Aurea'

Sambucus racemosa 'Sutherland Gold'

***S. r.* 'Tenuifolia'** A small, slow-growing shrub that forms a low mound of arching branches and has finely divided, fernlike leaves. It is as beautiful as a cut-leaved Japanese maple and a good substitute in alkaline soils. A good rock-garden plant.
Zone 4 US, 4b Can. 🏆

Santolina *Compositae*

Lavender cotton

Low-growing, mound-forming, evergreen subshrubs with dense, finely divided foliage that is gray, green, or silvery and dainty, buttonlike flower heads on tall stalks in midsummer. They need a sunny location in any well-drained soil. They are natives of the Mediterranean region, and there are about five species in all.

S. chamaecyparissus (Lavender cotton) A charming dwarf species, particularly valued for its woolly, silvery-hued, feathery foliage. Its flower heads are bright lemon yellow. S France, Pyrenees. In cultivation since the 16th century.
Zone 6 US, 7 Can. 🏆

Santolina chamaecyparissus

***S. c.* 'Nana'** A dwarfer, denser, more compact form, ideal for the rock garden.
Zone 6 US, 7 Can. 🏆

Santolina chamaecyparissus 'Nana'

S. pinnata A dwarf subshrub related to *S. chamaecyparissus* but differing in its longer, finely divided leaves and off-white flower heads. Italy.
Zone 6 US, 7 Can.

***S. p.* 'Edward Bowles'** A charming form, similar to 'Sulphurea' but with foliage that is more gray-green and flower heads of much paler yellow, almost cream.
Zone 6 US, 7 Can.

S. p.* subsp. *neapolitana A dwarf subshrub similar to *S. chamaecyparissus* but somewhat looser in growth and with longer, more feathery leaves. The flowers are bright lemon yellow. Italy.
Zone 6 US, 7 Can. 🏆

Santolina pinnata 'Edward Bowles'

***S. p.* 'Sulphurea'** A form with gray-green foliage and pale yellow flower heads.
Zone 6 US, 7 Can.

S. rosmarinifolia A dwarf species with threadlike, vivid green leaves. The flower heads are bright lemon yellow. SW Europe. In cultivation 1727.
Zone 7 US, 8 Can.

Santolina rosmarinifolia 'Primrose Gem'

***S. r.* 'Primrose Gem'** A lovely form only 12 in (30 cm) high, with pale primrose yellow flower heads. Originated before 1960 at Hillier Nurseries. *(See photo on p.565.)*
Zone 7 US, 8 Can. 🏆

Sapium *Euphorbiaceae*

A genus of 100 or more species of deciduous trees and shrubs, almost all from the tropics. They will grow in any well-drained, fertile soil and prefer a sunny location.

S. sebiferum (Chinese tallow tree, popcorn tree) A medium-sized tree with lustrous, light green, pointed oval leaves on red stalks. The foliage turns orange, red, or purplish in fall. The flowers are not showy, but the decorative fruit in fall is a three-lobed capsule with white seeds that resemble little popcorn kernels. The seeds yield a milky coating that is used like tallow for soap and candles. S China, Japan; naturalized in SE United States.
Zone 8 US, 9? Can.

Sarcococca *Buxaceae*

A genus of about 14 species, related to Buxus *and native to eastern and Southeast Asia. They are dwarf to small shrubs with glossy evergreen foliage. The small, white, fragrant male flowers open in late winter, with the tiny female ones occurring in the same cluster. They will grow in any fertile, well-drained soil but do especially well in alkaline ones; they need part to full shade. With one or two exceptions, they slowly reach 4–5 ft (1.2–1.5 m). They are excellent for cutting, as their foliage is attractive year-round and the fragrant flowers last well in a vase; they should be used selectively, however, as their perfume can be strong.*

S. confusa A dense, spreading, small shrub with elliptic, taper-pointed leaves and very fragrant, white flowers with cream anthers. It has black berries. China. In cultivation 1916.
Zone 7 US, 8 Can. 🏆

S. hookeriana (Himalayan sarcococca) An erectly growing small species with lance-shaped leaves, white flowers, and black berries. Himalaya.
Zone 6 US, 7 Can. 🏆

Sarcococca confusa

Sarcococca hookeriana

Sarcococca hookeriana var. *digyna*

S. h.* var. *digyna A slightly hardier small form with leaves that are more slender. The true plant has female flowers with two stigmas rather than three.
Zone 5 US, 6 Can. 🏆

S. h.* var. *humilis A dwarf, dense shrub that suckers to form clumps and is seldom more than 2 ft (60 cm) high. The male flowers have pink anthers, and the berries are black. It is suitable as ground cover. China. Introduced 1907.
Zone 6 US, 7 Can. 🏆

***S. h.* 'Purple Stem'** An attractive small shrub with the young stems, leaf stalks, and midribs flushed with purple.
Zone 6 US, 7 Can.

Sarcococca hookeriana 'Purple Stem'

Sarcococca hookeriana var. *humilis*

Sarcococca orientalis

S. orientalis A vigorous, upright small shrub with leaves that are three-veined, wedge shaped at the base, and pointed. The flowers are fragrant and the fruits are black. E China. Introduced 1980.
Zone 7? US, 8? Can.

S. ruscifolia var. chinensis A small, fairly slow growing variety of sweet box that is similar in general appearance to *S. confusa* but has dark red berries. C and W China.
Zone 7 US, 8 Can. 🏆

Sasa *Gramineae*
Bamboo

A genus of between 40 and 50 species of small, clump-forming evergreen bamboos, natives of Japan, Korea, and China. They have a low habit and relatively broad leaves. They are moisture lovers but will grow in good soil over limestone.

S. palmata A rampant bamboo that forms extensive clumps of green canes 6½–8 ft (2–2.5 m) high. The leaves are up to 14 in (35 cm) long by 3½ in (9 cm) wide, and the margins often wither during a hard winter. Too invasive for a small garden but an excellent shelter plant where there is enough room. Japan. Introduced 1889.
Zone 7 US, 8 Can. 🏆

Sasa ramosa

S. ramosa A dwarf, creeping species that quickly makes extensive mats of bright green foliage. The canes are 16 in–3½ ft (0.4–1.1 m) high, bright green at first but becoming deep olive green, and bear a solitary branch from each joint. The leaves are 2–6 in (5–15 cm) long by ½–¾ in (1–2 cm) wide and downy on both surfaces. It is too rampant for most gardens but makes an excellent ground cover where little else will grow, even in dense shade. Japan. Introduced 1892.
Zone 7 US, 8 Can.

Sasa veitchii

S. veitchii (Kumazasa, kuma bamboo) A small, dense species forming large clumps of deep purplish green, later purple, canes 2–4 ft (0.6–1.2 m) high. The leaves are 4–10 in (10–25 cm) long by 1–2½ in (2.5–6 cm) wide, withering and becoming pale straw-colored or whitish along the margins in fall and providing an attractive variegated effect that lasts throughout the winter. Invasive. Japan. Introduced 1880.
Zone 8 US, 9? Can.

Sassafras *Lauraceae*

A genus of three species of deciduous trees needing acidic soil and a slightly sheltered location.

S. albidum (Sassafras) A distinctive, aromatic, medium-sized, suckering tree. It is broadly conical and has zigzag branches that show up well in winter. The leaves vary in shape and may have one or two conspicuous lobes or none at all. They are dark green above, paler beneath, and change to red and orange-gold in fall. The flowers, which appear in late spring, are not very conspicuous, but the fruit stalk is bright red and stands out in late summer. The young growth is vulnerable to frost. E United States. Introduced 1633.
Zone 4 US, 5 Can.

Sassafras albidum

Saxegothaea *Podocarpaceae*

There is just one evergreen coniferous species in this genus, which was named after Albert of Saxe-Coburg-Gotha, prince consort of Queen Victoria.

S. conspicua (Prince Albert's yew) An unusual large shrub or small tree of loose habit, with laxly spreading branches

Saxegothaea conspicua

arranged in whorls of three or four and drooping branchlets. The linear leaves are up to $^3/_4$ in (2 cm) long, dark green, and marked with two blue bands beneath. They are rather twisted and are arranged on the lateral branches in two ranks. The fruits are up to $^3/_4$ in (2 cm) across, soft, and prickly. It will grow in any fertile, friable soil and does best in shade. Chile, Patagonia. Introduced 1847 by William Lobb.
Zone 8 US, 9? Can.

Schima *Theaceae*

A small genus of evergreen trees and shrubs that need acidic soil in a sheltered site. Now usually regarded as consisting of one variable species.

S. argentea A medium-sized to large, erect, bushy shrub with leaves that taper at both ends and are shiny dark green above and usually bloomy beneath. The fragrant cream flowers resemble small camellias, about $1^1/_2$ in (4 cm) wide, and are produced on the young wood in late summer. This distinctive member of the camellia family has reached 16 ft (5 m) at the Hillier Gardens and Arboretum in 40 years. China, Assam, Taiwan.
Zone 9 US

Schisandra *Schisandraceae*

A genus of some 25 species of evergreen and deciduous twining shrubs from Asia, with one species in North America. They bear clusters of flowers in the axils of the leaves, after which female plants bear long, pendulous spikes of attractive berries. They are suitable for growing on walls or fences or over shrubs and will grow well in any fertile, well-drained but moisture-retentive soil, preferably out of the hottest sun. Any pruning necessary for removing dead wood or for training should be done in late winter or early spring.

S. chinensis (Chinese magnolia vine) A medium-sized deciduous climber grown primarily for its bright red fruits in fall. The fragrant flowers are white to pink. China.
Zone 4 US, 5 Can.

S. grandiflora A medium-sized deciduous climber with fairly leathery, lanceolate leaves, 3–4 in (7.5–10 cm) long and with conspicuous veins. The flowers, $1–1^1/_4$ in (2.5–3 cm) across, are white or pale pink and are borne on drooping stalks in late spring and early summer. The berries are scarlet. Himalaya.
Zone 9 US

S. propinqua* var. *sinensis A medium-sized deciduous climber with short-stalked, orange flowers in late summer and fall. The leaves persist for a long time, and the berries are scarlet. China. Introduced 1907.
Zone 9? US, 9? Can.

Schisandra rubriflora

S. rubriflora A medium-sized deciduous climber closely related to *S. grandiflora* but with deep crimson flowers on pendulous stalks in late spring. The berries are scarlet. Himalayan region. Introduced 1908.
Zone 9 US

S. sphenanthera A vigorous, medium-sized deciduous climber with leaves broadest above the middle and flowers of a distinctive shade of orange-red, verging on terra-cotta, that are borne on slender stalks in late spring and early summer. The berries are scarlet. China. Introduced 1907 by Ernest Wilson.
Zone 7 US, 8 Can.

Schizophragma *Hydrangeaceae*

A genus of four species of deciduous ornamental climbers that support themselves by means of aerial roots. The small, creamy flowers are densely borne in large, flattened heads, each of which is attended by several large, cream, sterile flowers. They will grow in all types of soil and are suitable for shade, although they flower best in sun. While they eventually grow tall, they are slow starters and need a fair amount of encouragement in the early years. Some species are confused with Hydrangea anomala *subsp.* petiolaris.

Schizophragma hydrangeoides

S. hydrangeoides (Japanese hydrangea vine) A superb climber, to 30 ft (9 m). The leaves are toothed, and the flower heads are 8–10 in (20–25 cm) across with white or ivory bracts $1–1^1/_2$ in (2.5–4 cm) long. Japan.
Zone 4 US, 5 Can.

Schizophragma hydrangeoides 'Roseum'

***S. h.* 'Roseum'** A lovely form with rose-blushed bracts.
Zone 4 US, 5b Can.

S. integrifolium A climber that reaches 12 ft (3.5 m) and whose leaves are smooth edged or with just a few small, narrow teeth. The flower heads are often as much as 1 ft (30 cm) across, and the bracts can be $2^1/_2–3^1/_2$ in (6–9 cm) long. They are borne freely in midsummer. It is a magnificent species, larger in all its parts than *S. hy-*

Schizophragma integrifolium

drangeoides. C China. Introduced 1901 by Ernest Wilson.
Zone 7 US, 8 Can. 🏆

Sciadopitys *Taxodiaceae*

A genus of one evergreen coniferous species.

Sciadopitys verticillata

S. verticillata (Japanese umbrella pine) A slow-growing, hardy tree of medium size. It is dense and conical when young, usually with a single trunk, sometimes with several. The bark peels to reveal the reddish brown new bark. The branches are horizontal and bear lush clusters of rich, glossy green foliage. The apparently single linear leaves, up to 5 in (13 cm) long, are in fact fused pairs and are arranged in dense whorls like the spokes of an umbrella. The attractive cones, 2½–4 in (6–10 cm) long, are green at first and ripen to brown in the second year. Japan. Introduced 1861.
Zone 5 US, 6 Can. 🏆

Semiarundinaria *Gramineae*

A small genus of evergreen bamboos native to eastern Asia. They are moisture lovers but will grow in good soil over limestone.

Semiarundinaria fastuosa

S. fastuosa A hardy, vigorous, stiffly erect bamboo that forms tall, dense clumps of deep glossy green canes 14½–24 ft (4.5–7.5 m) high, which are useful as stakes. The leaves are 4–10 in (10–25 cm) long and up to 1 in (2.5 cm) wide. It is a distinctively handsome species that makes a good screen or tall hedge. Japan. Introduced 1892.
Zone 7 US, 8 Can. 🏆

Senecio *Compositae*

A very large genus of 1,500 or more species of annuals, perennials, shrubs, and climbers, widely distributed throughout the world. S. scandens *is the only climber generally available in cultivation. The shrubby members are mostly evergreen and bear heads or panicles of white or yellow daisy flowers in summer. They are all sun lovers and are excellent in coastal areas. However, with rare exceptions, the woody species will not tolerate low temperatures, although they resist wind well. Most of those listed below are from New Zealand.*

S. bidwillii A dwarf, evergreen, alpine shrub of compact, rigid habit that very slowly reaches 30 in (75 cm). The more or less elliptical leaves, up to 1 in (2.5 cm) long, are remarkably thick, shiny green above and covered beneath, like the stems, in a soft white or buff, woolly felt. The flowers are not very decorative. New Zealand.
Zone 9 US

S. compactus A small, compact evergreen shrub up to 3 ft (1 m) high, making a dense, broad mound. The oval leaves are up to 2 in (5 cm) long, wavy-edged, and white-felted beneath, as are the shoots and flower stalks. The flower heads are bright yellow. It is subject to injury in severe winters. See also *S.* Dunedin hybrids. North Island, New Zealand.
Zone 9 US

Senecio 'Drysdale'

***S.* 'Drysdale'** A small evergreen shrub similar to 'Sunshine' but with slightly larger flowers and scalloped leaves.
Zone 9? US

***S.* Dunedin hybrids** This name encompasses various hybrids and backcrosses that have occurred between *S. compactus*, *S. greyi*, and *S. laxifolius* and are now more commonly grown than any of the parents. The most frequently seen plant has been named

Senecio elaeagnifolius

'Sunshine'; it was previously grown as *S. greyi* and *S. laxifolius*, both of which are extremely rare in cultivation.
Zone 9 US

S. elaeagnifolius A medium-sized, rigid, dense evergreen shrub with oval, leathery leaves 3–6 in (7.5–15 cm) long. They are glossy above, and their undersides are thickly buff-felted, as are the young shoots and flower stalks. The flower heads are not very ornamental. It is an excellent coastal shrub. New Zealand.
Zone 9 US

S. greyi See *S.* 'Sunshine' and *S.* Dunedin hybrids.

Senecio heritieri

S. heritieri A small, loosely growing evergreen shrub with broad leaves 4–6 in (10–15 cm) long. The young stems and the leaf undersides are covered with a dense white felt. The flower heads are white and crimson with purple centers; are violet scented, recalling the popular cineraria; and are borne in large panicles from late spring to midsummer. It is suitable only for the mildest areas or the greenhouse. Tenerife. Introduced 1774.
Zone 10? US

S. laxifolius See *S.* 'Sunshine'.

***S.* 'Moira Read'** A small evergreen shrub similar to 'Sunshine' but whose leaves are blotched with creamy yellow.
Zone 9 US

S. monroi A small, dense shrub that often forms a broad dome, recognized by its oblong or oval, conspicuously undulate leaves. They are covered beneath with a dense white felt, as are the young shoots and

Senecio monroi

flower stalks. The yellow flower heads are in dense terminal clusters. New Zealand.
Zone 9 US 🏆

S. reinoldii (Muttonbird scrub) A medium-sized, dense, rounded evergreen shrub with thick, leathery, rounded leaves 2–5 in (5–13 cm) long, shining green above and felted below. The flowers are yellowish and not outstanding. It is nevertheless one of the best shrubs for coastal gardens in windy areas, as it tolerates sea spray. New Zealand.
Zone 9 US

Senecio reinoldii

S. scandens A fairly vigorous, semi-evergreen, semiwoody climber with stems up to 13 ft (4 m) long. The conspicuous small, bright yellow, short-rayed flower heads are produced in large panicles in autumn. It is best planted where it can scramble over bushes and into small, densely branched trees. It needs a sunny, sheltered site, and although it is frequently cut to the ground in winter, it will usually spring up again from the base. E Asia. Introduced 1895.
Zone 9 US

Senecio 'Sunshine'

***S.* 'Sunshine'** A gray shrub, making a mound up to 3 ft (1 m) high and 6½ ft (2 m) wide. The evergreen leaves are silvery gray when young and become green above. The flower heads are yellow and borne in large, dome-shaped clusters.
Zone 9 US

Senecio viravira

S. viravira (Argentine groundsel, dusty miller) A beautiful, lax, silvery white, medium-sized evergreen shrub with finely divided pinnate leaves. Its branches have a tendency to climb, and it can be grown against a wall, which also provides needed shelter. The flowers, borne in summer, are not ornamental, but it is grown for its striking foliage. Argentina. Introduced 1893.
Zone 9 US

Senna *Leguminosae*

A large genus of about 240 species of deciduous trees, shrubs, and herbs with a wide tropical and subtropical distribution. The leaves are evenly pinnate, and the pods produce the senna that is used medicinally. The following requires a warm, sheltered, sunny site or can be grown in a greenhouse.

Senna × floribunda

S. × floribunda A handsome, vigorous shrub whose leaves have 4–5 pairs of leaflets. The large flowers are a rich, deep yellow and are borne in terminal clusters in late summer and fall. It is widely naturalized in warm parts of the world. In cultivation c. 1800. Australia.
Zone 10? US

Sequoia *Taxodiaceae*
Redwood

A genus of one evergreen coniferous species.

S. sempervirens (Redwood, California redwood) A very large, narrow tree, over 350 ft (105 m) high and 28 ft (8.5 m) in diameter in its native forest but usually up to 100 ft (30 m) tall and 20 ft (6 m) wide in gardens. It has a thick, fibrous, reddish brown outer bark that is soft and spongy. The branches are slightly drooping, yew-like, and bear linear-oblong leaves in two ranks. It needs full sun and prefers a deep, well-drained, acid to neutral soil but will grow in an alkaline one if there is good soil depth. At the southern end of its native range, where it is dry, it depends on coastal

Sequoia sempervirens

fog for moisture, and it grows best in moist, cool areas. It needs deep, regular watering. The redwood is one of the longest-lived trees, one specimen having been dated 2,200 years old. N California to S Oregon.
Zone 7 US, 7b Can. 🏆

***S. s.* 'Adpressa'**, syn. *S. s.* 'Albospica' The tips of the young shoots are cream. It is

Sequoia sempervirens 'Adpressa'

Sequoia sempervirens 'Prostrata'

often grown as a dwarf shrub, but it will eventually make a large tree unless it is cut back frequently.
Zone 7 US, 8 Can.

***S. s.* 'Albospica'** See *S. s.* 'Adpressa'.

***S. s.* 'Prostrata'** A remarkable dwarf form with spreading branches that are thickly covered with comparatively broad, glaucous green, two-ranked leaves.
Zone 7 US, 8 Can.

Sequoiadendron *Taxodiaceae*

A genus of one evergreen coniferous species.

Sequoiadendron giganteum

S. giganteum (Giant sequoia, giant redwood) A very large tree that grows on the western slopes of the Sierra Nevada at altitudes of 4300–8000 ft (1310–2440 m). It reaches over 300 ft (91 m) tall and 30 ft (9 m) in diameter. It has the largest trunk girth of any conifer; the 'General Sherman' tree in Sequoia National Park, at 275 ft

(84 m) tall, has a girth of 82 ft (25 m). The giant sequoia has deeply furrowed, reddish brown outer bark, similar to that of *Sequoia sempervirens*. When young it is densely branched and conical; later the branches are more widely spaced and conspicuously downswept. Sometimes the trunk is clear of branches for a considerable distance from the ground. The leaves, which persist for up to four years, are awl shaped, up to 1/2 in (12 mm) long, and spirally arranged. It needs full sun and a deep, well-drained soil; it should be watered deeply in dry spells. It grows 2–3 ft (60–90 cm) per year. The oldest documented felled specimen was about 3,200 years old, making the giant sequoia among the oldest living trees. C California.
Zone 6 US, 6b Can. 🏆

***S. g.* 'Glaucum'** A narrowly conical large tree with bluish-green foliage.
Zone 6 US, 6b Can.

Sequoiadendron giganteum 'Pendulum'

***S. g.* 'Pendulum'** A tree with a unique appearance, sometimes assuming fantastic shapes, but usually forming a tall, narrow column with long branches hanging almost parallel to the trunk.
Zone 6 US, 6b Can.

Shepherdia *Elaeagnaceae*

A genus of three evergreen or deciduous shrubs from North America. Good for windbreaks and land reclamation, they are tolerant of dry soils high in salts.

S. argentea (Silver buffaloberry) A large shrub or small tree that has small thorns on the tips of its silvery branches. The deciduous leaves are silvery on both surfaces, and the entire plant appears gray from a distance. Flowers are small and yellow, while the berrylike, sour but edible fruits are orange-red with silvery scales. It can be sheared to form a hedge. Manitoba to Nevada. Introduced 1759.
Zone 2 US, 2 Can.

Sinarundinaria *Gramineae*

A genus of some 50 evergreen bamboos, natives of China and the Himalaya. They are moisture lovers but will grow in good soil over limestone.

S. anceps See *Yushania anceps*.

Sinarundinaria nitida

S. nitida, syn. *Arundinaria nitida* This beautiful, clump-forming species is often confused with *Thamnocalamus spathaceus* but has purple-flushed canes and narrower leaves. It is one of the most elegant and ornamental bamboos, with canes 10–13 ft (3–4 m) high or more, arching at the summits under the weight of foliage. The thin, delicate leaves are 2–3 in (5–8 cm) long by 1/4–1/2 in (6–12 mm) wide. It does best in light shade and makes an excellent specimen plant. It can also be grown in a container. China. In cultivation 1889.
Zone 4 US, 5 Can. 🏆

Sinocalycanthus *Calycanthaceae*

A genus of one deciduous species closely related to Calycanthus *and originally included in it.*

S. chinensis A shrub reaching about 10 ft (3 m) in height, with leaves up to 6 in (15 cm) long and glossy green, turning yellow in autumn. The nodding flowers, 2 3/4 in (7 cm) across, are borne singly at the ends of the shoots in early summer. They are composed of two whorls of about 10 tepals, the outer ones white, sometimes flushed pink, and the inner ones smaller, pale yellow, and white at the base with maroon markings. E China. Introduced 1983.
Zone 6? US, 7? Can.

Skimmia *Rutaceae*

A genus of four species of slow-growing, aromatic, evergreen shrubs or trees, natives of the Himalaya and East Asia. All those listed below, with the exception of S. japonica *subsp.* reevesiana, *bear male and female flowers on separate plants, and both sexes must be planted if the brightly colored berries, which persist throughout the winter, are to be produced. They are tolerant of shade and industrial pollution and are ideal for coastal locations. They prefer a moist, acidic soil amended with organic matter.*

S. anquetilia A small shrub that has previously been distributed as *S. laureola* female; the true *S. laureola* has been introduced but is rare in cultivation. *S. anquetilia* has pungently aromatic leaves, greenish yellow flowers, and bright red fruits; the true *S. laureola* is small and creeping, with cream or greenish white flowers and black berries. Himalaya. Introduced 1841.
Zone 9 US

***S.* × *confusa* 'Kew Green'** A small, mound-forming male shrub with broad

Skimmia × confusa 'Kew Green'

leaves. It has very large clusters of fragrant, creamy blooms and is the best of the genus for flowers.
Zone 6? US, 7? Can. 🏆

S. japonica (Japanese skimmia) A variable, small, densely branched, dome-shaped shrub with leathery leaves and dense terminal panicles of yellowish white, often fragrant flowers in mid- to late spring. On female plants they are followed by clusters of globular, bright red fruits. It is adaptable and will grow in alkaline or acid soil. The following forms are recommended.
Zone 6 US, 7 Can.

Skimmia japonica 'Fragrans'

***S. j.* 'Fragrans'** A free-flowering male clone bearing dense panicles of white flowers with a scent of lily-of-the-valley.
Zone 6 US, 7 Can. 🏆

***S. j.* 'Fructu-albo'** A rather weak, low-growing, compact female clone with small leaves and white flowers.
Zone 6 US, 7 Can.

Skimmia japonica 'Nymans'

***S. j.* 'Nymans'** An extremely free-fruiting form with comparatively large fruits.
Zone 6 US, 7 Can. 🏆

***S. j.* 'Red Riding Hood'** A dwarf, mound-forming shrub with small leaves. It is a female with red berries.
Zone 6 US, 7 Can.

Skimmia japonica subsp. *reevesiana* 'Robert Fortune'

***S. j.* subsp. *reevesiana* 'Robert Fortune'** This name applies to the commonly grown clone deriving from the original introduction. It is a dwarf shrub, rarely reaching the height of 3 ft (1 m), and forms a low, compact mound. The leaves are narrowly elliptic, often with a pale margin. The flowers are hermaphrodite, white, and in short terminal panicles in late spring. The matte, bright red berries are egg shaped and last throughout the winter and usually until the flowers appear again in spring. Unlike other forms of *S. japonica*, this plant will not grow well in alkaline soils. S China, SE Asia. Introduced 1849.
Zone 6 US, 7b Can. 🏆

***S. j.* 'Rogersii'** A dense, dwarf, slow-growing female with curved or twisted leaves and large red fruits.
Zone 6 US, 7 Can.

***S. j.* 'Rogersii Nana'** A free-flowering male clone, similar to 'Rogersii' but even dwarfer, slower growing, and with smaller leaves.
Zone 6 US, 7 Can.

Skimmia japonica 'Rubella'

***S. j.* 'Rubella'** A small male shrub with large, open panicles of red buds throughout the winter, opening in early spring into white, yellow-anthered flowers. It is especially valued in the winter garden.
Zone 6 US, 7 Can. 🏆

***S. j.* 'Ruby King'** A small male shrub with narrow, taper-pointed, dark green leaves and large, conical panicles of flowers from deep red buds.
Zone 6 US, 7 Can.

***S. j.* 'Veitchii'** A vigorous female clone with distinctly broad leaves and large bunches of brilliant orange-red fruits. It is usually grown as 'Foremanii'.
Zone 6 US, 7 Can.

Smilax *Smilacaceae*

A large genus of 200 or more species of evergreen and deciduous plants, the majority of them climbing. Their often prickly stems are tough and wiry, and they support themselves by means of tendrils. They are usually grown for their rich, often glossy, green foliage; the flowers are generally not conspicuous. They will grow in sun or shade in any ordinary soil, and some species can become invasive.

S. china A deciduous shrub with rounded, prickly, scrambling stems. The leaves are variable, usually roundish ovate with a heart-shaped base, often turning red in autumn. Greenish yellow flowers are borne in late spring, followed by bright red fruits. China, Japan, Korea. Introduced 1759.
Zone 8 US, 9? Can.

Solanum *Solanaceae*

A very large genus of about 1,500 species, mainly herbaceous plants but also encompassing some semievergreen or deciduous climbers, shrubs, and subshrubs, widely distributed throughout the world and including several, such as the potato (S. tuberosum), *that are economically important. The climbing members of the genus are excellent specimens for mild-climate gardens. They need full sun but adapt to most soils.*

***S. crispum* 'Glasnevin'** A vigorous, semievergreen climber with scrambling, normally herbaceous stems up to 20 ft (6 m) long. The flowers are very slightly fragrant, a little more than 1 in (2.5 cm) across, and similar to those of a potato but rich purple-blue with a bright yellow beak of stamens. They are borne very freely in loose clusters over a long season from midsummer well into fall. It is beautiful when trained on a wall or allowed to scramble over a fence or shed. It will take slightly cooler temperatures than *S. jasminoides*.
Zone 9 US 🏆

Solanum jasminoides 'Album'

***S. jasminoides* 'Album'** A fast-growing semievergreen climber with twining stems up to 30 ft (9 m) long in mild areas. The flowers are $^{3}/_{4}$ in (2 cm) across, white with a staminal beak, and profusely borne in loose clusters from midsummer until late fall. It benefits from the protection of a sunny wall.
Zone 9 US 🏆

Solanum laciniatum

S. laciniatum (Kangaroo apple) A beautiful deciduous subshrub with purple stems up to $6^{1}/_{2}$ ft (2 m) high. The leaves are lance shaped and deeply cut into irregular lobes. The very attractive flowers, violet with a yellow beak, are borne in loose clusters during summer. They are followed by small, egg-shaped fruits that change from green to

Solanum crispum 'Glasnevin'

yellow. It is a vigorous species for mild areas, where it sometimes seeds itself, or it can be grown in the greenhouse. The plant is poisonous. Australia.
Zone 9 US

Sollya *Pittosporaceae*

A genus of three species of beautiful evergreen climbers from southwest Australia suitable only for the mildest locations or the greenhouse. They require a sunny, sheltered location and well-drained soil.

S. heterophylla A beautiful plant with slender stems up to 6½ ft (2 m) or more. The leaves are usually ovate to lanceolate, 1–2 in (2.5–5 cm) long. Nodding clusters of sky blue flowers are freely borne during summer and fall. Introduced 1830.
Zone 10 US

Sophora *Leguminosae*

A genus of about 80 species of evergreen and deciduous trees, shrubs, and herbaceous perennials. The following are valued for their elegant pinnate leaves and bright floral display. They prefer full sun and a well-drained loam, either acid or slightly alkaline.

Sophora davidii

S. davidii A medium-sized to large deciduous shrub with gray-downy, later spiny, branches. The leaves have 7–10 pairs of leaflets, and the small, bluish white pea flowers are borne in short, terminal clusters in early summer. China. Introduced 1897.
Zone 5 US, 6 Can.

Sophora japonica

S. japonica (Japanese pagoda tree) A medium-sized to large, usually rounded deciduous tree with leaves up to 1 ft (30 cm) long, composed of 9–15 leaflets. The creamy pea flowers are in large, loose terminal clusters in late summer and fall but are not borne on young trees. China. Introduced 1753.
Zone 4 US, 5b Can. 🏆

***S. j.* 'Pendula'** A picturesque small weeping tree with stiffly drooping branchlets. It is an admirable lawn specimen and also forms a natural arbor.
Zone 4 US, 5b Can.

***S. j.* 'Regent'** A vigorous medium-sized shrub with glossy dark green leaves that flowers at a relatively early age.
Zone 4 US, 5 Can.

Sophora microphylla 'Sun King'

***S. microphylla* 'Sun King'** Although the species is a large, arching evergreen shrub, this is a bushier and somewhat more cold-tolerant form with small, pinnate leaves and elongated, large, bright yellow flowers that appear in early to late spring. At the Hillier Gardens and Arboretum in southern England, it has survived several cold winters in exposed locations.
Zone 9? US

S. prostrata A small evergreen shrub, occasionally prostrate in habit but usually forming a broad, rounded mound of wiry, interlacing stems. The leaves have between 6 and 8 pairs of tiny leaflets. The small, brownish yellow to orange pea flowers are borne singly or in clusters of 2–3 in late spring. New Zealand.
Zone 8 US, 9? Can.

Sophora tetraptera

S. tetraptera (Kowhai, New Zealand sophora) An evergreen large shrub or small tree with spreading or drooping branches covered with a yellow down when young; the leaves have 10–20 pairs of leaflets. The flowers are pea shaped but somewhat tubular, bright yellow, up to 2 in (5 cm) long,

and in drooping clusters in late spring. The seedpods look like rows of beads. New Zealand. Introduced 1772.
Zone 9 US 🏆

***S. t.* 'Grandiflora'** A form with large leaflets and slightly larger flowers.
Zone 9 US

Sorbaria *Rosaceae*

A genus of four to five handsome, vigorous deciduous shrubs with elegant pinnate leaves that distinguish the genus from Spiraea. *They have white or creamy flowers in terminal panicles during summer and early fall, and their brownish or reddish stems and seed heads are attractive even in winter. They thrive in moist, rich soil in full sun or part shade. The old flowering stems can be pruned hard in late winter or early spring to encourage strong, vigorous shoots.*

S. aitchisonii (Kashmir false spirea) An elegant medium-sized shrub with long, spreading branches that are reddish when young. The leaves have 11–23 sharply toothed and tapered leaflets, and the creamy flowers are borne in large, conical panicles in mid- to late summer. Afghanistan. Introduced 1895.
Zone 5 US, 6 Can. 🏆

S. arborea, syn. *S. kirilowii* A large, robust shrub with strong, spreading, arching stems and large leaves composed of 13–17 lance-shaped, slender-pointed leaflets that are downy beneath. The white flowers are borne in large, conical panicles at the ends of the current year's growth in mid- to late summer. C and W China. Introduced 1908.
Zone 5 US, 6 Can.

S. kirilowii See *S. arborea.*

Sorbaria arborea

Sorbaria aitchisonii

Sorbaria sorbifolia

S. sorbifolia (Ural false spirea) A small to medium-sized, suckering shrub with erect stems and leaves made up of 13–25 sharply pointed leaflets. The flowers are borne in narrow, erect panicles in mid- to late summer. N Asia. Introduced 1759.
Zone 2 US, 2 Can.

Sorbaria tomentosa

S. tomentosa (Lindley false spirea) A large, strong, spreading shrub bearing large leaves composed of 11–23 deeply toothed leaflets and yellowish white flowers. Himalaya.
Zone 8 US, 9 Can.

SORBUS

Rosaceae Mountain ash

NO MATTER what the size of your garden, it is a good practice to include at least a few shrubs and trees that provide interest in more than one season; this is especially true in small gardens, where every inch of space counts. *Sorbus* is one genus that provides ornamental features throughout the year — and does so without needing much care.

The genus includes about 100 deciduous trees and shrubs that are distributed throughout the Northern Hemisphere, and there are basically two distinct types of plants. The first type is the mountain ash, which is also the common name for *Sorbus*. These plants, such as *S. cashmiriana* and *S. vilmorinii,* have pinnate leaves with numerous leaflets, which give them a fern-like appearance when they are in leaf; in fall the leaves turn yellow and reddish. They bear clusters of attractive off-white flowers in spring, which are succeeded by berries that are most commonly bright red but may also be pink, orange, yellow, or white. The berries are often colorful by late summer and, if not eaten by birds, remain on the trees well into late fall or even winter. The one drawback of this type, however, is that it is very susceptible to fireblight.

Sorbus vilmorinii

The second type is known as the white-beam. These plants, including *S. intermedia* and *S. latifolia,* are quite different from those of the first type in that they have simple rather than pinnate leaves. These are usually toothed and sometimes lobed and are typically silvery or white on their undersides — a characteristic that gives the type its common name and also provides a lovely display when the foliage is stirred in a breeze. While the whitebeams are not as spectacular when in fruit, the bunches of red to brown fruits are attractive, and the fall foliage color ranges from eye-catching to dramatic. Whitebeams generally tolerate alkaline soil well and succeed in coastal locations, but they will suffer in areas with air pollution.

CARE AND CULTIVATION

Sorbus is easy to grow in any good, fertile, well-drained, slightly acidic soil and needs full sun, although the plants do not like intense summer heat. They should be mulched well and watered deeply during dry spells. When necessary, pruning should be done in late winter or early spring.

Like many other genera in the Rosaceae family, mountain ashes are susceptible to fireblight, whose symptoms include shriveled flowers and leaves and shoots that die back, possibly exuding a slime. The only solution is to dig out and dispose of the affected plant.

Any dead wood should be cut out as soon as possible, as coral-spot fungus can enter and spread quickly to healthy parts of the plant. Plants can also be infested with the larvae of the mountain ash sawfly, which cause defoliation; this pest can be controlled with insecticide.

S. alnifolia (Korean mountain ash) A small to medium-sized tree with attractive, smooth, gray bark and a dense, oval or round head of purplish brown branches. The lustrous green leaves are oval, strongly veined, and double-toothed, like those of a hornbeam, and turn scarlet or orange-brown in fall. It blooms in spring with flat clusters of white flowers and bears small, oval fruits that are bright orange to red. Japan, Korea, China. Introduced 1892.
Zone 3 US, 4 Can.

Sorbus aria

S. aria (Whitebeam) A small to medium-sized tree, with a somewhat rounded head of branches and clusters of creamy white flowers. The more or less oval leaves are grayish white at first, later bright green above but vividly silver-white beneath, and turn gold and russet in fall. The bunches of brown-speckled crimson fruits ripen in fall and are very attractive to birds. It grows well in limestone soils. The following forms are recommended. Europe.
Zone 3 US, 4 Can.

***S. a.* 'Chrysophylla'** A form whose leaves are yellowish throughout summer and are particularly effective in late spring. They become rich butter yellow in fall.
Zone 3 US, 4 Can.

***S. a.* 'Decaisneana'** See *S. a.* 'Majestica'.

***S. a.* 'Lutescens'** A form whose leaves are covered with a dense, creamy felt on the upper surfaces when young and turn gray-green by late summer. It is an outstanding tree in spring.
Zone 3 US, 4 Can. 🏆

***S. a.* 'Magnifica'** An upright tree with

Sorbus aria 'Chrysophylla'

Sorbus aria 'Lutescens'

Sorbus aria 'Majestica'

large, glossy green leaves and large clusters of red fruits.
Zone 3 US, 4 Can.

***S. a.* 'Majestica'**, syn. *S. a.* 'Decaisneana' (Majestic whitebeam) A handsome tree with larger, elliptic leaves that are 4–6 in (10–15 cm) long and larger fruits.
Zone 3 US, 4 Can. 🏆

Sorbus aucuparia

S. aucuparia (European mountain ash, rowan) A medium-sized tree whose leaves have 11–19 sharply toothed leaflets. The round fruits, which are bright orange-red and carried in large, dense bunches in late summer and fall, are very attractive to birds. It prefers well-drained acid to very acid soil and will not tolerate shallow, alkaline soil. Europe; cultivated in the United States since at least the 18th century.
Zone 3 US, 3 Can.

***S. a.* 'Aspleniifolia'**, syn. *S. a.* 'Laciniata' An elegant tree with deeply cut and toothed leaflets that give the leaves a fernlike effect.
Zone 3 US, 3 Can.

***S. a.* 'Beissneri'** A graceful tree with a

Sorbus aucuparia 'Beissneri'

dense head of erect branches. The young shoots and sometimes the leaf stalks are dark coral-red. The leaves are yellowish green, particularly when young, and the leaflets vary in shape, many having an attractive, fernlike appearance. Mature

bark is a warm copper or russet. In cultivation 1899.
Zone 3 US, 3 Can.

S. a. 'Cardinal Royal' An upright tree with a profusion of bright red berries. Introduced by Michigan State University.
Zone 4 US, 5 Can.

Sorbus aucuparia 'Edulis'

S. a. 'Edulis' A vigorous tree with larger leaves and broader, longer leaflets than the species. Its edible fruits are also larger and are carried in heavier bunches. Originated c. 1800.
Zone 3 US, 4 Can.

Sorbus aucuparia 'Fastigiata'

S. a. 'Fastigiata' A remarkable, slow-growing, columnar shrub or small tree that grows to about 16 ft (5 m), with stout, closely erect stems. The leaves are large and have 11–15 dark green leaflets. The large, red fruits are held in densely packed bunches.
Zone 3 US, 4 Can.

S. a. 'Laciniata' See *S. a.* 'Aspleniifolia'.

S. a. 'Pendula' (Weeping European mountain ash) In time this forms a small tree wider than it is tall. The pendulous branches are covered with fruit in fall.
Zone 3 US, 3 Can.

S. a. 'Rossica' (Russian mountain ash) A form whose leaves are entire below; it is not as susceptible to fireblight.
Zone 3 US, 3 Can.

Sorbus cashmiriana

S. cashmiriana (Kashmir mountain ash) A vigorous, small, open tree whose leaves have 17–19 strongly serrated leaflets. The buds are soft pink and open tinged with pink in late spring. The fruits are gleaming white with a pink tinge, 1/2 in (12 mm) across, and held on pink or red stalks in loose, drooping clusters that persist long after the leaves have fallen. Kashmir. In cultivation 1934.
Zone 4 US, 5 Can. 🏆

S. 'Chinese Lace' A small, upright tree whose leaves have deeply cut and divided leaflets that give a lacy effect. They turn purple in fall. The fruits are dark red.
Zone 4 US, 5 Can.

S. commixta (Japanese mountain ash) A small, variable tree that is columnar when young and broadens a little at maturity. Its leaves have 11–15 slender-pointed, serrated leaflets that are coppery when young, become glossy green, and then turn vivid yellow and red in fall. A good tree for group planting. Japan, Korea. In cultivation 1880.
Zone 5 US, 6 Can.

S. decora (Showy mountain ash) Perhaps the best North American species, this is a

Sorbus commixta

small, shrubby tree with large, showy fruits that persist well into winter. It is fairly resistant to fireblight. NE North America.
Zone 2 US, 2 Can.

S. discolor (Snowberry mountain ash) A small tree with round, white fruits that may be tinged yellow or pink in fall. N China.
Zone 5 US, 6 Can.

S. domestica (Service tree) A medium-sized tree with open, spreading branches; rough, scaly bark; and sticky winter buds. The pinnate leaves are composed of 13–21 leaflets and turn orange-red or yellow in fall; the pear- or apple-shaped fruits are 1–1 1/4 in (2.5–3 cm) long and green tinged with red. S and E Europe. Long cultivated.
Zone 6 US, 7 Can.

Sorbus 'Eastern Promise'

S. 'Eastern Promise' A small, oval-headed, upright tree. Its pinnate leaves have 15–19 leaflets that are dark green and arise from a reddish main axis. In fall they turn purple and then fiery orange. The

deep rose-pink fruits are borne in dense, hanging clusters that weigh down the branches.
Zone 4 US, 5 Can.

Sorbus 'Ethel's Gold'

***S.* 'Ethel's Gold'** A small tree with bright green, sharply serrated leaflets and bunches of golden amber fruits that persist into winter if not eaten by birds. Originated before 1959 at Hillier Nurseries.
Zone 4 US, 5 Can.

S. folgneri (Folgner mountain ash) A graceful, variable small tree, usually with spreading or arching branches. The leaves are oval or narrowly oval, double-toothed, dark green above, and white or gray-felted beneath; they usually turn color in fall. The dark red or purplish red fruits are variable in size and shape and are borne in drooping clusters. It is not troubled by spider mites, as other species sometimes are. C China. Introduced 1901.
Zone 3 US, 3 Can.

***S. f.* 'Lemon Drop'** A small tree with glossy, bright yellow fruits. Originated before 1950 at Hillier Nurseries.
Zone 4 US, 4b Can.

***S.* 'Ghose'** A small, upright tree. The large leaves have 15–19 sharply serrated leaflets and are dark matte green above, glaucous beneath, and rusty pubescent. The fruits are rose-red, small, and held in large, dense bunches that are persistent. Himalaya. Introduced by Hillier Nurseries.
Zone 6? US, 7? Can.

***S.* 'Golden Wonder'** A small, upright tree. Its leaves have 13–15 deep blue-green, sharply toothed leaflets that turn yellow and red in autumn. Golden yellow fruits are borne in large clusters in late summer and early fall.
Zone 4 US, 5 Can.

S. harrowiana A remarkable and distinctive large shrub or small tree with stout, ascending branches. The leaves are 8–12 in (20–30 cm) long and have 2–4 pairs of stalkless leaflets and a long-stalked terminal leaflet; the leaflets are 6–7 in (15–18 cm) long and up to 2 in (5 cm) wide. The small, dull white flowers are borne in large, flattened corymbs and are followed by equally small, pink or pearly white fruits. China. Trees raised from seed collected by George Forrest in 1912 proved very tender and died in mild winters. Conversely, trees from another collection made later survived harsher winters unharmed. Obviously, the provenance of the seed has a large influence on hardiness, and a zone rating cannot be given at this time.

Sorbus × *hostii*

S.* × *hostii A large shrub or small tree. The leaves are more or less oval, sharply toothed, green above, and gray-downy beneath. The pale pink flowers are followed by early-ripening, bright red fruits. Europe. In cultivation 1820.
Zone 5 US, 6 Can.

S. hupehensis A small but vigorous tree that develops a bold, compact head of ascending, purple-brown branches. The leaves, which have 11–17 leaflets, are large, distinctively blue-green above and downy-white beneath, and easily recognizable from a distance. The fruits are white or sometimes tinged with pink and are borne

Sorbus hupehensis

in loose, drooping bunches that persist into late winter. The leaves turn a beautiful red in fall. W China (Hupeh). Introduced 1910 by Ernest Wilson.
Zone 5 US, 6 Can. 🏆

Sorbus hupehensis var. *obtusa*

S. h.* var. *obtusa An attractive form with pink fruits and leaves that usually have 11 leaflets. Various selections have been made and named, including 'Pink Pagoda', 'Rosea', and 'Rufus'; they all have pink fruits and can be difficult to distinguish from the type.
Zone 5 US, 6 Can. 🏆

***S. hybrida* 'Gibbsii'** A small tree, to about 23 ft (7 m), with broad, ovate leaves that are divided at the base into 1–2 pairs of long leaflets and have a widely rounded apex. They are green above and gray-woolly below. The spherical, coral-red fruits are ½ in (12 mm) or a little more across and held in large clusters.
Zone 5 US, 6 Can. 🏆

Sorbus hybrida 'Gibbsii'

S. insignis A magnificent small tree that needs a reasonably sheltered site. It has stout, stiffly ascending branches and pinnate leaves, up to 10 in (25 cm) long, composed of 11–15 leaflets. The leaves stay on the tree for a long period and turn red in early winter. The small, oval, pink fruits are borne in large heads and persist into the early part of spring; they seem to hold little attraction for birds. Himalayan region. Introduced 1928.
Zone 9? US

Sorbus intermedia

S. intermedia (Swedish whitebeam) A small to medium-sized tree with a dense, usually rounded head of branches and leaves lobed in the lower half, coarsely toothed beyond, dark green and glossy above, and gray-woolly beneath. The orange-red fruits are ½ in (12 mm) wide and held in bunches. The following form is recommended. N Europe.
Zone 3 US, 4 Can.

***S. i.* 'Brouwers'** A selected form with ascending branches making an oval crown.
Zone 3 US, 4 Can. 🏆

Sorbus 'Joseph Rock'

***S.* 'Joseph Rock'** An outstanding small tree that has an erect head of branches. Its leaves have 15–19 leaflets that turn red, orange, copper, and purple in fall. The clusters of round fruits are creamy yellow at first and deepen to amber-yellow, remaining on the branches well after leaf drop. Unfortunately, it is very susceptible to fireblight. Although its origin remains a mystery, it could possibly be a form of a variable Chinese species.
Zone 4 US, 5 Can. 🏆

Sorbus × *kewensis*

S.* × *kewensis A first-class, free-fruiting small tree. The orange-red fruits are in large, heavy bunches and make for an attractive display in fall. Raised at Kew Gardens, England.
Zone 4? US, 5? Can. 🏆

Sorbus koehniana

S. koehniana A medium-sized shrub or small, elegant tree. Its leaves have 17–33 narrow, toothed leaflets, and the small, round, porcelain white fruits are held in slender, drooping clusters on red stalks. It is best grown as a shrub. C China. Introduced 1910 by Ernest Wilson.
Zone 4 US, 5 Can. 🏆

Sorbus latifolia

S. latifolia A small to medium-sized tree with downy young shoots and shaggy, peeling bark. The leaves are ovate or broadly elliptic, sharply lobed, glossy green above, and yellow felted beneath. The fruits are globular and russet-yellow with large, brownish speckles. Portugal to Germany.
Zone 5 US, 6 Can.

***S.* 'Leonard Messel'** A rather neglected form, this makes a splendid small tree with upright branches that form a dense, oval crown. The large leaves, which usually have 9–11 blue-green leaflets on a pink rachis, turn red and purple in fall. The distinctive,

Sorbus 'Leonard Messel'

bright pink fruits are borne in broad, hanging clusters. Raised 1949 by Col. L. C. R. Messel.

Zone 5? US, 6? Can.

S. megalocarpa A remarkable large shrub with large, more or less oval leaves that sometimes turn crimson in fall. The large flower buds open before the leaves in spring and form large, domed heads of cream flowers. The flowers should not be cut for decoration, as their smell is unpleasant. The fruits are large, about 1 in (2.5 cm) across, but are brown and not particularly attractive. W China. Introduced 1903 by Ernest Wilson.

Zone 6 US, 7 Can.

***S.* 'Pearly King'** A small tree with fernlike leaves consisting of 13–17 narrow, sharply toothed leaflets. The fruits are 5/8 in (15 mm) across and are rose, changing to white with a pink flush; they are held in large, loose, pendulous bunches. It is a hybrid of *S. vilmorinii*. Originated at Hillier Nurseries.

Zone 5 US, 6 Can.

S. reducta An unusual dwarf to small, suckering shrub that forms clumps of slender, erect stems 2–3 ft (60–90 cm) high. The leaves have red stalks and 13–15 leaflets that turn bronze and reddish purple in fall. The fruits are globular and white, flushed with rose. Some plants under this name are similar in leaf and fruit but grow on a single stem and do not sucker. China, N Myanmar. Introduced 1943.

Zone 4 US, 4b Can. 🏆

S. sargentiana (Sargent mountain ash) A magnificent species that slowly develops into a tree up to 30 ft (9 m) high and as much across with white-woolly young shoots and hairy flower clusters. The leaves are large and attractive, up to 1 ft (30 cm) long, and are composed of 7–11 slender-pointed leaflets, each 3–5 in (7.5–13 cm) long. The small, scarlet fruits are in large, rounded heads up to 6 in (15 cm) across and ripen late. The foliage turns a rich red in fall. The winter buds are large, sticky, and crimson. W China. Introduced 1908 by Ernest Wilson.

Sorbus reducta

Sorbus sargentiana

Zone 6? US, 7? Can. 🏆

***S.* 'Savill Orange'** A small tree with dense clusters of large, orange-red berries. It is a seedling of *S. aucuparia* 'Fructu-luteo'. Originated c. 1970 in the Valley Gardens, Windsor Great Park.

Zone 4 US, 4b Can.

S. scalaris A small tree with wide-spreading branches and neat, frondlike leaves composed of 21–33 narrow leaflets that turn red and purple in late fall. The fruits are small, red, and densely packed in flattened heads. China. Introduced 1904 by Ernest Wilson.

Sorbus scalaris

Zone 4 US, 4b Can. 🏆

S. serotina An upright, small tree somewhat like *S. decora* but with 13 leaflets, rather than 11–17. Foliage is dark green above and gray-green beneath, turns reddish brown in fall, and persists into winter. Japan. Introduced 1900.

Zone 3 US, 3b Can.

***S. a.* 'Sheerwater Seedling'** A vigorous, upright, small tree with a compact, egg-shaped head of ascending branches and large clusters of orange-red fruits.

Zone 3 US, 4 Can. 🏆

Sorbus 'Sunshine'

***S.* 'Sunshine'** A small tree, erect when young. The leaves have 7–8 pairs of leaflets, and the golden yellow fruits, held in large clusters, color before those of 'Joseph Rock', of which it is a seedling. Raised 1968 at Hillier Nurseries.

Zone 4? US, 5? Can.

***S. thibetica* 'John Mitchell'** This is a handsome, medium-sized to large tree that eventually develops a broad, rounded head. The mature leaves are large, about 6 in (15 cm) long and as much across. They are glossy dark green above and white-felted beneath. The fruit is gold to red and is borne in bunches.
Zone 5? US, 6? Can. 🏆

Sorbus × *thuringiaca* 'Fastigiata'

***S.* × *thuringiaca* 'Fastigiata'** A distinctive small tree with an egg-shaped head of closely packed, ascending branches. The leaves are narrow, divided at the base into 1–3 pairs of leaflets, dull green above and gray-felted below. The fruits are scarlet with a few brown flecks.
Zone 4 US, 5 Can.

Sorbus torminalis bark

S. torminalis (Chequer tree, wild service tree) An attractive medium-sized tree with ascending branches. The leaves are maple-like, ovate, sharply and conspicuously lobed, and glossy dark green above, turning bronze-yellow in fall. The fruits are elongated and russet-brown. Europe, Asia Minor, N Africa.
Zone 6 US, 7 Can.

S. ursina A distinctive, small, erect tree with stout, ascending branches and red buds. The leaves have 15–21 net-veined leaflets, and the fruits are white or pink-tinted and in dense bunches. Himalaya. Introduced 1950 by Col. Donald Lowndes.
Zone 6 US, 7 Can.

S. vestita (Himalayan whitebeam) A medium-sized tree, erect when young and spreading when older. The leaves are 6–10 in (15–25 cm) long, green above and silvery white or buff beneath. The fruits are green, speckled and flushed with warm brown, and resemble small crab apples or pears. A magnificent species with bold foliage and one of the handsomest of all hardy trees. Himalaya. Introduced 1820.
Zone 6? US, 7? Can.

S. vilmorinii (Vilmorin mountain ash) A beautiful medium-sized shrub or small tree.

Sorbus vilmorinii

The fernlike leaves, often in clusters, are composed of 11–31 small leaflets that turn red and purple in fall. The loose, drooping clusters of fruits are rose-red at first, gradually passing through shades of pink to white, flushed with light rose. It is a charming species, very suitable for a small garden. W China. Introduced 1889 by the Abbé Delavay. *(See also photo on p.577.)*
Zone 3 US, 3 Can. 🏆

S. wardii A rare tree with stiff, erect branches that give it a columnar habit. The elliptic to obovate leaves are green and ribbed above, thinly hairy beneath; young leaves are gray-downy. The globular fruits, borne in loose corymbs, are amber speckled with grayish brown. A specimen at the Hillier Gardens and Aboretum is growing vigorously and is over 30 ft (9 m) high. It is a beautiful silvery whitebeam for small gardens. Bhutan, Tibet. Introduced by Frank Kingdon-Ward.
Zone 5? US, 6? Can.

***S.* 'White Wax'** A small tree with a conical head of branches. The fernlike leaves have up to 23 oblong, sharply toothed leaflets, and the pure white fruits, 1/2 in (1 cm) across, are borne in drooping clusters.
Zone 4 US, 5 Can.

***S.* 'Wilfred Fox'** A handsome tree that is broadly columnar when young; it eventually becomes round headed and reaches 40 ft (12 m) tall. The elliptic leaves are 6–8 in (15–20 cm) long, shallowly lobed, and doubly serrated; they are glossy dark green above and grayish white tomentose below. The marblelike fruits are green at first, turning deep amber speckled with gray. It is named after the creator of Winkworth Arboretum, England.
Zone 6? US, 7? Can.

***S.* 'Winter Cheer'** A small to medium-sized, open-branched tree. The large, flat bunches of fruits are a warm chrome yellow at first, ripening to orange-red. They begin to color in early fall and persist well into winter. Raised 1959 by Hillier Nurseries.
Zone 4 US, 5 Can.

Spartium *Leguminosae*

A genus of one deciduous species, closely related to Cytisus *and* Genista.

S. junceum (Spanish broom) A vigorous shrub with a loose habit that has erect, green, rushlike stems up to 10 ft (3 m) high and small, inconspicuous, bluish green leaves. The large, fragrant, yellow pea flowers, 1 in (2.5 cm) long, are in loose, terminal clusters throughout summer and early fall. It thrives in well-drained soil and a sunny location and is an excellent shrub for coastal areas. Specimens in sheltered gardens are likely to become tall and leggy, but

Spartium junceum

they can be pruned hard in early spring as long as care is taken not to cut into the old, hard wood. It is difficult to transplant and should be raised from container-grown specimens. Mediterranean region. Introduced c. 1548.

Zone 7 US, 8 Can. 🏆

Spiraea *Rosaceae*

Spirea

A varied genus of deciduous flowering shrubs, many of which have attractive foliage and graceful habits. There are about 70 species in north-temperate regions. They are easy to grow in any moist, ordinary soil and a sunny or shady location, although a few turn yellow and fail in very shallow alkaline soil. Late-blooming types that flower on the current year's shoots, such as S. japonica, *can be pruned to the ground in early spring. Those that bloom early on the previous year's shoots, such as* S. × vanhouttei, *should be thinned out and have their old flowering shoots cut to within a short distance of the old wood immediately after flowering. Any specimens that suffer winter damage can be cut back almost to ground level in early spring.*

***S.* 'Arguta'** (Garland spirea) A dense, medium-sized shrub with graceful, slender branches and pure white flowers in small, flat clusters all along the branches in mid- to late spring. One of the most effective and free-flowering of the early spireas, although *S.* × *cinerea* 'Grefsheim' is considered to be a better plant. In cultivation before 1884.

Zone 2 US, 2b Can.

S. betulifolia A dwarf shrub, occasionally

Spiraea 'Arguta'

3 ft (1 m) high, forming mounds of reddish brown branches and rounded leaves. The white flowers are in dense, dome-shaped clusters, 1–2½ in (2.5–6 cm) across, and are borne in early summer. Small enough for a large rock garden. NE Asia, Japan. Introduced c. 1812.

Zone 4 US, 4b Can.

Spiraea × *billardii* 'Triumphans'

***S.* × *billardii* 'Triumphans'** A beautiful medium-sized shrub with erect stems bearing oblong to lance-shaped, sharply toothed leaves with grayish hairs and dense, conical panicles of purplish rose flowers in summer. It will not tolerate shallow, alkaline soil.

Zone 3 US, 3 Can.

***S. cantoniensis* 'Flore Pleno'** A wide-spreading, graceful form of Reeves' spirea. It grows up to 6½ ft (2 m) high and has slender arching branches, lance-shaped leaves, and double white flowers in rounded clusters along the branches in early summer.

Zone 6 US, 7 Can.

***S.* × *cinerea* 'Grefsheim'** A small, densely branched shrub that has downy, arching stems and narrow leaves. The small white flowers are profusely produced in dense clusters all along the branches toward the end of spring.

Zone 4 US, 4b Can. 🏆

Spiraea fritschiana

S. fritschiana A small, mound-forming shrub with blue-green leaves and white flowers that are tinged with pink and held in broad, dense terminal corymbs in early summer. Korea. Introduced 1976 by Carl Miller and Sir Harold Hillier.

Zone 6 US, 7 Can.

Spiraea japonica 'Albiflora'

***S. japonica* 'Albiflora'** A dwarf shrub of compact habit with white flowers in dense, terminal clusters from midsummer onward. Introduced before 1868.

Zone 4 US, 5 Can.

***S. j.* 'Anthony Waterer'** An excellent dwarf shrub for the front of the border or

Spiraea japonica 'Anthony Waterer'

for mass effect. The flowers are bright crimson and borne from midsummer onward; the foliage is occasionally variegated with cream and pink.
Zone 2 US, 2b Can. 🏆

***S. j.* 'Bullata'** A dwarf, slow-growing shrub with small, broad leaves that are puckered on their upper surfaces. The rose-crimson flowers are borne in terminal, flat-topped clusters in summer. Garden origin. Japan. In cultivation before 1881.
Zone 4 US, 4b Can.

Spiraea japonica 'Candlelight'

***S. j.* 'Candlelight'** A dwarf, compact, bushy shrub with buttery yellow young leaves that gradually turn deeper and make a good foil for the pink flowers from midsummer onward. It has good fall leaf color and does not revert.
Zone 4 US, 4b Can.

***S. j.* 'Crispa'** A dwarf shrub with glossy dark green leaves that are reddish purple when young and are deeply and sharply

Spiraea japonica 'Crispa'

toothed. The pink flowers are borne in large, flattened heads from midsummer onward.
Zone 2 US, 2b Can.

***S. j.* 'Dart's Red'** A plant that is similar to 'Anthony Waterer' and has flattened heads of deep red flowers but does not have variegated foliage.
Zone 3 US, 3 Can.

Spiraea japonica 'Firelight'

***S. j.* 'Firelight'** This is a dwarf shrub with arching branches whose young leaves are orange-red, deeper than those of 'Goldflame', of which it is a seedling. They turn bright orange-yellow, then pale green; in fall they turn a fiery red. The rose-pink flowers are borne from midsummer onward. It does not revert.
Zone 2 US, 2b Can.

***S. j.* 'Froebellii'** This shrub is similar to 'Anthony Waterer', but it grows somewhat taller and broader and it never has variegated foliage. It is one of the most popular

Spiraea japonica 'Goldmound'

forms. Raised 1892.
Zone 2 US, 2b Can.

***S. j.* 'Goldflame'** A very popular dwarf shrub. The young leaves emerge reddish orange in spring and become bright yellow, eventually turning green. The flowers are

Spiraea japonica 'Goldflame'

deep rose-red. All-green shoots should be removed.
Zone 2 US, 2b Can. 🏆

***S. j.* 'Goldmound'** A dwarf, compact shrub with yellow foliage, turning yellow-green when mature, and small heads of pink flowers from midsummer onward. Introduced by Perron Nurseries, Montreal, Quebec.
Zone 2 US, 2b Can. 🏆

***S. j.* 'Little Princess'** This shrub forms a low, dwarf mound with rose-crimson flowers from midsummer onward. *(See photo on p.586.)* Zone 3 US, 3 Can.

***S. j.* 'Macrophylla'** This is not the form to choose for flowers but it is perhaps the best

Spiraea japonica 'Little Princess'

spirea for fall color. The large, bullate leaves are reddish purple when young.
Zone 4 US, 4b Can.

***S. j.* 'Nana'** A superb dwarf shrub forming a dense mound 18–24 in (45–60 cm) high and somewhat more wide. It bears tiny heads of rose-pink flowers from midsummer onward. Good for planting in masses.
Zone 3 US, 3b Can. 🏆

Spiraea japonica 'Shirobana'

***S. j.* 'Shirobana'** This is an unusual dwarf form that produces a mixture of deep rose, pink, and white flowers on both the same and different heads. They are borne from midsummer onward. The foliage is an attractive dark green.
Zone 3 US, 3 Can. 🏆

S. nipponica This is one of the best shrubs for early-summer flowers. It is vigorous and medium-sized with a dense, bushy habit and has long, arching stems and leaves that are almost round. The clusters of small white flowers crowd the upper sides of the stout branches, and each flower lies immediately above a green bract. Japan. Introduced c. 1885.
Zone 3 US, 3 Can.

***S. n.* 'Halward Silver'** A free-flowering form that is smaller than the species and densely branched. Introduced by the Royal Botanic Gardens, Hamilton, Ontario.
Zone 3 US, 3 Can.

Spiraea nipponica 'Snowmound'

***S. n.* 'Snowmound'** A small, dense, mound-forming shrub with white flowers that crowd the upper sides of the branches in early summer, often hiding the stems almost entirely. Japan.
Zone 3 US, 3 Can. 🏆

Spiraea prunifolia

S. prunifolia (Bridalwreath) A dense shrub with arching branches up to $6^1/_2$ ft (2 m) high. The ovate leaves turn orange or red in fall. The white, double flowers are in tight, buttonlike clusters along the branches in mid- to late spring. It was introduced from Japan about 1845, before the inferior single form was discovered; the latter is named *S. p.* f. *simpliciflora.* The double form is sometimes listed as *S. p.* 'Plena' or 'Floreplena'.
Zone 3 US, 4 Can.

Spiraea thunbergii

S. thunbergii (Thunberg spirea) A popular, small to medium-sized, spreading, dense shrub with white flowers in numerous clusters along the branches in early and midspring, often hiding the stems. It is the earliest spirea to bloom. China, naturalized in Japan. Introduced c. 1863 from Japan.
Zone 3 US, 3 Can. 🏆

Spiraea × *vanhouttei*

***S. trilobata* 'Fairy Queen'** This forms a compact shrub about 3 ft (90 cm) tall and wide at maturity. The flat-topped clusters of white flowers appear from late spring to early summer and cover the branches. The dark green, three-lobed leaves make it one of the prettiest spireas when not in bloom.
Zone 2 US, 2b Can.

S.* × *vanhouttei (Vanhoutte spirea) A vigorous medium-sized shrub, up to 6½ ft (2 m) high, that has gracefully arching branches. The leaves are more or less rhomboidal, sometimes with 3–5 lobes, and the white flowers are borne in dense umbels along the branches in early summer. Garden origin before 1868.
Zone 3 US, 3 Can. 🏆

***S.* × *v.* 'Pink Ice'** A small shrub whose foliage is conspicuously flecked with creamy white. It is recently available and has not yet become widely popular.
Zone 3 US, 4 Can.

Stachyurus *Stachyuraceae*

This is the only genus in its family and consists of five or six deciduous species that are native to eastern Asia, only two of which are generally available. The stiffly pendulous flower clusters are formed in the leaf axils before the leaves drop in autumn, but the flowers do not open until early spring. Stachyurus *will grow in any fertile soil, in a sunny or partly shady location. It is good practice to prune old or weak shoots back to ground level, since new shoots are readily produced from the base.*

Stachyurus chinensis

S. chinensis A medium-sized to large shrub with purplish branchlets and fairly slender leaves. The drooping flower clusters are 4–5 in (10–13 cm) long and consist of 30–35 soft yellow, cup-shaped flowers. China. Introduced 1908 by Ernest Wilson.
Zone 9 US

***S. c.* 'Magpie'** The leaves of this medium-sized shrub are gray-green above with an irregular cream margin, splashed with pale green and tinted with rose-pink. It tends to produce shoots with all-white foliage. Originated c. 1945 at Hillier Nurseries.
Zone 9 US

Stachyurus praecox

S. praecox A medium-sized to large shrub with reddish brown branchlets. The leaves are more or less elliptical and are larger and broader than those of *S. chinensis*. The stiffly drooping flower clusters are 1½–2¾ in (4–7 cm) long and consist of 15–24 pale yellow, bell-shaped flowers. They open about two weeks earlier than those of *S. chinensis*, in early spring or even earlier in mild weather. Japan. Introduced 1864.
Zone 6 US, 7 Can. 🏆

Staphylea *Staphyleaceae*

Bladder nut

A genus of 11 deciduous species that are natives of temperate regions of the Northern Hemisphere. Their seeds are in curious, inflated, bladderlike capsules with 2–3 cells. They are easy to grow in any fertile soil in sun or part shade and need no regular pruning if given enough room to develop. Old, overgrown, or untidy specimens may be cut back hard in winter.

S. colchica A vigorous shrub with erect branches, reaching 11 ft (3.5 m) high. The leaves have 3–5 leaflets, and the white flowers are held in erect panicles up to 5 in (13 cm) long in late spring. The bladders are up to 4 in (10 cm) long. Caucasus. Introduced 1850.
Zone 4 US, 5 Can. 🏆

Staphylea colchica 'Hessei'

***S. c.* 'Hessei'** An attractive form whose flowers are flushed with red-purple.
Zone 4 US, 5 Can.

Staphylea holocarpa 'Rosea'

***S. holocarpa* 'Rosea'** A lovely large shrub or small tree. In mid- to late spring its branches are hung with drooping clusters of soft pink flowers. The bronze young leaves

Staphylea pinnata

age to blue-green. In cultivation 1908.
Zone 6 US, 7 Can.

S. pinnata A large, vigorous, erect shrub with leaves of 3–7 (usually 5) leaflets and white flowers in long, narrow, drooping panicles in late spring and early summer. Europe, Asia Minor. In cultivation 1596. *(Photo on p.587.)* Zone 6 US, 7 Can.

Stauntonia *Lardizabalaceae*

A genus of about six species of evergreen, twining shrubs closely related to Holboellia *and needing a warm, sheltered wall in full sun or part shade. They will thrive in ordinary soil.*

Stauntonia hexaphylla

S. hexaphylla (Japanese staunton vine) A strong climber, up to 33 ft (10 m) or more, with large leaves composed of 3–7 stalked, leathery, dark green leaflets. The fragrant flowers are 3/4 in (2 cm) across, with male and female in separate clusters. They are white, tinged with violet, and appear in spring. The edible, egg-shaped, pulpy, purple fruits are 1–2 in (2.5–5 cm) long and are produced only after a warm, dry summer. E Asia. Introduced 1874.
Zone 9 US

Stephanandra *Rosaceae*

A genus of four species of deciduous shrubs native to eastern Asia. Although they are of only subtle beauty in flower, their graceful habit and very attractive foliage earn them a place in the garden. They will grow in most soils in sun or part shade. The leaves are often richly colored in fall. Untidy specimens can be pruned back hard in early spring.

S. incisa (Cutleaf stephanandra) A small to medium-sized shrub of dense habit that has slender, brown, zigzag stems. The leaves are up to 3 in (7.5 cm) long, ovate, incisely toothed, and lobed. The greenish white flowers are borne in crowded, small panicles in the early days of summer. Japan, Korea. Introduced 1872.
Zone 4 US, 5 Can.

Stephanandra incisa 'Crispa'

***S. i.* 'Crispa'** A dwarf shrub with crinkled leaves, forming dense, low mounds. It makes a good ground cover or hedge. Originated c. 1930 in Denmark.
Zone 4 US, 5 Can.

Stephanandra tanakae

S. tanakae An elegant medium-sized shrub that produces long, arching, brown stems. The toothed leaves are more or less triangular, growing up to 5 in (13 cm) long, with 3–5 lobes. They produce good fall colors of red, orange, and yellow. The flowers are a little larger than those of *S. incisa* but are not showy. Japan. Introduced 1893.
Zone 4 US, 4b Can.

Stranvaesia

S. davidiana See *Photinia davidiana.*

Stewartia *Theaceae*

A genus of nine deciduous ornamental shrubs and trees related to Camellia. *They need a partly shaded site and a rich, moist, loamy, acidic soil; they grow particularly well when sheltered by other trees. All have exquisite, cup-shaped, solitary, white or cream flowers that are short-lived but produced in continuous succession over several weeks in mid- to late summer. The leaves turn purplish to orange-red in fall, and older specimens have attractive trunks and flaking bark similar to that of the sycamore. They resent being moved once planted and prefer to have their roots shaded from hot sun. Overshading can cause dead wood at the base, and removing this is virtually the only pruning required.*

S. malacodendron (Virginia stewartia) A beautiful large shrub, or occasionally a small tree, that produces flowers in the leaf

Stewartia malacodendron

axils; they are up to 4 in (10 cm) wide, with purple stamens. SE United States. In cultivation 1742.
Zone 7 US, 8 Can.

S. monadelpha (Tall stewartia) A large tree with attractive fall color and the smallest flowers among the stewartias. The flowers are 1–1 1/2 in (2.5–4 cm) across, with spreading petals. The stamens have violet

anthers. Japan, Korea. In cultivation 1903.
Zone 6 US, 7 Can.

S. ovata* var. *grandiflora (Showy stewartia) A large shrub or small tree with large flowers, up to 4 in (10 cm) wide, that have purple stamens. The foliage is orange to scarlet in fall, and the flaking bark is particularly attractive. SE United States.
Zone 5 US, 6 Can.

S. pseudocamellia (Japanese stewartia) A medium-sized to large tree with attractive, dark red, peeling bark. The flowers are 2–2½ in (5–6 cm) wide and have bright yellow anthers. The leaves turn purplish red in fall. Japan.
Zone 5 US, 6 Can. 🏆

S. p.* var. *koreana (Korean stewartia) A medium-sized tree with exceptionally bright orange-red fall color. The flowers are similar to those of other stewartias but open wider with spreading petals. Korea. Introduced 1917 by Ernest Wilson.
Zone 5 US, 6 Can. 🏆

Stewartia serrata

S. serrata A small tree with brown stems and leathery leaves. The flowers, 2–2½ in (5–6 cm) wide, are stained with red on the outside at the base and have yellow anthers. They open in early summer, before the other species. It has rich fall color. Japan. In cultivation before 1915.
Zone 6 US, 7 Can.

S. sinensis (Chinese stewartia) A large shrub or small tree with smooth, yellow bark that peels in fall to reveal the new gray bark. The flowers are up to 2 in (5 cm) wide and fragrant. It has rich fall color. C China. Introduced 1901 by Ernest Wilson.
Zone 5 US, 6 Can.

Styrax *Styracaceae*
Snowbell

A genus of some 100 species of evergreen and deciduous trees and shrubs, widely distributed in temperate and tropical regions of the Northern Hemisphere. They are distinguished in late spring and summer by their fragrant, bell-shaped, white flowers, which often hang below the leaves. They thrive in light, loamy, acidic soil in sun or part shade, and are good for small gardens. If pruning becomes necessary, it should be done in summer.

S. americanus (American snowbell) A medium-sized to large shrub with flowers

Stewartia monadelpha

Stewartia pseudocamellia

Stewartia pseudocamellia var. *koreana*

that hang below the branches in summer. SE United States. Introduced 1765.
Zone 5 US, 6 Can.

S. grandifolius Similar to *S. americanus* but it flowers earlier and has larger leaves. SE United States. Introduced 1765.
Zone 7 US, 8 Can.

Styrax japonica

S. japonica (Japanese snowbell) A beautiful large shrub or small tree with wide-spreading, almost horizontal, fanlike branches, often drooping at the tips. The leaves are fairly narrow and pointed, and the flowers, with a yellow beak of stamens, hang profusely all along the undersides of the branches in early summer. It is the most widely grown species and deservedly so, as it is both dainty and elegant. It is best planted where the flowers can be admired from below. Japan, Korea. Introduced 1862 by Richard Oldham.
Zone 4 US, 5b Can. 🏆

***S. j.* 'Pink Chimes'** A very free-flowering form with pale pink flowers that are deeper at the base. Raised before 1976 in Japan.
Zone 5 US, 6 Can.

Styrax obassia

S. obassia (Fragrant snowbell) A beautiful large shrub or small, round-headed tree with handsome, broad, almost rounded leaves 4–8 in (10–20 cm) long. The fragrant flowers are 1 in (2.5 cm) long and borne in long, lax, terminal racemes in early summer, although they are often hidden by the foliage. Japan. Introduced 1879 by Charles Maries.
Zone 5 US, 6 Can. 🏆

Sycopsis *Hamamelidaceae*

A genus of seven species of evergreen shrubs and trees, natives of the Himalaya. There is only one species in general cultivation. It prefers moisture-retentive, neutral or slightly acid soil but can grow over limestone as long as the soil is deep.

Sycopsis sinensis

S. sinensis A medium-sized to large shrub or small tree. The leaves are somewhat puckered and leathery. The flowers have no petals and consist of small clusters of yellow, red-anthered stamens, enclosed by chocolate brown, woolly scales. They open in late winter and early spring. C China. Introduced 1901 by Ernest Wilson.
Zone 8 US, 9? Can.

Symphoricarpos *Caprifoliaceae*

A genus of about 17 species of deciduous shrubs mainly from North America and Mexico, with one species in China. The flowers are bell shaped but small and not ornamental; the plants are grown primarily for their often abundant display of white or rose berries, which appear in fall and generally last well into winter, as they are left untouched by birds. Several are excellent for hedges, and all grow well in shade, even among the roots and under the drip line of overhanging trees. They will grow in all types of soil and may form clumps by suckering. Untidy specimens can be pruned back hard in early spring.

Symphoricarpos albus var. *laevigatus*

S. albus* var. *laevigatus (Snowberry) A vigorous shrub forming dense clumps up to 6½ ft (2 m) high. The elliptical leaves can grow to 3 in (7.5 cm) long, and the berries, borne profusely in fall, resemble glistening white marbles. *S. albus* is smaller and not as free-fruiting. W North America.
Zone 3 US, 3 Can.

***S.* × *chenaultii* 'Hancock'** A dense, dwarf, wide-spreading form of the chenault coralberry with pinkish berries that are purplish red on the exposed side. It makes a good ground cover, especially under trees. Introduced c. 1940 by Leslie Hancock, Woodland Nurseries, Mississauga, Ontario.
Zone 4 US, 5 Can.

S.* × *doorenbosii A useful group of attractive hybrids. Raised by Mr. Doorenbos in Holland.

***S.* × *d.* 'Magic Berry'** A small, compact, spreading shrub with large quantities of rose-pink berries.
Zone 4 US, 5 Can.

***S.* × *d.* 'Mother of Pearl'** A small, dense shrub with heavy crops of white, rose-flushed berries.
Zone 4 US, 5 Can.

***S.* × *d.* 'White Hedge'** A small, vigorous,

Symphoricarpos × *doorenbosii* 'Magic Berry'

upright shrub that freely produces erect clusters of small white berries.

Zone 4 US, 5 Can.

S. orbiculatus (Coralberry, Indian currant) A spreading, medium-sized shrub with arching branches and bluish foliage that turns a rusty red in fall. The pale yellow flowers are not conspicuous, but the fruit is like a raspberry except that the terminal berry is larger than the rest. E United States. Introduced 1727.

Zone 2 US, 2b Can.

***S. o.* 'Foliis Variegatis'** A graceful small shrub grown for its small, oval leaves that are irregularly margined with yellow.

Zone 3 US, 3 Can.

Symplocos *Symplocaceae*

A large genus of about 250 species of evergreen and deciduous trees and shrubs, widely distributed in tropical and subtropical regions, excluding Africa. Only one is generally grown. It requires an acidic soil and, if it is to bear fruits, a warm, sunny location.

S. paniculata (Asiatic sweetleaf, sapphire berry) A deciduous small to medium-sized shrub or small tree with finely toothed, oblong leaves and small, white, fragrant flowers borne in panicles in late spring and early summer. They are followed (particularly after a hot summer) by bright sapphire blue fruits that may persist into the winter; two or more plants are needed to ensure fertilization. Himalaya to Japan. Introduced 1871.

Zone 5 US, 6 Can.

Syringa *Oleaceae*

Lilac

A genus of very popular, hardy, deciduous shrubs and small trees that includes some of the most elegant, colorful, and fragrant woody plants flowering in late spring and early summer. The species, which are all single-flowered, are lesser known than the considerable number of large-flowered garden lilacs, and their fine qualities deserve much wider recognition. Lilacs do well in most well-drained soils, especially alkaline ones, and need full sun. Prune by removing the spent flower heads immediately after flowering; summer pinching of extra-strong shoots is desirable. Overcrowding of the branches allows mildew to thrive, and a little judicious thinning from time to time is good practice; plants should also be sited where there is good air circulation. Where the soil is shallow or otherwise poor, lilacs will respond well to mulching and feeding. Avoid locations where water collects in spring or the flowers will fail to open and the plants may even die.

Syringa × *chinensis* 'Saugeana'

***S.* × *chinensis* 'Saugeana'** A dense, bushy, medium-sized shrub with ovate leaves and large, drooping panicles of fragrant, lilac-red flowers in late spring. Raised c. 1809.

Zone 2 US, 2b Can.

***S.* × *hyacinthiflora* 'Esther Staley'** A large shrub with red buds that open to single pink flowers in late spring. In cultivation 1948.

Zone 2 US, 2b Can. 🏆

***S.* × *josiflexa* 'Bellicent'** A large shrub with deep green leaves and enormous panicles of clear rose-pink flowers. It is one of

Syringa × *hyacinthiflora* 'Esther Staley'

Syringa × *josiflexa* 'Bellicent'

Syringa julianae

the best forms of this excellent hybrid.

Zone 2 US, 2 Can. 🏆

S. julianae A choice, free-flowering, graceful shrub about 6½ ft (2 m) high and wide. It has privetlike leaves that are gray-downy on their undersides. The flowers are fragrant and pale lilac, from darker buds, and are borne in slender, upright panicles in late

spring and early summer. W China. Introduced 1900 by Ernest Wilson.
Zone 4 US, 5b Can.

S. laciniata (Cutleaf lilac) A graceful small shrub with three- to nine-lobed leaves and small panicles of lilac flowers in late spring. Turkey. Introduced 17th century.
Zone 4 US, 4b Can.

Syringa meyeri 'Palibin'

***S. meyeri* 'Palibin'** A slow-growing, eventually medium-sized shrub of dense habit. The pale lilac-pink flowers are borne in numerous elegant panicles, even on young plants. This is a lovely lilac that is suitable for the small garden.
Zone 2 US, 2b Can. 🏆

Syringa microphylla 'Superba'

***S. microphylla* 'Superba'** A very pretty, small-leaved shrub up to 6½ ft (2 m) high. The rosy pink flowers are abundantly borne in late spring and then intermittently until midfall. Raised in France.
Zone 3 US, 3 Can. 🏆

***S. patula* 'Miss Kim'** A small to medium-sized shrub with fragrant single flowers that are purple when in bud and upon opening and then fade to bluish ice white. They are borne in late spring to early summer. The leaves are dark green with wavy edges. A selection from wild source seed of *S. patula*, collected 1947 in Korea.
Zone 2 US, 2 Can. 🏆

S.* × *persica (Persian lilac) A slenderly branched shrub up to 8 ft (2.5 m) tall that is rounded and bushy. Leaves are lance shaped, and the fragrant pale lilac flowers are borne in small panicles in late spring.
Zone 2 US, 2b Can. 🏆

Syringa × *persica* 'Alba'

***S.* × *p.* 'Alba'** A form with white flowers.
Zone 2 US, 2b Can. 🏆

S.* × *prestoniae A race of extremely hardy, late-flowering lilacs that originated in Ottawa, Ontario. They are medium-sized to large shrubs with large panicles of flowers in late spring and early summer. Pink to salmon are the dominant colors.
Zone 2 US, 2 Can.

***S.* × *p.* 'Donald Wyman'** A popular form with long clusters of rosy pink flowers. In cultivation 1944.
Zone 2 US, 2 Can.

***S.* × *p.* 'Elinor'** A form with flowers that are dark purplish red in bud and open to pale lavender. They are borne in fairly erect panicles. In cultivation 1934.
Zone 2 US, 2 Can. 🏆

***S.* × *p.* 'Isabella'** A form whose purple flowers are borne in fairly erect panicles. This was the first of these hybrids and was named for the breeder, Isabella Preston, of

Syringa × *prestoniae* 'Elinor'

the Canadian Experiment Station in Ottawa, Ontario. In cultivation 1927.
Zone 2 US, 2 Can.

***S.* × *p.* 'James McFarlane'** Another popular form with upright spikes of pink flowers, darker in bud. In cultivation 1959.
Zone 2 US, 2 Can.

S. reticulata (Japanese tree lilac) A large shrub or small tree with large trusses of creamy white flowers that emit a strange scent quite unlike that of the common lilac and that open much later. The speckled bark adds winter interest. N Japan. Introduced 1876.
Zone 2 US, 2 Can.

***S. r.* 'Ivory Silk'** A more upright form usually grown as a tree. Introduced by Sheridan Nurseries, Ontario, Canada.
Zone 2 US, 2 Can.

Syringa sweginzowii 'Superba'

***S. sweginzowii* 'Superba'** A vigorous, elegant, medium-sized shrub with flesh pink, sweetly fragrant flowers borne in long,

loose panicles in late spring and early summer. W China. Introduced 1894.
Zone 3 US, 3 Can.

Syringa yunnanensis 'Rosea'

S. yunnanensis **'Rosea'** A superior form of the Yunnan lilac, this is a beautiful medium-sized to large shrub with attractive foliage and fragrant rose-pink flowers in long, slender panicles in early summer. Selected at Hillier Nurseries.
Zone 3 US, 3 Can.

CULTIVARS OF *SYRINGA VULGARIS*

Syringa vulgaris, the common or French lilac, is a large, vigorous, suckering shrub. Its flowers are richly scented and borne in dense, erect panicles in late spring. This European species has been the parent of a vast range of garden lilacs that are medium-sized to large shrubs or occasionally small trees, flowering in late spring and early summer. Flowers range in color from white and creamy yellow to red, blue, and purple and may be single or double. All are sweetly scented. Far too many cultivars with little to distinguish them have been named, and the following list includes only the best of them. After transplanting it takes 2–3 years before full flowering and size of truss are achieved. All the following are large shrubs and hardy to zones 2 US and Can.

SINGLE

***S.* 'Congo'** Rich lilac-red flowers in large, compact panicles, paling with age. In cultivation 1896.

***S.* 'Firmament'** Clear lilac-blue flowers, borne early. In cultivation 1932.

Syringa vulgaris 'Congo'

***S.* 'Massena'** Deep reddish purple flowers with large florets, borne in broad panicles. In cultivation 1923.

***S.* 'Maud Notcutt'** Pure white flowers in large panicles up to 1 ft (30 cm) long. In cultivation 1956. *(See photo on p.594.)*

***S.* 'Primrose'** Pale primrose yellow, only faintly scented flowers, which are borne in small, dense panicles. Originated 1949 as a sport in Holland.

Syringa vulgaris 'Firmament'

***S.* 'Sarah Sands'** A late-blooming form with deep reddish purple flowers. In cultivation 1943. *(See photo on p.594.)*

***S.* 'Sensation'** Purplish red florets edged with white, in large panicles. It is inclined to

Syringa vulgaris 'Massena'

Syringa vulgaris 'Maud Notcutt'

In cultivation 1910.

DOUBLE

S. **'Charles Joly'** Dark purplish red flowers, borne late. A reliable and popular lilac. In cultivation 1896.

S. **'Katherine Havemeyer'** Purple-lavender flowers, fading to pale lilac-pink, in broad, compact panicles. It is a first-class lilac. In cultivation 1922.

S. **'Krasavitsa Moskvy'** (Beauty of Moscow) Pale lavender buds open a pure white. A prolific bloomer and one of the best double whites. Introduced 1963 from Russia.

Syringa vulgaris 'Mrs. Edward Harding'

Syringa vulgaris 'Sensation'

revert and lose its variegation. In cultivation 1938.

S. **'Slater's Elegance'** This is a good white lilac with large individual flowers in medium-sized panicles. Introduced 1975 from Canada.

S. **'Vestale'** Pure white flowers in broad, densely packed panicles; a magnificent lilac.

Syringa vulgaris 'Mme. Lemoine'

S. **'Michel Buchner'** Pale rosy lilac flowers are borne in large, dense panicles. In cultivation 1885.

S. **'Mme. Antoine Buchner'** Rose-pink to rosy mauve flowers, borne late in loose, narrow panicles. In cultivation 1909.

S. **'Mme. Lemoine'** Flowers creamy yellow in bud, opening to pure white. An old and popular lilac. In cultivation 1890.

S. **'Mrs. Edward Harding'** A free-flowering form with claret red flowers shaded pink and borne late. In cultivation 1922.

S. **'Paul Thirion'** Flowers carmine in bud, opening to claret-rose and finally lilac-pink. They are borne late. In cultivation 1915.

S. **'Président Grévy'** Lilac-blue flowers in massive panicles. In cultivation 1886.

Syringa vulgaris 'Sarah Sands'

Syringa vulgaris 'Président Grévy'

T

Tamarix *Tamaricaceae*
Tamarisk

A genus of about 50 species of deciduous shrubs or small trees, native to Europe, Asia, and North Africa. They can resist strong winds and are so tolerant of salt that they survive along the edges of beaches. They need full sun and prefer well-drained, acidic soil but will tolerate most conditions except shallow soil over limestone. They are graceful and in some cases showy, with slender, whiplike branches and plumelike foliage. The tiny pink flowers are borne in slender racemes toward the ends of the branches, and these combine into large, feathery flower trusses that make a bold splash of color. The plants can become straggly, and pruning is necessary to maintain balance. Species that flower on growths of the current year should be pruned in late winter or early spring, while those that flower on the previous year's wood should be pruned immediately after flowering.

T. gallica (French tamarisk) A large, spreading shrub or small tree with dark purple-brown branches and sea green foliage. The pink flowers appear in summer and are crowded into lax, cylindrical racemes on shoots of the current year. SW Europe, especially along the Mediterranean coast.
Zone 6 US, 7 Can.
T. ramosissima (Five-stamen tamarisk) A large shrub or small tree with reddish brown branches and pink flowers in slender racemes in summer. They are borne on shoots of the current year. W and C Asia. Introduced c. 1885.
Zone 3 US, 3 Can.

Tamarix ramosissima

Tamarix ramosissima 'Rubra'

***T. r.* 'Rubra'** A splendid large shrub or small tree that is distinguished by darker flowers than the species.
Zone 3 US, 3 Can. 🏆

Tamarix tetrandra

T. tetrandra A large shrub with long, dark branches and green leaves. Light pink flowers in long panicles open in late spring or early summer on the previous year's wood. SE Europe, W Asia. Introduced 1821.
Zone 5 US, 6 Can. 🏆

Taxodium *Taxodiaceae*
Bald cypress

A genus of three species of deciduous coniferous trees from swampy areas in North and Central America. The linear leaves are either flattened or awl shaped, arranged in two opposite ranks on short deciduous branchlets that look like pinnate leaves. They prefer acidic conditions but can be grown in all soils except limestone. In waterlogged conditions they should be mound-planted.

Taxodium ascendens 'Nutans'

***T. ascendens* 'Nutans'** (Pond cypress) A beautiful, tall, columnar tree with shortly spreading or ascending branches. The thin, crowded branches are erect at first, later nodding, and are covered with adpressed, awl-shaped leaves up to 1/4 in (5 mm) long that turn brown in fall. In cultivation 1789.
Zone 5 US, 6 Can. 🏆
T. distichum (Bald cypress, swamp cypress) A beautiful large tree and the most suitable conifer for wet soil. It has fibrous, reddish brown bark and a strongly buttressed trunk. The leaves are 1/2–3/4 in (1–2 cm) long and turn bronze-yellow in fall. When grown near water, large specimens produce "knees" — woody growths from the roots that project aboveground and

look like termite hills. It is the dominant tree in the Florida Everglades. Introduced c. 1640 by John Tradescant.
Zone 4 US, 5 Can. 🏆

Taxus *Taxaceae*
Yew

A genus of about seven species of evergreen coniferous trees and shrubs widely distributed in north-temperate regions. They have linear leaves, either in two ranks or arranged radially, that are marked by two yellowish green or grayish brown bands on their undersides. The fruits, borne on female plants, have a brightly colored, fleshy cup (aril) that contains a single seed. The cup itself is the only part of a yew that is not poisonous. The yews are of great garden value and given good drainage are tolerant of most soils and conditions, even dry shade. They make good hedges and topiary. Yews are toxic if eaten.

Taxus baccata

T. baccata (Common yew, English yew) This is a small to medium-sized tree or large shrub with dark, almost black-green leaves up to 1¼ in (3 cm) long. The aril is red. It is usually found in the wild on limestone formations, and there are many garden forms. Europe, W Asia, Algeria.
Zone 5 US, 6 Can. 🏆

***T. b.* 'Adpressa Variegata'** A large shrub or small tree with leaves only ½ in (1 cm) long. It is a male form whose leaves unfold a mellow gold and then turn yellow; as the leaves age to green, the yellow remains at the margins. Also grown under the name 'Adpressa Aurea'. In cultivation 1866.
Zone 5 US, 6 Can. 🏆

***T. b.* 'Amersfoort'** A curious, small to medium-sized, open shrub with stiffly ascending branches covered with small, radially arranged leaves. It is most unlike a yew and resembles *Olearia nummulariifolia*.
Zone 5 US, 6 Can.

Taxus baccata 'Aurea'

***T. b.* 'Aurea'** (Golden yew) A large, compact shrub with erect, ascending branches. The leaves are gold at the margins and tips and have a green-gold midrib the first year; they turn green by their second year. In cultivation 1855.
Zone 5 US, 6 Can.

***T. b.* 'Dovastoniana'** (Westfelton yew) A distinctive, wide-spreading, small, elegant tree with tiers of long, horizontal branches and long, weeping branchlets. The leaves are black-green. It is a male form with occasional female branches. In cultivation 1777.
Zone 5 US, 6 Can. 🏆

***T. b.* 'Dovastoniana Aurea'** Similar in habit to *T. b.* 'Dovastoniana' but with leaves margined with bright yellow. It is a male form. In cultivation 1891.
Zone 5 US, 6 Can. 🏆

Taxus baccata 'Dovastoniana Aurea'

***T. b.* 'Elegantissima'** The most popular of the golden yews. It is a dense-growing, large bush with ascending branches and yellow young leaves that later turn straw yellow, with the color confined to the mar-

Taxus baccata 'Elegantissima'

Taxus baccata 'Fastigiata'

gin. It is a female form. In cultivation 1852.
Zone 5 US, 6 Can. 🏆

***T. b.* 'Fastigiata'** (Irish yew) A large female shrub of erect habit, making a dense, compact, broad column of closely packed branches. It is narrowly columnar when young. The leaves are black-green and arranged radially. Originally found 1778 in County Fermanagh, Ireland.
Zone 5 US, 6 Can. 🏆

Taxus baccata 'Fastigiata Aureomarginata'

***T. b.* 'Fastigiata Aureomarginata'** (Golden Irish yew) A male form similar to *T. b.* 'Fastigiata' except that the leaves have yellow margins. In cultivation 1880.
Zone 5 US, 6 Can.
🏆

***T. b.* 'Lutea'** A form with abundant yellow berries that are attractive against the dark green foliage. Discovered c. 1817 in Glasnevin, Ireland.
Zone 5 US, 6 Can.

***T. b.* 'Nutans'** A slow-growing, flat-topped

Taxus baccata 'Nutans'

bush with irregular leaves that are often small and scalelike. Zone 5 US, 6 Can.

***T. b.* 'Repandans'** A low-growing, often semiprostrate female bush with long, spreading branches that droop at the tips. An excellent ground-cover plant. In cultivation 1887.
Zone 5 US, 6 Can. 🏆

Taxus baccata 'Repandans'

Taxus baccata 'Repens Aurea'

***T. b.* 'Repens Aurea'** A low, spreading female bush with leaves margined in yellow when young, later turning to cream. It loses its color when in deep shade.
Zone 5 US, 6 Can. 🏆

***T. b.* 'Semperaurea'** A slow-growing, medium-sized, male bush with short, crowded, ascending branches. The unfolding leaves are a mellow gold, then turn a rusty yellow, which is retained. In cultivation 1908.
Zone 5 US, 6 Can. 🏆

Taxus baccata 'Semperaurea'

***T. b.* 'Standishii'** A small, dense, columnar female form of 'Fastigiata Aureomarginata' with erect, slow-growing branches and radially arranged, golden yellow leaves.
Zone 5 US, 6 Can. 🏆

Taxus baccata 'Standishii'

***T. cuspidata* 'Capitata'** (Upright Japanese yew) The most popular form of Japanese yew, this makes a tall, narrow tree with a central leader. There are both male and

female forms of this selection.
Zone 4 US, 4b Can.

***T.* × *media* 'Densiformis'** A female form with very dense foliage that makes a shrub up to 4 ft (1.2 m) tall and twice as wide. The needles are a bright green and retain their color well in winter.
Zone 4 US, 5 Can.

***T.* × *m.* 'Hicksii'** A broadly columnar, medium-sized to large female bush that makes an excellent hedge. It is similar to *T. baccata* 'Fastigiata' but has longer leaves, up to 1¼ in (3 cm).
Zone 4 US, 5 Can. 🏆

Tecomaria *Bignoniaceae*

A genus of one evergreen climbing species, related to Campsis.

T. capensis (Cape honeysuckle) A vigorous, self-clinging or twining climber up to 16 ft (5 m) high. The pinnate leaves have 5–9 toothed leaflets. The scarlet, trumpet-shaped flowers, 2 in (5 cm) long, appear in late summer. It is suitable only for mild climates and needs well-drained soil. In cold areas it makes an excellent greenhouse plant. E and S Africa. Introduced 1823.
Zone 9 US

Telopea *Proteaceae*
Waratah

A small Australasian genus of three or four evergreen species, most of which need a warm climate. The species below prefers moist but well-drained, acid soil.

Telopea truncata

T. truncata (Tasmanian waratah) A medium-sized to large shrub or occasionally a small tree. The flowers are rich crimson, in dense terminal heads in early summer. For its genus it is remarkably hardy and is at its hardiest when planted among other evergreens. Tasmania. Introduced 1930 by Harold Comber.
Zone 7 US, 8 Can.

Tetracentron *Tetracentraceae*

A genus of one deciduous species.

T. sinense A large shrub or small to medium-sized tree. The leaves are ovate or heart shaped, with long, slender points, and are tinted red when young. The flowers are minute and yellowish and drape the leafy branches in summer with dense, pendulous catkins. It prefers neutral or acid soil, although it has been grown successfully for a long time on the limestone at the Hillier Nurseries. Himalayan region. Introduced 1901 by Ernest Wilson.
Zone 7 US, 8 Can.

Tetradium *Rutaceae*

A genus of nine species of trees with pinnate leaves, now including Euodia. *They are related to* Phellodendron. *Those in cultivation are deciduous trees that will grow in all types of soil.*

Tetradium daniellii

T. daniellii, syn. *Euodia daniellii* A variable, fast-growing, small to medium-sized tree with large pinnate leaves and domed clusters of small, white, pungently scented flowers with yellow anthers, which are borne in late summer and early fall. Red to purplish or black fruits follow. China, Korea. Introduced 1905.
Zone 4 US, 5b Can.

Teucrium *Labiatae*
Germander

A genus of about 100 species of herbaceous shrubs, subshrubs, and perennials, widely distributed but concentrated in the Mediterranean region. The shrubby plants are grown for their flowers and foliage and require sun and well-drained soil. All have square stems and two-lipped flowers.

Teucrium chamaedrys

T. chamaedrys (Wall germander) A dwarf, bushy, aromatic, evergreen subshrub with a creeping rootstock and erect, hairy stems that are densely covered with small, toothed leaves. The flowers are rose-pink with darker veins, produced in whorls from midsummer to early fall. It is suitable for growing in wall nooks and can be sheared for a low edging. C and S Europe.
Zone 5 US, 6 Can.

T. fruticans (Shrubby germander) A small evergreen shrub whose stems and leaf undersides are covered with a dense, white felt. The pale blue flowers are borne in terminal racemes in summer. It needs a sunny, well-drained, sheltered location. S Europe, N Africa. Introduced 1714.
Zone 8 US, 9? Can.

***T. f.* 'Azureum'** A slightly more tender form with darker blue flowers that contrast better with the foliage.
Zone 9 US 🏆

T. subspinosum A very dwarf, gray, spiny shrublet of unusual appearance, with small, mauve-pink flowers produced in summer. An excellent plant for a rock garden or scree. Majorca.
Zone 9 US

Thamnocalamus *Gramineae*

A genus of six evergreen species of bamboo, natives of China, the Himalaya, and Africa. They are moisture lovers but will also grow in good soil that dries out in summer.

T. spathaceus, syn. *Arundinaria murielae* An elegant species, forming graceful, arching clumps 8–11 ft (2.5–3.5 m) or more high. The canes are bright green at first, maturing to dull yellow-green. The leaves are 2½–4 in (6–10 cm) long by ½–¾ in (1–2 cm) wide and bright pea green. This beautiful bamboo is considered one of the best species in cultivation. China. Introduced 1913 by Ernest Wilson.
Zone 6 US, 7 Can. 🏆

Thamnocalamus spathiflorus

T. spathiflorus, syn. *Arundinaria spathiflora* A beautiful, clump-forming species of neat, erect habit. The densely packed canes can reach 14½ ft (4.5 m) high but are more usually 8–10 ft (2.5–3 m). They are bright green, ripening to a pinkish purple on the exposed sides, and are white-bloomy during their first season. The leaves are 3–6 in (7.5–15 cm) long by ¼–½ in (6–12 mm) wide. It thrives in a little shade and shelter. NW Himalaya. Introduced 1882.
Zone 6 US, 7 Can.

Thuja *Cupressaceae*
Arborvitae

A genus of six species of evergreen coniferous trees and shrubs. They differ from Chamaecyparis *in that their foliage is usually aromatic and in the formation of the cones. Most form conical trees with small, scalelike, overlapping leaves in four ranks that are borne in large, flattened, fanlike sprays. Arborvitae will thrive in almost any soil as long as it is well drained. Two species —* T. occidentalis *and* T. plicata *— are excellent for hedges and screens, and a good number of cultivars are dwarf or slow-growing enough for use in the rock garden. There are several excellent colored forms. They are harmful if eaten.*

T. koraiensis (Korean arborvitae) A usually densely shrubby species that occasionally forms a small tree, with decurved branches and dark brown, peeling bark. The foliage is in large, flattened, frondlike sprays, green or sea green above, white beneath, and pungently aromatic when crushed. Korea. Introduced 1917.
Zone 5 US, 6 Can.

Thuja occidentalis 'Aureospicata'

T. occidentalis (American arborvitae, Eastern arborvitae, Eastern white cedar) A medium-sized, columnar tree with reddish brown, peeling bark. The branches are spreading and upwardly curved at the tips. The leaves, which have conspicuous resin glands, are dark green above, pale green beneath, and borne in numerous flattened sprays. They usually turn bronze in winter. The foliage smells pleasantly fruity when crushed. E North America. In cultivation 1534.
Zone 3 US, 3 Can.

***T. o.* 'Aureospicata'** A large, erect tree whose young shoots become yellow, intensified in winter to a soft gold.
Zone 3 US, 3 Can.

Thuja occidentalis 'Danica'

***T. o.* 'Danica'** A dense, compact, globular, dwarf bush with its foliage held in erect, flattened sprays.
Zone 3 US, 3 Can. 🏆

***T. o.* 'Emerald'** See *T. o.* 'Smaragd'.

***T. o.* 'Europe Gold'** A large shrub or small tree of narrowly conical habit with golden yellow foliage. *(See photo on p.600.)*
Zone 3 US, 3 Can.

***T. o.* 'Golden Globe'** A small, dense, rounded shrub with golden yellow foliage year-round. In cultivation 1965. *(See photo on p.600.)* Zone 3 US, 3 Can.

***T. o.* 'Hetz Midget'** A very slow-growing, dwarf, globular bush. Selected in the 1930s by Fairview Nursery, Fairview, Pa. *(See photo on p.600.)* Zone 3 US, 3 Can.

Thuja occidentalis 'Europe Gold'

Thuja occidentalis 'Golden Globe'

Thuja occidentalis 'Hetz Midget'

***T. o.* 'Holmstrup'** A slow-growing, medium-sized to large, narrowly conical bush of dense, compact habit. Its rich green foliage, held in vertically arranged sprays, is retained year-round. In cultivation 1951.
Zone 3 US, 3 Can. 🏆

***T. o.* 'Holmstrup Yellow'** A sport of 'Holmstrup' with golden yellow foliage. Raised before 1951 in Denmark.
Zone 3 US, 3 Can.

***T. o.* 'Little Giant'** A dense, dwarf, globular, slightly flat-topped bush with rich green foliage in crowded, crimped sprays. Introduced by McConnell Nursery, Canada.
Zone 3 US, 3 Can.

***T. o.* 'Lutea Nana'** A small, conical, dense bush whose foliage is yellow-green in summer and deep golden yellow in winter. In cultivation 1891.
Zone 3 US, 3 Can. 🏆

***T. o.* 'Nigra'** (Black cedar) A compact, upright form with very dark green foliage. It keeps its color well in winter, not turning a brownish green as many varieties do.
Zone 3 US, 4 Can.

***T. o.* 'Pyramidalis'** A large, fast-growing, upright, pyramidal shrub with bright green foliage. It withstands shearing and is popular for hedges.
Zone 3 US, 4 Can.

***T. o.* 'Rheingold'** A slow-growing, ovoid or conical bush, eventually growing into a medium-sized to large shrub. The foliage is mainly adult and is a rich, deep gold shading to amber, with reddish tints in summer. It is a very popular plant, providing perhaps the best mellow gold color to be found in winter. Young plants with juvenile foliage will in time revert to the form described here. First listed 1910 by Hesse Nurseries, Germany.
Zone 3 US, 3 Can. 🏆

Thuja occidentalis 'Rheingold'

Thuja occidentalis 'Sunkist'

***T. o.* 'Smaragd'**, syn. *T. o.* 'Emerald' A narrowly conical small tree with bright green foliage.
Zone 3 US, 3 Can. 🏆

***T. o.* 'Sunkist'** A dense, small, broadly conical, round-topped bush with golden yellow foliage in summer.
Zone 3 US, 3 Can.

***T. o.* 'Wansdyke Silver'** This is an attractive small, slow-growing bush making a conical shape. Its foliage is brightly

variegated with cream. In cultivation 1966.
Zone 3 US, 3 Can.

***T. o.* 'Wareana Lutescens'** A slow-growing, very compact, conical bush with short, thickened sprays of pale yellow foliage. In cultivation 1884.
Zone 3 US, 3 Can.

***T. o.* 'Woodwardii'** A dense, ovoid shrub, taller than broad, eventually reaching 3 ft (1 m) tall. Its foliage stays green in winter.
Zone 2 US, 2b Can.

***T. o.* 'Yellow Ribbon'** A medium-sized shrub that is narrowly conical in shape and has bright yellow foliage.
Zone 3 US, 3b Can.

T. orientalis (Oriental arborvitae) A large shrub or small tree with a dense, conical or columnar habit when young. The branches are erect and the leaves are borne in frond-like, vertical sprays. It is distinct in its rather formal habit, its cones, and the aroma of its foliage, which is weaker than in the other species. There are several forms suitable for rock gardens. China. Introduced c. 1690.
Zone 5 US, 6 Can.

***T. o.* 'Aurea Nana'** A dwarf, globular, dense bush with crowded, vertically arranged sprays of light yellow-green foliage. In cultivation 1804.
Zone 6 US, 7 Can. 🏆

***T. o.* 'Conspicua'** A medium-sized to large, dense, compact, conical shrub with gold foliage whose color is retained longer than most. In cultivation 1804.
Zone 5 US, 6 Can.

***T. o.* 'Elegantissima'** A medium-sized to large shrub with a dense, columnar habit and attractive golden yellow foliage, tinged with deeper gold, that turns green in winter. In cultivation 1858.
Zone 5 US, 6 Can. 🏆

***T. o.* 'Meldensis'** A dwarf, densely globular shrub with semijuvenile foliage that is sea green in summer and turns a warm yellow-brown in winter. Raised 1852.
Zone 5 US, 6 Can.

***T. o.* 'Rosedalis'** A dense, ovoid shrub with soft juvenile foliage. In early spring it is bright yellow; it changes by midsummer to sea green and by winter to bloomy plum-purple. In 15 years it is likely to reach 32 in (80 cm) high. In cultivation 1923.
Zone 5 US, 6 Can.

Thuja orientalis 'Elegantissima'

Thuja orientalis 'Rosedalis'

T. plicata (Western red cedar, giant arborvitae) A large, fast-growing tree with shredding bark and spreading branches. The leaves are bright glossy green above, faintly bloomy beneath, and are held in large, drooping sprays. They have a pleasant, fruity aroma when crushed. It makes a good hedge or screen and tolerates clipping, shade, and alkaline soil. W North America. Introduced 1853.
Zone 5 US, 6 Can. 🏆

Thuja plicata

Thuja plicata 'Aurea'

***T. p.* 'Aurea'** An outstanding medium-sized tree with rich gold foliage that is at its best in winter after frost.
Zone 5 US, 6 Can. 🏆

Thuja plicata 'Cuprea'

T. p. **'Cuprea'** A dense, very slow-growing, small, conical shrub, with the growths tipped in various shades of deep cream to gold. Good for the rock garden.
Zone 5 US, 6 Can.

T. p. **'Fastigiata'** A tall, narrowly columnar form with densely arranged, slender, ascending branches. It is excellent as a single specimen tree or for hedges, as it does not require much clipping. In cultivation 1867.
Zone 5 US, 6 Can. 🏆

T. p. **'Irish Gold'** A large tree similar to *T. p.* 'Zebrina' except that the foliage is more strongly flecked with a deeper yellow.
Zone 5 US, 6 Can. 🏆

Thuja plicata 'Rogersii'

T. p. **'Rogersii'** A slow-growing, compact, dwarf, conical bush with densely crowded gold and bronze foliage. It will grow to about 4 × 3 ft (1.2 × 1 m) in 30 years. In cultivation c. 1928.
Zone 5 US, 6 Can.

Thuja plicata 'Zebrina'

T. p. **'Semperaurescens'** A very vigorous large tree whose leaves and shoots are tinged with golden yellow and become bronze-yellow by winter. Ideal for use as a tall screen. In cultivation 1923.
Zone 5 US, 6 Can.

T. p. **'Stoneham Gold'** A slow-growing but eventually large shrub with a dense, narrowly conical habit. The foliage is bright gold, tipped with coppery bronze. It is a superb plant for a large rock garden. In cultivation 1948.
Zone 5 US, 6 Can. 🏆

Thuja plicata 'Stoneham Gold'

T. p. **'Zebrina'** A conical tree with sprays of green foliage banded with creamy yellow. It is a vigorous, large tree and one of the best variegated conifers, the densely crowded variegations giving a yellow effect to the whole tree. In cultivation 1868.
Zone 5 US, 6 Can.

Thujopsis *Cupressaceae*

A genus of one evergreen coniferous species, differing from Thuja *in that it has broader, flatter branchlets and larger leaves.*

T. dolobrata (False arborvitae) A distinctive, attractive large shrub or small to medium-sized tree with a dense, broadly conical habit. The branchlets are flattened

Thujopsis dolobrata 'Aurea'

and bear sprays of large, four-ranked, scale-like leaves that are shining dark green above and are marked with silver-white bands beneath. It produces cones up to ³/₄ in (2 cm) long. It thrives in all kinds of moist, well-drained soil, including shallow alkaline ones. Japan. Introduced 1853.
Zone 5 US, 6 Can. 🏆

***T. d.* 'Aurea'** A large shrub or small to medium-sized tree whose leaves are suffused with golden yellow. In cultivation 1866.
Zone 5 US, 6 Can.

***T. d.* 'Nana'** A dwarf, compact, spreading, flat-topped shrub. A good conifer for the rock garden. Introduced 1861.
Zone 5 US, 6 Can.

Tibouchina *Melastomataceae*

A large genus with about 350 species of evergreen and deciduous shrubs and subshrubs native to tropical America. The following is suitable only for warm climates.

T. semidecandra See *T. urvilleana.*

T. urvilleana, syn. *T. semidecandra* (Glory bush) A large evergreen shrub with four-angled stems and velvety-hairy, prominently veined leaves. The large, vividly royal purple flowers open from red buds and are produced continuously throughout summer and fall. Old plants may become straggly and should be pruned in early spring as needed. It makes an excellent greenhouse plant for cold climates. S Brazil. Introduced 1864.
Zone 10 US 🏆

Tibouchina urvilleana

Tilia *Tiliaceae*

Linden

A genus of about 45 species of deciduous trees from many parts of the north-temperate regions. They are easy to grow, and many develop into stately trees. They prefer fertile soil that is slightly acid to slightly alkaline and tolerate pollution. They benefit from being mulched and require deep watering during drought. Unless otherwise stated, all those below have clusters of small, fragrant, creamy yellow flowers freely borne in midsummer. If you keep bees, do not grow T. tomentosa *and its forms, as the flowers are toxic to them. Also do not plant* T. platyphyllos *where its branches will overhang parked cars or outdoor living areas, as aphids feeding on it drop a sticky honeydew.*

T. americana (American linden, basswood) A medium-sized tree with broad, green, coarsely toothed leaves up to 1 ft (30 cm) long. Its large leaves make it a striking tree, but they tend to become shredded if exposed to strong wind. E North America. Introduced 1752.
Zone 2 US, 2b Can.

Tilia cordata

T. cordata (Little-leaf linden) A medium-sized to large, rounded tree with heart-shaped, 2–3 in (5–7.5 cm) long, leathery leaves, glossy dark green above and pale green below with reddish brown axillary tufts. The spreading flower clusters appear in late summer, and the ivory flowers are sweetly scented. Europe.
Zone 3 US, 3 Can. 🏆

***T. c.* 'Greenspire'** A fast-growing, upright form that makes a narrowly oval crown. Selected before 1955 by Princeton Nurseries, New Jersey.
Zone 3 US, 3 Can. 🏆

Tilia × euchlora

T. × euchlora (Crimean linden) A medium-sized tree with rounded leaves that are shiny dark green above and paler beneath. It is elegant when young, with glossy leaves and arching branches, and becomes dense and twiggy with pendulous lower branches when mature. It is not affected by aphids, but its flowers tend to have a narcotic effect on bees. In cultivation 1860.
Zone 3 US, 3 Can. 🏆

Tilia × europaea

T. × europaea (European linden) A large, vigorous, long-lived tree with glabrous, greenish, zigzag shoots. The broadly ovate or rounded leaves are heart shaped at the base and sharply toothed. It has a densely suckering habit and attracts aphids.
Zone 3 US, 4 Can.

***T. × e.* 'Pallida'** (Kaiser linden) This is the

tree of Berlin's famous street Unter den Linden. The ascending branches form a broadly conical crown, and the leaves are yellowish green beneath.
Zone 3 US, 4 Can.

Tilia × europaea 'Wratislaviensis'

***T. × e.* 'Wratislaviensis'** (Warsaw linden) The leaves of this large tree are golden yellow when young and become green with age. It is a lovely tree whose young growths give the effect of a halo.
Zone 3 US, 4 Can. 🏆

***T.* 'Harold Hillier'** A handsome, vigorous, medium-sized, narrowly conical tree. The leaves vary in length up to 6 in (15 cm) and are maplelike, with three lobes, edged with bristle-tipped teeth. The fall color is a beautiful butter yellow. Raised 1973 by Nigel Muir.
Zone 5? US, 6? Can.

T. henryana A very rare, fall-flowering tree with wonderful broad, fringed leaves often brightly edged with carmine when young. Although medium-sized in the wild, it is very slow growing in cultivation. China.
Zone 6 US, 7 Can.

Tilia henryana

T. mongolica (Mongolian linden) A small, compact, rounded tree with dense, twiggy growth and reddish shoots. The pretty, ivylike leaves are up to 3 in (7.5 cm) long, on red stalks. They are coarsely toothed with 3–5 lobes, especially on young trees, and turn bright yellow in fall. Russia, Mongolia, N China. Introduced 1880.
Zone 3 US, 3b Can. 🏆

T. oliveri An elegant, medium-sized to large tree with shoots that are inclined to be pendulous. The leaves are dark green above and silvery white beneath. It is not troubled by aphids. C China. Introduced 1900 by Ernest Wilson.
Zone 6 US, 7 Can.

***T.* 'Petiolaris'** See *T. tomentosa* 'Petiolaris'.

T. platyphyllos (Broad-leaved linden, large-leaf linden) A large, vigorous tree with roundish leaves that are sharply toothed, shortly downy above and densely so beneath. The flowers appear toward the middle of summer. It suckers slightly and is prone to aphid infestations. Europe.
Zone 4 US, 5 Can.

Tilia platyphyllos

Tilia platyphyllos 'Aurea'

***T. p.* 'Aurea'** The young shoots of this large tree are yellow, becoming olive green. They are particularly notable in winter.
Zone 4 US, 5 Can.

***T. p.* 'Laciniata'** A small to medium-sized tree of dense, conical habit with leaves deeply and irregularly cut into rounded and taillike lobes.
Zone 4 US, 5 Can.

***T. p.* 'Prince's Street'** A vigorous, upright large tree with young shoots that are bright red in winter.
Zone 4 US, 5 Can.

***T. p.* 'Rubra'** (Red-twigged linden) The young shoots of this medium-sized tree are bright brownish red and are particularly effective in winter.
Zone 4 US, 4b Can.

T. tomentosa (Silver linden) A handsome large tree with a stately habit. The erect branches carry short-stalked, rounded, sharply toothed leaves, dark green above and silver-felted beneath; they are particularly effective when stirred by a breeze. It is not troubled by aphids, but the flowers are toxic to bees. SE and EC Europe. Introduced 1767.
Zone 4 US, 4b Can.

Tilia tomentosa

***T. t.* 'Brabant'** A large, upright tree that develops a dense, broadly conical crown. Selected in Holland. In cultivation 1970.
Zone 4 US, 4b Can. 🏆

***T. t.* 'Chelsea Sentinel'** A form that resembles *T. t.* 'Petiolaris' in its long-stalked leaves and attractively weeping branches, but it is distinctly columnar.
Zone 4 US, 4b Can.

Tilia tomentosa 'Petiolaris'

***T. t.* 'Petiolaris'**, syn. *T.* 'Petiolaris' (Weeping silver linden) One of the most beautiful of all large, weeping trees. It has graceful, downward-sweeping branches, and the leaves are long-stalked, rounded, toothed, and dark green above and white-felted beneath, making them especially attractive when stirred by a breeze. The flowers are richly scented but narcotic to bees. Origin uncertain; possibly from SE Europe and W Asia. In cultivation 1840.
Zone 4 US, 4b Can. 🏆

Toona *Meliaceae*

A genus of six species of evergreen and deciduous trees from China, Southeast Asia, and northern Australia; it is distinct from Cedrela, *which is now confined to eight species occurring in the tropical regions of the Americas. They thrive in most fertile, well-drained soils with plenty of sun. The following species resembles a more refined* Ailanthus altissima.

T. sinensis, syn. *Cedrela sinensis* (Chinese toon) A medium-sized, fast-growing deciduous tree with large, pinnate leaves that are often bronze when young. It has fragrant white flowers in panicles that are typically as long as 1 ft (30 cm) and lovely yellow tints in fall. China. Introduced 1862.
Zone 5 US, 6 Can.

***T. s.* 'Flamingo'** The young foliage of this medium-sized tree is bright pink and turns cream, then green.
Zone 5 US, 6 Can.

Torreya *Taxaceae*

A genus of about seven species of evergreen coniferous trees and shrubs, natives of eastern Asia and North America. The leaves are linear, rigid, and spine-tipped and are marked with two glaucous bands beneath; they are arranged spirally on leading shoots and are twisted on lateral shoots to appear in two ranks. The fruits are plumlike and fleshy, each containing a single seed. They are excellent trees in alkaline soil and will tolerate shade well.

T. californica (California nutmeg) A small to medium-sized, broadly conical to rounded tree that resembles a majestic yew. The leaves are rigid, up to 3 in (7.5 cm) long, shiny dark green above, and spine-tipped. The egg-shaped fruits are green and streaked with purple when ripe. California. Introduced 1851 by William Lobb.
Zone 8 US, 9? Can.

Trachelospermum *Apocynaceae*
Star jasmine

There are about 20 evergreen species in this genus; one is native to the southeastern United States and the rest are from East and Southeast Asia. These beautiful, self-clinging, twining climbers have sweetly scented, jasminelike flowers in mid- to late summer; the petals are slightly twisted and are arranged to form a star or pinwheel shape. When cut, the stems exude a milky sap. They will grow in any well-drained soil and need some shade in hot climates. They require support when young and are slow in getting established. Older specimens should be pruned occasionally to prevent excessive woodiness.

T. asiaticum (Yellow star jasmine) A densely leafy species that grows up to 20 ft (6 m) high and as much across. Its flowers, ¾ in (2 cm) across, are cream with a buff-yellow center and change to yellow. It is hardier, neater, and more compact than *T. jasminoides.* Japan, Korea.
Zone 7 US, 8 Can. 🏆

T. jasminoides (Chinese star jasmine) A rather slow-growing climber that reaches up to 30 ft (9 m) tall. The very fragrant flowers are 1 in (2.5 cm) across and white, becoming cream with age. It is suitable for a screen. Very popular in the South and California. China, Taiwan. Introduced 1844 by Robert Fortune.
Zone 9 US 🏆

Trachelospermum jasminoides 'Variegatum'

***T. j.* 'Japonicum'** A taller-growing selection with larger leaves than the form. When established it will cover a wall effectively.
Zone 9 US

***T. j.* 'Variegatum'** The leaves of this form are margined and blotched with cream and are often suffused with crimson in winter.
Zone 9 US 🏆

***T. j.* 'Wilsonii'** An unusual form whose leaves vary from ovate to slenderly lance shaped. They are attractively veined and often turn crimson in winter. China. Introduced by Ernest Wilson.
Zone 9 US

Trachycarpus *Palmae*

A genus of six species of evergreen palms with very large, fan-shaped leaves, natives of the Himalaya and eastern Asia. The following species is among the hardiest cultivated palms, but its leaves need protection from strong wind.

T. fortunei (Windmill palm) A small to medium-sized palm that will reach 40 ft (12 m) after many decades. It develops a single trunk that is thickly covered with the fibrous remains of old leaf sheaths. The

Trachycarpus fortunei

large, fan shaped leaves are 3–5 ft (1–1.5 m) wide and on long, stout stalks in a cluster from the top of the trunk; they persist for many years. The small, yellow flowers are borne in large, terminal, curving panicles in early summer. The fruits are like blue-black marbles. In favorable conditions it may self seed. China. Introduced 1830 by Philipp von Siebold and 1849 by Robert Fortune.
Zone 7 US, 8 Can. 🏆

Trochodendron *Trochodendraceae*

A genus of one evergreen species.

Trochodendron aralioides

T. aralioides (Wheel-stamen tree) A slow-growing large tree with a spreading head and aromatic bark. It has long-stalked, leathery leaves that are broadest above the middle, scalloped at the margins, and bright apple green or yellowish green; they are held in beautiful spiral whorls. The green flowers are borne in erect terminal clusters in spring and early summer and are ideal for flower arrangements. It grows in most fertile soils except shallow, alkaline ones and will grow in sun or shade. It is hardier than generally supposed. Japan, Taiwan, S Korea. In cultivation 1894.
Zone 8 US, 9? Can.

Tsuga *Pinaceae*
Hemlock

A genus of about 10 species of elegant, evergreen coniferous trees of broadly conical habit with spreading branches and gently drooping or arching branchlets. They are native to eastern Asia and North America. The leaves are short, narrow, and straight and appear to be in two ranks, except in T. mertensiana, *on which they are arranged radially. They take shade well and grow best in a moist, well-drained, loamy soil; they will not tolerate hot, dry summers.* T. canadensis *can be grown in moderately deep soil over limestone.*

T. canadensis (Canada hemlock, Eastern hemlock) A large tree, often with several main stems from near the base. The short needlelike leaves are glossy dark green above and bluish green, marked with two white bands, beneath. The cones persist in winter. E North America. Introduced 1736.
Zone 3 US, 4 Can.

***T. c.* 'Albospica'** A slow-growing, compact shrub that produces leaves with creamy white tips.
Zone 3 US, 4 Can.

***T. c.* 'Aurea'** A dwarf, slow-growing form with a compact, conical habit. Its leaves are broad and crowded and are golden yellow when unfolding, becoming greenish yellow.
Zone 3 US, 4 Can.

Tsuga canadensis 'Cole'

Tsuga canadensis 'Jeddeloh'

***T. c.* 'Bennett'** A slow-growing, dwarf shrub with a spreading habit and dense, crowded growth. In cultivation 1920.
Zone 3 US, 4 Can.

***T. c.* 'Cole'** A prostrate plant with long branches growing flattened along the

Tsuga canadensis 'Bennett'

Tsuga canadensis 'Pendula'

ground that spread over time to form carpets. Found 1929 in New Hampshire.

Zone 3 US, 4 Can.

***T. c.* 'Jeddeloh'** A compact dwarf shrub with arching branches. Selected in W Germany. In cultivation 1965.

Zone 3 US, 4 Can.

***T. c.* 'Pendula'** (Sargent weeping hemlock) A graceful form that develops into a low mound of overlapping, drooping branches; it is flat topped and often twice as broad as it is tall. One specimen reached $6^1/_2 \times 11$ ft (2×3.5 m) in 40 years. Introduced before 1876.

Zone 3 US, 4 Can.

T. diversifolia (Japanese hemlock) An excellent large, dense tree with a rounded habit that retains its foliage for up to 10 years; other hemlocks drop their needles after about 4 years. Young branchlets are pubescent and reddish brown, and the needles are notched. Japan.

Zone 5 US, 6 Can.

T. heterophylla (Western hemlock) A large, fast-growing tree, up to 100 ft (30 m), with gracefully spreading branches and a spirelike crown. The leaves are up to $^3/_4$ in (2 cm) long and marked with two white bands beneath. It makes an elegant specimen. W North America. Introduced 1851.

Zone 6 US, 7 Can.

***T. h.* 'Greenmantle'** A graceful, tall, narrow tree producing pendulous branches. Originated at Windsor Great Park, England. Named 1971.

Zone 6 US, 7 Can.

***T. mertensiana* 'Glauca'** A beautiful, slow-growing, spirelike tree with glaucous leaves that are radially arranged on the branchlets. In cultivation 1850.

Zone 5 US, 6 Can.

Tweedia

T. caerulea See *Oxypetalum caeruleum.*

U

Ugni

U. molinae See *Myrtus ugni.*

Ulex *Leguminosae*

Gorse, furze

A genus of about 20 species of spiny shrubs from western Europe and North Africa, some of which are naturalized in the United States. Vigorous but hard to establish, they do best in poor, acid soil. They have yellow flowers and can be grown as a hedge; they should be trimmed after flowering.

Ulex europaeus 'Flore Pleno'

***U. europaeus* 'Flore Pleno'** A densely branched, compact shrub that usually grows to no more than 5 ft (1.5 m); it is extremely spiny. The flowers are chrome yellow, semidouble, long lasting, and caramel-scented and almost completely cover the plants in mid- to late spring and later. Good for covering slopes. In cultivation 1828.

Zone 6 US, 7 Can.

***U. gallii* 'Mizen Head'** A dwarf shrub of prostrate habit with shoots that spread along the ground and deep yellow flowers in early fall.

Zone 9? US

Ulmus *Ulmaceae*

Elm

The elm population in Europe and North America was virtually wiped out by the mid-1970s as a result of bark beetles, which carry the spores of a virulent strain of fungal disease that blocks the conductive tissues of the trees. The disease is known as Dutch elm disease, because it was initially identified in the Netherlands. Asiatic elms are resistant to it.

The disease did not disappear when the trees died. Many trees regrew from suckers, and these show little sign of a problem until they become large enough to have thick, rugged bark, when they can become reinfected. If an elm is infected, which is evident first by yellowing leaves and then by the sudden death of a branch or larger portion of the tree, action should be taken immediately. When an individual branch is affected, it should be removed; if it is more than that, the tree should be felled, and its stump debarked or preferably removed.

Elms are noble trees that thrive in almost any soil and in any location, no matter how exposed. The small, reddish flowers are borne on bare twigs in spring.

U. americana (American elm) A large, noble, vase-shaped tree that has been decimated by Dutch elm disease. Isolated stands still exist in some areas on the prairies, where the bark beetles do not occur. Disease-resistant strains, sometimes hybrids with Asian species, are being developed, but it is too soon to tell if they will be successful. C and E North America.

Zone 2 US, 2 Can.

U. carpinifolia (Smoothleaf elm) A large, upright or pyramidal tree with slender branches and glossy green leaves that are smooth above and slightly downy on the veins below. S and C Europe.

Zone 5 US, 6 Can.

***U. c.* 'Dicksonii'** (Dickson's golden elm) A very slow-growing, narrowly upright, medium-sized to large tree with beautiful, bright golden yellow leaves. It appears to be unaffected by Dutch elm disease.

Zone 4 US, 5 Can.

Ulmus glabra 'Camperdownii'

Ulmus × *hollandica* 'Jaqueline Hillier'

***U. c.* 'Umbraculifera'** A form with a densely globe-shaped head.
Zone 4 US, 5 Can.

U. glabra (Wych elm, Scotch elm) A large, impressive tree that usually develops a dome-shaped crown with spreading branches that are arching or pendulous at their extremities. The large, short-stalked leaves are rough and coarsely toothed and turn yellow in fall. Europe, N and W Asia.
Zone 4 US, 5 Can.

***U. g.* 'Camperdownii'** (Camperdown elm) A small, neat, compact form with a rounded head and weeping branches that reach to the ground. In cultivation 1850.
Zone 4 US, 5 Can. 🏆

***U. g.* 'Lutescens'** A beautiful, free-growing form whose leaves are soft cream-yellow in spring and later become yellowish green.
Zone 4 US, 5 Can.

***U. g.* 'Pendula'** (Tabletop elm) A form with a flat-topped head whose branches spread horizontally and are pendulous at the ends.
Zone 4 US, 5 Can.

***U.* × *hollandica* 'Jaqueline Hillier'** A medium-sized to large, slow-growing, suckering, dense shrub with small, double-toothed leaves. Its neat, dense, closely packed habit makes it suitable as a low hedge. It appears to be resistant to Dutch elm disease.
Zone 4 US, 4b Can.

U. japonica (Japanese elm) A graceful small tree that appears immune to Dutch elm disease. NE Asia, Japan.
Zone 4 US, 4b Can.

***U. minor* 'Dampieri Aurea'** A narrowly conical, small tree whose crowded, broad leaves are suffused with golden yellow.
Zone 4 US, 5 Can.

U. parvifolia (Chinese elm) A medium-sized tree with downy young shoots. The leaves are small, leathery, and glossy green and persist halfway through the winter. The flowers are produced in early fall. It appears to be unaffected by Dutch elm disease. N and C China, Korea, Taiwan, Japan. Introduced 1794.
Zone 4 US, 5 Can.

***U. p.* 'Frosty'** A small, slow-growing, shrubby form whose tiny, neatly arranged leaves have margins and teeth that are frosted with white.
Zone 4 US, 5 Can.

***U. p.* 'Pendens'** A form with drooping shoots and semievergreen leaves in mild climates. It is popular in southern California.
Zone 4 US, 5 Can.

U. pumila (Siberian elm) A medium-sized tree with oval to lance-shaped, toothed leaves. It is well suited to the Midwest, as it is very tolerant of drought. N Asia. Introduced 1770.
Zone 3 US, 3b Can.

***U.* 'Sapporo Autumn Gold'** A fast-growing, medium-sized tree with glossy green leaves that are tinged red when young and turn yellow-green in fall. It is resistant to Dutch elm disease.
Zone 4 US, 4b Can.

Ulmus minor 'Dampieri Aurea'

V

Vaccinium *Ericaceae*

A genus of about 450 species of evergreen and deciduous shrubs with wide distribution. They are modestly beautiful flowering shrubs with fine fall color in the deciduous species and notable crops of berries, many of which are edible and important commercially. They need moist, acidic, well-drained soil and are tolerant of shade; they should be mulched to protect their shallow roots and retain moisture. Pruning is seldom necessary.

Vaccinium corymbosum

V. angustifolium (Lowbush blueberry) A low-growing deciduous shrub, up to 8 in (20 cm) tall, with small, smooth, lance-shaped leaves that turn bright scarlet in fall. It is grown commercially for its round, blue-black, edible fruits. NE North America.
Zone 2 US, 2 Can.

V. ashei (Rabbiteye blueberry) A large deciduous or evergreen shrub grown in the South in place of *V. corymbosum*. The flowers are white or pink to red and the edible fruits are black. SE United States.
Zone 8 US, 9 Can.

V. corymbosum (Highbush blueberry) A medium-sized to large deciduous shrub that forms a dense clump of erect, branching stems. The leaves are up to 3 in (8 cm) long and turn vivid scarlet and bronze in fall. The pale pink or white, urn-shaped flowers are borne in late spring. The edible large berries are black with a blue bloom. It is cultivated commercially, and named forms

Vaccinium cylindraceum

with superior fruit quality are now available; some are hybrids with other species. E North America. Introduced 1765.
Zone 3 US, 4 Can. 🏆

V. crassifolium (Creeping blueberry) An evergreen creeping shrub that forms a ground cover up to 6 ft (2 m) wide. It has small, elliptic leaves and tiny pink flowers in late spring. The edible fruits are purple-black. SE United States.
Zone 7 US, 8 Can.

V. cylindraceum A semievergreen species forming a medium-sized to large shrub. The cylindrical flowers are packed into short clusters along the previous year's branchlets in late summer and fall. They are red in bud, open to pale yellow-green tinged with red, and are followed by cylindrical, blue-black, bloomy berries. Azores.
Zone 10 US 🏆

V. delavayi (Delaway blueberry) A neat, compact, evergreen shrub, slowly reaching 2 ft (60 cm), that is densely set with small, boxlike, leathery leaves. The tiny, pink-tinged flowers are in clusters at the ends of the shoots in late spring or early summer. The round berries are purplish blue. China. Introduced before 1923 by George Forrest.
Zone 6 US, 7 Can.

V. floribundum A small evergreen shrub with red young growths and small, dark green leaves that are purplish red when young. They are densely set on the spray-like branches. The cylindrical, rose-pink flowers are in dense clusters in early summer, and the berries are red and edible. Andes of Ecuador. Introduced c. 1840.
Zone 9 US

Vaccinium glaucoalbum

V. glaucoalbum A suckering evergreen shrub that forms patches up to 6½ ft (2 m) high. The comparatively large leaves are more or less oval, gray-green above and vividly blue-white beneath. The cylindrical, pale pink flowers are borne in clusters among rosy, silvery white bracts in late spring and early summer. The berries are black with a blue bloom and last into winter. It may be damaged by frost at the limits of its range. Himalayan region. In cultivation 1900.
Zone 9 US 🏆

Vaccinium moupinense

V. macrocarpon (Cranberry) A prostrate evergreen shrublet with slender, wiry, creeping stems and small oval leaves. The flowers are small, drooping, and pink, with the petals curving back to reveal yellow anthers. They are carried in short clusters in summer. The fruits are red, globular, and edible but tart. It needs a moist, peaty, boggy soil. Selected clones are grown com-

Vaccinium nummularia

Vaccinium vitis-idaea 'Koralle'

mercially for cranberries. E North America. Introduced 1760.
Zone 2 US, 2 Can.

V. moupinense A neat, dwarf, evergreen shrub with a dense habit. It has narrow oval leaves and urn-shaped, mahogany red flowers that are borne on stalks of the same color in dense clusters in late spring and early summer. The rounded berries are purplish black. W China. Introduced 1909 by Ernest Wilson. *(See photo on p.609.)*
Zone 9 US

V. nummularia A compact evergreen shrub with bristly-hairy, arching shoots that are covered with a double row of small, leathery, rounded leaves. The small rose-red flowers are in dense clusters at the ends of the shoots in late spring and early summer and are followed by edible black berries. Himalaya. Introduced c. 1850.
Zone 7 US, 8 Can.

V. ovatum (Box blueberry) A medium-sized evergreen shrub grown for its foliage, which covers the downy branches thickly. The leathery leaves are bright coppery red when young and become lustrous dark green. The white or pink, bell-shaped flowers are in short clusters in late spring and early summer. The berries are red at first, ripening to black. W North America. Introduced 1826 by David Douglas.
Zone 6 US, 7 Can.

V. praestans (Cherry blueberry) A creeping deciduous shrub that forms dense patches 1–4 in (2.5–10 cm) high. The leaves, 1–2 in (2.5–5 cm) long, turn color in fall. The white to reddish, bell-shaped flowers are borne singly or in clusters of 2–3 in early summer. The large berries are globular, bright glossy red, fragrant, and sweetly edible. NE Asia, Japan. Introduced 1914.
Zone 4 US, 4b Can.

V. retusum A dwarf, slow-growing, evergreen shrub up to 3 ft (1 m) tall. It has stiff, downy shoots; small, leathery, oval leaves; and small, urn-shaped, pink flowers in late spring. E Himalaya. Introduced c. 1882.
Zone 8 US, 9? Can.

***V. vitis-idaea* 'Koralle'** A form of the mountain cranberry, this is a dwarf, creeping, evergreen shrub. The leaves are small and box-like, and the bell-shaped flowers are white tinged with pink and borne in short clusters from early to late summer. The large red berries are borne freely.
Zone 1 US, 1 Can. 🏆

Vestia *Solanaceae*

A genus of one evergreen species, related to Cestrum.

V. foetida A small, erect shrub whose leaves have an unpleasant smell when bruised. The flowers are nodding, tubular, pale yellow, and borne profusely from mid-spring to midsummer. They are followed by small yellow fruits. Chile. Introduced 1815.
Zone 9 US

Vestia foetida

Viburnum

Caprifoliaceae

While you will probably never see a border planted solely with viburnums, it would be entirely possible to do so and still achieve a beautiful display of diverse plants that offer many ornamental features.

There are about 150 species of evergreen and deciduous shrubs in the genus, with a very wide distribution in north-temperate regions. Their most noteworthy characteristic is their white or pink-tinged blooms, which generally appear between midwinter and late spring. The blooms come in three forms: globular "snowballs" of sterile flowers, flat clusters of fertile flowers, and flat clusters of fertile flowers surrounded by a ring of sterile flowers. They emit a strong, sweet perfume that is a welcome addition to the garden at any time; *V. carlesii* is the most fragrant species.

Viburnums also offer a range of attractive foliage. The evergreen *V.* × *burkwoodii*, for instance, has glossy leaves, while those of *V. carlesii* are soft and velvety. *V. trilobum* has broad, lobed, maplelike leaves, whereas *V. rhytidophyllum*, the aptly named leatherleaf viburnum, bears long, elliptic, leathery leaves that are deeply etched. In fall the foliage color rivals that of the Japanese maples. *V. lantanoides* turns deep red, for example, while *V. carlesii* changes to amber and soft red.

Additionally, many viburnums are excellent as fruiting shrubs, with clusters of large berries in a variety of colors. Most are red, including those of *V. dilatatum* and *V. trilobum*. *V. davidii* produces blue berries, and those of *V. opulus* 'Xanthocarpum' are a clear yellow. *V. lantana* and *V. plicatum* are among those that have red fruits maturing to black, and the berries of *V. lentago* change from yellowish green to red to blue-black. The fruits of *V. trilobum* are edible and can be used for making preserves. Fruits of all viburnums, however, are very attractive to birds, who can quickly pick a shrub clean.

Viburnums range in size from dwarfs like *V. farreri* 'Nanum' to the treelike *V. lentago*, which can reach 30 ft (9 m). One species, *V. plicatum*, has a distinctive horizontal branching habit. The form 'Mariesii' in particular has attractively tiered branches that make it stand out in the landscape.

Care and cultivation

Viburnums are vigorous and easy to grow, which in part accounts for their widespread popularity. They prefer deep, moisture-retentive but well-drained, slightly acidic to neutral soil in sun or part shade. *V. lantanoides* is one that needs acidic soil and a cool, shady location, like that of a woodland. Evergreens should be pruned in late spring and deciduous viburnums immediately after flowering.

Viburnums are of variable hardiness, and the evergreens are for the most part a little less hardy than the deciduous ones. Berry production is uncertain unless more than one clone of the same species is grown or related species flower at the same time as one another. The exception is *V. opulus*, although forms with sterile florets, such as *V. o.* 'Roseum', cannot bear fruits at all.

V. opulus often suffers from snowball aphid, which causes severe leaf curl, and the viburnum aphid feeds on many species, especially *V.* × *burkwoodii*, but causes little damage. Except for these pests, viburnums are remarkably trouble-free.

Viburnum × *bodnantense* 'Dawn'

V. betulifolium (Birchleaf viburnum) A large, erect shrub with coarsely toothed

Viburnum betulifolium

leaves and wide, flat heads of white flowers in early summer. It is beautiful in fall, when the long, swaying branches are heavy with bunches of fruits that resemble red currants and persist into winter. Young plants do not fruit freely, and a group of plants from different sources should be planted to ensure fruiting. W and C China. Introduced 1901 by Ernest Wilson.
Zone 5 US, 6 Can.

V. × bodnantense A vigorous, medium-sized to large shrub with densely packed clusters of sweetly scented, rose-tinted flowers that are freely produced over several weeks from midfall onward, well into winter. First raised 1933 at the Royal Botanic Garden, Edinburgh, and then 1935 at Bodnant Gardens. Zone 6 US, 7 Can.

***V. × b.* 'Charles Lamont'** A form with pure pink flowers like those of *V. farreri*. One of the original seedlings raised 1933 at the Royal Botanic Garden, Edinburgh.
Zone 6 US, 7 Can. 🏆

***V. × b.* 'Dawn'** This was the first named form of the cross, and it is considered one of the most beautiful. It has highly scented, rose-tinted flowers that darken with age. *(See photo on p.611.)*
Zone 6 US, 7 Can. 🏆

***V. × b.* 'Deben'** A lovely shrub with clusters of sweetly scented flowers that are pink in bud and open white during mild spells from midfall to midspring.
Zone 6 US, 7 Can. 🏆

V. × burkwoodii (Burkwood viburnum) A

Viburnum × bodnantense 'Charles Lamont'

Viburnum × bodnantense 'Deben'

beautiful medium-sized evergreen or semi-evergreen shrub. It inherits its fragrant, pink-budded, white flowers from *V. carlesii*, one of its parents. The leaves are glossy dark green above and brownish-gray-felted beneath. Flowering is from midwinter to late spring. The fruits are red changing to black. Raised c. 1924 at Burkwood and Skipworth Nursery, Kingston-on-Thames, England.
Zone 5 US, 6 Can.

***V. × b.* 'Anne Russell'** A pretty, more compact, less evergreen hybrid with clusters of fragrant flowers. Raised c. 1951.
Zone 5 US, 6 Can. 🏆

***V. × b.* 'Fulbrook'** A later-flowering form with clusters of comparatively large, sweetly scented flowers that are pink in bud and open white.
Zone 5 US, 6 Can. 🏆

***V. × b.* 'Park Farm Hybrid'** A vigorous medium-sized shrub, with a more spreading habit and slightly larger clusters of fragrant flowers in mid- to late spring.
Zone 5 US, 6 Can. 🏆

Viburnum × burkwoodii 'Anne Russell'

Viburnum × burkwoodii 'Park Farm Hybrid'

V. × carlcephalum (Fragrant snowball) A compact, medium-sized, deciduous shrub with rounded clusters up to 5 in (13 cm) across of relatively large, very fragrant, pink-budded, white flowers in late spring. The glossy leaves have good fall color, and

Viburnum × carlcephalum

the fruits are red, changing to black. Raised c. 1932.
Zone 5 US, 6 Can. 🏆

V. carlesii (Korean spice viburnum) This is one of the most deliciously scented shrubs. It is a medium-sized, rounded, deciduous shrub with ovate, velvety-downy leaves that color beautifully in fall. The rounded clusters of white flowers, borne in mid- and late spring, are pink in bud and emit a sweet, daphnelike fragrance. The fruits are blue-black and appear in summer. Korea. Introduced 1902.
Zone 4 US, 5b Can.

***V. c.* 'Aurora'** An outstanding selection with red buds opening to deliciously fragrant pink flowers.
Zone 4 US, 5b Can. 🏆

Viburnum carlesii 'Diana'

***V. c.* 'Diana'** A vigorous medium-sized form with pink flowers that open from reddish buds. Young foliage is tinged purple.
Zone 4 US, 5b Can. 🏆

Viburnum 'Chesapeake'

***V.* 'Chesapeake'** A small shrub that forms a mound broader than it is tall, with glossy, dark green, persistent leaves. The flowers are pink in bud, open white, and are followed by red fruits that turn black.
Zone 6 US, 7 Can.

Viburnum cinnamomifolium

V. cinnamomifolium A large evergreen shrub with large, leathery leaves and small, white flowers borne in flat clusters 4–6 in (10–15 cm) across in early summer. They are followed in fall by small, egg-shaped, shiny blue-black fruits. Will take part shade. China. Introduced 1904 by Ernest Wilson.
Zone 7 US, 8 Can. 🏆

V. davidii (David viburnum) A small, compact, evergreen shrub that forms a low, wide mound and makes a good ground cover. The large, narrowly oval leaves have three veins and are glossy dark green above, paler beneath. The flowers are small, dull white, and borne in terminal clusters in early summer, and the bright blue egg-shaped fruits are striking in winter. More than one specimen is needed to ensure pollination. W China. Introduced 1904 by Ernest Wilson.
Zone 7 US, 8 Can. 🏆

Viburnum davidii

V. dentatum (Arrowwood) A large, vigorous, deciduous shrub with glossy, bright red foliage in fall. Its showy fruits are blue-black. E United States.
Zone 3 US, 3 Can.

Viburnum dilatatum

V. dilatatum (Linden viburnum) A medium-sized deciduous shrub with oval to fairly rounded, coarsely toothed leaves and pure white, pungently scented flowers borne in trusses in late spring and early summer. The fall foliage is russet red, and the vivid red fruits often last well into winter. Japan. Introduced before 1875.
Zone 4 US, 5 Can.

***V.* 'Eskimo'** A small semievergreen shrub with leathery leaves and compact white flower heads, 3 in (7.5 cm) across, that look

Viburnum 'Eskimo'

like snowballs. They are borne in mid-spring, opening from pink-tinged cream buds. The fruits are red and turn black. Introduced by the U.S. National Arboretum, Washington, D.C.
Zone 5 US, 6 Can.

Viburnum farreri

V. farreri, syn. *V. fragrans* (Fragrant viburnum) A medium-sized to large deciduous shrub with stiff, erect branches but a broad, rounded outline as it ages. Its leaves are bronze when young. The scented flowers are in terminal and lateral clusters and open white from pink buds in early spring; buds need protection in cold climates. The red fruits are seldom produced. N China. Introduced 1910 by William Purdom and later by Reginald Farrer.
Zone 4 US, 5b Can. 🏆

***V. f.* 'Candidissimum'** A distinctive form with young leaves that are green, not bronze, and pure white flowers.
Zone 4 US, 5b Can.

Viburnum farreri 'Candidissimum'

Viburnum farreri 'Nanum'

***V. f.* 'Nanum'** A dense, dwarf form with a compact, moundlike habit. The flowers are pleasantly scented but sparsely produced.
Zone 4 US, 5b Can.

V. foetens A beautiful, fragrant, medium-sized, deciduous shrub of loose spreading habit with white flowers that are occasionally pink in bud and open from late winter to early spring. It tolerates part shade. W Himalaya. In cultivation 1937.
Zone 6 US, 7 Can.

Viburnum foetens

V. fragrans See *V. farreri.*

V. furcatum A large deciduous shrub with fairly rounded leaves up to 6 in (15 cm) long that are colorful over a long period in late summer and fall. The flowers appear in late spring and are in flattened, terminal clusters, surrounded by several ray florets, much like those of a lacecap hydrangea. The fruits are red and turn black. Japan, Taiwan. Introduced 1892.
Zone 6 US, 7 Can. 🏆

Viburnum furcatum

***V. × globosum* 'Jermyn's Globe'** A small to medium-sized, evergreen, rounded, dense shrub with leathery, narrow leaves and small white flowers in flattened clusters in late spring and often at other times of the year. The egg-shaped fruits are bluish black. Originated 1964 at Hillier's West Hill Nursery.
Zone 7? US, 8? Can.

Viburnum × globosum 'Jermyn's Globe'

V. grandiflorum A medium-sized deciduous shrub with fragrant white flowers that are flushed with rose and open in late winter to early spring. The fruits are blue-black to purple. Himalaya, W China.
Zone 7 US, 8 Can.

V. harryanum A medium-sized, dense, evergreen shrub with distinctive small, neat, round leaves, often in whorls of three. The small white flowers open in late spring, and the egg-shaped fruits are shiny black. China. Introduced 1904 by Ernest Wilson.
Zone 9 US

Viburnum henryi

V. henryi (Henry viburnum) A medium-sized, eventually large evergreen shrub with an open, erect habit. The fragrant white flowers are borne in pyramidal panicles in early summer and are followed by ellipsoid fruits that are bright red, then black. Introduced 1901 from China by Ernest Wilson. Zone 7 US, 8 Can.

Viburnum × hillieri 'Winton'

***V. × hillieri* 'Winton'** A medium-sized, semievergreen shrub with spreading and ascending branches and narrowly oval leaves that are copper-tinted when unfolding and suffused with bronze-red in winter. The creamy white flowers are profusely borne in panicles in early summer and are succeeded by red fruits that turn black. The hybrid, of which this is the original selected clone, arose 1950 at Hillier Nurseries. Zone 6 US, 7 Can. 🏆

V. japonicum (Japanese viburnum) A medium-sized, evergreen shrub with firm, leathery, often puckered leaves up to 6 in

Viburnum japonicum

(15 cm) long and 4 in (10 cm) wide. The fragrant white flowers are borne in dense, rounded trusses in early summer but not on young plants. The fruits are red. Japan. Introduced c. 1879 by Charles Maries. Zone 8 US, 9 Can.

Viburnum × juddii

V. × juddii (Judd viburnum) A small to medium-sized, bushy, deciduous shrub with freely produced terminal clusters of sweetly scented, pink-tinted white flowers in mid- to late spring. The fruits are red-black. It has a better constitution than *V. carlesii*, which is one of its parents, and is less prone to aphid attacks. Raised 1920 by William Judd at the Arnold Arboretum, Boston, Mass. Zone 4 US, 5 Can. 🏆

V. lantana (Wayfaring tree) A large, deciduous, treelike shrub with broadly ovate leaves. The young shoots are covered with a dense tomentum, sometimes turning dark crimson in fall. The creamy white flowers appear in late spring and early summer and are followed by oblong red fruits that mature to black. Tolerates dry and alkaline soils. C and S Europe, N Asia Minor, North Africa; naturalized in E United States. Zone 2 US, 2b Can.

Viburnum lantanoides

V. lantanoides (Hobblebush) A medium-sized shrub with fairly large, rounded leaves that turn claret in fall. The white flower heads resemble those of a lacecap hydrangea and appear in late spring and early summer. The red fruits turn blackish purple. It prefers woodland conditions and acid soil. E North America. Introduced 1820. Zone 2 US, 2b Can.

V. lentago (Nannyberry, sheepberry) A large, treelike, deciduous shrub with glossy green leaves that turn purple-red in fall. It produces large clusters of white flowers in spring, and its berries turn from yellowish green to red to blue-black. North America. Zone 3 US, 3 Can.

Viburnum macrocephalum 'Sterile'

V. macrocephalum **'Sterile'** A semi-evergreen, medium-sized, rounded form of the Chinese snowball. The flowers are in large, globular heads that resemble those of a mophead hydrangea. Garden origin. China. Introduced 1844. *(See photo on p.615.)*
Zone 6 US, 7 Can.

V. odoratissimum (Sweet viburnum) A large evergreen shrub with glossy, oval, leathery leaves. The fragrant white flowers are borne in large, conical panicles in summer, and the fruits are red, turning black. India to Japan. Introduced c. 1818.
Zone 8 US, 9 Can.

Viburnum opulus

Viburnum opulus 'Xanthocarpum'

V. opulus (European cranberry bush) A large, vigorous, deciduous shrub with five-lobed, maplelike leaves that turn red in fall and flattened clusters of white flowers in late spring, like those of a lacecap hydrangea. The red, translucent fruits last well into winter and have an unpleasant scent. It does best in boggy soil and tolerates urban sites. Europe, Asia, N Africa.
Zone 3 US, 3 Can.

V. o. **'Aureum'** A compact, medium-sized form with bright yellow leaves that turn green. It tends to burn in full sun.
Zone 3 US, 3 Can.

V. o. **'Compactum'** A small, dense shrub that flowers and fruits freely.
Zone 2 US, 2b Can. 🏆

V. o. **'Notcutt's Variety'** A large shrub with larger flowers and fruits.
Zone 2 US, 2 Can. 🏆

V. o. **'Roseum'**, syn. *V. o.* 'Sterile' (European snowball, guelder rose) A popular and attractive shrub whose cream flowers are gathered into conspicuous globular heads. The cultivar name relates to the fact that the individual florets resemble small, single roses. It is very vulnerable to infestations of plant lice.
Zone 2 US, 2b Can. 🏆

Viburnum opulus 'Roseum'

V. o. **'Sterile'** See *V. o.* 'Roseum'.

V. o. **'Xanthocarpum'** A medium-sized shrub with fruits that are pure, clear yellow at all stages, becoming a little darker and almost translucent when ripe.
Zone 2 US, 2b Can. 🏆

V. plicatum (Japanese snowball) A wide-spreading, medium-sized, deciduous shrub with a distinctive method of branching that gives it considerable architectural value. The branches are in layers, creating an attractive tiered effect over time, and the leaves are bright green and pleated. The inflorescences, which appear in late spring and early summer, are umbels of small, fertile, creamy flowers, surrounded by large, white ray florets, like those of a lacecap hydrangea. They are borne in double rows along the upper sides of the branches. The fruits are red, turning black, and the leaves are often tinted red to purple in fall. China, Japan, Taiwan. Introduced c. 1865.
Zone 5 US, 6 Can.

V. p. **'Grandiflorum'** A medium-sized shrub similar to *V. p.* 'Sterile' but with

Viburnum plicatum 'Grandiflorum'

larger heads of sterile white florets, flushed pink at the margins.
Zone 5 US, 6 Can. 🏆

***V. p.* 'Lanarth'** A fine medium-sized shrub, resembling *V. p.* 'Mariesii' but more

Viburnum plicatum 'Lanarth'

vigorous and less horizontally branched.
Zone 5 US, 6 Can.

***V. p.* 'Mariesii'** A superb medium-sized shrub with tiered branches and an abundance of flowers that when open make the bush seem to be covered with snow. The ray florets are relatively large, the leaves are colorful in fall, and the red fruits, held on red stalks, turn black.
Zone 4 US, 5b Can. 🏆

***V. p.* 'Nanum Semperflorens'**, syn. *V. p.* 'Watanabe' A slow-growing, small, dense form with white flowers borne over a long period in summer and fall. Found wild in Japan c. 1956 by Kanji Watanabe.
Zone 5 US, 6 Can.

***V. p.* 'Pink Beauty'** A charming selection

Viburnum plicatum 'Mariesii'

Viburnum plicatum 'Nanum Semperflorens'

Viburnum plicatum 'Pink Beauty'

whose white ray florets change to pink as they age. It is free-fruiting.
Zone 5 US, 6 Can. 🏆

***V. p.* 'Roseum'** A form whose florets open white and then change to a deep pink.
Zone 5 US, 6 Can.

***V. p.* 'Rowallane'** A medium-sized shrub similar to *V. p.* 'Lanarth' but a little less vigorous. The ray florets are larger, and it usually produces a good crop of fruits. It has good fall color.
Zone 5 US, 6 Can. 🏆

Viburnum plicatum 'Shasta'

***V. p.* 'Shasta'** A profusely flowering, wide-spreading form, like *V. p.* 'Lanarth' but with larger ray florets. The bright red fruits turn black. Raised 1970 in the United States.
Zone 4 US, 5b Can.

Viburnum plicatum 'Sterile'

***V. p.* 'Sterile'** (Japanese snowball) A popular, medium-sized, dense, spreading shrub. The white, sterile florets are concentrated in globular heads up to 3 in (7.5 cm) across, borne in a double row along the length of each arching branch in late spring and early summer. It is sometimes confused with *V. opulus* 'Sterile'. Garden origin. China. Introduced 1844 by Robert Fortune.
Zone 5 US, 6 Can.

***V. p.* 'Summer Snowflake'** A medium-sized shrub with tiered branches and lace-

Viburnum plicatum 'Summer Snowflake'

cap flower heads in late spring and onward through summer. The leaves turn red to purple in fall. Introduced c. 1980 by the University of British Columbia.
Zone 5 US, 6 Can.

V. p.* f. *tomentosum (Double-file viburnum) A large shrub with almost horizontal, overlapping branches. The creamy white flowers are in flat-topped clusters, arranged in two rows above the branches. The leaves turn wine red in fall, and the red fruits turn black. Introduced 1865 from China.
Zone 5 US, 6 Can.

***V. p.* 'Watanabe'** See *V. p.* 'Nanum Semperflorens'.

***V.* × *rhytidophylloides* 'Alleghany'** A large shrub with elliptical, leathery, dark green, puckered leaves; clusters of yellowish white flowers; and brilliant red fruits that ripen to black. Introduced by the U.S. National Arboretum, Washington, D.C.
Zone 4 US, 5 Can.

V. rhytidophyllum (Leatherleaf viburnum) A large, fast-growing, evergreen or semievergreen shrub with large, elliptic to oblong, crinkled leaves that are dark green above and densely gray-felted beneath. The small, creamy flowers are borne in stout, felty clusters in late spring. The oval fruits turn from red to black, but two or more plants are required for free fruiting. It is an excellent foliage shrub, creating the effect of a large-leaved rhododendron. China. Introduced 1900 by Ernest Wilson.
Zone 5 US, 6 Can.

Viburnum rhytidophyllum

Viburnum sargentii 'Onondaga'

***V. sargentii* 'Onondaga'** This large shrub is a form of the Sargent cranberry bush. The maplelike leaves are maroon when young, green when mature, and reddish purple in fall. The flowers are borne in lacecap heads, with the fertile flowers deep red in bud, surrounded by a loose ring of white, sterile flowers. Selected 1959 at the U.S. National Arboretum, Washington, D.C.
Zone 3 US, 3b Can. 🏆

Viburnum setigerum

V. setigerum (Tea viburnum) A distinctive, medium-sized, open, somewhat lax, deciduous shrub. The slender-pointed, slightly toothed leaves constantly change color, from blue-red through shades of green to orange-yellow in fall. The trusses of white flowers in early summer are followed by clusters of large, orange-yellow, somewhat flattened, oval fruits that mature to bright red. China. Introduced 1901 by Ernest Wilson.
Zone 5 US, 6 Can.

Viburnum tinus

V. sieboldii (Siebold viburnum) A large, treelike, deciduous shrub with long, elliptic, wrinkled leaves and round clusters of white flowers. The rosy red fruits are held on red stalks and turn black.
Zone 4 US, 5 Can.

V. tinus (Laurustinus) A medium-sized to large evergreen shrub with masses of glossy green, oval leaves. The flattened clusters of pink-budded, white flowers are borne continuously from late fall to early spring. The egg-shaped fruits are metallic blue and turn black. It makes an attractive informal hedge and tolerates shade. Mediterranean region. In cultivation since the late 16th century.
Zone 7 US, 8 Can.

***V. t.* 'Eve Price'** A dense, compact, medium-sized shrub with smaller leaves than the type. Its pink-tinged flowers open from carmine buds.
Zone 7 US, 8 Can. 🏆

***V. t.* 'French White'** A vigorous medium-sized to large shrub that bears large heads of white flowers.
Zone 7 US, 8 Can.

Viburnum tinus 'Eve Price'

Viburnum tinus 'French White'

Viburnum tinus 'Gwenllian'

***V. t.* 'Gwenllian'** A compact, medium-sized form with small leaves. The flowers are deep pink in bud and open to white with a pink flush on the backs of the lobes.
Zone 7 US, 8 Can. 🏆

***V. t.* 'Lucidum'** This is a vigorous medium-sized to large shrub with relatively large leaves and flower heads that are larger

Viburnum tinus 'Lucidum'

than those of the type and open white in early to midspring.
Zone 7 US, 8 Can.

Viburnum tinus 'Purpureum'

***V. t.* 'Purpureum'** A medium-sized to large shrub with very dark green leaves that are tinted purple when young.
Zone 7 US, 8 Can.

Viburnum tinus 'Variegatum'

***V. t.* 'Variegatum'** A medium-sized shrub with leaves variegated with creamy yellow.
Zone 8 US, 9? Can.

V. trilobum (Highbush cranberry, American cranberry bush) A tall, usually slender shrub with maplelike leaves and white flowers in early summer. The edible bright red berries in summer persist well into winter. E North America. Introduced 1812.
Zone 2 US, 2 Can.

***V. t.* 'Compactum'** This dwarf form grows only about 6 ft (1.8 m) tall and can be used for a hedge.
Zone 2 US, 2 Can.

Viburnum wrightii 'Hessei'

***V. t.* 'Wentworth'** This form was selected for its larger fruits and better fall color.
Zone 2 US, 2 Can.

***V. wrightii* 'Hessei'** A dwarf form of the Wright viburnum with broad, ovate, prettily veined leaves and clusters of white flowers in late spring, followed by red fruits in fall. It is an excellent shrub for the front of the border.
Zone 5 US, 6 Can.

Vinca *Apocynaceae*

Periwinkle

A genus of seven species of herbaceous plants and evergreen shrubs that are natives of Europe, North Africa, and western and central Asia. The following are vigorous, evergreen, trailing shrubs that make extensive carpets and are ideal as ground cover in sun or shade. They grow in all fertile soils. The shoots root as they go but not very deeply, and the plants can easily be controlled by cutting back the stems in late winter.

Vinca major

V. major (Big periwinkle) A rampant, arching, trailing species that roots only at the tips of the shoots. The leaves are up to 3 in (7.5 cm) long, and the flowers are bright blue, 1½ in (4 cm) across, and borne in the leaf axils in late spring and early summer. C and S Europe, North Africa.
Zone 6 US, 7 Can.

Vinca major 'Maculata'

***V. m.* 'Maculata'** The leaves have a central blotch of greenish yellow, which becomes more noticeable on young plants in open locations.
Zone 6 US, 7 Can.

***V. m.* 'Variegata'** The leaves are blotched and margined with cream. The plant is as vigorous as the green form.
Zone 6 US, 7 Can. 🏆

V. minor (Common periwinkle, myrtle) A familiar ground cover with long, trailing stems that root at intervals and leaves up to 2 in (5 cm) long. It bears bright blue flowers, 1 in (2.5 cm) wide, singly on the leaf

Vinca major 'Variegata'

Vinca minor

axils of short, erect shoots from midspring to early summer and then intermittently until fall. Europe, W Asia.
Zone 3 US, 3 Can. 🏆

Vinca minor 'Argenteo-variegata'

***V. m.* 'Argenteo-variegata'** Leaves are variegated with cream and flowers are blue.
Zone 3 US, 3b Can. 🏆

***V. m.* 'Atropurpurea'** A form with deep plum-purple flowers.
Zone 3 US, 4 Can. 🏆

***V. m.* 'Aureovariegata'** The leaves are blotched with yellow and the flowers are blue.
Zone 3 US, 4 Can.

***V. m.* 'Azurea Flore Pleno'** A form with sky blue, double flowers.
Zone 3 US, 3 Can. 🏆

Vinca minor 'Gertrude Jekyll'

***V. m.* 'Gertrude Jekyll'** A form with glistening white flowers.
Zone 3 US, 4 Can. 🏆

Vinca minor 'La Grave'

***V. m.* 'La Grave'** The flowers of this form are azure blue, larger than those of the type. 'Bowles' Variety' is now regarded as a synonym for this plant.
Zone 3 US, 3 Can. 🏆

***V. m.* 'Multiplex'** A form with plum-purple, double flowers.
Zone 3 US, 3b Can.

Vitex *Verbenaceae*
Chaste tree

Of the some 250 species in this genus, the few that are grown in cool-temperate gardens are deciduous and are valued for their aromatic foliage and scented flowers. In maritime locations they need good drainage and full sun to ripen their growth and maximize flowering. They are excellent against a sunny wall. Old flowering shoots can be pruned in either late winter or very early spring. At the northern limits of the range, the tops may die back, but new shoots will emerge in spring.

Vitex agnus-castus

V. agnus-castus (Lilac chaste tree) An attractive, spreading, aromatic, medium-sized shrub with pairs of leaves consisting of 5–7 short-stalked leaflets. The fragrant violet flowers are held in slender racemes at the ends of the current year's shoots in early to midfall. Mediterranean region to C Asia. In cultivation since 1570.
Zone 6 US, 7 Can.

Vitex agnus-castus f. *alba*

V. a.* f. *alba A medium-sized shrub with white flowers.
Zone 6 US, 7 Can.

Vitis *Vitaceae*
Grape

This genus comprises about 60 species of climbers that support themselves by twining tendrils. They are widely distributed throughout the north-temperate regions, particularly in North America. Some of them are grown for their fruits, used for table grapes and in wine making, although many of them are grown for their ornamental value. They often have flaking bark and are variable in leaf, with several species showing fall color. Most are vigorous and can be trained to cover walls, pergolas, arches, and fences. They will tolerate a variety of conditions but grow best in well-drained, fertile soil, preferably in full sun or light shade. The small, greenish flowers are in panicles or racemes in summer and are not particularly beautiful, although they are followed after hot, dry seasons by bunches of small grapes.

Vitis 'Brant'

***V.* 'Brant'** This vine reaches a height of 30 ft (9 m), if provided with a suitable support, and produces cylindrical bunches of sweet, aromatic, dark purple-black grapes that are bloomy when ripe. The attractive, deeply three- to five-lobed leaves turn dark red and purple in fall, with greenish or yellow veins. It is not a form of the common grape vine but a seedling of multiple parentage. It is now very hard to find commercially. Raised early 1860s in Canada by Charles Arnold.
Zone 7? US, 8? Can. 🏆

Vitis coignetiae

V. coignetiae (Crimson glory vine) This is one of the most spectacular vines and can reach up to 50 ft (15 m). The leaves often measure 1 ft (30 cm) across and are heart shaped at the base, with 3–5 shallow lobes and a rust-colored felt beneath. The fruits are black with a purple bloom. The leaves turn crimson and scarlet in fall and put on a magnificent display. The best color occurs where the soil is poor or the root run is restricted, as when the plant is grown on a wall. Japan, Korea. In cultivation c. 1875.
Zone 4 US, 5 Can. 🏆

V. pulchra A large climber with reddish shoots and coarsely toothed leaves up to 6 in (15 cm) wide. The young leaves are reddish and the fall foliage is bright scarlet. It is possibly a hybrid of *V. coignetiae.* In cultivation 1880.
Zone 5 US, 6 Can.

V. vinifera (Vine grape) Although this is the species from which the finest wine-grape varieties are selected, some forms are

Vitis vinifera

Vitis vinifera 'Apiifolia'

ornamental. The following are recommended. S and C Europe.

***V. v.* 'Apiifolia'** A large, attractive plant with deeply divided leaves.
Zone 5 US, 6 Can.

***V. v.* 'Fragola'** A large, unusual form with small fruits that have a musky flavor somewhat like strawberries or gooseberries.
Zone 5 US, 6 Can.

***V. v.* 'Incana'** (Dusty miller grape) The three-lobed or unlobed leaves of this medium-sized climber are gray-green and covered with a white, cobwebby down. It has black fruits.
Zone 5 US, 6 Can.

Vitis vinifera 'Purpurea'

***V. v.* 'Purpurea'** (Teinturier grape) The leaves of this medium-sized climber are claret red at first and become a deep wine-purple. It is most effective when grown among shrubs that have silver foliage. *Teinturier* is French for "dyer."
Zone 5 US, 6 Can. 🏆

W

Wattaka

W. sinensis See *Dregea sinensis*.

Weigela *Caprifoliaceae*

A genus of about 10 species of deciduous flowering shrubs from temperate eastern Asia. They are very ornamental and easily grown, reaching an average height of 6 1/2 ft (2 m). They are ideal for urban gardens and other areas where there may be air pollution. The tubular, foxglovelike flowers appear primarily in late spring and early summer all along the shoots of the previous year. Occasionally a small second crop of flowers is produced in late summer or early fall. They grow in any reasonably fertile soil. Old flowering shoots should be thinned out and cut back to within a short distance of the old wood immediately after flowering.

Weigela florida

W. florida (Old-fashioned weigela) A medium-sized shrub with ovate-oblong to obovate, tapering leaves. The funnel-shaped flowers are reddish or rose-pink on the outside, paler within. It is the most popular species and is the parent of many hybrids. Japan, Korea, Manchuria, N China. Introduced 1845 by Robert Fortune.
Zone 4 US, 5 Can.

***W. f.* 'Foliis Purpureis'** A slower-growing, dwarf form of compact habit that has purple-flushed leaves and pink flowers.
Zone 4 US, 4b Can. 🏆

***W. f.* 'Variegata'** A compact, small to medium-sized shrub with leaves edged with cream and rose-pink flowers.
Zone 4 US, 5 Can. 🏆

W. f.* var. *venusta A graceful shrub with dense clusters of pale purple-pink flowers.
Zone 4 US, 5 Can.

Weigela florida 'Versicolor'

***W. f.* 'Versicolor'** A small to medium-sized shrub with creamy white flowers, changing to red.
Zone 4 US, 5 Can.

***W. hortensis* 'Nivea'** A beautiful small to medium-sized shrub with leaves that are densely white-downy beneath. It bears large white flowers. In cultivation 1870.
Zone 7 US, 8 Can.

W. middendorffiana (Middendorf weigela) A small, compact shrub with flaking bark and bell-shaped, sulphur yellow flowers with dark orange markings on the lower lobes; they are produced in mid- to late spring. It is best grown in a cool, moist, sheltered, partly shady site. Japan, N China,

Weigela praecox 'Variegata'

Manchuria. Introduced 1850.
Zone 4 US, 5 Can.

***W. praecox* 'Fleur de Mai'** A small shrub with profuse purplish pink flowers that are white streaked with pink inside.
Zone 5 US, 6 Can.

***W. p.* 'Variegata'** A small shrub with leaves variegated with creamy white and large, honey-scented, rose-pink flowers with yellow markings in the throat in midspring.
Zone 5 US, 6 Can. 🏆

HYBRIDS

The following is a selection of hardy hybrids that flower on old wood in late spring and early summer and often a second time in early fall. The flowering stems should be shortened or removed immediately after flowering.

Weigela 'Abel Carrière'

***W.* 'Abel Carrière'** A medium-sized shrub with many large, bright rose-carmine flowers, flecked gold in the throat. Buds are purple-carmine. In cultivation 1876.
Zone 4 US, 5 Can. 🏆

Weigela 'Bristol Ruby'

***W.* 'Bristol Ruby'** A vigorous, erect, medium-sized shrub with an abundance of ruby red flowers.
Zone 4 US, 5 Can.

Weigela 'Eva Rathke'

***W.* 'Eva Rathke'** A slow-growing, compact, medium-sized shrub bearing bright red-crimson flowers with straw-colored anthers that are borne over a long season.
Zone 4 US, 5 Can.

***W.* 'Java Red'** A compact shrub quite similar to *W. florida* 'Foliis Purpureis' but with red rather than pink flowers.
Zone 4 US, 5 Can.

***W.* 'Minuet'** A free-flowering dwarf shrub with dark red blooms produced over a long period and purple-tinged foliage. Introduced by Agriculture Canada, Ottawa.
Zone 3 US, 4 Can.

***W.* 'Mont Blanc'** A vigorous medium-sized shrub with large, fragrant, white flowers. It is perhaps the best white weigela. In cultivation 1898.
Zone 4 US, 5 Can. 🏆

***W.* 'Newport Red'**, syn. *W.* 'Vanicek' A superb medium-sized shrub, similar to 'Eve Rathke' but with larger, lighter red flowers.

Weigela 'Mont Blanc'

Weigela 'Rubidor'

Found by V. A. Vanicek of Newport, R.I.
Zone 4 US, 5 Can.

***W.* 'Pink Princess'** A taller selection from Iowa State University that has lilac-pink flowers.
Zone 4 US, 5 Can.

***W.* 'Red Prince'** A brother to 'Pink Princess' that bears bright red flowers over a long period.
Zone 4 US, 5 Can.

***W.* 'Rubidor'** A small shrub with yellow or green leaves that have broad yellow margins and carmine flowers. It is likely to burn if planted in full sun. *(See photo on p.623.)*
Zone 4 US, 5 Can.

***W.* 'Rumba'** A compact form with dark red flowers and light green foliage. It is very hardy.
Zone 3 US, 3b Can.

***W.* 'Vanicek'** See *W.* 'Newport Red'.

Wisteria *Leguminosae*

A genus of about 10 species of deciduous twiners that are native to eastern Asia and North America. These are among the most beautiful of all climbers, producing long, distinctive racemes of white, pink, blue, or mauve pea flowers in late spring and early summer and often repeating later in the year. The pinnate leaves are also very attractive.

Wisterias should be planted in full sun and good, fertile, loamy, well-drained soil. They are excellent for growing on walls and pergolas, and they can even be carefully trained into small standards. Large, vigorous specimens may require an annual hard pruning in late winter to keep them within bounds, and this can be followed in late summer by a second pruning that consists of shortening the leafy shoots to five or six buds. Pruning early in the life of the plant should, however, be concentrated on forming a strong framework of primary branches.

There are basically two types of wisterias: those that twine from left to right, such as W. sinensis, *and those that twine from right to left, such as* W. floribunda *and* W. venusta.

Cultivars have proliferated in recent years, and new forms often emerge with little to distinguish them from established ones. It is best to select forms that have proved themselves over time and to buy plants that have been vegetatively propagated instead of seedlings, which may not flower for many years. Wisterias are toxic if eaten.

W. floribunda (Japanese wisteria) A lovely climber up to 30 ft (9 m) high with leaves consisting of 13–19 leaflets. The fragrant, violet-blue or bluish purple flowers are held in slender racemes, up to 18 in (45 cm) long, that emerge with the leaves and open from the base upward. The stems twine in a clockwise direction. The following forms are recommended. Japan. Introduced 1830 by Philipp von Siebold.
Zone 5 US, 6 Can.

Wisteria floribunda 'Alba'

***W. f.* 'Alba'** The flowers are white with a lilac tint on the keel. They are borne in racemes 18–24 in (45–60 cm) long.
Zone 5 US, 6 Can. 🏆

***W. f.* 'Lawrence'** A form with pale blue flowers with a white keel. It is the hardiest wisteria.
Zone 4 US, 5 Can.

W. f.* f. *macrobotrys A group of forms with racemes to 1–3 ft (30–90 cm) or more. 'Multijuga', the most common, has fragrant lilac flowers tinged blue-purple. It is best grown on a pergola or arch to allow for the long flower clusters.
Zone 4 US, 5b Can. 🏆

Wisteria floribunda f. *macrobotrys*

Wisteria floribunda 'Rosea'

***W. f.* 'Rosea'** The flowers of this form are in long racemes and are pale rose, tipped with purple.
Zone 4 US, 5b Can. 🏆

Wisteria sinensis

W. sinensis (Chinese wisteria) This is perhaps the most popular wisteria and the largest, reaching 60–100 ft (18–30 m) with suitable support. The elegant leaves have 9–13 elliptic to elliptic-oblong leaflets. The fragrant mauve or deep lilac flowers, 1 in (2.5 cm) long, are borne before the leaves appear in late spring. They are produced in racemes 8–12 in (20–30 cm) long, and all the flowers open simultaneously; they are followed by velvety seedpods. The stems twine in a counterclockwise direction. Unlike *W. floribunda*, it often has a small second flush of flowers later in the summer. China. Introduced 1816 from a garden in Canton, China.
Zone 5 US, 6 Can.

***W. s.* 'Alba'** A form with white flowers.
Zone 5 US, 6b Can.

Wisteria sinensis 'Alba'

***W. s.* 'Black Dragon'** The flowers are double and dark purple, but many of the plants in cultivation appear to be *W. floribunda* 'Violacea Plena'.
Zone 5 US, 6 Can.

***W. s.* 'Caroline'** A form with deep blue-purple, very fragrant flowers.
Zone 5 US, 6 Can.

***W. s.* 'Jako'** A form with very fragrant white flowers.
Zone 5 US, 6 Can.

***W. s.* 'Plena'** A form with double, rosette-shaped, lilac flowers.
Zone 5 US, 6 Can.

Wisteria venusta

W. venusta (Silky wisteria) A vigorous climber reaching up to 30 ft (9 m) high. The leaves consist of 9–13 ovate to oval, downy leaflets. In late spring and early summer it bears slightly fragrant white flowers, which are the largest in the genus; they are in racemes that are 4–6 in (10–15 cm) long. The seedpods are velvety. Introduced before 1912 from Japan, where it is known only in cultivation.
Zone 6 US, 7 Can.

Xanthoceras *Sapindaceae*

A genus of one deciduous species that is related to Koelreuteria *but quite different in its general appearance.*

Xanthoceras sorbifolium

X. sorbifolium (Yellowhorn) A beautiful large shrub or small tree with lustrous, dark green, pinnate leaves composed of 9–17 leaflets. The flowers are 1 in (2.5 cm) wide and borne in late spring in erect clusters, like those of a horse chestnut. They are sweetly scented and white with a carmine eye that fades to soft carmine. It requires sun and warmth to ripen its growth and flower well and can be grown in all types of fertile soil, although it can also take a shady, moist location. N China. Introduced 1866.
Zone 4 US, 4b Can.

Xanthorhiza *Ranunculaceae*

A genus of one deciduous species. Although it is related to the buttercup family, it is very different in general appearance from other family members.

Xanthorhiza simplicissima

X. simplicissima (Yellow-root) A small, suckering shrub that eventually makes a clump of erect stems up to 3 ft (1 m) high. It has very attractive pinnate leaves, composed of 3–5 oval to lance-shaped, deeply toothed, bright green leaflets that turn red-orange to bronze, often with a purple tinge, in fall. The tiny, delicate, deep purple flowers appear in loose, drooping panicles with the leaves in early to mid-spring. The roots and inner bark are bright yellow. It thrives in moist clay but dislikes shallow, alkaline soil. Overgrown plants can be cut back to the ground in spring and mulched. It is useful as ground cover. E United States. Introduced 1776.
Zone 4 US, 5 Can.

Y

Yucca *Agavaceae*

This genus comprises about 40 species of evergreens that are native to semiarid regions of Central America, Mexico, and the United States. They produce rosettes or clumps of narrow, swordlike, usually rigid leaves and tall, candelabrum-like panicles of large, nodding, waxy, bell-shaped flowers; they are of great architectural value in the landsape. Several species are hardy in all but really cold conditions and prefer a hot, dry, well-drained location in full sun. They are well suited to gardens in coastal areas, and some make good container specimens.

Yucca filamentosa

Y. filamentosa (Adam's needle) A stemless species with dense clumps of spreading or erect, lance-shaped, slightly bloomy leaves. There are many curly white threads along the leaf margins. The creamy flowers, each 2–3 in (5–7.5 cm) long, are borne in erect, conical panicles 3–6½ ft (1–2 m) high in mid- to late summer, even on young plants. It is a source of fiber used in making rope. SE United States. In cultivation 1675.
Zone 3 US, 4 Can. 🏆

***Y. f.* 'Bright Edge'** This is a small shrub with leaves that have a narrow, golden yellow margin.
Zone 3 US, 4 Can. 🏆

***Y. f.* 'Variegata'** The leaves of this small shrub are margined with cream.
Zone 3 US, 4 Can. 🏆

Y. flaccida A stemless, low-growing yucca

Yucca filamentosa 'Bright Edge'

Yucca filamentosa 'Variegata'

that forms tufts of long, lance-shaped leaves. The terminal part of each leaf bends downward, and the margins have thin, curly white threads. The creamy flowers are 2–2½ in (5–6.5 cm) long and borne in erect, downy panicles 2–4 ft (0.6–1.2 m) high in mid- to late summer. It spreads by short growths at the base. The following forms

are recommended. SE United States. Introduced 1816.
Zone 3 US, 4 Can.

Yucca flaccida 'Golden Sword'

***Y. f.* 'Golden Sword'** A striking form whose leaves have a broad central band of creamy yellow.
Zone 3 US, 4 Can. 🏆

Yucca flaccida 'Ivory'

Yucca glauca

***Y. f.* 'Ivory'** A small shrub producing large panicles of creamy white flowers stained with green.
Zone 3 US, 4 Can. 🏆

Y. glauca (Spanish bayonet, soapweed) A low-growing, short-stemmed species with a compact, rounded head of linear, grayish green leaves that are margined with white and edged with a few threads. The greenish white flowers, 2–3 in (5–7.5 cm) long, are borne in an erect raceme 3–5 ft (1–1.5 m) high in mid- to late summer, but plants do not flower until mature.
Zone 3 US, 3 Can.

Yucca gloriosa

Y. gloriosa (Spanish dagger, mound-lily yucca) A shrub that reaches 8 ft (2.5 m), with a stout stem and few or no branches; at the limits of its range, it many not have a stem. The leaves are stiff, bloomy green, up to 2 ft (60 cm) long by 3–4 in (7.5–10 cm) wide, and produced in a dense, terminal head. The leaf spine tips are sharp. The flowers are large, up to 4 in (10 cm) wide, and greenish white, sometimes tinged with red on the outside. They are carried in an erect, crowded, conical panicle, 3–6½ ft (1–2 m) high, from midsummer to early fall. SE United States. In cultivation c. 1550.
Zone 6 US, 7 Can. 🏆

Yucca gloriosa 'Variegata'

***Y. g.* 'Variegata'** The leaves of this form are dramatically margined and striped with creamy yellow that fades to cream on the older leaves.
Zone 6 US, 7 Can. 🏆

Yucca recurvifolia

Y. recurvifolia A medium-sized species, usually with a short stem and several branches. The tapered leaves, 2–3 ft (60–90 cm) long, are blue-bloomy at first and become green as they age. All but the central, upper leaves are characteristically downward-curved. The creamy flowers are in dense, erect panicles 2–3 ft (60–90 cm) or more high in late summer. Its leaves are not

as sharply pointed as those of *Y. gloriosa.* It is suitable for urban gardens. SE United States. Introduced 1794.
Zone 6 US, 7 Can. 🏆

Y. whipplei (Our Lord's candle) A stemless

Yucca whipplei

species that develops into a dense, globular clump of long, narrow, rigid, spine-tipped leaves that are finely toothed and blue-bloomy. The large, fragrant flowers are greenish white to cream, edged with purple. They are in a densely packed panicle at the end of an erect, 6½–11 ft (2–3.5 m) scape (stalk) in late spring and early summer. Although it can withstand frost, this magnificent species is best grown only in sunny locations in very mild areas; it needs very well drained soil. W California, Baja, Mexico. Introduced 1854.
Zone 8 US, 9 Can.

Yushania *Gramineae*

A genus of two evergreen species of bamboo from eastern Asia.

Y. anceps, syn. *Arundinaria anceps, Sinarundinaria anceps* A beautiful but rampant species that is suitable for screens and hedges in large gardens. The mature canes are straight, erect, and glossy deep green and reach a height of 10–11 ft (3–3.5 m) or more in mild places. The arching tips bear masses of glossy green leaves, 4–6 in (10–15 cm) long and ½ in (12 mm) wide. The canes can be used for stakes. N Himalaya. Introduced 1865.
Zone 9 US 🏆

Z

Zanthoxylum *Rutaceae*

A genus of about 200 species of deciduous trees and shrubs found largely in warm regions of the world. Most have spiny branches and aromatic leaves. The flowers are small, but the compound leaves are always attractive and in some species are as beautiful as the fronds of a fern; in others they have the spectacular appeal of the tree of heaven, Ailanthus altissima. *The fruits may be jet black or bright red. They are easy to grow in any ordinary soil in sun or shade.*

Z. americanum (Prickly ash, toothache tree) A large, rather gaunt shrub or short-stemmed tree with short, stout thorns and leaves that are composed of 5–11 more or less oval leaflets. The small, yellowish green flowers are in short clusters in spring and are followed by jet black fruits. The twigs and fruits are said to have been chewed by Native Americans to alleviate toothache, as the acrid juice has a numbing effect. It is very hardy. E North America. Introduced c. 1740.
Zone 3 US, 3 Can.

Zanthoxylum piperitum

Z. piperitum (Japan pepper) A neat, medium-sized shrub with pairs of flattened spines and attractive pinnate leaves composed of 11–23 stalkless, broadly lance-shaped or fairly oval leaves. Small, greenish yellow flowers, produced on the old wood in late spring or early summer, are followed by small, reddish fruits with black seeds used as a pepper in Japan. Leaves turn a rich yellow in fall. Japan, Korea, Manchuria, China. In cultivation 1877.
Zone 6 US, 7 Can.

Zauschneria *Onagraceae*

A genus of four species of dwarf deciduous subshrubs or perennials. They require a warm, sunny, and, most important, well-drained location and are good specimens for the rock garden. Although they are not rated as very hardy, they can in fact be grown in areas that are colder than the zones indicated, as long as they do not have to tolerate wet, heavy soil. Known as California fuchsias, they are not fuchsias at all but belong to the same plant family.

***Z. californica* 'Dublin'**, syn. *Z. c.* 'Glasnevin' A bushy subshrub with several erect stems that are covered with narrow, downy, gray-green leaves. The tubular, fuchsia-like flowers are red with a scarlet tube and are borne in long, loose spikes over a long period from late summer to midfall.
Zone 8 US, 9 Can. 🏆

***Z. c.* 'Glasnevin'** See *Z. c.* 'Dublin'.

Zauschneria californica subsp. *mexicana*

Z. c.* subsp. *mexicana A plant similar to *Z. c.* 'Dublin' but with broad, green leaves.
Zone 8 US, 9? Can.

Z. cana, syn. *Z. microphylla* A dwarf subshrub with linear gray leaves and loose spikes of red, scarlet-tubed flowers in late summer and fall. California.
Zone 9 US 🏆

Z. microphylla See *Z. cana*.

Zelkova *Ulmaceae*

A genus of five species of smooth-barked deciduous trees or, rarely, shrubs; one species is native to Crete and the rest are from Asia. They are related to Ulmus *but do not suffer from Dutch elm disease. They thrive in deep, moist, loamy soil and are fairly tolerant of shade, wind, and drought. The small, greenish flowers and the fruits that follow are unremarkable and of little ornamental value. Nevertheless, zelkovas are neat, handsome plants that are useful as shade trees.*

Z. carpinifolia (Elm zelkova) A large, long-lived, slow-growing tree that can reach up to 100 ft (30 m) high. The bark is smooth and gray like that of a beech but peels in irregular flakes with age. The trunk is generally short, soon giving way to numerous erect, crowded branches that form a characteristically dense, conical head. In old trees the trunk is often buttressed. The dark green leaves, which grow up to 3 in (7.5 cm) long, are more or less elliptical, coarsely toothed, and rough. They are borne on hairy shoots and turn orange-brown in fall. Caucasus, N Iran. Introduced 1760.
Zone 6 US, 7 Can.

Z. serrata (Japanese zelkova) A medium-sized, occasionally large, graceful, wide-spreading tree with a rounded crown and smooth, gray, later flaking bark. The leaves are more or less slenderly oval, up to $4^{3}/_{4}$ in (12 cm) long, and edged with slender-pointed, coarse teeth. In fall they turn bronze or red. Japan, Korea, Taiwan, China. Introduced 1861.
Zone 4 US, 5b Can. 🏆

Zelkova serrata

Zelkova carpinifolia

***Z. s.* 'Green Vase'** The vase shape of this form makes it a good substitute for the American elm. Fast growing when young.
Zone 4 US, 5b Can.

***Z. s.* 'Village Green'** This form was selected for its straight trunk and resistance to Dutch elm disease. It has red fall foliage.
Zone 5 US, 6 Can.

Zenobia *Ericaceae*

A genus of one deciduous or semievergreen species.

Zenobia pulverulenta

Z. pulverulenta (Dusty zenobia) A beautiful small shrub with a loose, graceful, slightly upright habit and arching stems. It has bloomy young shoots and bloomy, more or less oblong, shallowly toothed leaves that are gray to gray-green and turn red in fall. The bloom tends to be more conspicuous on young leaves and gradually fades with age. The white, bell-shaped flowers are similar to those of a large lily-of-the-valley and smell like anise; they are held in pendulous clusters in early to midsummer. It prefers a sandy, acidic soil and part shade. It should be pruned occasionally to maintain its rounded shape and to prevent it from growing too tall. SE United States. Introduced 1801.
Zone 5 US, 6 Can.

Index

This is an index of common names, gardening terms, and techniques. Italic page numbers refer to photographs and illustrations

Picture Acknowledgments

The roman numerals i to vii following a page reference identify the position of the photograph on the page. Starting at the top of the left-hand column with i, the numerals are allocated in sequential order running vertically from the top to the bottom of each column. For example, on page 269 shown below, the top picture in the left column is 269i, the centre column picture is 269iv and the bottom right picture is 269vi. Jacket photographs are also used in the book and are credited beside the relevant page reference using the same system.

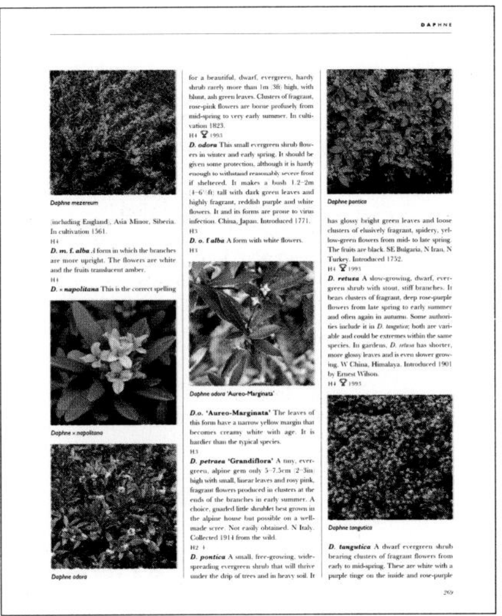

DAPHNE

Daphne mezereum

(including England), Asia Minor, Siberia. In cultivation 1561.
H4
D. m.* f. *alba A form in which the branches are more upright. The flowers are white and the fruits translucent amber.
H4
D.* × *napolitana This is the correct spelling

Daphne × napolitana

Daphne odora

for a beautiful, dwarf, evergreen, hardy shrub rarely more than 1m (3ft) high, with blunt, ash green leaves. Clusters of fragrant, rose-pink flowers are borne profusely from mid-spring to very early summer. In cultivation 1823.
H4 🏆 1993
D. odora This small evergreen shrub flowers in winter and early spring. It should be given some protection, although it is hardy enough to withstand reasonably severe frost if sheltered. It makes a bush 1.2–2m (4–6½ft) tall with dark green leaves and highly fragrant, reddish purple and white flowers. It and its forms are prone to virus infection. China, Japan. Introduced 1771.
H3
D. o.* f. *alba A form with white flowers.
H3

Daphne odora 'Aureo-Marginata'

***D.o.* 'Aureo-Marginata'** The leaves of this form have a narrow yellow margin that becomes creamy white with age. It is hardier than the typical species.
H3
***D. petraea* 'Grandiflora'** A tiny, evergreen, alpine gem only 5–7.5cm (2–3in) high with small, linear leaves and rosy pink, fragrant flowers produced in clusters at the ends of the branches in early summer. A choice, gnarled little shrublet best grown in the alpine house but possible on a well-made scree. Not easily obtained. N Italy. Collected 1914 from the wild.
H2 ‡
D. pontica A small, free-growing, wide-spreading evergreen shrub that will thrive under the drip of trees and in heavy soil. It

Daphne pontica

has glossy bright green leaves and loose clusters of elusively fragrant, spidery, yellow-green flowers from mid- to late spring. The fruits are black. SE Bulgaria, N Iran, N Turkey. Introduced 1752.
H4 🏆 1993
D. retusa A slow-growing, dwarf, evergreen shrub with stout, stiff branches. It bears clusters of fragrant, deep rose-purple flowers from late spring to early summer and often again in autumn. Some authorities include it in *D. tangutica*; both are variable and could be extremes within the same species. In gardens, *D. retusa* has shorter, more glossy leaves and is even slower growing. W China, Himalaya. Introduced 1901 by Ernest Wilson.
H4 🏆 1993

Daphne tangutica

D. tangutica A dwarf evergreen shrub bearing clusters of fragrant flowers from early to mid-spring. These are white with a purple tinge on the inside and rose-purple

269

Andrew Lawson 19; 38; 48; 55; 60ii; 119i; 120ii; 125v; 128iv; 133iv; 136ii; 137ii; 141i, iii, v; 143iv; 144iii; 145ii; 146ii, iv; 147v; 153ii; 161iv; 162ii; 164i, iii; 167ii, iii; 168ii, v, vi; 169iv, v; 172i, ii; 185iv; 186i; 187i, v; 188vi; 189iv; 191v; 192i; 193iv, v; 197i; 200iii, vi; 204i, iv; 205iv; 215iv; 216i; 217iii; 219vii; 222i (also jacket front ix); 223ii, iv; 224iv; 225iii; 226i, iii, iv; 227iv; 229v; 231ii; 235iv; 237i; 238i, ii; 241iii; 242iii; 245i, iii; 254iii; 255ii; 264i; 265v; 266i; 267i; 273v; 279i; 291iii; 293iii; 296iii; 299ii; 300i, vi; 302iv; 304ii; 305ii, iv; 307iv; 308iii; 316i, 318v, vi; 325iv; 326iv, v; 329ii; 333ii, iii, iv; 334i; 335ii; 340i; 343iv, v; 347i, v; 353iii; 358i, iv; 359iii; 361i; 366i, iii; 367i, v; 369ii; 381iii, v; 382i; iii; 383iii, v; 413iii; 416ii; 418ii, v; 419i; 424ii, iii; 425iv; 428vi; 430iii; 432i; 433ii; 434iii; 438ii; 445iv; 446vii; 447v; 451iv; 452iii; 453i; 456ii; 457i, ii; 458i, ii; 459i; 466vi; 467ii; 470i, vi; 472iii; 474iii; 484ii; 485ii; 486i; 487i; 489iii; 495i; 499ii; 503i; 506v; 525ii; 537ii, iv; 538ii; 539iii, v; 542iii; 544i, iv; 545i, iii; 546iii, iv; 550ii; 551iii; 554i, ii; 558ii, iv; 560i, iii; 562ii, iii, iv; 563i, iv, vi; 564i, ii; 566v; 568i; 570i; 574ii; 575i, ii; 576iii; 577i; 579iv; 581iii; 584ii; 585vi; 591iv; 593iv; 595i; 596v; 597i; 598iii; 600iv, v; 603iv; 607i; 610ii; 611i; 612iii; 614i, iii; 617vii; 618v; 619vi; 620i; 621iv; 622i; 624i, iii; 625ii; 626iv

Brian Carter/Garden Picture Library 119iv; 128ii; 133ii; 139ii; 154i; 174i; 177i; 179i; 180i; 184ii; 185v; 186iii; 193iii; 201ii; 231iv; 245v; 262iv; 264iii; 268iv; 276ii; 277iv; 283iv; 300v; 309iii, iv (also jacket back vii); 314iii, 320iii; 321i; 322iii; 324vi; 328vi; 336iii; 338i; 340iii, iv; 347iv; 348i, iii; 351ii; 369iii; 370iii; 389v; 391i; 392iii; 398iv; 402iv; 406i; 411v; 413i; 414v; 415iv; 419ii; 420i, iv; 426iv; 432ii; 442v; 444iii; 448iii; 449v; 450iii; 455iv; 460i; 462i; 466ii; 468ii, vi; 470ii; 473i; 491ii; 497i; 498ii; 501iii; 505iii; 506ii; 507i; 510i, v; 513iv; 514i; 517ii; 518i; 519iv; 520i, ii; 521ii; 522v; 523ii; 526i; 529i; 530ii; 532i; 533iv; 535iii; 536i; 537iii; 539ii; 540iv; 543v; 544iii; 546i; 548iii; 549ii; 555iii; 565vi; 567i, iv; 570v; 574i; 584iii; 587ii; 593iii; 594i; 595iv; 596iii; 597v; 598i; 599ii; 603ii; 615v; 618iv

Brigitte Thomas/Garden Picture Library 18; 31i, ii; 64 (also jacket front ii); 67; 116-7; 120iv, v; 133vi; 202iv, 385ii; 446v; 463ii; 475ii; 551i

Bob Challinor/Garden Picture Library 221i; 299i, 536ii

Christopher Fairweather/Garden Picture Library 161i; 183ii; 189v; 206i; 245ii; 246i; 303iii; 332iii; 391iii; 423ii; 439i; 442vi; 460iv; 499iii; 501ii; 503iv, v; 514ii; 516iv; 522iv, vi; 525i; 607ii; 618i; 623iv

Christopher Gallagher/Garden Picture Library 17

Clay Perry/Garden Picture Library 24

Clive Nichols 618ii

Clive Nichols/Garden Picture Library 269v; 278iii; 356ii; 426iii; 579iii (also jacket back ii)

David Askham/Garden Picture Library 243i; 386ii; 478ii; 516v; 520v; 581v; 582iii; 608i

David England/Garden Picture Library 269i; 336ii; 337ii, iv; 558i

David Russell/Garden Picture Library 122iii; 125vi; 220ii; 225ii; 231iii; 263ii; 268i; 299iv; 355ii; 384iv; 385i; 411iv; 539iv; 592ii

Densey Clyne/Garden Picture Library 185i; 547iii

Didier Willery/Garden Picture Library 62; 129iv; 131iv; 136iii; 138ii; 143ii; 156iii; 160iv; 161ii; 163iv; 183iv; 193ii; 197iv; 208iii; 242i; 243v; 258iii; 259iii; 263iv; 271i; 272vi; 273iii, vi; 299iii (also jacket front iv); 344i; 345iv; 379ii; 395iv; 402iii; 428ii; 435iii; 458iii; 463iv; 466v; 467v; 468i; 471i; 474ii; 492iii; 499i; 531ii; 543iii; 550v; 554iii; 559iii, v; 561i; 564iv; 578iv; 581ii; 582iv; 590iv; 592iii; 594iv (also jacket front viii); 604ii, iii; 608ii; 612vi; 617ii; 623i; 629iii

Eric Crichton 142ii; 147ii; 149iii; 159iii; 163v; 170iii; 173ii; 174ii, v; 175ii; 178i; 185ii; 188v; 193i; 195iv; 206iv; 215iii; 223i; 230v; 235iii; 239ii; 244iii; 252iii; 259iv; 260i; 261ii; 262v; 266ii; 270iii; 274ii; 277i; 283iii; 285ii; 286iii; 288v; 290iii; 291i, v; 293iv; 298i; 303iv; 304i; 305iii; 312i; 316v; 317iii; 320ii; 324v; 325ii; 330ii; 335v; 336iii; 337i, 341ii, iii; 342i; 343i; 345iii; 348iv; 349iv; 350i; 351i; 358v; 365i; 368i, iii; 370iv; 371iii; 373ii; 376i; 377ii; 380i; 381ii; 383ii; 384i; 387i; 390ii; 394iii; 399v; 400i (also jacket back ix); 403iv; 404iv; 408ii, iii; 409iii; 414iii; 416iii, iv; 418i, iii; 419iv;

420iii, v; 421ii; 425ii, iii; 427i, iv; 431i; 434i; 436iii, iv; 442iv; 443iii; 449iii, vi; 451i; 452i; 454ii; 461i; 462iv; 463iii; 466iii; 468iii, iv; 469iii; 471ii, iv, v; 472i; 476ii; 485iii, iv; 488i; 490iii; 492v; 493iii; 494ii; 496i; 500i; 504i; 505i; 507ii; 508iv; 509i; 512ii, iii; 513i; 518iii, iv; 519ii; 521iii; 526v; 528iii; 535v; 536iii; 538iv; 541i; 542ii; 545ii; 546ii; 547v; 549i; 550iii; 552i; 553iii; 557ii; 559ii; 563ii; 565iii; 569i; 570iv; 575iv; 578i; 580ii; 586iv; 587iii; 588ii; 590ii; 593ii; 594v, vi (also jacket spine); 596ii; 597iii; 601i; 603iii; 606i; 614iv; 615i; 620vi; 621ii, v; 623iii; 627iv; 629ii

Garden Picture Library 234iii

Harry Smith Collection 124iv; 125iv; 127i; 130i; 131vi; 132ii; 135iii; 136iv, v; 138iv; 139iv; 141ii; 146iii; 147iv; 154ii; 163i; 164ii, v, vi; 166i; 168i, iii; 171i; 172iv; 175iii; 176ii, iv; 184v (also jacket front xi); 185iii, vi; 186iv; 187ii; 188ii, iii; 190v; 192iv; 196i; 199ii; 204iii; 206ii; 215ii; 217ii; 218v; 219ii; 220iii (also jacket front iii); 233iv; 234i, iii; 235i; 236iii; 247iii; 248iv, v; 250i; 252v; 253iii, v; 254ii; 261iii; 262i, iii; 264ii; 265ii; 267iv; 269iii; 270iv; 271ii; 272i, iv; 273ii; 274iii, iv; 275ii; 278i; 279iii; 280ii; 284v; 285iii, vi; 288vi; 289v; 297iii; 301iii; 302vi; 305i; 306i; 309ii; 310i, ii, iii; 311iv; 313v; 315iii; 317i; 325iii; 327i, iv; 330iii; 336i, iv; 337iii; 338ii; 341i; 343iii; 355iv; 359iv; 371i; 373i, iii; 384iii; 386i; 388i; 389iii, iv; 390i, iii; 391ii; 393ii, v; 394i, ii, v; 395iii, v; 399iii; 402i; 403i, iii; 404i; 407ii, iii; 409i; 411i, ii; 415i; 416i; 429iii; 435iv; 440iii; 441iii, vi; 442vii; 455iii; 456iii; 463v; 467iii, iv; 469i; 475iii; 479i; 480i; 482ii, iv; 488ii; 489ii; 490i, ii; 491i, iii; 492i, ii; 493i, ii; 494i; 496iii; 497iii; 498i; 500ii, iii; 502i, ii, iii; 503ii; 504ii; 506i, iii; 507iv (also jacket front v); 508i, ii, iii; 509ii; 511vi; 513iii; 514iv, vi; 515i, ii, iii, iv, v; 516i; 517iii, v; 518v; 519iii; 521i; 522iii; 523vi; 524i, ii, iii, v; 525v; 526ii; 528i, ii; 531iv; 534ii; 535ii; 539i; 552ii; 553iv; 555i; 559i; 561ii, iii; 563vii; 570iii; 573ii; 576iv; 581vi; 582ii; 583i; 589ii; 595ii; 610iii; 613ii, v, vi; 617iv; 619v; 620v; 623v

Henj Dijkman/Garden Picture Library 476i

Howard Rice/Garden Picture Library 160i; 205i; 225v; 251i; 254iv; 311v; 357i; 538iii; 556i; 557i; 564v; 591v; 615iv

Jane Legate/Garden Picture Library 617iii

Jerry Pavia/Garden Picture Library 236i; 283ii; 366ii; 525iv; 610i

Jill Hedges Garden Archive 3; 5

Joanne Pavia/Garden Picture Library 240iv

John Ferro Sims/Garden Picture Library 462ii; 578vi

John Glover 20i,ii; 21; 27; 35; 36i, ii; 39; 71; 79; 83; 84; 85ii, iii; 88i, ii, iii; 95i, ii, iii; 98i, ii, iii; 102i, ii, iii; 103i, ii, iii; 105i, ii

John Glover/Garden Picture Library 16; 122v; 127iv; 131i; 132i, iv; 133i; 134i; 137i, iii; 140i; 141iv; 142i; 143i; 146i, v; 148i; 160iii; 161v; 162i; 176i; 177ii; 178iii; 179ii; 181i, 184i, iv; 188iv; 191ii; 194iii; 195i; 200v; 205ii; 216ii; 219i; 223iii; 225i; 230i; 242ii; 246iv; 248ii; 250ii; 254i; 262ii; 265i, iii; 266iii, iv; 267ii; 269vi; 271iii; 275iv; 281i; 283v; 284i, iv, vi; 285v; 288ii, iii, vii; 290ii; 292ii; 294i; 301ii; 304iii; 316ii; 318iv; 321iii; 323iii; 324iv; 326i; 328i; 332iv; 334ii, vi; 338iii; 346i, iii; 361iii; 364iii; 367iii; 370ii; 372ii; 376iv; 383i; 388iii; 389i, ii, vi; 392i, iv; 393i, iii; 395ii; 396iii; 398v; 401v; 406ii, iii; 411iii; 418iv; 421i; 427iii (also jacket back x); 440i; 441ii; 443i; 460iii; 462iii; 463i; 464ii, v; 466i; 467vi; 469ii; 470iii, iv, v; 472ii; 476iv, v; 478iii; 483i; 484iii; 496ii; 497iv; 505ii, iv, v, vi; 510iii; 511ii, iii, iv; 513ii; 521iv; 523iii, iv; 525iii; 527ii; 529ii; 532ii; 545iv; 547iv; 560ii; 561iv; 566iii, vi; 568ii; 573iv; 580i; 581iv; 586i, iii, v, vi; 587iv, v; 588iv; 591i; 592i; 593i; 597iv; 601iv; 604v; 605i; 612ii; 613i; 614ii, v, vi; 620iv; 621iii, iv; 622ii; 624iv (also jacket front i); 625i; 626i, iii; 627vi; 628ii; 629i

John Hillier 143ii; 286vi; 398i; 399v; 405i; 416iv; 555i; 566iv; 569iv,v; 576i; 579i; 588i

Jonathan Weaver/Garden Picture Library 523i

J S Sira/Garden Picture Library 140iii, iv; 169i, ii, iii; 190vii; 191i, iii; 220iv; 224i; 245iv; 279iv; 315i; 323vi; 324iii; 346iv; 369i; 396ii; 397i; 401iv; 420ii; 423i, v; 424i; 425i; 437i; 441iv; 442i; 443ii; 444ii; 449ii; 475i; 476iii; 506iv; 538v; 548i; 574iii; 581i; 594ii; 598ii; 603i; 612i; 627iii

Juliette Wade/Garden Picture Library 130iii; 159ii; 160v; 162iii; 224iii; 243iv; 268iii; 495ii

Karin Craddock/Garden Picture Library 295ii; 587i

Lamontagne/Garden Picture Library 130ii; 184iii (also jacket front vi), vi; 190ii; 192ii; 196iv; 202i; 226ii; 248iii; 255i; 302ii; 345iii; 384v; 391iv; 435ii; 494iii; 543iv; 547ii; 595iii

Linda Burgess/Garden Picture Library 318iii; 452iv; 459ii; 624ii

Marijke Heuff/Garden Picture Library 28; 227iii; 578v; 620iv

Mayer/Le Scanff/Garden Picture Library 347ii; 558iii

Mel Watson/Garden Picture Library 460ii

Michael Howes/Garden Picture Library 23

Neil Holmes/Garden Picture Library 29; 139iii; 156i; 157i; 158i, ii; 162iv; 170ii; 171iv; 216v; 218iii; 234ii; 241ii; 323ii; 325v; 326ii; 329iv, v; 358iii; 371ii; 383iv; 464i; 467i; 477ii; 478i; 523v; 565i; 594iii

Nigel Kemp/Garden Picture Library 309v

Noel Kavanagh/Garden Picture Library 42; 392v; 543ii

Philippe Bonduel/Garden Picture Library 553ii

Photos Horticultural 154iii

Reader's Digest 135ii; 140ii; 156v; 158iv; 175i; 195iii; 200ii; 201iii; 236ii; 244iv; 255v; 261i; 264iv; 336v; 337v; 344iv; 345i; 346ii; 348ii, v; 349iii; 352i, v; 353vi; 359ii; 361ii; 362iii; 365ii; 379iii; 398i, vi; 405ii; 406v; 415v; 427ii; 428i

Robert Estall/Garden Picture Library 448iv

Roger Hyam/Garden Picture Library 14-15; 471iii; 497ii

Ron Evans/Garden Picture Library 501i; 578iii

Ron Sutherland/Garden Picture Library 247ii; 309i; 484i; 628i

Stephen Jury/Garden Picture Library 547i

Steven Wooster/Garden Picture Library 37; 75; 125i; 257iii

Sue Atkinson 198i

Sunniva Harte/Garden Picture Library 430i; 433i; 543i

Vaughan Fleming/Garden Picture Library 426i; 446vi; 596i

Zara McCalmont/Garden Picture Library 357iii